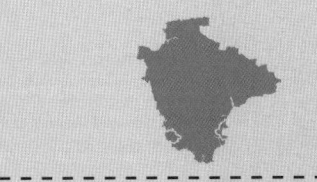

LOCAL EXPLORER

DEVON

& PLYMOUTH

www.philips-maps.co.uk

Published by Philip's, a division of
Octopus Publishing Group Ltd
www.octopusbooks.co.uk
Carmelite House, 50 Victoria Embankment,
London EC4Y 0DZ
An Hachette UK Company
www.hachette.co.uk

First edition 2024
First impression 2024
DEVEA

ISBN 978-1-84907-645-6

© Philip's 2024

This product includes mapping data licensed from Ordnance Survey® with the permission of the Controller of His Majesty's Stationery Office. © Crown copyright 2024. All rights reserved. Licence number 100011710.

Photographic acknowledgements:
Alamy Stock Photo: /Susie Kearley III top; /Terry Mathews II top; /Christopher Nicholson II bottom; /Realimage front cover; /Sebastian Wasek III bottom.

Printed in China

CONTENTS

II **Best places to visit**

IV **Key to map pages**

VI **Route planning**

X **Key to map symbols**

1 **Street maps** at 1¾ inches to 1 mile

150 **Street maps** at 3½ inches to 1 mile

261 **Street maps** of Exeter and Plymouth at 7 inches to 1 mile

264 **Index** of towns, villages, streets, hospitals, industrial estates, railway stations, schools, shopping centres, universities and places of interest

Best places to visit

Outdoors

Dartmoor National Park Large national park known for its dramatic scenery of high open moorland and hilltop tors (granite outcrops), a major draw for walkers. The moor encompasses many attractive market towns, among them **Moretonhampstead**, **Okehampton** and **Tavistock**. Picturesque villages include **Lustleigh** and **Widecombe in the Moor**. The latter is famous for the late Gothic St Pancras Church, known as the Cathedral of the Moor for its 120-foot tower. **Buckfast Abbey** welcomes visitors to its church and gardens. Within the national park's boundaries are lakes and reservoirs, popular for water sports, and it is home to herds of ponies, known to have grazed here for over 3,000 years. There are visitor centres in Postbridge, Princetown and Haytor. 🖳 www.buckfast.org.uk
🖳 www.dartmoor.gov.uk
🖳 https://visitdartmoor.co.uk **128 A8**

Exmoor National Park National park in north Devon and Somerset, a landscape of moorland, woodland and rolling hills, popular with walkers. It is home to wild red deer and endangered Exmoor ponies. It has a dramatic rugged coastline overlooking the Bristol Channel. On the coast is the attractive fishing village of **Lynmouth** (location of a National Park Visitor Centre), which is connected to **Lynton** above by a Victorian, water-powered funicular railway. The nearby **Valley of Rocks** is famous for its feral goats grazing on the precipitous cliffs. 🖳 www.exmoor-nationalpark.gov.uk **151 C6**

Hembury Fort Remains of a large Iron Age hill fort. Archaeological finds suggest that the Romans also occupied the site. Walkers are rewarded with far-reaching views over the surrounding Area of Outstanding Natural Beauty, the **Blackdown Hills**. 🖳 http://www.hemburyfort.co.uk **84 F6**

Jurassic Coast Area of coastline stretching from Exmouth in Devon to Studland Bay in Dorset, famous for its typically red

▲ Lundy

cliffs, rock formations and caves, and for the plentiful fossils, which date from the Triassic, Jurassic and Cretaceous periods. It is a UNESCO World Heritage Site. Worth visiting along the coast are the pretty village of Beer; Seaton, for the heritage **Seaton Tramway**; and the seaside towns of Sidmouth and Budleigh Salterton. 🖳 www.jurassiccoast.org
🖳 www.tram.co.uk

Lundy Granite island off the north coast of Devon, about three miles long and half a mile wide accessible by boat from either Bideford or Ilfracombe. It is a popular location for birdwatching, diving, climbing, fishing and walking. There are also talks, guided walks and snorkel safaris. 🖳 www.landmarktrust.org.uk **14**

Lydford Gorge Deep river gorge on the edge of Dartmoor. It is an area of temperate rainforest and ancient woodland. Walking trails lead through lush vegetation to the high Whitelady Waterfall and dramatic Devil's Cauldron pothole. **Lydford Castle**, in the nearby village of Lydford, is a 13th-century tower built as a prison. *Lydford* 🖳 www.nationaltrust.org.uk 🖳 www.english-heritage.org.uk **107 E3**

North Devon Coast Area of Outstanding Natural Beauty, some of the most attractive coastal scenery in Devon, with dramatic cliffs, rocky coves and long sandy beaches backed by rolling hills and wooded valleys. Towns in the area include **Ilfracombe**, with its attractive harbour and 14th-century chapel, and **Bideford**, a historic port on the estuary of the River Torridge. The coast is known for its picturesque villages, of which some of the most popular are **Lee**, **Croyde**, **Appledore** and **Clovelly**. Sandy beaches, popular with families and surfers, include Woolacombe, Saunton Sands and Westward Ho! 🖳 www.northdevon-aonb.org.uk

▼ Dartmouth Castle

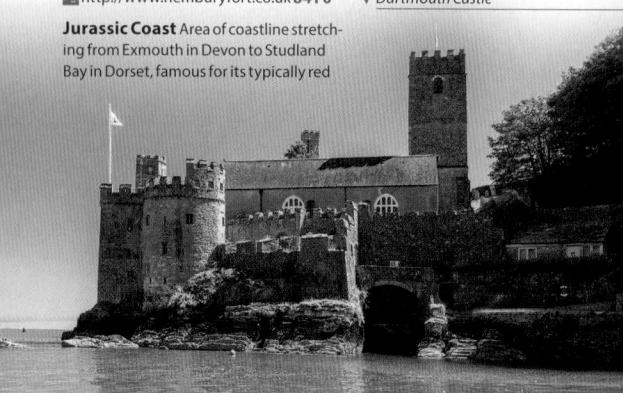

Okehampton Castle Ruined castle on a ridge above the River Okement. Built by the Normans, this large castle was converted into an impressive private residence in the 13th and 14th centuries, before being abandoned in the 16th. There are walks in the surrounding woodland. *Okehampton* 🖳 www.english-heritage.org.uk **170 A3**

RHS Garden Rosemoor More than 65 acres of formal and informal gardens surrounded by woodland. It is particularly well known for its two rose gardens and its 'hot' garden, so called for the vibrantly colourful planting, and 'cool' garden, which has a contrastingly calmer palette and water feature. There is also a lake, arboretum, winter garden and more. *Great Torrington* 🖳 www.rhs.org.uk **159 D2**

Upper Plym Valley Large area of Dartmoor National Park managed by English Heritage. It is an area filled with evidence of Bronze Age settlements, including fragments of walls and round-houses, earth banks known as reaves, and stone rows. *Yelverton* 🖳 www.english-heritage.org.uk **132 D7**

Towns & villages

Brixham Picturesque town at the southern end of what is known as the 'English Riviera' on the South Devon coast. It is one of the UK's busiest fishing ports, with a flourishing fish market, and is thought to have been a fishing centre since its foundation in Saxon times. Colourful fishermen's cottages overlook the harbour, and are best viewed on boat trips, many of which can be taken on board heritage trawlers. Within the busy harbour is a replica of Sir Francis Drake's flagship, the **Golden Hind**. Visitors can explore the ship and learn about Devon-born Drake's circumnavigation of the globe. **Brixham Heritage Museum** is devoted to local history and culture. Its varied collection ranges from archaeological finds, to World War 2 memorabilia, to the story of the fish hawker women. On the headland just outside Brixham is **Berry Head National Nature Reserve**, popular for its dramatic sea views, well-preserved Napoleonic-era fortifications, lighthouse and seabird colonies. There is a visitors centre. 🖳 www.goldenhind.co.uk 🖳 www.brixhammuseum.uk **230 E3**

Dartmouth Historic port town on the estuary of the River Dart. It is well known for its association with the Royal Navy: all its officers train at the **Britannia Royal Naval College**, which can be visited on tours. Dartmouth developed as a port under the Normans. Its centre is full of narrow medieval lanes and listed buildings, including the 17th-century Butterwalk, a row of merchants' houses, location of the **Dartmouth Museum**, which relates the history of the town. On the harbourfront, the remains of a Tudor fort, **Bayard's Cove Fort**, can be explored. Just outside town, **Dartmouth Castle**, together with Kingswear Castle on the opposite bank, guards the entrance to the estuary. Dartmouth lies within the **South Devon Area of Outstanding Natural Beauty**, which has sandy beaches, rugged coastline and attractive villages to explore. 🖳 https://discoverdartmouth.com/info/visitor-centre **233 E3**

Exeter Historic cathedral city on the River Exe, the county town of Devon. **Exeter Cathedral** dominates the heart of the city. Its massive square towers are Norman, but the rest of the cathedral was built in the 14th century. It is particularly admired for the unusually long, stone-vaulted ceiling above the nave and quire, as well as the stone carving on the West Front and throughout the building, and an Astronomical Clock. Nearby, the **Royal Albert Memorial Museum and Art Gallery**, has a large and varied collection, encompassing fine and decorative arts, local history and archaeology, world cultures and natural sciences. Underneath the High Street are underground passageways, dating from the 14th century, through which fresh water used to be brought into the city. They can be visited on tours. Much of Exeter's old city walls are intact; trail leaflets and information boards guide visitors to the remaining sections. Exeter Quay, a short distance from the city centre, is a popular leisure area. The old **Custom House**, built in 1680, hosts cultural events and exhibitions, as well as a permanent display and audio-visual presentation on the history of the quay. 🖳 www.visitexeter.com **261 B4**

Plymouth Port city on the Tamar estuary, on the south coast of Devon. It played a major role in the UK's maritime history. It is also home to the UK's largest naval base, and was badly damaged by bombing during World War 2. On the waterfront is the 17th-century fortress known as the **Royal Citadel**; still in use by the military, it can be visited on tours. The Citadel overlooks the Hoe, a large park with open lawns, statues and **Smeaton's Tower**. This 18th-century lighthouse has been restored and offers fantastic views from its former lantern room. The old city centre, known as the Barbican, has historic buildings and cobbled streets and lies between two harbours. The **Mayflower Museum** tells the story of the Pilgrims' journey and has an intricate model of the ship. The history of this area of Plymouth can be explored in the **Elizabethan House**. On the other side of Sutton Harbour is the **National Marine Aquarium**, the UK's largest aquarium. The **Box Museum and Art Gallery** relates the history of Plymouth and displays artefacts from some of the many journeys that started from here. **Drake's Island** can be reached by boat. It has an interesting military history, with cannons and tunnels to explore. 🖳 www.visitplymouth.co.uk 🖳 www.theboxplymouth.com 🖳 www.national-aquarium.co.uk **262 C1**

Tiverton Attractive market town on the River Exe in Mid Devon. It was a hub of the local woollen cloth industry in the 16th to 18th centuries. **Tiverton Museum of Mid Devon Life** is devoted to the history of the town and surrounding area, with displays about farming, transport, home life, and local industries such as brewing, weaving and lace making. **Tiverton Castle** dates from the 12th century, although it has been substantially altered over the centuries. Visitors can explore the castle and gardens. **St Peter's** and **St George's** churches are both Grade 1 listed. St Peter's is particularly noted for the ornately carved Greenway Chapel, which dates from 1517. St George's Church is considered to be one of the best examples

of a Georgian church, having been very little altered since the early 18th century. On the outskirts of Tiverton is the **Grand Western Canal**, which is now a country park and nature reserve. Trips can taken on horse-drawn barges, and the towpath is popular with walkers and cyclists 🖥 www.tivertonmuseum.org.uk 🖥 www.tivertoncastle.com **161 D3**

Torquay Traditional seaside resort and port in South Devon, on what is known as the 'English Riviera'. It has a large well-protected harbour and is known for its sandy beaches, notably Torre Abbey Sands, Babbacombe and Oddicombe, which is reached by the 1920s Babbacombe Cliff Railway. The town's oldest building, **Torre Abbey** is an art gallery and museum housed in a 12th-century former monastery. **Torquay Museum** has galleries devoted to local history as well as Ancient Egypt and Agatha Christie, one of Torquay's most famous residents. **Babbacombe Model Village** has hundreds of detailed miniature buildings and people from different eras. Nearby, **Bygones** is a museum of mainly Victorian life, in which visitors can walk up an authentic street of shops, visit period rooms and see a steam train and exhibitions devoted to wartime Britain. **Kents Cavern** is an extensive system of caves of archaeological and geological significance. 🖥 www.torre-abbey.org.uk 🖥 www.kents-cavern.co.uk **220 B2**

Totnes Historic market town overlooked by a Norman motte-and-bailey castle, **Totnes Castle**, which has far-reaching views from its stone keep. The town has well-preserved buildings from Tudor times onwards, notably a fine 15th-century parish church, a Tudor Butterwalk arcade, and merchants' houses from the 16th and 17th centuries. **Totnes Museum** is based in an Elizabethan manor house and garden. There are children's activities and talks. Bogan House, in a well-preserved medieval merchant's house, is home to the **Fashion & Textiles Museum**, which exhibits clothes, accessories and hats from the extensive Devonshire Collection of Period Costume. 🖥 www.english-heritage.org.uk 🖥 www.totnesmuseum.org **223 E6**

Buildings

A La Ronde Sixteen-sided cottage built in the 18th century for two women travellers. Its unusual design extends to the interior of the house, including a central octagonal hall, and the collections – mementoes from their travels – on view. *Exmouth* 🖥 www.nationaltrust.org.uk **196 A3**

Berry Pomeroy Castle Partially ruined castle surrounding the remains of a grand Elizabethan mansion. The defensive gatehouse dates from the 15th century and has an interesting wall painting from this period. The surrounding woodlands are popular with walkers. *Totnes* 🖥 www.english-heritage.org.uk **217 D1**

Buckland Abbey Former Cistercian Abbey, which became a grand Tudor house, occupied by two famous explorers, Richard Grenville and later Francis Drake. Remains of the Tudor house can be seen in the Great Hall and kitchen. Surrounding the abbey are gardens and woodlands, with a natural play area. There is a well-preserved medieval Tithe Barn. *Yelverton* 🖥 www.nationaltrust.org.uk **126 C1**

Castle Drogo Castle designed by renowned 20th-century architect Edwin Lutyens and built in the 1910s and 1920s, overlooking the Teign Gorge. The gardens retain their original design, with lawns, terraces and a rose garden. Walking routes above the gorge give views over Dartmoor; there are also paths within the shelter of the gorge. *Moretonhampstead* 🖥 www.nationaltrust.org.uk **96 C1**

Coleton Fishacre Arts and Crafts-style country house and garden on the South Devon coast. The interiors are Art Deco, with furniture typical of the period. As well as the formal dining room, saloon and library, bedrooms and servants' quarters can be seen. The gardens, in a sheltered valley leading to the sea, are highly regarded for their exotic plants, as well as woodland and wildflowers. *Kingswear* 🖥 www.nationaltrust.org.uk **234 F2**

Hartland Abbey Attractive country house, founded as a monastery in the 12th century, located within grounds leading down to the Nort Devon coast. *Hartland* 🖥 www.hartlandabbey.com **22 C4**

Knightshayes Gothic Revival house designed by Victorian architect William Burges. The interior is also neo-Gothic, with extravagant carving and a medieval-inspired Great Hall. The gardens encompass formal and woodland gardens and include terraces, a kitchen garden and a Garden in the Wood. *Tiverton* 🖥 www.nationaltrust.org.uk **49 C2**

Powderham Castle Castle, gardens and deer park on the River Exe. Dating from the late 14th century, the castle can be explored on guided tours. The grounds include a rose garden, an American garden with 18th-century Belvedere tower, and a 'secret' garden with an adventure play area and pets corner. *Exeter* 🖥 www.powderham.co.uk **194 F4**

▼ *Brixham harbour*

Museums & galleries

The Burton Art galleries, museum and community venue, established in 1951 to house the collection of local artist Hubert Coop. It now displays a wide-ranging collection of paintings, ceramics and artefacts mainly related to Bideford and the surrounding area. *Bideford* 🖥 www.burtonartgallery.co.uk **157 A3**

Coldharbour Mill Well-preserved woollen mill, which opened in 1797 and still produces yarn today. Visitors can see the period machinery, much of it still in operation, steam engines and boilers, which are fired up on steaming days. The grounds contain a mill pond and large water wheel. *Uffculme* 🖥 www.coldharbourmill.org.uk **66 A7**

Dartmoor Prison Museum Museum exploring the history of Dartmoor Prison, founded in 1806. Based in the old dairy building, the museum has artefacts relating to all areas of prison life. It remains a functioning prison. *Princetown* 🖥 www.dartmoor-prison.co.uk **119 A1**

Dingles Fairground Museum Collection of heritage fairground rides and associated artefacts. A large Museum Hall displays fairground artwork and other memorabilia. The hands-on Rides Hall contains traditional restored fairground rides for visitors to enjoy. *Lifton* 🖥 www.dinglesfhc.co.uk **106 A5**

Moretonhampstead Motor Museum Collection of more than 150 vintage and classic vehicles. *Moretonhampstead* 🖥 www.moretonmotormuseum.co.uk **111 E4**

Museum of Dartmoor Life Museum housed in an early 19th-century mill, exploring the history of Dartmoor. *Okehampton* 🖥 www.dartmoorlife.org.uk **170 B5**

Topsham Museum Museum primarily concerned with the maritime history of Topsham, a small town on the Exe Estuary with a long history as a fishing port, shipyard and exporting point for the cloth trade. 🖥 https://topshammuseum.org.uk **182 F4**

Family activities

Beer Quarry Caves Complex of underground man-made tunnels, the result of 2,000 years of quarrying for beer stone, a type of stone frequently used in churches, including Exeter Cathedral. 🖥 www.beerquarrycaves.co.uk **191 A5**

Dartmoor Zoo 33-acre zoo on the edge of Dartmoor National Park. It has a wide variety of species, from invertebrates to large mammals, and is particularly well known for its big cats. *Sparkwell* 🖥 www.dartmoorzoo.org.uk **133 A1**

Dartmouth Steam Railway 7-mile heritage railway which connects the resorts of Torbay to Kingswear where the ferry crosses to Dartmouth. In the summer there is the possibility of combining a rail

▲ *Lynton & Lynmouth Cliff Railway*

journey with a trip on the paddle steamer Kingswear Castle. *Paignton & Kingswear* 🖥 www.dartmouthrailriver.co.uk **234 A4**

Morwellham Quay Restored Victorian village and former copper mine, now an open air museum within the UNESCO Cornwall and West Devon Mining Landscape World Heritage Site. A narrow gauge railway takes visitors deep into the mine and into the village, with its restored miners' cottages, quay, docks and ship. There is a Victorian farm and nature reserve. *Tavistock* 🖥 www.morwellham-quay.co.uk **125 E4**

Paignton Zoo Large zoo and botanical gardens, with a wide variety of species housed in enclosures designed to be as close to their natural habitat as possible. The more than 2,000 species range from rhinos and lions to storks and frogs. 🖥 www.paigntonzoo.org.uk **225 F4**

River Dart Country Park Activity park within Dartmoor National Park. Among the many outdoor activities are adventure play areas, an assault course, zip wires and bike park, as well as woodland walks and a tree trail. *Ashburton* 🖥 https://riverdart.co.uk **130 D5**

South Devon Railway Heritage railway that runs beside the River Dart between Buckfastleigh and Totnes. Restored steam and diesel locomotives pull vintage carriages along the 7-mile route. Near Totnes station is **Totnes Rare Breeds Farm**. Next to Buckfastleigh station is **Dartmoor Otters and Butterflies**. 🖥 www.southdevonrailway.co.uk **236 D5, 215 E4 & 223 C7**

Watermouth Castle Victorian castle and family theme park overlooking Watermouth Cove. Within the castle are old-fashioned games, rooms displayed as they were in Victorian times, and a water show. The landscaped gardens contain many children's rides and activities, among them a carousel, swing boats, crazy golf and a toboggan run. *Ilfracombe* 🖥 www.watermouthcastle.com **2 D4**

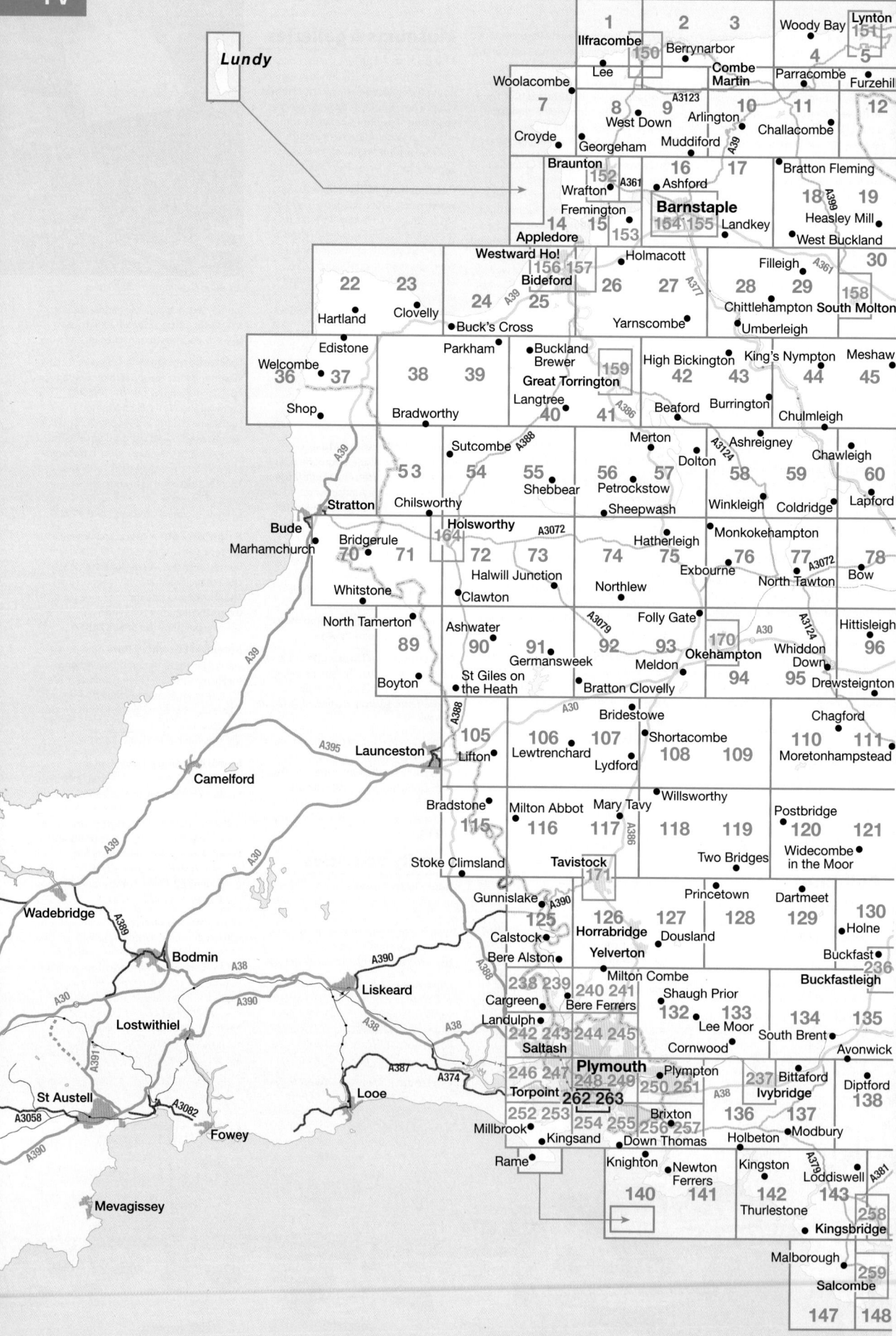

IV

Lundy

1 Ilfracombe
2 Berrynarbor
3
Woody Bay
151 Lynton
150
Lee
Combe Martin
4 Parracombe
5 Furzehill
Woolacombe
7
8 West Down
9 A3123
10 Arlington
11 Challacombe
12
Croyde
Georgeham
Muddiford
A39
Braunton
152 A361
16 Ashford
17
Bratton Fleming
18 A399 19
Wrafton
Fremington
Barnstaple
Heasley Mill
14
15 153
154 155 Landkey
West Buckland
Appledore
Westward Ho!
156 157
Holmacott
Filleigh A361
30
Bideford
26
27 A377
28
29 Chittlehampton South Molton
158
22
23
24
25
Yarnscombe
Umberleigh
Hartland
Clovelly
Buck's Cross
Buckland Brewer
High Bickington
King's Nympton
Meshaw
Welcombe
Edistone
Parkham
159
42
43
44
45
36
37
38
39
Great Torrington
Beaford
Burrington
Chulmleigh
Shop
Bradworthy
Langtree
40
41 A386
Merton
Ashreigney
Chawleigh
53
54
55 Shebbear
56 Petrockstow
57 Dolton
A312A 58
59
60 Lapford
Sutcombe A388
Winkleigh
Coldridge
Stratton
Chilsworthy
Sheepwash
Bude
Holsworthy
A3072
Monkokehampton
77 A3072
78
Marhamchurch
Bridgerule
164
72
73
74
Hatherleigh
75
76
North Tawton
Bow
70
71
Exbourne
Whitstone
Halwill Junction
Northlew
North Tamerton
Ashwater
Folly Gate
Hittisleigh
89
90
91
Germansweek
92
93
170 A30
A3124
96
Boyton
St Giles on the Heath
Meldon
Okehampton
Whiddon Down
Drewsteignton
Bratton Clovelly
94
95
Bridestowe
Chagford
105
106
107
Shortacombe
110
111
Lifton
Lewtrenchard
108
109
Moretonhampstead
Launceston
Lydford
Camelford
Willsworthy
Bradstone
Milton Abbot
Mary Tavy
Postbridge
115
116
117
118
119
120
121
Stoke Climsland
A386
Two Bridges
Widecombe in the Moor
Tavistock
171
Princetown
Dartmeet
Gunnislake A390
125
126
127
128
129
130 Holne
Calstock
Horrabridge
Dousland
Buckfast
Bere Alston
Yelverton
Buckfastleigh
236
Milton Combe
238 239
240 241
Shaugh Prior
132
133
134
135
Cargreen
Bere Ferrers
Lee Moor
Landulph
242 243
244 245
Cornwood
South Brent
Avonwick
Saltash
Plymouth
Plympton
237 Bittaford
Diptford
246 247
248 249
250 251
A38
Ivybridge
138
Torpoint
262 263
Brixton
136
137 Modbury
252 253
254 255
256 257
Holbeton
Millbrook
Down Thomas
Kingston
Loddiswell A379 A381
Kingsand
Knighton
Newton Ferrers
142
143
258
Rame
140
141
Thurlestone
Kingsbridge
Malborough
259
Salcombe
147
148

Wadebridge
Bodmin
Liskeard
Lostwithiel
St Austell
Looe
Fowey
Mevagissey

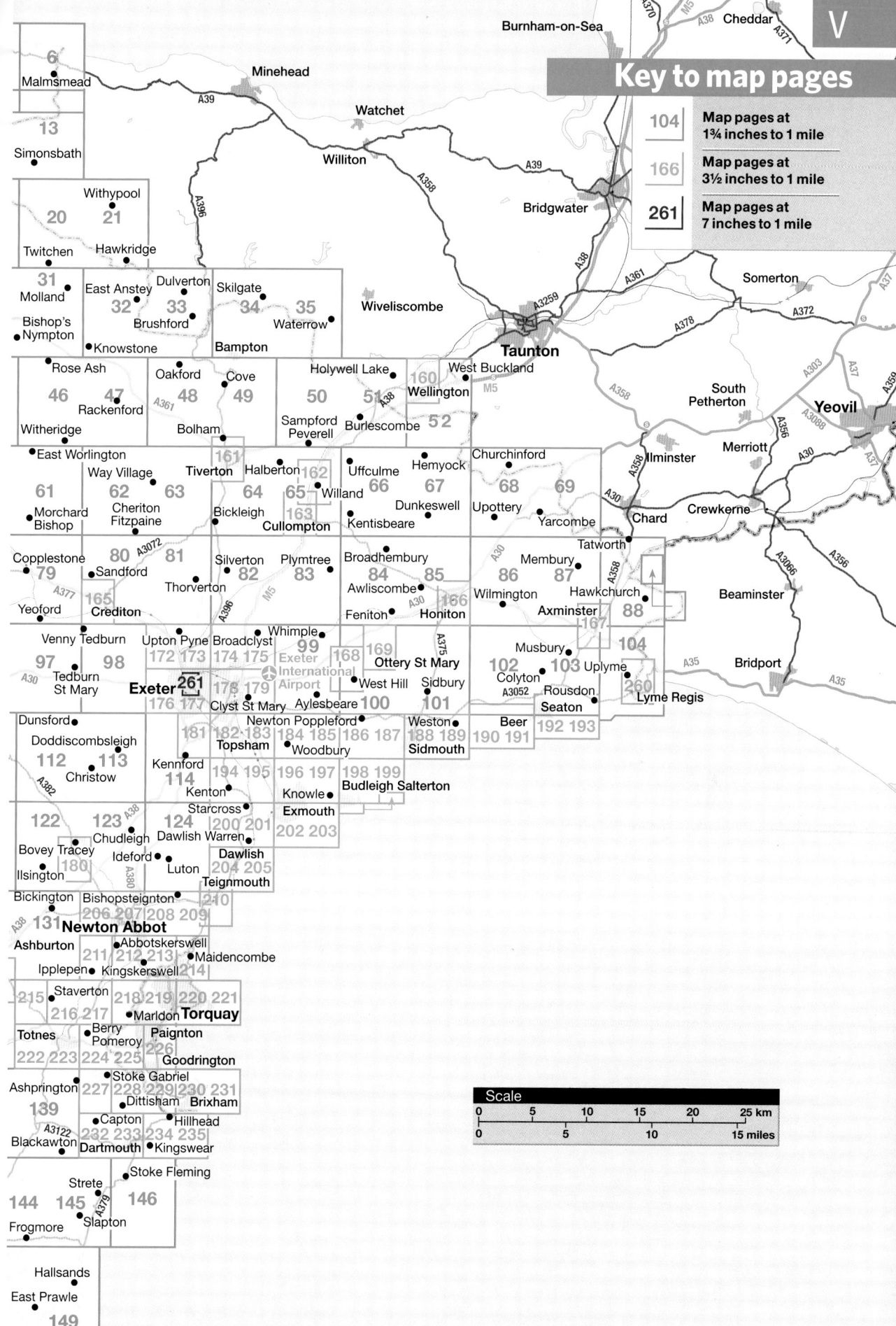

Key to map pages

104	Map pages at 1¾ inches to 1 mile
166	Map pages at 3½ inches to 1 mile
261	Map pages at 7 inches to 1 mile

Burnham-on-Sea
Cheddar

Minehead
Watchet
Williton
Bridgwater

Somerton

Yeovil

6 Malmsmead

13 Simonsbath

20 Twitchen
21 Withypool
Hawkridge

31 Molland
32 East Anstey
33 Dulverton
34 Skilgate
35 Waterrow

Wiveliscombe

Taunton
West Buckland
160 Wellington
South Petherton
Merriott

Bishop's Nympton
Knowstone
Brushford
Bampton

46 Rose Ash
47 Rackenford
48 Oakford
49 Cove
50 Holywell Lake
51 52
Sampford Peverell
Burlescombe

Witheridge
Bolham

Ilminster

61 Morchard Bishop
62 Cheriton Fitzpaine
63 Way Village
East Worlington
161 Tiverton
64 Halberton
65 Willand
66 Uffculme
67 Hemyock
68 Churchinford
69
Chard
Crewkerne

162
163 Cullompton
Bickleigh
Kentisbeare
Dunkeswell
Upottery
Yarcombe

79 Copplestone
80 Sandford
81 Thorverton
82 Silverton
83 Plymtree
84 Broadhembury
85
Awliscombe
86 Wilmington
87 Membury
88 Hawkchurch
Tatworth
Beaminster

165 Crediton
Yeoford
166 Honiton
Feniton
167 Axminster
Bridport

97 Venny Tedburn
98 Tedburn St Mary
Upton Pyne
172 173 Broadclyst
174 175
99 Whimple
168 169 Ottery St Mary
West Hill
Sidbury
102 Colyton
103 Uplyme
Musbury
104
360 Lyme Regis

Exeter 261
Exeter International Airport
176 177 178 179
Clyst St Mary
Aylesbeare
100 101
Rousdon
Seaton
Beer

112 Dunsford
Doddiscombsleigh
113 Christow
181 Newton Poppleford
182 183 184 185 186 187
Topsham
Woodbury
188 189 Sidmouth
Weston
190 191
192 193

122 123 124
Kennford
114
Kenton
Starcross
194 195 196 197 198 199
Knowle
Budleigh Salterton
202 203 Exmouth
200 201

Bovey Tracey
180 Ideford
Chudleigh
Luton
204 205 Dawlish
210 Teignmouth
Dawlish Warren

Ilsington
Bickington
131 Newton Abbot
Bishopsteignton
206 207 208 209

Ashburton
211 212 213 Abbotskerswell
214 Maidencombe
Ipplepen
Kingskerswell

215 216 217 Staverton
218 219 220 221
Marldon Torquay
Totnes
Berry Pomeroy
Paignton
222 223 224 225 226 Goodrington

Ashprington
139 227 228 229 230 231
Stoke Gabriel
Dittisham
Brixham

Blackawton
232 233 234 235
Capton
Dartmouth
Hillhead
Kingswear

Strete
144 145 146
Frogmore
Slapton
Stoke Fleming

Hallsands
East Prawle
149

Scale					
0	5	10	15	20	25 km
0		5	10		15 miles

Route planning

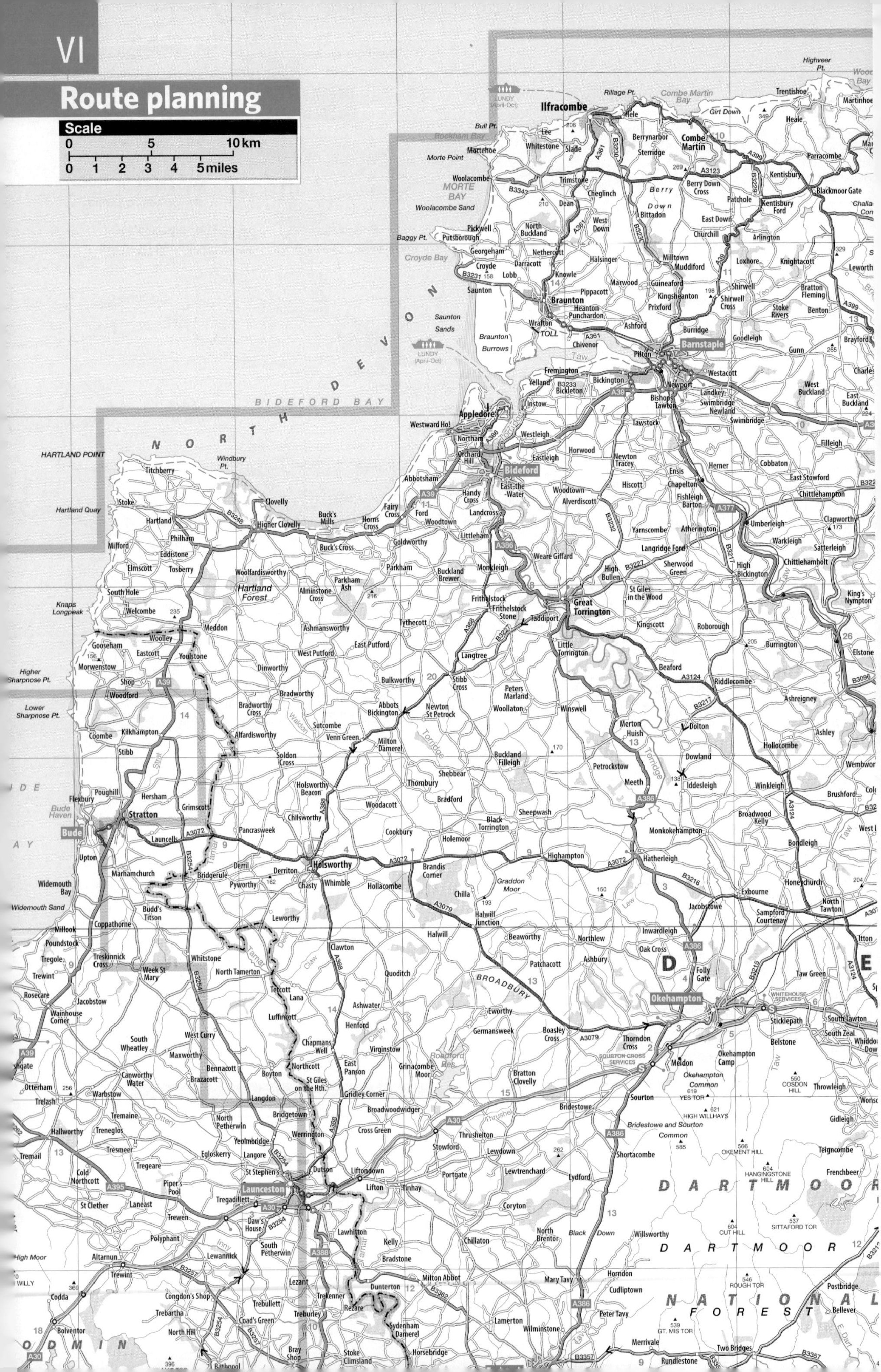

Scale

```
0          5          10km
0  1  2  3  4  5miles
```

NORTH DEVON

BIDEFORD BAY

HARTLAND POINT

DARTMOOR

DARTMOOR NATIONAL FOREST

BODMIN

Ilfracombe · Combe Martin · Barnstaple · Braunton · Appledore · Bideford · Great Torrington · Bude · Stratton · Holsworthy · Launceston · Okehampton

Lundy (April-Oct)

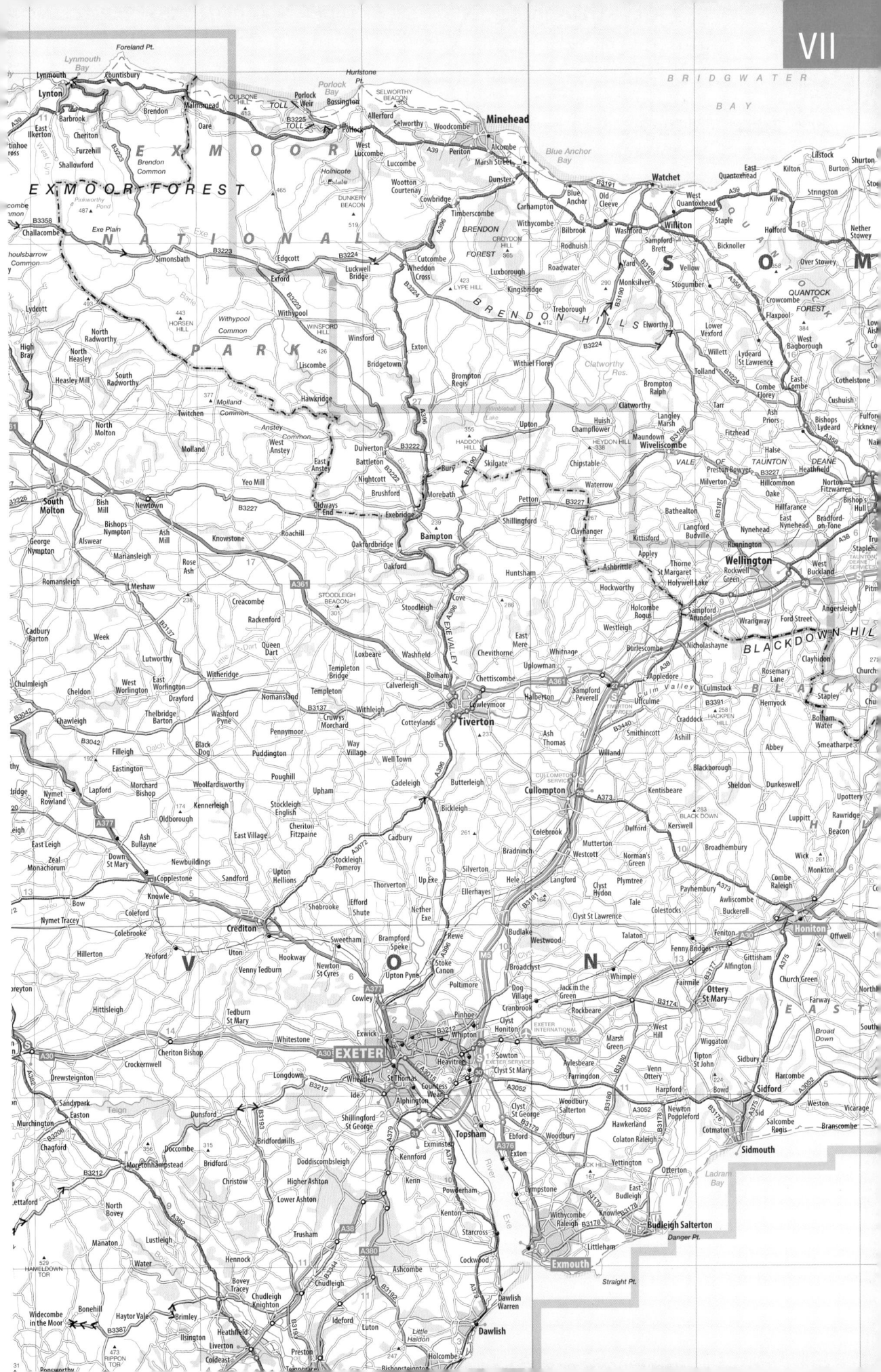
BRIDGWATER
BAY
Foreland Pt.
Lynmouth Bay
Lynmouth
Lynton
Countisbury
Hurlstone Pt.
Porlock Bay
Porlock Weir
Porlock
Bossington
Selworthy Beacon
Allerford
Selworthy
Woodcombe
Minehead
Alcombe
Blue Anchor Bay
Watchet
Culbone Hill
TOLL
Malmsmead
Brendon
Oare
Barbrook
East Ilkerton
Cheriton
Furzehill
Shallowford
Brendon Common
EXMOOR
EXMOOR FOREST
Pinkworthy Pond
Exe Plain
Challacombe
NATIONAL
PARK
West Luccombe
Holnicote Estate
Luccombe
Wootton Courtenay
Dunkery Beacon
Cowbridge
Timberscombe
Periton
Marsh Street
Dunster
Carhampton
Blue Anchor
Old Cleeve
Withycombe
Bilbrook
Washford
Williton
Sampford Brett
Rodhuish
Roadwater
Yard
Monksilver
Vellow
Stogumber
BRENDON FOREST
Croydon Hill
Luxborough
Kingsbridge
Treborough
BRENDON HILLS
Elworthy
Simonsbath
Edgcott
Exford
Cutcombe
Wheddon Cross
Luckwell Bridge
Lype Hill
Withypool
Withypool Common
Horsen Hill
Winsford Hill
Winsford
Exton
Bridgetown
Liscombe
Hawkridge
Withiel Florey
Brompton Regis
Clatworthy Res.
Brompton Ralph
Clatworthy
Lydcott
High Bray
North Radworthy
North Heasley
South Radworthy
Heasley Mill
Twitchen
Molland Common
Anstey Common
West Anstey
East Anstey
North Molton
Molland
Dulverton
Battleton
Nightcott
Brushford
Haddon Hill
Wimbleball Lake
Upton
Huish Champflower
Heydon Hill
Skilgate
Bury
Chipstable
Waterrow
Petton
Morebath
Exebridge
Oldways End
Yeo Mill
South Molton
Bish Mill
Newtown
Bishops Nympton
Ash Mill
George Nympton
Alswear
Knowstone
Roachill
Oakfordbridge
Bampton
Shillingford
Clayhanger
Marianslelgh
Rose Ash
Romansleigh
Meshaw
Oakford
Ashbrittle
Huntsham
Hockworthy
Creacombe
Rackenford
Stoodleigh Beacon
Stoodleigh
Cove
EXE VALLEY
Cadbury Barton
Week
Queen Dart
Loxbeare
Washfield
East Mere
Chevithorne
Whitnage
Uplowman
Lutworthy
Witheridge
Templeton Bridge
Calverleigh
Bolham
Chettiscombe
Chulmleigh
Cheldon
West Worlington
East Worlington
Drayford
Nomansland
Templeton
Cowleymoor
Tiverton
Halberton
Sampford Peverell
Chawleigh
Thelbridge Barton
Washford Pyne
Cruwys Morchard
Withleigh
Cotteylands
Black Dog
Pennymoor
Ash Thomas
Filleigh
Eastington
Puddington
Way Village
Well Town
Willand
Lapford
Morchard Bishop
Woolfardisworthy
Poughill
Cadeleigh
Butterleigh
Cullompton
Nymet Rowland
Kennerleigh
Stockleigh English
Upham
Bickleigh
Oldborough
Ash Bullayne
East Village
Cheriton Fitzpaine
Cadbury
Bradninch
Colebrook
East Leigh
Zeal Monachorum
Down St Mary
Newbuildings
Stockleigh Pomeroy
Copplestone
Sandford
Upton Hellions
Thorverton
Up Exe
Silverton
Ellerhayes
Hele
Bow
Knowle
Coleford
Shobrooke
Efford
Shute
Nether Exe
Nymet Tracey
Colebrooke
Crediton
Sweetham
Brampford Speke
Rewe
Hillerton
Yeoford
Uton
Hookway
Newton St Cyres
Venny Tedburn
Upton Pyne
Stoke Canon
Cowley
Poltimore
Hittisleigh
Tedburn St Mary
Pinhoe
Exwick
Whitestone
Cheriton Bishop
EXETER
Crockernwell
Drewsteignton
Longdown
Whipton
Heavitree
Sowton
Clyst Honiton
Exeter International
Exeter Services
Clyst St Mary
Wheatley
St Thomas
Ide
Alphington
Countess Wear
Sandypark
Easton
Teign
Murchington
Chagford
Dunsford
Shillingford St George
Exminster
Topsham
Doccombe
Bridford
Bridfordmills
Moretonhampstead
Christow
Doddiscombsleigh
Kennford
Kenn
Higher Ashton
Lower Ashton
North Bovey
Lustleigh
Manaton
Trusham
Powderham
Kenton
Starcross
Hennock
Ashcombe
Cockwood
Hameldown Tor
Bovey Tracey
Chudleigh
Chudleigh Knighton
Dawlish Warren
Dawlish
Widecombe in the Moor
Bonehill
Haytor Vale
Brimley
Ilsington
Heathfield
Liverton
Coldeast
Ideford
Luton
Little Haldon
Preston
Teigngrace
Holcombe
Bishopsteignton
Rippon Tor
Ponsworthy
Ebford
Exton
Lympstone
Woodbury
Woodbury Salterton
Clyst St George
Withycombe Raleigh
Exmouth
Littleham
Straight Pt.
Budleigh Salterton
Danger Pt.
Knowle
East Budleigh
Otterton
Yettington
Black Hill
Colaton Raleigh
Hawkerland
Newton Poppleford
Harpford
Venn Ottery
Farringdon
Aylesbeare
Marsh Green
West Hill
Rockbeare
Jack in the Green
Cranbrook
Dog Village
Broadclyst
Whimple
Budlake
Westwood
Talaton
Clyst St Lawrence
Clyst Hydon
Plymtree
Langford
Mutterton
Westcott
Norman's Green
Dulford
Kerswell
Broadhembury
Tale
Payhembury
Colestocks
Awliscombe
Buckerell
Feniton
Fenny Bridges
Gittisham
Alfington
Fairmile
Ottery St Mary
Honiton
Offwell
Church Green
Farway
EAST
Wiggaton
Tipton St John
Sidbury
Bowd
Sidford
Harcombe
Weston
Salcombe Regis
Sid
Cotmaton
Sidmouth
Ladram Bay
Branscombe
Vicarage
Kentisbeare
Black Down
Blackborough
Sheldon
Dunkeswell
Luppitt
Upottery
Rawridge
Beacon
Wick
Monkton
Combe Raleigh
Abbey
Smeatharpe
Bolham Water
Hemyock
Stapley
Culmstock
Craddock
Hackpen Hill
Ashill
Smithincott
Uffculme
Culm Valley
Appledore
Burlescombe
Westleigh
Holcombe Rogus
Nicholashayne
BLACKDOWN HILLS
Clayhidon
Rosemary Lane
Sampford Arundel
Wrangway
Ford Street
Angersleigh
Holywell Lake
Rockwell Green
Wellington
Thorne St Margaret
Appley
Kittisford
Runnington
West Buckland
Langford Budville
Nynehead
Bathealton
Milverton
Hillcommon
Oake
Hillfarance
Bradford-on-Tone
East Nynehead
Norton Fitzwarren
Bishop's Hull
Heathfield
Halse
TAUNTON DEANE
VALE OF
Preston Bowyer
Maundown
Wiveliscombe
Langley Marsh
Fitzhead
Ash Priors
Bishops Lydeard
Tarr
Combe Florey
East Combe
Tolland
Lydeard St Lawrence
Willett
Lower Vexford
West Bagborough
QUANTOCK FOREST
Crowcombe
Flaxpool
Bicknoller
Over Stowey
Nether Stowey
Holford
Staple
Kilve
West Quantoxhead
East Quantoxhead
Kilton
Lilstock
Burton
Stringston
Shurton
Cothelstone
Cushuish
Fulford
Pickney
Tiverton Services
Cullompton Services
Taunton Deane Services
V
O
N
S
O
M

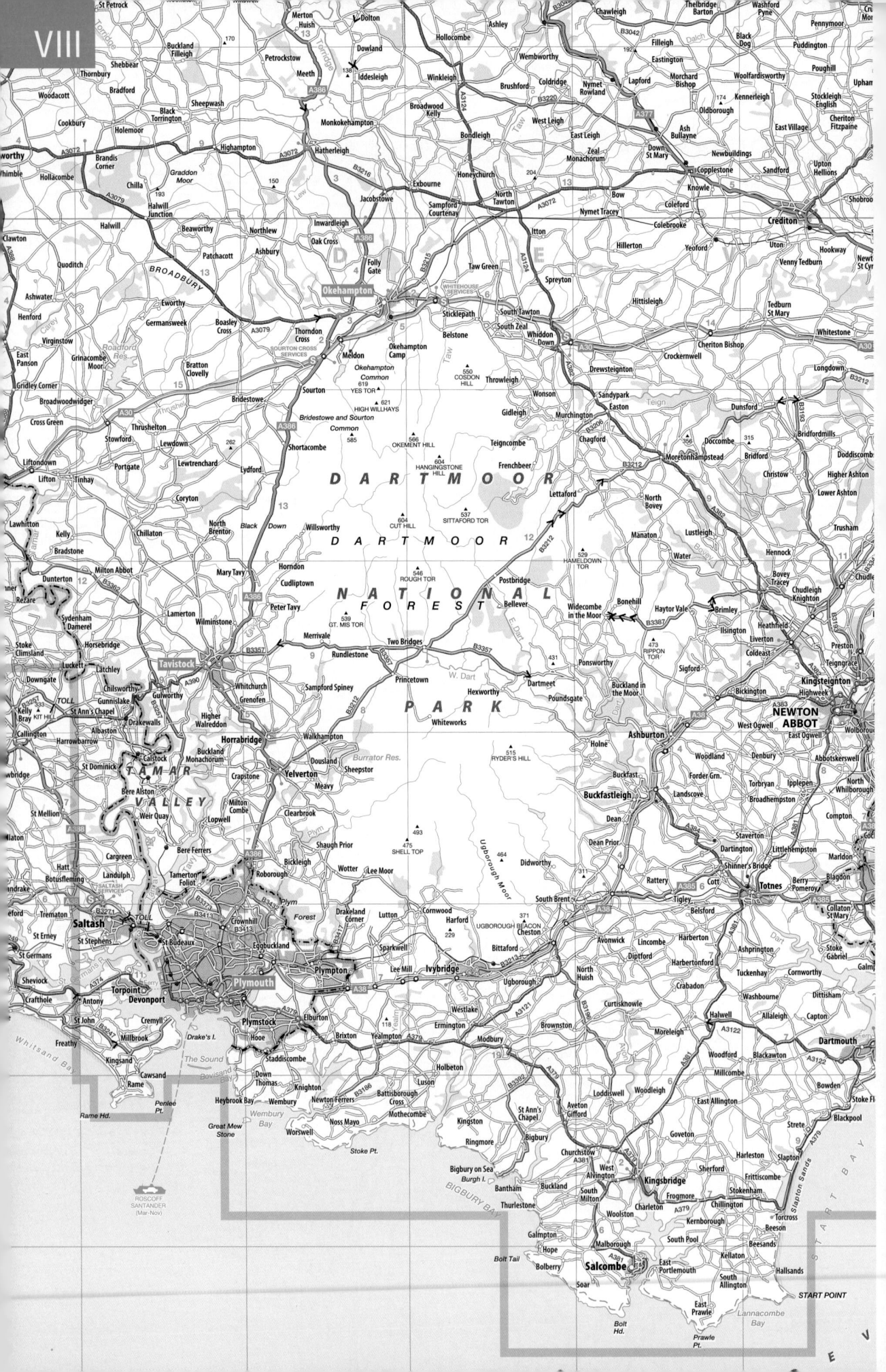

St Petrock
Merton
Huish
Dolton
Ashley
Chawleigh
Thelbridge Barton
Washford Pyne
Pennymoor
Buckland Filleigh
170
Petrockstow
Dowland
Hollocombe
B3042
Filleigh
Black Dog
Puddington
Shebbear
Thornbury
Meeth
138
Iddesleigh
Winkleigh
Wembworthy
192
Eastington
Lapford
Morchard Bishop
Woolfardisworthy
Poughill
Bradford
A386
Brushford
Coldridge
Nymet Rowland
174
Kennerleigh
Stockleigh English
Woodacott
Sheepwash
Black Torrington
Monkokehampton
A3124
Broadwood Kelly
B3220
Oldborough
Cheriton Fitzpaine
Cookbury
Holemoor
West Leigh
A377
Ash Bullayne
East Village
worthy
A3072
Highampton
A3072
Hatherleigh
Bondleigh
East Leigh
Down St Mary
Newbuildings
Upton Hellions
Brandis Corner
Zeal Monachorum
204
Copplestone
Sandford
Hollacombe
Graddon Moor
150
B3216
Honeychurch
Knowle
Chilla
193
Exbourne
North Tawton
A3072
Bow
Coleford
Halwill Junction
A3079
Jacobstowe
Sampford Courtenay
Nymet Tracey
Crediton
Halwill
Inwardleigh
Colebrooke
Beaworthy
Northlew
Oak Cross
Itton
Clawton
A386
Hillerton
Yeoford
Uton
Hookway
Patchacott
Ashbury
Folly Gate
B3215
A3124
Quoditch
Taw Green
Venny Tedburn
BROADBURY
Spreyton
Ashwater
Okehampton
WHITEHOUSE SERVICES
Hittisleigh
Tedburn St Mary
Eworthy
Henford
Sticklepath
South Tawton
Germansweek
Boasley Cross
A3079
Thorndon Cross
Belstone
South Zeal
Whiddon Down
A30
Cheriton Bishop
Whitestone
Virginstow
Meldon
Okehampton Camp
Crockernwell
East Panson
Grinacombe Moor
Roadford Res.
SOURTON CROSS SERVICES
Bratton Clovelly
Okehampton Common
550 COSDON HILL
Drewsteignton
Longdown
619 YES TOR
Throwleigh
B3212
Gridley Corner
Sourton
621 HIGH WILLHAYS
Wonson
Sandypark
Teign
Broadwoodwidger
Bridestowe
Easton
Dunsford
A30
A382
Bridestowe and Sourton Common
Gidleigh
Murchington
B3193
Cross Green
Thrushelton
A386
B3206
Stowford
585
566 OKEMENT HILL
Chagford
356
Doccombe
315
Bridfordmills
Lewdown
262
Shortacombe
Teigncombe
Moretonhampstead
Bridford
Doddiscombsleigh
Portgate
Lewtrenchard
Lydford
604 HANGINGSTONE HILL
Frenchbeer
B3212
Christow
Higher Ashton
Liftondown
Lifton
Tinhay
DARTMOOR
Lettaford
Lower Ashton
Coryton
604 CUT HILL
537 SITTAFORD TOR
North Bovey
Lawhitton
North Brentor
Black Down
Willsworthy
Trusham
Kelly
Chillaton
DARTMOOR
Manaton
Lustleigh
Bradstone
B3212
529 HAMELDOWN TOR
Water
Hennock
Horndon
546 ROUGH TOR
Bovey
Milton Abbot
Mary Tavy
Dunterton
B3362
Cudliptown
NATIONAL
Postbridge
Bovey Tracey
Chudleigh Knighton
Rezare
A386
FOREST
Bellever
Widecombe in the Moor
Bonehill
Haytor Vale
Brimley
Sydenham Damerel
Lamerton
Peter Tavy
539 GT. MIS TOR
B3387
Wilminstone
Heathfield
Ilsington
Stoke Climsland
Horsebridge
Merrivale
Two Bridges
B3357
473 RIPPON TOR
Liverton
Preston
Tavistock
B3357
Rundlestone
E. Dart
Ponsworthy
431
Coldeast
Teigngrace
Luckett
Latchley
W. Dart
Sigford
A382
Downgate
A390
Princetown
Dartmeet
Buckland in the Moor
Kingsteignton
Chilsworthy
Whitchurch
Sampford Spiney
Hexworthy
Bickington
Highweek
Kelly Bray
Gunnislake
333 KIT HILL
TOLL
Gulworthy
Grenofen
B3212
PARK
Poundsgate
A383
NEWTON ABBOT
St Ann's Chapel
Drakewalls
Higher Walreddon
Whiteworks
A38
West Ogwell
Callington
Albaston
Walkhampton
Ashburton
East Ogwell
Harrowbarrow
Horrabridge
Holne
515 RYDER'S HILL
Calstock
Buckland Monachorum
Dousland
Burrator Res.
Woodland
Denbury
Abbotskerswell
St Dominick
TAMAR
Sheepstor
Buckfast
Forder Grn.
Ipplepen
Crapstone
Yelverton
Meavy
Torbryan
North Whilborough
Bere Alston
VALLEY
Milton Combe
Buckfastleigh
Landscove
Broadhempston
Weir Quay
Clearbrook
St Mellion
Lopwell
Dean
Compton
A388
Plym
493
Ugborough Moor
Staverton
Shaugh Prior
475 SHELL TOP
Dean Prior
Dartington
Littlehempston
Cargreen
Bere Ferrers
A386
464
Marldon
Roborough
Bickleigh
Didworthy
311
Shinner's Bridge
Hatt
Landulph
Wotter
Lee Moor
Berry Pomeroy
Blagdon
Botusfleming
Tamerton Foliot
Rattery
Cott
SALTASH SERVICES
Plym
A385
Totnes
A385
B3373
South Brent
Collaton St Mary
B3432
Tigley
Trematon
B3271
Saltash
B3413
Crownhill
Drakeland Corner
Lutton
Cornwood
A38
Belsford
TOLL
Forest
371
B3417
Harford
UGBOROUGH BEACON
Cheston
229
A381
St Erney
St Stephens
St Budeaux
Eggbuckland
Avonwick
Lincombe
Harberton
Dart
Sparkwell
Bittaford
Stoke Gabriel
St Germans
Diptford
Ashprington
Plympton
Lee Mill
Ivybridge
B3213
Harbertonford
Sheviock
A374
Torpoint
Plymouth
North Huish
Tuckenhay
Cornworthy
Crafthole
Devonport
A38
Ugborough
Crabadon
Antony
Erme
Washbourne
Dittisham
Cremyll
A379
Elburton
Westlake
Curtisknowle
St John
Plymstock
A3121
Halwell
Allaleigh
Capton
B3247
Drake's I.
118
Yealm
Ermington
Brownston
Millbrook
Hooe
Brixton
Yealmpton
A379
B3196
A3122
Freathy
Modbury
Moreleigh
Whitsand Bay
The Sound
Staddiscombe
Woodford
Blackawton
Dartmouth
Kingsand
19
A379
A3122
Cawsand
Bovisand Bay
Down Thomas
Holbeton
Millcombe
Rame
Knighton
Luson
A381
Bowden
Penlee Pt.
Heybrook Bay
Wembury
Newton Ferrers
B3186
B3392
Loddiswell
Woodleigh
Battisborough Cross
Stoke Fleming
Rame Hd.
Wembury Bay
Mothecombe
St Ann's Chapel
Aveton Gifford
East Allington
Great Mew Stone
Noss Mayo
Kingston
Blackpool
Worswell
Strete
Ringmore
Avon
Bigbury
Goveton
Stoke Pt.
Churchstow
A381
A379
Bigbury on Sea
Burgh I.
West Alvington
Harleston
Slapton
Sherford
Kingsbridge
Frittiscombe
BIGBURY BAY
Bantham
Buckland
South Milton
Frogmore
Stokenham
ROSCOFF SANTANDER (Mar-Nov)
Thurlestone
Charleton
A379
Chillington
Slapton Sands
START BAY
Woolston
Torcross
Kernborough
Beeson
Galmpton
South Pool
Beesands
Malborough
Hope
Bolt Tail
A381
Kellaton
Bolberry
Salcombe
East Portlemouth
Hallsands
South Allington
Soar
START POINT
East Prawle
Lannacombe Bay
Bolt Hd.
Prawle Pt.

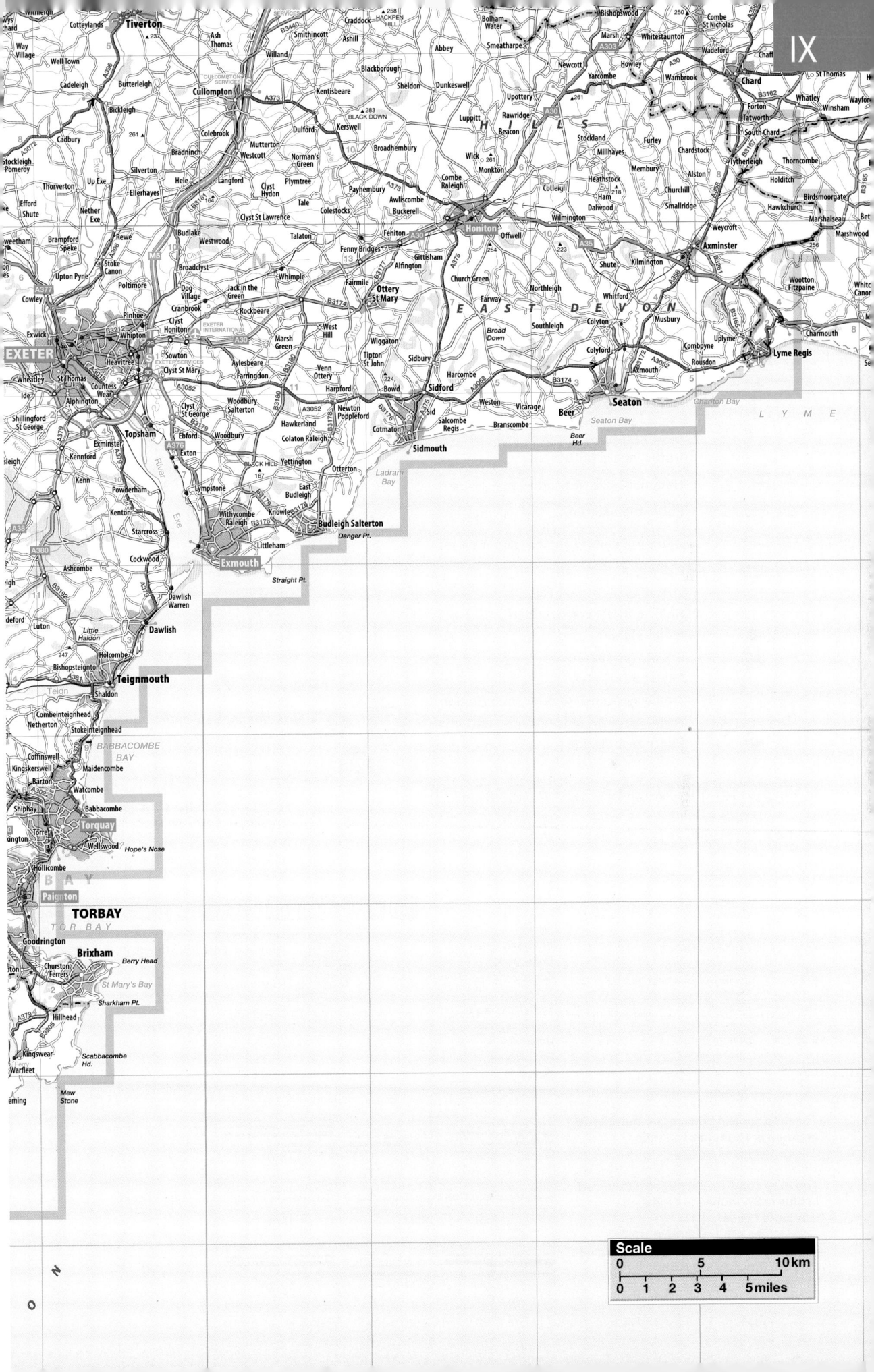

IX
Tiverton
Cotteylands
Way Village
Well Town
Cadeleigh
Butterleigh
Bickleigh
Cadbury
Stockleigh Pomeroy
Thorverton
Up Exe
Silverton
Efford
Shute
Nether Exe
Ellerhayes
Brampford Speke
Rewe
Stoke Canon
Upton Pyne
Poltimore
Cowley
Exwick
Pinhoe
Whipton
EXETER
Heavitree
Wheatley
St Thomas
Countess Wear
Alphington
Ide
Shillingford St George
Exminster
Kennford
Kenn
Powderham
Kenton
Starcross
Cockwood
Ashcombe
Dawlish Warren
Dawlish
Luton
Little Haldon
Holcombe
Bishopsteignton
Teignmouth
Teign
Shaldon
Combeinteignhead
Netherton
Stokeinteignhead
BABBACOMBE BAY
Coffinswell
Kingskerswell
Maidencombe
Barton
Watcombe
Shiphay
Babbacombe
Torquay
Torre
Wellswood
Hope's Nose
Hollicombe
Paignton
TORBAY
TOR BAY
Goodrington
Brixham
Berry Head
Churston Ferrers
St Mary's Bay
Sharkham Pt.
Hillhead
Kingswear
Scabbacombe Hd.
Warfleet
Mew Stone
Ash Thomas
Cullompton
Colebrook
Bradninch
Mutterton
Westcott
Hele
Langford
Clyst Hydon
Plymtree
Budlake
Westwood
Broadclyst
Clyst St Lawrence
Dog Village
Jack in the Green
Whimple
Cranbrook
Rockbeare
Clyst Honiton
EXETER INTERNATIONAL
Sowton
Clyst St Mary
Aylesbeare
Farringdon
Marsh Green
West Hill
Topsham
Clyst St George
Ebford
Woodbury
Woodbury Salterton
Exton
Lympstone
Withycombe Raleigh
Exmouth
Littleham
Straight Pt.
BLACK HILL
Yettington
East Budleigh
Knowle
Budleigh Salterton
Danger Pt.
Otterton
Ladram Bay
Hawkerland
Colaton Raleigh
Newton Poppleford
Harpford
Venn Ottery
Tipton St John
Wiggaton
Bowd
Sidbury
Sidford
Sid
Salcombe Regis
Sidmouth
Cotmaton
Ottery St Mary
Fairmile
Fenny Bridges
Feniton
Alfington
Gittisham
Talaton
Payhembury
Colestocks
Tale
Awliscombe
Buckerell
Norman's Green
Dulford
Kerswell
Kentisbeare
BLACK DOWN
Broadhembury
Blackborough
Sheldon
Willand
Smithincott
Ashill
Craddock
HACKPEN HILL
Bolham Water
Abbey
Smeatharpe
Dunkeswell
Luppitt
Rawridge
Beacon
Upottery
Wick
Monkton
Combe Raleigh
Honiton
Offwell
Church Green
Farway
Broad Down
Southleigh
Northleigh
Harcombe
Weston
Branscombe
Vicarage
Beer
Beer Hd.
Seaton
Seaton Bay
Colyton
Colyford
Axmouth
Whitford
Shute
Kilmington
Musbury
Combpyne
Rousdon
Uplyme
Lyme Regis
Charlton Bay
LYME
Charmouth
Wootton Fitzpaine
EAST DEVON
HILLS
Wilmington
Cotleigh
Dalwood
Ham
Heathstock
Millhayes
Stockland
Membury
Furley
Smallridge
Churchill
Chardstock
Axminster
Weycroft
Alston
Hawkchurch
Birdsmoorgate
Marshalsea
Marshwood
Holditch
Thorncombe
Tytherleigh
South Chard
Tatworth
Forton
Chard
Whatley
Winsham
Wambrook
Howley
Yarcombe
Newcott
Marsh
Whitestaunton
Wadeford
Combe St Nicholas
Bishopswood
St Thomas
Scale
0 5 10km
0 1 2 3 4 5 miles

Key to map symbols

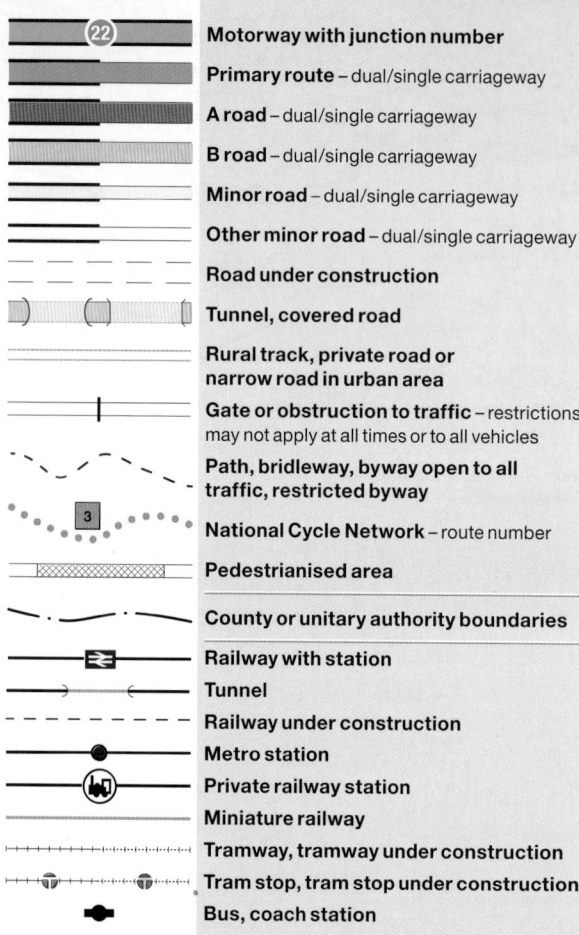

	Motorway with junction number
	Primary route – dual/single carriageway
	A road – dual/single carriageway
	B road – dual/single carriageway
	Minor road – dual/single carriageway
	Other minor road – dual/single carriageway
	Road under construction
	Tunnel, covered road
	Rural track, private road or narrow road in urban area
	Gate or obstruction to traffic – restrictions may not apply at all times or to all vehicles
	Path, bridleway, byway open to all traffic, restricted byway
	National Cycle Network – route number
	Pedestrianised area
	County or unitary authority boundaries
	Railway with station
	Tunnel
	Railway under construction
	Metro station
	Private railway station
	Miniature railway
	Tramway, tramway under construction
	Tram stop, tram stop under construction
	Bus, coach station

	Ambulance station
	Coastguard station
	Fire station
	Police station
	Accident and Emergency entrance to hospital
H	Hospital
+	Place of worship
i	Information centre
P	Shopping centre, parking
P&R PO	Park and Ride, Post Office
	Camping site, caravan site
	Golf course, picnic site
Church ROMAN FORT	Non-Roman antiquity, Roman antiquity
Univ	Important buildings, schools, colleges, universities and hospitals
	Woods, built-up area
River Medway	Water name
	River, weir
	Stream
	Canal, lock, tunnel
	Water
	Tidal water
58 87 246	Adjoining page indicators and overlap bands – the colour of the arrow and band indicates the scale of the adjoining or overlapping page (see scales below)

The dark grey border on the inside edge of some pages indicates that the mapping does not continue onto the adjacent page

The small numbers around the edges of the maps identify the 1-kilometre National Grid lines

Enlarged maps only

	Railway or bus station building
	Place of interest
	Parkland

Abbreviations

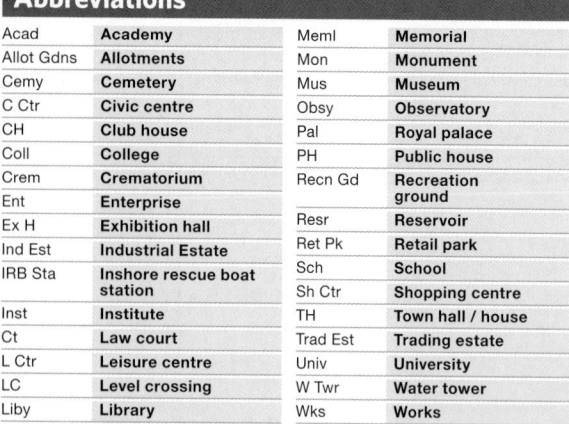

Acad	Academy	Meml	Memorial
Allot Gdns	Allotments	Mon	Monument
Cemy	Cemetery	Mus	Museum
C Ctr	Civic centre	Obsy	Observatory
CH	Club house	Pal	Royal palace
Coll	College	PH	Public house
Crem	Crematorium	Recn Gd	Recreation ground
Ent	Enterprise	Resr	Reservoir
Ex H	Exhibition hall	Ret Pk	Retail park
Ind Est	Industrial Estate	Sch	School
IRB Sta	Inshore rescue boat station	Sh Ctr	Shopping centre
Inst	Institute	TH	Town hall / house
Ct	Law court	Trad Est	Trading estate
L Ctr	Leisure centre	Univ	University
LC	Level crossing	W Twr	Water tower
Liby	Library	Wks	Works
Mkt	Market	YH	Youth hostel

The map scale on the pages numbered in green is 1¾ inches to 1 mile
2.76 cm to 1 km • 1:36 206

The map scale on the pages numbered in blue is 3½ inches to 1 mile
5.52 cm to 1 km • 1:18 103

The map scale on the pages numbered in red is 7 inches to 1 mile
11.04 cm to 1 km • 1:9051

A   B   C   D   E   F

8
51
7
50
6
49
5
48

150

ILFRACOMBE

Ferry P
Lundy (summer only)

The Outfalls
Brandy Cove
Point

Mus
Liby

GRANVILLE RD
WILDER RD
HIGH ST
PO
A399
Sch

TORRS PK

PO

HIGHFIELD RD
MARLBOROUGH RD
Sch

Flat Point

Torrs
Park

H
Sch

Shag Point

LANGLEIGH LA
SOUTH VIEW

ST BRANNOCK'S RD

4

Bull
Point

Pensport
Rock

Lee Bay

South West Coast Path

LANGLEIGH PK

Langleigh

27

SLADE RD
SLADE RD
CAIRNSIDE

FURZE HILL RD

Tarka Trail

HORNE LA

LOWER
GREYSTONE

Whitestone
Farm

• Mast
Higher
Slade

BROOKDALE PARK RD

47

P

Lee

PH

Lincombe

CAIRNSIDE

3

P

HIGHER SLADE RD

Lower
Slade

SLADE VALLEY RD

Hotel

+

Higher
Warcombe

8

Pludd

SLADE CL

46

NORTH
MORTE
RD

Dumage
Barton

Windcutter
Hill

Lower
Campscott

DISSUE LA

P

Mullacott

A361

2

CHANNEL
VIEW

Easewell

BOROUGH VALLEY

DIBBON'S LA

Slade
Resrs

X

Mortehoe

WARCOMBE LA

Shaftsboro
Farm

Middle
Campscott

150

45

SHAFTSBOROUGH LA

Higher
Campscott

Holiday
Park

1 COMMERCIAL POINT
2 WILDERBROOK WAY

MORTEHOE STATION RD

P

Little Shelfin
Farm

PH

Mullacott Cross
Ind Est

1

SEYMOUR BGLWS 1
SEYMOUR VILLAS 2

SANDY LA

Borough
Cross

Borough
Farm

Bickenbridge

B3343
MULLACOTT
CROSS

A3123

HEADLANDS VIEW AVE
HARTLAND VIEW RD

LEE CROSS
WOOLACOMBE
STATION RD

Pool
Farm

POOL LA

B3343

A361

44

46   A   47   B   48   C   49   D   50   E   51   F

7

8

2

For full street detail of the
highlighted area see page 150.

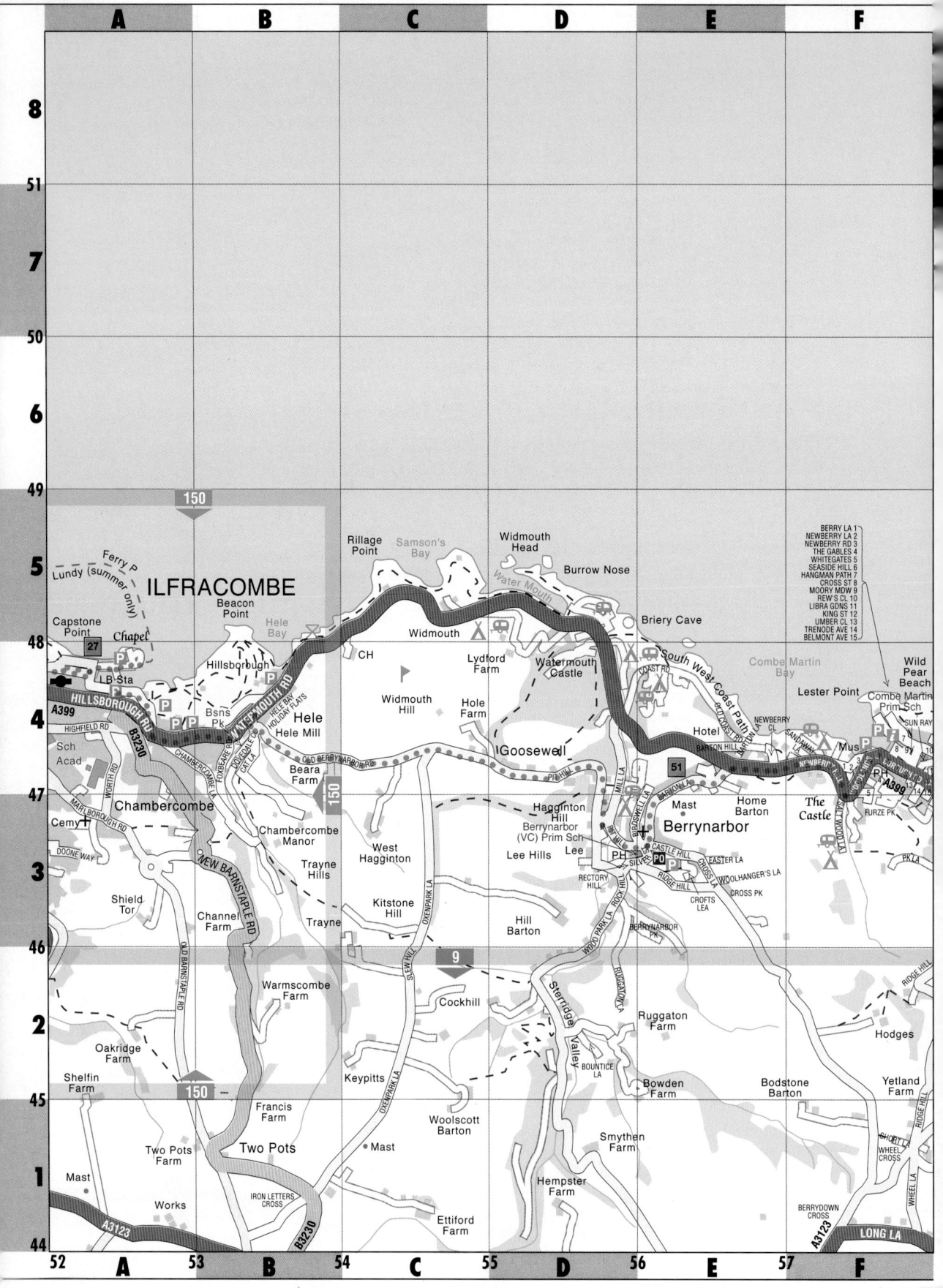

Scale: 1¾ inches to 1 mile

0   ¼   ½   mile

0   250m   500m   750m   1 km

8

51

7

50

6

49

5

48

4

47

3

46

2

45

1

44

A   B   C   D   E   F

52   53   54   55   56   57

150

ILFRACOMBE

Rillage Point

Samson's Bay

Widmouth Head

Burrow Nose

BERRY LA 1
NEWBERRY LA 2
NEWBERRY RD 3
THE GABLES 4
WHITEGATES 5
SEASIDE HILL 6
HANGMAN PATH 7
CROSS ST 8
MOORY MDW 9
REW'S CL 10
LIBRA GDNS 11
KING ST 12
UMBER CL 13
TRENODE AVE 14
BELMONT AVE 15

Lundy (summer only)

Ferry P

Beacon Point

Hele Bay

Water Mouth

Widmouth

Briery Cave

Combe Martin Bay

Wild Pear Beach

Capstone Point

Chapel

27

CH

Lydford Farm

Watermouth Castle

South West Coast Path

Lester Point

Comba Martin Prim Sch

LB Sta

Hillsborough

Hillsborough

Widmouth Hill

Hole Farm

Coast Rd

Hotel

NEWBERRY CL

SUN RAY

HILLSBOROUGH RD

A399

Bsns Pk

HELE BAY HOLIDAY FLATS

Goosewell

Barton Hill Rd

Mus

PH

A399

HIGHFIELD RD

B3230

LYNMOUTH RD

Hele

Hele Mill

OLD BERRYNARBOR RD

NEWBERRY LA

Home Barton

The Castle

FURZE PK

Sch Acad

WORTH RD

CHAMBERCOMBE LA

Beara Farm

150

Mast

Berrynarbor

PK LA

Chambercombe

Cemy

MARLBOROUGH RD

Chambercombe Manor

West Hagginton

Hagginton Hill

Berrynarbor (VC) Prim Sch

Lee

Mast

CASTLE HILL

EASTER LA

WOOLHANGER'S LA

DOONE WAY

NEW BARNSTAPLE RD

Trayne Hills

Lee Hills

PH

SILVER

PO

RECTORY HILL

RIDGE HILL

CROSS PK

Shield Tor

Channel Farm

Kitstone Hill

Trayne

Hill Barton

WOOD PARK LA

ROCK HILL

BERRYNARBOR PK

CROFTS LEA

RIDGE HILL

OLD BARNSTAPLE RD

SLEW HILL

OXENPARK LA

9

Cockhill

Sterridge Valley

RUGGATON LA

Ruggaton Farm

Hodges

Warmscombe Farm

BOUNTICE LA

Bowden Farm

Bodstone Barton

Yetland Farm

Oakridge Farm

150

Keypitts

Smythen Farm

SHORT WHEEL CROSS

Shelfin Farm

Francis Farm

OXENPARK LA

Woolscott Barton

Hempster Farm

WHEEL LA

RIDGE HILL

Mast

Two Pots Farm

Two Pots

Mast

Ettiford Farm

BERRYDOWN CROSS

LONG LA

Works

IRON LETTERS CROSS

A3123

B3230

A3123

For full street detail of the highlighted area see page 150.

1

9

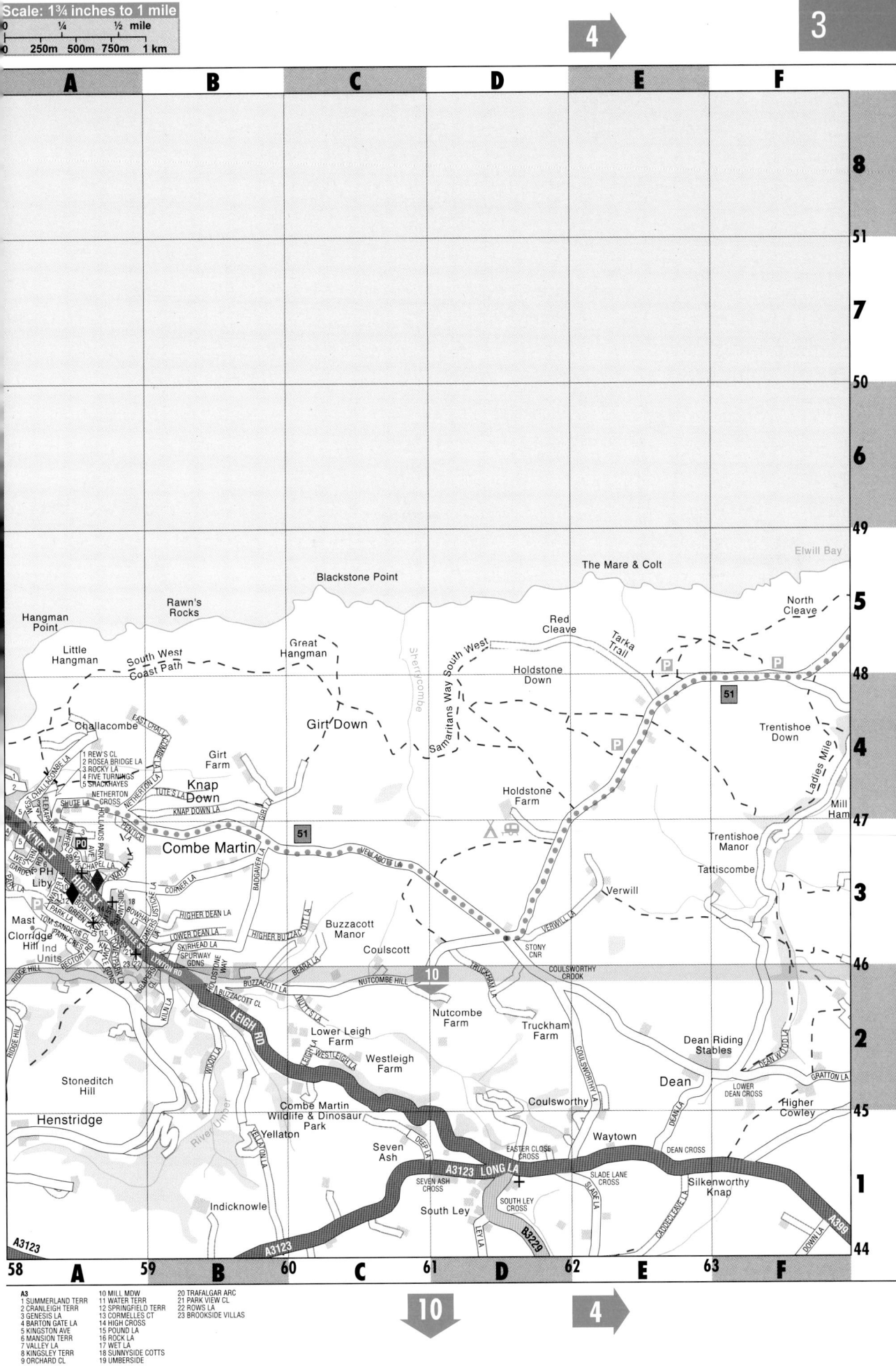

A   B   C   D   E   F

8

51

7

50

6

49

5

48

4

47

3

46

2

45

1

44

Hangman
Point

Little
Hangman

Rawn's
Rocks

Blackstone Point

The Mare & Colt

Elwill Bay

North
Cleave

Red
Cleave

Tarka
Trail

South West
Coast Path

Great
Hangman

Girt Down

Samaritans Way South West

Holdstone
Down

Trentishoe
Down

Challacombe

EAST CHALLA

Girt
Farm

Knap
Down

Ladies Mile

Mill
Ham

1 REW'S CL
2 ROSEA BRIDGE LA
3 ROCKY LA
4 FIVE TURNINGS
5 SHACKHAYES

NETHERTON
CROSS

SHUTE LA

TUTE'S LA

KNAP DOWN LA

Holdstone
Farm

51

Trentishoe
Manor

Tattiscombe

PO

PH
Liby

HIGH ST

Combe Martin

HIGHER DEAN LA

LOWER DEAN LA

BADGAVER LA

NEW RD

Buzzacott
Manor

Coulscott

Verwill

VERWILL LA

STONY
CNR

Mast

Clorridge
Hill
Ind
Units

RIDGE HILL

LEIGH RD

WOOD LA

SKIRHEAD LA
SPURWAY
GDNS

BUZZACOTT LA

HIGHER BUZZA

BEARA LA

NUTT'S LA

NUTCOMBE HILL

10

TRUCKHAM LA

COULSWORTHY
CROOK

46

Stoneditch
Hill

Henstridge

River Umber

FELLACOTT LA

BUZZACOTT CL

KILN LA

WESTLEIGH LA

Lower Leigh
Farm

Westleigh
Farm

Nutcombe
Farm

Truckham
Farm

COULSWORTHY LA

DEAN LA

DEAN WOOD LA

Dean Riding
Stables

Dean

LOWER
DEAN CROSS

Higher
Cowley

GRATTON LA

Combe Martin
Wildlife & Dinosaur
Park

Yellaton

Seven
Ash

DEEP LA

Coulsworthy

EASTER CLOSE
CROSS

Waytown

SLADE LANE
CROSS

SLADE LA

DEAN CROSS

Silkenworthy
Knap

CADDECLEAVE LA

A3123

SEVEN ASH
CROSS

A3123

South Ley

LONG LA

SOUTH LEY
CROSS

LEY LA

B3229

Indicknowle

A3123

DOWN LA

A399

A3
1 SUMMERLAND TERR
2 CRANLEIGH TERR
3 GENESIS LA
4 BARTON GATE LA
5 KINGSTON AVE
6 MANSION TERR
7 VALLEY LA
8 KINGSLEY TERR
9 ORCHARD CL

10 MILL MDW
11 WATER TERR
12 SPRINGFIELD TERR
13 CORMELLES CT
14 HIGH CROSS
15 POUND LA
16 ROCK LA
17 WET LA
18 SUNNYSIDE COTTS
19 UMBERSIDE

20 TRAFALGAR ARC
21 PARK VIEW CL
22 ROWS LA
23 BROOKSIDE VILLAS

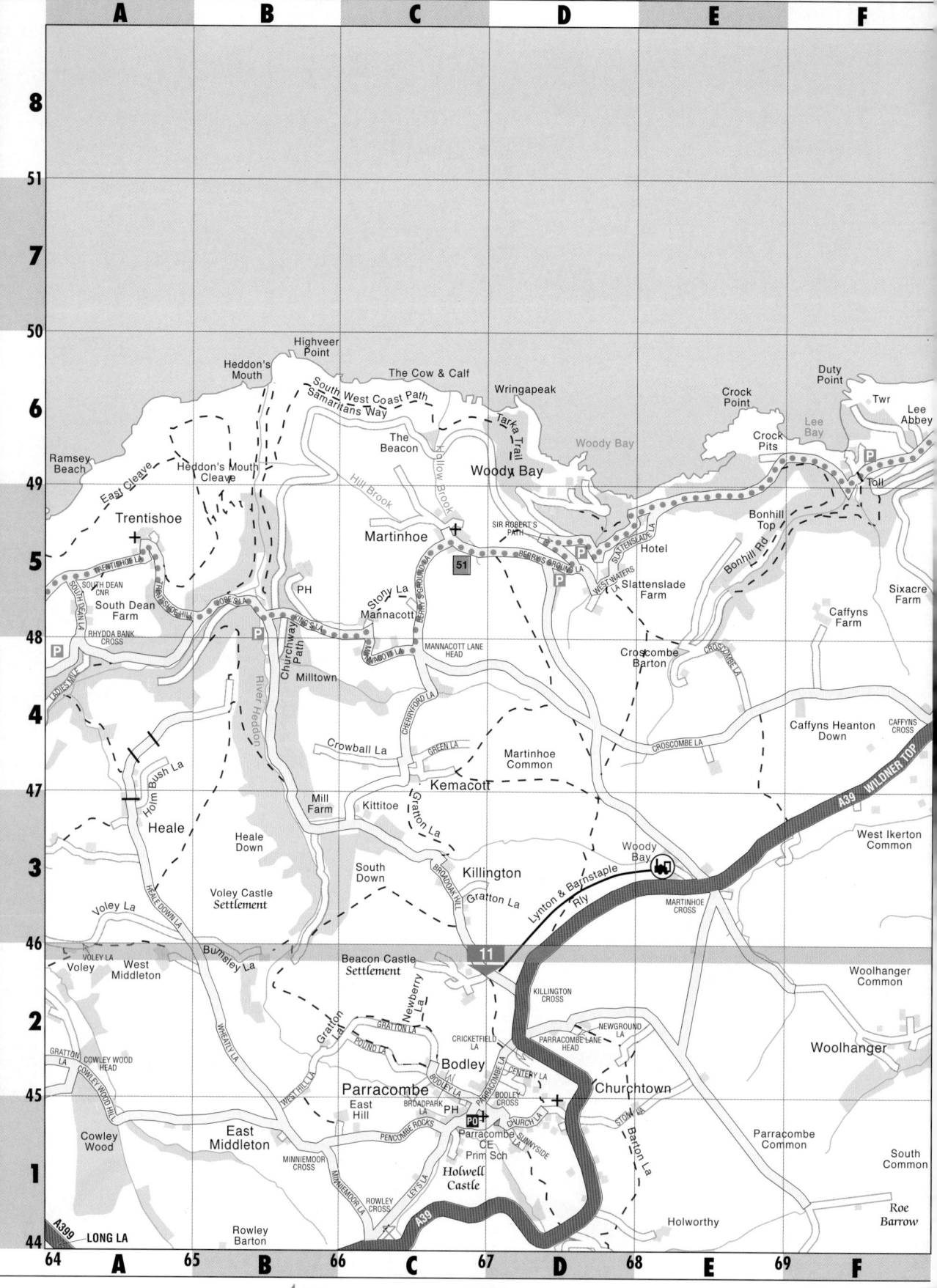

A   B   C   D   E   F

8

51

7

50

6

49

5

48

4

47

3

46

2

45

1

44

Ramsey Beach

East Cleave

Trentishoe

TRENTISHOE LA

SOUTH DEAN CNR

South Dean Farm

SOUTH DEAN LA

RHYDDA BANK CROSS

P

LADIES MILE

Heddon's Mouth Cleave

Heddon's Mouth

Highveer Point

The Cow & Calf

South West Coast Path
Samaritans Way

The Beacon

Hill Brook

Hollow Brook

Tarka Trail

Wringapeak

Woody Bay

Woody Bay

Crock Point

Crock Pits

Lee Bay

Duty Point

Twr

Lee Abbey

Martinhoe

Sir Robert's Path

BERRYS GROUND LA

51

P

West Waters La

Slattenslade Farm

Hotel

Bonhill Top

Bonhill Rd

SLATTENSLADE LA

Sixacre Farm

Caffyns Farm

Croscombe Barton

CROSCOMBE LA

Caffyns Heanton Down

Caffyns Cross

Stony La

Mannacott

PH

Churchway Path

KING SLA

River Heddon

Milltown

Mannacott Lane Head

CHERRYFORD LA

GREEN LA

Crowball La

Martinhoe Common

Holm Bush La

Heale

Heale Down

Mill Farm

Kittitoe

GRATTON LA

Kemacott

Killington

BROADOAK HILL

Gratton La

Lynton & Barnstaple Rly

Woody Bay

Martinhoe Cross

CROSCOMBE LA

A39 WILDNER TOP

West Ikerton Common

Voley La

HEALE DOWN LA

Voley Castle Settlement

South Down

Burnsley La

Beacon Castle Settlement

11

Killington Cross

Woolhanger Common

Voley La

Voley

West Middleton

WHEATLY LA

GRATTON LA

Newberry La

GRATTON LA

CRICKETFIELD LA

Bodley

PARRACOMBE LA

NEWGROUND LA

Parracombe Lane Head

Woolhanger

GRATTON LA

Cowley Wood Head

COWLEY WOOD HILL

POUND LA

WEST HILL LA

East Hill

BODLEY LA

BROADPARK LA

PH

Bodley Cross

PENTERY LA

CHURCH LA

Parracombe

Churchtown

STOW LA

BARTON LA

Parracombe Common

Cowley Wood

East Middleton

PENCOMBE ROCKS

P

Parracombe CE Prim Sch

SUNNYSIDE LA

LEYS LA

Holwell Castle

South Common

MINNIEMOOR LA

Minniemoor Cross

Rowley Cross

Holworthy

Roe Barrow

A399

LONG LA

Rowley Barton

A38

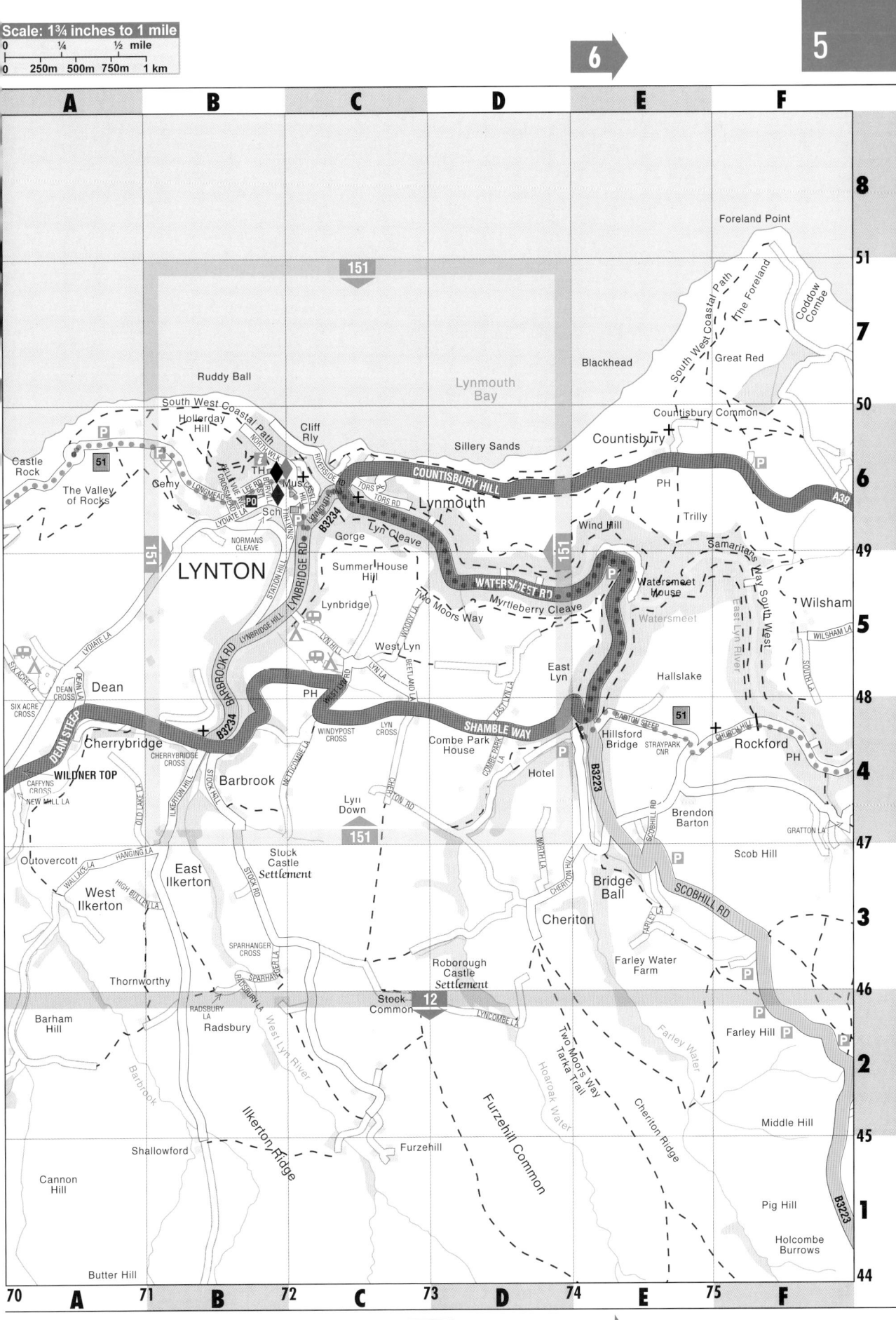

A   B   C   D   E   F

8

51

7

Foreland Point

151

50

South West Coastal Path

Trne Foreland

Coddow Combe

Ruddy Ball

Blackhead

Great Red

Lynmouth Bay

Countisbury Common

South West Coastal Path

Hollerday Hill

Cliff Rly

Countisbury

6

A39

Sillery Sands

COUNTISBURY HILL

PH

Castle Rock

51

Cerny

Mus

PO

Sch

Lynmouth

TORS RD

Gorge

Lyn Cleave

Wind Hill

Trilly

Samaritans Way South West

The Valley of Rocks

151

WATERSMEET RD

Watersmeet House

49

LYNTON

Summer House Hill

Myrtleberry Cleave

Watersmeet

Wilsham

WILSHAM LA

Lynbridge

Two Moors Way

West Lyn

East Lyn

Hallslake

5

East Lyn River

48

BARBROOK RD

LYNBRIDGE HILL

PH

SHAMBLE WAY

BARTON STEEP

51

CHURCH LA

Rockford

PH

Dean

LYDIATE LA

DEAN STEEP

Cherrybridge

CHERRYBRIDGE CROSS

WINDYPOST CROSS

Combe Park House

Hillsford Bridge

STRAYPARK CNR

Six Acre Cross

DEAN CROSS

Barbrook

Lyn Cross

Hotel

B3223

Brendon Barton

GRATTON LA

4

WILDNER TOP

CAFFYNS CROSS

NEW MILL LA

OLD LAKE LA

STOCK HILL

Lyn Down

CHERITON RD

SCOBHILL RD

Scob Hill

47

ILKERTON HILL

METTICOMBE LA

151

Stock Castle Settlement

NORTH LA

Bridge Ball

Cheriton

FARLEY LA

TIMBERS RD

Outovercott

HANGING LA

WALLACK LA

East Ilkerton

HIGH BULLEN LA

STOCK RD

SPARHANGER CROSS

SPARHANGER LA

Roborough Castle Settlement

LYNCOMBE LA

Farley Water Farm

3

West Ilkerton

Thornworthy

RADSBURY LA

Radsbury

West Lyn River

Stock Common

12

Cheriton Ridge

46

Barham Hill

Barbrook

Ilkerton Ridge

Two Moors Way Tarka Trail

Farley Water

Farley Hill

2

Hoaroak Water

Middle Hill

45

Shallowford

Furzehill

Furzehill Common

Pig Hill

B3223

Cannon Hill

1

Butter Hill

Holcombe Burrows

44

70   A   71   B   72   C   73   D   74   E   75   F

For full street detail of the highlighted area see page 151.

12

6

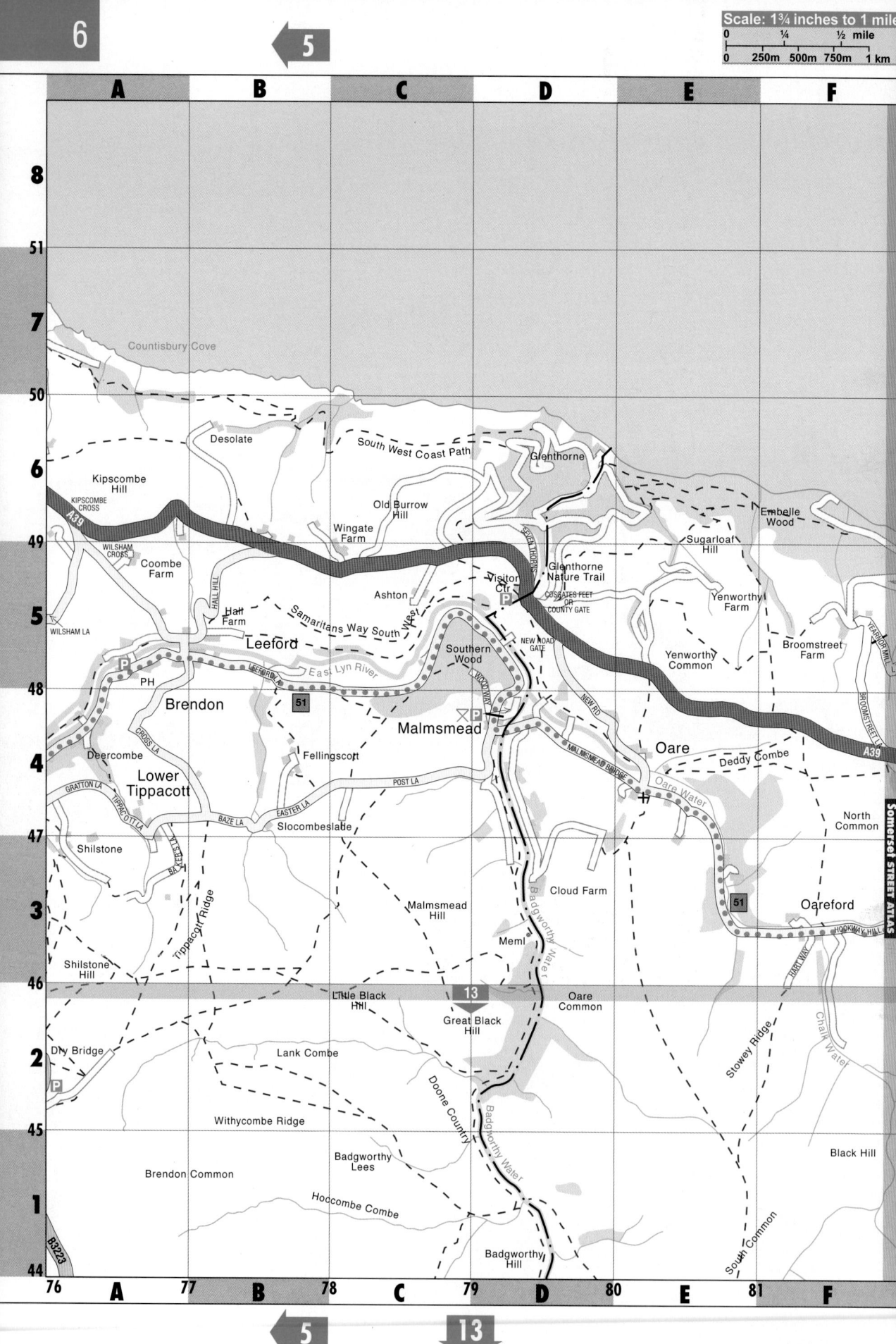

A   B   C   D   E   F

8

51

7

Countisbury Cove

50

6

Desolate

South West Coast Path

Glenthorne

Kipscombe Hill

Old Burrow Hill

Embelle Wood

KIPSCOMBE CROSS

49

A39

WILSHAM CROSS

Wingate Farm

Sugarloaf Hill

Coombe Farm

HALL HILL

Ashton

Glenthorne Nature Trail

Yenworthy Farm

SEVEN THORNS

Visitor Ctr
P

5

Hall Farm

Samaritans Way South

West

COSGATES FEET OR COUNTY GATE

Yenworthy Common

Broomstreet Farm

WILSHAM LA

Leeford

Southern Wood

NEW ROAD GATE

48

P
PH

LEEFORD

East Lyn River

WOODWAY

BROOMSTREET LA

51

NEW RD

Brendon

Malmsmead

P

Oare

A39

4

CROSS LA

Fellingscott

MALMSMEAD BRIDGE

Deddy Combe

Deercombe

POST LA

Oare Water

GRATTON LA

Lower Tippacott

BAZE LA

EASTER LA

Slocombeslade

North Common

TIPPACOTT LA

Shilstone

47

BA EEL'S LA

Tippacott Ridge

Malmsmead Hill

Oareford

51

HOOKWAY HILL

3

Shilstone Hill

Cloud Farm

Meml

HARTWAY

Chalk Water

46

Little Black Hill

13

Oare Common

Dry Bridge

2

Lank Combe

Great Black Hill

Stowey Ridge

P

Doone Country

45

Withycombe Ridge

Badgworthy Lees

Badgworthy Water

Black Hill

1

Brendon Common

Hoccombe Combe

South Common

B3223

Badgworthy Hill

44

76   A   77   B   78   C   79   D   80   E   81   F

5   13

Somerset STREET ATLAS

Morte
Point

HEADLAND CT 1
KINEVOR CL 2
MORTEHOE STATION RD 3
ADA S TERR 4

Mortehoe

PH
PO

Cemy
Mortehoe
Her Ctr

Grunta
Beach
CASTLE
ROCK
Grunta
Pool
SHARP ROCK S
UPPPER CLAYPARK 6
Hotel
Barricane
Beach

CROSSWAYS
CT

LOWER CLAYPARK

Woolacombe

Meml
ARLINGTON PL 1
THE GROVE 2
ARLINGTON RD 3
FROG ST 4
MILL LA 6
HUNTER LA 5
WEST RD 7
RAWNSLEY LA 8
FAIRHOLME RD 9
SPRINGFIELD RD 10
SANDY LANE CT 11
CLIFFSIDE 12

BEACH RD
BARTON RD
SOUTH ST

P
PO

Hotel

Dunes

P

Mill
Rock

CHALLACOMBE
HILL

Potter's
Hill

MARINE DR

278

Woolacombe
Down

Morte
Bay

Woolacombe Sand

Black
Rock

Putsborough
Sand

DOWN LA

Whiting
Hole

Long
Bar

Vention

Pickwell

South West Coast Path

Baggy
Point

Croyde
Hoe

Ramson La

CLIFTON
CT

VENTON RD

P

Manor
House

Putsborough

Middleborough
Hill

Middlehill La

BROADWAY LA

MIDDLEBOROUGH LA

New
La

STENTAWAY LA

MEADOW LA

COMBAS LA

PUTSBOROUGH RD

Croyde
Bay

P

Hotel

TOM'S
FIELD

Ora Hill

Croyde

North
Hole

MOOR LA

PARK CR

MOOR

LANE HEAD CL

ORA CL

PENNY
HILL

MILLERS
BROOK

Forda
Hill

FROGSTREET HILL

BEACH RD

Croyde Bay

CROYDE
SANDS
BGLWS

P
PH

ST MARY'S RD

CLOUTMAN'S

HOBB'S HILL

GEORGEHAM RD

HOLE CLEAVE RD

Cross

South
Hole
Farm

Dunes

WEST GOVER LA

SANDY LA

PATHDOWN

MILKARA LA

B3231

COTT LA

ORCHARD CR

CROYDE RD

P

P

Chapel

SOMETHING LA

WITHY LA

LANGFIELD

1 ORA STONE PK
2 BONNICOTT LA
3 LEADENGATE FIELDS
4 LEADENGATE CL
5 SANDY WAY
6 ST HELEN'S CL
7 HOME FARM CL
8 WATERY LA
9 MYRTLE FARM VIEW
10 SEA BIRDS PK
11 BAY VIEW CL

Saunton
Down

B3231

8

14

8

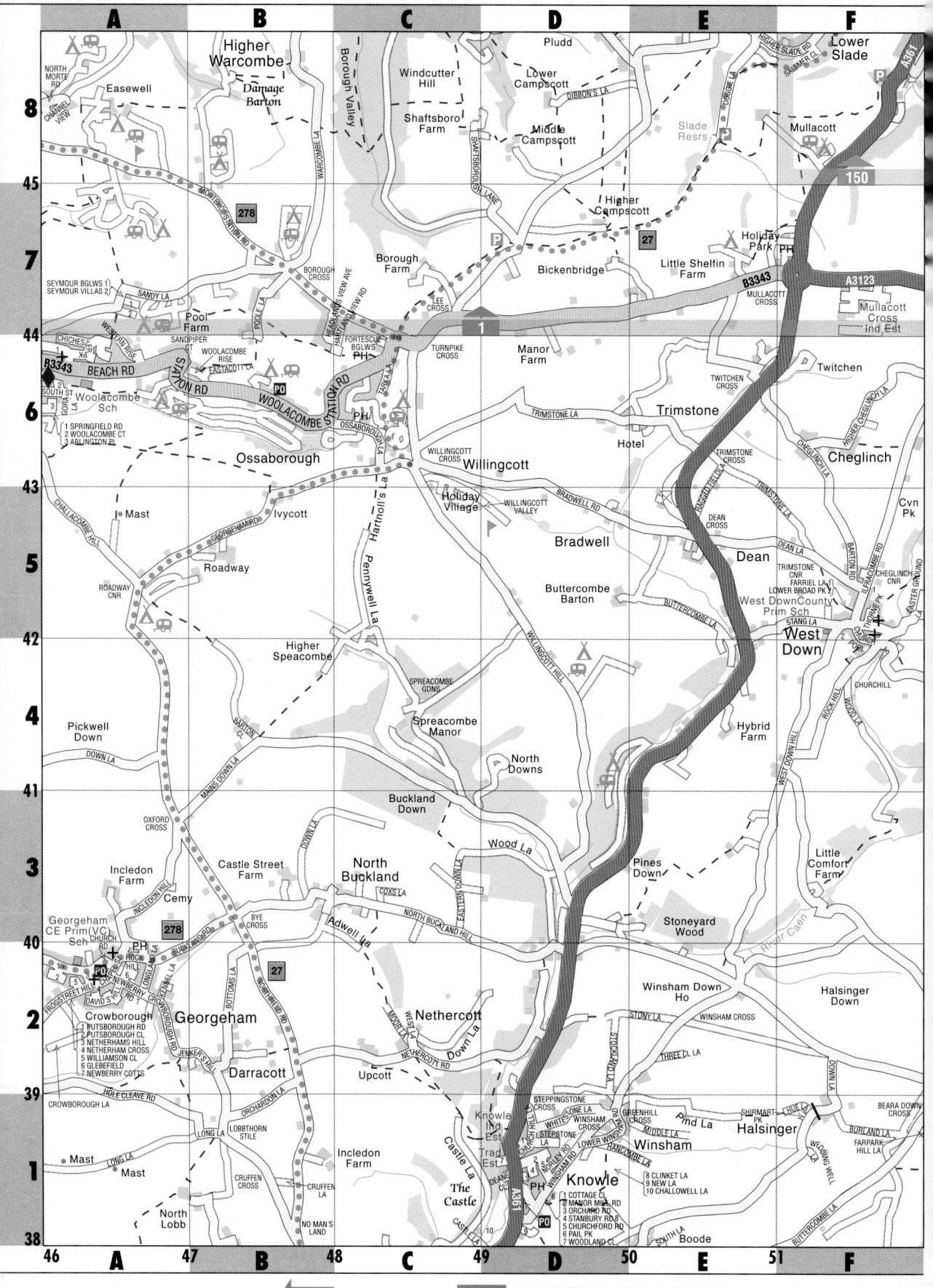

Scale: 1¾ inches to 1 mile

0   ¼   ½   mile
0 250m 500m 750m 1 km

A   B   C   D   E   F

8   North Morte Rd   Easewell   Higher Warcombe   Damage Barton   Borough Valley   Windcutter Hill   Shaftsboro Farm   Pludd   Lower Campscott   Middle Campscott   Higher Slade Rd   Lower Slade   Slade Resrs   Mullacott   P

45   Channel View   278   Borough Cross   Headland View Ave   Hartland View Rd   Borough Farm   Higher Campscott   27   P   Little Shelfin Farm   Holiday Park   PH   150

7   Seymour Bglws 1   Seymour Villas 2   Sandy La   Poole La   Lee Cross   Bickenbridge   B3343   Mullacott Cross   A3123

44   Chiches   B3343   Sandpiper Ct   Fortescue Bglws   PH   Turnpike Cross   Manor Farm   Twitchen Cross   Twitchen   Mullacott Cross Ind Est

6   Beach Rd   South St   Woolacombe Sch   1 Springfield Rd   2 Woolacombe Ct   3 Ablington Pl   Station Rd   Woolacombe Rise   Eastacott La   PO   Woolacombe   PH   Ossaborough La   Willingcott Cross   Willingcott   Hotel   Trimstone   Trimstone Cross   Higher Cheglinch La   Cheglinch

43   Challacombe Hill   Mast   Ossaborough   George Nympton Rd   Ivycott   Hartnol La   Holiday Village   Willingcott Valley   Bradwell Rd   Bradwell   Dean Cross   Dean   Cragged Field   Dean La   Cvn Pk

5   Roadway Cnr   Roadway   Pennywell La   Buttercombe Barton   Buttercombe La   Dean   Trimstone Cnr   Farriel La   Lower Broad Pk   West Down County Prim Sch   Stang La   Ilfracombe Rd   Cheglinch Cnr   Foster Ground

42   Higher Speacombe   Spreacombe Gdns   Spreacombe Manor   West Down   Churchill

4   Pickwell Down   Barton La   Mains Down La   Down La   North Downs   Willingcott Hill   Hybrid Farm   West Down Hill   Rock Hill   Wood La   Churchill

41   Oxford Cross   Buckland Down   Wood La   Pines Down   Little Comfort Farm

3   Incledon Farm   Incledon Hill   Cemy   Castle Street Farm   North Buckland   Coxs La   Eastern Down La   Stoneyard Wood   River Caen   Halsinger Down

40   Georgeham CE Prim(VC) Sch   Church Rd   Rock Hill   PH   278   Bye Cross   Adwell La   North Buckland Hill   Down La

2   Crowborough   1 Putsborough Rd   2 Putsborough Cl   3 Netherhams Hill   4 Netherham Cross   5 Williamson Cl   6 Glebefield   7 Newberry Cotts   Frogstreet Hill   David's Hill   PO   Newberry Rd   Crowborough Rd   Longland La   Buckland Rd   Jenkins Hill   Georgeham   27   Bottoms La   Northfield La   Nethercott   West La   Moor La   Nethercott Rd   Down La   Stony La   Winsham Down Ho   Winsham Cross   Three Cl La   Down La   Halsinger

39   Crowborough La   Hole Cleave Rd   Darracott   Orchardon La   Upcott   Steppingstone Cross   One La   Church La   Whites Stepstone   Stony La   Greenhill Cross   Middle La   Lower Winsham   Shirmart Pk   Blue La   Halsinger   Beara Down La

1   Mast   Long La   Mast   Lobbthorn Stile   Cruffen Cross   Incledon Farm   No Man's Land   Knowle Ind Est   Trad Est   Castle La   Deane La   The Castle   Castle La   PH   A361   PO   10   Knowle   1 Cottage Cl   2 Manor Mill   3 Orchard Rd   4 Stanbury Rd   5 Churchford Rd   6 Pail Pk   7 Woodland Cl   8 Clinket La   9 New La   10 Challowell La   Winsham   South La   Boode   Buttercombe La   Farpark Hill La   Wedding Well   Burland La

38   North Lobb   Cruffen La

46   A   47   B   48   C   49   D   50   E   51   F

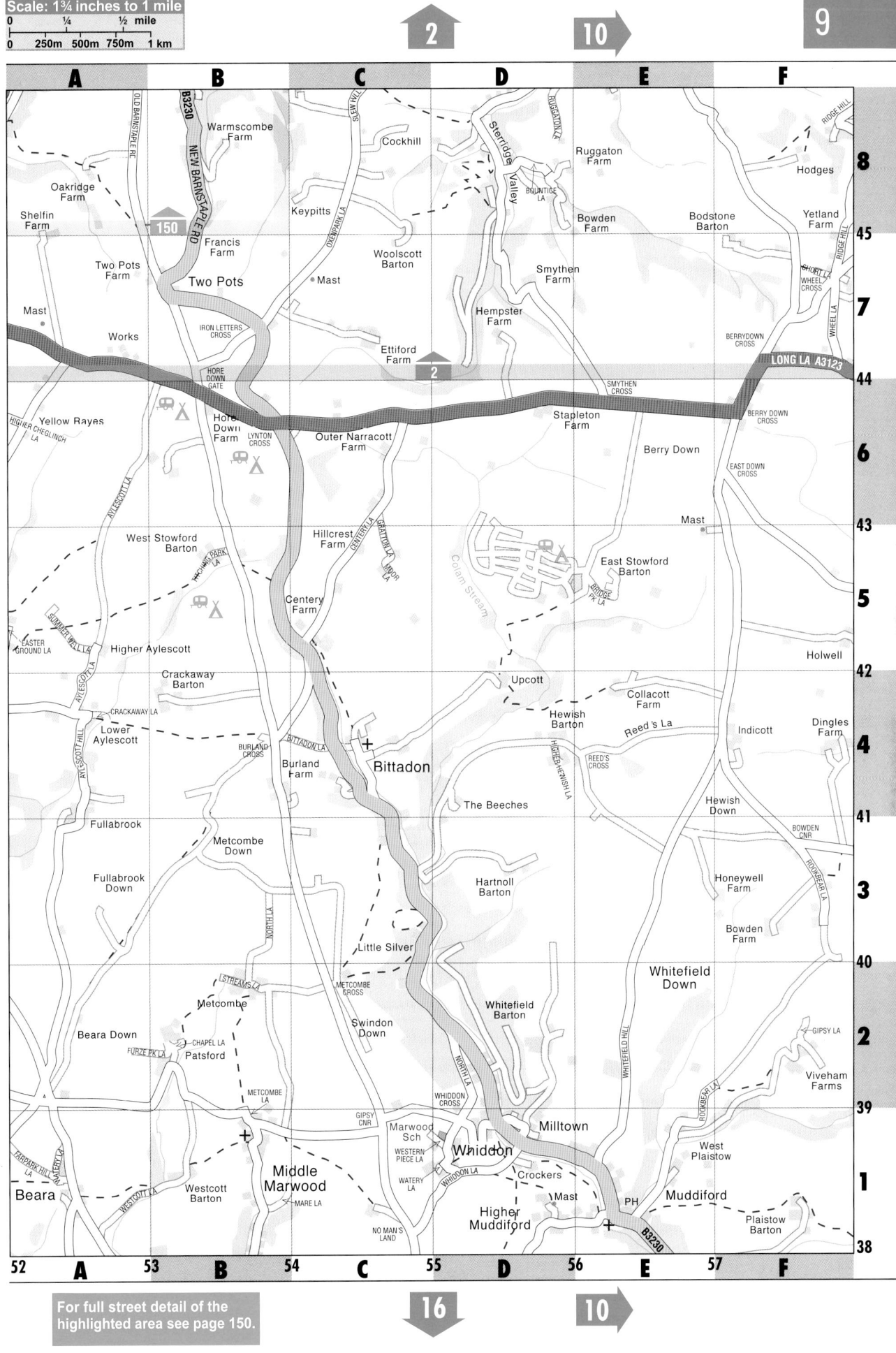

Scale: 1¾ inches to 1 mile

0   ¼   ½   mile
0   250m   500m   750m   1 km

2

10

| A | B | C | D | E | F |

8

Ridge Hill

Old Barnstaple Rd
B3230
New Barnstaple Rd

Warmscombe Farm
Cockhill
Sterridge Valley
Ruggaton La
Ruggaton Farm
Hodges

Oakridge Farm
Keypitts
Bountice La
Bowden Farm
Bodstone Barton
Yetland Farm
45

Shelfin Farm
150
Francis Farm
Woolscott Barton
Smythen Farm
Short La
Wheel Cross
Wheel La
7

Two Pots Farm
Two Pots
Mast
Hempster Farm
Berrydown Cross

Mast
Works
Iron Letters Cross
Ettiford Farm
2
Smythen Cross
Long La A3123
44

Hore Down Gate

Higher Cheglinch La
Yellow Rayes
Hore Down Farm
Lynton Cross
Outer Narracott Farm
Stapleton Farm
Berry Down Cross
6

Berry Down
East Down Cross

Aylescott La
West Stowford Barton
Hillcrest Farm
Centery La
Grattons La
Moor La
Colam Stream
Bridge Pk La
East Stowford Barton
Mast
43

Hatching Park La
Centery Farm
Holwell
5

Summerwell La
Easter Ground La
Higher Aylescott
Upcott
42

Aylescott Hill
Crackaway Barton
Hewish Barton
Collacott Farm
Reed's La
Indicott
Dingles Farm

Lower Aylescott
Crackaway La
Burland Cross
Bittadon La
Bittadon
Higher Hewish La
Reed's Cross
Hewish Down
4

Fullabrook
Burland Farm
Bowden Cnr
41

Metcombe Down
The Beeches
Honeywell Farm
Rockbear La

Fullabrook Down
Hartnoll Barton
Bowden Farm
3

North La
Little Silver
Whitefield Down
40

Streams La
Metcombe Cross
Gipsy La
2

Beara Down
Chapel La
Patsford
Swindon Down
Whitefield Barton
Whitefield Hill
Viveham Farms

Furze Pk La
Metcombe La
Gipsy Cnr
North La
Whiddon Cross
Milltown
Rockbear La
39

Tarpark Hill La
Watery La
Marwood Sch
Western Piece La
Whiddon La
Whiddon
Crockers
West Plaistow
Muddiford
1

Beara
Westcott La
Westcott Barton
Middle Marwood
Mare La
Watery La
Mast
PH
B3230
Plaistow Barton

No Man's Land
Higher Muddiford
38

| 52 | A | 53 | B | 54 | C | 55 | D | 56 | E | 57 | F |

16

10

For full street detail of the highlighted area see page 150.

150

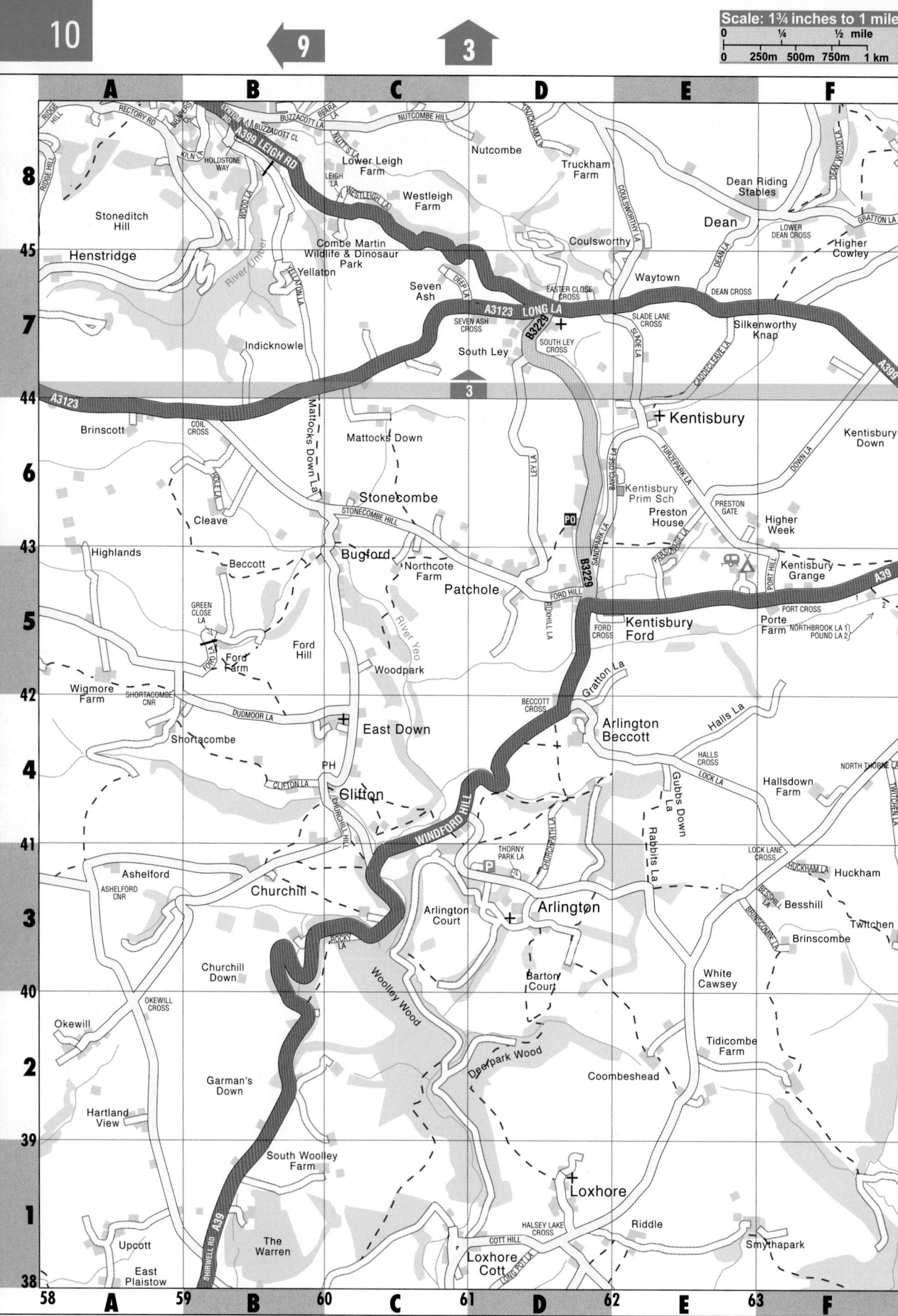

Scale: 1¾ inches to 1 mile
Stoneditch Hill
Henstridge
Lower Leigh Farm
Westleigh Farm
Combe Martin Wildlife & Dinosaur Park
Yellaton
Nutcombe
Truckham Farm
Coulsworthy
Dean Riding Stables
Dean
Higher Cowley
Waytown
Seven Ash
Indicknowle
South Ley
Silkenworthy Knap
Brinscott
Mattocks Down
Kentisbury
Kentisbury Down
Stonecombe
Cleave
Kentisbury Prim Sch
Preston House
Higher Week
Highlands
Beccott
Bugford
Northcote Farm
Patchole
Kentisbury Grange
Ford Hill
Ford Farm
Kentisbury Ford
Porte Farm
Woodpark
Wigmore Farm
East Down
Shortacombe
Arlington Beccott
Hallsdown Farm
Clifton
Ashelford
Churchill
Arlington Court
Arlington
Huckham
Besshill
Twitchen
Brinscombe
Churchill Down
Woolley Wood
Barton Court
White Cawsey
Okewill
Deerpark Wood
Tidicombe Farm
Garman's Down
Coombeshead
Hartland View
South Woolley Farm
Loxhore
Riddle
Upcott
The Warren
Loxhore Cott
Smythapark
East Plaistow

9
3
9
17

Scale: 1¾ inches to 1 mile

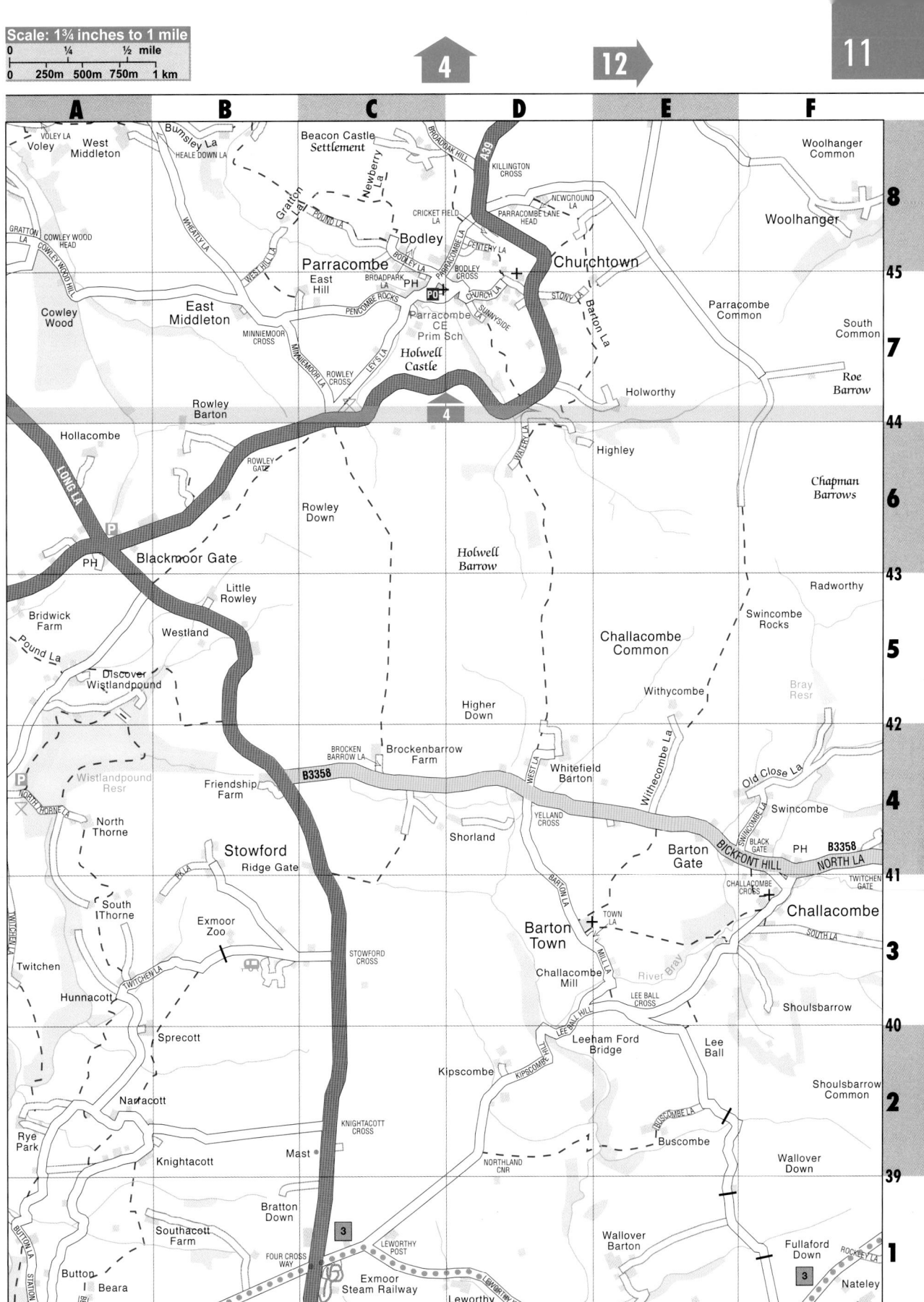

0 ¼ ½ mile
0 250m 500m 750m 1 km
4
12
A B C D E F
Voley
West Middleton
Bumsley La
Beacon Castle Settlement
Newberry La
Gratton La
Woolhanger Common
Woolhanger
Bodley
Parracombe
Churchtown
East Hill
PH
PO
East Middleton
Cowley Wood
Parracombe CE Prim Sch
Holwell Castle
Barton La
Parracombe Common
South Common
Roe Barrow
Holworthy
Rowley Barton
Hollacombe
Highley
LONG LA
Chapman Barrows
Rowley Down
P
PH
Blackmoor Gate
Holwell Barrow
Little Rowley
Radworthy
Bridwick Farm
Westland
Swincombe Rocks
Pound La
Challacombe Common
Discover Wistlandpound
Withycombe
Bray Resr
Higher Down
Brockenbarrow Farm
Whitefield Barton
B3358
Wistlandpound Resr
Friendship Farm
Withecombe La
Old Close La
Swincombe
North Thorne
Shorland
Stowford
Ridge Gate
Barton Gate
PH
B3358
NORTH LA
BICKFONT HILL
Challacombe
South Thorne
Exmoor Zoo
Barton Town
Twitchen
Challacombe Mill
River Bray
Hunnacott
Shoulsbarrow
Sprecott
Leeham Ford Bridge
Lee Ball
Kipscombe
Shoulsbarrow Common
Narracott
Rye Park
Buscombe
Mast
Knightacott
Wallover Down
Bratton Down
3
Southacott Farm
Wallover Barton
Fullaford Down
3
Button
Beara
Exmoor Steam Railway
Leworthy
Nateley
Fullaford
A399
A39
8 45 7 44 6 43 5 42 4 41 3 40 2 39 1 38
64 65 66 67 68 69
18
12

Scale: 1¾ inches to 1 mile

0   ¼   ½ mile

0   250m 500m 750m 1 km

A   B   C   D   E   F

Barham Hill

Thornworthy

RADSBURY LA

Radsbury

Stock Common

LYNCOMBE LA

Farley Water

Farley Hill

P

B3223

P

P

8

Ilkerton Ridge

West Lyn River

Furzehill

Furzehill Common

Two Moors Way

Tarka Trail

Hoaroak Water

Cheriton Ridge

Middle Hill

B3223

45

Shallowford

7

Cannon Hill

Pig Hill

Holcombe Burrows

44

Butter Hill

5

6

Saddle Gate

Thorn Hill

Hoaroak

Benjamy

Clannon Ball

Long Stone

Winaway

Hoar Oak Tree

43

Longstone Barrow

The Chains

Hoaroak Hill

5

Wood Barrow

Pinkery Pond

42

Broad Mead

Pinkworthy

Chains Barrow

Tarka Trail

Exe Plain

4

Yarbury Combe

North Ridge Common

Breakneck Hole

Pinkery Farm

Macmillan Way West

Exe Head

Dure Down

Twitchen Farm

B3358

NORTH LA

41

Old Close Bottom

Edgerley Stone

Goat Hill

Driver

Titchcombe

Tangs Bottom

Duredon Farm

3

SOUTH LA

Roosthitchen

40

Weirs Combe

Hearlake

Kennels

Acklands

River Barle

COBHAM FARM LA

2

Sloley Stone

Shoulsbarrow Common

Mole's Chamber

Great Vintcombe

Smallacombe

Cornham Farm

B3358

Shoulsbury Castle

3

Ricksy Ball

39

Henthitchen

Two Moors Way

1

ROCKLEY LA

Bray Common

Setta Barrow

Squallacombe

Horcombe

Rockley Farm

38

70   A   71   B   72   C   73   D   74   E   75   F

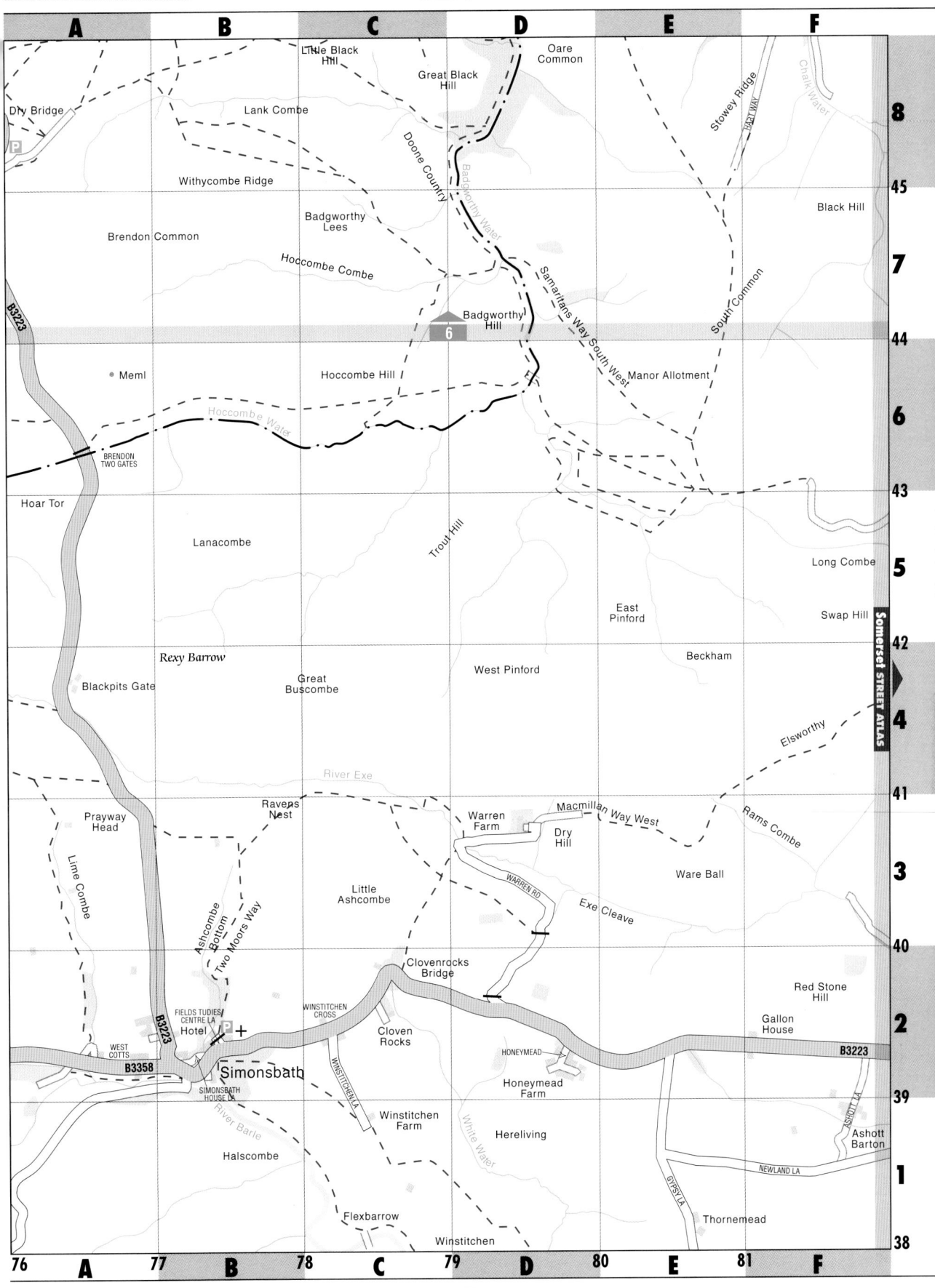

A   B   C   D   E   F

Dry Bridge

P

Little Black Hill

Great Black Hill

Oare Common

Lank Combe

Stowey Ridge

HAZEL WAY

Chalk Water

8

Withycombe Ridge

Doone Country

Badgworthy Water

45

Black Hill

Brendon Common

Badgworthy Lees

7

Hoccombe Combe

Samaritans Way South West

South Common

44

B3223

Badgworthy Hill

6

Meml

Hoccombe Hill

Manor Allotment

6

Hoccombe Water

43

Brendon Two Gates

Hoar Tor

Lanacombe

Trout Hill

Long Combe

5

Rexy Barrow

East Pinford

Swap Hill

42

Blackpits Gate

Great Buscombe

West Pinford

Beckham

Somerset STREET ATLAS

4

Elsworthy

River Exe

41

Prayway Head

Ravens Nest

Warren Farm

Macmillan Way West

Rams Combe

Lime Combe

Dry Hill

Ware Ball

3

Little Ashcombe

WARREN RD

Exe Cleave

40

Ashcombe Bottom

Two Moors Way

Clovenrocks Bridge

Red Stone Hill

FIELDS TUDIES CENTRE LA

WINSTITCHEN CROSS

Cloven Rocks

HONEYMEAD

Gallon House

B3223

2

B3223

WEST COTTS

Hotel P

Simonsbath

WINSTITCHEN LA

Honeymead Farm

B3358

SIMONSBATH HOUSE LA

39

River Barle

Winstitchen Farm

Hereliving

White Water

Ashott Barton

ASHOTT LA

Halscombe

GYPSY LA

NEWLAND LA

Thornemead

1

Flexbarrow

Winstitchen

38

76   A   77   B   78   C   79   D   80   E   81   F

Scale: 1¾ inches to 1 mile

| 0 | ¼ | ½ | mile |
| 0 | 250m | 500m | 750m | 1 km |

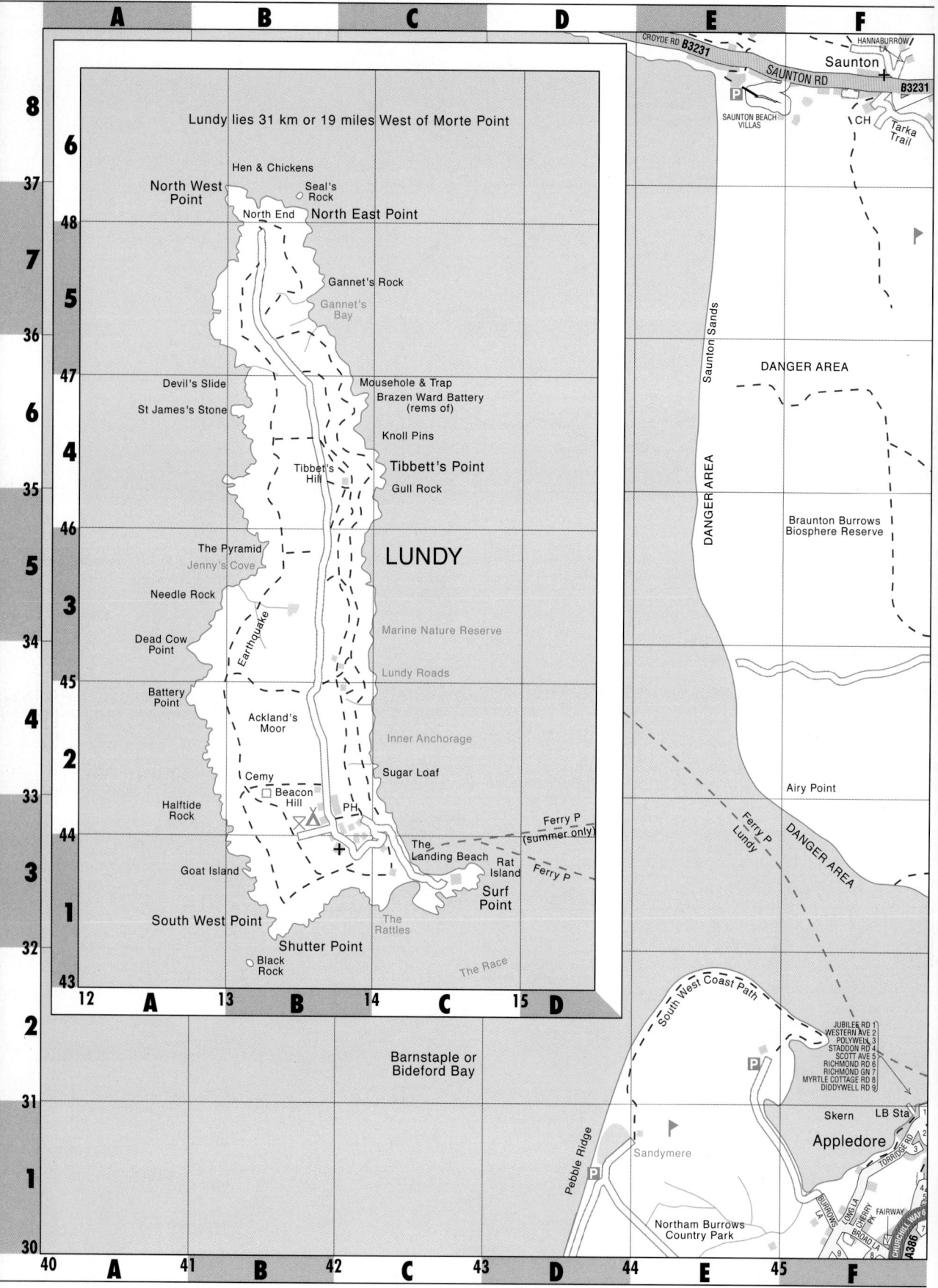

Lundy lies 31 km or 19 miles West of Morte Point

CROYDE RD B3231

SAUNTON RD

Saunton

HANNABURROW LA

B3231

Tarka Trail

CH

SAUNTON BEACH VILLAS

Hen & Chickens

North West Point

Seal's Rock

North End

North East Point

Gannet's Rock

Gannet's Bay

Saunton Sands

DANGER AREA

Devil's Slide

St James's Stone

Mousehole & Trap

Brazen Ward Battery (rems of)

Knoll Pins

DANGER AREA

Tibbet's Hill

Tibbett's Point

Gull Rock

Braunton Burrows Biosphere Reserve

The Pyramid

Jenny's Cove

LUNDY

Needle Rock

Earthquake

Marine Nature Reserve

Dead Cow Point

Lundy Roads

Battery Point

Ackland's Moor

Inner Anchorage

Airy Point

DANGER AREA

Cemy

Sugar Loaf

Beacon Hill

PH

Ferry P Lundy

Halftide Rock

Ferry P (summer only)

Goat Island

The Landing Beach

Rat Island

Ferry P

South West Point

Surf Point

Ferry P Lundy

DANGER AREA

Shutter Point

The Rattles

Black Rock

The Race

South West Coast Path

Barnstaple or Bideford Bay

JUBILEE RD 1
WESTERN AVE 2
POLYWELL 3
STADDON RD 4
SCOTT AVE 5
RICHMOND RD 6
RICHMOND GN 7
MYRTLE COTTAGE RD 8
DIDDYWELL RD 9

Skern

LB Sta

Appledore

Pebble Ridge

Sandymere

Northam Burrows Country Park

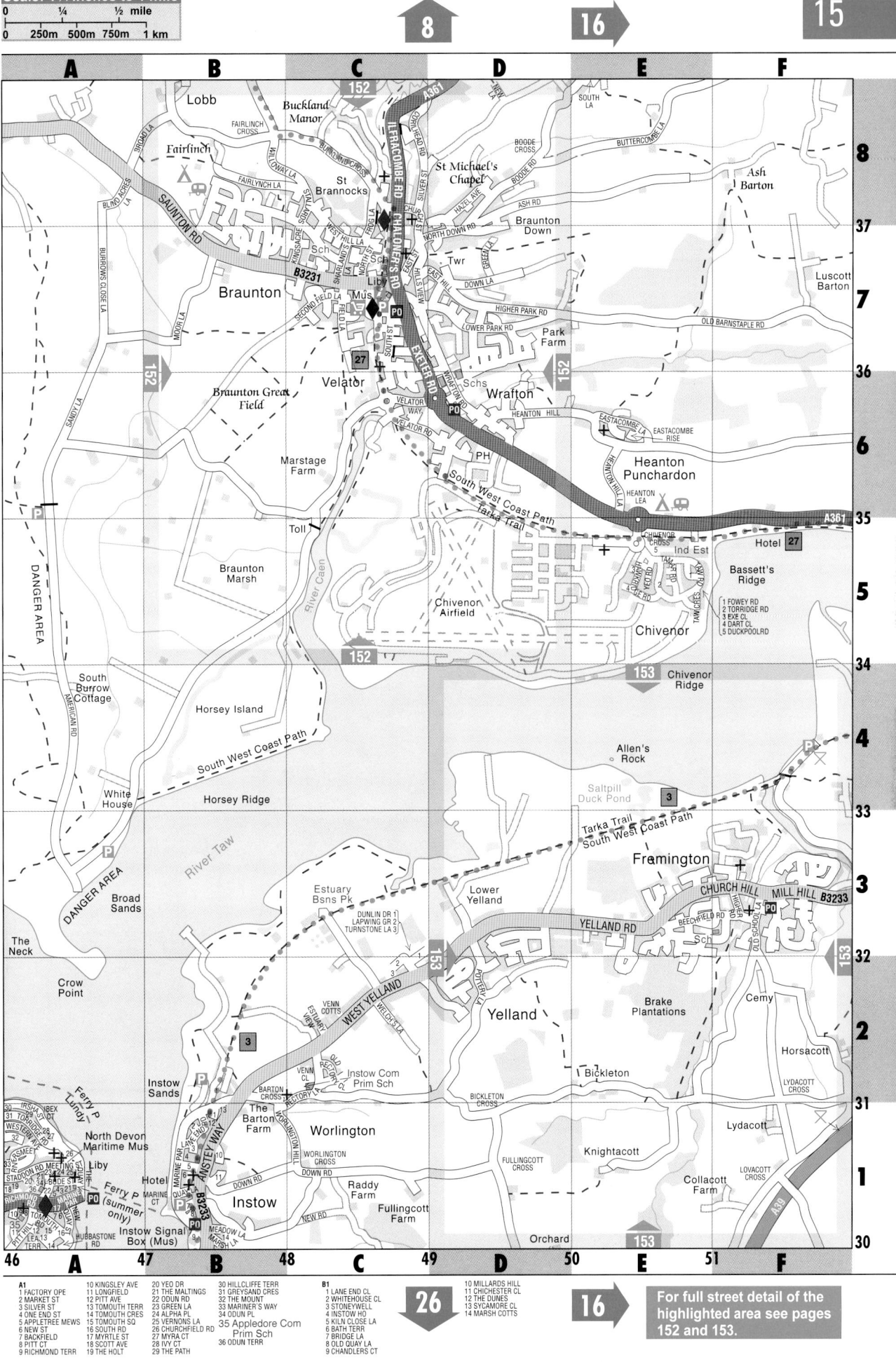

Scale: 1¾ inches to 1 mile

0   ¼   ½ mile
0 250m 500m 750m 1 km

A   **B**   **C**   **D**   **E**   **F**

Lobb

Buckland Manor

Fairlinch

Fairlinch Cross

St Brannocks

St Michael's Chapel

Braunton Down

South La

Boode Cross

Ash Barton

Luscott Barton

Braunton

Old Barnstaple Rd

Mus

Liby

Sch

Velator

Wrafton

Park Farm

Braunton Great Field

Marstage Farm

Heanton Hill

Eastacombe Rise

Heanton Punchardon

Heanton Lea

Bassett's Ridge

1 FOWEY RD
2 TORRIDGE RD
3 EXE CL
4 DART CL
5 DUCKPOOL RD

Hotel 27

Toll

Braunton Marsh

River Caen

Chivenor Airfield

Chivenor

Chivenor Cross

Ind Est

South Burrow Cottage

American Rd

153 Chivenor Ridge

Horsey Island

South West Coast Path

Allen's Rock

Saltpill Duck Pond 3

P

White House

Horsey Ridge

Tarka Trail
South West Coast Path

Framington

Church Hill Mill Hill B3233

River Taw

DANGER AREA

Broad Sands

Estuary Bsns Pk

Lower Yelland

Yelland Rd

Higher

Old School Rd

Beechfield Rd

Sch

The Neck

Crow Point

DUNLIN DR 1
LAPWING GR 2
TURNSTONE LA 3

153

West Yelland

Yelland

Brake Plantations

Cemy

Horsacott

Venn Cotts

Instow Com Prim Sch

Bickleton

Lydacott Cross

Instow Sands

Barton Cross

The Barton Farm

Worlington

Bickleton Cross

Knightacott

Lydacott

North Devon Maritime Mus

Liby

Ferry P (summer only)

Hotel

Instow

Worlington Cross

Raddy Farm

Down Rd

Fullingcott Cross

Fullingcott Farm

Collacott Farm

Lovacott Cross

Instow Signal Box (Mus)

New Rd

Meadow La

Orchard

153

46   **A**   **47**   **B**   **48**   **C**   **49**   **D**   **50**   **E**   **51**   **F**

A1
1 FACTORY OPE
2 MARKET ST
3 SILVER ST
4 ONE END ST
5 APPLETREE MEWS
6 NEW ST
7 BACKFIELD
8 PITT CT
9 RICHMOND TERR

10 KINGSLEY AVE
11 LONGFIELD
12 PITT AVE
13 TOMOUTH TERR
14 TOMOUTH CRES
15 TOMOUTH SQ
16 SOUTH RD
17 MYRTLE ST
18 SCOTT AVE
19 THE HOLT

20 YEO DR
21 THE MALTINGS
22 ODUN RD
23 GREEN LA
24 ALPHA PL
25 VERNONS LA
26 CHURCHFIELD RD
27 MYRA CT
28 IVY CT
29 THE PATH

30 HILLCLIFFE TERR
31 GREYSAND CRES
32 THE MOUNT
33 MARINER'S WAY
34 ODUN PL
35 Appledore Com Prim Sch
36 ODUN TERR

B1
1 LANE END CL
2 WHITEHOUSE CL
3 STONEYWELL
4 INSTOW HO
5 KILN CLOSE LA
6 BATH TERR
7 BRIDGE LA
8 OLD QUAY LA
9 CHANDLERS CT

10 MILLARDS HILL
11 CHICHESTER CL
12 THE DUNES
13 SYCAMORE CL
14 MARSH COTTS

For full street detail of the highlighted area see pages 152 and 153.

A   B   C   D   E   F

8

Marwood
WIGLEY CROSS
Pippacott
Whitehall
Marwood Hill Gdns
Guineaford
Kennacot Farm
Quarry
Plaistow Mills
B3230
Sloley Barton

37

Lee House
Kingsheanton
Broomhill Farm
Hotel
North Hill
SOUTH VIEW
PH
MEREWOOD CL
Prixford
Broomhill Sculpture Gardens

7

OLD BARNSTAPLE RD
Mainstone
WATERLAKE LA
Waterlake
Knowl Water
PRIXFORD
Varley Farm
Bradiford Water
South Hill

36

NORTH LA
Blakewell
Hartpiece Farm

6

WINDY CROSS
West Ashford
Horridge
STRAND CL
GRATTAN LA
LOOKOUT COTTS
Tutshill
B3230
SHIRWELL RD
Burridge
Roborough
fort

35

A361
LIMEKILN LA
ASHFIELD LA
Ashford
ASHFIELD LA
STRAND LA
FIELD LA
LONG LA
Upcott
HIGHER NEWCLOSE LA
Pilland
UPCOTT HILL
154
Bradiford House
Westaway
SHIRWELL CROSS
ROBOROUGH RD
Raleigh House
155
SMOKY HOUSE LA

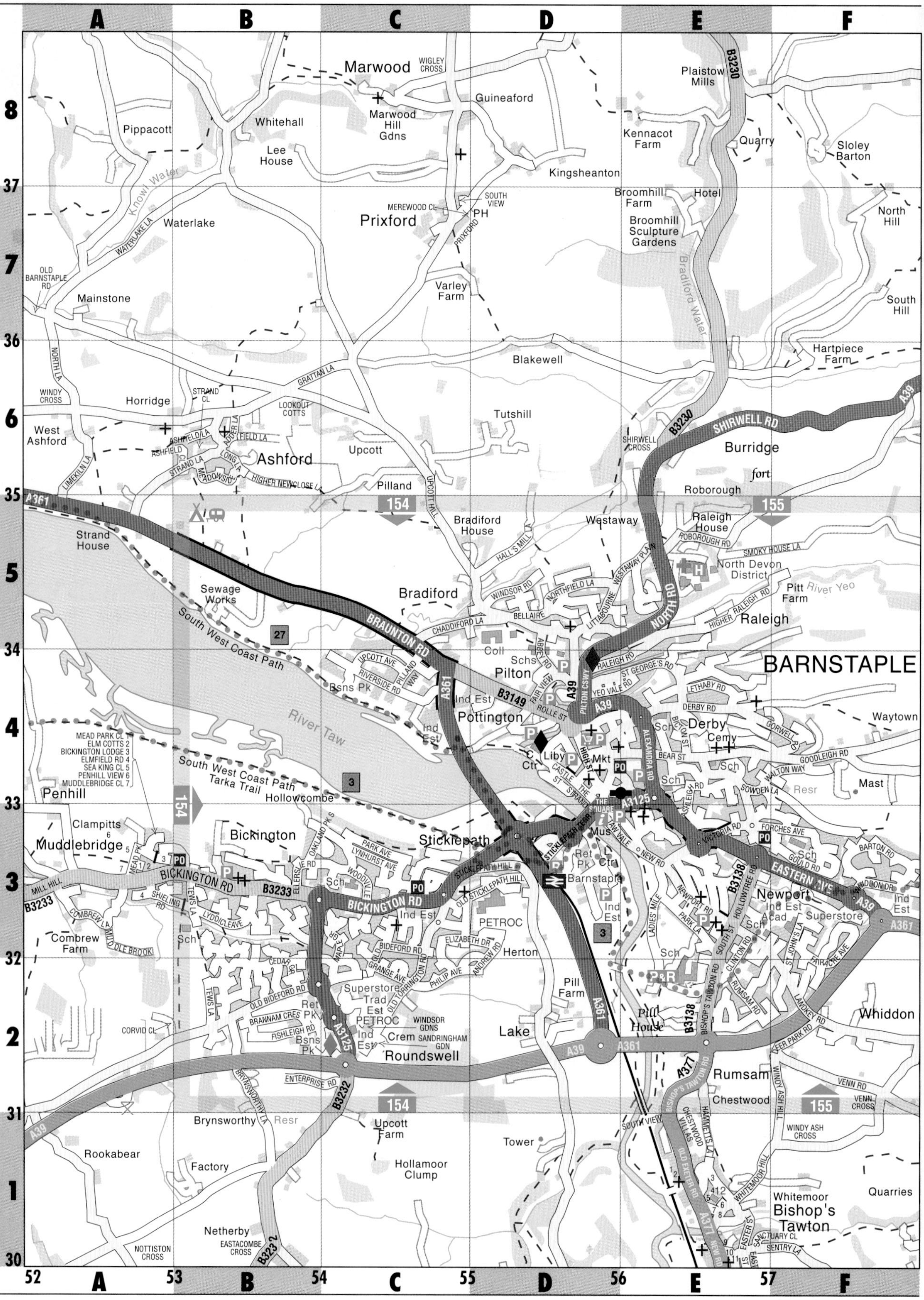

Strand House
HALL'S MILL
BRAUNTON RD
Bradiford
WINDSOR RD
NORTHFIELD LA
North Devon District
H
Pitt Farm
River Yeo
Raleigh

5

Sewage Works
South West Coast Path
27
CHADDIFORD LA
BELLAIRE
LITTABOURNE
WESTAWAY PLAIN
HIGHER RALEIGH RD

34

UPCOTT AVE
RIVERSIDE RD
PILLAND WAY
Bsns Pk
Coll
Schs
Pilton
FAIR VIEW
ABBEY RD
RALEIGH RD
ST GEORGE'S RD
NORTH RD
LETHABY RD
BARNSTAPLE
River Taw
B3149
ROLLE ST
YEO VALE RD
A39
PILTON CSWY
DERBY RD

4

MEAD PARK CL 1
ELM COTTS 2
BICKINGTON LODGE 3
ELMFIELD RD 4
SEA KING CL 5
PENHILL VIEW 6
MUDDLEBRIDGE CL 7
South West Coast Path Tarka Trail
3
Hollowcombe
Pottington
Ind Est
Ind Est
C Ctr
Liby
CASTLE ST
HIGH ST
Mkt
PO
P
BEAR ST
Sch
Derby
Cemy
GORWELL RD
Waytown
WALTON WAY
GOODLEIGH RD
Resr
Mast

33

Penhill
Clampitts
Muddlebridge
Bickington
154
OAKLAND PK
PARK AVE
LYNHURST AVE
ELLERSLEA
WOODVILLE
Sticklepath
Mus
THE SQUARE
A3125
NEW RD
SOWDEN LA
Sch
FORCHES AVE
PO
BARTON RD

3

MILL HILL
B3233
MEAD LA
PO
BICKINGTON RD
B3233
TEWS LA
SHIELING LA
LYDDICLEAVE
Sch
Ind Est
PETROC
OLD STICKLEPATH HILL
STICKLEPATH HILL
Barnstaple
Ret Pk Ctr
Ind Est
Herton
P
Newport
Ind Est
Acad
Superstore
B3138
EASTERN AVE
ABBON DR
A39
A361

Combrew LA
MIDDLE BROOK
Combrew Farm
CEDAR LA
MAPLE LA
BRANNAM CRES
FISHLEIGH RD
OLD BIDEFORD RD
BIDEFORD RD
ELIZABETH DR
ANDREW RD
PHILIP AVE
LADIES MILE
NEWPORT RD
PARK LA
CLINTON RD
SOUTH RD
HOLLOWTREE RD
FAIR ACRE AVE
HACKNEY RD
Whiddon

2

CORVID CL
TEWS LA
Ret Pk
Superstore
Trad Est
PETROC
Ind Est
Crem
Bsns Pk
A3125
GRANGE AVE
DORRINGTON RD
WINDSOR GDNS
SANDRINGHAM GDN
Roundswell
Lake
Pill Farm
Pill House
B3138
Rumsam
Chestwood
155
VENN RD
VENN CROSS
WINDY ASH CROSS

31

A39
ENTERPRISE RD
BRYNSWORTHY LA
B3232
Brynsworthy
Resr
154
Upcott Farm
A39
A361
BISHOP'S TAWTON RD
CHESTWOOD VILLAS
OLD EXETER RD
SOUTH VIEW
HARTNELLS LA
DEER PARK RD
A377
DEER PARK HILL

1

Rookabear
Factory
Hollamoor Clump
Tower
WHITEMOOR HILL
Whitemoor
Bishop's Tawton
EASTER'S LA
SANCTUARY CL
Quarries
WINDY ASH CROSS

30

NOTTISTON CROSS
Netherby
EASTACOMBE CROSS
B3232
A377
SENTRY LA
SOUTH VIEW

52   53   54   55   56   57

A   B   C   D   E   F

1 LAW VIEW
2 HIGHFIELD TERR
3 MOUNT PLEASANT
4 DEER WOOD VIEW
5 LAW MEMORIAL HO
6 CROSS FARM CT
7 SCHOOL LA
8 SANDERS LA
9 ROSE COTTS
10 VILLAGE ST
11 THE SQUARE
12 Bishop's Tawton Prim Sch

For full street detail of the highlighted area see pages 154 and 155.

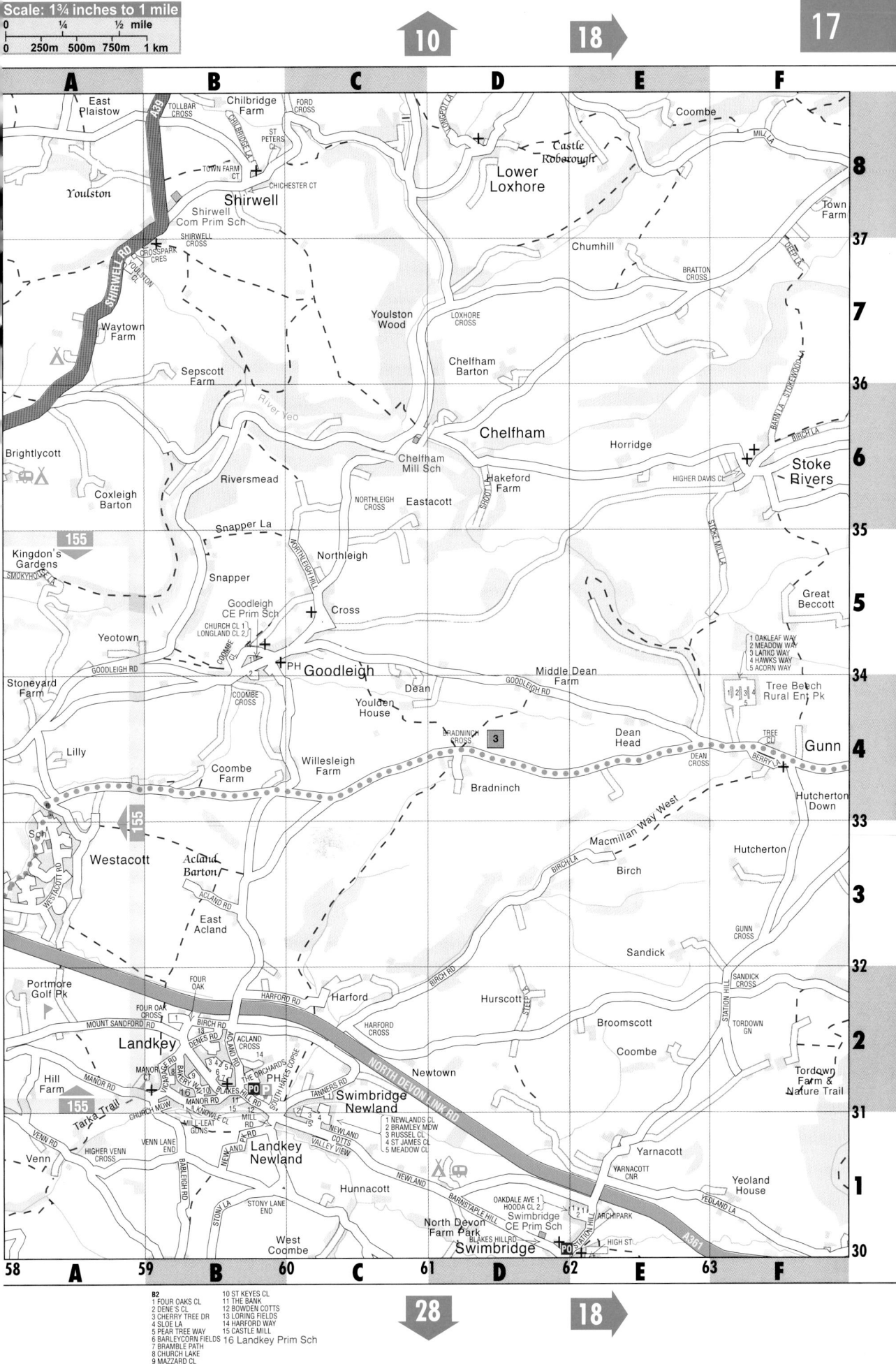

East Plaistow
Youlston
Chilbridge Farm
Ford Cross
Tollbar Cross
St Peters Cl
Town Farm Ct
Chichester Ct
Shirwell
Shirwell Com Prim Sch
Crosspark Cres
Shirwell Cross
Castle Roborough
Lower Loxhore
Coombe
Mill La
Town Farm
Chumhill
Bratton Cross
Waytown Farm
Youlston Wood
Loxhore Cross
Chelfham Barton
Sepscott Farm
River Yeo
Chelfham
Brightlycott
Coxleigh Barton
Riversmead
Chelfham Mill Sch
Hakeford Farm
Northleigh Cross
Eastacott
Horridge
Higher Davis Cl
Stoke Rivers
Barnla
Birch La
Kingdon's Gardens
155
Snapper La
Snapper
Northleigh
Northleigh Hill
Cross
Great Beccott
1 OAKLEAF WAY
2 MEADOW WAY
3 LATIG WAY
4 HAWKS WAY
5 ACORN WAY
Yeotown
Goodleigh CE Prim Sch
CHURCH CL 1
LONGLAND CL 2
PH
Goodleigh
GOODLEIGH RD
Dean
Youlden House
Middle Dean Farm
GOODLEIGH RD
Tree Beech Rural Ent Pk
Stoneyard Farm
Coombe Cross
Bradninch Cross
3
Dean Head
Dean Cross
TREE CL
Gunn
BERRY CL
Lilly
Coombe Farm
Willesleigh Farm
Bradninch
155
Macmillan Way West
Hutcherton Down
Westacott
Sch
Acland Barton
East Acland
ACLAND RD
Birch La
Birch
Hutcherton
Sandick
Gunn Cross
Portmore Golf Pk
FOUR OAK
FOUR OAK CROSS
MOUNT SANDFORD RD
BIRCH RD
DENES CL
ACLAND RD
HARFORD RD
Harford
Harford Cross
Hurscott
Broomscott
Coombe
STEEP
Sandick Cross
STATION HILL
TORDOWN GN
Landkey
MANOR RD
BARLEY WAY
MANOR RD
PH
ACLAND CROSS
14
THE ORCHARDS
SOUTH HAYES COPSE
Newtown
Tordown Farm & Nature Trail
Hill Farm
MANOR RD
CHURCH MDW
16
PO
P
TANNERS RD
Swimbridge Newland
NORTH DEVON LINK RD
155
VENN RD
HIGHER VENN CROSS
VENN LANE END
BARLEIGH RD
KNOWLE
MILL RD
NEWLAND
MILL LEAT GDNS
1 NEWLANDS CL
2 BRAMLEY MDW
3 RUSSEL CL
4 ST JAMES CL
5 MEADOW CL
NEWLAND COTTS
VALLEY VIEW
Yarnacott
YARNACOTT CNR
Tarka Trail
Venn
Landkey Newland
STONY LA
Hunnacott
STONY LANE END
NEWLAND
BARNSTAPLE HILL
North Devon Farm Park
OAKDALE AVE 1
HOODA CL 2
Swimbridge CE Prim Sch
ARCHPARK
Yeoland House
YEOLAND LA
YARNACOTT
West Coombe
BLAKES HILL RD
Swimbridge
PO
HIGH ST
A361

B2
1 FOUR OAKS CL
2 DENE'S CL
3 CHERRY TREE DR
4 SLOE LA
5 PEAR TREE WAY
6 BARLEYCORN FIELDS
7 BRAMBLE PATH
8 CHURCH LAKE
9 MAZZARD CL
10 ST KEYES CL
11 THE BANK
12 BOWDEN COTTS
13 LORING FIELDS
14 HARFORD WAY
15 CASTLE MILL
16 Landkey Prim Sch

Scale: 1¾ inches to 1 mile

0   ¼   ½ mile
0 250m 500m 750m 1 km

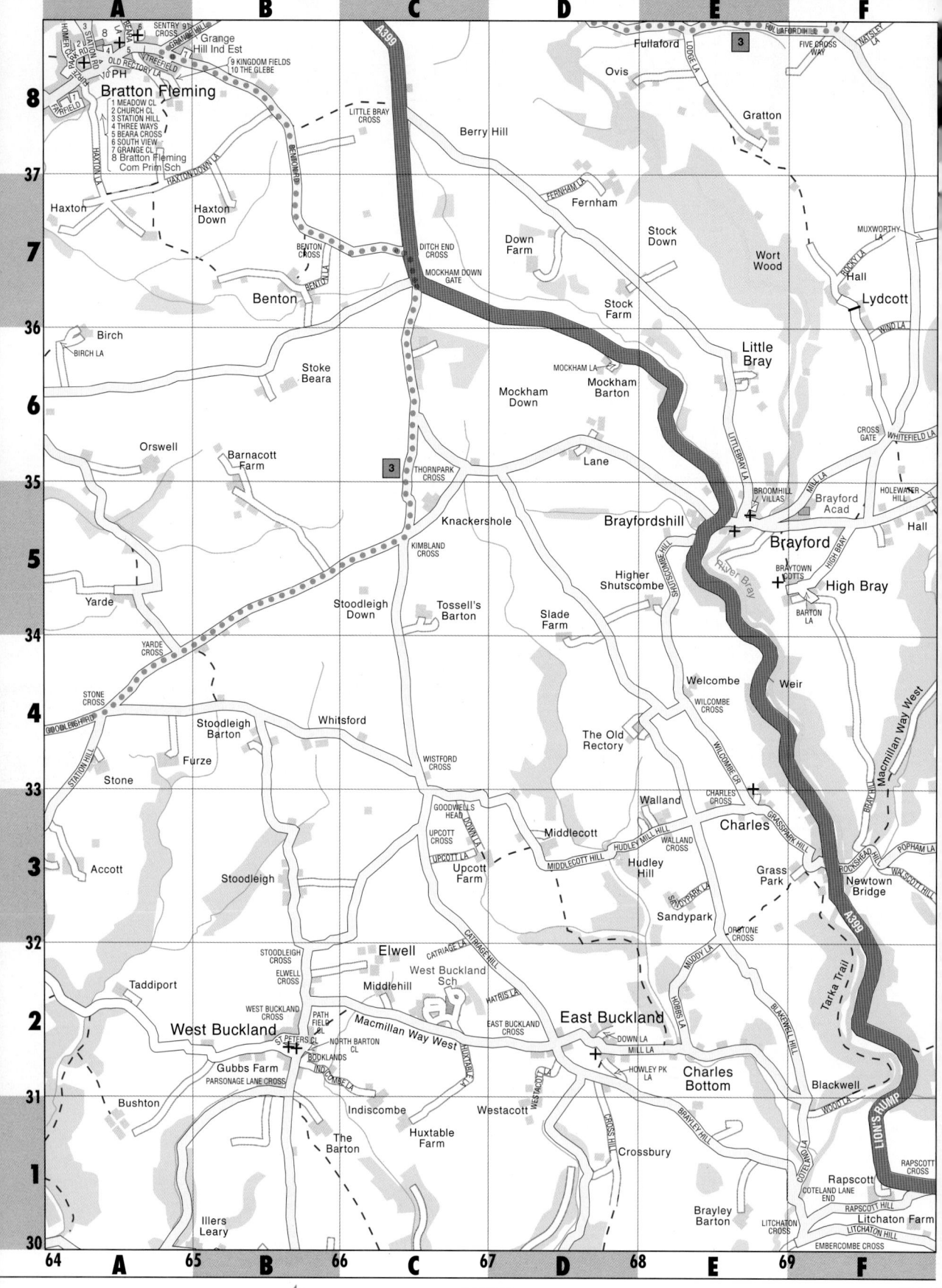

A399

Fullaford
3
Five Cross Way

Ovis
Gratton

Berry Hill

Little Bray Cross

Fernham

Down Farm

Stock Down

Wort Wood

Hall
Lydcott

Ditch End Cross

Mockham Down Gate

Stock Farm

Little Bray

Mockham La

Mockham Barton

Mockham Down

Cross Gate
Whitefield La

Thornpark Cross
3

Knackershole

Lane

Brayfordshill

Broomhill Villas

Brayford Acad

Brayford

Holewater Hill
Hall

Kimbland Cross

Higher Shutscombe

Braytown Cotts

High Bray

Barton La

Stoodleigh Down

Tossell's Barton

Slade Farm

Welcombe
Wilcombe Cross

Weir

Macmillan Way West

Yarde Cross

Stone Cross

Whitsford

The Old Rectory

Wilcombe Cr

Stoodleigh Barton

Furze

Wistford Cross

Walland

Charles Cross

Charles

Grasspark Hill

Stone

Accott

Stoodleigh

Goodwell's Head

Upcott Cross

Upcott La

Upcott Farm

Middlecott

Middlecott Hill

Hudley Mill Hill

Walland Cross

Hudley Hill

Sandypark

Grass Park

Orrtone Cross

Newtown Bridge

Rockshead

Popham La

Wagscott Hill

Tarka Trail

Stoodleigh Cross

Elwell Cross

Elwell

West Buckland Sch

Middlehill

Catriage Hill

Carriage Hill

Downta La

East Buckland Cross

East Buckland

Down La

Mill La

Hobbs La

Moody La

Blackmell Hill

Taddiport

West Buckland Cross

Path Field Cl

Peters Cl

North Barton Cl

Macmillan Way West

Hatris La

Buckland La

Westacott La

Charles Bottom

Brayley Hill

Blackwell

Lion's Rump

West Buckland

Gubbs Farm

Parsonage Lane Cross

Bocklands

Indiscombe La

Howley Pk La

Coteland La

Woodta La

Rapscott Cross

Bushton

Indiscombe

Huxtable Farm

Westacott

Cross La

Crossbury

Coteland Lane End

Rapscott

Rapscott Hill

Litchaton Farm

The Barton

Brayley Barton

Litchaton Cross

Litchaton Hill

Embercombe Cross

Illers Leary

Bratton Fleming area inset:
Homer Park
Station Rd
Sentry Cross
Fortescue Hill
Grange Hill Ind Est
Grange Hill
Treefield
Old Rectory La
PH
9 Kingdom Fields
10 The Glebe
Haxton Down La
Bratton Fleming
1 MEADOW CL
2 CHURCH CL
3 STATION HILL
4 THREE WAYS
5 BEARA CROSS
6 SOUTH VIEW
7 GRANGE CL
8 BRATTON FLEMING COM PRIM SCH

Haxton

Haxton Down

Benmead Rd

Benton Cross

Benton La

Benton

Birch
Birch La

Stoke Beara

Orswell

Barnacott Farm

Yarde

Oxenbridge

Station Hill

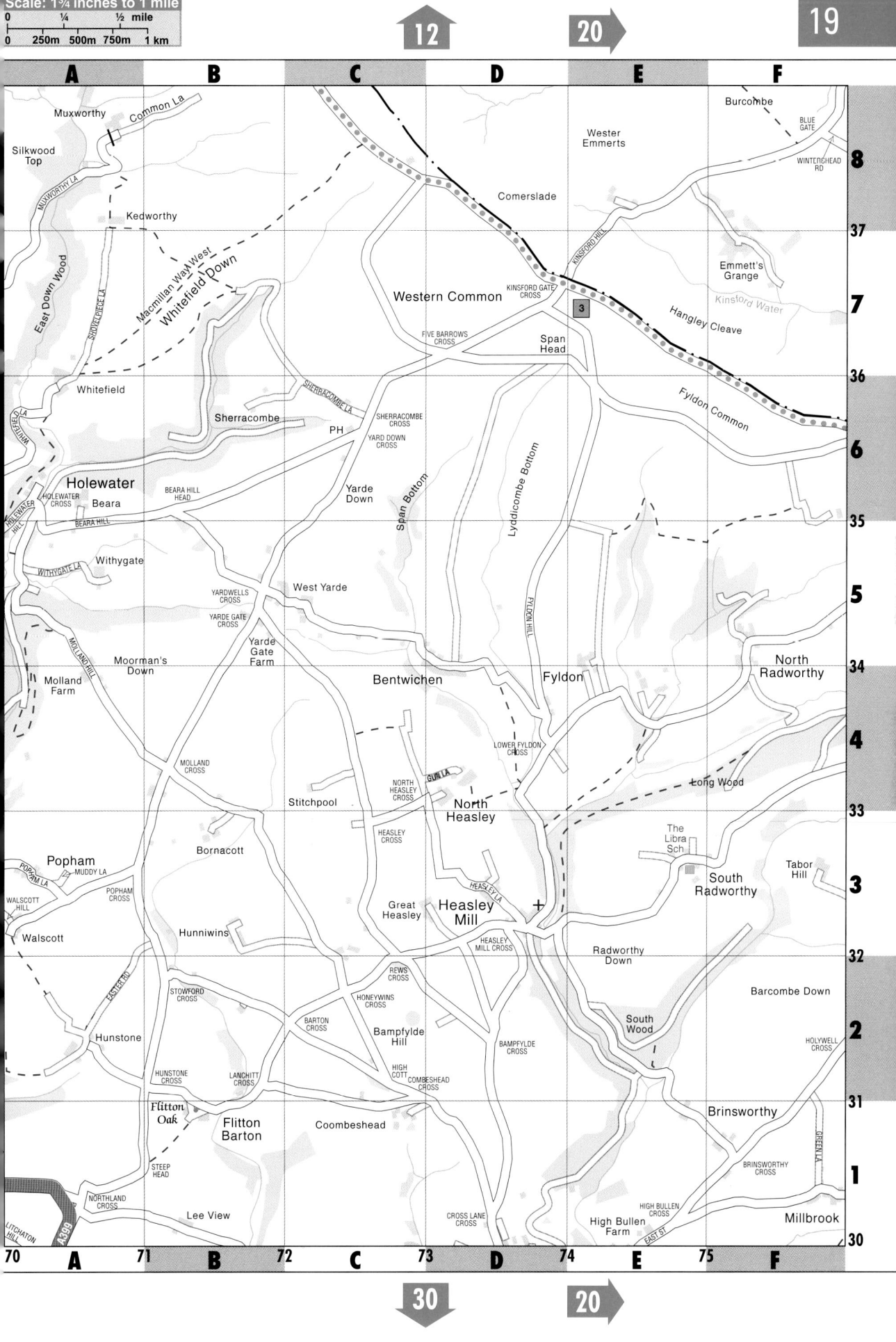

Scale: 1¾ inches to 1 mile
0 ¼ ½ mile
0 250m 500m 750m 1 km
12
20
A B C D E F
8
37
7
36
6
35
5
34
4
33
3
32
2
31
1
30
70 71 72 73 74 75
Muxworthy
Common La
Silkwood Top
MUXWORTHY LA
Kedworthy
East Down Wood
SHOVEPIECE LA
Macmillan Way West
Whitefield Down
Whitefield
WHITEFIELD LA
Sherracombe
SHERRACOMBE LA
PH
Holewater
HOLEWATER CROSS
HOLEWATER HILL
Beara
BEARA HILL HEAD
BEARA HILL
Withygate
WITHYGATE LA
Molland Farm
MOLLAND HILL
Moorman's Down
YARDWELLS CROSS
YARDE GATE CROSS
Yarde Gate Farm
West Yarde
Yarde Down
SHERRACOMBE CROSS
YARD DOWN CROSS
Span Bottom
Western Common
FIVE BARROWS CROSS
KINSFORD GATE CROSS
Span Head
Comerslade
Wester Emmerts
Burcombe
BLUE GATE
WINTERCHEAD RD
KINSFORD HILL
Emmett's Grange
Kinsford Water
Hangley Cleave
3
Fyldon Common
Lyddicombe Bottom
FYLDON HILL
Fyldon
Bentwichen
North Radworthy
LOWER FYLDON CROSS
GUN LA
NORTH HEASLEY CROSS
North Heasley
Long Wood
MOLLAND CROSS
Stitchpool
HEASLEY CROSS
Bornacott
Popham
POPHAM LA
MUDDY LA
POPHAM CROSS
WALSCOTT HILL
Walscott
Hunniwins
Great Heasley
Heasley Mill
HEASLEY LA
HEASLEY MILL CROSS
The Libra Sch
South Radworthy
Tabor Hill
Radworthy Down
Barcombe Down
EASTER RD
STOWFORD CROSS
REWS CROSS
HONEYWINS CROSS
BARTON CROSS
Bampfylde Hill
BAMPFYLDE CROSS
South Wood
HOLYWELL CROSS
Hunstone
HUNSTONE CROSS
LANCHITT CROSS
HIGH COTT
COMBESHEAD CROSS
Brinsworthy
Flitton Oak
Flitton Barton
Coombeshead
GREEN LA
BRINSWORTHY CROSS
STEEP HEAD
NORTHLAND CROSS
A399
LITCHATON HILL
Lee View
CROSS LANE CROSS
HIGH BULLEN CROSS
High Bullen Farm
EAST ST
Millbrook
30
20

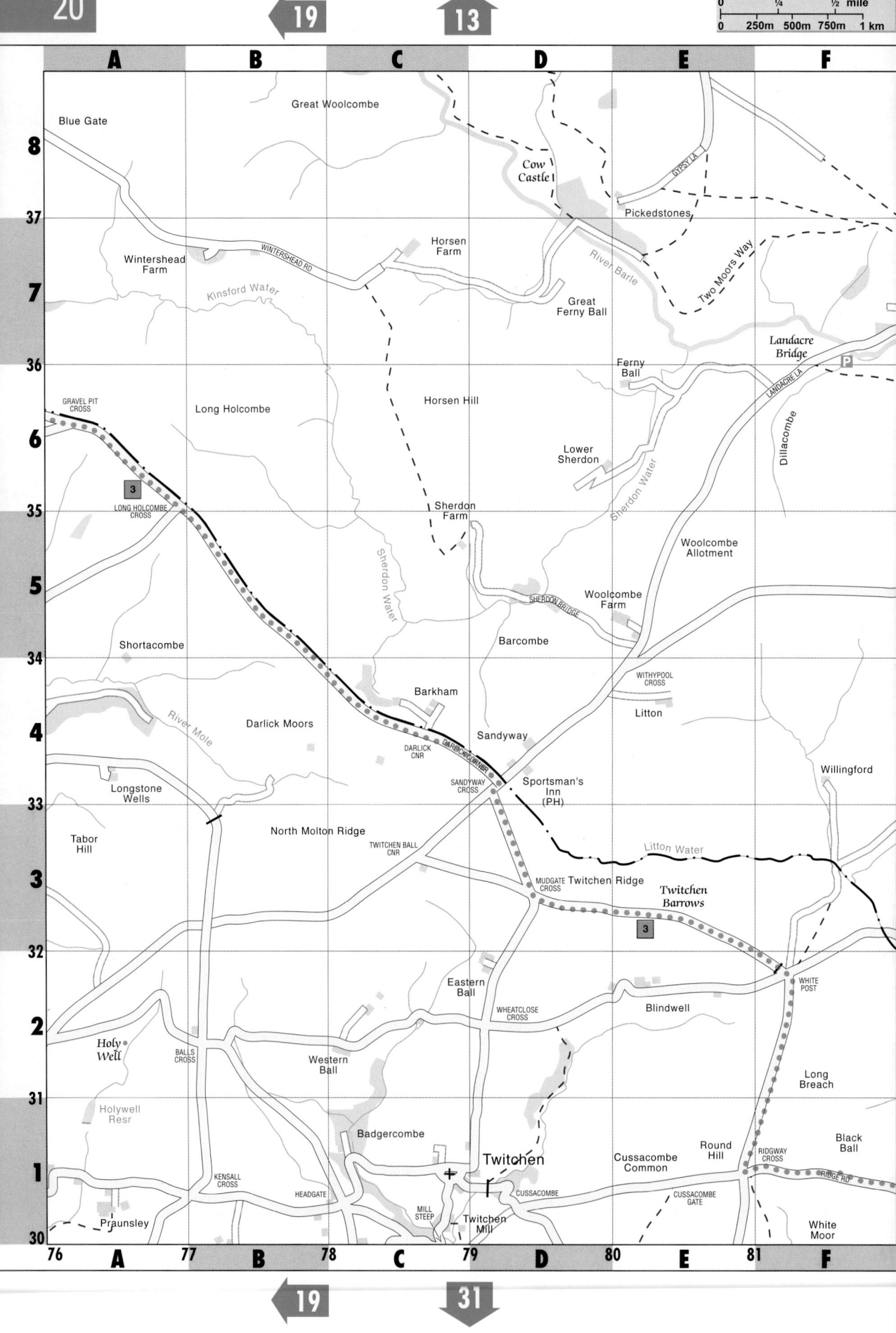

Scale: 1¾ inches to 1 mile

0   ¼   ½   mile
0   250m   500m   750m   1 km

A   B   C   D   E   F

8   Blue Gate

Great Woolcombe

Cow Castle

Pickedstones

GYPSY LA

37   Wintershead Farm

WINTERSHEAD RD

Horsen Farm

River Barle

Two Moors Way

Landacre Bridge

7   Kinsford Water

Great Ferny Ball

LANDACRE LA

36   Ferny Ball

Dillacombe

Gravel Pit Cross

Long Holcombe

Horsen Hill

Lower Sherdon

6

3

Long Holcombe Cross

Sherdon Farm

Sherdon Water

35

Woolcombe Allotment

Shortacombe

Sherdon Water

Woolcombe Farm

5

Sherdon Bridge

34   Barcombe

WITHYPOOL CROSS

River Mole

Darlick Moors

Barkham

Sandyway

Litton

4

DARLICK CNR

LIMPING COMBE

Sandyway Cross

Willingford

Longstone Wells

North Molton Ridge

Sportsman's Inn (PH)

33   Tabor Hill

TWITCHEN BALL CNR

Litton Water

3

Mudgate Cross

Twitchen Ridge

Twitchen Barrows

3

32

White Post

Eastern Ball

Blindwell

2   Holy Well

BALLS CROSS

WHEATCLOSE CROSS

Long Breach

31

Western Ball

Black Ball

Holywell Resr

Badgercombe

Cussacombe Common

Round Hill

RIDGWAY CROSS

1   KENSALL CROSS

Twitchen

Cussacombe

RIDGE RD

Praunsley

HEADGATE

MILL STEEP

Twitchen Mill

CUSSACOMBE GATE

White Moor

30

76   A   77   B   78   C   79   D   80   E   81   F

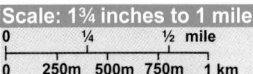

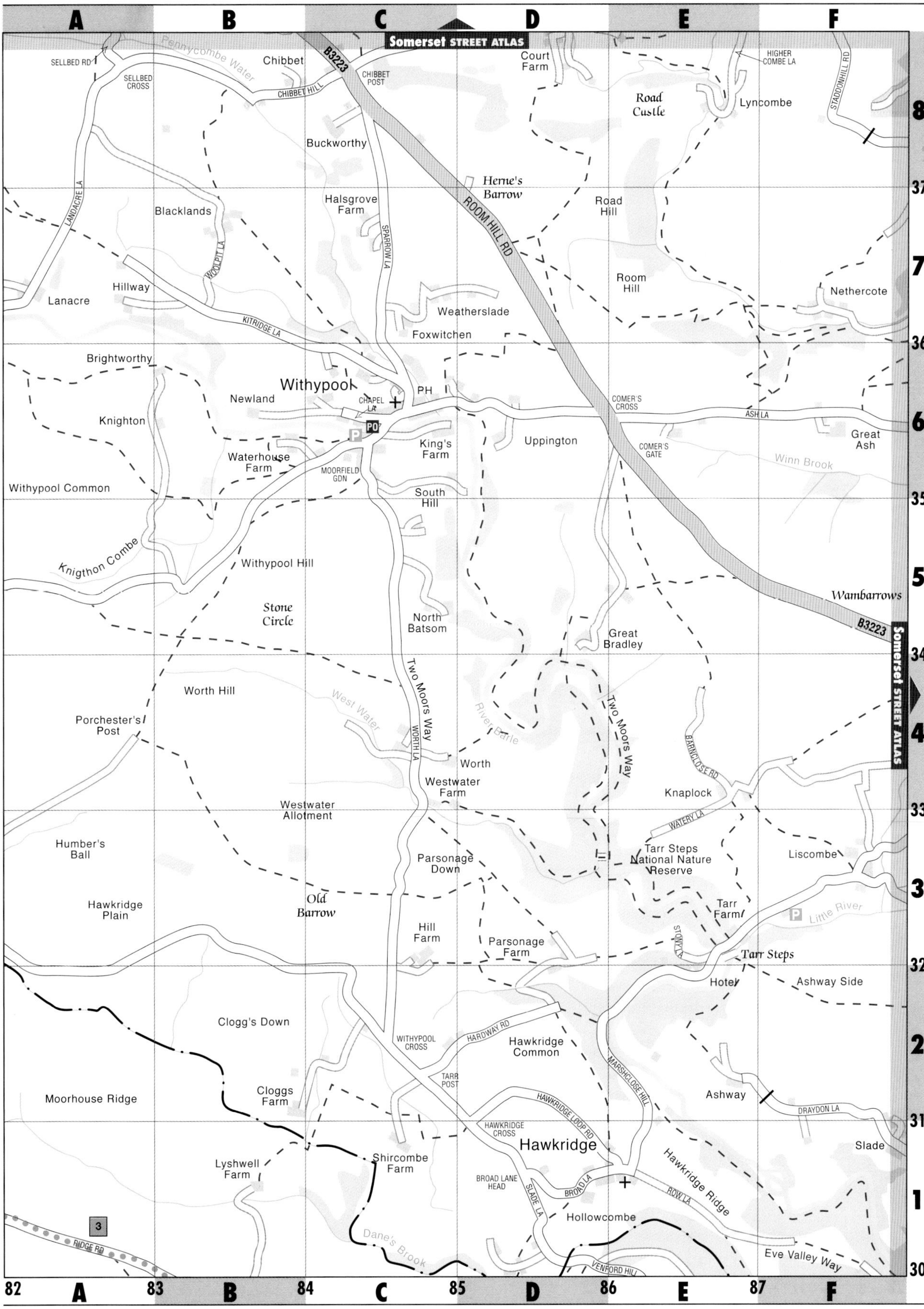

A **B** **C** **D** **E** **F**

Somerset STREET ATLAS

SELLBED RD
SELLBED CROSS
Pennycombe Water
Chibbet
CHIBBET HILL
CHIBBET POST
Court Farm
HIGHER COMBE LA
STADDONHILL RD
8

Buckworthy
Road Castle
Lyncombe
37

Blacklands
Halsgrove Farm
Herne's Barrow
ROOM HILL RD
Road Hill
7

Lanacre
Hillway
WOOLCOTT LA
KITRIDGE LA
SPARROW LA
Weatherslade
Foxwitchen
Room Hill
Nethercote
36

LANDACRE LA
Brightworthy
Withypool
Newland
CHAPEL LA
PH
PO
Comer's Cross
ASH LA
6

Knighton
Waterhouse Farm
MOORFIELD GDN
King's Farm
Uppington
Comer's Gate
Winn Brook
Great Ash
35

Withypool Common
Knigthon Combe
Withypool Hill
South Hill
Stone Circle
North Batsom
Two Moors Way
WORTH LA
Great Bradley
Two Moors Way
Wambarrows
B3223
5

Worth Hill
West Water
River Barle
Knaplock
BARNICLOSE RD
Somerset STREET ATLAS
34

Porchester's Post
Westwater Allotment
Worth
Westwater Farm
WATERY LA
Liscombe
4

Humber's Ball
Old Barrow
Parsonage Down
Tarr Steps National Nature Reserve
Tarr Farm
P Little River
33

Hawkridge Plain
Hill Farm
Parsonage Farm
SLADE LA
Tarr Steps
Hotel
Ashway Side
3

Clogg's Down
WITHYPOOL CROSS
HARDWAY RD
Hawkridge Common
MARSHCLOSE HILL
Ashway
DRAYDON LA
32

Moorhouse Ridge
Cloggs Farm
TARR POST
HAWKRIDGE LOOP RD
Hawkridge Ridge
Slade
2

Lyshwell Farm
Shircombe Farm
HAWKRIDGE CROSS
Hawkridge
BROAD LANE HEAD
SLADE LA
BROAD LA
ROW LA
31

RIDGE RD
Dane's Brook
Hollowcombe
VENFORD HILL
Eve Valley Way
1

30

Scale: 1¾ inches to 1 mile

0   ¼   ½ mile
0 250m 500m 750m 1 km

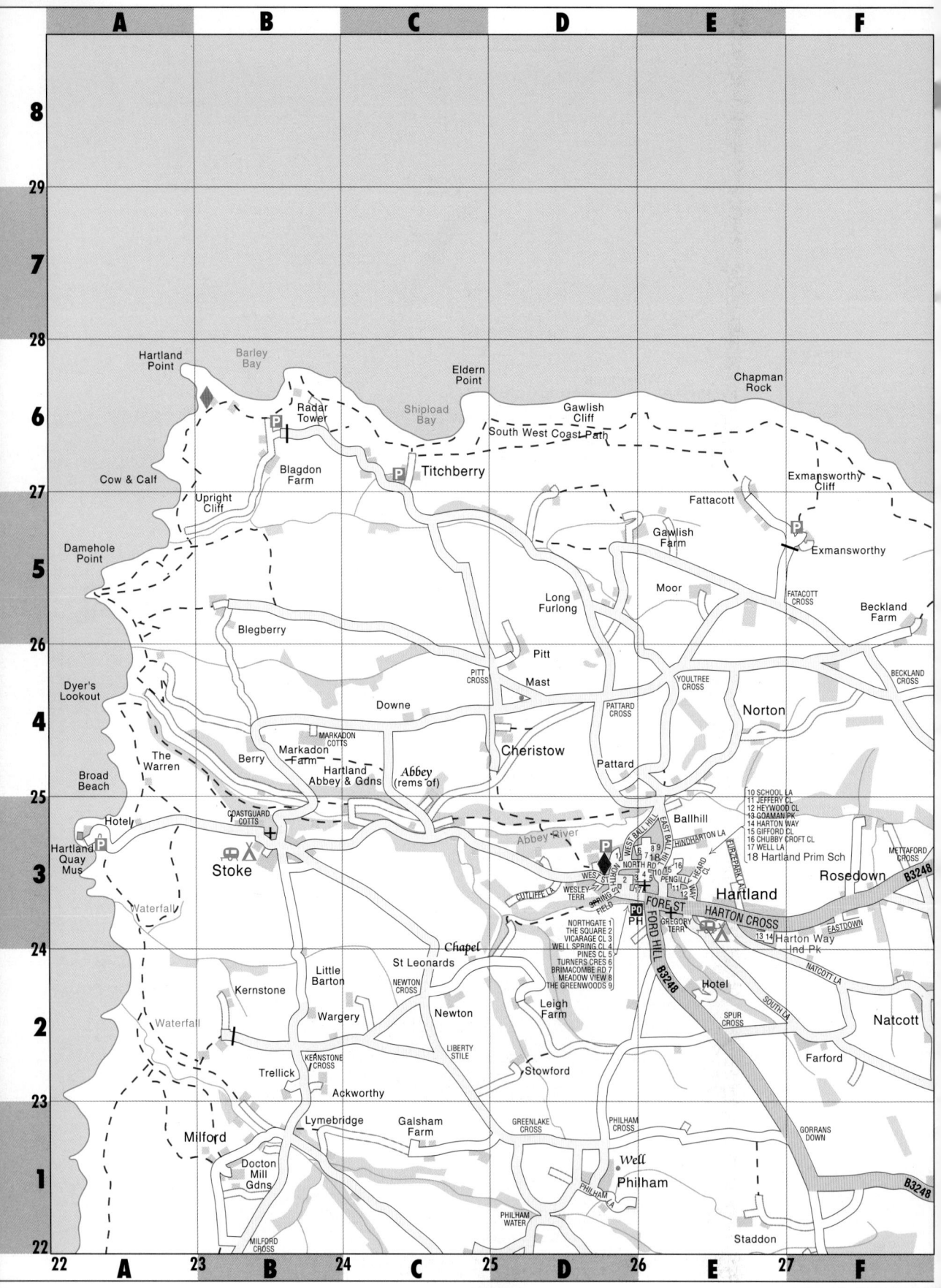

Hartland Point
Barley Bay
Radar Tower
Blagdon Farm
Cow & Calf
Upright Cliff
Damehole Point
Blegberry
Dyer's Lookout
The Warren
Berry
Broad Beach
Hotel
Hartland Quay Mus
Stoke
COASTGUARD COTTS
Waterfall
Markadon Farm
MARKADON COTTS
Hartland Abbey & Gdns
Abbey (rems of)
Downe
Pitt Cross
Mast
Pitt
Cheristow
Shipload Bay
Eldern Point
South West Coast Path
Gawlish Cliff
Titchberry
Fattacott
Gawlish Farm
Moor
Long Furlong
Chapman Rock
Exmansworthy Cliff
Exmansworthy
FATACOTT CROSS
Beckland Farm
BECKLAND CROSS
Norton
YOULTREE CROSS
PATTARD CROSS
Pattard
Ballhill
WEST BALL HILL
EAST BALL HILL
HINDHARTON LA
FIRZEPARK LA
Hartland
Rosedown
METTAFORD CROSS
B3248
HARTON CROSS
EASTDOWN
Harton Way Ind Pk
Hotel
SPUR CROSS
SOUTH LA
NATCOTT LA
Natcott
Farford
GORRANS DOWN
B3248
Staddon
Philham
PHILHAM WATER
PHILHAM LA
Well
GREENLAKE CROSS
PHILHAM CROSS
Galsham Farm
Lymebridge
Docton Mill Gdns
MILFORD CROSS
Milford
Trellick
KERNSTONE CROSS
Ackworthy
Kernstone
Wargery
Little Barton
St Leonards
NEWTON CROSS
Newton
LIBERTY STILE
Leigh Farm
Stowford
Chapel
Waterfall

10 SCHOOL LA
11 JEFFERY CL
12 HEYWOOD CL
13 GOAMAN PK
14 HARTON WAY
15 GIFFORD CL
16 CHUBBY CROFT CL
17 WELL LA
18 Hartland Prim Sch

NORTHGATE 1
THE SQUARE 2
VICARAGE CL 3
WELL SPRING CL 4
PINES CL 5
TURNERS CRES 6
BRIMACOMBE RD 7
MEADOW VIEW 8
THE GREENWOODS 9

WESLEY TERR
CUTLIFFE LA
NORTH RD
WEST ST
SPRINGFIELD
FORD HILL
FOREST ST
PO
PH
GREGORY TERR
PENGILLY WAY
Abbey River

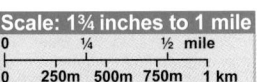

A   **B**   **C**   **D**   **E**   **F**

8

29

7

28

6

27

Beckland Bay   Windbury Point

Blackchurch Rock

5

Mouth Mill

Brownsham

P

26

Snaxland

South West Coast Path

Wood Rock

4

Highdown Cottage   Yapham Farm

Clovelly Court Gdns

Gallant Rock

HIGHDOWN CROSS

YAPHAM CROSS

25

UNDERDOWN   B3237

Hescott Farm

P

LB Sta

PH   Clovelly

Velly

Visitor Centre

HIGH ST

Mettaford Farm

LIGHTHOUSE CROSS

Chapel

SLERRA

Clovelly Prim Sch

Wrinkleberry

Slerra

Bight a Doubleyou

3

WRINKLEBERRY

Hugglepit

WINSWORTHY

BURSCOTT

THE HOBBY   The Hobby

Lower Bight of Fernham

TURNPIKE CL

24

Highford Farm

STOOP

Higher Clovelly

Holloford Farm

Eastacott

2

Warmleigh Farm

Clovelly Dykes

B3248   B3237

WOOLFARDISWORTHY CROSS

Hobby Lodge

Clovelly Cross

ATLANTIC HIGHWAY   DOWNLAND CROSS

Burnstone

A39

Mast

23

BAXWORTHY CROSS

DOWNLAND CROSS

Wr Twr

Milky Way Adventure Pk

1

B3248

A39

STITWORTHY CROSS

Thornery

Slade Farm

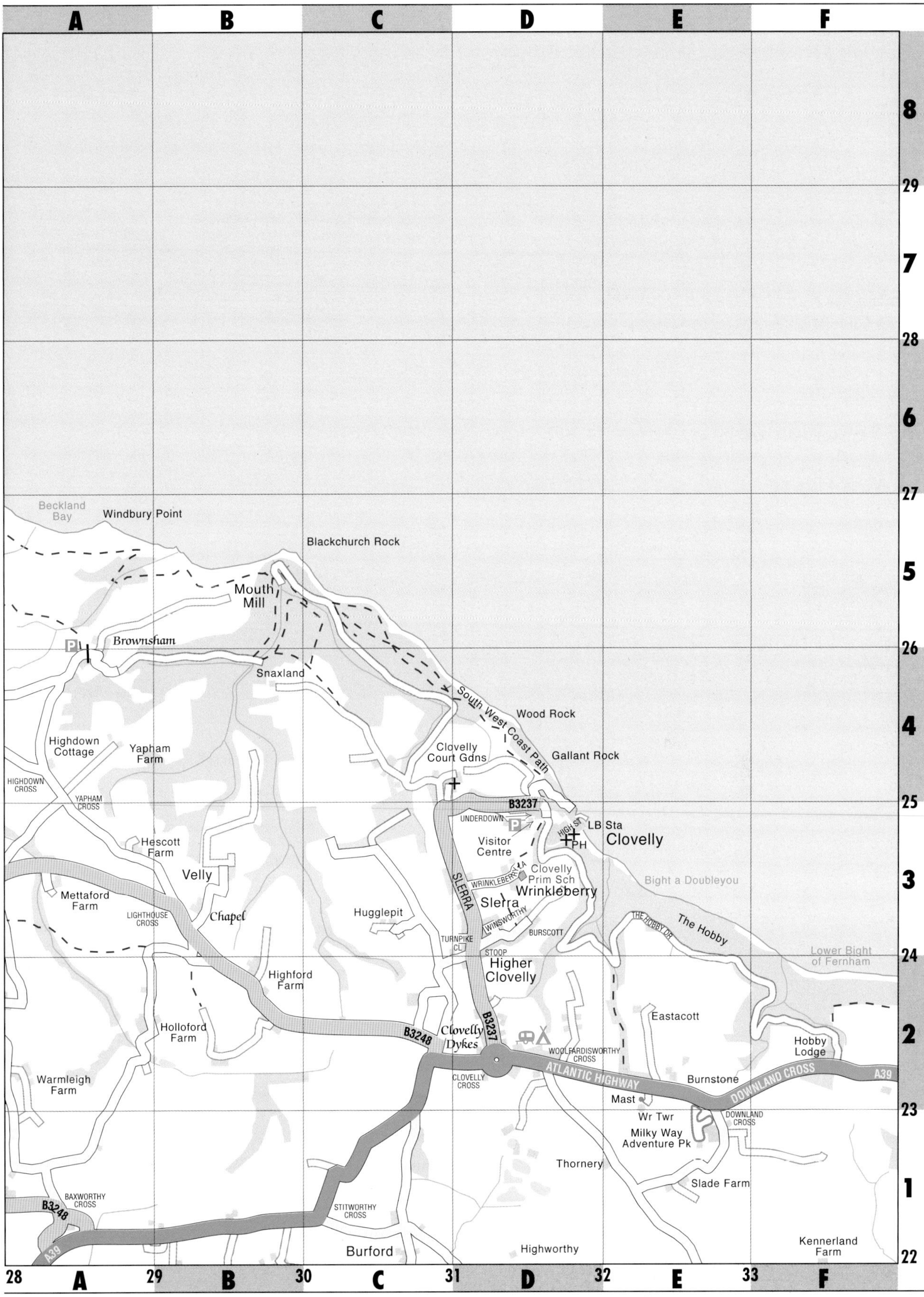

Burford

Highworthy

Kennerland Farm

22

28   **A**   29   **B**   30   **C**   31   **D**   32   **E**   33   **F**

Scale: 1¾ inches to 1 mile
0   ¼   ½   mile
0   250m 500m 750m 1 km

A   B   C   D   E   F

8

29

7

28

6

27

5

26

4

25

3

24

2

23

1

22

Babbacombe Mouth
Babbacombe Cliff
Higher Rowden
Portledge
Chiddlecombe
Gauter Point
Castle
Peppercombe
Gilscott
South West Coast Path
Sloo
Northway
Buck's Mills
Hoops PH
PH
Horns Cross
Holwell
Holiday Village
Atlantic Acad
Watershute
Waytown
Goldworthy
DOTHERIDGE LA
Buck's Cross
Cemy
WALLAND DR
Walland
Foxdown Manor
Bitworthy
Limebury
Broad Parkham
Newhaven
BREWERS HILL
PARKHAM CROSS
ATLANTIC HIGHWAY
A39

34   A   35   B   36   C   37   D   38   E   39   F

Scale: 1¾ inches to 1 mile
0 ¼ ½ mile
0 250m 500m 750m 1 km

14
26

A B C D E F

8
Northam Burrows Country Park
Westward Ho!
CH
Diddywell
Sch
APPLEDORE RD
JACKETS LA
PEBBLERIDGE RD
VENTON DR
GOLF LINKS RD
KINGSLEY RD
BEACH RD
AVON LA
TORVILLE PK
TADWORTHY RD
LAKENHAM HILL
TOWER ST
NORTH ST
CROSS ST
FORE ST
DIDDYWELL RD
HIGHBURY HILL
LONG LA
TAYLOR DR
DENESHAY DR
CHURCHILL WAY
BIDNA LA
WINDMILL LA
PO
NELSON RD
ATLANTIC WAY
MERLEY RD
STANWELL HILL

29
Mermaid's Pool
BAY VIEW RD
Mast
Buckleigh
CORNBOROUGH RD
BENSON DR
GOATS HILL RD
CLEVELANDS PK
GLUDEN RD
CHOPE RD
DADDON HILL
HEYWOOD RD
B3236

7
Northam
South West Coast Path
DURRANT LA
Port Hill
PH
Pusehill
PUSEHILL RD
BUCKLEIGH RD
SILFORD RD
LENWOOD RD
RALEIGH HILL
LIMERS LA
LOWER GRIPE
Cornborough

28
Silford
A39
Orchard Hill
ORCHARD HILL
Torridge Bridge
Raleigh Hill
RALEIGH HILL
Kenwith
Abbotsham Court
FIRST RALEIGH
Ferry P
CHANTERS RD
PARK LA
NORTHAM RD
KINGSLEY RD

6
Rickard's Down
ROCK LA
Combe Walker
Combe
Shamland
BIDEFORD
Sch
Mus
NORTHDOWN RD
Greencliff
Rixlade
Abbotsham
PH
OSBORNE LA
WATER PARK RD
LANE FIELD RD
SLADE
NORTH RD
LIME GR
MILL ST
PITT LA
THE QUAY
A386
BARNSTAPLE ST

27
BACK LA
PUMP LA
PO
Farm Pk
Sch
GLEBE HOUSES
ATLANTIC HIGHWAY
Winsford
ABBOTSHAM RD
BELVOIR RD
HIGH ST
OLD TOWN
MEDDON ST
GRANGE RD
Coll
ROYSTON RD
Moreton Park
LAUREL AVE
MORETON PARK RD
STUCLEY RD
PYNES LA
CAPERN RD
TORRINGTON LA
CLIFTON ST
Westacott

5
156
157
Sch
MEADOW PK
HAMILTON CL
SPEEDWELL CL
ROWE CL
STRATHMORE CT
NEW RD
Old Ford House
Kynock Ind Est
Bowood
ABBOTSHAM CROSS
Kingdon Ent Pk
ADAMS CT
CLOVELLY RD
Cemy
MARLEN CT
WHITING CL
NUTTABERRY BGLWS
Cockington Farm
Babbacombe Farm
GIPSY LA
Superstore
STANWELL HILL
Atlantic Village Outlet Shopping
Adjavin Farm
SCRATCHFACE LA
FARM RD
Caddsdown Ind Pk
Caddsdown
BUCKLAND RD
Fletcher Ind Est
River Torridge
Tarka Trail

26
1 GRENVILLE ESTATE CRES
2 RICHARD CL
3 PYNES WLK
4 THE GRENVILLE EST
5 BOWDEN GN
6 BUCKLAND CL
7 HANDY CROSS

1 ATLANTIC PK WAY
2 PINCOMBE RD
3 SAMS CL
4 DADDON CL

1 CHESTNUT DR
2 WILLOW GR
3 CEDAR WAY
4 LOMBARD CL
5 BEECH BANK
6 BRENNACOTT RD
7 HIGH PARK CL
8 BRENNACOTT PL
9 Clovelly Road Ind Est

Upcott Farm
UPCOTT HILL
COACH DR
Knotty Corner

4
High Park
Hallsannery
Ford
Jennetts Resr
TOM'S LA
Winscott
Fairy Cross
Littleham Court
Ashridge

25
PORTLEDGE PL
CHURCH PK
DUNN LA
LITTLEHAM CROSS
Moorhead
Yeo Vale
Woodtown
MOUNT PLEASANT
ALTAMIRA COTTS
APP'S LA
SCRATCHFACE LA
Heale House
CHURCH LA
Littleham
A388
A386

3
Rollstone
Alwington
BOUNDSTONE CTS
Hooper's Water Farm
Edge Mill
DOTHERIDGE LA
River Yeo
Bulland
South Yeo
Annery

24
Tuckingmill
ORLEIGH CT
ORLEIGH MILL WLK
Orleigh Mills
Howley
Beara Farm
Halsbury
Saltrens
LEE AVE

2
23
1
22

40 A 41 B 42 C 43 D 44 E 45 F

40
26
For full street detail of the highlighted area see pages 156 and 157.

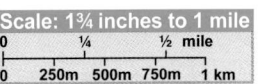

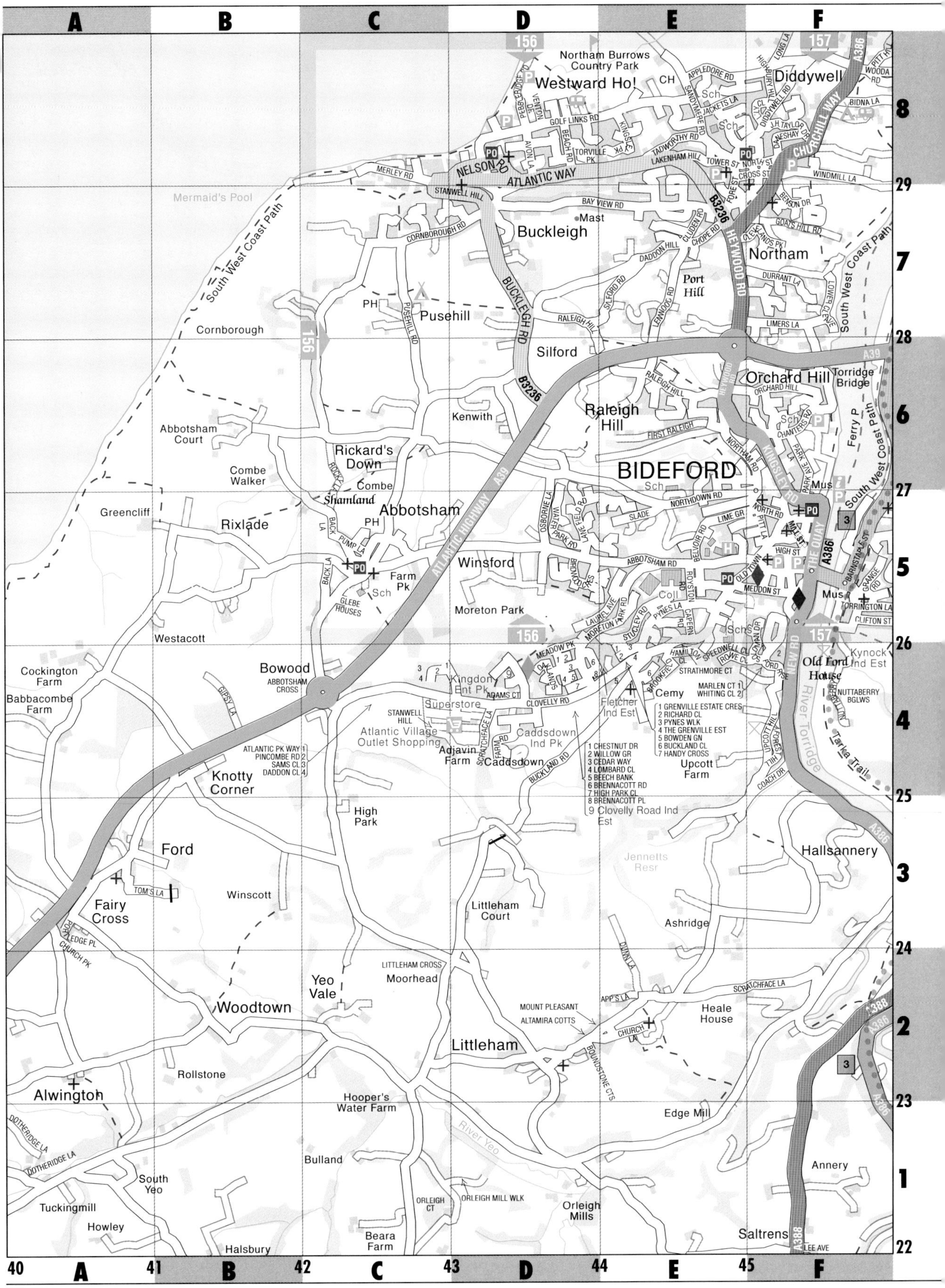

A   B   C   D   E   F

157
B3233
WOODA RD
BIDNA LS
Shipyard
Ferry P
WINTONILLA
South West Coast Path
River Torridge
South West Coast Path
8

29

PH
Westleigh
3
LANGMEAD
Tapeley Park & Gardens
Huish
Combe
Treyhill
BARNACOTT CROSS
Orchard Farm
Huish Moor
Knowle Farm
Mast
Holmacott
Brookham
Masts
LITCHARDON CROSS
HOLMACOTT CROSS
Voscombe
VOSCOMBE CROSS

7

B3233
CRAMPIT
Ball Hill
BLACKGATE CROSS
Bradavin Farm
Eastleigh Manor
HORWOOD CROSS
Pyewell
Horwood
East Barton Farm
LOVACOTT GR
N1

28

A39
Southcott
COBLEY LA
Eastleigh
Blackdown La
West Barton Farm
Boskins

6

27

Cemy
OLD BARNSTAPLE RD
Pillhead
Weach Barton
Ashridge

5

East-the-Water
MINES RD
MANTED ST
Schl
BROADLANDS
TORRINGTON LA
MINES RD
YRES CL
Little Pillhead
Webbery Cross
Webbery House
Buddacombe
Bulworthy

26

PO
BRECON CL
ABBOTS DR
TRENTICL
MONK'S CL
COATES RD
ALVERDISCOTT RD
157
Warmington
CHUBB RD
CHURCHILL RD
CHOPES CL
LITTLE CT
LCRES
Woodtown
BOUNDARY PK
Stony Cross

4

BARTON HO 1
GOAMAN RD 2
CLIVEDEN RD 3
TENACOTT HTS 4
FULFORD CL 5
OCHIL CL 6
WICKHAM CL 7
Alverdiscott Road Ind Est
GAMMATON RD
Woodville Farm
Gammaton
Gammaton Resrs
Alverdiscott
B3232

25

PAPACOTT LA
Tennacott Farm
Beara
Gammaton Moor
GAMMATON MOOR CROSS
Brownscombe
Haddacott
HADDACOTT CROSS
Garnacott Farm

3

A386
Pillmouth
Tarka Trail
Oldiscleave Farm
GUSCOTT LA
FORCE LA
Guscott
Huntshaw Water

24

Landcross
A386
River Torridge

2

Hallspill
Netherdowns
Little Weare Barton
Huxhill
TWITCHEN CROSS
HUNTSHAW MOOR CROSS

23

A386
ANNERY KILN COTTS
Venton
Huntshaw
Knockworthy Farm
KNOCKWORTHY CROSS

1

Tarka Trail
The Hill
CHURCHVIEW
Weare Giffard
3
TAVERN GDNS
Park
Southcott Barton
Huntshaw Mill Bridge
Berry Castle
Woodhouse Farm
FOXES CROSS
Waggadon
DARRACOTT

22

46   A   47   B   48   C   49   D   50   E   51   F

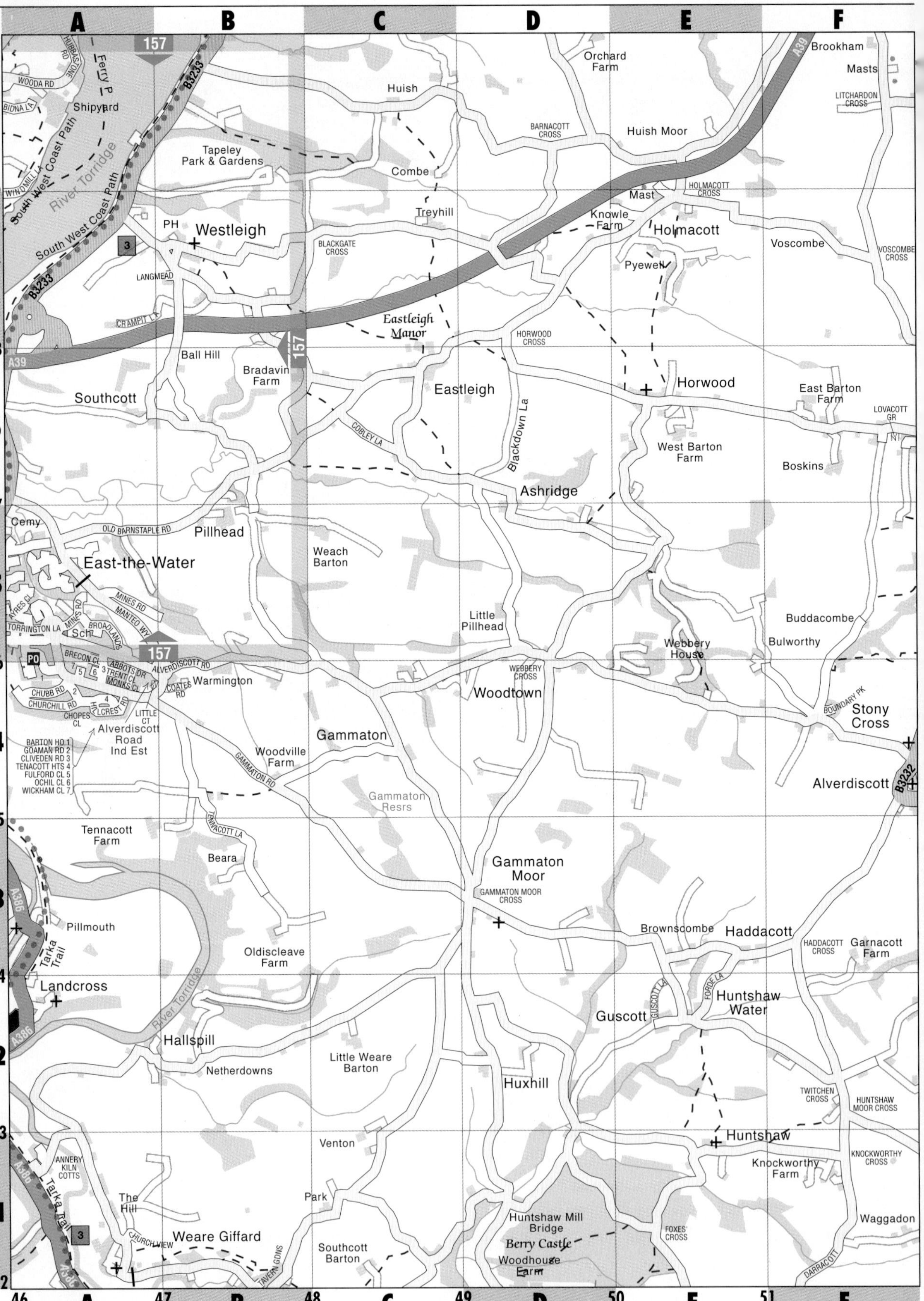

For full street detail of the highlighted area see page 157.

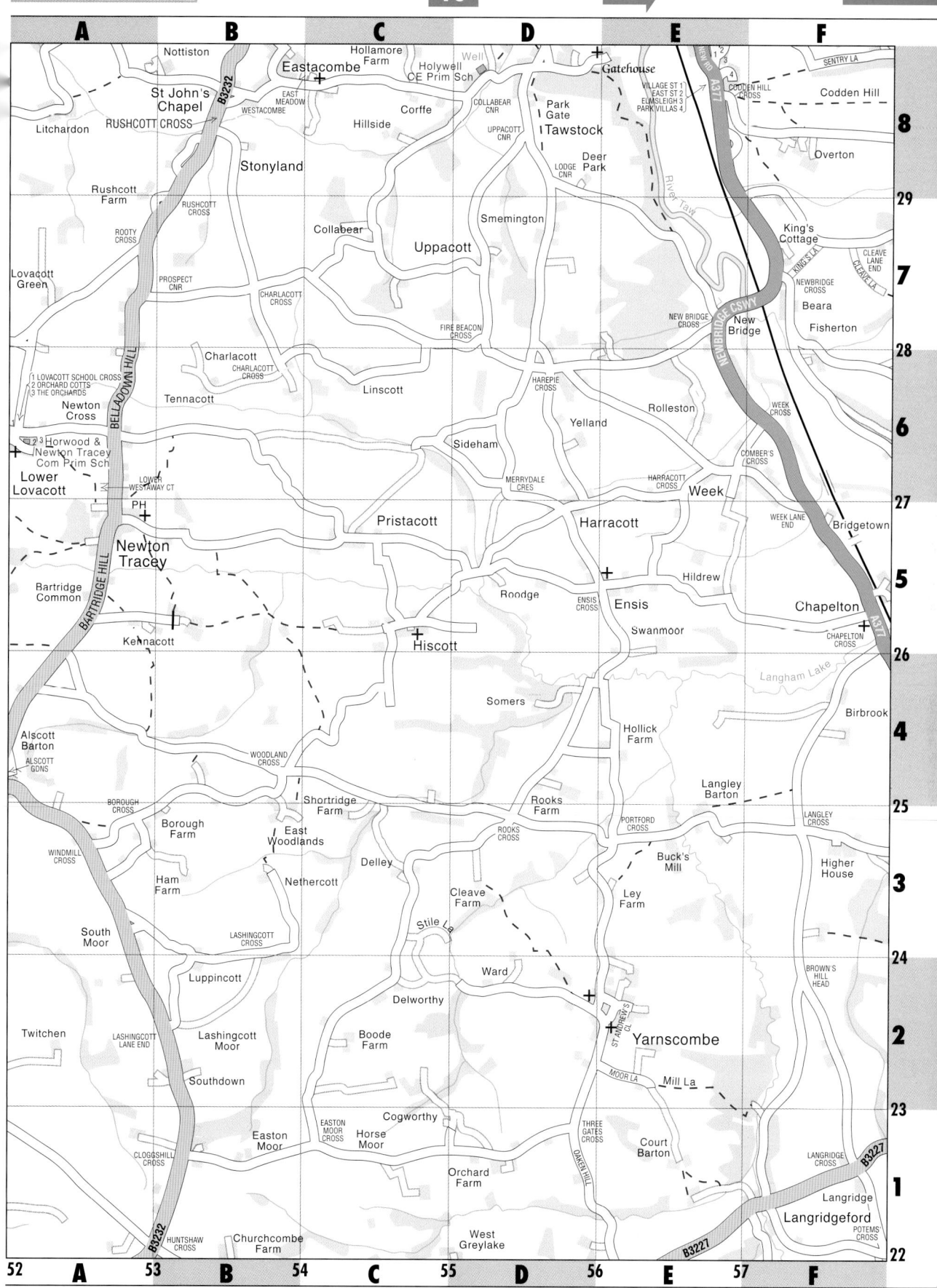

A   B   C   D   E   F

SENTRY LA

Nottiston

St John's Chapel
RUSHCOTT CROSS

Eastacombe

Hollamore Farm

Well

Holywell CE Prim Sch

Gatehouse

CODDEN HILL CROSS

Codden Hill

Litchardon

EAST MEADOW
WESTACOMBE

Corffe

COLLABEAR CNR

Park Gate

Tawstock

VILLAGE ST 1
EAST ST 2
ELMSLEIGH 3
PARK VILLAS 4

8

Hillside

UPPACOTT CNR

Overton

Stonyland

Rushcott Farm

RUSHCOTT CROSS

Collabear

Smemington

LODGE CNR

Deer Park

River Taw

29

ROOTY CROSS

Uppacott

King's Cottage

7

Lovacott Green

PROSPECT CNR

CHARLACOTT CROSS

FIRE BEACON CROSS

NEW BRIDGE CROSS

NEWBRIDGE CROSS

CLEAVE LANE END

CLEAVE LA

28

Charlacott

New Bridge

Beara

Fisherton

1 LOVACOTT SCHOOL CROSS
2 ORCHARD COTTS
3 THE ORCHARDS

CHARLACOTT CROSS

Linscott

HAREPIE CROSS

Rolleston

WEEK CROSS

6

Newton Cross

Tennacott

Yelland

NEWBRIDGE CSWY

Horwood & Newton Tracey Com Prim Sch

Sideham

MERRYDALE CRES

HARRACOTT CROSS

COMBER'S CROSS

27

Lower Lovacott

LOWER WESTAWAY CT

PH

Pristacott

Harracott

Week

WEEK LANE END

Bridgetown

Newton Tracey

Roodge

ENSIS CROSS

Ensis

Hildrew

Chapelton

5

Bartridge Common

Kennacott

Hiscott

Swanmoor

CHAPELTON CROSS

A377

BARTRIDGE HILL

BELLADOWN HILL

B3232

Somers

Langham Lake

26

Alscott Barton

WOODLAND CROSS

Hollick Farm

Birbrook

4

ALSCOTT GDNS

Langley Barton

BOROUGH CROSS

Shortridge Farm

Rooks Farm

PORTFORD CROSS

LANGLEY CROSS

25

WINDMILL CROSS

Borough Farm

East Woodlands

Delley

ROOKS CROSS

Buck's Mill

Higher House

3

Ham Farm

Nethercott

Cleave Farm

Ley Farm

South Moor

LASHINGCOTT CROSS

Stile La

Ward

BROWN'S HILL HEAD

24

Luppincott

Delworthy

ST ANDREW'S CL

2

Twitchen

LASHINGCOTT LANE END

Lashingcott Moor

Boode Farm

Yarnscombe

MOOR LA

Mill La

Southdown

Cogworthy

23

CLOGGSHILL CROSS

Easton Moor

EASTON MOOR CROSS

Horse Moor

THREE GATES CROSS

Court Barton

LANGRIDGE CROSS

B3227

1

B3232

HUNTSHAW CROSS

Churchcombe Farm

Orchard Farm

West Greylake

OAKEN HILL

B3227

Langridge

Langridgeford

POTEMS CROSS

22

52   A   53   B   54   C   55   D   56   E   57   F

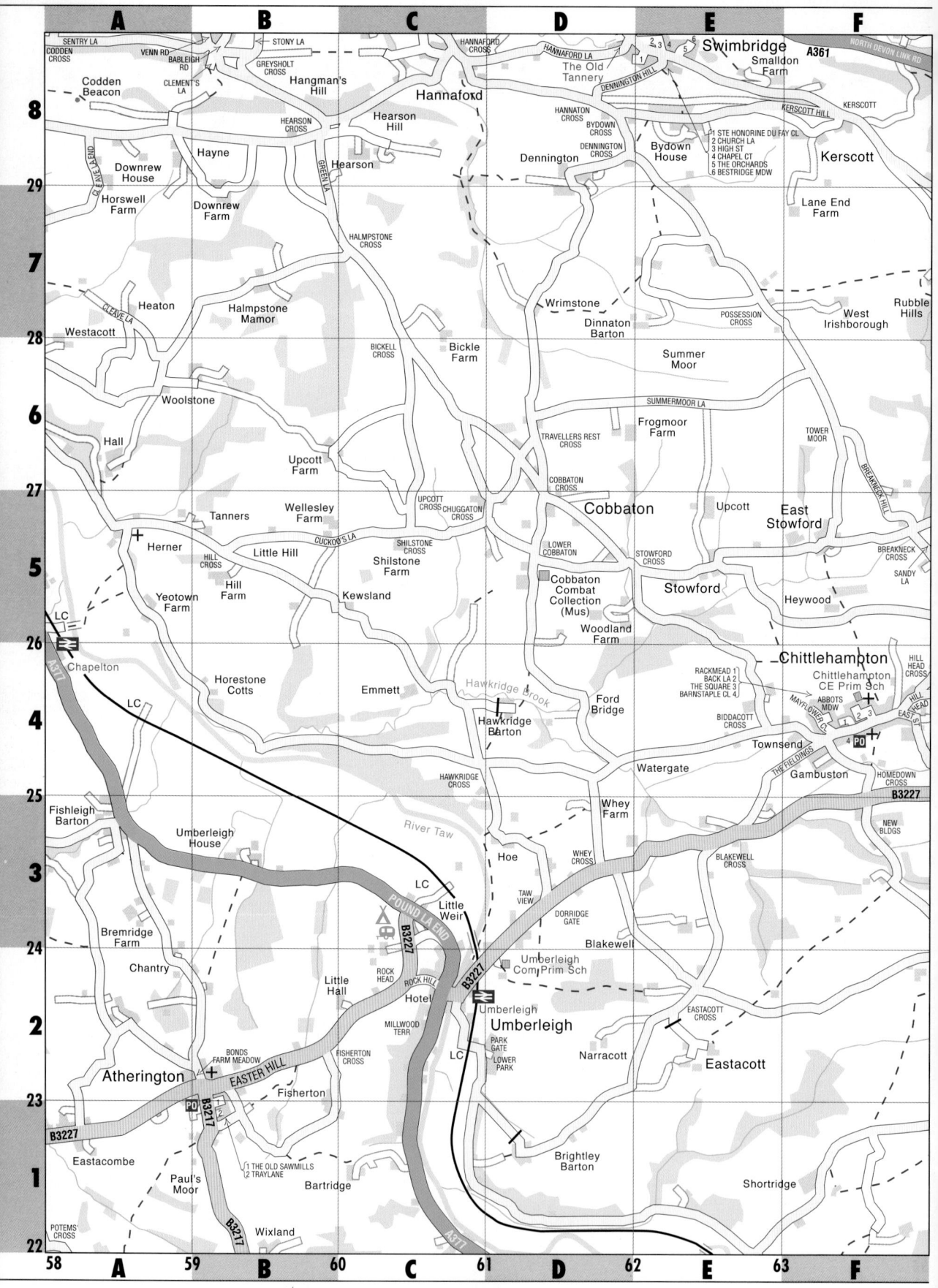

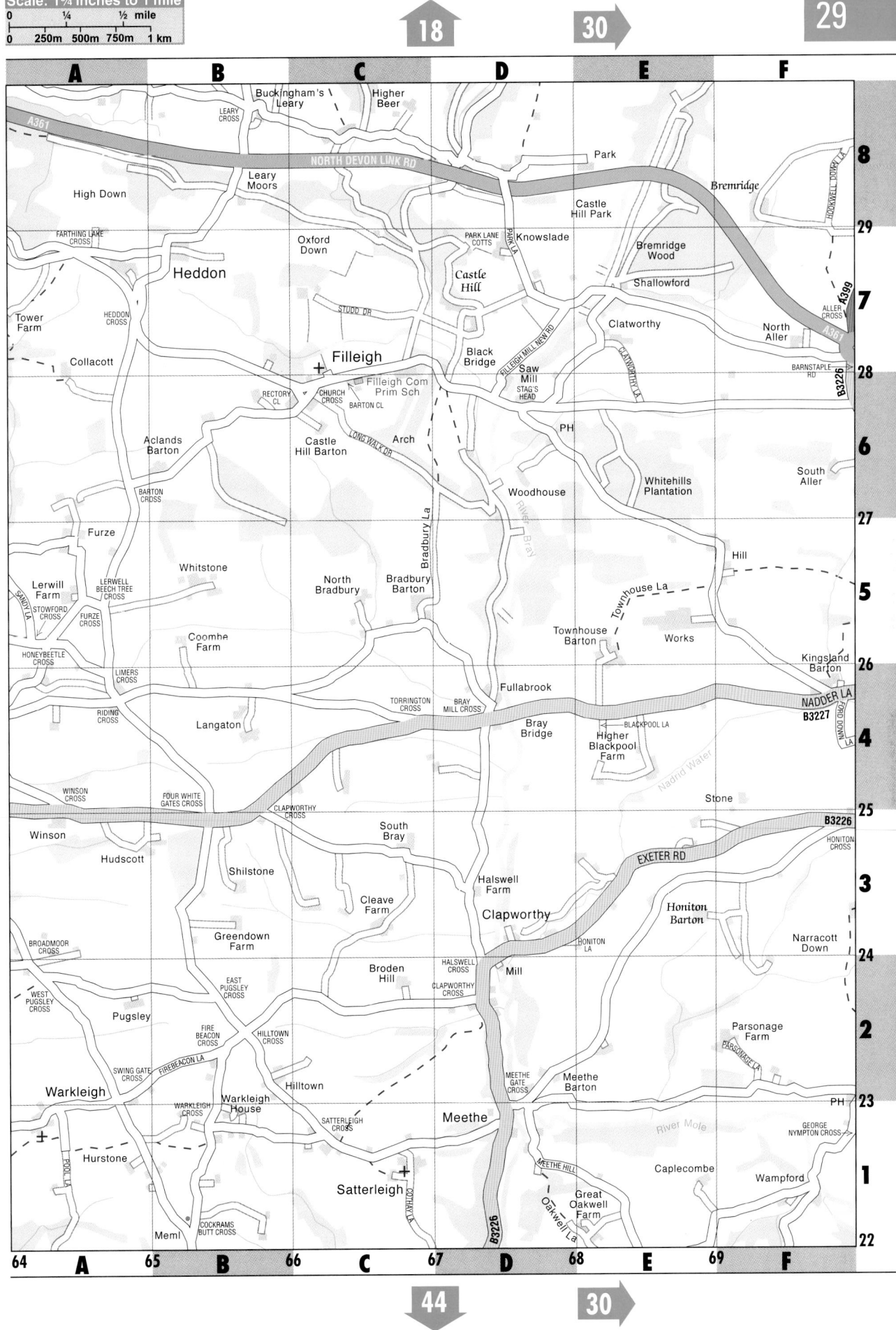

A   B   C   D   E   F

A361
NORTH DEVON LINK RD
Buckingham's Leary
LEARY CROSS
Higher Beer
Park
Bremridge
HOCKWELL DOWN LA

High Down
Leary Moors
Castle Hill Park
Bremridge Wood
8
29
FARTHING LAKE CROSS
Oxford Down
Park Lane Cotts
PARK LA
Knowslade
Shallowford
A399

Heddon
HEDDON CROSS
Castle Hill
Clatworthy
ALLER CROSS
North Aller
A361
7
28

Tower Farm
Collacott
STUDD DR
Filleigh
Black Bridge
FILLEIGH MILL NEW RD
Saw Mill
STAG'S HEAD
CLATWORTHY LA
BARNSTAPLE RD
B3226

RECTORY CL
CHURCH CROSS
Filleigh Com Prim Sch
BARTON CL
PH
6

Aclands Barton
Castle Hill Barton
LONG WALK DR
Arch
Woodhouse
Whitehills Plantation
South Aller
27

BARTON CROSS
Bradbury La
River Bray
Hill
5

Furze
Whitstone
North Bradbury
Bradbury Barton
Townhouse La
Townhouse Barton
Works
26

Lerwill Farm
SANDY LA
LERWELL BEECH TREE CROSS
STOWFORD CROSS
FURZE CROSS
Coombe Farm
Fullabrook
Kingsland Barton
NADDER LA
B3227
CHOWN LA
4

LIMERS CROSS
HONEYBEETLE CROSS
TORRINGTON CROSS
BRAY MILL CROSS
Bray Bridge
BLACKPOOL LA
Higher Blackpool Farm

RIDING CROSS
Langaton
Stone
25

WINSON CROSS
FOUR WHITE GATES CROSS
CLAPWORTHY CROSS
South Bray
EXETER RD
B3226
HONITON CROSS
3

Winson
Hudscott
Shilstone
Cleave Farm
Halswell Farm
Clapworthy
Honiton Barton
Narracott Down
24

BROADMOOR CROSS
Greendown Farm
EAST PUGSLEY CROSS
Broden Hill
HALSWELL CROSS
HONITON LA
Mill
CLAPWORTHY CROSS
Parsonage Farm
PARSONAGE LA
2

WEST PUGSLEY CROSS
Pugsley
FIRE BEACON CROSS
HILLTOWN CROSS
Meethe Barton
PH
23

Warkleigh
SWING GATE CROSS
FIREBEACON LA
WARKLEIGH CROSS
Warkleigh House
Hilltown
SATTERLEIGH CROSS
MEETHE GATE CROSS
Meethe
George Nympton Cross

Hurstone
POOL LA
COTHAY LA
Satterleigh
Great Oakwell Farm
MEETHE HILL
OAKWELL LA
Caplecombe
Wampford
1

Meml
COCKRAMS BUTT CROSS
B3226
River Mole
22

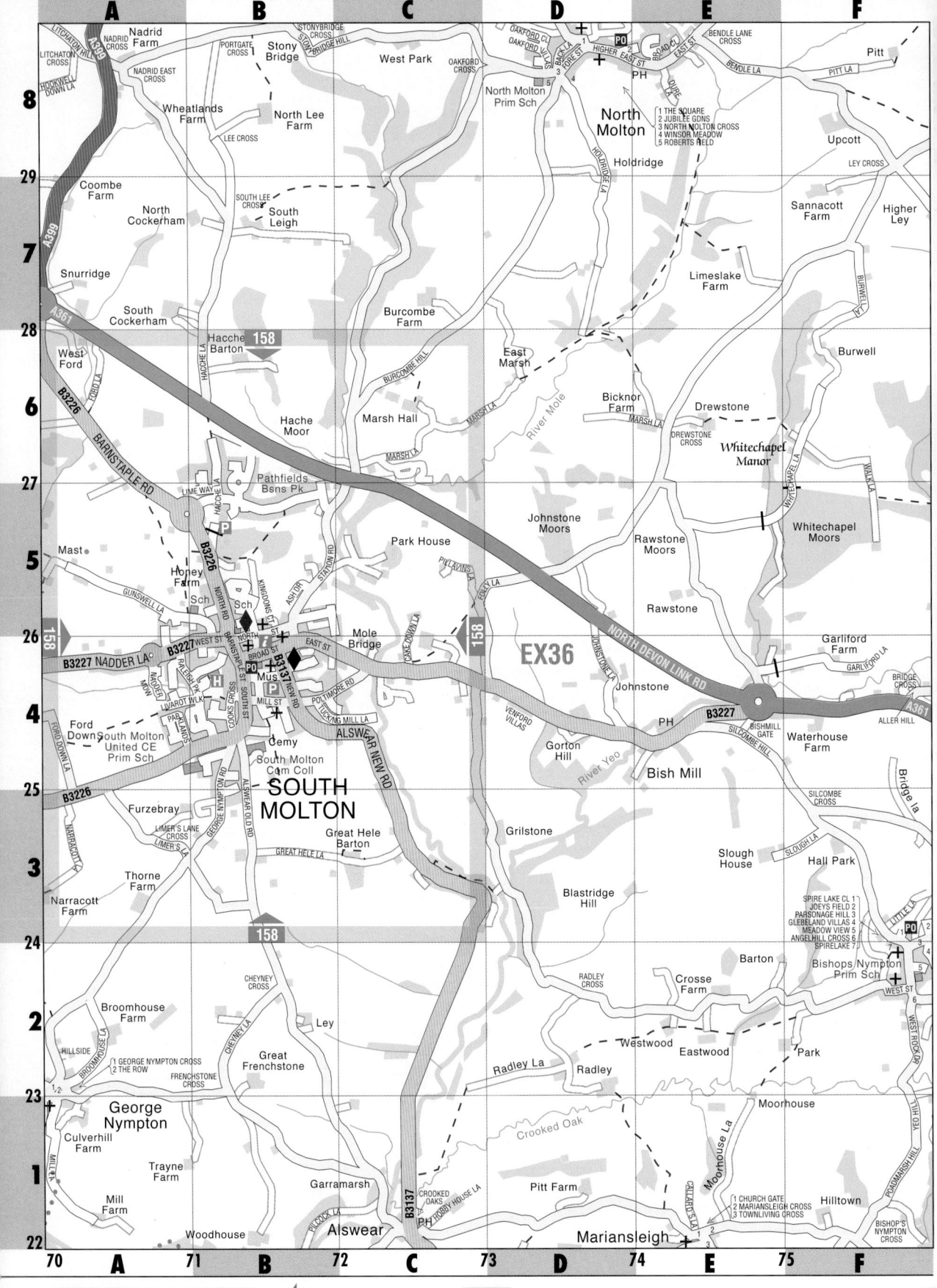

29
19

Scale: 1¾ inches to 1 mile

0   ¼   ½   mile
0   250m 500m 750m 1 km

South Molton / North Molton area

Litchaton Cross
Litchaton Hill
A399
Nadrid Cross
Nadrid Farm
Hookwell Down La
Portgate Cross
Stonybridge Cross
Stony Bridge
Stonybridge Hill
West Park
Oakford Cross
Oakford Cl
Oakford Villas
Back La
Fore St
Road Cl
East St
Bendle Lane Cross
Bendle La
Pitt
Pitt La
North Molton Prim Sch
North Molton
1 THE SQUARE
2 JUBILEE GDNS
3 NORTH MOLTON CROSS
4 WINSOR MEADOW
5 ROBERTS FIELD
Ley Cross
Upcott
Nadrid East Cross
Wheatlands Farm
North Lee Farm
Lee Cross
Holdridge
Holdridge La
Sannacott Farm
Higher Ley
Coombe Farm
North Cockerham
South Lee Cross
South Leigh
Ure
Snurridge
A361
Limeslake Farm
Burwell La
South Cockerham
West Ford
A361
Hacche La
Hacche Barton
158
Burcombe Farm
Burcombe Hill
Marsh La
East Marsh
River Mole
Bicknor Farm
Marsh La
Drewstone
Whitechapel Manor
Burwell
B3226
Cobda La
Barnstaple Rd
Hache Moor
Marsh Hall
Marsh La
Drewstone Cross
Whitechapel La
Walk La
Mast
Lime Way
Hacche La
Pathfields Bsns Pk
Park House
Pillavins
Johnstone Moors
Rawstone Moors
Whitechapel Moors
Honey Farm
B3226
North Rd
Kingsnoms Ct
Ash Dr
Station Rd
Folly La
Gunswell La
Sch
Sch
Mole Bridge
Cake Down La
158
Rawstone
Garliford Farm
158
West St
B3227
Barnstaple St
Broad St
East St
Christone La
Johnstone
EX36
NORTH DEVON LINK RD
Garliford Cross
Bridge Cross
B3227 Nadder La
PO
Mus
New Rd
Poltimore Rd
South St
Mill St
B3137
Aller Hill
A361
H
Cooks Cross
Tucking Mill La
Venford Villas
PH
B3227
Bishmill Gate
Silcombe Hill
Waterhouse Farm
Ford Down
South Molton United CE Prim Sch
Labot Wlk
Cemy
Alswear New Rd
Gorton Hill
River Yeo
Bish Mill
Cowley
South Molton Com Coll
Cemy
SOUTH MOLTON
George Nympton Rd
Alswear Old Rd
Furzebray
Great Hele Barton
Great Hele La
Grilstone
Slough House
Slough La
Silcombe Cross
Hall Park
Bridge La
Limer's Lane Cross
Limer's La
Blastridge Hill
Narracott
Thorne Farm
Narracott Farm
158
Radley Cross
Crosse Farm
Barton
Spire Lake Cl 1
Joeys Field 2
Parsonage Hill 3
Glebeland Villas 4
Meadow View 5
Angelhill Cross 6
Spirelake 7
Little La
PO
Bishops Nympton Prim Sch
West St
Broomhouse La
Broomhouse Farm
Cheyney Cross
Cheyney La
Ley
Westwood
Eastwood
Park
West Rd
Hillside
1 GEORGE NYMPTON CROSS
2 THE ROW
Great Frenchstone
Frenchstone Cross
Radley La
Radley
Moorhouse La
Moorhouse
TTH LA
½
George Nympton
Mill La
Culverhill Farm
Trayne Farm
Garramarsh
Crooked Oak
Pitt Farm
Callard's La
Moorhouse La
1 CHURCH GATE
2 MARIANSLEIGH CROSS
3 TOWNLIVING CROSS
Hilltown
Pogmarsh La
Bishop's Nympton Cross
Mill Farm
Woodhouse
Pilcock La
Alswear
B3137
Crooked Oaks
Hobby House La
PH
Mariansleigh

29
45
For full street detail of the highlighted area see page 158.

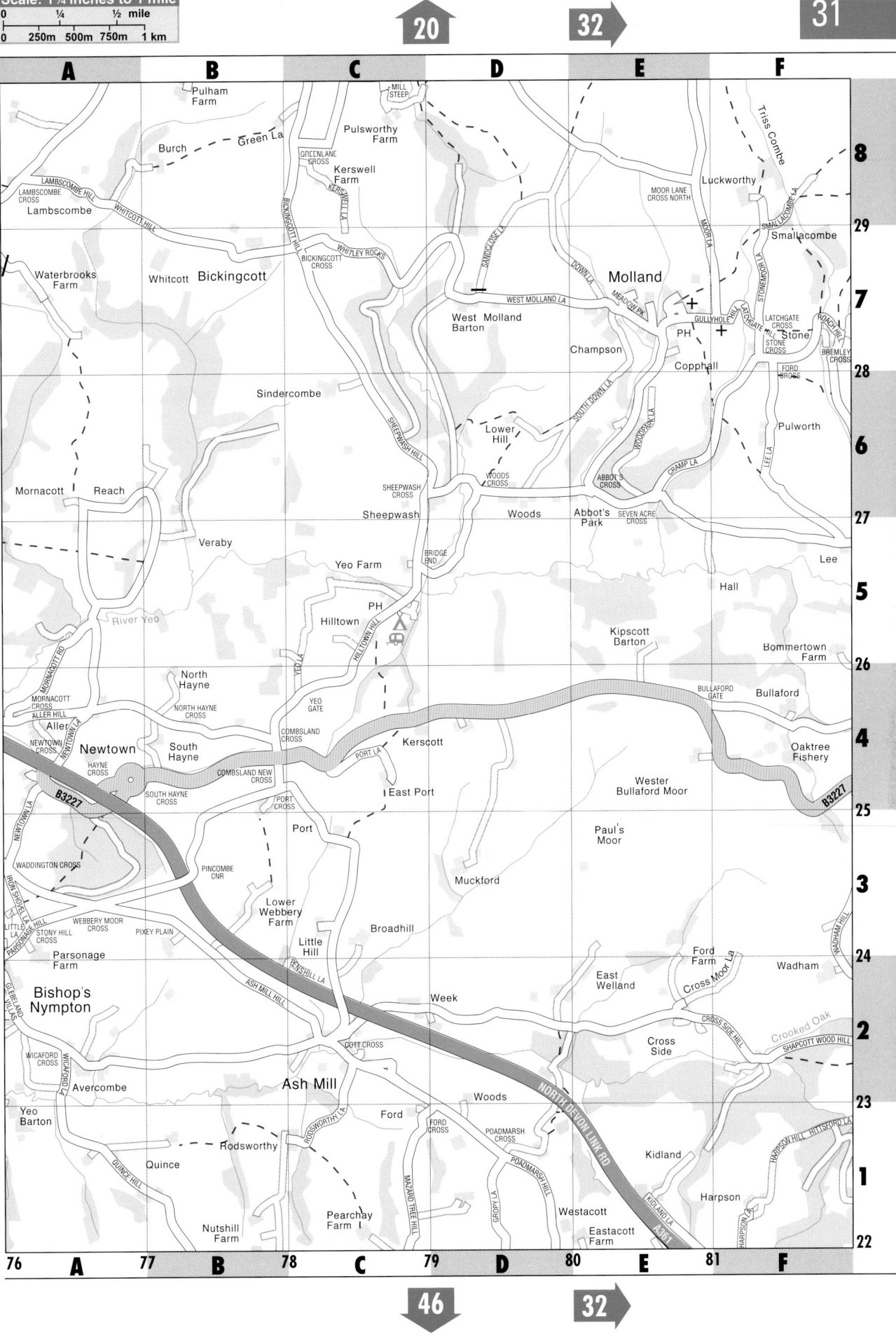
Scale: 1¾ inches to 1 mile
0 ¼ ½ mile
0 250m 500m 750m 1 km
20
32
A B C D E F
Pulham Farm
MILL STEEP
Pulsworthy Farm
Triss Combe
Burch
Green La
GREENLANE CROSS
Kerswell Farm
KERSWELL LA
Luckworthy
MOOR LANE CROSS NORTH
LAMBSCOMBE HILL
LAMBSCOMBE CROSS
Lambscombe
WHITCOTT HILL
BICKINGCOTT HILL
WHITLEY ROCKS
BICKINGCOTT CROSS
SANDCLOSE LA
MOOR LA
SMALLACOMBE LA
Smallacombe
Waterbrooks Farm
Whitcott
Bickingcott
DOWN LA
Molland
MEADOW PK
STONEMOOR LA
WEST MOLLAND LA
West Molland Barton
GULLYHOLE HILL
LATCHGATE HILL
LATCHGATE CROSS
Stone
STONE CROSS
ROACH HILL
BREMLEY CROSS
PH
Champson
Copphall
FORD CROSS
Sindercombe
SOUTH DOWN LA
WOODPARK LA
Pulworth
Lower Hill
SHEEPWASH HILL
CRAMP LA
LEE LA
WOODS CROSS
ABBOT'S CROSS
Mornacott
Reach
SHEEPWASH CROSS
Sheepwash
Woods
Abbot's Park
SEVEN ACRE CROSS
Veraby
BRIDGE END
Yeo Farm
Lee
Hall
PH
River Yeo
Hilltown
HILLTOWN HILL
Kipscott Barton
MORNACOTT RD
YEO LA
Bommertown Farm
North Hayne
MORNACOTT CROSS
ALLER HILL
NORTH HAYNE CROSS
YEO GATE
BULLAFORD GATE
Bullaford
Aller
NEWTOWN LA
NEWTOWN CROSS
Newtown
South Hayne
COMBSLAND CROSS
Kerscott
PORT LA
Oaktree Fishery
HAYNE CROSS
COMBSLAND NEW CROSS
East Port
Wester Bullaford Moor
B3227
SOUTH HAYNE CROSS
PORT CROSS
Port
Paul's Moor
WADDINGTON CROSS
PINCOMBE CNR
Muckford
IRON SHOVEL LA
Lower Webbery Farm
LITTLE LA
PARSONAGE HILL
WEBBERY MOOR CROSS
STONY HILL CROSS
PIXEY PLAIN
Broadhill
Little Hill
WADHAM HILL
Parsonage Farm
Ford Farm
Wadham
BENSHILL LA
East Welland
Cross Moor La
Bishop's Nympton
GLEBELAND VILLAS
ASH MILL HILL
Week
CROSS SIDE HILL
Crooked Oak
SHAPCOTT WOOD HILL
Cross Side
WICAFORD CROSS
WICAFORD LA
COTT CROSS
Avercombe
Ash Mill
NORTH DEVON LINK RD
Woods
Yeo Barton
RODSWORTHY LA
Ford
FORD CROSS
PODMARSH CROSS
HARPSON HILL
HITTSFORD LA
Rodsworthy
Kidland
Quince
QUINCE HILL
MAZARD TREE HILL
PODMARSH HILL
GROPY LA
Harpson
KIDLAND LA
Nutshill Farm
Pearchay Farm
Westacott
Eastacott Farm
HARPSON LA
A361
8 29 7 28 6 27 5 26 4 25 3 24 2 23 1 22
76 77 78 79 80 81
46
32

← 31
↑ 21

Scale: 1¾ inches to 1 mile

0   ¼   ½ mile
0   250m   500m   750m   1 km

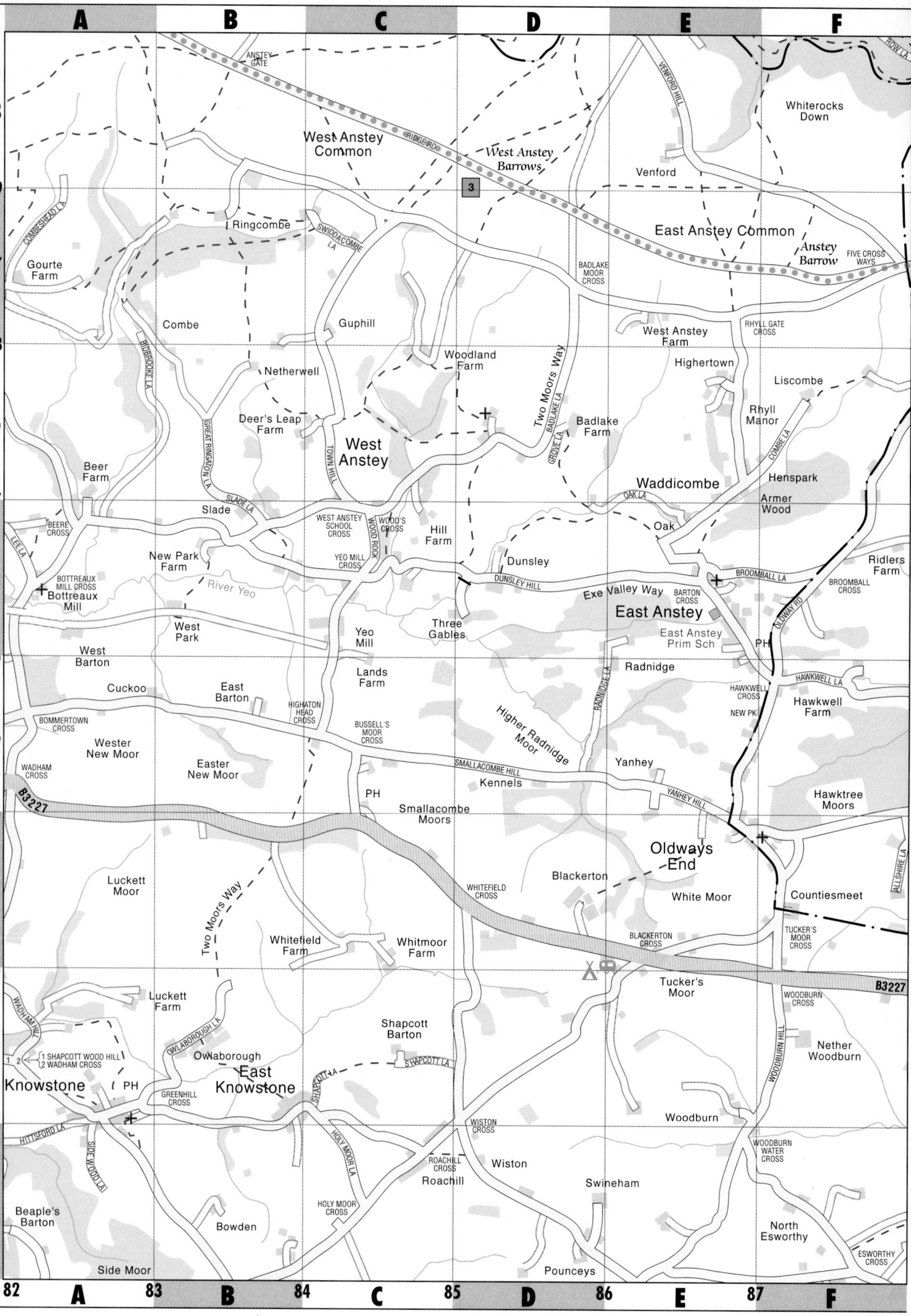

A   B   C   D   E   F

8

Anstey Gate

Whiterocks Down

RIDGE RD

West Anstey Common

West Anstey Barrows

Venford

ROW LA

VENFORD HILL

29

3

East Anstey Common

Anstey Barrow

Five Cross Ways

Ringcombe

SWINACOMBE LA

Badlake Moor Cross

West Anstey Farm

RHYLL GATE CROSS

7

Gourte Farm

COMBESHEAD LA

BIDBROOKE LA

Combe

Guphill

Woodland Farm

Highertown

Liscombe

28

Netherwell

TWO MOORS WAY

GROVE LA

BADLAKE LA

Rhyll Manor

COMBE LA

Deer's Leap Farm

Badlake Farm

Henspark

6

GREAT RINGION LA

TOWN HILL

West Anstey

Waddicombe

Armer Wood

Beer Farm

Slade

SLADE LA

OAK LA

Oak

27

BEERE CROSS

WEST ANSTEY SCHOOL CROSS

WOOD'S CROSS

Hill Farm

Dunsley

BROOMBALL LA

Ridlers Farm

LEE LA

New Park Farm

WOOD ROCK

YEO MILL CROSS

DUNSLEY HILL

OLDWAY RD

BROOMBALL CROSS

5

BOTTREAUX MILL CROSS

River Yeo

Exe Valley Way

BARTON CROSS

East Anstey

Bottreaux Mill

West Park

Yeo Mill

Three Gables

East Anstey Prim Sch

PH

26

West Barton

Lands Farm

Radnidge

HAWKWELL LA

Cuckoo

East Barton

RADNIDGE LA

HAWKWELL CROSS

Hawkwell Farm

BOMMERTOWN CROSS

HIGHATON HEAD CROSS

BUSSELL'S MOOR CROSS

Higher Radnidge Moor

NEW PK

4

WADHAM CROSS

Wester New Moor

Easter New Moor

SMALLACOMBE HILL

Yanhey

Hawktree Moors

Kennels

25

B3227

PH

Smallacombe Moors

YANHEY HILL

Oldways End

Luckett Moor

TWO MOORS WAY

Blackerton

White Moor

Countiesmeet

3

WHITEFIELD CROSS

BLACKERTON CROSS

TUCKER'S MOOR CROSS

ALLSHIRE LA

Luckett Farm

Whitefield Farm

Whitmoor Farm

WOODBURN CROSS

24

WADHAM HILL

OWLABOROUGH LA

Shapcott Barton

Tucker's Moor

B3227

2

1 SHAPCOTT WOOD HILL
2 WADHAM CROSS

Owlaborough

East Knowstone

SHAPCOTT LA

Nether Woodburn

Knowstone

PH

GREENHILL CROSS

SHAPCOTT LA

WOODBURN HILL

Woodburn

23

HITTSFORD LA

SIDE WOOD LA

HOLY MOOR LA

WISTON CROSS

WOODBURN WATER CROSS

Beaple's Barton

ROACHILL CROSS

Wiston

Swineham

North Esworthy

1

Bowden

HOLY MOOR CROSS

Roachill

ESWORTHY CROSS

22

Side Moor

Pounceys

82   A   83   B   84   C   85   D   86   E   87   F

34

A B C D E F

Somerset STREET ATLAS

A396 Dunster

Brewer's Castle
ROW LA
Mounsey Castle
HINHAM LA
ASHWICK LA
Draydon Farm
DRAYDON LA
MARSH HILL
B3223
HIGHER COMBE RD
Court Down
Stockham
STOCKHAM HILL
A396
Oxgrove Farm
8
Marsh Hill House
New Invention
Hinam Farm
LOOSEALL LA
Northcombe
NORTHCOMBE LA
MARSHBRIDGE CROSS
Northmoor
Barlynch Farm
29
BUNNT BURROW'S TRACK
LOUISA GATE
HINHAM LA
CHILCOTT CROSS
NORTHMOOR HILL
NORTHMOOR RD
NEWGATE CROSS
HOLLAM CROSS
HOLLAM LA
Barlynch Woods
MINEHEAD LA
HINAM CROSS
Exe Valley Way
Old Shute
Oldberry Castle
Holla m House
B3223
1 EXMOOR GDNS
2 THE PADDOCK
3 BANK SQ
4 FORE ST
5 UNION ST
6 CHURCH LA
7 VICARAGE HILL
8 BRIDGE ST
9 BARNSCLOSE N
10 HERBERT HO
11 BARNSCLOSE
12 BARNSCLOSE W
13 RUDY LA
HELEBALL LA
7
Bury Hill
BURY HILL
SHELDON'S LA
CHILCOTT LA
OLDSHUTE LA
THE GARDENS
WEIR HEAD COTTS
HANOVER CT
Old Berry Farm
PO
TOWN MARSH
BEECH TREE CROSS
OLDBERRY LA
KEMPS WAY
LADY ST
HIGH ST
PH
HOLLAM DR
Hele Bridge
28
Chilcott
3
Liby & Visitor Ctr
P
KING'S CNR
GREAT MDW
JURY RD
JURY HILL
B3222
MACHINE CROSS
CAWKETT LA
Cawkett Farm
OLD RD
Wilway
ANDREW'S HILL CROSS
WILWAY LA
ANDREW
COTTAGE LA
B3222
CHAPEL ST
ROSEMARY LA
FISHERS MEAD
AMORY RD
BATH MEADOW DR
PIXTON WAY
VALENTINES
MUSGRAVES
LADY VICTORIA'S DR
MILLHAM LA
BARNES CLOSE MEAD
Dulverton
6
BURY RD
Streamcombe
COMBE LA
Barns Close Ind Est
ALLERS VIEW
THREE GATES CROSS
CLAYFORD RD
BATTLETON
Pixton Park
27
STREAMCOMBE LA
All Saints 14 CE Sch
Dulverton Mid 15 & Com Sch
Beasley Farm
River Barle
Bury Castle
Bere
Barle Ent Ctr
LADYHARRIS LA
ACLANDS DR
Combe
Weir House
DYEHOUSE CROSS
DYEHOUSE LA
Knowle Farm
Gulland
CLAYFORD LA
Clayford
Allers Wood
5
Pixy Copse
BEER LA
POOLE HILL
Pixton Hill
Beer Moors
IRON POST
Mast
3
Brockey River
Ashill
Venn
THE GREEN
Perry Farm
26
HAWKWELL LA
Brushford
ELLERSDOWN LA
West Knowle
Nightcott
NIGHTCOTT LA
BRUSHFORD NEW RD
MARKET CL
PERRY NEW RD
SILVERDALE CL
River Exe
DENNINGTON LA
Exe Valley Way
LANGALLER HILL
4
MOOR LA
1 NICHOLAS CL
2 POUNDSCLOSE
TWELVE ACRE POST
Langaller Farm
Kents Hill
Hulverton Hill
Poole Farm
CROFT LA
RIPHAY CORNER
25
Upcott
Exebridge Ind Est
ALLSHIRE LA
TRACKFORDMOOR CROSS
Croft
Riphay Barton
RIPHAY CROSS
MILL LA
RIVER VIEW
Wind Pump
Rocks
Fishery
Sowerhill
Exebridge
3
Langridge
Wilsons Farm
Den Brook
HELE MANOR LA
B3222
PH
Hele Manor Farm
Higher Grants Farm
BLIGHTS HILL
24
West Tapps
GRANT'S HILL
Red Deer Farm
Great Highleigh
2
East Tapps
Western Farm
EAST TAPPS LA
NEW LA
Combe Water
Mast
23
Combe Head
BLACKALLER LA
Newhouse Farm
Hutswell Farm
East Loosemoor
OLDBARN LA
East Mildon
1
West Mildon
Benshayes Farm
HIGH BOLHAM
B3227
A396
SOUTH MOLTON RD
Ford Farm
Westbrook Farmhouse
B3227
22

88 A 89 B 90 C 91 D 92 E 93 F

48

34

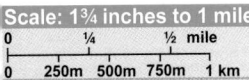

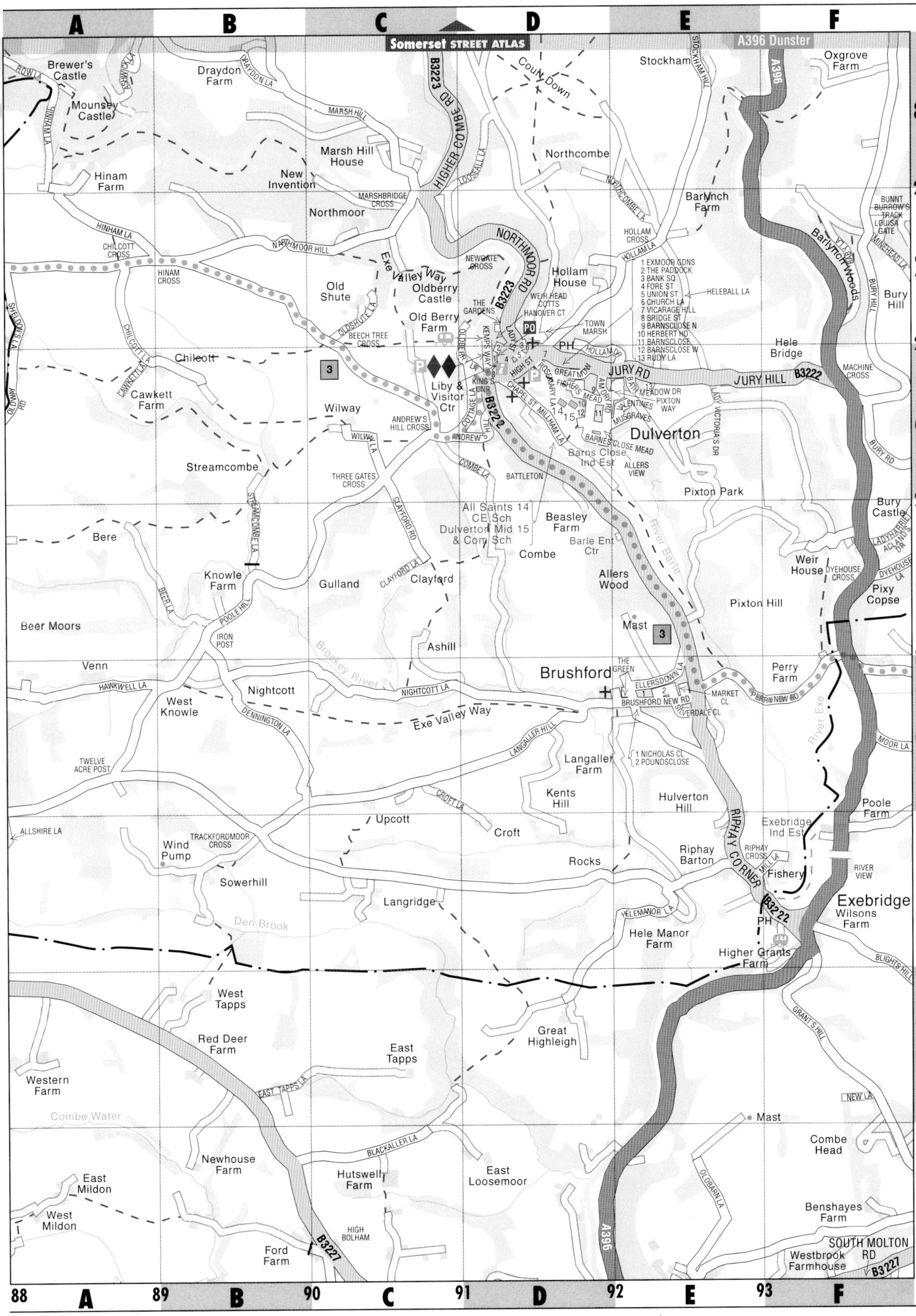

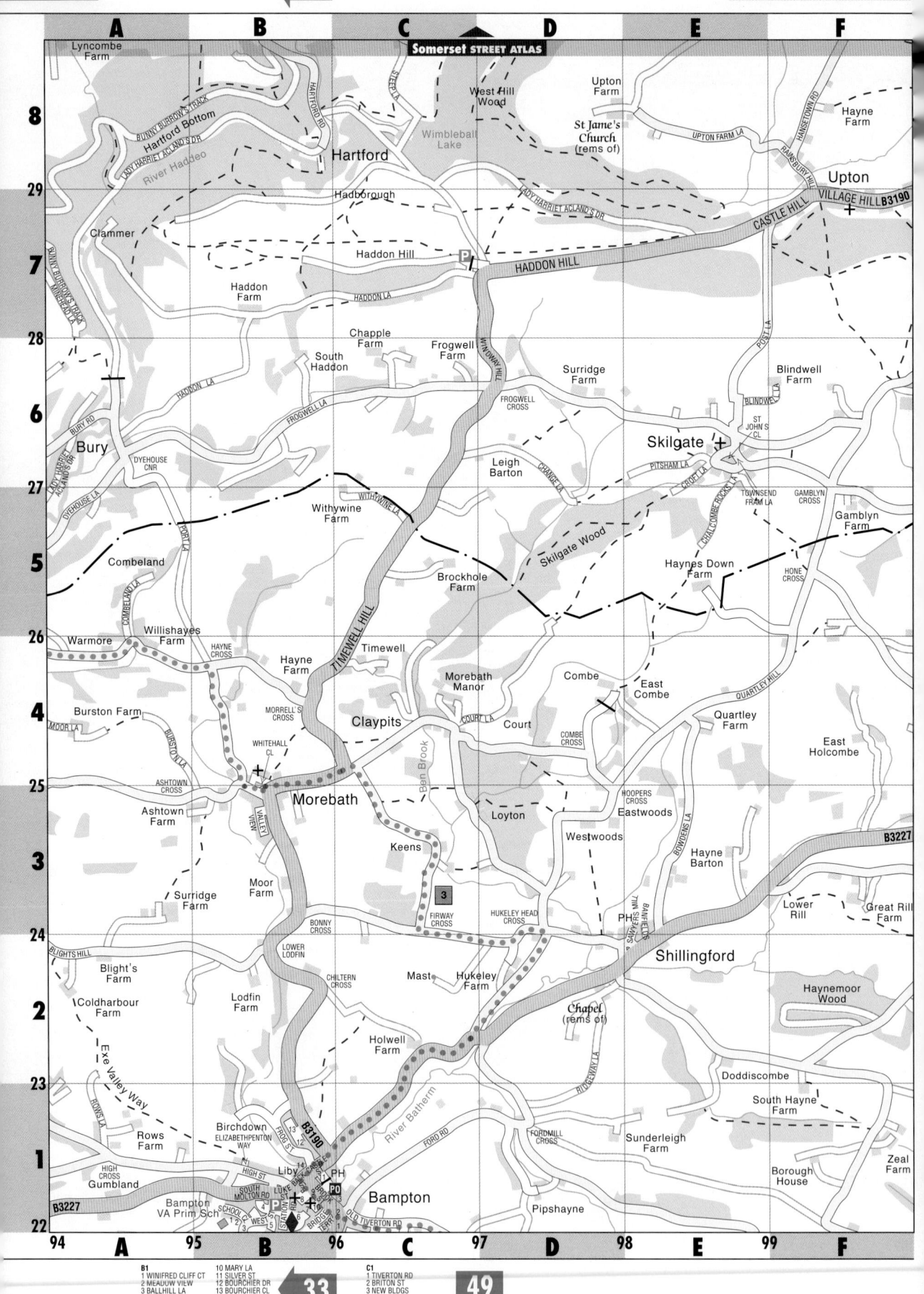

Scale: 1¾ inches to 1 mile

0   ¼   ½   mile
0 250m 500m 750m 1 km

A   B   C   D   E   F

Somerset STREET ATLAS

Lyncombe Farm

West Hill Wood

Upton Farm

Hayne Farm

8

Hartford Bottom

River Haddeo

Wimbleball Lake

St Jame's Church (rems of)

UPTON FARM LA

Upton

Hartford

29

Hadborough

LADY HARRIET ACLAND'S DR

CASTLE HILL

VILLAGE HILL B3190

Clammer

Haddon Hill

P

HADDON HILL

7

Haddon Farm

HADDON LA

Surridge Farm

Blindwell Farm

28

Chapple Farm

Frogwell Farm

FROGWELL LA

WINDMILL HILL

Frogwell Cross

ST JOHN'S CL

Skilgate

6

Bury

South Haddon

HADDON LA

DYEHOUSE CNR

Leigh Barton

CHANGE LA

PITSHAM LA

CROFT LA

TOWNSEND FARM LA

GAMBLYN CROSS

27

DYEHOUSE LA

WITHYWINE LA

Withywine Farm

Skilgate Wood

Haynes Down Farm

HONE CROSS

Gamblyn Farm

5

Combeland

Brockhole Farm

COMBELAND LA

PORLA

TIMEWELL HILL

Warmore

Willishayes Farm

HAYNE CROSS

Hayne Farm

Timewell

Combe

East Combe

Quartley Farm

QUARTLEY HILL

26

Burston Farm

MOOR LA

BURSTON LA

MORRELL'S CROSS

Claypits

Morebath Manor

COURT LA

Court

COMBE CROSS

East Holcombe

4

WHITEHALL CL

ASHTOWN CROSS

VALLEY VIEW

Morebath

HOOPERS CROSS

Eastwoods

BOWDENS LA

Hayne Barton

25

Ashtown Farm

Keens

Loyton

Westwoods

B3227

3

Surridge Farm

Moor Farm

3

FIRWAY CROSS

HUKELEY HEAD CROSS

SAWYERS MILL

PH

BANFIELDS

Lower Rill

Great Rill Farm

24

BONNY CROSS

Shillingford

BLIGHTS HILL

LOWER LODFIN

CHILTERN CROSS

Mast

Hukeley Farm

RIDGEWAY LA

Haynemoor Wood

2

Blight's Farm

Lodfin Farm

Holwell Farm

Chapel (rems of)

Doddiscombe

23

Coldharbour Farm

Exe Valley Way

River Batherm

FORDMILL CROSS

South Hayne Farm

Zeal Farm

ROWS LA

FORD RD

Sunderleigh Farm

Borough House

1

Rows Farm

Birchdown

ELIZABETHPENTON WAY

B3190

FROG LA

HIGH ST

Liby

PH

PO

Bampton

Pipshayne

HIGH CROSS

Gumbland

SOUTH MOLTON RD

SCHOOL

P

OLD TIVERTON RD

22

B3227

Bampton VA Prim Sch

94   A   95   B   96   C   97   D   98   E   99   F

B1
1 WINIFRED CLIFF CT
2 MEADOW VIEW
3 BALLHILL LA
4 MARKET CL
5 LORDS MEADOW LA
6 BARNHAY
7 CHURCH TERR
8 NEWTON SQ
9 FORE ST

10 MARY LA
11 SILVER ST
12 BOURCHIER DR
13 BOURCHIER CL
14 NEWTON CT

C1
1 TIVERTON RD
2 BRITON ST
3 NEW BLDGS

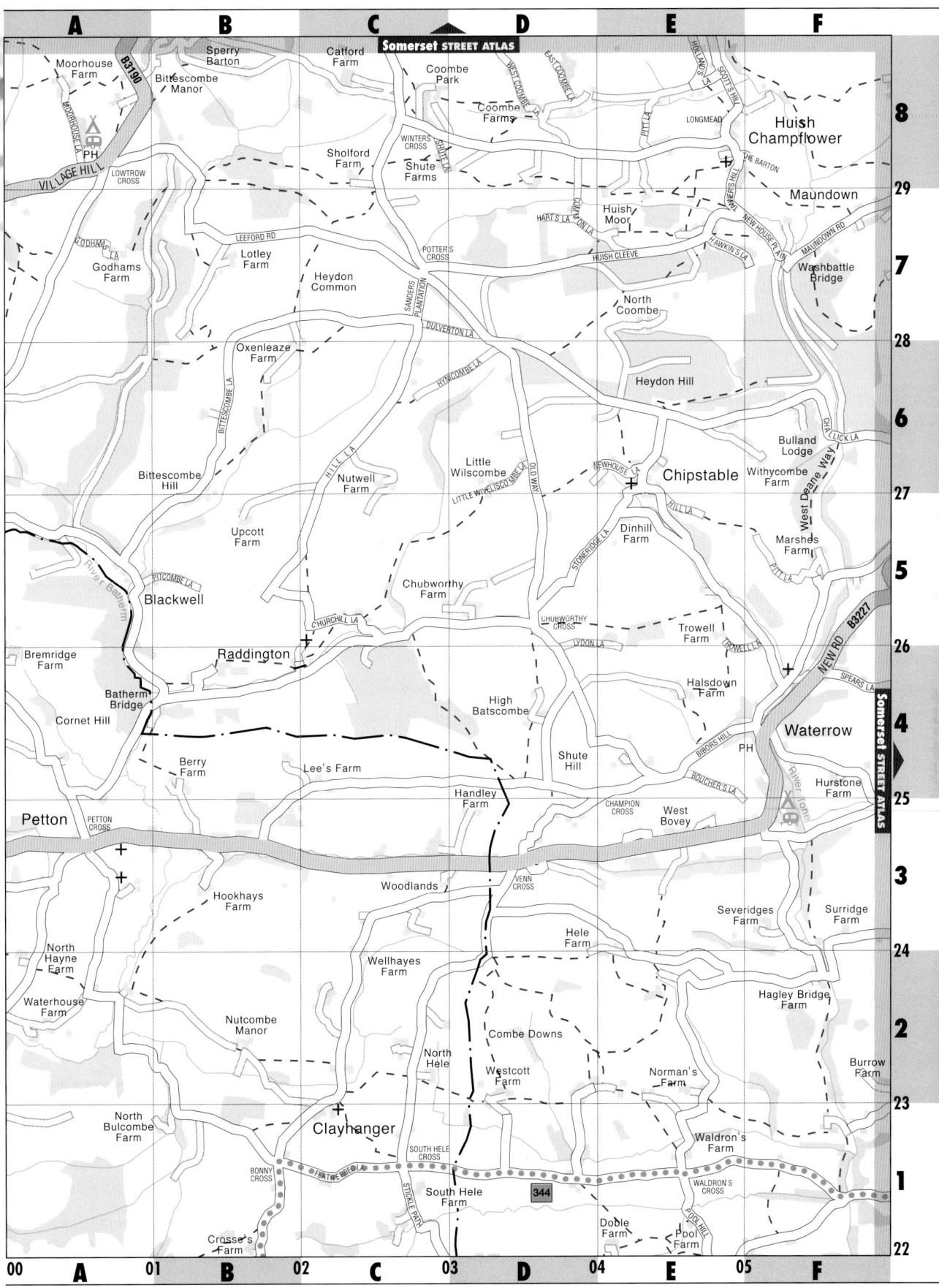

Scale: 1¾ inches to 1 mile

0   ¼   ½ mile
0 250m 500m 750m 1 km

Moorhouse Farm
B3190
Sperry Barton
Catford Farm
Coombe Park
Coombe Farms
WEST COOMBE LA
EAST COOMBE LA
HOLLIN'S LA
SCOTT'S LA
Huish Champflower
LONGMEAD
Maundown
Bittescombe Manor
MOORHOUSE LA
PH
VILLAGE HILL
LOWTROW CROSS
Sholford Farm
WINTERS CROSS
Shute Farms
SHUTE LA
PITT LA
THE BARTON
HAWKIN'S LA
NEW HOUSE PK LA
MAUNDOWN RD
Washbattle Bridge
RODHAM LA
LEEFORD RD
Lotley Farm
POTTER'S CROSS
HART'S LA
COMMON LA
Huish Moor
HUISH CLEEVE
Godhams Farm
Heydon Common
SANDERS PLANTATION
DULVERTON LA
North Coombe
BITTESCOMBE LA
Oxenleaze Farm
HYNCOMBE LA
Heydon Hill
HILL LA
Nutwell Farm
Little Wilscombe
LITTLE WILSCOMBE LA
OLD WAY
NEWHOUSE LA
Chipstable
Bulland Lodge
CHALLICK LA
West Deane Way
Bittescombe Hill
Upcott Farm
Withycombe Farm
STONERIDGE LA
Dinhill Farm
HILL LA
Marshes Farm
PITT LA
PITCOMBE LA
River Batherm
Blackwell
CHURCHILL LA
Chubworthy Farm
Chubworthy Cross
LYDON LA
Trowell Farm
TROWELL LA
NEW RD
B3227
Bremridge Farm
Raddington
Halsdown Farm
SPEARS LA
Batherm Bridge
High Batscombe
BIBOR'S HILL
PH
Waterrow
Cornet Hill
Shute Hill
BOUCHER'S LA
Hurstone Farm
Berry Farm
Lee's Farm
Handley Farm
CHAMPION CROSS
West Bovey
River Tone
Petton
PETTON CROSS
Woodlands
VENN CROSS
Severidges Farm
Surridge Farm
Hookhays Farm
Hele Farm
North Hayne Farm
Wellhayes Farm
Hagley Bridge Farm
Waterhouse Farm
Combe Downs
Nutcombe Manor
North Hele
Westcott Farm
Norman's Farm
Burrow Farm
North Bulcombe Farm
Clayhanger
SOUTH HELE CROSS
Waldron's Farm
BONNY CROSS
FEN THE ROAD LA
STICKLE PATH
South Hele Farm
344
WALDRON'S CROSS
Crosse's Farm
Doble Farm
POOL HILL
Pool Farm

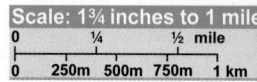

Scale: 1¾ inches to 1 mile

0   ¼   ½ mile
0 250m 500m 750m 1 km

A **B** **C** **D** **E** **F**

8
21
7
20
6
19
5
18
4
17
3
16
2
15
1
14

16 **A** 17 **B** 18 **C** 19 **D** 20 **E** 21 **F**

Mast
Nabor Point
Embury Beacon
Embury Beach
Knaps Head
The Hermitage
Welcombe Mouth
Marsland Mouth
Gull Rock
Marsland Cliff
Marsland Manor
Cornakey Cliff
South West Coast Path
Yeol Mouth
Cornakey Farm
Cory
Henna Cliff
Westcott Farm
Well
Hawker's Hut
Morwenstow
Vicarage Cliff
CROSSTOWN
Lucky Hole
Crosstown PH
Higher Sharpnose Point
The Tidna
BARN HILL
CROSSWATER
HORSE RD
Tonacombe
WOODVILLE CROSS
STANBURY CROSS
WOODVILLE RD

Cornwall STREET ATLAS

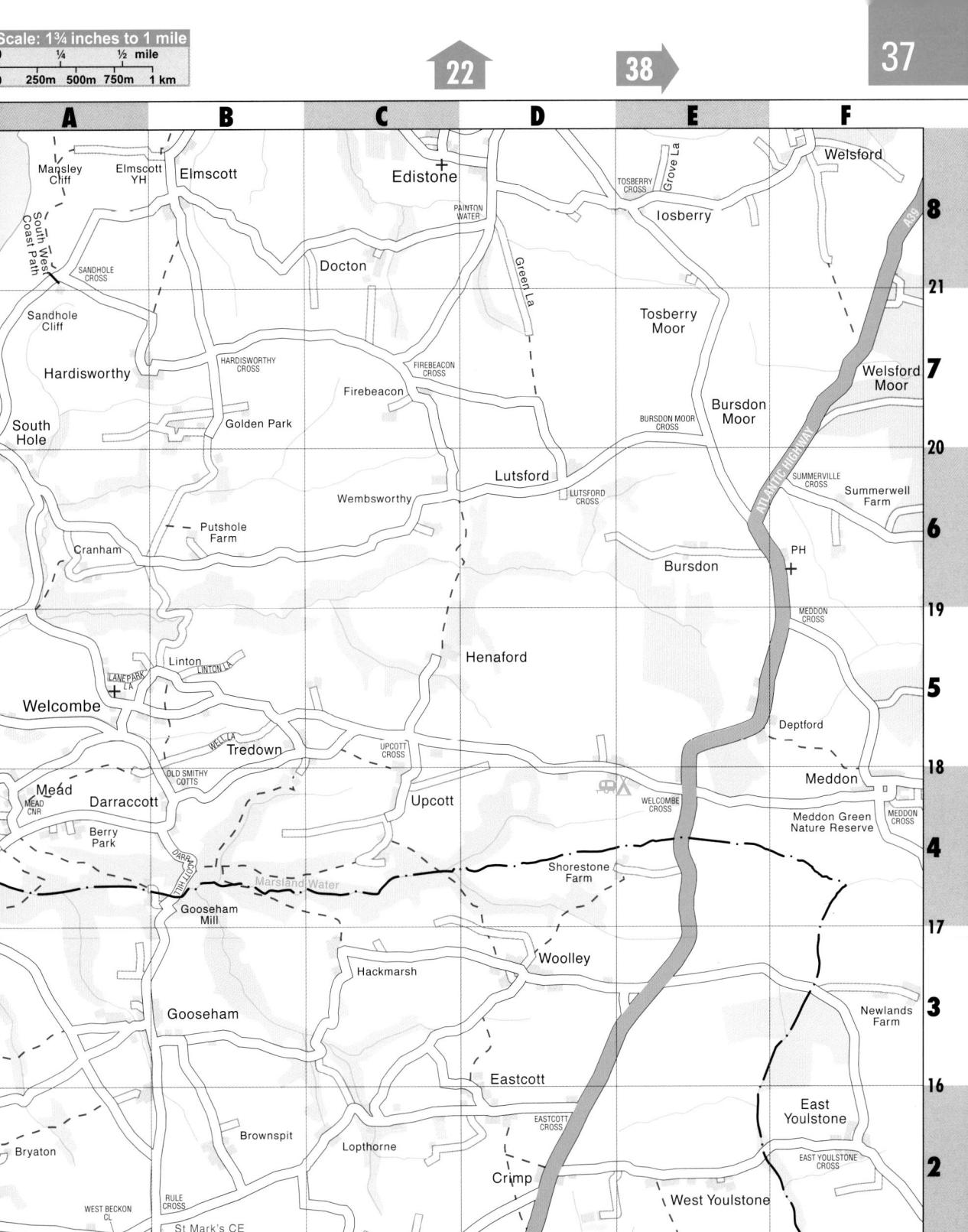

A   B   C   D   E   F

8
21
7
20
6
19
5
18
4
17
3
16
2
15
1
14

Mansley Cliff
Elmscott YH
Elmscott
Edistone
Welsford
Iosberry
Tosberry Cross
Grove La

South West Coast Path
SANDHOLE CROSS
Docton
PAINTON WATER
Tosberry Moor
Welsford Moor

Sandhole Cliff
Hardisworthy
HARDISWORTHY CROSS
Firebeacon
FIREBEACON CROSS
Green La
Bursdon Moor
BURSDON MOOR CROSS
Summerville Cross
Summerwell Farm

Hardisworthy
Golden Park
Firebeacon
Lutsford

South Hole
Wembsworthy
Lutsford
LUTSFORD CROSS
Bursdon
PH

Cranham
Putshole Farm
Henaford
Meddon Cross

Linton
LINTON LA
Deptford

Welcombe
LANE PARK LA
Tredown
WELL LA
UPCOTT CROSS
Meddon

Mead
MEAD CNR
Darraccott
OLD SMITHY COTTS
Upcott
WELCOMBE CROSS
Meddon Green Nature Reserve
MEDDON CROSS

Berry Park
DARRACOTT HILL
Marsland Water
Shorestone Farm

Gooseham Mill

Hackmarsh
Woolley
Newlands Farm

Gooseham

Brownspit
Lopthorne
Eastcott
EASTCOTT CROSS
East Youlstone

Bryaton
Crimp
West Youlstone
EAST YOULSTONE CROSS

WEST BECKON CL
RULE CROSS
St Mark's CE Prim Sch
MOSWENNA RD
FURZE GDNS
HAWKERS DR
SARGENTS MDW
River Tamar

Shop
THE STOWE
Ruxmoor
Milton

WOODVILLE RD
Darzle Farm
Middlefields
Wrasford Moor

ATLANTIC HIGHWAY
A39

Cornwall STREET ATLAS
A39 Bude (A3072)

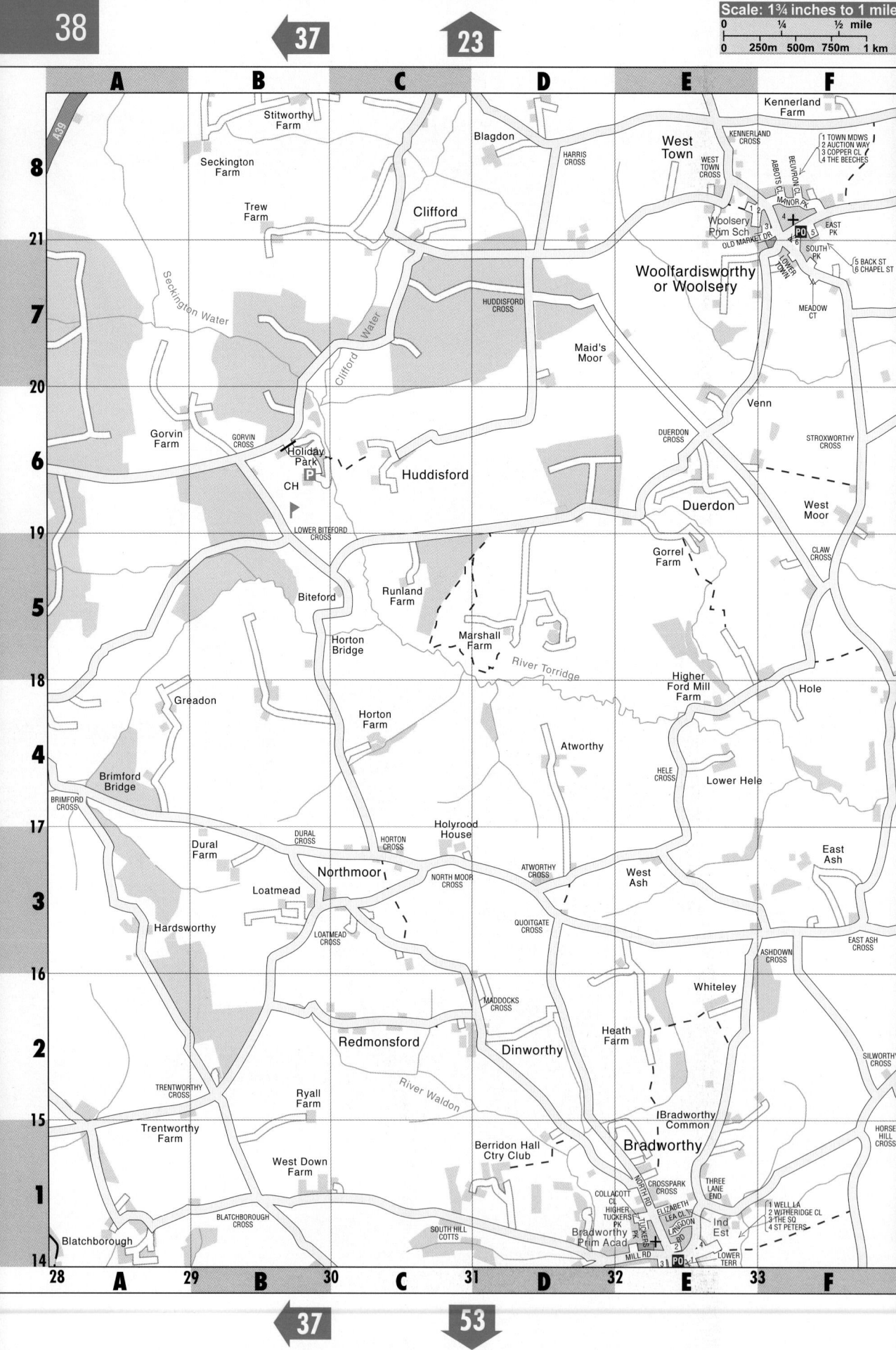

Scale: 1¾ inches to 1 mile

0   ¼   ½   mile

0   250m 500m 750m 1 km

A   B   C   D   E   F

8

21

7

20

6

19

5

18

4

17

3

16

2

15

1

14

A39

Stitworthy
Farm

Seckington
Farm

Trew
Farm

Blagdon

Clifford

HARRIS
CROSS

Kennerland
Farm

West
Town

KENNERLAND
CROSS

WEST
TOWN
CROSS

1 TOWN MDWS
2 AUCTION WAY
3 COPPER CL
4 THE BEECHES

Woolsery
Prim Sch

ABBOTS CL

BEUVRON CL

MANOR PK

PO

1
4
3
5
6

EAST
PK

5 BACK ST
6 CHAPEL ST

OLD MARKET DR

LOWER TOWN

SOUTH
PK

MEADOW
CT

Woolfardisworthy
or Woolsery

Seckington Water

HUDDISFORD
CROSS

Maid's
Moor

Venn

STROXWORTHY
CROSS

Clifford Water

Gorvin
Farm

GORVIN
CROSS

Holiday
Park

CH
P

Huddisford

DUERDON
CROSS

Duerdon

West
Moor

CLAW
CROSS

LOWER BITEFORD
CROSS

Biteford

Runland
Farm

Gorrel
Farm

Marshall
Farm

River Torridge

Higher
Ford Mill
Farm

Hole

Horton
Bridge

Greadon

Horton
Farm

Atworthy

HELE
CROSS

Lower Hele

East
Ash

Brimford
Bridge

BRIMFORD
CROSS

DURAL
CROSS

HORTON
CROSS

Holyrood
House

Dural
Farm

Northmoor

NORTH MOOR
CROSS

ATWORTHY
CROSS

West
Ash

ASHDOWN
CROSS

EAST ASH
CROSS

Loatmead

QUOITGATE
CROSS

Hardsworthy

LOATMEAD
CROSS

MADDOCKS
CROSS

Redmonsford

Dinworthy

Heath
Farm

Whiteley

SILWORTHY
CROSS

TRENTWORTHY
CROSS

Ryall
Farm

River Waldon

Bradworthy
Common

Bradworthy

HORSE
HILL
CROSS

Trentworthy
Farm

West Down
Farm

Berridon Hall
Ctry Club

THREE
LANE
END

CROSSPARK
CROSS

1 WELL LA
2 WITHERIDGE CL
3 THE SQ
4 ST PETERS

Blatchborough

BLATCHBOROUGH
CROSS

SOUTH HILL
COTTS

Bradworthy
Prim Acad

COLLACOTT
CL
HIGHER
TUCKERS
PK

NORTH RD

TUCKERS PK

ELIZABETH
LEA CL

LANGDON

MILL RD

PO

Ind
Est

LOWER
TERR

28   A   29   B   30   C   31   D   32   E   33   F

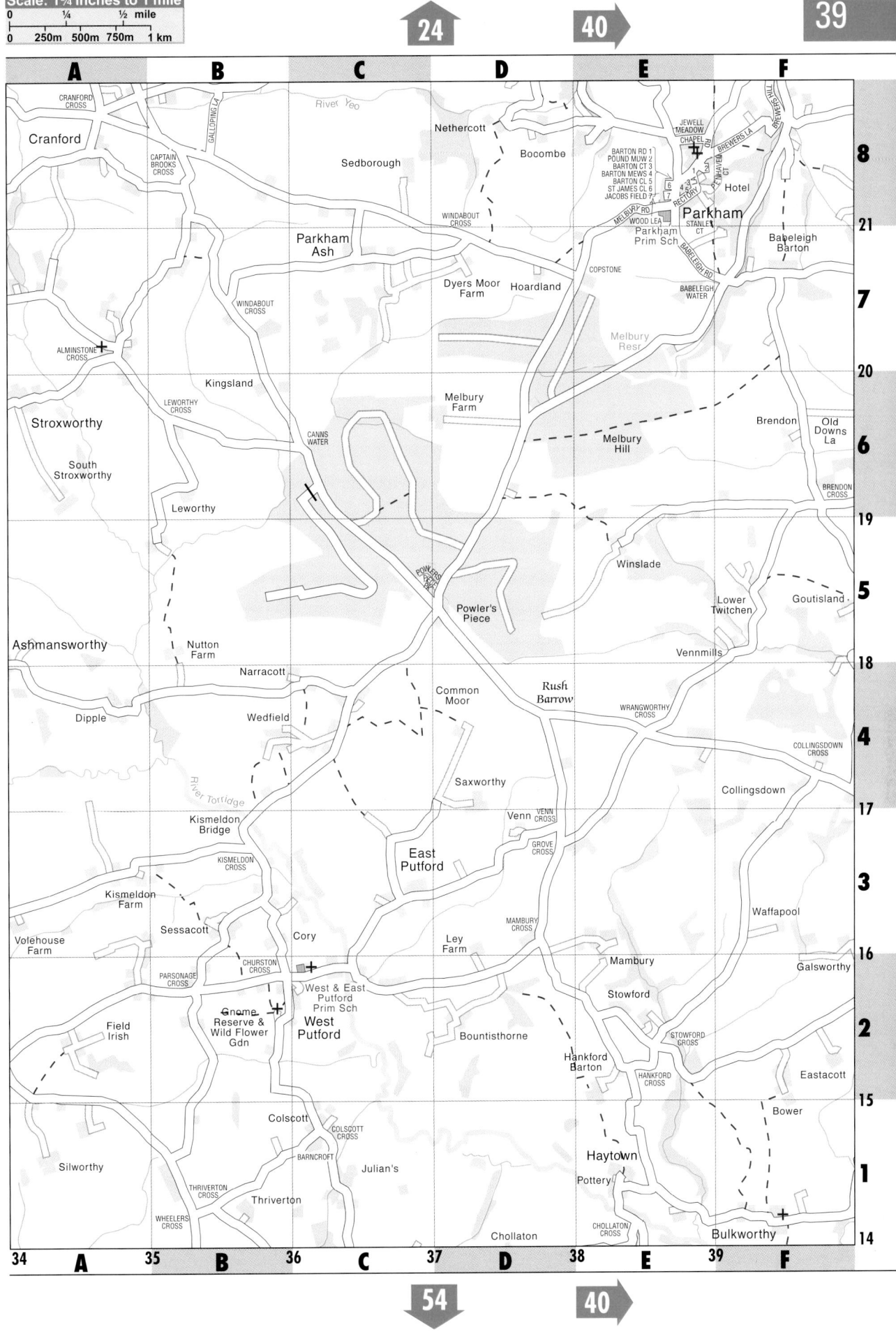

A B C D E F

8
21
7
20
6
19
5
18
4
17
3
16
2
15
1
14

CRANFORD CROSS

Cranford

CAPTAIN BROOKS CROSS

GALDIPING LA

River Yeo

Nethercott

Sedborough

Bocombe

JEWELL MEADOW CHAPEL

BARTON RD 1
POUND MUW 2
BARTON CT 3
BARTON MEWS 4
BARTON CL 5
ST JAMES CL 6
JACOBS FIELD 7

BREWERS LA

Hotel

Parkham

WOOD LEA

MELBURY RD
Parkham Prim Sch

STANLEY CT

Babeleigh Barton

Parkham Ash

WINDABOUT CROSS

Dyers Moor Farm

Hoardland

Copstone

BABELEIGH RD

BABELEIGH WATER

Melbury Resr

ALMINSTONE CROSS

WINDABOUT CROSS

Kingsland

Melbury Farm

Melbury Hill

Brendon

Old Downs La

Stroxworthy

LEWORTHY CROSS

CANNS WATER

BRENDON CROSS

South Stroxworthy

Leworthy

Winslade

Lower Twitchen

Goutisland

POWLER'S PIECE

Powler's Piece

Vennmills

Ashmansworthy

Nutton Farm

Narracott

Common Moor

Rush Barrow

WRANGWORTHY CROSS

COLLINGSDOWN CROSS

Dipple

Wedfield

Saxworthy

Venn

VENN CROSS

Collingsdown

River Torridge

Kismeldon Bridge

GROVE CROSS

KISMELDON CROSS

East Putford

MAMBURY CROSS

Waffapool

Kismeldon Farm

Sessacott

Cory

Ley Farm

Mambury

Galsworthy

Volehouse Farm

PARSONAGE CROSS

CHURSTON CROSS

West & East Putford Prim Sch

Stowford

STOWFORD CROSS

Field Irish

Gnome Reserve & Wild Flower Gdn

West Putford

Bountisthorne

Hankford Barton

HANKFORD CROSS

Eastacott

Bower

Colscott

COLSCOTT CROSS

BARNCROFT

Julian's

Haytown

Pottery

Silworthy

THRIVERTON CROSS

Thriverton

Chollaton

CHOLLATON CROSS

Bulkworthy

WHEELERS CROSS

A   B   C   D   E   F

Looseham

Halsbury
Barton

Bowden

Orchard
Farm

SALTRENS

Ley
Farm

Stone

Burrow

MONKLEIGH MILL LA

Upcott

Petticombe
Manor

Monkleigh
Prim Sch

21

Cabbacott

TOWER HILL

BOWDEN
CROSS

CAPERN
PK

CASTLE
MDW

5 RICKARDS ROW
6 SOUTHWOOD MDWS
7 ROLLES TERR
8 GREENINGS RD
9 ORLEIGH CL
10 NORTHWOOD LA
11 HILLPARK
12 Buckland Brewer
   Com Prim Sch

Venton
Farm

LOXDOWN
RD

Monkleigh

BUCKLAND VIEW 1
BABLEIGH CL 2
ASHTONS COTTS 3
TUCKERS PK 4

BARTON RD

10
6
8
9
12
11
5

HILTON RD

P

PH

7

PH

Buckland
Brewer

Higher
Culleigh

Gorwood
Farm

GORWOOD RD

CATSBOROUGH
CROSS

20

Park
Farm

Great
Gorwood

Bearah
Farm

MILL LA

Old Downs La

SCRATCHFACE LA

Thorne
Farm

MILL LA

Horwood
Barton

6

Frithelstock
Stone

Bilsford

Hele

Ash
Farms

CHURCH LA

MEADOWSTONE
CL

BACK LA

19

Buda

Craneham

Cemy

HELE LA

5

Lydeland Water

Smythacott

Stretchacott

18

Hembury
Castle

Knaworthy

Eckworthy

HEMBURY
CROSS

Ashbury

Southcott

SOUTHCOTT
CROSS

4

Tythecott

Hollamoor

B3227

Veilstone

Milford

Silklands

Cholash
Farm

Bibbear
Farm

Southcott

Wooda

3

Thornhillhead

THORNHILLHEAD

Buda

Langtree
Com Prim Sch

SOUTHLANDS
DR

Thorne
Moor

Wtr
Twr

LATCH LA

FORE ST

THE
CRESCENT

PH

16

Holwell
Farm

WONDERS
CNR

DRAGON MILL

CHURCH
LA

CHURCH
MDW

Langtree

Withacott

Watertown

LANGTREEWOOD

R LA

COLLACOTT
CROSS

MARKET
FIELD

PH

15

B3221

1 ELM CL
2 BEECH RD
3 WILLOW GR

HEATHLAND
VIEW

Putshole

Burstone

Stibb
Cross

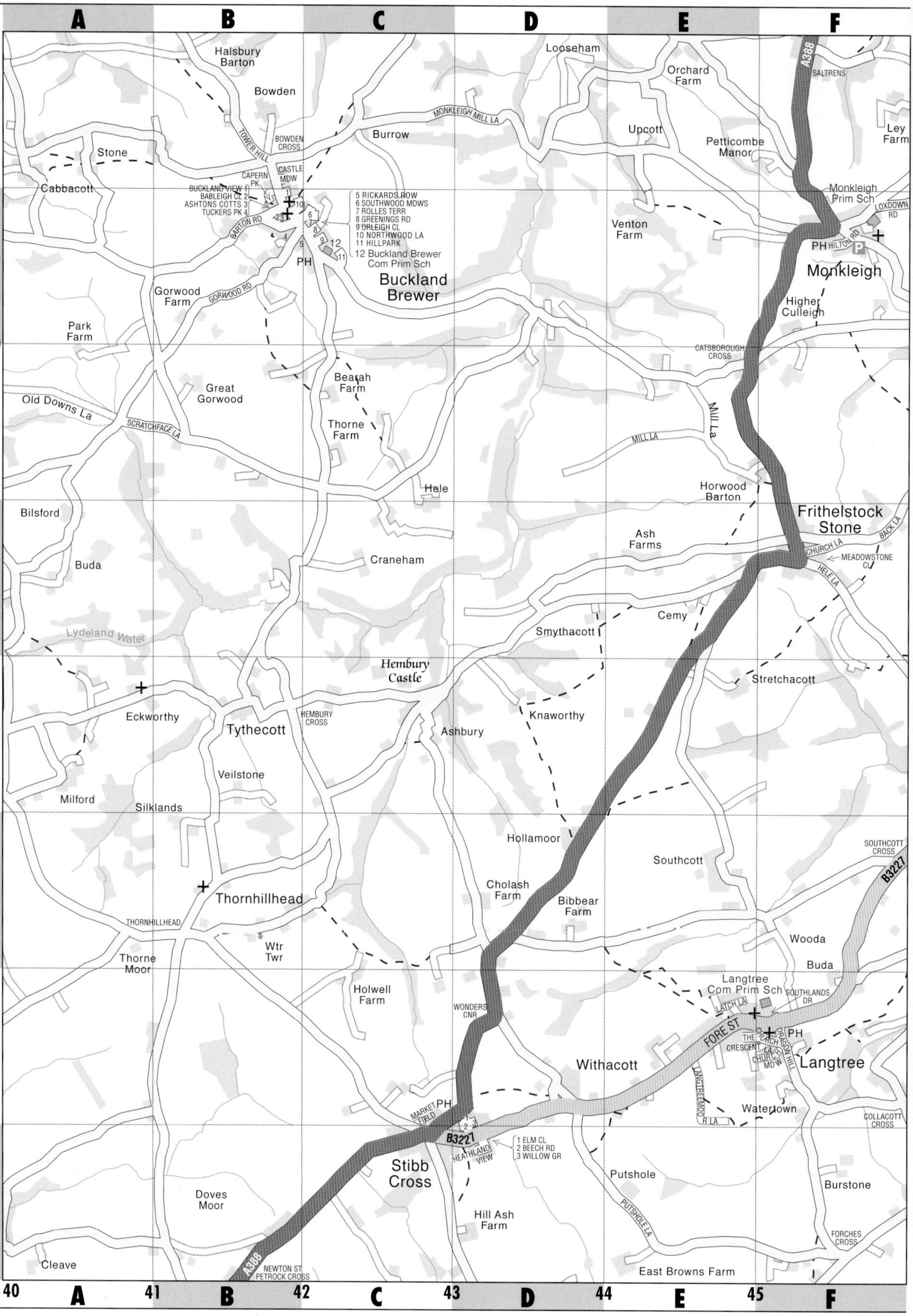

Doves
Moor

PUTSHOLE LA

1

Hill Ash
Farm

East Browns Farm

FORCHES
CROSS

A386

NEWTON ST
PETROCK CROSS

14

Cleave

Scale: 1¾ inches to 1 mile

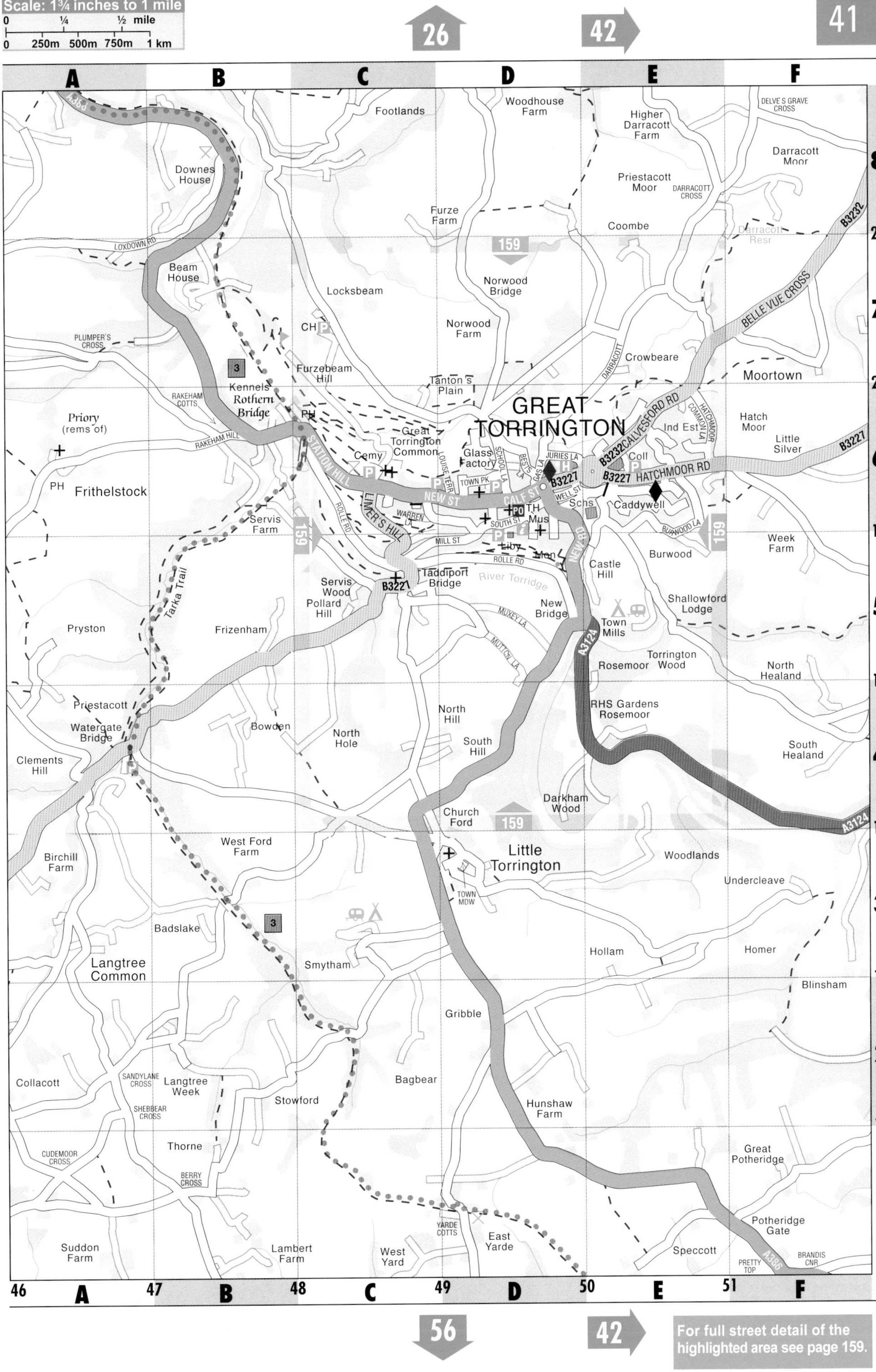

0 ¼ ½ mile
0 250m 500m 750m 1 km

26 42 **41**

A B C D E F

8
Footlands
Woodhouse Farm
Higher Darracott Farm
DELVE'S GRAVE CROSS
Darracott Moor
21
Downes House
Furze Farm
Priestacott Moor
DARRACOTT CROSS
Darracott Resr
B3232
159
LOXDOWN RD
Beam House
Locksbeam
Norwood Bridge
Coombe
BELLE VUE CROSS
7
PLUMPER'S CROSS
CH
Furzebeam Hill
Norwood Farm
Crowbeare
Moortown
20
3
Kennels Rothern Bridge
RAKEHAM COTTS
Tanton's Plain
DARRACOTT
CALVESFORD RD
Hatch Moor
Little Silver
B3227
Priory (rems of)
RAKEHAM HILL
PH
Great Torrington Common
GREAT TORRINGTON
B3232
Ind Est
HATCHMOOR COMMON LA
6
PH
Frithelstock
STATION HILL
Cemy
Glass Factory
SCHOOL LA
JURIES LA
Coll
B3227
HATCHMOOR RD
B3227
Servis Farm
159
ROLLE RD
LIMER'S HILL
TOWN PK
CALF ST
WELL ST
Caddywell
BURWOOD LA
19
WARREN
NEW ST
SOUTH ST
PO
TH
Mus
Schs
Week Farm
Tarka Trail
MILL ST
Liby
Men
NEW RD
Burwood
159
Servis Wood Pollard Hill
B3227
Taddiport Bridge
ROLLE RD
River Torridge
Castle Hill
Shallowford Lodge
5
Pryston
Frizenham
New Bridge
MUXEY LA
A3124
Town Mills
Torrington Wood
North Healand
18
Priestacott
Bowden
MUTTON LA
North Hill
RHS Gardens Rosemoor
Rosemoor
4
Watergate Bridge
North Hole
South Hill
South Healand
Clements Hill
West Ford Farm
Church Ford
159
Darkham Wood
A3124
17
Birchill Farm
Little Torrington
Woodlands
Undercleave
3
Badslake
3
Smytham
TOWN MDW
Hollam
Homer
Blinsham
16
Langtree Common
Gribble
Bagbear
2
Collacott
SANDYLANE CROSS
Langtree Week
Stowford
Hunshaw Farm
Great Potheridge
15
SHEBBEAR CROSS
Thorne
CUDEMOOR CROSS
BERRY CROSS
Potheridge Gate
1
Suddon Farm
Lambert Farm
West Yard
YARDE COTTS
East Yarde
Speccott
PRETTY TOP
A386
BRANDIS CNR
14

46 A 47 B 48 C 49 D 50 E 51 F

56 42

For full street detail of the highlighted area see page 159.

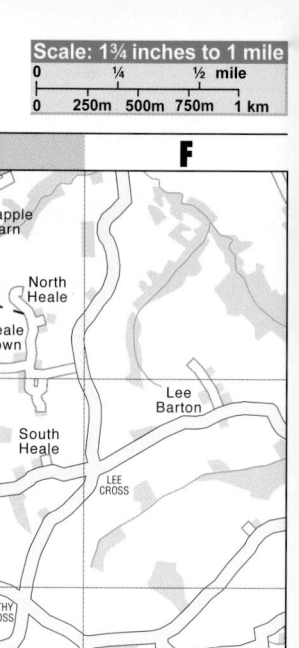

Scale: 1¾ inches to 1 mile

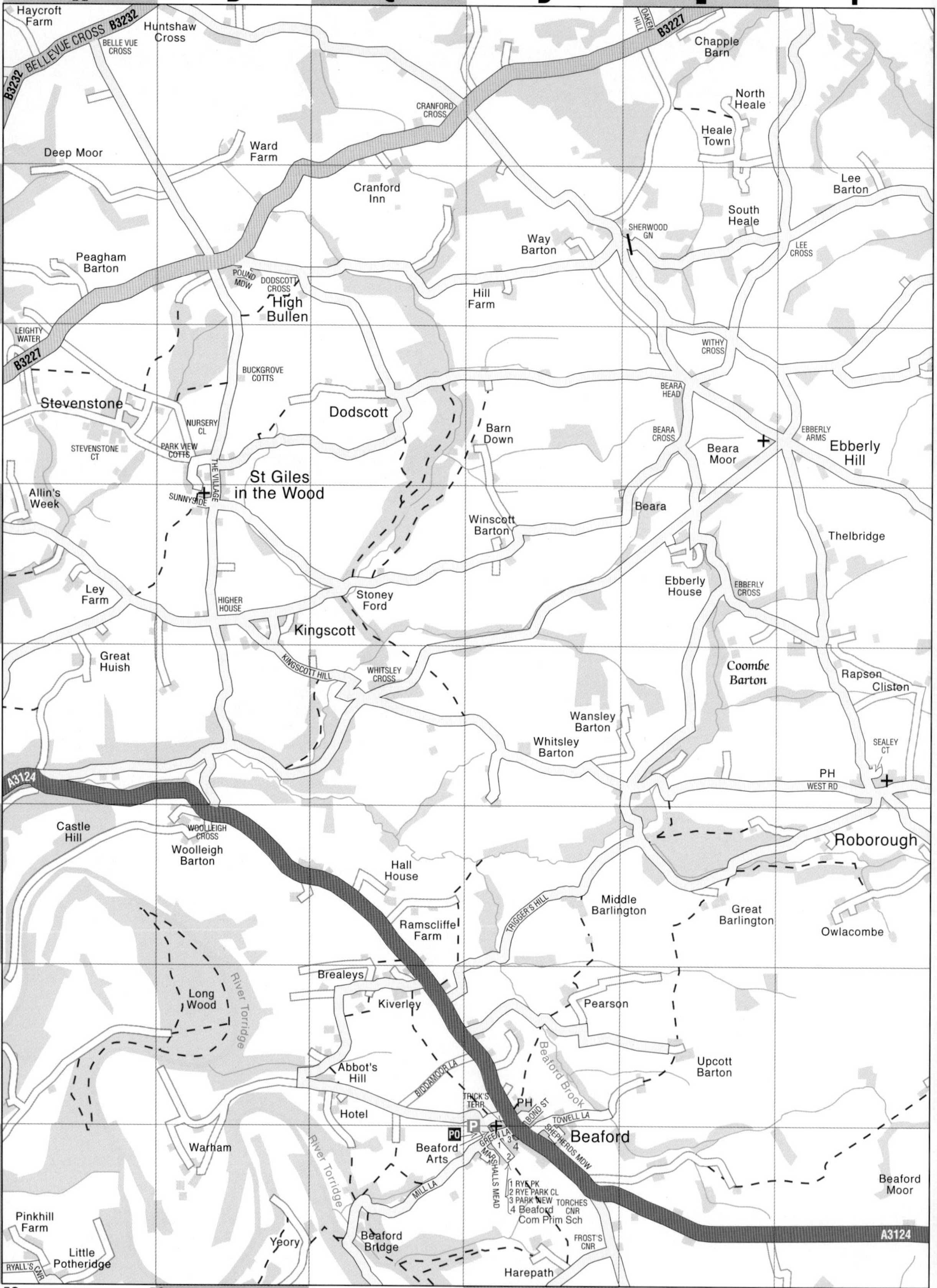

0   ¼   ½   mile
0   250m   500m   750m   1 km

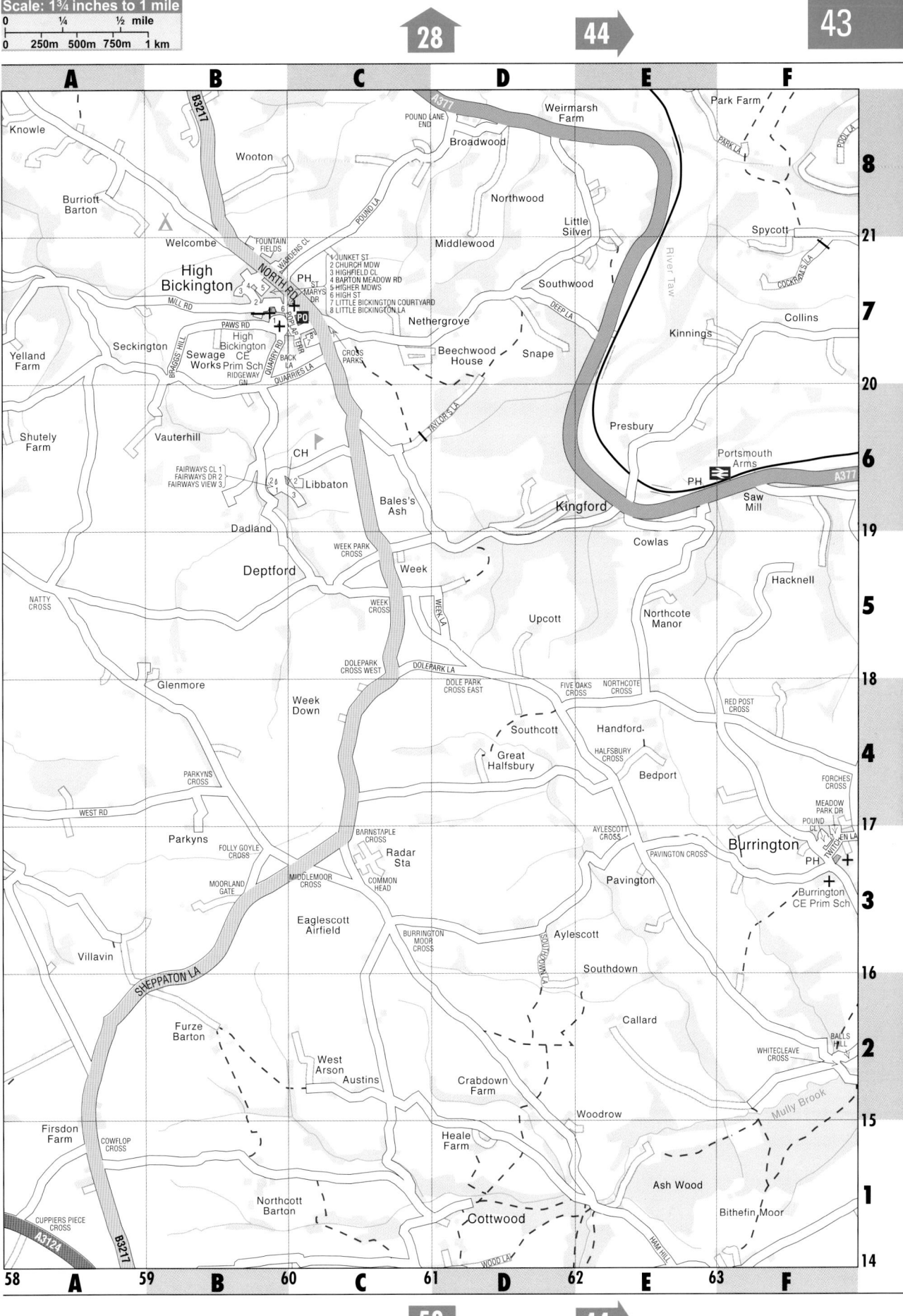

A   B   C   D   E   F

Knowle

Burriott
Barton

B3217

Wooton

Welcombe

FOUNTAIN
FIELDS

WARDENS CL

POUND LA

A371

POUND LANE
END

Broadwood

Weirmarsh
Farm

Park Farm

PARK LA

8

21

High
Bickington

NORTH RD

PH
ST
MARYS
DR

1 JUNKET ST
2 CHURCH MDW
3 HIGHFIELD CL
4 BARTON MEADOW RD
5 HIGHER MDWS
6 HIGH ST
7 LITTLE BICKINGTON COURTYARD
8 LITTLE BICKINGTON LA

PO

Northwood

Middlewood

Little
Silver

Southwood

DEEP LA

River Taw

Spycott

COCKRAILS LA

Collins

7

MILL RD

Yelland
Farm

Seckington

BRAGGS HILL

Sewage
Works

High
Bickington
CE
Prim Sch

RIDGEWAY
GN

QUARRY RD

BACK
LA

QUARRIES LA

CROSS
PARKS

Nethergrove

Beechwood
House

Snape

Kinnings

Presbury

20

Shutely
Farm

Vauterhill

CH

FAIRWAYS CL 1
FAIRWAYS DR 2
FAIRWAYS VIEW 3

Libbaton

TAYLOR'S LA

Bales's
Ash

Kingford

Cowlas

Portsmouth
Arms

PH

Saw
Mill

A377

6

19

Dadland

Deptford

WEEK PARK
CROSS

Week

WEEK LA

Northcote
Manor

Hacknell

5

NATTY
CROSS

WEEK
CROSS

Upcott

Glenmore

Week
Down

DOLEPARK
CROSS WEST

DOLEPARK LA

DOLE PARK
CROSS EAST

FIVE OAKS
CROSS

NORTHCOTE
CROSS

RED POST
CROSS

18

PARKYNS
CROSS

Southcott

Great
Halfsbury

HALFSBURY
CROSS

Handford

Bedport

FORCHES
CROSS

4

WEST RD

Parkyns

FOLLY GOYLE
CROSS

BARNSTAPLE
CROSS

Radar
Sta

COMMON
HEAD

AYLESCOTT
CROSS

PAVINGTON CROSS

Pavington

MEADOW
PARK DR

POUND
CL

TWITCHEN LA

Burrington

PH

Burrington
CE Prim Sch

17

3

MOORLAND
GATE

MIDDLEMOOR
CROSS

Eaglescott
Airfield

BURRINGTON
MOOR
CROSS

Aylescott

SOUTHCOTT LA

Southdown

16

Villavin

SHEPPATON LA

Furze
Barton

West
Arson

Austins

Crabdown
Farm

Woodrow

Callard

WHITECLEAVE
CROSS

BALLS
HILL

Mully Brook

2

15

Firsdon
Farm

COWFLOP
CROSS

Northcott
Barton

Heale
Farm

Cottwood

Ash Wood

HAM HILL

Bithefin Moor

1

CUPPIERS PIECE
CROSS

A3124

B3217

WOOD LA

14

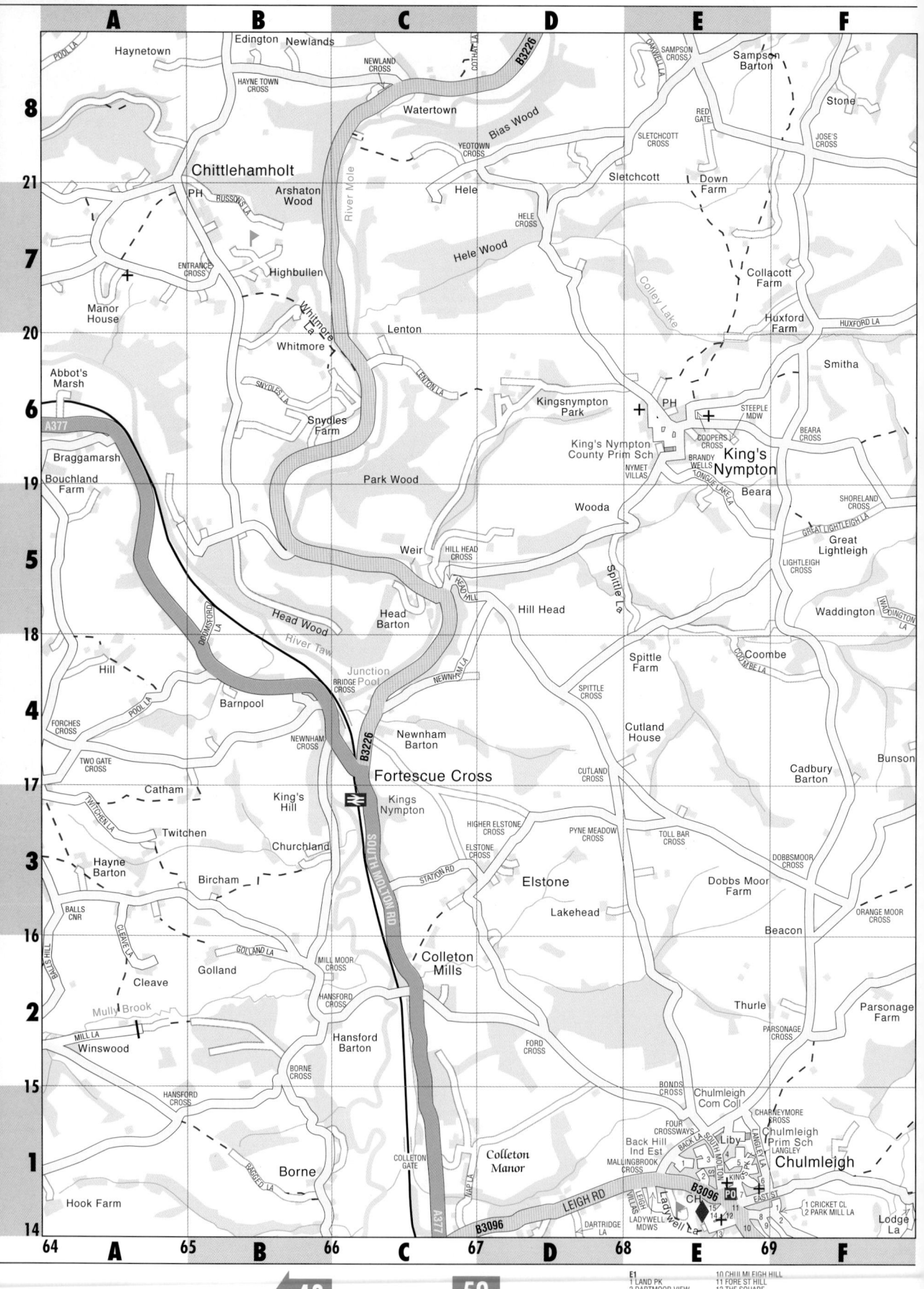

Scale: 1¾ inches to 1 mile
0   ¼   ½ mile
0 250m 500m 750m 1 km

Column labels (top): A B C D E F

Row labels (left): 8 21 7 20 6 19 5 18 4 17 3 16 2 15 1 14

Haynetown
Edington Newlands
Hayne Town Cross
Newland Cross
B3226
COTTA LA
Sampson Cross
DANIELLA
Sampson Barton
Stone
Watertown
Bias Wood
Yeotown Cross
Red Gate
Sletchcott Cross
Jose's Cross
Chittlehamholt
PH RUSSOL'S LA
Arshaton Wood
River Mole
Hele
Hele Cross
Sletchcott
Down Farm
Collacott Farm
Coley Lake
Highbullen
ENTRANCE CROSS
Hele Wood
Huxford Farm
Huxford La
Manor House
Whitmore La
Lenton
Smitha
Abbot's Marsh
SNYDLE'S LA
Whitmore
LENTON LA
Kingsnympton Park
PH
STEEPLE MDW
COOPERS CROSS
Beara Cross
A377
Snydles Farm
King's Nympton County Prim Sch
King's Nympton
Braggamarsh
Park Wood
Wooda
NYMET VILLAS
BRANDY WELLS
Beara
Bouchland Farm
Shoreland Cross
GREAT LIGHTLEIGH LA
Hill
Weir
HILL HEAD CROSS
HEAD MILL
Hill Head
Great Lightleigh
LIGHTLEIGH CROSS
DRONSFORD LA
Head Wood
Head Barton
SPITTLE LA
Waddington
WADDINGTON LA
River Taw
Junction Pool
Spittle Farm
Coombe
COOMBE LA
BRIDGE CROSS
NEWNH'M LA
POOL LA
Barnpool
NEWNH'M LA
Spittle Cross
Cutland House
Cadbury Barton
Bunson
FORCHES CROSS
NEWNHAM CROSS
B3226
Newnham Barton
CUTLAND CROSS
TWO GATE CROSS
Fortescue Cross
TWITCHEN LA
Catham
King's Hill
Kings Nympton
Higher Elstone Cross
Pyne Meadow Cross
Toll Bar Cross
DOBBSMOOR CROSS
Hayne Barton
Twitchen
Churchland
ELSTONE CROSS
Dobbs Moor Farm
ORANGE MOOR CROSS
BALLS CNR
Bircham
STATION RD
Elstone
SOUTH MOLTON RD
BALLS HILL
CLEAVE LA
GOLLAND LA
MILL MOOR CROSS
Lakehead
Beacon
Cleave
Golland
HANSFORD CROSS
Colleton Mills
Thurle
Parsonage Farm
MULLY BROOK
MILL LA
Winswood
HANSFORD CROSS
BORNE CROSS
Hansford Barton
FORD CROSS
PARSONAGE CROSS
BONDS CROSS
Chulmleigh Com Coll
CHARNEYMORE CROSS
RAGGED LA
Borne
COLLETON GATE
Colleton Manor
FOUR CROSSWAYS
Back Hill Ind Est
Chulmleigh Prim Sch
Liby
LANGLEY
Chulmleigh
Hook Farm
TAR LA
A377
B3096
LEIGH RD
DARTRIDGE LA
MALLINGBROOK CROSS
LEIGH VILLAS
LADYWELL MDWS
Ladywell La
CH
PO
EAST ST
Cricket Cl
Park Mill La
Lodge La

E1
1 LAND PK
2 DARTMOOR VIEW
3 FOUR WAYS DR
4 THREE CROSSWAYS
5 BEACON RISE
6 LANGLEY GDNS
7 ROYAL CHARTER PK
8 WINDY CROSS
9 EGYPT LA
10 CHULMLEIGH HILL
11 FORE ST HILL
12 THE SQUARE
13 ROCK HILL
14 NEW ST
15 CHURCH CL

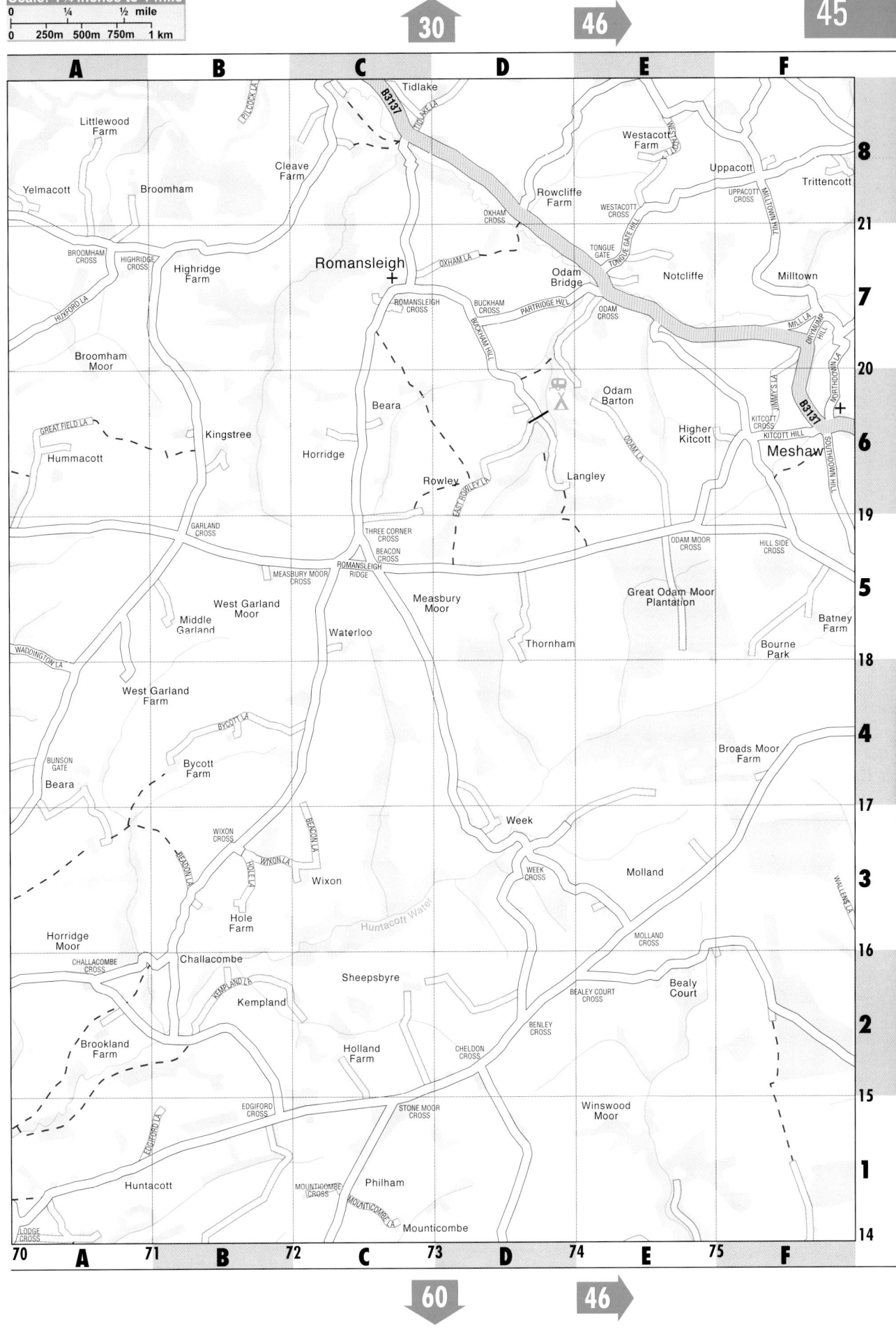
Scale: 1¾ inches to 1 mile
0 ¼ ½ mile
0 250m 500m 750m 1 km
30
46
A B C D E F
Tidlake
B3137
TIDLAKE LA
PILCOCK LA
Littlewood Farm
Westacott Farm
WESTACOTT LA
Uppacott
Trittencott
Cleave Farm
Yelmacott
Broomham
Rowcliffe Farm
UPPACOTT CROSS
MILLTOWN HILL
OXHAM CROSS
WESTACOTT CROSS
TONGUE GATE HILL
BROOMHAM CROSS
HIGHRIDGE CROSS
Highridge Farm
Romansleigh
OXHAM LA
TONGUE GATE
Odam Bridge
Notcliffe
Milltown
HUXFORD LA
ROMANSLEIGH CROSS
BUCKHAM CROSS
PARTRIDGE HILL
ODAM CROSS
MILL LA
DRYMUMP HILL
BUCKHAM HILL
Broomham Moor
NORTHDOWN LA
JIMMY'S LA
Beara
Odam Barton
GREAT FIELD LA
Kingstree
Higher Kitcott
KITCOTT CROSS
KITCOTT HILL
Meshaw
Hummacott
Horridge
ODAM LA
SOUTHDOWN HILL
Rowley
EAST ROWLEY LA
Langley
GARLAND CROSS
THREE CORNER CROSS
BEACON CROSS
ODAM MOOR CROSS
HILL SIDE CROSS
MEASBURY MOOR CROSS
ROMANSLEIGH RIDGE
Measbury Moor
Great Odam Moor Plantation
West Garland Moor
Middle Garland
Batney Farm
Waterloo
Thornham
Bourne Park
WADDINGTON LA
West Garland Farm
BYCOTT LA
Broads Moor Farm
BUNSON GATE
Bycott Farm
Beara
Week
WIXON CROSS
BEACON LA
BEADON LA
WIXON LA
HOLE LA
WEEK CROSS
Molland
Wixon
WALLENS LA
Hole Farm
Huntacott Water
Horridge Moor
MOLLAND CROSS
CHALLACOMBE CROSS
Challacombe
Sheepsbyre
KEMPLAND LA
Kempland
BEALEY COURT CROSS
Bealy Court
BENLEY CROSS
Brookland Farm
Holland Farm
CHELDON CROSS
EDGIFORD CROSS
STONE MOOR CROSS
Winswood Moor
EDGIFORD LA
Huntacott
MOUNTICOMBE CROSS
Philham
MOUNTICOMBE LA
Mounticombe
LODGE CROSS
70 71 72 73 74 75
8 21 7 20 6 19 5 18 4 17 3 16 2 15 1 14
60
46

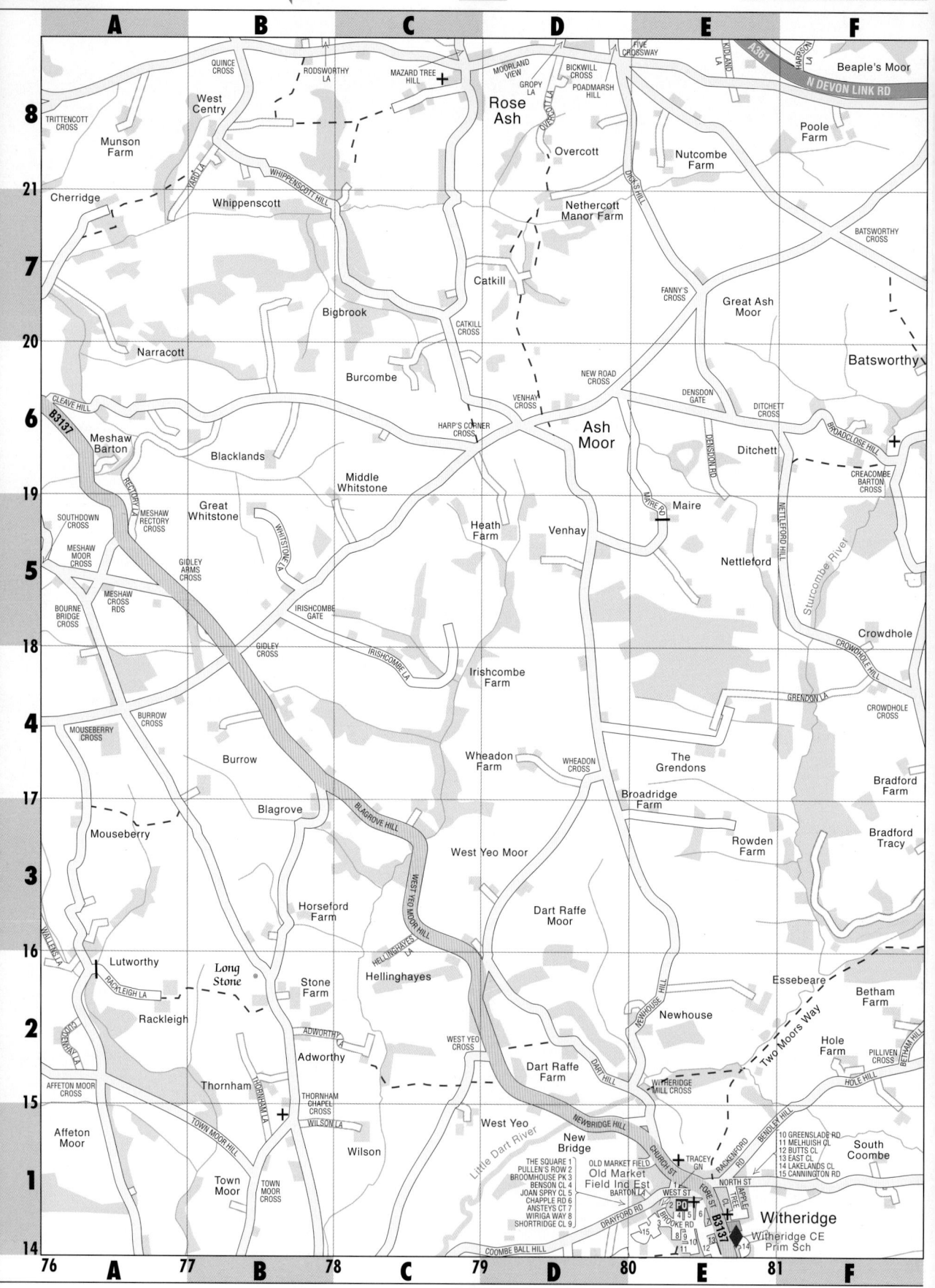

Scale: 1¾ inches to 1 mile

0 ¼ ½ mile

0 250m 500m 750m 1 km

A B C D E F

8

21

7

20

6

19

5

18

4

17

3

16

2

15

1

14

76 A 77 B 78 C 79 D 80 E 81 F

Trittencott Cross
Munson Farm
Cherridge
West Centry
Quince Cross
Rodsworthy La
Mazard Tree Hill
Moorland View
Rose Ash
Five Crossway
Gropy La
Bickwill Cross
Poadmarsh Hill
Beaple's Moor
Overcott
Nutcombe Farm
Poole Farm
N DEVON LINK RD
A361
KIDLAND LA
HARSON LA
Whippenscott
Whippenscott Hill
YARD LA
Nethercott Manor Farm
Batsworthy Cross
Catkill
Narracott
Bigbrook
Catkill Cross
Fanny's Cross
Great Ash Moor
Batsworthy
Burcombe
New Road Cross
Densdon Gate
Ditchett Cross
Broadclose Hill
Cleave Hill
B3137
Meshaw Barton
Blacklands
Harp's Corner Cross
Venhay Cross
Ash Moor
Densdon Gate
Ditchett
Creacombe Barton Cross
Southdown Cross
Rectory La
Meshaw Rectory Cross
Great Whitstone
Middle Whitstone
Heath Farm
Venhay
Maire
MIRE RD
DENSDON RD
Nettleford
NETTLEFORD HILL
Sturcombe River
Meshaw Moor Cross
Gidley Arms Cross
Whitstone La
Irishcombe Gate
Nettleford
Bourne Bridge Cross
Meshaw Cross Rds
Gidley Cross
Irishcombe La
Irishcombe Farm
Crowdhole
CROWDHOLE HILL
Mouseberry Cross
Burrow Cross
Blagrove Hill
Wheadon Farm
Wheadon Cross
The Grendons
GRENDON LA
Crowdhole Cross
Mouseberry
Burrow
Blagrove
West Yeo Moor
Broadridge Farm
Bradford Farm
Rowden Farm
Bradford Tracy
WEST YEO MOOR HILL
Dart Raffe Moor
WALLENS LA
Lutworthy
Long Stone
Horseford Farm
HELLINGHAYES LA
Stone Farm
Hellinghayes
NEWHOUSE HILL
Newhouse
Essebeare
Two Moors Way
Betham Farm
RACKLEIGH LA
Rackleigh
ADWORTHY
West Yeo Cross
DART HILL
Witheridge Mill Cross
Hole Farm
Hole Hill
PILLIVEN LA
BETHAM LA
DRUID LA
AFFETON MOOR LA
Affeton Moor Cross
Thornham
THORNHAM LA
Adworthy
Thornham Chapel Cross
WILSON LA
NEWBRIDGE HILL
West Yeo
New Bridge
Tracey Gn
CHURCH ST
RACKENFORD RD
BENDLEY HILL
10 GREENSLADE RD
11 MELHUISH CL
12 BUTTS CL
13 EAST CL
14 LAKELANDS CL
15 CANNINGTON RD
South Coombe
Affeton Moor
TOWN MOOR HILL
Wilson
Little Dart River
THE SQUARE 1
PULLEN'S ROW 2
BROOMHOUSE PK 3
BENSON CL 4
JOAN SPRY CL 5
CHAPPLE RD 6
ANSTEYS CT 7
WIRIGA WAY 8
SHORTRIDGE CL 9
Old Market Field
Old Market Field Ind Est
BARTON LA
WEST ST
FORE ST
NORTH ST
APPLE TREE
B3137
Witheridge
Witheridge CE Prim Sch
Town Moor
TOWN MOOR CROSS
DRAYFORD RD
COOMBE BALL HILL
PO

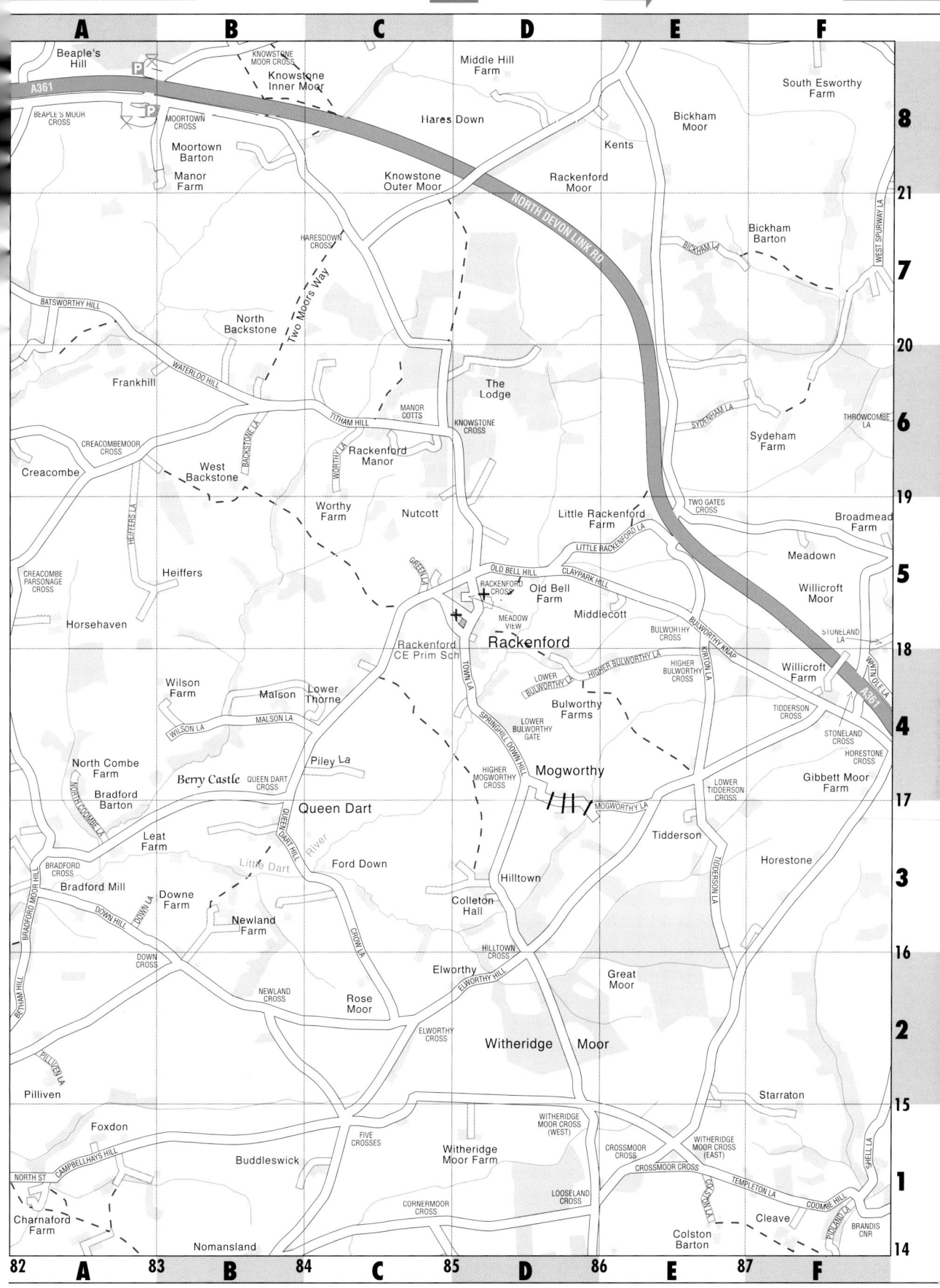

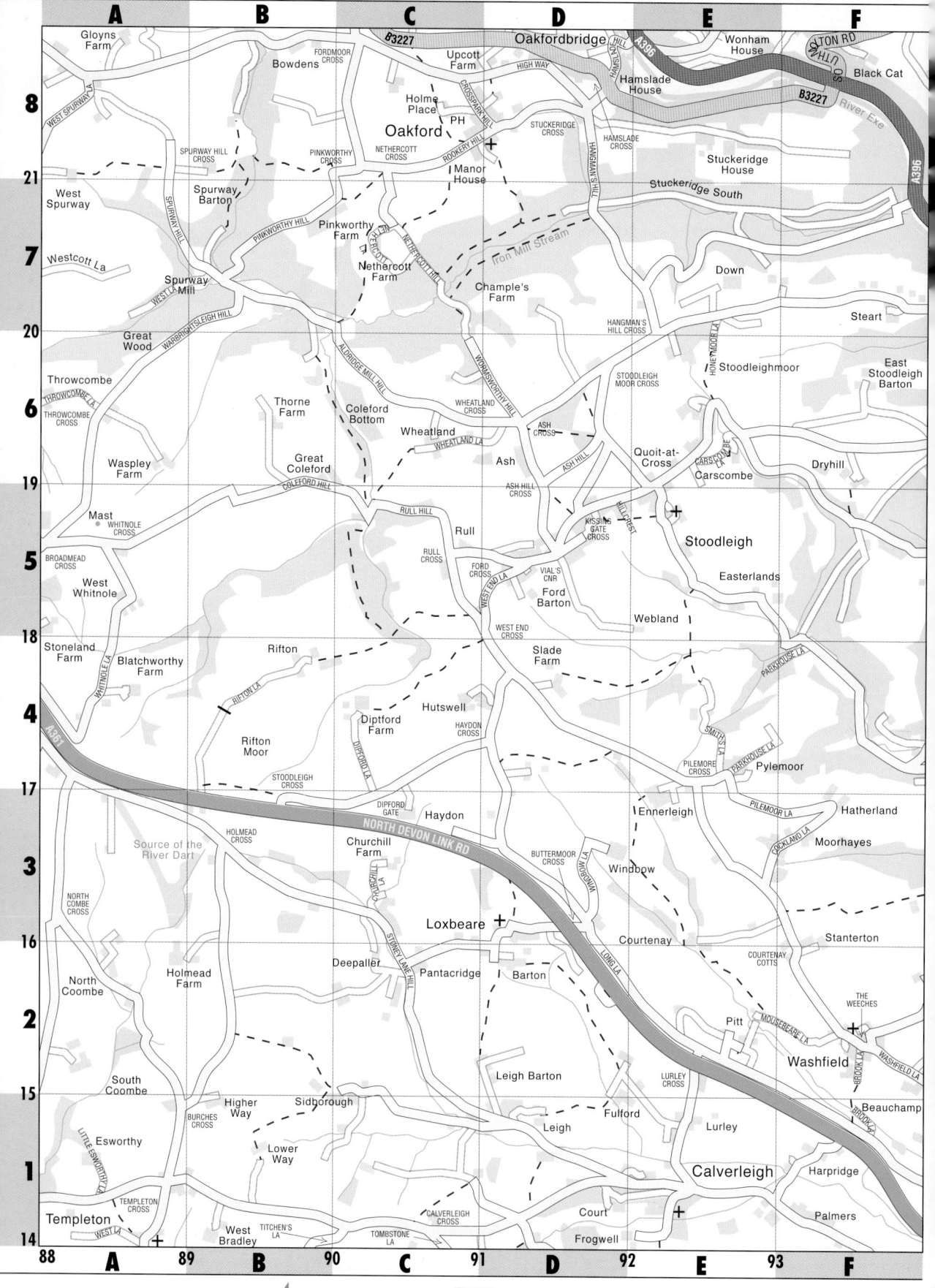

Scale: 1¾ inches to 1 mile

0   ¼   ½ mile
0   250m   500m   750m   1 km

8
Gloyns Farm
Bowdens
Fordmoor Cross
B3227
Oakfordbridge
Wonham House
Holton Rd
Black Cat
SOUTH
A396
WEST SPURWAY LA
Upcott Farm
High Way
Hamslade House
B3227
River Exe

Holme Place
Oakford
PH
Crosspark Hill
Stuckeridge Cross
Hamslade Cross
Stuckeridge House
A396

21
West Spurway
Spurway Hill Cross
Pinkworthy Cross
Nethercott Cross
Rookery Hill
Manor House
Hangman's Hill
Stuckeridge South

7
Westcott La
Spurway Barton
Pinkworthy Hill
Pinkworthy Farm
Nethercott Hill
Nethercott Farm
Iron Mill Stream
Chample's Farm
Down
Steart
Spurway Mill
WEST LA
SPURWAY HILL

20
Great Wood
WARBRIGHTSLEIGH HILL
Hangman's Hill Cross
HONEYMOOR LA
Stoodleighmoor
East Stoodleigh Barton

6
Throwcombe
THROWCOMBE LA
Throwcombe Cross
Thorne Farm
Coleford Bottom
ALDRIDGE MILL HILL
Wheatland
WHEATLAND LA
Wheatland Cross
Ash Cross
Stoodleigh Moor Cross
Quoit-at-Cross
CARSCOMBE LA
Carscombe
Dryhill
Waspley Farm
Great Coleford
COLEFORD HILL
Ash
Ash Hill
WOMBSWORTHY HILL

19
Mast
WHITNOLE CROSS
WHITNOLE LA
Rull Hill
Rull
Ash Hill Cross
HILL CREST
KISSING GATE CROSS
Stoodleigh
Easterlands

5
Broadmead Cross
West Whitnole
Rull Cross
Ford Cross
WEST END LA
Ford Barton
VIAL'S CNR
Webland
PARKHOUSE LA

18
Stoneland Farm
Blatchworthy Farm
Rifton
RIFTON LA
West End Cross
Slade Farm

4
A361
Rifton Moor
DIPFORD LA
Diptford Farm
Hutswell
Haydon Cross
SMITH'S LA
Pilemore Cross
PARKHOUSE LA
Pylemoor

17
Stoodleigh Cross
Dipford Gate
Haydon
NORTH DEVON LINK RD
Ennerleigh
PILEMOOR LA
Hatherland

3
Source of the River Dart
Holmead Cross
Churchill Farm
CHURCH LA
Buttermoor Cross
PT MORHAM
Windbow
COCKLAND LA
Moorhayes
North Combe Cross

16
North Coombe
Holmead Farm
STONEY LANE HILL
Deepaller
Pantacridge
Barton
LONG LA
Loxbeare
Courtenay
Courtenay Cotts
Stanterton

2
South Coombe
BURCHES CROSS
Higher Way
Sidborough
Leigh Barton
LURLEY CROSS
Pitt
MOUSEBEARE LA
THE WEECHES
Washfield
BROOK LA
WASHFIELD LA

15
Esworthy
LITTLE ESWORTHY LA
Lower Way
Leigh
Fulford
Lurley
Beauchamp
BROOK LA

1
Templeton
Templeton Cross
WEST LA
West Bradley
TITCHEN'S LA
TOMBSTONE LA
Calverleigh Cross
Court
Frogwell
Calverleigh
Harpridge
Palmers

14

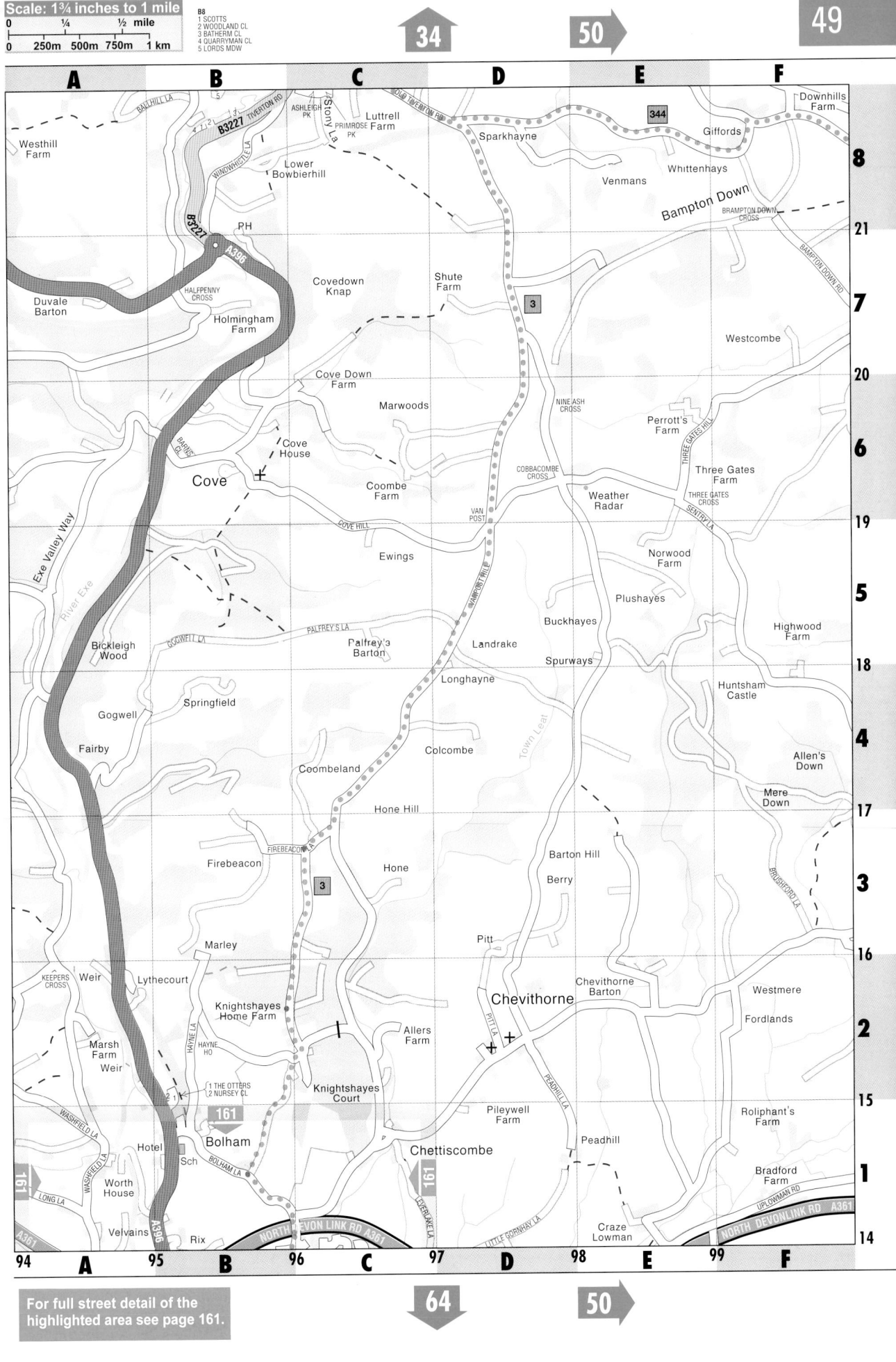

Scale: 1¾ inches to 1 mile

0   ¼   ½ mile

0   250m 500m 750m 1 km

B8
1 SCOTTS
2 WOODLAND CL
3 BATHERM CL
4 QUARRYMAN CL
5 LORDS MDW

34

50

A B C D E F

Westhill Farm

BAILHILL LA

B3227 TIVERTON RD

ASHLEIGH PK

Stony LA

Luttrell Farm

PRIMROSE PK

OLD TIVERTON RD

Sparkhayne

344

Giffords

Downhills Farm

Lower Bowbierhill

WINDWHISTLE LA

Venmans

Whittenhays

Bampton Down

BRAMPTON DOWN CROSS

BAMPTON DOWN RD

8

21

PH

B3227

A396

HALFPENNY CROSS

Covedown Knap

Shute Farm

3

Westcombe

7

Duvale Barton

Holmingham Farm

BARNS CL

Cove Down Farm

Marwoods

NINE ASH CROSS

Perrott's Farm

THREE GATES HILL

Three Gates Farm

20

6

Cove House

Cove

Coombe Farm

COBBACOMBE CROSS

Weather Radar

THREE GATES CROSS

SENTRY LA

Exe Valley Way

COVE HILL

VAN POST

Norwood Farm

19

River Exe

Ewings

Plushayes

5

Bickleigh Wood

GOGWELL LA

PALFREY'S LA

Palfrey's Barton

Landrake

Buckhayes

Spurways

Highwood Farm

18

Gogwell

Springfield

Longhayne

Town Leat

Huntsham Castle

4

Fairby

Colcombe

Coombeland

Allen's Down

17

Hone Hill

Mere Down

BRUSHFORD LA

3

Firebeacon

FIREBEACON LA

3

Hone

Barton Hill

Berry

16

Marley

Pitt

PITT LA

Chevithorne Barton

Westmere

2

KEEPERS CROSS

Weir

Lythecourt

HAYNE LA

Knightshayes Home Farm

HAYNE HO

Allers Farm

Chevithorne

Fordlands

15

Marsh Farm

Weir

1 THE OTTERS
2 NURSEY CL

161

Knightshayes Court

Pileywell Farm

PEADHILL LA

Roliphant's Farm

WASHFIELD LA

LONG LA

Hotel

Sch

BOLHAM LA

Bolham

Chettiscombe

161

LOWERLAKE LA

Peadhill

LITTLE GORNHAY LA

Craze Lowman

UPLOWMAN RD

NORTH DEVON LINK RD A361

Bradford Farm

1

161

Worth House

A396

Velvains

Rix

NORTH DEVON LINK RD A361

14

94 A 95 B 96 C 97 D 98 E 99 F

64

50

For full street detail of the highlighted area see page 161.

49
35

Scale: 1¾ inches to 1 mile

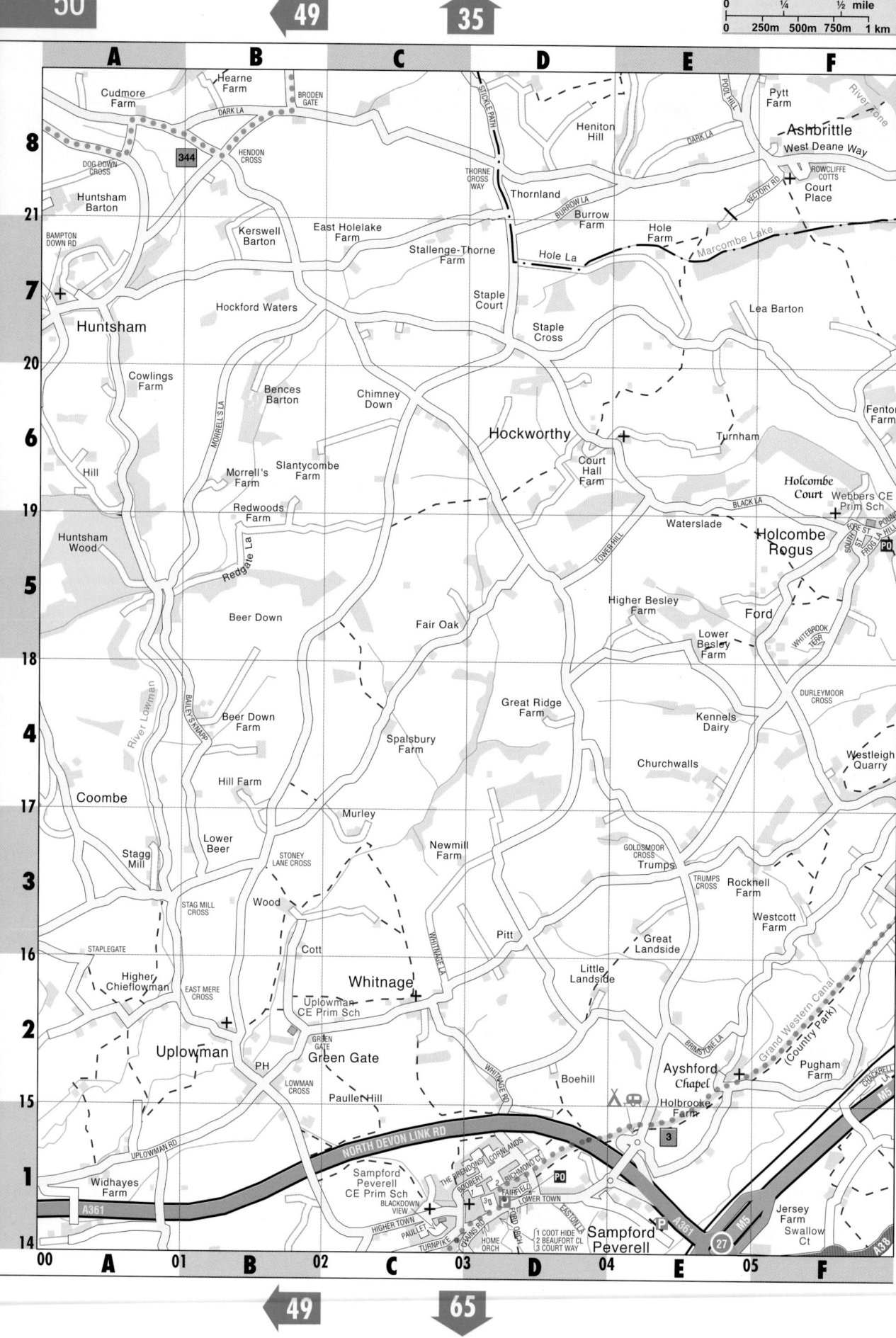
Cudmore Farm
Hearne Farm
Broden Gate
Dark La
Dog Down Cross
Hendon Cross
344
Huntsham Barton
Bampton Down Rd
Kerswell Barton
East Holelake Farm
Stallenge-Thorne Farm
Stickle Path
Thorne Cross Way
Thornland
Burrow La
Burrow Farm
Hole La
Heniton Hill
Pool Hill
Hole Farm
Marcombe Lake
Pytt Farm
Ashbrittle
West Deane Way
River Tone
Rowcliffe Cotts
Court Place
Rectory Rd
Huntsham
Hockford Waters
Staple Court
Staple Cross
Lea Barton
Cowlings Farm
Bences Barton
Chimney Down
Morrell's La
Hockworthy
Court Hall Farm
Turnham
Fenton Farm
Hill
Morrell's Farm
Slantycombe Farm
Redwoods Farm
Holcombe Court
Webbers CE Prim Sch
Black La
Waterslade
Holcombe Rogus
Pound
Fore St
South St
Frog La
Hill
PO
Huntsham Wood
Redgate La
Tower Hill
Beer Down
Fair Oak
Higher Besley Farm
Ford
Lower Besley Farm
Whitebrook Terr
River Lowman
Bailey's Knapp
Great Ridge Farm
Durleymoor Cross
Beer Down Farm
Spalsbury Farm
Kennels Dairy
Churchwalls
Westleigh Quarry
Hill Farm
Coombe
Murley
Lower Beer
Newmill Farm
Stagg Mill
Stoney Lane Cross
Goldsmoor Cross
Trumps
Trumps Cross
Rockhell Farm
Stag Mill Cross
Wood
Westcott Farm
Staplegate
Cott
Pitt
Whitnage La
Great Landside
Higher Chieflowman
East Mere Cross
Whitnage
Little Landside
Grand Western Canal (Country Park)
Uplowman CE Prim Sch
Uplowman
PH
Green Gate
Green Gate
Brimstone La
Ayshford Chapel
Pugham Farm
Lowman Cross
Paullet Hill
Whitnage Rd
Boehill
Holbrooke Farm
Chackrell La
M5
Uplowman Rd
North Devon Link Rd
3
Sampford Peverell CE Prim Sch
The Brendons
Cornlands
Boobery
Richmond Ct
Fairfield
Widhayes Farm
A361
Blackdown View
Higher Town
Paullet
Turnpike
Chains Rd
Home Orch
Ford Orch
Lower Town
Easton La
1 Coot Hide
2 Beaufort Cl
3 Court Way
Sampford Peverell
A361
M5
27
Jersey Farm
Swallow Ct
A38
A
B
C
D
E
F
8
21
7
20
6
19
5
18
4
17
3
16
2
15
1
14
00
01
02
03
04
05

49
65

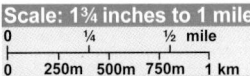

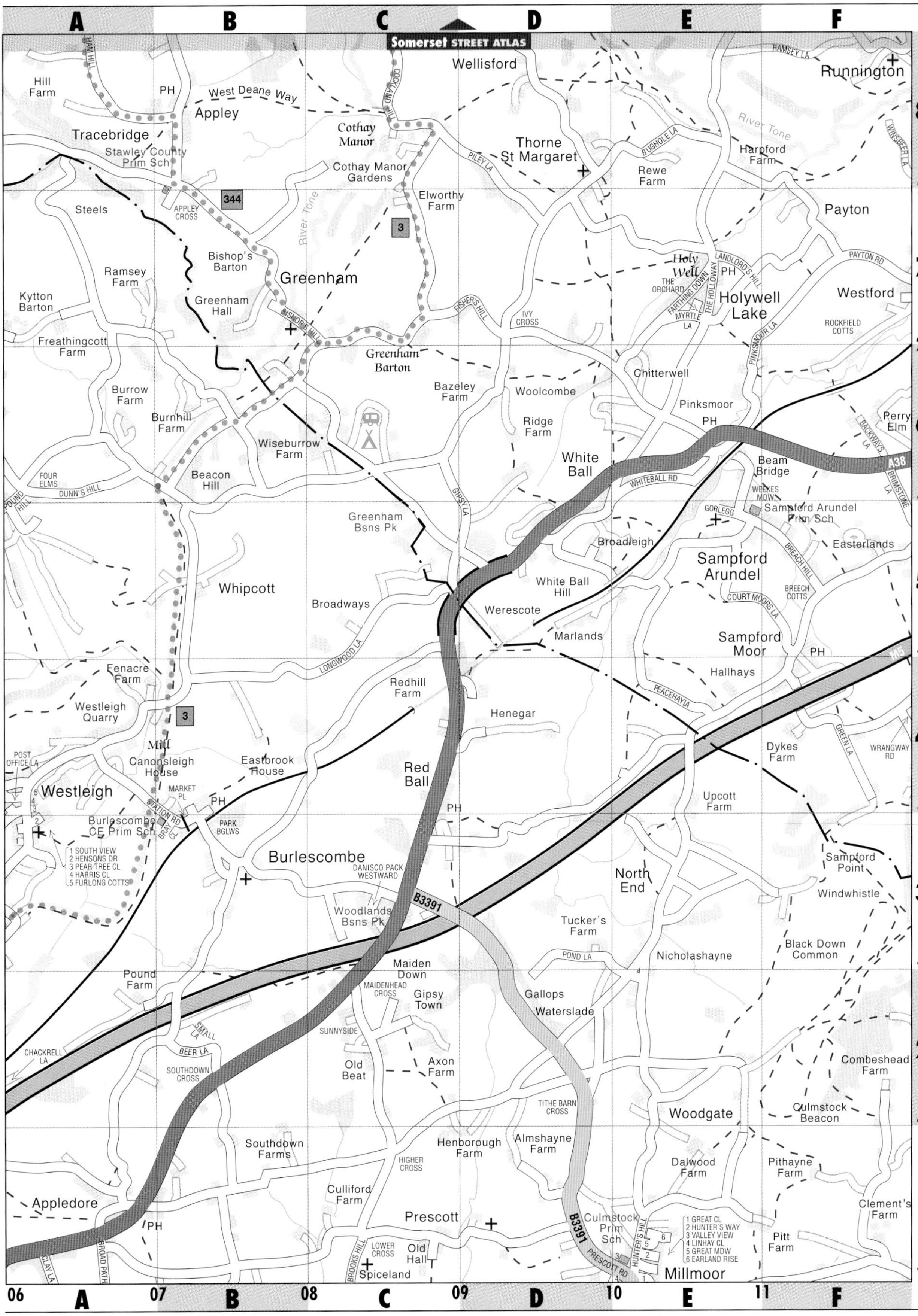

Scale: 1¾ inches to 1 mile

| 0 | | ¼ | | ½ mile |
| 0 | 250m | 500m | 750m | 1 km |

52

Somerset STREET ATLAS

A · **B** · **C** · **D** · **E** · **F**

8
21
7
20
6
19
5
18
4
17
3
16
2
15
1
14

Hill Farm
Tracebridge
Stawley County Prim Sch
Steels
Appley
West Deane Way
Wellisford
Runnington
Ramsey La
River Tone
Cothay Manor
Thorne St Margaret
Bughole La
Harpford Farm
Rewe Farm
Payton
Payton Rd
Chinsbeer La
Appley Cross
344
Cothay Manor Gardens
Elworthy Farm
Pilley La
Fisher Hill
Holy Well
The Orchard
Myrtle La
Farthing Down
The Holloway
Landlord's Hill
PH
Holywell Lake
Westford
Rockfield Cotts
Kytton Barton
Ramsey Farm
Bishop's Barton
Greenham
3
Greenham Hall
Ivy Cross
Pinksmoor La
Pinksmoor
PH
Chitterwell
Perry Elm
Backways La
Freathingcott Farm
Burrow Farm
Burnhill Farm
Wiseburrow Farm
Beacon Hill
Greenham Barton
Bazeley Farm
Ridge Farm
Woolcombe
White Ball
Whiteball Rd
Broadleigh
Gorlegg
Sampford Arundel Prim Sch
Weekes Mdw
Easterlands
A38 Grimstone
Four Elms
Pound Hill
Dunn's Hill
Greenham Bsns Pk
Gipsy La
White Ball Hill
Werescote
Sampford Arundel
Court Moors La
Breach Hill
Breech Cotts
Whipcott
Broadways
Longwood La
Marlands
PH
Sampford Moor
M5
Fenacre Farm
Westleigh Quarry
3
Redhill Farm
Henegar
Hallhays
Peachayla
Green La
Dykes Farm
Wrangway Rd
Post Office La
Mill
Canonsleigh House
Eastbrook House
Red Ball
Upcott Farm
Westleigh
Station Rd
Market Pl
PH
Park Bglws
PH
Burlescombe CE Prim Sch
1 SOUTH VIEW
2 HENSONS DR
3 PEAR TREE CL
4 HARRIS CL
5 FURLONG COTTS
Burlescombe
Danisco Pack Westward
North End
Sampford Point
Windwhistle
Black Down Common
Pound Farm
Woodlands Bsns Pk
B3391
Maiden Down
Maidenhead Cross
Gipsy Town
Tucker's Farm
Pond La
Nicholashayne
Combeshead Farm
Chackrell La
Small La
Beer La
Southdown Cross
Sunnyside
Old Beat
Axon Farm
Gallops Waterslade
Tithe Barn Cross
Woodgate
Culmstock Beacon
Appledore
PH
Broad Path
Southdown Farms
Higher Cross
Culliford Farm
Henborough Farm
Almshayne Farm
Dalwood Farm
Pithayne Farm
Clement's Farm
Clay La
Prescott
Brooks Hill
Lower Cross
Spiceland
Old Hall
B3391
Prescott Rd
Culmstock Prim Sch
Hunter's Hill
1 GREAT CL
2 HUNTER'S WAY
3 VALLEY VIEW
4 LINHAY CL
5 GREAT MDW
6 EARLAND RISE
6
Millmoor
Pitt Farm

06 · **A** · **07** · **B** · **08** · **C** · **09** · **D** · **10** · **E** · **11** · **F**

66
52

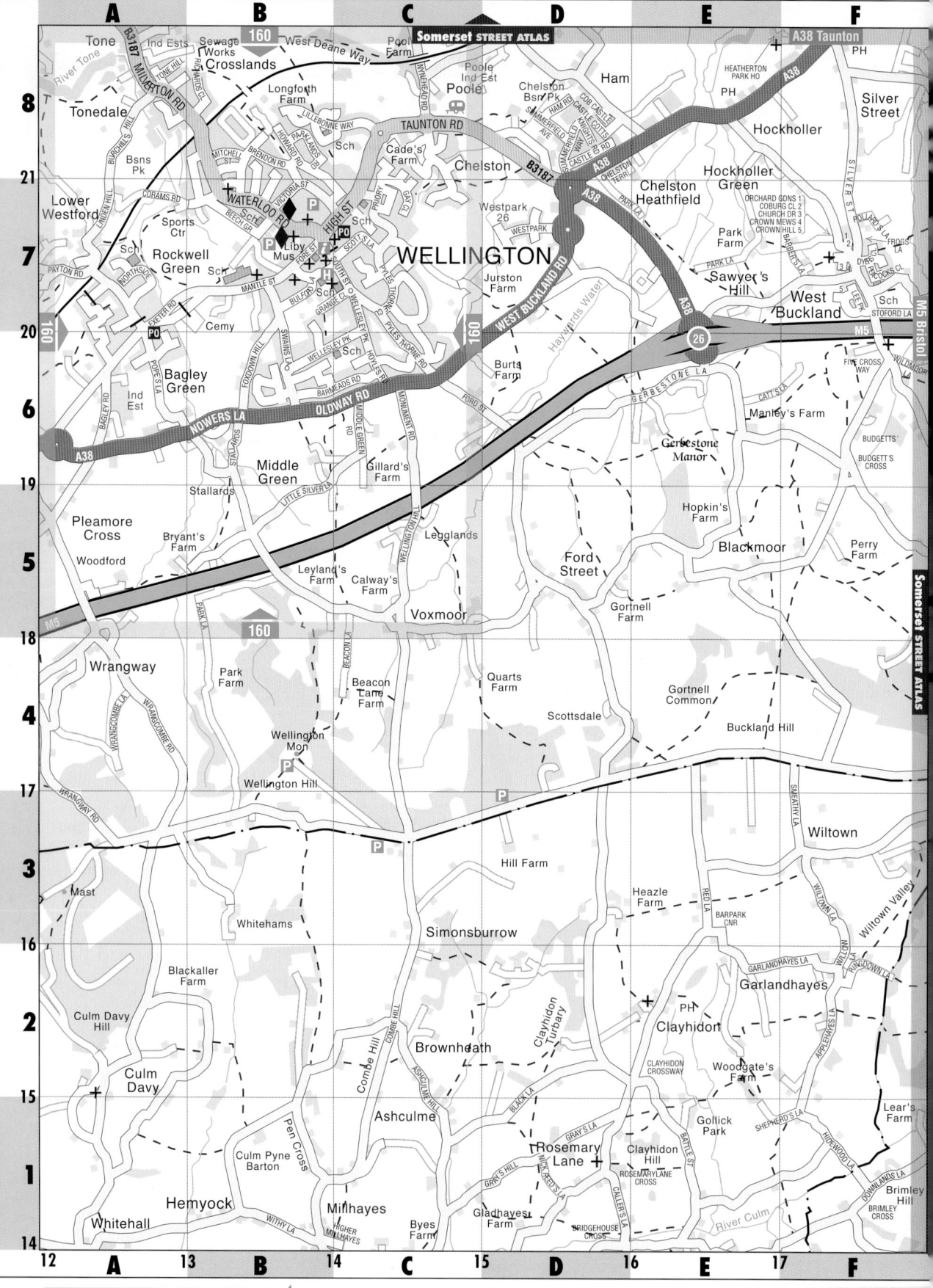

51

Scale: 1¾ inches to 1 mile

0 ¼ ½ mile
0 250m 500m 750m 1 km

Somerset STREET ATLAS

Tone
Ind Ests
Sewage
Works
Crosslands
West Deane Way
Poole
Farm
Poole
Ind Est
Poole
Ham
HEATHERTON
PARK HO
PH
PH
Silver
Street
River Tone
Tonedale
Longforth
Farm
TAUNTON RD
Chelston
Bsn Pk
Hockholler
A38
B3187
MILVERTON RD
MITCHELL ST
BRENDON RD
HOWARD RD
PARK LANDS CL
LILLEBONNE WAY
Sch
Cade's
Farm
Chelston
B3187
Hockholler
Green
Lower
Westford
Bsns
Pk
BURCHILLS HILL
CORAMS RD
WATERLOO RD
BEECH GR
VICTORIA ST
HIGH ST
Sch
PRIORY
GAS CT
Chelston
Heathfield
ORCHARD GDNS 1
COBURG CL 2
CHURCH DR 3
CROWN MEWS 4
CROWN HILL 5
Park
Farm
Sch
Rockwell
Green
P
Liby
Mus
P
PO
WELLINGTON
Westpark
26
WESTPARK
PARK LA
Sawyer's
Hill
West
Buckland
Sch
PAYTON RD
EXETER RD
NORTHCSE
MANTLE ST
BULFORD
GRANGE CL
SOUTH ST
SCOTT'S LN
SOUTH ST
WELLESLEY PK
THORNE
WEST BUCKLAND RD
Jurston
Farm
WEST BUCKLAND RD
M5
M5 Bristol
Cemy
PO
SWAINS LO
FOXDOWN HILL
WELLESLEY LO
BARMEADS RD
Sch
PYLES MORNE RD
HOYLES RD
MONUMENT RD
Hayward's Water
Burts
Farm
160
Haywards Water
GERBESTONE LA
Five Cross
Way
WILDMOOR
160
Bagley
Green
Ind
Est
NOWERS LA
OLDWAY RD
STALLARDS
MIDDLE GREEN
FORD ST
26
Manley's Farm
CATT'S LA
BUDGETTS'
BUDGETT'S
CROSS
A38
Middle
Green
Stallards
LITTLE SILVER LA
Gillard's
Farm
WELLINGTON HILL
Gerbestone
Manor
Hopkin's
Farm
Blackmoor
Perry
Farm
Pleamore
Cross
Woodford
Bryant's
Farm
Leyland's
Farm
Calway's
Farm
Legglands
Ford
Street
Gortnell
Farm
M5
160
Voxmoor
Wrangway
Park
Farm
BEACON LA
Beacon
Lane
Farm
Quarts
Farm
Gortnell
Common
Buckland Hill
WRANGCOMBE LA
WRANGCOMBE LA
PARK LA
Wellington
Mon
Wellington Hill
P
Scottsdale
SMEATHY LA
Wiltown
WRANGWAY RD
P
Hill Farm
Heazle
Farm
RED LA
BARPARK
CNR
WILTON LA
Wiltown Valley
Mast
Whitehams
Simonsburrow
GARLANDHAYES LA
Garlandhayes
RINGDOWN LA
Blackaller
Farm
COMBE HILL
PH
Clayhidon
Woodgate's
Farm
APPLECATES LA
Culm Davy
Hill
Clayhidon
Turbary
CLAYHIDON
CROSSWAY
Lear's
Farm
Culm
Davy
Brownheath
GRAY'S LA
BLACK LA
Ashculme
Gollick
Park
SHEPHERD'S LA
HORWOOD LA
Brimley
Hill
PEN CROSS
ASHCULME HILL
GRAY'S HILL
RED LA
Rosemary
Lane
Clayhidon
Hill
ROSEMARYLANE
CROSS
BATTLE ST
DOWNLANDS LA
Brimley
Cross
Culm Pyne
Barton
Hemyock
Millhayes
WITHY LA
HIGHER
MILLHAYES
Byes
Farm
Gladhayes
Farm
CALLER LA
BRIDGEHOUSE
CROSS
River Culm
Whitehall

51   67

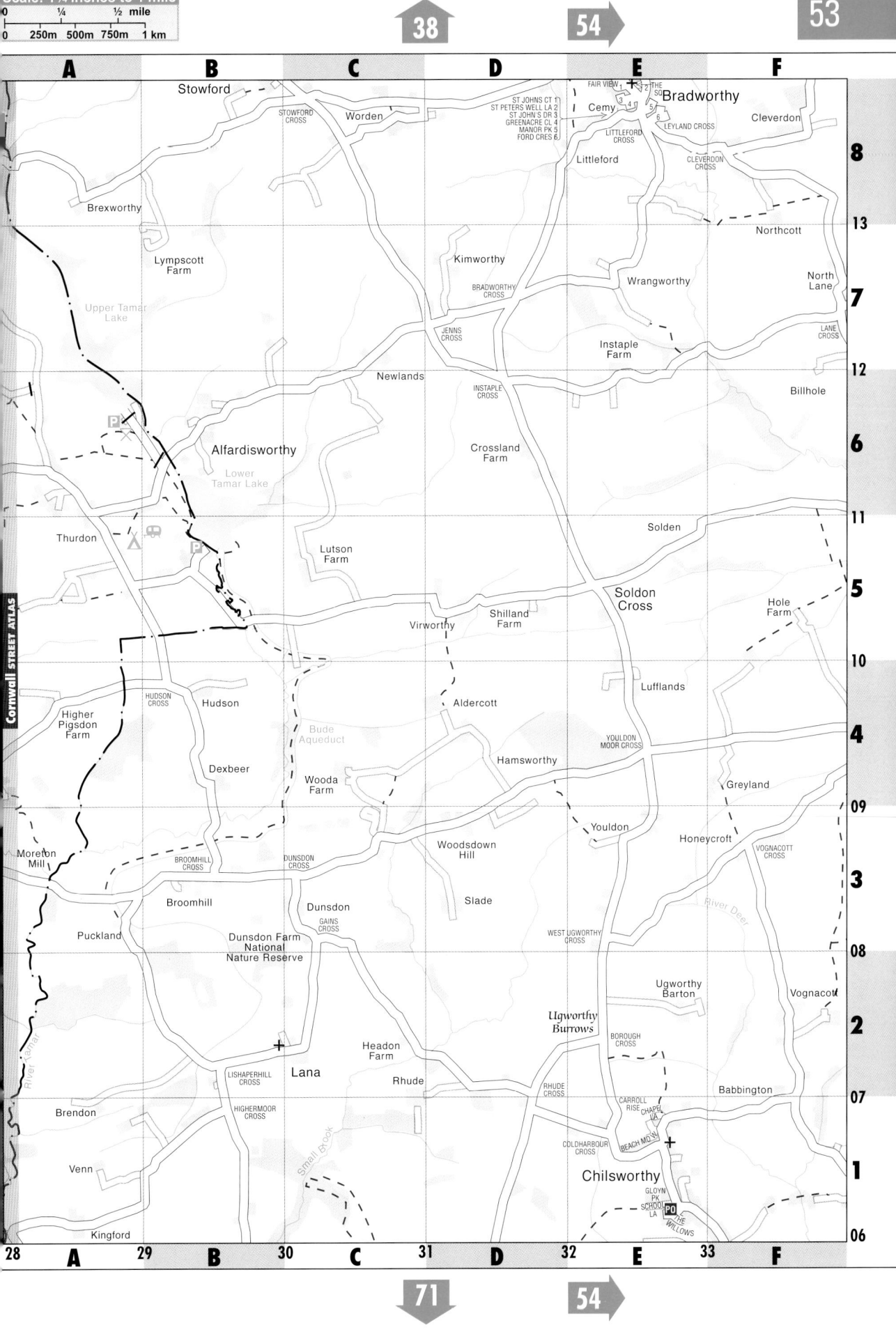

Stowford

STOWFORD CROSS
Worden

FAIR VIEW
Cemy
THE SQ
Bradworthy
Cleverdon

ST JOHNS CT 1
ST PETERS WELL LA 2
ST JOHN S DR 3
GREENACRE CL 4
MANOR PK 5
FORD CRES 6

LEYLAND CROSS

LITTLEFORD CROSS

CLEVERDON CROSS

Brexworthy

Littleford

Northcott

Lympscott Farm

Kimworthy

Wrangworthy

North Lane

Upper Tamar Lake

BRADWORTHY CROSS

LANE CROSS

JENNS CROSS

Instaple Farm

Newlands

INSTAPLE CROSS

Billhole

Alfardisworthy

Crossland Farm

Lower Tamar Lake

Solden

Thurdon

Lutson Farm

Hole Farm

Soldon Cross

Virworthy

Shilland Farm

Higher Pigsdon Farm

HUDSON CROSS
Hudson

Aldercott

Lufflands

Bude Aqueduct

YOULDON MOOR CROSS

Greyland

Dexbeer

Wooda Farm

Hamsworthy

Moreton Mill

Woodsdown Hill

Youldon

Honeycroft

VOGNACOTT CROSS

BROOMHILL CROSS

DUNSDON CROSS

Slade

River Deer

Puckland

Broomhill

Dunsdon

WEST UGWORTHY CROSS

GAINS CROSS

Dunsdon Farm National Nature Reserve

Ugworthy Barton

Vognacott

Ugworthy Burrows

BOROUGH CROSS

LISHAPERHILL CROSS

Lana

Headon Farm

Rhude

RHUDE CROSS

Babbington

Brendon

HIGHERMOOR CROSS

CARROLL RISE
CHAPEL LA
BEACH MD

Venn

COLDHARBOUR CROSS

Chilsworthy

GLOYN PK SCHOOL LA
PO
THE WILLOWS

Kingford

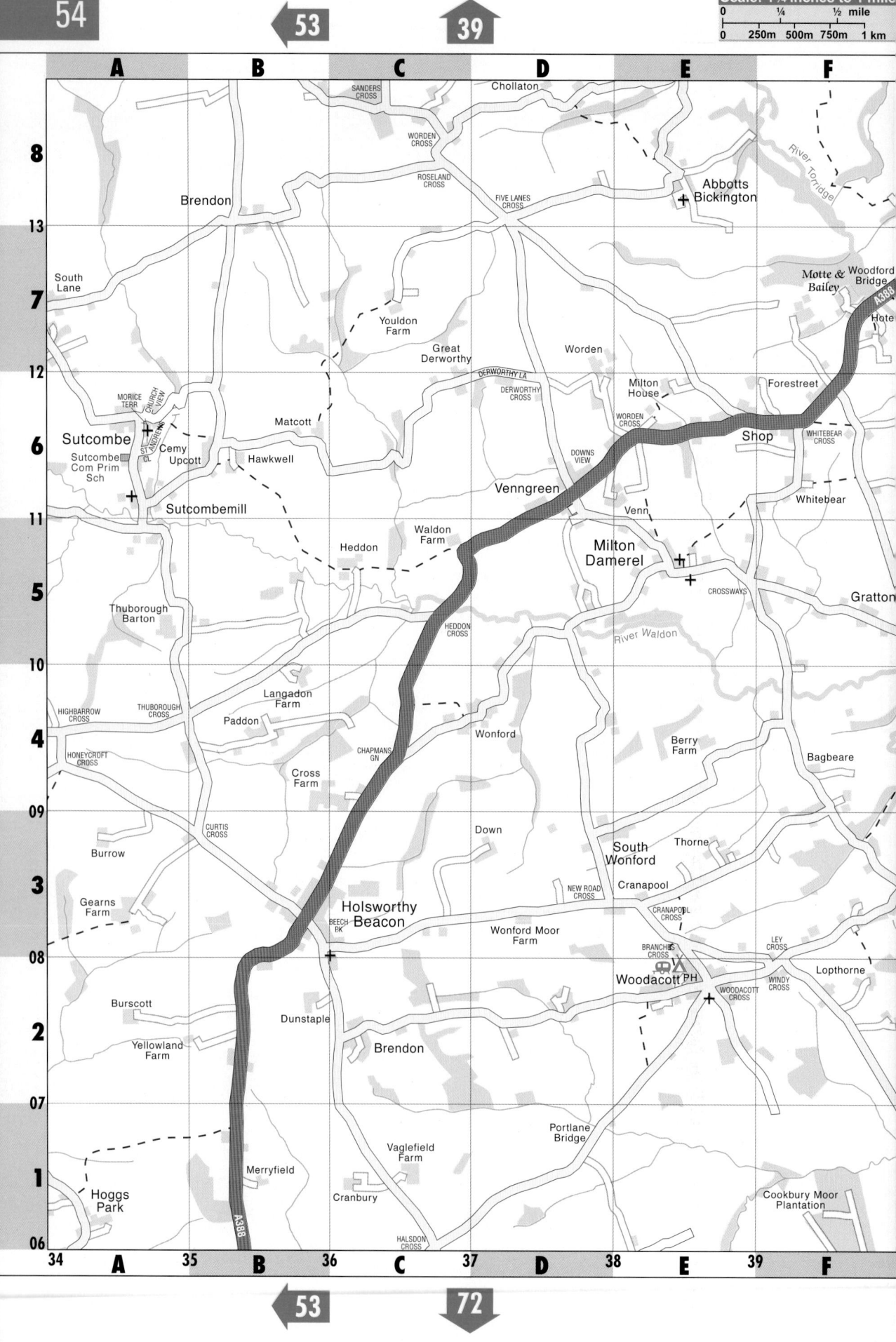
53
39
Scale: 1¾ inches to 1 mile
0 ¼ ½ mile
0 250m 500m 750m 1 km
A B C D E F
Sanders Cross
Chollaton
Worden Cross
River Torridge
Roseland Cross
Five Lanes Cross
Abbotts Bickington
Brendon
South Lane
Motte & Bailey
Woodford Bridge
A388
Hote
Youldon Farm
Great Derworthy
Worden
Derworthy La
Derworthy Cross
Milton House
Forestreet
Morice Terr
Church View
Matcott
Worden Cross
St Andrews Cl
Sutcombe
Cemy
Upcott
Hawkwell
Downs View
Shop
Whitebear Cross
Sutcombe Com Prim Sch
Venngreen
Whitebear
Sutcombemill
Venn
Waldon Farm
Heddon
Milton Damerel
Crossways
Gratton
Thuborough Barton
Heddon Cross
River Waldon
Langadon Farm
Highbarrow Cross
Thuborough Cross
Paddon
Wonford
Berry Farm
Honeycroft Cross
Chapmans Gn
Bagbeare
Cross Farm
Curtis Cross
Down
South Wonford
Thorne
Burrow
Cranapool
New Road Cross
Gearns Farm
Holsworthy Beacon
Beech Pk
Cranapool Cross
Wonford Moor Farm
Branches Cross
Ley Cross
Lopthorne
Woodacott
PH
Windy Cross
Woodacott Cross
Burscott
Dunstaple
Yellowland Farm
Brendon
Portlane Bridge
Vaglefield Farm
Merryfield
Cranbury
Hoggs Park
Cookbury Moor Plantation
Halsdon Cross
A388
8 13 7 12 6 11 5 10 4 09 3 08 2 07 1 06
34 35 36 37 38 39
53
72

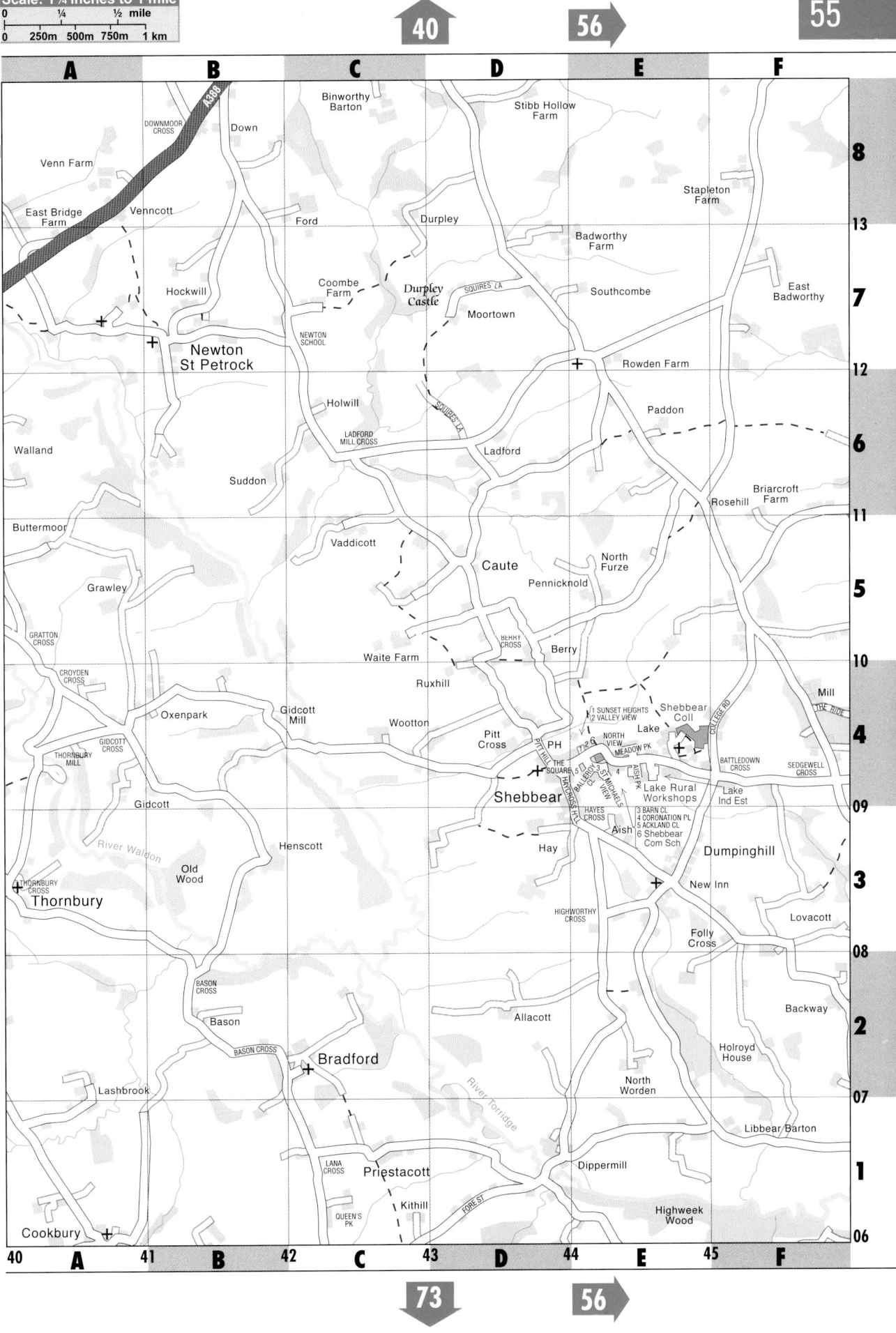
Scale: 1¾ inches to 1 mile
0 ¼ ½ mile
0 250m 500m 750m 1 km
40
56
A B C D E F
8
13
7
12
6
11
5
10
4
09
3
08
2
07
1
06
40 A 41 B 42 C 43 D 44 E 45 F
73
56
A388
DOWNMOOR CROSS
Down
Binworthy Barton
Stibb Hollow Farm
Venn Farm
Stapleton Farm
East Bridge Farm
Venncott
Ford
Durpley
Badworthy Farm
Coombe Farm
Durpley Castle
SQUIRES' LA
Southcombe
East Badworthy
Hockwill
Moortown
NEWTON SCHOOL
Newton St Petrock
Rowden Farm
Holwill
SQUIRES' LA
Paddon
Walland
LADFORD MILL CROSS
Ladford
Suddon
Briarcroft Farm
Rosehill
Buttermoor
Vaddicott
Caute
North Furze
Pennicknold
Grawley
GRATTON CROSS
BERRY CROSS
Berry
Waite Farm
CROYDEN CROSS
Ruxhill
Mill
THE RIDE
Oxenpark
Gidcott Mill
Wootton
1 SUNSET HEIGHTS
2 VALLEY VIEW
Shebbear Coll
COLLEGE RD
Pitt Cross
PH
Lake
NORTH VIEW
MEADOW PK
GIDCOTT CROSS
THORNBURY MILL
PITT HILL
THE SQUARE
BALLEROY CL
ST MICHAELS VIEW
AISH PK
BATTLEDOWN CROSS
SEDGEWELL CROSS
Lake Rural Workshops
Lake Ind Est
Gidcott
Shebbear
HAYCROSS HILL
HAYES CROSS
3 BARN CL
4 CORONATION PL
5 ACKLAND CL
6 Shebbear Com Sch
Aish
River Waldon
Henscott
Hay
Dumpinghill
Old Wood
THORNBURY CROSS
Thornbury
New Inn
HIGHWORTHY CROSS
Lovacott
Folly Cross
BASON CROSS
Backway
Allacott
Bason
Holroyd House
BASON CROSS
Bradford
North Worden
Lashbrook
River Torridge
Libbear Barton
LANA CROSS
Priestacott
Dippermill
Kithill
FORE ST
QUEEN'S PK
Highweek Wood
Cookbury

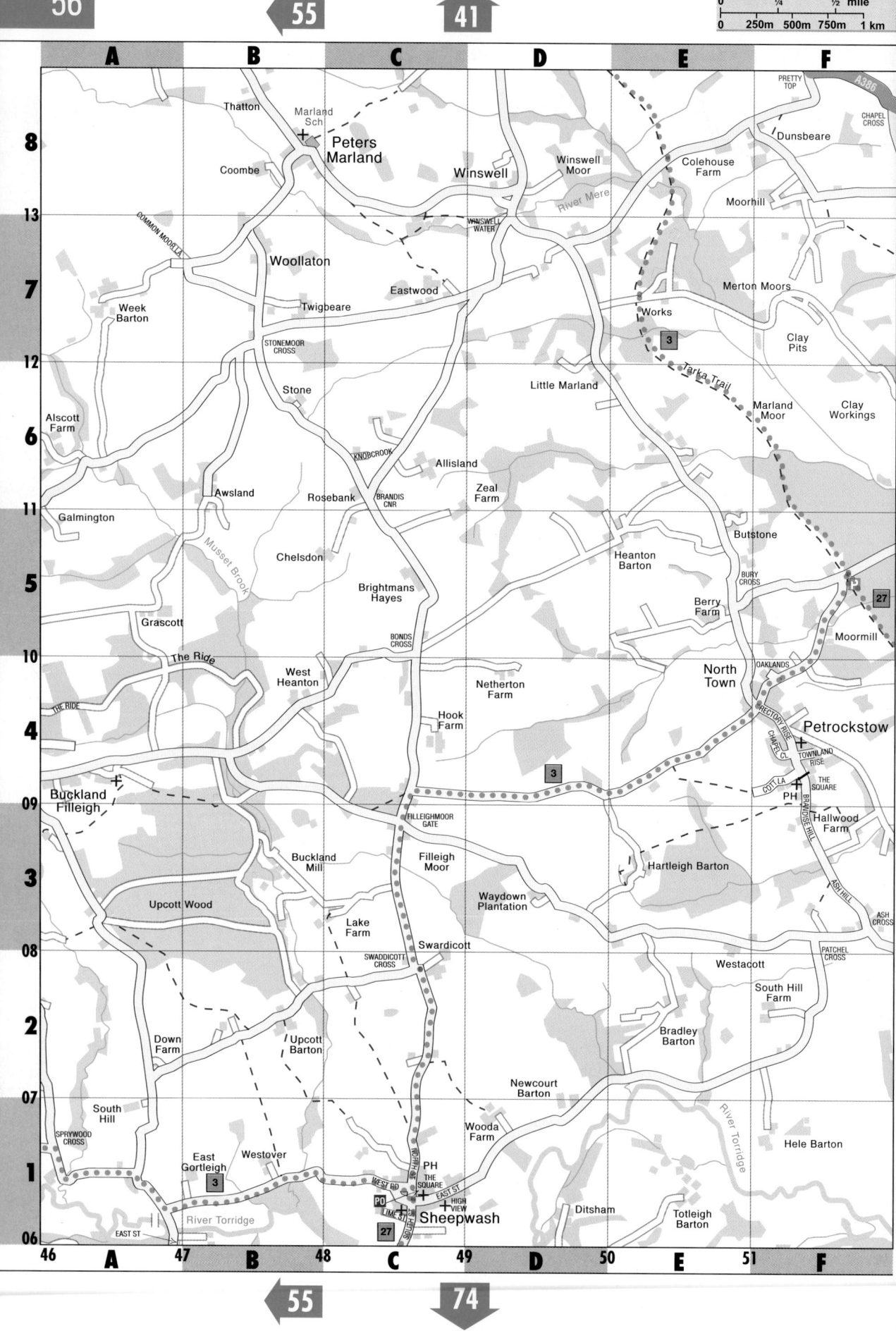

55
41

Scale: 1¾ inches to 1 mile

0   ¼   ½ mile
0 250m 500m 750m 1 km

A   B   C   D   E   F

PRETTY TOP
A386
CHAPEL CROSS
Thatton
Marland Sch
Peters Marland
Winswell
Winswell Moor
Dunsbeare
Colehouse Farm
Moorhill
Coombe
River Mere
8
13
COMMON MOOR LA
Woollaton
Eastwood
Winswell Water
Merton Moors
Works
3
Clay Pits
7
Week Barton
Twigbeare
STONEMOOR CROSS
Tarka Trail
12
Stone
Little Marland
Marland Moor
Clay Workings
Alscott Farm
6
KNOBCROOK
Allisland
Zeal Farm
Awsland
BRANDIS CNR
Butstone
Galmington
Rosebank
11
Chelsdon
Heanton Barton
BURY CROSS
27
Brightmans Hayes
Berry Farm
Moormill
5
Grascott
BONDS CROSS
North Town
OAKLANDS
Petrockstow
The Ride
West Heanton
Netherton Farm
RECTORY RISE
CHAPEL CL
TOWNLAND RISE
10
THE RIDE
Hook Farm
3
COTT LA
THE SQUARE
PH
4
Buckland Filleigh
FILLEIGHMOOR GATE
Filleigh Moor
BRANDIS HILL
Hallwood Farm
09
Buckland Mill
Waydown Plantation
Hartleigh Barton
ASH HILL
3
Upcott Wood
Lake Farm
Swardicott
ASH CROSS
Down Farm
SWADDICOTT CROSS
Westacott
PATCHEL CROSS
2
Upcott Barton
South Hill Farm
08
Bradley Barton
Newcourt Barton
River Torridge
07
South Hill
Wooda Farm
Hele Barton
SPRYWOOD CROSS
East Gortleigh
Westover
PH
THE SQUARE
EAST ST
Ditsham
Totleigh Barton
1
3
WEST RD
NORTH ST
HIGH VIEW
PO
LIME ST
Sheepwash
06
EAST ST
River Torridge
27

46   A   47   B   48   C   49   D   50   E   51   F

55
74

42 58

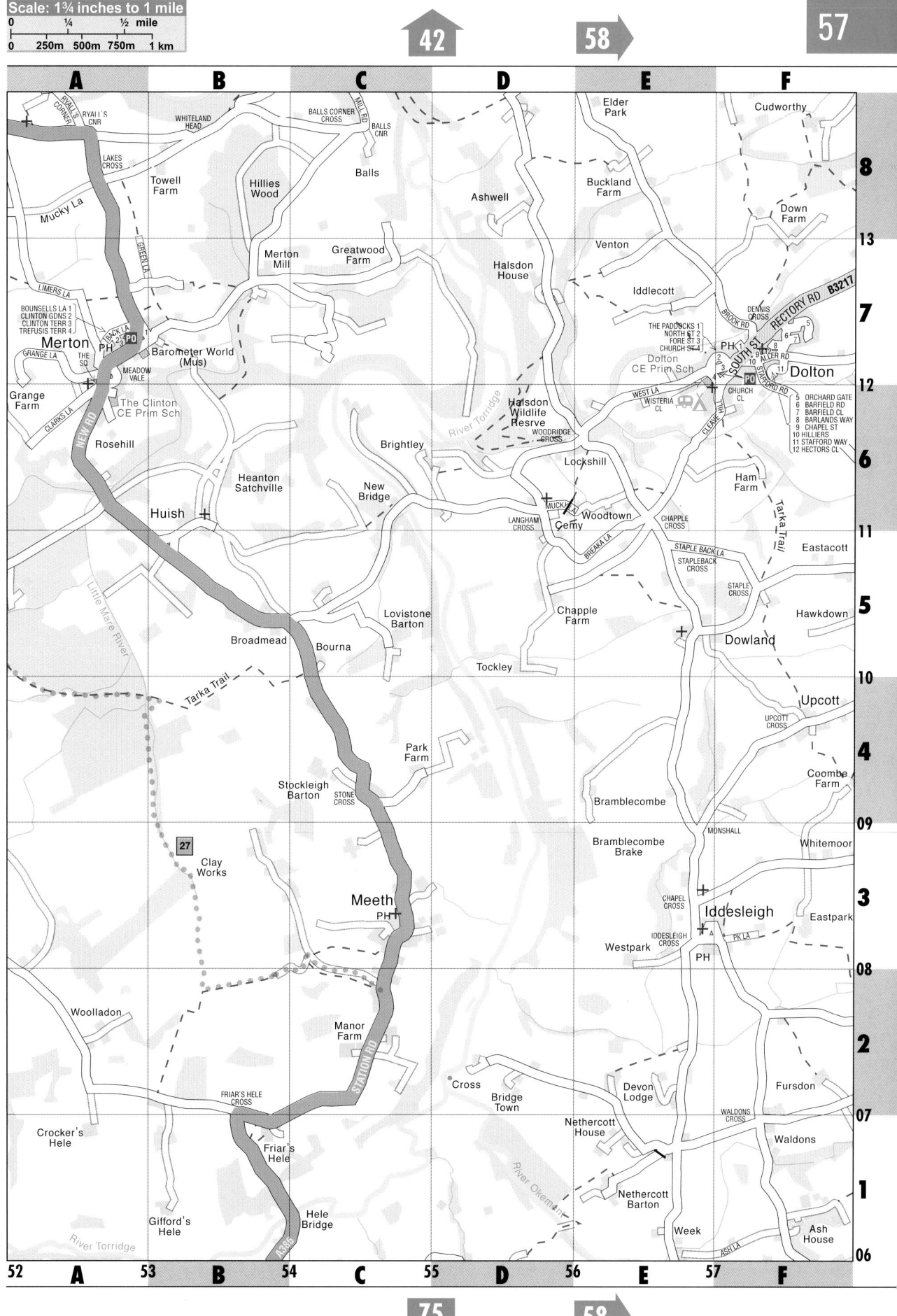

Scale: 1¾ inches to 1 mile
0 ¼ ½ mile
0 250m 500m 750m 1 km
Merton
Grange Farm
The Clinton CE Prim Sch
Rosehill
Barometer World (Mus)
Towell Farm
Hillies Wood
Merton Mill
Balls
Greatwood Farm
Ashwell
Halsdon House
Elder Park
Buckland Farm
Venton
Iddlecott
Cudworthy
Down Farm
Dolton
Dolton CE Prim Sch
Halsdon Wildlife Resrve
River Torridge
Brightley
New Bridge
Heanton Satchville
Huish
Lockshill
Woodtown
Cemy
Ham Farm
Tarka Trail
Eastacott
Hawkdown
Chapple Farm
Dowland
Lovistone Barton
Broadmead
Bourna
Tockley
Upcott
Park Farm
Stockleigh Barton
Coombe Farm
Bramblecombe
Bramblecombe Brake
Whitemoor
Clay Works
Meeth
Iddesleigh
Eastpark
Westpark
Little Mare River
Woolladon
Manor Farm
Cross
Bridge Town
Devon Lodge
Fursdon
Nethercott House
Waldons
Crocker's Hele
Friar's Hele
Nethercott Barton
River Okement
Gifford's Hele
Hele Bridge
Week
Ash House
River Torridge
NEW RD
STATION RD
A386
B3217
RECTORY RD
SOUTH ST

75 58

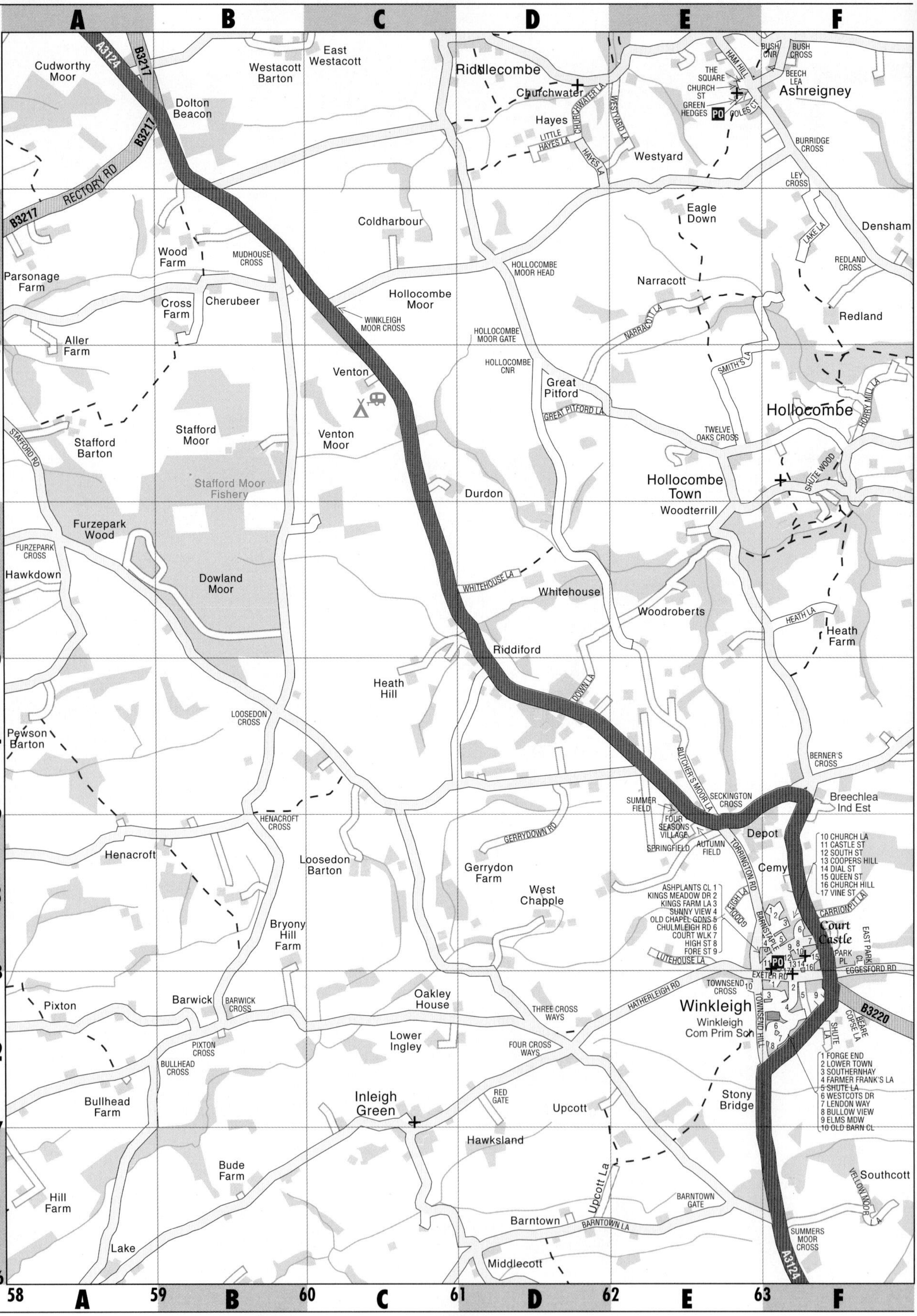

Scale: 1¾ inches to 1 mile

0   ¼   ½   mile
0   250m   500m   750m   1 km

A   B   C   D   E   F

8

Cudworthy Moor

B3217

Dolton Beacon

Westacott Barton

East Westacott

Riddlecombe

Churchwater

CHURCHWATER LA

WESTYARD LA

HAM HILL

THE SQUARE

BUSH CNR

BUSH CROSS

BEECH LEA

Ashreigney

CHURCH ST
GREEN HEDGES
COLES CT
PO

BURRIDGE CROSS

13

B3217

RECTORY RD

Hayes

LITTLE HAYES LA

HAYES LA

Westyard

LEY CROSS

LAKE LA

Densham

7

Wood Farm

MUDHOUSE CROSS

Cherubeer

Coldharbour

Hollocombe Moor

HOLLOCOMBE MOOR HEAD

Eagle Down

Narracott

REDLAND CROSS

Redland

Parsonage Farm

Cross Farm

12

Aller Farm

WINKLEIGH MOOR CROSS

HOLLOCOMBE MOOR GATE

HOLLOCOMBE CNR

NARRACOTT LA

SMITH'S LA

Hollocombe

Stafford Barton

Venton

Great Pitford

GREAT PITFORD LA

TWELVE OAKS CROSS

SHUTE WOOD

PORKY MILL LA

6

Stafford Moor

Venton Moor

Durdon

Hollocombe Town

Woodterrill

Stafford Road

Stafford Moor Fishery

WHITEHOUSE LA

Whitehouse

Woodroberts

HEATH LA

Heath Farm

11

Furzepark Wood

Dowland Moor

Riddiford

5

FURZEPARK CROSS

Hawkdown

Heath Hill

IDONA LA

BUTCHER'S MOOR LA

SECKINGTON CROSS

BERNER'S CROSS

Breechlea Ind Est

10

LOOSEDON CROSS

SUMMER FIELD

FOUR SEASONS VILLAGE

Depot

TORRINGTON RD

Cemy

10 CHURCH LA
11 CASTLE ST
12 SOUTH ST
13 COOPERS HILL
14 DIAL ST
15 QUEEN ST
16 CHURCH HILL
17 VINE ST

4

Pewson Barton

HENACROFT CROSS

GERRYDOWN RD

Springfield

Autumn Field

Court Castle

EAST PARK

EGGESFORD RD

09

Henacroft

Loosedon Barton

Gerrydon Farm

West Chapple

ASHPLANTS CL 1
KINGS MEADOW DR 2
KINGS FARM LA 3
SUNNY VIEW 4
OLD CHAPEL GDNS 5
CHULMLEIGH RD 6
COURT WLK 7
HIGH ST 8
FORE ST 9

BARNSTAPLE ST

FORGE LA

PARK PL

PO

CARRION LA

B3220

3

Bryony Hill Farm

LUTEHOUSE LA

EXETER RD

TOWNSEND CROSS

Winkleigh

Winkleigh Com Prim Sch

HATHERLEIGH RD

SHUTE LA

BARE CORSE LA

8

Pixton

Barwick

BARWICK CROSS

Oakley House

THREE CROSS WAYS

Stony Bridge

TOWNSEND HILL

1 FORGE END
2 LOWER TOWN
3 SOUTHERNHAY
4 FARMER FRANK'S LA
5 SHUTE LA
6 WESTCOTS DR
7 LENDON WAY
8 BULLOW VIEW
9 ELMS MDW
10 OLD BARN CL

2

PIXTON CROSS

BULLHEAD CROSS

Lower Ingley

FOUR CROSS WAYS

RED GATE

Upcott

VELLOWMOOR

Southcott

Bullhead Farm

Inleigh Green

Hawksland

07

Bude Farm

A3124

1

Hill Farm

Lake

UPCOTT LA

Barntown

BARNTOWN LA

BARNTOWN GATE

SUMMERS MOOR CROSS

Middlecott

06

58   A   59   B   60   C   61   D   62   E   63   F

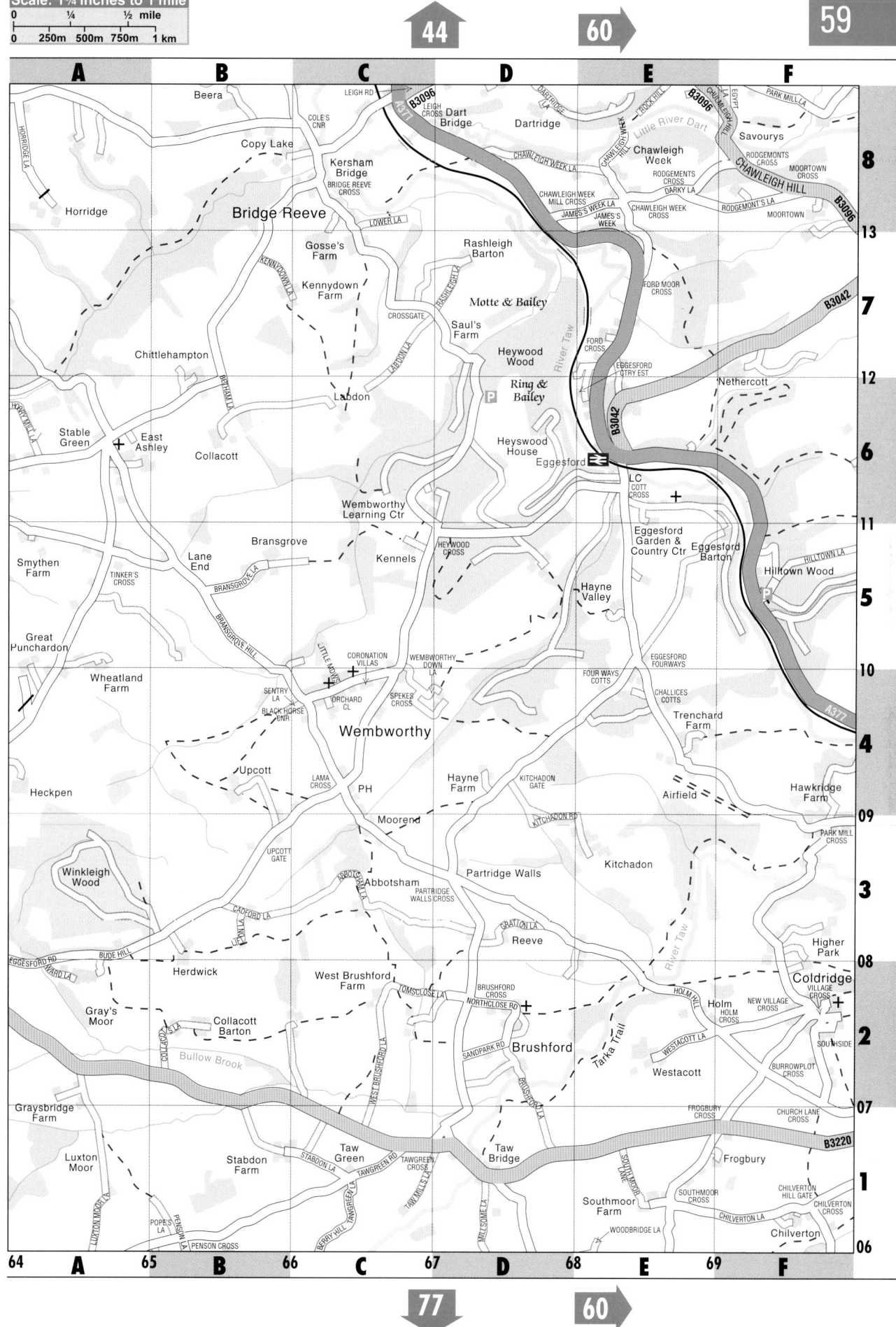

Beera

Copy Lake

HORRIDGE LA

Horridge

COLE'S CNR

LEIGH RD

B3096

A3111

LEIGH CROSS

Dart Bridge

Dartridge

DARTRIDGE

Little River Dart

ROCK HILL

B3096

CHAWLEIGH HILL

EGYPT HILL

PARK MILL LA

Savourys

RODGEMONTS CROSS

Moortown CROSS

CHAWLEIGH HILL

B3096

8

13

Kersham Bridge

BRIDGE REEVE CROSS

Bridge Reeve

Gosse's Farm

LOWER LA

Kennydown Farm

KENNYDOWN LA

CHAWLEIGH WEEK LA

Chawleigh Week

CHAWLEIGH WEEK MILL CROSS

James's Week

RODGEMONTS CROSS

DARKY LA

Chawleigh Week CROSS

JAMES'S WEEK

RODGEMONT'S LA

Moortown

Rashleigh Barton

RASHLEIGH LA

Motte & Bailey

Chittlehampton

CROSSGATE

Saul's Farm

Heywood Wood

LABDON LA

BETHAM LA

Labdon

Ring & Bailey

River Taw

FORD MOOR CROSS

B3042

7

12

FORD CROSS

EGGESFORD QTRY EST

Nethercott

B3042

Stable Green

East Ashley

Collacott

P

Heyswood House

Eggesford

LC COTT CROSS

Eggesford Garden & Country Ctr

Eggesford Barton

HILLTOWN LA

Hilltown Wood

6

11

Wembworthy Learning Ctr

Bransgrove

HEYWOOD CROSS

Kennels

Hayne Valley

P

5

Smythen Farm

TINKER'S CROSS

Lane End

BRANSGROVE LA

BRANSGROVE HILL

CORONATION VILLAS

LITTLE MOOR

Wembworthy DOWN LA

FOUR WAYS COTTS

Eggesford FOURWAYS

CHALLICES COTTS

A377

10

Great Punchardon

Wheatland Farm

SENTRY LA

ORCHARD CL

BLACK HORSE CNR

SPEKES CROSS

Wembworthy

Trenchard Farm

4

Heckpen

Upcott

LAMA CROSS

PH

Hayne Farm

KITCHADON GATE

Airfield

Hawkridge Farm

09

Moorend

KITCHADON RD

Kitchadon

PARK MILL CROSS

Winkleigh Wood

UPCOTT GATE

CADFORD LA

ABBOTSHAM LA

Abbotsham

Partridge WALLS CROSS

Partridge Walls

CRATION LA

3

08

EGGESFORD RD

WARD LA

BUDE HILL

Herdwick

Reeve

Higher Park

Coldridge Village CROSS

Gray's Moor

COLLACOTT LA

Collacott Barton

Bullow Brook

West Brushford Farm

TOMSCLOSE LA

Brushford CROSS

NORTHCLOSE RD

HOLM HILL

Holm HOLM CROSS

NEW Village CROSS

SOUTHSIDE

2

Graysbridge Farm

WEST BRUSHFORD LA

SANDPARK RD

Brushford

BRUSFORD LA

Tarka Trail

River Taw

WESTACOTT LA

Westacott

BURROWPLOT CROSS

CHURCH LANE CROSS

07

Luxton Moor

LUXTON MOOR LA

Stabdon Farm

STABDON LA

TAWGREEN LA

Taw Green

TAWGREEN CROSS

TAW MILLS LA

Taw Bridge

WILLSOME LA

SOUTHMOOR LA

Southmoor Farm

SOUTHMOOR CROSS

CHILVERTON LA

Frogbury

FROGBURY CROSS

CHILVERTON HILL GATE

CHILVERTON CROSS

B3220

Chilverton

POPE'S LA

PENSON LA

BERRY HILL

PENSON CROSS

WOODBRIDGE LA

1

06

A B C D E F

Affeton Barton
Gatehouse
Stone Barton
Cheldon House
Winswood
Affeton Castle Cross
Affeton Hill
Stonemill Farm
Dockworthy Cross
Cheldon
East Cheldon Farm
Hobsehill Cross
Chawleigh
Little Dart River
Cheldon Cross
Horse Hill
Hollow Tree Cross
B3096
B3042
BELLEVUE
70 STEPS
SCHOOL CL
PO
PH
BUTTS CL
BLACKWALLS LA
Leigh
Andrew's La
East Leigh
West Burridge Cross
Burridge
Cobley Farm
Round Ash
PORTSMOUTH ARMS CROSS
WATERING PK LA
SHOOTING LA
LEACHES LA
COOPER'S CROSS
LEIGH LA
LABBETT'S CROSS
Pouncers
Burridge Moor Cross
Cobley La
Tween Moor Cross
B3042
Southcott
CLOEPARK LA
SOUTHCOTT CROSS
FIDDLE LA
BOX'S CNR
Nutson
Duckham
Pouncers Cross
Deneridge Cross
Northlake
HILLTOWN LA
East Hilltown
CARPENTER'S CROSS
Fiddlecott
CARPENTER'S LA
Toatley Farm
DUCKHAM LA
Handsford Farm
Filleigh Moor Cross
Filleigh
Deneridge Hill
Broomsmead
Cleave
Chenson Farm
Tonyfield Farm
Bowerthy
BOWERTHY LA
LOWER FORCHES CROSS
HIGHER FORCHES CROSS
Cobley
Broadridge Farm
Chenson
A377
LC
Tarka Trail
TONYFIELD WOOD CROSS
Bowerthy Wood
River Taw
NYMET BRIDGE CROSS
Nymet Bridge
RENSEY LA
Rensey
Hole
Eastington
COBLEY LA
Broadridge La
Clotworthy Farm
Hele Farm
Lapfordwood House
WEST LA
Parsonage Farm
Lapford Com Prim Sch
EASTINGTON CROSS
Eastington Hill
Wigham
Nymet House
River Yeo
Lapford
PROSPECT WAY
MOORLAND VIEW
3
1
2
ORCHARD CROSS
Calves Bridge
Chillingford
Nymet Rowland
EGGESFORD CROSS
HIGHER LEY
POPE'S LA
ORCHARD WAY
PH
1 PARK RD
2 PARK MEADOW CL
3 WESTGATE
4 CHURCH CL
Back La
Barris
Lapford
PH
HIGHFIELD
CROWSE LA
BIRCH LA
MIDDLECOTT LA
BRIDGE MDW CL
Lapford Cross
AMBROSIA CL
YEO VALE CROSS
LAPFORD CROSS
Rudge
Rudge Rew
Upcott
Coldridge Barton
Cleaveanger
Yeo Vale Ind Est
KELLAND CROSS
KELLAND HILL
Chapel
Bury Cross
HALL LA
Easton Barton
Pepper Lake
B3220
HOBBYMOOR CROSS
Aller Bridge
CLEAVEANGER LA
Furzedown Farm
EDGERLEY CROSS
Kelland Barton
Bury Barton
Bradiford Farm
A377
PISSLETON LA
DOWN HILL
Gillscott Farm
GILLSCOTT CROSS
BLACKDITCH CROSS
BIRCH LA
Pennycotts
Perryhouse La
B3220

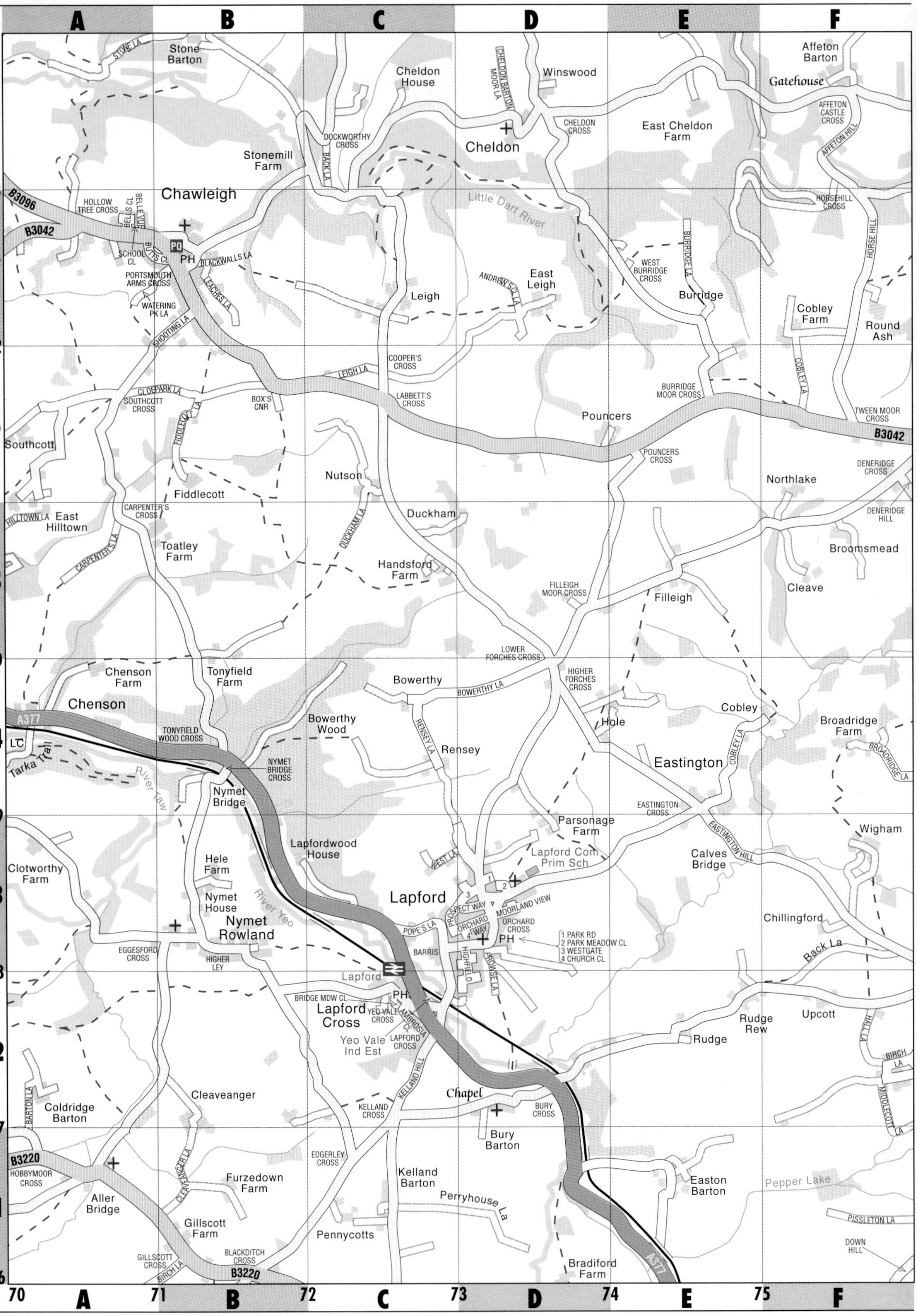

8 13 7 12 6 11 5 10 4 09 3 08 2 07 1 06

70 71 72 73 74 75

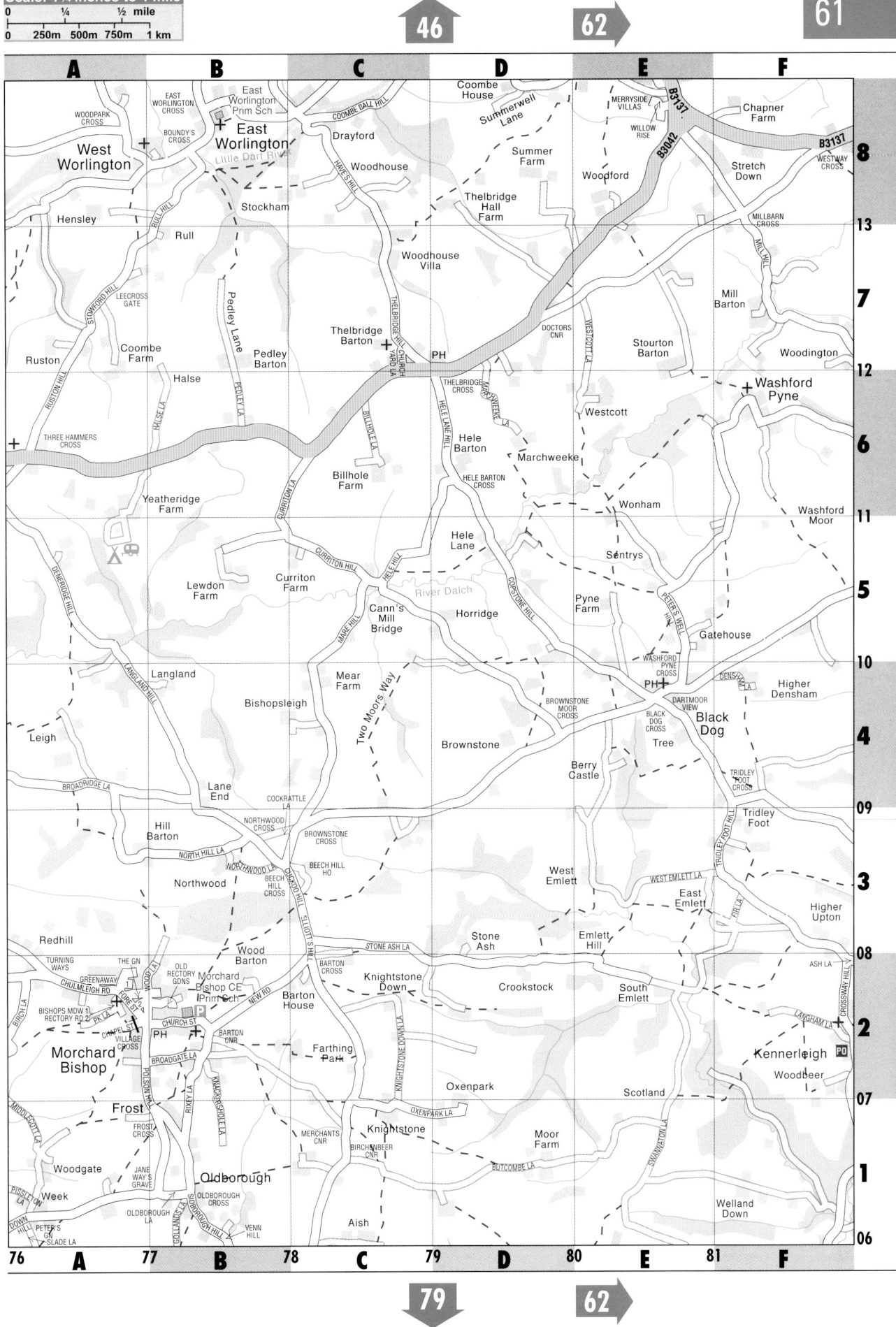

Scale: 1¾ inches to 1 mile

0   ¼   ½   mile
0   250m   500m   750m   1 km

A   B   C   D   E   F

46   62

WOODPARK CROSS

West Worlington

EAST WORLINGTON CROSS

East Worlington Prim Sch

East Worlington

BOUNDY'S CROSS

COOMBE BALL HILL

Coombe House

Summerwell Lane

MERRYSIDE VILLAS

WILLOW RISE

B3137

B3042

Chapner Farm

8

Hensley

Rull

STOCKFORD HILL

LEECROSS GATE

Drayford

Woodhouse

Stockham

Summer Farm

Woodford

Stretch Down

WESTWAY CROSS

B3137

13

Ruston

Coombe Farm

RUSTON HILL

HALSE LA

PEDLEY LA

Pedley Lane

Rull

Halse

Pedley Barton

Woodhouse Villa

Thelbridge Hall Farm

Thelbridge Barton

PH

THELBRIDGE HILL

CHURCH YARD LA

BILLHOLE LA

DOCTORS CNR

WESTCOTT LA

Mill Barton

MILLBARN CROSS

MILL HILL

Woodington

7

Three Hammers Cross

Yeatheridge Farm

Billhole Farm

Thelbridge Cross

HELE LANE HILL

MARCHWEEKE LA

Hele Barton

Stourton Barton

Washford Pyne

12

CURRITON LA

HELE HILL

Hele Barton Cross

Marchweeke

Westcott

Washford Moor

6

Langland

DENERIDGE HILL

LANGLAND HILL

Lewdon Farm

Curriton Farm

CURRITON HILL

Cann's Mill Bridge

LARGE HILL

Hele Lane

River Dalch

Horridge

COPSTONE HILL

Sentrys

Wonham

Pyne Farm

PETER'S WELL

Gatehouse

Washford Pyne Cross

PH

Higher Densham

DENSHAM LA

11

5

Leigh

Bishopsleigh

Mear Farm

Two Moors Way

Brownstone

Brownstone Moor Cross

Black Dog Cross

DARTMOOR VIEW

Black Dog

Tree

10

BROADRIDGE LA

Lane End

COCKRATTLE LA

Berry Castle

TRIDLEY FOOT CROSS

Tridley Foot

TRIDLEY FOOT HILL

4

Hill Barton

NORTH HILL LA

NORTHWOOD CROSS

Brownstone Cross

NORTHWOOD LA

BEECH HILL CROSS

CHAGFORD HILL

BEECH HILL HO

West Emlett

WEST EMLETT LA

East Emlett

FIR LA

Higher Upton

09

Redhill

Northwood

Wood Barton

SLIOTT'S HILL

STONE ASH LA

BARTON CROSS

Stone Ash

Emlett Hill

ASH LA

CROSSWAY HILL

3

TURNING WAYS

CHULMLEIGH RD

GREENAWAY

THE GN

FORE ST

OLD RECTORY GDNS

Morchard Bishop CE Prim Sch

NEW RD

Knightstone Down

Crookstock

South Emlett

LANGHAM LA

08

BIRCH LA

BISHOPS MDW

RECTORY RD

PK LA

CHAPEL ST

Morchard Bishop

VILLAGE CROSS

PH

BROADGATE LA

RIXEY LA

CHURCH ST

Barton House

BARTON CNR

KNIGHTSTONE DOWN LA

Farthing Park

Scotland

Kennerleigh

PO

Woodbeer

2

Frost

FROST CROSS

POLSON HILL

KNACKERSHOLE LA

MERCHANTS CNR

BIRCHANBEER CNR

Oxenpark

OXENPARK LA

Moor Farm

SWANNATON LA

07

MIDDLESCOTT LA

Woodgate

JANE WAY'S GRAVE

Oldborough

OLDBOROUGH CROSS

OLDBOROUGH LA

SIDBOROUGH HILL

Knightstone

BUTCOMBE LA

Welland Down

1

Week

PISSLEY LA

DOWN HILL

PETER'S GN

SLADE LA

VENN HILL

Aish

06

76   A   77   B   78   C   79   D   80   E   81   F

79   62

Scale: 1¾ inches to 1 mile

0 ¼ ½ mile
0 250m 500m 750m 1 km

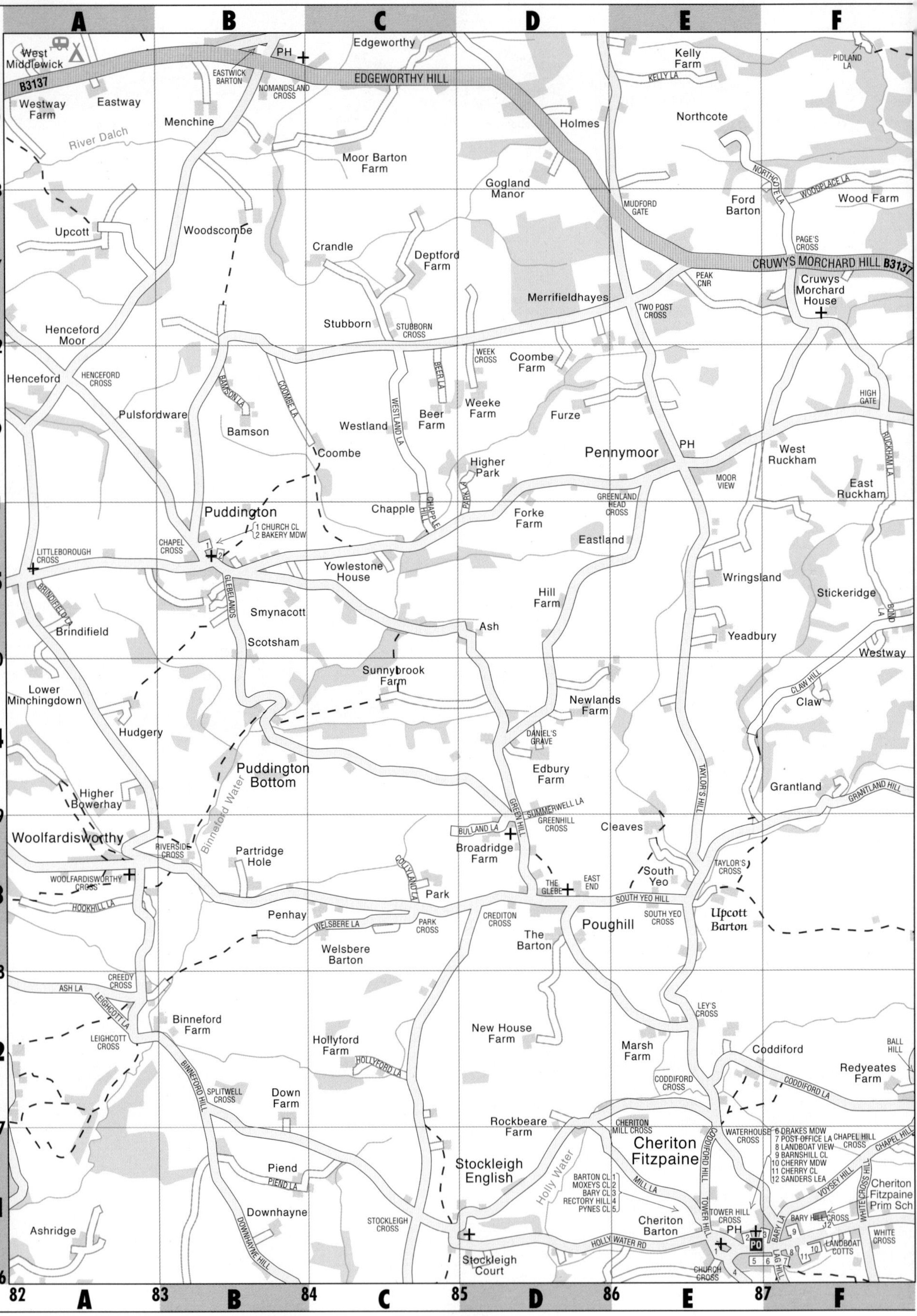

A B C D E F

8

West Middlewick
Westway Farm
Eastway
B3137
Menchine
Eastwick Barton
Nomandsland Cross
PH
Edgeworthy
EDGEWORTHY HILL
Holmes
Kelly Farm
Northcote
KELLY LA
PIDLAND LA
NORTHCOTE LA

13

River Dalch
Woodscombe
Moor Barton Farm
Gogland Manor
Mudford Gate
Ford Barton
WOODPLACE LA
Wood Farm
PAGE'S CROSS

7

Upcott
Crandle
Deptford Farm
Merrifieldhayes
PEAK CNR
CRUWYS MORCHARD HILL B3137
Cruwys Morchard House

12

Henceford Moor
Stubborn
Stubborn Cross
Week Cross
Coombe Farm
TWO POST CROSS

6

Henceford
Henceford Cross
Pulsfordware
Bamson
BAMSON LA
COOMBE LA
Westland
WESTLAND LA
Beer Farm
BEER LA
Weeke Farm
Furze
Pennymoor
PH
MOOR VIEW
West Ruckham
HIGH GATE
East Ruckham
BUCKLAND LA

11

Coombe
Puddington
Chapple
CHAPPLE HILL
PARK LA
Higher Park
Forke Farm
GREENLAND HEAD CROSS
Eastland
Wringsland
Stickeridge

5

Littleborough Cross
Chapel Cross
1 CHURCH CL
2 BAKERY MDW
Yowlestone House
GLEBELANDS
Smynacott
Scotsham
Ash
Hill Farm
Yeadbury
ROAD

10

Brindifield
BRINDIFIELD LA
Lower Minchingdown
Hudgery
Sunnybrook Farm
Newlands Farm
DANIEL'S GRAVE
Claw
CLAW HILL
Westway

4

Higher Bowerhay
Puddington Bottom
Binneford Water
Edbury Farm
GREEN HILL
SUMMERWELL LA
Greenhill Cross
TAYLOR'S HILL
Grantland
GRANTLAND HILL

09

Woolfardisworthy
Riverside Cross
Partridge Hole
BULLAND LA
Broadridge Farm
Cleaves
South Yeo
Taylor's Cross

3

Woolfardisworthy Cross
HOOKHILL LA
Penhay
WELSBERE LA
Park
PARK CROSS
CREDITON CROSS
The Glebe
EAST END
SOUTH YEO HILL
Poughill
SOUTH YEO CROSS
Upcott Barton

08

ASH LA
CREEDY CROSS
Welsbere Barton
The Barton
LEY'S CROSS

2

LEIGHCOTT LA
LEIGHCOTT CROSS
Binneford Farm
BINNEFORD HILL
Hollyford Farm
HOLLYFORD LA
New House Farm
Marsh Farm
Coddiford
CODDIFORD CROSS
CODDIFORD LA
BALL HILL
Redyeates Farm

07

SPLITWELL CROSS
Down Farm
Rockbeare Farm
CHERITON MILL CROSS
WATERHOUSE CROSS
Cheriton Mill Cross
6 DRAKES MDW
7 POST-OFFICE LA
8 LANDBOAT VIEW
9 BARNSHILL CL
10 CHERRY MDW
11 CHERRY CL
12 SANDERS LEA
CHAPEL HILL

1

Ashridge
Piend
PIEND LA
Stockleigh English
Holly Water
Cheriton Fitzpaine
MILL LA
BARTON CL 1
MOXEYS CL 2
BARY CL 3
RECTORY HILL 4
PYNES CL 5
Cheriton Barton
BARY HILL CROSS
Cheriton Fitzpaine Prim Sch
VOYSEY HILL
WHITECROSS HILL
TOWER HILL
PH
PO
Landboat Cotts
WHITE CROSS

Downhayne
DOWNHAYNE HILL
Stockleigh Cross
Stockleigh Court
HOLLY WATER RD
CHURCH CROSS
CODDIFORD HILL

06

82 A 83 B 84 C 85 D 86 E 87 F

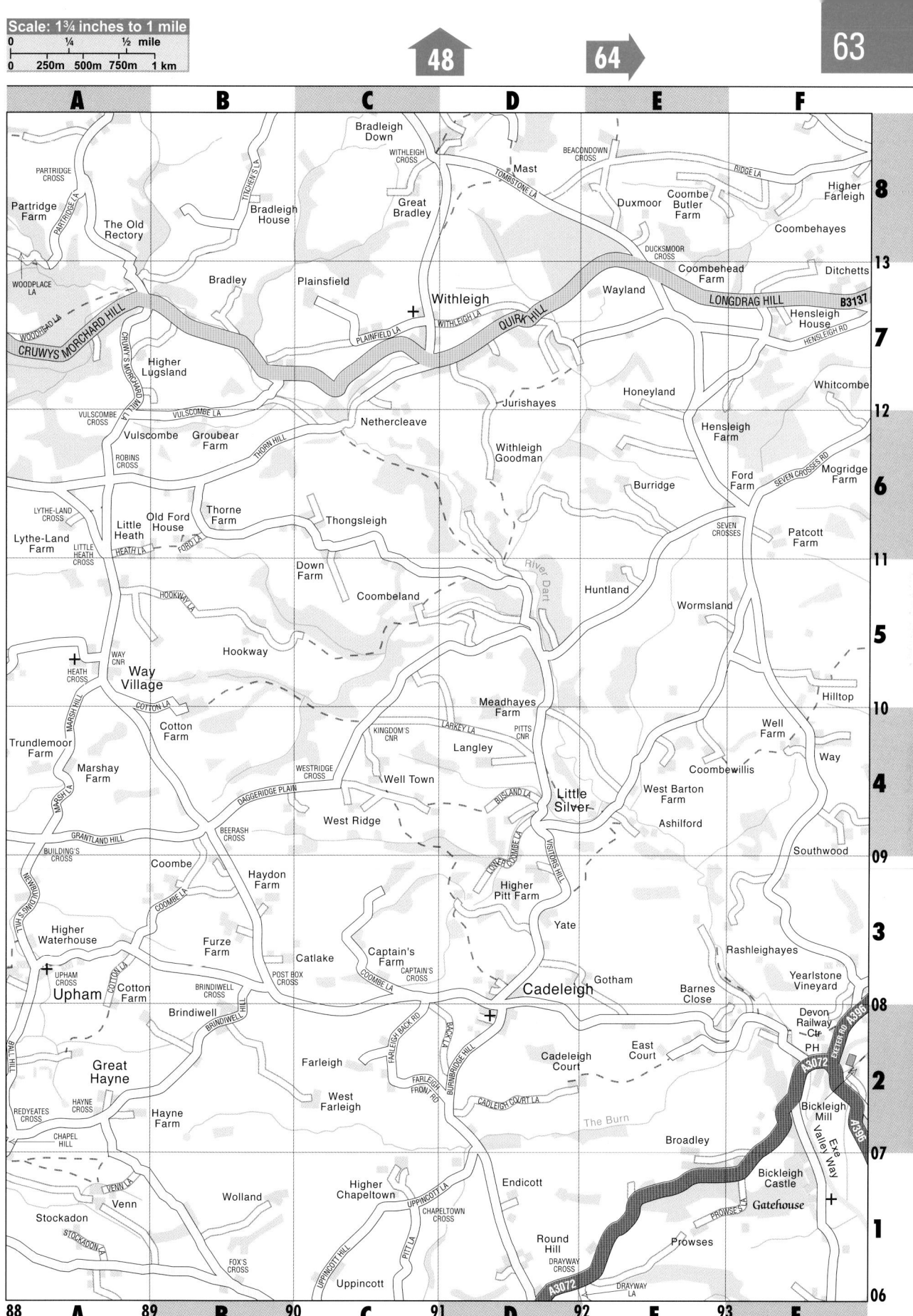

PARTRIDGE CROSS
Partridge Farm
PARTRIDGE LA
The Old Rectory
Bradleigh House
TITCHEN'S LA
Bradleigh Down
WITHLEIGH CROSS
Great Bradley
Mast
TOMBSTONE LA
BEACONDOWN CROSS
Duxmoor
Coombe Butler Farm
RIDGE LA
Higher Farleigh
Coombehayes
8
DUCKSMOOR CROSS
WOODPLACE LA
Bradley
Plainsfield
Withleigh
Wayland
Coombehead Farm
LONGDRAG HILL
B3137
Ditchetts
13
WOODRIDGE LA
CRUWYS MORCHARD HILL
CRUWYS MORCHARD WAY
Higher Lugsland
PLAINFIELD LA
WITHLEIGH LA
QUIRK HILL
Hensleigh House
HENSLEIGH RD
7
VULSCOMBE CROSS
VULSCOMBE LA
Nethercleave
Jurishayes
Honeyland
Hensleigh Farm
Whitcombe
12
Vulscombe
Groubear Farm
THORN HILL
Withleigh Goodman
Ford Farm
SEVEN CROSSES RD
Mogridge Farm
6
ROBINS CROSS
Burridge
Patcott Farm
LYTHE-LAND CROSS
Little Heath
Old Ford House
Thorne Farm
Thongsleigh
HEATH LA
FORD LA
SEVEN CROSSES
11
Lythe-Land Farm
LITTLE HEATH CROSS
Down Farm
River Dart
Huntland
Wormsland
HOOKWAY LA
Coombeland
Hilltop
5
Hookway
WAY CNR
Well Farm
Way
HEATH CROSS
MARSH HILL
Way Village
COTTON LA
Meadhayes Farm
LARKEY LA
PITTS CNR
Coombewillis
10
Trundlemoor Farm
Cotton Farm
KINGDOM'S CNR
Langley
West Barton Farm
Well Town
Little Silver
Ashilford
4
Marshay Farm
WESTRIDGE CROSS
BUSLAND LA
Southwood
09
MARSH LA
DAGGERIDGE PLAIN
West Ridge
LONG LA
COOMBE LA
VISITORS HILL
GRANTLAND HILL
BEERASH CROSS
Higher Pitt Farm
BUILDING'S CROSS
Coombe
Haydon Farm
Yate
Rashleighayes
3
NEWBURY DOWN HILL
COOMBE LA
Furze Farm
Catlake
Captain's Farm
Gotham
Yearlstone Vineyard
08
Higher Waterhouse
COTTON LA
POST BOX CROSS
CAPTAIN'S CROSS
Cadeleigh
Barnes Close
Devon Railway Ctr PH
EXETER RD A396
UPHAM CROSS
Cotton Farm
BRINDIWELL CROSS
COOMBE LA
A3072
Upham
Brindiwell
BRINDIWELL HILL
Cadeleigh Court
East Court
Bickleigh Mill
A396
2
Great Hayne
Farleigh
FARLEIGH BACK RD
BURNBRIDGE HILL
PITT LA
CADELEIGH COURT LA
The Burn
Exe Valley Way
HAYNE CROSS
West Farleigh
FARLEIGH FROM RD
Broadley
Bickleigh Castle
07
REDYEATES CROSS
Hayne Farm
Gatehouse
CHAPEL HILL
VENN LA
Wolland
Higher Chapeltown
UPPINGCOTT LA
Endicott
PROWSE'S LA
Prowses
1
Venn
CHAPELTOWN CROSS
Round Hill
Stockadon
STOCKADON LA
UPPINGCOTT HILL
PITT LA
FOX'S CROSS
Uppincott
DRAYWAY CROSS
A3072
DRAYWAY LA
06

88   A   89   B   90   C   91   D   92   E   93   F

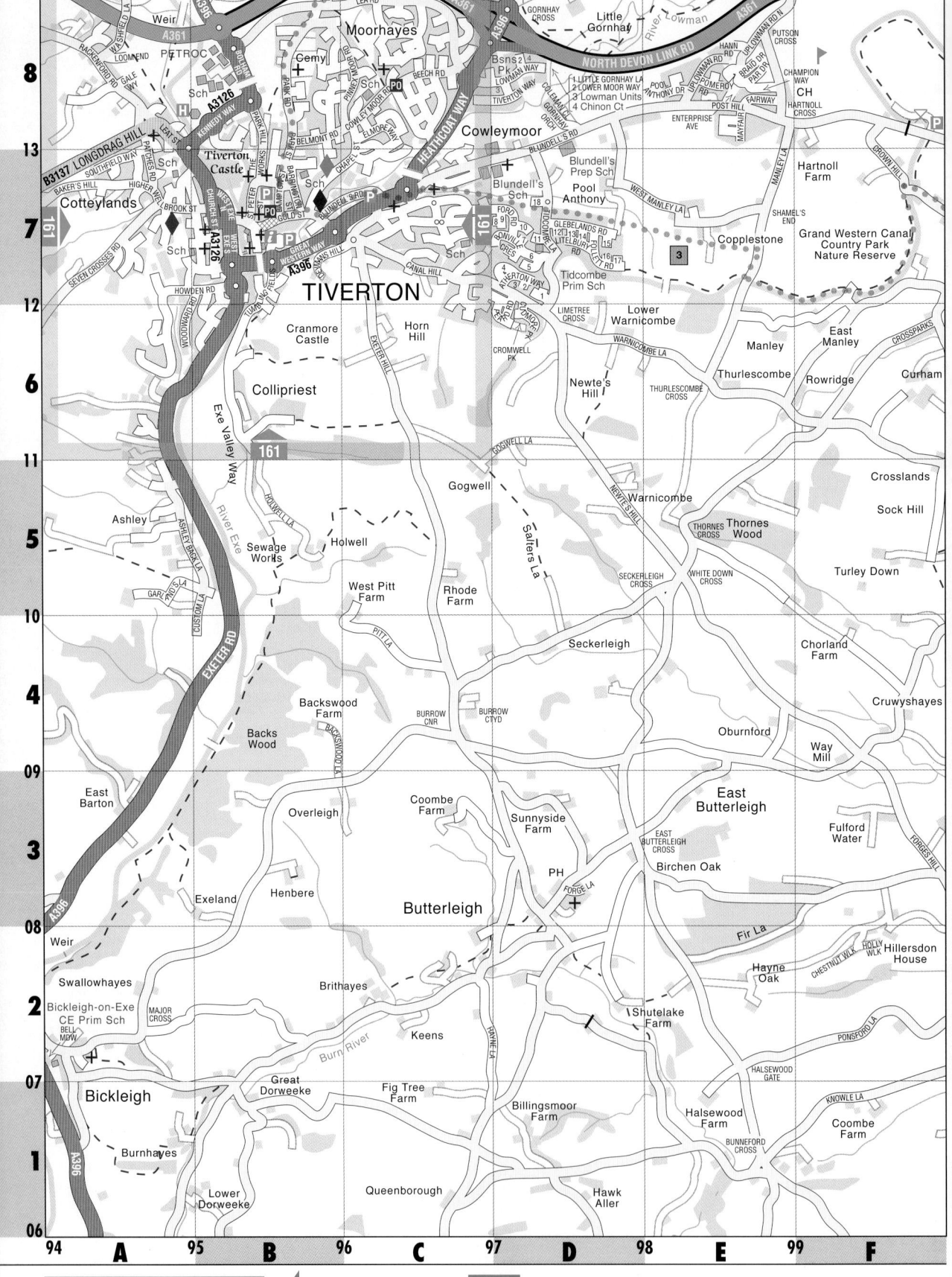

D7
1 LIME TREE MEAD
2 RENNIE RD
3 WESLEY CL
4 FRANCIS CRES
5 CHILCOTT CL
6 MARINA WAY

7 CHICHESTER PL
8 COLERIDGE RD
9 PUGSLEY RD
10 STARKEY CL
11 TIDCOMBE CL
12 ST LAWRENCE CL
13 RAYER RD

14 POLWHELE RD
15 WESTCOTT RD
16 RYDER CL
17 RIPPON CL
18 TIDCOMBE WLK

Scale: 1¾ inches to 1 mile
0   ¼   ½   mile
0 250m 500m 750m 1 km

TIVERTON

Moorhayes

Cowleymoor

Little Gornhay

NORTH DEVON LINK RD

Tiverton Castle

Cotteylands

Cranmore Castle

Horn Hill

Collipriest

Blundell's Prep Sch
Pool Anthony
Copplestone
Grand Western Canal Country Park Nature Reserve

Hartnoll Farm

Lower Warnicombe

Manley

East Manley

Thurlescombe

Rowridge

Curham

Exe Valley Way

Gogwell

Warnicombe

Crosslands

Sock Hill

Ashley

Sewage Works

Holwell

West Pitt Farm

Rhode Farm

Salters La

Newte's Hill

Thornes Cross

Thornes Wood

Turley Down

Seckerleigh

Chorland Farm

Backswood Farm

Backs Wood

Burrow CNR

Burrow CTYD

Oburnford

Way Mill

Cruwyshayes

East Barton

Overleigh

Coombe Farm

Sunnyside Farm

East Butterleigh

Fulford Water

Exeland

Henbere

Butterleigh

Birchen Oak

Fir La

Hayne Oak

Hillersdon House

Swallowhayes

Bickleigh-on-Exe CE Prim Sch

Brithayes

Keens

Shutelake Farm

Bickleigh

Great Dorweeke

Fig Tree Farm

Billingsmoor Farm

Halsewood Farm

Coombe Farm

Burnhayes

Lower Dorweeke

Queenborough

Hawk Aller

Bunneford Cross

For full street detail of the highlighted area see page 161.

Scale: 1¾ inches to 1 mile

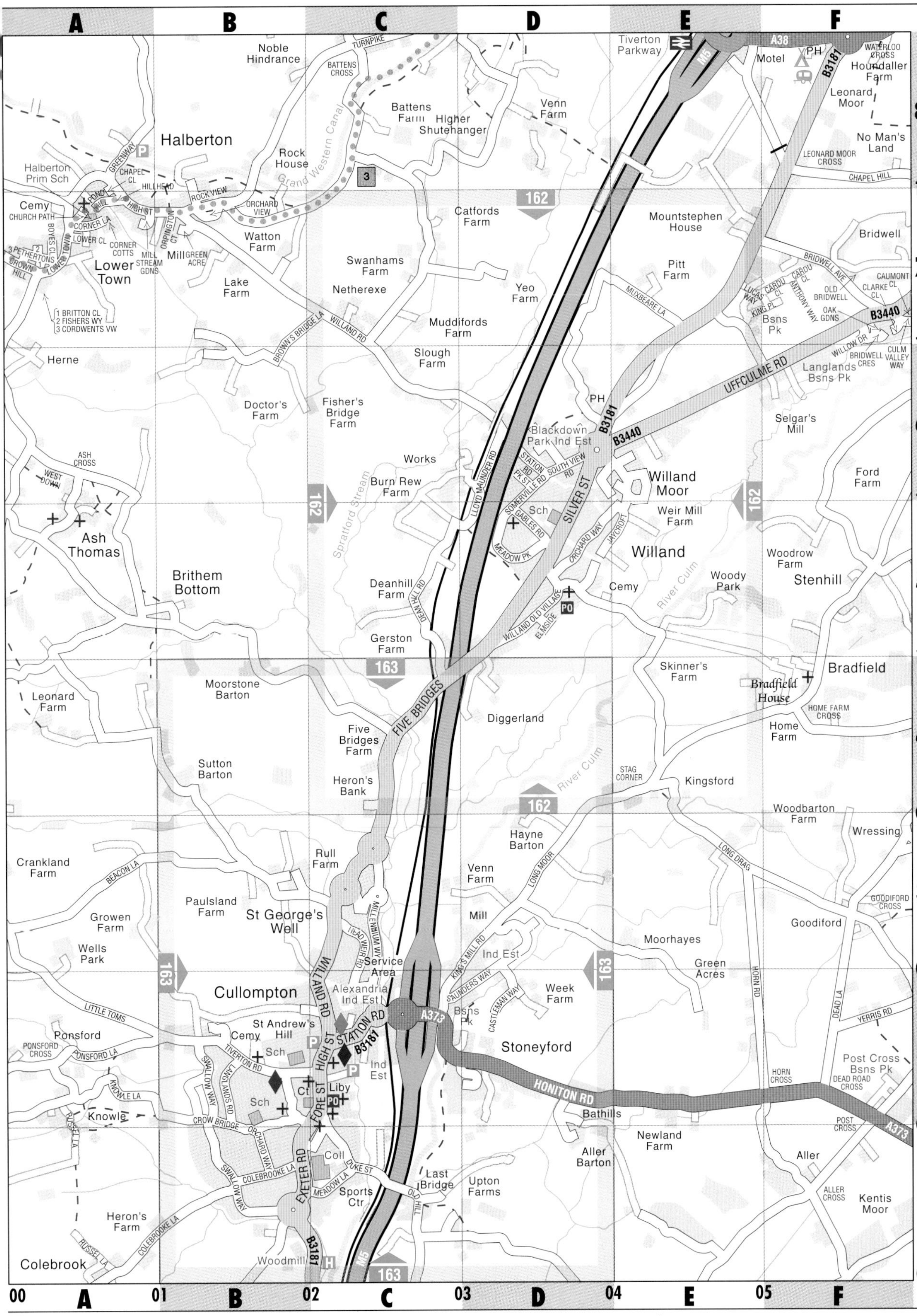

0   ¼   ½ mile
0   250m   500m   750m   1 km

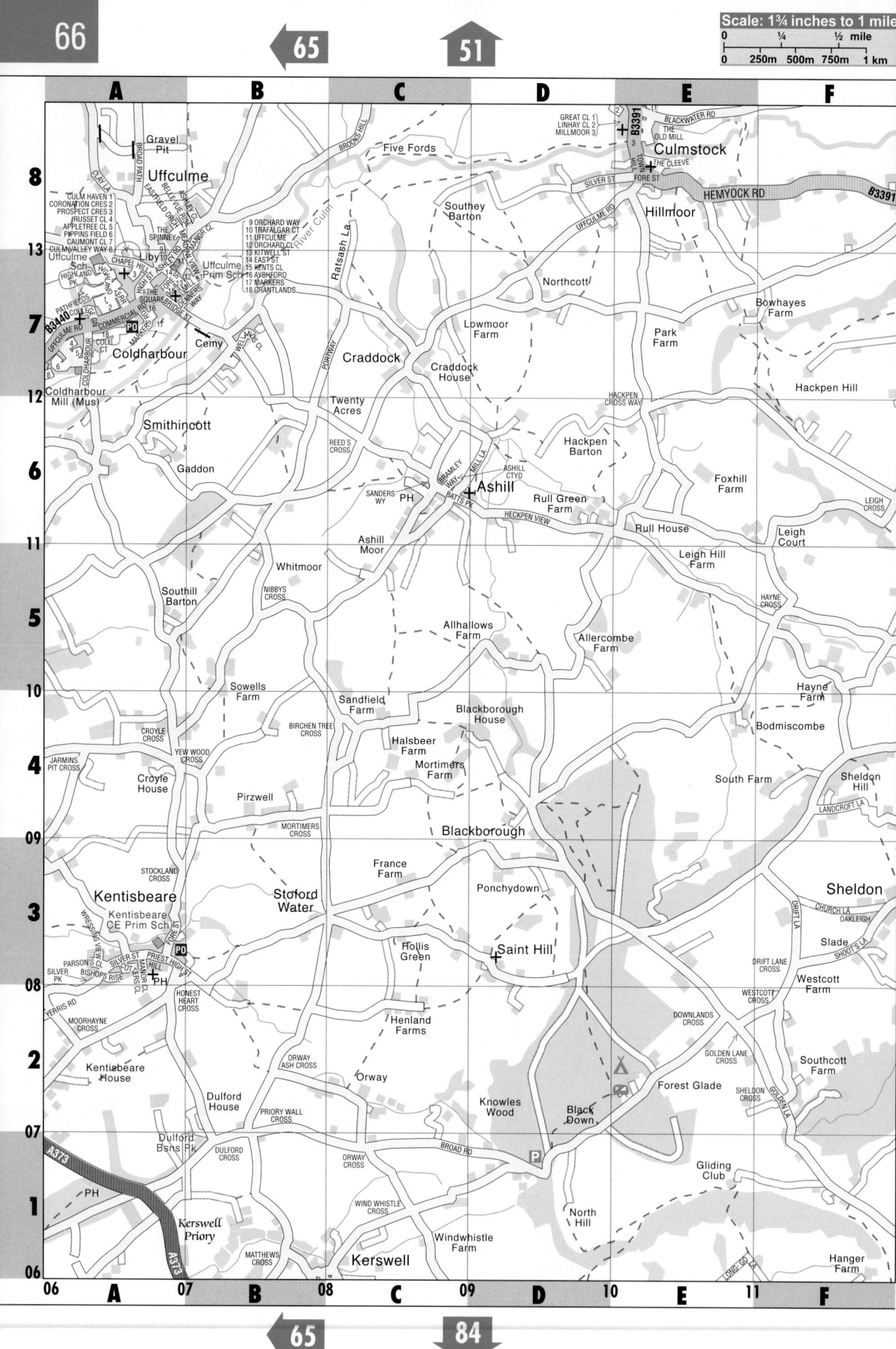

A   B   C   D   E   F

8

Gravel Pit
BROAD PATH
Uffculme
CLAY LA
ASHLEY CL

Five Fords
BROOKS HILL
River Culm

GREAT CL 1
LINHAY CL 2
MILLMOOR 3

BLACKWATER RD
THE OLD MILL
Culmstock
THE CLEEVE
B3391
SILVER ST
FORE ST

B3391

13
CULM HAVEN 1
CORONATION CRES 2
PROSPECT CRES 3
RUSSEL CL 4
APPLETREE CL 5
PIPPINS FIELD 6
CAUMONT CL 7
CULM VALLEY WAY 8
Uffculme
Sch
HIGHLAND
PK

BELLE VUE DR
EASTFIELD ORCH
MEADOW HILL
MANOR CL

CHAPEL HILL
HIGHLANDS
Liby 10
Uffculme
Prim Sch
THE SPINNEY

9 ORCHARD WAY
10 TRAFALGAR CT
11 UFFCULME
12 ORCHARD CL
13 KITWELL ST
14 EAST ST
15 KENTS CL
16 ASHFORD
17 MARKERS
18 GRANTLANDS

HEMYOCK RD
Hillmoor

Northcott

Bowhayes Farm

7
B3440
UFFCULME RD
Coldharbour
COLL CT
CHURCH RD
PO
MARKET
Cemy
WELL CL

Southey Barton

Lowmoor Farm

Park Farm

RATSASH LA

Craddock

Craddock House

HACKPEN CROSS WAY

Hackpen Hill

12
Coldharbour Mill (Mus)

Smithincott

Gaddon

Twenty Acres

REED'S CROSS

PORTWAY

Hackpen Barton

Foxhill Farm

LEIGH CROSS

6
Southill Barton

Whitmoor

NIBBYS CROSS

BRAMLEY WAY
BATTS PK
SANDERS WY
PH
Ashill
MILL LA

ASHILL CTYD
HECKPEN VIEW
Rull Green Farm
Rull House

Leigh Hill Farm

Leigh Court

HAYNE CROSS

11
Ashill Moor

5
Sowells Farm

Allhallows Farm

Allercombe Farm

Hayne Farm

CROYLE CROSS
YEW WOOD CROSS
BIRCHEN TREE CROSS

Sandfield Farm

Blackborough House

Bodmiscombe

10

JARMINS PIT CROSS

Halsbeer Farm

South Farm

Sheldon Hill

LANDCROFT LA

4
Croyle House
Pirzwell

Mortimers Farm

MORTIMERS CROSS

Blackborough

DRIFT LA
CHURCH LA
OAKLEIGH
Sheldon

09

3
Kentisbeare
Kentisbeare
CE Prim Sch
FORE ST

STOCKLAND CROSS

Stoford Water

France Farm

Ponchydown

Slade
SHOOTS LA

DRIFT LANE CROSS

WESTCOTT CROSS
Westcott Farm

PARSON'S CL
SILVER CT
MANOR CL
KENTS CL
PRIEST HIGH ST
PO
PH
Hollis Green
Saint Hill

WRESSING VIEW
SILVER ST
BISHOPS RISE
HONEST HEART CROSS

DOWNLANDS CROSS
SHELDON CROSS

SILVER PK

GOLDEN LANE CROSS

Southcott Farm

08
YERRIS RD
MOORHAYNE CROSS

Henland Farms

Forest Glade
GOLDEN LA

2
Kentisbeare House

ORWAY ASH CROSS
Orway

Knowles Wood

Black Down

Dulford House

PRIORY WALL CROSS

07

A373
PH

Dulford Bsns Pk
DULFORD CROSS

ORWAY CROSS

BROAD RD
P

Gliding Club

1

Kerswell Priory

MATTHEWS CROSS

WIND WHISTLE CROSS

Windwhistle Farm

North Hill

LONG CO LA
Hanger Farm

06
A373

Kerswell

06   A   07   B   08   C   09   D   10   E   11   F

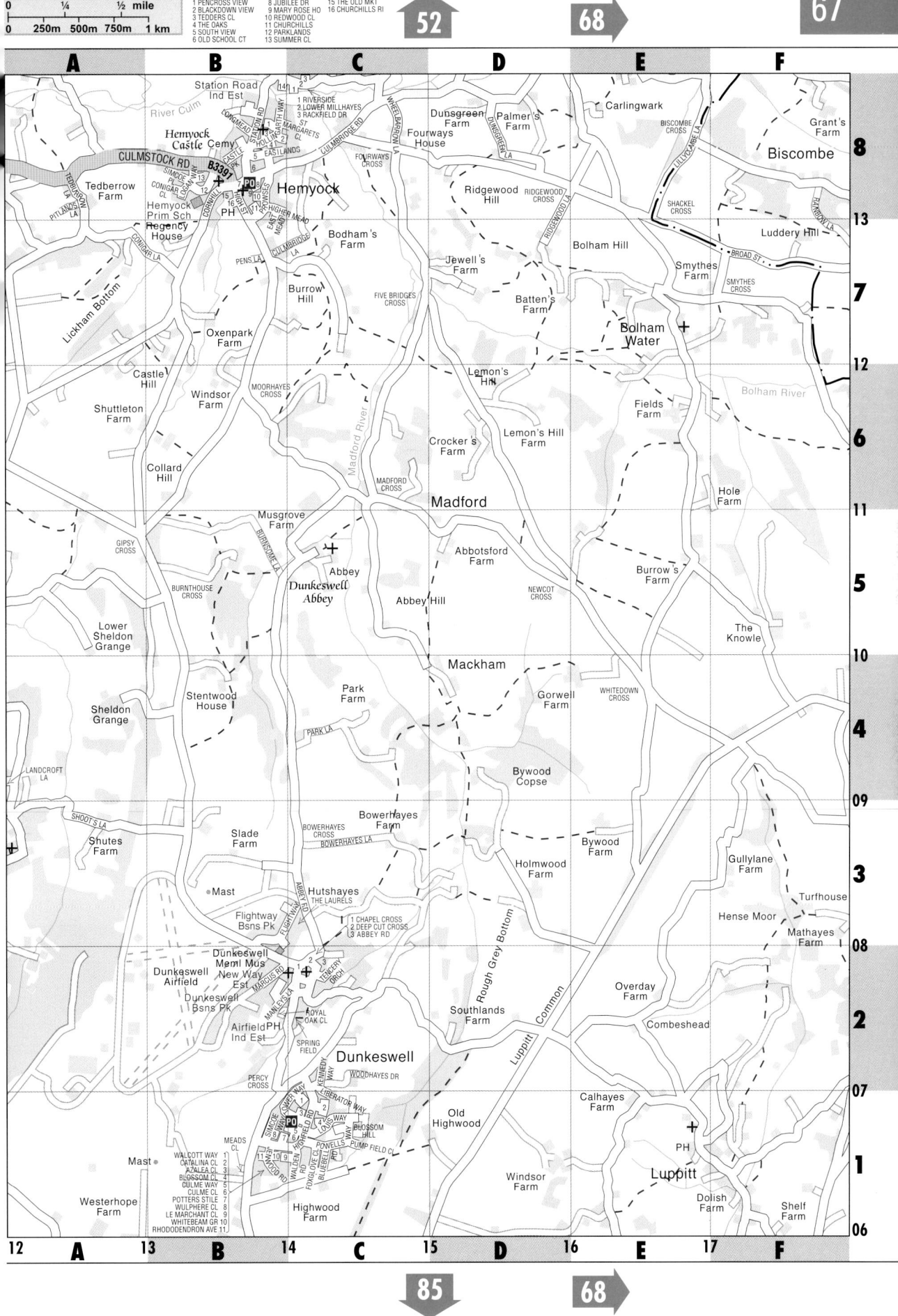

Scale: 1¾ inches to 1 mile

0   ¼   ½ mile

0 250m 500m 750m 1 km

B8
1 PENCROSS VIEW
2 BLACKDOWN VIEW
3 TEDDERS CL
4 THE OAKS
5 SOUTH VIEW
6 OLD SCHOOL CT
7 FORE ST
8 JUBILEE DR
9 MARY ROSE HO
10 REDWOOD CL
11 CHURCHILLS
12 PARKLANDS
13 SUMMER CL
14 MILL LEAT
15 THE OLD MKT
16 CHURCHILLS RI

52   68

Station Road Ind Est
River Culm
Hemyock Castle Cemy
CULMSTOCK RD
Tedberrow Farm
Hemyock Prim Sch
Regency House
B3391
PH
PO
Hemyock
Lickham Bottom
Oxenpark Farm
Burrow Hill
Bodham's Farm
Dunsgreen Farm
Palmer's Farm
Fourways House
Fourways Cross
Ridgewood Hill
Ridgewood Cross
Carlingwark
Biscombe Cross
SHACKEL CROSS
Luddery Hill
Biscombe
Bolham Hill
Smythes Farm
BROAD ST
Smythes Cross
Jewell's Farm
Five Bridges Cross
Batten's Farm
Bolham Water
Castle Hill
Windsor Farm
Shuttleton Farm
Collard Hill
Moorhayes Cross
Madford River
Lemon's Hill
Crocker's Farm
Lemon's Hill Farm
Fields Farm
Bolham River
Hole Farm
Madford Cross
Madford
Gipsy Cross
Musgrove Farm
Burnthouse Cross
Abbey
Dunkeswell Abbey
Abbey Hill
Abbotsford Farm
Newcot Cross
Burrow's Farm
The Knowle
Lower Sheldon Grange
Sheldon Grange
Stentwood House
Park Farm
Mackham
Gorwell Farm
Whitedown Cross
Landcroft La
Shoot S La
Shutes Farm
Slade Farm
Bowerhayes Cross
Bowerhayes Farm
Bywood Copse
Bywood Farm
Park La
Holmwood Farm
Gullylane Farm
Turfhouse
Hense Moor
Mathayes Farm
Mast
Hutshayes
The Laurels
Flightway Bsns Pk
1 CHAPEL CROSS
2 DEEP CUT CROSS
3 ABBEY RD
Rough Grey Bottom
Luppitt Common
Dunkeswell Meml Mus
New Way Est
Dunkeswell Airfield
Dunkeswell Bsns Pk
Airfield PH
Ind Est
Royal Oak Cl
Spring Field
Southlands Farm
Overday Farm
Combeshead
Percy Cross
Dunkeswell
Woodhayes Dr
Kennedy Way
Liberator Way
Blossom Hill
Pump Field Cl
Old Highwood
Calhayes Farm
Luppitt
PH
Meads Cl
PO
Westerhope Farm
Mast
Highwood Farm
Highwood
Windsor Farm
Dolish Farm
Shelf Farm

1 WALCOTT WAY
2 CATALINA CL
3 AZALEA CL
4 BLOSSOM CL
5 CULME WAY
6 CULME CL
7 POTTERS STILE
8 WULPHERE CL
9 LE MARCHANT CL
10 WHITEBEAM GR
11 RHODODENDRON AVE

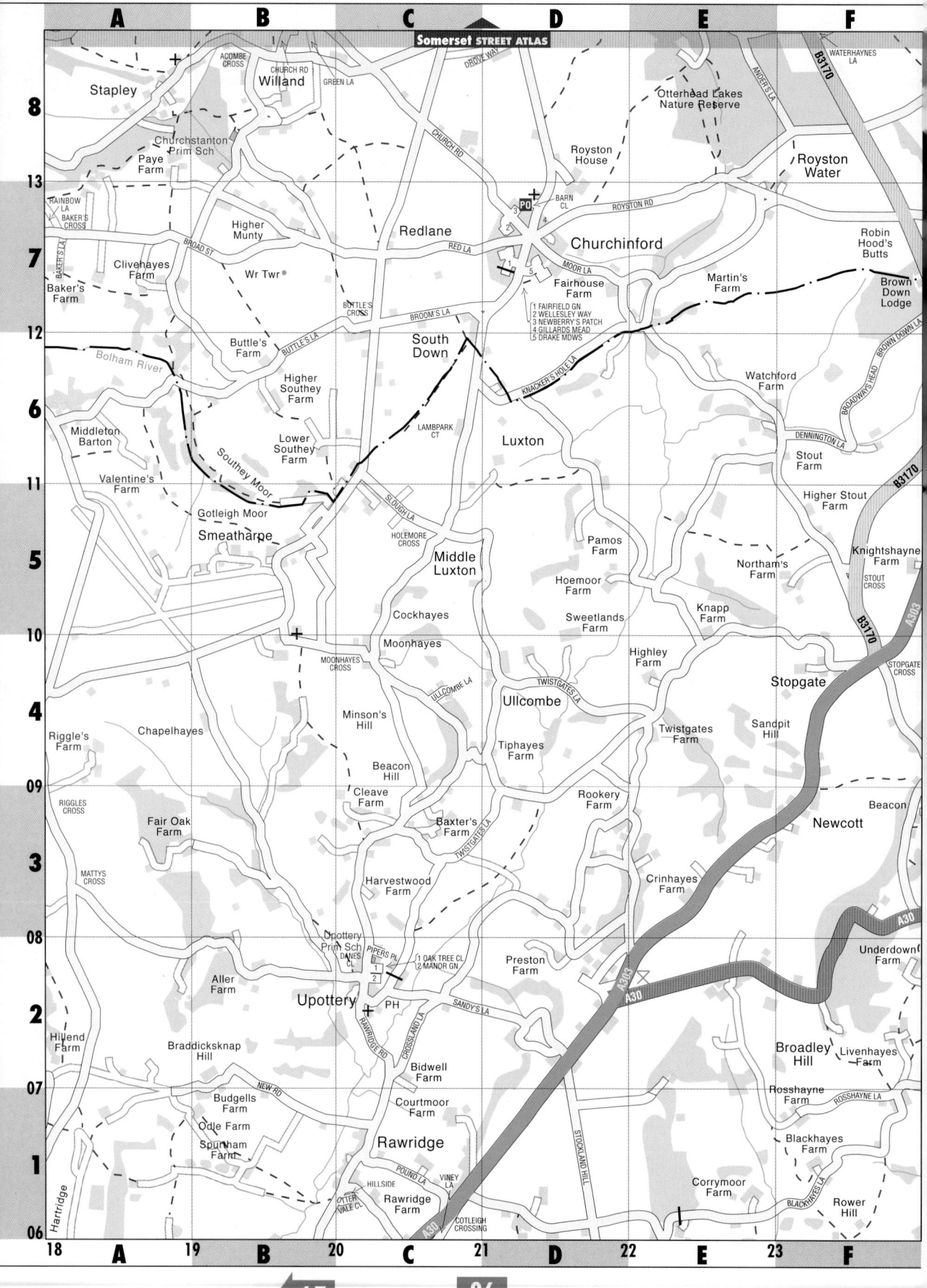

Scale: 1¾ inches to 1 mile

0   ¼   ½   mile
0 250m 500m 750m 1 km

Somerset STREET ATLAS

A   B   C   D   E   F

8

Stapley
ACOMBE CROSS
Willand
CHURCH RD
GREEN LA
DROVE WAY
Otterhead Lakes
Nature Reserve
ANDER'S LA
WATERHAYNES LA
B3170

Churchstanton
Prim Sch
Paye
Farm
CHURCH RD
Royston
House
Royston
Water

13

RAINBOW
LA
BAKER'S
CROSS
Higher
Munty
BROAD ST
Redlane
RED LA
BARN
CL
PO
ROYSTON RD
Robin
Hood's
Butts

7

BAKER'S LA
Clivehayes
Farm
Wr Twr
Churchinford
Fairhouse
Farm
MOOR LA
Martin's
Farm
Brown
Down
Lodge

Baker's
Farm
BUTTLE'S
CROSS
BROOM'S LA
1 FAIRFIELD GN
2 WELLESLEY WAY
3 NEWBERRY'S PATCH
4 GILLARDS MEAD
5 DRAKE MDWS

12

Buttle's
Farm
BUTTLE'S LA
South
Down
KNACKER'S HOLE LA
Watchford
Farm
BROWN DOWN LA

Bolham River
Higher
Southey
Farm
LAMBPARK
CT
Luxton
DENNINGTON LA
Stout
Farm
B3170

6

Middleton
Barton
Lower
Southey
Farm
Southey Moor
Higher
Stout
Farm

11

Valentine's
Farm
Gotleigh Moor
SLOUGH LA
Knightshayne
Cross
STOUT
CROSS

Smeatharpe
HOLEMORE
CROSS
Middle
Luxton
Pamos
Farm
Northam's
Farm

5

Hoemoor
Farm
Knapp
Farm

Cockhayes
Sweetlands
Farm

10

Moonhayes
MOONHAYES
CROSS
Highley
Farm
Stopgate
STOPGATE
CROSS

4

Riggle's
Farm
Chapelhayes
Minson's
Hill
ULLCOMBE LA
Ullcombe
TWISTGATES LA
Twistgates
Farm
Sandpit
Hill
A303

RIGGLES
CROSS
Tiphayes
Farm
Beacon

09

Fair Oak
Farm
Cleave
Farm
Beacon
Hill
Rookery
Farm
Newcott

3

MATTYS
CROSS
Baxter's
Farm
TWISTGATES LA
Crinhayes
Farm

Harvestwood
Farm

08

Upottery
Prim Sch
DANES
CL
PIPERS PL
1 OAK TREE CL
2 MANOR GN
Preston
Farm
A303
Underdown
Farm

Aller
Farm
1
2
SANDY'S LA

2

Upottery
PH
CROSSLAND LA
Broadley
Hill
Livenhayes
Farm

Hillend
Farm
RAWRIDGE RD
Rosshayne
Farm
ROSSHAYNE LA

07

Braddicksknap
Hill
Bidwell
Farm
NEW RD
Budgells
Farm
Courtmoor
Farm
STOCKLAND HILL
Blackhayes
Farm

Odle Farm
Spurham
Farm

1

Rawridge
HILLSIDE
POUND LA
VINEY
LA
Corrymoor
Farm
BLACKHAYES LA
Rower
Hill

Hartridge
OTTER
VALE CL
Rawridge
Farm
COTLEIGH
CROSSING
A30

06

18   A   19   B   20   C   21   D   22   E   23   F

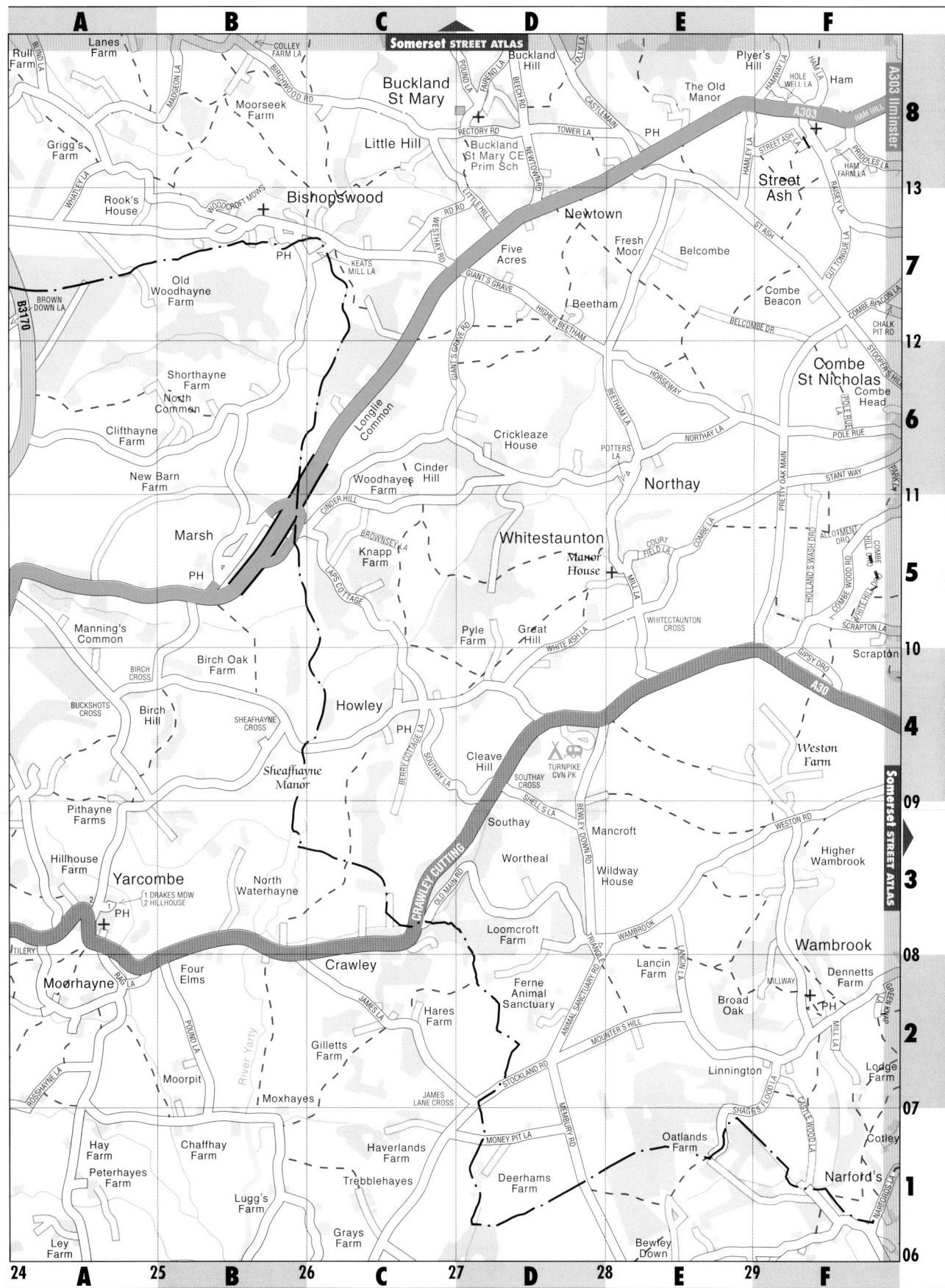

Scale: 1¾ inches to 1 mile

0   ¼   ½ mile
0   250m 500m 750m 1 km

A B C D E F

Somerset STREET ATLAS

A303 Ilminster

8 13 7 12 6 11 5 10 4 09 3 08 2 07 1 06

Somerset STREET ATLAS

Labels (left to right, top to bottom):

Lanes Farm
Bull Farm
Bindon La
COLLEY FARM LA
Buckland Hill
Plyer's Hill
HA LA
HARWAY LA
HOLE WELL LA
Ham
The Old Manor
Griffchwood RD
Moorseek Farm
MARDEON LA
Buckland St Mary
HAMLEY LA
HAM LA
A303
HAM HILL
BRIDDLES LA
Grigg's Farm
Little Hill
RECTORY RD
Buckland St Mary CE Prim Sch
TOWER LA
CASTLEMAN
PH
Street Ash
ST ASH
HAM FARM LA
RAISEY LA
WHITLEY LA
Rook's House
Bishopswood
PH
KEATS MILL LA
WESTHAY RD
RD RD
LITTLE HILL
POUND LA
FARLEIGH LA
TALY LA
BEECH RD
NEWTOWN RD
Newtown
Fresh Moor
Belcombe
Combe Beacon
STREET ASH
CUTT TONGUE LA
COMBE BEACON LA
B3170
BROWN DOWN LA
Old Woodhayne Farm
Five Acres
GIANT'S GRAVE RD
GIANT'S GRAVE
Higher Beetham
Beetham
BELCOMBE DR
STOOPER'S HILL
CHALK PIT RD
Combe St Nicholas
Combe Head
POLE RUE LA
Shorthayne Farm
North Common
Longlie Common
HORSEWAY
BEETHAM LA
Cricklease House
POTTERS LA
NORTHAY LA
Pole Rue
PRETTY OAK MAIN
STANT WAY
PARK LA
Clifthayne Farm
New Barn Farm
CINDER HILL
Cinder Hill
Woodhayes Farm
Northay
COMBE LA
ALLOTMENT DRO
COMBE WOOD RD
COMBE
LAPS COTTAGE
BROWNSEY LA
Marsh
Knapp Farm
Whitestaunton
Manor House
COURT FIELD LA
MILL LA
WHITECTAUNTON CROSS
HOLLAND S WASH DRO
POTTER'S LA
Scrapton
SCRAPTON LA
PH
Manning's Common
BIRCH CROSS
Birch Oak Farm
Howley
Pyle Farm
Great Hill
WHITE ASH LA
GIPSY DRO
A30
Buckshots Cross
Birch Hill
SHEAFHAYNE CROSS
PH
BERRY COTTAGE LA
SOUTHAY LA
Cleave Hill
SOUTHAY CROSS
TURNPIKE CVN PK
Weston Farm
Pithayne Farms
Sheafhayne Manor
SHELL'S LA
Southay
Mancroft
BEWLEY DOWN RD
WESTON RD
Higher Wambrook
Hillhouse Farm
Yarcombe
North Waterhayne
Wortheal
Wildway House
1 DRAKES MDW
2 HILLHOUSE
PH
TILERY
Moorhayne
BAG LA
Four Elms
POUND LA
River Yarty
Crawley
JAMES LA
CRAWLEY CUTTING
OLD MAIN RD
Loomcroft Farm
WAMBROOK
Lancin Farm
LANCIN LA
MILLWAY
Dennetts Farm
PH
Wambrook
GREEN KNAP
Hares Farm
Ferne Animal Sanctuary
ANIMAL SANCTUARY RD
FRIARY LA
MOUNTER'S HILL
Broad Oak
MILL LA
Moorpit
Gilletts Farm
Moxhayes
JAMES LANE CROSS
STOCKLAND RD
MEMBURY RD
Linnington
FLOOD LA
CASTLE WOOD LA
Lodge Farm
Hay Farm
Chaffhay Farm
MONEY PIT LA
Oatlands Farm
SHAG'S LA
Cotley
BOSSHAYNE LA
Peterhayes Farm
Haverlands Farm
Trebblehayes
Deerhams Farm
Narford's
NARFORD'S LA
Lugg's Farm
Ley Farm
Grays Farm
Bewley Down

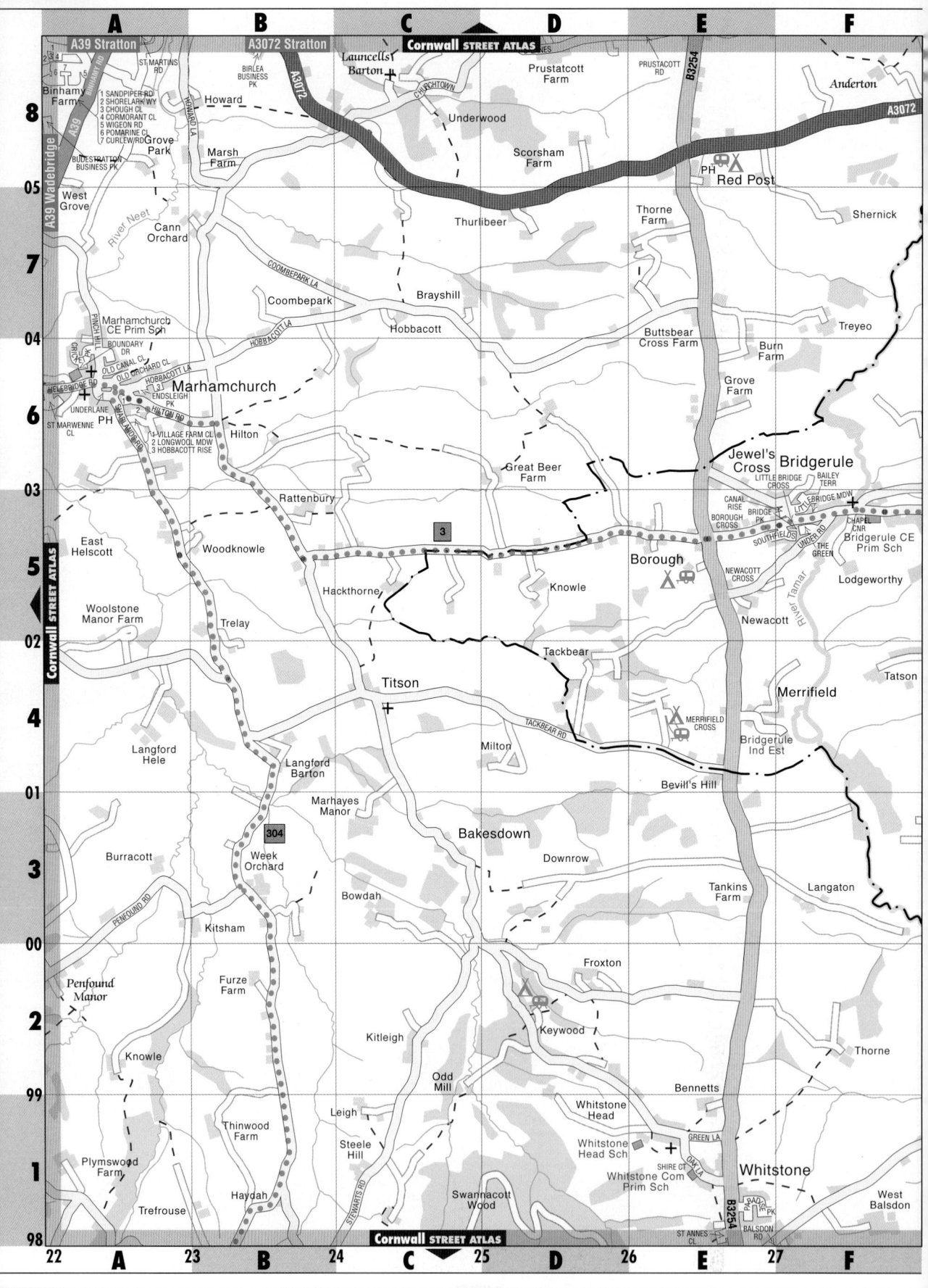

0   ¼   ½ mile
0   250m 500m 750m 1 km

A   B   C   D   E   F

A39 Stratton
A3072 Stratton
Cornwall STREET ATLAS

8

Binhamy Farm
St Martins Rd
Birlea Business Pk
Launcells Barton
Churchtown
Prustacott Farm
Prustacott Rd
B3254
Anderton
A3072

1 SANDPIPER RD
2 SHORELARK WY
3 CHOUGH CL
4 CORMORANT CL
5 WIGEON RD
6 POMARINE CL
7 CURLEW RD
Howard
Grove Park
Budestratton Business Pk
Underwood
Scorsham Farm
PH
Red Post

Marsh Farm
West Grove
A39 Wadebridge
River Neet
Cann Orchard
Thurlibeer
Thorne Farm
Shernick

05

7

Coombepark La
Coombepark
Brayshill
Buttsbear Cross Farm
Burn Farm
Treyeo

04

Marhamchurch CE Prim Sch
Boundary Dr
Old Canal Dr
Old Orchard Cl
Hobbacott La
Hobbacott
Hobbacott
Grove Farm

6

Pinch Hill
Endsleigh Pk
Marhamchurch
Hilton Rd
Hilton
Jewel's Cross
Bridgerule
Little Bridge Cross
Bailey Terr

Melbridge Rd
Underlane
St Marwenne Cl
PH
1 VILLAGE FARM CL
2 LONGWOOL MDW
3 HOBBACOTT RISE
Great Beer Farm
Canal Rise
Bridge Pk
Little Bridge Mdw
Chapel Cnr
Bridgerule CE Prim Sch

03

Rattenbury
Borough Cross
Southfields
Under Rd
The Green

East Helscott
Woodknowle
3
Newacott Cross
Lodgeworthy

5

Hackthorne
Knowle
Borough
Newacott

Woolstone Manor Farm
Trelay
Titson
Tackbear
River Tamar
Tatson

02

Merrifield

4

Langford Hele
Langford Barton
Milton
Tackbear Rd
Merrifield Cross
Bridgerule Ind Est

01

Marhayes Manor
Bevill's Hill

Burracott
304
Week Orchard
Bakesdown
Downrow
Tankins Farm
Langaton

3

Bowdah

Penfound Rd
Kitsham

00

Penfound Manor
Furze Farm
Froxton

2

Knowle
Kitleigh
Keywood
Thorne

Odd Mill
Bennetts

99

Thinwood Farm
Leigh
Whitstone Head
Green La
Whitstone

Stewarts Rd
Steele Hill
Whitstone Head Sch
Shire Ct
Oak La
West Balsdon

1

Plymswood Farm
Whitstone Com Prim Sch
B3254

Trefrouse
Haydah
Swannacott Wood
St Annes Cl
Balsdon Rd

98

Cornwall STREET ATLAS

22   A   23   B   24   C   25   D   26   E   27   F

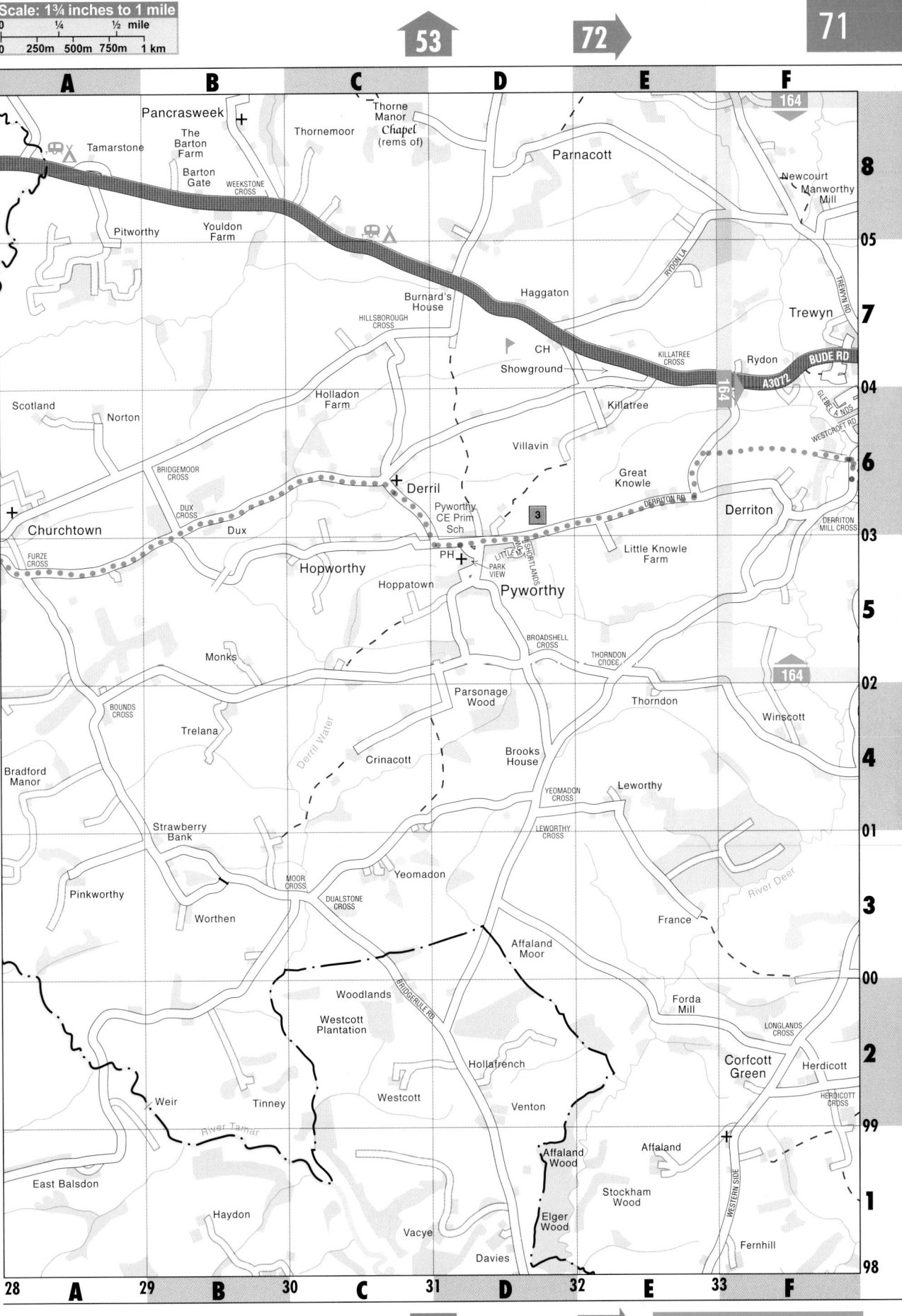

Scale: 1¾ inches to 1 mile

0   ¼   ½ mile
0   250m 500m 750m 1 km

A   B   C   D   E   F

Tamarstone

Pancrasweek

The Barton Farm

Barton Gate

Thornemoor

Thorne Manor Chapel (rems of)

Parnacott

Newcourt

Manworthy Mill

Pitworthy

Youldon Farm

WEEKSTONE CROSS

Haggaton

Trewyn

Burnard's House

HILLSBOROUGH CROSS

CH

Showground

KILLATREE CROSS

Rydon

BUDE RD

A3072

WESTCROFT RD

Scotland

Norton

Holladon Farm

Villavin

Killatree

Great Knowle

Derriton

DERRITON MILL CROSS

BRIDGEMOOR CROSS

DUX CROSS

Derril

Pyworthy CE Prim Sch

3

DERRITON RD

Churchtown

FURZE CROSS

Dux

Hopworthy

PH

LITTLE KNOWLE

PARK VIEW

SHORTLANDS

Pyworthy

Little Knowle Farm

Hoppatown

BROADSHELL CROSS

THORNDON CROSS

Monks

Parsonage Wood

Thorndon

Winscott

BOUNDS CROSS

Trelana

Derril Water

Crinacott

Brooks House

YEOMADON CROSS

Leworthy

LEWORTHY CROSS

Bradford Manor

Strawberry Bank

Pinkworthy

Worthen

MOOR CROSS

DUALSTONE CROSS

Yeomadon

River Deer

France

Affaland Moor

Forda Mill

LONGLANDS CROSS

Woodlands

BRIDGERULE RD

Westcott Plantation

Hollafrench

Corfcott Green

Herdicott

HERDICOTT CROSS

Weir

Tinney

Westcott

Venton

River Tamar

Affaland Wood

Affaland

WESTERN SIDE

East Balsdon

Haydon

Vacye

Elger Wood

Stockham Wood

Fernhill

Davies

28   A   29   B   30   C   31   D   32   E   33   F

A B C D E F

HOLSWORTHY

164
A388

Blagdonmoor Wharf
Arscott
Arliemoor Farm
Halsdon Barton
Cookbury Moor Plantation

New Market Rd
Quagmire La
River Tamar Way
Holsworthy Ind Est
Dol La
Canal Rd
Cemy
Lamerton
Lakes
Upcott Cross
3
Upcott
Cookbury Wick

Sch
North Rd
Waterloo Farm
Herdwicke
Crossparks Cross
Crossparks
Simpson
Anvil Cnr
Stapledon Cotts
Stapledon

A388
Liby
Windmill Rd
164
Belle Vue
Bodmin St
Fore St
Mus
Southcoombe Farm
Combesdown Cross
West Coombe Farm
Eastacombe
Beaconsfield Cross
Fernlea Farm
A3072

Undor La
Uplands Terr
Ruby Cl
Whimble Hill
Staddon Rd
Staddon Cross
Hollacombe Cross

Whimble Cross
Winterland La
Whimble
Staddon
Hollacombe
Hayne Barton
Claw Moor Plantation

Chasty
Keephill
Tredown
Little Claw Moor

Southcott Farm
Headon Cross
Headon
Hillside Cross

Ratherton
Moorhay

Winscott Cross
Common Moor
East Statfold

164
Holsworthy Woods
Whitecroft
Arscott

Sillick Moor
Claw Bridge
Clawford Cross
Forda
Bendibus Hill

North Down
Langdon
Clawford Vineyard & Fisheries
Middlecroft
Bendibus Cross
Haye Farm

East Down
Tinacre
Eastacombe
Grendisworthy Farm
Oak Cottage Cross
Hunscott Farm

Town Farm
Clawton
Buckhorn
Burrow Farm

Hotel
Claw Pk
Sprys Shop Cross
Sandymoor Cross

Clawton Prim Sch
North Beer
Heggadon

River Claw
Beer Hill
South Beer
Swingdon
Braddon

Kennicott
Kennacott Cross
A388

34 35 36 37 38 39

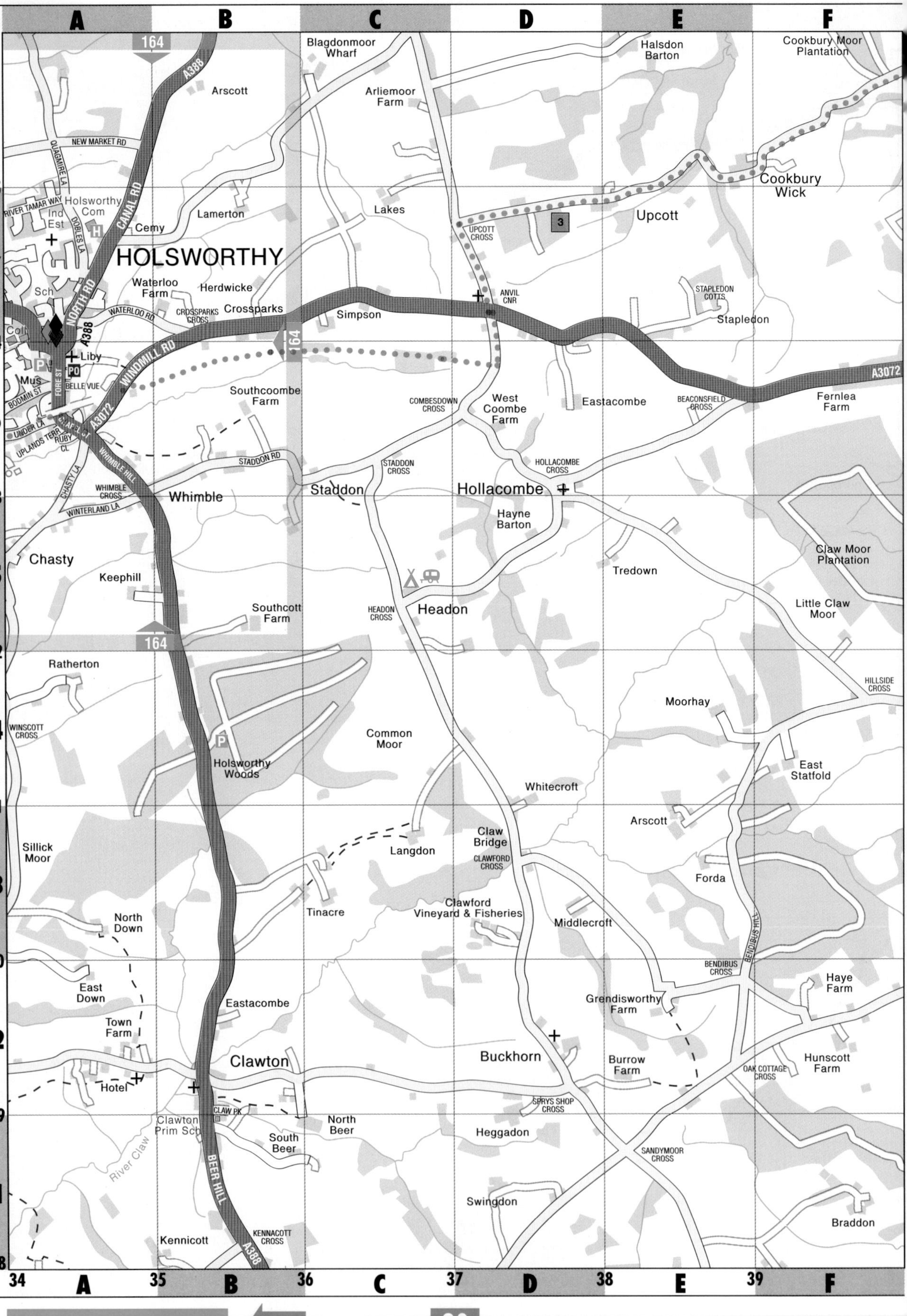

For full street detail of the highlighted area see page 164.

71 90

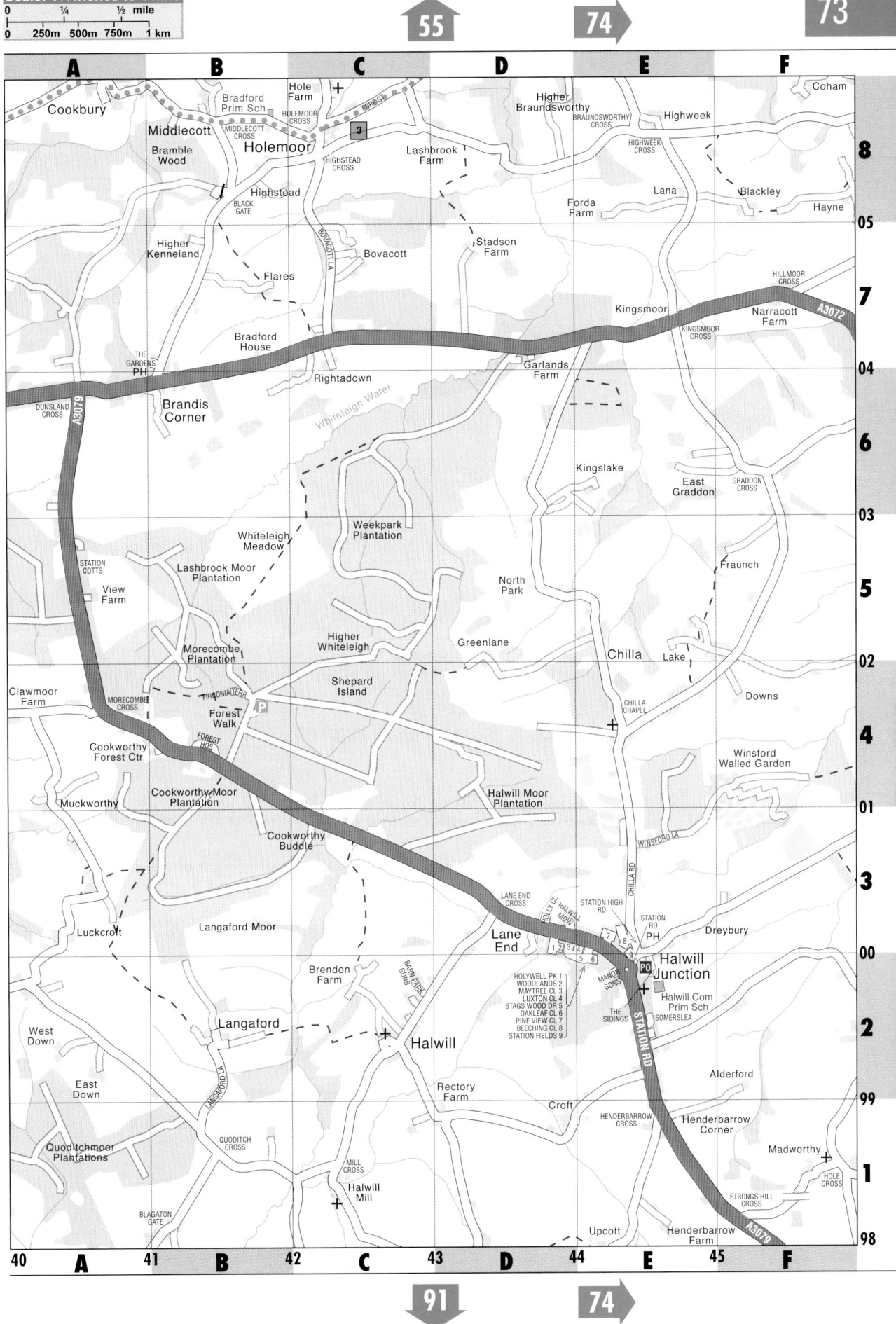

Scale: 1¾ inches to 1 mile

0 ¼ ½ mile
0 250m 500m 750m 1 km

A B C D E F

Cookbury
Middlecott
Bradford Prim Sch
Hole Farm
Holemoor
HOLEMOOR CROSS
3
MIDDLECOTT CROSS
Bramble Wood
Highstead
Highstead Cross
Lashbrook Farm
Higher Braundsworthy
BRAUNDSWORTHY CROSS
Highweek
Coham
HIGHWEEK CROSS

8

BLACK GATE
Higher Kenneland
Bovacott
Stadson Farm
Forda Farm
Lana
Blackley
Hayne

05

Flares
HILLMOOR CROSS

7

THE GARDENS PH
Bradford House
Rightadown
Kingsmoor
KINGSMOOR CROSS
Narracott Farm
A3072

04

DUNSLAND CROSS
A3079
Brandis Corner
Whiteleigh Water
Garlands Farm

6

Kingslake
East Graddon
GRADDON CROSS

03

STATION COTTS
View Farm
Whiteleigh Meadow
Lashbrook Moor Plantation
Weekpark Plantation
North Park
Fraunch

5

Morecombe Plantation
Higher Whiteleigh
Greenlane
Chilla
Lake

02

Clawmoor Farm
MORECOMBE CROSS
FIRSTONIA TERR
P Forest Walk
Shepard Island
CHILLA CHAPEL
Downs

4

FOREST HO
Cookworthy Forest Ctr
Muckworthy
Cookworthy Moor Plantation
Halwill Moor Plantation
Winsford Walled Garden

01

Cookworthy Buddle
WINSFORD LA

3

Luckcroft
Langaford Moor
LANE END CROSS
HOLLY CL
HALWILL MDW
STATION HIGH RD
CHILLA RD
STATION RD PH
Dreybury

Lane End
1 2 3 4
5 6
MANOR GDNS
PO
Halwill Junction

00

Brendon Farm
BARN PARK GDNS
HOLYWELL PK 1
WOODLANDS 2
MAYTREE CL 3
LUXTON CL 4
STAGS WOOD DR 5
OAKLEAF CL 6
PINE VIEW CL 7
BEECHING CL 8
STATION FIELDS 9
THE SIDINGS
Halwill Com Prim Sch
SOMERSLEA

West Down
Langaford
LANGAFORD LA
Halwill
Alderford

2

East Down
Rectory Farm
Croft
HENDERBARROW CROSS
Henderbarrow Corner

99

Quoditchmoor Plantations
QUODITCH CROSS
Madworthy
HOLE CROSS

MILL CROSS
Halwill Mill
STRONGS HILL CROSS

1

BLAGATON GATE
Upcott
Henderbarrow Farm
A3079

98

40 A 41 B 42 C 43 D 44 E 45 F

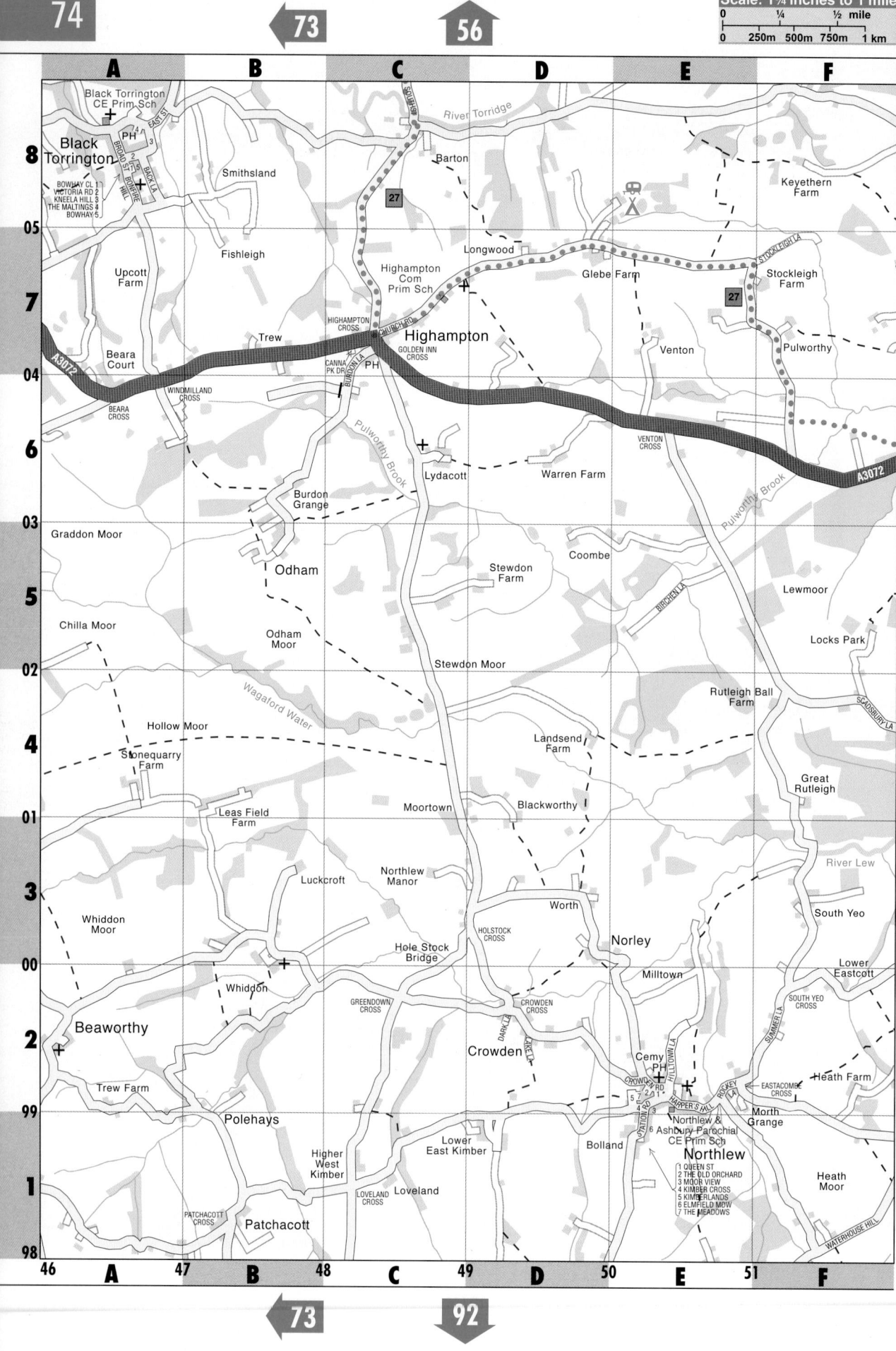

A B C D E F

8

05

7

04

6

03

5

02

4

01

3

00

2

99

1

98

Black Torrington
CE Prim Sch
PH
Black Torrington
BOWHAY CL 1
VICTORIA RD 2
KNEELA HILL 3
THE MALTINGS 4
BOWHAY 5
EAST ST
BROAD ST
BOWRIE HILL
BACK LA

Smithsland

Fishleigh

Upcott Farm

Beara Court

Beara Cross

Windmilland Cross

A3072

River Torridge

Barton

27

Highampton Com Prim Sch

Longwood

Glebe Farm

Keyethern Farm

Stockleigh Farm

27

STOCKLEIGH LA

Trew

Highampton Cross

CHURCH RD

Highampton

Golden Inn Cross

CANNA PK DR

BURDON LA

PH

Venton

Venton Cross

Pulworthy

Pulworthy Brook

A3072

Pulworthy Brook

Lydacott

Warren Farm

Burdon Grange

Graddon Moor

Odham

Coombe

Stewdon Farm

Lewmoor

Locks Park

Chilla Moor

Odham Moor

Stewdon Moor

Wagaford Water

Rutleigh Ball Farm

SCADSBURY LA

Hollow Moor

Stonequarry Farm

Landsend Farm

Great Rutleigh

River Lew

Leas Field Farm

Moortown

Blackworthy

Luckcroft

Northlew Manor

Worth

Norley

South Yeo

BIRCHEN LA

Whiddon Moor

Hole Stock Bridge

HOLSTOCK CROSS

Milltown

Lower Eastcott

SOUTH YEO CROSS

SUMMER LA

Whiddon

GREENDOWN CROSS

CROWDEN CROSS

Crowden

Cemy
PH

HILLTOWN LA

Heath Farm

EASTACOMBE CROSS

Morth Grange

Beaworthy

DARK LA

CROWDEN RD

HARPER'S HILL

ROCKEY LA

Trew Farm

Polehays

Lower East Kimber

Bolland

Northlew & Ashbury Parochial CE Prim Sch

Northlew

STATION RD

Heath Moor

Higher West Kimber

Loveland Cross

Loveland

1 QUEEN ST
2 THE OLD ORCHARD
3 MOOR VIEW
4 KIMBER CROSS
5 KIMBERLANDS
6 ELMFIELD MDW
7 THE MEADOWS

Patchacott Cross

Patchacott

WATERHOUSE HILL

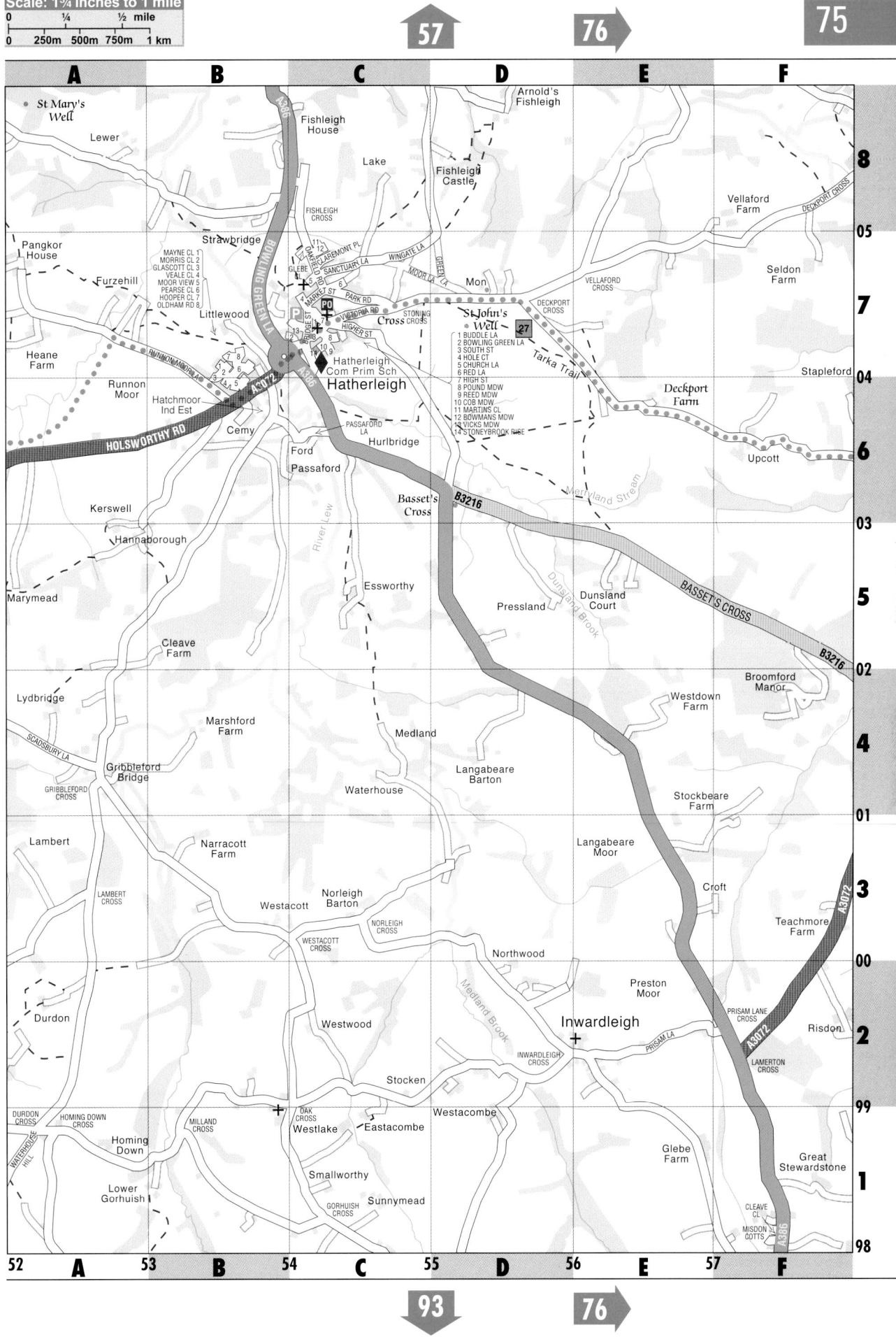

St Mary's Well

Lewer

Pangkor House

Furzehill

Heane Farm

Runnon Moor

Hatchmoor Ind Est

HOLSWORTHY RD

Littlewood

Strawbridge

MAYNE CL 1
MORRIS CL 2
GLASCOTT CL 3
VEALE CL 4
MOOR VIEW 5
PEARSE CL 6
HOOPER CL 7
OLDHAM RD 8

RUNNON MOOR AVE

A3072

A386

BOWLING GREEN LA

Cemy

Ford

Passaford

Kerswell

Hannaborough

Marymead

Fishleigh House

Lake

Fishleigh Cross

FISHLEIGH CROSS

CLAREMONT PL
SANCTUARY LA
MARKET ST
PARK RD
VICTORIA RD
HIGHER ST
STONING CROSS
MOOR LA

GLEBE

P
PO

Hatherleigh Com Prim Sch

Hatherleigh

PASSAFORD LA

Hurlbridge

Basset's Cross

Essworthy

Cleave Farm

River Lew

Arnold's Fishleigh

Fishleigh Castle

WINGATE LA

GREEN LA

Mon

St John's Well
Cross

27

1 BUDDLE LA
2 BOWLING GREEN LA
3 SOUTH ST
4 HOLE CT
5 CHURCH LA
6 RED LA
7 HIGH ST
8 POUND MDW
9 REED MDW
10 COB MDW
11 MARTINS CL
12 BOWMANS MDW
13 VICKS MDW
14 STONEYBROOK RISE

Tarka Trail

DECKPORT CROSS

VELLAFORD CROSS

Deckport Farm

B3216

Merryland Stream

Dunsland Brook

Dunsland Court

Pressland

Westdown Farm

Vellaford Farm

Seldon Farm

Stapleford

Upcott

BASSET'S CROSS

B3216

Broomford Manor

Lydbridge

SCADSBURY LA

Gribbleford Bridge

GRIBBLEFORD CROSS

Lambert

LAMBERT CROSS

Durdon

DURDON CROSS

HOMING DOWN CROSS

WATERHOUSE HILL

Homing Down

Lower Gorhuish

Marshford Farm

Narracott Farm

Westacott

WESTACOTT CROSS

Milland Cross

OAK CROSS

Westlake

Smallworthy

GORHUISH CROSS

Medland

Waterhouse

Norleigh Barton

NORLEIGH CROSS

Northwood

Westwood

Stocken

Eastacombe

Sunnymead

Langabeare Barton

Langabeare Moor

Medland Brook

Inwardleigh

INWARDLEIGH CROSS

Westacombe

Stockbeare Farm

Croft

Preston Moor

Glebe Farm

PRISAM LA

PRISAM LANE CROSS

LAMERTON CROSS

A3072

Teachmore Farm

Risdon

Great Stewardstone

CLEAVE CL

MISDON COTTS

A386

8 05 7 04 6 03 5 02 4 01 3 00 2 99 1 98

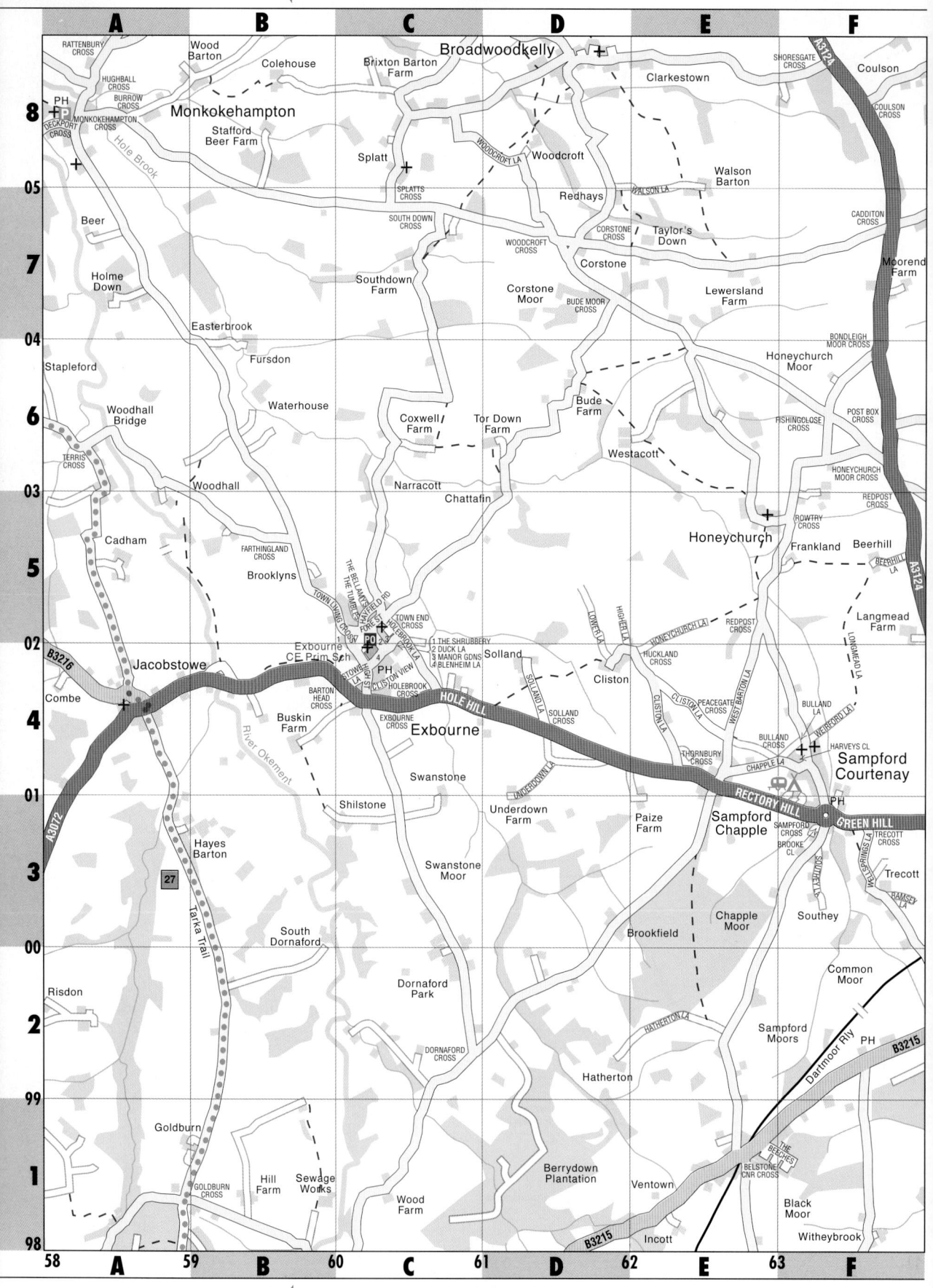

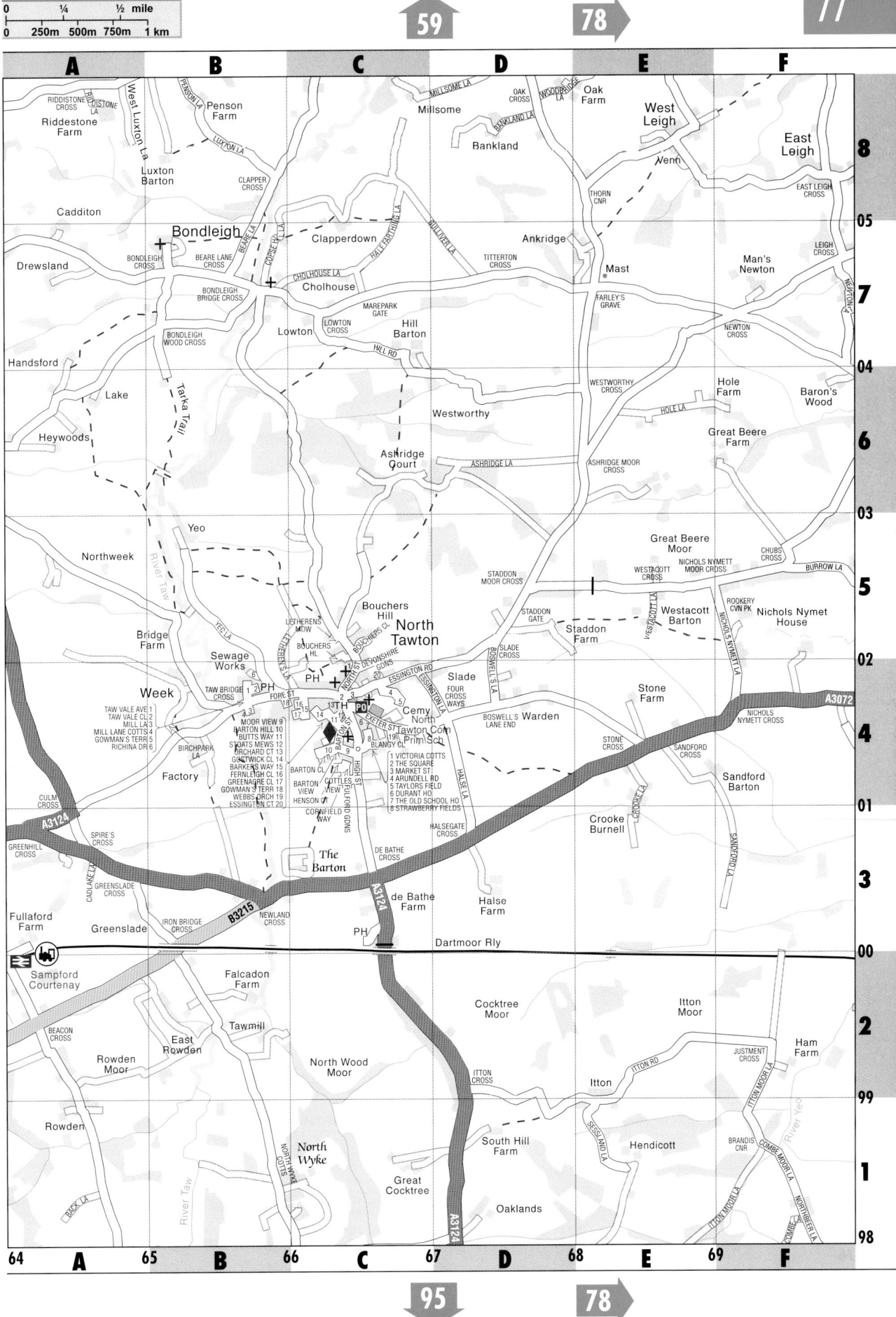

Scale: 1¾ inches to 1 mile

0   ¼   ½ mile
0   250m 500m 750m 1 km

A   B   C   D   E   F

RIDDISTONE CROSS
West Luxton La
Penson La
Penson Farm
Riddestone Farm
Riddestone La
Millsome La
Oak Cross
Woodbridge La
Oak Farm
West Leigh
East Leigh

Luxton La
Luxton Barton
Clapper Cross
Bankland La
Bankland
Venn
East Leigh Cross

8

Cadditon

Thorn Cnr
Leigh Cross

05

Bondleigh
Clapperdown
Half Earthing La
Gulliver La
Titterton Cross
Ankridge
Mast
Man's Newton

Drewsland
Bondleigh Cross
Beare Lane Cross
Copse Pk La
Beare La
Cholhouse La
Cholhouse
Farley's Grave
Newton Cross

7

Bondleigh Bridge Cross
Marepark Gate
Lowton Cross
Hill Barton
Newton La

Handsford
Bondleigh Wood Cross
Lowton
Hill Rd
Westworthy Cross
Hole Farm
Baron's Wood

04

Lake
Tarka Trail
Hill Barton
Westworthy
Hole La

Heywoods

Great Beere Farm

6

Ashridge Court
Ashridge La
Ashridge Moor Cross

03

Yeo
River Taw
Staddon Moor Cross
Great Beere Moor
Nichols Nymett Moor Cross
Chubs Cross
Burrow La

Northweek
Yeo La
Bouchers Hill
North Tawton
Staddon Gate
Westacott Cross
Westacott Barton
Rookery Cvn Pk
Nichols Nymet House

5

Bridge Farm
Letherens Mdw
Bouchers Cl
North St
Devonshire Gdns
Essington Rd
Slade
Staddon Farm
Nichols Nymett La

Sewage Works
Bouchers Hl
PH
Slade Cross
Boswell's La

02

Week
Taw Bridge Cross
Forest St
PH
Cemy
North Tawton Com Prim Sch
Four Cross Ways
Stone Farm

TAW VALE AVE 1
TAW VALE CL 2
MILL LA 3
MILL LANE COTTS 4
GOWMAN'S TERR 5
RICHINA DR 6
Birchpark La
TH
PO
Exeter St
Boswell's Warden Lane End
Nichols Nymett Cross

A3072

4

MOOR VIEW 9
BARTON HILL 10
BUTTS WAY 11
STOATS MEWS 12
ORCHARD CT 13
GOTTWICK CL 14
BARKERS WAY 15
FERNLEIGH CL 16
GREENACRE CL 17
GOWMAN'S TERR 18
WEBBS ORCH 19
ESSINGTON CT 20
Factory
Barton Cl
Barton View
Blancy Cl
Cottles View
Henson Ct
Cornfield Way

High St
Fulford Gdns
1 VICTORIA COTTS
2 THE SQUARE
3 MARKET ST
4 ARUNDELL RD
5 TAYLORS FIELD
6 DURANT HO
7 THE OLD SCHOOL HO
8 STRAWBERRY FIELDS
Stone Cross
Sandford Cross
Sandford Barton

Culm Cross
Halse La
Crooke Burnell
Cadleck La
Sandford La

01

Greenhill Cross
A3124
Spire's Cross
Cadlake Cross
Greenslade Cross
The Barton
De Bathe Cross
Halsegate Cross

3

Fullaford Farm
Greenslade
Iron Bridge Cross
B3215
Newland Cross
de Bathe Farm
Halse Farm
PH
Dartmoor Rly

00

Sampford Courtenay
Beacon Cross
Falcadon Farm
Cocktree Moor
Itton Moor
Ham Farm

2

Rowden Moor
East Rowden
Tawmill
North Wood Moor
Justment Cross

99

Rowden
North Wyke Cotts
Itton Cross
Itton Rd
Itton
Sessland La
Itton Moor La
Brandis Cnr
River Yeo

1

North Wyke
Great Cocktree
South Hill Farm
Hendicott
Combe Moor La
Northern La

Oaklands
A3124

98

64   A   65   B   66   C   67   D   68   E   69   F

77
60

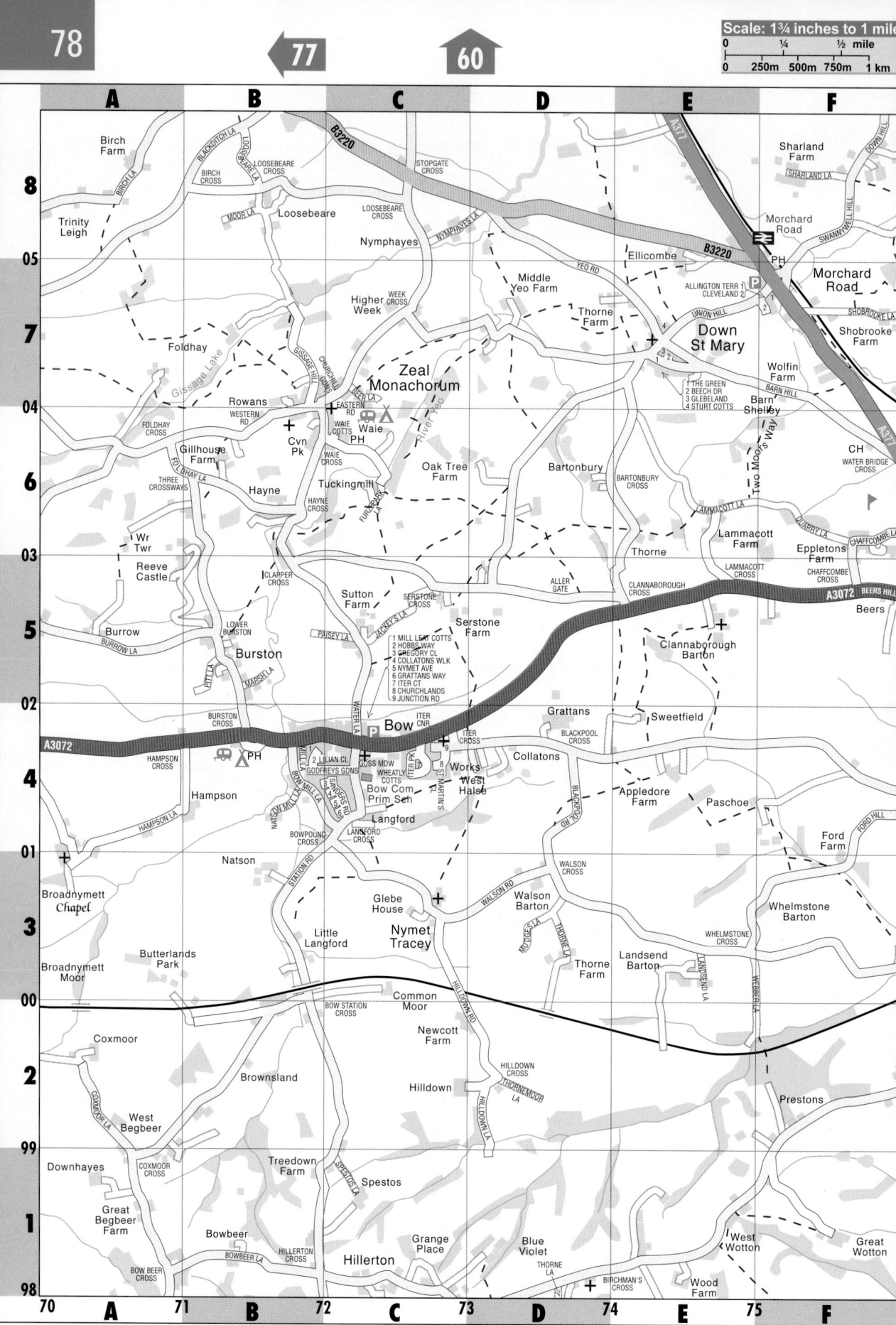
Scale: 1¾ inches to 1 mile
0 ¼ ½ mile
0 250m 500m 750m 1 km
A
B
C
D
E
F
Birch Farm
BIRCH LA
BLACKDITCH LA
LOOSEBEARE LA
BIRCH CROSS
LOOSEBEARE CROSS
B3220
STOPGATE CROSS
A377
Sharland Farm
SHARLAND LA
DOWN HILL
8
Trinity Leigh
MOOR LA
Loosebeare
LOOSEBEARE CROSS
Nymphayes
NYMPHAYES LA
Morchard Road
SWANNYWELL HILL
05
Ellicombe
B3220
PH
Morchard Road
Middle Yeo Farm
YEO RD
ALLINGTON TERR 1
CLEVELAND 2
Higher Week
WEEK CROSS
Thorne Farm
UNION HILL
SHOBROOKE LA
7
Foldhay
Down St Mary
Shobrooke Farm
Gissage Lake
GISSAGE HILL
CHURCHILL GDNS
Zeal Monachorum
Wolfin Farm
BEER LA
1 THE GREEN
2 BEECH DR
3 GLEBELAND
4 STURT COTTS
BARN HILL
04
Rowans
WESTERN RD
EASTERN RD
Barn Shelley
FOLDHAY CROSS
Cvn Pk
WAIE COTTS
Waie
PH
River Yeo
Two Moors Way
Gillhouse Farm
WAIE CROSS
CH
FOLDHAY LA
Oak Tree Farm
Bartonbury
WATER BRIDGE CROSS
6
THREE CROSSWAYS
Tuckingmill
BARTONBURY CROSS
Hayne
HAYNE CROSS
FURZE PARK LA
LAMMACOTT LA
QUARRY LA
CHAFFCOMBE LA
Wr Twr
Lammacott Farm
03
Thorne
Eppletons Farm
Reeve Castle
CLAPPER CROSS
LAMMACOTT CROSS
CHAFFCOMBE CROSS
ALLER GATE
CLANNABOROUGH CROSS
A3072
BEERS HILL
Sutton Farm
SERSTONE CROSS
Beers
5
Burrow
LOWER BURSTON
JACKEY'S LA
Serstone Farm
BURROW LA
PAISEY LA
1 MILL LEAT COTTS
2 HOBBS WAY
3 GREGORY CL
4 COLLATONS WLK
5 NYMET AVE
6 GRATTANS WAY
7 ITER CT
8 CHURCHLANDS
9 JUNCTION RD
Clannaborough Barton
Burston
PITT LA
MARSH LA
02
Grattans
Sweetfield
BURSTON CROSS
WATER LA
Bow
ITER CNR
A3072
ITER CROSS
BLACKPOOL CROSS
HAMPSON CROSS
PH
MILL LA
LILIAN CL
GOSS MDW
Collatons
GODFREYS GDNS
WHEATLY COTTS
ITER PK
Works
4
ST MARTIN'S CL
West Halse
Hampson
BOW MILL LA
SANDERS RD
Bow Com Prim Sch
BLACKPOOL RD
Appledore Farm
Paschoe
NATSON MILL LA
Langford
HAMPSON LA
BOWPOUND CROSS
LANGFORD CROSS
FORD HILL
Ford Farm
01
Natson
WALSON CROSS
STATION RD
Broadnymett Chapel
WALSON RD
Glebe House
Walson Barton
Whelmstone Barton
3
MUDGES LA
THORNE LA
Little Langford
Nymet Tracey
WHELMSTONE CROSS
Butterlands Park
Landsend Barton
Broadnymett Moor
Thorne Farm
LANDSEND LA
WEBBER LA
00
Common Moor
BOW STATION CROSS
HILLDOWN RD
Newcott Farm
Coxmoor
2
Brownsland
HILLDOWN CROSS
THORNEMOOR LA
Hilldown
Prestons
COXMOOR LA
West Begbeer
HILLDOWN LA
99
Downhayes
COXMOOR CROSS
Treedown Farm
SPESTOS LA
Spestos
1
Great Begbeer Farm
West Wotton
Great Wotton
Bowbeer
Grange Place
Blue Violet
BOWBEER LA
HILLERTON CROSS
Hillerton
THORNE LA
BIRCHMAN'S CROSS
BOW BEER CROSS
Wood Farm
98
70
71
72
73
74
75

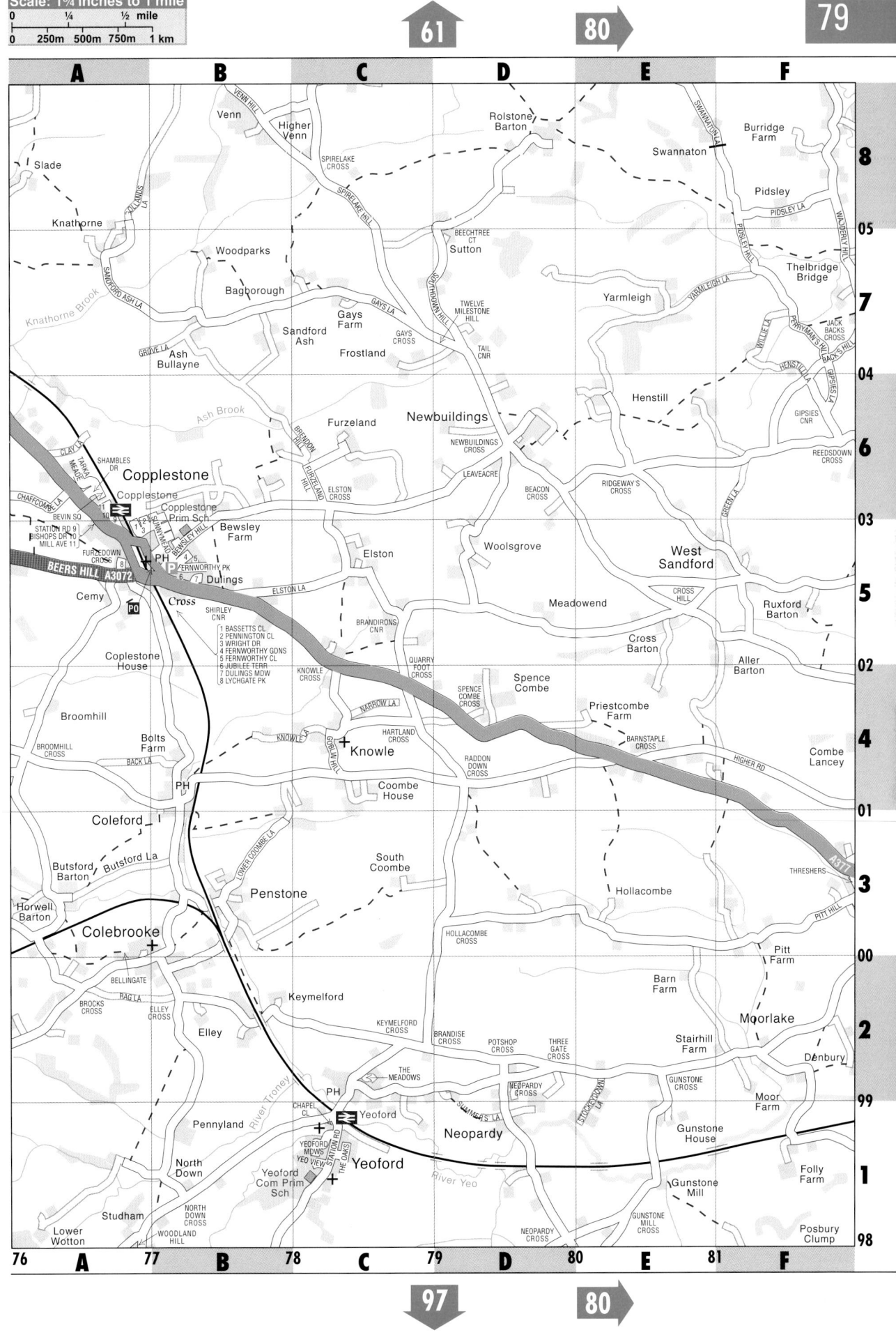

Scale: 1¾ inches to 1 mile
0 ¼ ½ mile
0 250m 500m 750m 1 km
61
80
A
B
C
D
E
F
Venn
VENN HILL
Higher Venn
SPIRELAKE CROSS
SPIRELAKE HILL
Rolstone Barton
SWANNATON LA
Burridge Farm
Swannaton
Slade
Pidsley
PIDSLEY LA
GILLANDS LA
Knathorne
BEECHTREE CT
Sutton
PIDSLEY HILL
WADDERLY HILL
Woodparks
Thelbridge Bridge
SANDFORD ASH LA
Bagborough
Yarmleigh
YARMLEIGH LA
Knathorne Brook
GAYS LA
Gays Farm
Sandford Ash
TWELVE MILESTONE HILL
SOUTHDOWN HILL
JACK BACKS CROSS
PERRYMAN'S HILL
WILLIE LA
GAYS CROSS
Frostland
GROVE LA
Ash Bullayne
TAIL CNR
BACK'S HILL
HENSTILL LA
GIPSIES LA
Henstill
Ash Brook
Furzeland
Newbuildings
GIPSIES CNR
BRENDON HILL
NEWBUILDINGS CROSS
REEDSDOWN CROSS
CLAY LA
TARKA MEADE
SHAMBLES DR
Copplestone
FURZELAND HILL
LEAVEACRE
BEACON CROSS
RIDGEWAY'S CROSS
Copplestone
ELSTON CROSS
CHAFFCOMBE LA
Copplestone Prim Sch
GREEN LA
BEVIN SQ
STATION RD 9
BISHOPS DR 10
MILL AVE 11
SUNNYMEAD
BEWSLEY HILL
Bewsley Farm
Elston
Woolsgrove
West Sandford
FURZEDOWN CROSS
PH
FERNWORTHY PK
BEERS HILL A3072
Dulings
ELSTON LA
CROSS HILL
Cemy
PO
Cross
Meadowend
Ruxford Barton
SHIRLEY CNR
1 BASSETTS CL
2 PENNINGTON CL
3 WRIGHT DR
4 FERNWORTHY GDNS
5 FERNWORTHY CL
6 JUBILEE TERR
7 DULINGS MDW
8 LYCHGATE PK
BRANDIRONS CNR
Cross Barton
Coplestone House
QUARRY FOOT CROSS
Aller Barton
KNOWLE CROSS
Spence Combe
SPENCE COMBE CROSS
NARROW LA
Priestcombe Farm
Broomhill
Bolts Farm
HARTLAND CROSS
BARNSTAPLE CROSS
BROOMHILL CROSS
KNOWLE LA
GOBLIN HILL
Knowle
Combe Lancey
BACK LA
RADDON DOWN CROSS
HIGHER RD
PH
Coombe House
Coleford
PH
LOWER COOMBE LA
South Coombe
Butsford Barton
Butsford La
A377
THRESHERS
Horwell Barton
Penstone
Hollacombe
PITT HILL
Colebrooke
HOLLACOMBE CROSS
Pitt Farm
BELLINGATE
Barn Farm
RAG LA
Keymelford
BROCKS CROSS
ELLEY CROSS
Moorlake
Elley
KEYMELFORD CROSS
BRANDISE CROSS
POTSHOP CROSS
THREE GATE CROSS
Stairhill Farm
Denbury
THE MEADOWS
NEOPARDY CROSS
GUNSTONE CROSS
River Troney
PH
STOCKSDOWN LA
Moor Farm
CHAPEL CL
SUMMERS LA
Yeoford
Pennyland
Neopardy
Gunstone House
YEOFORD MDWS
YEO VIEW
STATION RD
THE OAKS
North Down
Yeoford
Yeoford Com Prim Sch
River Yeo
Folly Farm
Gunstone Mill
Studham
NORTH DOWN CROSS
GUNSTONE MILL CROSS
Lower Wotton
WOODLAND HILL
NEOPARDY CROSS
Posbury Clump
8
05
7
04
6
03
5
02
4
01
3
00
2
99
1
98
76
77
78
79
80
81
97
80

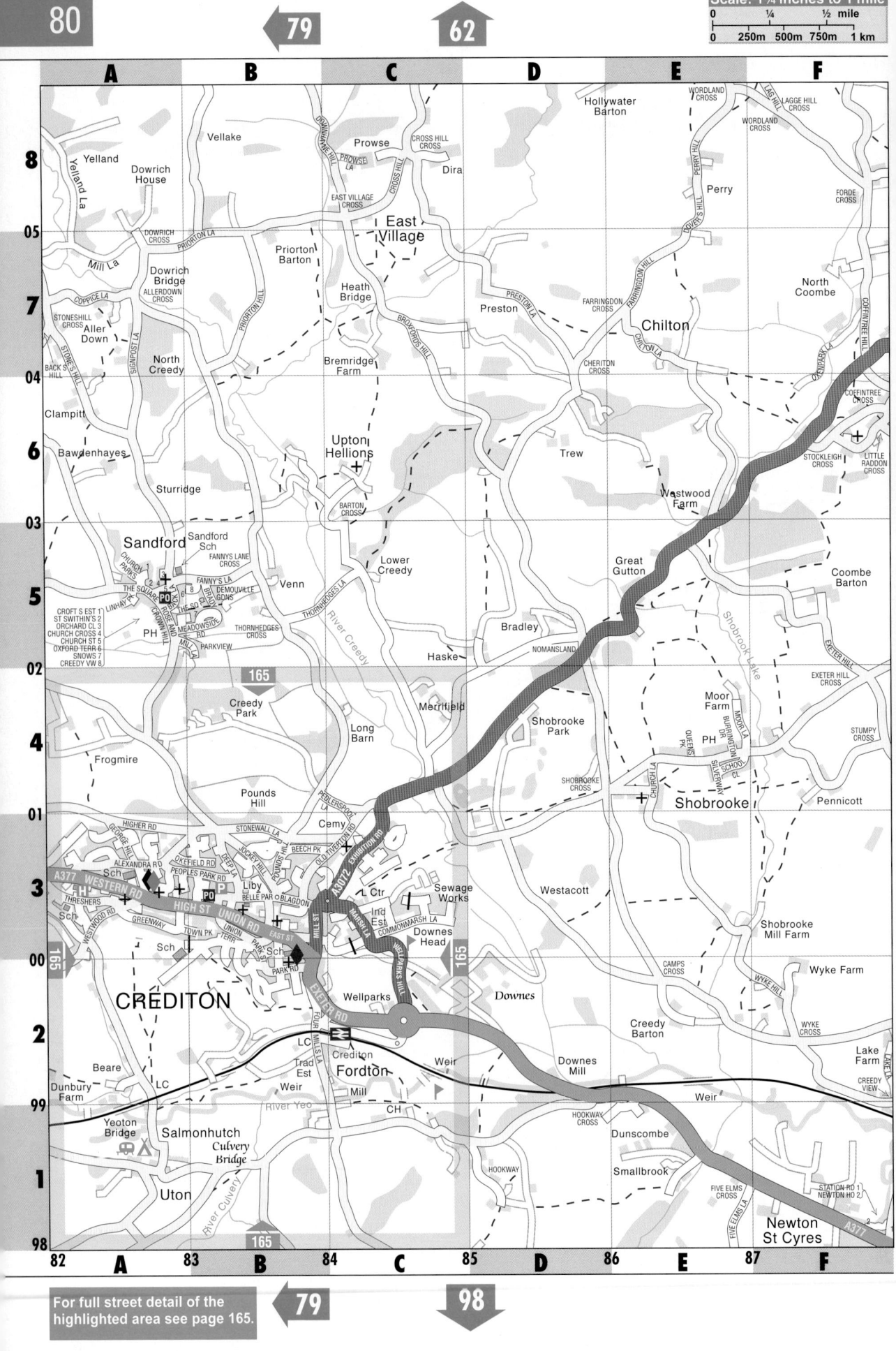

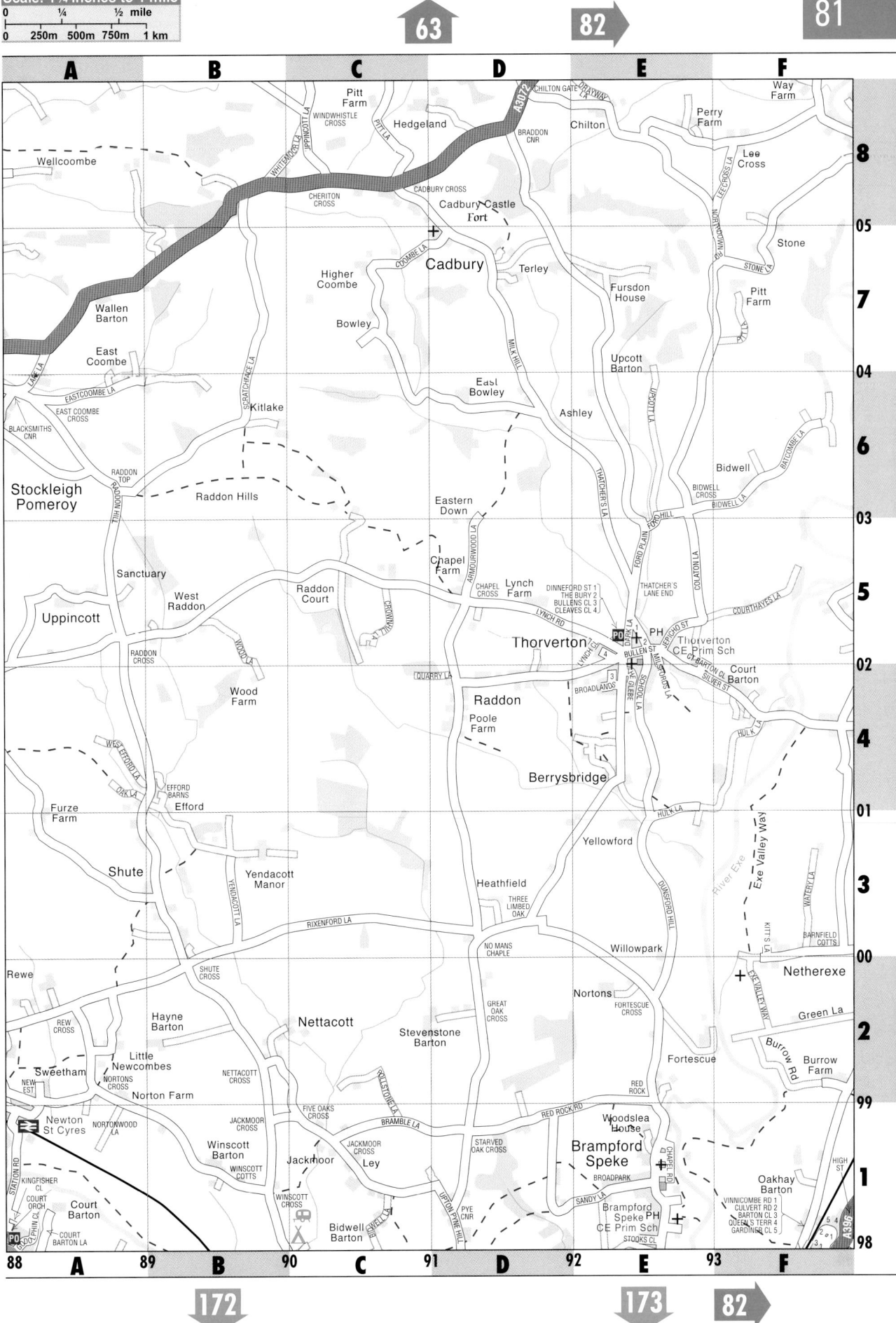

A **B** **C** **D** **E** **F**

Wellcoombe

Wallen Barton

East Coombe

EASTCOOMBE LA

BLACKSMITHS CNR

Stockleigh Pomeroy

Sanctuary

Uppincott

West Efford LA

OAK LA

Furze Farm

Shute

Rewe

NEW EST

Sweetham

NORTONS CROSS

Newton St Cyres

KINGFISHER CL

COURT ORCH

Court Barton

PO

COURT BARTON LA

STATION RD

NORTONWOOD LA

Hayne Barton

Little Newcombes

Norton Farm

REW CROSS

Pitt Farm

WINDWHISTLE CROSS

WHITEMOOR LA

UPPINCOTT LA

PITT LA

Hedgeland

Cheriton Cross

CADBURY CROSS

Higher Coombe

Bowley

Kitlake

SCRATCHFACE LA

Raddon Hills

RADDON TOP

RADDON HILL

West Raddon

RADDON CROSS

Raddon Court

CROWN LA

Wood Farm

WOOD LA

Efford

EFFORD BARNS

Yendacott Manor

YENDACOTT LA

RIXENFORD LA

SHUTE CROSS

Nettacott

NETTACOTT CROSS

Winscott Barton

WINSCOTT COTTS

Jackmoor

WINSCOTT CROSS

JACKMOOR CROSS

FIVE OAKS CROSS

RAILSTONE LA

Bidwell Barton

CYDER LA

Jackmoor Ley

JACKMOOR CROSS

BRAMBLE LA

Stevenstone Barton

Raddon Court

CHAPEL FARM

Chapel Farm

ARMOURWOOD LA

East Bowley

Eastern Down

Chapel Cross

CHAPEL LA

Lynch Farm

Lynch Cross

LYNCH RD

Raddon

Poole Farm

Heathfield

THREE LIMBED OAK

NO MANS CHAPLE

Great Oak Cross

STARVED OAK CROSS

UPTON PYNE HILL

A3072

CHILTON GATE

BRADDON CNR

Cadbury Cross

Cadbury Castle Fort

Cadbury

COOMBE LA

Terley

Ashley

MILK HILL

THATCHER'S LA

Chilton

Fursdon House

Upcott Barton

UPCOTT LA

FORD HILL

FORD PLAIN

Bidwell Cross

Bidwell

BIDWELL LA

Thatcher's Lane End

COLATON LA

DINNEFORD ST 1
THE BURY 2
BULLENS CL 3
CLEAVES CL 4

Thorverton

PO

PH

BULLENS CL

PARK LA

LYNCH CL

SCHOOL LA

GLEBE LA

BROADLANDS

QUARRY LA

Berrysbridge

HULK LA

Yellowford

DUNSFORD HILL

Willowpark

Nortons

FORTESCUE CROSS

Fortescue

RED ROCK

RED ROCK RD

SANDY LA

Brampford Speke

BROADPARK

CHAPEL RD

Woodslea House

Brampford Speke CE Prim Sch

PH

STOOKS CL

Way Farm

Perry Farm

Lee Cross

LEE CROSS LA

NEWTON LA

Stone

STONE CT

Pitt Farm

PITT LA

BATCOMBE LA

Thorverton CE Prim Sch

EPCOMB ST

GT BARTON CL

Court Barton

SILVER ST

MILLMOORS LA

COURTHAYES LA

Netherexe

CE VALLEY WAY

KITT'S LA

WATERY LA

BARNFIELD COTTS

Green La

BURROW RD

Burrow Farm

Exe Valley Way

River Exe

Oakhay Barton

VINNICOMBE RD 1
CULVERT RD 2
BARTON CL 3
QUEEN'S TERR 4
GARDINER CL 5

HIGH ST

A396

88 89 90 91 92 93

A **B** **C** **D** **E** **F**

8
05
7
04
6
03
5
02
4
01
3
00
2
99
1
98

A   B   C   D   E   F

8

05

7

04

6

03

5

02

01

4

00

3

2

99

1

98

94   A   95   B   96   C   97   D   98   E   99   F

Copenhagen
A396
Burn
STONE LA
Leigh Barton
Southcombe
Mast
Stokehouse
Chapelhaies
Trinity
COLEBROOKE LA
Gingerland
Bagmore
TRINITY COTTS
BAGMORE HILL
Ravenshayes
Land Farm
CHRIST CROSS
Tedbridge
FORWARD GN
Rode Moors
WEEK CROSS
KERDISHAYES LA
ASH CROSS
HEN'S LA
Chitterley Bsns Ctr
COOMBE LA
Coblands Farm
Roach
CHRISTCROSS LA
Rhode Farm
BEACON CROSS
Castle Hill
Bradninch
PH
FORE ST
Woods La
COBLANDS CROSS
Ash Farm
ROACH LA
Yarde Downs
YARD DOWN LA
COPDOWN LA
PEAKFIELD CROSS WAYS
PETER ST 1
BEACON RD 2
MILLWAY 3
MILLWAY GDNS 4
CEMETERY LA 5
KENSHAM CL 6
PASSMORE RD 7
BOWLEY MDW 8
BEACON HILL
PO
Cemy
Jenny's Portion
Livinghayes
GREENSLINCH LA
Greenslinch
Caseberry
CASEBERRY LA
WEST END RD
BARNS CL
WESTFIELD
CHARWELL MDW
The Duchy Sch
9 JUBILEE RD
10 LANDUNVEZ RD
SILVERDALE 1
HIGH BULLEN 2
PRISPEN VIEW 3
PRISPEN DR 4
APPLEMEDE 5
PARSONAGE LA 6
DAVIES CL 7
FRENCH CL 8
WYNDHAM RD 9
PRISPEN HO
OLD BUTTERLEIGH RD
HIGH ST
TIVERTON RD
LIVINGSHAYES RD
Silverton CE Prim Sch
1 HILLCREST RD
2 OAK CL
PARK RD
COTT LA
Ford
Stockwell
Moorland
Hele Payne
Mill
KING ST 10
ORCHARD LA 11
MEADOW LEA 12
THE MEAD 13
ST ANNES PL 14
ST MARYS VIEW 15
PH
SCHOOL RD
CHURCH RD
COACH RD
Silverton
RED CROSS
STOCKWELL CROSS
WORTH LA
Hele
STATION RD
PH
LC
M5
UPEXE LA
PO
TUNS LA
EXETER RD
Up Exe
KENSOM HILL
QUARRY LA
BARTON LA
HAYNE LA
Hayne House
ELLERHAYES
Strathculm
STRATHCULM RD
SIDMOUTH RD
Rudway Barton
PH
STUMPY CROSS
Dunsmore
Singelton Park
LEASE HILL
PENSTONE BARNS
BEARE SQ
Broomhill
Old Heazille Farm
Flock Mill
River Culm
LEASE COTTS
Paper Mills
BRIDGE LA
BRIDGE CL
Beare
Lower Comberoy Farm
FROGMORE CROSS
P
Heazille Barton
REWE CT
Killerton Park
Killerton House
BEARE LA
Hollis Head
Rewe
Bridge
Columbjohn
COLUMBJOHN CROSS
THE CLOSE
GREEN LA
REWE BARS
REWE CROSS
DANES CROSS
WATERY LA
Budlake
Sprydon Plantation
REWES CROSS
P
P
P
Ratcliffes
DANES HILL
Danes Wood
P
FRANCIS COURT COTTS
Budlake Old Post Office
Francis Court Farm
Newhall Farm
Ashclyst Forest Wlks
P
Sandy La
Brookleigh
Bussells
Belfield House
Cutton
Hay House
LONGMEADOW
Chillacombe Farm
GIPSY CNR
Burrow Farm
River Clyst
A396
Stoke Canon
GARDINER CL
Sandy La
BOWLS CROSS
M5
MOOREDSE LA
MOOR LA
B3181
Beaumont
BURROW CROSS

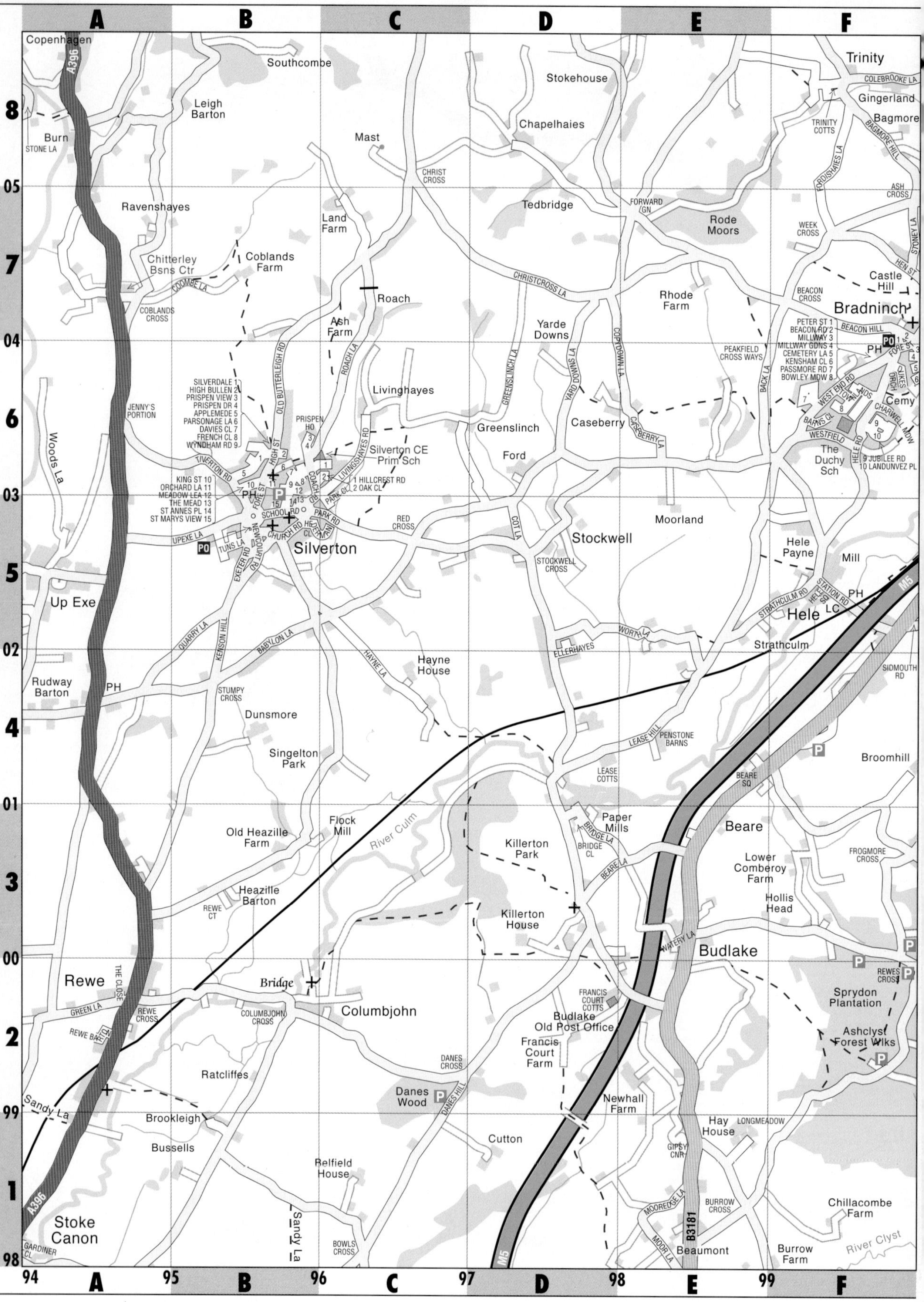

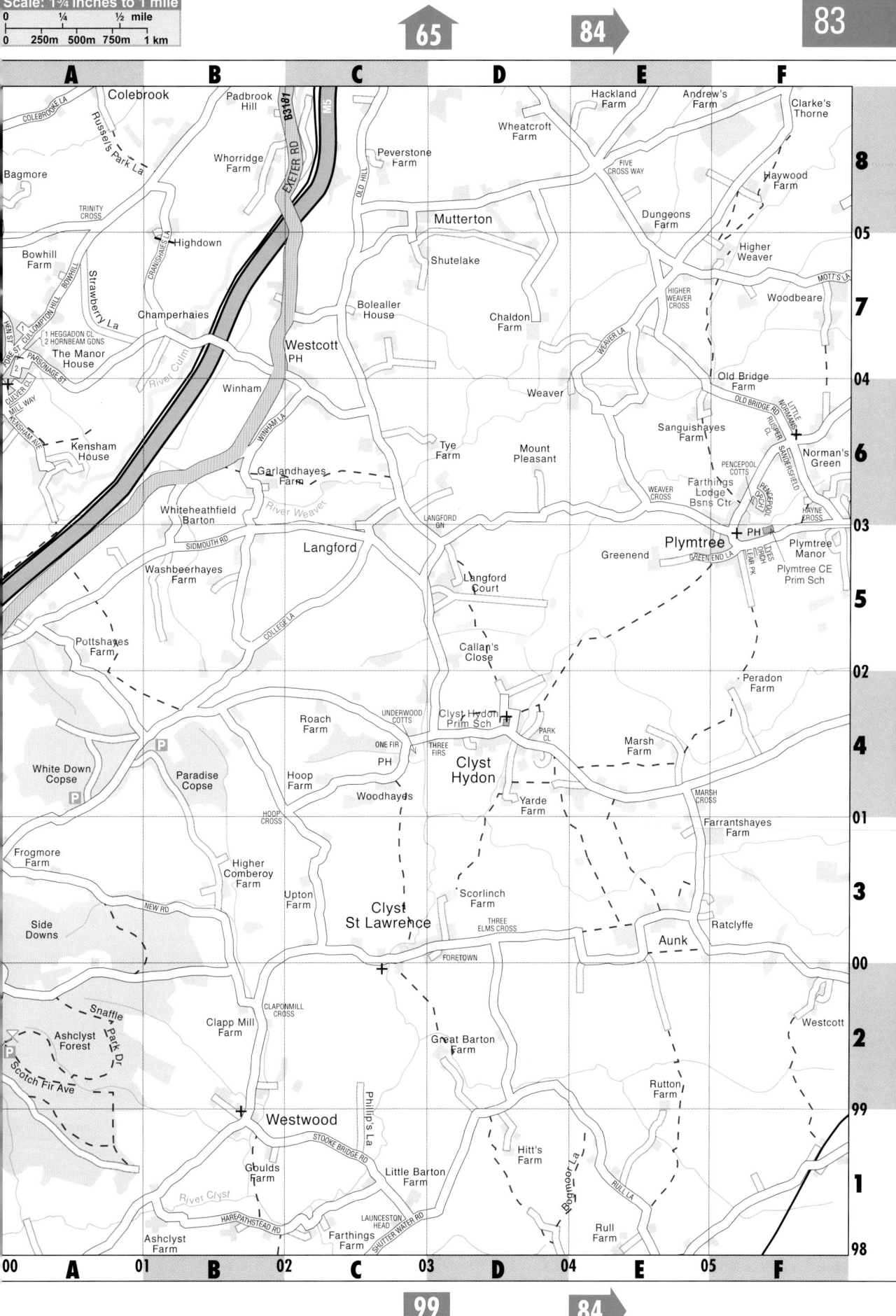

Scale: 1¾ inches to 1 mile

0 ¼ ½ mile
0 250m 500m 750m 1 km

Colebrook

Bagmore

Padbrook Hill

Colebrook La

Russel's Park La

Whorridge Farm

TRINITY CROSS

Highdown

Bowhill Farm

Strawberry La

Champerhaies

The Manor House

1 HEGGADON CL
2 HORNBEAM GDNS

Kensham House

Winham

Westcott PH

Peverstone Farm

Mutterton

Shutelake

Bolealler House

Chaldon Farm

Weaver

Tye Farm

Mount Pleasant

Garlandhayes Farm

Whiteheathfield Barton

River Weaver

Langford GN

Langford

Washbeerhayes Farm

SIDMOUTH RD

Langford Court

Pottshayes Farm

COLLEGE LA

Callan's Close

Roach Farm

UNDERWOOD COTTS

Clyst Hydon Prim Sch

PARK CL

ONE FIR PH

THREE FIRS

Clyst Hydon

White Down Copse

Paradise Copse

Hoop Farm

Woodhayes

Yarde Farm

HOOP CROSS

Frogmore Farm

NEW RD

Higher Comberoy Farm

Upton Farm

Clyst St Lawrence

Scorlinch Farm

THREE ELMS CROSS

Ratclyffe

Side Downs

FORETOWN

Aunk

Snaffle Park Dr

Ashclyst Forest

CLAPONMILL CROSS

Clapp Mill Farm

Great Barton Farm

Scotch Fir Ave

Westwood

Philip's La

Rutton Farm

Westcott

Goulds Farm

STOOKE BRIDGE RD

Little Barton Farm

Hitt's Farm

Bogmoor La

RULL LA

Rull Farm

River Clyst

HAREPATHSTEAD RD

Ashclyst Farm

Farthings Farm

LAUNCESTON HEAD

SHUTTER WATER RD

Hackland Farm

Andrew's Farm

Clarke's Thorne

Wheatcroft Farm

FIVE CROSS WAY

Haywood Farm

Dungeons Farm

Higher Weaver

HIGHER WEAVER CROSS

WEAVER LA

Woodbeare

MOTT'S LA

Old Bridge Farm

OLD BRIDGE RD

LITTLE NORMANS

RUSPER CL

SAUNDERSFIELD

Sanguishayes Farm

WEAVER CROSS

Farthings Lodge Bsns Ctr

PENCEPOOL COTTS

PENCEPOOL

Norman's Green

HAYNE CROSS

Plymtree

Greenend

GREEN END LA

LYES ORCH

LEAR PK

PH

Plymtree Manor

Plymtree CE Prim Sch

Peradon Farm

Marsh Farm

MARSH CROSS

Farrantshayes Farm

EXETER RD

B3181

M5

River Culm

WINHAM LA

OLD HILL

HEN ST

PINE ST

PASSMORE ST

CRANSHAIES LA

BOWHILL

COLLOMPTON HILL

MILL WAY

KENSHAM AVE

CULVER

84

83 66

Scale: 1¾ inches to 1 mile

0   ¼   ½ mile
0 250m 500m 750m 1 km

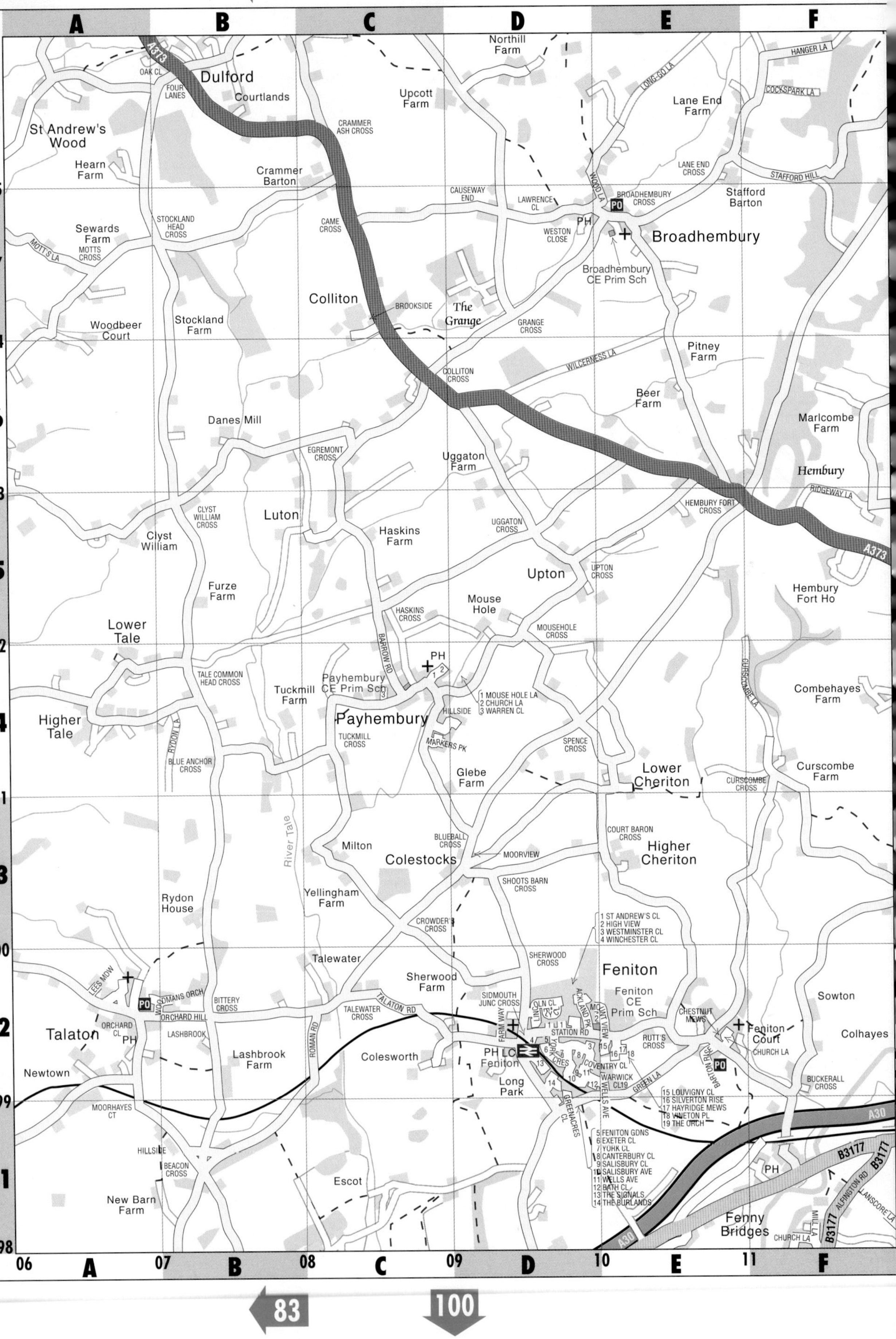

A B C D E F

8
St Andrew's Wood
Dulford
Courtlands
Hearn Farm
Crammer Barton
Crammer Ash Cross
Upcott Farm
Northill Farm
Lane End Farm
Hanger La
Cockspark La
Long Go La
Woodla

05
Sewards Farm
Stockland Head Cross
Came Cross
Causeway End
Lawrence Cl
Broadhembury Cross
Lane End Cross
Stafford Hill
Stafford Barton
Motts La
Motts Cross
Weston Close
PH
PO
Broadhembury

7
Woodbeer Court
Stockland Farm
Colliton
Brookside
The Grange
Grange Cross
Broadhembury CE Prim Sch
Pitney Farm
Marlcombe Farm

04
Colliton Cross
Wilcerness La
Beer Farm
Hembury

6
Danes Mill
Egremont Cross
Uggaton Farm
Hembury Fort Cross
Ridgeway La
A373

03
Clyst William Cross
Luton
Haskins Farm
Uggaton Cross
Upton
Upton Cross
Hembury Fort Ho

5
Clyst William
Furze Farm
Haskins Cross
Mouse Hole
Mousehole Cross

Lower Tale
Tale Common Head Cross
Tuckmill Farm
Payhembury CE Prim Sch
PH
1 Mouse Hole La
2 Church La
3 Warren Cl
Combehayes Farm
Chriscombe La

02
Higher Tale
Rydon La
Blue Anchor Cross
Payhembury
Hillside
Tuckmill Cross
Markers Pk
Spence Cross
Lower Cheriton
Curscombe Cross
Curscombe Farm

4
Glebe Farm
Court Baron Cross

01
Milton
Blueball Cross
Colestocks
Moorview
Higher Cheriton

3
Rydon House
Yellingham Farm
Shoots Barn Cross
Crowder Cross
1 St Andrew's Cl
2 High View
3 Westminster Cl
4 Winchester Cl

00
Talewater
Sherwood Cross
Sherwood Farm
Sidmouth Junc Cross
Feniton
Feniton CE Prim Sch
Chestnut Mews
Sowton
Lees Mdw
Womans Orch
Orchard Hill
Talaton Rd
Roman Rd
Talewater Cross
Station Rd
Farm Way
Feniton Court
Church La
Colhayes

2
Talaton
PO
Orchard Cl
PH
Lashbrook
Bittery Cross
Colesworth
PH
Feniton
Warwick Cl
Coventry Cl
Rutt's Cross
Buckerall Cross

Newtown
Lashbrook Farm
Long Park
15 Louvigny Cl
16 Silverton Rise
17 Hayridge Mews
18 Weston Pl
19 The Orch

99
Moorhayes Ct
Greenacres Cl
5 Feniton Gdns
6 Exeter Cl
7 York Cl
8 Canterbury Cl
9 Salisbury Cl
10 Salisbury Ave
11 Wells Ave
12 Bath Cl
13 The Signals
14 The Burlands
A30
B3117

1
Hillside
Beacon Cross
Escot
PH
Fenny Bridges
Alfington Rd
Llanscore La
Mill La
Church La

New Barn Farm

98
06 A 07 B 08 C 09 D 10 E 11 F

83 100

River Tale

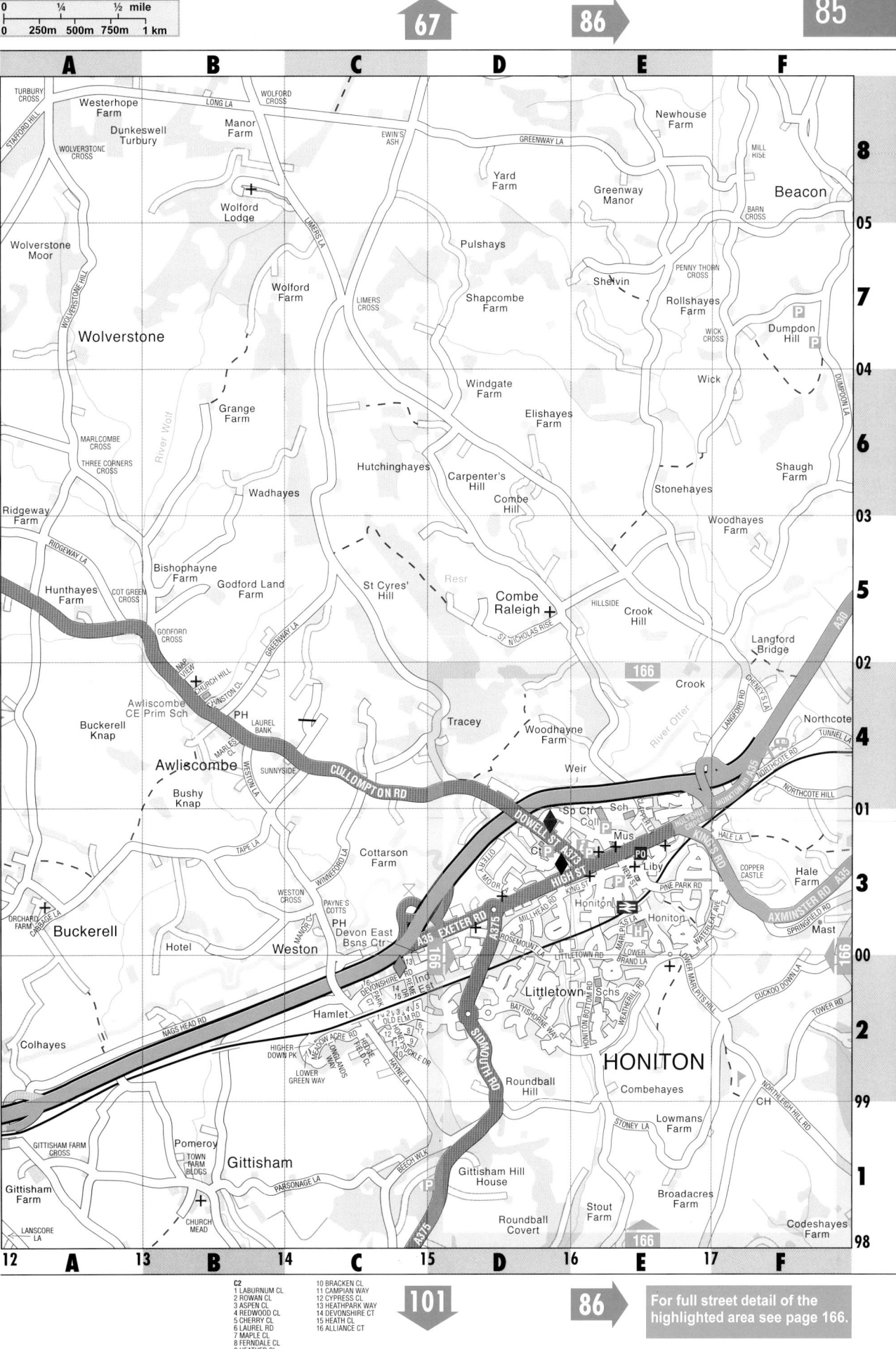
Scale: 1¾ inches to 1 mile
0 ¼ ½ mile
0 250m 500m 750m 1 km
67
86
A
B
C
D
E
F
TURBURY CROSS
STAFFORD HILL
Westerhope Farm
Dunkeswell Turbury
WOLVERSTONE CROSS
LONG LA
WOLFORD CROSS
Manor Farm
EWIN'S ASH
GREENWAY LA
Newhouse Farm
MILL RISE
Beacon
Yard Farm
Greenway Manor
Wolford Lodge
LIMERS LA
BARN CROSS
Wolverstone Moor
WOLVERSTONE HILL
Pulshays
PENNY THORN CROSS
Shelvin
Wolford Farm
LIMERS CROSS
Shapcombe Farm
Rollshayes Farm
Wolverstone
WICK CROSS
Dumpdon Hill
Wick
DUMPDON LA
Windgate Farm
Grange Farm
River Wolf
Elishayes Farm
MARLCOMBE CROSS
THREE CORNERS CROSS
Hutchinghayes
Carpenter's Hill
Shaugh Farm
Wadhayes
Combe Hill
Stonehayes
Ridgeway Farm
Woodhayes Farm
RIDGEWAY LA
Bishophayne Farm
Godford Land Farm
St Cyres' Hill
Resr
Hunthayes Farm
COT GREEN CROSS
Combe Raleigh
HILLSIDE
Crook Hill
GODFORD CROSS
GREENWAY LA
ST NICHOLAS RISE
Langford Bridge
A30
NAP VIEW
CHURCH HILL
JOHNSTON CL
166
Crook
CHENEY'S LA
Awliscombe CE Prim Sch
PH
LAUREL BANK
Buckerell Knap
Tracey
Woodhayne Farm
River Otter
LANGFORD RD
Northcote
TUNNEL LA
MARLES CL
NORTHCOTE RD
Awliscombe
WESTON LA
SUNNYSIDE
CULLOMPTON RD
Weir
Bushy Knap
NORTHCOTE HILL
MONKTON RD
A35
Sp Ctr
Sch
CLAPPER LA
Coll
DOWELL ST
A373
HOLYSHUTE CROSS
KING'S RD
HALE LA
TAPE LA
Cottarson Farm
WINNEFORD LA
Ct
Mus
PO
Liby
NEW ST
OTTERY MOOR
HIGH ST
COPPER CASTLE
Hale Farm
PINE PARK RD
KING ST
WESTON CROSS
PAYNE'S COTTS
MILL HEAD RD
Honiton
AXMINSTER RD
ORCHARD FARM
CABBAGE LA
Buckerell
MANOR CL
PH
Devon East Bsns Ctr
EXETER RD
A375
MARLPITS LA
WATERLEAT AVE
SPRINGFIELD RD
Mast
Hotel
Weston
ROSEMOUNT LA
LITTLETOWN RD
LOWER BRAND LA
DEVONSHIRE RD
PARK CT
FERNE DR
Ind Est
Littletown
HONITON BOTTOM RD
Schs
WEATHERILL RD
LOWER MARLPITS HILL
CUCKOO DOWN LA
TOWER RD
Hamlet
OLD ELM RD
BATTISHORNE WAY
NAGS HEAD RD
MEADOW ACRE RD
HIGHER DOWN PK
LONGLANDS WAY
HEDGE FIELD CL
HONEYSUCKLE DR
SIDMOUTH RD
Colhayes
LOWER GREEN WAY
HAYNE LA
HONITON
Roundball Hill
Combehayes
NORTHLEIGH HILL RD
CH
STONEY LA
Lowmans Farm
GITTISHAM FARM CROSS
Pomeroy
TOWN FARM BLDGS
Gittisham
BEECH WLK
Gittisham Hill House
Gittisham Farm
PARSONAGE LA
Broadacres Farm
LANSCORE LA
CHURCH MEAD
Roundball Covert
Stout Farm
Codeshayes Farm
8
05
7
04
6
03
5
02
4
01
3
00
2
99
1
98
12
13
14
15
16
17
C2
1 LABURNUM CL
2 ROWAN CL
3 ASPEN CL
4 REDWOOD CL
5 CHERRY CL
6 LAUREL RD
7 MAPLE CL
8 FERNDALE CL
9 HEATHER CL
10 BRACKEN CL
11 CAMPIAN WAY
12 CYPRESS CL
13 HEATHPARK WAY
14 DEVONSHIRE CT
15 HEATH CL
16 ALLIANCE CT
101
86
For full street detail of the highlighted area see page 166.

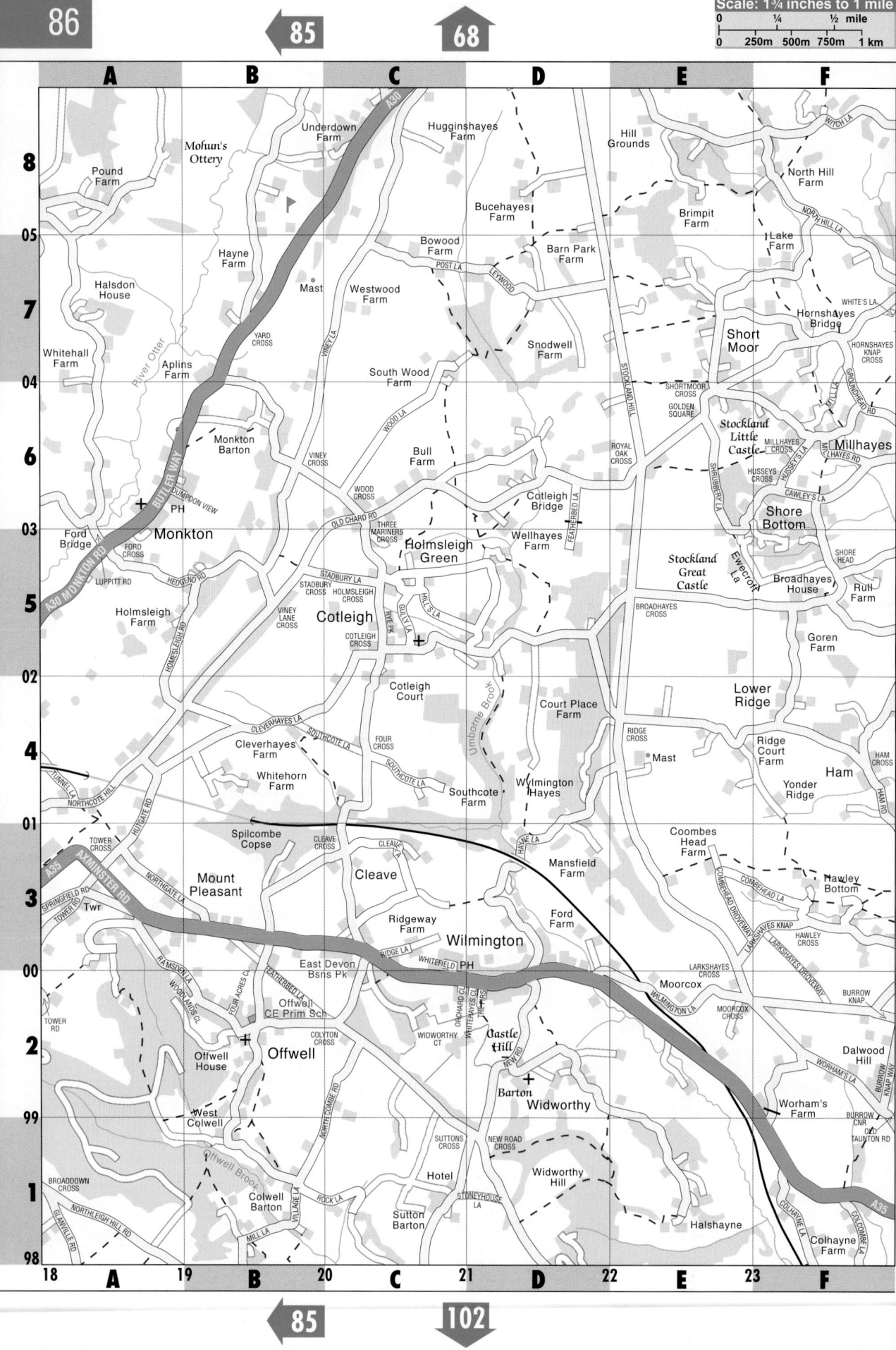

Scale: 1¾ inches to 1 mile

0   ¼   ½   mile

0   250m   500m   750m   1 km

A   B   C   D   E   F

Pound Farm

Mohun's Ottery

Underdown Farm

Hugginshayes Farm

Hill Grounds

North Hill Farm

Halsdon House

Hayne Farm

Mast

Westwood Farm

Bowood Farm

POST LA

Barn Park Farm

LEYWOOD

Brimpit Farm

Lake Farm

WITCH LA

NORTH HILL LA

Whitehall Farm

River Otter

Aplins Farm

YARD CROSS

VINEY LA

South Wood Farm

Snodwell Farm

STOCKLAND HILL

WHITE'S LA

Short Moor

Hornshayes Bridge

HORNSHAYES KNAP CROSS

Monkton Barton

VINEY CROSS

WOOD LA

Bull Farm

ROYAL OAK CROSS

SHORTMOOR CROSS

GOLDEN SQUARE

Stockland Little Castle

MILLHAYES CROSS

GROUNDHEAD RD

MILLHAYES RD

Millhayes

BUTLER WAY

DUMPDON VIEW

PH

WOOD CROSS

OLD CHARD RD

THREE MARINERS CROSS

Holmsleigh Green

Wellhayes Farm

FEATHERBED LA

Cotleigh Bridge

SHRUBBERY LA

HUSSEYS CROSS

HUSSEY'S LA

CAWLEY'S LA

Shore Bottom

SHORE HEAD

Ford Bridge

A30 MONKTON RD

Monkton

FORD CROSS

LUPPITT RD

HEDGEND RD

STADBURY LA

STADBURY CROSS

HOLMSLEIGH CROSS

VINEY LANE CROSS

Cotleigh

HILL'S LA

PYE PK

GULLY LA

Stockland Great Castle

BROADHAYES CROSS

Ewecroft

Broadhayes House

Rull Farm

HOLMSLEIGH RD

Holmsleigh Farm

COTLEIGH CROSS

Cotleigh Court

Umborne Brook

Court Place Farm

Goren Farm

CLEVERHAYES LA

SOUTHCOTE LA

FOUR CROSS

RIDGE CROSS

Lower Ridge

Ridge Court Farm

HAM CROSS

A35 AXMINSTER RD

TUNNEL LA

NORTHCOTE HILL

Cleverhayes Farm

Whitehorn Farm

SOUTHCOTE LA

Southcote Farm

Wylmington Hayes

Mast

Ham

HAM RD

Yonder Ridge

TOWER CROSS

Spilcombe Copse

CLEAVE CROSS

CLEAVE

HAYNE LA

Mansfield Farm

Coombes Head Farm

COMBEHEAD DROVEWAY

COMBEHEAD LA

Hawley Bottom

SPRINGFIELD RD

NORTHGATE LA

HUTGATE RD

Mount Pleasant

Cleave

Ridgeway Farm

RIDGE LA

Wilmington

Ford Farm

WHITEFIELD PH

LARKSHAYES KNAP

LARKSHAYES DROVEWAY

Hawley Cross

Twr

TOWER RD

RAMSDEN LA

WOODLANDS CL

FOUR ACRES CL

FEATHERBED LA

East Devon Bsns Pk

ORCHARD CL

WHITEHAYES CL

NEW RD

Moorcox

WALMINGTON LA

LARKSHAYES CROSS

MOORCOX CROSS

BURROW KNAP

TOWER RD

Offwell House

Offwell CE Prim Sch

COLYTON CROSS

WIDWORTHY CT

Castle Hill

Dalwood Hill

WORHAM'S LA

BURROW KNAP WAY

Offwell

NORTH COMBE RD

Barton

Widworthy

Worham's Farm

BURROW CNR

OLD TAUNTON RD

West Colwell

VILLAGE LA

ROCK LA

Widworthy Hill

A35

COLHAYNE LA

COLCOMBE LA

BROADDOWN CROSS

Offwell Brook

Colwell Barton

MILL LA

SUTTONS CROSS

Hotel

NEW ROAD CROSS

STONEYHOUSE LA

Halshayne

Colhayne Farm

NORTHLEIGH HILL RD

GLANVILLE RD

Sutton Barton

A   B   C   D   E   F

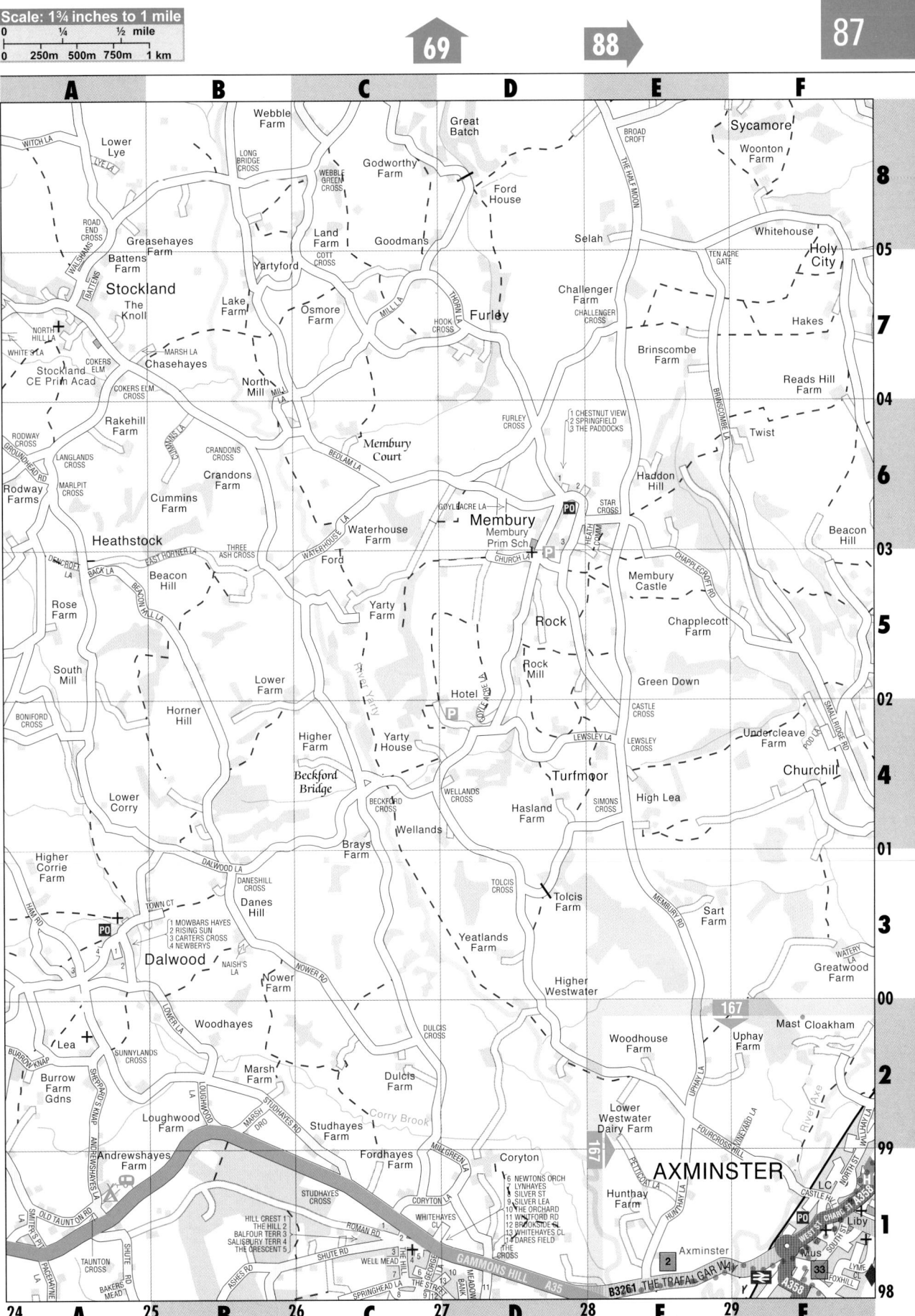

69

88

A   B   C   D   E   F

8

Webble Farm

Sycamore

Woonton Farm

Broad Croft

Lower Lye

WITCH LA
LYE LA

Godworthy Farm

Great Batch

THE HALF MOON

Whitehouse

05

ROAD END CROSS

Greasehayes Farm

Land Farm

Ford House

Selah

Holy City

WALSHAMS
NORTH HILL LA
WHITE ST LA
BATTENS

Battens Farm

Yartyford

Goodmans

TEN ACRE GATE

7

Stockland

The Knoll

Lake Farm

Osmore Farm

COTT CROSS
MILL LA

Furley

Challenger Farm

Brinscombe Farm

Hakes

COKERS ELM

Chasehayes

North Mill

HOOK CROSS
THORN LA

CHALLENGER CROSS

Reads Hill Farm

04

Stockland CE Prim Acad

COKERS ELM CROSS

MARSH LA

MILL LA

BRINSCOMBE LA

Twist

6

Rakehill Farm

CUMMINS LA

Crandons Cross

Membury Court

BEDLAM LA

FURLEY CROSS

1 CHESTNUT VIEW
2 SPRINGFIELD
3 THE PADDOCKS

Haddon Hill

RODWAY CROSS
GROUNDHEAD RD
LANGLANDS CROSS

Crandons Farm

WATERHOUSE LA

STAR CROSS

Beacon Hill

Rodway Farms

MARLPIT CROSS

Cummins Farm

Waterhouse Farm

GOYLEACRE LA

PO

Membury

HEATH SQUM

Membury Castle

03

Heathstock

THREE ASH CROSS

Ford

CHURCH LA

Membury Prim Sch

P

CHAPPLECROFT RD

5

DENCROFT LA
BACK LA
EAST HORNER LA

Beacon Hill

Yarty Farm

Rock

Chapplecott Farm

Rose Farm

BEACON HILL LA

GOYLE TREE LA

Rock Mill

Green Down

02

South Mill

Horner Hill

Lower Farm

Higher Farm

Hotel

P

LEWSLEY LA

CASTLE CROSS

LEWSLEY CROSS

Undercleave Farm

POD LA
SMALLRIDGE RD

Churchill

4

BONIFORD CROSS

RIVER YARTY

Yarty House

Beckford Bridge

BECKFORD CROSS

WELLANDS CROSS

Turfmoor

High Lea

SIMONS CROSS

01

Lower Corry

DALWOOD LA

Brays Farm

Wellands

Hasland Farm

DANESHILL CROSS

MEMBURY RD

Sart Farm

3

Higher Corrie Farm

PO

Danes Hill

1 MOWBARS HAYES
2 RISING SUN
3 CARTERS CROSS
4 NEWBERYS

NOWER RD

Yeatlands Farm

TOLCIS CROSS

Tolcis Farm

WATERY LA

Greatwood Farm

HAM RD

TOWN CT

Dalwood

NAISH'S LA

Nower Farm

Higher Westwater

00

Lea

Woodhayes

SUNNYLANDS CROSS

LOWER LA

DULCIS CROSS

167

Woodhouse Farm

Mast Cloakham

Uphay Farm

River Axe

2

BURROW KNAP

SHEPARD'S KNAP

Burrow Farm Gdns

Marsh Farm

Dulcis Farm

UPHAY LA

Lower Westwater Dairy Farm

167

99

Loughwood Farm

LOUGHWOOD
MARSH DRO
STUDHAYES RD

Studhayes Farm

Corry Brook

MILL GREEN LA

Coryton

167

PETTICOAT LA

FOURCROSSHILL
VINEYARD LA

AXMINSTER

CASTLE HILL
NORTH ST
WILLHAY LA

LC

Liby

ANDREWSHAYES LA

Andrewshayes Farm

STUDHAYES CROSS

Fordhayes Farm

CORYTON LA

WHITEHAYES CL

6 NEWTONS ORCH
7 LYNHAYES
8 SILVER ST
9 SILVER LEA
10 THE ORCHARD
11 WHITFORD RD
12 BROOKSIDE SL
13 WHITEHAYES CL
14 OARES FIELD

Hunthay Farm

Axminster

2

PO

WEST ST
SOUTH ST
CHARD ST
A358

Mus

33

LYME CL
FOXHILL

1

OLD TAUNTON RD
SMITHS PL
PACKENAYNE

TAUNTON CROSS

SHUTE RD
ASHES RD
BAKERS MEAD

HILL CREST 1
THE HILL 2
BALFOUR TERR 3
SALISBURY TERR 4
THE CRESCENT 5

ROMAN RD

WHITEHAYES CL

STUDHAYES CROSS

SHUTE RD

WELL MEAD

SPRINGHEAD LA

THE HILL

GEORGE
MEADOW BANK

THE STREET

GAMMONS HILL

A35

B3261 THE TRAFALGAR WAY

A358

98

24   A   25   B   26   C   27   D   28   E   29   F

103

88

For full street detail of the highlighted area see page 167.

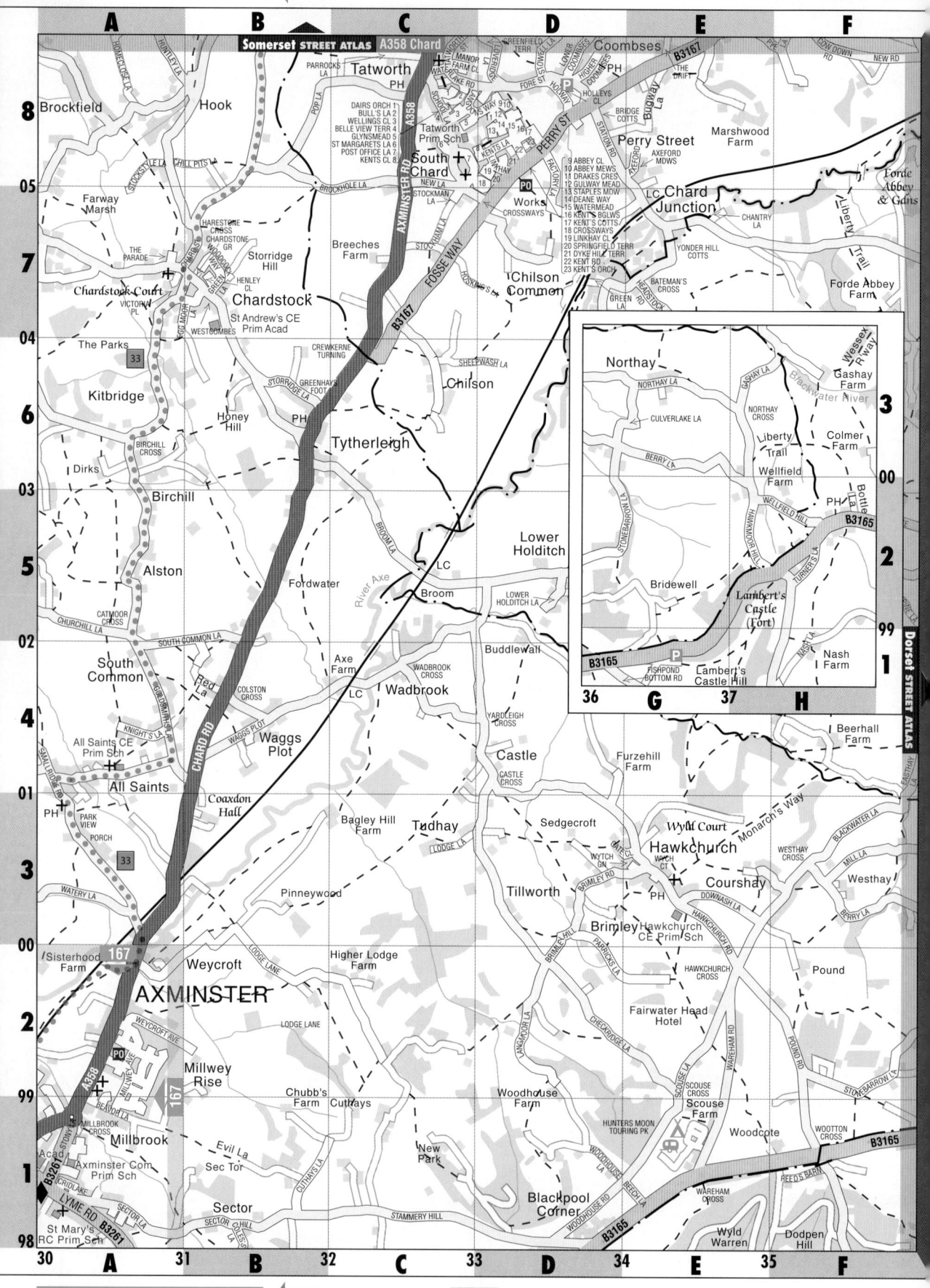

87

Scale: 1¾ inches to 1 mile

0   ¼   ½   mile
0 250m 500m 750m 1 km

Somerset STREET ATLAS A358 Chard

Dorset STREET ATLAS

87

104

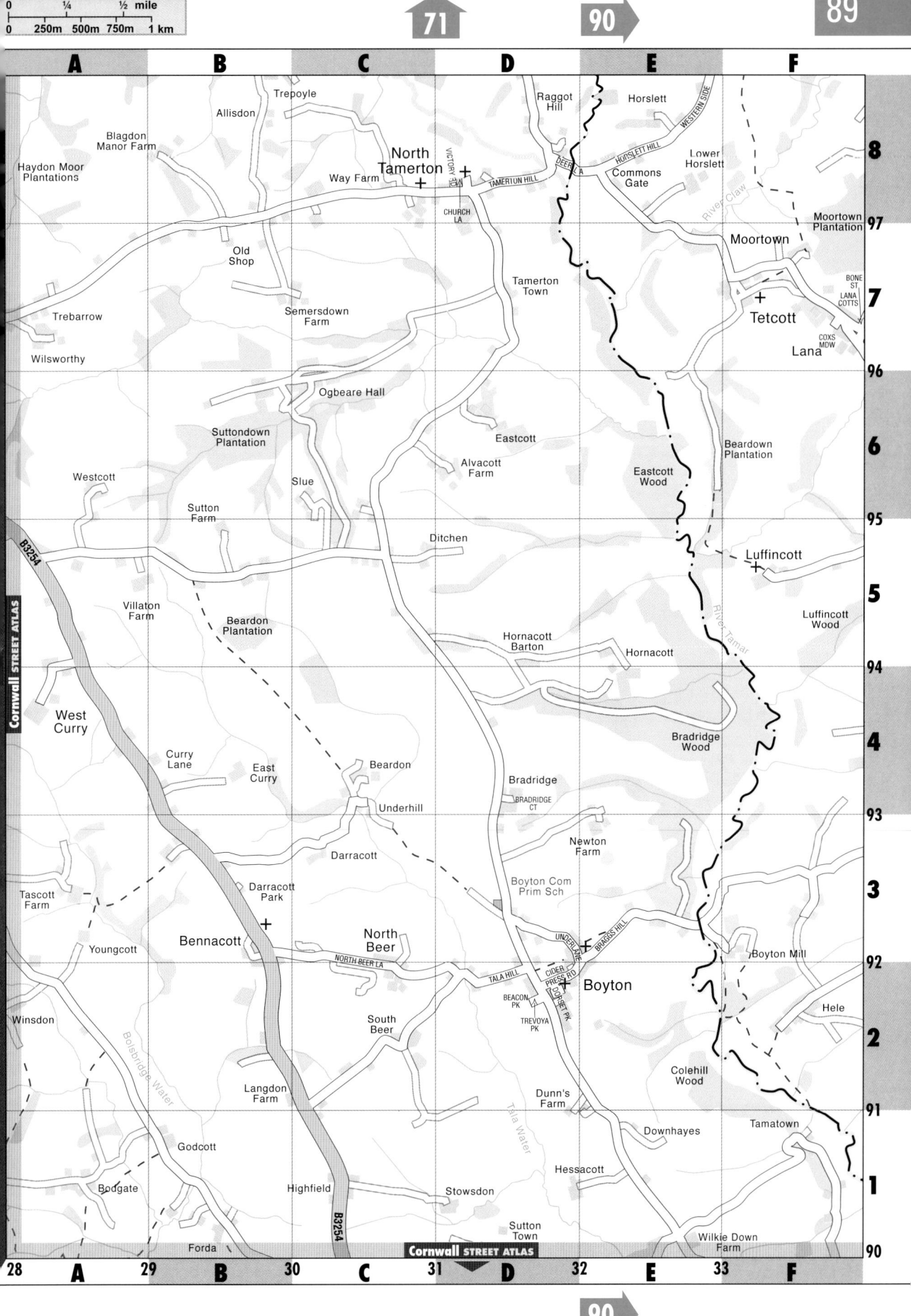
Trepoyle
Allisdon
Raggot Hill
Horslett
Blagdon Manor Farm
Haydon Moor Plantations
North Tamerton
Way Farm
VICTORY RD
CHURCH LA
TAMERTON HILL
DEER LA
HORSLETT HILL
WESTERN SIDE
Lower Horslett
Commons Gate
River Claw
Moortown Plantation
Moortown
Old Shop
Tamerton Town
BONE ST
LANA COTTS
Tetcott
Trebarrow
Semersdown Farm
COXS MDW
Lana
Wilsworthy
Ogbeare Hall
Suttondown Plantation
Eastcott
Alvacott Farm
Beardown Plantation
Eastcott Wood
Westcott
Slue
Sutton Farm
Ditchen
Luffincott
B3254
Villaton Farm
Beardon Plantation
Luffincott Wood
Hornacott Barton
Hornacott
River Tamar
West Curry
Bradridge Wood
Curry Lane
East Curry
Beardon
Bradridge
BRADRIDGE CT
Underhill
Newton Farm
Darracott
Tascott Farm
Darracott Park
Boyton Com Prim Sch
Bennacott
North Beer
UNDERLANE
BRAGGS HILL
Youngcott
NORTH BEER LA
TALA HILL
CIDER PRESS RD
Boyton
Boyton Mill
BEACON PK
DORSET PK
TREVOYA PK
Winsdon
Bolsbridge Water
South Beer
Hele
Colehill Wood
Langdon Farm
Dunn's Farm
Tala Water
Downhayes
Tamatown
Godcott
Hessacott
Bodgate
Highfield
Stowsdon
Sutton Town
Wilkie Down Farm
Forda
Cornwall STREET ATLAS

Scale: 1¾ inches to 1 mile

0   ¼   ½   mile

0   250m   500m   750m   1 km

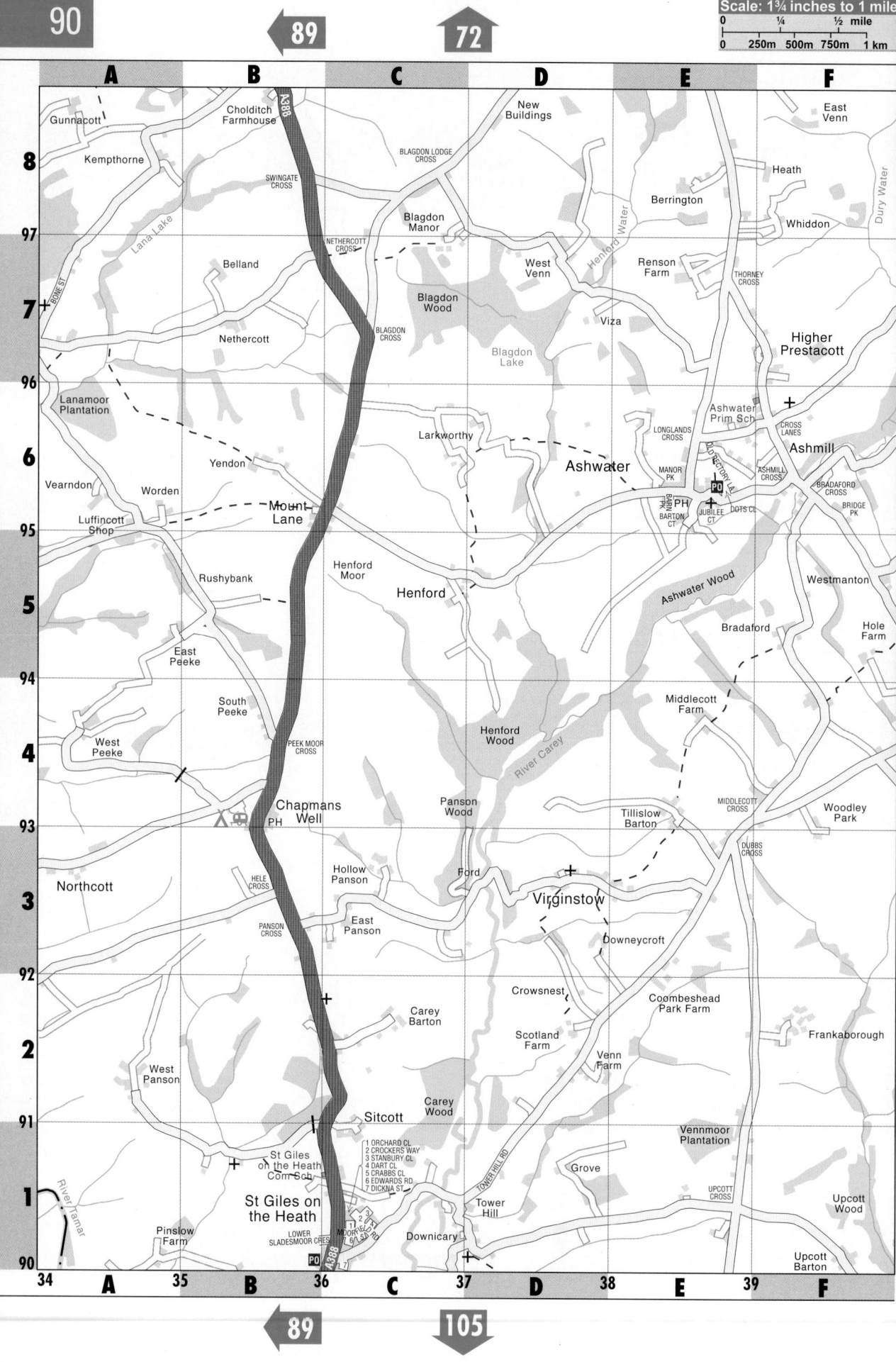

A   B   C   D   E   F

8

97

7

96

6

95

5

94

4

93

3

92

2

91

1

90

34   A   35   B   36   C   37   D   38   E   39   F

Gunnacott
Kempthorne
Choldith Farmhouse
SWINGATE CROSS
Blagdon Manor
New Buildings
BLAGDON LODGE CROSS
East Venn
Heath
Whiddon
Dury Water
NETHERCOTT CROSS
Belland
Blagdon Wood
West Venn
Berrington
Renson Farm
THORNEY CROSS
BONE ST
Nethercott
BLAGDON CROSS
Blagdon Lake
Viza
Higher Prestacott
Lanamoor Plantation
Larkworthy
Ashwater
Ashwater Prim Sch
CROSS LANES
Yendon
LONGLANDS CROSS
MANOR PK
ASHMILL CROSS
Ashmill
Vearndon
Worden
Mount Lane
BARTON PK
PH
BARTON CT
PO
JUBILEE CT
DOTS CL
BRADAFORD CROSS
BRIDGE PK
Luffincott Shop
Henford Moor
PH
Rushybank
Henford
Ashwater Wood
Westmanton
East Peeke
South Peeke
Bradaford
Hole Farm
PEEK MOOR CROSS
Henford Wood
Middlecott Farm
West Peeke
River Carey
MIDDLECOTT CROSS
Woodley Park
Chapmans Well
PH
Panson Wood
Tillislow Barton
DUBBS CROSS
Northcott
HELE CROSS
Hollow Panson
Ford
Virginstow
PANSON CROSS
East Panson
Downeycroft
Carey Barton
Crowsnest
Coombeshead Park Farm
Frankaborough
West Panson
Scotland Farm
Venn Farm
Carey Wood
Vennmoor Plantation
Sitcott
1 ORCHARD CL
2 CROCKERS WAY
3 STANBURY CL
4 DART CL
5 CRABBS CL
6 EDWARDS RD
7 DICKNA ST
Grove
UPCOTT CROSS
Upcott Wood
St Giles on the Heath Com Sch
River Tamar
St Giles on the Heath
LOWER SLADESMOOR CRES
MOORFIELD
Downicary
TOWER HILL RD
Tower Hill
Upcott Barton
Pinslow Farm
PO
A388

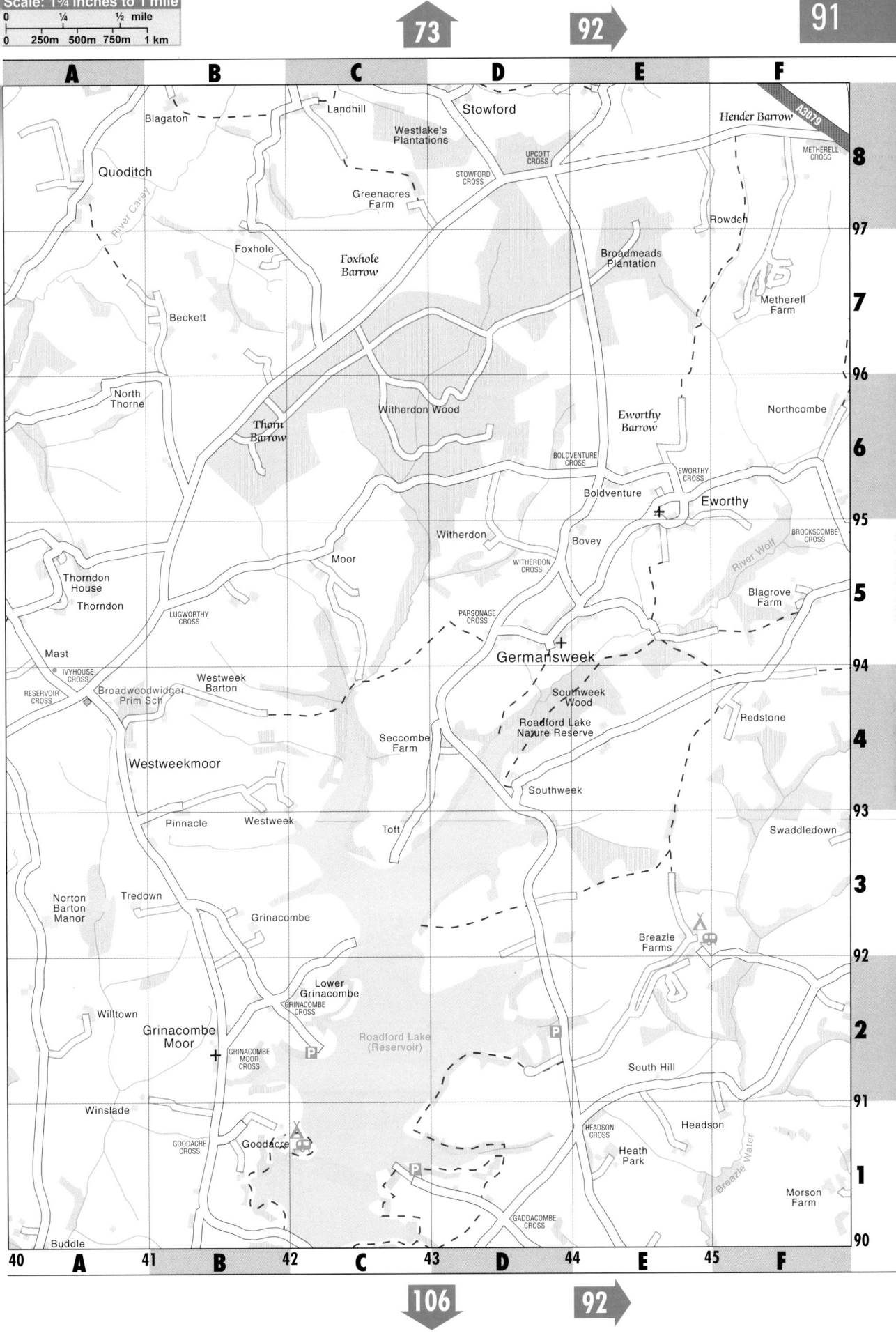

Scale: 1¾ inches to 1 mile

0   ¼   ½ mile
0 250m 500m 750m 1 km

Quoditch

Blagaton

Landhill

Westlake's
Plantations

Stowford

Hender Barrow

METHERELL
CROSS

River Carey

Foxhole

Greenacres
Farm

UPCOTT
CROSS

STOWFORD
CROSS

Rowden

97

North
Thorne

Beckett

Foxhole
Barrow

Broadmeads
Plantation

Metherell
Farm

7

96

Thorn
Barrow

Witherdon Wood

Eworthy
Barrow

Northcombe

6

Thorndon
House

Thorndon

Moor

Witherdon

BOLDVENTURE
CROSS

Boldventure

Bovey

Eworthy
EWORTHY
CROSS

Eworthy

95

River Wolf

BROCKSCOMBE
CROSS

Mast

IVYHOUSE
CROSS

LUGWORTHY
CROSS

WITHERDON
CROSS

Blagrove
Farm

5

RESERVOIR
CROSS

Broadwoodwidger
Prim Sch

Westweek
Barton

PARSONAGE
CROSS

Germansweek

Southweek
Wood

94

Redstone

Westweekmoor

Seccombe
Farm

Roadford Lake
Nature Reserve

4

Pinnacle

Westweek

Southweek

93

Swaddledown

Tredown

Toft

Norton
Barton
Manor

Grinacombe

Breazle
Farms

3

92

Willtown

Lower
Grinacombe

GRINACOMBE
CROSS

Roadford Lake
(Reservoir)

South Hill

2

Grinacombe
Moor

GRINACOMBE
MOOR
CROSS

Headson

Winslade

GOODACRE
CROSS

Goodacre

HEADSON
CROSS

Heath
Park

Breazle Water

91

Morson
Farm

1

Buddle

GADDACOMBE
CROSS

90

A   B   C   D   E   F

40   41   42   43   44   45

A   B   C   D   E   F

A3079

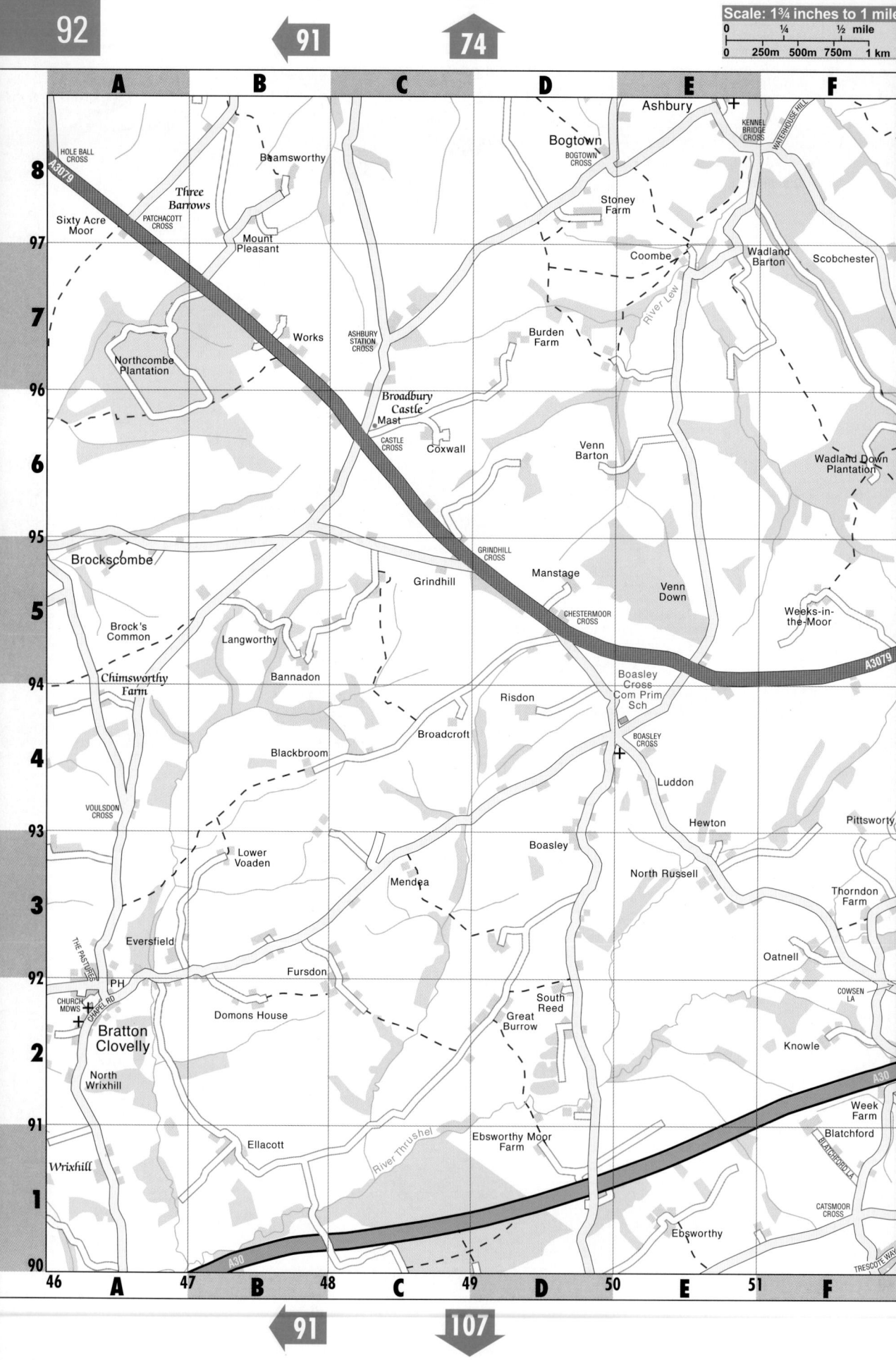

Scale: 1¾ inches to 1 mile

0 ¼ ½ mile
0 250m 500m 750m 1 km

A B C D E F

Ashbury

Bogtown

Bogtown Cross

Kennel Bridge Cross

Waterhouse Hill

8 A3079
Hole Ball Cross

Beamsworthy

Three Barrows

Patchacott Cross

Mount Pleasant

Stoney Farm

Coombe

Wadland Barton

Scobchester

97 Sixty Acre Moor

7 Northcombe Plantation

Works

Ashbury Station Cross

Burden Farm

River Lew

96 Broadbury Castle
Mast

Castle Cross

Coxwall

Venn Barton

Wadland Down Plantation

6

Grindhill Cross

Manstage

Venn Down

Weeks-in-the-Moor

95 Brockscombe

Grindhill

Chestermoor Cross

5 Brock's Common

Langworthy

Bannadon

A3079

Boasley Cross Com Prim Sch

94 Chimsworthy Farm

Risdon

Boasley Cross

Broadcroft

Luddon

4 Blackbroom

Hewton

Pittsworthy

Voulsdon Cross

Boasley

North Russell

Thorndon Farm

93

3 Lower Voaden

Mendea

Oatnell

Cowsen La

Eversfield

Fursdon

South Reed

Knowle

92 The Pastures

PH

Church Mdws

Chapel Rd

Domons House

Great Burrow

2 Bratton Clovelly

North Wrixhill

A30

Week Farm

Blatchford

Blatchford La

91 Wrixhill

Ellacott

River Thrushel

Ebsworthy Moor Farm

Catsmoor Cross

1 Ebsworthy

Trescote Way

90
46 A 47 B 48 C 49 D 50 E 51 F

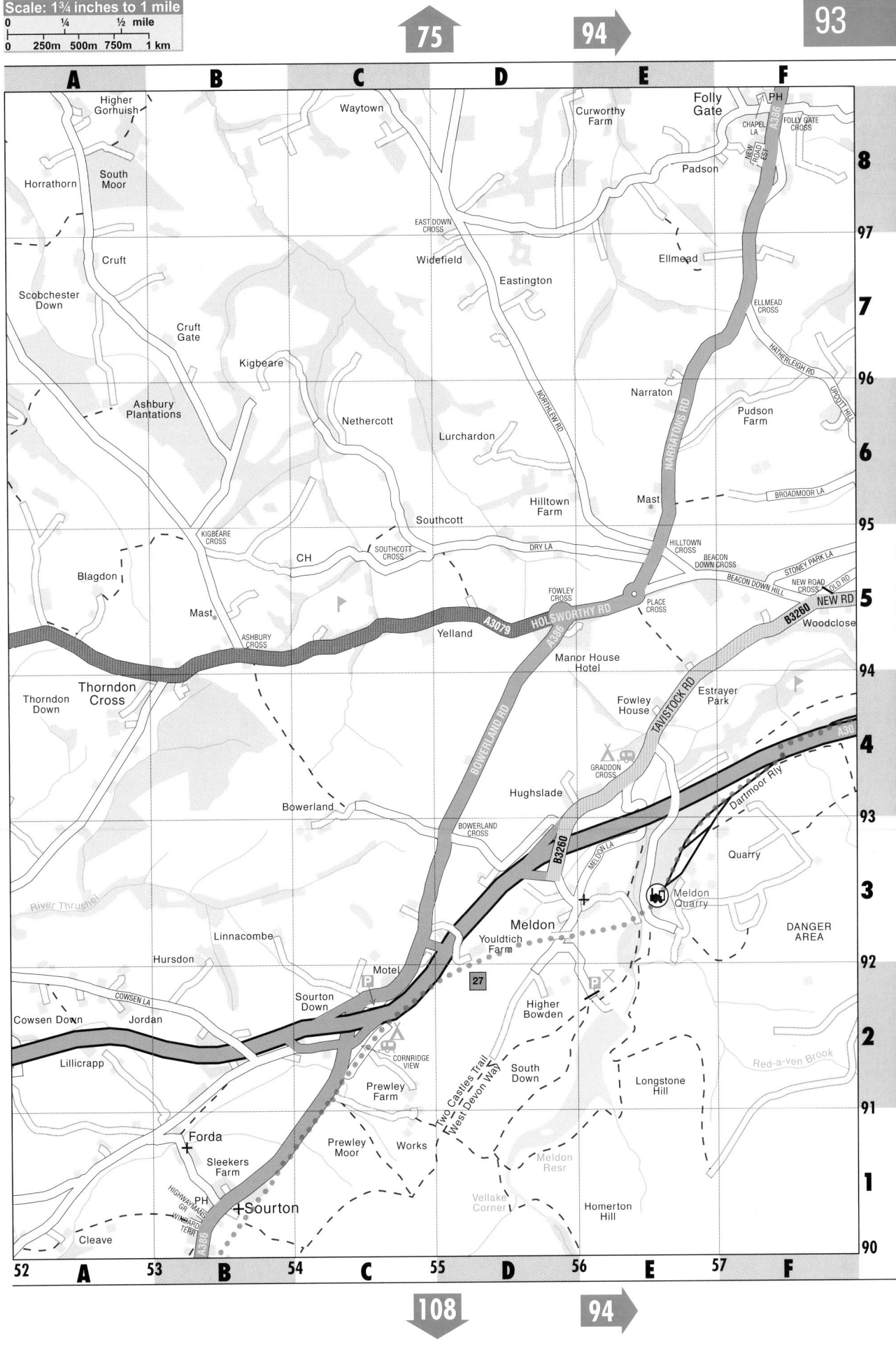

Scale: 1¾ inches to 1 mile

0   ¼   ½   mile

0   250m   500m   750m   1 km

75   94

8

97

7

96

6

95

5

94

4

93

3

92

2

91

1

90

A   B   C   D   E   F

Higher Gorhuish

South Moor

Horrathorn

Cruft

Scobchester Down

Cruft Gate

Kigbeare

Ashbury Plantations

Nethercott

Waytown

Widefield

Eastington

Lurchardon

Hilltown Farm

Southcott

Kigbeare Cross

Blagdon

CH

SOUTHCOTT CROSS

Mast

DRY LA

FOWLEY CROSS

PLACE CROSS

Yelland

A3079   HOLSWORTHY RD

A386

BOWERLAND RD

Thorndon Cross

Thorndon Down

Bowerland

BOWERLAND CROSS

Manor House Hotel

Fowley House

Hughslade

GRADDON CROSS

Curworthy Farm

Folly Gate

PH

CHAPEL LA

NEW ROAD ESTD   A386

FOLLY GATE CROSS

Padson

Ellmead

ELLMEAD CROSS

HATHERLEIGH RD

UPCOTT HILL

Narraton

Pudson Farm

BROADMOOR LA

Mast

Hilltown Cross

BEACON DOWN CROSS

STONEY PARK LA

NEW ROAD CROSS

OLD RD

BEACON DOWN HILL

NEW RD

B3260   Woodclose

Estrayer Park

NARRATONS RD

TAVISTOCK RD

A30

Dartmoor Rly

Quarry

Meldon Quarry

DANGER AREA

B3260

MELDON LA

Meldon

Youldtich Farm

Linnacombe

Hursdon

Motel

Sourton Down

Cowsen Down

COWSEN LA

Jordan

Lillicrapp

River Thrushel

27

CORNRIDGE VIEW

Prewley Farm

Prewley Moor

Works

Two Castles Trail   West Devon Way

Higher Bowden

South Down

Longstone Hill

Red-a-ven Brook

Meldon Resr

Vellake Corner

Homerton Hill

Forda

Sleekers Farm

PH

HIGHWAYMANS GR

WINGARD TERR

A386

Sourton

Cleave

52   A   53   B   54   C   55   D   56   E   57   F

Scale: 1¾ inches to 1 mile

0   ¼   ½   mile
0   250m   500m   750m   1 km

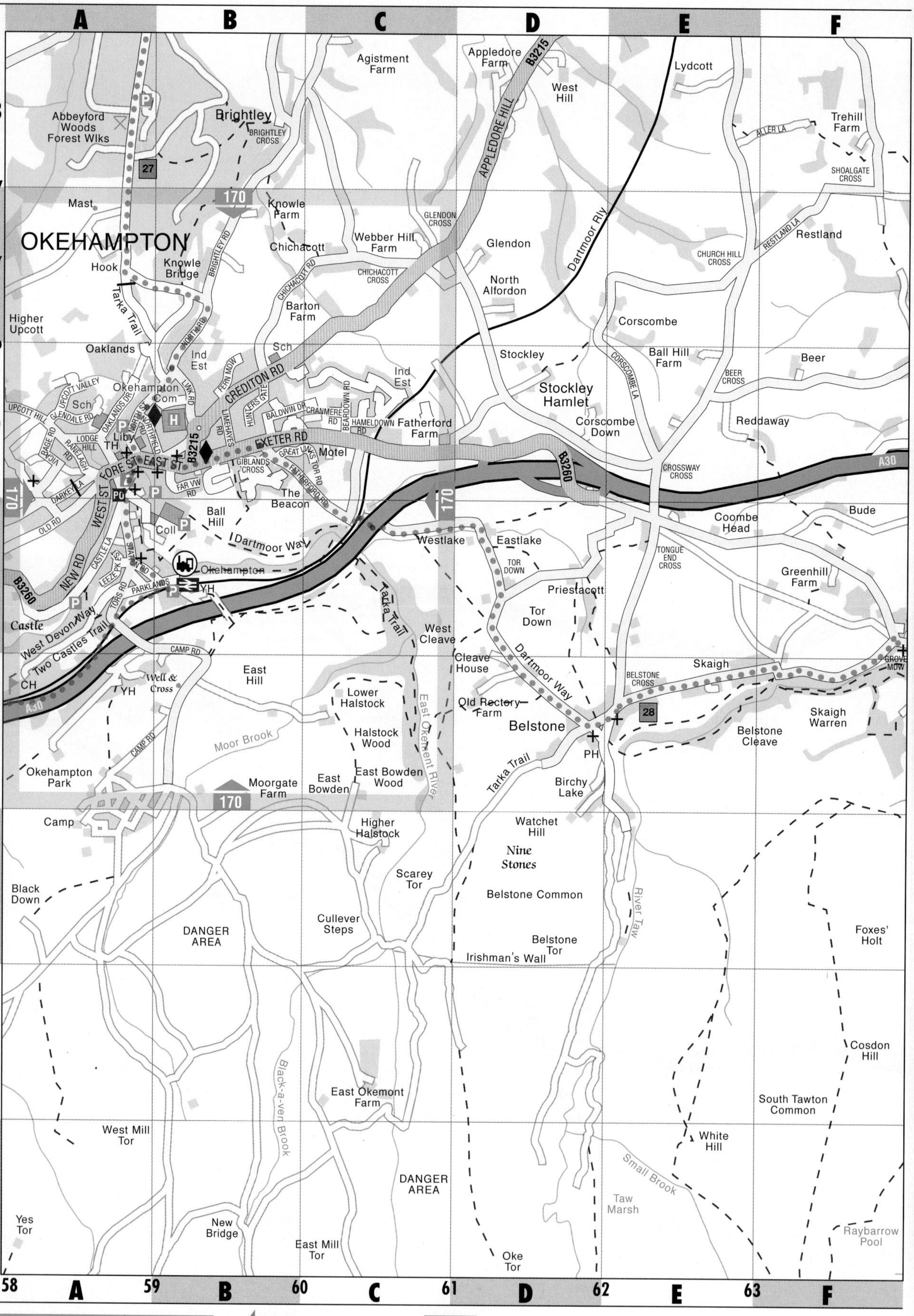

A   B   C   D   E   F

8

Abbeyford Woods Forest Wlks

Brightley

BRIGHTLEY CROSS

Agistment Farm

Appledore Farm

West Hill

Lydcott

Trehill Farm

ALLER LA

SHOALGATE CROSS

27

97

170

Mast

Knowle Farm

Chichacott

Webber Hill Farm

GLENDON CROSS

Glendon

CHURCH HILL CROSS

RESTLAND LA

Restland

7

OKEHAMPTON

Hook

Knowle Bridge

CHICHACOTT RD

CHICHACOTT CROSS

North Alfordon

Corscombe

Beer

BEER CROSS

Tarka Trail

Barton Farm

Sch

Ind Est

Stockley

Ball Hill Farm

CORSCOMBE LA

96

Higher Upcott

Oaklands

Ind Est

Stockley Hamlet

Corscombe Down

Reddaway

UPCOTT HILL

Sch

Okehampton Com

CREDITON RD

FERN MDW

BALDWIN DR

CRANMERE RD

HAMELDOWN RD

Fatherford Farm

B3260

CROSSWAY CROSS

A30

6

UPCOTT VALLEY

GLENDALE RD

LODGE HILL

EAGLE RD

RANDELL

TH

Liby

H

OAKLANDS DR

BRIGHTLEY RD

MILL RD

EAST ST

B3215

EXETER RD

HIGH ST

KERSLAKE

GREAT LINKS TOR RD

GIBLANDS CROSS

FATHERFORD RD

Motel

TONGUE END CROSS

Coombe Head

Bude

95

170

B3260

NEW RD

WEST ST

FORE ST

PO

DARKEY LA

CASTLE LA

LEET RD

FAR VW RD

Ball Hill

The Beacon

Coll

Dartmoor Way

Westlake

Eastlake

TOR DOWN

Priestacott

Tor Down

BELSTONE CROSS

Skaigh

Greenhill Farm

GROVE MDW

5

Castle

West Devon Way

Two Castles Trail

CH

A30

Okehampton

YH

Tarka Trail

West Cleave

Cleave House

Dartmoor Way

94

CAMP RD

East Hill

Lower Halstock

Halstock Wood

Old Rectory Farm

Belstone

PH

28

Belstone Cleave

Skaigh Warren

93

Okehampton Park

Camp

170

Moorgate Farm

East Bowden

East Bowden Wood

Higher Halstock

Watchet Hill

Nine Stones

Birchy Lake

Moor Brook

River Taw

Black Down

Black-a-ven Brook

Scarey Tor

Belstone Common

Foxes' Holt

3

DANGER AREA

Cullever Steps

Belstone Tor

Irishman's Wall

East Okemont River

Cosdon Hill

2

West Mill Tor

East Okemont Farm

White Hill

South Tawton Common

91

Small Brook

Yes Tor

New Bridge

East Mill Tor

DANGER AREA

Oke Tor

Taw Marsh

Raybarrow Pool

90

58   A   59   B   60   C   61   D   62   E   63   F

For full street detail of the highlighted area see page 170.

93

109

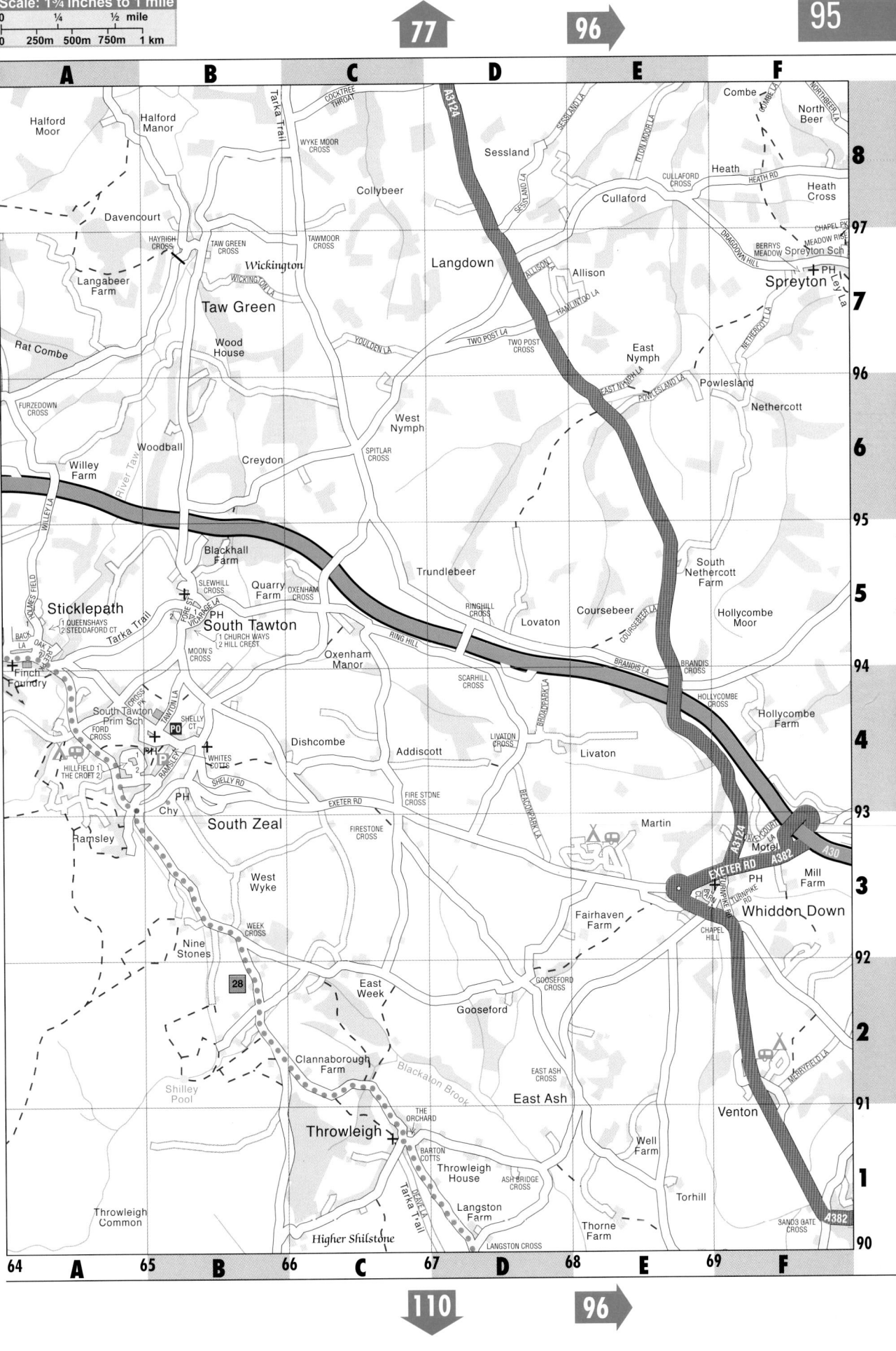
Scale: 1¾ inches to 1 mile
77
96
A B C D E F
Halford Moor
Halford Manor
Davencourt
Langabeer Farm
Taw Green
Wickington
Wood House
Rat Combe
Collybeer
Sessland
Cullaford
Heath
Heath Cross
Combe
North Beer
Langdown
Allison
Spreyton
Spreyton Sch
East Nymph
Powlesland
Nethercott
West Nymph
Woodball
Willey Farm
Creydon
Blackhall Farm
Quarry Farm
Sticklepath
South Tawton
Trundlebeer
Lovaton
Coursebeer
South Nethercott Farm
Hollycombe Moor
Oxenham Manor
Finch Foundry
South Tawton Prim Sch
Dishcombe
Addiscott
Livaton
Hollycombe Farm
South Zeal
Ramsley
Martin
Motel
Mill Farm
Whiddon Down
West Wyke
Fairhaven Farm
Nine Stones
East Week
Gooseford
Clannaborough Farm
Shilley Pool
Throwleigh
East Ash
Venton
Well Farm
Throwleigh House
Langston Farm
Torhill
Thorne Farm
Throwleigh Common
Higher Shilstone
Tarka Trail
A3124
A30
A382
110
96

95
78

Scale: 1¾ inches to 1 mile

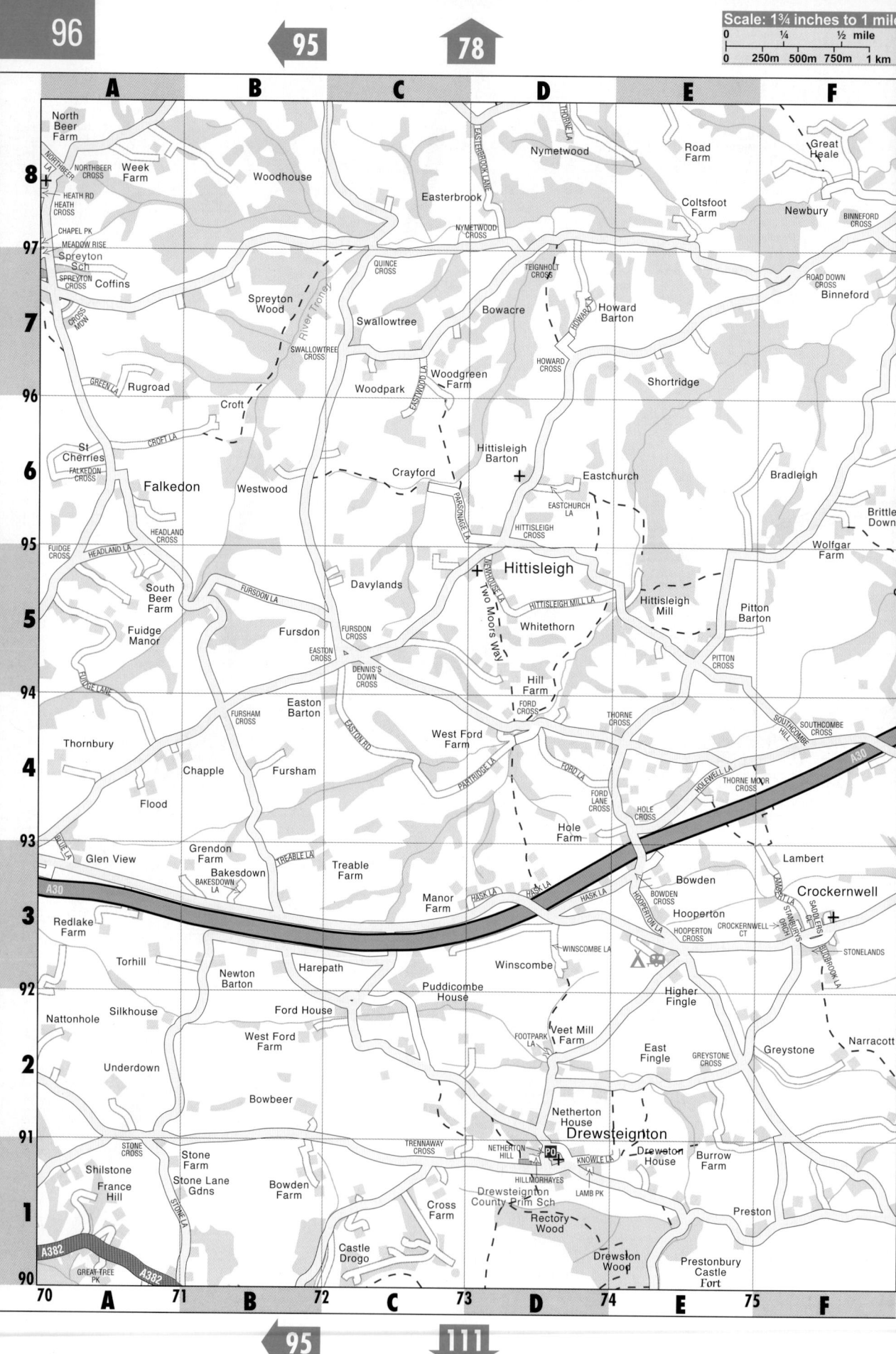
North Beer Farm
Week Farm
Woodhouse
Easterbrook
Nymetwood
Road Farm
Great Heale
Coltsfoot Farm
Newbury
Spreyton Sch
Coffins
Spreyton Wood
River Troney
Swallowtree
Bowacre
Howard Barton
Binneford
Rugroad
Croft
Woodpark
Woodgreen Farm
Shortridge
St Cherries
Falkedon
Westwood
Crayford
Hittisleigh Barton
Eastchurch
Bradleigh
Brittle Down
Wolfgar Farm
Hittisleigh
Davylands
South Beer Farm
Two Moors Way
Whitethorn
Hittisleigh Mill
Pitton Barton
Fuidge Manor
Fursdon
Hill Farm
Easton Barton
Thornbury
West Ford Farm
Chapple
Fursham
Flood
Hole Farm
Glen View
Grendon Farm
Bakesdown
Treable Farm
Lambert
Bowden
Crockernwell
Redlake Farm
Manor Farm
Hooperton
Torhill
Newton Barton
Harepath
Winscombe
Puddicombe House
Higher Fingle
Nattonhole
Silkhouse
Ford House
West Ford Farm
Veet Mill Farm
East Fingle
Greystone
Narracott
Underdown
Bowbeer
Netherton House
Drewsteignton
Drewston House
Burrow Farm
Shilstone
Stone Farm
France Hill
Stone Lane Gdns
Bowden Farm
Cross Farm
Drewsteignton County Prim Sch
Rectory Wood
Preston
Castle Drogo
Drewston Wood
Prestonbury Castle Fort
A30
A382

95
111

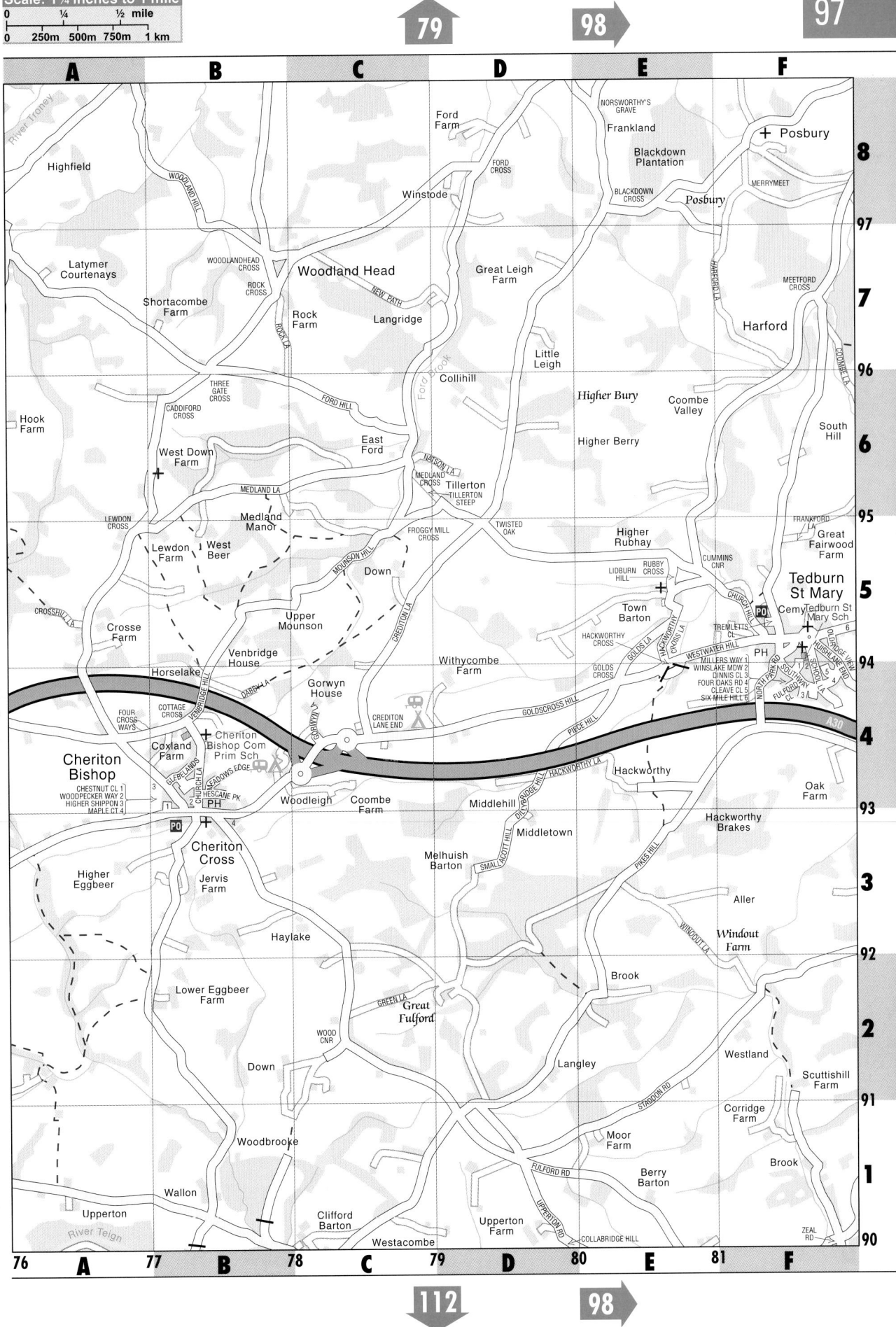

A   B   C   D   E   F

River Troney

Highfield

Latymer Courtenays

Shortacombe Farm

Hook Farm

West Down Farm

WOODLAND HILL

WOODLANDHEAD CROSS

ROCK CROSS

THREE GATE CROSS

CADDIFORD CROSS

ROCK LA

Rock Farm

FORD HILL

Woodland Head

NEW PATH

Langridge

East Ford

Ford Farm

Winstode

FORD CROSS

Ford Brook

Collihill

Great Leigh Farm

Little Leigh

Higher Bury

Higher Berry

NORSWORTHY'S GRAVE

Frankland

Blackdown Plantation

BLACKDOWN CROSS

Posbury

MERRYMEET

Posbury

HARFORD LA

Harford

MEETFORD CROSS

COOMBE LA

Coombe Valley

South Hill

8

97

7

96

6

LEWDON CROSS

CROSSHILL LA

Crosse Farm

MEDLAND LA

Lewdon Farm

West Beer

Medland Manor

MOUNSON HILL

Down

Upper Mounson

NATSON LA

MEDLAND CROSS

Tillerton

TILLERTON STEEP

FROGGY MILL CROSS

CREDITON LA

TWISTED OAK

Higher Rubhay

LIDBURN HILL

RUBBY CROSS

CUMMINS CNR

Town Barton

HACKWORTHY CROSS

GOLDS CROSS

GOLDS LA

HACKWORTHY LA

FRANKFORD LA

Great Fairwood Farm

Tedburn St Mary

CHURCH HILL

PO

Cemy

Tedburn St Mary Sch

TREMLETTS

WESTWATER HILL

MILLERS WAY 1
WINSLAKE MDW 2
DINNIS CL 3
FOUR OAKS RD 4
CLEAVE CL 5
SIX MILE HILL 6

PH

NORTH PARK RD

FULFORD CL

OLD LODGE VEN

OLD LAKE END

SCHOOL

95

5

94

Venbridge House

Horselake

VENBRIDGE HILL

DABB LA

Gorwyn House

GORWYN LA

CREDITON LANE END

Withycombe Farm

GOLDSCROSS HILL

PURCE HILL

HACKWORTHY LA

Hackworthy

A30

4

FOUR CROSS WAYS

Coxland Farm

COTTAGE CROSS

CHURCH LA

GLEBELANDS

Cheriton Bishop Com Prim Sch

MEADOWS EDGE

HESCANE PK

Woodleigh

Coombe Farm

Middlehill

Middletown

DILLBRIDGE HILL

SMALLACOTT HILL

Melhuish Barton

Hackworthy Brakes

Oak Farm

93

Cheriton Bishop

CHESTNUT CL 1
WOODPECKER WAY 2
HIGHER SHIPPON 3
MAPLE CT 4

PO

PH

Cheriton Cross

Jervis Farm

PIKES HILL

Aller

Windout Farm

3

Higher Eggbeer

Haylake

WINDOUT RD

92

Lower Eggbeer Farm

Down

GREEN LA

Great Fulford

WOOD CNR

Brook

Langley

STADDON RD

Westland

Scuttishill Farm

Corridge Farm

Brook

2

91

Woodbrooke

Wallon

Clifford Barton

Westacombe

FULFORD RD

Upperton Farm

UPPERTON RD

Moor Farm

Berry Barton

COLLABRIDGE HILL

ZEAL RD

1

90

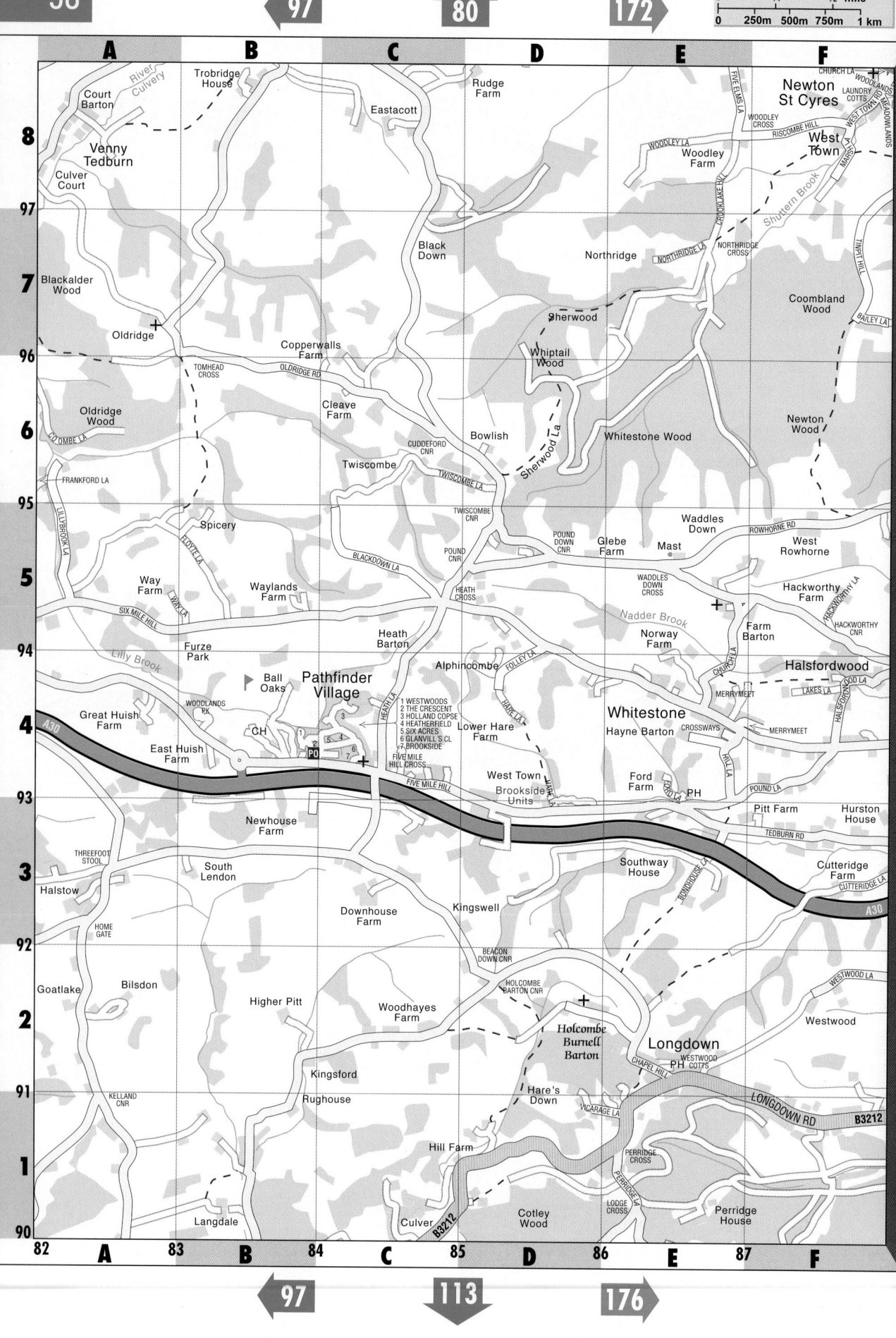

97
80
172

Scale: 1¾ inches to 1 mile
0   ¼   ½   mile
0   250m   500m   750m   1 km

A   B   C   D   E   F

8
97
7
96
6
95
5
94
4
93
3
92
2
91
1
90

82   A   83   B   84   C   85   D   86   E   87   F

River Culvery
Court Barton
Venny Tedburn
Culver Court
Trobridge House
Eastacott
Rudge Farm
Newton St Cyres
West Town
Church La
Laundry Cotts
Woodlands
West Town
Marsh
Five Elms La
Brooklake Hill
Woodley Cross
Riscombe Hill
Woodley La
Woodley Farm
Shutern Brook
Northridge
Northridge La
Northridge Cross
Tinpit Hill
Bailey La
Coombland Wood
Blackalder Wood
Oldridge
Copperwalls Farm
Tomhead Cross
Oldridge Rd
Black Down
Sherwood
Whiptail Wood
Sherwood La
Whitestone Wood
Newton Wood
Oldridge Wood
Coombe La
Cleave Farm
Cuddeford Cnr
Bowlish
Frankford La
Twiscombe
Twiscombe La
Twiscombe Cnr
Waddles Down
Rowhorne Rd
West Rowhorne
Lillybrook La
Spicery
Blackdown La
Pound Cnr
Pound Down Cnr
Glebe Farm
Mast
Hackworthy Farm
Hackworthy La
Hackworthy Cnr
Way Farm
Waylands Farm
Heath Cross
Waddles Down Cross
Nadder Brook
Farm Barton
Flote La
Six Mile Hill
Luck La
Furze Park
Heath Barton
Alphincombe
Folley La
Norway Farm
Church La
Halsfordwood
Lakes La
Wood La
Lilly Brook
Ball Oaks
Woodlands Pk
Pathfinder Village
Heath La
Hare La
Lower Hare Farm
Whitestone
Hayne Barton
Crossways
Merrymeet
Merrymeet
Halsdon La
Great Huish Farm
CH
PO
1 Westwoods
2 The Crescent
3 Holland Copse
4 Heatherfield
5 Six Acres
6 Glanvill's Cl
7 Brookside
Five Mile Hill Cross
West Town
Brookside Units
Five Mile Hill
Ford Farm
Ford La
PH
Pound La
Pitt Farm
Hurston House
East Huish Farm
Lane La
A30
Threefoot Stool
Newhouse Farm
South Lendon
Downhouse Farm
Kingswell
Southway House
Bondhouse La
Tedburn Rd
Cutteridge Farm
Cutteridge La
A30
Halstow
Home Gate
Beacon Down Cnr
Goatlake
Bilsdon
Higher Pitt
Woodhayes Farm
Holcombe Barton Cnr
Holcombe Burnell Barton
Longdown
PH
Cotts
Westwood La
Westwood
Kelland Cnr
Kingsford
Rughouse
Hare's Down
Chapel Hill
Westwood Cotts
Vicarage La
Longdown Rd
B3212
Hill Farm
Perridge Cross
Perridge La
Langdale
Culver
B3212
Cotley Wood
Lodge Cross
Perridge House

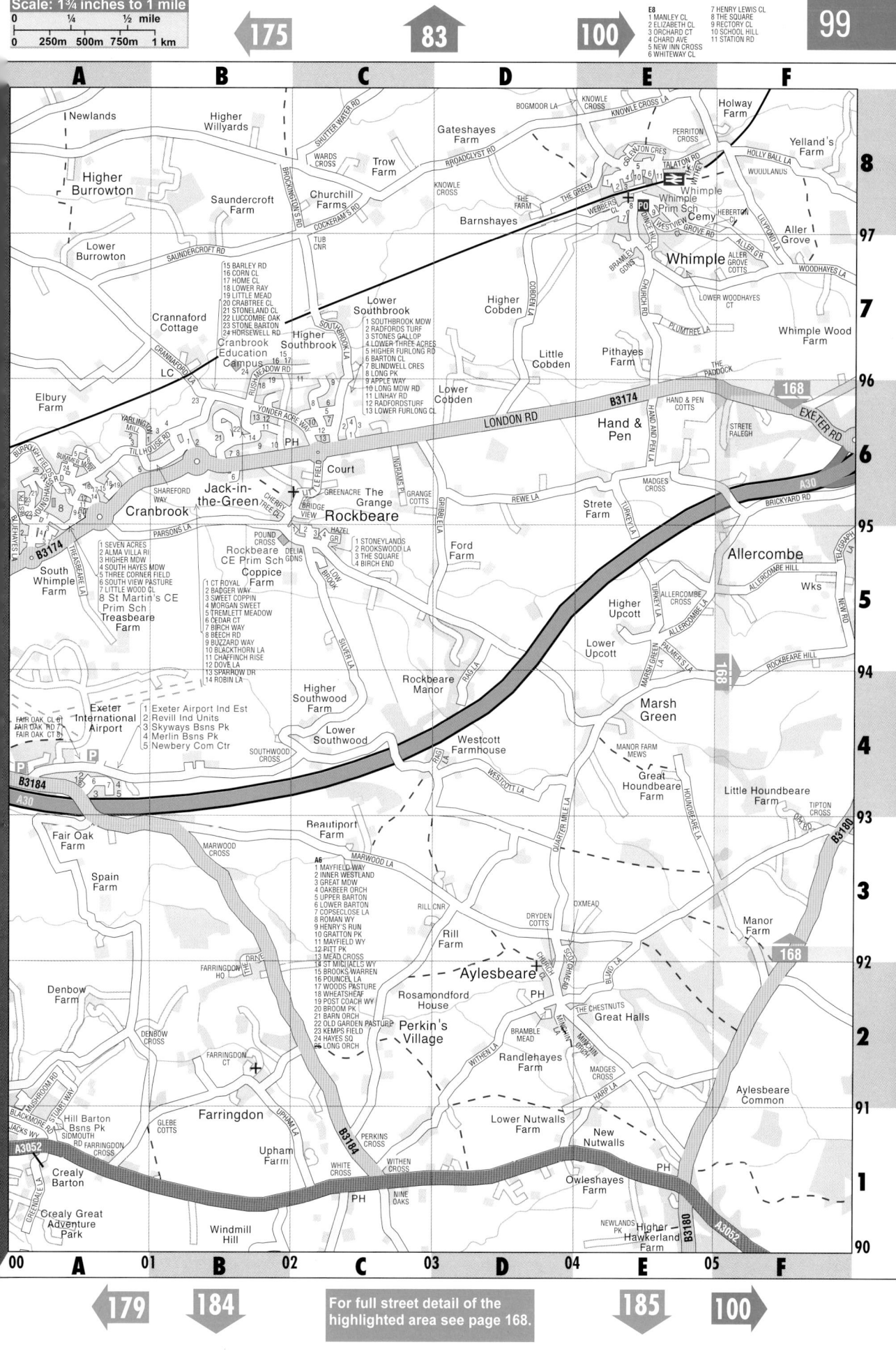

E8
1 MANLEY CL
2 ELIZABETH CL
3 ORCHARD CT
4 CHARD AVE
5 NEW INN CROSS
6 WHITEWAY CL

7 HENRY LEWIS CL
8 THE SQUARE
9 RECTORY CL
10 SCHOOL HILL
11 STATION RD

Newlands

Higher Willyards

Bogmoor La

Knowle Cross

Knowle Cross La

Holway Farm

Higher Burrowton

Saundercroft Farm

Gateshayes Farm

Broadclyst Rd

Perriton Cross

Yelland's Farm

Lower Burrowton

Shutter Water Rd

Wards Cross

Churchill Farms

Trow Farm

Knowle Cross

The Farm

Osmon Cres

Talaton Rd

Holly Ball La

Woodlands

Barnshayes

The Green

Webbers Cl

Whimple Prim Sch

Whimple Cemy

Heberton Cl

Aller Grove

Cockeram's Rd

Saundercroft Rd

Tub Cnr

Whimple

Aller Grove Cotts

97

Crannaford Cottage

15 BARLEY RD
16 CORN CL
17 HOME CL
18 LOWER RAY
19 LITTLE MEAD
20 CRABTREE CL
21 STONELAND CL
22 LUCCOMBE OAK
23 STONE BARTON
24 HORSEWELL RD

Lower Southbrook

1 SOUTHBROOK MDW
2 RADFORDS TURF
3 STONES GALLOP
4 LOWER THREE ACRES
5 HIGHER FURLONG RD
6 BARTON CL
7 BLINDWELL CRES
8 LONG PK
9 APPLE WAY
10 LONG MDW RD
11 LINHAY RD
12 RADFORDSTURF
13 LOWER FURLONG CL

Higher Cobden

Church Rd

Lower Woodhayes Ct

Whimple Wood Farm

Woodhayes La

7

Elbury Farm

Cranbrook Education Campus

Higher Southbrook

Southbrook La

Rushmead Rd

Little Cobden

Cobden La

Lower Cobden

Pithayes Farm

Plumtree La

The Paddock

168

Exeter Rd

96

Yarlington Mill

Crannaford La

Till House Rd

Yonder Acre Wy

London Rd

B3174

Hand & Pen

Hand & Pen La

Hand & Pen Cotts

Strete Ralegh

6

Burrow Fields

Young Hayes Rd

Submill Mdw

Shareford Way

Jack-in-the-Green

Cherry Tree Cl

Greenacre

Court

Bridge View

Ingrams La

The Grange

Grange Cotts

Rewe La

Madges Cross

Brickyard Rd

A30

95

Bluehayes La

Treasbeare La

B3174

South Whimple Farm

Cranbrook

Parsons La

Rockbeare

1 SEVEN ACRES
2 ALMA VILLA RI
3 HIGHER MDW
4 SOUTH HAYES MDW
5 THREE CORNER FIELD
6 SOUTH VIEW PASTURE
7 LITTLE WOOD CL
8 St Martin's CE Prim Sch

Treasbeare Farm

Pound Cross

Rockbeare CE Prim Sch

Coppice Farm

Delia Gdns

Hazel Gr

Low Brook

1 STONEYLANDS
2 ROOKSWOOD CL
3 THE SQUARE
4 BIRCH END

Ford Farm

Gribble La

Strete Farm

Turkey La

Allercombe Hill

Allercombe

Telegraph La

New Rd

Wks

5

1 CT ROYAL
2 BADGER WAY
3 SWEET COPPIN
4 MORGAN SWEET
5 TREMLETT MEADOW
6 CEDAR CT
7 BIRCH WAY
8 BEECH RD
9 BUZZARD WAY
10 BLACKTHORN LA
11 CHAFFINCH RISE
12 DOVE LA
13 SPARROW DR
14 ROBIN LA

Silver La

Rag La

Higher Upcott

Lower Upcott

Turkey La

Palmers La

Allercombe Cross

Allercombe La

Rockbeare Hill

168

94

Exeter Airport Ind Est
Revill Ind Units
Skyways Bsns Pk
Merlin Bsns Pk
Newbery Com Ctr

Higher Southwood Farm

Lower Southwood

Rockbeare Manor

Westcott Farmhouse

Marsh Green

Manor Farm Mews

Great Houndbeare Farm

Little Houndbeare Farm

Tipton Cross

B3180

93

P

Exeter International Airport

FAIR OAK CL 6
FAIR OAK RD 7
FAIR OAK 8

1 EXETER AIRPORT IND EST
2 REVILL IND UNITS
3 SKYWAYS BSNS PK
4 MERLIN BSNS PK
5 NEWBERY COM CTR

Southwood Cross

Westcott La

Rag La

Quarter Mile La

Houndbeare La

Manor Farm

4

P

B3184

A30

Fair Oak Farm

Marwood Cross

Beautiport Farm

Marwood La

Dryden Cotts

Oxmead

168

92

Spain Farm

A6
1 MAYFIELD WAY
2 INNER WESTLAND
3 GREAT MDW
4 OAKBEER ORCH
5 UPPER BARTON
6 LOWER BARTON
7 COPSECLOSE LA
8 ROMAN WY
9 HENRY'S RUN
10 GRATTON PK
11 MAYFIELD WY
12 PITT PK
13 MEAD CROSS
14 ST MICHAELS CL
15 BROOKS WARREN
16 POUNCEL LA
17 WOODS PASTURE
18 WHEATSHEAF
19 POST COACH WY
20 BROOM PK
21 BARN ORCH
22 OLD GARDEN PASTURE
23 KEMPS FIELD
24 HAYES SQ
25 LONG ORCH

Rill Cnr

Rill Farm

Aylesbeare

PH

Church La

Great Halls

Withen La

Millchin Orch

Manor Farm

3

Denbow Farm

Farringdon Ho

Denbow Cross

Farringdon Ct

Rosamondford House

Perkin's Village

Bramble Mead

The Chestnuts

Randlehayes Farm

Madges Cross

Harp La

Aylesbeare Common

2

Blackmore Rd

Mushroom Rd

Start Way

Jacks Wy

Hill Barton Bsns Pk

Sidmouth Rd

Glebe Cotts

Farringdon

Upham La

B3184

Upham Farm

Perkins Cross

White Cross

Withen La

Lower Nutwalls Farm

New Nutwalls

PH

B3180

91

A3052

Crealy Barton

Greendale La

Farringdon Cross

Windmill Hill

PH

Nine Oaks

PH

Oweshayes Farm

Newlands Pk

Higher Hawkerland

A3052

1

Crealy Great Adventure Park

90

00 A 01 B 02 C 03 D 04 E 05 F

179

184

For full street detail of the highlighted area see page 168.

185

100

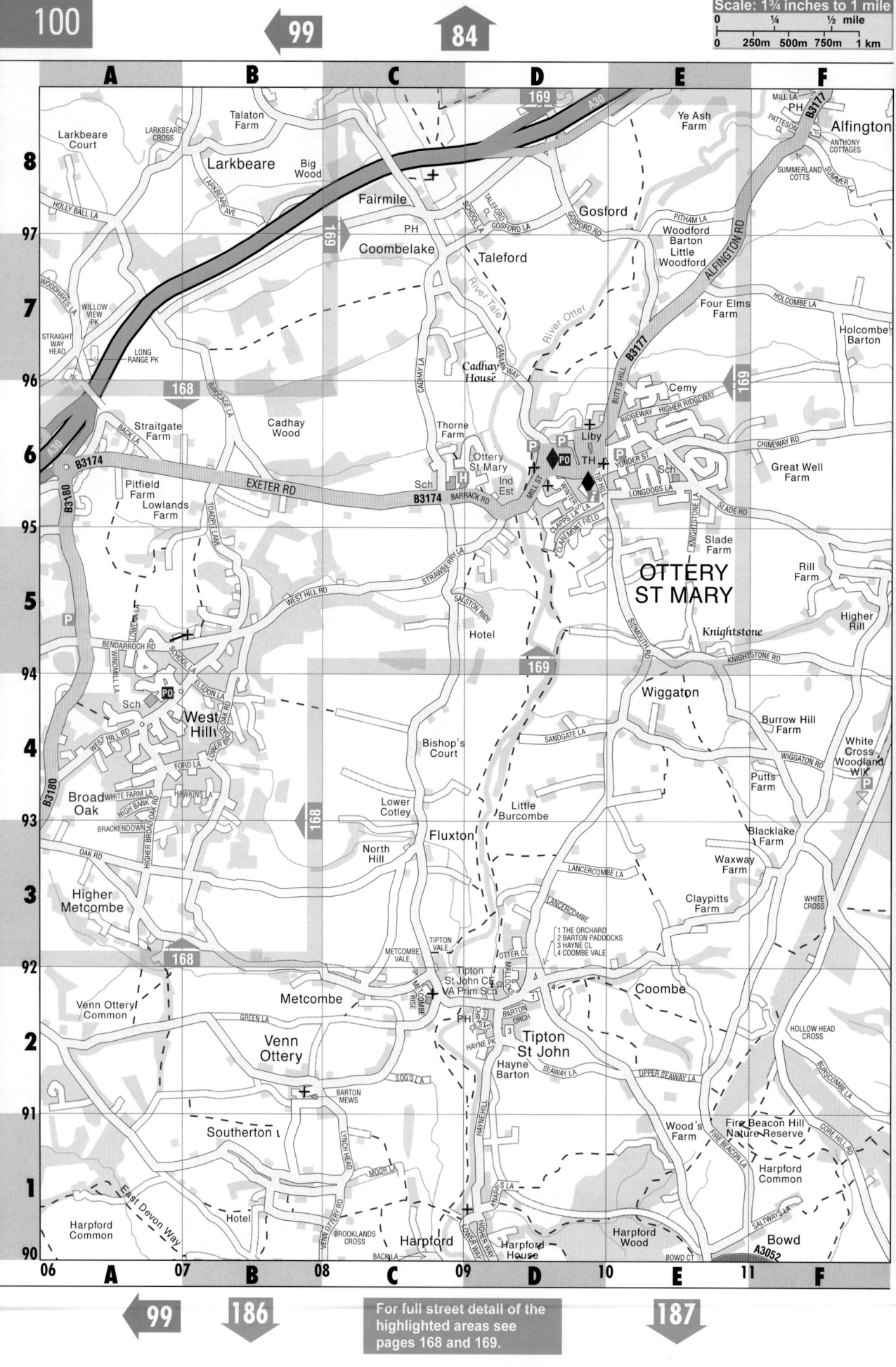

Scale: 1¾ inches to 1 mile

99
84
99
186
187

Alfington

Larkbeare Court
Larkbeare Cross
Talaton Farm
Larkbeare
Big Wood
Ye Ash Farm

HOLLY BALL LA
WILLOW VIEW PK
Fairmile
Coombelake
PH
Gosford
Woodford Barton
Little Woodford
MILL LA
PH
PATTESON CL
ANTHONY COTTAGES
SUMMERLAND COTTS

STRAIGHT WAY HEAD
LONG RANGE PK
168
Cadhay Wood
Thorne Farm
Taleford
Cadhay House
PITHAM LA
Four Elms Farm
HOLCOMBE LA
Holcombe Barton

Straitgate Farm
BACK LA
BIRDCAGE LA
EXETER RD
B3174
Ottery St Mary
Ind Est
169
HIGHER RIDGEWAY
Cemy
CHINEWAY RD
Great Well Farm

Pitfield Farm
Lowlands Farm
Sch
BARRACK RD
B3174
Liby
TH
YONDER ST
Sch
LONGDOGS LA
SLADE RD

TOADPIT LANE
WEST HILL RD
STRAWBERRY LA
SALSTON RIDE
Hotel
OTTERY ST MARY
Knightstone
KNIGHTSTONE RD
Slade Farm
Rill Farm
Higher Rill

BENDARROCH RD
LOWER BR
SCHOOL LA
ELSDON LA
Sch
PO
West Hill
Wiggaton
Burrow Hill Farm
WIGGATON RD
White Cross Woodland Wlk

WEST HILL RD
FORD LA
HAWKINS LA
Bishop's Court
SANDGATE LA
Putts Farm

B3180
Broad Oak
WHITE FARM LA
HIGH BANK RD
HIGHER BROAD OAK RD
BRACKENDOWN
Lower Cotley
Little Burcombe
LANCERCOMBE LA
Blacklake Farm
Waxway Farm
White Cross

OAK RD
North Hill
Fluxton
LANCERCOMBE LA
Claypitts Farm

Higher Metcombe
168
METCOMBE VALE
TIPTON VALE
1 THE ORCHARD
2 BARTON PADDOCKS
3 HAYNE CL
4 COOMBE VALE
Coombe
HOLLOW HEAD CROSS

Venn Ottery Common
GREEN LA
Metcombe
METCOMBE RISE
PH
Tipton St John CE VA Prim Sch
BARTON ORCH
Tipton St John
SEAWAY LA
UPPER SEAWAY LA

Venn Ottery
SOG'S LA
HAYNE HILL
Hayne Barton
Wood's Farm
FIRE BEACON LA
Fire Beacon Hill Nature Reserve
CORE HILL RD
BURSCOMBE LA

BARTON MEWS
Southerton
LYNCH HEAD
MOOR LA
KNAPP'S LA
Harpford Common
SALTWAYS LA

East Devon Way
Harpford Common
YEW OTTERY RD
BROOKLANDS CROSS
Hotel
BACK LA
Harpford
LOWER WAY
HIGHER WAY
Harpford House
Harpford Wood
BOWD CT
Bowd
A3052

For full street detail of the highlighted areas see pages 168 and 169.

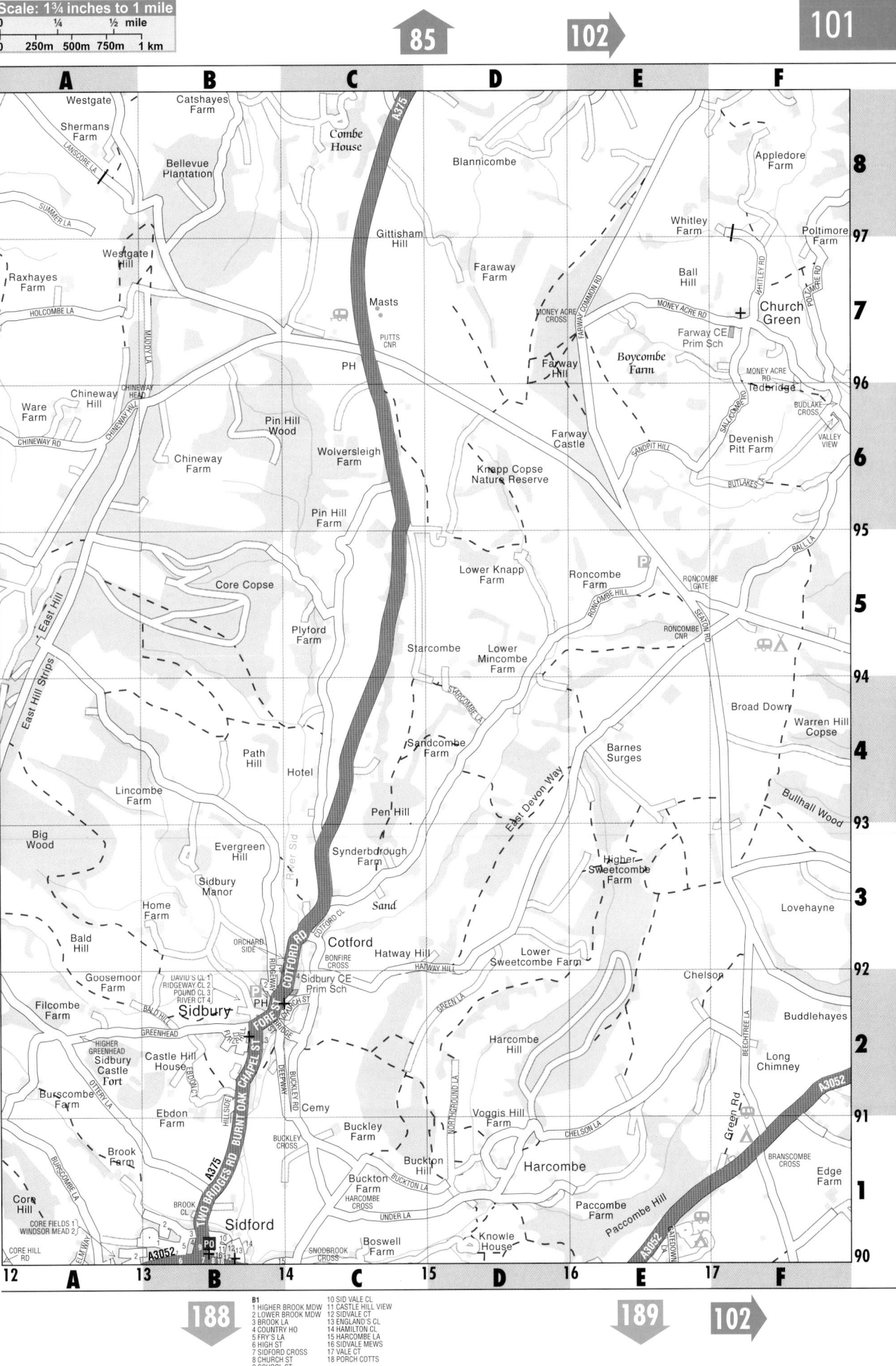

Scale: 1¾ inches to 1 mile

85 102

B1
1 HIGHER BROOK MDW
2 LOWER BROOK MDW
3 BROOK LA
4 COUNTRY HO
5 FRY'S LA
6 HIGH ST
7 SIDFORD CROSS
8 CHURCH ST
9 SCHOOL ST
10 SID VALE CL
11 CASTLE HILL VIEW
12 SIDVALE CT
13 ENGLAND'S CL
14 HAMILTON CL
15 HARCOMBE LA
16 SIDVALE MEWS
17 VALE CT
18 PORCH COTTS

Scale: 1¾ inches to 1 mile

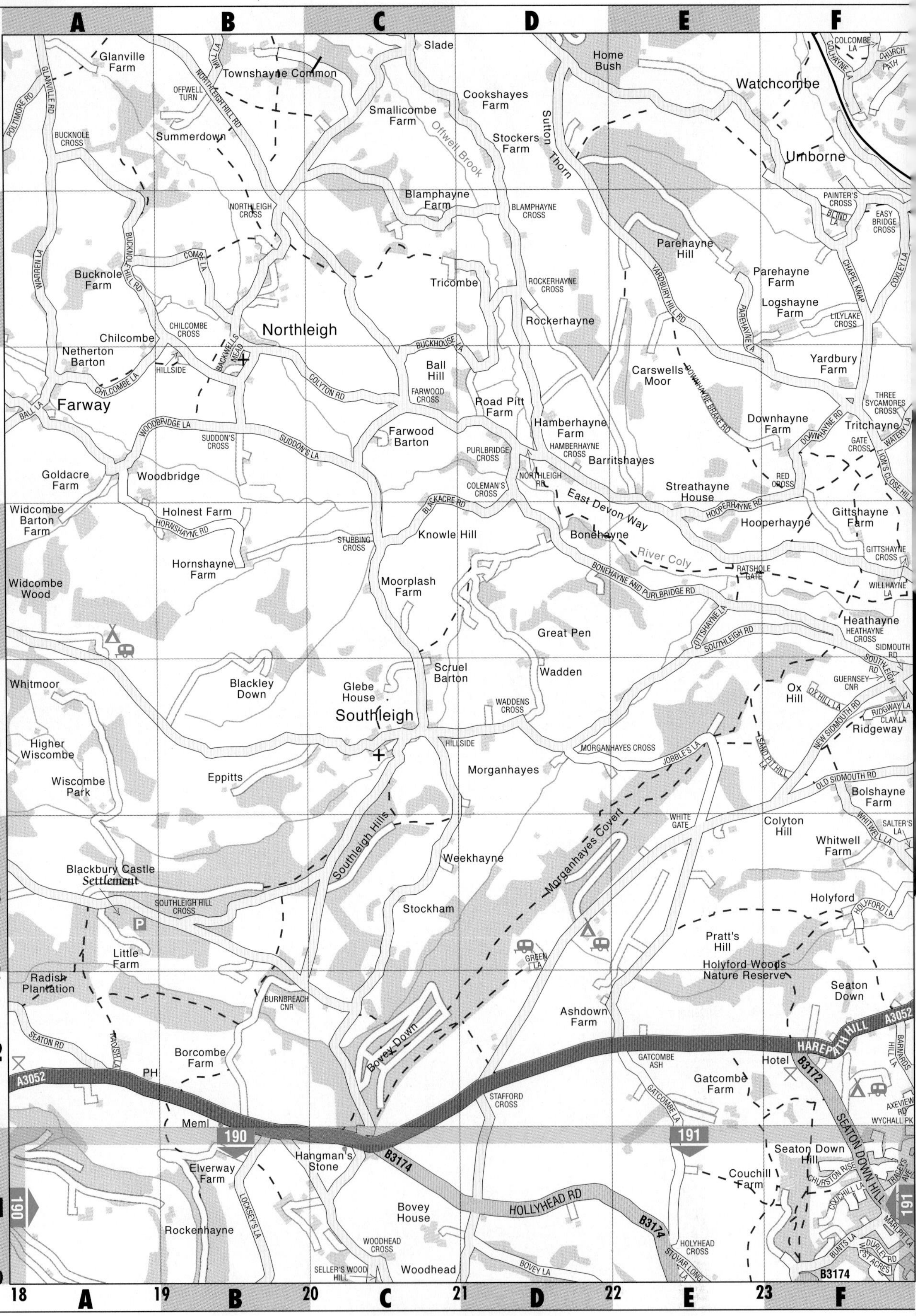

0   ¼   ½   mile
0 250m 500m 750m 1 km

A   B   C   D   E   F

8
Glanville Farm
Townshayne Common
Slade
Cookshayes Farm
Home Bush
Watchcombe
OFFWELL TURN
Smallicombe Farm
Stockers Farm
Sutton Thorn
Summerdown
Oftwell Brook
COLCOMBE LA
COLRAINE LA
CHURCH PATH

97
Blamphayne Farm
Blamphayne Cross
NORTHLEIGH CROSS
PAINTER'S CROSS
BLIND LA
EASY BRIDGE CROSS

7
Bucknole Farm
Tricombe
Rockerhayne Cross
Rockerhayne
Parehayne Hill
Parehayne Farm
Logshayne Farm
PAREHAYNE LA
YARDBURY HILL RD
LILYLAKE CROSS
COXLEY LA
CHAPEL KNAP

96
Chilcombe
CHILCOMBE CROSS
Northleigh
Netherton Barton
HILLSIDE
BUCKWELL HEAD
BUCKHOUSE LA
Ball Hill
Carswells Moor
Yardbury Farm
THREE SYCAMORES CROSS
BONHAYNE BRAKE RD

6
Farway
BALL LA
WOODBRIDGE LA
COLYTON RD
Farwood Barton
FARWOOD CROSS
Road Pitt Farm
Hamberhayne Farm
Hamberhayne Cross
Barritshayes
Downhayne Farm
Tritchayne
GATE CROSS
WATER LA
LION'S CLOSE HILL
CHILCOMBE LA

95
Goldacre Farm
Woodbridge
SUDDON'S CROSS
SUDDON'S LA
PURLBRIDGE CROSS
COLEMAN'S CROSS
NORTHLEIGH RD
East Devon Way
Streathayne House
Hooperhayne
Gittshayne Farm
RED CROSS
HOOPERHAYNE LA
GITTSHAYNE CROSS

Widcombe Barton Farm
Holnest Farm
HORNSHAYNE RD
BLACKACRE RD
Knowle Hill
Bonehayne
River Coly
RATSHOLE GATE
WILLHAYNE LA

5
Widcombe Wood
Hornshayne Farm
STUBBING CROSS
Moorplash Farm
BONEHAYNE AND PURLBRIDGE RD
SOUTHLEIGH LA
Heathayne
HEATHAYNE CROSS
SIDMOUTH RD

94
Whitmoor
Blackley Down
Glebe House
Scruel Barton
Great Pen
Wadden
SOUTHLEIGH RD
Ox Hill
OXHILL LA
GUERNSEY CNR

4
Higher Wiscombe
Southleigh
Eppitts
HILLSIDE
WADDENS CROSS
Morganhayes
MORGANHAYES CROSS
Morganhayes Covert
JOBBLE'S LA
WHITE GATE
Ridgeway
CLAYLA
RIDGWAY LA
NEW SIDMOUTH RD
OLD SIDMOUTH RD
SALTER'S LA
SAND PIT HILL

93
Wiscombe Park
Southleigh Hills
Colyton Hill
Whitwell Farm
Bolshayne Farm
WHITWELL LA

3
Blackbury Castle Settlement
SOUTHLEIGH HILL CROSS
Weekhayne
Stockham
Pratt's Hill
Holyford
Holyford Woods Nature Reserve
Seaton Down
HOLYFORD LA

92
Radish Plantation
Little Farm
BURNBREACH CNR
GREEN LA
Ashdown Farm

2
SEATON RD
Borcombe Farm
Bovey Down
PH
STAFFORD CROSS
Gatcombe Ash
Gatcombe Farm
Hotel
HAREPATH HILL
A3052
A3052
B3172
AXEVIEW RD
WYCHALL LA
BARNARDS HILL LA

91
Meml
190
STAFFORD CROSS
191
Seaton Down Hill
SEATON DOWN HILL
CHURSTON RISE

1
190
Elverway Farm
Hangman's Stone
B3174
Bovey House
HOLLYHEAD RD
B3174
Couchill Farm
COVCHILL LA
MARSH LA
TRACEYS
191
Rockenhayne
LOOSEYS LA
WOODHEAD CROSS
SELLER'S WOOD HILL
Woodhead
BOVEY LA
STOVAR LONG LA
HOLYHEAD CROSS
MARSH LA
BRUNTS LA
DURLEY RD
WEST ACRES
B3174

90
18   A   19   B   20   C   21   D   22   E   23   F

For full street detail of the highlighted area see pages 190 and 191.

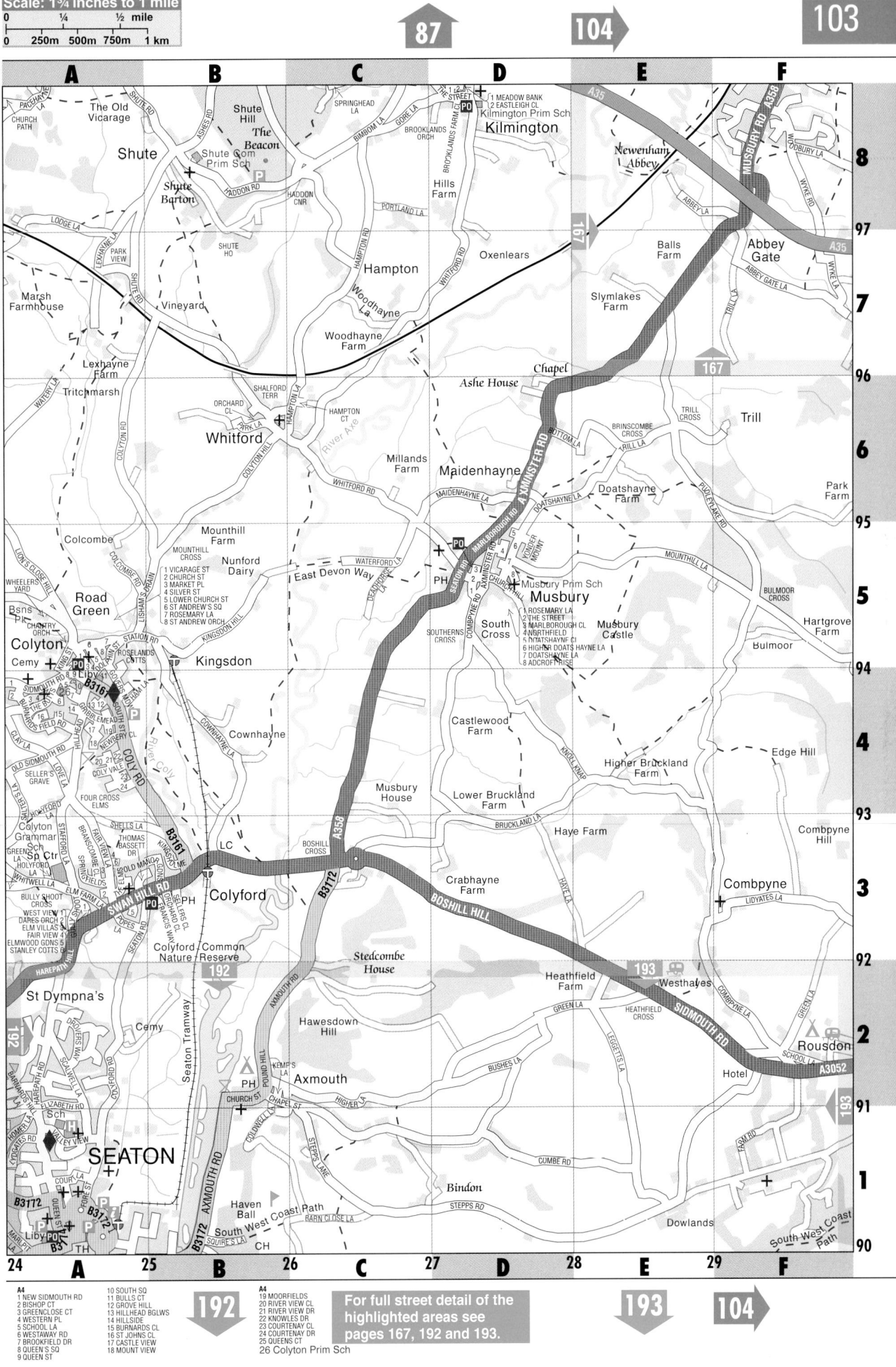

Scale: 1¾ inches to 1 mile
0 ¼ ½ mile
0 250m 500m 750m 1 km
87
104
103
A B C D E F
Shute
The Old Vicarage
Shute Hill
The Beacon
Shute Com Prim Sch
Shute Barton
Springhead La
Bimbom La
Gore La
Brooklands Orch
1 Meadow Bank
2 Eastleigh Cl
Kilmington Prim Sch
Kilmington
Hills Farm
Newenham Abbey
Mushury Rd
A358
A35
Woodbury La
Abbey La
Wyke Rd
Haddon Rd
Haddon Cnr
Portland La
Lodge La
Church Path
Lexhayne La
Park View
Shute Ho
Shute Rd
Hampton Rd
Whitford Rd
Hampton
Oxenlears
Balls Farm
Abbey Gate
Abbey Gate La
Trill La
Slymlakes Farm
Marsh Farmhouse
Vineyard
Woodhayne La
Woodhayne Farm
Lexhayne Farm
Tritchmarsh
Watery La
Chapel
Ashe House
167
Shalford Terr
Orchard Cl
Park La
Hampton La
Hampton Ct
River Axe
Whitford
Colyton Rd
Colyton Hill
Millands Farm
Maidenhayne
Axminster Rd
Bottom La
Brinscombe Cross
Trill Cross
Trill
Park Farm
Whitford Rd
Maidenhayne La
Doatshayne La
Doatshayne Farm
Pudleylake Rd
Mounthill Farm
Mounthill Cross
Colcombe
Colcombe Rd
Lion's Close Hill
Nunford Dairy
Waterford La
East Devon Way
Deadhorse La
Marlborough Rd
Seaton Rd
Yonder Mount
Mounthill La
Wheelers Yard
1 Vicarage St
2 Church St
3 Market Pl
4 Silver St
5 Lower Church St
6 St Andrew's Sq
7 Rosemary La
8 St Andrew Orch
Road Green
Lisham's Drain
Kingsdon Hill
Bsns Pk
Chantry Orch
Station Rd
Colyton
Cemy
Liby
B3161
Roselands Cotts
Kingsdon
Musbury Prim Sch
Musbury
1 Rosemary La
2 The Street
3 Marlborough Cl
4 Northfield
5 Doatshayne Cl
6 Higher Doats Hayne La
7 Doatshayne La
8 Adcroft Rise
South Cross
Southerns Cross
Combpyne Rd
Church Hill
Musbury Castle
Bulmoor Cross
Hartgrove Farm
Bulmoor
Castlewood Farm
Cownhayne La
Cownhayne
River Coly
Coly Rd
Newbery Cl
Old Sidmouth Rd
Seller's Grave
Love La
Coly Vale
Clay La
Four Cross Elms
Knoll Knap
Higher Bruckland Farm
Edge Hill
Musbury House
Lower Bruckland Farm
Bruckland La
Haye Farm
Combpyne Hill
Colyton Grammar Sch
Shells La
Thomas Bassett Dr
Stafford La
Branscombe Cl
Fair View La
Springfields
Kingston
Old Manor
Sp Ctr
Holyford La
Whitwell La
Elm Farm La
Swan Hill Rd
Bully Shoot Cross
West View
Dares Orch
Elm Villas
Fair View
Elmwood Gdns
Stanley Cotts
LC
Boshill Cross
A358
B3172
Colyford
PH
Sellers Cl
Orchard Cl
Francis Way
Seaton Rd
Popes La
Crabhayne Farm
Boshill Hill
Haye La
Combpyne
Lidyates La
Colyford Common Nature Reserve
192
Stedcombe House
Heathfield Farm
193
Westhayes
Harepath Hill
St Dympna's
Axmouth Rd
Green La
Heathfield Cross
Leggetts La
Sidmouth Rd
Combpyne La
Hawesdown Hill
Cemy
Seaton Tramway
Droviers Way
Scalwell La
Colyford Rd
Barnards Hill
Harepath Rd
Elizabeth Rd
Pound Hill
Kemp's La
Axmouth
Bushes La
School La
Rousdon
A3052
Hotel
Church St
Chapel St
Higher La
Sch
Homer La
Valley View
Lydgates Rd
SEATON
Coldwell La
Stepps Lane
Combe Rd
Farm Rd
Bindon
Court La
Fore St
Queen St
B3172
Axmouth Rd
Haven Ball
South West Coast Path
Barn Close La
Stepps Rd
Dowlands
Marlpit
Squire's La
CH
TH
24 25 26 27 28 29
A4
1 New Sidmouth Rd
2 Bishop Ct
3 Greenclose Ct
4 Western Pl
5 School La
6 Westaway Rd
7 Brookfield Dr
8 Queen's Sq
9 Queen St
10 South Sq
11 Bulls Ct
12 Grove Hill
13 Hillhead Bglws
14 Hillside
15 Burnards Cl
16 St Johns Cl
17 Castle View
18 Mount View
A4
19 Moorfields
20 River View Cl
21 River View Dr
22 Knowles Dr
23 Courtenay Cl
24 Courtenay Dr
25 Queens Ct
26 Colyton Prim Sch
192
For full street detail of the highlighted areas see pages 167, 192 and 193.
193
104

Scale: 1¾ inches to 1 mile

0   ¼   ½   mile
0   250m   500m   750m   1 km

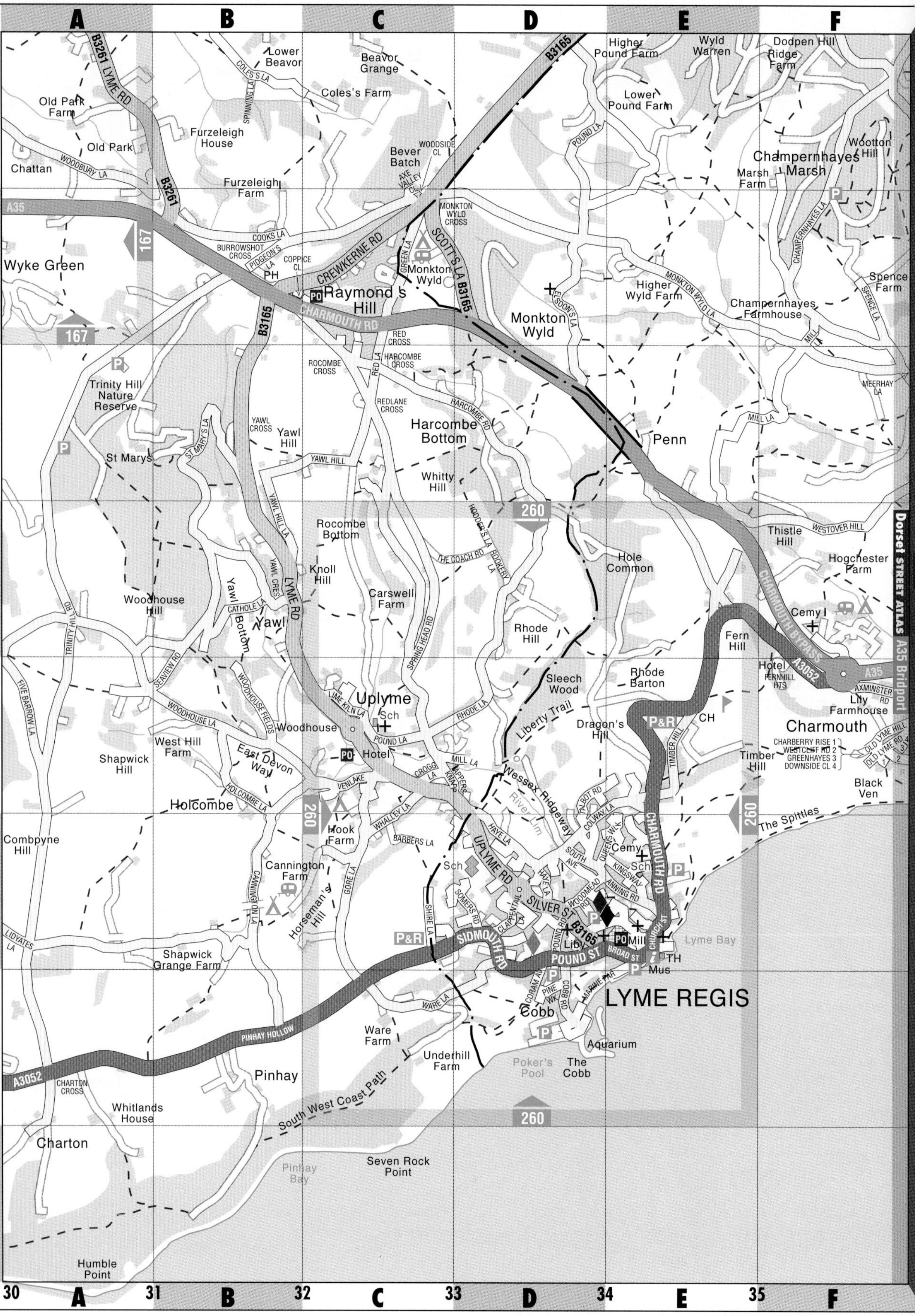

A   B   C   D   E   F

8
Old Park Farm
Old Park
Chattan
WOODBURY LA
B3261 LYME RD
Furzeleigh House
COLE'S LA
COLE'S LA DINNIUS
Lower Beavor
Beavor Grange
Coles's Farm
Furzeleigh Farm
WOODSIDE CL
Bever Batch
AXE VALLEY CL
B3165
Higher Pound Farm
Lower Pound Farm
POUND LA
Wyld Warren
Dodpen Hill Ridge Farm
Wootton Hill
Champernhayes Marsh
Marsh Farm

97
A35
B3261
BURROWSHOT CROSS
COOKS LA
PIDGEON'S LA
PH
CREWKERNE RD
COPPICE CL
PO
Raymond's Hill
GREEN LA
Monkton Wyld
SCOTT'S LA B3165
MONKTON WYLD CROSS
EASONS LA
Monkton Wyld
Higher Wyld Farm
MONKTON WYLD LA
Champernhayes Farmhouse
CHAMPERNHAYES LA
Spence Hill
SPENCE LA
MILL LA
MEERHAY LA
P

7
Wyke Green
167
167
CHARMOUTH RD
B3165
RED CROSS
HARCOMBE CROSS
Penn

96
Trinity Hill Nature Reserve
RED LA
ROCOMBE CROSS
REDLANE CROSS
HARCOMBE RD
Harcombe Bottom
Whitty Hill
Hole Common
260
WESTOVER HILL
Thistle Hill
Hogchester Farm

6
P
St Marys
ST MARY'S LA
YAWL CROSS
Yawl Hill
YAWL HILL
LYME RD
THE COACH RD
ROOKERY
HARCOMBE LA
Cemy
CH
Dorset STREET ATLAS A35 Bridport

95
Woodhouse Hill
YAWL HILL LA
YAWL CRES
Knoll Hill
Rocombe Bottom
Carswell Farm
SPRING HEAD RD
Rhode Hill
A35

5
FIVE BARROW LA
TRINITY HILL RD
CATHOLE LA
Yawl Bottom
Yawl
Sleech Wood
Liberty Trail
Rhode Barton
Dragon's Hill
Fern Hill
Hotel FERNHILL HTS
CHARMOUTH BYPASS B3052
AXMINSTER RD
Lily Farmhouse

94
SEAVIEW RD
WOODHOUSE LA
WOODHOUSE FIELDS
Uplyme
Sch
LYME KILN LA
Woodhouse
RHODE LA
P&R
CH
Charmouth
CHARBERRY RISE 1
WESTCLIFF RD 2
GREENHAYES 3
DOWNSIDE CL 4
OLD LYME RD

4
Shapwick Hill
West Hill Farm
East Devon Way
HOLCOMBE LA
VENLAKE
PO
Hotel
POUND LA
MILL LA
Wessex Ridgeway
River Lim
TIMBER HILL
Timber Hill
Black Ven

93
Combpyne Hill
WOODHOUSE LA
Holcombe
260
CROGG
KIPPERS LA
WHALLEY LA
BARBERS LA
Hook Farm
TALBOT RD
COLWAY LA
Cemy
Sch
260
The Spittles
P

3
LIDYATES LA
CANNINGTON LA
Cannington Farm
Horseman's Hill
GORE LA
SHIRE LA
Sch
SOMERS RD
HAYE LA
HAYE LA
CLAPPENTAIL
POUND RD
Sch
SILVER ST
SOUTH AVE
QUEENS
KINGSWAY
CHARMOUTH RD
Lyme Bay

92
Shapwick Grange Farm
WARE LA
SIDMOUTH RD
P&R
Ware Farm
UPLYME RD
POUND ST
Lib
COBB RD
PINE WK
BROAD ST
POUND ST
PO
Mus
LYME REGIS
TH
i

2
A3052
CHARTON CROSS
PINHAY HOLLOW
Pinhay
Underhill Farm
Cobb
Poker's Pool
Aquarium
The Cobb
P

91
Whitlands House
South West Coast Path
Seven Rock Point
260

1
Charton
Pinhay Bay

90
Humble Point

A   B   C   D   E   F
30   31   32   33   34   35

For full street detail of the highlighted areas see pages 167 and 260.

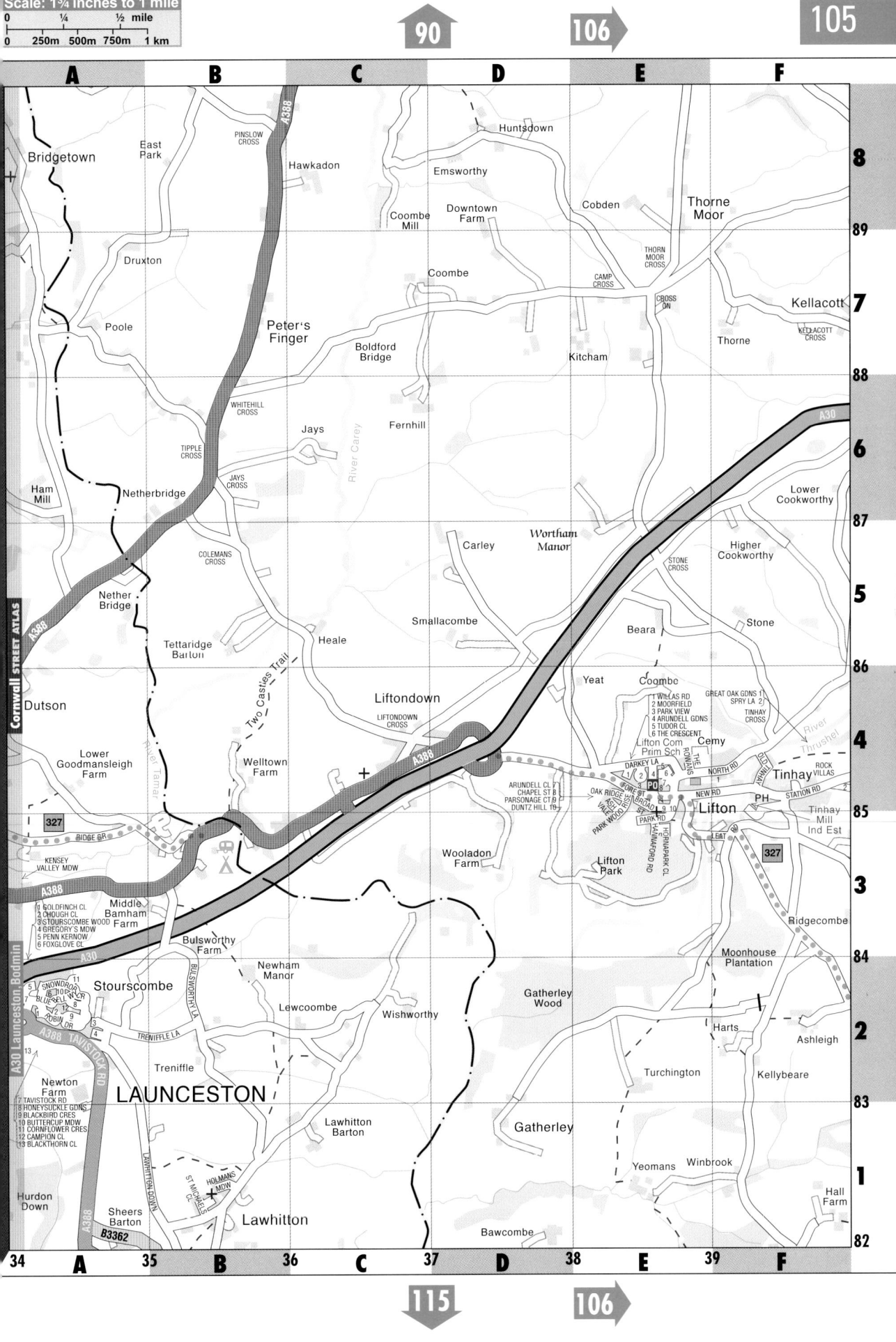

A   B   C   D   E   F

Bridgetown

East Park

PINSLOW CROSS

A388

Hawkadon

Huntsdown

Emsworthy

Downtown Farm

Cobden

Thorne Moor

8

Druxton

Coombe Mill

Coombe

CAMP CROSS

THORN MOOR CROSS

CROSS DN

89

Kellacott

7

Poole

Peter's Finger

Boldford Bridge

Kitcham

Thorne

KELLACOTT CROSS

Ham Mill

WHITEHILL CROSS

Netherbridge

TIPPLE CROSS

JAYS CROSS

Jays

River Carey

Fernhill

Wortham Manor

A30

Lower Cookworthy

88

Nether Bridge

COLEMANS CROSS

Carley

Higher Cookworthy

STONE CROSS

6

5

Cornwall STREET ATLAS

A388

Tettaridge Barton

Heale

Smallacombe

Beara

STONE

Stone

87

Dutson

Two Castles Trail

Liftondown

LIFTONDOWN CROSS

Yeat

Coombe

1 WILLAS RD
2 MOORFIELD
3 PARK VIEW
4 ARUNDELL GDNS
5 TUDOR CL
6 THE CRESCENT

GREAT OAK GDNS 1
SPRY LA 2

TINHAY CROSS

Cemy

River Thrushel

86

Lower Goodmansleigh Farm

River Tamar

Welltown Farm

A388

Lifton Com Prim Sch

DARKEY LA
THE ROMANS

NORTH RD

4

327

RIDGE GR

KENSEY VALLEY MDW

Wooladon Farm

ARUNDELL CL 7
CHAPEL ST 8
PARSONAGE CT 9
DUNTZ HILL 10

OAK RIDGE
PARK WOOD RISE
FORE ST
BROAD ST
PO

PARK RD

Lifton

PH

STATION RD

Tinhay

ROCK VILLAS

Tinhay Mill Ind Est

85

A30 Launceston Bodmin

A30

A388

1 GOLDFINCH CL
2 CHOUGH CL
3 STOURSCOMBE WOOD
4 GREGORY'S MDW
5 PENN KERNOW
6 FOXGLOVE CL

Middle Bamham Farm

Bulsworthy Farm

Lifton Park

HARNAFORD RD

HORNAPARK CL

327

Ridgecombe

3

Newham Manor

Moonhouse Plantation

84

5 SNOWDROP
6 BLUEBELL WLK
ROBIN DR

11
10
12
9

Stourscombe

BULSWORTHY LA

Lewcoombe

Wishworthy

Gatherley Wood

Harts

Ashleigh

2

Newton Farm

TRENIFFLE LA

Treniffle

Kellybeare

Turchington

7 TAVISTOCK RD
8 HONEYSUCKLE GDNS
9 BLACKBIRD CRES
10 BUTTERCUP MDW
11 CORNFLOWER CRES
12 CAMPION CL
13 BLACKTHORN CL

LAUNCESTON

Lawhitton Barton

Gatherley

83

Hurdon Down

A388

Sheers Barton

B3362

LAWHITTON DOWN

ST MICHAELS CL

HOLMANS MDW

Lawhitton

Bawcombe

Yeomans

Winbrook

Hall Farm

1

82

34   A   35   B   36   C   37   D   38   E   39   F

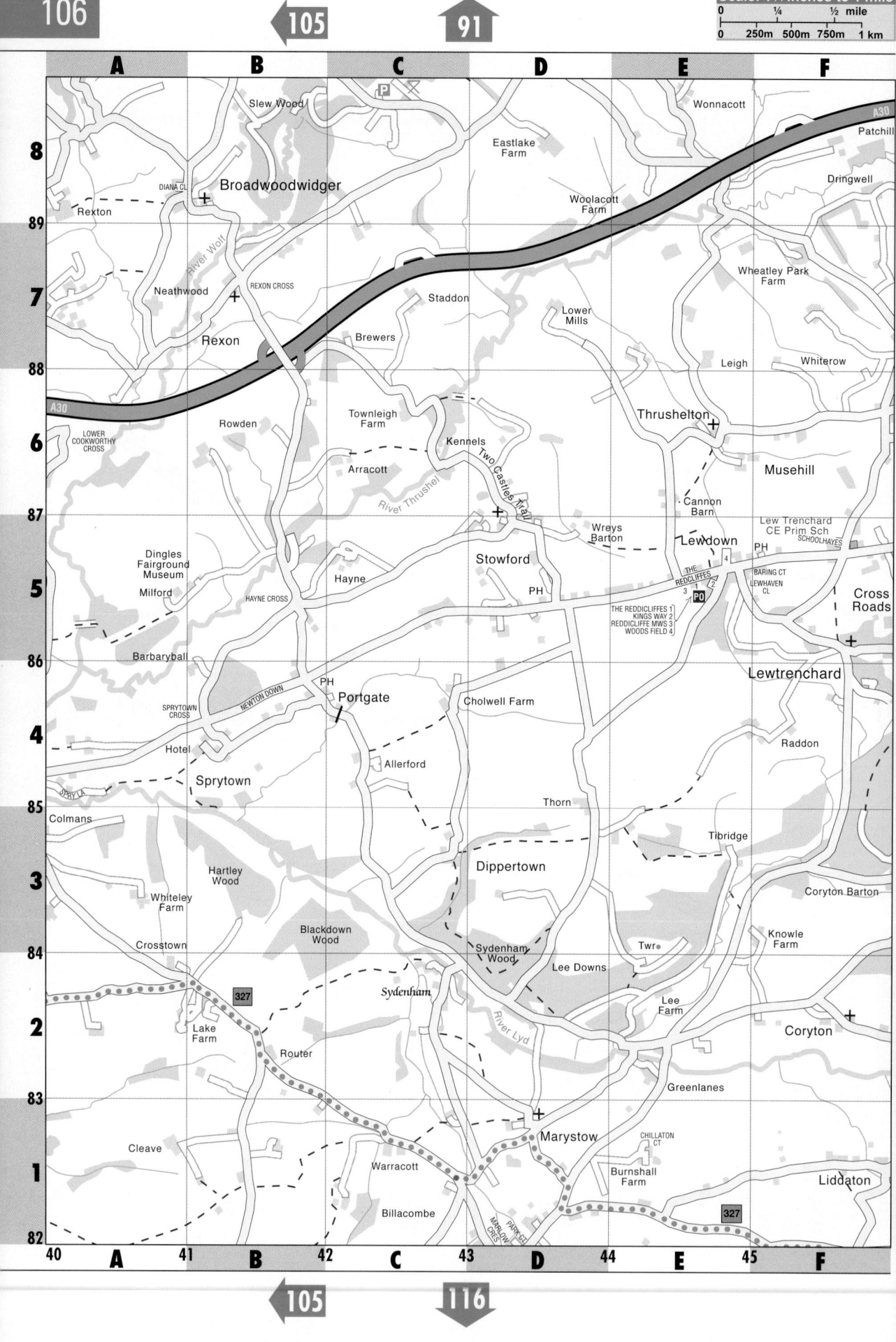

105
91

Scale: 1¾ inches to 1 mile

0   ¼   ½ mile

0   250m 500m 750m 1 km

A   B   C   D   E   F

A30

Wonnacott

Patchill

Slew Wood

Eastlake
Farm

Woolacott
Farm

Dringwell

8

DIANA CL

Broadwoodwidger

Rexton

Wheatley Park
Farm

89

River Wolf

REXON CROSS

7

Neathwood

Rexon

Staddon

Lower
Mills

Leigh

Whiterow

Brewers

88

A30

Rowden

Townleigh
Farm

Kennels

Thrushelton

Musehill

6

LOWER
COOKWORTHY
CROSS

River Thrushel

Two Castles Trail

Arracott

Cannon
Barn

Lew Trenchard
CE Prim Sch
SCHOOLHAYES

87

Dingles
Fairground
Museum

Hayne

Stowford

Wreys
Barton

Lewdown

PH

THE
REDDICLIFFES

BARING CT
LEWHAVEN
CL

4

Milford

HAYNE CROSS

PH

PO

Cross
Roads

5

THE REDDICLIFFES 1
KINGS WAY 2
REDDICLIFFE MWS 3
WOODS FIELD 4

86

Barbaryball

NEWTON DOWN

PH

Portgate

Cholwell Farm

Lewtrenchard

SPRYTOWN
CROSS

Hotel

Allerford

Raddon

4

VERY LA

Sprytown

Thorn

Tibridge

85

Colmans

Hartley
Wood

Dippertown

Coryton Barton

3

Whiteley
Farm

Blackdown
Wood

Sydenham
Wood

Twr

Knowle
Farm

84

Crosstown

Lee Downs

327

Lake
Farm

Router

Sydenham

Lee
Farm

Coryton

2

River Lyd

Greenlanes

83

Cleave

Marystow

CHILLATON
CT

Liddaton

Warracott

Burnshall
Farm

1

Billacombe

PARK

MARLOW
CRES

327

82

40   A   41   B   42   C   43   D   44   E   45   F

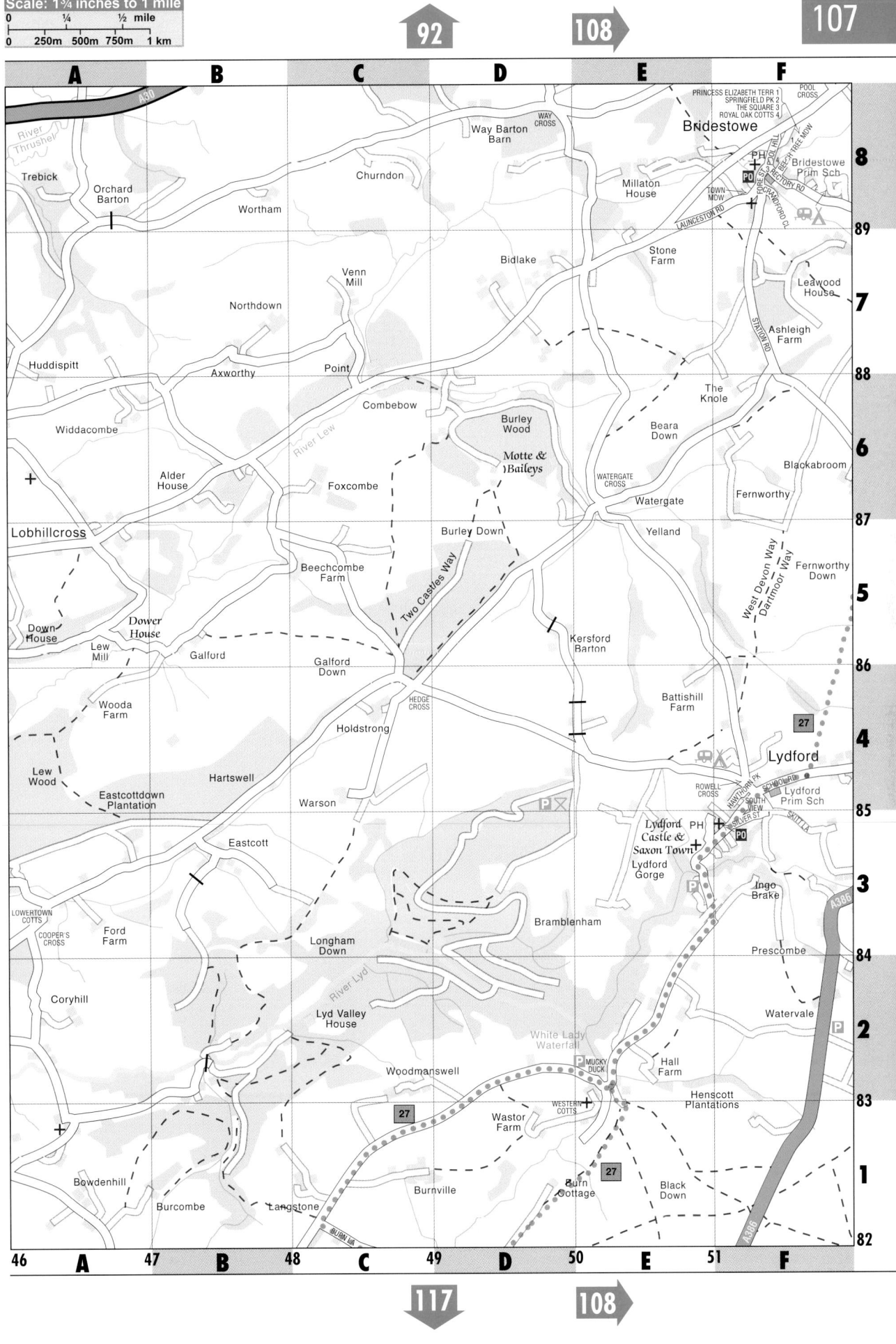

Scale: 1¾ inches to 1 mile

0   ¼   ½ mile
0 250m 500m 750m 1 km

92
108

A | B | C | D | E | F

8
89
7
88
6
87
5
86
4
85
3
84
2
1
82

Way Barton
Barn

WAY
CROSS

PRINCESS ELIZABETH TERR 1
SPRINGFIELD PK 2
THE SQUARE 3
ROYAL OAK COTTS 4

POOL
CROSS

Bridestowe

Bridestowe
Prim Sch

PH
PO

BEECH TREE MDW

OLD HILL

RECTORY RD

CRANFORD CL

TOWN
MDW

LAUNCESTON RD

Trebick

Orchard
Barton

Wortham

Churndon

Bidlake

Millaton
House

Stone
Farm

STATION RD

Leawood
House

Venn
Mill

Northdown

Ashleigh
Farm

Huddispitt

Axworthy

Point

Combebow

River Lew

Burley
Wood

Motte &
Baileys

Beara
Down

The
Knole

Widdacombe

Alder
House

Foxcombe

WATERGATE
CROSS

Watergate

Blackabroom

Fernworthy

Lobhillcross

Beechcombe
Farm

Burley Down

Two Castles Way

Yelland

West Devon Way
Dartmoor Way

Fernworthy
Down

Down
House

Dower
House

Galford

Galford
Down

Kersford
Barton

Battishill
Farm

27

Lew
Mill

HEDGE
CROSS

Holdstrong

Lydford

Wooda
Farm

Lydford
Prim Sch

Lew
Wood

Hartswell

Warson

ROWELL
CROSS

SOUTH
VIEW

SCHOOL RD

SKITTLA

HAWTHORN PK

Lydford
Castle &
Saxon Town

PH
PO

SILVER ST

Eastcottdown
Plantation

Eastcott

Lydford
Gorge

Ingo
Brake

Lowertown
Cotts

Cooper's
Cross

Ford
Farm

Longham
Down

Bramblenham

Prescombe

Coryhill

River Lyd

Watervale

Lyd Valley
House

White Lady
Waterfall

MUCKY
DUCK

Hall
Farm

Henscott
Plantations

Woodmanswell

27

Wastor
Farm

WESTERN
COTTS

Bowdenhill

Burcombe

Langstone

BURN LA

Burnville

Burn
Cottage

27

Black
Down

A386

A30

A386

A386

River
Thrushel

117
108

46 | 47 | 48 | 49 | 50 | 51
A | B | C | D | E | F

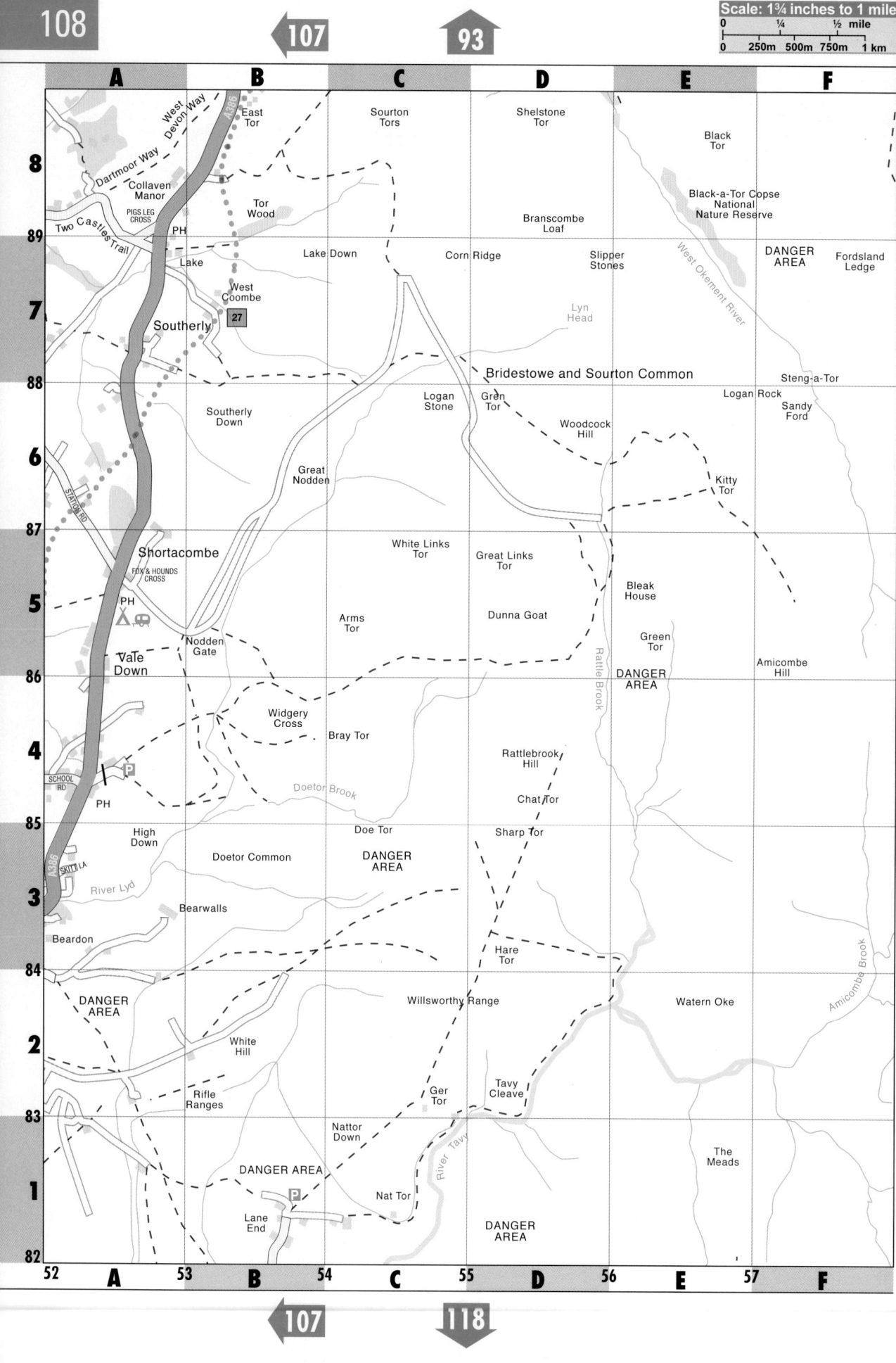

Scale: 1¾ inches to 1 mile

0   ¼   ½ mile
0 250m 500m 750m 1 km

A **B** **C** **D** **E** **F**

West Devon Way

A386

East Tor

Sourton Tors

Shelstone Tor

Black Tor

8

Dartmoor Way

Collaven Manor

PIGS LEG CROSS

Tor Wood

Black-a-Tor Copse National Nature Reserve

Two Castles Trail

PH

Lake Down

Branscombe Loaf

89

Lake

Corn Ridge

Slipper Stones

West Okement River

DANGER AREA

Fordsland Ledge

West Coombe

27

Bridestowe and Sourton Common

7

Southerly

Steng-a-Tor

88

Logan Stone

Gren Tor

Logan Rock

Sandy Ford

STATION RD

Southerly Down

Woodcock Hill

6

Great Nodden

Kitty Tor

87

White Links Tor

Great Links Tor

Shortacombe

FOX & HOUNDS CROSS

Bleak House

5

PH

Arms Tor

Dunna Goat

Green Tor

Amicombe Hill

86

Nodden Gate

Rattle Brook

DANGER AREA

Vale Down

Widgery Cross

Bray Tor

Rattlebrook Hill

4

Doetor Brook

P

Chat Tor

SCHOOL RD

PH

Doe Tor

Sharp Tor

85

High Down

Doetor Common

DANGER AREA

A386

SKITT LA

River Lyd

Hare Tor

3

Bearwalls

Beardon

84

DANGER AREA

Willsworthy Range

Watern Oke

Amicombe Brook

White Hill

2

Rifle Ranges

Ger Tor

Tavy Cleave

83

Nattor Down

River Tavy

The Meads

DANGER AREA

1

P

Nat Tor

Lane End

DANGER AREA

82

52 **A** **53** **B** **54** **C** **55** **D** **56** **E** **57** **F**

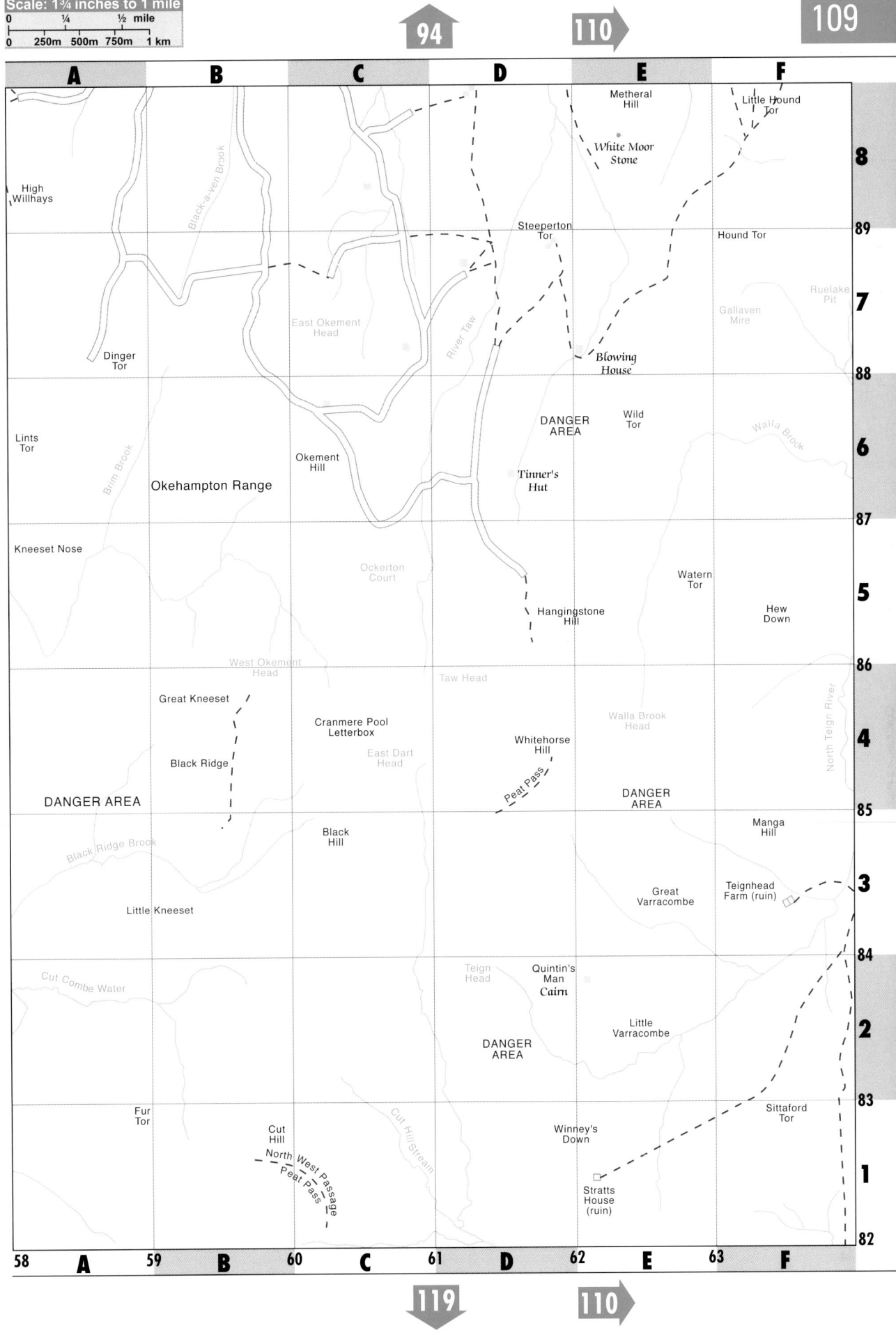

A   B   C   D   E   F

High
Willhays

Black-a-ven Brook

Metheral
Hill

Little Hound
Tor

8

White Moor
Stone

Steeperton
Tor

89

Hound Tor

East Okement
Head

Dinger
Tor

River Taw

Ruelake
Pit

7

Gallaven
Mire

Blowing
House

88

Lints
Tor

Brim Brook

DANGER
AREA

Wild
Tor

Walla Brook

6

Okehampton Range

Okement
Hill

Tinner's
Hut

87

Kneeset Nose

Ockerton
Court

Watern
Tor

5

Hangingstone
Hill

Hew
Down

West Okement
Head

Taw Head

86

Great Kneeset

Cranmere Pool
Letterbox

Walla Brook
Head

North Teign River

4

Black Ridge

East Dart
Head

Whitehorse
Hill

Peat Pass

DANGER
AREA

DANGER AREA

85

Black
Hill

Manga
Hill

Black Ridge Brook

Little Kneeset

Great
Varracombe

Teignhead
Farm (ruin)

3

84

Cut Combe Water

Teign
Head

Quintin's
Man
Cairn

Little
Varracombe

2

DANGER
AREA

83

Fur
Tor

Cut Hill Stream

Winney's
Down

Sittaford
Tor

Cut
Hill

North West Passage
Peat Pass

1

Stratts
House
(ruin)

82

58   A   59   B   60   C   61   D   62   E   63   F

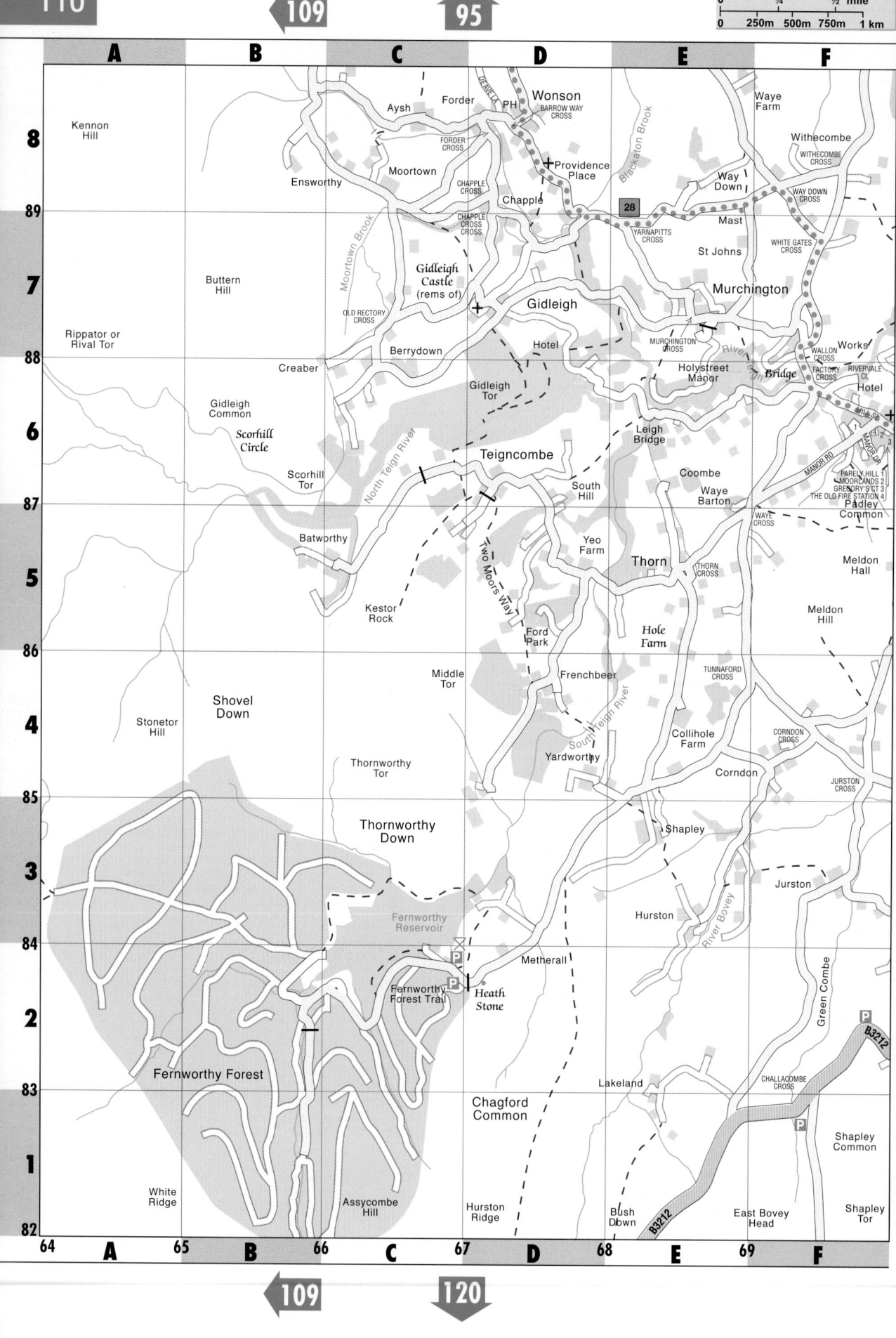

109
95

Scale: 1¾ inches to 1 mile

0 ¼ ½ mile
0 250m 500m 750m 1 km

A **B** **C** **D** **E** **F**

Kennon Hill

Aysh Forder PH Wonson
Barrow Way Cross
Waye Farm

Forder Cross
Moortown
Providence Place
Withecombe
Withecombe Cross

Ensworthy
Chapple Cross
Chapple
Way Down
Way Down Cross
Mast

89

Chapple Cross Cross
28
Yarnapitts Cross
White Gates Cross

Buttern Hill

Gidleigh Castle (rems of)
Gidleigh
St Johns
Murchington

7

Old Rectory Cross
Hotel
Murchington Cross
Wallon Cross
Works

Rippator or Rival Tor
Berrydown
Holystreet Manor
Factory Cross
Bridge
Rivervale CL
Hotel

Creaber
88

Gidleigh Common
Gidleigh Tor
Leigh Bridge
Mile St
Padley Common

Scorhill Circle
Teigncombe
South Hill
Coombe
Waye
Manor Rd
Parely Hill
Moorlands 2
Gregory's Ct 3
The Old Fire Station 4

6

Scorhill Tor
North Teign River
Yeo Farm
Waye Barton
Waye Cross

87

Batworthy
Kestor Rock
Two Moors Way
Thorn
Thorn Cross
Meldon Hall

5

Ford Park
Frenchbeer
Hole Farm
Tunnaford Cross
Meldon Hill

86

Shovel Down
Middle Tor
Yardworthy
South Teign River
Collihole Farm
Corndon Cross
Jurston Cross

4

Stonetor Hill
Thornworthy Tor
Corndon

85

Thornworthy Down
Shapley

3

Fernworthy Reservoir
Hurston
River Bovey
Jurston

84

Metherall
Green Combe

Fernworthy Forest Trail
Heath Stone
B3212

2

Lakeland
Challacombe Cross
Shapley Common

83

Fernworthy Forest
Chagford Common

White Ridge
Assycombe Hill
Hurston Ridge
Bush Down
B3212
East Bovey Head
Shapley Tor

82

64 65 66 67 68 69

A **B** **C** **D** **E** **F**

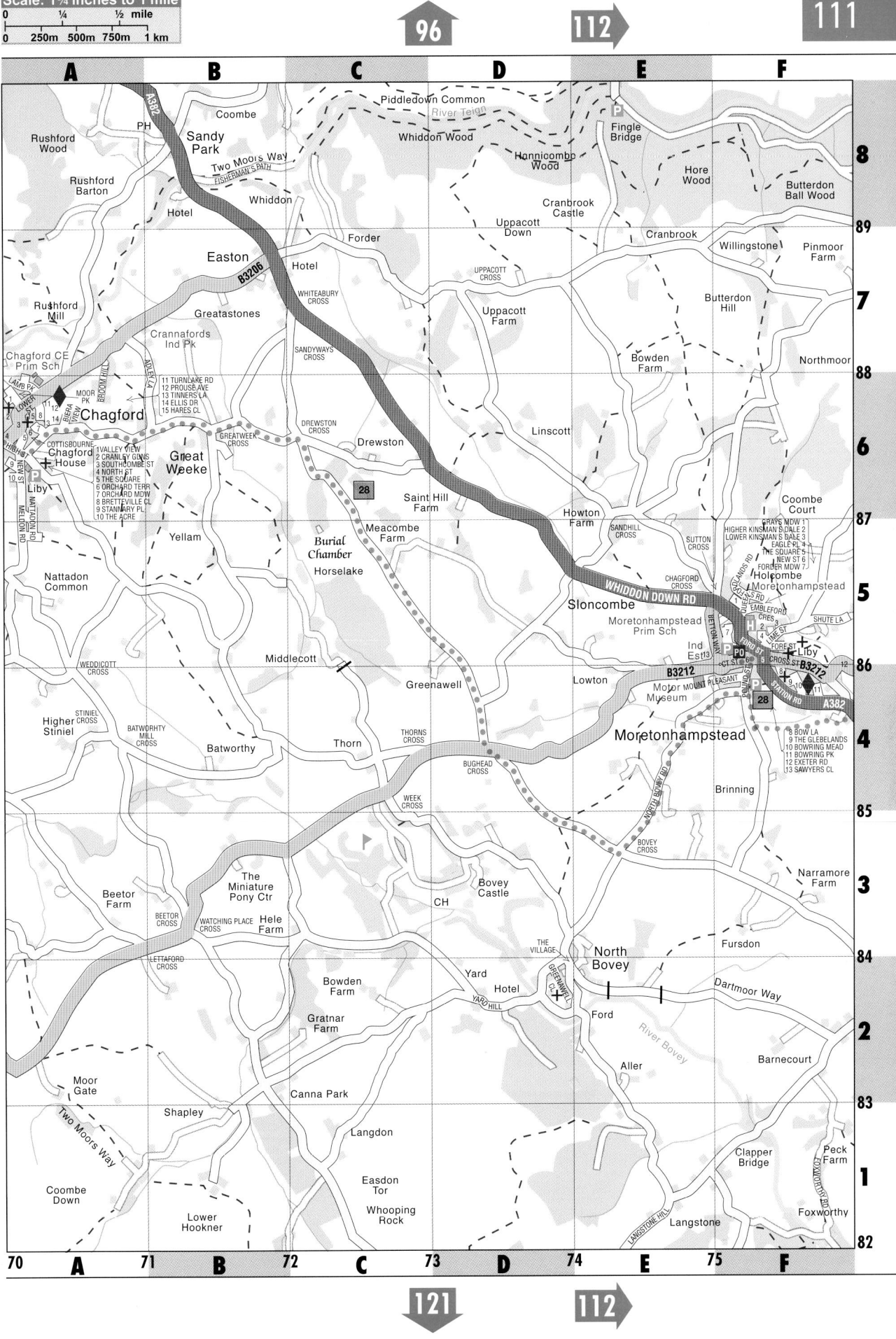

Scale: 1¾ inches to 1 mile

0   ¼   ½ mile
0   250m 500m 750m 1 km

96
112

A   B   C   D   E   F

Rushford
Wood

Piddledown Common
River Teign

Coombe

Sandy
Park

Whiddon Wood

P
Fingle
Bridge

Hannicombo
Wood

Hore
Wood

Butterdon
Ball Wood

8

Rushford
Barton

PH

Two Moors Way
FISHERMAN'S PATH

Hotel

Whiddon

Whiddon

Forder

Uppacott
Down

Cranbrook
Castle

Cranbrook

Willingstone

Pinmoor
Farm

89

Easton

B3206

Hotel

WHITEABURY
CROSS

UPPACOTT
CROSS

Uppacott
Farm

Butterdon
Hill

7

Rushford
Mill

Greatastones

SANDYWAYS
CROSS

Bowden
Farm

Northmoor

88

Chagford CE
Prim Sch

Crannafords
Ind Pk

11 TURNLAKE RD
12 PROUSE AVE
13 TINNERS LA
14 ELLIS DR
15 HARES CL

MOOR
PK

Chagford

Drewston
Cross

DREWSTON
CROSS

Drewston

Linscott

Coombe
Court

6

Libry

Chagford
House

1 VALLEY VIEW
2 CRANLSY GDNS
3 SOUTHCOMBE ST
4 NORTH ST
5 THE SQUARE
6 ORCHARD TERR
7 ORCHARD MDW
8 BRETTEVILLE CL
9 STANNARY PL
10 THE ACRE

Great
Weeke

GREATWEEK
CROSS

28

Saint Hill
Farm

Howton
Farm

SANDHILL
CROSS

SUTTON
CROSS

GRAYS MDW 1
HIGHER KINSMAN S DALE 2
LOWER KINSMAN S DALE 3
EAGLE PL 4
THE SQUARE 5
NEW ST 6
FORDER MDW 7

87

Yellam

Burial
Chamber

Meacombe
Farm

CHAGFORD
CROSS

Holcombe

Moretonhampstead

Nattadon
Common

Horselake

Sloncombe

Moretonhampstead
Prim Sch

EMBLEFORD
CRES

H

Libry
B3212

5

WEDDICOTT
CROSS

Middlecott

Greenawell

Lowton

Ind
Est13

PO
P

CROSS ST

FORE ST

B3212

12

86

Higher
Stiniel

STINIEL
CROSS

BATWORTHY
MILL CROSS

Batworthy

Thorn

THORNS
CROSS

Motor
Museum

MOUNT PLEASANT

P
28

A382

8 BOW LA
9 THE GLEBELANDS
10 BOWRING MEAD
11 BOWRING PK
12 EXETER RD
13 SAWYERS CL

4

Beetor
Farm

BEETOR
CROSS

The
Miniature
Pony Ctr

WEEK
CROSS

BUGHEAD
CROSS

Moretonhampstead

Brinning

85

WATCHING PLACE
CROSS

Hele
Farm

CH

Bovey
Castle

BOVEY
CROSS

Narramore
Farm

3

LETTAFORD
CROSS

Bowden
Farm

Yard
Hotel

THE
VILLAGE

GREENWELL
CL

North
Bovey

Fursdon

Dartmoor Way

84

Moor
Gate

Gratnar
Farm

YARD HILL

Ford

Aller

River Bovey

Barnecourt

2

Two Moors Way

Shapley

Canna Park

Langdon

83

Coombe
Down

Lower
Hookner

Easdon
Tor

Whooping
Rock

Clapper
Bridge

Peck
Farm

FOXWORTHY RD

Foxworthy

1

LANGSTONE HILL

Langstone

82

70   A   71   B   72   C   73   D   74   E   75   F

121
112

Scale: 1¾ inches to 1 mile

0 ¼ ½ mile

0 250m 500m 750m 1 km

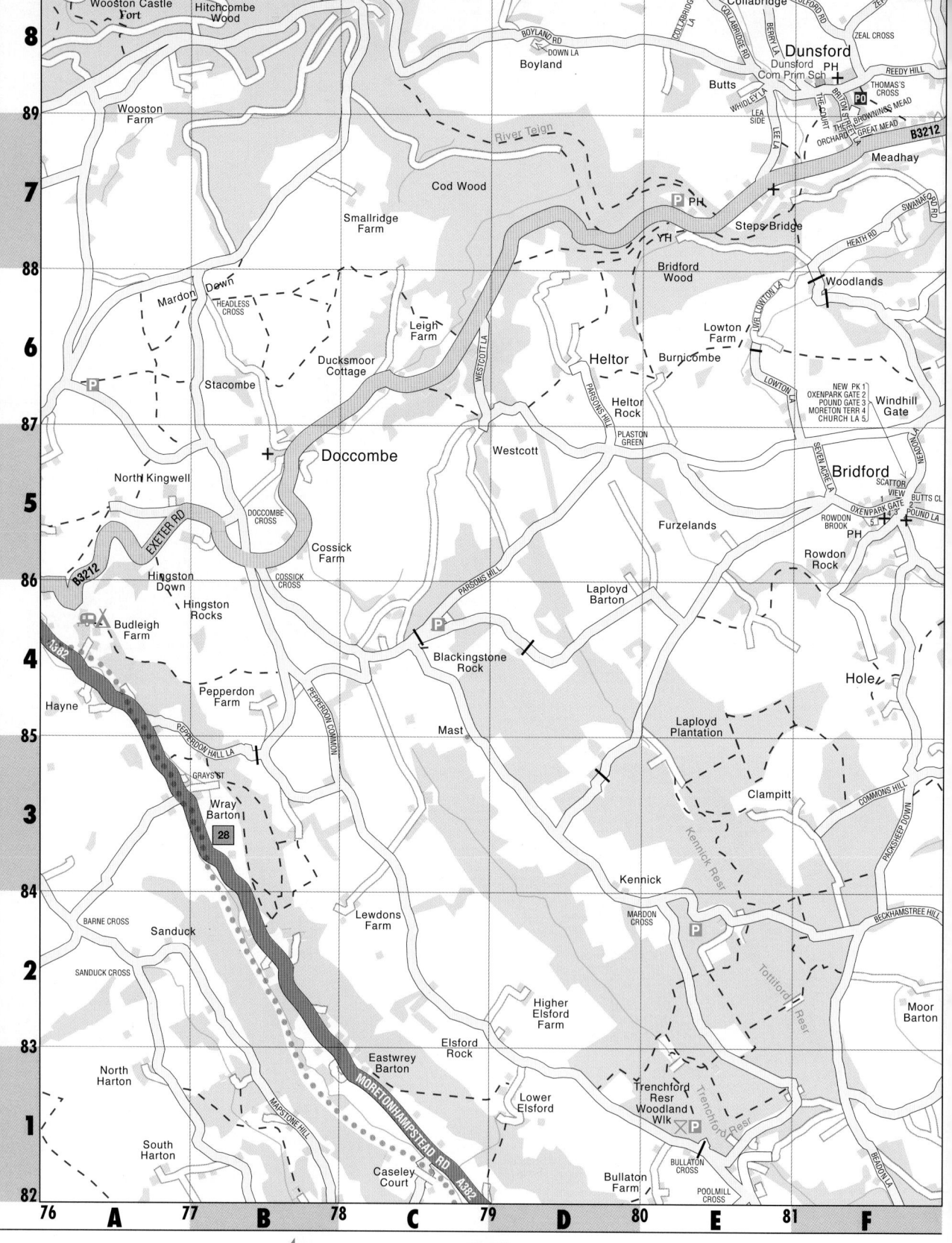

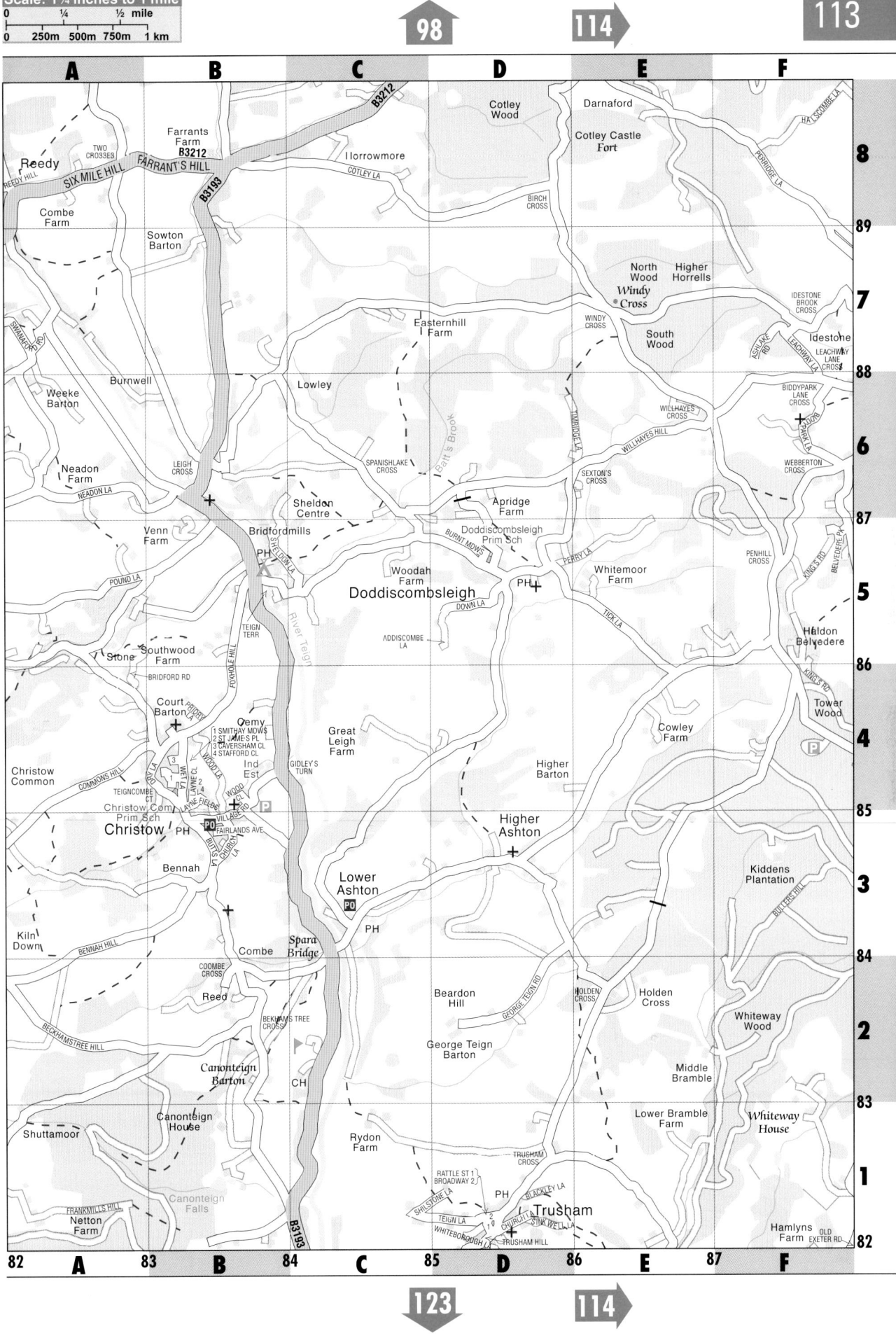

A   B   C   D   E   F

8

89

7

88

6

87

5

86

4

85

3

84

2

83

1

82

Reedy

SIX MILE HILL

REEDY HILL

TWO CROSSES

Combe Farm

Sowton Barton

Farrants Farm
B3212

FARRANT'S HILL

B3193

Horrowmore

COTLEY LA

B3212

Cotley Wood

Darnaford

Cotley Castle Fort

HATSCOMBE LA

PERRIDGE LA

Weeke Barton

Burnwell

Easternhill Farm

North Wood

Higher Horrells

Windy Cross

IDESTONE BROOK CROSS

Neadon Farm

NEADON LA

Lowley

Windy Cross

South Wood

ASHLAKE RD

LEACHWAY LA

LEACHWAY LANE CROSS

Idestone

Venn Farm

LEIGH CROSS

Spanishlake Cross

Batt's Brook

WILLHAYES CROSS

BIDDYPARK LANE CROSS

PARK LA

Webberton Cross

Sheldon Centre

Bridfordmills

SHELDON LA

PH

Apridge Farm

Doddiscombsleigh Prim Sch

WILL HAYES HILL

SEXTON'S CROSS

TUBRIDGE LA

POUND LA

PRIORY

Southwood Farm

BRIDFORD RD

Stone

FOXHOLE HILL

River Teign

TEIGN TERR

BURNT MOWS

Woodah Farm

Doddiscombsleigh

PERRY LA

PH

Whitemoor Farm

PENHILL CROSS

KING'S RD

BELVEDERE RD

Court Barton

Cemy

1 SMITHAY MOWS
2 ST JAME S PL
3 CAVERSHAM CL
4 STAFFORD CL

DOWN LA

ADDISCOMBE LA

TICK LA

Haldon Belvedere

Christow Common

COMMONS HILL

Great Leigh Farm

GIDLEY'S TURN

Higher Barton

Cowley Farm

P

Tower Wood

Christow Com Prim Sch

Christow

PH

PO

BURY LA

WET LA CL

LAYNE CL

WOOD LA

LAYNE FIELDS

WOOD

Ind Est

VILLAGE RD

FAIRLANDS AVE

CHURCH LA

P

Higher Ashton

Kiddens Plantation

BULLERS HILL

Bennah

BUTTS LA

KINGS RD

Kiln Down

BENNAH HILL

Combe

Spara Bridge

Lower Ashton

PO

PH

Beardon Hill

GEORGE TEIGN RD

Holden Cross

Holden Cross

Whiteway Wood

COOMBE CROSS

Reed

BEKHAMS TREE CROSS

George Teign Barton

Middle Bramble

BECKHAMSTREE HILL

Canonteign Barton

CH

Lower Bramble Farm

Whiteway House

Canonteign House

Rydon Farm

TRUSHAM CROSS

Shuttamoor

FRANKMILLS HILL

Netton Farm

Canonteign Falls

B3193

RATTLE ST 1
BROADWAY 2

SHILSTONE LA

TEIGN LA

WHITEBOROUGH LA

PH

BLACKLEY LA

CHURCH LA

SINK WELL LA

Trusham

TRUSHAM HILL

Hamlyns Farm

OLD EXETER RD

82   A   83   B   84   C   85   D   86   E   87   F

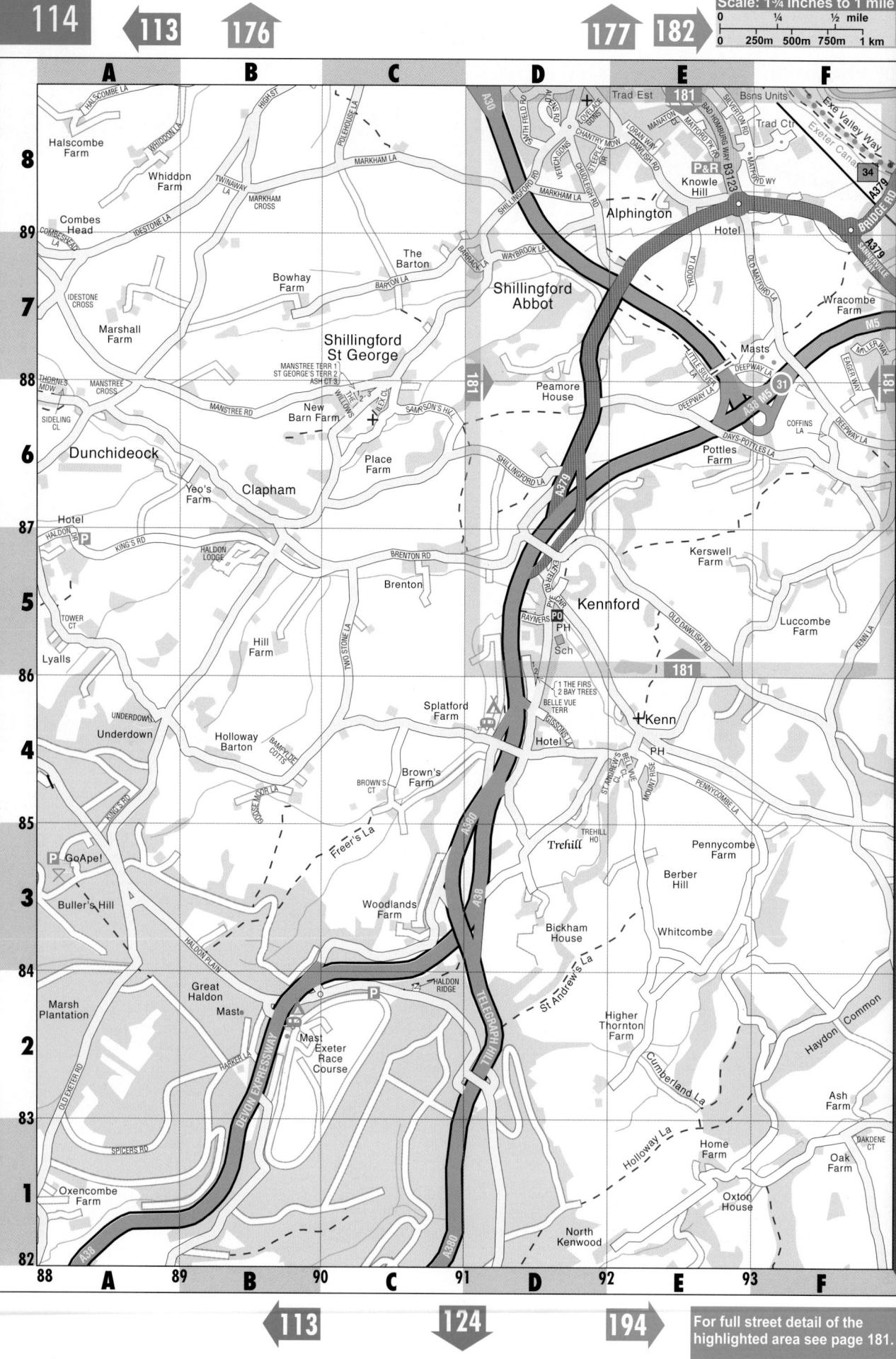

114
113
176
177
182

Scale: 1¾ inches to 1 mile
0   ¼   ½   mile
0   250m   500m   750m   1 km

A   B   C   D   E   F

8
Halscombe Farm
Halscombe La
Whiddon Farm
Whiddon La
High St
Markham La
Polehouse La
Trad Est
181
Bsns Units
Exe Valley Way
Exeter Canal
34

89
Combes Head
Combeshead La
Idestone La
Twinaway La
Markham Cross
The Barton
Barton La
Barrack La
Waybrook La
Shillingford Rd
Chudleigh Rd
Chantry Mdw
Steele Dr
Dawlish Rd
Knowle Hill
P&R
Alphington
Hotel
B3123
Bad Homburg Way
Silverton Rd
Matford Pk Rd
Matford Rd Wy
Trad Ctr
A379
Sannerville Way
A379

7
Idestone Cross
Bowhay Farm
Markham La
Shillingford Abbot
Little Silver
Masts
M5
Wracombe Farm
M5
Butler Way
Exxcet Way
181

Marshall Farm
Shillingford St George
Manstree Terr 1
St George's Terr 2
Ash Ct 3

88
Thornes Mdw
Manstree Cross
Manstree Rd
The Willows
Ilex Cl
New Barn Farm
Samson's Hil
Shillingford La
181
Peamore House
Deepway La
31
A38 M5
Coffins La
Deepway La

Sideling Cl

6
Dunchideock
Yeo's Farm
Clapham
Place Farm
A379
Pottles Farm
Days-Pottles La

87
Hotel
Haldon
P
King's Rd
Haldon Lodge
Brenton Rd
Exeter Rd
Kerswell Farm

5
Tower Ct
Lyalls
Hill Farm
Brenton
Two Stone La
Rayners
PH
Sch
PO
Kennford
Old Dawlish Rd
Luccombe Farm
Kenn La

86
181

Underdown

4
Underdown
Holloway Barton
Bampfylde Cotts
Goosemoor La
Splatford Farm
Brown's Ct
Brown's Farm
Hotel
Rissons Cl
1 The Firs
2 Bay Trees
Belle Vue Terr
Kenn
PH
St Andrew's Cl
Belle Vue
Mount Rise
Pennycombe La

85
King's Rd
Freer's La
A38
Trehill
Trehill Ho
Pennycombe Farm
Berber Hill

3
Buller's Hill
P
GoApe!
Haldon Plain
Woodlands Farm
A38
Bickham House
Whitcombe
Haydon Common

84
Marsh Plantation
Great Haldon
Haldon Ridge
P
Telegraph Hill
St Andrew's La
Higher Thornton Farm
Ash Farm

2
Old Exeter Rd
Harcer La
Devon Expressway
Mast
Mast
Exeter Race Course
A380
Cumberland La
Oakdene Ct

83
Spicers Rd
Holloway La
Home Farm
Oak Farm

1
Oxencombe Farm
A380
North Kenwood
Oxton House

82
A38

88   A   89   B   90   C   91   D   92   E   93   F

113
124
194

For full street detail of the highlighted area see page 181.

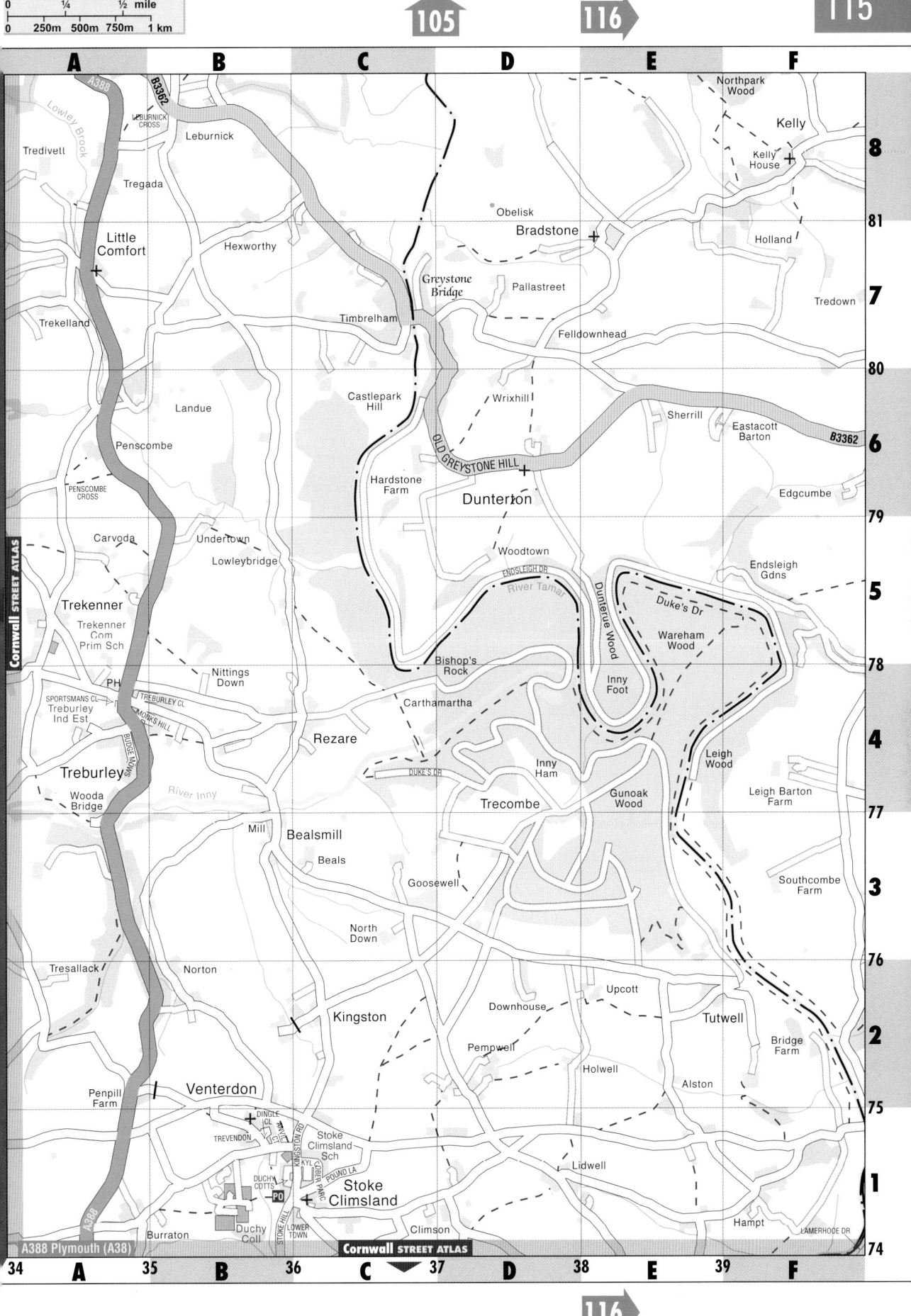

Cornwall STREET ATLAS

A388
B3362
LEBURNICK CROSS
Tredivett
Lowley Brook
Leburnick
Little Comfort
Tregada
Hexworthy
Tregada
Trekelland
Timbrelham
Greystone Bridge
Obelisk
Bradstone
Northpark Wood
Kelly
Kelly House
Holland
Pallastreet
Tredown
Felldownhead
Landue
Penscombe
Castlepark Hill
Wrixhill
Sherrill
Eastacott Barton
Edgcumbe
B3362
PENSCOMBE CROSS
Hardstone Farm
OLD GREYSTONE HILL
Dunterton
Carvoda
Undertown
Lowleybridge
Woodtown
Endsleigh Gdns
ENDSLEIGH DR
Trekenner
River Tamar
Duke's Dr
Trekenner Com Prim Sch
Dunterue Wood
Wareham Wood
Nittings Down
Bishop's Rock
Inny Foot
Leigh Wood
PH
TREBURLEY CL
MONKS HILL
Carthamartha
Treburley Ind Est
SPORTSMANS CL
Rezare
Inny Ham
Gunoak Wood
Leigh Barton Farm
BUDGE DOWNS
Treburley
River Inny
Trecombe
Wooda Bridge
Mill
Bealsmill
Beals
Goosewell
Southcombe Farm
DUKE'S DR
Tresallack
Norton
North Down
Upcott
Kingston
Downhouse
Tutwell
Pempwell
Bridge Farm
Penpill Farm
Holwell
Alston
Venterdon
DINGLE CL
TREVENDON
Stoke Climsland Sch
Lidwell
KINGSTON RD
POUND LA
COBER PARC
KYL
DUCHY CDTTS
PO
Stoke Climsland
Hampt
LAMERHOOE DR
Burraton
Duchy Coll
STOKE HILL
LOWER TOWN
Climson

Scale: 1¾ inches to 1 mile
0 ¼ ½ mile
0 250m 500m 750m 1 km

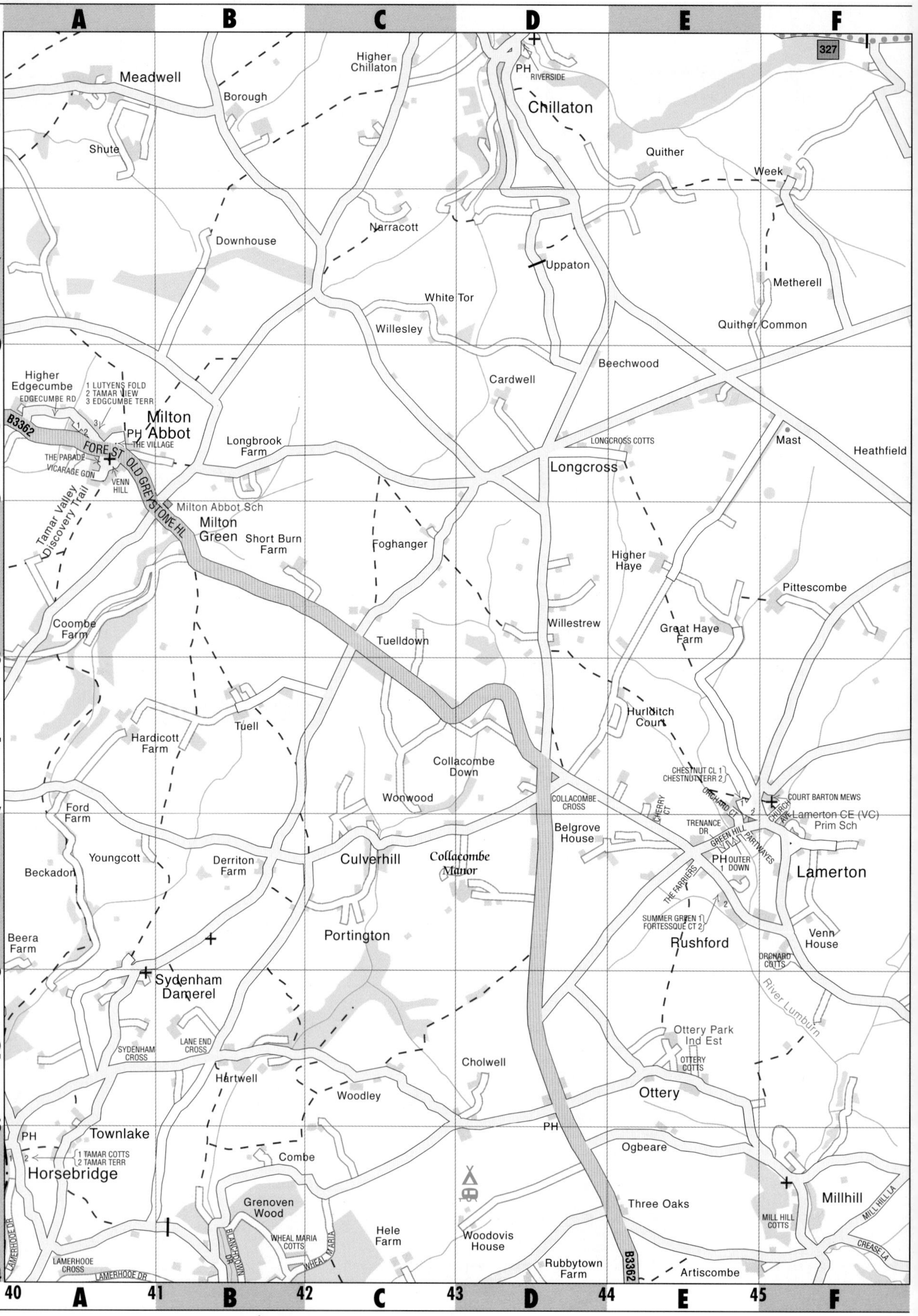

A B C D E F

8
81
7
80
6
79
5
78
4
77
3
76
2
75
1
74

Meadwell
Borough
Higher Chillaton
Chillaton
PH RIVERSIDE
327
Quither
Week
Shute
Downhouse
Narracott
Uppaton
Metherell
White Tor
Quither Common
Willesley
Beechwood
Cardwell
Higher Edgecumbe
EDGECUMBE RD
1 LUTYENS FOLD
2 TAMAR VIEW
3 EDGCUMBE TERR
B3362
Milton Abbot
PH
FORE ST
THE VILLAGE
THE PARADE
VICARAGE GDN
VENN HILL
OLD GREYSTONE HL
Longbrook Farm
Longcross
LONGCROSS COTTS
Mast
Heathfield
Tamar Valley Discovery Trail
Milton Abbot Sch
Milton Green
Short Burn Farm
Foghanger
Higher Haye
Pittescombe
Coombe Farm
Tuelldown
Willestrew
Great Haye Farm
Hardicott Farm
Tuell
Collacombe Down
Wonwood
Hurlditch Court
CHESTNUT CL 1
CHESTNUT TERR 2
COURT BARTON MEWS
Ford Farm
Youngcott
Derriton Farm
Culverhill
Collacombe Cross
Collacombe Manor
Belgrove House
CHERRY CT
ORCHARD CT
CHURCH
Lamerton CE (VC) Prim Sch
Beckadon
Portington
TRENANCE DR
GREEN HILL
PARTWAYS
PH OUTER 1 DOWN
Lamerton
Beera Farm
THE FARRIERS
SUMMER GREEN 1
FORTESSQUE CT 2
Rushford
Venn House
ORCHARD COTTS
Sydenham Damerel
Cholwell
Ottery Park Ind Est
OTTERY COTTS
River Lumburn
LANE END CROSS
SYDENHAM CROSS
Hartwell
Woodley
Ottery
PH
Townlake
PH
Combe
Ogbeare
Millhill
1 TAMAR COTTS
2 TAMAR TERR
Horsebridge
Grenoven Wood
WHEAL MARIA COTTS
Hele Farm
Woodovis House
Three Oaks
MILL HILL COTTS
MILL HILL LA
LAMERHOOE DR
LAMERHOOE CROSS
LAMERHOOE DR
BLANCHDOWN DR
WHEAL MARIA
Rubbytown Farm
B3362
Artiscombe
CREASE LA

40 41 42 43 44 45

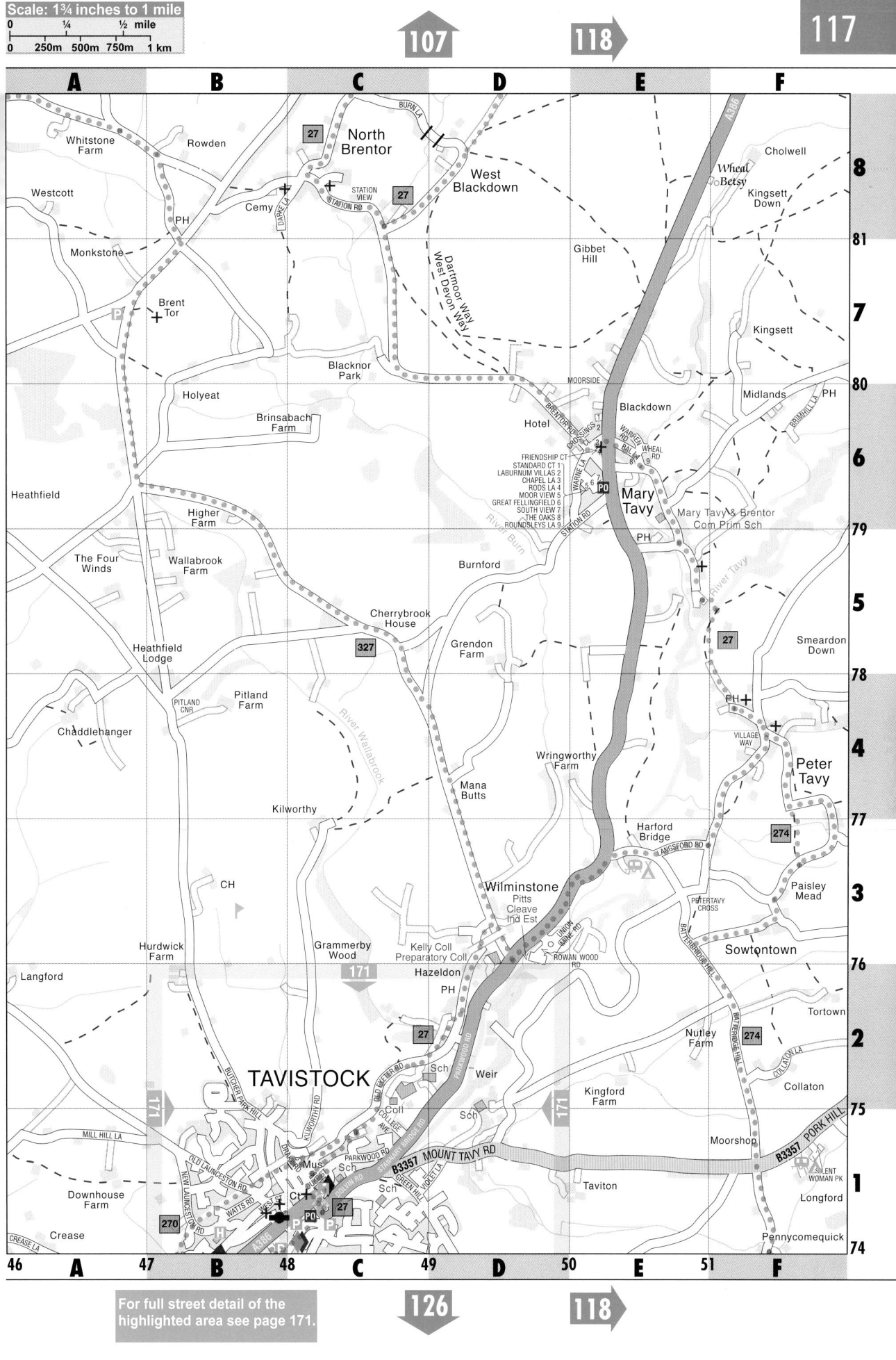

Scale: 1¾ inches to 1 mile

0   ¼   ½ mile
0 250m 500m 750m 1 km

107

118

117

A B C D E F

8
81
7
80
6
79
5
78
4
77
3
76
2
75
1
74

Whitstone Farm
Rowden
27
North Brentor
BURN LA
West Blackdown
Wheal Betsy
Cholwell
Kingsett Down

Westcott
Cemy
DARKE LA
STATION VIEW
27
STATION RD
Gibbet Hill
Kingsett

Monkstone
PH
Brent Tor
P
Midlands
PH

Blacknor Park
MOORSIDE
Blackdown
BRIMHILL

Holyeat
Hotel
BRENTOR RD
CROSSINGS
WARNE LA
WARREN RD
WHEAL RD
WHEAL BAL

Heathfield
Brinsabach Farm
FRIENDSHIP CT 1
STANDARD CT 1
LABURNUM VILLAS 2
CHAPEL LA 3
RODS LA 4
MOOR VIEW 5
GREAT FELLINGFIELD 6
SOUTH VIEW 7
THE OAKS 8
ROUNDSLEYS LA 9
PO
Mary Tavy
Mary Tavy & Brenter Com Prim Sch

Higher Farm
River Burn
STATION RD
Burnford
PH
River Tavy

The Four Winds
Wallabrook Farm
327
Cherrybrook House
Grendon Farm
27
Smeardon Down

Chaddlehanger
Heathfield Lodge
PITLAND CNR
Pitland Farm
River Wallabrook
PH
VILLAGE WAY
Peter Tavy
274

Kilworthy
Mana Butts
Wringworthy Farm
Paisley Mead

Langford
Hurdwick Farm
CH
Grammerby Wood
171
Kelly Coll Preparatory Coll
Hazeldon
PH
Wilminstone
Pitts Cleave Ind Est
Harford Bridge
LANGSFORD RD
PETERTAVY CROSS
Sowtontown
BATTERIDGE HILL
COLLATON LA
Tortown
Collaton

Mill Hill La
TAVISTOCK
BUTCHER PARK HILL
171
KILWORTHY RD
OLD EXETER RD
27
Sch
UNION LANE RD
ROWAN WOOD RD
Weir
171
Kingford Farm
27
Nutley Farm
274
Moorshop
B3357 PORK HILL

Downhouse Farm
270
Crease
NEW LAUNCESTON RD
OLD LAUNCESTON RD
WATTS RD
Mus
COLLEGE AVE
PARKWOOD RD
SPRINGHILL CROSS RD
GREEN HILL
Sch
Sch
B3357 MOUNT TAVY RD
Taviton
Kingford Farm
LENT WOMAN PK
Longford
Pennycomequick

CREASE LA
PO
27
A386
H
Ct

46 A 47 B 48 C 49 D 50 E 51 F

126

118

For full street detail of the highlighted area see page 171.

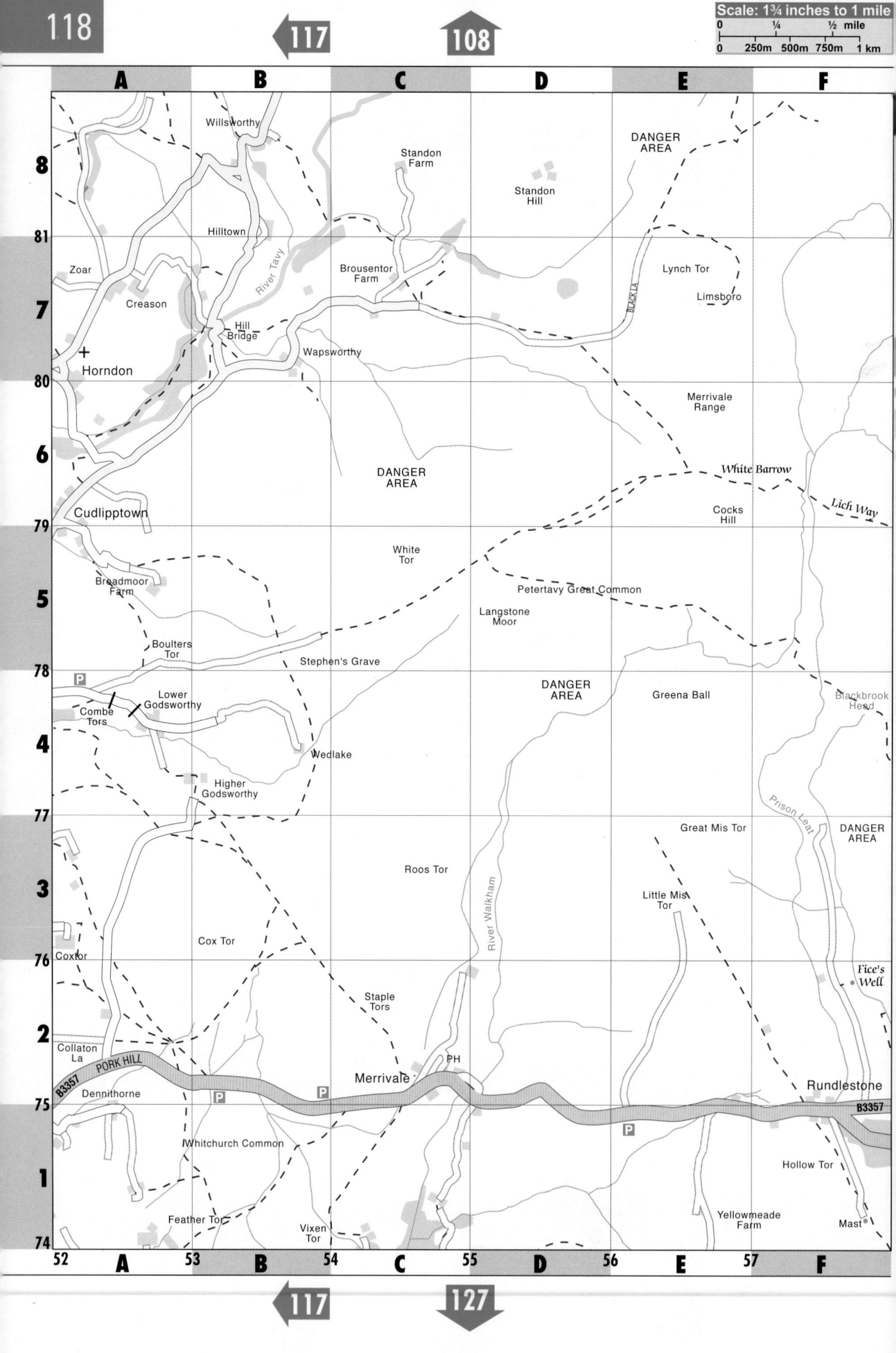

118

117

108

Scale: 1¾ inches to 1 mile

0   ¼   ½ mile
0   250m 500m 750m 1 km

A   B   C   D   E   F

8

Willsworthy

Standon
Farm

DANGER
AREA

Standon
Hill

81

Hilltown

River Tavy

Brousentor
Farm

Lynch Tor

Limsboro

BLACKLA

Zoar

7

Creason

Hill
Bridge

Wapsworthy

80

Horndon

Merrivale
Range

6

DANGER
AREA

White Barrow

Lich Way

Cudlipptown

Cocks
Hill

79

White
Tor

Broadmoor
Farm

Petertavy Great Common

5

Langstone
Moor

Boulters
Tor

Stephen's Grave

78

P

DANGER
AREA

Greena Ball

Blackbrook
Head

Combe
Tors

Lower
Godsworthy

4

Wedlake

Higher
Godsworthy

Great Mis Tor

DANGER
AREA

Prison Leat

77

Roos Tor

Little Mis
Tor

River Walkham

3

Cox Tor

Coxtor

76

Fice's
Well

Staple
Tors

2

Collaton
La

PORK HILL

PH

Merrivale

Rundlestone

B3357

Dennithorne

P

P

B3357

75

P

Whitchurch Common

Hollow Tor

1

Feather Tor

Vixen
Tor

Yellowmeade
Farm

Mast

74

52   A   53   B   54   C   55   D   56   E   57   F

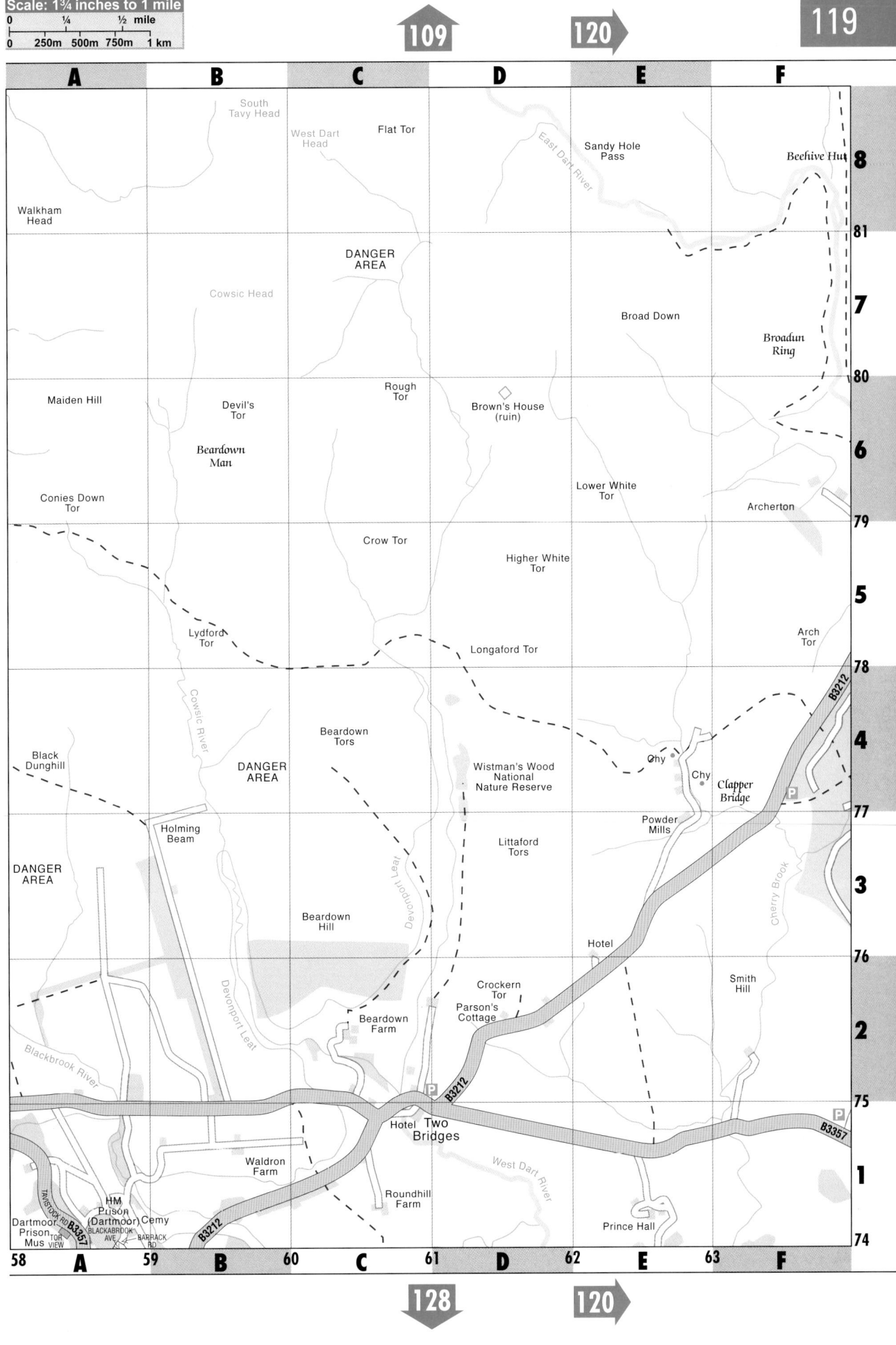

A   B   C   D   E   F

8

South Tavy Head

West Dart Head

Flat Tor

East Dart River

Sandy Hole Pass

Beehive Hut

81

Walkham Head

DANGER AREA

7

Cowsic Head

Broad Down

Broadun Ring

80

Maiden Hill

Devil's Tor

Rough Tor

Brown's House (ruin)

6

Beardown Man

Lower White Tor

Archerton

Conies Down Tor

79

Crow Tor

Higher White Tor

Arch Tor

5

Lydford Tor

Longaford Tor

78

B3212

Black Dunghill

Beardown Tors

Chy

4

Chy

Clapper Bridge

P

77

DANGER AREA

Holming Beam

Wistman's Wood National Nature Reserve

Powder Mills

Cherry Brook

DANGER AREA

Littaford Tors

3

Devonport Leat

Beardown Hill

76

Devonport Leat

Hotel

Smith Hill

2

Crockern Tor

Parson's Cottage

Beardown Farm

Blackbrook River

Beardown Farm

B3212

75

P

Hotel   Two Bridges

P

B3357

1

Waldron Farm

West Dart River

74

Roundhill Farm

TAVISTOCK RD

HM Prison (Dartmoor) Cemy

Prince Hall

Dartmoor Prison Mus

B3357

BLACKBROOK AVE

TOR VIEW

BARRACK RD

B3212

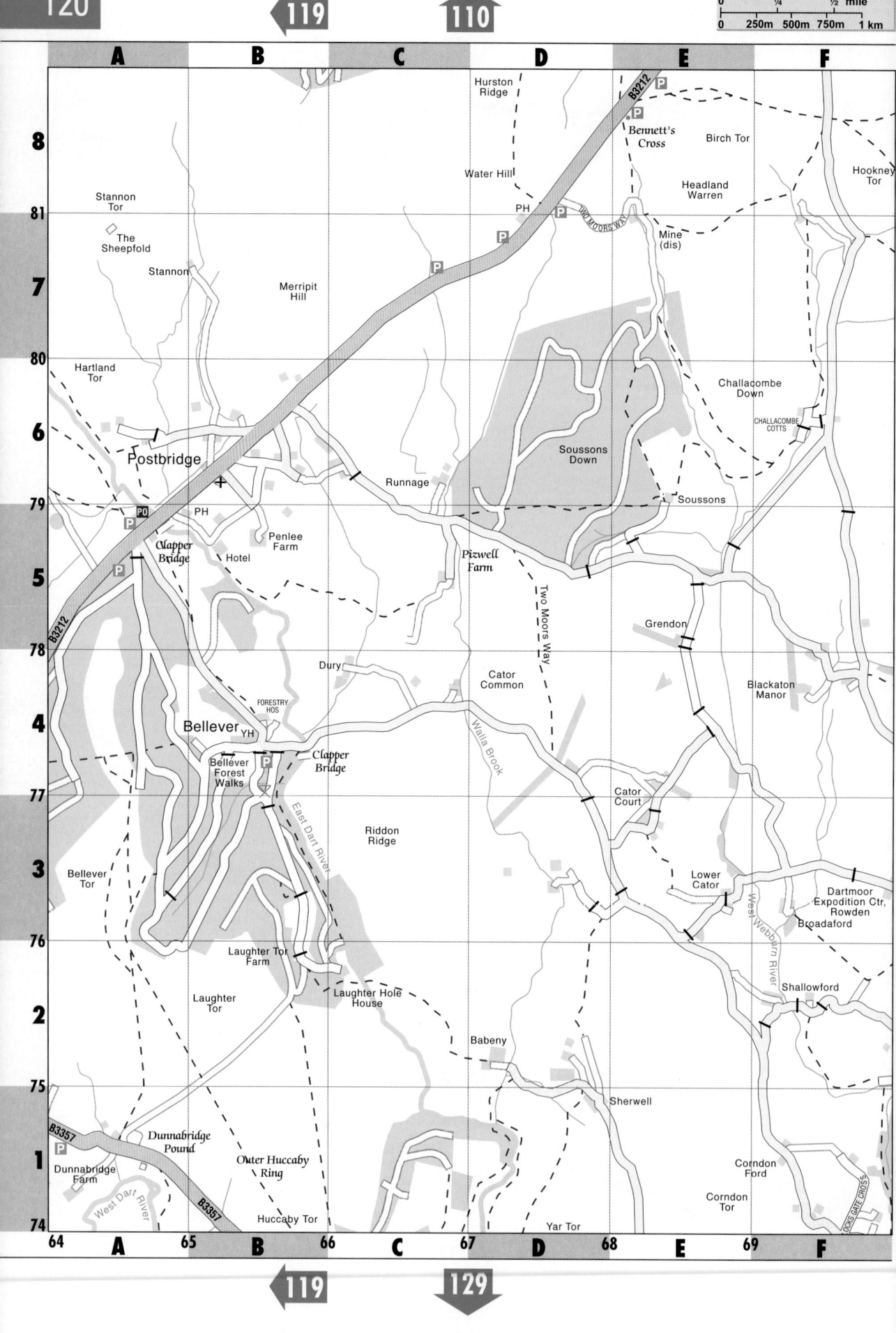

Scale: 1¾ inches to 1 mile

0   ¼   ½ mile
0 250m 500m 750m 1 km

A   B   C   D   E   F

8

81

7

80

6

79

5

78

4

77

3

76

2

75

1

74

Stannon Tor

The Sheepfold

Stannon

Hartland Tor

Postbridge

PO
PH
P
Clapper Bridge
Penlee Farm
Hotel
P

B3212

Bellever
YH
Bellever Forest Walks
P
Clapper Bridge

East Dart River

Bellever Tor

Laughter Tor Farm

Laughter Tor

Laughter Hole House

B3357
P
Dunnabridge Pound
Dunnabridge Farm
West Dart River
B3357
Outer Huccaby Ring
Huccaby Tor

Hurston Ridge

Water Hill

PH
P
P

B3212
Bennett's Cross
Birch Tor

Headland Warren

TWO MOORS WAY

Mine (dis)

Merripit Hill

Runnage

Soussons Down

Soussons

Pizwell Farm

Two Moors Way

Dury

FORESTRY HOS

Cator Common

Walla Brook

Riddon Ridge

Babeny

Yar Tor

Grendon

Blackaton Manor

Cator Court

Lower Cator

West Webburn River

Sherwell

Challacombe Down

CHALLACOMBE COTTS

Hookney Tor

Shallowford

Dartmoor Expedition Ctr, Rowden
Broadaford

Corndon Ford

Corndon Tor

BXS GATE CROSS

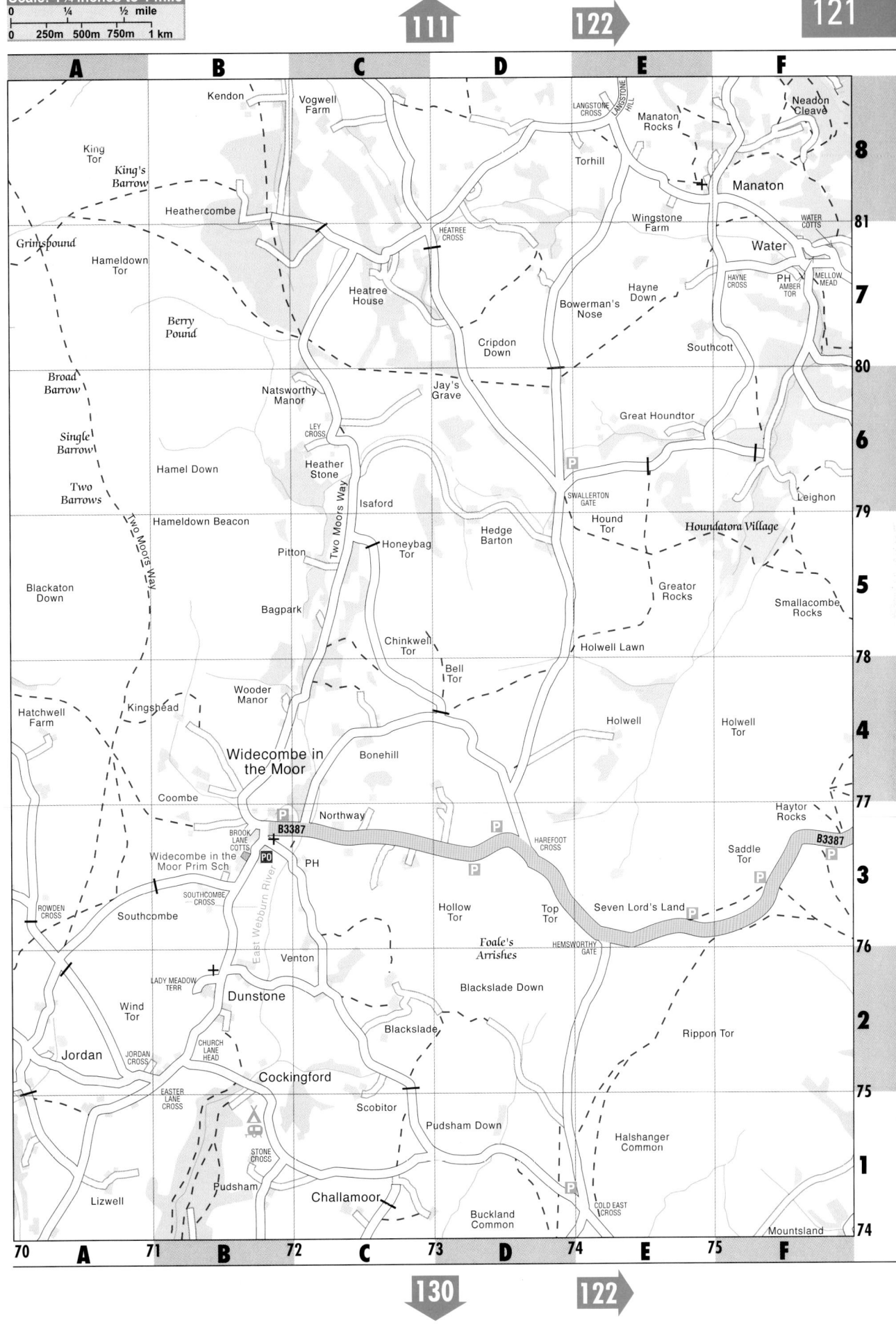

Scale: 1¾ inches to 1 mile

0   ¼   ½ mile
0   250m 500m 750m 1 km

↑ 111   → 122

A **B** **C** **D** **E** **F**

Kendon
Vogwell Farm
Langstone Cross
LANGSTONE HILL
Manaton Rocks
Neadon Cleave

8

King Tor
King's Barrow
Torhill
Manaton

Heathercombe
Heatree Cross
Wingstone Farm
Water COTTS

81

Grimspound
Hamel Down Tor
Heatree House
Bowerman's Nose
Hayne Down
Hayne Cross
PH AMBER TOR
MELLOW MEAD

7

Broad Barrow
Berry Pound
Cripdon Down
Southcott
Water

Single Barrow
Natsworthy Manor
Jay's Grave
Great Houndtor

80

6

Two Barrows
LEY CROSS
Heather Stone
SWALLERTON GATE
Leighon

Hamel Down
Isaford
Hound Tor
Houndatora Village

79

Blackaton Down
Hameldown Beacon
Pitton
Honeybag Tor
Hedge Barton
Greator Rocks
Smallacombe Rocks

5

Two Moors Way
Bagpark
Chinkwell Tor
Holwell Lawn

78

Hatchwell Farm
Kingshead
Wooder Manor
Bell Tor
Holwell
Holwell Tor

4

Widecombe in the Moor
Bonehill
Haytor Rocks

77

Coombe
P
Northway
P
Saddle Tor
B3387

BROOK LANE COTTS
B3387
HAREFOOT CROSS
P

Widecombe in the Moor Prim Sch
PO
PH
P
Top Tor
Seven Lord's Land
P

3

ROWDEN CROSS
Southcombe
SOUTHCOMBE CROSS
Hollow Tor
HEMSWORTHY GATE

East Webburn River
Venton
Foale's Arrishes

76

Wind Tor
LADY MEADOW TERR
Dunstone
Blackslade Down
Rippon Tor

2

Jordan
JORDAN CROSS
CHURCH LANE HEAD
Cockingford
Blackslade

EASTER LANE CROSS
Scobitor
Pudsham Down
Halshanger Common

75

STONE CROSS
Challamoor
COLD EAST CROSS
P

1

Pudsham
Lizwell
Buckland Common
Mountsland

74

70 **A** **71** **B** **72** **C** **73** **D** **74** **E** **75** **F**

↓ 130   → 122

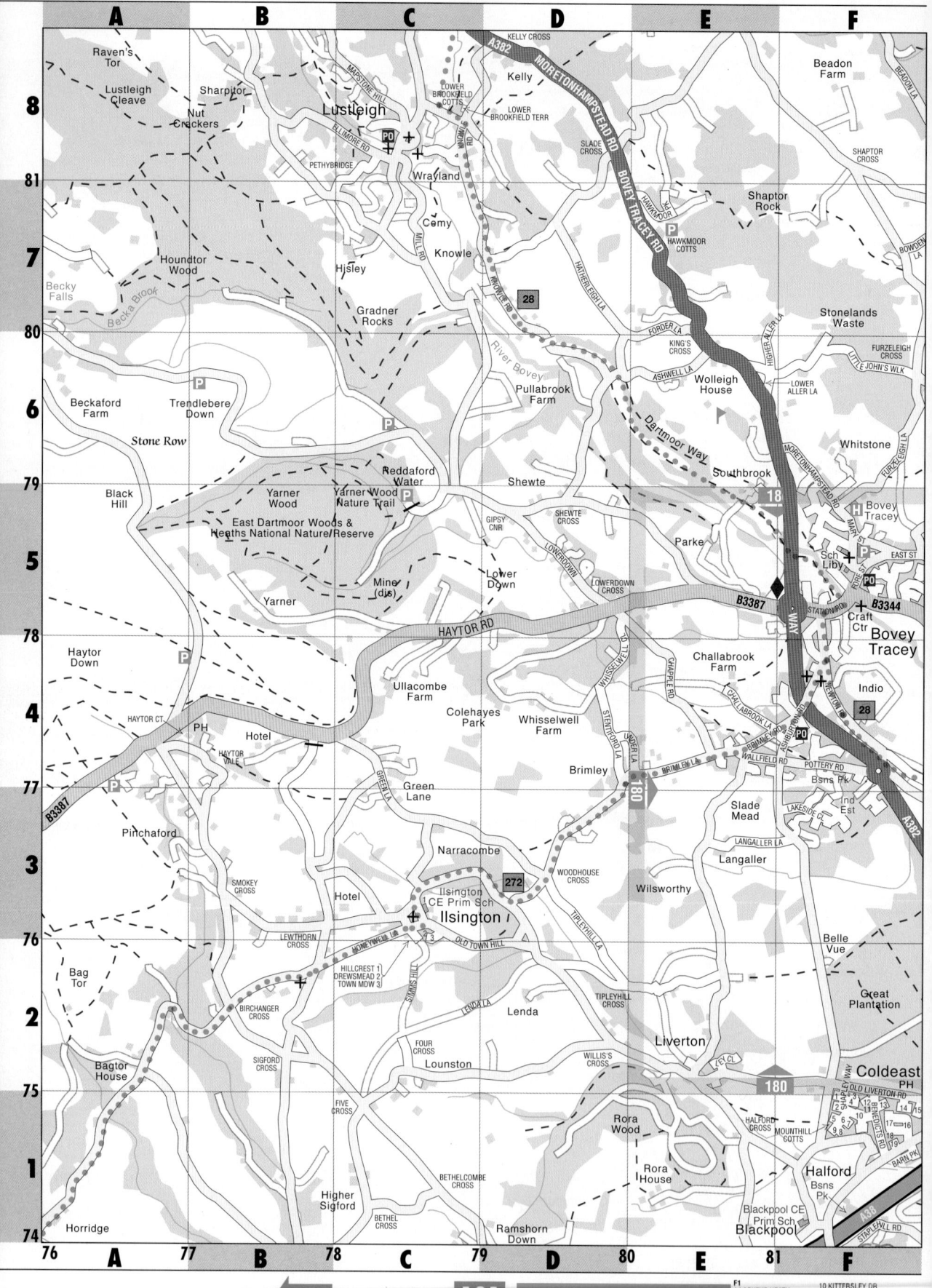

Scale: 1¾ inches to 1 mile

0   ¼   ½   mile
0   250m   500m   750m   1 km

For full street detail of the highlighted area see page 180.

F1
1 LASKEYS HEATH
2 TAYLORS NEWTAKE
3 LEAT MDW
4 ROWELLS MEAD
5 BEAUMONT CL
6 DIVETT DR
7 MUNRO MEAD
8 POMEROY PL
9 FLOWERS MDW
10 KITTERSLEY DR
11 CHAPEL LA
12 BEANHAY CL
13 BENLEARS ACRE
14 BICKFORDS GN
15 SUMMERLANDS CT
16 SUMMERHILL RD
17 SUMMERHILL CRES
18 SUMMERHILL CL
19 BENEDICTS CL

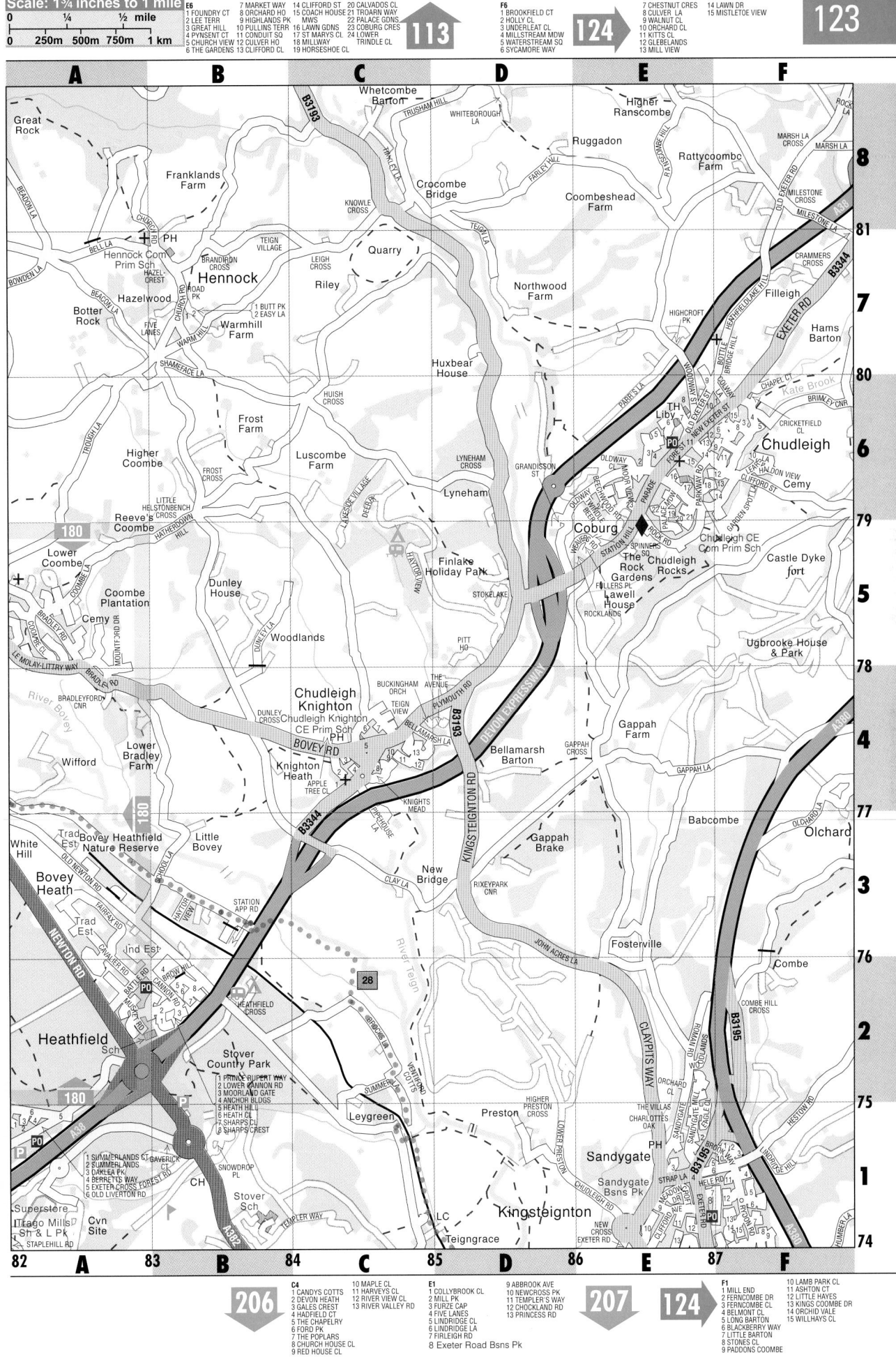

123
Scale: 1¾ inches to 1 mile
0 ¼ ½ mile
0 250m 500m 750m 1 km
E6
1 FOUNDRY CT
2 LEE TERR
3 GREAT HILL
4 PYNSENT CT
5 CHURCH VIEW
6 THE GARDENS
7 MARKET WAY
8 ORCHARD HO
9 HIGHLANDS PK
10 PULLINS TERR
11 CONDUIT SQ
12 CULVER HO
13 CLIFFORD CL
14 CLIFFORD ST
15 COACH HOUSE MWS
16 LAWN GDNS
17 ST MARYS CL
18 MILLWAY
19 HORSESHOE CL
20 CALVADOS CL
21 TROARN WAY
22 PALACE GDNS
23 COBURG CRES
24 LOWER TRINDLE CL
113
F6
1 BROOKFIELD CT
2 HOLLY CL
3 UNDERLEAT CL
4 MILLSTREAM MDW
5 WATERSTREAM SQ
6 SYCAMORE WAY
124
7 CHESTNUT CRES
8 CULVER LA
9 WALNUT CL
10 ORCHARD CL
11 KITTS CL
12 GLEBELANDS
13 MILL VIEW
14 LAWN DR
15 MISTLETOE VIEW
A B C D E F
Great Rock
Whetcombe Barton
B3193
TRUSHAM HILL
WHITEBOROUGH LA
Higher Ranscombe
Ruggadon
Rattycoombe Farm
MARSH LA CROSS
MARSH LA
Franklands Farm
Crocombe Bridge
Coombeshead Farm
MILESTONE CROSS
MILESTONE LA
A38
KNOWLE CROSS
BEADON LA
PH
Quarry
BELL LA
Hennock Com Prim Sch
TEIGN VILLAGE
BRANDIRON CROSS
LEIGH CROSS
CRAMMERS CROSS
B3344
Hennock
Riley
Northwood Farm
Filleigh
BOWDEN LA
HAZEL-CREST
ROAD PK
Hazelwood
Botter Rock
BEACON LA
1 BUTT PK
2 EASY LA
Warmhill Farm
HIGHCROFT PK
EXETER RD
Hams Barton
FIVE LANES
WARM HILL
SHAMEFACE LA
Huxbear House
CHAPEL CT
Kate Brook
BRIMLEY CNR
HUISH CROSS
PARR'S LA
TH
Liby
CRICKETFIELD CL
Frost Farm
PO
Chudleigh
Higher Coombe
Luscombe Farm
LYNEHAM CROSS
GRANDISSON ST
OLDWAY CL
HALDON VIEW
CLIFFORD ST
Cemy
FROST CROSS
Lyneham
LITTLE HELSTONBENCH CROSS
Reeve's Coombe
HATHERDOWN HILL
180
Coburg
ROCK RD
STATION HILL
Chudleigh CE Com Prim Sch
Lower Coombe
Finlake Holiday Park
SPINNERS SQ
The Rock Gardens
Chudleigh Rocks
Castle Dyke fort
Coombe Plantation
Dunley House
STOKELAKE
FULLERS PL
Lawell House
ROCKLANDS
Cemy
BRADLEY RD
MOUNTFORD DR
DUNLEY LA
Woodlands
PITT HO
Ugbrooke House & Park
LE MOLAY-LITTRY WAY
BUCKINGHAM ORCH
THE AVENUE
PLYMOUTH RD
Chudleigh Knighton
River Bovey
BRADLEYFORD CNR
DUNLEY CROSS
Chudleigh Knighton CE Prim Sch
TEIGN VIEW
DEVON EXPRESSWAY
B3193
Gappah Farm
A380
BOVEY RD
BELLAMARSH LA
Bellamarsh Barton
GAPPAH CROSS
Wifford
Lower Bradley Farm
Knighton Heath
APPLE TREE CL
KINGSTEIGNTON RD
GAPPAH LA
KNIGHTS MEAD
PIPEHOUSE LA
Babcombe
OLCHARD LA
White Hill
Trad Est
Bovey Heathfield Nature Reserve
Little Bovey
B3344
Gappah Brake
Olchard
Bovey Heath
OLD NEWTON RD
SCHOOL LA
New Bridge
CLAY LA
RIXEYPARK CNR
FAIRFAX RD
Trad Est
HAYTOR VIEW
STATION APP RD
NEWTON RD
CAVALIER RD
Ind Est
JOHN ACRES LA
Fosterville
BROW HILL
BATTLE RD
CANNON RD
28
River Teign
Combe
HEATHFIELD CROSS
COMBE HILL CROSS
B3195
CLAYPITS WAY
ROMAN RD
Heathfield
Sch
Stover Country Park
BROCKS LA
VENTIFORD COTTS
1 PRINCE RUPERT WAY
2 LOWER CANNON RD
3 MOORLAND GATE
4 ANCHOR BLDGS
5 HEATH HILL
6 HEATH CL
7 SHARPS CL
8 SHARPS CREST
180
SUMMER LA
ORCHARD RD
HIGHER PRESTON CROSS
Preston
THE VILLAS
CHARLOTTES OAK
HESTOW RD
Leygreen
P
A38
PO
PH
1 SUMMERLANDS CT
2 SUMMERLANDS
3 OAKLEA PK
4 BERRETTS WAY
5 EXETER CROSS
6 OLD LIVERTON RD
GAVERICK CT
FOREST RD
LOWER PRESTON
Sandygate
BROOK WAY
LINDRIDGE HILL
SNOWDROP PL
CH
Sandygate Bsns Pk
STRAP LA
HELE RD
Stover Sch
CHUDLEIGH RD
CLIFFORD AVE
EXETER RD
Superstore
Trago Mills Sh & L Pk
Cvn Site
TEMPLER WAY
LC
Kingsteignton
NEW CROSS
EXETER RD
PO
HUMBER LA
STAPLEHILL RD
A382
Teigngrace
A380
82 83 84 85 86 87
8 81 7 80 6 79 5 78 4 77 3 76 2 75 1 74
206
C4
1 CANDYS COTTS
2 DEVON HEATH
3 GALES CREST
4 HADFIELD CT
5 THE CHAPELRY
6 FORD PK
7 THE POPLARS
8 CHURCH HOUSE CL
9 RED HOUSE CL
10 MAPLE CL
11 HARVEYS CL
12 RIVER VIEW CL
13 RIVER VALLEY RD
E1
1 COLLYBROOK CL
2 MILL PK
3 FURZE CAP
4 FIVE LANES
5 LINDRIDGE CL
6 LINDRIDGE LA
7 FIRLEIGH RD
8 Exeter Road Bsns Pk
9 ABBROOK AVE
10 NEWCROSS PK
11 TEMPLER'S WAY
12 CHOCKLAND RD
13 PRINCESS RD
207
124
F1
1 MILL END
2 FERNCOMBE DR
3 FERNCOMBE CL
4 BELMONT CL
5 LONG BARTON
6 BLACKBERRY WAY
7 LITTLE BARTON
8 STONES CL
9 PADDONS COOMBE
10 LAMB PARK CL
11 ASHTON CT
12 LITTLE HAYES
13 KINGS COOMBE DR
14 ORCHID VALE
15 WILLHAYS CL

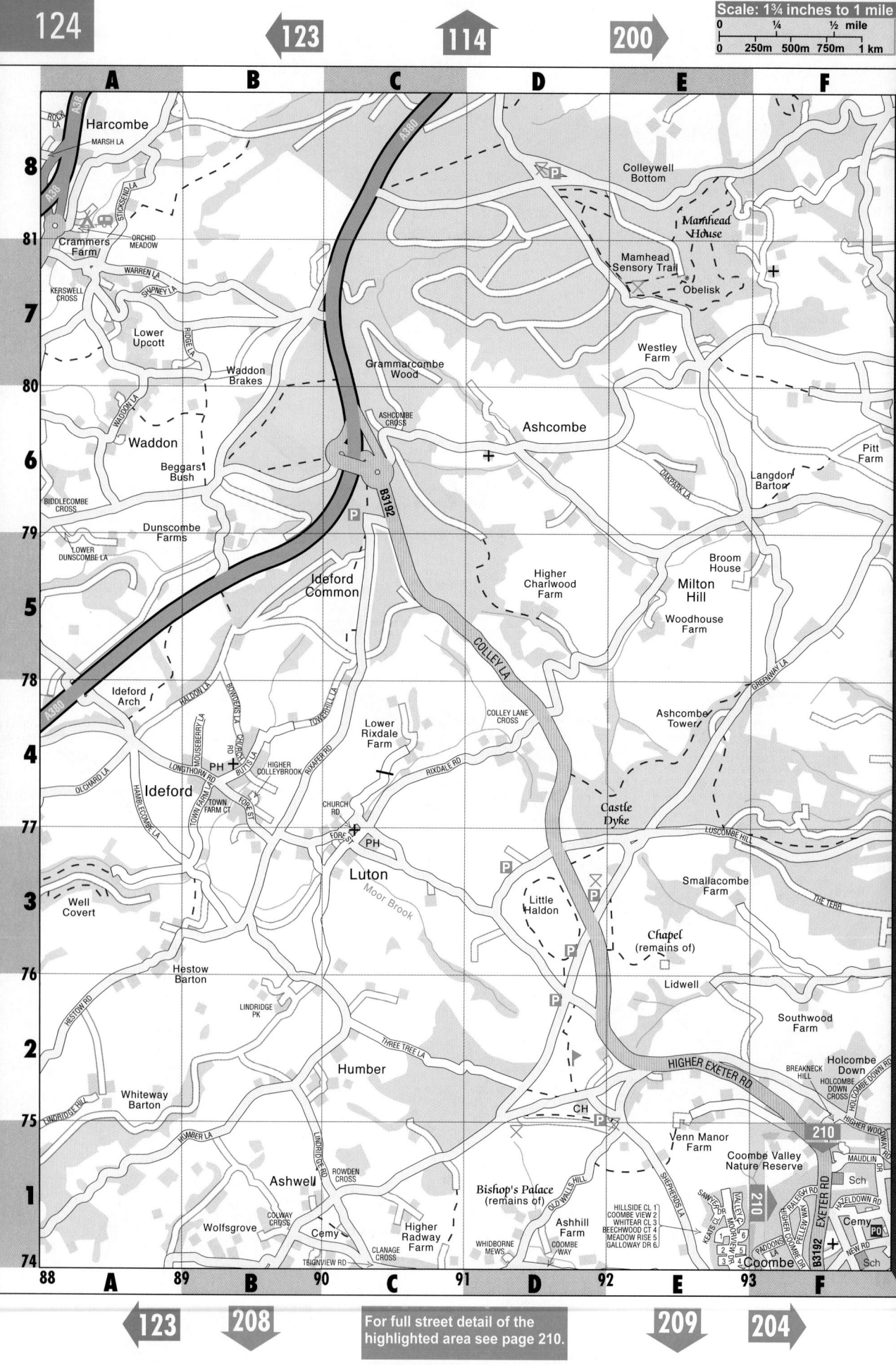

Scale: 1¾ inches to 1 mile

0 ¼ ½ mile
0 250m 500m 750m 1 km

A B C D E F

Harcombe
MARSH LA
ROCK LA
Crammers Farm
ORCHID MEADOW
WARREN LA
KERSWELL CROSS
SHIPNEY LA
STICKSENILA
Lower Upcott
Waddon Brakes
RIDGE LA
Grammarcombe Wood
ASHCOMBE CROSS
Colleywell Bottom
Mamhead House
Mamhead Sensory Trail
Obelisk
Westley Farm

8

81

7

Waddon
Beggars Bush
BIDDLECOMBE CROSS
WADDON LA
Dunscombe Farms
LOWER DUNSCOMBE LA
Ashcombe
Higher Charlwood Farm
Broom House
Milton Hill
Woodhouse Farm
DARKPARK LA
Langdon Barton
Pitt Farm

80

6

79

B3192

Ideford Common
Ideford Arch
A380
HALDON LA
BOWDENS LA
CHURCH RD
LONGTHORN RD
HOUSEBERRY LA
TOWER HILL LA
RIXAFER RD
Lower Rixdale Farm
Colley Lane Cross
COLLEY LA
Ashcombe Tower
GREENWAY LA
LUSCOMBE HILL

78

5

4

Ideford
HAMBLECOMBE LA
OLCHARD LA
TOWN FARM LA
BUTTS LA
FORE ST
PH
Higher Colleybrook
RIXDALE RD
Castle Dyke
Smallacombe Farm
THE TERR

77

3

CHURCH RD
FORE ST
PH
Luton
Moor Brook
Little Haldon
Chapel (remains of)
Lidwell
Southwood Farm

76

2

Hestow Barton
HESTOW RD
LINDRIDGE PK
THREE TREE LA
Humber
HIGHER EXETER RD
BREAKNECK HILL
Holcombe Down
HOLCOMBE DOWN CROSS
HOLCOMBE LA

75

Whiteway Barton
LINDRIDGE HILL
HUMBER LA
LINDRIDGE LA
Ashwell
ROWDEN CROSS
Venn Manor Farm
Coombe Valley Nature Reserve
SHEPHERDS LA
210
HIGHER WOODWAY RD
MAUDLIN
Sch

1

Wolfsgrove
COLWAY CROSS
Cemy
TEIGNVIEW RD
CLANAGE CROSS
Higher Radway Farm
Bishop's Palace (remains of)
WHIDBORNE MEWS
OLD WELLS HILL
Ashhill Farm
COOMBE WAY
SAWTER DR
KENT'S LA
MALEY CL
MOORVIEW DR
210
RALEIGH RD
PELLEW WAY
PADDONS LA
EXETER RD
HAZELDOWN RD
Cemy
PO
Coombe
NEW RD
B3192
Sch

74

HILLSIDE CL 1
COOMBE VIEW 2
WHITEAR CL 3
BEECHWOOD CT 4
MEADOW RISE 5
GALLOWAY DR 6.

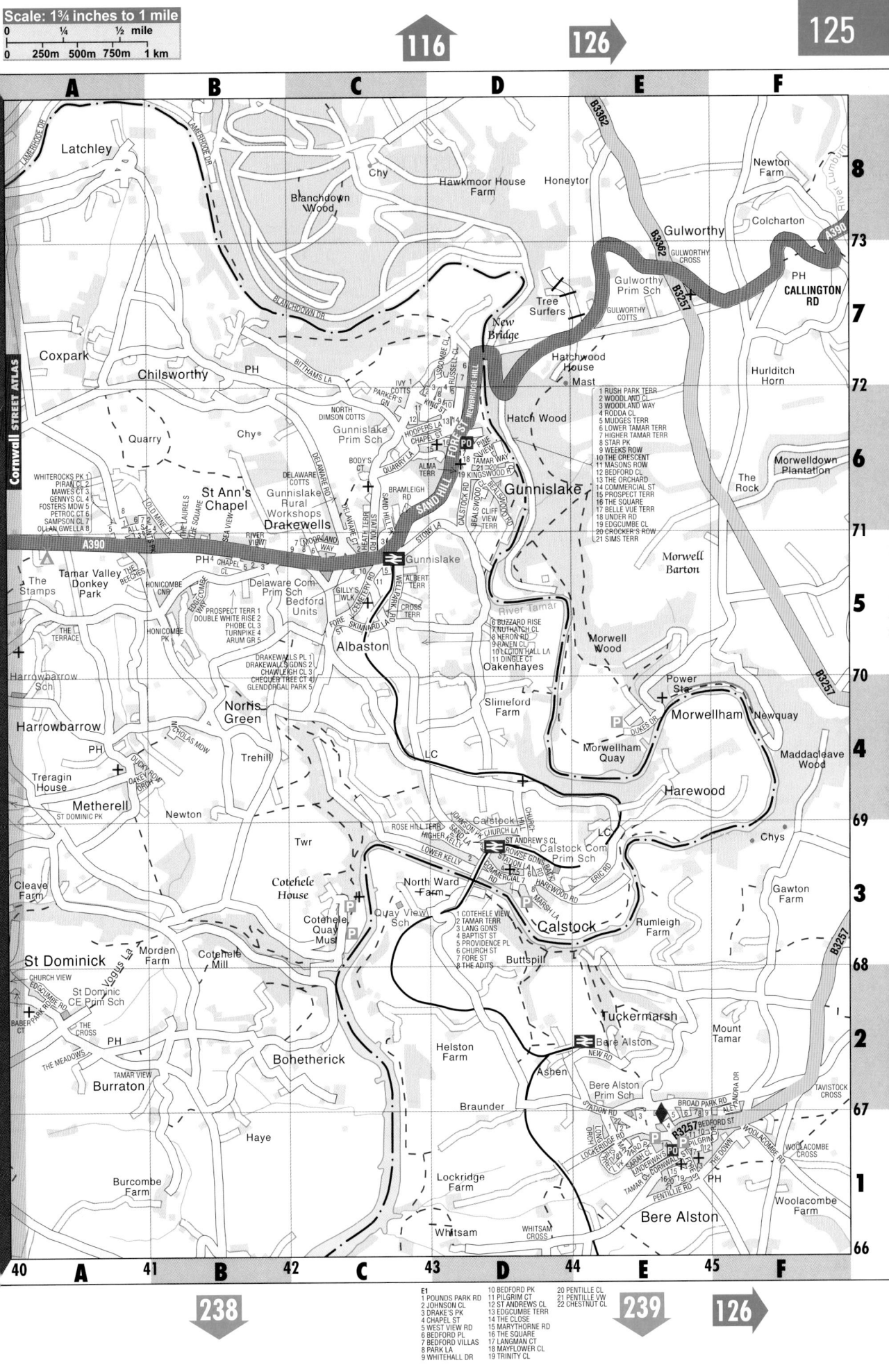

Cornwall STREET ATLAS

Latchley

Blanchdown Wood

Chy

Hawkmoor House Farm

Honeytor

Newton Farm

Colcharton

Gulworthy

River Lumburn

B3362

Gulworthy Cross

B3257

CALLINGTON RD

PH

Hurlditch Horn

Coxpark

Chilsworthy

PH

Quarry

Chy

North Dimson Cotts

Gunnislake Prim Sch

St Ann's Chapel

Delaware Cotts

Gunnislake Rural Workshops

Drakewells

A390

Tamar Valley Donkey Park

The Stamps

Honicombe CNR

Honicombe Pk

WHITEROCKS PK 1
PIRAN CL 2
MAWES CT 3
GENNYS CL 4
FOSTERS MDW 5
PETROC CT 6
SAMPSON CL 7
OLLAN GWELLA 8

PROSPECT TERR 1
DOUBLE WHITE RISE 2
PHOBE CL 3
TURNPIKE 4
ARUM GR 5

DRAKEWALLS PL 1
DRAKEWALLS GDNS 2
CHAWLEIGH CL 3
CHEQUER TREE CT 4
GLENDORGAL PARK 5

Albaston

Harrowbarrow Sch

Harrowbarrow

PH

Treragin House

Metherell

ST DOMINIC PK

Newton

Norris Green

Trehill

NICHOLAS MDW

DUCKY ROW

OAKEY LA

New Bridge

Tree Surfers

SAND HILL FORE ST NEWBRIDGE HILL

Gunnislake

Hatch Wood

Mast

Hatchwood House

Gulworthy Prim Sch

Gulworthy Cotts

STAR PK

1 RUSH PARK TERR
2 WOODLAND CL
3 WOODLAND WAY
4 RODDA CL
5 MUDGES TERR
6 LOWER TAMAR TERR
7 HIGHER TAMAR TERR
8 STAR PK
9 WEEKS ROW
10 THE CRESCENT
11 MASONS ROW
12 BEDFORD CL
13 THE ORCHARD
14 COMMERCIAL ST
15 PROSPECT TERR
16 THE SQUARE
17 BELLE VUE TERR
18 UNDER RD
19 EDGCUMBE CL
20 CROCKER'S ROW
21 SIMS TERR

Morwell Barton

Morwelldown Plantation

The Rock

Morwell Wood

6 BUZZARD RISE
7 NUTHATCH CL
8 HERON RD
9 RAVEN CL
10 LEGION HALL LA
11 DINGLE CT

Oakenhayes

Slimeford Farm

LC

Power Sta

Morwellham

Newquay

Morwellham Quay

Harewood

Maddacleave Wood

B3257

Cleave Farm

St Dominick

St Dominic CE Prim Sch

BABER CT
EDGCUMBE RD
PARK RD
THE CROSS
PH
THE MEADOWS

Cotehele House

Cotehele Quay Mus

Cotehele Mill

Morden Farm

Bohetherick

Burraton

Haye

TAMAR VIEW

Twr

St Andrew's CL

ROSE HILL TERR
HIGHER KELLY
LOWER KELLY

SAND LA
JOHNSON PK
ROWSE GDNS
STATION LA
COMMERCIAL RD

North Ward Farm

Quay View Sch

1 COTEHELE VIEW
2 TAMAR TERR
3 LANG GDNS
4 BAPTIST ST
5 PROVIDENCE PL
6 CHURCH ST
7 FORE ST
8 THE ADITS

Calstock

CHURCH LA

Calstock Com Prim Sch

LC

Chys

Gawton Farm

ERIC RD

HAREWOOD RD

MARSH LA

Rumleigh Farm

Buttspill

Tuckermarsh

Mount Tamar

Helston Farm

Bere Alston

Ashen

NEW RD

Bere Alston Prim Sch

BROAD PARK RD

FLORA DR

Tavistock Cross

Braunder

STATION RD

LONG ORCH

B3257

BEDFORD ST

WOOLACOMBE RD

Woolacombe Cross

Lockridge Farm

Burcombe Farm

Whitsam

WHITSAM CROSS

UNDERWAYS

TAMAR CL

PENTILLIE RD

PH

Bere Alston

Woolacombe Farm

20 PENTILLE CL
21 PENTILLE VW
22 CHESTNUT CL

E1
1 POUNDS PARK RD
2 JOHNSON CL
3 DRAKE'S PK
4 CHAPEL ST
5 WEST VIEW RD
6 BEDFORD PL
7 BEDFORD VILLAS
8 PARK LA
9 WHITEHALL DR
10 BEDFORD PK
11 PILGRIM CT
12 ST ANDREWS CL
13 EDGCUMBE TERR
14 THE CLOSE
15 MARYTHORNE RD
16 THE SQUARE
17 LANGMAN CT
18 MAYFLOWER CL
19 TRINITY CL

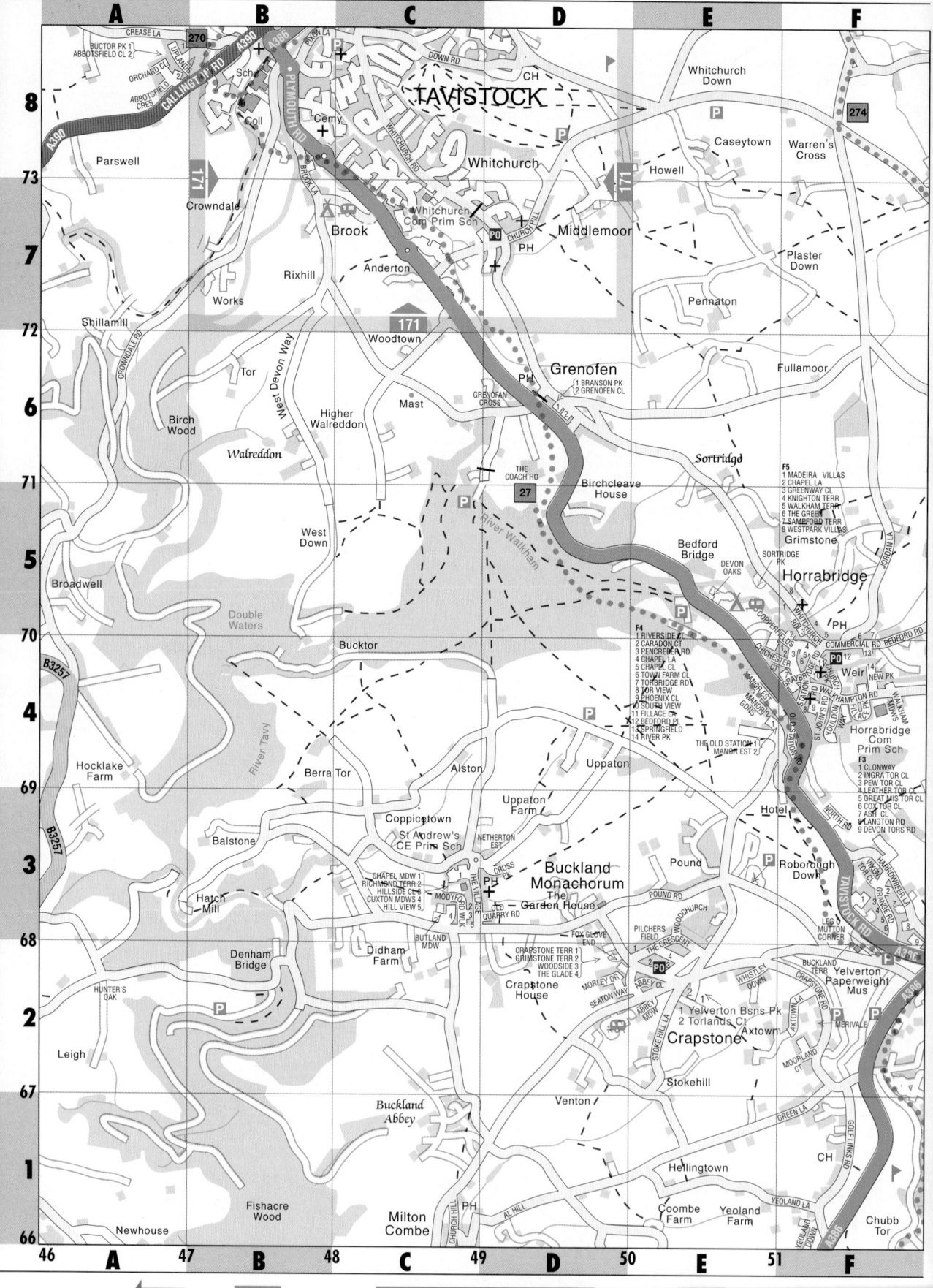

Scale: 1¾ inches to 1 mile

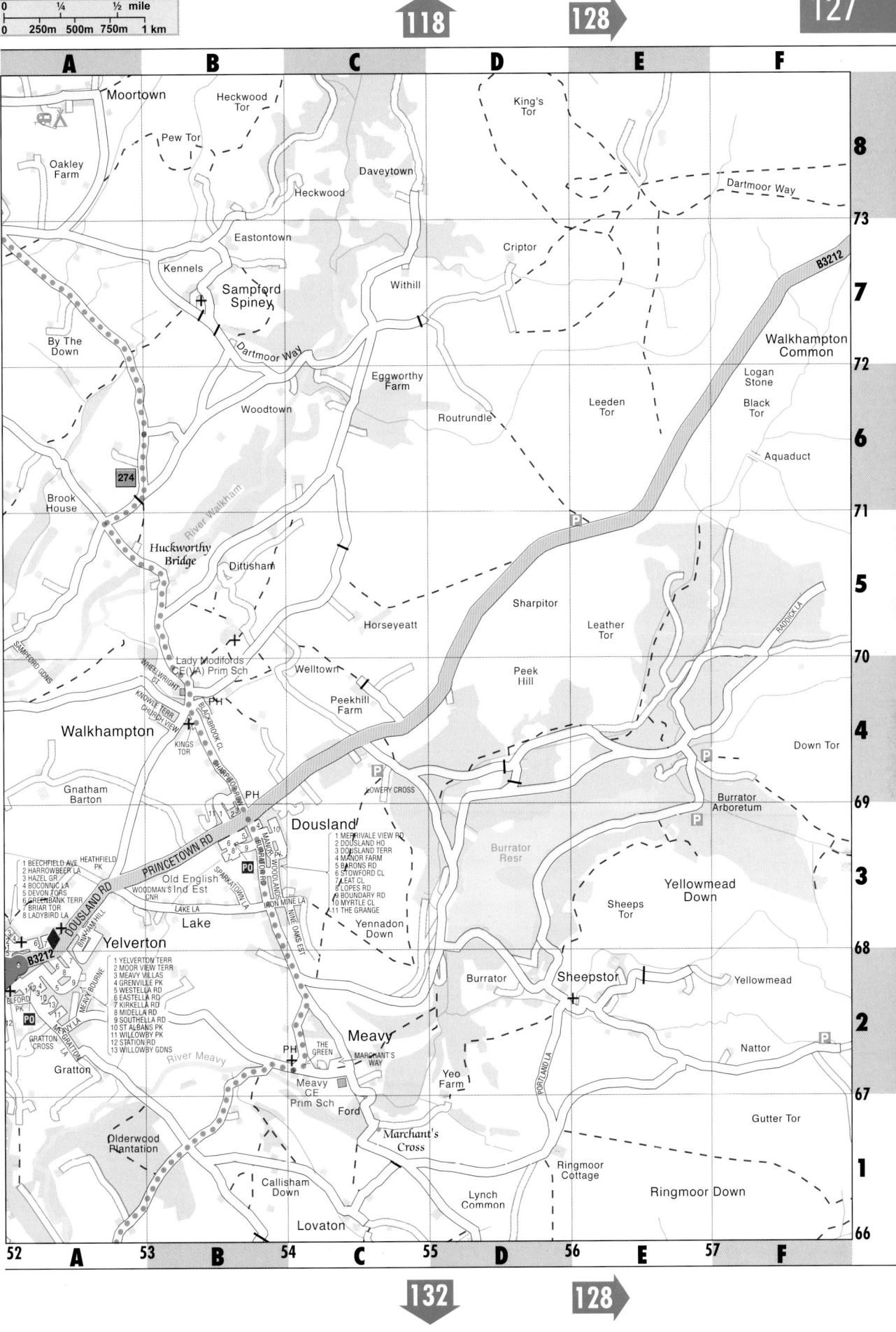

A B C D E F

8
73
7
72
6
71
5
70
4
69
3
68
2
67
1
66

Moortown
Heckwood Tor
Pew Tor
Heckwood
Oakley Farm
Daveytown
King's Tor
Dartmoor Way
Criptor
Eastontown
Kennels
Withill
Sampford Spiney
By The Down
Dartmoor Way
Walkhampton Common
Logan Stone
Black Tor
Eggworthy Farm
Woodtown
Routrundle
Leeden Tor
Aquaduct
Brook House
River Walkham
Huckworthy Bridge
Dittisham
Sharpitor
Leather Tor
Down Tor
Horseyeatt
Lady Modifords CE(VA) Prim Sch
Welltown
Peek Hill
SAMPFORD GDNS
WHEELWRIGHT CT
KNOWLE TERR
CHURCH VIEW
BLACKBROOK CL
Walkhampton
Peekhill Farm
KINGS TOR
PH
Gnatham Barton
SHARP TOR CL
PH
Lowery Cross
Burrator Resr
Yellowmead Down
Burrator Arboretum
Sheeps Tor
1 BEECHFIELD AVE
2 HARROWBEER LA
3 HAZEL GR
4 BOCONNIC LA
5 DEVON TORS
6 GREENBANK TERR
7 BRIAR TOR
8 LADYBIRD LA
HEATHFIELD PK
Dousland
1 MERRIVALE VIEW RD
2 DOUSLAND HO
3 DOUSLAND TERR
4 MANOR FARM
5 BARONS RD
6 STOWFORD CL
7 LEAT CL
8 LOPES RD
9 BOUNDARY RD
10 MYRTLE CL
11 THE GRANGE
PRINCETOWN RD
DOUSLAND RD
Old English
Woodman's Ind Est
WOODMAN'S CNR
LAKE LA
SPARKATOWN LA
MANOR RD
WOODLANDS
IRON MINE LA
NINE OAKS EST
PO
Lake
Yennadon Down
Yelverton
1 YELVERTON TERR
2 MOOR VIEW TERR
3 MEAVY VILLAS
4 GRENVILLE PK
5 WESTELLA RD
6 EASTELLA RD
7 KIRKELLA RD
8 MIDELLA RD
9 SOUTHELLA RD
10 ST ALBANS PK
11 WILLOWBY PK
12 STATION RD
13 WILLOWBY GDNS
B3212
BINKHAM HILL
MEAVY BOURNE
MEAVY LA
MEGRATTON
PO
GRATTON CROSS
Gratton
River Meavy
Meavy
PH
THE GREEN
MARCHANT'S WAY
Burrator
Sheepstor
Yellowmead
Nattor
Yeo Farm
PORTLAND LA
Meavy CE Prim Sch
Ford
Marchant's Cross
Gutter Tor
Olderwood Plantation
Callisham Down
Lynch Common
Ringmoor Cottage
Ringmoor Down
Lovaton

RADDICK LA
274

127 119

Scale: 1¾ inches to 1 mile

0   ¼   ½   mile
0   250m   500m   750m   1 km

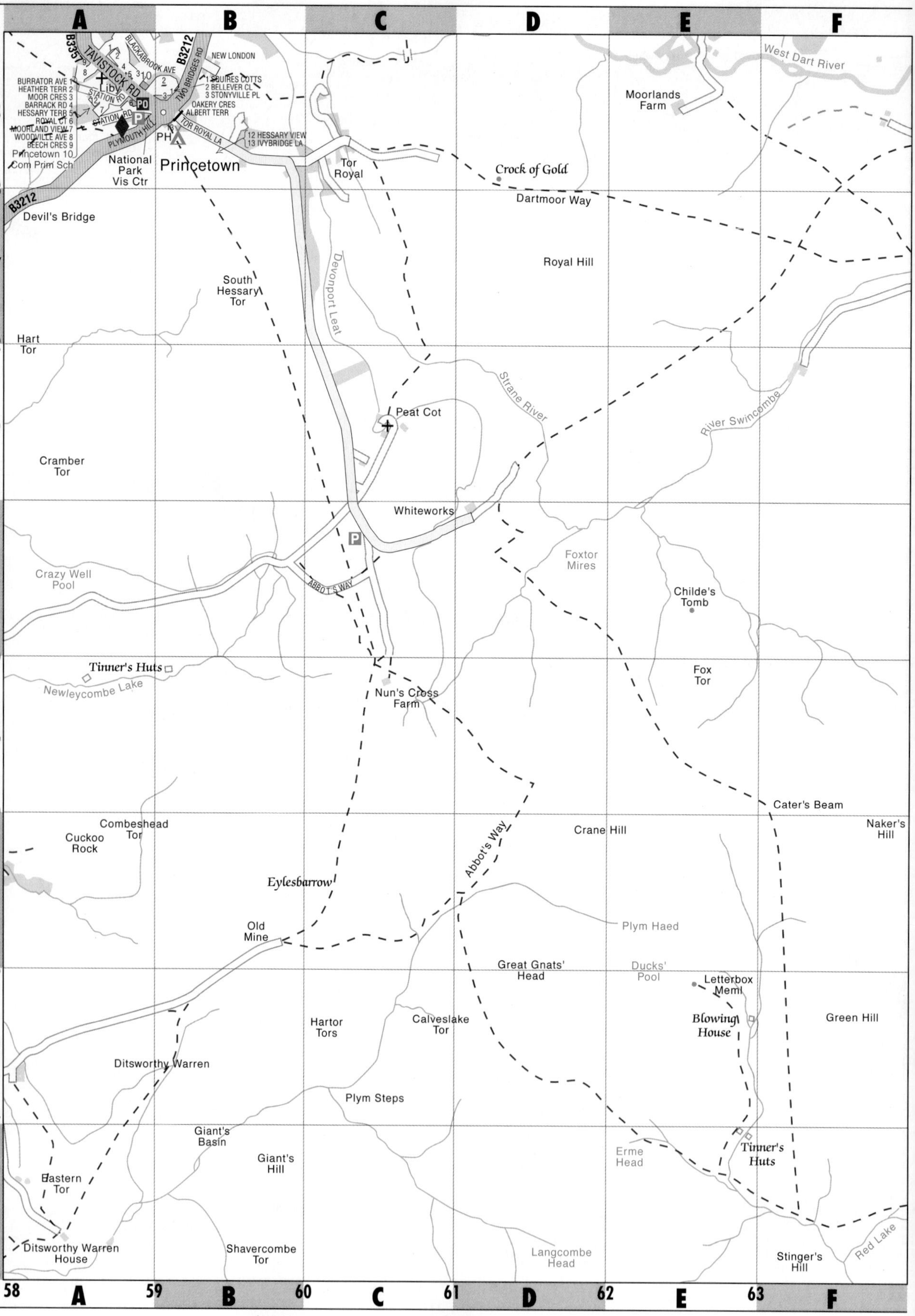

A   B   C   D   E   F

West Dart River

B3357
TAVISTOCK RD
BLACKABROOK AVE
B3212
TWO BRIDGES RD
NEW LONDON

8

BURRATOR AVE 1
HEATHER TERR 2
MOOR CRES 3
BARRACK RD 4
HESSARY TERR 5
ROYAL CI 6
MOORLAND VIEW 7
WOODVILLE AVE 8
BEECH CRES 9
Princetown 10
Com Prim Sch

1 SQUIRES COTTS
2 BELLEVER CL
3 STONYVILLE PL
OAKERY CRES
ALBERT TERR
12 HESSARY VIEW
13 IVYBRIDGE LA

Moorlands Farm

STATION RD
PO
P
PLYMOUTH HILL
Lib
P
PH
TOR ROYAL LA

National Park Vis Ctr

Princetown

Tor Royal

Crock of Gold

73

Dartmoor Way

B3212

Devil's Bridge

Royal Hill

7

South Hessary Tor

Devonport Leat

72

Hart Tor

Strane River

6

Peat Cot

River Swincombe

Cramber Tor

71

Whiteworks

Foxtor Mires

5

P

ABBOT'S WAY

Childe's Tomb

Crazy Well Pool

70

Fox Tor

Tinner's Huts

Newleycombe Lake

Nun's Cross Farm

4

69

Cater's Beam

Combeshead Tor

Cuckoo Rock

Crane Hill

Naker's Hill

3

Eylesbarrow

Abbot's Way

Plym Haed

Old Mine

68

Great Gnats' Head

Ducks' Pool

Letterbox Meml

Green Hill

2

Hartor Tors

Calveslake Tor

Blowing House

Ditsworthy Warren

Plym Steps

67

Giant's Basin

Giant's Hill

Erme Head

Tinner's Huts

1

Eastern Tor

Ditsworthy Warren House

Shavercombe Tor

Langcombe Head

Stinger's Hill

Red Lake

66

58   A   59   B   60   C   61   D   62   E   63   F

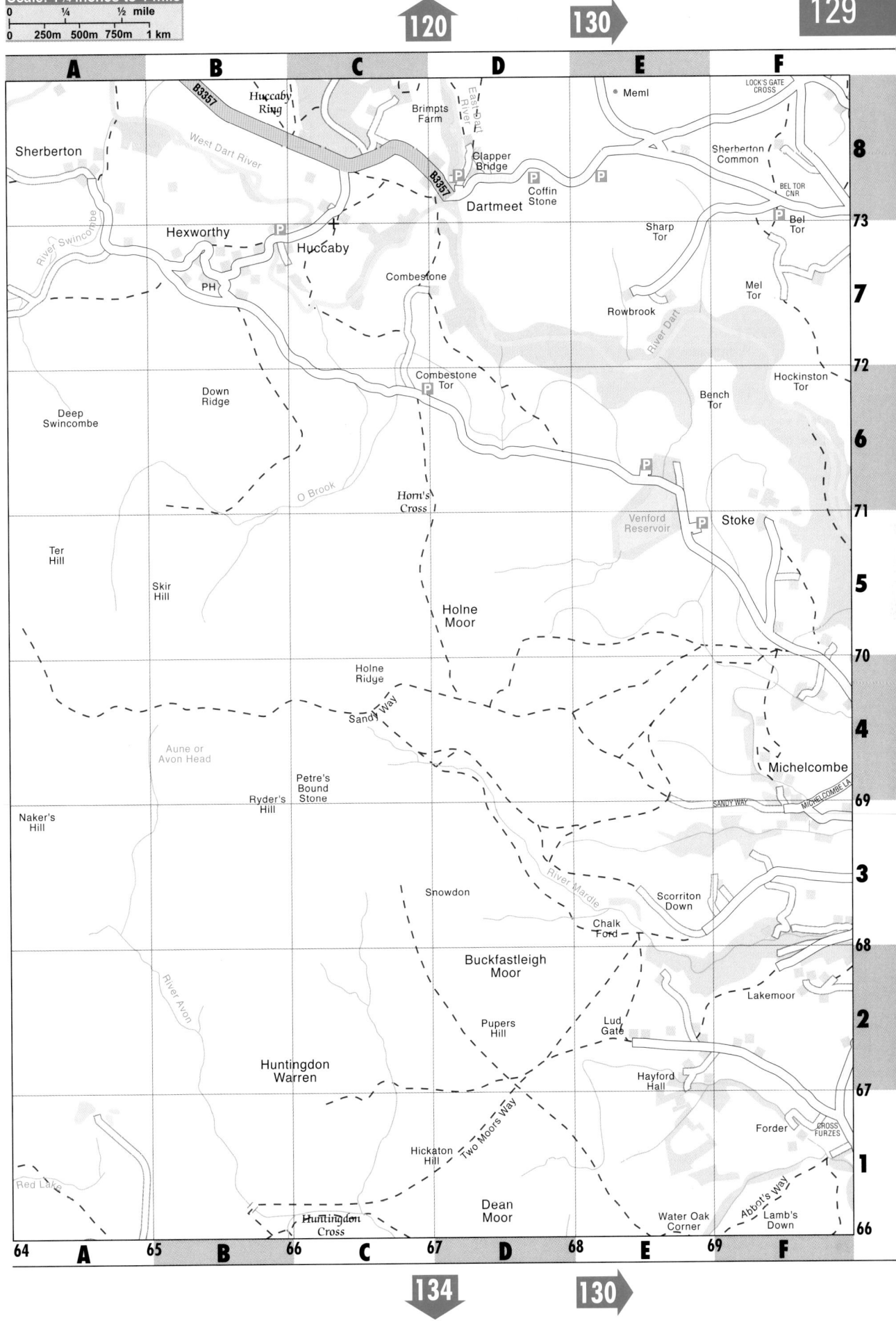

Scale: 1¾ inches to 1 mile

0   ¼   ½ mile
0 250m 500m 750m 1 km

120
130

A   B   C   D   E   F

Sherberton

B3357

Huccaby Ring

West Dart River

Brimpts Farm

East Dart River

Meml

LOCK'S GATE CROSS

Sherberton Common

BEL TOR CNR

8

Hexworthy

P

B3357

Clapper Bridge

P

Coffin Stone

P

Dartmeet

Sharp Tor

Bel Tor

73

Huccaby

PH

P

River Swincombe

Combestone

Rowbrook

Mel Tor

7

Down Ridge

Combestone Tor

P

River Dart

Hockinston Tor

72

Deep Swincombe

O Brook

Horn's Cross

Bench Tor

6

Ter Hill

Skir Hill

Holne Moor

Venford Reservoir

P

Stoke

71

Holne Ridge

Sandy Way

5

Aune or Avon Head

Petre's Bound Stone

Ryder's Hill

Michelcombe

70

Naker's Hill

Snowdon

River Mardle

Sandy Way

MICHELCOMBE LA

4

Scorriton Down

Chalk Ford

69

River Avon

Buckfastleigh Moor

Pupers Hill

Lud Gate

Lakemoor

3

Huntingdon Warren

Hayford Hall

Forder

CROSS FURZES

68

Two Moors Way

Hickaton Hill

Dean Moor

Water Oak Corner

Abbot's Way

Lamb's Down

2

Red Lake

Huntingdon Cross

1

64   A   65   B   66   C   67   D   68   E   69   F

134
130

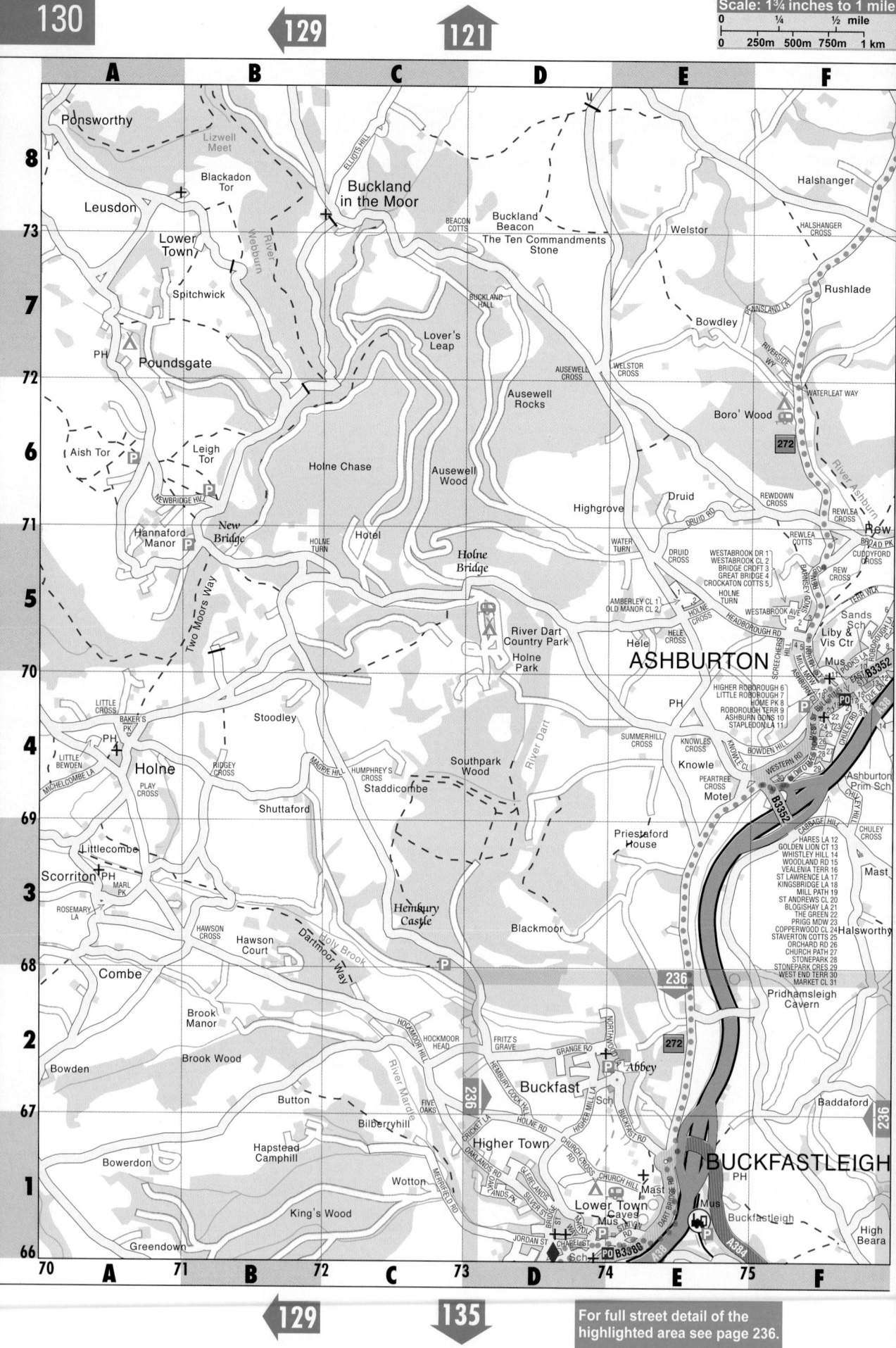

Scale: 1¾ inches to 1 mile

0   ¼   ½   mile
0 250m 500m 750m 1 km

A B C D E F

8

Ponsworthy

Lizwell
Meet

Blackadon
Tor

Buckland in the Moor

Halshanger

Leusdon

ELLIOTS HILL

73

BEACON
COTTS

Buckland
Beacon

Welstor

HALSHANGER
CROSS

Lower
Town

The Ten Commandments
Stone

Rushlade

Spitchwick

BUCKLAND
HALL

LANSLAND LA

7

Bowdley

RIVERSIDE WY

PH

Lover's
Leap

WATERLEAT WAY

Poundsgate

Ausewell
CROSS

WELSTOR
CROSS

Boro' Wood

272

72

River Ashburn

Ausewell
Rocks

Aish Tor

P

Leigh
Tor

Holne Chase

Ausewell
Wood

Druid

REWDOWN
CROSS

Highgrove

REWLEA
CROSS

Rew

P

NEWBRIDGE HILL

6

DRUID RD

REWLEA
COTTS

BROAD PK

CUDDYFORD
CROSS

71

Hannaford
Manor

New
Bridge

HOLNE
TURN

Hotel

Holne
Bridge

WATER
TURN

DRUID
CROSS

Holne
Turn

WESTABROOK DR 1
WESTABROOK CL 2
BRIDGE CROFT 3
GREAT BRIDGE 4
CROCKATON COTTS 5

REW
CROSS

Sands
Sch

Liby &
Vis Ctr

Mus

B3352

P

Two Moors Way

AMBERLEY CL 1
OLD MANOR CL 2

WESTABROOK AVE

HEADBOROUGH RD

HELE
CROSS

5

HOLNE
TURN

BARNSEY RD

POOLS CL

LOVE LA

River Dart Country Park

Hele

ASHBURTON

PO

70

River Dart

Holne
Park

WATER
CROSS

HIGHER ROBOROUGH 6
LITTLE ROBOROUGH 7
HOME PK 8
ROBOROUGH TERR 9
ASHBURN GDNS 10
STAPLEDON LA 11

A38

LITTLE
CROSS

BAKER'S
PK

Stoodley

PH

SUMMERHILL
CROSS

KNOWLES
CROSS

BOWDEN HILL

KNOWLE CL

WESTERN RD

MILL RD

CHILLEY RD

12
13
28
25

Ashburton
Prim Sch

4

LITTLE
BEWDEN

PH

RIDGEY
CROSS

MAGPIE HILL

HUMPHREY'S
CROSS

Southpark
Wood

Knowle

PEARTREE
CROSS

Motel

30

B3352

CHULEY
CROSS

Mast

Holne

PLAY
CROSS

Staddicombe

CABBAGE HILL

HARES LA 12
GOLDEN LION CT 13
WHISTLEY HILL 14
WOODLAND RD 15
VEALENIA TERR 16
ST LAWRENCE LA 17
KINGSBRIDGE LA 18
MILL PATH 19
ST ANDREWS CL 20
BLOGISHAY LA 21
THE GREEN 22
PRIGG MDW 23
COPPERWOOD CL 24
STAVERTON COTTS 25
ORCHARD RD 26
CHURCH PATH 27
STONEPARK 28
STONEPARK CRES 29
WEST END TERR 30
MARKET CL 31

MICHELCOMBE LA

69

Shuttaford

Priestaford
House

Halsworthy

3

Littlecombe

Scorriton

PH

MARL
PK

Hembury
Castle

Blackmoor

ROSEMARY
LA

HAWSON
CROSS

Hawson
Court

Holy Brook

Dartmoor Way

P

236

Pridhamsleigh
Cavern

68

Combe

River Mardle

272

2

Brook
Manor

HOCKMOOR HILL

Hockmoor
Head

FRITZ'S
GRAVE

GRANGE RD

NORTHWOOD

Abbey

Bowden

Brook
Wood

FIVE
OAKS

236

CRICKET LA

Buckfast

Sch

HIGHER MILL LA

BUCKFAST RD

Baddaford

236

67

Button

Bilberryhill

HEMBURY COCK HILL

Holne Rd

CHURCH
CROSS

HOLNE RD

Higher
Town

Bowerdon

Hapstead
Camphill

OAKLANDS RD

MERRIFIELD RD

SILVER ST

GLEBELANDS

CHURCH HILL

CHURCH
CROSS

Mast

BUCKFASTLEIGH

PH

1

King's Wood

Wotton

SANDS PK

JORDAN ST

CHAPEL ST

Lower Town
Caves
Mus

DART BRIDGE RD

Mus

P

Buckfastleigh

High
Beara

66

Greendown

PO

B3380

A38

Sch

B3380

A384

70 A 71 B 72 C 73 D 74 E 75 F

For full street detail of the
highlighted area see page 236.

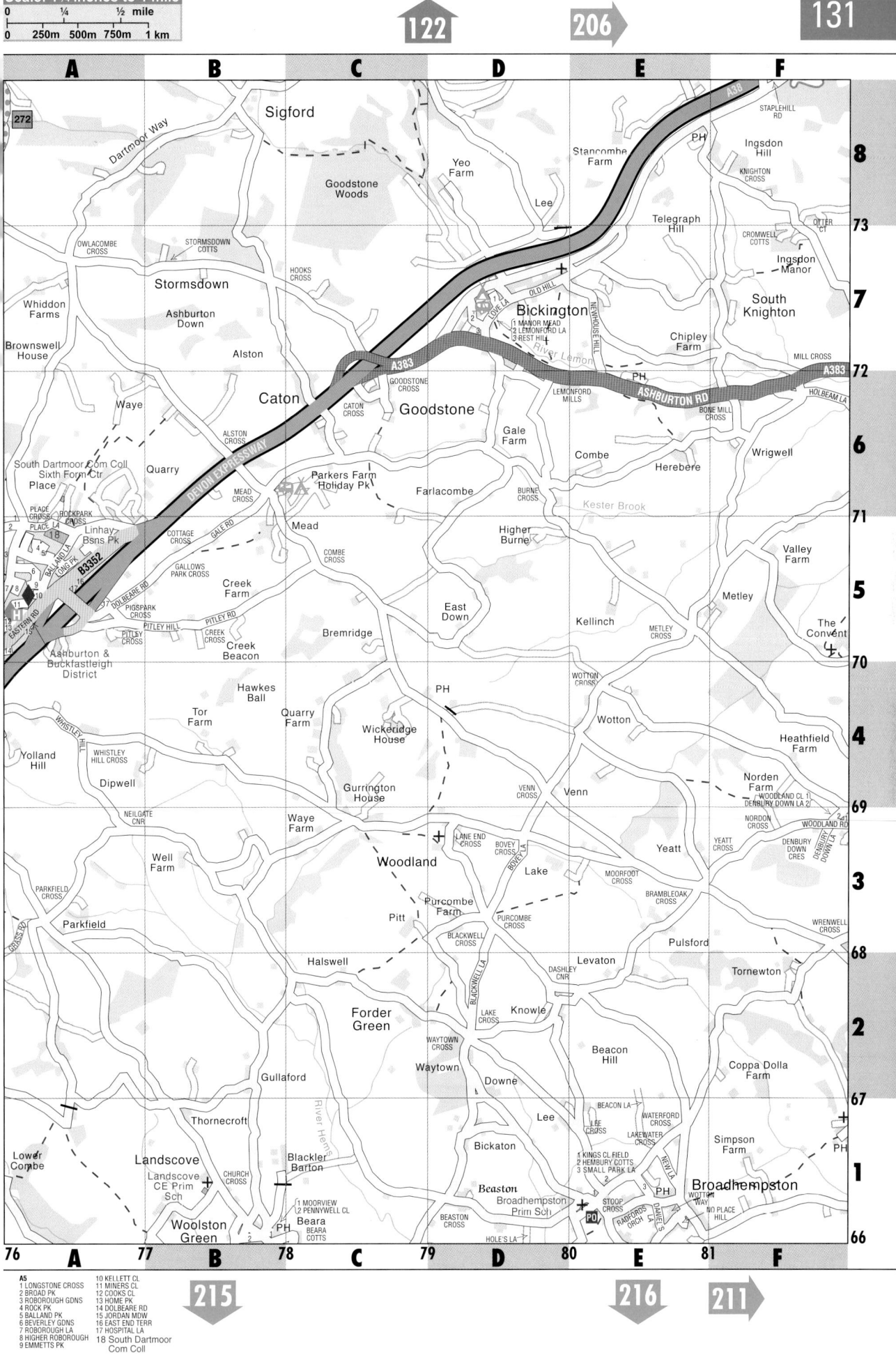

Scale: 1¾ inches to 1 mile
0   ¼   ½ mile
0   250m 500m 750m 1 km

122

206

131

A B C D E F

272

Sigford

Dartmoor Way

Goodstone
Woods

Yeo
Farm

Lee

Stancombe
Farm

PH

Ingsdon
Hill

STAPLEHILL
RD

8

Telegraph
Hill

KNIGHTON
CROSS

73

CROMWELL
COTTS

OTTER
CT

Owlacombe
Cross

Stormsdown

STORMSDOWN
COTTS

Ashburton
Down

HOOKS
CROSS

Bickington

1 MANOR MEAD
2 LEMONFORD LA
3 REST HILL

Old Hill
LOVE LA

NEWHOUSE HILL

Chipley
Farm

South
Knighton

Ingsdon
Manor

7

Whiddon
Farms

Alston

MILL CROSS

Brownswell
House

Caton

A383

Goodstone
Cross

CATON
CROSS

Goodstone

River Lemon

LEMONFORD
MILLS

PH

ASHBURTON RD

BONE MILL
CROSS

A383

HOLBEAM LA

72

Waye

ALSTON
CROSS

Gale
Farm

Combe

Herebere

Wrigwell

Quarry

South Dartmoor Com Coll
Sixth Form Ctr
Place

MEAD
CROSS

Parkers Farm
Holiday Pk

Farlacombe

BURNE
CROSS

Kester Brook

6

71

PLACE
CROSS

ROCKPARK
CROSS

COTTAGE
CROSS

GALE RD

Mead

COMBE
CROSS

Higher
Burne

Valley
Farm

PLACE

Linhay
Bsns Pk

GALLOWS
PARK CROSS

Metley

B3352

DOLBEARE RD

PIGSPARK
CROSS

Creek
Farm

East
Down

Kellinch

METLEY
CROSS

The
Convent

5

EASTERN RD

PITLEY HILL

PITLEY RD

Bremridge

70

Ashburton &
Buckfastleigh
District

PITLEY HILL

CREEK
CROSS

Creek
Beacon

PH

WOTTON
CROSS

Hawkes
Ball

Tor
Farm

Quarry
Farm

Wickeridge
House

Wotton

Heathfield
Farm

4

Yolland
Hill

WHISTLEY
HILL CROSS

Dipwell

Gurrington
House

VENN
CROSS

Venn

Norden
Farm

WOODLAND CL 1
DENBURY DOWN LA 2

69

NEILGATE
CNR

Waye
Farm

LANE END
CROSS

BOVEY
CROSS

BOVEY LA

Yeatt

NORDON
CROSS

YEATT
CROSS

DENBURY
DOWN
CRES

WOODLAND RD

DENBURY DOWN LA

Well
Farm

Lake

MOORFOOT
CROSS

BRAMBLEOAK
CROSS

3

PARKFIELD
CROSS

Woodland

Pitt

Purcombe
Farm

PURCOMBE
CROSS

Pulsford

WRENWELL
CROSS

Parkfield

BLACKWELL
CROSS

Levaton

Tornewton

68

CROSS RD

Halswell

BLACKWELL LA

LAKE
CROSS

DASHLEY
CNR

Knowle

Forder
Green

WAYTOWN
CROSS

Beacon
Hill

Coppa Dolla
Farm

2

Gullaford

Waytown

Downe

67

Lower
Combe

Thornecroft

River Hems

Blackler
Barton

Lee

Simpson
Farm

BEACON LA

LEE
CROSS

WATERFORD
CROSS

PH

1

Landscove

Landscove
CE Prim
Sch

CHURCH
CROSS

1 MOORVIEW
2 PENNYWELL CL

Bickaton

1 KINGS CL FIELD
2 HEMBURY COTTS
3 SMALL PARK LA

LAKEWATER
CROSS

NEW LA

Broadhempston

WOTTON
WAY

Woolston
Green

PH

Beara

BEARA
COTTS

Beaston

Broadhempston
Prim Sch

BEASTON
CROSS

PO

STOOP
CROSS

RADFORDS
ORCH

DANIEL'S
LA

NO PLACE
HILL

66

HOLE'S LA

A5
1 LONGSTONE CROSS
2 BROAD PK
3 ROBOROUGH GDNS
4 ROCK PK
5 BALLAND PK
6 BEVERLEY GDNS
7 ROBOROUGH LA
8 HIGHER ROBOROUGH
9 EMMETTS PK
10 KELLETT CL
11 MINERS CL
12 COOKS CL
13 HOME PK
14 DOLBEARE RD
15 JORDAN MDW
16 EAST END TERR
17 HOSPITAL LA
18 South Dartmoor
Com Coll

241
127
245
250
251

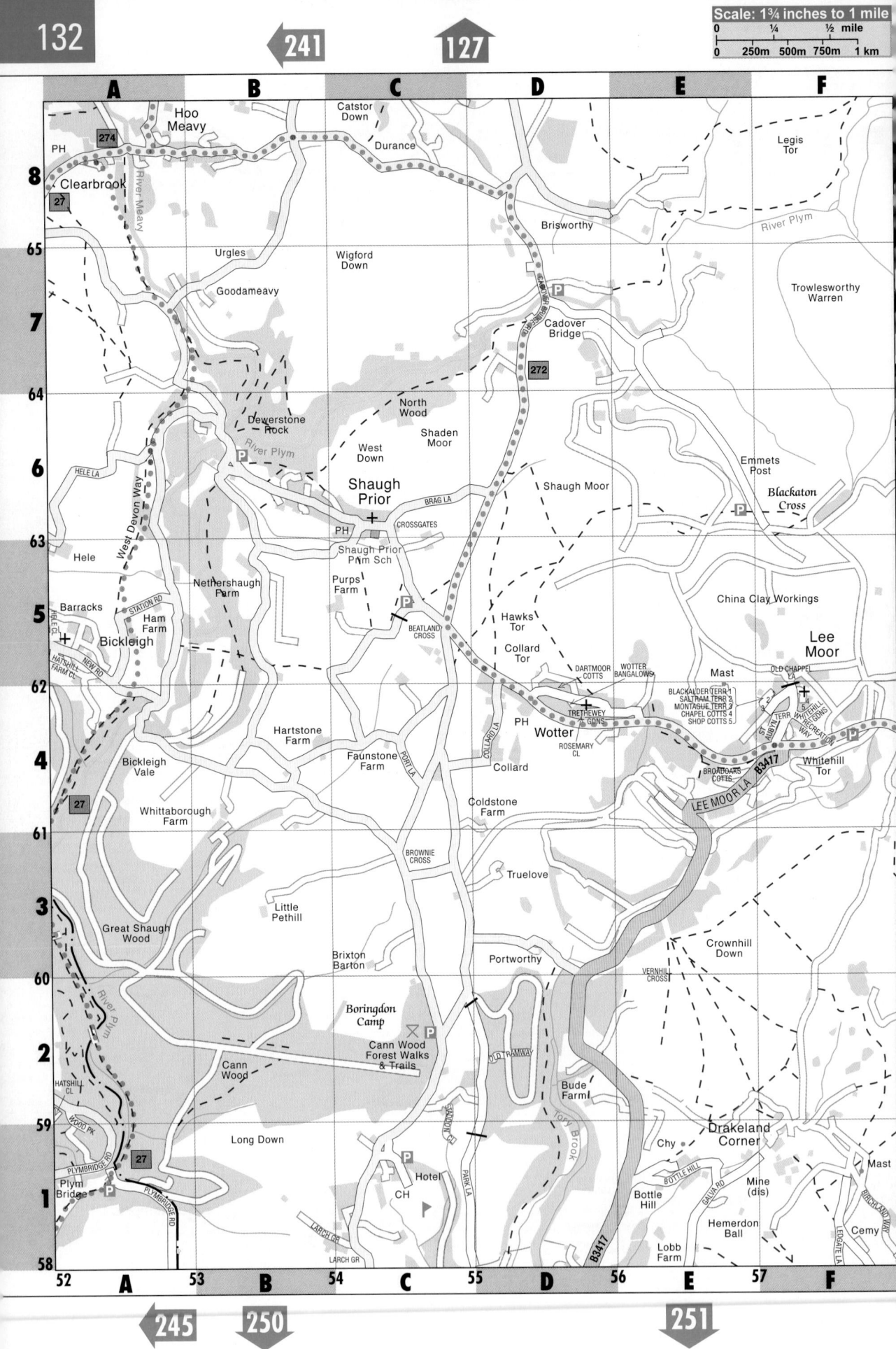
Scale: 1¾ inches to 1 mile
0 ¼ ½ mile
0 250m 500m 750m 1 km
Hoo Meavy
Clearbrook
PH
River Meavy
Catstor Down
Durance
Legis Tor
Brisworthy
River Plym
Urgles
Wigford Down
Goodameavy
Trowlesworthy Warren
Cadover Bridge
North Wood
Dewerstone Rock
Shaden Moor
West Down
River Plym
Shaugh Prior
BRAG LA
CROSSGATES
Shaugh Moor
Emmets Post
Blackaton Cross
HELE LA
West Devon Way
Hele
Shaugh Prior Prim Sch
Purps Farm
Nethershaugh Farm
China Clay Workings
Barracks
STATION RD
Ham Farm
Bickleigh
BEATLAND CROSS
Hawks Tor
Collard Tor
Lee Moor
Mast
OLD CHAPEL LA
DARTMOOR COTTS
WOTTER BANGALOWS
BLACKALDER TERR 1
SALTRAM TERR 2
MONTAGUE TERR 3
CHAPEL COTTS 4
SHOP COTTS 5
TRETHEWEY GDNS
ROSEMARY CL
Wotter
Hartstone Farm
Faunstone Farm
PORT LA
COLLARD LA
Collard
ST AUBYN TERR
WHITEHILL
RECREATION WAY
BROADOAKS COTTS
LEE MOOR LA
B3417
Whitehill Tor
Bickleigh Vale
Coldstone Farm
Whittaborough Farm
BROWNIE CROSS
Truelove
Little Pethill
Great Shaugh Wood
Crownhill Down
Brixton Barton
Portworthy
VERNHILL CROSS
River Plym
Boringdon Camp
Cann Wood Forest Walks & Trails
OLD TRAMWAY
Cann Wood
HATSHILL CL
Bude Farm
Tory Brook
Long Down
WOOD PK
Drakeland Corner
Chy
PLYMBRIDGE RD
Hotel
Mast
Plym Bridge
CH
BOTTLE HILL
GALVA RD
Mine (dis)
Bottle Hill
Hemerdon Ball
Cemy
BIRCHLAND WAY
LARCH GR
PARK LA
STADDON CL
Lobb Farm
LEDGATE LA
A B C D E F
52 53 54 55 56 57
58 59 60 61 62 63 64 65
1 2 3 4 5 6 7 8
274 27 272

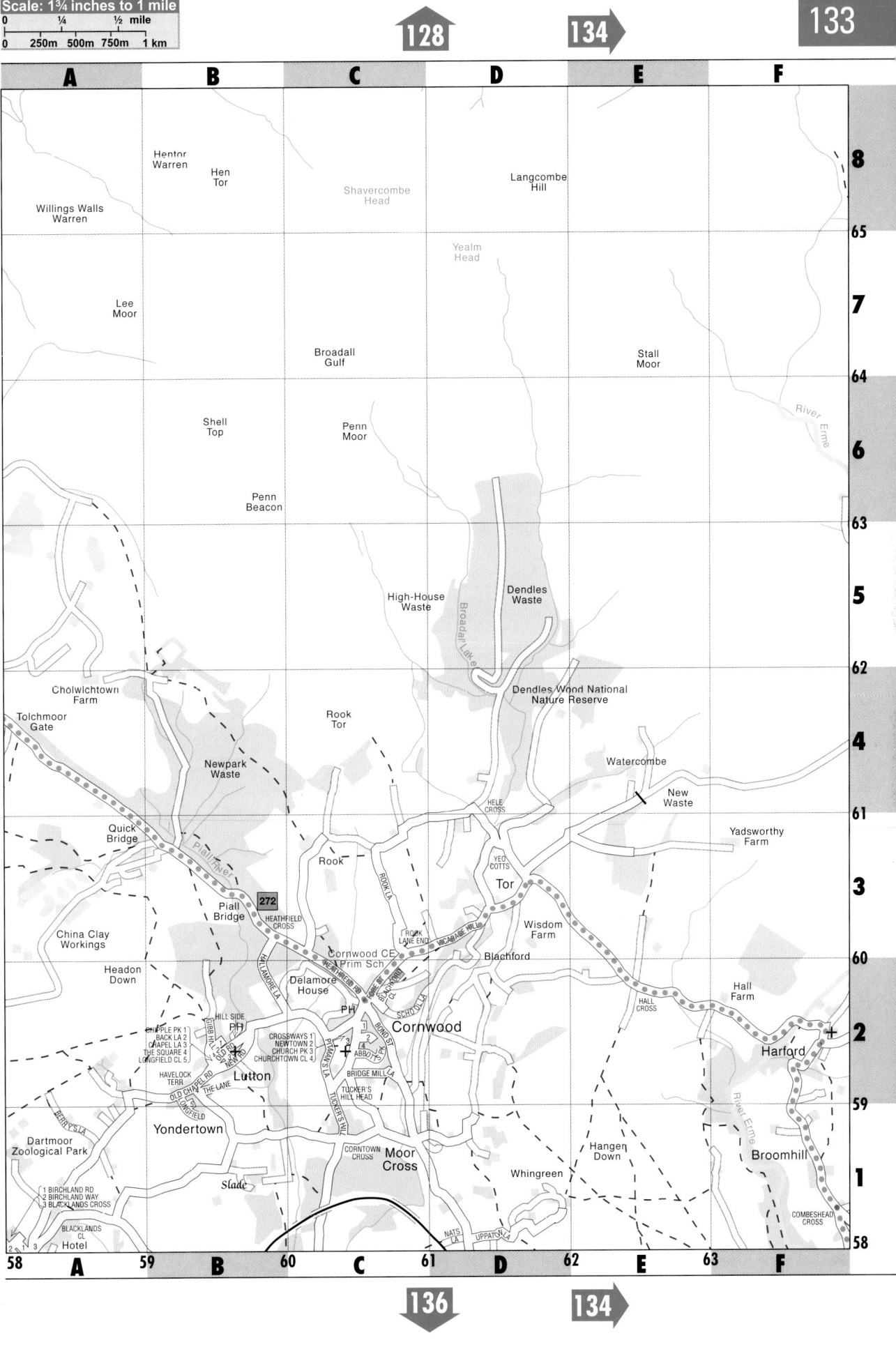

Scale: 1¾ inches to 1 mile

0   ¼   ½ mile

0   250m 500m 750m 1 km

128
134
136
134

A   B   C   D   E   F

Hentor
Warren

Hen
Tor

Shavercombe
Head

Langcombe
Hill

8

Willings Walls
Warren

65

Lee
Moor

Yealm
Head

7

Broadall
Gulf

Stall
Moor

64

River Erme

Shell
Top

Penn
Moor

6

Penn
Beacon

63

High-House
Waste

Dendles
Waste

5

Broadall Lake

62

Cholwichtown
Farm

Dendles Wood National
Nature Reserve

Tolchmoor
Gate

Rook
Tor

Watercombe

4

Newpark
Waste

New
Waste

61

HELE
CROSS

Quick
Bridge

Yadsworthy
Farm

Plym Leat

Rook

YEO
COTTS

Tor

3

China Clay
Workings

Piall
Bridge

272

HEATHFIELD
CROSS

ROOK LA

ROOK
LANE END

VICARAGE HILL

Wisdom
Farm

Hall
Farm

60

Headon
Down

Cornwood CE
Prim Sch

Blachford

HALL
CROSS

Delamore
House

PH

Cornwood

Harford

2

HILL SIDE
PH

BOND ST

SCHOOL LA

CHIPPLE PK 1
BACK LA 2
CHAPEL LA 3
THE SQUARE 4
LONGFIELD CL 5

CROSSWAYS 1
NEWTOWN 2
CHURCH PK 3
CHURCHTOWN CL 4

ABBOTTS

Lutton

HAVELOCK
TERR

OLD CHAPEL RD

THE LANE

LONGFIELD

BRIDGE MILL LA

TUCKER'S
HILL HEAD

River Erme

59

BERRYS LA

Dartmoor
Zoological Park

Yondertown

TUCKER'S WY

CORNTOWN
CROSS

Moor
Cross

Hangen
Down

Broomhill

1

1 BIRCHLAND RD
2 BIRCHLAND WAY
3 BLACKLANDS CROSS

Slade

Whingreen

COMBESHEAD
CROSS

BLACKLANDS
CL

Hotel

NATS
LA

UPPATON LA

58

58   A   59   B   60   C   61   D   62   E   63   F

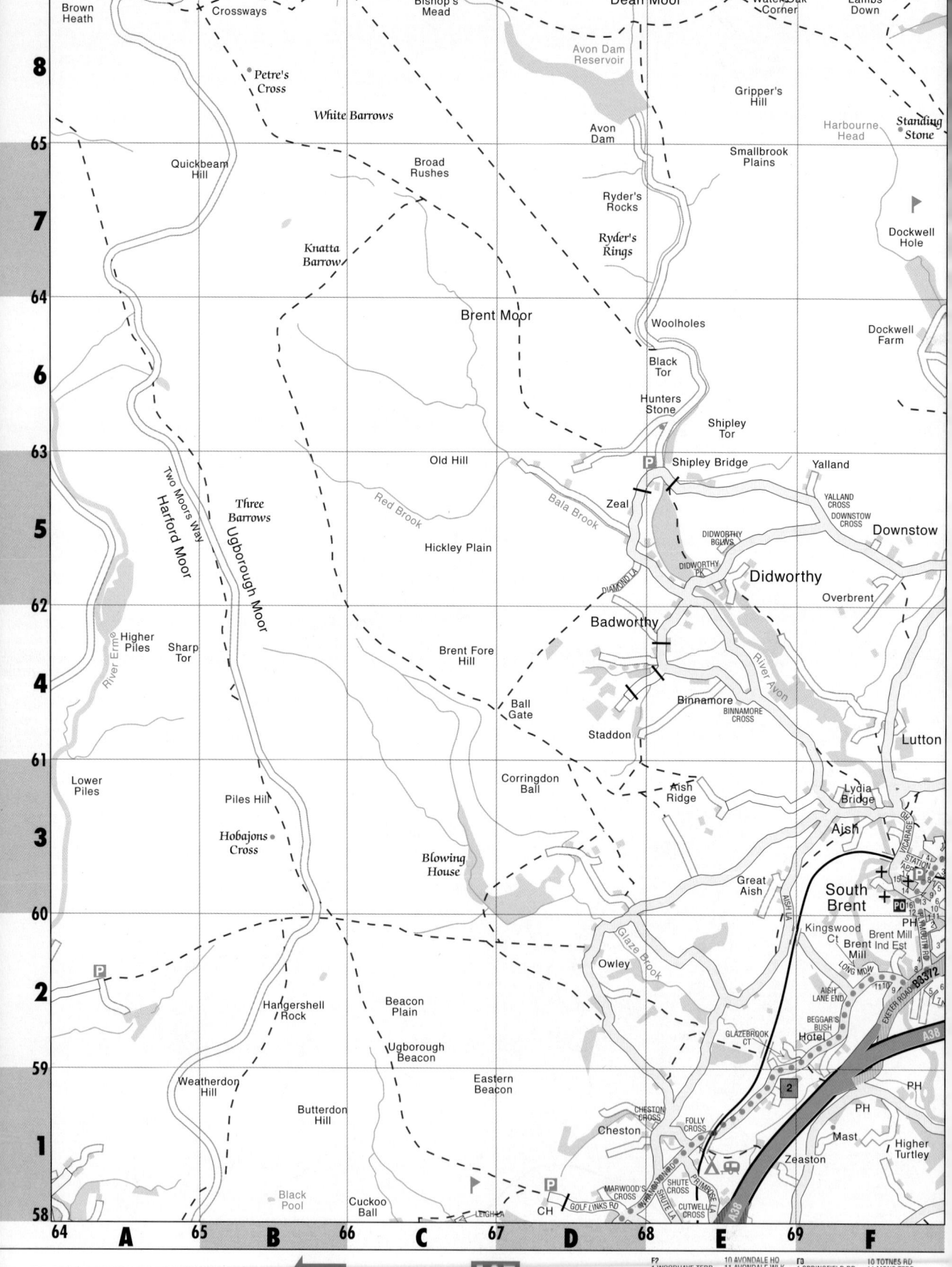

Scale: 1¾ inches to 1 mile

0   ¼   ½   mile
0   250m 500m 750m 1 km

Brown Heath
Crossways
Bishop's Mead
Dean Moor
Water Oak Corner
Lambs Down

Petre's Cross
White Barrows
Avon Dam Reservoir
Gripper's Hill
Harbourne Head
Standing Stone

Quickbeam Hill
Broad Rushes
Avon Dam
Smallbrook Plains
Dockwell Hole

Knatta Barrow
Ryder's Rocks
Ryder's Rings

Brent Moor
Woolholes
Dockwell Farm

Two Moors Way
Harford Moor
Three Barrows
Ugborough Moor
Black Tor
Hunters Stone
Shipley Tor

Old Hill
Red Brook
Bala Brook
Zeal
Shipley Bridge
Yalland
YALLAND CROSS
DOWNSTOW CROSS
Downstow

Higher Piles
Sharp Tor
Hickley Plain
DIDWORTHY BGLWS
DIDWORTHY PK
Didworthy
Overbrent

River Erme
Brent Fore Hill
Badworthy
Binnamore
BINNAMORE CROSS
Lutton

Lower Piles
Ball Gate
Staddon

Piles Hill
Corringdon Ball
Aish Ridge
Lydia Bridge
Aish

Hobajons Cross
Blowing House
Great Aish
South Brent

Kingswood Ct
Brent Mill
Brent Ind Est
Mill

Glaze Brook
Owley
LONG MDW
AISH LANE END
883572
EXETER ROAD
A38

Hangershell Rock
Beacon Plain
GLAZEBROOK CT
Beggar's Bush
Hotel

Weatherdon Hill
Ugborough Beacon
Eastern Beacon
2
PH

Butterdon Hill
CHESTON CROSS
FOLLY CROSS
Zeaston
Mast
Higher Turtley

Black Pool
Cuckoo Ball
Cheston
MARWOOD'S CROSS
SHUTE CROSS
GOLF LINKS RD
CUTWELL CROSS
LEIGH
CH

F2
1 WOODHAYE TERR
2 WOODHAYE CL
3 CLOBELLS
4 BEACON TERR
5 ST MICHAELS TERR
6 CORN PK
7 GREENFIELD DR
8 BEACON VIEW
9 NEW ORCHARD

10 AVONDALE HO
11 AVONDALE WLK

F3
1 SPRINGFIELD RD
2 HILLSIDE
3 BISHOPS MEAD
4 BROOKWOOD CL
5 ASHWOOD
6 CHAPEL FIELDS
7 BALMORAL LA
8 STATION RD
9 MANOR CT

10 TOTNES RD
11 MONS TERR
12 CLIFTON TERR
13 FORE ST
14 CHURCH ST
15 WELLINGTON SQ
16 STOCKBRIDGE LA
17 OLD STATION YARD

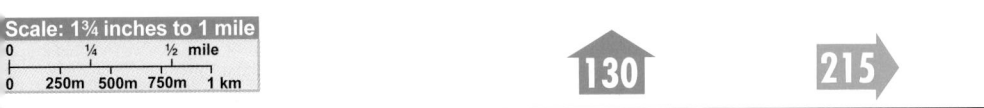

Scale: 1¾ inches to 1 mile

0 — ¼ — ½ mile
0 — 250m — 500m — 750m — 1 km

135

130 **215**

BUCKFASTLEIGH

Austin's Bridge
Higher Beara Cross
Green Lane End
Green La
Kilbury Manor
Wallaford Down
Wallaford
WALLAFORD RD
Bigadon House
Rill Wood
Loverscombe
Mast
Rill
Weston
Skerraton Down
Skerraton
Dean Wood
Higher Dean
Lower Dean
Luscombe
Reddacleave Kiln Cross
Deancombe
Whitehead's Cross
Cuming Farm
Addislade
Nurston
Butts Cross
Pennywell Farm & Wildlife Ctr
Gidley Bridge
Moorshead Cross
Dean Prior
Smallacombe Cross
Bukamore
Brownston Farm
Eden Farm
Clampits Stile
Bulkamore Ct
Yelland Farm
Zempson
Zempson Cross
Dean Cross
Tordean
Dean Lane End
Yelland Cross
Lower Bulkamore Cross
Brownston Cross
Willing Cross
Bloody Pool
Bowdown Cross
Yelland Bglws
Higher Bulkamore Cross
Gingaford Cross
Willing Gate
Stippadon
Harbourneford
Drybridge Cross
Almshouse Cross
Willing
Harbourneford Cross
White-Oxen Manor
Whiteoxen Cross
Crabbers Cross
Carden Pk
Penswell Cross
Baera Common
Higher Beara
Marley Farm
Syon Abbey
Rattery
Leigh Cross
Leigh Grange
Forder La
Forder
The Dower Ho
Mill Cross
Brooking
Tigley Cross
Hillside
Stidston La
Marley Head
Smalla
Culver La
Venton
Tigley
Harwell La
Stidson Cross
Stidston
A385
Edeswell Farm
Venton Cross
Palstone
Crowder Mdw
New Cross
Lisburne
Harbourne River
Hazard Old Hazard Cotts
Exeter Rd
Webland La
Wonton
Bluepost
Langford
Barleycombe Farm
Wonton Cross
Shorter Cross
Moore
Horsebrook Avonwick
Charford Cross
Charford Manor
Elwell
Kerswill Cross
Kerswill
East Moore Cross
Lincombe
Larcombe End
West Leigh Cross

1 Courtenay Pk
2 Shipley Cl
3 Pool Pk
4 Avon Cl
5 Totnes Rd
6 Clobells
7 Sanderspool Cross
8 Higher Gn
9 Noland Pk
10 Kerrics La
11 Brent Mill
12 Corn Pk
13 Kerries Ct
14 Crowder Cross
15 South Brent Prim Sch

16 Fairfield
17 Middle Green
18 Lower Green

1 The Orchard
2 Avonwick Gn
3 Higher Moor

River Avon

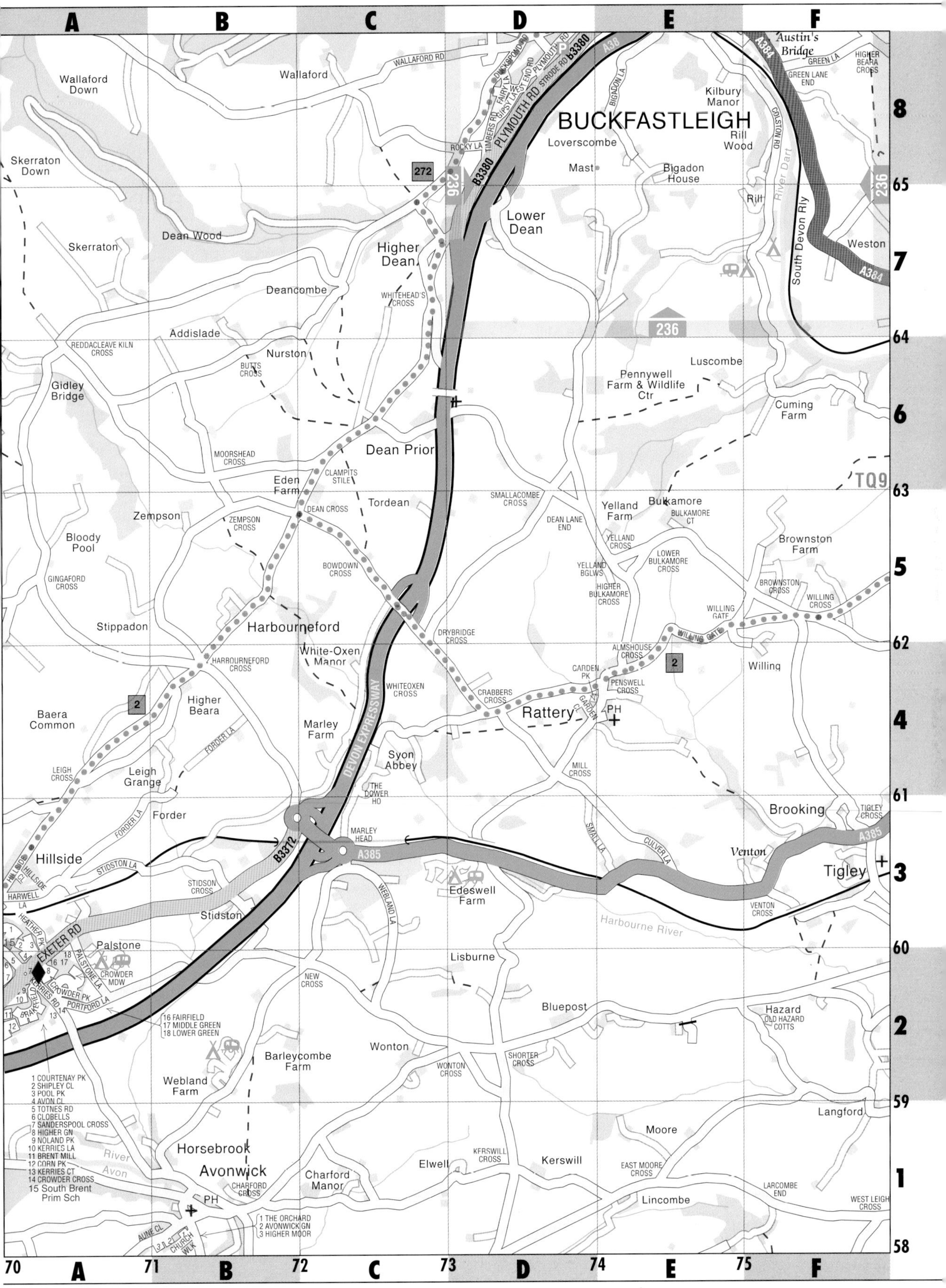

138 **222**

For full street detail of the highlighted area see page 236.

136

251

133

Scale: 1¾ inches to 1 mile
0   ¼   ½ mile
0   250m 500m 750m 1 km

A   B   C   D   E   F

8

1 BIRCHLAND WAY
2 NEWTON'S ROW
3 FAIRWAY GDNS

Sparkwell
MOLL TALL'S CROSS
Sparkwell All Saints Prim Sch
Venton Farm

Woodburn Farm

Sherrell Farm

Pit Hill Farm

237

Great Stert

Fardel

CH

Henlake Down

57

IVYBRIDGE

Venton

Cadleigh Lodge

237

Mount Pleasant

ZETH HILL LA

7

HOLLYBERRY RD
HARRIS WAY

Hitchcombe

Lee Mill

Cadleigh Cross

St Austin's Priory

Woodland
Pk Sch
Cemy
Sch

Col

RICHMOND PL

BEECH RD

WOODLAND RD

Blachford Rd
Crescent Rd
Station Rd

56

Lee Mill

NORTH RD
Lee Mill Ind Est

CADLEIGH LA

Western Rd

P PO PH
L Ctr
2

Woolcombe La

HAZELDENE CL 1
BUTTSFORD TERR 2
THE AVE 3

BOTTLE PK
HENRY CL

EAST WAY

PH

2

Cadleighpark

1 KINGSLEY CL
2 CADLEIGH CL
3 STRASHLEIGH VIEW
4 OAK CT
5 PENNANT WAY
6 ASH CT
7 ABBOTS CL
8 VICTORIA COTTS
9 JULIAN COTTS

B3213

Ind Est

OLD TURNPIKE RD

DEVON EXPRESSWAY

WARREN LA

Drew

Newlands

6

A38

RECYCLING WAY

Motel

Smithaleigh

Sewage Works

Hunsdon Farm

HUNSDON RD

Cleeve House

Yeolands

COWSELL LA
KEATON LA

River Erme

Ford Farm
Collaford Farm Bsns Units

Challonsleigh

Strashleigh

55

Southwood Wood

Swainstone

Brook Farm

West Worthele

COLE LA

East Worthele

Choakford Farm

New England Quarry

5

West Pitton House

NEW ENGLAND RD

NEW ENGLAND WAY

Popple's Bridge

Fursdon

237

KEATON LA

EAST PITTON BARNS

Coyton

Tod Moor

Mast

54

East Pitton Farm

Lotherton Bridge

WINSOR CROSS

LEY CROSS

TELEGRAPH CROSS

Westlake

CHURCH ST
IVYBRIDGE RD

4

Treby Farm

Airstrip (dis)

River Yealm

Winsor

GRASSY LA

KNAP CROSS

BURRATON CROSS

Luson

WHIPPLE'S CROSS

Preston Farm

Ermington Prim Sch

PH

53

Yeo Farm

Worston

WILBURTON CROSS

28

Burraton

Langbrook

LANGBROOK CROSS

Ermington

WOOD VIEW TERR

BACK LA

3

Stoneycross

YEO PK

Orchard Farm

ORCHARD HILL LA

Wilburton Farm

Langbrook

Clickland

Long Brook

Hollowcombe

HOLLOWCOMBE CROSS

A3121

River Erme

TOTNES RD

PARKHILL COTTS 1
CHAPEL ST 2
THE SQUARE 3
SCHOOL RD 4
ERME SIDE COTTS 5
FAWNS CL 6
ERME PK 7
TOWN HILL 8

52

ELM TREE PK
A379
MARKET ST
MILL LEAT CL

Yealmbridge

Courtyard Cotts

Waye Farmhouse

MODBURY CROSS

Sexton

Sequer's Bridge

GOUTSFORD GATE

Erme Pk

RIDGE LA

A379

NEW RD
TORR BRIDGE PK
RIVERSIDE WLK

Yealmpton

Dunstone

Butland Wood

MOORSHEAD CROSS

Flete House

Goutsford Bridge

2

CHAPEL RD
PLOUGHMAN WAY
CREAMERY CL
ROCKDALE RD

Torr

Ramsland

Hole

BLUEGATE HILL

LONDON RD

1 CHURCH PARK RD
2 TORR LA
3 HILLSIDE WAY
4 TORR FARM COTTS

Little Orcheton

51

B3186
TWO CROSSES

Crebar

Ford

1 THE DRIVE
2 EASTERNTOWN
3 ORCHARD COTTS
4 MASONS YARD
5 HOLBETON SCH

Ashridge

1

LOLESBURY CROSS

MARLAND CROSS

Holbeton

HUXHAM'S CROSS
BRET RD

PO
PH

LUSON CROSS

P

BROWNSWELLA

50

Luson

GARDEN CL

58   A   59   B   60   C   61   D   62   E   63   F

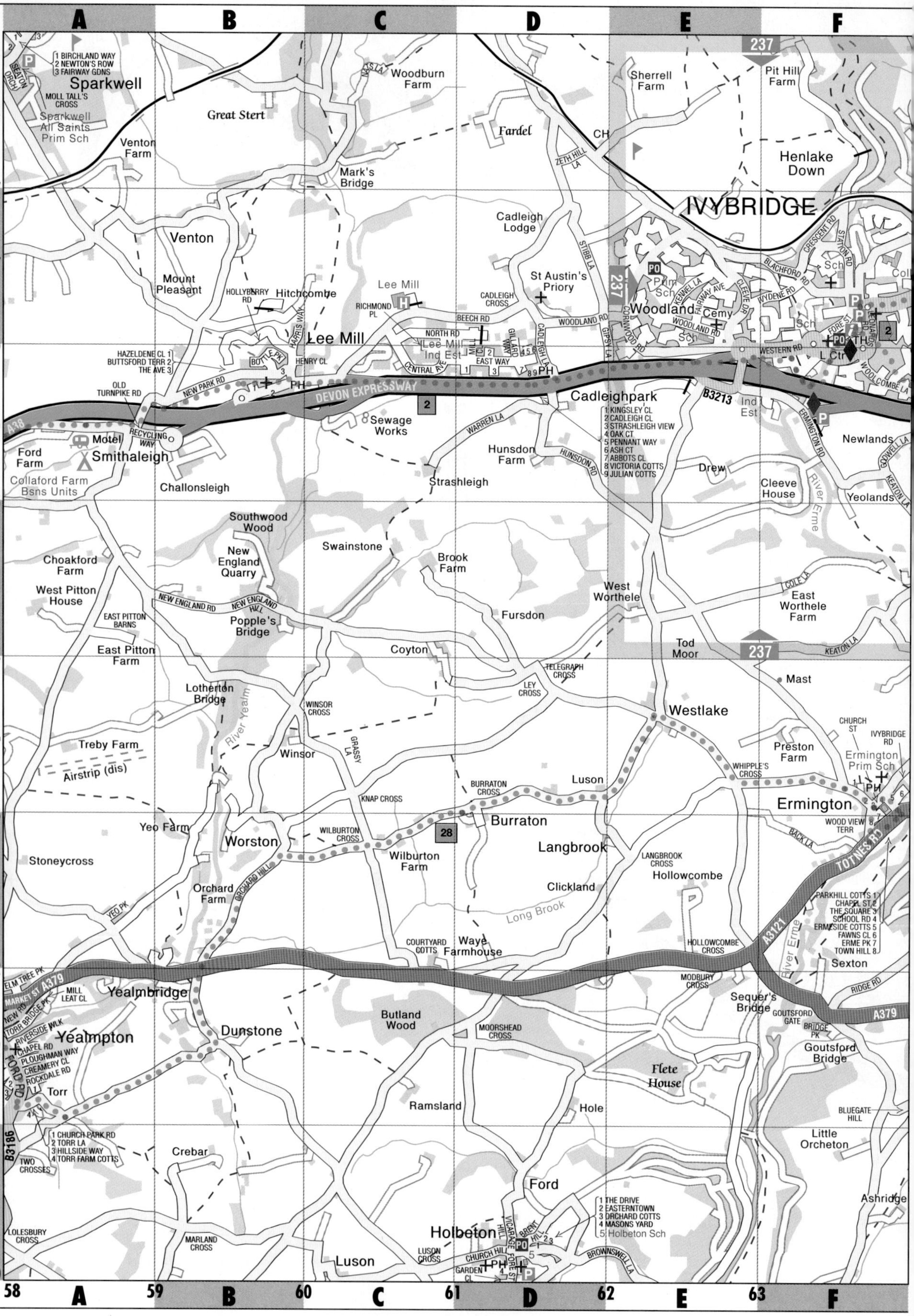

257

141

For full street detail of the highlighted area see page 237.

142

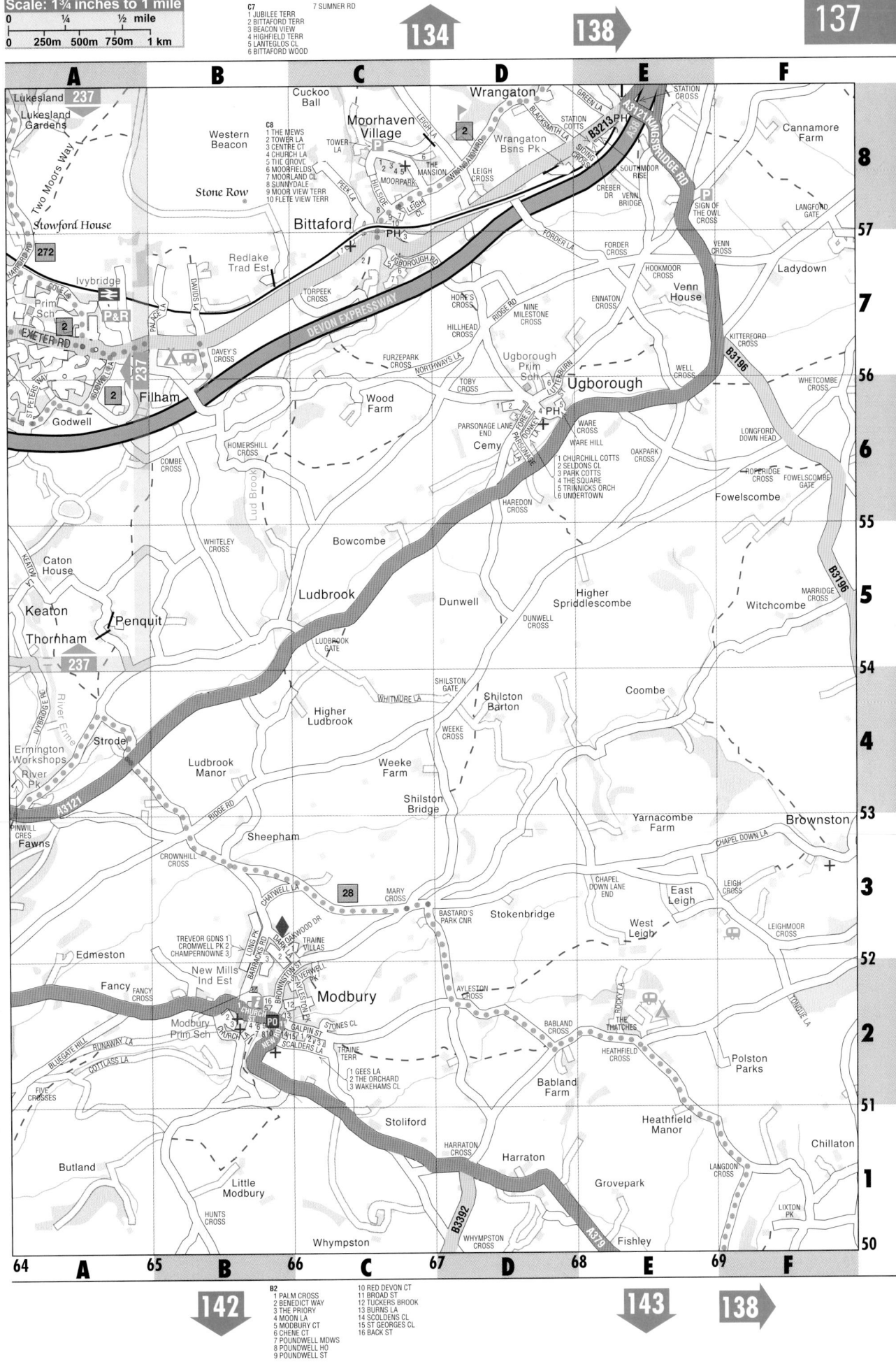

Scale: 1¾ inches to 1 mile

0 ¼ ½ mile
0 250m 500m 750m 1 km

137

134

138

C7
1 JUBILEE TERR
2 BITTAFORD TERR
3 BEACON VIEW
4 HIGHFIELD TERR
5 LANTEGLOS CL
6 BITTAFORD WOOD

7 SUMNER RD

C8
1 THE MEWS
2 TOWER LA
3 CENTRE CT
4 CHURCH LA
5 THE GROVE
6 MOORFIELDS
7 MOORLAND CL
8 SUNNYDALE
9 MOOR VIEW TERR
10 FLETE VIEW TERR

Lukesland
Lukesland Gardens
Two Moors Way
Stowford House
Ivybridge
Prim Sch
P&R
Filham
EXETER RD
St PETER's WAY
Godwell
Redlake Trad Est
PALACE LA
DAVIDS LA
TORPEEK CROSS
DAVEY'S CROSS

Western Beacon
Stone Row
Bittaford
Moorhaven Village
MOORPARK
TOWER LA
PEEK LA
PH
LEIGH LA
PHILSILL

Cuckoo Ball
Wrangaton
Wrangaton Bsns Pk
BLACKSMITH LA
WRANGATON RD
LEIGH LA
LEIGH CL
The Mansion

DEVON EXPRESSWAY
UGBOROUGH RD
FORDER LA

Wood Farm
COMBE CROSS
HOMERSHILL CROSS
Lud Brook
WHITELEY CROSS

FURZEPARK CROSS
NORTHWAYS LA
TOBY CROSS
HILLHEAD CROSS
HONE'S CROSS
RIDGE RD
NINE MILESTONE CROSS

Ugborough Prim Sch
Ugborough
PH
PARSONAGE LANE END
FORE ST
LUTTERBURN ST
LIVERTON
Cemy
WARE ST
WARE HILL
HAREDON CROSS

1 CHURCHILL COTTS
2 SELDONS CL
3 PARK COTTS
4 THE SQUARE
5 TRINNICKS ORCH
6 UNDERTOWN

STATION COTTS
STATION CROSS
SIDING CROSS
CREBER DR
VENN BRIDGE
SOUTHMOOR RISE
GREEN LA
B3213
A3121 KINGSBRIDGE RD

STATION CROSS
SIGN OF THE OWL CROSS
FORDER CROSS
HOOKMOOR CROSS
ENNATON CROSS
Venn House
VENN CROSS
WELL CROSS
KITTERFORD CROSS
B3196

Cannamore Farm
LANGFORD GATE
Ladydown
WHETCOMBE CROSS
LONGFORD DOWN HEAD
ROPERIDGE CROSS
FOWELSCOMBE GATE
Fowelscombe
MARRIDGE CROSS
Witchcombe
B3196

Bowcombe
Ludbrook
Dunwell
Higher Spriddlescombe
DUNWELL CROSS
Coombe

LUDBROOK GATE
Keaton
Thornham
Penquit
Caton House

WHITMORE LA
SHILSTON GATE
Shilston Barton
WEEKE CROSS
Higher Ludbrook
Weeke Farm
Shilston Bridge

Ermington Workshops
River Pk
River Erme
A3121
Strode
RIDGE RD
Ludbrook Manor
Sheepham
CROWNHILL CROSS
Fawns
PINWILL CRES

Yarnacombe Farm
Brownston
CHAPEL DOWN LA
CHAPEL DOWN LANE END
East Leigh
West Leigh
LEIGH CROSS
LEIGHMOOR CROSS

CHATWELL LA
28
MARY CROSS
BASTARD'S PARK CNR
Stokenbridge
AYLESTON CROSS
BABLAND CROSS
THE THATCHES
Heathfield CROSS
Polson Parks

Edmeston
Fancy
FANCY CROSS
New Mills Ind Est
TREVOR GDNS 1
CROMWELL PK 2
CHAMPERNOWNE 3
BARRACKS RD
KING PK
OAKWOOD DR
BROWNSTON ST
SILVERWELL
Modbury
Modbury Prim Sch
PO
CHURCH ST
GALPIN ST
STONES CL
SCALDERS LA
TRAINE TERR
TRAINE VILLAS

1 GEES LA
2 THE ORCHARD
3 WAKEHAMS CL

Butland
Little Modbury
HUNTS CROSS
Stoliford
Whympston
WHYMPSTON CROSS
HARRATON CROSS
Harraton
Grovepark
Fishley
Babland Farm
Heathfield Manor
Chillaton
LIXTON PK
LANGDON CROSS
BLUEGATE HILL
RUNAWAY LA
COTTLASS LA
FIVE CROSSES
NEW RD
B3392
A379
ROCKHILL
LONGIE LA

237 272 2 237 2
8 57 7 56 6 55 5 54 4 53 3 52 2 51 1 50

B2
1 PALM CROSS
2 BENEDICT WAY
3 THE PRIORY
4 MOON LA
5 MODBURY CT
6 CHENE CT
7 POUNDWELL MDWS
8 POUNDWELL HO
9 POUNDWELL ST
10 RED DEVON CT
11 BROAD ST
12 TUCKERS BROOK
13 BURNS LA
14 SCOLDENS CL
15 ST GEORGES CL
16 BACK ST

64 A 65 B 66 C 67 D 68 E 69 F

137
135

Scale: 1¾ inches to 1 mile

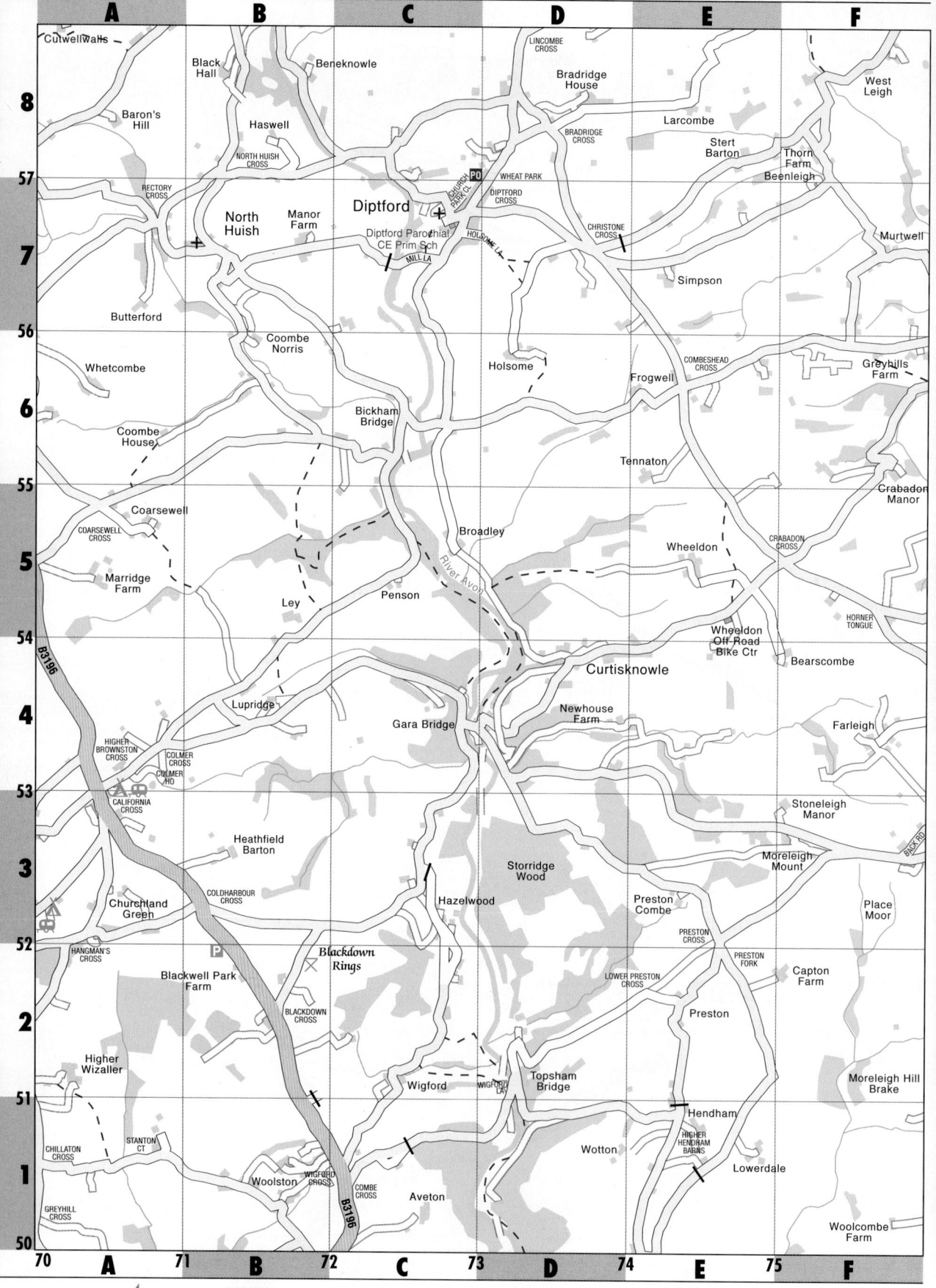
Cutwellwalls
Black Hall
Beneknowle
Baron's Hill
Haswell
NORTH HUISH CROSS
LINCOMBE CROSS
Bradridge House
BRADRIDGE CROSS
Larcombe
Stert Barton
Thorn Farm
Beenleigh
West Leigh
RECTORY CROSS
North Huish
Manor Farm
Diptford
PO
CHURCH PARK CL
WHEAT PARK
DIPTFORD CROSS
Diptford Parochial CE Prim Sch
HOLSOME LA
MILL LA
CHRISTONE CROSS
Murtwell
Simpson
Butterford
Coombe Norris
Whetcombe
Holsome
COMBESHEAD CROSS
Frogwell
Greyhills Farm
Bickham Bridge
Coombe House
Tennaton
Crabadon Manor
Coarsewell
COARSEWELL CROSS
Broadley
Wheeldon
CRABADON CROSS
Marridge Farm
River Avon
Penson
Ley
HORNER TONGUE
Wheeldon Off-Road Bike Ctr
Bearscombe
B3196
Curtisknowle
Lupridge
Newhouse Farm
Gara Bridge
Farleigh
HIGHER BROWNSTON CROSS
COLMER CROSS
COLMER HO
CALIFORNIA CROSS
Stoneleigh Manor
Heathfield Barton
BACK RD
Moreleigh Mount
Storridge Wood
Hazelwood
COLDHARBOUR CROSS
Churchland Green
Preston Combe
Place Moor
PRESTON CROSS
HANGMAN'S CROSS
Blackdown Rings
PRESTON FORK
Capton Farm
Blackwell Park Farm
LOWER PRESTON CROSS
BLACKDOWN CROSS
Preston
Higher Wizaller
Topsham Bridge
Wigford
WIGFORD LA
Moreleigh Hill Brake
Hendham
HIGHER HENDHAM BARNS
STANTON CT
CHILLATON CROSS
Wotton
Lowerdale
Woolston
WIGFORD CROSS
COMBE CROSS
Aveton
B3196
GREYHILL CROSS
Woolcombe Farm
A B C D E F
8 57 7 56 6 55 5 54 4 53 3 52 2 51 1 50
70 71 72 73 74 75

137
143
144

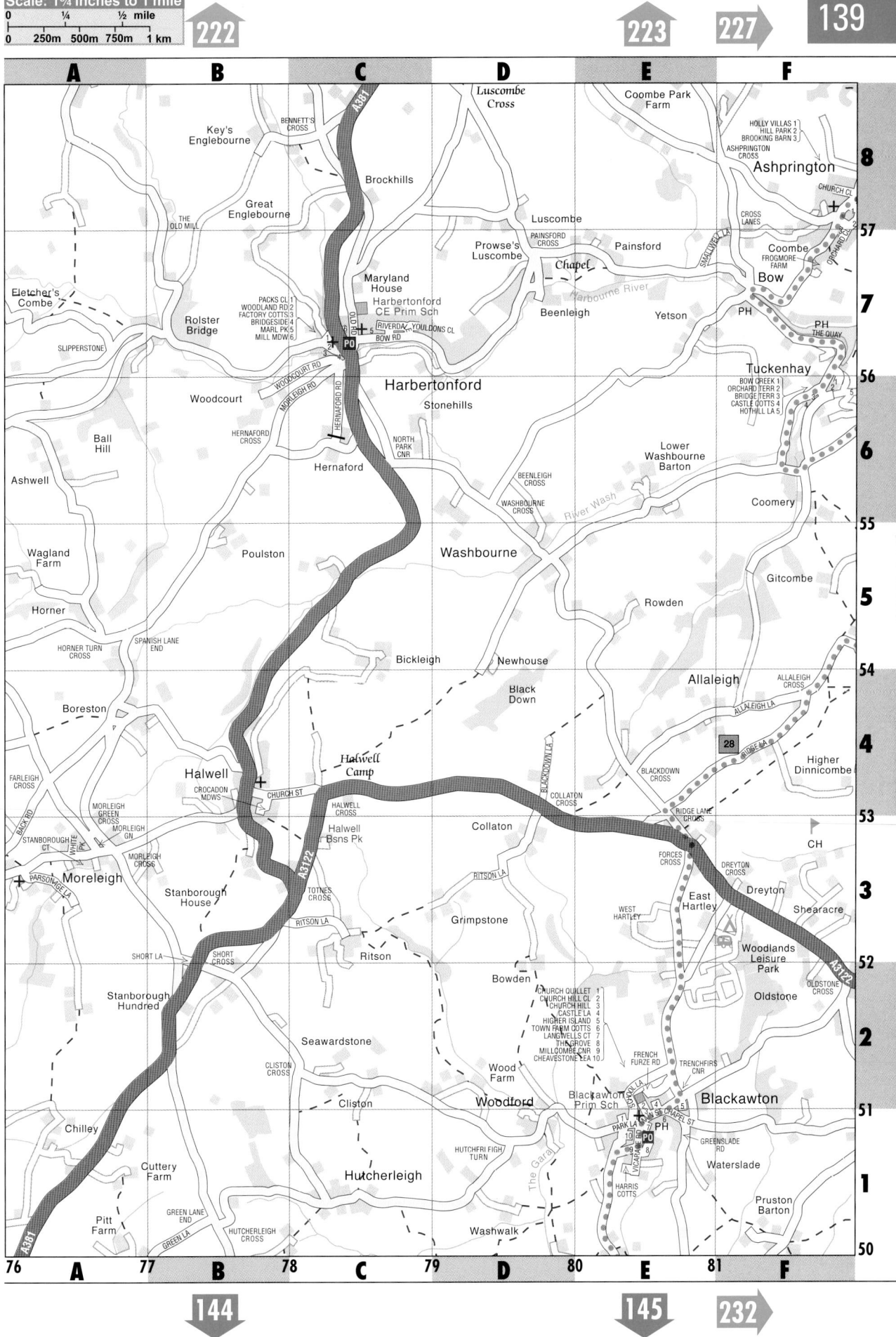
Scale: 1¾ inches to 1 mile
0 ¼ ½ mile
0 250m 500m 750m 1 km
222
223
227
144
145
232
A B C D E F
8 57 7 56 6 55 5 54 4 53 3 52 2 51 1 50
76 77 78 79 80 81
Luscombe Cross
Coombe Park Farm
HOLLY VILLAS 1
HILL PARK 2
BROOKING BARN 3
ASHPRINGTON CROSS
Ashprington
CHURCH CL
Key's Englebourne
BENNETT'S CROSS
A381
Brockhills
Great Englebourne
THE OLD MILL
Luscombe
PAINSFORD CROSS
Painsford
Prowse's Luscombe
Chapel
SMALLWELL LA
CROSS LANES
Coombe
FROGMORE FARM
ORCHARD CL
Bow
Maryland House
Harbertonford CE Prim Sch
Harbourne River
Beenleigh
Yetson
PH
Fletcher's Combe
PACKS CL 1
WOODLAND RD 2
FACTORY COTTS 3
BRIDGESIDE 4
MARL PK 5
MILL MDW 6
Rolster Bridge
OLD RD
RIVERDALE
YOULDONS CL
BOW RD
PO
THE QUAY
SLIPPERSTONE
WOODCOURT RD
MORLEIGH RD
Harbertonford
Tuckenhay
BOW CREEK 1
ORCHARD TERR 2
BRIDGE TERR 3
CASTLE COTTS 4
HOTHILL LA 5
Woodcourt
HERNAFORD RD
Stonehills
Ball Hill
HERNAFORD CROSS
NORTH PARK CNR
Lower Washbourne Barton
Hernaford
Ashwell
BEENLEIGH CROSS
Coomery
WASHBOURNE CROSS
River Wash
Wagland Farm
Poulston
Washbourne
Gitcombe
Rowden
Horner
HORNER TURN CROSS
SPANISH LANE END
Bickleigh
Newhouse
Black Down
Allaleigh
ALLALEIGH CROSS
ALLALEIGH LA
Boreston
28
RIDGE LA
Higher Dinnicombe
BLACKDOWN LA
Halwell Camp
FARLEIGH CROSS
Halwell
CROCADON MDWS
CHURCH ST
BLACKDOWN CROSS
COLLATON CROSS
RIDGE LANE CROSS
MORLEIGH GREEN CROSS
HALWELL CROSS
BACK RD
Halwell Bsns Pk
Collaton
CH
STANBOROUGH CT
WHITE PK
MORLEIGH GN
MORLEIGH CROSS
A3122
FORCES CROSS
DREYTON CROSS
PARSONAGE LA
Moreleigh
RITSON LA
East Hartley
Dreyton
Stanborough House
TOTNES CROSS
WEST HARTLEY
Shearacre
Grimpstone
RITSON LA
Woodlands Leisure Park
SHORT LA
SHORT CROSS
Ritson
Bowden
OLDSTONE CROSS
Stanborough Hundred
CHURCH QUILLET 1
CHURCH HILL CL 2
CHURCH HILL 3
CASTLE LA 4
HIGHER ISLAND 5
TOWN FARM COTTS 6
LANGWELLS CT 7
THE GROVE 8
MILLCOMBE CNR 9
CHEAVESTONE LEA 10
Oldstone
Seawardstone
FRENCH FURZE RD
TRENCHFIRS CNR
CLISTON CROSS
Wood Farm
Blackawton Prim Sch
SCHOOL LA
Blackawton
Clistom
Woodford
PARK LA
MAIN ST
CHAPEL ST
Chilley
HUTCHERLEIGH TURN
The Gara
VICARAGE RD
GREENSLADE RD
Waterslade
Cuttery Farm
Hutcherleigh
HARRIS COTTS
Pruston Barton
GREEN LANE END
Pitt Farm
GREEN LA
HUTCHERLEIGH CROSS
Washwalk

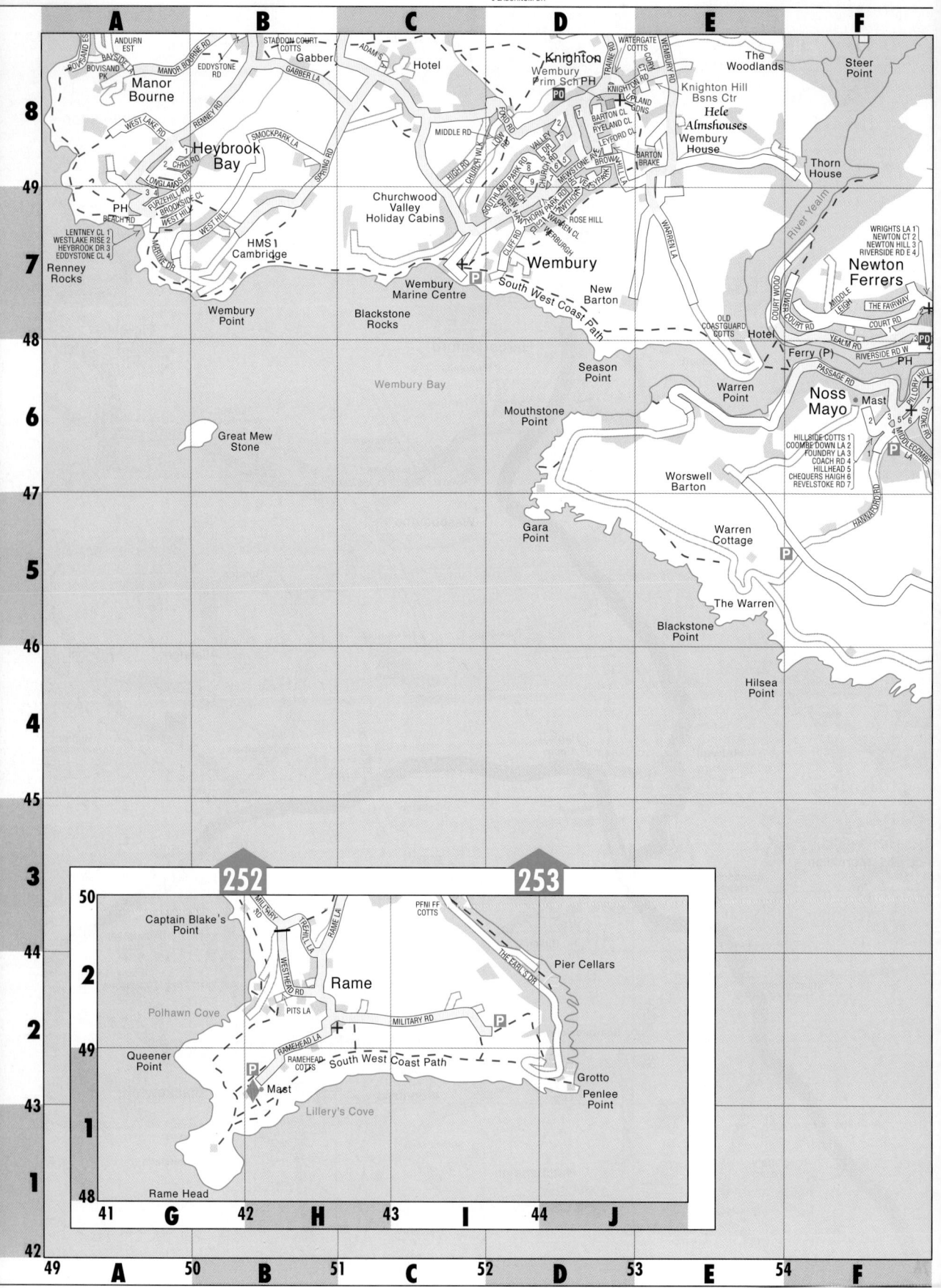

Scale: 1¾ inches to 1 mile

D8
1 WEMBURY MDW
2 HIGHFIELD DR
3 CROSS PARK RD
4 CROSSWAYS
5 COLLIERS CL
6 LABURNUM DR
7 SEA VIEW DR
8 SOUTHLAND PARK CRES
9 HILLCREST CL

0   ¼   ½ mile
0   250m   500m   750m   1 km

Manor Bourne
Heybrook Bay
Renney Rocks
HMS Cambridge
Wembury Point
Blackstone Rocks
Wembury Marine Centre
Wembury Bay
Great Mew Stone

Gabber
Hotel
Churchwood Valley Holiday Cabins
Knighton
Wembury Prim Sch
Hele Almshouses
Wembury House
Knighton Hill Bsns Ctr
The Woodlands
Steer Point
Thorn House
Wembury
New Barton
South West Coast Path
Rose Hill
Season Point
Mouthstone Point
Warren Point
Worswell Barton
Gara Point
Warren Cottage
The Warren
Blackstone Point
Hilsea Point
Newton Ferrers
Noss Mayo
Ferry (P)
Hotel
Mast

WRIGHTS LA 1
NEWTON CT 2
NEWTON HILL 3
RIVERSIDE RD E 4

HILLSIDE COTTS 1
COOMBE DOWN LA 2
FOUNDRY LA 3
COACH RD 4
HILLHEAD 5
CHEQUERS HAIGH 6
REVELSTOKE RD 7

LENTNEY CL 1
WESTLAKE RISE 2
HEYBROOK DR 3
EDDYSTONE CL 4

Captain Blake's Point
Polhawn Cove
Queener Point
Rame
Rame Head
Lillery's Cove
Mast
South West Coast Path
Pier Cellars
Grotto
Penlee Point

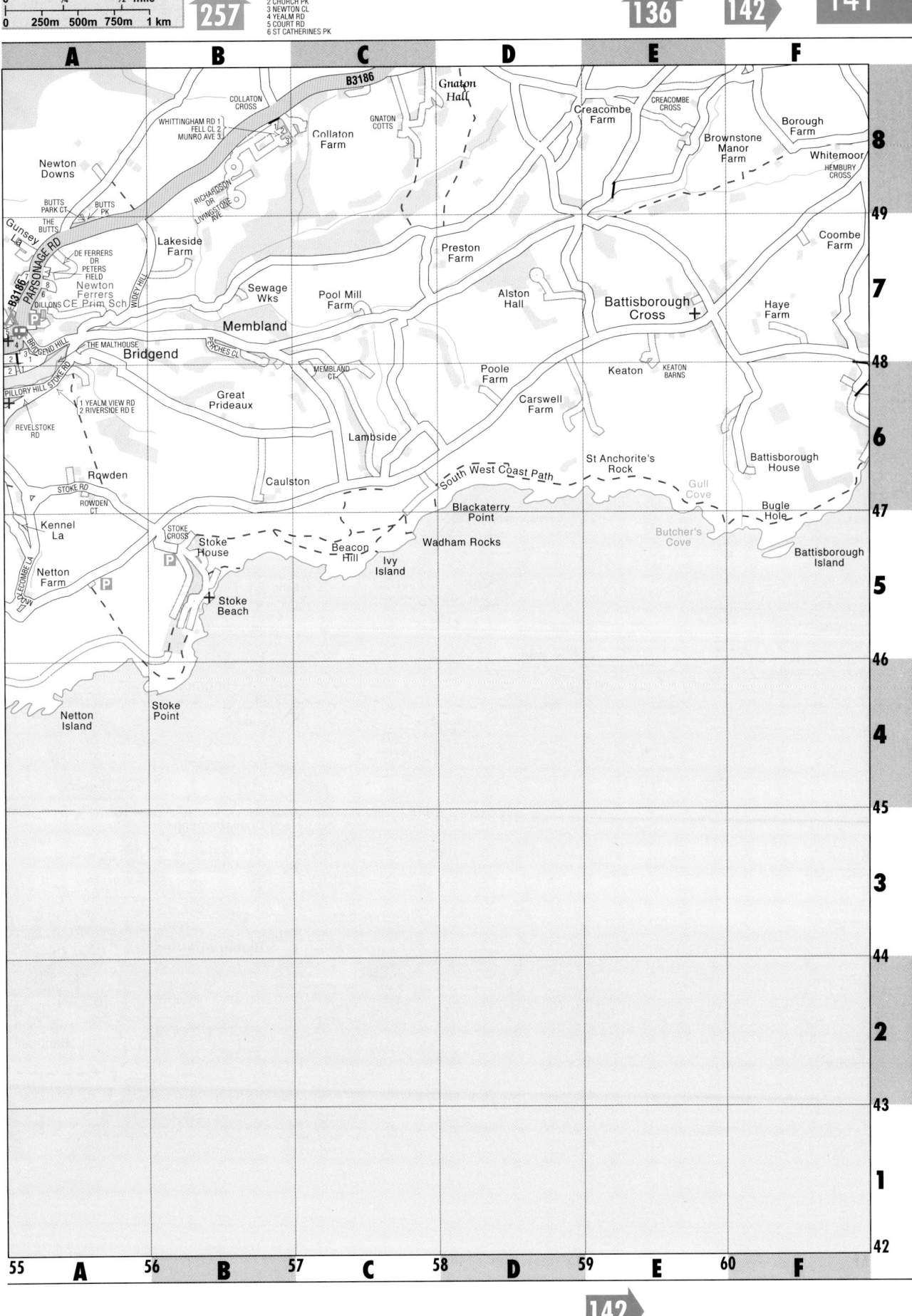

Scale: 1¾ inches to 1 mile

0   ¼   ½ mile
0 250m 500m 750m 1 km

257

A8
1 CHURCH PARK RD
2 CHURCH PK
3 NEWTON CL
4 YEALM RD
5 COURT RD
6 ST CATHERINES PK

7 MEADOW CL
8 ARCHERS CT

136   142   141

B3186
Collaton
Cross
Gnaton
Hall
WHITTINGHAM RD 1
FELL CL 2
MUNRO AVE 3
Collaton
Farm
GNATON
COTTS
Creacombe
Farm
Creacombe
Cross
Borough
Farm
Newton
Downs
Brownstone
Manor
Farm
Whitemoor
HEMBURY
CROSS
BUTTS
PARK CT
BUTTS
PK
RICHARDSON
DR
LIVINGSTONE
AVE
THE
BUTTS
Gunsey
La
Lakeside
Farm
Preston
Farm
Coombe
Farm
B3186
PARSONAGE RD
DE FERRERS
DR
PETERS
FIELD
Newton
Ferrers
DILLONS CE Prim Sch
WIDEY HILL
Sewage
Wks
Pool Mill
Farm
Alston
Hall
Battisborough
Cross
Haye
Farm
Membland
THE MALTHOUSE
PEACHES CL
BRIDGEND HILL
Bridgend
Membland
CT
Poole
Farm
Keaton
KEATON
BARNS
PILLORY HILL STOKE RD
1 YEALM VIEW RD
2 RIVERSIDE RD E
Great
Prideaux
Carswell
Farm
Battisborough
House
REVELSTOKE
RD
Lambside
St Anchorite's
Rock
Gull
Cove
Rowden
Caulston
South West Coast Path
Blackaterry
Point
Bugle
Hole
STOKE RD
ROWDEN
CT
STOKE CROSS
Stoke
House
Butcher's
Cove
Battisborough
Island
Kennel
La
Beacon
Hill
Wadham Rocks
MELCOMBE LA
Netton
Farm
Stoke
Beach
Ivy
Island
Netton
Island
Stoke
Point

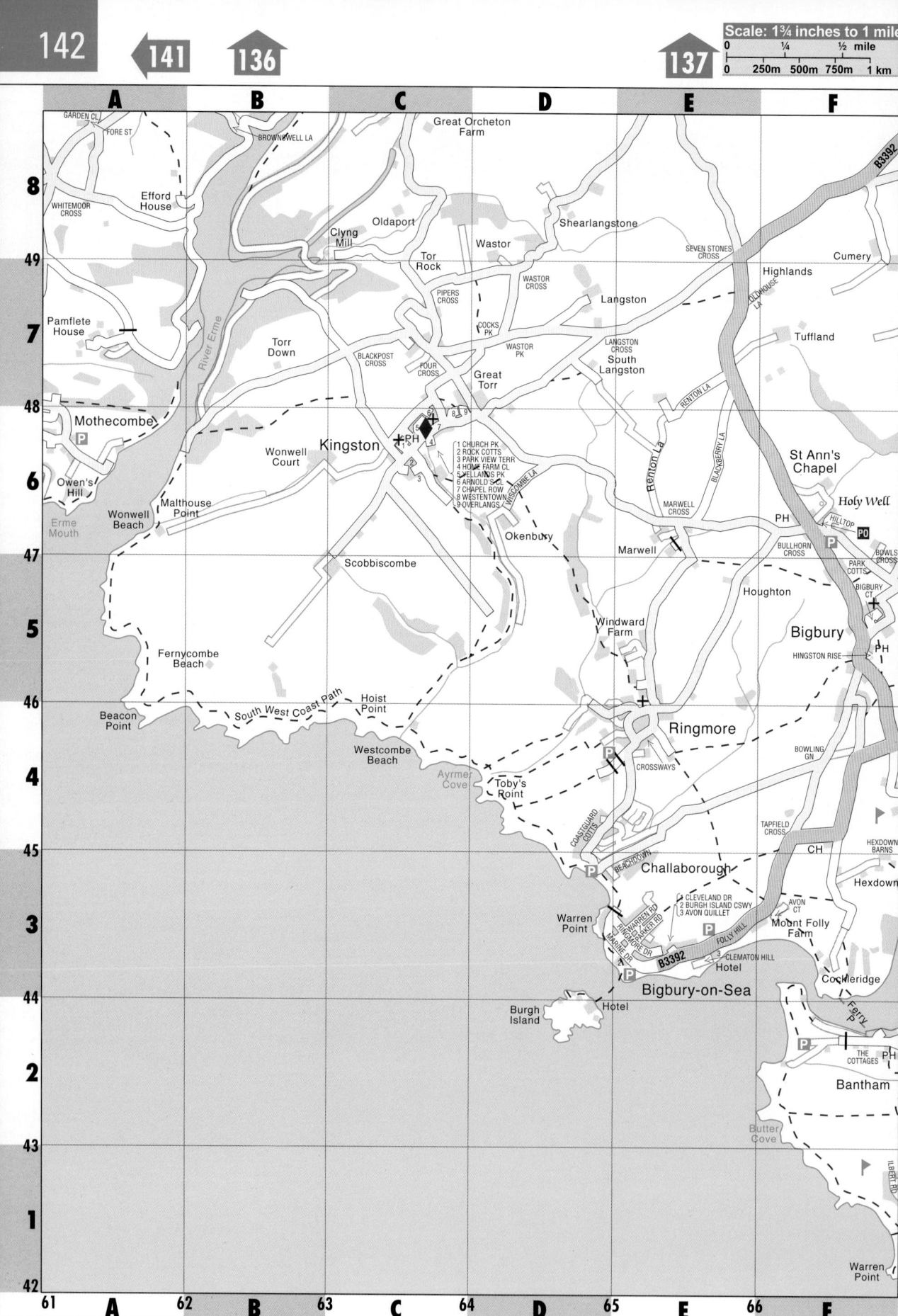

GARDEN CL
FORE ST
WHITEMOOR CROSS
Efford House
BROWNSWELL LA
Great Orcheton Farm
B3392

Clyng Mill
Oldaport
Shearlangstone
Seven Stones Cross
Highlands
Cumery

Wastor
Wastor Cross
Tor Rock
Pipers Cross
Langston
Oldhouse LA
Tuffland

Pamflete House
Torr Down
COCKS PK
Blackpost Cross
Four Cross
WASTOR PK
Langston Cross
South Langston
Renton LA
St Ann's Chapel

Mothecombe
Wonwell Court
Kingston
PH
Great Torr
Blackberry LA
Holy Well
HILLTOP
PO

Owen's Hill
Wonwell Beach
Malthouse Point
Erme Mouth
Okenbury
WISCOMBE LA
Marwell Cross
PH
BULLHORN CROSS
PARK COTTS
BOWLS CROSS
BIGBURY CT

1 CHURCH PK
2 ROCK COTTS
3 PARK VIEW TERR
4 HOME FARM CL
5 YELLANDS PK
6 ARNOLD SCL
7 CHAPEL ROW
8 WESTENTOWN
9 OVERLANGS

Scobbiscombe
Marwell
Houghton
Bigbury
PH

Fernycombe Beach
Windward Farm
Hingston Rise

South West Coast Path
Hoist Point
Ringmore
BOWLING GN

Beacon Point
Westcombe Beach
Ayrmer Cove
Toby's Point
CROSSWAYS
TAPFIELD CROSS
CH
HEXDOWN BARNS

COASTGUARD COTTS
BEACHDOWN
Challaborough
Hexdown

Warren Point
CLEVELAND DR
1 CLEVELAND DR
2 BURGH ISLAND CSWY
3 AVON QUILLET
AVON CT
Mount Folly Farm

MARINE DR
WARREN RD
SHARLAND RD
CEMETERY RD
B3392
FOLLY HILL
Clematon Hill
Hotel
Cockleridge
Ferry P

Bigbury-on-Sea
Burgh Island
Hotel
Butter Cove
THE COTTAGES
PH
Bantham

ILBERT RD
Warren Point

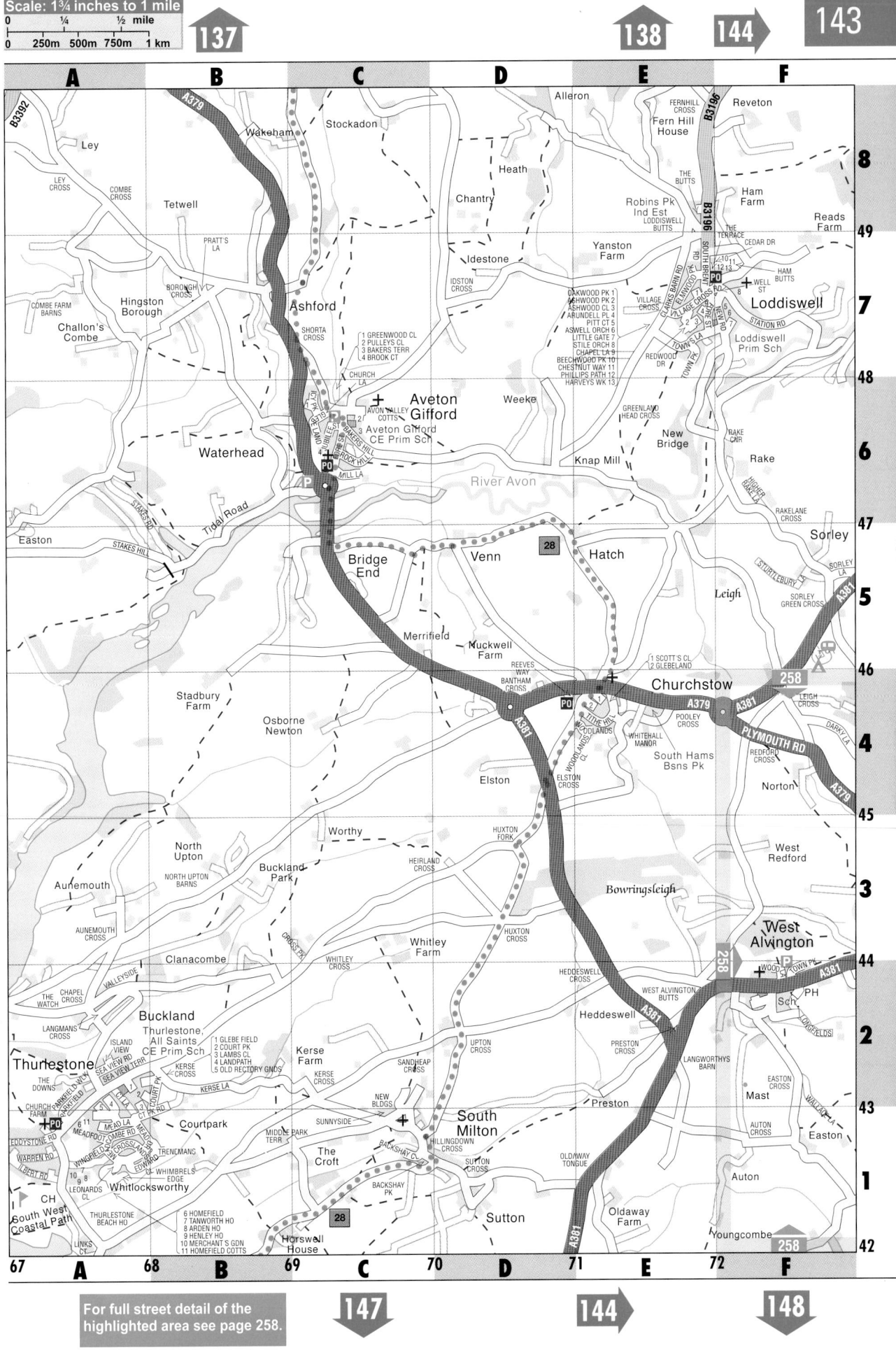

Scale: 1¾ inches to 1 mile

0   ¼   ½   mile
0   250m 500m 750m 1 km

137

138 144

143

B3392
Ley
LEY CROSS
COMBE CROSS
Tetwell
Hingston Borough
COMBE FARM BARNS
Challon's Combe
BOROUGH CROSS
PRATT'S LA
A379
Wakeham
Stockadon
Alleron
FERNHILL CROSS
Reveton
Fern Hill House
THE BUTTS
B3196
Heath
Ham Farm
Chantry
Robins Pk Ind Est
LODDISWELL BUTTS
Reads Farm
Idestone
THE TERRACE
CEDAR DR
Ashford
IDSTON CROSS
Yanston Farm
PO
HAM BUTTS
WELL ST
SHORTA CROSS
CHURCH LA
Village CROSS
Loddiswell
STATION RD
Aveton Gifford
Weeke
Loddiswell Prim Sch
Waterhead
Aveton Gifford CE Prim Sch
AVON VALLEY COTTS
PO
Knap Mill
New Bridge
GREENLAND HEAD CROSS
Rake
MILL LA
River Avon
RAKE CNR
HIGHER RAKE LA
Easton
STAKES HILL
Tidal Road
Venn
28
Hatch
Sorley
RAKELANE CROSS
STURTLEBURY LA
SORLEY LA
Bridge End
Leigh
SORLEY GREEN CROSS
A381
Stadbury Farm
Merrifield
Muckwell Farm
REEVES WAY
BANTHAM CROSS
Churchstow
258
LEIGH CROSS
Osborne Newton
PO
A379
A381
PLYMOUTH RD
DARKY LA
REDFORD CROSS
Worthy
Elston
ELSTON CROSS
WOODLANDS CL
WHITEHALL MANOR
South Hams Bsns Pk
Norton
A379
North Upton
Buckland Park
NORTH UPTON BARNS
HUXTON FORK
HEIRLAND CROSS
West Redford
Aunemouth
Bowringsleigh
AUNEMOUTH CROSS
Clanacombe
WHITLEY CROSS
Whitley Farm
HUXTON CROSS
HEDDESWELL CROSS
West Alvington
258
A381
VALLEYSIDE
THE CHAPEL WATCH CROSS
CRASS PK
WEST ALVINGTON BUTTS
WOODTOWN PK
LANGMANS CROSS
Buckland
Thurlestone, All Saints CE Prim Sch
Kerse Farm
Heddeswell
Preston CROSS
LONGFIELDS
Thurlestone
ISLAND VIEW
SEA VIEW RD
KERSE CROSS
KERSE LA
UPTON CROSS
Preston
Langworthys Barn
EASTON CROSS
Mast
THE DOWNS
Courtpark
MIDDLE PARK TERR
New Bldgs
SANDHEAP CROSS
South Milton
Auton CROSS
Easton
CHURCH FARM
The Croft
Sunnyside
HILLINGDOWN CROSS
OLDAWAY TONGUE
Auton
South West Coastal Path
Whitlocksworthy
Backshay CL
BACKSHAY PK
SUTTON CROSS
Sutton
Oldaway Farm
Youngcombe
28
Horswell House
A381
258

For full street detail of the highlighted area see page 258.

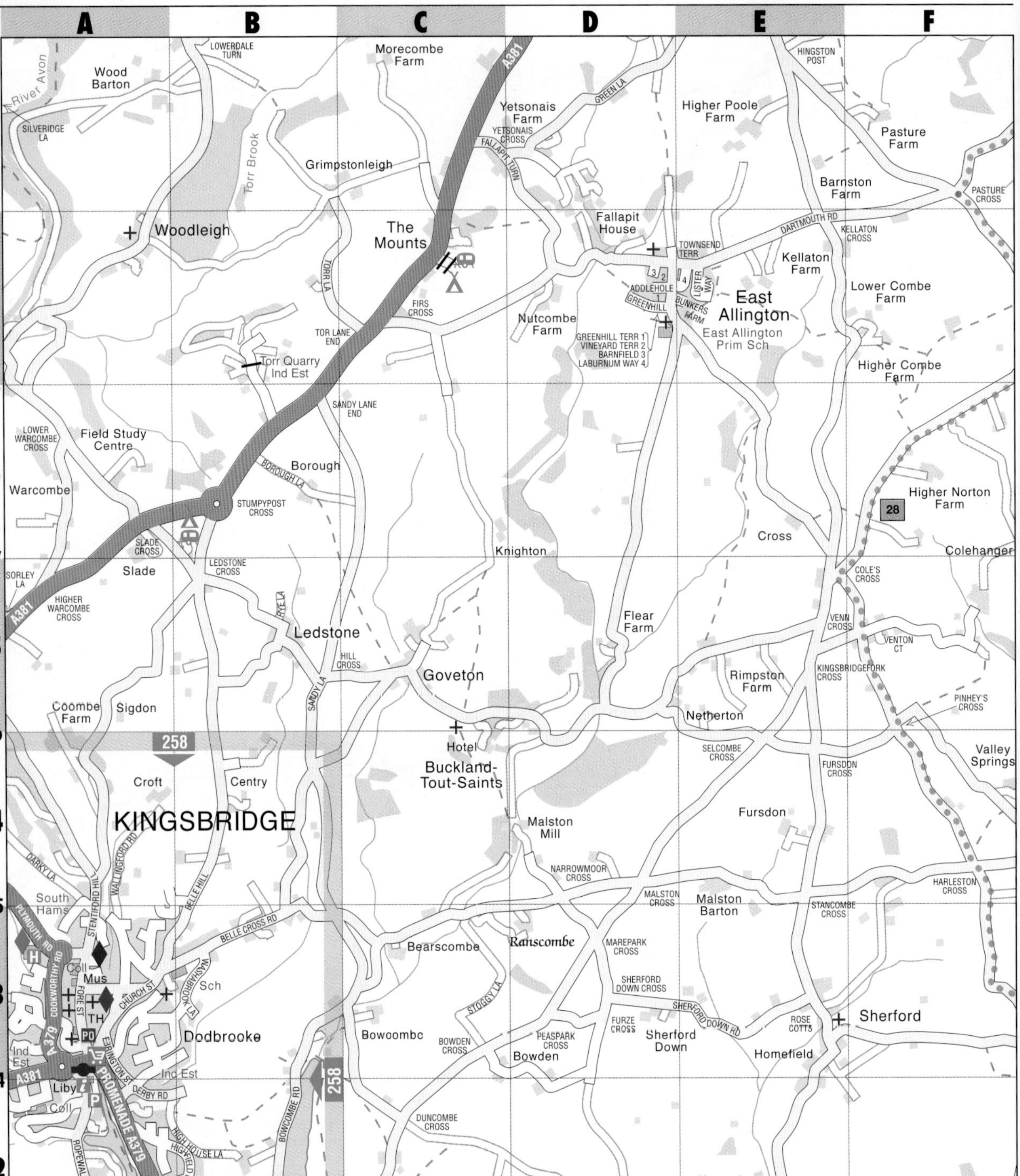

143 138 139

A B C D E F

River Avon
Wood Barton
SILVERIDGE LA
LOWERDALE TURN
Morecombe Farm
A381
HINGSTON POST
Woodleigh
Grimpstonleigh
Yetsonais Farm
Yetsonais Cross
Green La
Higher Poole Farm
Pasture Farm
Barnston Farm
PASTURE CROSS
The Mounts
FALLAPIT TURN
Fallapit House
Townsend Terr
DARTMOUTH RD
Kellaton Cross
Kellaton Farm
Lower Combe Farm
Torr Brook
TORR LA
Firs Cross
Nutcombe Farm
Addlehole
Greenhill
BUNKERS
USTER WAY
East Allington
East Allington Prim Sch
Higher Combe Farm
TOR LANE END
Torr Quarry Ind Est
Greenhill Terr 1
Vineyard Terr 2
Barnfield 3
Laburnum Way 4
SANDY LANE END
Borough
BOROUGH LA
Lower Warcombe Cross
Field Study Centre
Warcombe
Knighton
Cross
Higher Norton Farm
28
Colehanger
STUMPYPOST CROSS
SLADE CROSS
SORLEY LA
A381
HIGHER WARCOMBE CROSS
Slade
LEDSTONE CROSS
Flear Farm
COLE'S CROSS
VENN CROSS
VENTON CT
Coombe Farm
Sigdon
Ledstone
LIFE LA
Goveton
HILL CROSS
SANDLA
Rimpston Farm
Netherton
KINGSBRIDGEFORK
Valley Springs
PINHEY'S CROSS
258
Croft
Centry
Hotel
Buckland-Tout-Saints
SELCOMBE CROSS
FURSDON CROSS
Fursdon
KINGSBRIDGE
Malston Mill
NARROWMOOR CROSS
MALSTON CROSS
Malston Barton
STANCOMBE CROSS
HARLESTON CROSS
DARKY LA
PLYMOUTH RD
STEWTHORD HILL
WALLINGFORD RD
South Hams
BELLE HILL
BELLE CROSS RD
Sch
Bearscombe
Ranscombe
MAREPARK CROSS
ROSE COTTS
Sherford
Mus
COLL
TH
CHURCH ST
WASHABROOK LA
STOGGS LA
SHERFORD DOWN RD
SHERFORD DOWN CROSS
Sherford Down
COOKWORTHY RD
FORE ST
PO
Dodbrooke
Bowoombe
BOWDEN CROSS
PEASPARK CROSS
FURZE CROSS
Homefield
A379
ERMINGTON
Ind Est
Bowden
Ind Est
A381
Liby
Coll
DERBY RD
258
DUNCOMBE CROSS
PROMENADE RD
BOWCOMBE RD
Keynedon Barton
Coombe Park
ROPEWALK
HIGH HOUSE LA
HIGHFIELD DR
Southville
The Grange
1 Herons Reach
2 West Charleton Ct
3 Saunders Way
4 Charleton Court Barns
East Charleton
Frogmore
PH
OLD FROGMORE RD
PRIMROSE CL
PORT LANE CL
SHINDLE PK
A379
Hotel
EMBANKMENT RD
A379
Park Farm
Cemy
Ferry P (Summer only)
CHARLETON WAY
COMPTON CL
LIFE LA
DANIEL'S LA
EAST FARM
APPLE TREE CL
Mill Farm
Coombe Mdws
ROBINS FIELD
CURLEW DR
Kingsbridge Estuary
Sewage Works
Charleton CE Prim Sch
SOCKLEMANS CL
MARSH LA
BRIDGETT LA
ORCHARD CL
WILLOWS
CREEK CL
Winslade Manor
COPPERFIELD
LOO CROSS
258
West Charleton
Frogmore Creek
ORCHARD VIEW
WINSLADE CL 2
WINSLADE CT

143 148 149

For full street detail of the highlighted area see page 258.

73 A 74 B 75 C 76 D 77 E 78 F

8 49 7 48 6 47 5 46 4 45 3 44 2 43 1 42

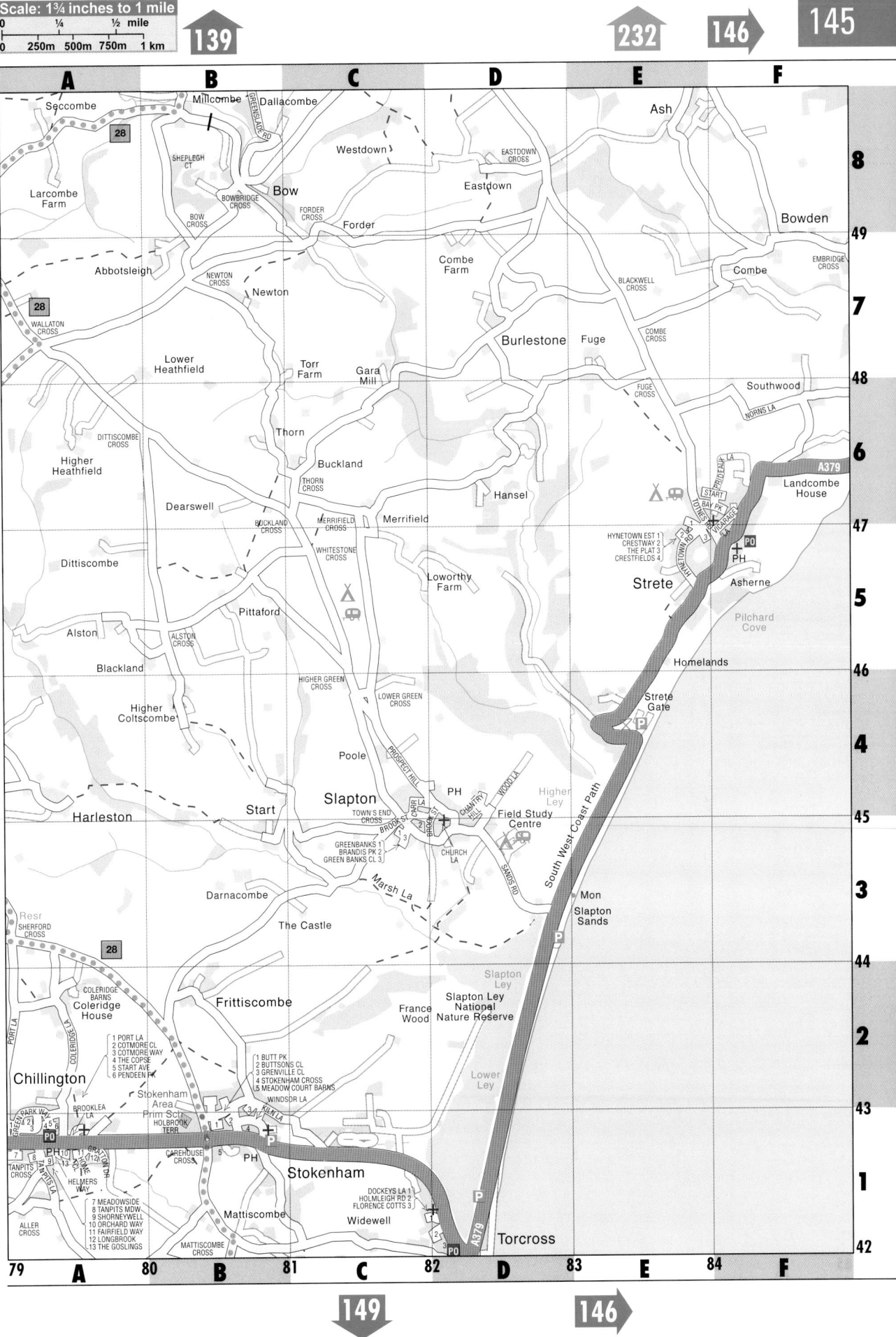

Scale: 1¾ inches to 1 mile

0   ¼   ½ mile
0   250m 500m 750m 1 km

139
232 146
149
146

A   B   C   D   E   F

8
49
7
48
6
47
5
46
4
45
3
44
2
43
1
42

Seccombe
Millcombe   Dallacombe
28
SHEPLEGH CT
Larcombe Farm
BOWBRIDGE CROSS
Bow
BOW CROSS
FORDER CROSS
Westdown
Forder
Eastdown
EASTDOWN CROSS
Ash
Bowden
Abbotsleigh
NEWTON CROSS
Newton
Combe Farm
BLACKWELL CROSS
Combe
EMBRIDGE CROSS
28
WALLATON CROSS
Lower Heathfield
TORR FARM
Gara Mill
Burlestone
Fuge
COMBE CROSS
Southwood
NORNS LA
DITTISCOMBE CROSS
Thorn
FUGE CROSS
A379
Higher Heathfield
Buckland
THORN CROSS
Hansel
PRIDEAUX LA
START
TOTNES RD
BAY PK
Landcombe House
Dearswell
BUCKLAND CROSS
MERRIFIELD CROSS
Merrifield
HYNETOWN EST 1
CRESTWAY 2
THE PLAT 3
CRESTFIELDS 4
HYNETOWN RD
PO
PH
Dittiscombe
WHITESTONE CROSS
Loworthy Farm
Strete
Asherne
Pittaford
Alston
ALSTON CROSS
Pilchard Cove
Blackland
HIGHER GREEN CROSS
LOWER GREEN CROSS
Homelands
Higher Coltscombe
Poole
Strete Gate
PROSPECT HILL
PH
WOOD LA
Higher Ley
P
Harleston
Start
Slapton
TOWN'S END CROSS
CARR LA
CHANTRY HILL
BROOK ST
Field Study Centre
South West Coast Path
GREENBANKS 1
BRANDIS PK 2
GREEN BANKS CL 3
CHURCH LA
Darnacombe
Marsh La
SANDS RD
Mon Slapton Sands
The Castle
P
COLERIDGE BARNS
Coleridge House
Frittiscombe
France Wood
Slapton Ley National Nature Reserve
Slapton Ley
PORT LA
COLERIDGE LA
1 PORT LA
2 COTMORE CL
3 COTMORE WAY
4 THE COPSE
5 START AVE
6 PENDEEN PK
1 BUTT PK
2 BUTTSONS CL
3 GRENVILLE CL
4 STOKENHAM CROSS
5 MEADOW COURT BARNS
WINDSOR LA
Lower Ley
Chillington
GREEN PARK WAY
BROOKLEA LA
Stokenham Area Prim Schl
HOLBROOK TERR
KILN LA
P
PO
PH
GRATTON DR
TANPITS LA
CAREHOUSE CROSS
PH
Stokenham
DOCKEYS LA 1
HOLMLEIGH RD 2
FLORENCE COTTS 3
P
TANPITS CROSS
Helmers Way
7 MEADOWSIDE
8 TANPITS MDW.
9 SHORNEYWELL
10 ORCHARD WAY
11 FAIRFIELD WAY
12 LONGBROOK
13 THE GOSLINGS
Mattiscombe
Widewell
A379
PO
Torcross
ALLER CROSS
MATTISCOMBE CROSS

Resr
SHERFORD CROSS
28

Scale: 1¾ inches to 1 mile

0   ¼   ½   mile

0   250m 500m 750m   1 km

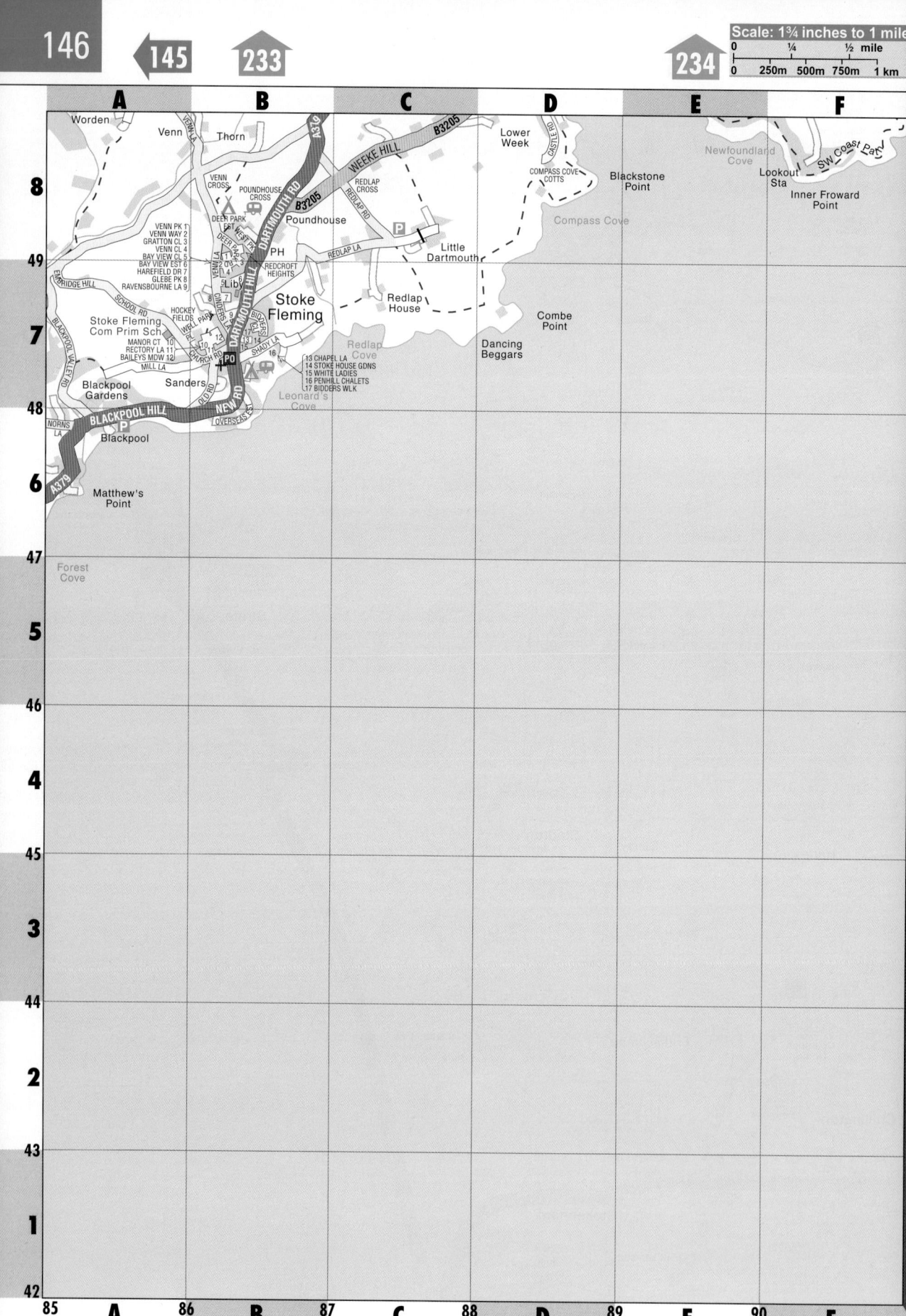

Worden

Venn

Thorn

VENN LA

B3205

WEEKE HILL

Lower
Week

Newfoundland
Cove

SW Coast Path

VENN
CROSS

POUNDHOUSE
CROSS

A379

B3205

REDLAP
CROSS

COMPASS COVE
COTTS

Blackstone
Point

Lookout
Sta

Inner Froward
Point

8

DEER PARK

DARTMOUTH RD

REDLAP RD

CASTLE RD

Compass Cove

VENN PK 1
VENN WAY 2
GRATTON CL 3
VENN CL 4
BAY VIEW CL 5

PH

Poundhouse

REDLAP LA

P

Little
Dartmouth

49

DEER PARK

DARTMOUTH HILL

REDCROFT
HEIGHTS

EMBRIDGE HILL

SCHOOL RD

BAY VIEW EST 6
HAREFIELD DR 7
GLEBE PK 8
RAVENSBOURNE LA 9

5 Lib

Stoke
Fleming

Redlap
House

HOCKEY
FIELDS

WELL PARK

CHURCH RD

LATIMER LA

CHIDERS LA

Stoke Fleming
Com Prim Sch

7

BLACKPOOL VALLEY RD

MANOR CT 10
RECTORY LA 11
BAILEYS MDW 12

10

12

Combe
Point

BIG BEERS LA

SHADY LA

Redlap
Cove

Dancing
Beggars

MILL LA

11

13

14

15

PO

16

13 CHAPEL LA
14 STOKE HOUSE GDNS
15 WHITE LADIES
16 PENHILL CHALETS
17 BIDDERS WLK

Sanders

17

Blackpool
Gardens

Leonard's
Cove

48

NORNS
LA

BLACKPOOL HILL

NEW RD

OLD RD

OVERSEAS LA

P

Blackpool

6

A379

Matthew's
Point

47

Forest
Cove

5

46

4

45

3

44

2

43

1

42

85   86   87   88   89   90

Scale: 1¾ inches to 1 mile

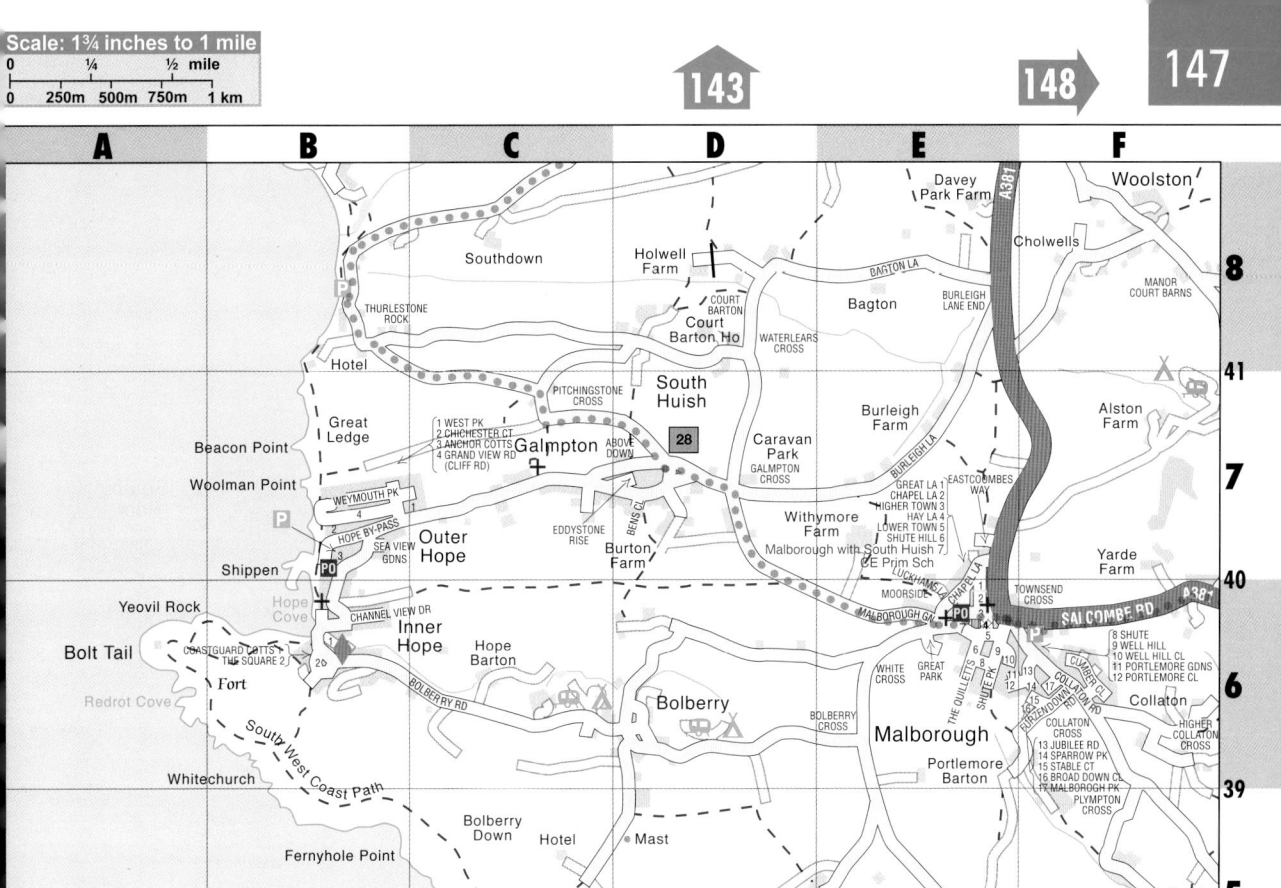

Woolston
Davey Park Farm
Cholwells
Southdown
Holwell Farm
Bagton
Court Barton Ho
South Huish
Galmpton
Outer Hope
Inner Hope
Hope Barton
Bolberry
Malborough
Portlemore Barton
Bolt Tail
Beacon Point
Woolman Point
Shippen
Yeovil Rock
Redrot Cove
Whitechurch
South West Coast Path
Bolberry Down
Fernyhole Point
Slippery Point
West Cliff
Mast
Hazel Tor
Catholl Cliff
Lantern Rock
Soar Mill Cove
Soar
Rew
Combe
Collaton
Alston Farm
Yarde Farm
Burleigh Farm
Caravan Park
Withymore Farm
Burton Farm
Great Ledge
Hotel
The Warren
Steeple Cove
Off Cove
SALCOMBE RD
A381

143
148
148

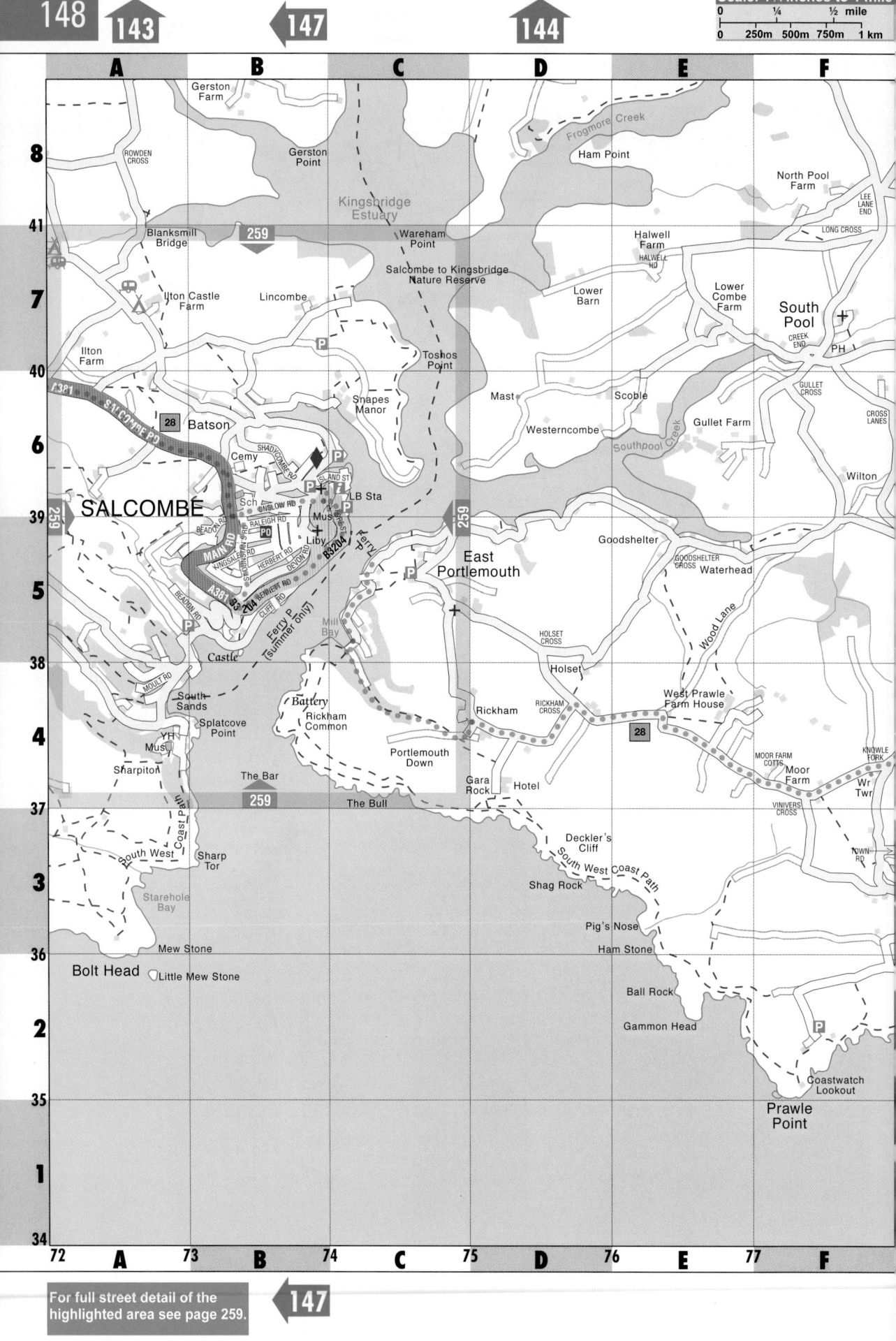

Scale: 1¾ inches to 1 mile

0   ¼   ½ mile
0 250m 500m 750m 1 km

8

41

259

7

40

6

39

259

5

38

4

37

3

36

2

35

1

34

A   B   C   D   E   F

Gerston Farm

Gerston Point

Kingsbridge Estuary

Frogmore Creek

Ham Point

North Pool Farm

LEE LANE END

LONG CROSS

Blanksmill Bridge

Wareham Point

Salcombe to Kingsbridge Nature Reserve

Halwell Farm

HALWELL HO

Lower Combe Farm

South Pool

CREEK END

PH

Ilton Castle Farm

Lincombe

Lower Barn

Ilton Farm

A381

Toshos Point

Mast

Scoble

GULLET CROSS

CROSS LANES

SALCOMBE RD

28

Batson

Snapes Manor

Westerncombe

Gullet Farm

Wilton

Cemy

SHADYCOMBE RD

ISLAND ST

Southpool Creek

SALCOMBE

Sch

ONSLOW RD

LB Sta

Goodshelter

GOODSHELTER CROSS

Waterhead

BEADON RD

MAIN RD

RALEIGH RD

Mus

PO

Liby

East Portlemouth

KINGSALE RD

HERBERT RD

DEVON RD

B3204

Wood Lane

A381

FORTESCUE RD

BENNETT RD

CLIFF RD

Ferry P (Summer only)

259

Holset Cross

Holset

Goodshelter

Castle

MOULT RD

Mill Bay

Rickham

RICKHAM CROSS

West Prawle Farm House

South Sands

Battery

Rickham Common

28

MOOR FARM COTTS

Moor Farm

KNOWLE FORK

Splatcove Point

YH Mus

Gara Rock

Hotel

Wr Twr

Sharpiton

The Bar

259

Portlemouth Down

VINIVERS CROSS

TOWN RD

The Bull

South West Coast Path

Deckler's Cliff

South West Coast Path

Sharp Tor

Shag Rock

Starehole Bay

Pig's Nose

Mew Stone

Ham Stone

Bolt Head

Little Mew Stone

Ball Rock

Gammon Head

Coastwatch Lookout

Prawle Point

72   A   73   B   74   C   75   D   76   E   77   F

For full street detail of the highlighted area see page 259.

147

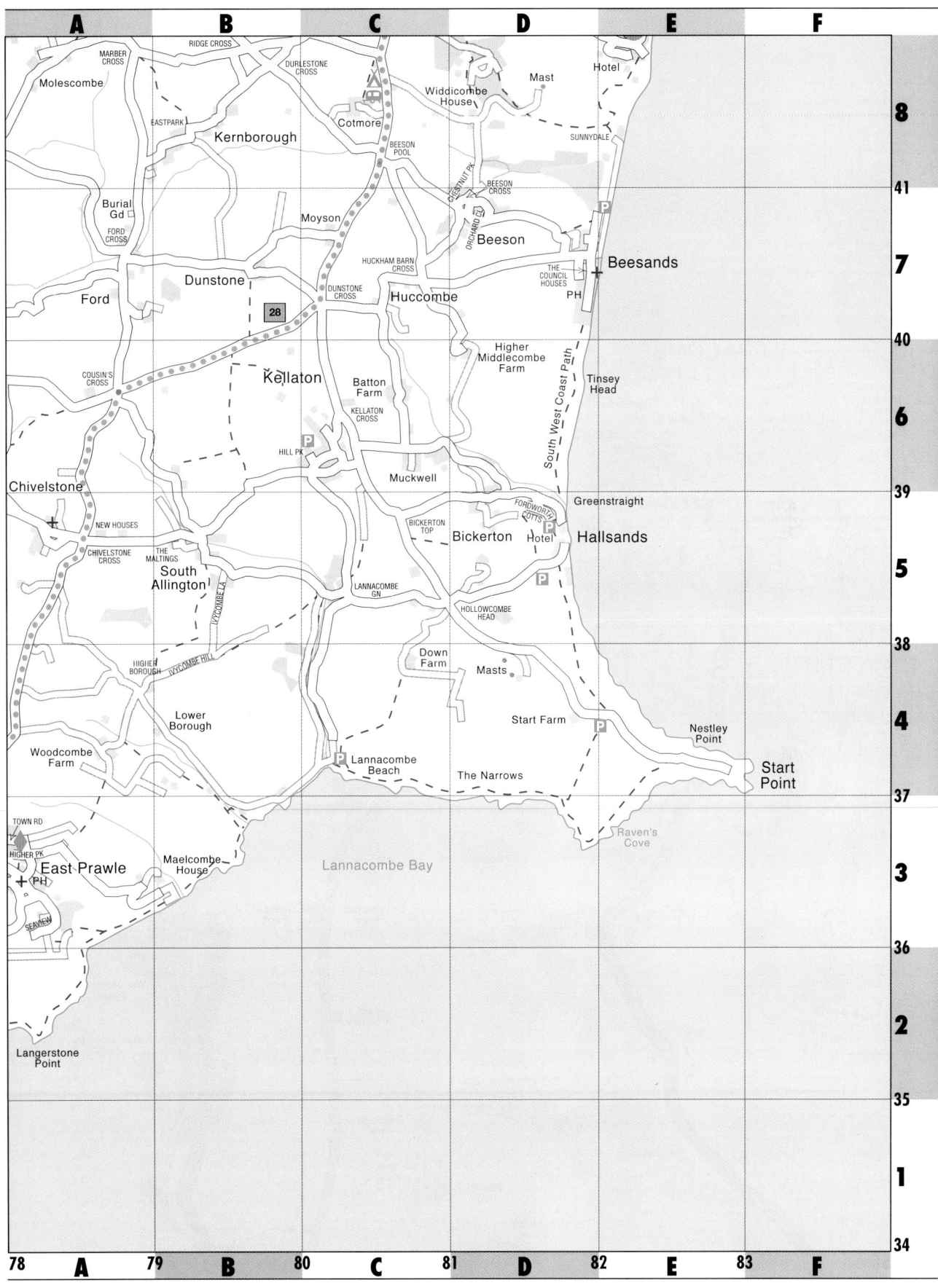

Scale: 1¾ inches to 1 mile

0 ¼ ½ mile

0 250m 500m 750m 1 km

144

145

149

A B C D E F

8

41

7

40

6

39

5

38

4

37

3

36

2

35

1

34

MARBER CROSS

Molescombe

RIDGE CROSS

DURLESTONE CROSS

Mast

Hotel

Widdicombe House

Cotmore

Kernborough

EASTPARK

BEESON POOL

SUNNYDALE

Burial Gd

FORD CROSS

Moyson

CHESTNUT PK

BEESON CROSS

ORCHARD

Beeson

Dunstone

HUCKHAM BARN CROSS

DUNSTONE CROSS

THE COUNCIL HOUSES

Beesands

Ford

28

Huccombe

PH

Higher Middlecombe Farm

Tinsey Head

COUSIN'S CROSS

Kellaton

Batton Farm

KELLATON CROSS

South West Coast Path

Chivelstone

HILL PK

Muckwell

Greenstraight

NEW HOUSES

FORDWORTH COTTS

CHIVELSTONE CROSS

THE MALTINGS

BICKERTON TOP

Bickerton

Hotel

Hallsands

South Allington

IVYCOMBE LA

LANNACOMBE GN

HIGHER BOROUGH

IVYCOMBE HILL

HOLLOWCOMBE HEAD

Down Farm

Masts

Lower Borough

Start Farm

Nestley Point

Woodcombe Farm

Lannacombe Beach

The Narrows

Start Point

TOWN RD

HIGHER PK

Maelcombe House

Lannacombe Bay

Raven's Cove

East Prawle

PH

SEAVIEW

Langerstone Point

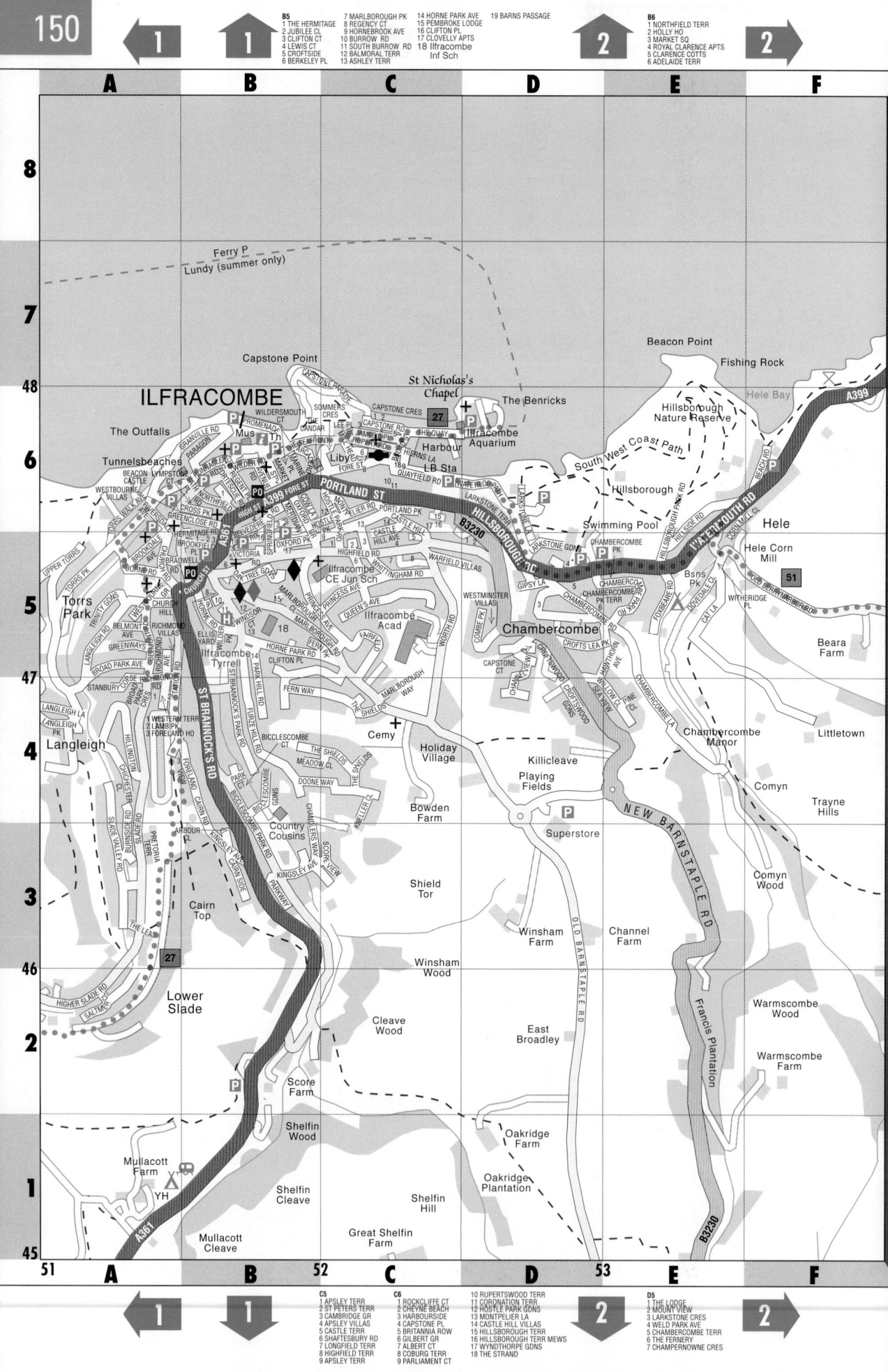
B5
1 THE HERMITAGE
2 JUBILEE CL
3 CLIFTON CT
4 LEWIS CT
5 CROFTSIDE
6 BERKELEY PL
7 MARLBOROUGH PK
8 REGENCY CT
9 HORNEBROOK AVE
10 BURROW RD
11 SOUTH BURROW RD
12 BALMORAL TERR
13 ASHLEY TERR
14 HORNE PARK AVE
15 PEMBROKE LODGE
16 CLIFTON PL
17 CLOVELLY APTS
18 Ilfracombe Inf Sch
19 BARNS PASSAGE
B6
1 NORTHFIELD TERR
2 HOLLY HO
3 MARKET SQ
4 ROYAL CLARENCE APTS
5 CLARENCE COTTS
6 ADELAIDE TERR
ILFRACOMBE
Ferry P
Lundy (summer only)
Capstone Point
St Nicholas's Chapel
The Benricks
Ilfracombe Aquarium
Harbour
LB Sta
The Outfalls
Tunnelsbeaches
Mus
Th
Liby
Beacon Point
Fishing Rock
Hele Bay
Hillsborough Nature Reserve
South West Coast Path
Hillsborough
Swimming Pool
Hele
Hele Corn Mill
Bsns Pk
Beara Farm
PORTLAND ST
HILLSBOROUGH RD
WATERMOUTH RD
A399
A361
B3230
Torrs Park
Ilfracombe CE Jun Sch
Ilfracombe Acad
Ilfracombe Tyrrell
Chambercombe
Langleigh
Cemy
Holiday Village
Killicleave
Playing Fields
Chambercombe Manor
Littletown
Comyn
Trayne Hills
Bowden Farm
Superstore
Country Cousins
Shield Tor
Cairn Top
Comyn Wood
Winsham Farm
Channel Farm
Winsham Wood
Lower Slade
NEW BARNSTAPLE RD
OLD BARNSTAPLE RD
ST BRANNOCK'S RD
Cleave Wood
East Broadley
Warmscombe Wood
Warmscombe Farm
Francis Plantation
Score Farm
Shelfin Wood
Oakridge Farm
Mullacott Farm
YH
Oakridge Plantation
Shelfin Cleave
Shelfin Hill
Great Shelfin Farm
Mullacott Cleave
C5
1 APSLEY TERR
2 ST PETERS TERR
3 CAMBRIDGE GR
4 APSLEY VILLAS
5 CASTLE TERR
6 SHAFTESBURY RD
7 LONGFIELD TERR
8 HIGHFIELD TERR
9 APSLEY TERR
C6
1 ROCKCLIFFE CT
2 CHEYNE BEACH
3 HARBOURSIDE
4 CAPSTONE PL
5 BRITANNIA ROW
6 GILBERT GR
7 ALBERT CT
8 COBURG TERR
9 PARLIAMENT CT
10 RUPERTSWOOD TERR
11 CORONATION TERR
12 HOSTLE PARK GDNS
13 MONTPELIER LA
14 CASTLE HILL VILLAS
15 HILLSBOROUGH TERR
16 HILLSBOROUGH TERR MEWS
17 WYNDTHORPE GDNS
18 THE STRAND
D5
1 THE LODGE
2 MOUNT VIEW
3 LARKSTONE CRES
4 WELD PARK AVE
5 CHAMBERCOMBE TERR
6 THE FERNERY
7 CHAMPERNOWNE CRES

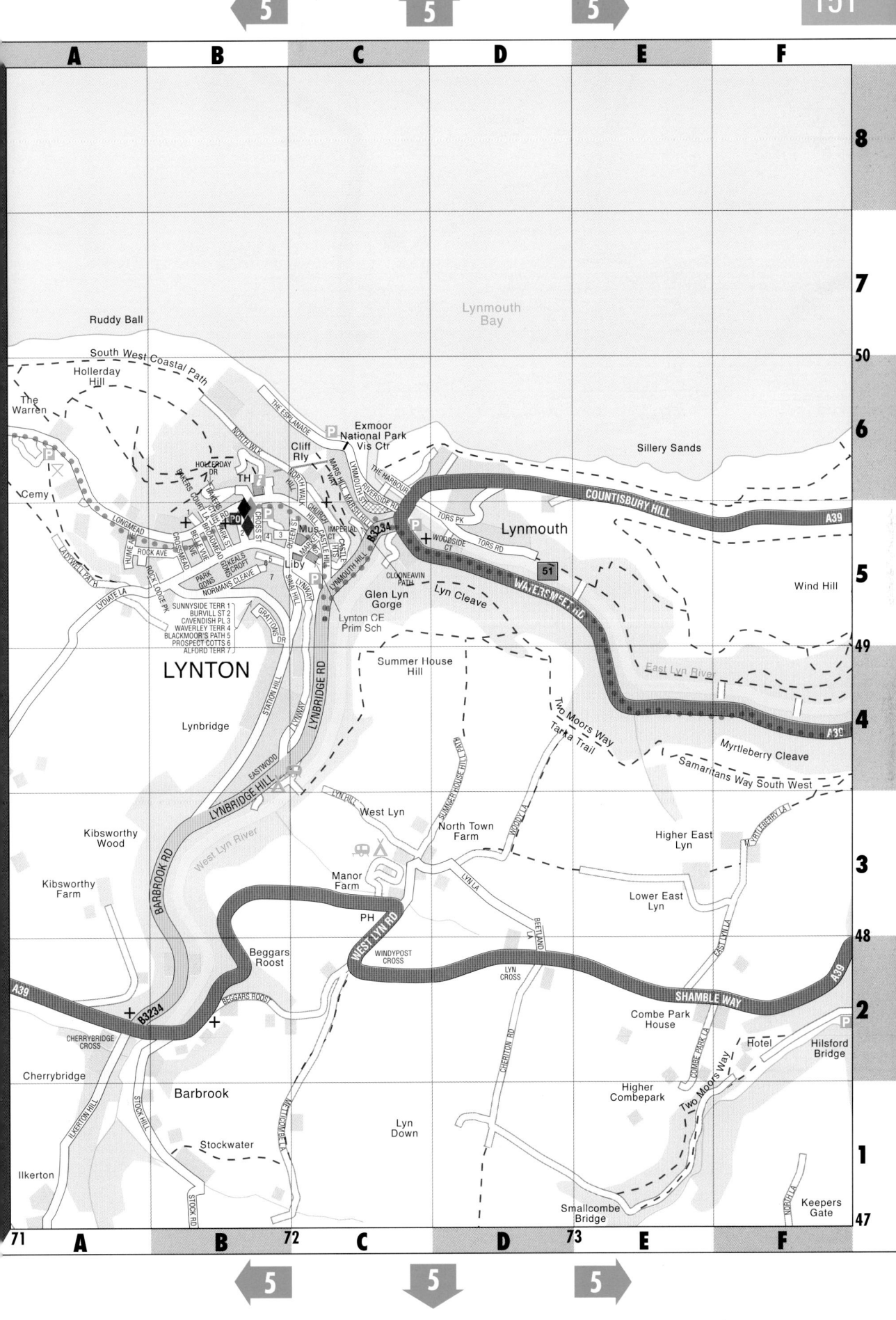
Ruddy Ball
South West Coastal Path
Hollerday Hill
The Warren
Lynmouth Bay
Exmoor National Park Vis Ctr
Cliff Rly
Sillery Sands
Cemy
TH
Mus
Liby
Lynmouth
COUNTISBURY HILL
A39
WATERSMEET RD
Glen Lyn Gorge
Lyn Cleave
Lynton CE Prim Sch
Wind Hill
LYNTON
Summer House Hill
East Lyn River
Two Moors Way
Tarka Trail
Myrtleberry Cleave
Samaritans Way South West
Lynbridge
LYNBRIDGE RD
LYNBRIDGE HILL
West Lyn
North Town Farm
Kibsworthy Wood
West Lyn River
Higher East Lyn
Kibsworthy Farm
Manor Farm
Lower East Lyn
BARBROOK RD
PH
WEST LYN RD
Beggars Roost
WINDYPOST CROSS
LYN CROSS
SHAMBLE WAY
B3234
Combe Park House
Hotel
Hilsford Bridge
CHERRYBRIDGE CROSS
Cherrybridge
Barbrook
Higher Combepark
Lyn Down
Stockwater
Ilkerton
Smallcombe Bridge
Keepers Gate
SUNNYSIDE TERR 1
BURVILL ST 2
CAVENDISH PL 3
WAVERLEY TERR 4
BLACKMOOR'S PATH 5
PROSPECT COTTS 6
ALFORD TERR 7
A B C D E F
8 7 6 5 4 3 2 1
50 49 48 47
71 72 73

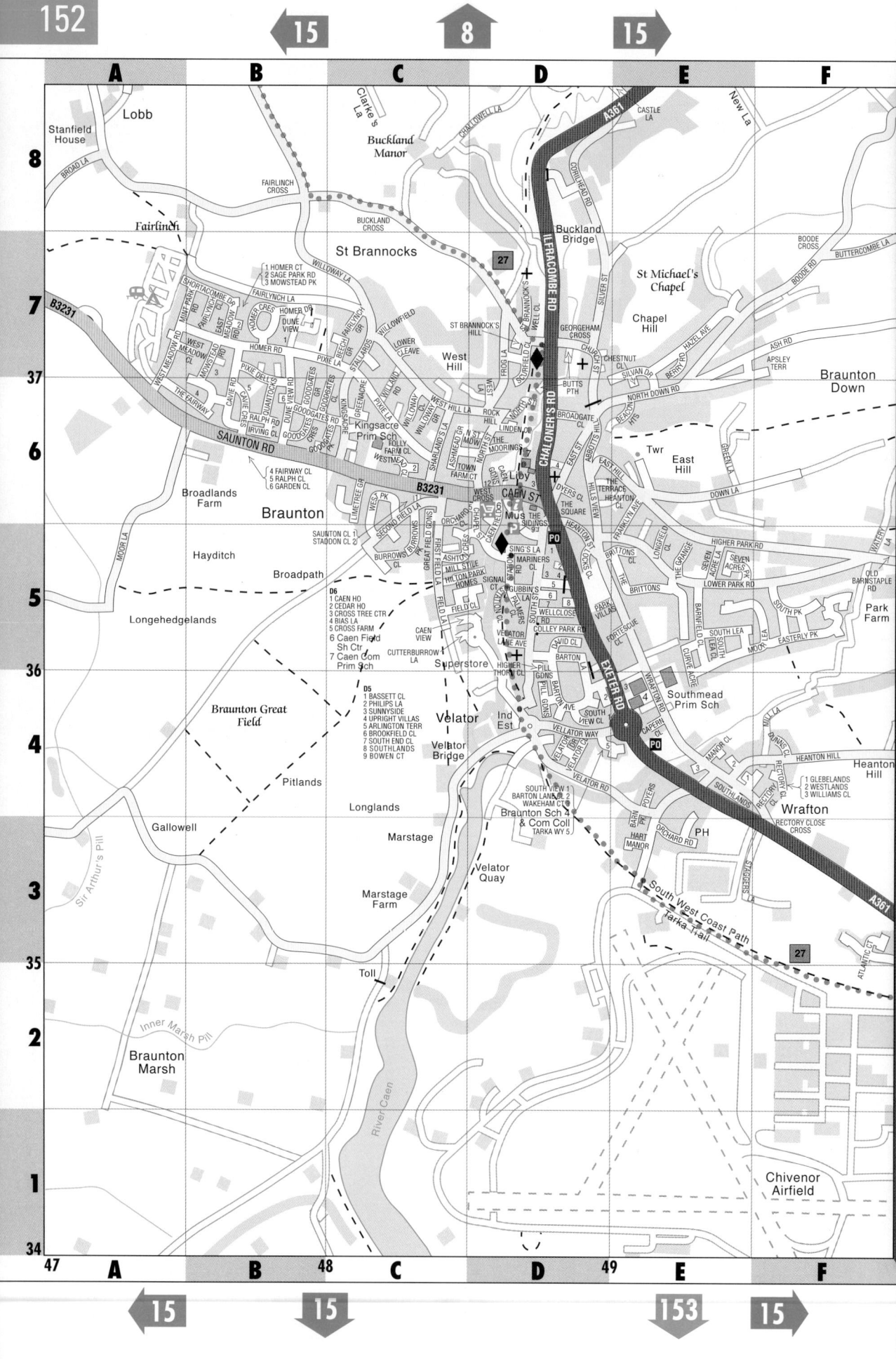

A B C D E F

Lobb
Stanfield House
Broad La
Fairlinch
B3231

St Brannocks
Buckland Manor
Fairlinch Cross
Buckland Cross
Willoway La

Clarke's La
Challowell La
A361
Castle La
New La

Buckland Bridge
St Michael's Chapel
Boode Cross
Buttercombe La

27
St Brannock's Hill
Well Cl
Georgeham Cross
Chapel Hill
Braunton Down

Kingsacre Prim Sch
West Hill
Chestnut
Silvan Dr
Berry Rd
Hazel Ave
Ash Rd
Apsley Terr

Saunton Rd
Broadlands Farm
Braunton
North Down Rd
Beacon Hts
East Hill
Twr

Hayditch
Broadpath
Longehedgelands
Caen St
Mus
PO
The Square
Heanton Ave
Franklin Ave
Higher Park Rd
Seven Acres
Lower Park Rd

D6
1 CAEN HO
2 CEDAR HO
3 CROSS TREE CTR
4 BIAS LA
5 CROSS FARM
6 Caen Field Sh Ctr
7 Caen Com Prim Sch

Caen View
Cutterburrow La
Superstore
Mariners Cl
Wellclose
Colley Park Rd
South Pk
Park Farm
Old Barnstaple Rd

D5
1 BASSETT CL
2 PHILIPS LA
3 SUNNYSIDE
4 UPRIGHT VILLAS
5 ARLINGTON TERR
6 BROOKFIELD CL
7 SOUTH END CL
8 SOUTHLANDS
9 BOWEN CT

Braunton Great Field
Velator
Ind Est
Exeter Rd
Southmead Prim Sch

Pitlands
Velator Bridge
Longlands
Gallowell
Marstage
Heanton Hill
Wrafton

1 GLEBELANDS
2 WESTLANDS
3 WILLIAMS CL

Rectory Close Cross

Sir Arthur's Pill
Marstage Farm
Velator Quay
South West Coast Path
Tarka Trail
27

Toll
35
Inner Marsh Pill
Braunton Marsh

Chivenor Airfield

River Caen

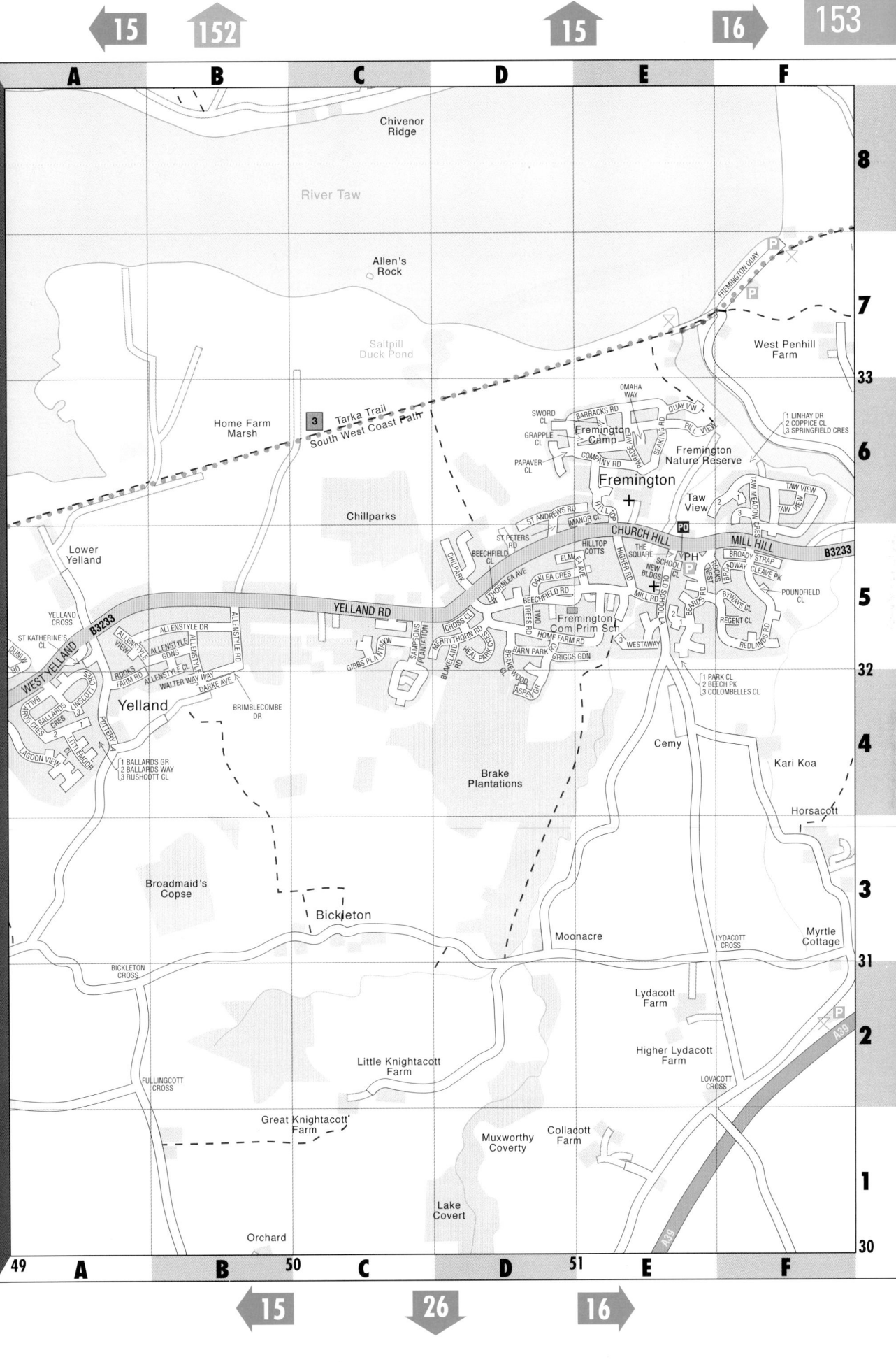

A B C D E F

8

Chivenor
Ridge

River Taw

Allen's
Rock

7

33

Saltpill
Duck Pond

West Penhill
Farm

3 Tarka Trail
Home Farm
Marsh
South West Coast Path

SWORD
CL

OMAHA
WAY

BARRACKS RD
QUAY VW

1 LINHAY DR
2 COPPICE CL
3 SPRINGFIELD CRES

6

Fremington
Camp

GRAPPLE
CL

SEARING RD

PILL VIEW

Fremington
Nature Reserve

PAPAVER
CL

COMPANY RD

Fremington

Chillparks

Taw
View

TAW MEADOW CRES
TAW VIEW
TAW VIEW
TAW

ST ANDREWS RD
MANOR CL

CHURCH HILL

MILL HILL

B3233

Lower
Yelland

ST PETERS
RD

CHILPARK

HILLTOP
SCOTTS

HIGHER RD

THE
SQUARE

PO
SCHOOL
NEW
BLDGS

PH
BROADY STRAP
CLEAVE PK

5

YELLAND CROSS

B3233

ALLENSTYLE RD

BEECHFIELD

THORNLEA AVE

OAKLEA CRES

ELM CL

MILL RD

HILL CL

BEARD RD

REGENT CL

POUNDFIELD
CL

ST KATHERINE'S
CL

YELLAND RD

BEECHFIELD RD

BYWAYS CL

REDLANDS RD

32

ALLENSTYLE VIEW
ALLENSTYLE DR
ALLENSTYLE GDNS
ALLENSTYLE CL
ALLENSTYLE

ROOKS
FARM RD

GIBBS PLA

SAMPSONS PLANTATION

TWO
TREES RD

Fremington
Com Prim Sch

1 PARK CL
2 BEECH PK
3 COLOMBELLES CL

WEST YELLAND
Yelland

WALTER WAY WAY
DARKE AVE

BRIMBLECOMBE
DR

BLAKELAND RD
BARNYTHORN RD
HEAL PARK

HOME FARM RD
BRAKE WOOD RD
ASPEN

BARN PARK

GRIGGS GDN

WESTAWAY

POTTERY LA

1 BALLARDS GR
2 BALLARDS WAY
3 RUSHCOTT CL

BALLARDS
CRES

LAGOON VIEW

Cemy

Kari Koa

4

Brake
Plantations

Horsacott

3

Broadmaid's
Copse

Bickleton

Moonacre

LYDACOTT
CROSS

Myrtle
Cottage

31

BICKLETON
CROSS

Lydacott
Farm

2

FULLINGCOTT
CROSS

Little Knightacott
Farm

Higher Lydacott
Farm

LOVACOTT
CROSS

A39

Great Knightacott
Farm

Muxworthy
Coverty

Collacott
Farm

1

Orchard

Lake
Covert

30

A6
1 ST GEORGE'S TERR
2 LANSDOWN TERR
3 VERONA CT
4 GRANGE CT
5 CARRINGTON TERR
6 PORTLAND BLDGS
7 HIGHER MAUDLIN ST
8 NEW BLDGS
9 MAGDALENE LAWN
10 RICHMOND WLK

A7
1 CLAUDE DIX CL
2 CHARLES HUDSON LA
3 RALEIGH COTTS
4 OSWALD BROWNING WAY
5 MASEFIELD AVE
6 WORDSWORTH AVE
7 PILTON LAWN

16

B5
1 SABRE WLK
2 METEOR WLK
3 NORTH GARRON
4 THE FIRS
5 RAVELIN GDNS
6 GOODLEIGH RD

17

17

A4
1 KILN LA
2 BRANNAMS SQ
3 CERAMIC TERR
4 PENROSE ALMSHOUSES
5 LOWER CHURCH ST
6 HIGHER CHURCH ST
7 SALEM ALMSHOUSES
8 SALEM ST
9 BARBICAN PL
10 WOODLAND CT
11 PULCHRASS ST
12 SUMMERLAND PL
13 BRANNAMS CT
14 TAW CT
15 TRINITY PL
16 SANDERLING CL
17 CHESTER TERR
18 CARLTON TERR
19 PORTLAND CT
20 DUNRAVEN
21 GLEN LYN
22 TREMERE CT
23 PARK TERR
24 ROCK PARK TERR
25 NORFOLK TERR

A5
1 LOWER GAYDON ST
2 GROSVNER ST
3 GROSVENOR CT
4 GROSVENOR TERR
5 BARUM MEWS
6 QUEEN'S HO
7 HARDAWAY HEAD
8 SILVER ST
9 ALBERT LA
10 BELLE MEADOW RD
11 BULLER RD
12 BEDFORD ST
13 FORT TERR
14 EBBERLY CT
15 ALEXANDRA CT
16 TROUVILLE
17 MEDARD HO
18 CALVADOS
19 NORMANDY HO
20 Ashleigh CE (VC) Prim Sch

16

B3
1 BOWERING CT
2 WATER LANE CL
3 MONTERY PL
4 WATER LANE COTTS
5 HOLLOWTREE CT
6 COT MANOR
7 CONGRAM'S CL
8 ABYSSINIA TERR
9 ABYSSINIA CT
10 EDDY'S LA
11 CLINTON TERR
12 CORPORATION ST
13 CORPORATION TERR
14 CORPORATION CRES
15 CLARENCE PL
16 SYCAMORE PK

17

17

B4
1 WEST VIEW CT
2 LAUDERDALE
3 NORTH GREEN
4 FORCHES GREEN FLATS
5 SOUTH GREEN
6 CLAYFIELD VILLAS
7 VICTORIA CL
8 BROOKDALE TERR

25 ⟵
14 ⬆

F7
1 COWPARK TERR
2 MORWENNA TERR
3 SPRINGFIELD TERR
4 CHAPEL HO
5 ADMIRALS CT
6 THE SQUARE

7 ST MARGARET'S CT
8 MONDEVILLE WAY
9 ST TERESA'S CT
10 DIDDYWELL RD

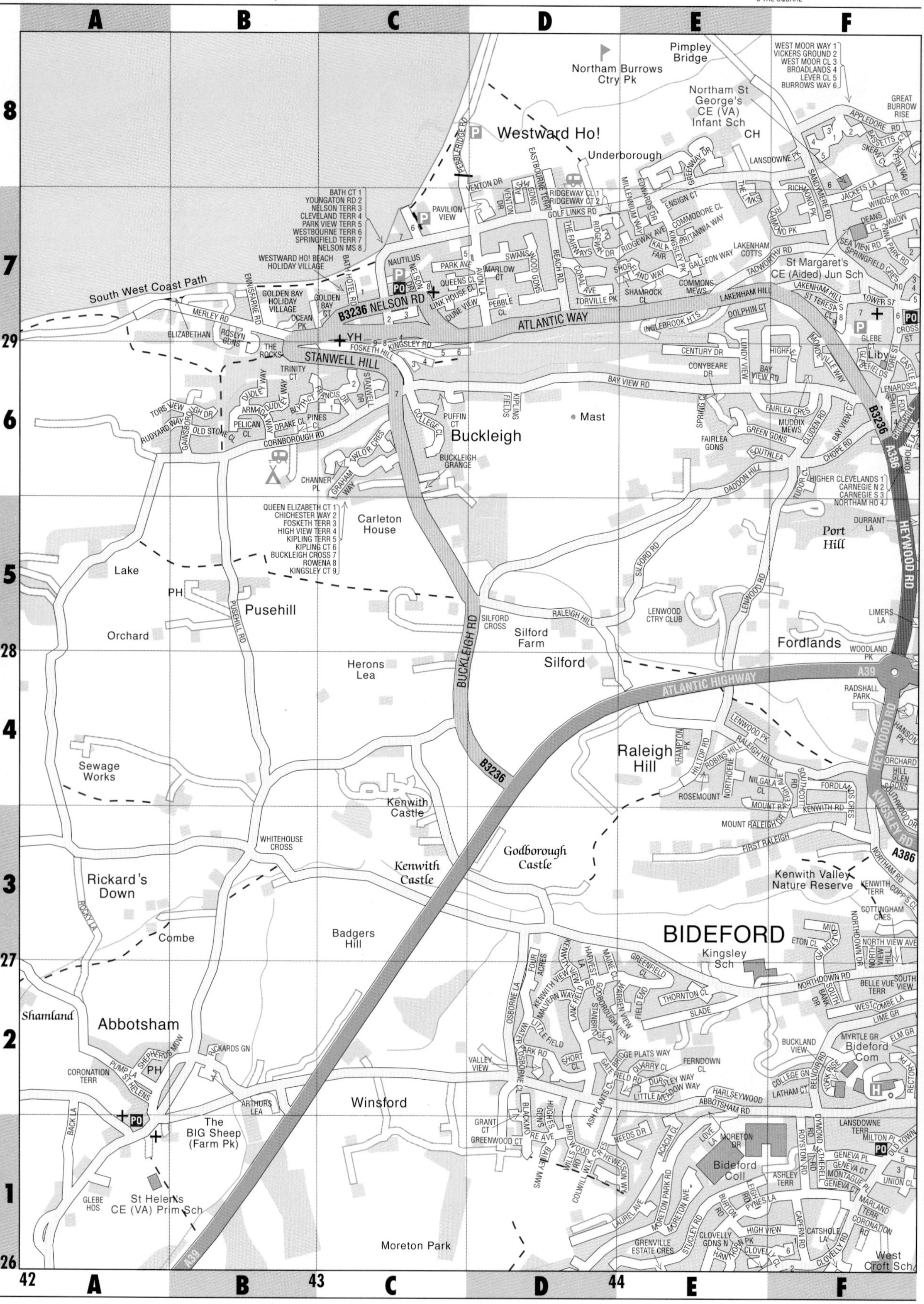

A B C D E F

8

Northam Burrows Ctry Pk

Pimpley Bridge

Westward Ho!

WEST MOOR WAY 1
VICKERS GROUND 2
WEST MOOR CL 3
BROADLANDS 4
LEVER CL 5
BURROWS WAY 6

GREAT BURROW RISE

Northam St George's CE (VA) Infant Sch

CH

Underborough

APPLEDORE RD

BATH CT 1
YOUNGATON RD 2
NELSON TERR 3
CLEVELAND TERR 4
PARK VIEW TERR 5
WESTBOURNE TERR 6
SPRINGFIELD TERR 7
NELSON MS 8

LANSDOWNE PK

JACKETS LA

WINDSOR RD

7

PAVILION VIEW

RIDGEWAY CL 1
RIDGEWAY CT 2

GOLF LINKS RD

St Margaret's CE (Aided) Jun Sch

NAUTILUS

Park Ave

SWANSWOOD GDNS

MARLOW

QUEENS CL

LAKENHAM COTTS

SPRINGFIELD CRES

TOWER ST

South West Coast Path

Westward Ho! Beach Holiday Village

WESTWARD HO! BEACH HOLIDAY VILLAGE

NELSON RD B3236

LINK HOUSE CL

DUNE VIEW

PEBBLE CL

ATLANTIC WAY

SHAMROCK CL

COMMONS MEWS

LAKENHAM HILL

ST TERESA'S CT

GLEBE

Liby

CROSS ST

GOLDEN BAY HOLIDAY VILLAGE

MERLEY RD

ROSLYN GDNS

OCEAN PK

Elizabethan

The Rocks

GOLDEN BAY CT

YH

STANWELL HILL

KINGSLEY RD

29

CENTURY DR

CONYBEARE DR

BAY VIEW RD

DOLPHIN CT

MONDEVILLE WAY

BAYFIELD

CASTLE

6

TORS VIEW

RUDYARD WAY

OLD STONE

PELICAN CL

CORNBOROUGH RD

DRAKE CL

TRINITY CT

BLYTH CT

FRANCIS

DUDLEY WAY

ARMADA

PINES

TAYLORS CRES

GRAHAM WAY

CHANNEL VIEW

BUCKLEIGH GRANGE

COLLEGE CL

Buckleigh

PUFFIN CT

KIPLING FIELDS

Mast

SPRINGCL

MUDDIX MEWS

GREEN GDNS

FAIRLEA CRES

FAIRLEA GDNS

DUTHLEA

BAK VIEW CL

CHOPE RD

B3236

A386

HEYWOOD RD

HIGHER CLEVELANDS 1
CARNEGIE N 2
CARNEGIE S 3
NORTHAM HO 4

DURRANT LA

Port Hill

QUEEN ELIZABETH CT 1
CHICHESTER WAY 2
FOSKETH TERR 3
HIGH VIEW TERR 4
KIPLING TERR 5
KIPLING CT 6
BUCKLEIGH CROSS 7
ROWENA 8
KINGSLEY CT 9

Carleton House

5

Lake

PH

PUSEHILL RD

Pusehill

BUCKLEIGH RD

Silford Cross

SILFORD RD

Silford Farm

RALEIGH HILL

Silford

LENWOOD CTRY CLUB

LENWOOD RD

LIMERS LA

Fordlands

WOODLAND PK

A39

28

Orchard

Herons Lea

ATLANTIC HIGHWAY

RADSHALL PARK

HANSON RD

ORCHARD

HILL GLEN

COLTHOUSE DR

4

Sewage Works

B3236

HAMPTON PK

LENWOOD PK

RALEIGH HILL

Raleigh Hill

ROBINS CL

NORTHCOTE

HILLTOP RD

NILGALA CL

SOUTHCOTT

FORDLANDS CRES

KINGSLEY DR

A386

WHITEHOUSE CROSS

Kenwith Castle

ROSEMOUNT

MOUNT RD

MOUNT RALEIGH

KENWITH RD

KINGSLEY DR

Godborough Castle

FIRST RALEIGH

MOUNT RALEIGH

3

Rickard's Down

ROCK LA

Kenwith Castle

Godborough Castle

Kenwith Valley Nature Reserve

KENWITH TERR

KENWITH CORPS CL

COTTINGHAM CRES

MID

NORTHDOWN DR

NORTH VIEW AVE

27

Combe

Badgers Hill

BIDEFORD

Kingsley Sch

NORTHDOWN RD

BELLE VUE TERR

WESTCOMBE LA

SOUTH VIEW

Shamland

Abbotsham

RICKARDS GN

OSBORNE LA

KENWITH VIEW

KENWITH WAY

MALVERN WAY

FOUR ACRES

WITHY CL

WATTS RD

HARVEST LA

MAINE CL

WARREN VIEW

GODBOROUGH VIEW

STANBROOK CL

GREENFIELD

THORNTON CL

LAWN END

FIELD END

SLADE

SOUTH BANK

BUCKLAND VIEW

MYRTLE GR

Bideford Com

ELM GR

2

CORONATION TERR

PUMP LA

ST HELENS

SHEPHERDS MDW

PH

ARTHURS LEA

Winsford

VALLEY VIEW

SHORT CL

PARK RD

FIELD RD

BRIDGE PLATS WAY

DURSLEY WAY

FERNDOWN CL

LITTLE MEADOW

MEADOW WAY

HARLSEYWOOD

ABBOTSHAM RD

LATHAM CT

COLLEGE RD

LANSDOWNE TERR

MILTON CL

DIMOND CL

ROYSTON RD

GENEVA CT

GENEVA PL

MARLAND TERR

MONTAGUE PL

Bideford Coll

H

PO

1

GLEBE HOS

St Helen's CE (VA) Prim Sch

The BIG Sheep (Farm Pk)

GRANT CT

GREENWOOD CT

NEEDS DR

LOVE LA

MORETON DR

ASHLEY TERR

Bideford Coll

GERMER PINES LA

HIGH VIEW

CAPERN RD

CATSHOLE LA

UNION CL

PO

BACK LA

GEENVILLE ESTATE CRES

GRENVILLE ESTATE CRES

MORETON PARK DR

STUCKLEY RD

BURTON LA

LAUREL AVE

ACACIA RD

CLOVELLY RD

CLOVELLY GDNS N

HAWKINS PK

CLOVELLY

CORONATION RD

West Croft Sch

26

Moreton Park

42 A 43 B 44 C D E F

F1
1 WATERLOO TERR
2 CLOVELLY GDNS S
3 WESTCROFT CT
4 TRAFALGAR PL
5 MEDDON ST
6 BACKABOROUGH LA

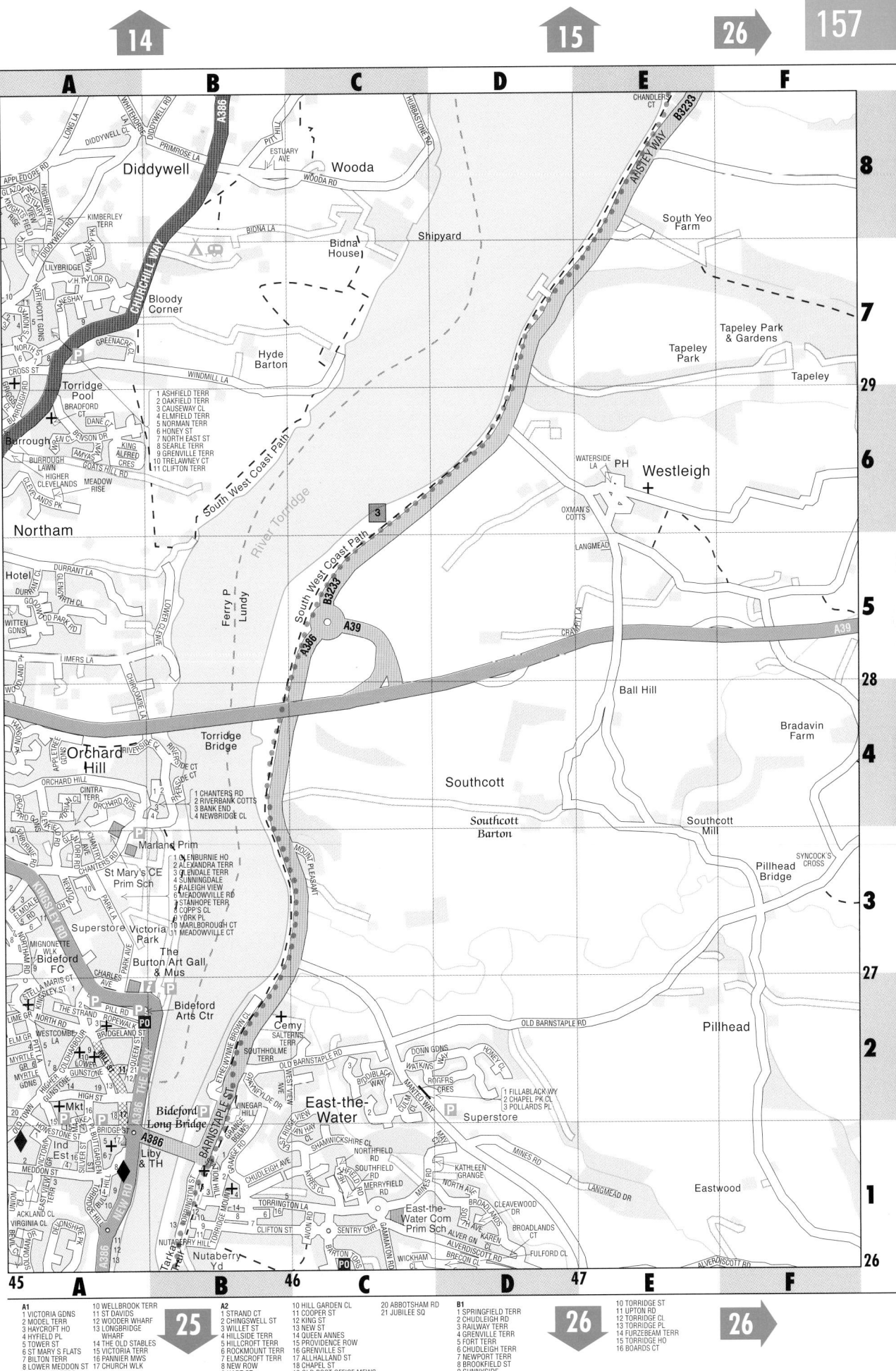

Diddywell

Wooda

Shipyard

Bidna House

Bloody Corner

Hyde Barton

South Yeo Farm

Tapeley Park & Gardens

Tapeley Park

Tapeley

Torridge Pool

Burrough

Northam

Westleigh

Oxman's Cotts

Langmead

Waterside La   PH

South West Coast Path

River Torridge

Ferry P Lundy

Hotel

Ball Hill

Bradavin Farm

Torridge Bridge

Orchard Hill

Southcott

Southcott Barton

Southcott Mill

Pillhead Bridge

Syncock's Cross

Marland Prim

St Mary's CE Prim Sch

Superstore

Victoria Park

The Burton Art Gall & Mus

Bideford FC

Bideford Arts Ctr

Cemy

Pillhead

Old Barnstaple Rd

Mkt

Ind Est

Liby & TH

Bideford Long Bridge

East-the-Water

Superstore

Eastwood

East-the-Water Com Prim Sch

Nutaberry Yd

Street index boxes on map:

1 ASHFIELD TERR
2 OAKFIELD TERR
3 CAUSEWAY CL
4 ELMFIELD TERR
5 NORMAN TERR
6 HONEY ST
7 NORTH EAST ST
8 SEARLE TERR
9 GRENVILLE TERR
10 TRELAWNEY CT
11 CLIFTON TERR

1 CHANTERS RD
2 RIVERBANK COTTS
3 BANK END
4 NEWBRIDGE CL

1 GLENBURNIE HO
2 ALEXANDRA TERR
3 GLENDALE TERR
4 SUNNINGDALE
5 RALEIGH VIEW
6 MEADOWVILLE RD
7 STANHOPE TERR
8 COPP'S CL
9 YORK PL
10 MARLBOROUGH CT
11 MEADOWVILLE CT

1 FILLABLACK WY
2 CHAPEL PK CL
3 POLLARDS PL

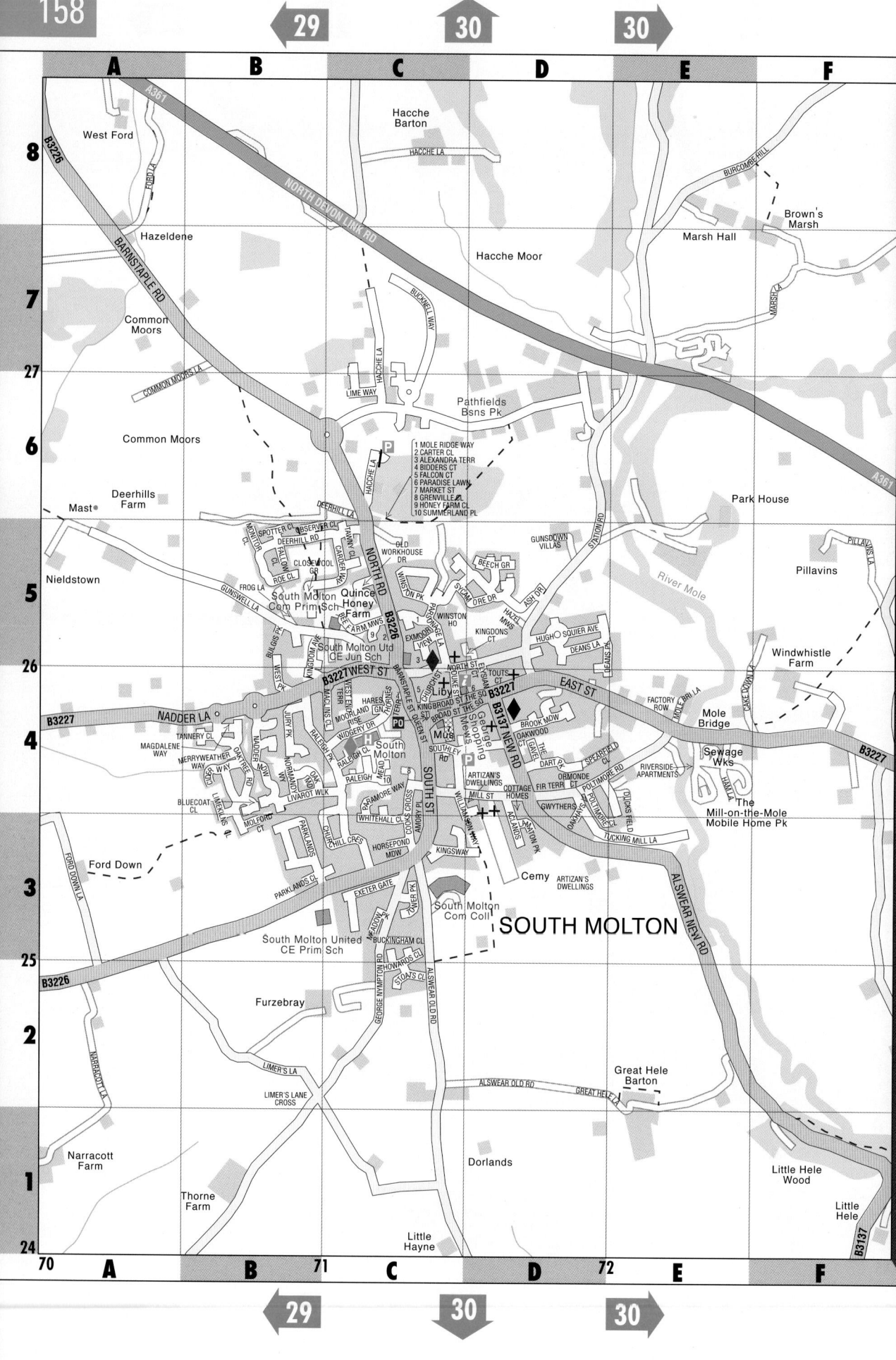

29
30
30

West Ford

Hacche
Barton

HACCHE LA

Marsh Hall

Brown's
Marsh

BURCOMBE HILL

MARSH LA

Hazeldene

Hacche Moor

FORD LA

BARNSTAPLE RD

A361

B3226

Common
Moors

BUCKNELL WAY

HACCHE LA

COMMON MOORS LA

LIME WAY

Pathfields
Bsns Pk

A361

Park House

Common Moors

Deerhills
Farm

Mast

1 MOLE RIDGE WAY
2 CARTER CL
3 ALEXANDRA TERR
4 BIDDERS CT
5 FALCON CT
6 PARADISE LAWN
7 MARKET ST
8 GRENVILLE PL
9 HONEY FARM CL
10 SUMMERLAND PL

DEERHILL LA

HACCHE LA

STATION RD

Gunsdown
Villas

River Mole

Pillavins

PILLAVINS LA

Nieldstown

SPOTTER CL
MONITOR CL
DEERHILL RD
OBSERVER CL
FALCON CL
HAWK CL
CARDEN WAY
ROE CL
CLOSE WOOL GR

NORTH RD

HAZEL CL
ORE DR

OLD
WORKHOUSE
DR

BEECH GR

SYCAM

ASH DR

Windwhistle
Farm

MOLE CRI LA

CAKE DOWN LA

FROG LA

South Molton
Com Prim Sch

Quince
Honey
Farm

WESSON PK

WINSTON
HO

EXMOOR CL

KINGDONS
CT

HUGH SQUIER AVE

DEANS LA

GUNSWELL LA

BULGIS PK

B3226

FARM MWS

PARSONAGE LA

WEST PK

South Molton Utd
CE Jun Sch

VIEW

B3227 WEST ST

PARTRIDGE LA

TOUTS
NOBLES CL

EAST ST

FACTORY
ROW

Mole
Bridge

B3227

NADDER LA

TANNERY CL

JURY PK

HARES
MOORLAND
RISE

WEST END
TERR

MAC LNS
GOLDGN

THORNES

BARNSTAPLE ST

QUEEN ST

B3227

BROAD ST

B3227

KINGBROAD ST THE SQ

Lib

Mus

George
Shopping
Mews

BROOK MDW

OAKWOOD

SOUTHLEY

B3137 NEW RD

SPEARFIELD

RIVERSIDE
APARTMENTS

Sewage
Wks

B3227

Magdalene
Way

MERRYWEATHER
WAY

NADDER MDW

OAK TREE RD

NORMANDY
WAY

RALEIGH RD

NIDGERY DR

OLD RD

PO

South
Molton

MEAD CL
RALEIGH

OAKWOOD
GATE

THE
DART
ORMONDE

CT

POLTIMORE RD

OLDS FIELD

The
Mill-on-the-Mole
Mobile Home Pk

BLUECOAT
CL

LIMERS CL

MOLFORD
CT

PARAMORE WAY

WHITEHALL CL

CHURCH HILL CR'S

COOKS CROSS

AMORY PL

SOUTH ST

ARTIZAN'S
DWELLINGS

MILL ST

GWYTHERS

COTTAGE
FIR TERR
HOMES

POLTIMORE
OAKLANDS

TUCKING MILL LA

Ford Down

FORD DOWN LA

PARKLANDS

HORSEPOND
MDW

WILLIAMS WAY

LANTON PK

AC MDS

KINGSWAY

Cemy

Artizan's
Dwellings

ALSWEAR NEW RD

PARKLANDS CL

EXETER GATE

TOWER PK

Little
Hayne

GEORGE WYMPTON RD

BUCKINGHAM CL

HOWARDS CL

SLOAN'S CL

ALSWEAR OLD RD

South Molton Com Coll

SOUTH MOLTON

B3226

South Molton United
CE Prim Sch

Furzebray

LIMER'S LA

LIMER'S LANE
CROSS

ALSWEAR OLD RD

Great Hele
Barton

GREAT HELE LA

Little Hele
Wood

Little
Hele

B3137

Narracott
Farm

NARRACOTT LA

Thorne
Farm

Dorlands

A

B

C

D

E

F

8

7

27

6

5

26

4

3

25

2

1

24

70

71

72

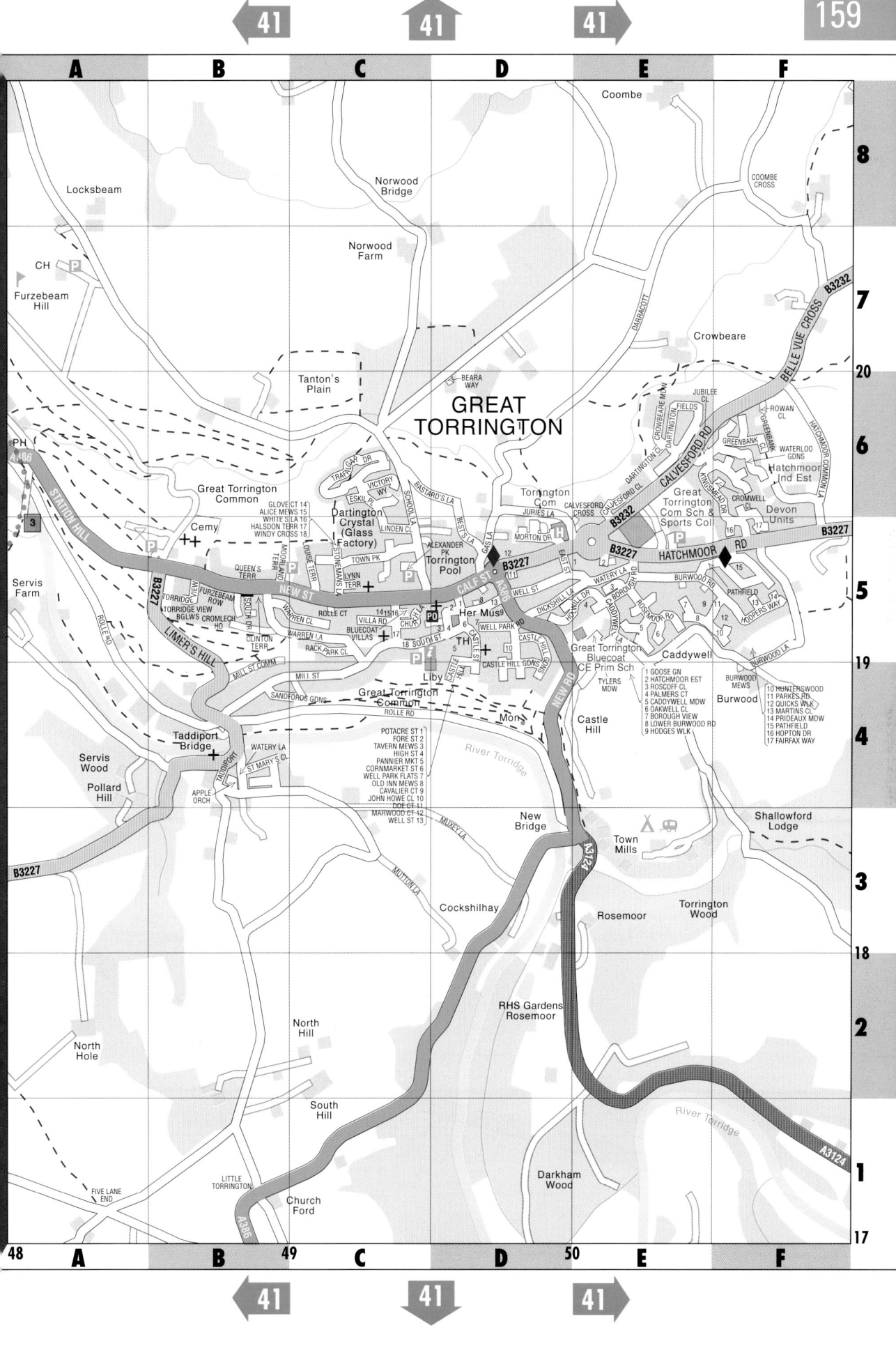
41
41
41
A
B
C
D
E
F
8
7
20
6
5
19
4
3
18
2
1
17
48
49
50
Coombe
COOMBE CROSS
Locksbeam
Norwood Bridge
Norwood Farm
CH
Furzebeam Hill
Crowbeare
DARRACOTT
B3232
BELLE VUE CROSS
Tanton's Plain
BEARA WAY
GREAT TORRINGTON
JUBILEE CL
FIELDS
ROWAN CL
GREENBANK
WATERLOO GDNS
HATCHMOOR COMMON LA
Hatchmoor Ind Est
DARTINGTON CL
CALVESFORD RD
GREENBANK CL
CROMWELL CL
KINGSMEAD DR
Devon Units
PH
A386
STATION HILL
Great Torrington Common
TRAFALGAR DR
VICTORY WY
ESKIL PL
SCHOOL LA
BASTARD'S LA
Torrington Com
JURIES LA
CALVESFORD CROSS
CALVESFORD CL
Great Torrington Com Sch & Sports Coll
GLOVE CT 14
ALICE MEWS 15
WHITE'S LA 16
HALSDON TERR 17
WINDY CROSS 18
Dartington Crystal (Glass Factory)
LINDEN CL
BESTS LA
MORTON DR
B3227
Cemy
ALEXANDER PK
TOWN PK
Torrington Pool
GAS LA
HATCHMOOR RD
Servis Farm
QUEEN'S TERR
MOORLAND TERR
LOUISE TERR
STONEMANS LA
LYNN TERR
NEW ST
CALF ST
WELL ST
EAST ST
WATERY LA
BURWOOD RD
PATHFIELD
HOOPERS WAY
FURZEBEAM ROW
TORRIDGE VIEW
TORRIDGE VIEW BGLWS
CROMLECH HO
SOUTH DR
WARREN CL
ROLLE CT
VILLA RD
CHURCH LA
PO
Her Mus
DICKSHILL LA
HOWELL DR
BOROUGH RD
ROSEMOOR RD
CADDYWELL LA
ROLLE RD
CLINTON TERR
WARREN LA
BLUECOAT VILLAS
SOUTH ST
WELL PARK RD
CASTLE HILL GDNS
TH
CASTLE ST
RACK PARK CL
LIMER'S HILL
MILL ST COMM
MILL ST
Liby
CASTLE HILL
CASTLE HILL GDNS
Great Torrington Bluecoat CE Prim Sch
Caddywell
BURWOOD LA
TYLERS MDW
1 GOOSE GN
2 HATCHMOOR EST
3 ROSCOFF CL
4 PALMERS CT
5 CADDYWELL MDW
6 OAKWELL CL
7 BOROUGH VIEW
8 LOWER BURWOOD RD
9 HODGES WLK
BURWOOD MEWS
Burwood
10 HUNTERSWOOD
11 PARKES RD
12 QUICKS WLK
13 MARTINS CL
14 PRIDEAUX MDW
15 PATHFIELD
16 HOPTON DR
17 FAIRFAX WAY
SANDFORDS GDNS
Great Torrington Common
ROLLE RD
Mon
NEW RD
Castle Hill
Taddiport Bridge
WATERY LA
ST MARY'S CL
TADDIPORT
APPLE ORCH
Servis Wood
Pollard Hill
POTACRE ST 1
FORE ST 2
TAVERN MEWS 3
HIGH ST 4
PANNIER MKT 5
CORNMARKET ST 6
WELL PARK FLATS 7
OLD INN MEWS 8
CAVALIER CT 9
JOHN HOWE CL 10
DOE CT 11
MARWOOD CT 12
WELL ST 13
River Torridge
MUXEY LA
New Bridge
Town Mills
Shallowford Lodge
B3227
MUTTON LA
A3124
Cockshilhay
Rosemoor
Torrington Wood
RHS Gardens Rosemoor
North Hill
North Hole
South Hill
River Torridge
A3124
FIVE LANE END
LITTLE TORRINGTON
Church Ford
A386
Darkham Wood

◄ 51
52 ►

A B C D E F

Somerset STREET ATLAS

Tone

B3187

Lowmoor Ind Est

Sewage Works

West Deane Way

JOHN COLE CL 1
FOLLETT CL 2
PROCTOR RD 3
TREDWIN CL 4
MAURICE JENNINGS DR 5

Long Copse

Blackham Copse

Poole Farm

Tonedale Ind Est

Crosslands

Longforth Farm

PALMERS MEAD

LUKES CL

Poole Ind Est

WELLINGTON

Poole

THOMAS FOX RD

WHARF COTTS

FIVE HOS

GARDEN TERR

CRESSLANDS

STONE EIGH

RICHARDS CL

CANAL CL

WARDLEWORTH

TAUNTON RD

CADES GDNS

CADESIDE CVN SITE

B3187

Tonedale

GREGORYS GRES

Factory

RICE

LILLEBONNE WAY

BLACKDOWN MDW

Tonedale Bsns Pk

Works

STATION RD

HOLYOAKE ST

QUANTOCK RD

BRENDON RD

Isambard Kingdom Brunel Prim Sch

STEDHAMS CL

Drake's Place

PRIORY CT

RIVERSIDE

Riverside

SPRINGFIELD RD

HIGH PATH

MITCHELL ST

SEYMOUR ST

OWEN ST

IVY HO

BOVET ST

GEORGE ST

PENNY LA

PARK LANDS RD

HOWARD CL

HOWARD ST

DRAKES PK N

DRAKES

St John's CE Prim Sch

HIGH ST

PRIORY

THE OLD VICARAGE

1 PEAR TREE WAY
2 DAMSON CRES

Lower Westford

Tonedale Farm

WINGSEELD LA

LINDEN HILL

CORAMS LA

RIVERSIDE

Sports Ctr

BEECH GR

THE GABLES

WATERLOO RD

POPHAM FLATS

LANCEY CL

WHITE HART LA

ALEXANDRA RD

LONGFORTH RD

BURGAGE

NORTH ST

BAKER'S LA

BECKWELL

MITCHELL'S POOL

Bsns Pk

JURSTON LA

Jurston Farm

LINDEN HILL

LOWER WESTFORD

FOX CL

BURGHILL RD

ORCHARD CL

ALLENDALE CL

BROOK MDWS RD

Rockwell Green CE Prim Sch

Court Fields Com Sch

HYACINTH TERR

COURT DR

MANTLE ST

BULFORD

Mus

Lby

PO

SQUIRRE

CLIFFORD MEWS

Wellington Jun Sch

Wellington Com

THE PADDOCKS

Wellington Sch

LABURNUM RD

BEECH TERR

Beech Grove Prim Sch

WESTFORD CT

WATER PATH

PAYTON RD

WESTFORD RD

GREENWAY RD

ROCKWELL GN

NORTHSIDE RD

DAKEN GROUND

THE WILLOWS

ROCKWELL GATE

EXETER RD

HILLY HEAD

Cemy

TRINITY CL

TRINITY TERR

ROOKERY TERR 1
COURT TERR 2
TRINITY ROW 3

CRANFORD AV

TUDOR PL

MARTINS CL

WALKERS GATE

MYSFORD

EIGHT ACRE LA

MORNINGTON PK

WELLESLEY PK

PYLES THORN

HAWTHORNE RD

SANFORD MWS

JURSTON FIELDS

KENYON

JURSTON CT

Rockwell Green

Frank Webber Rd

LOWER FOXMOOR

EXETER RD

ANDREW ALLAN RD

GILLARDS CL

PO

FOXDOWN HO

SWAINS LA

SWAINS

CORNER CL

ARDWYN

Wellesley Park Prim Sch

HOYLES CL

WEBBERS RD

DAMSON CRES

OAKFIELD

PYLES THORNE

OLDWAY HO

WEST BUCKLAND RD

A38

Wellington Relief Rd

EXETER ROAD CVN PK

BLACKDOWN RD

POPES LA

FARTHING'S PITTS

FOXDOWN HILL

COX RD

IMMENSTADT WAY

THE BRAMBLES

BLACKBERRY

ELWORTHY DR

JOHN HILL

FORD ST

OLDWAY RD

PYLES THORNE

OLDWAY RD

Pitt Farm

BARRINGTON WAY

OTTIE ELIZABETH CL

ROSE CL

HOBBS CL

BAGLEY RD

Ryelands Farm Ind Est

Blackboy Farm

BURROUGH

ROPE WLK

BARN MEADS RD

MIDDLE GREEN RD

Robin's Close

Ford Farm

Burts Farm

Bagley Green

A38

Bagley Farm

Wellington Relief Rd

STANDIX

Stallards

Standle

Middle Green Farm

Middle Green

Gillard's Farm

Woodlands

M5

BRIMSTONE LA

Pleamore Cross

Greenacres

Little Silver La

Middle Green

Robin's Close

Legglands

Bryant's Farm

Leyland's Farm

Calway's Farm

WRANGCOMBE RD

Woodford

Long Wood

WELLINGTON HILL

BEECH CL

Briscoe House

Higher Woodford

Voxmoor

PARK LA

12 A 13 B C 14 D E F

◄ 51
52
52 ►

D5
1 THE GARDENS
2 CHAMPFORD MEWS
3 POUND TERR
4 MARTINS BLDGS
5 IMPROVEMENT PL
6 WILLCOCKS CL
7 LABURNUM COTTS
8 JUBILEE CT

D6
1 THE LAWN
2 BEECH CT
3 BELVEDERE CT
4 OLD CT MWS
5 CORNHILL

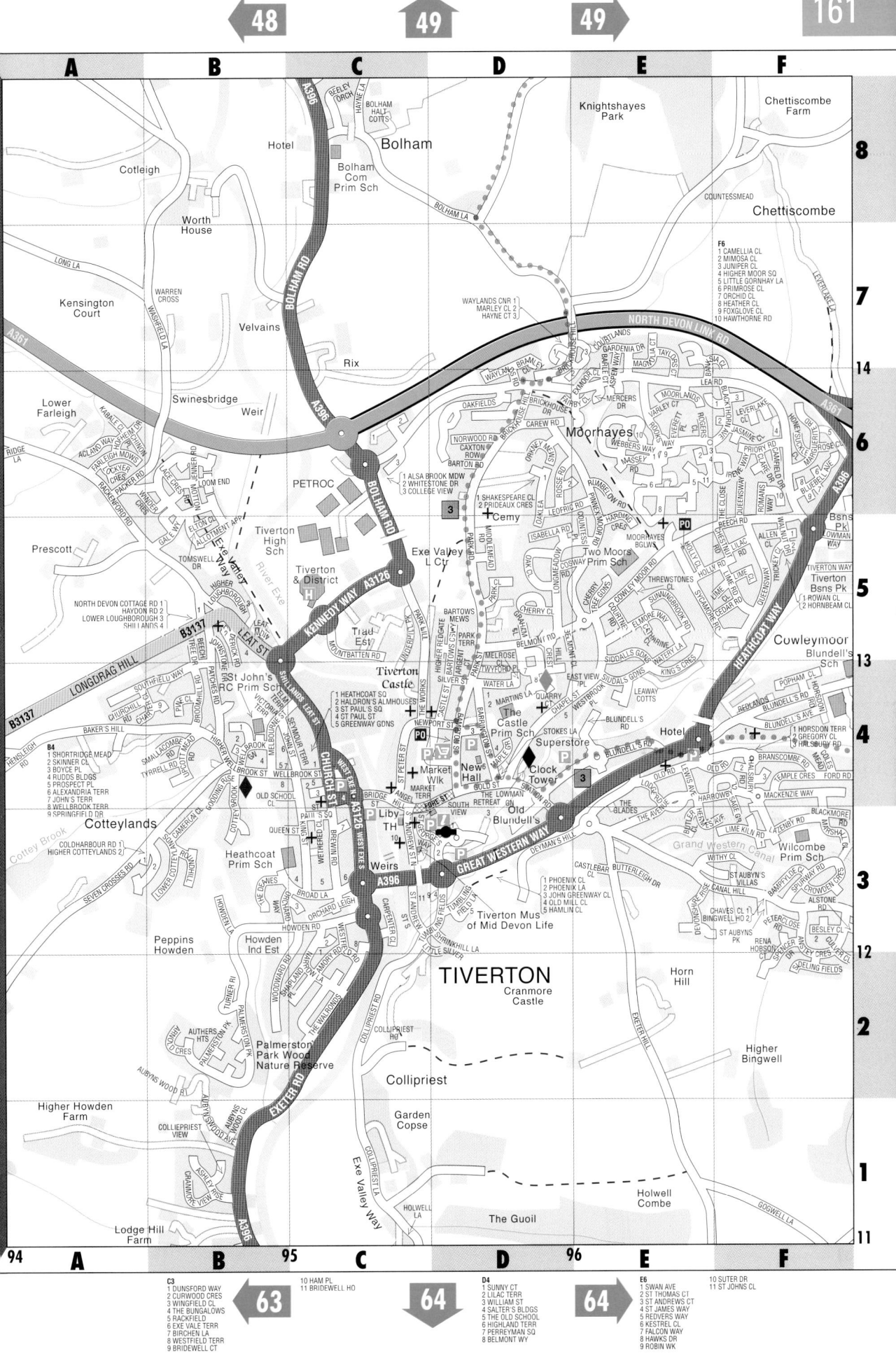

F6
1 CAMELLIA CL
2 MIMOSA CL
3 JUNIPER CL
4 HIGHER MOOR SQ
5 LITTLE GORNHAY LA
6 PRIMROSE CL
7 ORCHID CL
8 HEATHER CL
9 FOXGLOVE CL
10 HAWTHORNE RD

WAYLANDS CNR 1
MARLEY CL 2
HAYNE CT 3

1 ALSA BROOK MDW
2 WHITESTONE DR
3 COLLEGE VIEW

1 SHAKESPEARE CL
2 PRIDEAUX CRES

NORTH DEVON COTTAGE RD 1
HAYDON RD 2
LOWER LOUGHBOROUGH 3
SHILLANDS 4

B4
1 SHORTRIDGE MEAD
2 SKINNER CL
3 BOYCE PL
4 RUDDS BLDGS
5 PROSPECT PL
6 EXE VALE TERR
7 JOHN'S TERR
8 ALEXANDRIA TERR
9 WELLBROOK TERR
10 SPRINGFIELD TERR

COLDHARBOUR RD 1
HIGHER COTTEYLANDS 2

1 HEATHCOAT SQ
2 HALDRON'S ALMHOUSES
3 ST PAUL'S SQ
4 GT PAUL ST
5 GREENWAY GDNS

1 PHOENIX CL
2 PHOENIX LA
3 JOHN GREENWAY CL
4 OLD MILL CL
5 HAMLIN CL

C3
1 DUNSFORD WAY
2 CURWOOD CRES
3 WINGFIELD CL
4 THE BUNGALOWS
5 RACKFIELD
6 EXE VALE TERR
7 BIRCHEN LA
8 WESTFIELD TERR
9 BRIDEWELL CT

10 HAM PL
11 BRIDEWELL HO

D4
1 SUNNY CT
2 LILAC TERR
3 WILLIAM ST
4 SALTER'S BLDGS
5 THE OLD SCHOOL
6 HIGHLAND TERR
7 PERREYMAN SQ
8 BELMONT WY

E6
1 SWAN AVE
2 ST THOMAS CT
3 ST ANDREWS CT
4 ST JAMES WAY
5 REDVERS WAY
6 KESTREL CL
7 FALCON WAY
8 HAWKS DR
9 ROBIN WK

10 SUTER DR
11 ST JOHNS CL

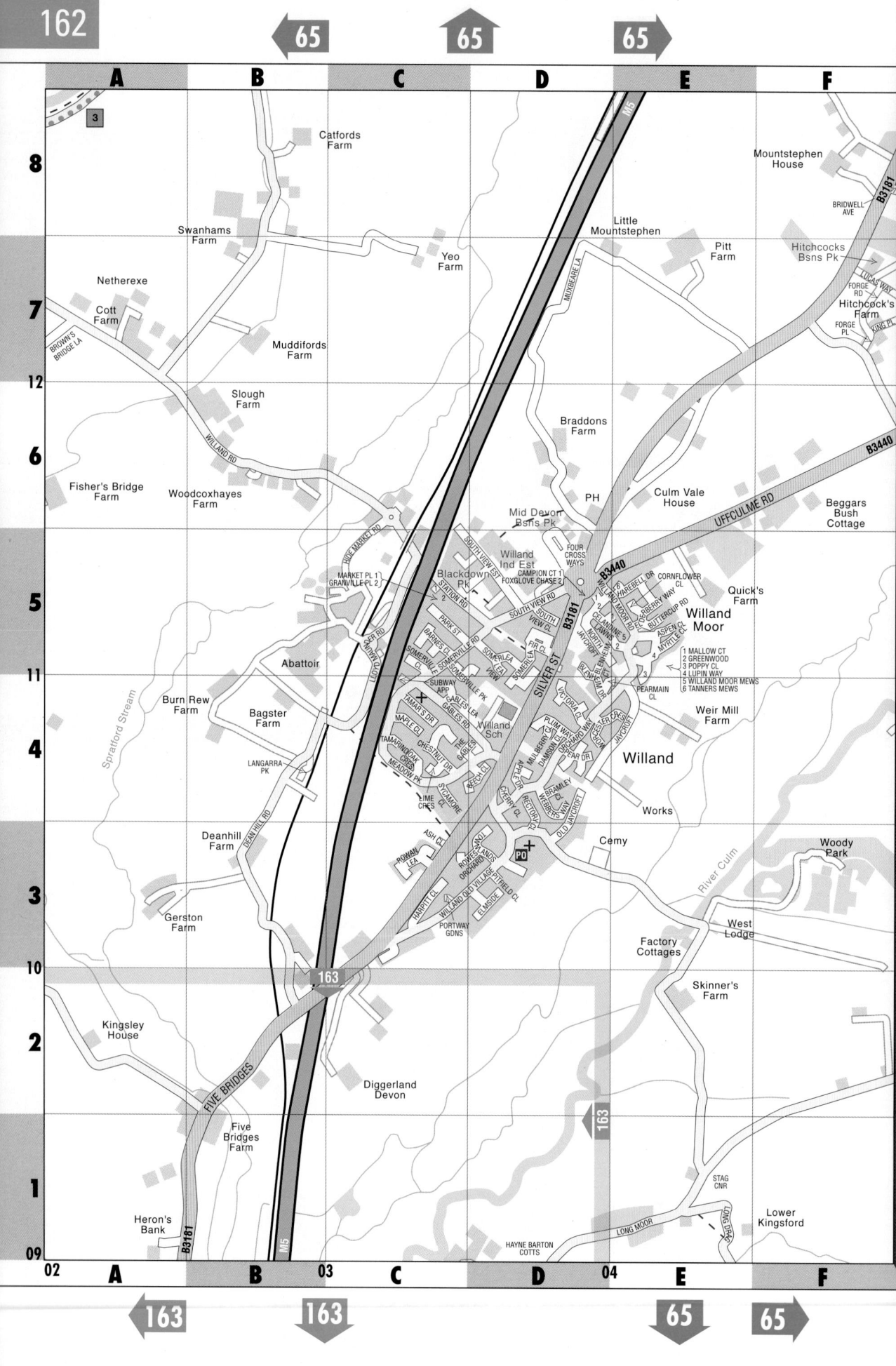

A B C D E F

8

Mountstephen
House

Catfords
Farm

BRIDWELL
AVE

B3181

Little
Mountstephen

Pitt
Farm

Hitchcocks
Bsns Pk

Swanhams
Farm

Yeo
Farm

FORGE
RD

LUCK'S WAY

Hitchcock's
Farm

7

Netherexe

FORGE
PL

KING PL

Cott
Farm

Muddifords
Farm

BROWN'S BRIDGE LA

12

Slough
Farm

Braddons
Farm

B3440

6

WILLAND RD

PH

Culm Vale
House

Fisher's Bridge
Farm

Woodcoxhayes
Farm

UFFCULME RD

Beggars
Bush
Cottage

Mid Devon
Bsns Pk

FOUR
CROSS
WAYS

Willand
Ind Est

B3440

Quick's
Farm

MARKET PL 1
GRANVILLE PL 2

SOUTH VIEW

Blackdown
Pk

CAMPION CT 1
FOXGLOVE CHASE 2

Willand
Moor

5

STATION RD

RIDGE MARKET RD

SOUTH VIEW RD

SOUTH VIEW CL

B3181

1 MALLOW CT
2 GREENWOOD
3 POPPY CL
4 LUPIN WAY
5 WILLAND MOOR MEWS
6 TANNERS MEWS

Abattoir

PARK ST

SOMERVILLE
CL

SOMERVILLE RD

FIR CL

SILVER ST

11

BARNES CL

SOMERLEA
VIEW

SOMERLEA

PEARMAIN
CL

Weir Mill
Farm

Burn Rew
Farm

SUBWAY
APP

GABLES LEA

Willand
Sch

VICTORIA CL

Bagster
Farm

TAMAR DR

MAPLE CL

THE
GABLES

Willand

Works

LANGARRA
PK

TAMARIND
CRES

OAK
MEADOW PK

CHESTNUT DR

MILBERRY CL

PLUM WAY

DAMSON CL

BRAMLEY
CL

4

SYCAMORE

BEECH CL

ORCHARD DR

RECTORY CL

OLD JAYCROFT

DEAN HILL RD

LIME
CRES

CHERRY CL

VERBERS WAY

Cemy

3

ASH CL

ROWAN
LEA

ROWE CL
ORCHARD

WILLAND OLD VILLAGE

STHFIELD CL

ELMSIDE

Factory
Cottages

West
Lodge

Woody
Park

Deanhill
Farm

HARRITT CL

PO

PORTWAY
GDNS

River Culm

Gerston
Farm

163

Skinner's
Farm

10

Kingsley
House

2

Spratford Stream

FIVE BRIDGES

Diggerland
Devon

163

STAG
CNR

Lower
Kingsford

1

Heron's
Bank

Five
Bridges
Farm

M5

HAYNE BARTON
COTTS

LONG MOOR

LONG DRG

09

65 65 162 162

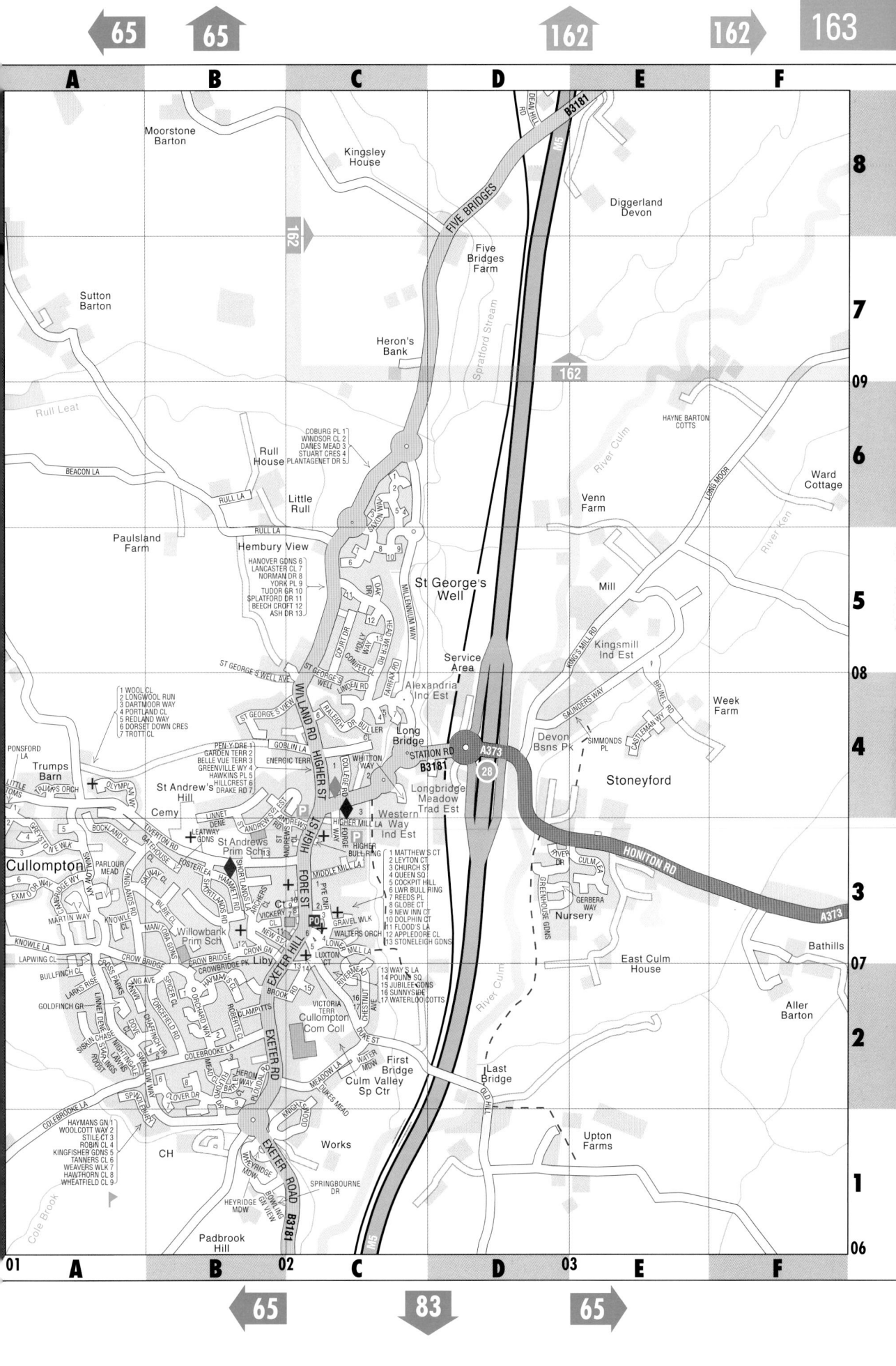

A
B
C
D
E
F
8
7
09
6
5
08
4
3
07
2
1
06
01
02
03
Moorstone Barton
Kingsley House
DEAN HILL RD
B3181
M5
Diggerland Devon
FIVE BRIDGES
162
Five Bridges Farm
Sutton Barton
Spratford Stream
Heron's Bank
162
Rull Leat
HAYNE BARTON COTTS
River Culm
COBURG PL 1
WINDSOR CL 2
DANES MEAD 3
STUART CRES 4
PLANTAGENET DR 5
Rull House
BEACON LA
Ward Cottage
LONG MOOR
Little Rull
RULL LA
Venn Farm
River Ken
SAXON WAY
Paulsland Farm
Hembury View
HANOVER GDNS 6
LANCASTER CL 7
NORMAN DR 8
YORK PL 9
TUDOR GR 10
SPLATFORD DR 11
BEECH CROFT 12
ASH DR 13
St George's Well
Mill
OAK DR
MILLENNIUM WAY
KING'S MILL RD
COURT DR
HOLLY WAY
HEAD WEIR RD
Kingsmill Ind Est
CONIFER CL
FAIRFAX RD
Service Area
ST GEORGE'S WELL AVE
ST GEORGE'S WELL
LINDEN RD
Alexandria Ind Est
BRUNEL RD
Week Farm
1 WOOL CL
2 LONGWOOL RUN
3 DARTMOOR WAY
4 PORTLAND CL
5 REDLAND WAY
6 DORSET DOWN CRES
7 TROTT CL
WILLAND RD
ST GEORGE'S VIEW
RALEIGH DR
BULLER CL
SAUNDERS WAY
CASTLEMAN WY
Long Bridge
Devon Bsns Pk
SIMMONDS PL
PONSFORD LA
PEN-Y-DRE 1
GARDEN TERR 2
BELLE VUE TERR 3
GREENVILLE WY 4
HAWKINS PL 5
HILLCREST 6
DRAKE RD 7
GOBLIN LA
HIGHER ST
ENERGIC TERR
WHITTON WAY
STATION RD
A373
B3181
28
Trumps Barn
COLLEGE RD
Stoneyford
LITTLE TOMS
TRUMPS ORCH
OLYMPIAN WY
St Andrew's Hill
Longbridge Meadow Trad Est
Cemy
LINNET DENE
ST ANDREWS EST
Western Way Ind Est
HIGHER MILL LA
GREYSTONE WLK
BOCKLAND CL
LEATWAY GDNS
St Andrews Prim Sch
HIGH ST
FORGE WAY
HIGHER BULL RING
TIVERTON RD
GATEHOUSE CL
1 MATTHEW'S CT
2 LEYTON CT
3 CHURCH ST
4 QUEEN SQ
5 COCKPIT HILL
6 LWR BULL RING
7 REEDS PL
8 GLOBE CT
9 NEW INN CT
10 DOLPHIN CT
11 FLOOD'S LA
12 APPLEDORE CL
13 STONELEIGH GDNS
RIVER DR
CULM LEA
HONITON RD
Cullompton
PARLOUR MEAD
SWALLOW WAY
FOSTERLEA
HAMMETT RD
SHORTLANDS LA
SHORTLANDS RD
MIDDLE MILL LA
FORE ST
CAMBRIDGE WY
EXMOOR WAY
LANGLANDS RD
SALWAY CL
ARCHERS CT
PYE CNR
GREENHOUSE GDNS
GERBERA WAY
Nursery
A373
MARTIN WAY
KNOWLE CL
BILBIE CL
VICKERY CL
GRAVEL WLK
PO
KNOWLE LA
MANITOBA GDNS
Willowbank Prim Sch
NEW ST
WALTERS ORCH
LOWER MILL LA
Bathills
LAPWING CL
CROW BRIDGE
CROW GN
Liby
LUXTON CT
East Culm House
BULLFINCH CL
CROSS PARKS
CROWBRIDGE PK
EXETER HILL
13 WAY'S LA
14 POUND SQ
15 JUBILEE GDNS
16 SUNNYSIDE
17 WATERLOO COTTS
LARKS RISE
HAYMANS CL
RIVERMEAD
GOLDFINCH GR
LINNET DENE
SPICER CL
ORCHARD WAY
BROOK RD
CHESTNUT AVE
River Culm
Aller Barton
CLAMPITTS
VICTORIA TERR
Cullompton Com Coll
SISKIN CHASE
NIGHTINGALE
DOVE
FORGEFIELD RD
CHAFFINCH DR
ROBERTS CL
DUKE ST
EXETER RD
COLEBROOKE LA
WATER MDW
First Bridge
Last Bridge
HERON WAY
MEADOW LA
DUKES MEAD
Culm Valley Sp Ctr
CLOVER DR
SPINDLEBURY
OLD HILL
COLEBROOKE LA
KNIGHTSWOOD
HAYMANS GN 1
WOOLCOTT WAY 2
STILE CT 3
ROBIN CL 4
KINGFISHER GDNS 5
TANNERS CL 6
WEAVERS WLK 7
HAWTHORN CL 8
WHEATFIELD CL 9
Works
Upton Farms
CH
HEYRIDGE MDW
EXETER ROAD
SPRINGBOURNE DR
Cole Brook
HEYRIDGE MDW
BOWLING GN VIEW
B3181
Padbrook Hill
M5

65 83 65

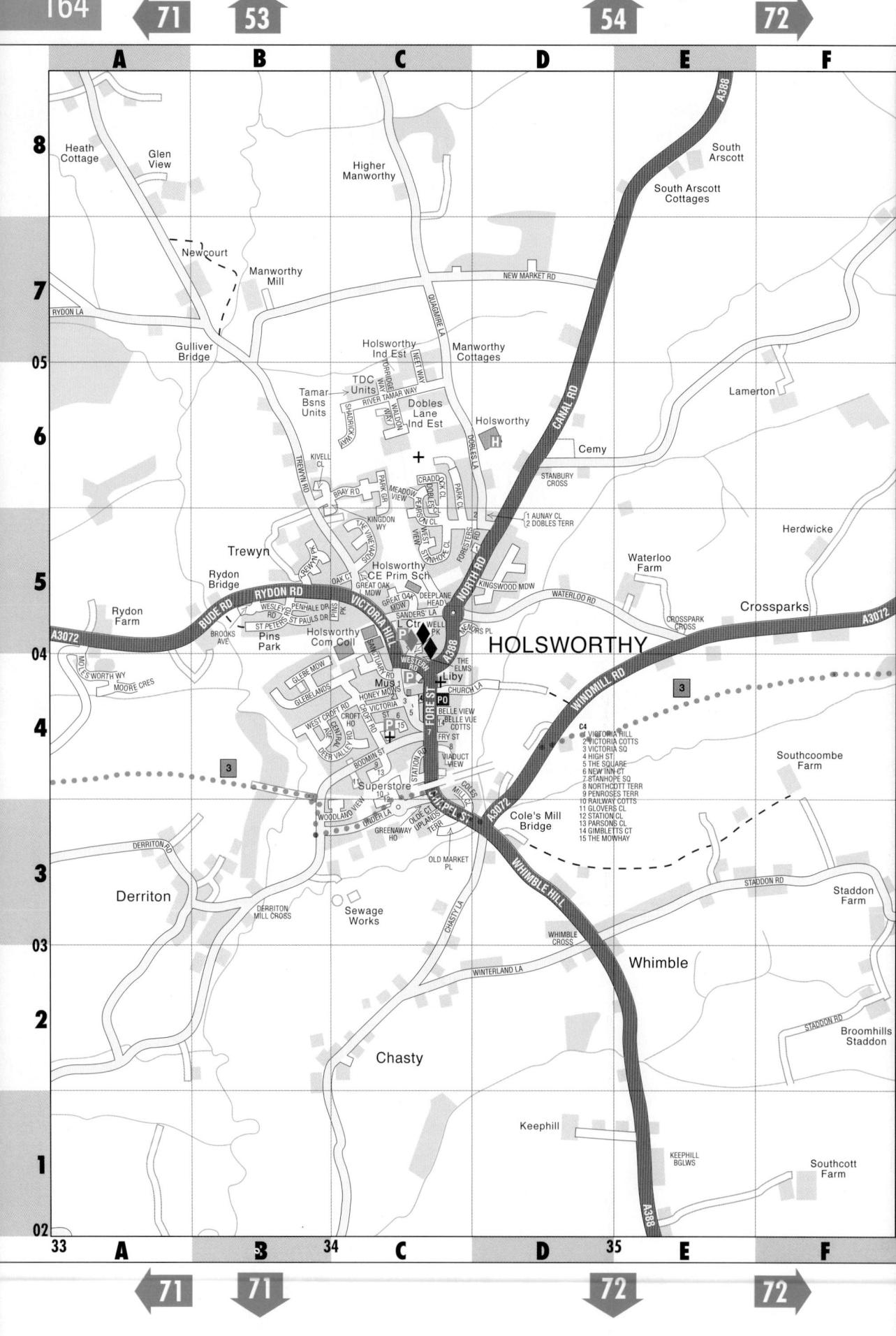

HOLSWORTHY

C4
1 VICTORIA HILL
2 VICTORIA COTTS
3 VICTORIA SQ
4 HIGH ST
5 THE SQUARE
6 NEW INN CT
7 STANHOPE SQ
8 NORTHCOTT TERR
9 PENROSES TERR
10 RAILWAY COTTS
11 GLOVERS CL
12 STATION CL
13 PARSONS CL
14 GIMBLETTS CT
15 THE MOWHAY

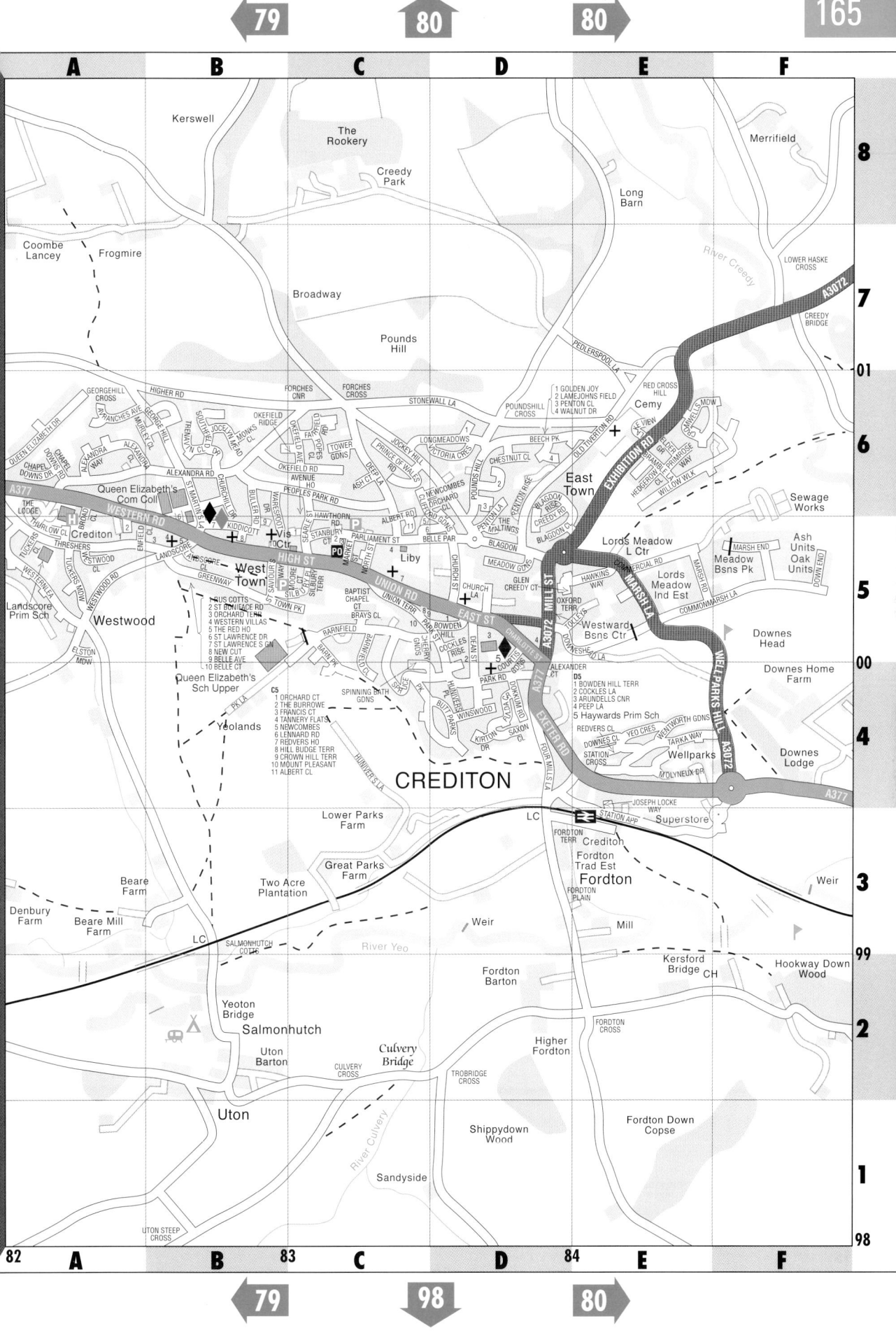

Kerswell

The Rookery

Merrifield

Creedy Park

Long Barn

River Creedy

LOWER HASKE CROSS

Coombe Lancey

Frogmire

A3072

CREEDY BRIDGE

Broadway

Pounds Hill

GEORGEHILL CROSS

HIGHER RD

FORCHES CNR

FORCHES CROSS

STONEWALL LA

PEDLERSPOOL LA

RED CROSS HILL

Cemy

1 GOLDEN JOY
2 LAMEJOHNS FIELD
3 PENTON CL
4 WALNUT DR

POUNDSHILL CROSS

LONGMEADOWS

BEECH PK

CHESTNUT CL

OLD TIVERTON RD

SE VIEW

EXHIBITION RD

CARVELLS MDW

Sewage Works

QUEEN ELIZABETH DR

BRANCHES AVE

GEORGE HILL

MUTLEY CL

OKEFIELD RIDGE

OKEFIELD RD

JOCKEY HILL

TOWER GDNS

VICTORIA CRES

POUNDS HILL

PENTON RISE

East Town

HEDGEROW CL

PRIMROSE WAY

WILLOW WLK

Ash Units Oak Units

QEII QUEEN ELIZABETH'S
Com Coll

WESTERN RD

Crediton

A377

THE LODGE

THURLOW CL

ENFIELD CL

CHURCHILL DR

ST MARTIN'S LA

BULLER RD

KIDDICOTT

NEWCOMBES

ALBERT RD

THE MALTINGS

Lords Meadow L Ctr

MARSH END

Meadow Bsns Pk

MARSH RD

Lords Meadow Ind Est

COMMONMARSH LA

Downes Head

West Town

HIGH ST

UNION RD

Liby

CHURCH ST

CHURCH LA

Glen Creedy

OXFORD TERR

Westward Bsns Ctr

A3072

MILL ST

HAWKINS WAY

Downes Home Farm

Landscore Prim Sch

Westwood

LANDSCORE

GREENWAY

TOWN PK

BAPTIST CHAPEL CT

BRAYS CL

BOWDEN HILL

COCKLES RISE

DEAN ST

PARK RD

COURTIS GDNS

Alexander

D5
1 BOWDEN HILL TERR
2 COCKLES LA
3 ARUNDELLS CNR
4 PEEP LA
5 Haywards Prim Sch

A377

EXETER RD

FOUR MILLS LA

WENTWORTH GDNS

YEO CRES

TARKA WAY

Wellparks

WELLPARKS HILL

A3072

Downes Lodge

Queen Elizabeth's Sch Upper

ELSTON MDW

Yeolands

C5
1 ORCHARD CT
2 THE BURROWE
3 FRANCIS CT
4 TANNERY FLATS
5 NEWCOMBES
6 LENNARD RD
7 REDVERS HO
8 HILL BUDGE TERR
9 CROWN HILL TERR
10 MOUNT PLEASANT
11 ALBERT CL

SPINNING BATH GDNS

HUNTERS LA

WINSWOOD

KIRTON DR

SAXON CL

REDVERS CL

DOWNES CL

STATION CROSS

MOLYNEUX DR

CREDITON

Lower Parks Farm

Great Parks Farm

LC

FORDTON TERR

STATION APP

JOSEPH LOCKE WAY

Superstore

Crediton

Fordton Trad Est

Fordton

Weir

Beare Farm

Two Acre Plantation

LC

SALMONHUTCH COTTS

Weir

Mill

Kersford Bridge   CH

Hookway Down Wood

Denbury Farm

Beare Mill Farm

River Yeo

Fordton Barton

FORDTON CROSS

Yeoton Bridge

Salmonhutch

Uton Barton

CULVERY CROSS

Culvery Bridge

TROBRIDGE CROSS

Higher Fordton

Uton

River Culvery

Shippydown Wood

Fordton Down Copse

Sandyside

UTON STEEP CROSS

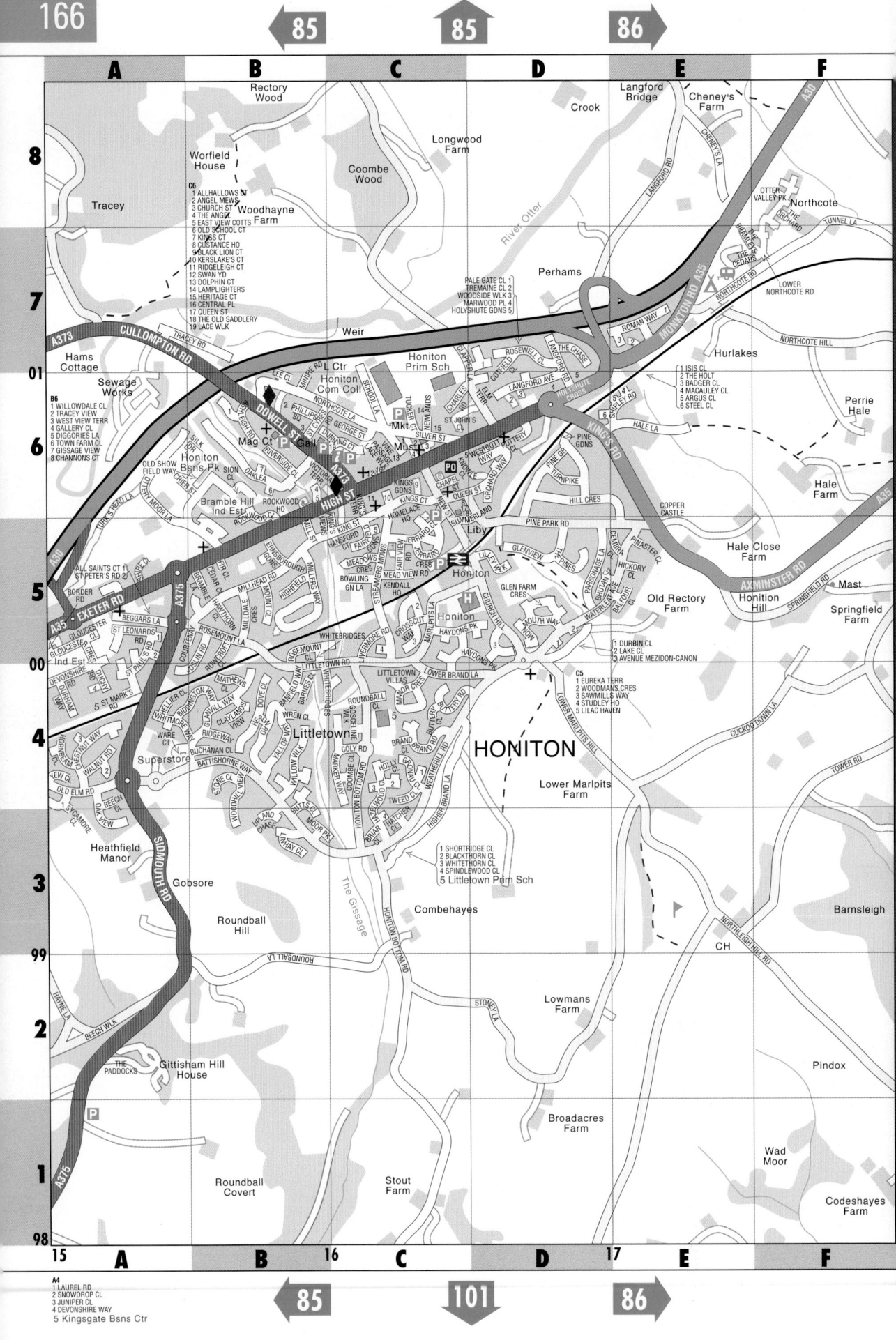
85
85
86
A
B
C
D
E
F
8
7
01
6
5
00
4
3
99
2
1
98
15
16
17
Rectory Wood
Worfield House
Coombe Wood
Longwood Farm
Crook
Langford Bridge
Cheney's Farm
Tracey
Woodhayne Farm
River Otter
Perhams
Northcote
Hams Cottage
Sewage Works
Weir
Honiton Prim Sch
L Ctr
Honiton Com Coll
Hurlakes
Perrie Hale
Hale Farm
Mag Ct
Gall
Mkt
Mus
Liby
Honiton Bsns Pk
Bramble Hill Ind Est
Honiton
Hale Close Farm
Honiton Hill
Mast
Springfield Farm
Old Rectory Farm
Ind Est
Littletown
Superstore
HONITON
Lower Marlpits Farm
Heathfield Manor
Gobsore
Roundball Hill
The Gissage
Combehayes
Barnsleigh
CH
Lowmans Farm
Gittisham Hill House
Pindox
Broadacres Farm
Wad Moor
Roundball Covert
Stout Farm
Codeshayes Farm
A373
A30
A35
A375
CULLOMPTON RD
DOWELL ST
HIGH ST
EXETER RD
KING'S RD
MONKTON RD
AXMINSTER RD
SIDMOUTH RD
HONITON BOTTOM RD
NORTHCOTE HILL
NORTHCOTE RD
LOWER NORTHCOTE RD
TUNNEL LA
HALE LA
PINE PARK RD
HILL CRES
CUCKOO DOWN LA
TOWER RD
NORTHLEIGH HILL RD
LOWER MARLPITS HILL
STONEY LA
ROUNDBALL LA
HAYNE LA
BEECH WLK
THE PADDOCKS
C6
1 ALLHALLOWS CT
2 ANGEL MEWS
3 CHURCH ST
4 THE ANGEL
5 EAST VIEW COTTS
6 OLD SCHOOL CT
7 KINGS CT
8 CUSTANCE HO
9 BLACK LION CT
10 KERSLAKE'S CT
11 RIDGELEIGH CT
12 SWAN YD
13 DOLPHIN CT
14 LAMPLIGHTERS
15 HERITAGE CT
16 CENTRAL PL
17 QUEEN ST
18 THE OLD SADDLERY
19 LACE WLK
B6
1 WILLOWDALE CL
2 TRACEY VIEW
3 WEST VIEW TERR
4 GALLERY CL
5 DIGGORIES LA
6 TOWN FARM CL
7 GISSAGE VIEW
8 CHANNONS CT
PALE GATE CL 1
TREMAINE CL 2
WOODSIDE WLK 3
MARWOOD PL 4
HOLYSHUTE GDNS 5
1 ISIS CL
2 THE HOLT
3 BADGER CL
4 MACAULEY CL
5 ARGUS CL
6 STEEL CL
1 DURBIN CL
2 LAKE CL
3 AVENUE MEZIDON-CANON
C5
1 EUREKA TERR
2 WOODMANS CRES
3 SAWMILLS WAY
4 STUDLEY HO
5 LILAC HAVEN
1 SHORTRIDGE CL
2 BLACKTHORN CL
3 WHITETHORN CL
4 SPINDLEWOOD CL
5 Littletown Prim Sch
ALL SAINTS CT 1
ST PETER'S RD 2
A4
1 LAUREL RD
2 SNOWDROP CL
3 JUNIPER CL
4 DEVONSHIRE WAY
5 Kingsgate Bsns Ctr
85
101
86

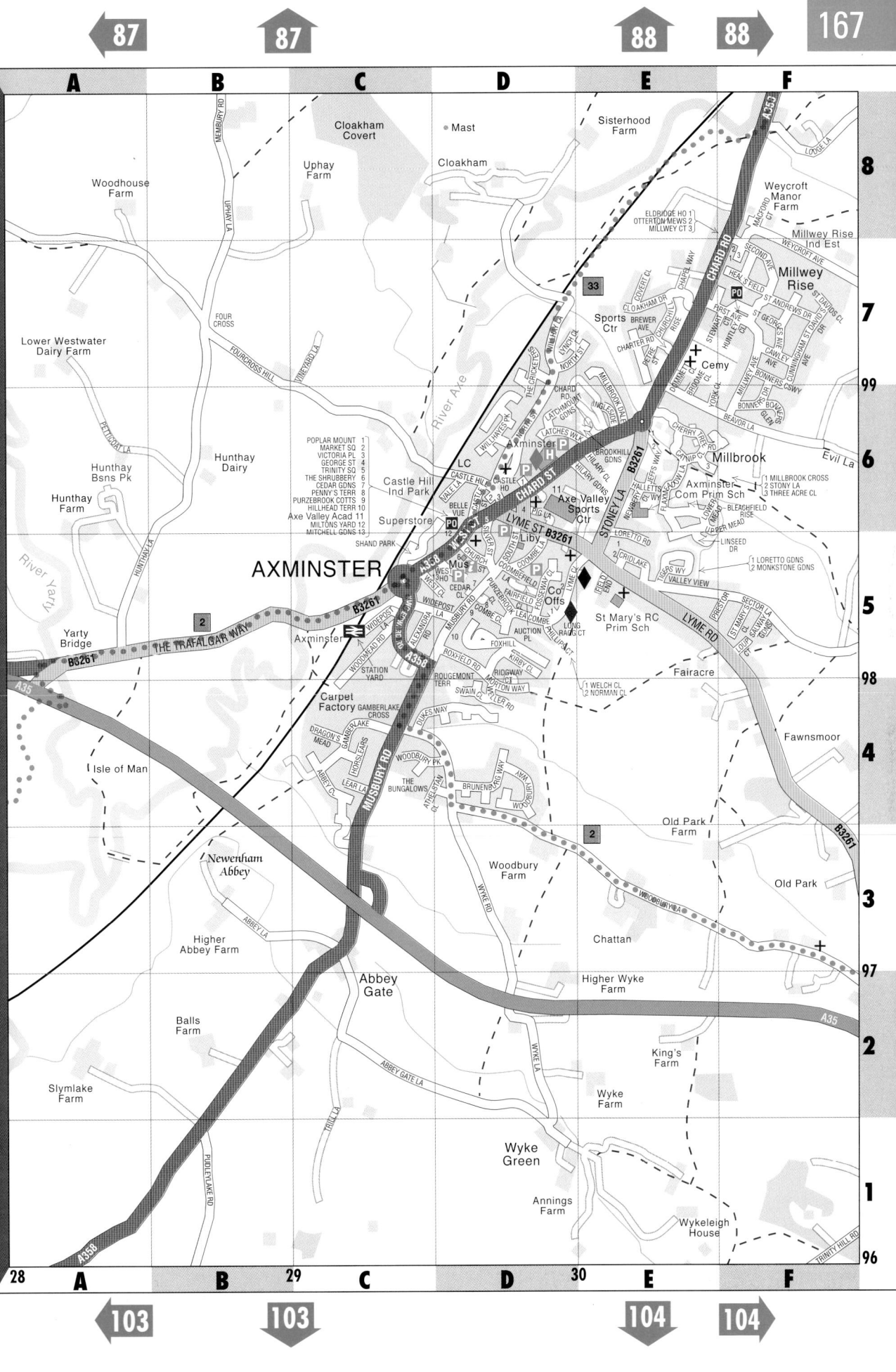

AXMINSTER

POPLAR MOUNT 1
MARKET SQ 2
VICTORIA PL 3
GEORGE ST 4
TRINITY SQ 5
THE SHRUBBERY 6
CEDAR GDNS 7
PENNY'S TERR 8
PURZEBROOK COTTS 9
HILLHEAD TERR 10
Axe Valley Acad 11
MILTONS YARD 12
MITCHELL GDNS 13

ELDRIDGE HO 1
OTTERTON MEWS 2
MILLWEY CT 3

1 MILLBROOK CROSS
2 STONY LA
3 THREE ACRE CL

1 LORETTO GDNS
2 MONKSTONE GDNS

1 WELCH CL
2 NORMAN CL

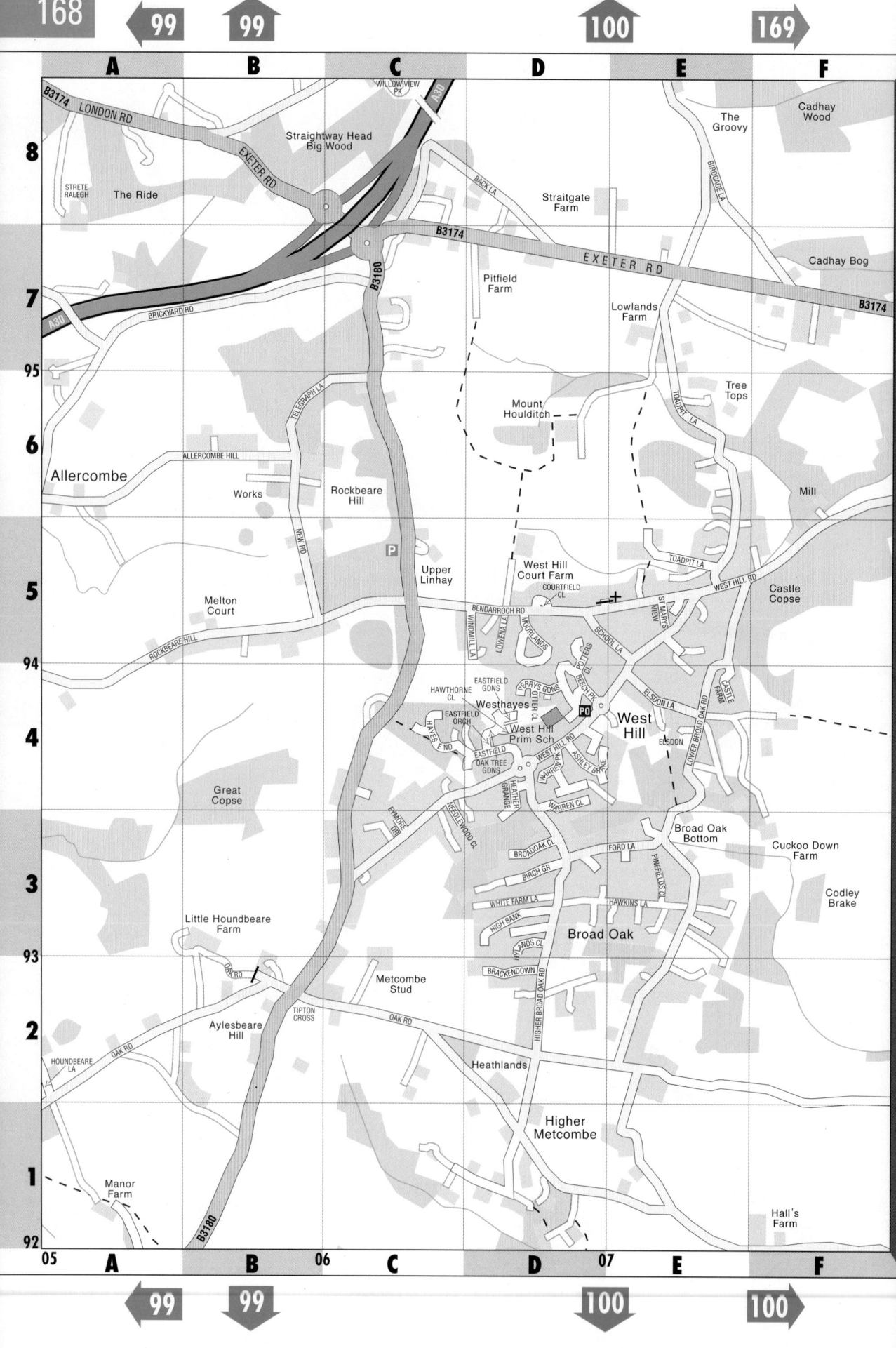

8

7

95

6

5

94

4

3

93

2

1

92

B3174 LONDON RD
STRETE RALEGH
The Ride
EXETER RD
A30
Straightway Head
Big Wood
WILLOW VIEW PK
A30
BACK LA
Straitgate Farm
The Groovy
Cadhay Wood
B3174
EXETER RD
B3174
Cadhay Bog
A30 BRICKYARD RD
B3180
Pitfield Farm
Lowlands Farm
BRIDGARE LA
Allercombe
ALLERCOMBE HILL
TELEGRAPH LA
Works
Rockbeare Hill
Mount Houlditch
TOADPIT LA
Tree Tops
Mill
NEW RD
Melton Court
ROCKBEARE HILL
P
Upper Linhay
West Hill Court Farm
COURTFIELD CL
TOADPIT LA
WEST HILL RD
Castle Copse
BENDARROCH RD
WINDMILL LA
LOWER LA
MOORLANDS
ST MARY'S VIEW
SCHOOL LA
ELSDON LA
CASTLE FARM
HAWTHORNE CL
EASTFIELD GDNS
PARRYS GDNS
OTTER CL
BECH PK
POTTERS
West Hill Prim Sch
Westhayes
EASTFIELD ORCH
West Hill RD
PO
West Hill
ELSDON LA
ELSDON
LOWER BROAD OAK RD
EASTFIELD
HAYES E ND
OAK TREE GDNS
WARREN PK
ASHLEY BRKE
Great Copse
FIVMORE DRR
NEEDLEWOOD CL
HEATHER GRANGE
WARREN CL
Broad Oak Bottom
Cuckoo Down Farm
Codley Brake
Little Houndbeare Farm
OAK RD
BROADOAK CL
BIRCH GR
FORD LA
PINEFIELDS CT
HAWKINS LA
WHITE FARM LA
HIGH BANK
Broad Oak
Metcombe Stud
OAK RD
HIGHER BROAD OAK RD
NDS CL
BRACKENDOWN
TIPTON CROSS
Aylesbeare Hill
HOUNDBEARE LA
OAK RD
Heathlands
Higher Metcombe
Manor Farm
B3180
Hall's Farm

05 A B 06 C D 07 E F

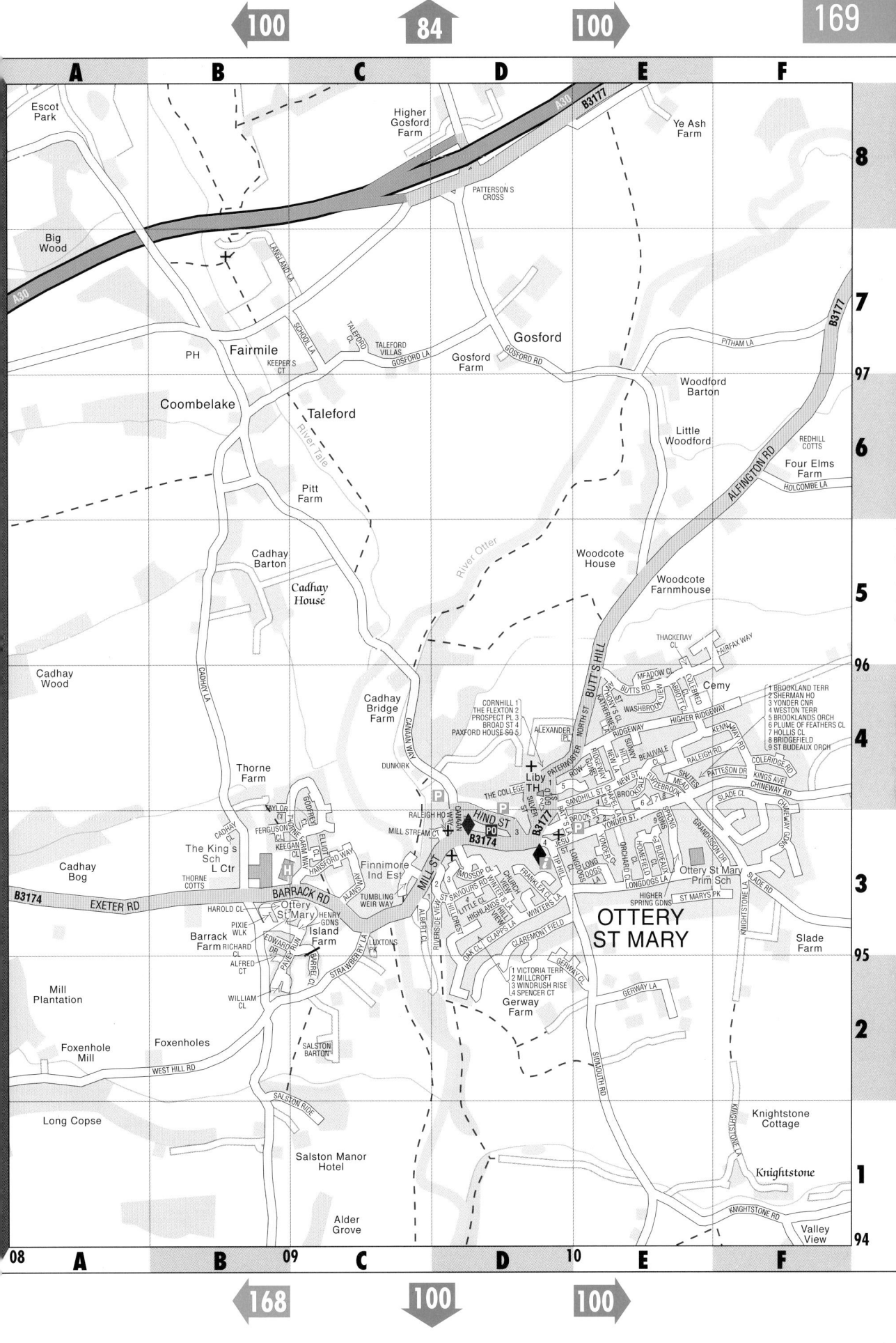

Grid columns: A B C D E F (top and bottom)
Grid rows: 8 97 7 6 5 96 4 95 3 2 1 94

Map labels:

Escot Park
Big Wood
A30
Fairmile
PH
Coombelake
Cadhay Wood
Cadhay Bog
B3174
Mill Plantation
Foxenhole Mill
Long Copse
Foxenholes
WEST HILL RD
SALSTON RISE
Salston Manor Hotel
Alder Grove
Barrack Farm
HAROLD CL
EXETER RD
BARRACK RD
Thorne Farm
THORNE COTTS
The King's Sch L Ctr
Ottery St Mary
Island Farm
HENRY GDNS
PIXIE WLK
RICHARD CL
ALFRED CT
WILLIAM CL
EDWARD DR
PARK RD
LAUREL CL
STRAWBERRY LA
FINNIMORE IND EST
TUMBLING WEIR WAY
LUXTONS PK
SALSTON BARTON
CADHAY CL
TAYLOR CL
GODFREY CL
FERGUSON CL
KEEGAN CL
ELLIOT CL
HANSFORD WAY
THORNE FARM WAY
ALANS CL
MILL ST
CADHAY LA
CANAAN WAY
DUNKIRK
Cadhay Barton
Cadhay House
Pitt Farm
River Tale
Taleford
SCHOOL LA
TALEFORD CL
TALEFORD VILLAS
LANGDALE LA
KEEPER'S CT
Higher Gosford Farm
B3177
A30
PATTERSON'S CROSS
Gosford
Gosford Farm
GOSFORD LA
GOSFORD RD
Ye Ash Farm
Woodford Barton
Little Woodford
PITHAM LA
ALFINGTON RD
REDHILL COTTS
Four Elms Farm
HOLCOMBE LA
B3177
Woodcote House
Woodcote Farmhouse
River Otter
Cadhay Bridge Farm
CORNHILL 1
THE FLEXTON 2
PROSPECT PL 3
BROAD ST 4
PAXFORD HOUSE SQ 5
ALEXANDER PL
THACKERAY
FAIRFAX WAY
Cemy
MEADOW CL
COLE RD
BUTT'S HILL
NORTH ST
KATHERINE CL
BUTTS RD
YONDER ST
WASHBROOK
HIGHER RIDGEWAY
RIDGEWAY
BEAUVALE
RALEIGH RD
KENNAWAY RD
COLERIDGE RD
KINGS AVE
CHINEWAY RD
PATTESON DR
SLADE CL
SLADE RD
Slade Farm
Ottery St Mary Prim Sch
ST MARYS PK
HIGHER SPRING GDNS
GRANDISSON DR
KNIGHTSTONE LA
1 BROOKLAND TERR
2 SHERMAN HO
3 YONDER CNR
4 WESTON TERR
5 BROOKLANDS ORCH
6 PLUME OF FEATHERS CL
7 HOLLIS CL
8 BRIDGEFIELD
9 ST BUDEAUX ORCH
Liby
TH
THE COLLEGE
PATERNOSTER ROW
NEW ST
SANDHILL ST
SILVER ST
HIND ST
B3177
B3174
RALEIGH HO
MILL STREAM CT
PO
LONGDOGS LA
BROOK ST
SPRING CL
CHINEWAY GDNS
RICHARD CL
S BUDEAUX CL
YONDER ST
TIP HILL
CHURCH
FRANKLEA CL
WINTERS LA
TIMOSSOP CL
ST SAVIOURS RD
LITTLE CL
SMITH ST
CLAPPS LA
WINTERS CL
RIVERSIDE VIEW
ALBERT CL
OAK CL
HIGHLANDS
VIEW
BROADS CL
CLAREMONT FIELD
GERWAY CL
GERWAY LA
Gerway Farm
1 VICTORIA TERR
2 MILLCROFT
3 WINDRUSH RISE
4 SPENCER CT
OTTERY ST MARY
SIDMOUTH RD
Knightstone Cottage
KNIGHTSTONE LA
KNIGHTSTONE RD
Knightstone
Valley View

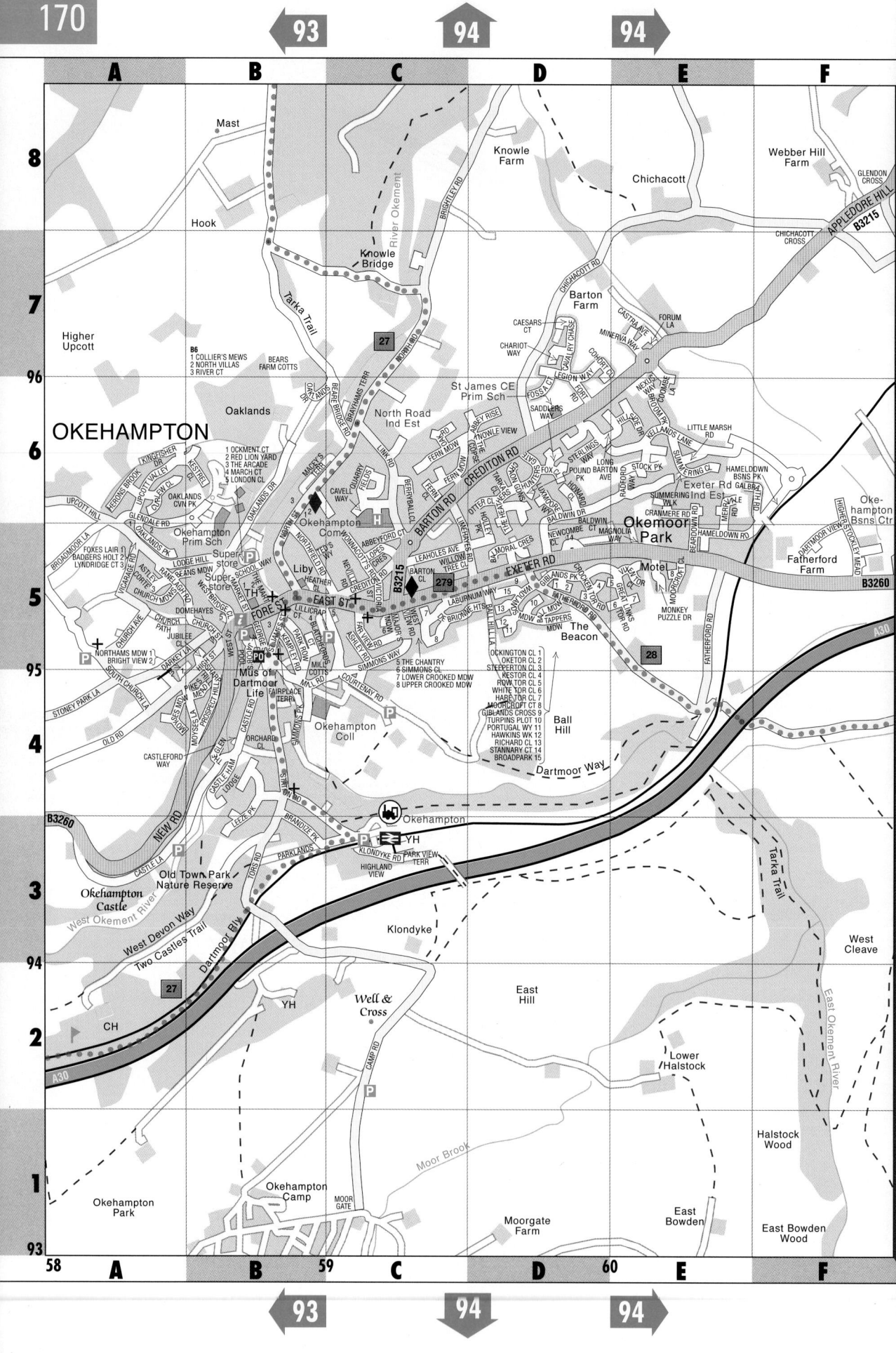
93
94
94
A
B
C
D
E
F
8
7
96
6
5
95
4
3
94
2
1
93
58
59
60
Mast
Hook
Knowle Farm
Chichacott
Webber Hill Farm
GLENDON CROSS
APPLEDORE HILL
B3215
CHICHACOTT CROSS
River Okement
BRIGHTLEY RD
Knowle Bridge
Tarka Trail
CHICHACOTT RD
Barton Farm
Higher Upcott
27
NORTH RD
CAESARS CT
CHARIOT WAY
CAVALRY CHASE
CASTRA AVE
FORUM LA
MINERVA WAY
COHORT CL
LEGION WAY
FORT RD
FOSSA CL
B6
1 COLLIER'S MEWS
2 NORTH VILLAS
3 RIVER CT
BEARS FARM COTTS
OAKLANDS DR
BEARE BRIDGE RD
BRAYHAMS TERR
St James CE Prim Sch
SADDLERS WAY
NEXUS WAY
BROOM PK
COOMBE LA
Oaklands
North Road Ind Est
LITTLE MARSH RD
KELLANDS LANE
OKEHAMPTON
ABBEY RISE
KNOWLE VIEW
HILLSIDE DR
STERLINGS WAY
LONG BARTON AVE
POUND PK
FOX CL
STOCK PK
SUMMERING CL
HAMELDOWN BSNS PK
CREDITON RD
1 OCKMENT CT
2 RED LION YARD
3 THE ARCADE
4 MARCH CT
5 LONDON CL
KINGFISHER DR
HERONS BROOK
UPCOTT VALLEY
CURLEW CL
KESTREL CL
OAKLANDS CVN PK
UPCOTT HILL
GLENDALE RD
OAKLANDS PK
Okehampton Prim Sch
MACEY'S TERR
QUARRY FIELDS
CAVELL WAY
LINK RD
BERRYBALL CL
FERN MDW
BARTON RD
OTTER CL
HOLLEY PK
THE HEATHERS
HUNTERS GATE
LUXMORE WAY
HOWARD CL
RADFORD WAY
Exeter Rd Ind Est
SUMMERING WLK
GALBRAITH RD
MERRIVALE
Oke-hampton Bsns Ctr
HIGHER STOCKLEY MEAD
DARTMOOR VIEW
Okehampton Com
H
WONNACOTTS RD
ABBEYFORD CT
LEAHOLES AVE
WILLOW TREE CL
LIMEHAYES RD
BALDWIN DR
NEWCOMBE CL
BALDWIN CT
MAGNOLIA WAY
Okemoor Park
CRANMERE RD
BEARDOWN RD
HAMELDOWN RD
BROADMOOR LA
FOXES LAIR 1
BADGERS HOLT 2
LYNDRIDGE CT 3
VICARAGE RD
ASTLEY CORTE
RANELAGH RD
LODGE HILL
BEANS MDW
Super-store
SCHOOL WAY
Liby
NORTHFIELD RD
TED'S WAY
LOPES CRES
BALMORAL CRES
EXETER RD
Motel
MOORCROFT CL
Fatherford Farm
B3260
CHURCH MDWS
WESTBRIDGE CL
TH
THE MARKET ST
HEATHER CL
NEVILLE RD
CREDITON RD
VICTORIA ST
B3215
BARTON CL
279
LABURNUM WAY
GIBLANDS PK
CROOKEN TOR RD
VIXEN TOR CL
GREAT LINKS TOR RD
MONKEY PUZZLE DR
FORE ST
EAST ST
LILLICRAP CT
BLATCHFORDS CT
DOMEHAYES
CHURCH RD
CHURCH PATH
JUBILEE CL
CHURCH AVE
WEST ST
GEORGE ST
ST JAMES ST
KEMPLEY RD
PARK ROW
ASHLEY RD
FAR VIEW RD
MAJOR'S MDW
WEST VIEW RD
BRIONNE HTS
BALL HILL LA
BALL MDW
TAPPERS MDW
The Beacon
FATHERFORD RD
FATHERFORD RD
A30
28
NORTHAMS MDW 1
BRIGHT VIEW 2
DARKEY LA
HIGH ST
MILL COTTS
SIMMONS WAY
5 THE CHANTRY
6 SIMMONS CL
7 LOWER CROOKED MDW
8 UPPER CROOKED MDW
OCKINGTON CL 1
OKETOR CL 2
STEEPERTON CL 3
KESTOR CL 4
ROW TOR CL 5
WHITE TOR CL 6
HARE TOR CL 7
MOORCROFT CT 8
GIBLANDS CROSS 9
TURPINS PLOT 10
PORTUGAL WY 11
HAWKINS WK 12
RICHARD CL 13
STANNARY CT 14
BROADPARK 15
STONEY PARK LA
SOUTH CHURCH LA
POOL
JACOB'S
PO
Mus of Dartmoor Life
MILL RD
COURTENAY RD
FAIRPLACE TERR
Okehampton Coll
Ball Hill
OLD RD
PIKES MEAD
PROSPECT HILL
MOYSES MDW
MOYSES LA
CASTLE RD
SIMMONS PK
ORCHARD CL
CASTLEFORD WAY
THE GLEN
CASTLE HAM
LODGE
Dartmoor Way
STATION RD
Okehampton
LEEZE PK
BRANDIZE PK
B3260
NEW RD
YH
PARKLANDS
KLONDYKE RD
PARK VIEW TERR
HIGHLAND VIEW
TORS RD
CASTLE LA
Old Town Park Nature Reserve
Okehampton Castle
West Okement River
West Devon Way
Two Castles Trail
Dartmoor Rly
Klondyke
Tarka Trail
West Cleave
East Hill
27
YH
Well & Cross
CH
East Okement River
Lower Halstock
CAMP RD
Halstock Wood
Moor Brook
Okehampton Camp
MOOR GATE
Okehampton Park
Moorgate Farm
East Bowden
East Bowden Wood
93
94
94

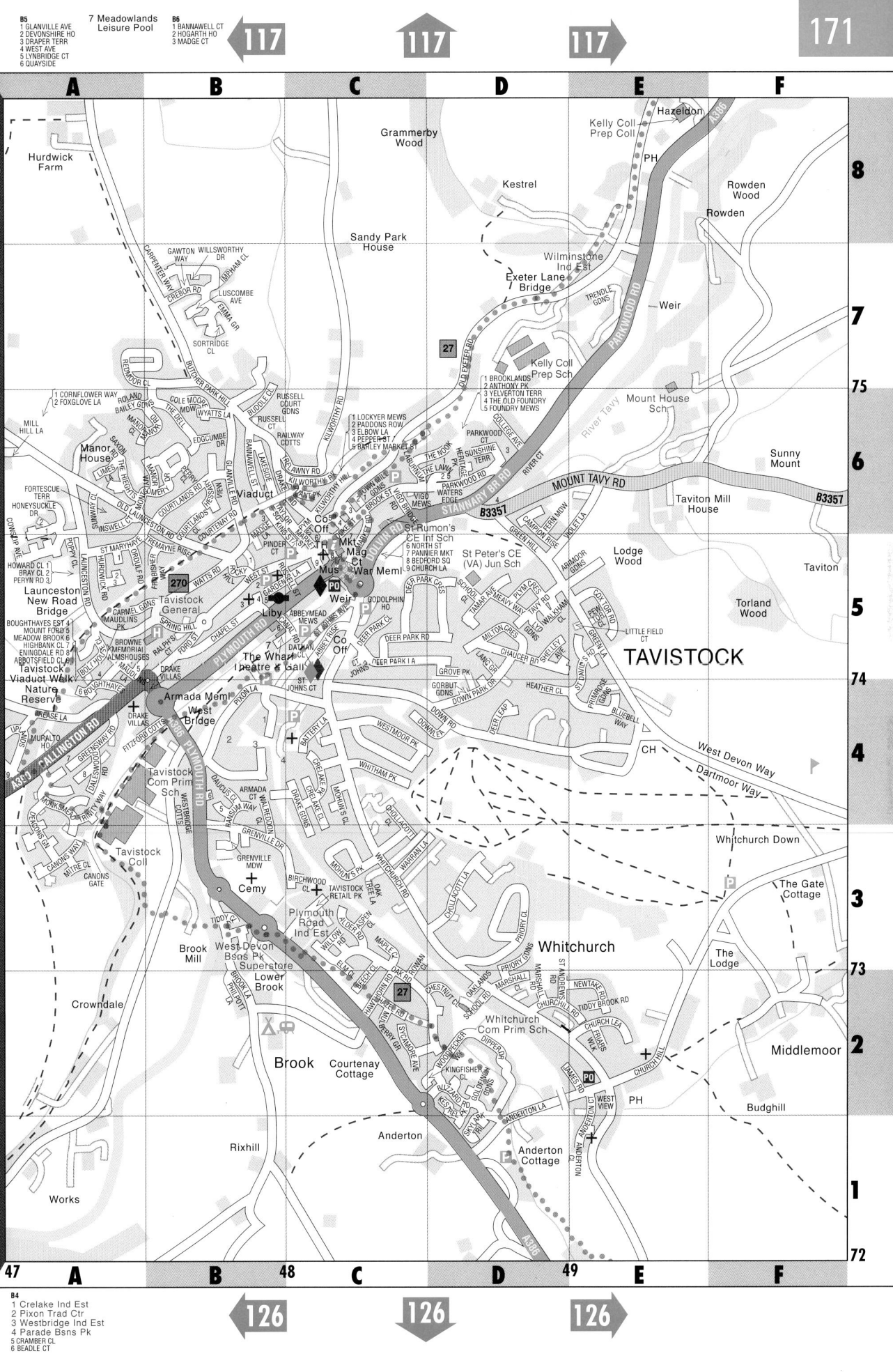

B5
1 GLANVILLE AVE
2 DEVONSHIRE HO
3 DRAPER TERR
4 WEST AVE
5 LYNBRIDGE CT
6 QUAYSIDE

7 Meadowlands
Leisure Pool

B6
1 BANNAWELL CT
2 HOGARTH HO
3 MADGE CT

117   117   117

B4
1 Crelake Ind Est
2 Pixon Trad Ctr
3 Westbridge Ind Est
4 Parade Bsns Pk
5 CRAMBER CL
6 BEADLE CT

126   126   126

98
81

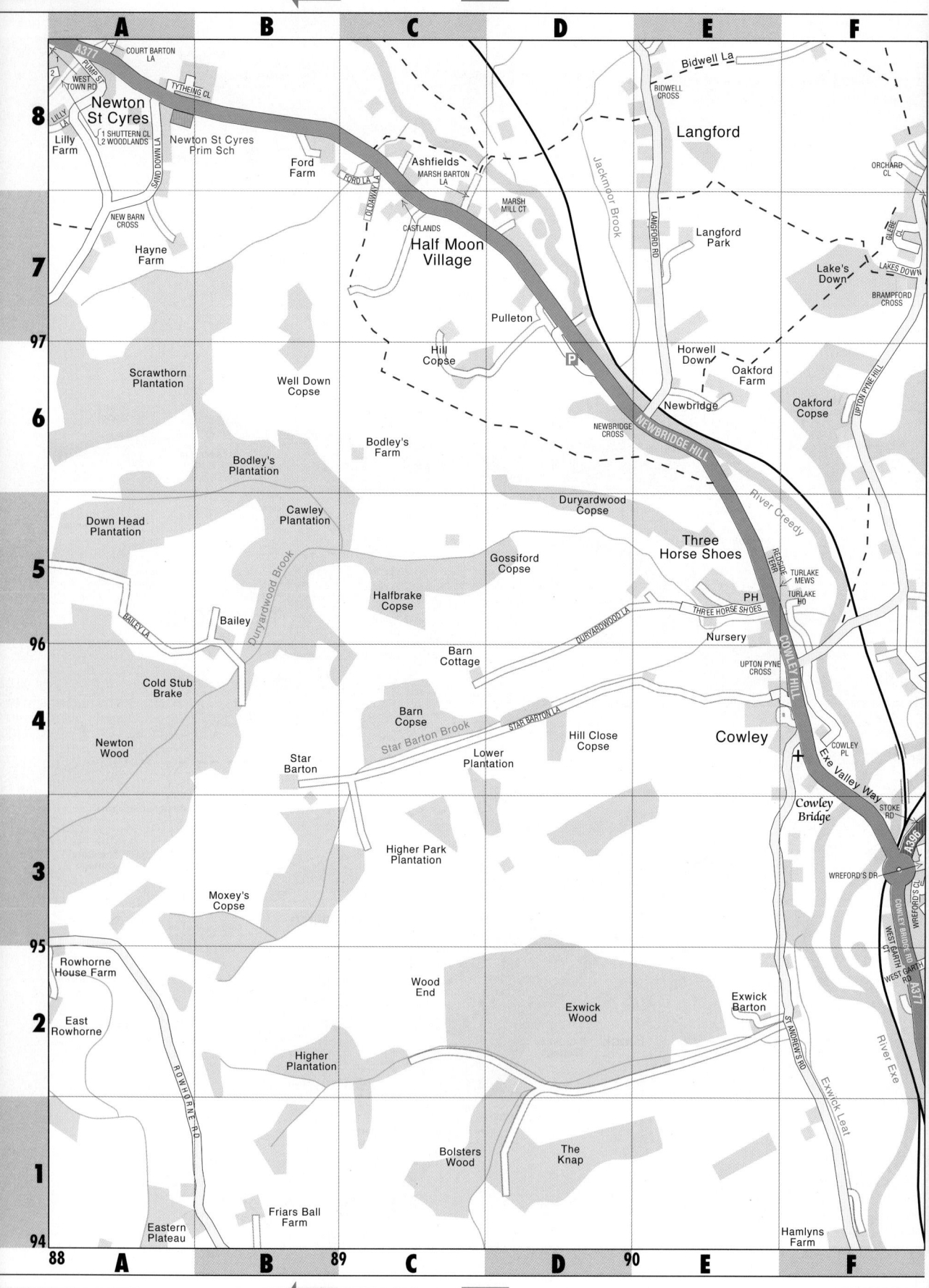
A
B
C
D
E
F
A377
COURT BARTON LA
PUMP ST
WEST TOWN RD
TYTHEING CL
Newton St Cyres
LILLY LA
1 SHUTTERN CL
2 WOODLANDS
Lilly Farm
Newton St Cyres Prim Sch
SAND DOWN LA
Ford Farm
FORD LA
OLDAWAY LA
Ashfields
MARSH BARTON LA
MARSH MILL CT
CASTLANDS
Half Moon Village
Bidwell La
BIDWELL CROSS
Langford
Jackmoor Brook
LANGFORD RD
Langford Park
ORCHARD CL
GLEBE CL
Lake's Down
LAKES DOWN
BRAMPFORD CROSS
NEW BARN CROSS
Hayne Farm
Pulleton
Hill Copse
Horwell Down
Oakford Farm
Newbridge
NEWBRIDGE CROSS
NEWBRIDGE HILL
UPTON PYNE HILL
Oakford Copse
Scrawthorn Plantation
Well Down Copse
Bodley's Farm
Bodley's Plantation
Cawley Plantation
Down Head Plantation
Duryardwood Copse
River Creedy
Three Horse Shoes
Gossiford Copse
REDSIDE TERR
TURLAKE MEWS
TURLAKE HO
PH
THREE HORSE SHOES
Halfbrake Copse
Duryardwood Brook
Bailey
BAILEY LA
DURYARDWOOD LA
Nursery
Barn Cottage
UPTON PYNE CROSS
COWLEY HILL
Cold Stub Brake
Barn Copse
Star Barton Brook
STAR BARTON LA
Hill Close Copse
Cowley
COWLEY PL
Newton Wood
Star Barton
Lower Plantation
Exe Valley Way
Cowley Bridge
STOKE RD
A396
Higher Park Plantation
WREFORD'S DR
WREFORD'S CL
Moxey's Copse
COWLEY BRIDGE RD
WEST GARTH CT
WEST GARTH RD
A377
Rowhorne House Farm
Wood End
Exwick Wood
Exwick Barton
East Rowhorne
ST ANDREW'S RD
River Exe
Higher Plantation
ROWHORNE RD
Exwick Leat
Bolsters Wood
The Knap
Friars Ball Farm
Eastern Plateau
Hamlyns Farm
8
7
97
6
5
96
4
3
95
2
1
94
88
89
90

98
176

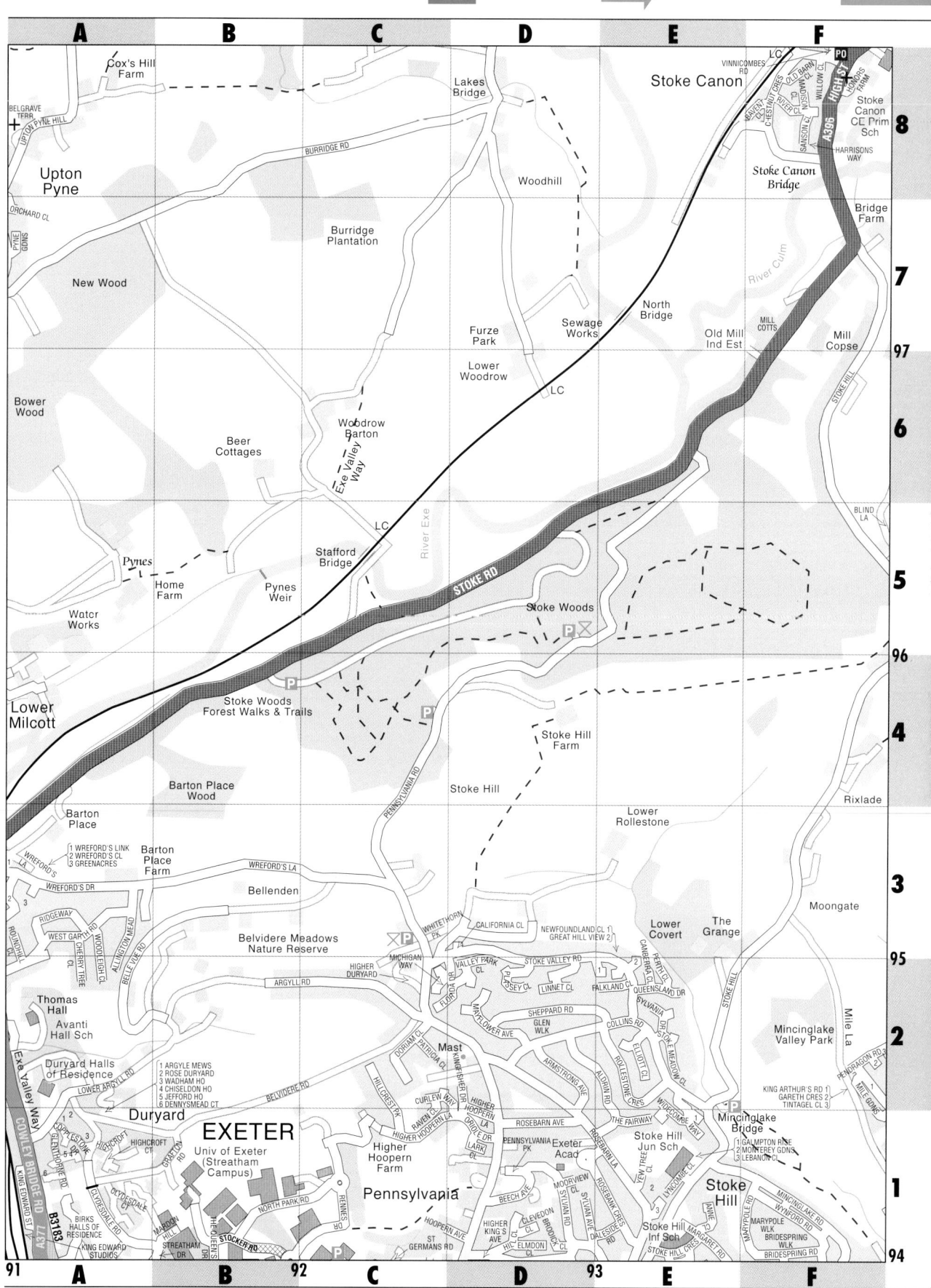
Cox's Hill Farm
Lakes Bridge
Stoke Canon
Upton Pyne
BURRIDGE RD
Woodhill
Stoke Canon CE Prim Sch
Stoke Canon Bridge
Bridge Farm
Burridge Plantation
New Wood
River Culm
North Bridge
Sewage Works
Furze Park
Old Mill Ind Est
Mill Copse
Lower Woodrow
Bower Wood
Woodrow Barton
Beer Cottages
Exe Valley Way
River Exe
Stafford Bridge
Pynes
Home Farm
Pynes Weir
STOKE RD
Water Works
Stoke Woods
Stoke Woods Forest Walks & Trails
Lower Milcott
Stoke Hill Farm
Barton Place Wood
Stoke Hill
PENNSYLVANIA RD
Barton Place
Lower Rollestone
Rixlade
Barton Place Farm
WREFORD'S LA
Bellenden
Moongate
Lower Covert
The Grange
Belvidere Meadows Nature Reserve
ARGYLL RD
Thomas Hall
Avanti Hall Sch
Mincinglake Valley Park
Mile La
Duryard Halls of Residence
Mast
Duryard
EXETER
Univ of Exeter (Streatham Campus)
Higher Hoopern Farm
Exeter Acad
Stoke Hill Jun Sch
Mincinglake Bridge
Pennsylvania
Stoke Hill
Stoke Hill Inf Sch
BIRKS HALLS OF RESIDENCE
COWLEY BRIDGE RD
A377
B3183
A396
HIGH ST

173
82

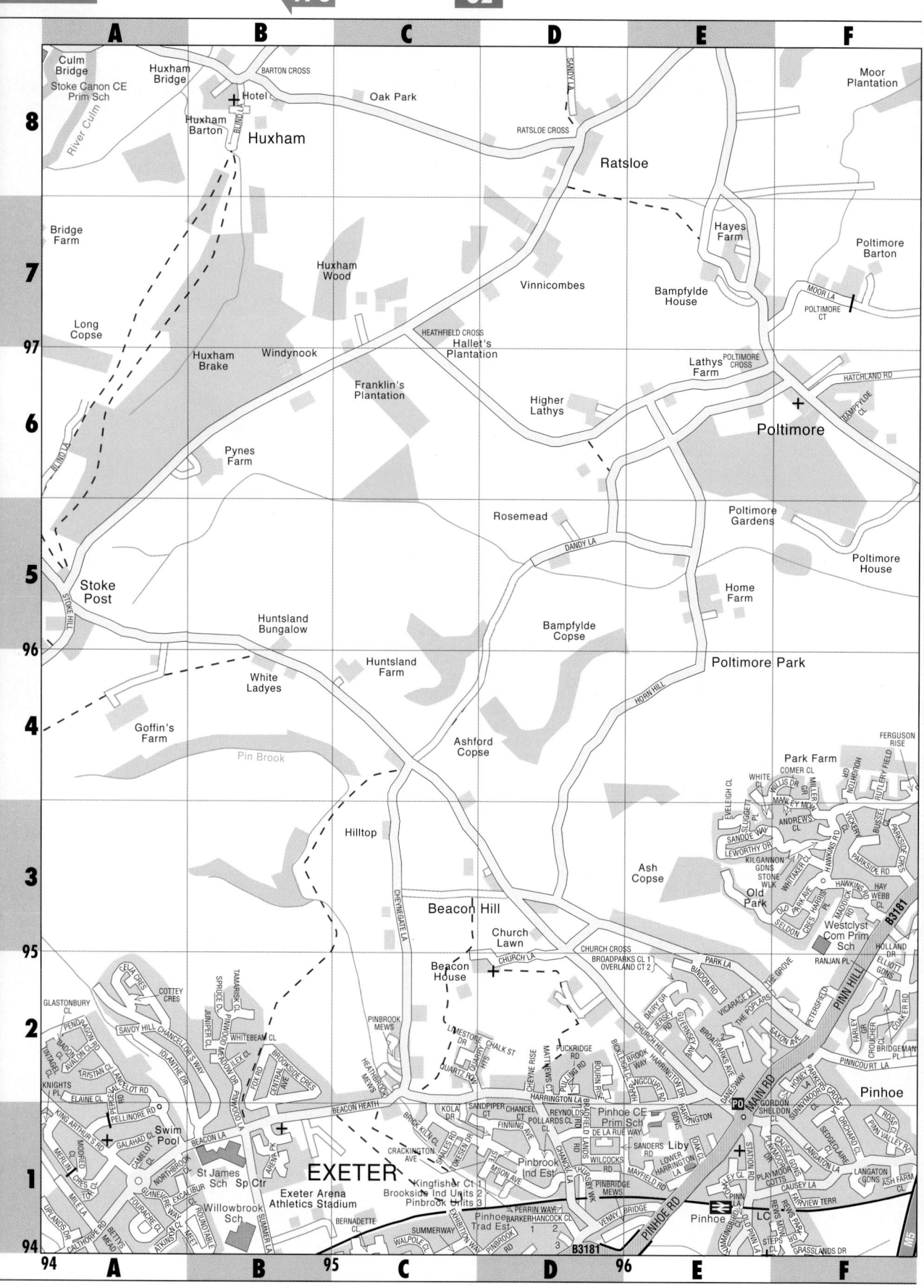
Culm Bridge
Stoke Canon CE Prim Sch
Huxham Bridge
BARTON CROSS
Hotel
Oak Park
Huxham Barton
Huxham
River Culm
RATSLOE CROSS
Ratsloe
Moor Plantation
Bridge Farm
Huxham Wood
Hayes Farm
Poltimore Barton
Vinnicombes
Bampfylde House
MOOR LA
POLTIMORE CT
Long Copse
HEATHFIELD CROSS
Hallet's Plantation
Huxham Brake
Windynook
Lathys Farm
POLTIMORE CROSS
HATCHLAND RD
Franklin's Plantation
Higher Lathys
BAMPFYLDE CL
Poltimore
Pynes Farm
BLIND LA
Rosemead
Poltimore Gardens
DANDY LA
Poltimore House
Stoke Post
Home Farm
STOKE HILL
Huntsland Bungalow
Bampfylde Copse
Huntsland Farm
Poltimore Park
White Ladyes
HORN HILL
Goffin's Farm
Ashford Copse
FERGUSON RISE
Pin Brook
Park Farm
Hilltop
Ash Copse
Beacon Hill
Old Park
Westclyst Com Prim Sch
Church Lawn
CHURCH CROSS
Beacon House
CHURCH LA
PARK LA
PINN HILL
B3181
EXETER
Exeter Arena Athletics Stadium
St James Sch
Sp Ctr
Swim Pool
Willowbrook Sch
Pinhoe CE Prim Sch
Pinbrook Ind Est
Pinhoe Trad Est
Kingfisher Ct 1
Brookside Ind Units 2
Pinbrook Units 3
Liby
Pinhoe
PINHOE RD
MAIN RD
M5
BEACON HEATH
BEACON LA
HARRINGTON LA
CHEYNEGATE LA
GLASTONBURY CL
COTTEY CRES
CELIA CRES
SAVOY HILL
CHANCELLOR'S WAY
IOLANTHE DR
PINWOOD LA
FOX RD
BROOKSIDE CRES
CENTRAL AVE
PINBROOK MEWS
HEATHBROOK MEWS
LIMESTONE DR
CHALK ST
QUARTZ RD
CHEYNE RISE
MATTHEWS CT
PUCKRIDGE RD
PULLING RD
BOURN RISE
BICKLEIGH CL
BRADFIELD LANDS
CHURCH HILL
HARRINGTON DR
DAIRY GR
JERSEY RD
GUERNSEY AVE
BINDON RD
VICARAGE LA
THE POPLARS
THE GROVE
BROADPARKS AVE
PETERSFIELD
SAXON AVE
DANESWAY
STATION RD
PINNCOURT LA
BRIDGEMAN PL
SUMMERWAY
WALPOLE CL
EXHIBITION WAY
PERRIN WAY
PINBRIDGE MEWS
VENNY BRIDGE
GRASSLANDS DR
ELAINE CL
KNIGHTS PL
KING ARTHUR'S RD
MERLIN CRES
MILE LA
UPLANDS DR
CALTHORPE RD
BETTYS MEAD
ATKINSON CL
FOURACRE CL
GALAHAD CL
PELLINORE RD
CAMELOT CL
NORTHBROOK CL
EXCALIBUR CL
ROUNDTABLE MEET
SUMMER LA
ARENA PK
BERNADETTE CL
CRACKINGTON AVE
SANDPIPER CT
CHANCEL CT
FINNING AVE
POLLARDS CL
REYNOLDS CL
KOLA DR
DE LA RUE WAY
SANDERS RD
WILCOCKS RD
LOWER HARRINGTON LA
MAYFIELD RD
OAK CL
HANCOCK CL
BARKER
PINHOE RD
B3181
94
95
96

173
178

A   B   C   D   E   F

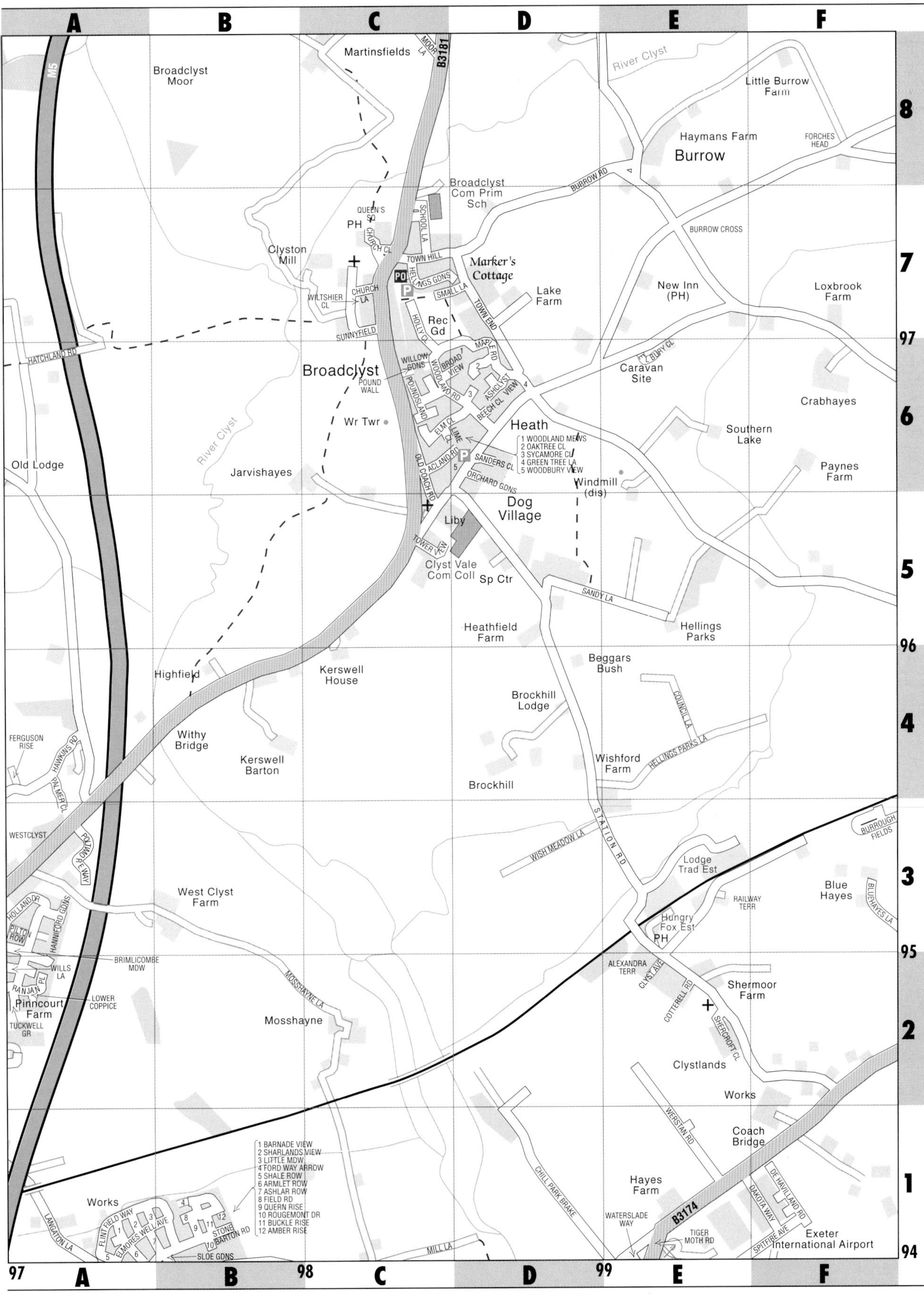

8
Martinsfields
Broadclyst
Moor
River Clyst
Little Burrow
Farm
Haymans Farm
Burrow
FORCHES
HEAD

7
QUEEN'S
SQ
PH
Clyston
Mill
CHURCH CL
SCHOOL LA
Broadclyst
Com Prim
Sch
BURROW RD
BURROW CROSS
Marker's
Cottage
New Inn
(PH)
Loxbrook
Farm

97
WILTSHIER
CL
CHURCH
LA
PO P
TOWN HILL
HOLLIES GDNS
SMALL LA
Lake
Farm
FT. BURY CL
Caravan
Site

6
HATCHLAND RD
SUNNYFIELD
Broadclyst
POUND
WALL
Wr Twr
Jarvishayes
River Clyst
WILLOW
GDNS
WOODLAND RD
BROAD
VIEW
MARSH RD
ASHCLYST
BEECH CL VIEW
Heath
1 WOODLAND MEWS
2 OAKTREE CL
3 SYCAMORE CL
4 GREEN TREE LA
5 WOODBURY VIEW
Crabhayes
Southern
Lake
Paynes
Farm

Old Lodge
ELM CL
LNK
OLD COACH RD
P
SANDERS CL
ORCHARD GDNS
Windmill
(dis)
Dog
Village

5
TOWER VW
Liby
Clyst Vale
Com Coll
Sp Ctr
SANDY LA
Hellings
Parks

96
Heathfield
Farm
Beggars
Bush

4
FERGUSON
RISE
Highfield
Kerswell
House
Brockhill
Lodge
Wishford
Farm
HELLINGS PARKS LA
COUNCIL LA

HAWKINS RD
PALMER CL
Withy
Bridge
Kerswell
Barton
Brockhill
STATION RD
BURROUGH
FIELDS

WESTCLYST
POWDERHAM WAY
West Clyst
Farm
Lodge
Trad Est
RAILWAY
TERR
Blue
Hayes
BLUEHAYES LA

3
HOLLAND DR
HANNIFORD GDNS
PILTON
ROW
BRIMLICOMBE
MDW
Hungry
Fox Est
PH

95
WILLS
LA
RANJAN
LOWER
COPPICE
Mosshayne
MOSSHAYNE LA
ALEXANDRA
TERR
CLYST AVE
Shermoor
Farm
COTTERELL RD
SHERGROFT CL

2
Pinncourt
Farm
TUCKWELL
GR
Clystlands
Works
WENSUM RD
Coach
Bridge
DE HAVILLAND RD

1
Works
LANGATON LA
FLINTFIELD WAY
ELMORES WELL AVE
STONE
BARTON RD
SLOE GDNS
1 BARNADE VIEW
2 SHARLANDS VIEW
3 LITTLE MDW
4 FORD WAY ARROW
5 SHALE ROW
6 ARMLET ROW
7 ASHLAR ROW
8 FIELD RD
9 QUERN RISE
10 ROUGEMONT DR
11 BUCKLE RISE
12 AMBER RISE
CHILL PARK BRAKE
MILL LA
Hayes
Farm
WATERSLADE
WAY
B3174
TIGER
MOTH RD
DAKOTA WAY
SPITFIRE AVE
Exeter
International Airport

94
97   A   98   B   C   98   D   99   E   F

98
172

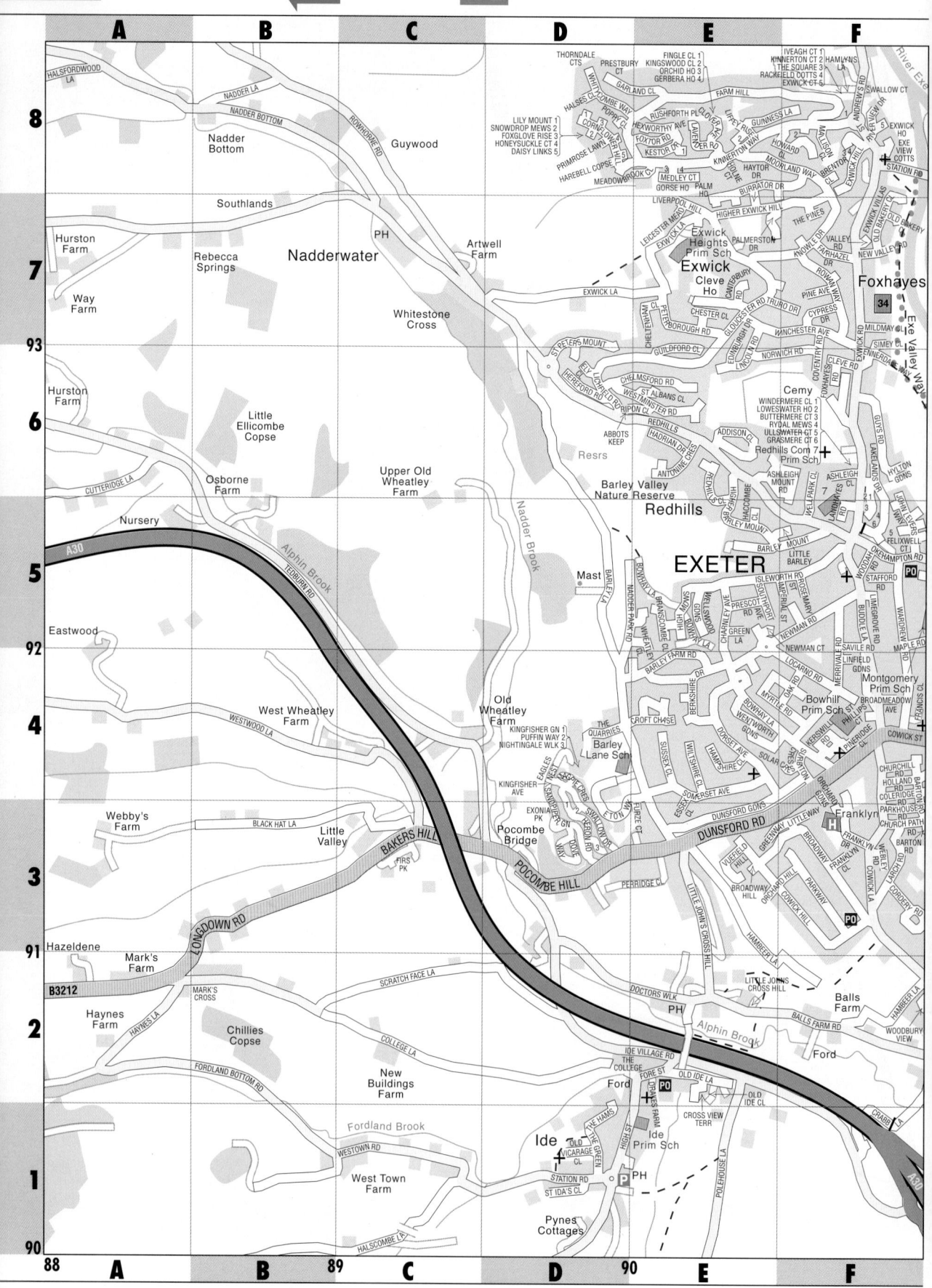
A
B
C
D
E
F
8
7
93
6
5
92
4
3
91
2
1
90
88
89
90
River Exe
HALSFORDWOOD LA
NADDER LA
NADDER BOTTOM
Nadder Bottom
ROWHORNE RD
Guywood
Southlands
PH
Hurston Farm
Rebecca Springs
Nadderwater
Artwell Farm
Way Farm
Whitestone Cross
Hurston Farm
Little Ellicombe Copse
Upper Old Wheatley Farm
Osborne Farm
CUTTERIDGE LA
Nursery
A30
Alphin Brook
TEDBURN RD
Nadder Brook
Mast
Eastwood
West Wheatley Farm
WESTWOOD LA
Old Wheatley Farm
Webby's Farm
BLACK HAT LA
Little Valley
BAKERS HILL
FIRS PK
POCOMBE HILL
Pocombe Bridge
LONGDOWN RD
Hazeldene
Mark's Farm
B3212
MARK'S CROSS
SCRATCH FACE LA
Haynes Farm
HAYNES LA
Chillies Copse
COLLEGE LA
FORDLAND BOTTOM RD
New Buildings Farm
Fordland Brook
WESTOWN RD
West Town Farm
HALSCOMBE LA
Pynes Cottages
Ide
Ide Prim Sch
Ford
FORE ST
OLD IDE LA
OLD IDE CL
CROSS VIEW TERR
IDE VILLAGE RD
THE COLLEGE
DRAKES FARM
HIGH ST
THE HAMS
THE GREEN
OLD VICARAGE CL
STATION RD
ST IDA'S CL
POLEHOUSE LA
DOCTORS WLK
Alphin Brook
BALLS FARM RD
Balls Farm
Ford
WOODBURY VIEW
HAMBEER LA
CRABB LA
LITTLE JOHNS CROSS HILL
LITTLE JOHN'S CROSS HILL
HAMBEER LA
THORNDALE CTS
PRESTBURY CT
FINGLE CL 1
KINGSWOOD CL 2
ORCHID HO 3
GERBERA HO 4
IVEAGH CT 1
KINNERTON CT 2
THE SQUARE 3
RACKFIELD COTTS 4
EXWICK CT 5
HAMLYNS LA
SWALLOW CT
GARLAND CL
FARM HILL
RUSHFORTH PL
GUINNESS LA
LILY MOUNT 1
SNOWDROP MEWS 2
FOXGLOVE RISE 3
HONEYSUCKLE CT 4
DAISY LINKS 5
PRIMROSE LAWN
HAREBELL COPSE
MEADOWBROOK CL
MEDLEY CT
GORSE HO
PALM HO
KESTOR DR
FOXTOR RD
HEXWORTHY AVE
KINNERTON WAY
HAYTOR DR
BURRATOR DR
MOORLAND WAY
HOWARD CL
MALLISON CL
BRENTOR CL
EXWICK HILL
RIVER VIEW DR
EXWICK HO
EXE VIEW COTTS
STATION RD
LIVERPOOL HILL
HIGHER EXWICK HILL
THE PINES
LEICESTER MEAD
EXWICK LA
Exwick Heights Prim Sch
Exwick
PALMERSTON DR
KNOWLE DR
VALLEY RD
FAIRHAZEL DR
NEW VALLEY RD
OLD BAKERY CL
EXWICK VILLAS
Foxhayes
34
Cleve Ho
CANTERBURY RD
TRURO DR
PINE AVE
ROWAN WAY
CYPRESS DR
EXWICK LA
CHESTER CL
PETERBOROUGH RD
CHELTENHAM CL
GLOUCESTER RD
WINCHESTER AVE
MILDMAY CL
SIMEY CL
Exe Valley Way
ENNERDALE WAY
ST PETERS MOUNT
GUILDFORD CL
EDINBURGH DR
LINCOLN RD
NORWICH RD
COVENTRY RD
FOXHAYES RD
CLEVE RD
EXWICK RD
ELY CL
HEREFORD RD
LICHFIELD RD
CHELMSFORD RD
ST ALBANS CL
WESTMINSTER RD
RIPON CL
Cemy
WINDERMERE CL 1
LOWESWATER HO 2
BUTTERMERE CT 3
RYDAL MEWS 4
ULLSWATER CT 5
GRASMERE CT 6
ABBOTS KEEP
REDHILLS
HADRIAN DR
ADDISON CL
Redhills Com Prim Sch
Resrs
ANTONINE CRES
GUYS RD
LAKELANDS DR
HYLTON GDNS
ASHLEIGH MOUNT RD
ASHLEIGH CL
WELL PARK CL
LANDHAYES RD
Barley Valley Nature Reserve
Redhills
HIGHER BARLEY MOUNT
HACCOMBE CL
BARLEY MOUNT
LITTLE BARLEY
FELIXWELL CT
OKEHAMPTON RD
WOODAH RD
STAFFORD RD
EXETER
PO
BARLEY LA
BOWHAY LA
NADDER PARK RD
ISLEWORTH RD
ROSEMARY ST
PRESCOT RD
SOUTHPORT AVE
IMPERIAL ST
WELLSWOOD GDNS
CHARNLEY AVE
GREEN LA
NEWMAN RD
NEWMAN CT
BUDDLE LA
LIMEGROVE RD
WARDREW RD
SAVILE RD
MAPLE RD
LINFIELD GDNS
MERRIVALE RD
BRANSCOMBE CL
WHEATLEY CL
BARLEY FARM RD
BERKSHIRE DR
LOCARNO RD
MYRTLE RD
OAK RD
Montgomery Prim Sch
Bowhill Prim Sch
BROADMEADOW AVE
ST PHILLIPS CT
FRANCIS CL
COWICK ST
CROFT CHASE
BOWHAY LA
WENTWORTH GDNS
KERSWILL RD
PINERIDGE CL
THE QUARRIES
Barley Lane Sch
KINGFISHER GN 1
PUFFIN WAY 2
NIGHTINGALE WLK 3
SUSSEX CL
WILTSHIRE CL
DORSET AVE
HAMPSHIRE CL
SOLAR CRES
SIDMOUTH RD
KINGFISHER AVE
EAGLES NEST
SANDPIPER GN
MAGPIE CRES
EXONIA PK
SWALLOW DR
HERON RD
DOVE WAY
ETON WLK
FURZE CT
SOMERSET AVE
ESSEX CL
DUNSFORD GDNS
DUNSFORD RD
ORCHARD GDNS
CHURCHILL RD
HOLLAND RD
COLERIDGE RD
BARTON RD
PARKHOUSE RD
CHURCH PATH RD
Franklyn
LITTLEWAY
GREENWAY
BROADWAY
FRANKLYN DR
FRANKLYN CL
WEBLEY RD
COWICK LA
BARTON RD
LARCH RD
VUEFIELD HILL
BROADWAY HILL
ORCHARD HILL
PARKWAY
COWICK HILL
CORDERY RD
PERRIDGE CL
A30

98
114

173
178

A5
1 EMMANUEL CL
2 EMMANUEL RD
3 LANDSCORE RD
4 CAMBRIDGE ST
5 CORNWALL ST
6 CLARENCE RD

7 CLEVELAND ST
8 OKEHAMPTON PL
9 PRINCESS ALEXANDRA CT
10 SWAN MAISONETTES
11 Montgomery
  Prim Sch

D8
1 VICTORIA RD
2 WILLOW WLK
3 NEW BLDGS
4 BRIDGE COTTS
5 ROSEWOOD TERR
6 ALMSHOUSES

E7
1 WATERMORE CT
2 PROSPECT GDNS
3 SYDENHAM HO
4 NICHOLS WY

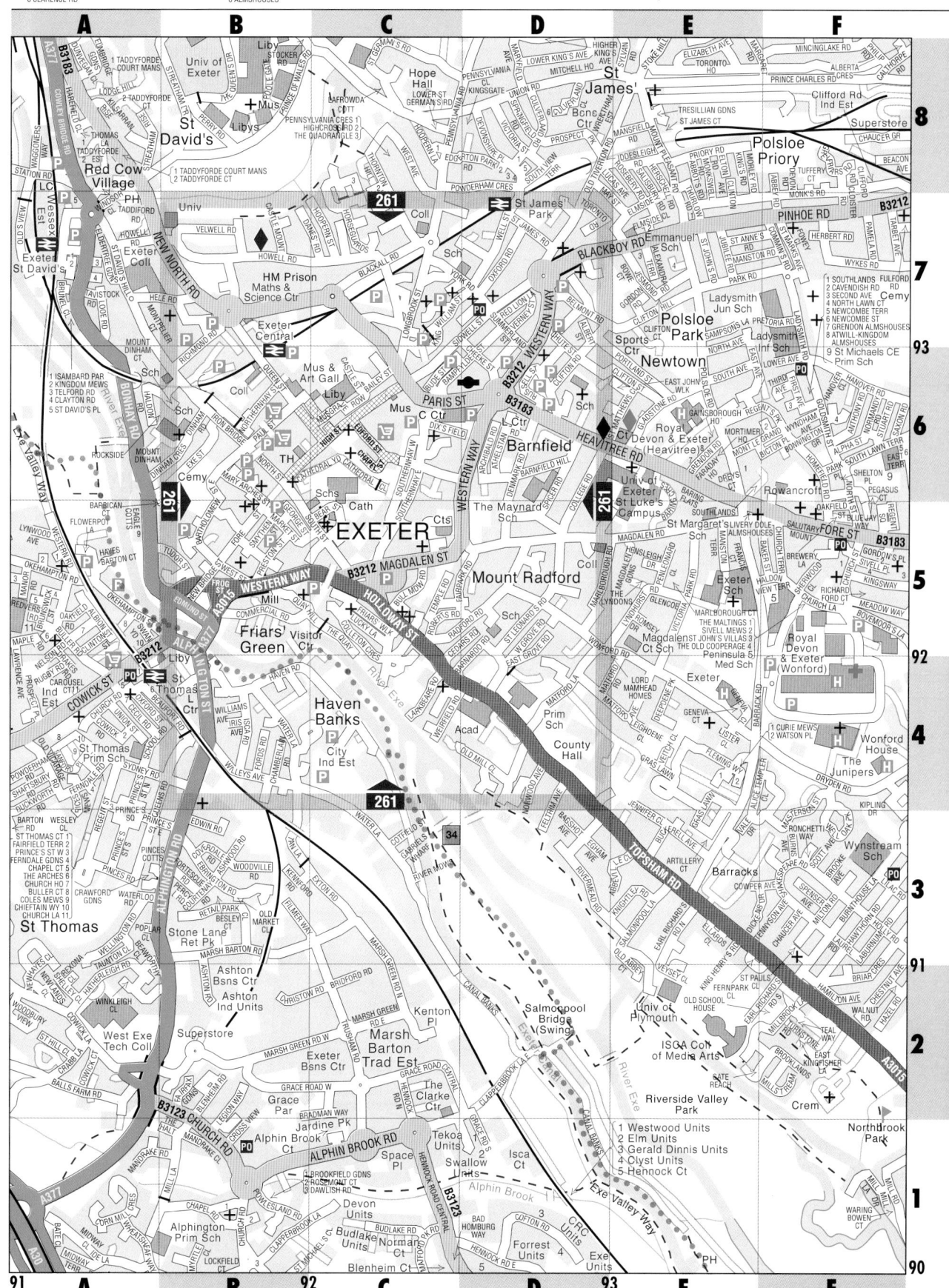

For full street detail of the highlighted area see page 261.

177
174

C8
1 MARK TWAIN HO
2 FLAYES ALMSHOUSES
3 PEEL ROW
4 ROYSTON CT
5 THE SEASONS
6 WILLOWBROOK AVE

7 MARGARET CT

E8
1 HARTS CL
2 MONKERTON CT
3 BAZLEY SQ
4 HILL TOP RD
5 VICTORIA RD
6 POLTIMORE DR

7 PINNBRIDGE CT
8 DENARIUS RD
9 SOLIDUS RD

F8
1 TITHEBARN LA
2 BATTLE ABBEY WAY
3 WHEAT BELT RISE
4 GRAMBEL RISE
5 ST NICHOLAS CL
6 CROOK COPSE

7 NURSERY GDNS

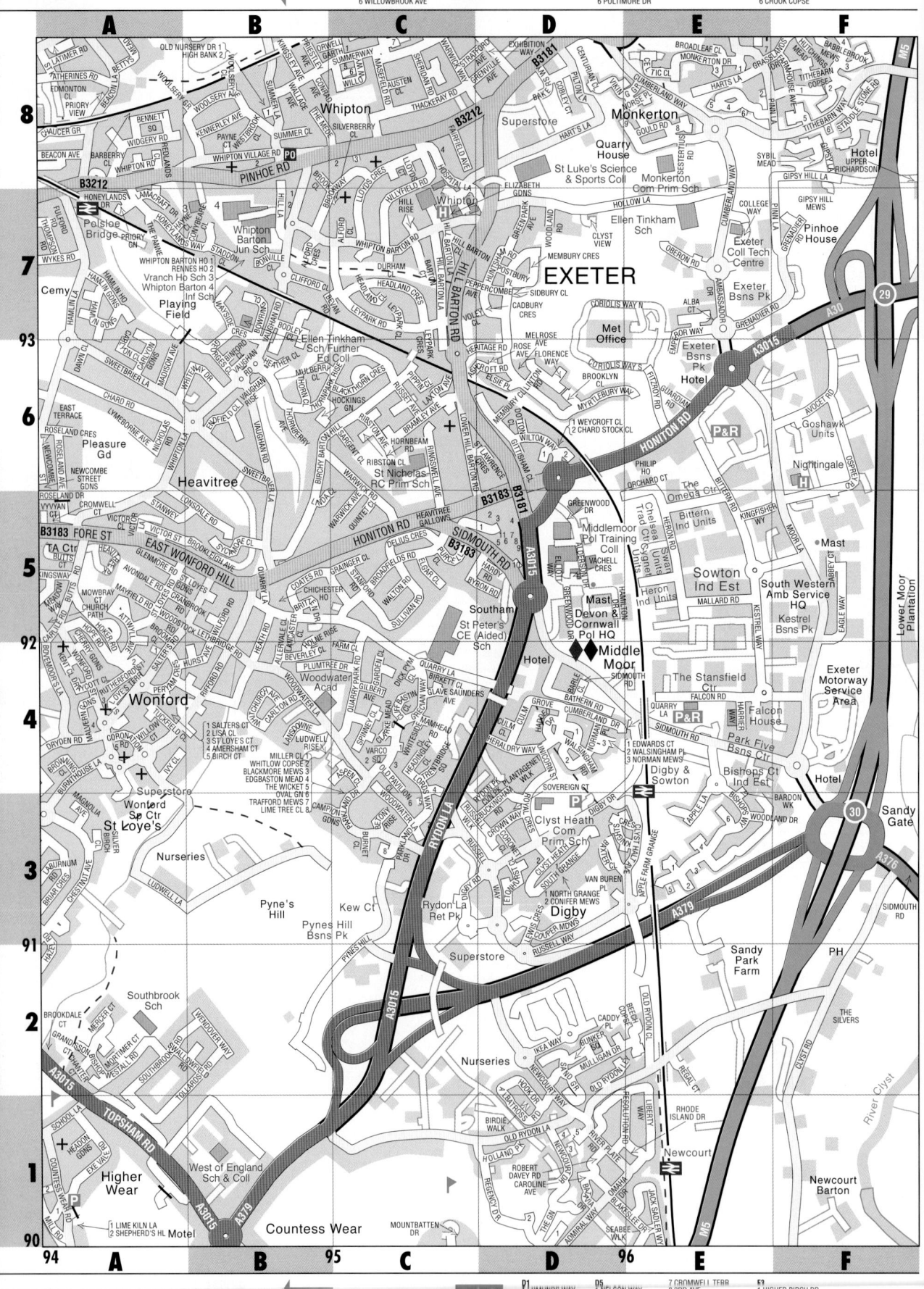

D1
1 EDMUNDS WAY
2 CATHERINES CL
3 MONTAGU CL
4 DUKES WLK
5 JUTLAND WAY

D5
1 NELSON WAY
2 WELLINGTON CL
3 THE SQUARE
4 ALEXANDER WLK
5 DRAKE AVE
6 MONTGOMERY RD

7 CROMWELL TERR
8 3RD AVE
9 MARLBOROUGH DR
10 BADGER CL
11 RINGSWELL PK

F3
1 HIGHER BIRCH DR
2 BRIDGE VIEW CL
3 BISHOPS VIEW
4 SANDY VIEW
5 ORCH CRES
6 SANDSTONE CL

175
99

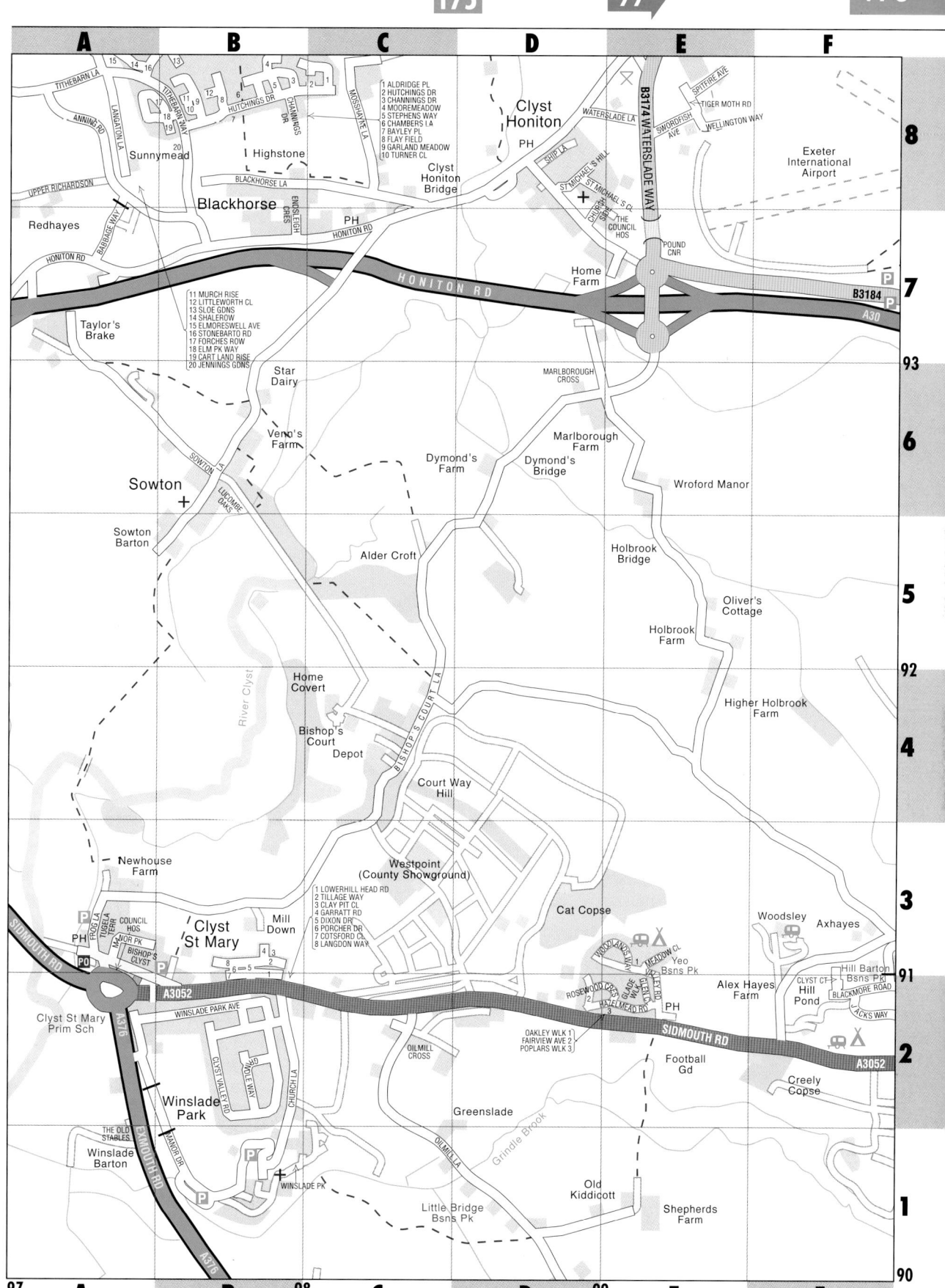
Clyst Honiton
Exeter International Airport
Sunnymead
Highstone
Blackhorse
Redhayes
Clyst Honiton Bridge
HONITON RD
B3174 WATERSLADE WAY
B3184
A30
Home Farm
POUND CNR
Taylor's Brake
Star Dairy
MARLBOROUGH CROSS
Marlborough Farm
Venn's Farm
Dymond's Farm
Dymond's Bridge
Wroford Manor
Sowton
Sowton Barton
Alder Croft
Holbrook Bridge
Oliver's Cottage
Holbrook Farm
Home Covert
Bishop's Court
Depot
Higher Holbrook Farm
Court Way Hill
Westpoint (County Showground)
Newhouse Farm
Clyst St Mary
Mill Down
Cat Copse
Woodsley
Axhayes
Yeo Bsns Pk
Alex Hayes Farm
Hill Barton Bsns Pk
Hill Pond
SIDMOUTH RD
A3052
Clyst St Mary Prim Sch
Winslade Park
Winslade Barton
OILMILL CROSS
Football Gd
Creely Copse
Greenslade
Grindle Brook
Old Kiddicott
Shepherds Farm
Little Bridge Bsns Pk
EXMOUTH RD
A376
River Clyst
1 ALDRIDGE PL
2 HUTCHINGS DR
3 CHANNINGS DR
4 MOOREMEADOW
5 STEPHENS WAY
6 CHAMBERS LA
7 BAYLEY PL
8 FLAY FIELD
9 GARLAND MEADOW
10 TURNER CL
11 MURCH RISE
12 LITTLEWORTH CL
13 SLOE GDNS
14 SHALEROW
15 ELMORESWELL AVE
16 STONEBARTO RD
17 FORCHES ROW
18 ELM PK WAY
19 CART LAND RISE
20 JENNINGS GDNS
1 LOWERHILL HEAD RD
2 TILLAGE WAY
3 CLAY PIT CL
4 GARRATT RD
5 DIXON DR
6 PORCHER DR
7 COTSFORD CL
8 LANGDON WAY
OAKLEY WLK 1
FAIRVIEW AVE 2
POPLARS WLK 3
97
98
99
90
91
92
93

183
99

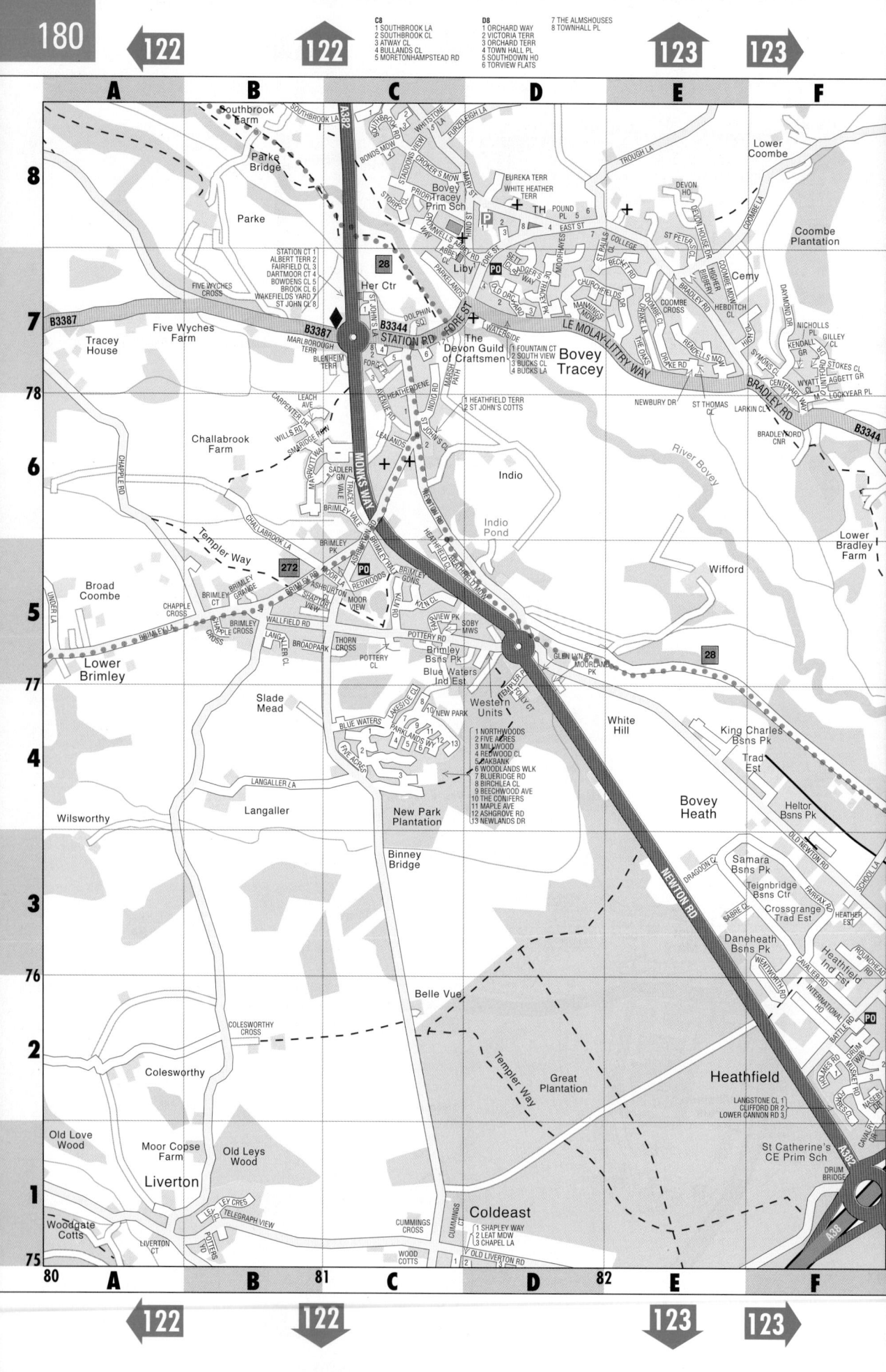
122
122
C8
1 SOUTHBROOK LA
2 SOUTHBROOK CL
3 ATWAY CL
4 BULLANDS CL
5 MORETONHAMPSTEAD RD
D8
1 ORCHARD WAY
2 VICTORIA TERR
3 ORCHARD TERR
4 TOWN HALL PL
5 SOUTHDOWN HO
6 TORVIEW FLATS
7 THE ALMSHOUSES
8 TOWNHALL PL
123
123
A
B
C
D
E
F
8
7
78
6
5
77
4
3
76
2
1
75
80
81
82
Southbrook Farm
Parke Bridge
Parke
Lower Coombe
Coombe Plantation
Bovey Tracey Prim Sch
EUREKA TERR
WHITE HEATHER TERR
POUND PL
TH
EAST ST
Liby
Her Ctr
Cemy
STATION CT 1
ALBERT TERR 2
FAIRFIELD CL 3
DARTMOOR CT 4
BOWDENS CL 5
BROOK CL 6
WAKEFIELDS YARD 7
ST JOHN CL 8
FIVE WYCHES CROSS
B3387
Tracey House
Five Wyches Farm
MARLBOROUGH TERR
BLENHEIM TERR
STATION RD
B3344
The Devon Guild of Craftsmen
1 FOUNTAIN CT
2 SOUTH VIEW
3 BUCKS CL
4 BUCKS LA
Bovey Tracey
LE MOLAY-LITTRY WAY
BRADLEY RD
NEWBURY DR
ST THOMAS CL
LARKIN CL
BRADLEYFORD CNR
1 HEATHFIELD TERR
2 ST JOHN'S COTTS
Challabrook Farm
MONKS WAY
Indio
Indio Pond
River Bovey
Lower Bradley Farm
Templer Way
Wifford
Broad Coombe
CHAPPLE CROSS
Lower Brimley
BRIMLEY BSNS PK
Blue Waters Ind Est
GLEN LYN PK
MOORLAND PK
Slade Mead
Western Units
White Hill
King Charles Bsns Pk
Trad Est
1 NORTHWOODS
2 FIVE ACRES
3 MILLWOOD
4 REDWOOD CL
5 OAKBANK
6 WOODLANDS WLK
7 BLUERIDGE RD
8 BIRCHLEA CL
9 BEECHWOOD AVE
10 THE CONIFERS
11 MAPLE AVE
12 ASHGROVE RD
13 NEWLANDS DR
LANGALLER LA
Wilsworthy
Langaller
New Park Plantation
Bovey Heath
Heltor Bsns Pk
Binney Bridge
NEWTON RD
Samara Bsns Pk
Teignbridge Bsns Ctr
Crossgrange Trad Est
Daneheath Bsns Pk
Heathfield Ind Est
Belle Vue
COLESWORTHY CROSS
Colesworthy
Great Plantation
Heathfield
LANGSTONE CL 1
CLIFFORD DR 2
LOWER CANNON RD 3
Old Love Wood
Moor Copse Farm
Old Leys Wood
Liverton
St Catherine's CE Prim Sch
DRUM BRIDGE
A382
A38
Woodgate Cotts
TELEGRAPH VIEW
CUMMINGS CROSS
Coldeast
1 SHAPLEY WAY
2 LEAT MDW
3 CHAPEL LA
WOOD COTTS
OLD LIVERTON RD
122
122
123
123

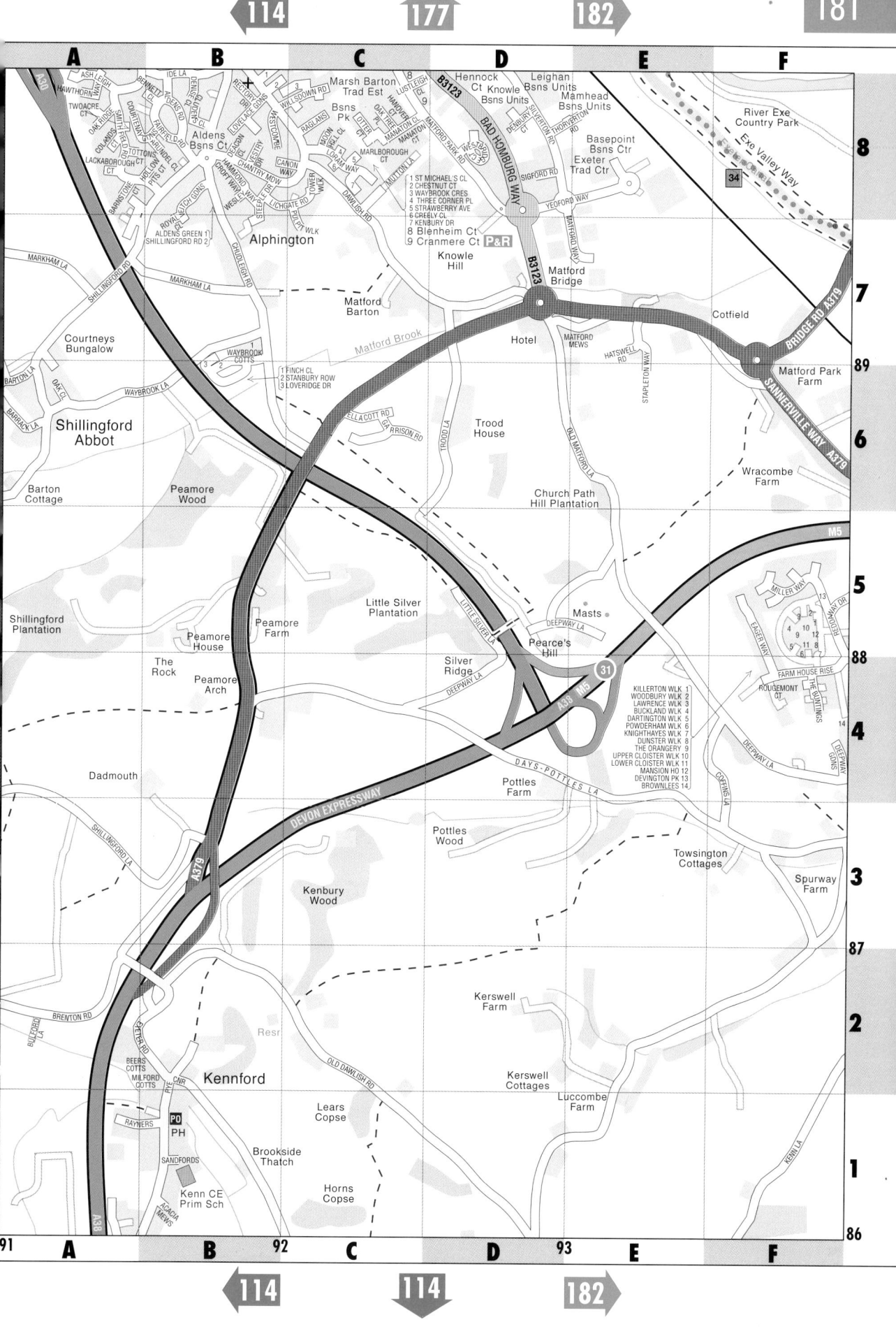

A   B   C   D   E   F

8

Marsh Barton Trad Est

Hennock Ct
Knowle Leighan Bsns Units
Mamhead Bsns Units

River Exe Country Park

Exe Valley Way

34

Bsns Pk

Aldens Bsns Ct

Basepoint Bsns Ctr
Exeter Trad Ctr

Marlborough Ct

1 ST MICHAEL'S CL
2 CHESTNUT CT
3 WAYBROOK CRES
4 THREE CORNER PL
5 STRAWBERRY AVE
6 CREELY CL
7 KENBURY DR
8 BLENHEIM CT
9 CRANMERE CT

P&R

Alphington

ALDENS GREEN 1
SHILLINGFORD RD 2

Knowle Hill

Matford Bridge

7

MARKHAM LA

Courtneys Bungalow

Matford Barton

Matford Brook

Hotel

Matford Mews

Cotfield

BRIDGE RD A379

Matford Park Farm

89

1 FINCH CL
2 STANBURY ROW
3 LOVERIDGE DR

WAYBROOK LA

HATSWELL RD

SANNERVILLE WAY A379

Trood House

Shillingford Abbot

GARRISON RD

Trood La

STAPLETON WAY

Old Matford La

6

Barton Cottage

Peamore Wood

Church Path Hill Plantation

Wracombe Farm

Shillingford Plantation

Peamore House

Little Silver Plantation

M5

5

The Rock

Peamore Farm

Peamore Arch

Little Silver La

Masts

Deepway La

MILLER WAY

88

Dadmouth

Silver Ridge

Pearce's Hill

Deepway La

31

A38 M5

KILLERTON WLK 1
WOODBURY WLK 2
LAWRENCE WLK 3
BUCKLAND WLK 4
DARTINGTON WLK 5
POWDERHAM WLK 6
KNIGHTHAYES WLK 7
DUNSTER WLK 8
THE ORANGERY 9
UPPER CLOISTER WLK 10
LOWER CLOISTER WLK 11
MANSION HO 12
DEVINGTON PK 13
BROWNLEES 14

ROUGEMONT CT

THE BUNTINGS

FARM HOUSE RISE

EAGER WAY

DEEPWAY GDNS

4

DAYS-POTTLES LA

Pottles Farm

Towsington Cottages

COFFINS LA

Spurway Farm

3

DEVON EXPRESSWAY

A379

Pottles Wood

87

Kenbury Wood

SHILLINGFORD LA

2

BRENTON RD

Resr

OLD DAWLISH RD

Kerswell Farm

KENN LA

BULLFORD LA

BEERS COTTS
MILFORD COTTS

EXETER RD

PYE CNR

Kennford

Kerswell Cottages

Luccombe Farm

1

RAYNERS

PO PH

SANDFORDS

Lears Copse

Brookside Thatch

Horns Copse

A38

Kenn CE Prim Sch

ACACIA MEWS

86

181
178

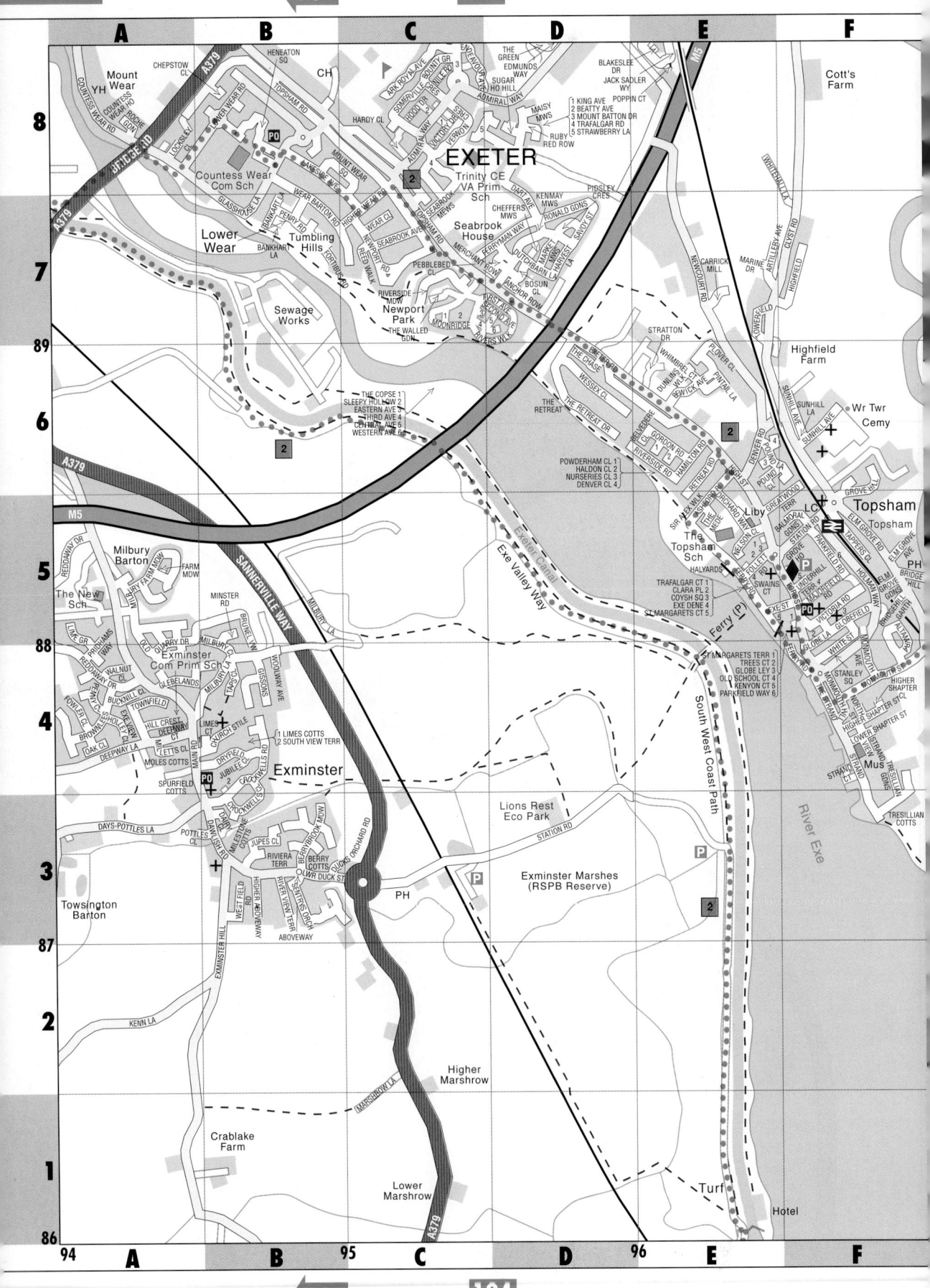
EXETER
Topsham
Exminster
Mount Wear
Countess Wear Com Sch
Lower Wear
Tumbling Hills
Sewage Works
Newport Park
Trinity CE VA Prim Sch
Seabrook House
Highfield Farm
Cott's Farm
Wr Twr
Cemy
The Topsham Sch
Milbury Barton
The New Sch
Exminster Com Prim Sch
Lions Rest Eco Park
Exminster Marshes (RSPB Reserve)
Towsington Barton
Higher Marshrow
Crablake Farm
Lower Marshrow
Turf
Hotel
South West Coast Path
Exe Valley Way
Exeter Canal
River Exe
SANNERVILLE WAY
A379
M5

181
194

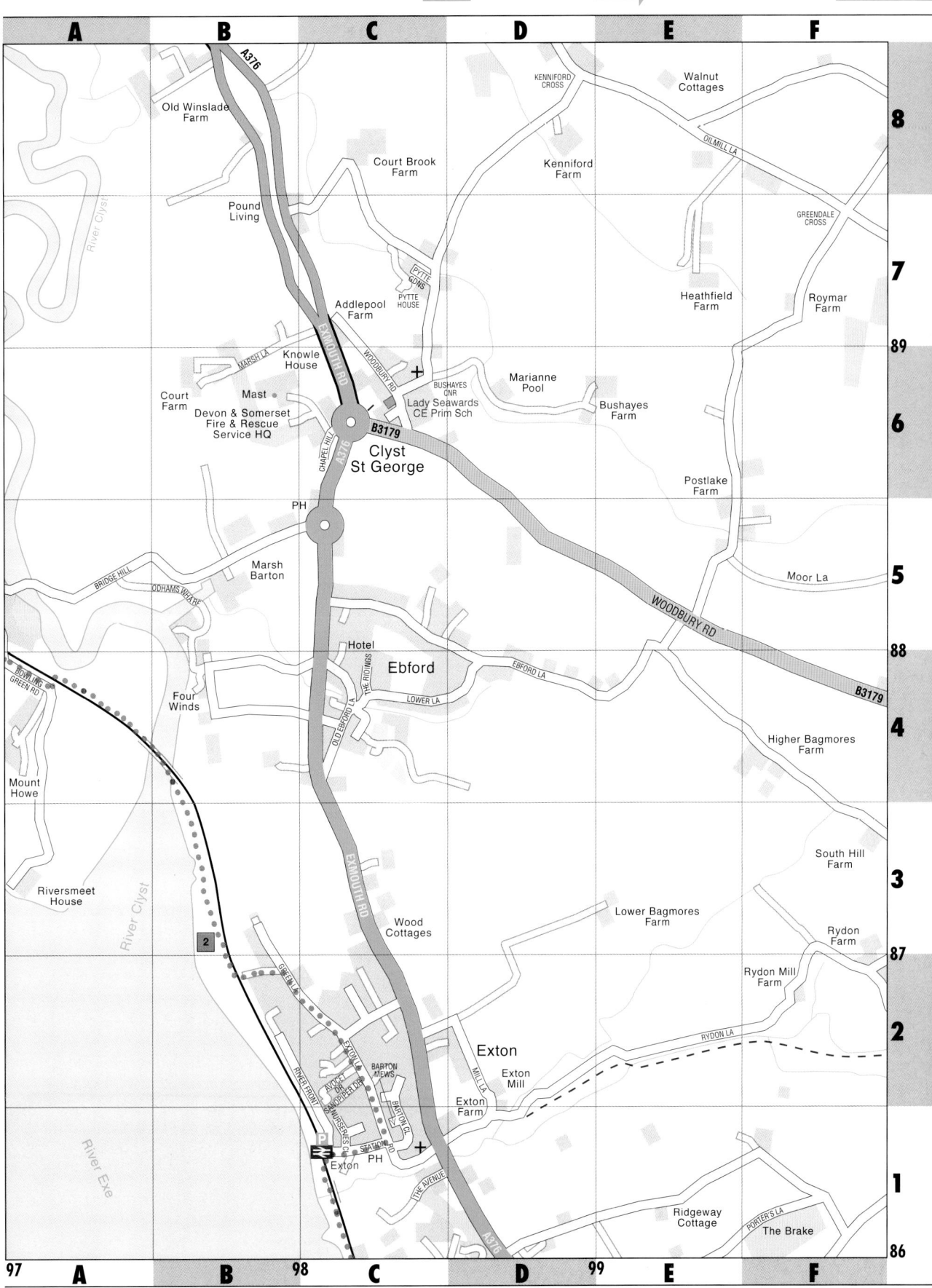
A
B
C
D
E
F
8
7
89
6
5
88
4
3
87
2
1
86
97
98
99
A376
Old Winslade Farm
Court Brook Farm
Kenniford Cross
Walnut Cottages
Oilmill La
Kenniford Farm
Pound Living
River Clyst
Greendale Cross
Pytte Gdns
Pytte House
Addlepool Farm
Heathfield Farm
Roymar Farm
Marsh La
Knowle House
Exmouth Rd
Woodbury Rd
Bushayes Cnr
Marianne Pool
Court Farm
Mast
Lady Seawards CE Prim Sch
Bushayes Farm
Devon & Somerset Fire & Rescue Service HQ
B3179
Chapel Hill
Clyst St George
Postlake Farm
PH
Marsh Barton
Moor La
Bridge Hill
Odhams Wharf
Woodbury Rd
Hotel
Ebford
Ebford La
The Ridings
Lower La
B3179
Bowling Green Rd
Four Winds
Old Ebford La
Higher Bagmores Farm
Mount Howe
Exmouth Rd
South Hill Farm
Riversmeet House
River Clyst
Wood Cottages
Lower Bagmores Farm
Rydon Farm
2
Green La
Rydon Mill Farm
Rydon La
Exton La
Barton Mews
Exton
River Front
Avocet Dr
Sandpiper Dr
Exton Mill
Mill La
Exton Farm
Barton Cl
Nursery Cl
Station Rd
P
PH
Exton
River Exe
The Avenue
Ridgeway Cottage
Porter's La
The Brake
A376

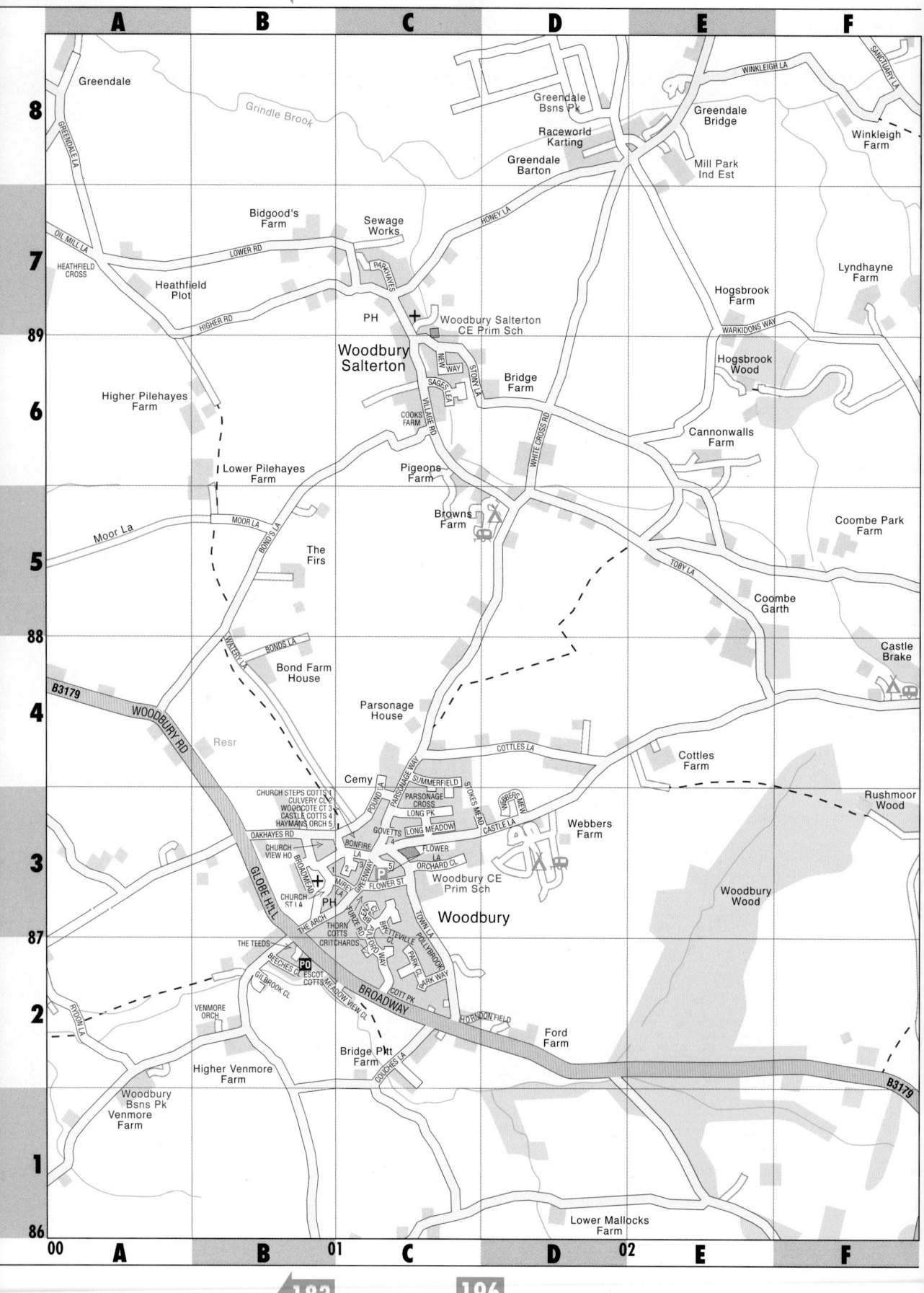

A   B   C   D   E   F

8

7

89

6

5

88

4

3

87

2

1

86

00   A   B   01   C   D   02   E   F

Greendale

Grindle Brook

Greendale Bsns Pk

Raceworld Karting

Greendale Barton

Greendale Bridge

Mill Park Ind Est

WINKLEIGH LA

Winkleigh Farm

SANCTUARY LA

Oil Mill La

GREENDALE LA

Bidgood's Farm

Sewage Works

LOWER RD

HIGHER RD

HONEY LA

PARKHAYES

PH

Woodbury Salterton CE Prim Sch

Woodbury Salterton

NEW WAY

SAGES LEA

STONY LA

VILLAGE RD

COOKS FARM

Bridge Farm

WHITE CROSS RD

Hogsbrook Farm

WARKIDONS WAY

Hogsbrook Wood

Lyndhayne Farm

Heathfield Cross

Heathfield Plot

Higher Pilehayes Farm

Lower Pilehayes Farm

MOOR LA

BOND'S LA

Moor La

The Firs

Pigeons Farm

Browns Farm

Cannonwalls Farm

TOBY LA

Coombe Park Farm

Coombe Garth

WATER LA

BONDS LA

Bond Farm House

Parsonage House

B3179

WOODBURY RD

Resr

Castle Brake

Rushmoor Wood

Cemy

COTTLES LA

Cottles Farm

PASSAGE WAY

SUMMERFIELD

Parsonage Cross

STOKES MEAD

HARPERS VIEW

Webbers Farm

CASTLE LA

Woodbury Wood

Church Steps Cotts 1
Culvery Cl 2
Woodcote Ct 3
Castle Cotts 4
Haymans Orch 5

POUND LA

LONG PK

GOVETTS

LONG MEADOW

Oakhayes Rd

Church View Ho

BONFIRE LA

GREENWAY

MIRE'S LA

FLOWER ST

FLOWER LA

ORCHARD CL

Woodbury CE Prim Sch

GLOBE HILL

BROADMEAD

CHURCH ST 1 4

PH

THE ARCH

THORN COTTS

PURZE RD

BETTEVILLE WAY

TOWN LA

ANTONY WAY

Woodbury

The Teeds

CRITCHARDS

PO

BEECHES CL

ESCOT COTTS

GILBROOK CL

MEADOW VIEW CL

POLLYBROOK

PARK LA

PARK PK

CARK WAY

BROADWAY

ECOTT CL

HORNDON FIELD

Ford Farm

B3179

Venmore Orch

PYDON LA

Higher Venmore Farm

Bridge Platt Farm

COUCHES LA

Woodbury Bsns Pk
Venmore Farm

Lower Mallocks Farm

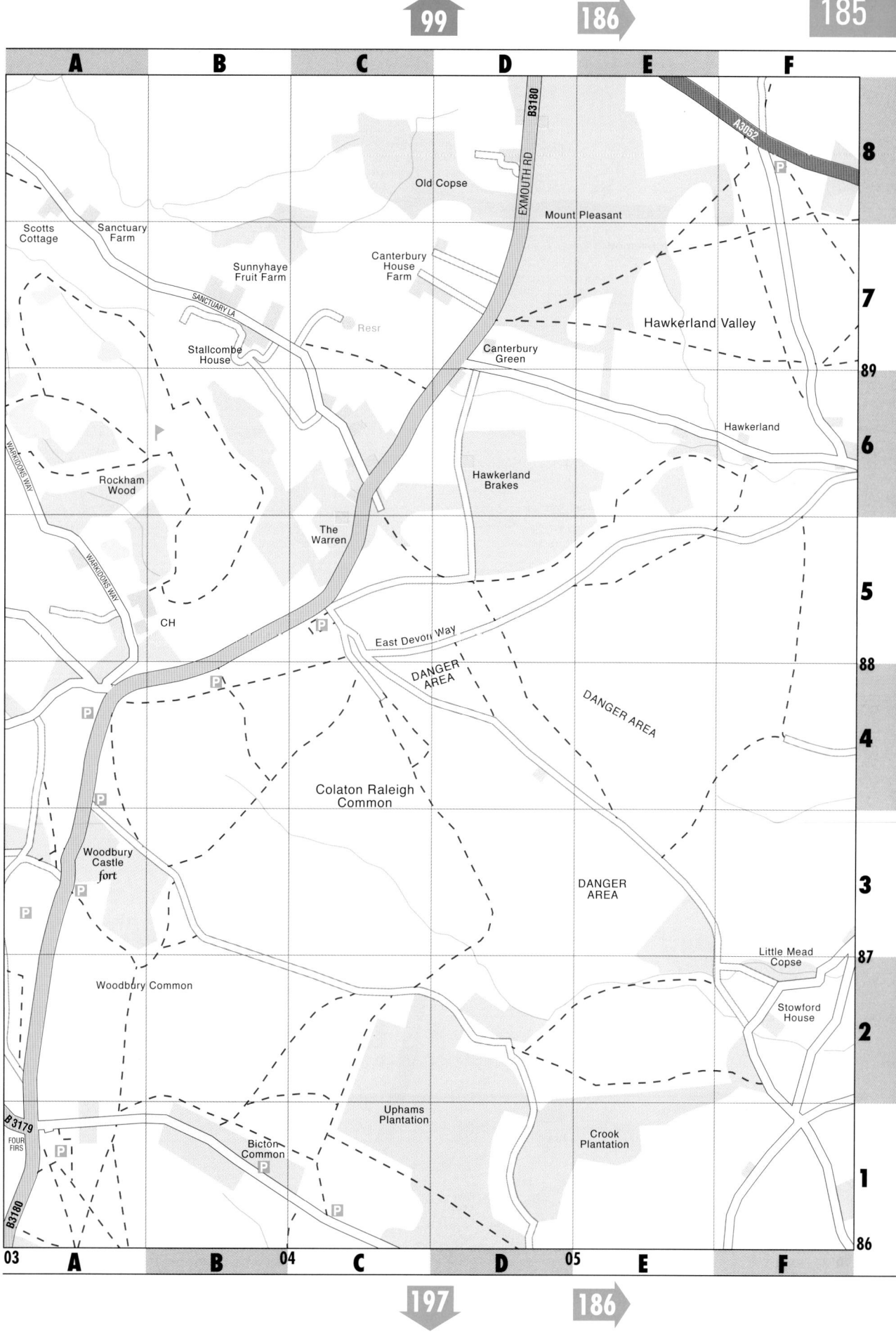

A B C D E F

B3180

EXMOUTH RD

A3052

Old Copse

Mount Pleasant

Scotts
Cottage

Sanctuary
Farm

Sunnyhaye
Fruit Farm

Canterbury
House
Farm

SANCTUARY LA

Resr

Stallcombe
House

Canterbury
Green

Hawkerland Valley

WARNDONS WAY

Hawkerland

Rockham
Wood

Hawkerland
Brakes

The
Warren

CH

East Devon Way

DANGER
AREA

DANGER AREA

Colaton Raleigh
Common

DANGER
AREA

Little Mead
Copse

Woodbury
Castle
fort

Stowford
House

Woodbury Common

B 3179

FOUR
FIRS

Uphams
Plantation

Crook
Plantation

Bicton
Common

B3180

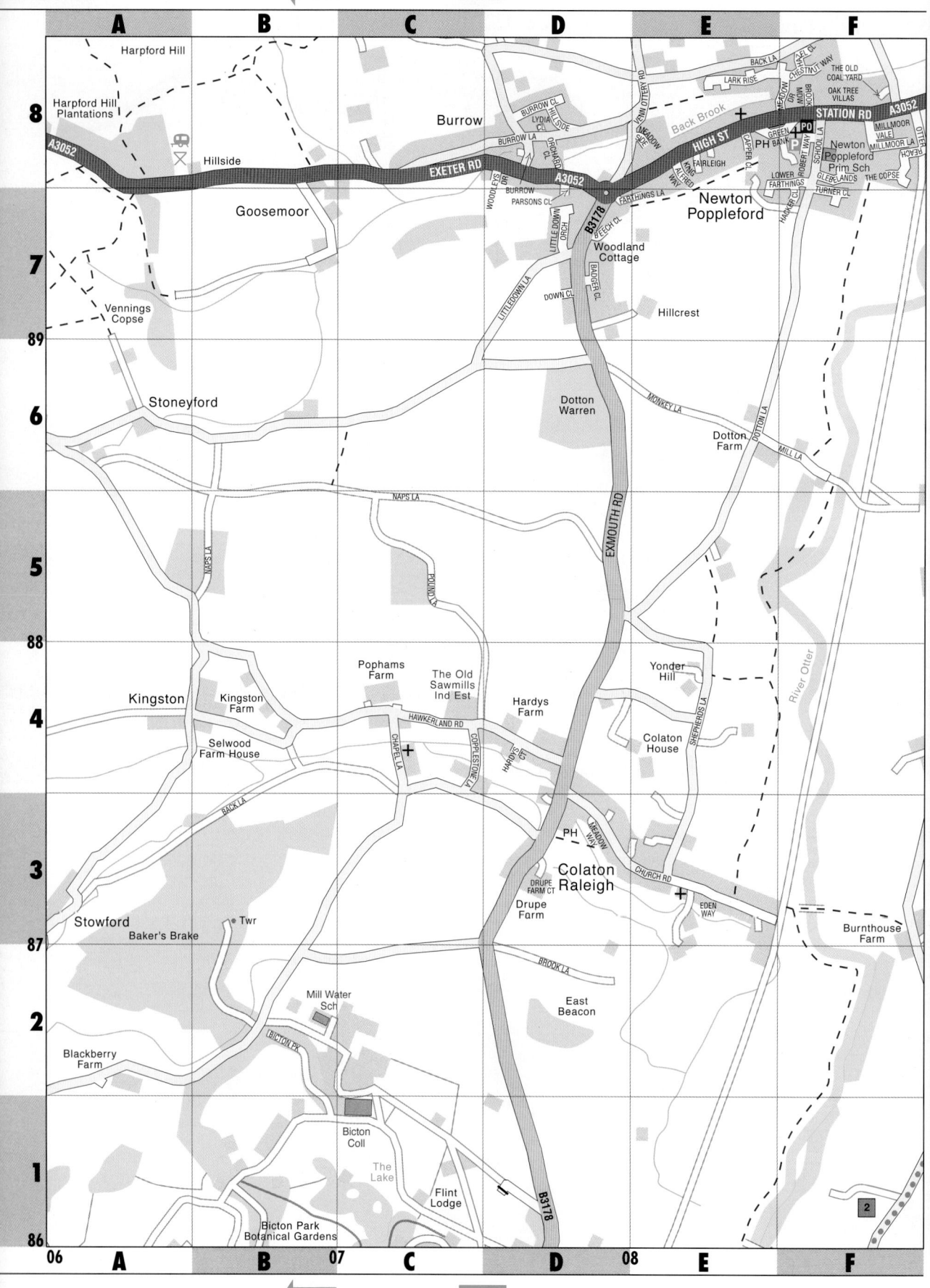

Harpford Hill

Harpford Hill Plantations

Hillside

Burrow

BURROW CL
LYDIA CL
BURROW LA
ORCHARD CL
WOODLEYS DR
BURROW PARSONS CL

Goosemoor

EXETER RD

A3052

LITTLE DOWN ORCH

LITTLEDOWN LA

DOWN CL

BADGER CL

BACK LA
LARK RISE
CHESTNUT WAY
CHAPEL CL
BROOK MDW
THE OLD COAL YARD

OAK TREE VILLAS

STATION RD
A3052

MILLMOOR VALE
MILLMOOR LA
THE COPSE
REACH

HIGH ST
VENN OTTERY RD
MEADOW RI
KING ALFRED WAY
FAIRLEIGH
PH
GREEN BANK
CAPPER CL
LOWER FARTHINGS
ROBERT WAY
HARPER CL
SCHOOL LA
GLEBELANDS
TURNER CL

PO
P

Newton Poppleford Prim Sch

Newton Poppleford

FARTHINGS LA
BEECH CL
B3178

Vennings Copse

Woodland Cottage

Hillcrest

Stoneyford

NAPS LA

NAPS LA

FOUNDRY LA

Dotton Warren

MONKEY LA

Dotton Farm

DOTTON LA

MILL LA

EXMOUTH RD

River Otter

Kingston

Kingston Farm

Selwood Farm House

Pophams Farm

HAWKERLAND RD

CHAPEL LA

COPPLESTONE LA

The Old Sawmills Ind Est

Hardys Farm

HARDYS CT

Yonder Hill

SHEPHERDS LA

Colaton House

BACK LA

Stowford

Baker's Brake

Twr

MEADOW WAY

PH

Colaton Raleigh

DRUPE FARM CT

Drupe Farm

CHURCH RD

BROOK LA

EDEN WAY

Burnthouse Farm

Mill Water Sch

BICTON PK

Blackberry Farm

East Beacon

Bicton Coll

The Lake

Flint Lodge

B3178

Bicton Park Botanical Gardens

2

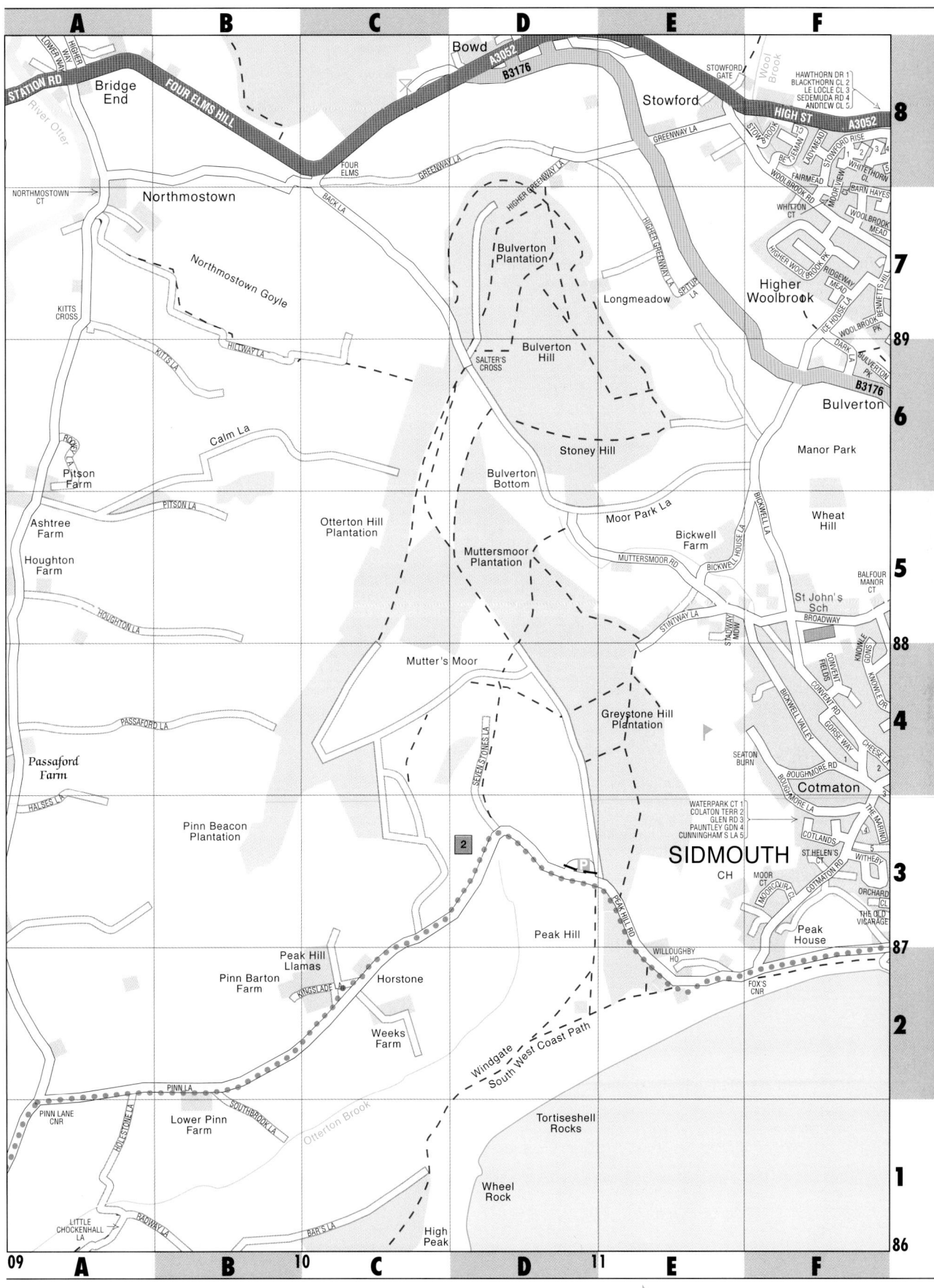

A B C D E F

8
7
89
6
5
88
4
88
3
87
2
1
86

STATION RD
HIGHER WAY
LOWER WAY
Bridge End
FOUR ELMS HILL
River Otter
Bowd
A3052
B3176
STOWFORD GATE
Stowford
Wool Brook
HAWTHORN DR 1
BLACKTHORN CL 2
LE LOCLE CL 3
SEDEMUDA RD 4
ANDREW CL 5
HIGH ST
A3052
NORTHMOSTOWN CT
Northmostown
FOUR ELMS
BACK LA
GREENWAY LA
Greenway La
HIGHER GREENWAY LA
SIDUP LA
LADY MEAD
STOWFORD RISE
WHITETHORN CL
FAIRMEAD
MOORVIEW
BARN HAYES
Northmostown Goyle
KITTS CROSS
HILLWAY LA
Bulverton Plantation
Longmeadow
HIGHER GREENWAY LA
Higher Woolbrook
WHITTON CT
HIGHER WOOLBROOK
RIDGEWAY
BENNETTS HILL
ICE HOUSE LA
WOOLBROOK PK
KITTS LA
Calm La
SALTER'S CROSS
Bulverton Hill
WOOLBROOK MEAD
DARK LA
BULVERTON PK
B3176
Bulverton
ROCK LA
Pitson Farm
PITSON LA
Stoney Hill
Manor Park
Ashtree Farm
Houghton Farm
HOUGHTON LA
Otterton Hill Plantation
Bulverton Bottom
Muttersmoor Plantation
Moor Park La
MUTTERSMOOR RD
Bickwell Farm
BICKWELL HOUSE LA
BICKWELL LA
Wheat Hill
St John's Sch
BALFOUR MANOR CT
Broadway
PASSAFORD LA
Mutter's Moor
STINTWAY LA
STACKWAY MDW
CONVENT FIELDS
CONVENT RD
KNOWLE GDNS
KNOWLE DR
Passaford Farm
HALSES LA
Greystone Hill Plantation
SEATON BURN
BICKWELL VALLEY
GORSE WAY
CHEESE LA
Pinn Beacon Plantation
SEVEN STONES LA
WATERPARK CT 1
COLATON TERR 2
GLEN RD 3
PAUNTLEY GDN 4
CUNNINGHAM S LA 5
ROUGHMORE RD
Cotmaton
THE MARINO
COTLANDS
ST HELEN'S CT
WITHEBY
2
P
SIDMOUTH
CH
MOOR CT
MOORCURL
COTMATON RD
ORCHARD CL
THE OLD VICARAGE
Peak Hill
PEAK HILL RD
Peak House
Peak Hill Llamas
Pinn Barton Farm
KINGSLADE LA
Horstone
WILLOUGHBY HO
FOX'S CNR
HOLESTONE LA
Weeks Farm
Windgate
South West Coast Path
PINN LANE CNR
PINN LA
SOUTHBROOK LA
Lower Pinn Farm
Otterton Brook
BAR'S LA
Tortiseshell Rocks
Wheel Rock
LITTLE CHOCKENHALL LA
BADWAY LA
High Peak

09 A B 10 C D 11 E F

188

A7
1 St Nicholas
CE Prim Sch

B7
1 RALEIGH HO
2 OLD FARM BGLWS
3 Manstone
Workshops

187

101

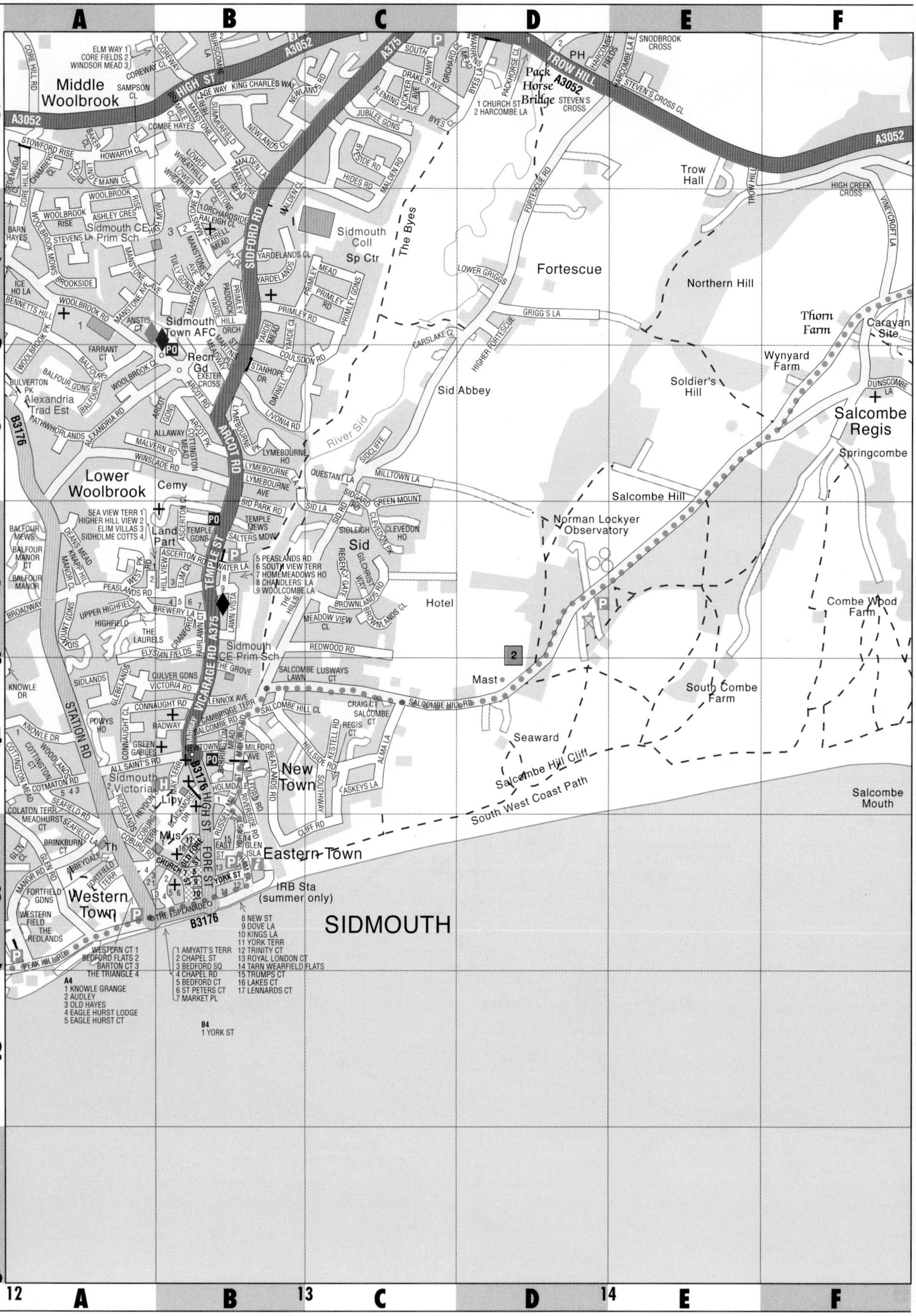

8 NEW ST
9 DOVE LA
10 KINGS LA
11 YORK TERR
1 AMYATT'S TERR   12 TRINITY CT
2 CHAPEL ST   13 ROYAL LONDON CT
3 BEDFORD SQ   14 TARN WEARFIELD FLATS
4 CHAPEL RD   15 TRUMPS CT
5 BEDFORD CT   16 LAKES CT
6 ST PETERS CT   17 LENNARDS CT
7 MARKET PL

A4
1 KNOWLE GRANGE
2 AUDLEY
3 OLD HAYES
4 EAGLE HURST LODGE
5 EAGLE HURST CT

WESTERN CT 1
BEDFORD FLATS 2
BARTON CT 3
THE TRIANGLE 4

B4
1 YORK ST

SEA VIEW TERR 1
HIGHER HILL VIEW 2
ELIM VILLAS 3
SIDHOLME COTTS 4

5 PEASLANDS RD
6 SOUTH VIEW TERR
7 HOMEMEADOWS HO
8 CHANDLERS LA
9 WOOLCOMBE LA

SIDMOUTH

A **B** **C** **D** **E** **F**

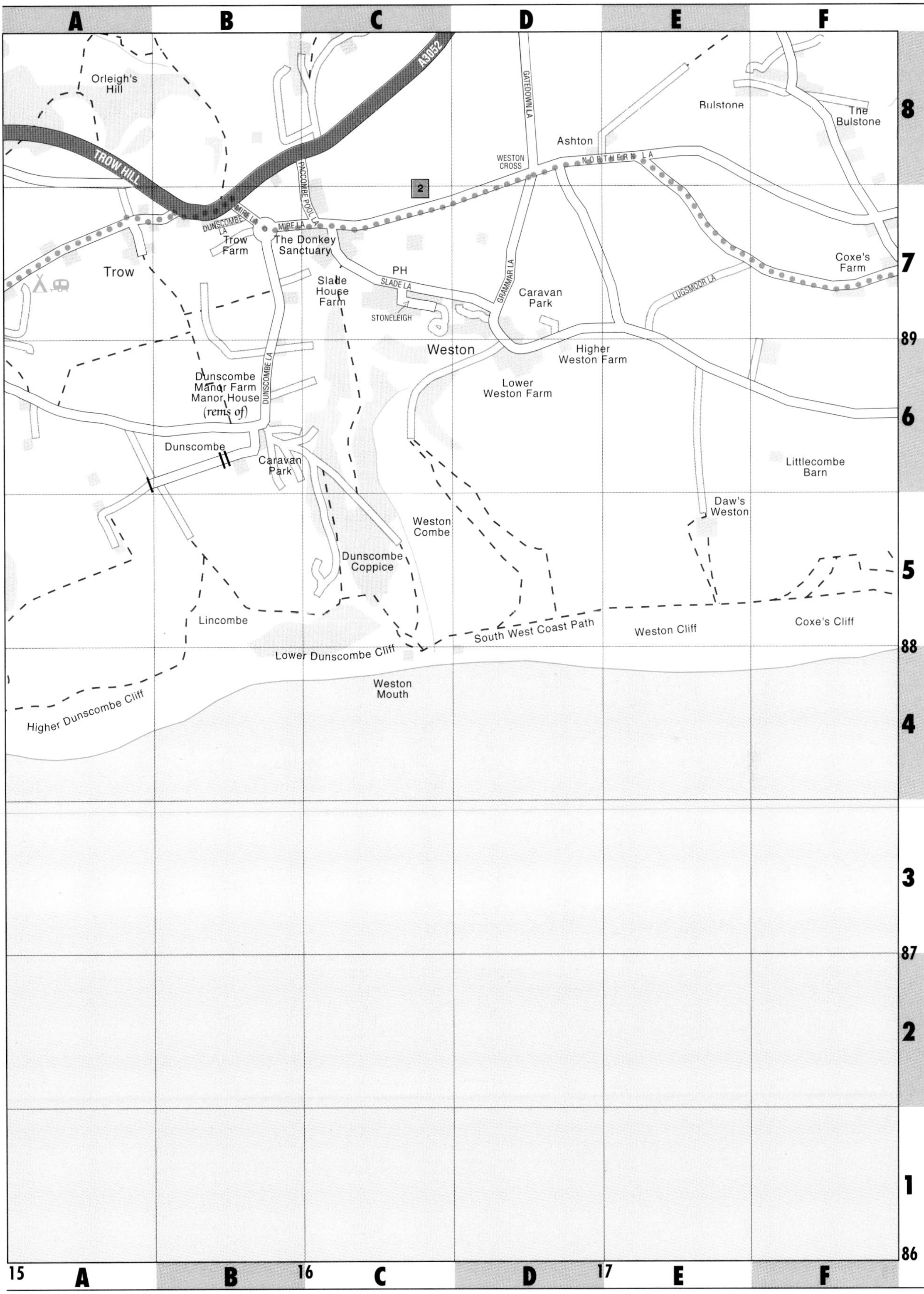

8

Orleigh's Hill

Bulstone

The Bulstone

Ashton

Weston Cross

A3052

GATEDOWN LA

NORTHERN LA

Coxe's Farm

7

TROW HILL

DUNSCOMBE LA

PACCOMBE HOLL

MIRE LA

Trow Farm

The Donkey Sanctuary

Trow

Slade House Farm

SLADE LA

PH

STONELEIGH

GRAMMAR LA

Caravan Park

LUGSMOOR LA

89

Weston

Higher Weston Farm

Dunscombe Manor Farm Manor House (rems of)

DUNSCOMBE LA

Lower Weston Farm

6

Littlecombe Barn

Dunscombe

Caravan Park

Daw's Weston

Weston Combe

Dunscombe Coppice

5

Lincombe

South West Coast Path

Weston Cliff

Coxe's Cliff

Lower Dunscombe Cliff

88

Weston Mouth

Higher Dunscombe Cliff

4

3

87

2

1

86

15 **A** **B** **16** **C** **D** **17** **E** **F**

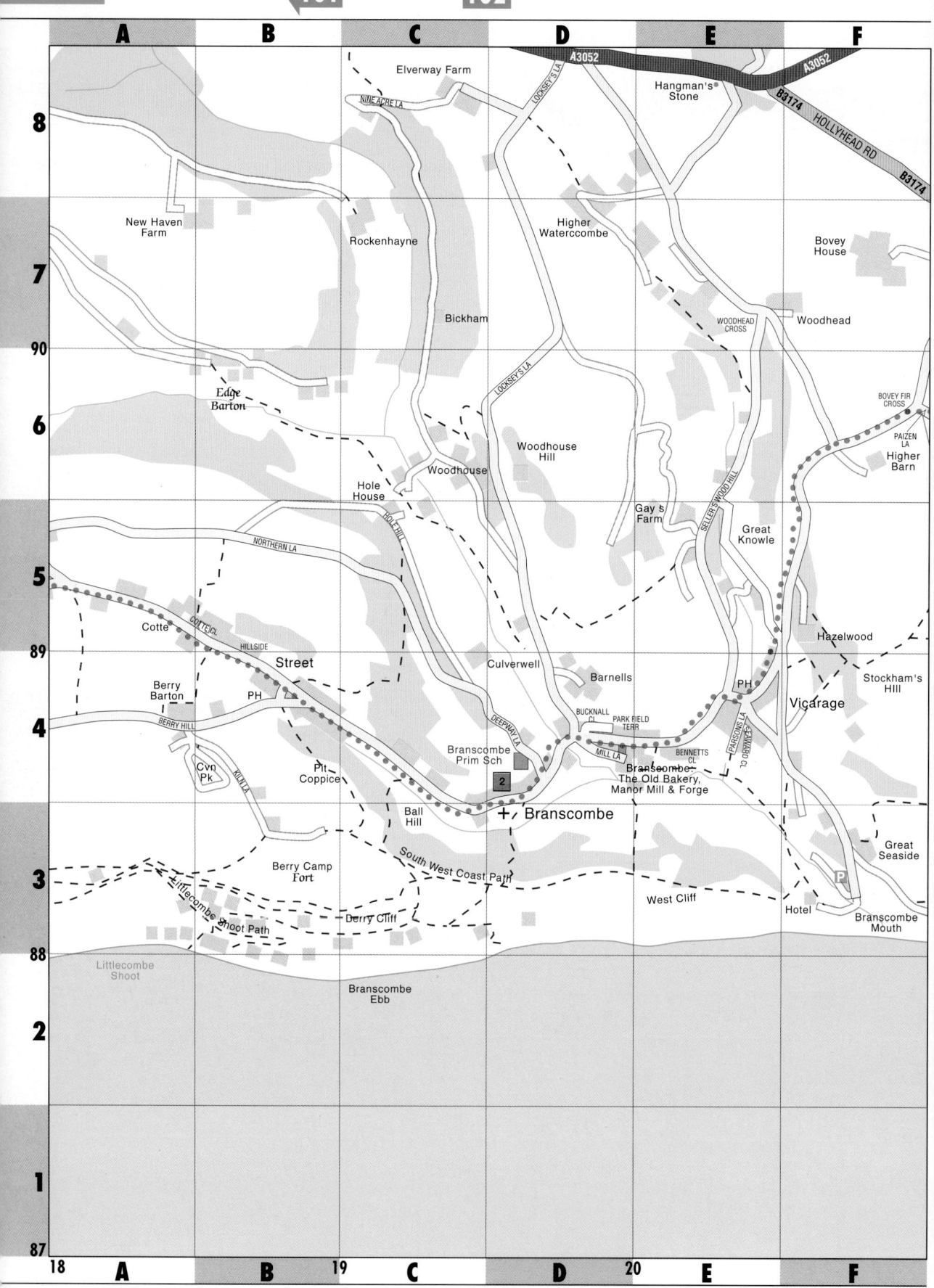

A   B   C   D   E   F

A3052   Hangman's   A3052
Stone   B3174

8   Elverway Farm   HOLLYHEAD RD

NINE ACRE LA

LOCKSEY'S LA   B3174

New Haven   Higher   Bovey
Farm   Watercombe   House

7   Rockenhayne

WOODHEAD   Woodhead
CROSS

Bickham

90   BOVEY FIR
CROSS

Edge   LOCKSEY'S LA   PAIZEN
Barton   LA
6   Higher
Woodhouse   Barn
Hole   Hill   Woodhouse
House   Gay's
Farm   Great
NORTHERN LA   Knowle

5   Cotte   HOLE HILL   Hazelwood

COTTEICL   SELLERS WOOD HILL
HILLSIDE   Culverwell   Barnells
89   Street   Stockham's
Berry   PH   BUCKNALL   PARK FIELD   PH   Vicarage   Hill
Barton   CL   TERR

4   BERRY HILL   DEEPWAY LA   MILL LA   BENNETTS   PARSONS LA
CL   CL

Cvn   Branscombe   Branscombe: TO BWAY
Pk   KILN LA   Prim Sch   The Old Bakery,
Pit   2   Manor Mill & Forge
Coppice   Ball   Branscombe
Hill   ✚   Great
Seaside
3   Berry Camp   South West Coast Path   West Cliff   P
Fort   Hotel   Branscombe
Littlecombe Shoot Path   Derry Cliff   Mouth

88   Littlecombe
Shoot   Branscombe
Ebb

2

1

87
18   A   19   B   C   20   D   E   F

189

A B C D E F
8 7 6 5 4 3 2 1
90 89 88 87
21 22 23
Couchill Farm
HOLLYHEAD RD
GATCOMBE LA
HOLLYHEAD CROSS
BOVEY LA
STOVAR LONG LA
PAIZEN LA
Beer YH
PEAZEN FLATS
RATTENBURY COTTS
TOWNSEND
B3174
COURT BARTON
HILL
BERRY LA
NEW RD
HIGHFIELD TERR 1
MARMORA TERR 2
GORDON TERR 3
ROSE COTTS 4
PIONEER COTTS 5
WEST VIEW 6
THE SQUARE 7
BARNARDS FARM 8
BERRY HILL 9
Mast
CLINTON RISE
QUARRY COTTS
QUARRY LA
Pecorama Pleasure Gdns
ASH HILL CT
Beer CE Prim Sch
CAUSEWAY
LONG HILL
Beer Quarry Caves
Beer Heights Light Rly
SHORT FURLONG
BARLINE
Cemy
CHURCH HILL
FORE ST
NEW CUT
PO
Beer
Marine House at Beer
DOLPHIN RD
STOVAR LONG LA
CLAPP'S LA
PIPPINS
HIGHER MDWS
THE MEADOWS
UNDERLEYS
WEST UNDERLEYS
MARE LA
LANEHEAD RD
LANEHEAD
SOUTHDOWN CL
SOUTHDOWN RD
COMMON LA
SEA HILL
SEA VIEW TERR
Beer Roads
PARK RD
COMMON HILL
LITTLE LA
Friar's Park Farm
South Down Farm
Mast
Arratt's Hill
The Hall
South Down Common
South West Coast Path
East Cliff
Hookend Cliff
Under Hookend
Hookend Beach
Sherborne Rocks
Beer Head
B3172
SEATON DOWN HILL
HONEY DITCHES DR
ROMAN WAY
VENBOROUGH CL
CONSTANTINE CL
BRAMBLE ACRE
BOSWELL WAY
UPPER CHURSTON RISE
CHURSTON RISE
SEATON DOWN CL
AUGUSTINE CL
STOWFORD HTS
ALBION CL
TRACEYS AVE
LYDGATES RD
COUCHILL LA
COUCHILL DR
MERROW DOWN DR
HOMER LA
SEATON DOWN RD
MARLPIT LA
GREENWAY
FREMINGTON RD
BUNTS LA
MARLPIT CL
DURLEY RD
WEST ACRES
ALLEYN CT
PADDOCK
SANDS CT
HIGHCLIFFE CRES
WESSITERS
BEER RD
B3174
HIGHCLIFFE CL
OLD BEER RD
HIGHCLIFFE CT
SEAFORTH LODGE
OLD BEER RD
THE GLEN
BEER HILL
Seaton Hole

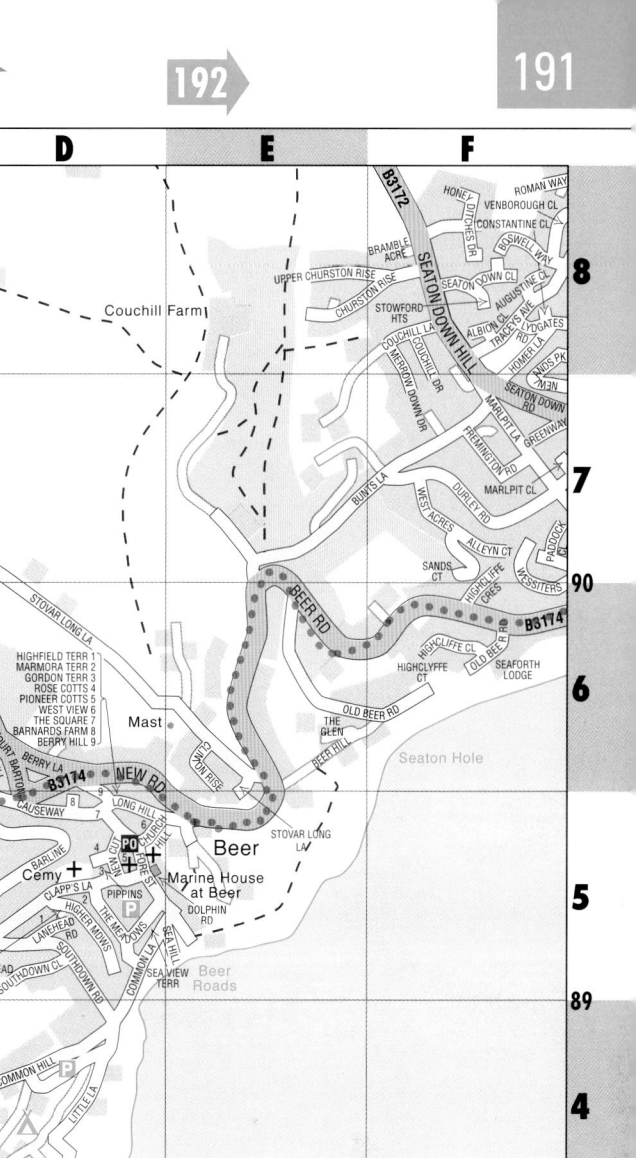

◁ 102
103 ▲

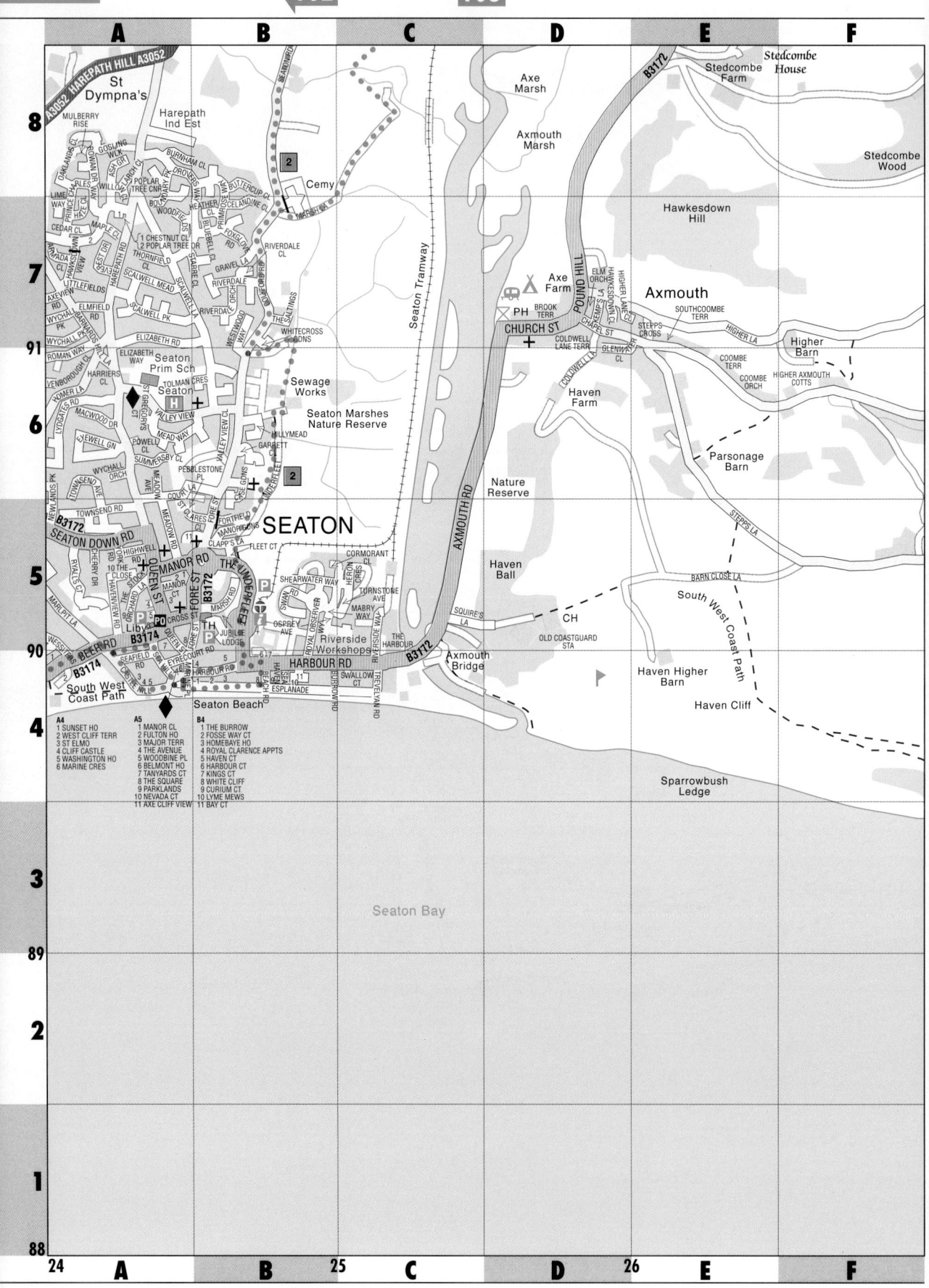

Seaton

A4
1 SUNSET HO
2 WEST CLIFF TERR
3 ST ELMO
4 CLIFF CASTLE
5 WASHINGTON HO
6 MARINE CRES

A5
1 MANOR CL
2 FULTON HO
3 MAJOR TERR
4 THE AVENUE
5 WOODBINE PL
6 BELMONT HO
7 TANYARDS CT
8 THE SQUARE
9 PARKLANDS
10 NEVADA CT
11 AXE CLIFF VIEW

B4
1 THE BURROW
2 FOSSE WAY CT
3 HOMEBAYE HO
4 ROYAL CLARENCE APPTS
5 HAVEN CT
6 HARBOUR CT
7 KINGS CT
8 WHITE CLIFF
9 CURIUM CT
10 LYME MEWS
11 BAY CT

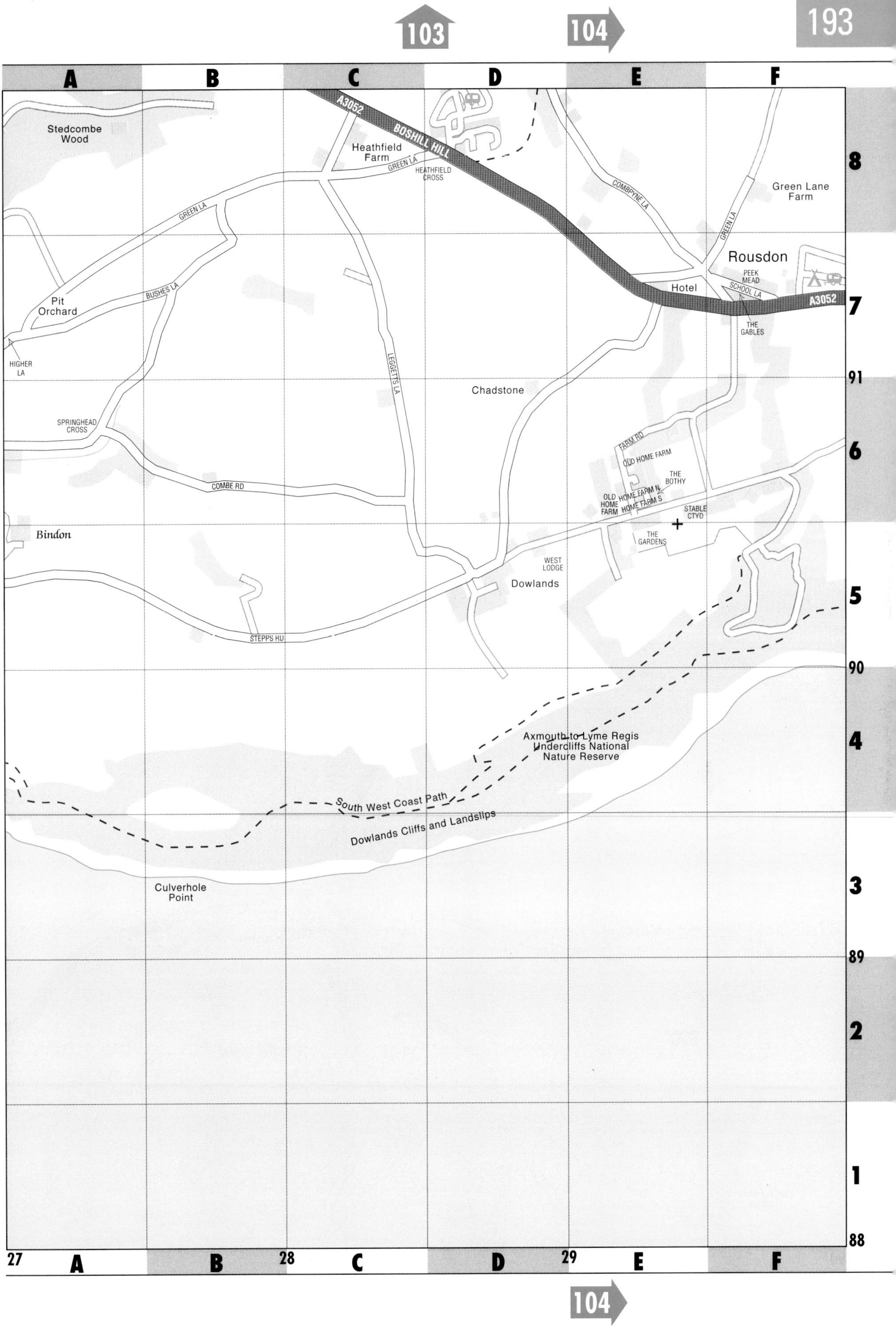

A B C D E F

8

Stedcombe
Wood

A3052 BOSHILL HILL

Heathfield
Farm

GREEN LA

GREEN LA

HEATHFIELD
CROSS

COMBPYNE LA

Green Lane
Farm

GREEN LA

Rousdon

PEEK
MEAD

Hotel

SCHOOL LA

A3052

7

GREEN LA

BUSHES LA

Pit
Orchard

THE
GABLES

HIGHER
LA

91

SPRINGHEAD
CROSS

LEGGETTS LA

Chadstone

6

COMBE RD

FARM RD

OLD HOME FARM

THE
BOTHY

OLD
HOME
FARM

HOME FARM N

HOME FARM S

STABLE
CTYD

Bindon

THE
GARDENS

WEST
LODGE

5

Dowlands

STEPPS HU

90

Axmouth to Lyme Regis
Undercliffs National
Nature Reserve

4

South West Coast Path

Dowlands Cliffs and Landslips

Culverhole
Point

3

89

2

1

88

114
182

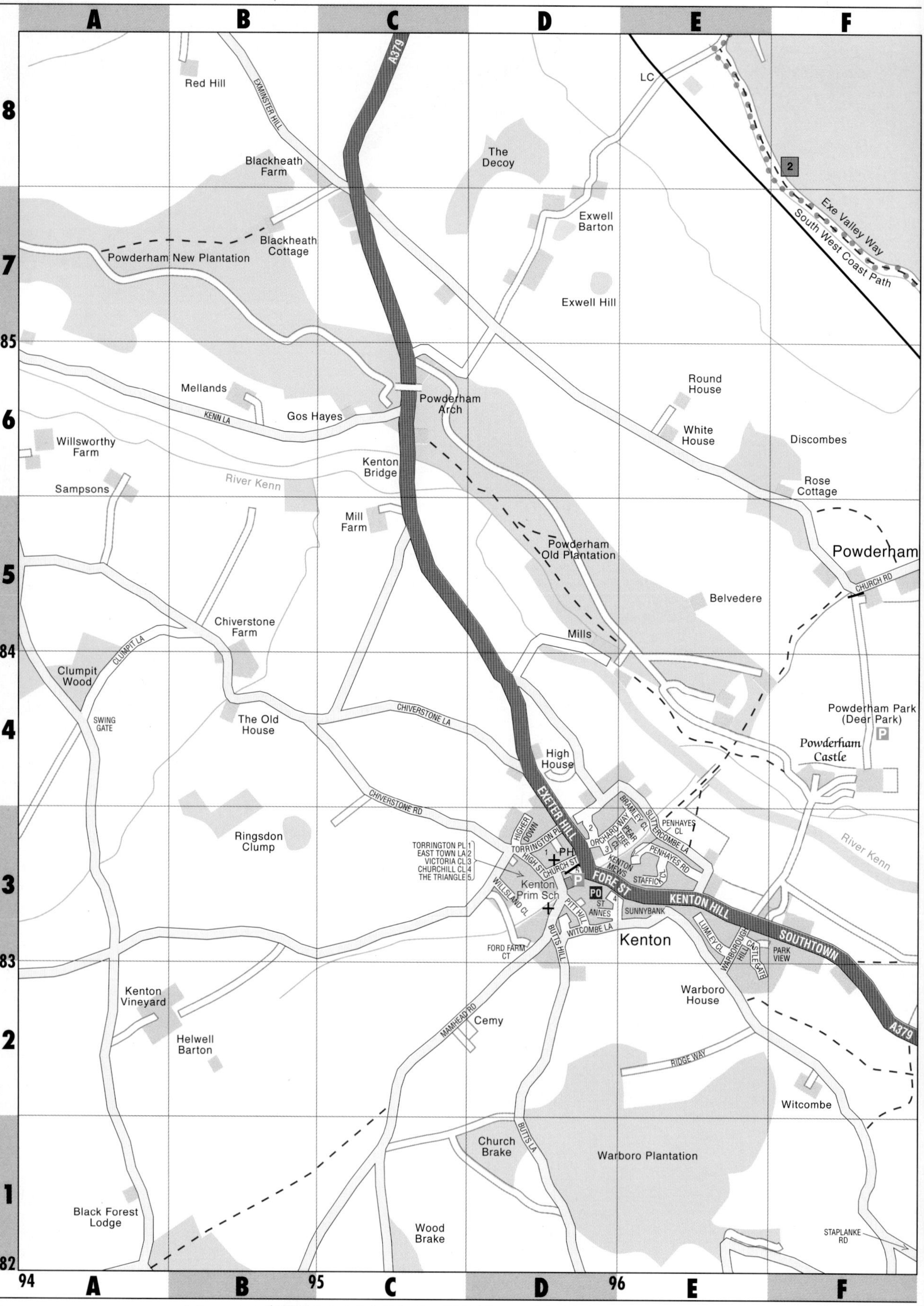

8

Red Hill

A379

LC

2

Exe Valley Way

South West Coast Path

Blackheath Farm

The Decoy

7

Powderham New Plantation

Blackheath Cottage

Exwell Barton

Exwell Hill

85

Mellands

KENN LA

Gos Hayes

Powderham Arch

Round House

White House

Discombes

6

Willsworthy Farm

River Kenn

Kenton Bridge

Rose Cottage

Sampsons

Mill Farm

Powderham Old Plantation

Powderham

5

Chiverstone Farm

Mills

CHURCH RD

Belvedere

84

Clumpit Wood

CLUMPIT LA

The Old House

CHIVERSTONE LA

High House

Powderham Park (Deer Park)

P

4

SWING GATE

Powderham Castle

River Kenn

Ringsdon Clump

CHIVERSTONE RD

EXETER HILL

HIGHER DOWN

BRAMLEY CT

ORCHARD WAY

SLITTERCOMBE LA

PENHAYES CL

KENTON MEWS

PENHAYES RD

STAFFICK

3

TORRINGTON PL 1
EAST TOWN LA 2
VICTORIA CL 3
CHURCHILL CL 4
THE TRIANGLE 5

HIGH ST

CHURCH ST

FORE ST

KENTON HILL

SOUTHTOWN

PH

P

Kenton Prim Sch

WILL ST

LAND CL

PITT WLL

WITCOMBE LA

PO

ST ANNES

SUNNYBANK

LUMLEY CL

WARBORO

CASTLE GATE

PARK VIEW

Kenton

A379

83

FORD FARM CT

BUTTS HILL

Warboro House

Kenton Vineyard

MAMHEAD RD

Cemy

BUTTS LA

RIDGE WAY

Witcombe

2

Helwell Barton

Church Brake

Warboro Plantation

1

Black Forest Lodge

Wood Brake

STAPLANKE RD

82

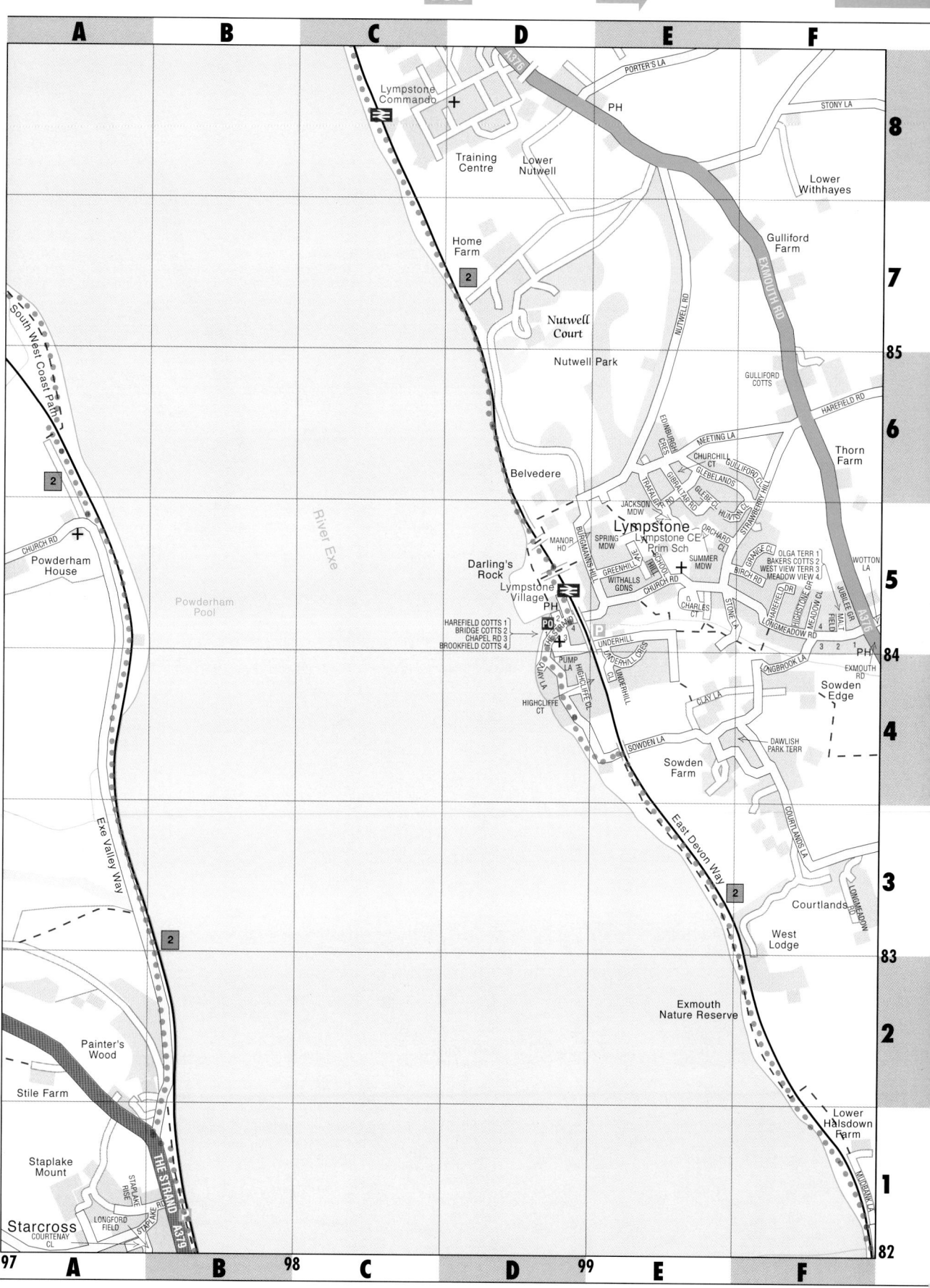

A   B   C   D   E   F

8
7
85
6
5
84
4
3
83
2
1
82

Lympstone Commando

Training Centre

Lower Nutwell

PORTER'S LA

PH

STONY LA

Lower Withhayes

Home Farm

2

Gulliford Farm

EXMOUTH RD

Nutwell Court

Nutwell Park

NUTWELL RD

HAREFIELD RD

Gulliford Cotts

South West Coast Path

River Exe

Belvedere

EDINBURGH CRES

MEETING LA

CHURCHILL CT

GLEBELANDS

GULLIFORD CL

Thorn Farm

2

Powderham House

CHURCH RD

Powderham Pool

Darling's Rock

Lympstone Village

PH

MANOR HO

BIRCHMANS HILL

SPRING MDW

JACKSON MDW

Lympstone

Lympstone CE Prim Sch

ORCHARD CL

SUMMER MDW

STRAWBERRY HILL

OLGA TERR 1

BAKERS COTTS 2

WEST VIEW TERR 3

MEADOW VIEW 4

WOTTON LA

JUBILEE GR

A376

5

PO

HAREFIELD COTTS 1

BRIDGE COTTS 2

CHAPEL RD 3

BROOKFIELD COTTS 4

PUMP LA

CLAY LA

HIGHCLIFFE CL

UNDERHILL

UNDERHILL LANES

GREENHILL

WITHALLS GDNS

CHURCH RD

CHARLES CT

STONE A

HAREFIELD DR

HIGHSTONE DR

MEADOW CL

LONGMEADOW RD

MALT FIELD

3 2 1

PH

84

EXMOUTH RD

Sowden Edge

LONGBROOK LA

CLAY LA

HIGHCLIFFE CT

SOWDEN LA

Sowden Farm

DAWLISH PARK TERR

East Devon Way

COURTLANDS LA

2

Courtlands

LONGMEADOW

West Lodge

Exe Valley Way

2

Exmouth Nature Reserve

Painter's Wood

Stile Farm

Lower Halsdown Farm

MINERVA CL

Staplake Mount

THE STRAND A379

STAPLAKE RISE

STAPLAKE LA

Starcross

COURTENAY CL

LONGFORD FIELD

97   A   B   98   C   D   99   E   F

195
184

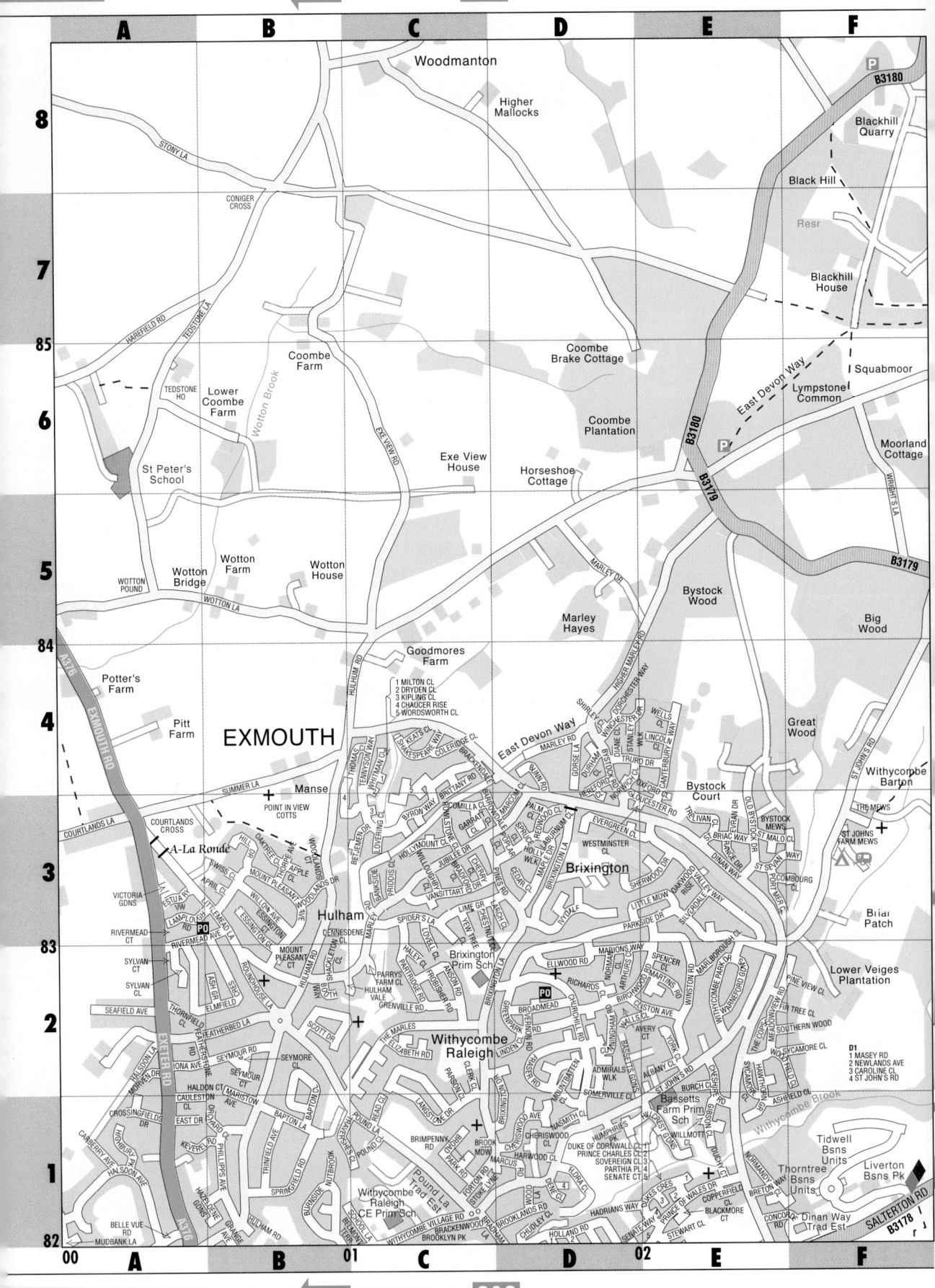
A
B
C
D
E
F
8
7
85
6
5
84
4
3
83
2
1
82
00
01
02
Woodmanton
Higher Mallocks
B3180
Blackhill Quarry
Black Hill
Resr
Blackhill House
STONY LA
CONIGER CROSS
HAREFIELD RD
TEDSTONE LA
Coombe Farm
Coombe Brake Cottage
East Devon Way
Squabmoor
Lympstone Common
TEDSTONE HO
Lower Coombe Farm
Wotton Brook
EXE VIEW RD
Coombe Plantation
B3180
Moorland Cottage
St Peter's School
Exe View House
Horseshoe Cottage
B3179
WRIGHT'S LA
MARLEY DR
B3179
WOTTON POUND
Wotton Bridge
Wotton Farm
Wotton House
WOTTON LA
Bystock Wood
Marley Hayes
Big Wood
A376
Potter's Farm
Goodmores Farm
HULHAM RD
HIGHER MARLEY RD
1 MILTON CL
2 DRYDEN CL
3 KIPLING CL
4 CHAUCER RISE
5 WORDSWORTH CL
EXMOUTH RD
Pitt Farm
EXMOUTH
East Devon Way
Great Wood
MARLEY RD
Withycombe Barton
ST JOHN'S RD
SUMMER LA
Manse
Bystock Court
COURTLANDS LA
POINT IN VIEW COTTS
THE MEWS
ST JOHNS FARM MEWS
COURTLANDS CROSS
A-La Ronde
Brixington
VICTORIA GDNS
Hulham
RIVERMEAD CT
Briar Patch
Brixington Prim Sch
SYLVAN CT
SYLVAN CL
Lower Veiges Plantation
SEAFIELD AVE
Withycombe Raleigh
D1
1 MASEY RD
2 NEWLANDS AVE
3 CAROLINE CL
4 ST JOHN'S RD
Bassetts Farm Prim Sch
Withycombe Brook
Tidwell Bsns Units
Thorntree Bsns Units
Liverton Bsns Pk
EXETER RD
Pound La Trad Est
Withycombe Raleigh CE Prim Sch
Dinan Way Trad Est
SALTERTON RD
B3178
BELLE VUE RD
MUDBANK LA
A376

195
202

185

198

A B C D E F
8 7 85 6 5 84 4 3 83 2 1 82
03 04 05
Kerslake Farm
Yettington
Bearden Barn
East Devon Way
SHEIRS ORCH
SHORTLANDS
Thorn Tree Plantation
Sand & Gravel Quarry
Tucker's Plants
Island Plantation
Hayes Barton (Home of Sir Walter Raleigh)
Washmoor Farm
SAWMILL LA
Sawmill Resr
Fryingpans
HAYES LA
Wheathill Plantation
East Budleigh Common
Hayeswood Cottage
Hayes Wood
Squabmoor Plantation
Bystock Fishponds
Hayeswood La
Withycombe Raleigh Common
ST JOHN'S RD
SHORTWOOD LA
Squabmoor Resr
Homeleigh
THE COMMON
Exmouth Archery Club
Dalditch Plantation
Shortwood Common
Dalditch Farm
Tidwell House
DALDITCH LA
Shortwood House
OUTER TING TONG
INNER TING TONG
BEARS LA
Dalditch Common
Long Orchard
B3178
KNOWLE MEWS
Knowle House
EVANS FIELD
DEEPWAYS
HOOKER CL
BARN LA
FORGE CL
Leeford Plantations
Knowle
TREWINS
SHORTWOOD CL
DUKE'S RD
QUEEN'S RD
GREENWAY LA
GREENHAVEN
COPPLEDOWN GDNS
HIGHER BEDLANDS
BEDLANDS LA
CLINTON CL
KNOWLE HILL
B3179
Leeford
ROLLE COTTS
KNOWLE VILLAGE
PH
St Peter's CE (Aided) Prim Sch
MOORHAVEN 1
CLINTON TERR 2
MOOR LA
Liverton Farm
Recycling Ctr
Knowle Hill Plantation
KNOWLE CNR
KNOWLE RD
Little Knowle
DARK LA
MOORMEAD
LIVERTON HILL
MOUNTAIN HILL
SALTERTON RD
PARK LODGE
LITTLE KNOWLE CT
PARK LA
CLYST HAYES GDNS
FAIRLEA CT
MEADOW CL
CASTLE LA
Bushy House
LANSDOWNE RD
EXMOUTH RD
HALSE HILL
LITTLE KNOWLE
MOORLANDS RD
MONTAGUE GDNS
WEST HILL LA
MEADOW RD
Mountain Farm
Quentance Farm

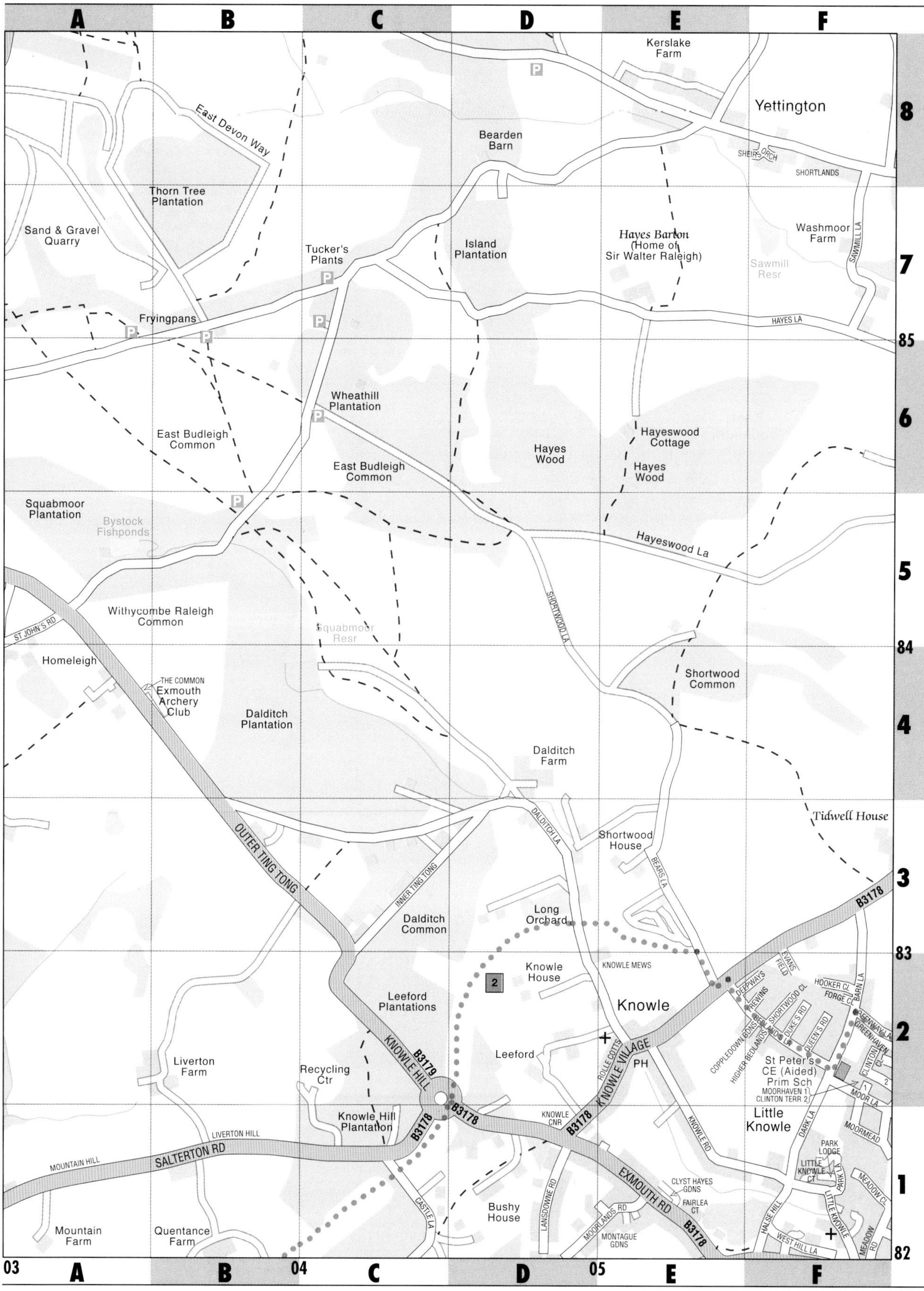

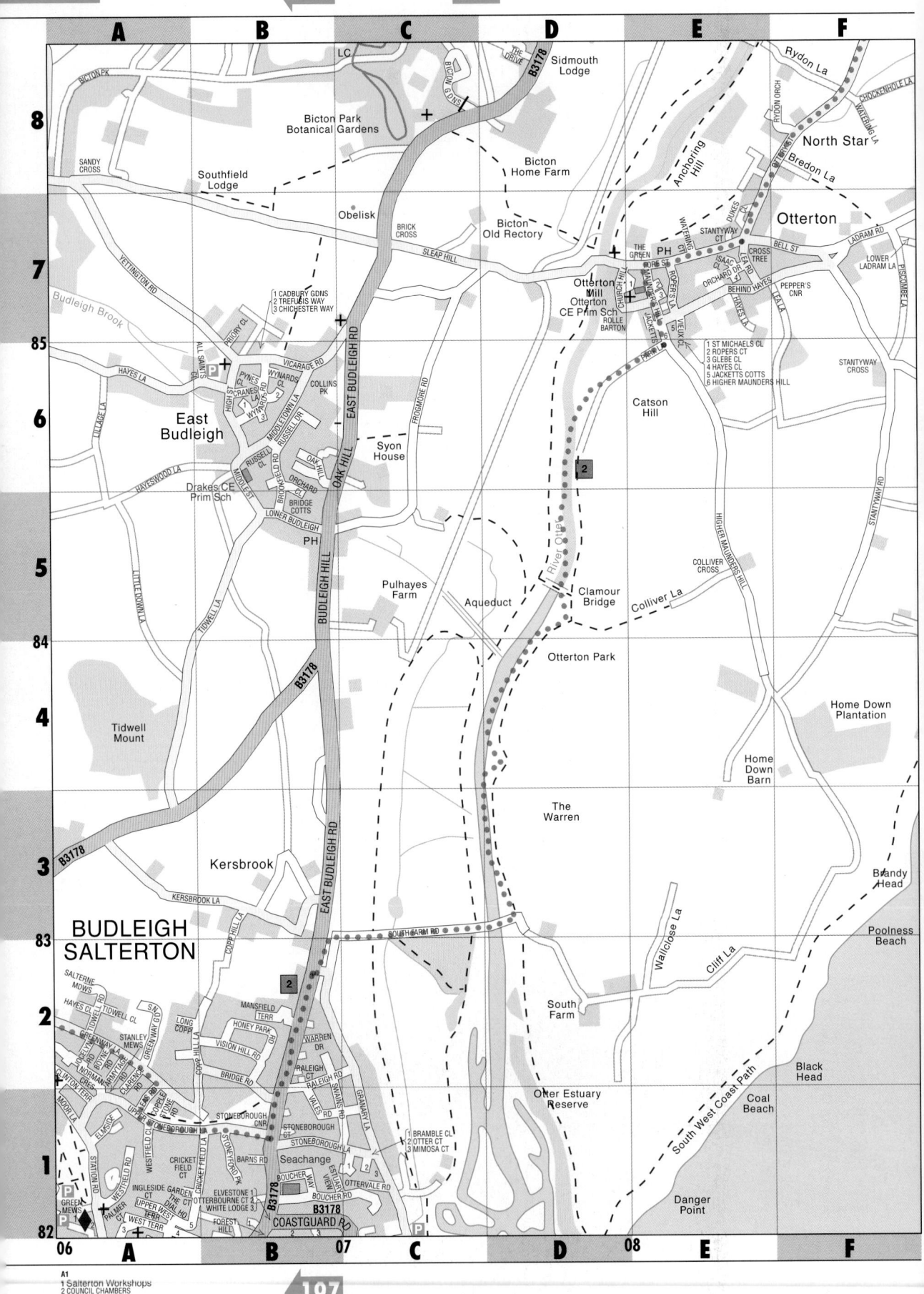

Map labels:

A B C D E F

8 7 85 6 5 84 5 84 4 3 83 2 1 82

Bicton Pk
Bicton Park Botanical Gardens
Southfield Lodge
Sandy Cross
Obelisk
Brick Cross
Sleap Hill
Sidmouth Lodge
The Drive
Bicton Home Farm
Bicton Old Rectory
Rydon La
Rydon Orch
Chockenhole La
Watering La
North Star
Bredon La
Otterton
Anchoring Hill
Stantyway Ct
Bell St
Ladram Rd
Lower Ladram La
Piscombe La
The Green
PH
Otterton Mill
Otterton
Otterton CE Prim Sch
Rolle Barton
Cross Tree
Pepper's Cnr
Behind Hayes
1 St Michaels Cl
2 Ropers Ct
3 Glebe Cl
4 Hayes Cl
5 Jacketts Cotts
6 Higher Maunders Hill
Stantyway Cross
Catson Hill
Stantyway Rd
Budleigh Brook
Yettington Rd
1 Cadbury Gdns
2 Trefusis Way
3 Chichester Way
Priory Cl
All Saints
Vicarage Rd
Collins Pk
East Budleigh Rd
Syon House
Frogmore Rd
Higher Maunders Hill
Colliver Cross
Colliver La
Hayes La
Lillage La
Pynes Cl
Wynards Cl
Middletown La
Oak Hill
Russell Cl
Russell Rd
Bridge Cotts
Lower Budleigh
PH
Drakes CE Prim Sch
Hayeswood La
Tidwell La
Littletown La
Budleigh Hill
B3178
Tidwell Mount
Pulhayes Farm
Aqueduct
Clamour Bridge
River Otter
Otterton Park
Home Down Plantation
Home Down Barn
Kersbrook
Kersbrook La
Copp Hill La
East Budleigh Rd
The Warren
Wallcose La
Cliff La
Brandy Head
Poolness Beach
B3178
BUDLEIGH SALTERTON
Salterne Mews
Hayes Cl
Tidwell Cl
Greenway
Stanley Mews
Mansfield Terr
Honey Park
Vision Hill Rd
Bridge Rd
Warren Dr
Raleigh Ct
Raleigh Rd
Swans Rd
Granary La
Stoneborough Cnr
Stoneborough Ct
Stoneborough La
Barns Rd
Seachange
1 Bramble Cl
2 Otter Ct
3 Mimosa Ct
South Farm
Otter Estuary Reserve
Black Head
Coal Beach
South West Coast Path
Danger Point
Clinton Terr
Moor La
Elmside
Station Rd
Green Mews
Cricket Field Ct
Ingleside Garden
Upper West Terr
West Terr
Palmer Cl
Elvstone Ct
White Lodge
Forest Hill
Boucher Way
Ottervale Rd
Boucher Rd
COASTGUARD RD
B3178

A1
1 Salterton Workshops
2 Council Chambers
3 The Lawn
4 East Terr
5 Chapel Hill

06 07 08

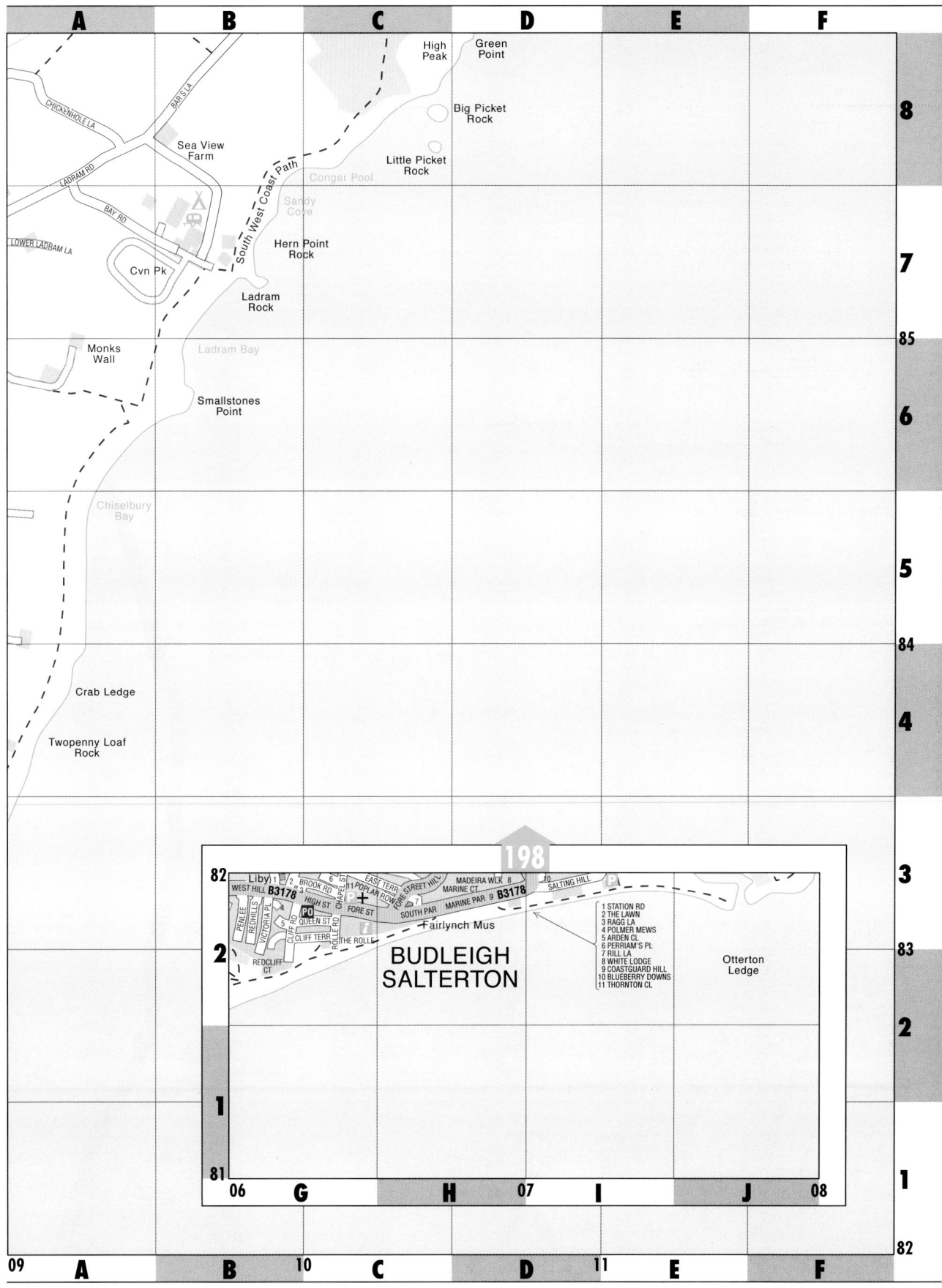

CHICKENHOLE LA

LADRAM RD

BAR'S LA

Sea View
Farm

BAY RD

South West Coast Path

Conger Pool

High
Peak

Green
Point

Big Picket
Rock

Little Picket
Rock

Sandy
Cove

LOWER LADRAM LA

Cvn Pk

Hern Point
Rock

Ladram
Rock

Monks
Wall

Ladram Bay

Smallstones
Point

Chiselbury
Bay

Crab Ledge

Twopenny Loaf
Rock

Liby

WEST HILL

B3178

PENLEE
REDHILLS

VICTORIA PL

PO

QUEEN ST

REDCLIFF
CT

CLIFF TERR

HIGH ST

BROOK RD

CHAPEL ST

ROLLE RD

CLIFF RD

THE ROLLE

FORE ST

EAST TERR

STREET HILL

FORE ST

POPLAR ROW

SOUTH PAR

MADEIRA WLK

MARINE CT

MARINE PAR

Fairlynch Mus

B3178

SALTING HILL

BUDLEIGH
SALTERTON

1 STATION RD
2 THE LAWN
3 RAGG LA
4 POLMER MEWS
5 ARDEN CL
6 PERRIAM'S PL
7 RILL LA
8 WHITE LODGE
9 COASTGUARD HILL
10 BLUEBERRY DOWNS
11 THORNTON CL

Otterton
Ledge

198

09   10   11

124
194

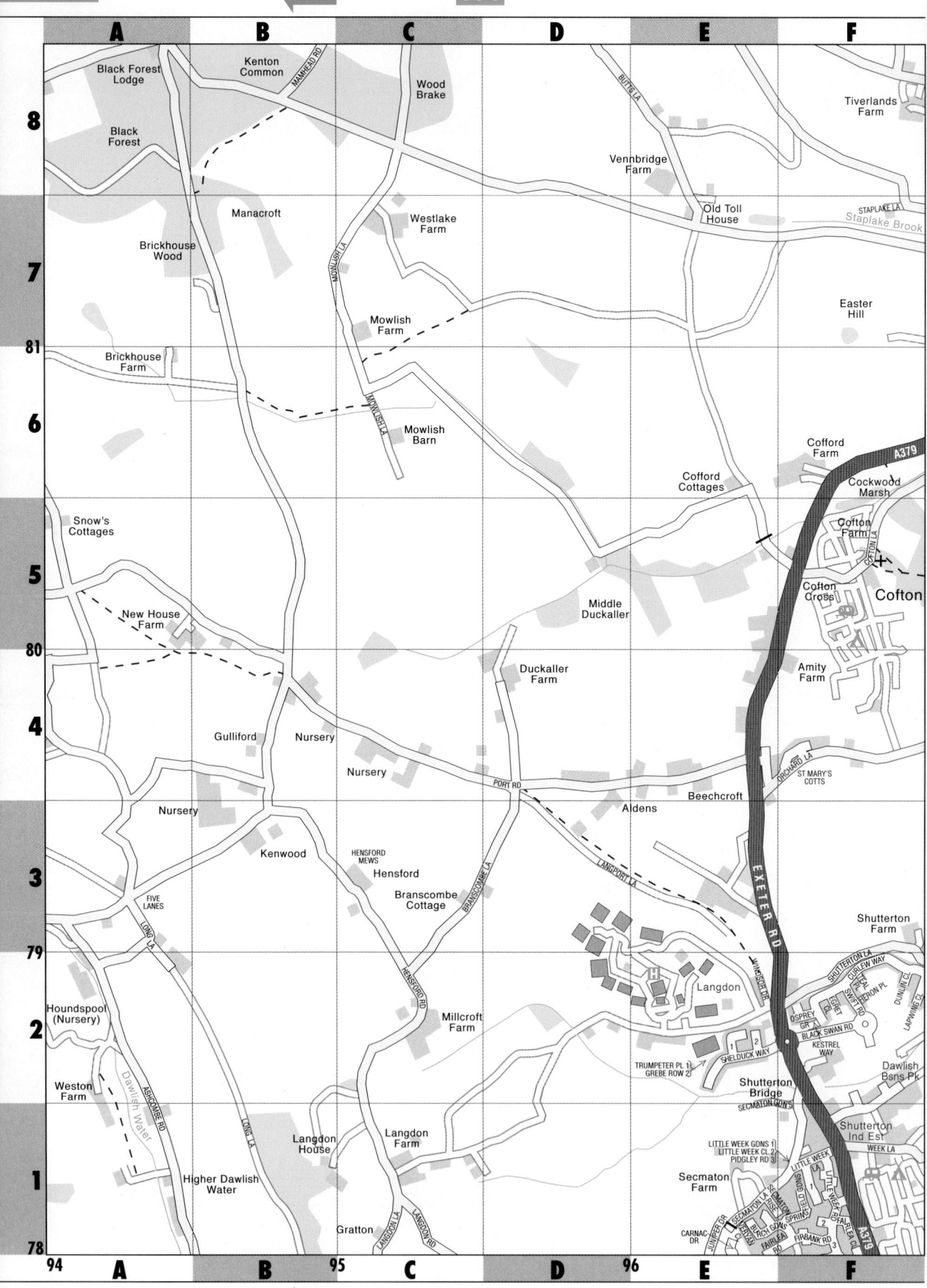
A B C D E F
8 7 81 6 5 80 4 3 79 2 1 78
94 95 96
Black Forest Lodge
Kenton Common
MAMHEAD RD
Wood Brake
Black Forest
Tiverlands Farm
BUTTS LA
Vennbridge Farm
Manacroft
Westlake Farm
Old Toll House
STAPLAKE LA
Staplake Brook
Brickhouse Wood
MOWLISH LA
Easter Hill
Mowlish Farm
Brickhouse Farm
Mowlish Barn
Cofford Farm
A379
Cofford Cottages
Cockwood Marsh
Snow's Cottages
Cofton Farm
COFTON LA
Cofton Cross
Cofton
Middle Duckaller
New House Farm
Duckaller Farm
Amity Farm
Gulliford
Nursery
Nursery
ORCHARD LA
ST MARY'S COTTS
PORT RD
Beechcroft
Nursery
Aldens
Kenwood
HENSFORD MEWS
Hensford
LANGPORT LA
EXETER RD
Branscombe Cottage
BRANSCOMBE LA
FIVE LANES
Shutterton Farm
LONG LA
SHUTTERTON LA
CURLEW WAY
Langdon
WINDSOR DR
HENSFORD RD
TEAL PL
SWIFT RD
FERON PL
DUNLIN CL
LAPWING CL
EGRET CL
Houndspool (Nursery)
Millcroft Farm
OSPREY GR
BLACK SWAN RD
KESTREL WAY
SHELDUCK WAY
TRUMPETER PL 1
GREBE ROW 2
Weston Farm
Dawlish Water
Shutterton Bridge
Dawlish Bsns Pk
ASHCOMBE RD
SECMATON GDNS
LONG LA
Langdon House
Langdon Farm
Shutterton Ind Est
LITTLE WEEK GDNS 1
LITTLE WEEK CL 2
PIDGLEY RD 3
WEEK LA
LITTLE WEEK LA
Higher Dawlish Water
Secmaton Farm
SECMATON LA
SECMATON RISE
SPRINGFIELD GDNS
LITTLE WEEK RD
FAIRLEA CL
CARNAC DR
JUNIPER DR
BIRCH GDNS
FAIRLEA RD
FIRBANK RD
Gratton
LANGDON LA
LANGDON RD

124
204

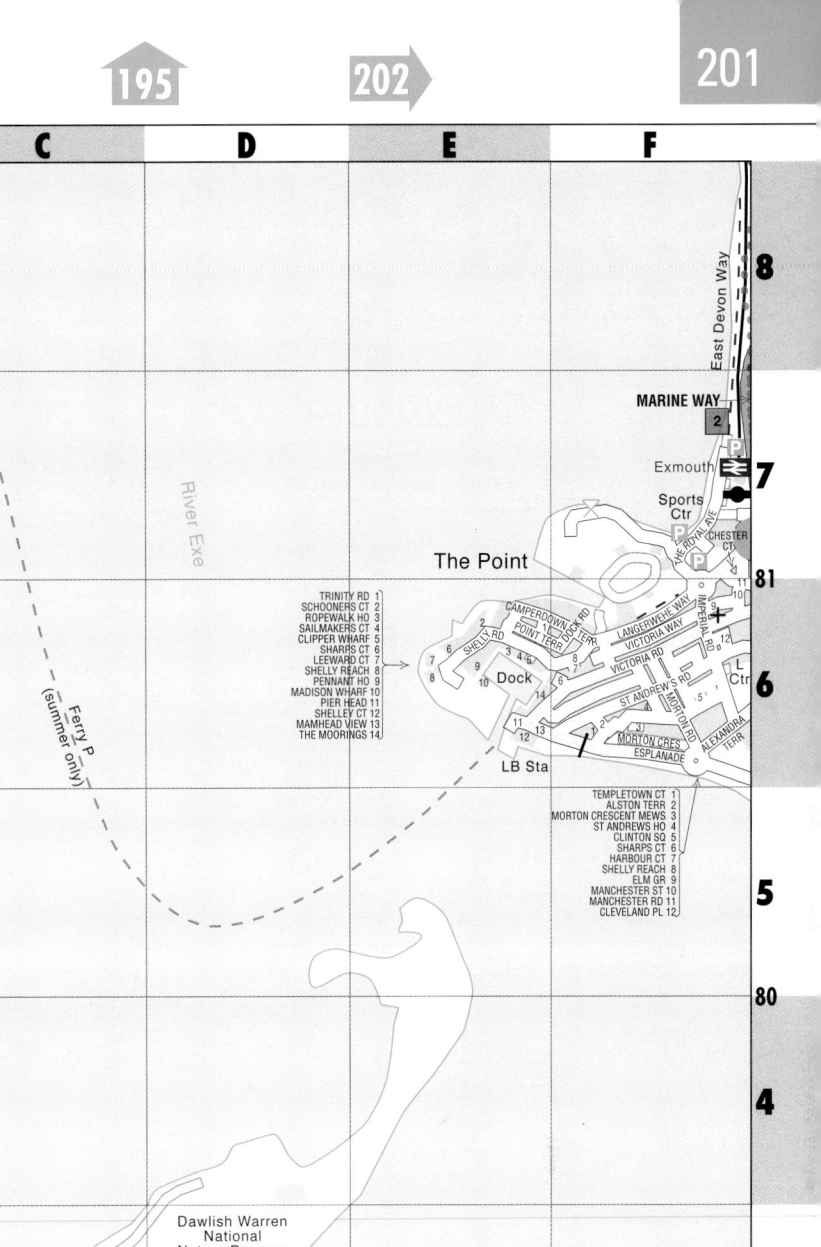

A B C D E F

Starcross

DREW'S CL 1
COOKSON'S RD 2
BRUMFI RD 3
THE GEORGIAN HO 4
COURTENAY TERR 5
WARBORO TERR 6
CORONATION TERR 7
CHURCH FLATS 8
ALEXANDRA MEWS 9
CHAPPLE CL 10
BISHOPS CL 11
STAPLAKE RD 12

Starcross

Jetty

Staplake

STAPLAKE LA

Old Staplake
Farm

EASTER HILL LA

Southbrook

EXETER RD

Westwood

COFTON LA
CHURCH RD

PH

Cockwood Prim Sch

Cockwood

KENBURY
CRES

South West
Coast Path

Eastdon

ORCHARD LA

Eastdon
Wood

Eastdon
House

1 LAPWING CL
2 AVOCET PL
3 TURNSTONE CL
4 CURLEW WAY

SHUTTERTON LA
MILLIN WAY

SHERWELL CL

POPULAR LA

SYCAMORE AVE

RIVERSIDE HAZELWOOD DR

BRACKEN WAY

Holiday
Ctr

Dawlish
Warren

WEEK LA

MOUNT PLEASANT RD

WARREN RD

Langstone Cliff

River Exe

Ferry P
(summer only)

The Point

TRINITY RD 1
SCHOONERS CT 2
ROPEWALK HO 3
SAILMAKERS CT 4
CLIPPER WHARF 5
SHARPS CT 6
LEEWARD CT 7
SHELLY REACH 8
PENNANT HO 9
MADISON WHARF 10
PIER HEAD 11
SHELLEY CT 12
MAMHEAD VIEW 13
THE MOORINGS 14

SHELLY RD

Dock

LB Sta

CAMPERDOWN
POINT TERR

LANGERWEHE WAY
VICTORIA WAY

VICTORIA RD

ST ANDREWS RD

MORTON CRES
ESPLANADE

ALEXANDRA TERR

TEMPLETOWN CT 1
ALSTON TERR 2
MORTON CRESCENT MEWS 3
ST ANDREWS HO 4
CLINTON SQ 5
SHARPS CT 6
HARBOUR CT 7
SHELLY REACH 8
ELM GR 9
MANCHESTER ST 10
MANCHESTER RD 11
CLEVELAND PL 12

MARINE WAY

East Devon Way

Exmouth

Sports
Ctr

CHESTER CT

Dawlish Warren
National
Nature Reserve

Visitor
Ctr

CH

1 HAZELWOOD PK
2 THE BUNGALOWS
3 PINE TREE CL
4 PALM CT

Dawlish
Warren

DEVON
VIEW

LEE
CLIFF
PK

BEACH RD

A7
1 GEORGE ST
2 SHUTE MEADOW ST
3 CHARLES ST
4 STAPLES MEWS
5 GLENORCHY CT
6 ALBION CT
7 HENRIETTA PL
8 HENRIETTA RD
9 ALBION TERR
10 PALACE COTTS
11 ALL SAINTS MEWS

201
196

EXMOUTH

Littleham

A6
1 CHAPEL ST
2 MAGNOLIA WLK
3 LOWER FORE ST
4 MARGARET ST
5 UNION ST
6 VICTORIA PL
7 HELENA PL
8 KING ST
9 UPPER CHURCH ST
10 MAGNOLIA HO
11 QUEEN ST
12 QUEEN'S CT
13 TOWER ST
14 CRITERION PL
15 CHAPEL HILL
16 BEACON HILL
17 ALEXANDRA TERR
18 LITTLE BICTON CT
19 THE OLD WEIGHBRIDGE
20 ST SAVIOURS HO
21 DRAY CT
22 ADMIRALS CT
23 PRINCES CT
24 The Beacon CE VA
   Prim Sch
25 MYRTLE ROW
26 THE STRAND

B6
1 MONTPELLIER CT
2 ASHLEY HO
3 HIGHFIELD CT
4 HAMILTON CT
5 MAGNOLIA CT

A B C D E F

B3178 WEST HILL
LITTLEHAM
CHURCH
PATH

Quentance
Farm

Knowle Hill
Plantations

West Down

LITTLEHAM CHURCH PATH

WEST HILL GDNS

CASTLE LA

SHERBROOK CL

NORTHVIEW RD

CH

8

CASTLE
COTTS

West Down
Beacon

South West Coast Path

ST MARGARET'S VIEW

Woodlands
Farm

7

RODNEY CL

81

WEST DOWN LA

World of
Country Life

6

ORCHARD CL

West Down
Farm

CEDARS

The Floors

Crowden
Point

GORE LA

MEADOW CRES

WEST DOWN VIEW

Littleham
Cove

Holiday
Park

5

80

DANGER AREA

Otter
Cove

DANGER
AREA

4

Sandy
Bay

Straight Point
Rifle Range

DANGER AREA

Straight
Point

3

79

2

1

78

03 A 04 B C 05 D E F

124
200

D6
1 PENFIELD GDNS
2 RED LION PL
3 SIDNEY CT
4 HOOPERN TERR
5 MANOR CT
6 FREDERICK TERR
7 SCHOOL HILL
8 QUEEN LA
9 STOCKTON LA
10 HATCHER ST
11 BLACKSWAN PL
12 LUSCOMBE TERR
13 PRIORY PARK RD
14 HALDON TERR
15 ORCHARD GDNS
16 PRINCES ST
17 KING ST
18 ALBERT ST
19 TOWN TREE HILL
20 GOLDEN TERR
21 OLD MANOR CT
22 WEDLAKE MEWS
23 ALEXANDER RD
24 BROOKLANDS
25 LAWN TERR

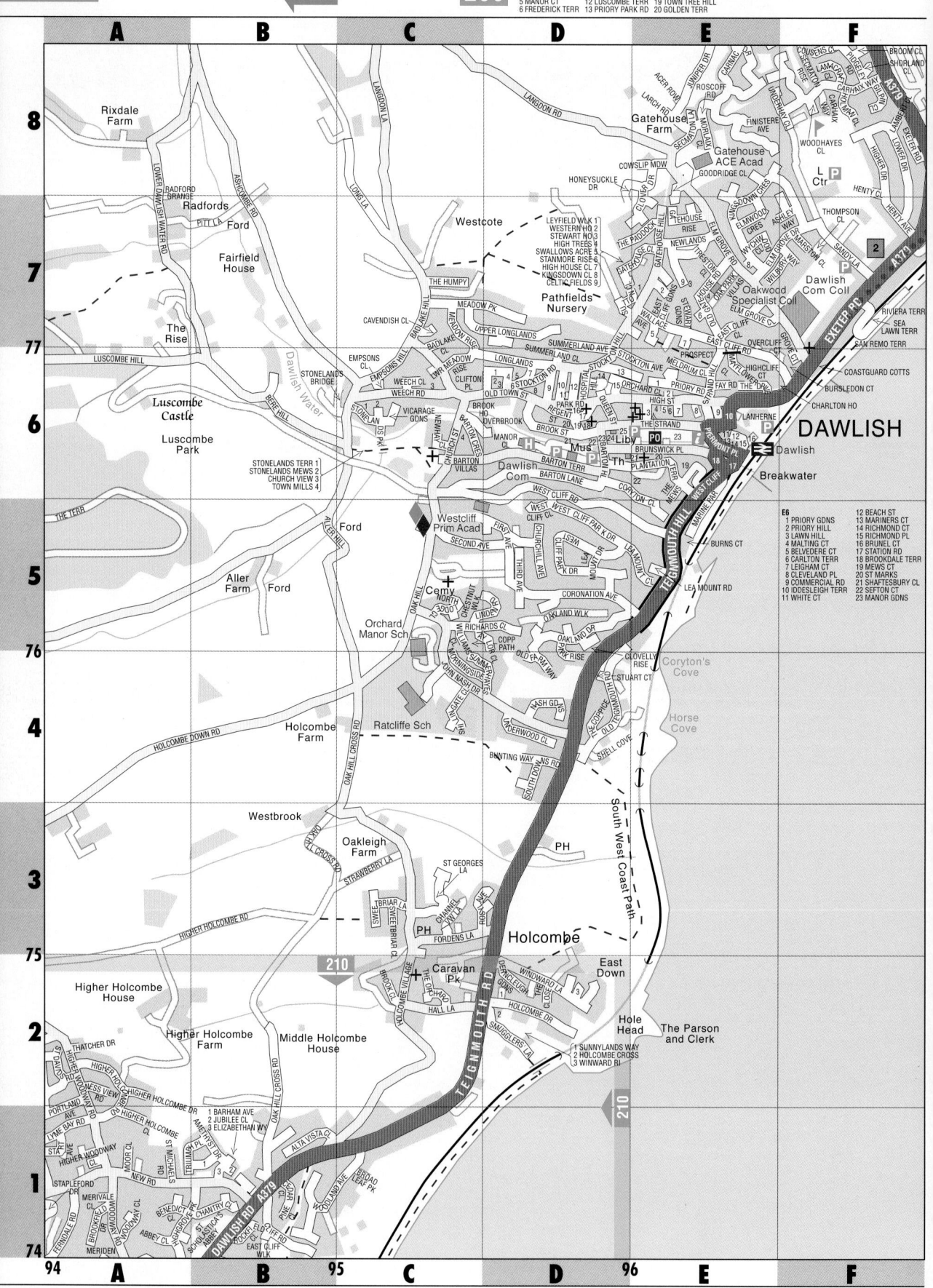

E6
1 PRIORY GDNS
2 PRIORY HILL
3 LAWN HILL
4 MALTING CT
5 BELVEDERE CT
6 CARLTON TERR
7 LEIGHAM CT
8 CLEVELAND PL
9 COMMERCIAL RD
10 IDDESLEIGH TERR
11 WHITE CT
12 BEACH ST
13 MARINERS CT
14 RICHMOND CL
15 RICHMOND PL
16 BRUNEL CT
17 STATION RD
18 BROOKDALE TERR
19 MEWS CT
20 ST MARKS
21 SHAFTESBURY CL
22 SEFTON CT
23 MANOR GDNS

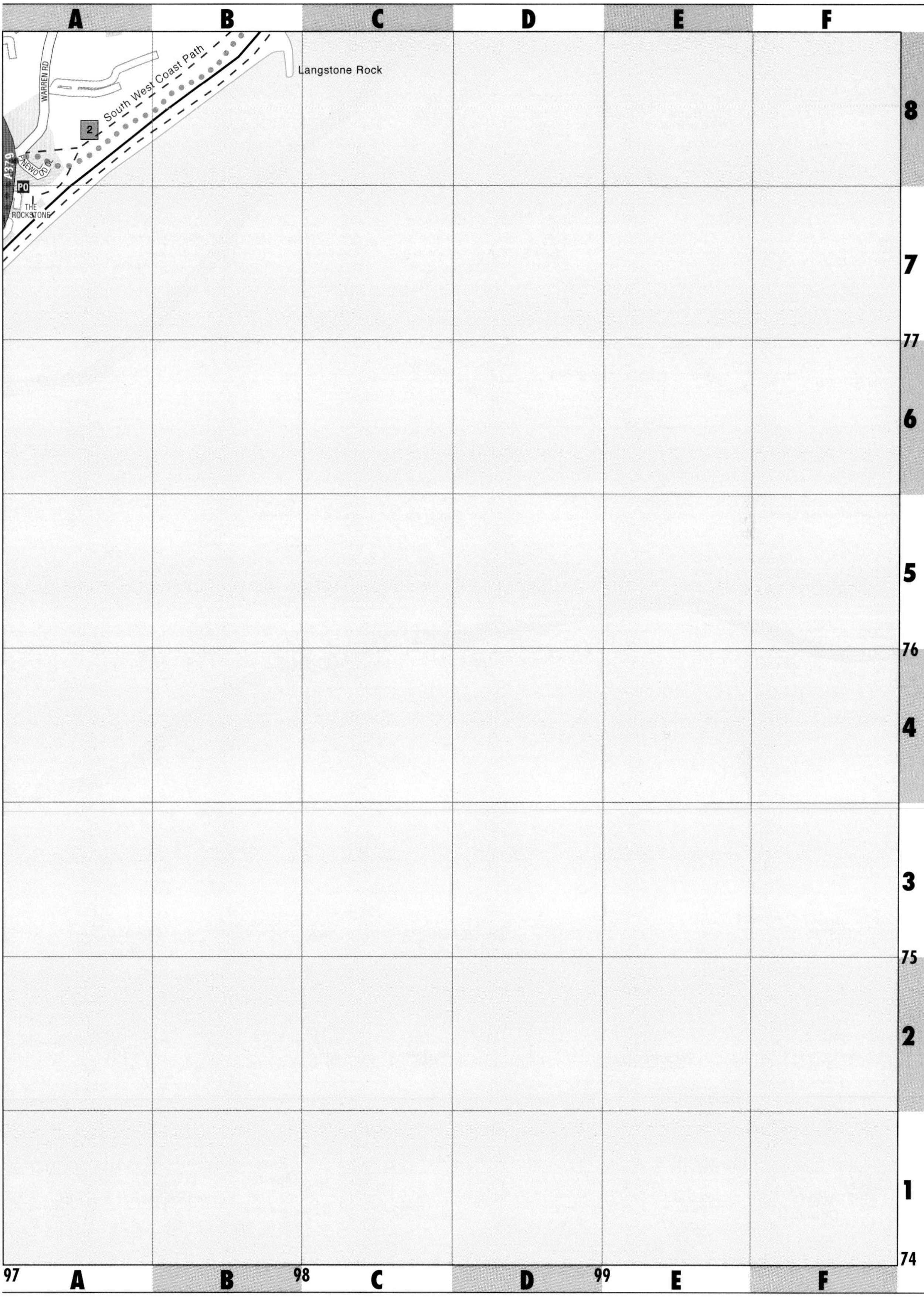

A B C D E F

8

7

77

6

5

76

4

3

75

2

1

74

WARREN RD

South West Coast Path

Langstone Rock

2

A379

PO

THE
ROCKSTONE

97 A B 98 C D 99 E F

131
123

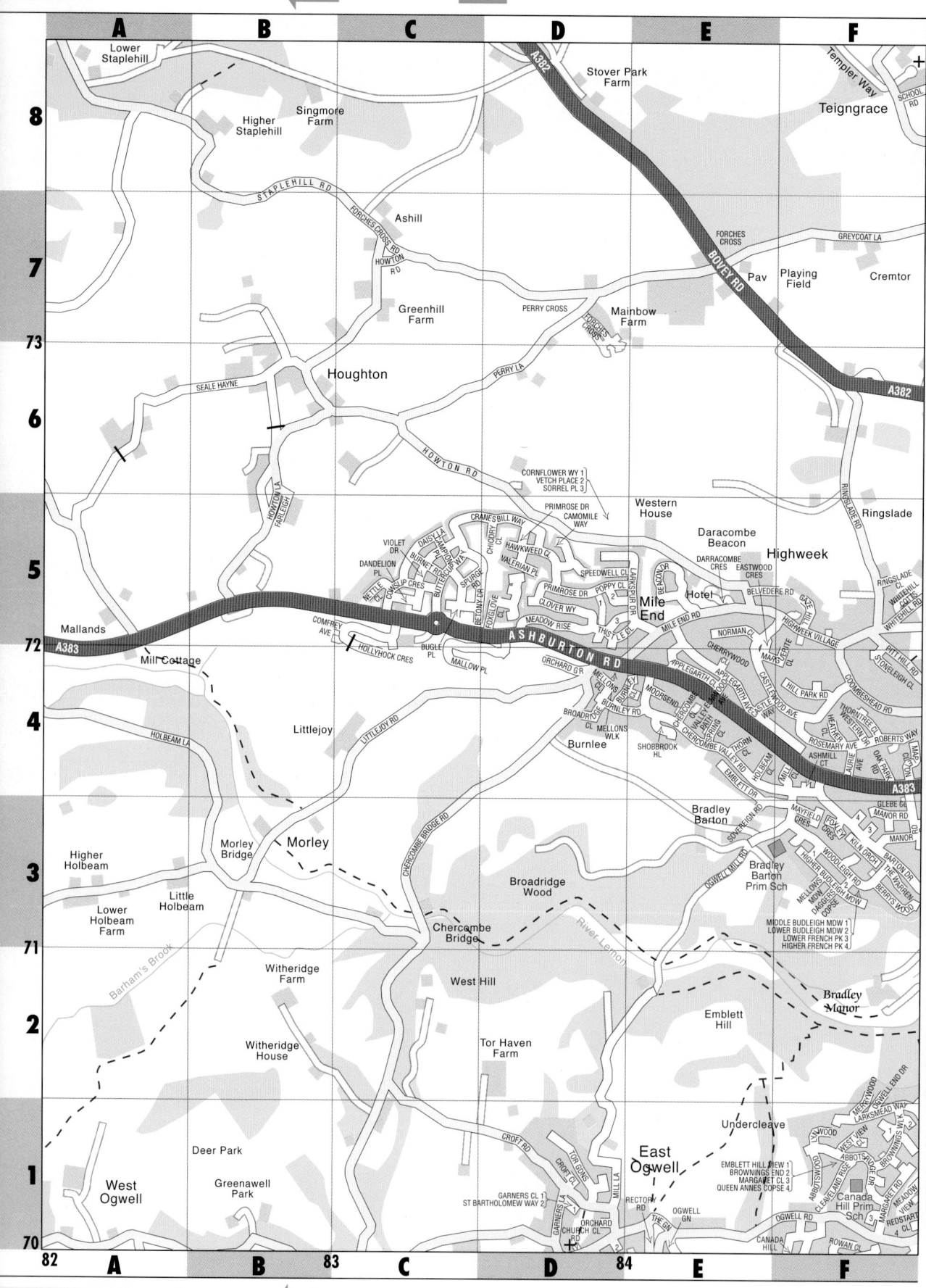
Lower Staplehill
Higher Staplehill
Singmore Farm
Stover Park Farm
Templer Way
Teigngrace
STAPLEHILL RD
Ashill
FORCHES CROSS RD
HOWTON RD
FORCHES CROSS
BOVEY RD
GREYCOAT LA
Pav
Playing Field
Cremtor
Greenhill Farm
PERRY CROSS
Mainbow Farm
Houghton
SEALE HAYNE
PERRY LA
A382
HOWTON LA
FARLEIGH
CORNFLOWER WY 1
VETCH PLACE 2
SORREL PL 3
Western House
RINGSLADE RD
Ringslade
Daracombe Beacon
Highweek
Mallands
A383
Mill Cottage
ASHBURTON RD
Mile End
Hotel
Littlejoy
LITTLEJOY RD
HOLBEAM LA
Burnlee
Bradley Barton
Morley
Morley Bridge
Higher Holbeam
Little Holbeam
Lower Holbeam Farm
Broadridge Wood
CHERCOMBE BRIDGE RD
Chercombe Bridge
River Lemon
Barham's Brook
Witheridge Farm
West Hill
Bradley Barton Prim Sch
Bradley Manor
Emblett Hill
Witheridge House
Tor Haven Farm
Undercleave
East Ogwell
Deer Park
West Ogwell
Greenawell Park
Canada Hill Prim Sch
CROFT RD
OGWELL RD

131
211

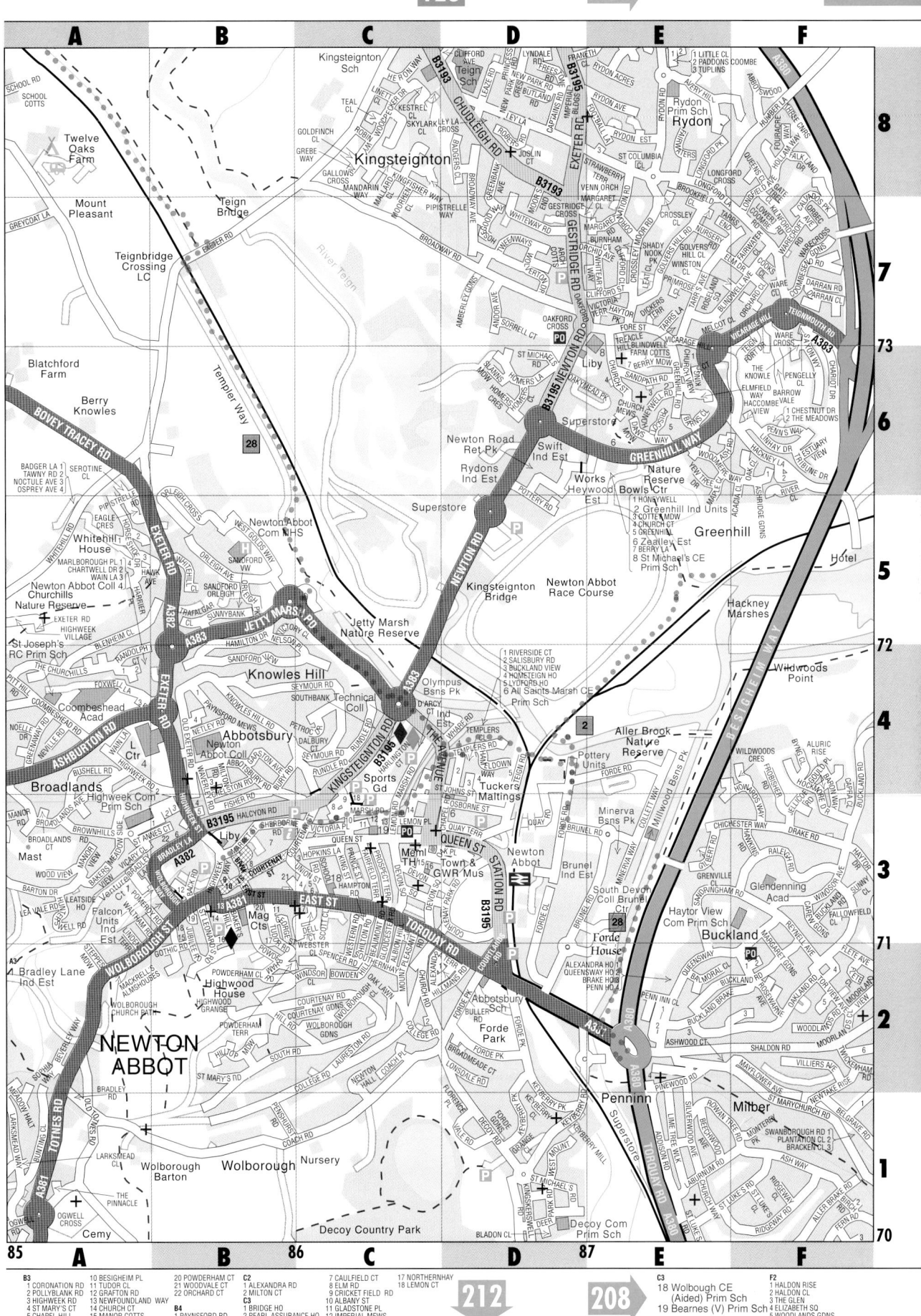

207
124

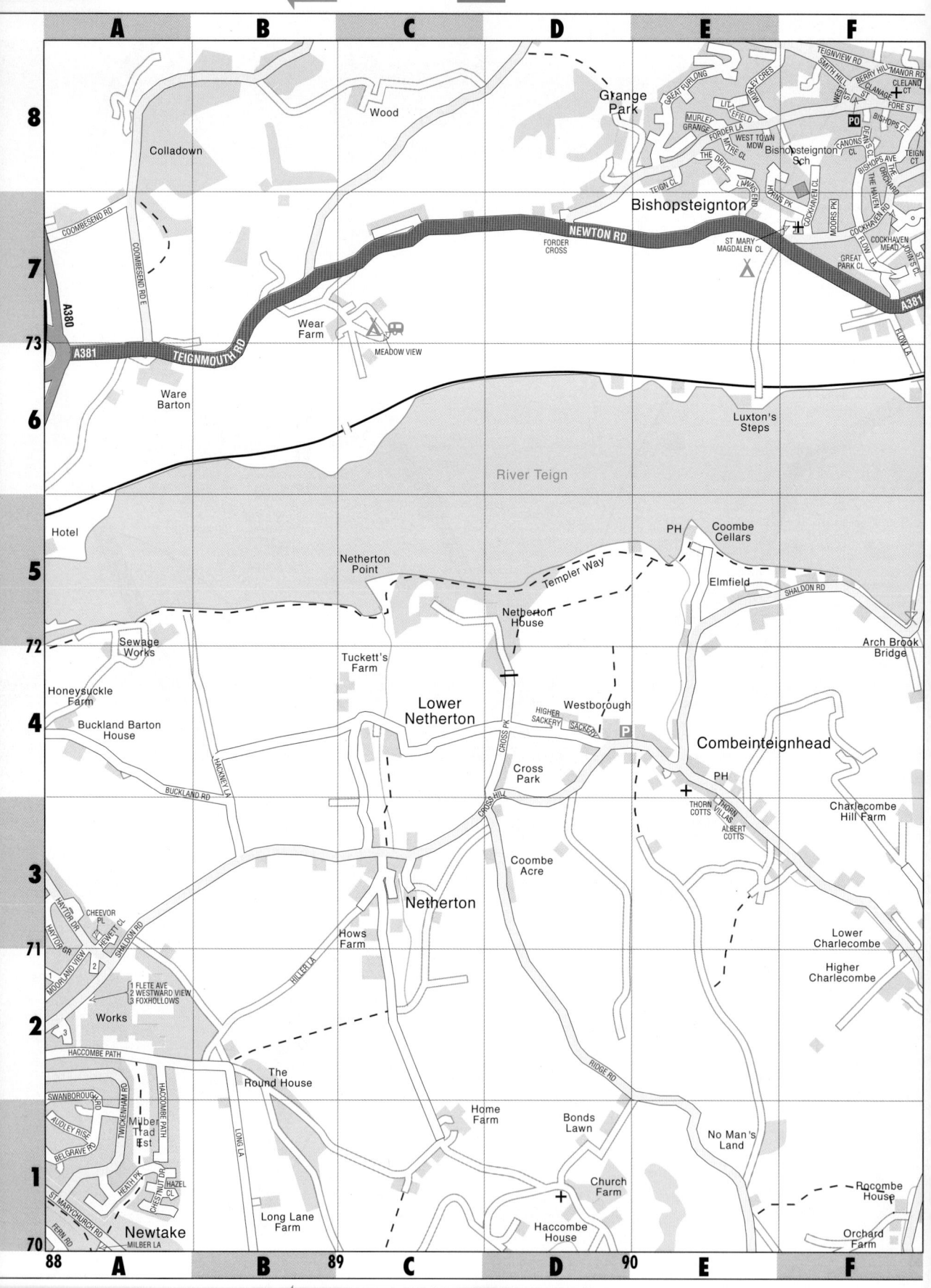
A
B
C
D
E
F
8
7
73
6
5
72
4
3
71
2
1
70
88
89
90
Wood
Grange Park
Colladown
Bishopsteignton
Bishopsteignton Sch
COOMBESEND RD
COOMBESEND RD E
NEWTON RD
FORDER CROSS
ST MARY MAGDALEN CL
A380
A381
TEIGNMOUTH RD
Wear Farm
MEADOW VIEW
Ware Barton
Luxton's Steps
River Teign
Hotel
PH
Coombe Cellars
Netherton Point
Templer Way
Elmfield
SHALDON RD
Netherton House
Sewage Works
Tuckett's Farm
Arch Brook Bridge
Honeysuckle Farm
Lower Netherton
Westborough
Buckland Barton House
HIGHER SACKERY
SACKERY
CROSS PK
Combeinteignhead
Cross Park
BUCKLAND RD
HACKNEY LA
CROSS HILL
THORN COTTS
THORN VILLAS
ALBERT COTTS
Charlecombe Hill Farm
Coombe Acre
Netherton
Hows Farm
HILLER LA
Lower Charlecombe
Higher Charlecombe
1 FLETE AVE
2 WESTWARD VIEW
3 FOXHOLLOWS
Works
HACCOMBE PATH
The Round House
RIDGE RD
SWANBOROUGH RD
TWICKENHAM RD
HACCOMBE PATH
Home Farm
Bonds Lawn
No Man's Land
AUDLEY RISE
Milber Trad Est
BELGRAVE RD
LONG LA
Church Farm
Rocombe House
HEATH PK
HAZEL CL
CHESTNUT DR
ST MARYCHURCH RD
Long Lane Farm
Haccombe House
Orchard Farm
FERN RD
Newtake
MILBER LA
HAYTOR DR
CHEEVOR PL
HEWETT CL
HAYTOR GR
SHALDON RD
MOORLAND VIEW
TEIGNVIEW RD
SMITH HILL
BERRY HILL
MANOR RD
CLANAGE
CLELAND CT
FORE ST
GREAT FURLONG
MURLEY CRES
LITTLEFIELD
MURLEY GRANGE
FORDER LA
WEST TOWN MDW
MYRTLE CL
BISHOPS CT
CANONS CL
DEAN'S CL
BISHOPS AVE
THE ORCHARD
TEIGN CT
THE DRIVE
TEIGN CL
LAWNSEND
HORNS PK
COCKHAVEN CL
MOORS PK
THE HAVEN
COCKHAVEN RD
COCKHAVEN MEAD
GREAT PARK CL
FLOW LA
JOHN'S CL
WEST ST
PO
P

207
213

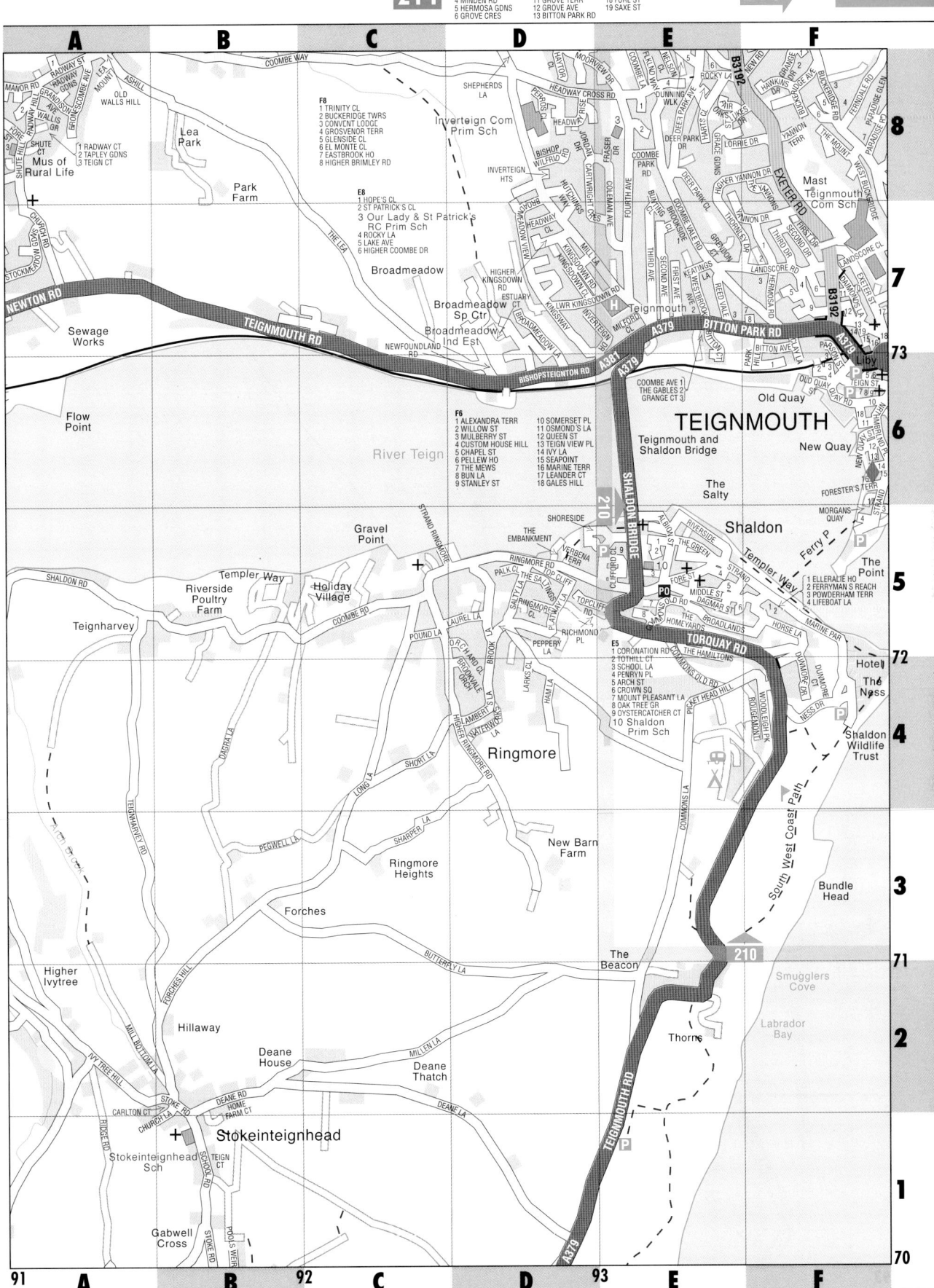

F7
1 UPPER HERMOSA RD
2 ROPE WLK
3 ELMHURST CT
4 MINDEN RD
5 HERMOSA GDNS
6 GROVE CRES
7 QUINNEL HO
8 CHELSEA PL
9 GLOUCESTER RD
10 BOSCAWEN PL
11 GROVE TERR
12 GROVE AVE
13 BITTON PARK RD
14 DOUGLAS HO
15 ST JAMES 'S PREC
16 ST JAMES HO
17 SPERANZA GR
18 FORE ST
19 SAXE ST

124 124 204

B6
1 TRINITY CL
2 BUCKERIDGE TWRS
3 CONVENT LODGE
4 GROSVENOR TERR
5 GLENSIDE CL
6 EL MONTE CL
7 EASTBROOK HO
A
B
C
D
E
F
8
7
74
6
5
73
4
3
72
2
1
71
93
94
95
Higher Holcombe House
Holcombe
Caravan Pk
East Down
Hole Head
Higher Holcombe Farm
Middle Holcombe House
Hazeldown Sch
Cemy
Trinity Sch
Our Lady & St Patricks RC Prim Sch
Mast
Teignmouth Com Sch
Sprey Point
Station Yd Bsns Pk
Outdoor Pool
Teignmouth
TEIGNMOUTH
Liby
Mus
Old Quay
New Quay
Teignmouth Pier
Teignmouth and Shaldon Bridge
River Teign
The Salty
Shaldon Prim Sch
Shaldon
IRB Sta
The Point
Ferry P
Templer Way
Hotel
The Ness
Shaldon Wildlife Trust
South West Coast Path
Bundle Head
HIGHER EXETER RD
EXETER RD
BITTON PARK RD
DAWLISH RD
TEIGNMOUTH RD
SHALDON BRIDGE
TORQUAY RD
A379
A381
B3192
HEATHLANDS RISE 1
HEATHLANDS CT 2
SHACKLETON WK 1
CHICHESTER CL 2
1 SOPER WLK
2 SOPER RD
3 DUNNING WLK
4 DUNNING RD
1 DERNCLEUGH GDNS
2 SUNNYLANDS WAY
3 HOLCOMBE CROSS
1 HOPE'S CL
2 ST PATRICK'S CL
3 DUNNING WLK
1 CHILTON AVE
2 BRUNEL CL
3 BARNPARK CL
4 BARNSLEY DR
5 LIVINGSTONE RD
C5
1 BARNSLEY CL
2 LOWER BRIMLEY CL
3 ALWYNS CL
4 HAMBLETON HO
5 ALWYNS CT
6 BELGRAVE TERR
7 ABBEYFIELD HO
8 GLADSTONE TERR
9 SALISBURY TERR
10 SHUTE HILL CRES
11 HEYWOODS CL
12 GLENDARAGH RD
13 LOWER BROOK ST
14 ALBERTA CT
15 MERE LA
16 BROOK ST
17 CLIFTON HO
1 COOMBE AVE
2 INVERTEIGN DR
3 THE GABLES
4 GRANGE CT
C4
1 ORCHARD HO
2 BICKFORD LA
3 STATION RD
4 HOLLANDS RD
5 POUND LA
6 REGENTS GDNS
7 FRENCH ST
8 FORE ST
9 CLAMPET LA
10 ORCHARD GDNS
11 GEORGE ST
12 BANK ST
13 WELLINGTON ST
14 WATERLOO ST
15 TRIANGLE PL
16 THE TRIANGLE
17 COURTENAY PL
18 REGENT ST
19 BATH TERR
20 CARLTON PL
21 POWDERHAM CT
22 DOLPHIN CT
23 MARINA CT
1 ELLERALIE HO
2 FERRYMAN S REACH
B4
1 ALEXANDRA TERR
2 WILLOW ST
3 MULBERRY ST
4 CUSTOM HOUSE HILL
5 CHAPEL ST
6 PELLEW HO
7 THE MEWS
8 BUN LA
9 WEDGWOOD CT
10 STANLEY ST
11 SOMERSET PL
12 OSMOND S LA
13 QUEEN ST
14 TEIGN VIEW PL
15 IVY LA
16 SEAPOINT
17 MARINE TERR
18 LEANDER CT
19 CHAPEL ST
B5
1 UPPER HERMOSA RD
2 ROPE WLK
3 ELMHURST CT
4 MINDEN RD
5 HERMOSA GDNS
6 GROVE CRES
7 QUINNEL HO
8 CHELSEA PL
9 GLOUCESTER RD
10 BOSCAWEN PL
11 GROVE TERR
12 GROVE AVE
13 BITTON PARK RD
14 DOUGLAS HO
15 ST JAME'S PREC
16 ST JAMES' HO
17 SPERANZA GR
18 ST JAMES MEWS
19 FORE ST
20 SAXE ST
A3
1 CORONATION RD
2 TOTHILL CT
3 SCHOOL LA
4 PENRYN PL
5 ARCH ST
6 CROWN SQ
7 MOUNT PLEASANT LA
8 OAK TREE GR
9 OYSTERCATCHER CT

209 209

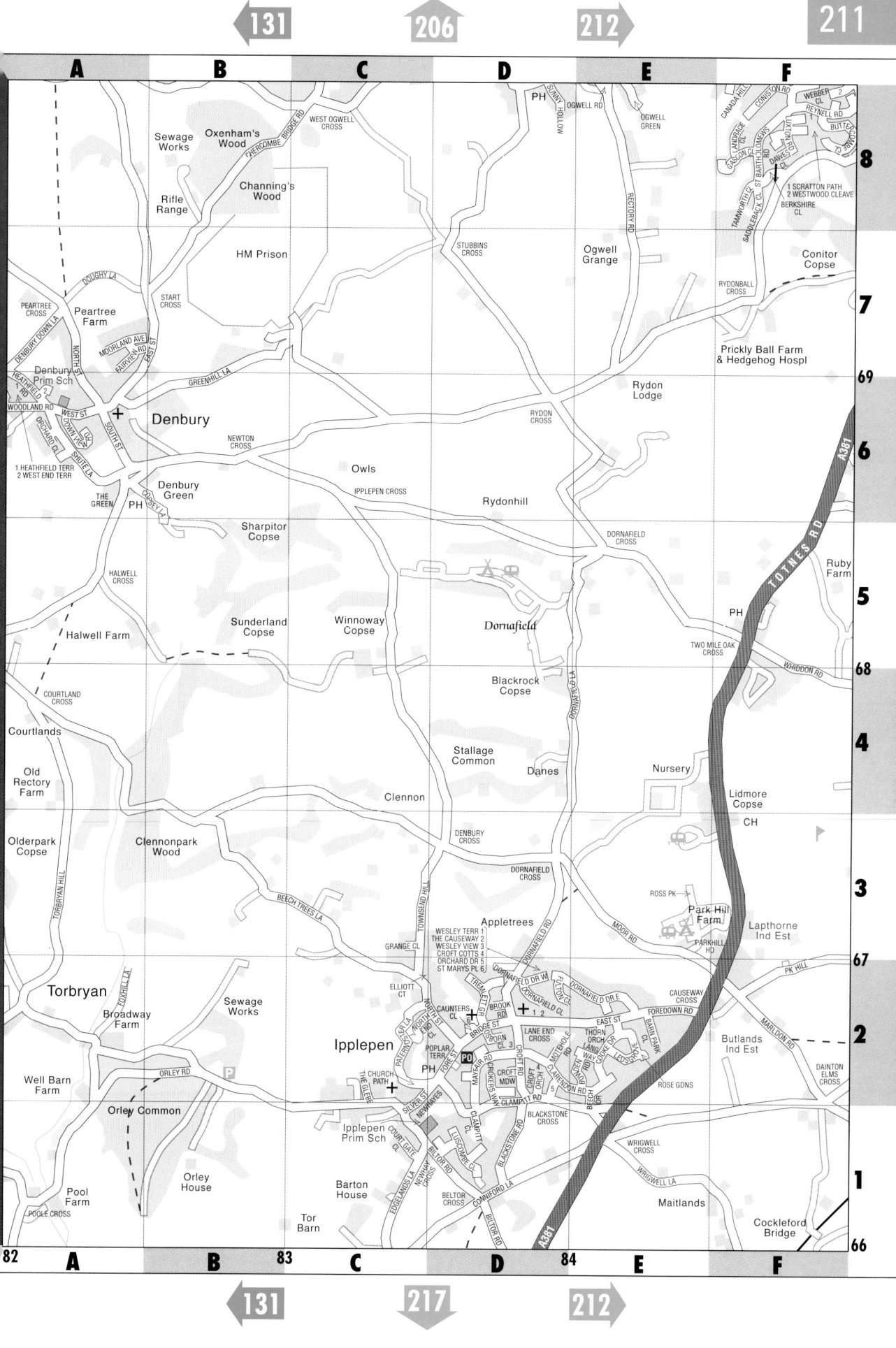

A

Sewage Works
Oxenham's Wood
Rifle Range
Channing's Wood
Peartree Cross
Peartree Farm
Doughy La
Moorland Ave
Fairyel Rd
Denbury Prim Sch
Heathfield Rd
Woodland Rd
Orchard Cl
West St
Down Cl
South St
Shute La
1 Heathfield Terr
2 West End Terr
THE GREEN
Denbury Green
PH
Cosey La
Halwell Cross
Halwell Farm
Courtland Cross
Courtlands
Old Rectory Farm
Olderpark Copse
Clennonpark Wood
Torbryan Hill
Beech Trees La
Foxhill La
Torbryan
Broadway Farm
Sewage Works
Well Barn Farm
Orley Rd
Orley Common
Orley House
Pool Farm
Poole Cross

B

West Ogwell Cross
Fercombe
Bridge Rd
HM Prison
Start Cross
Greenhill La
Newton Cross
Denbury
Sharpitor Copse
Sunderland Copse
Winnoway Copse
Ippelpen Cross
Owls

C

Stubbins Cross
Rydon Cross
Rydonhill
Dornafield
Blackrock Copse
Stallage Common
Danes
Clennon
Denbury Cross
Grange Cl
Townsend Hill
Appletrees
Wesley Terr 1
The Causeway 2
Wesley View 3
Croft Cotts 4
Orchard Dr 5
St Marys Pl 6
Elliott Ct
Caunters Cl
North End Cl
Paterns La
Clifa La
Ipplepen
Poplar Terr
PH
Church Path
Silver St
Newhayes
The Glebe
Ipplepen Prim Sch
Courtgate Cl
Barton House
Tor Barn
Edgelands La
Newway Cross
Beltor Rd
Beltor Cross
Luscombe Cl
Clampitt Cl
Clampitt Rd
Coniford La

D

PH
Sunny Hollow
Ogwell Rd
Ippelpen Cross
Dornafield Cross
Dornafield La
Dornafield Cross
Wesley
Treacle Gn
Brook Rd
Bridge St
Croft Rd
Croft Mdw
Lane End Cross
Crokers Way
Blackstone Rd
Blackstone Cross
Motehole Rd
Clarendon Rd
Billton Rd

E

Ogwell Green
Ogwell Grange
Rectory Rd
Rydon Lodge
Dornafield Cross
Dornafield Dr W
Dornafield Rd
Moor Rd
Parkhill Rd
Dornafield Dr E
East St
Thorn Orch Cl
Lang Way
Caring Rd
Foredown Rd
Barn Park
Beech Rd
Rose Gdns
Wrigwell Cross
Wrigwell La
Maitlands

F

Canada Hill
Coniston Rd
Webber Cl
Reynell Rd
Buttock Cl
Gascoyne Cl
Gardrange Cl
Tamworth Cl
Saddleback Cl
St Bartholomews
Dawes Rd
Dixon Cl
Berkshire Cl
1 Scratton Path
2 Westwood Cleave
Conitor Copse
Rydonball Cross
Prickly Ball Farm & Hedgehog Hospl
A381
Totnes Rd
Two Mile Oak Cross
Ruby Farm
PH
Whiddon Rd
Lidmore Copse
CH
Nursery
Ross Pk
Park Hill Farm
Parkhill
Lapthorne Ind Est
Pk Hill
Causeway Cross
Marldon Rd
Butlands Ind Est
Dainton Elms Cross
Cockleford Bridge

Grid rows: 8, 7, 69, 6, 5, 68, 4, 3, 67, 2, 1, 66

211 207

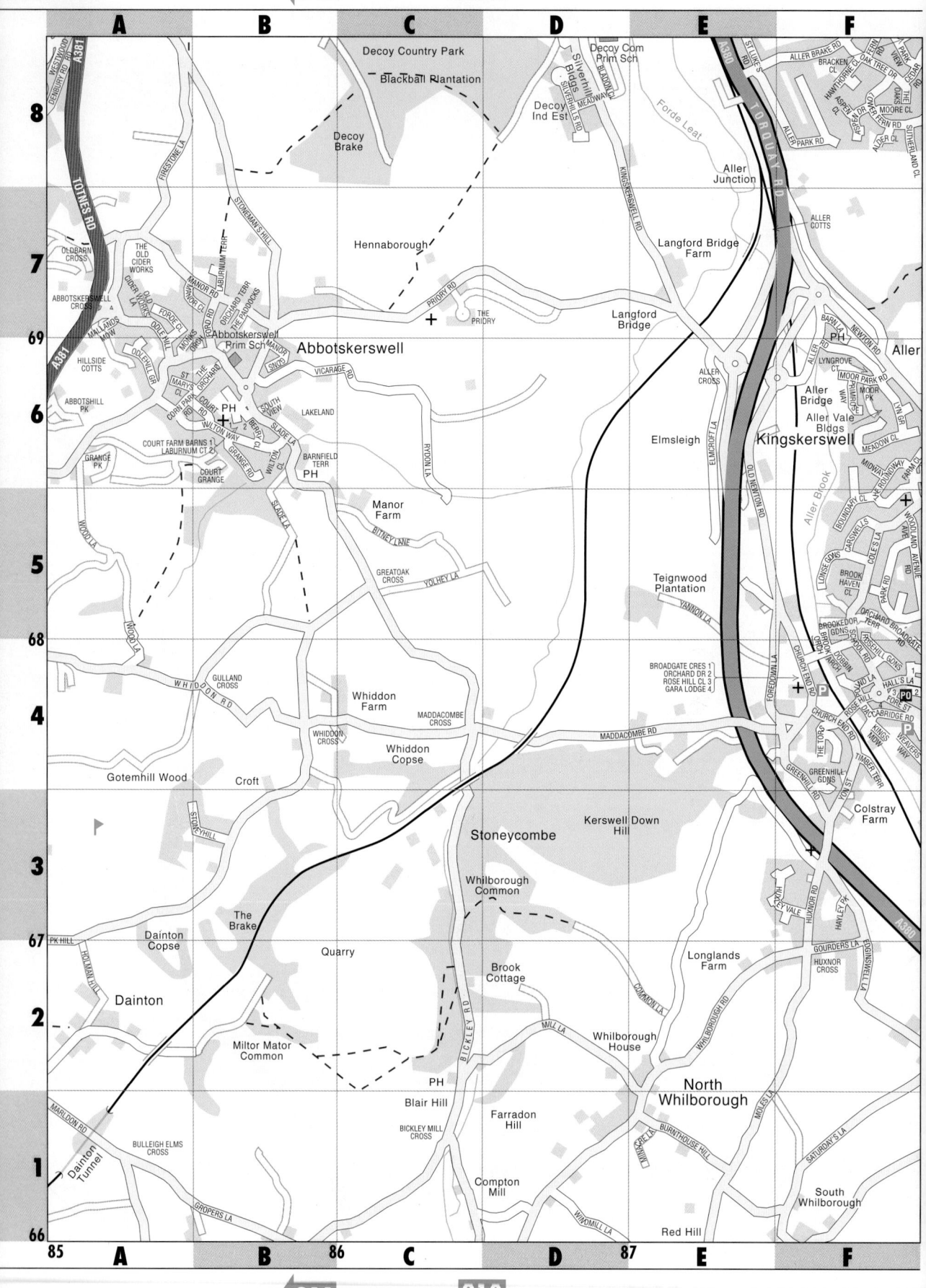

Decoy Country Park
Blackball Plantation
Decoy Brake
Decoy Com Prim Sch
Silverhills Bldgs
Decoy Ind Est
Forde Leat
Aller Junction
TORQUAY RD
TOTNES RD
A381
A380
Hennaborough
Langford Bridge Farm
Langford Bridge
THE PRIORY
PRIORY RD
Abbotskerswell
Abbotskerswell Prim Sch
STONEMAN'S HILL
LAKELAND
VICARAGE RD
RYDON LA
Elmsleigh
Kingskerswell
Aller
Aller Bridge
Aller Vale Bldgs
ALLER CROSS
ALLER COTTS
Manor Farm
BITNEY LANE
GREATOAK CROSS
YOLHEY LA
Teignwood Plantation
YANNON LA
Whiddon Farm
WHIDDON RD
GULLAND CROSS
MADDACOMBE CROSS
MADDACOMBE RD
WHIDDON CROSS
Whiddon Copse
Gotemhill Wood
Croft
Stoneycombe
Kerswell Down Hill
Colstray Farm
Whilborough Common
The Brake
Dainton Copse
Quarry
Brook Cottage
Longlands Farm
Dainton
Miltor Mator Common
BICKLEY RD
MILL LA
Whilborough House
North Whilborough
Blair Hill
Farradon Hill
BICKLEY MILL CROSS
BULLEIGH ELMS CROSS
Dainton Tunnel
Compton Mill
South Whilborough
Red Hill
GROPERS LA
WINDMILL LA
BURNTHOUSE HILL
SATURDAY'S LA
MOLES LA
WHILBOROUGH RD
COMMON LA
HUXNOR CROSS
GOURDERS LA
BROADGATE CRES 1
ORCHARD DR 2
ROSE HILL CL 3
GARA LODGE 4
A B C D E F
8 7 69 6 5 68 4 3 67 2 1 66
85 86 87

211 218

208
214

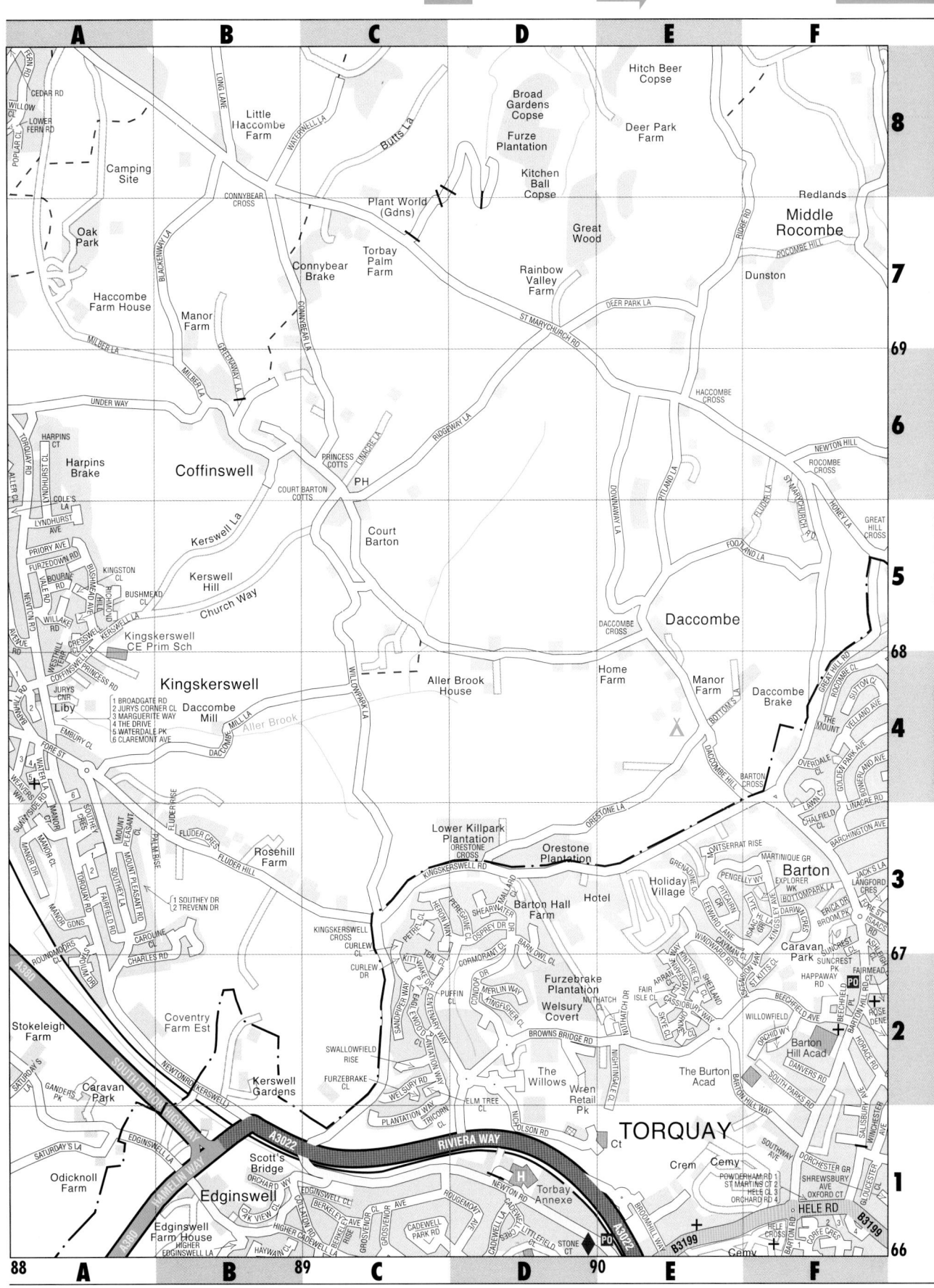
Little Haccombe Farm
Camping Site
Oak Park
Haccombe Farm House
Manor Farm
Connybear Brake
Torbay Palm Farm
Plant World (Gdns)
Broad Gardens Copse
Furze Plantation
Kitchen Ball Copse
Hitch Beer Copse
Deer Park Farm
Great Wood
Rainbow Valley Farm
Redlands
Middle Rocombe
Dunston
Harpins Brake
Coffinswell
Court Barton
Kerswell Hill
Kingskerswell CE Prim Sch
Kingskerswell
Daccombe Mill
Aller Brook House
Home Farm
Daccombe
Manor Farm
Daccombe Brake
Lower Killpark Plantation
Orestone Plantation
Rosehill Farm
Barton Hall Farm
Hotel
Holiday Village
Barton
Caravan Park
Furzebrake Plantation
Welsury Covert
Coventry Farm Est
Stokeleigh Farm
Caravan Park
Kerswell Gardens
The Willows
Wren Retail Pk
The Burton Acad
Barton Hill Acad
TORQUAY
Odicknoll Farm
Scott's Bridge
Edginswell
Edginswell Farm House
Torbay Annexe
Crem
Cemy
RIVIERA WAY
SOUTH DEVON HIGHWAY
HAMELIN WAY
1 BROADGATE RD
2 JURYS CORNER CL
3 MARGUERITE WAY
4 THE DRIVE
5 WATERDALE PK
6 CLAREMONT AVE
1 SOUTHEY DR
2 TREVENN DR
POWDERHAM RD 1
ST MARTINS CT 2
HELE CL 3
ORCHARD RD 4

219
214

213
209

A
B
C
D
E
F
8
7
69
6
5
68
4
3
67
2
1
66
91
92
93
A379
HIGHER COMMONS
POOLS WEIR
STOKE RD
Lower Gabwell
WHITEWAY LA
Higher Gabwell
Hafod Farm
Herring Cove
KIRTONS RD
GABWELL HILL
GABWELL LA
RIDGE RD
STOKE RD
Mackerel Cove
Higher Rocombe Barton
ASHACRE CROSS
Ross Hill
Blackaller's Cove
LONGPARK HILL
NEWTON HILL
Maidencombe
MAIDENCOMBE CROSS
STEEP HILL
TEIGNMOUTH RD
BRIM HILL
PH
Maidencombe Beach
BARTON HILL
HIGHER ROCOMBE
SLADNOR PARK RD
ORESTONE DR
SLADNOR PK
South West Coast Path
Babbacombe Bay
CLADDON LA
ROCK HOUSE LA
BARRADON CL
GOLDEN PK AVE
Great Hill
SOUTHERN CL
SEYMOUR DR
MAIDENCOMBE HO
Rock House
BOWERLAND AVE
BRAESIDE RD
PADACRE RD
MERRIVALE CL
KINGSGATE CL
ASHLEY PRIORS LA
WATCOMBE HEIGHTS RD
SWEDWELL RD
HELENS MEAD CL
HELENS MEAD RD
PEASLAND RD
BOVE PARK RD
COKER AVE
SWEDWELL LA
LINACRE RD
SCORESBY CL
Valley of Rocks
Whitsand Beach
Watcombe Head
BARCHINGTON AVE
GARD CL
PRINCE CHARLES CT
LEA RD
PO
HEAVISIDE CL
STEPS LA
THE CONIFERS
Watcombe Prim Sch
Mayfield Sch
Watcombe Beach
JACK'S LA
MOOR LA
WATCOMBE BEACH RD
MINCENT CL
MINCENT HILL
Combe Pafford Sch
STEPS CROSS
CHURCH RD
SUSSEX CL
WILLOW AVE
WHEATCOMBE CT
SMALLDON LA
Smugglers' Hole
ST AUGUSTINES CL
ISAACS RD
EDGELEY RD
STARPITTEN LA W
WESLEY MEWS
ORANGE GR
CLENNON LA
CLENNON CT
Watcombe
Playing Field
EASTERFIELD LA
TORQUAY
Shag Cliff
FALLOWAY CL
HALSTEADS RD
COLERIDGE CT
FORE ST
1 STADDON GDNS
2 CORNFIELD GN
3 SWEB ENTRANCE
4 SOVEREIGN MWS
HAPPAWAY RD
Ind Est
GARTH RD
FIRLANDS RD
IDEWELL RD
PAVOR RD
GRASMERE CL
Roundhouse Point
LUMMATON CROSS
COMBE RD
BIGBURY WAY
Petit Tor Beach
1 STABLE LA
2 HILLY GARDENS RD
3 PETIT WELL LA
4 ST MARY'S CT
5 CHARLOTTE CT
6 THE PADDOCK
7 PETITOR MEWS
8 CAMPION CT
9 CHURCH RD
Combe Pafford
Playing Field
B3199
LUMMATON PL
ST MARYCHURCH RD
Petit Tor
St Marychurch
St Marychurch CE Prim Sch
CH
Petit Tor Point
COMBE PK
COMBE LA
TEIGNMOUTH RD
WINSTONE AVE
LICHFIELD AVE
SHREWSBURY AVE
TRURO
LINCOLN GN
WESTERN RD
TRUMLANDS RD
CARY CASTLE DR
PETITOR RD
REDCLIFFE RD
THE LINKS
Cuthbert Mayne Sch
CUTHBERT CL
BRADLEY PARK RD
ROWLEY RD
B3199

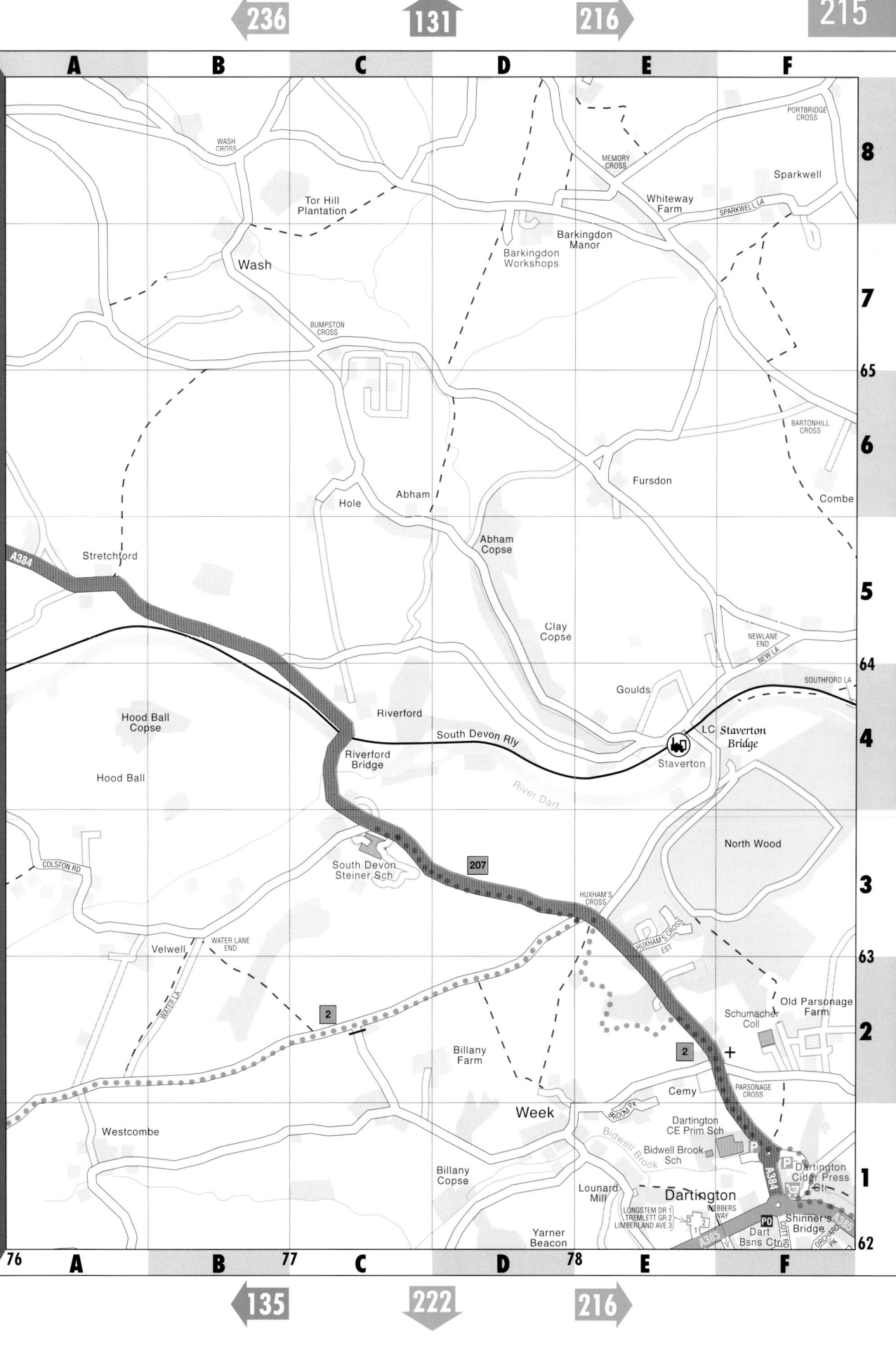

A   B   C   D   E   F

8
7
65
6
5
64
4
3
63
2
1
62

PORTBRIDGE CROSS
WASH CROSS
MEMORY CROSS
Sparkwell
Tor Hill Plantation
Whiteway Farm
SPARKWELL LA
Barkingdon Manor
Wash
Barkingdon Workshops
BUMPSTON CROSS
BARTONHILL CROSS
Fursdon
Combe
Hole
Abham
Abham Copse
Stretchford
A384
NEWLANE END
NEW LA
Clay Copse
SOUTHFORD LA
Hood Ball Copse
Riverford
Goulds
LC
Staverton Bridge
South Devon Rly
Staverton
Riverford Bridge
Hood Ball
River Dart
North Wood
COLSTON RD
207
South Devon Steiner Sch
HUXHAM'S CROSS
Velwell
WATER LANE END
HUXHAM'S CROSS EST
Old Parsonage Farm
WATER LA
2
Schumacher Coll
2
Billany Farm
+
PARSONAGE CROSS
Cemy
Westcombe
Week
BROOK PK
Dartington CE Prim Sch
P
Bidwell Brook Sch
P
Dartington Cider Press Ctr
Billany Copse
Bidwell Brook
Lounard Mill
A384
Yarner Beacon
Dartington
WEBBERS WAY
LONGSTEM DR 1
TREMLETT GR 2
LIMBERLAND AVE 3
PO
Dart Bsns Ctr
Shinner's Bridge
ORCHARD PK
A385

215
131

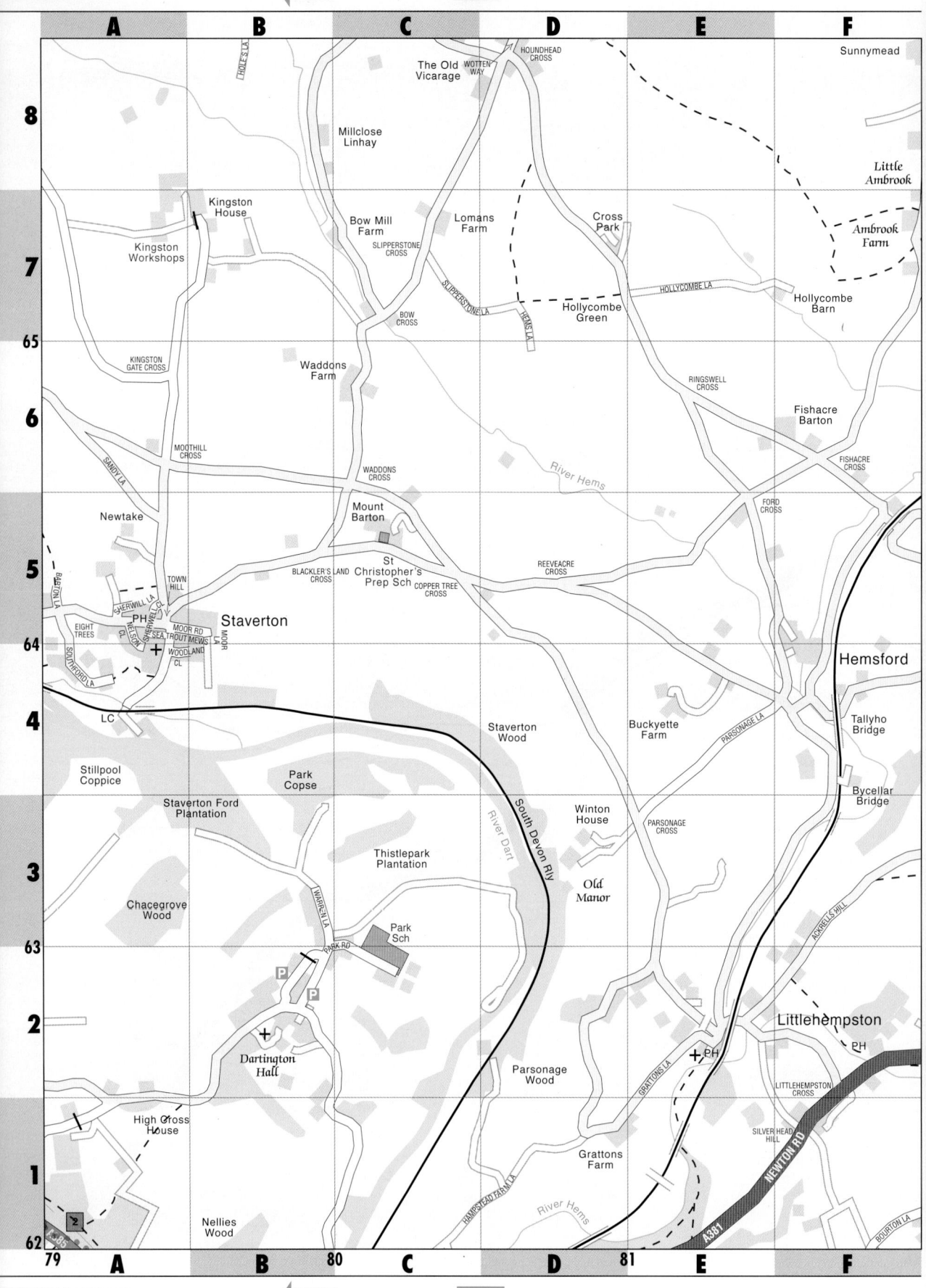
A
B
C
D
E
F
The Old Vicarage
WOTTEN WAY
HOUNDHEAD CROSS
Sunnymead
HOLE'S LA
Millclose Linhay
Little Ambrook
Kingston House
Kingston Workshops
Bow Mill Farm
Lomans Farm
Cross Park
Ambrook Farm
SLIPPERSTONE CROSS
SLIPPERSTONE LA
HEMS LA
HOLLYCOMBE LA
Hollycombe Green
Hollycombe Barn
BOW CROSS
KINGSTON GATE CROSS
Waddons Farm
RINGSWELL CROSS
Fishacre Barton
MOOTHILL CROSS
SANDY LA
WADDONS CROSS
River Hems
FISHACRE CROSS
Newtake
Mount Barton
FORD CROSS
BARTON LA
TOWN HILL
BLACKLER'S LAND CROSS
St Christopher's Prep Sch
COPPER TREE CROSS
REEVEACRE CROSS
SHERWILL LA
SHERWILL CL
PH
EIGHT TREES
NELSON CL
MOOR RD
SEA TROUT MEWS
WOODLAND CL
MOOR LA
Staverton
SOUTHFORD LA
Hemsford
LC
Staverton Wood
Buckyette Farm
PARSONAGE LA
Tallyho Bridge
Stillpool Coppice
Park Copse
Staverton Ford Plantation
South Devon Rly
River Dart
Winton House
PARSONAGE CROSS
Bycellar Bridge
Thistlepark Plantation
Old Manor
Chacegrove Wood
WARREN LA
Park Sch
PARK RD
ACKRELLS HILL
P
P
Littlehempston
PH
Dartington Hall
Parsonage Wood
GRATTONS LA
LITTLEHEMPSTON CROSS
High Cross House
SILVER HEAD HILL
NEWTON RD
Grattons Farm
HAMPSTEAD FARM LA
River Hems
A381
BOURTON LA
Nellies Wood
8
7
65
6
5
64
4
3
63
2
1
62
79
80
81

215
223

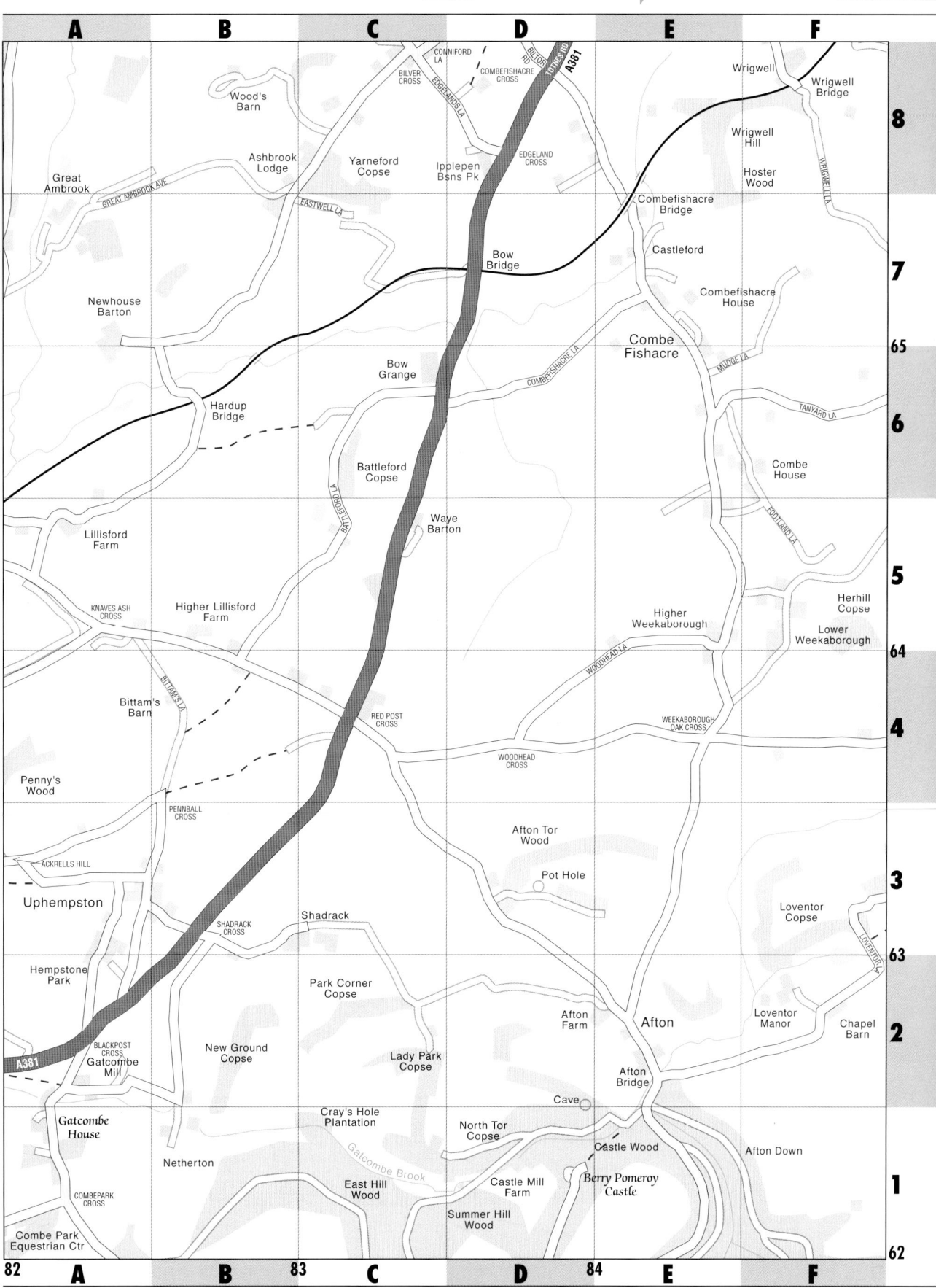

211 218

A B C D E F

8
7
65
6
5
64
4
3
63
2
1
62

224 218

Wrigwell
Wrigwell
Bridge
Wrigwell
Hill
Hoster
Wood
Combefishacre
Bridge
Castleford
Combefishacre
House
MUDGE LA
TANYARD LA
Combe
Fishacre
Combe
House
FOOTLAND LA
Herhill
Copse
Lower
Weekaborough
Higher
Weekaborough
WOODHEAD LA
WEEKABOROUGH
OAK CROSS
Loventor
Copse
LOVENTOR LA
Loventor
Manor
Chapel
Barn
Afton
Afton Bridge
Afton Down
Castle Wood
Berry Pomeroy
Castle
Afton Farm
Cave
Afton Tor
Wood
Pot Hole
North Tor
Copse
Castle Mill
Farm
Summer Hill
Wood
Woodhead
Cross
Red Post
Cross
Waye
Barton
Battleford
Copse
BATTLEFORD LA
Bow
Grange
Bow
Bridge
Ipplepen
Bsns Pk
Edgeland
Cross
EDGELANDS LA
Combefishacre
Cross
Conniford
La
Bilver
Cross
A381
BILTOR RD
TOTNES RD
Yarneford
Copse
Ashbrook
Lodge
Wood's
Barn
Great
Ambrook
GREAT AMBROOK AVE
EASTWELL LA
Newhouse
Barton
Hardup
Bridge
Lillisford
Farm
Higher Lillisford
Farm
Knaves Ash
Cross
BITTAM'S LA
Bittam's
Barn
Penny's
Wood
PENNBALL
CROSS
ACKRELLS HILL
Uphempston
Hempstone
Park
Shadrack
Cross
Shadrack
Park Corner
Copse
Lady Park
Copse
Cray's Hole
Plantation
Gatcombe Brook
East Hill
Wood
New Ground
Copse
Netherton
BLACKPOST
CROSS
Gatcombe
Mill
A381
Gatcombe
House
COMBEPARK
CROSS
Combe Park
Equestrian Ctr

82 83 84

217
212

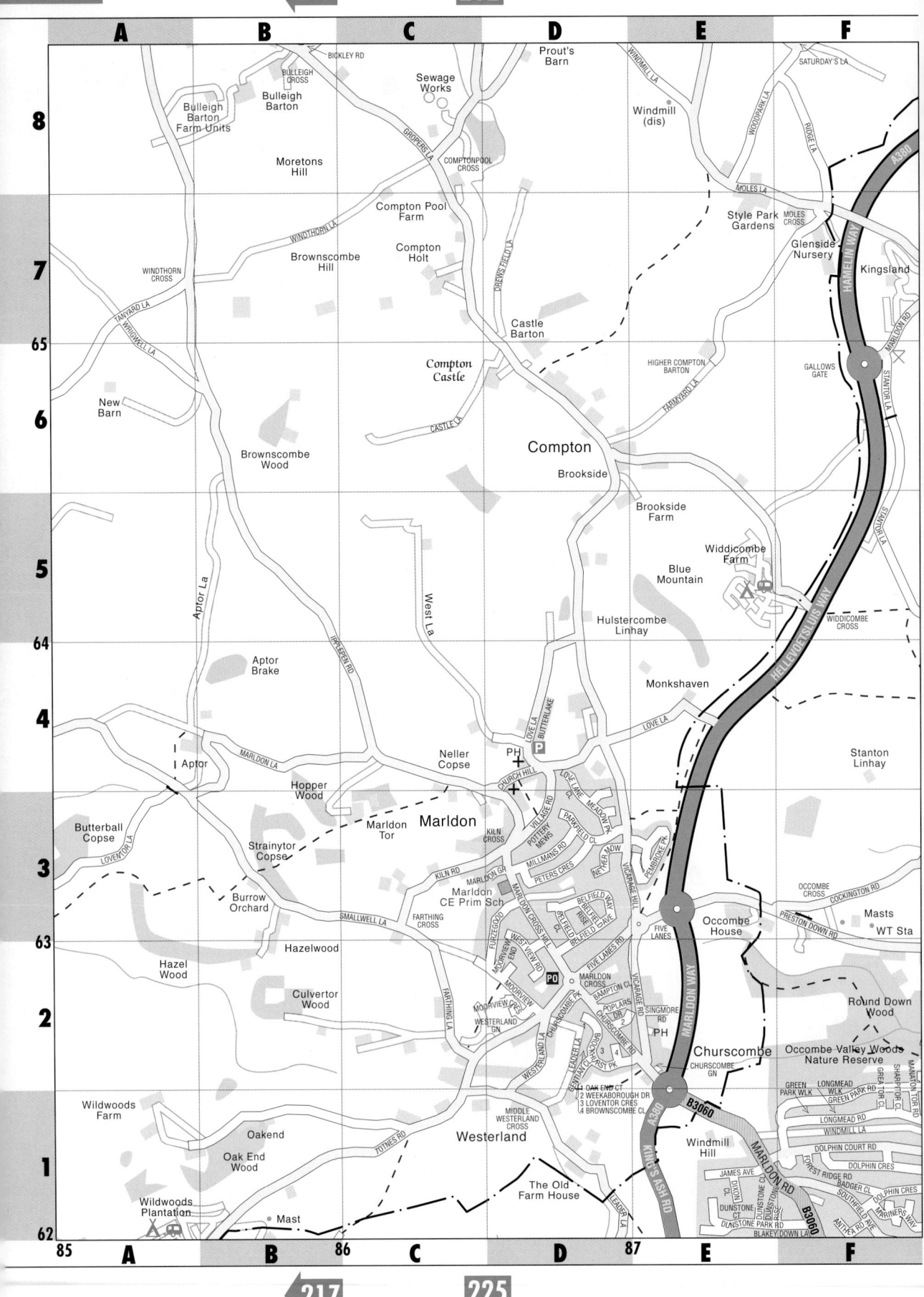
A
B
C
D
E
F
8
7
65
6
5
64
4
3
63
2
1
62
85
86
87
BICKLEY RD
BULLEIGH CROSS
Bulleigh Barton
Bulleigh Barton Farm Units
Sewage Works
Prout's Barn
WINDMILL LA
Windmill (dis)
SATURDAY'S LA
WOODPARK LA
RIDGE LA
A380
Moretons Hill
GROPERS LA
COMPTONPOOL CROSS
Compton Pool Farm
MOLES LA
Style Park Gardens
MOLES CROSS
WINDTHORN LA
Compton Holt
Glenside Nursery
HAMELIN WAY
Kingsland
WINDTHORN CROSS
Brownscombe Hill
DREWS FIELD LA
TANYARD LA
WRIGWELL LA
Castle Barton
MARLDON RD
Compton Castle
HIGHER COMPTON BARTON
GALLOWS GATE
STANTOR LA
New Barn
FARMYARD LA
CASTLE LA
Compton
Brownscombe Wood
Brookside
Brookside Farm
Widdicombe Farm
Blue Mountain
West La
Aptor La
HELLEVOETSLUIS WAY
WIDDICOMBE CROSS
Hulstercombe Linhay
Aptor Brake
IPPLEPEN RD
Monkshaven
LOVE LA
BUTTERLAKE
PH
P
Neller Copse
Aptor
MARLDON LA
Stanton Linhay
CHURCH HILL
Hopper Wood
MEADOW PK
Butterball Copse
Marldon Tor
Marldon
VILLAGE RD
POTTERY MEWS
KILN CROSS
PARKFIELD CL
LOVENTOR LA
Strainytor Copse
MILLMANS RD
NETHER MDW
PEMBROKE PK
KILN RD
PETERS CRES
MARLDON GR
VICARAGE HILL
Marldon CE Prim Sch
OCCOMBE CROSS
COCKINGTON RD
Burrow Orchard
BELFIELD WAY
BELFIELD RISE
BELFIELD AVE
SMALLWELL LA
FARTHING CROSS
FURZEGOOD
MARLDON CROSS HILL
FIVE LANES
Occombe House
PRESTON DOWN RD
Masts
WT Sta
Hazelwood
MOORVIEW END
WEST VIEW RD
FIVE LANES RD
Hazel Wood
PO
MARLDON CROSS
BAMPTON CL
Culvertor Wood
MOORVIEW
FARTHING LA
CHURSCOMBE PK
POPLARS DR
SINGMORE RD
Round Down Wood
MOORVIEW CRES
WESTERLAND GN
CHURSCOMBE RD
PH
MARLDON WAY
WESTERLAND LA
LEADER LA
BROCKHURST PK
Churscombe
Occombe Valley Woods Nature Reserve
CHURSCOMBE GN
GENTIAN CL
1 OAK END CT
2 WEEKABOROUGH DR
3 LOVENTOR CRES
4 BROWNSCOMBE CL
GREEN PARK WLK
LONGMEAD WLK
GREEN PARK RD
GREATOR CL
SHAPTOR CL
MANATON TOR RD
Wildwoods Farm
MIDDLE WESTERLAND CROSS
B3060
LONGMEAD RD
Oakend
Westerland
WINDMILL LA
Windmill Hill
TOTNES RD
KING'S ASH RD
DOLPHIN COURT RD
Oak End Wood
MARLDON RD
DOLPHIN CRES
FOREST RIDGE RD
The Old Farm House
JAMES AVE
BADGER CL
DIXON CL
DUNSTONE CL
DOLPHIN CRES
SOUTHFIELD AVE
Wildwoods Plantation
Mast
LEADER LA
DUNSTONE CT
DUNSTONE RISE
MARINERS WAY
DUNSTONE PARK RD
ANTHEA RD
BLAKEY DOWN LA
B3060

217
225

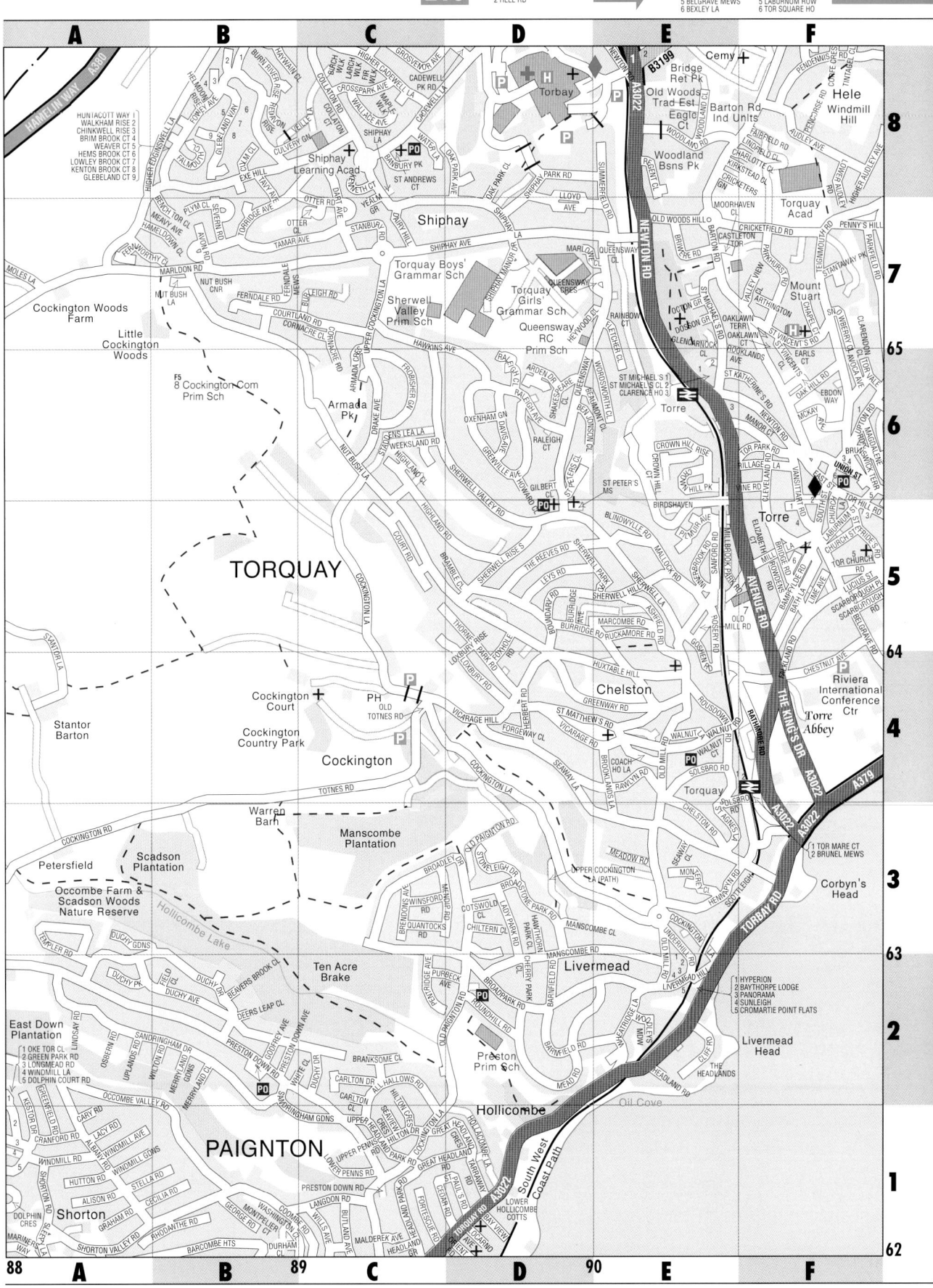

219

213 | E7
1 Torre CE Prim Sch
E8
1 Riviera Way
2 Hele Rd

220

F5
1 LANSDOWNE RD
2 LANSDOWNE LA
3 ZION RD
4 PRESTBURY PK
5 BELGRAVE MEWS
6 BEXLEY LA

F6
1 COLLEGE CT
2 MATHEW HO
3 HOMEPALMS HO
4 BRUNSWICK SQ
5 LABURNUM ROW
6 TOR SQUARE HO

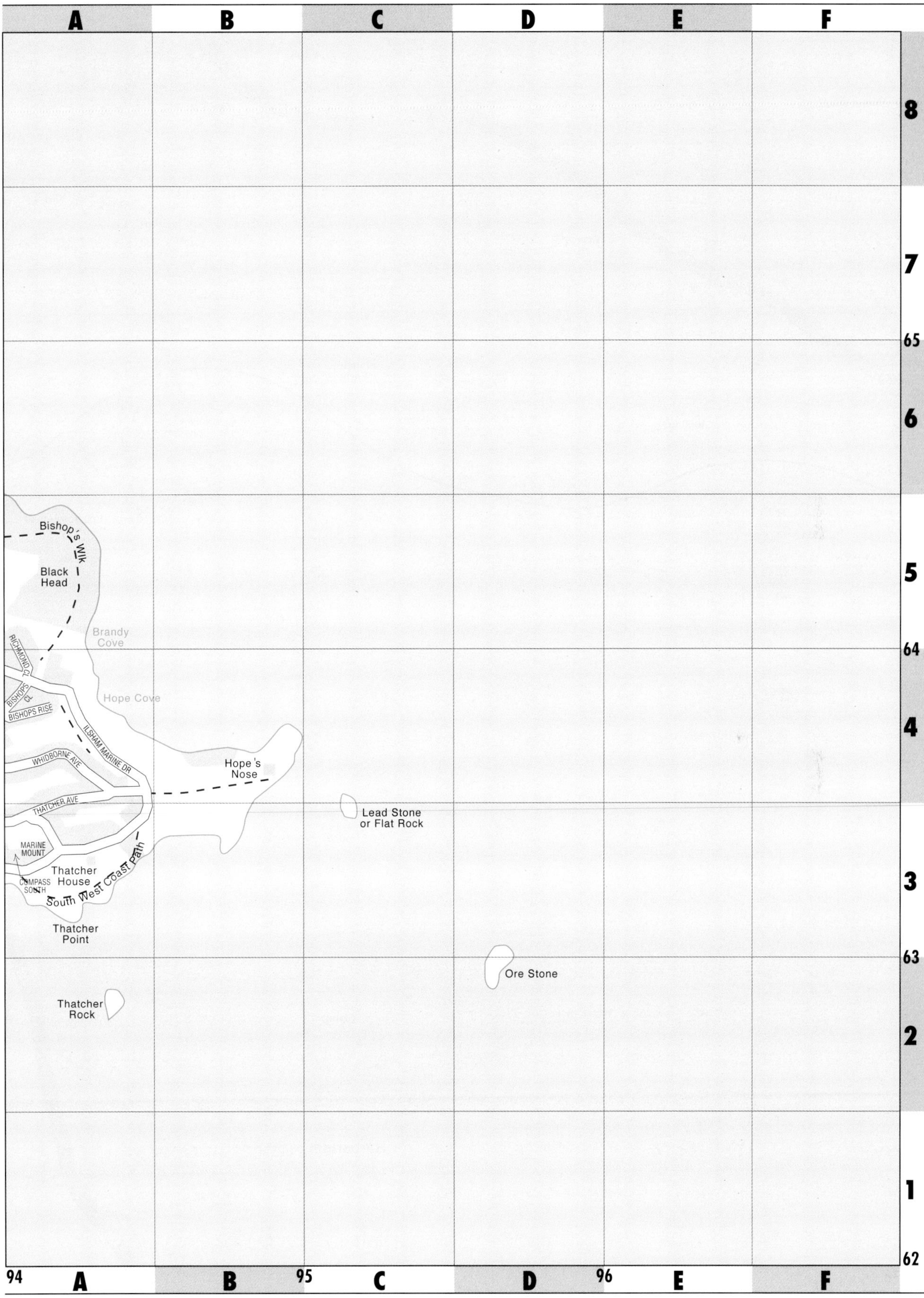

	A	B	C	D	E	F	

8

7

65

6

Bishop's Wlk
Black Head
5

Brandy Cove
64

Hope Cove
4

RICHMOND CL
BISHOPS CL
BISHOPS RISE
ILSHAM MARINE DR
WHIDBORNE AVE
Hope's Nose

THATCHER AVE
Lead Stone or Flat Rock
MARINE MOUNT
COMPASS SOUTH
Thatcher House
South West Coast Path
3

Thatcher Point
63

Ore Stone
Thatcher Rock
2

1

62

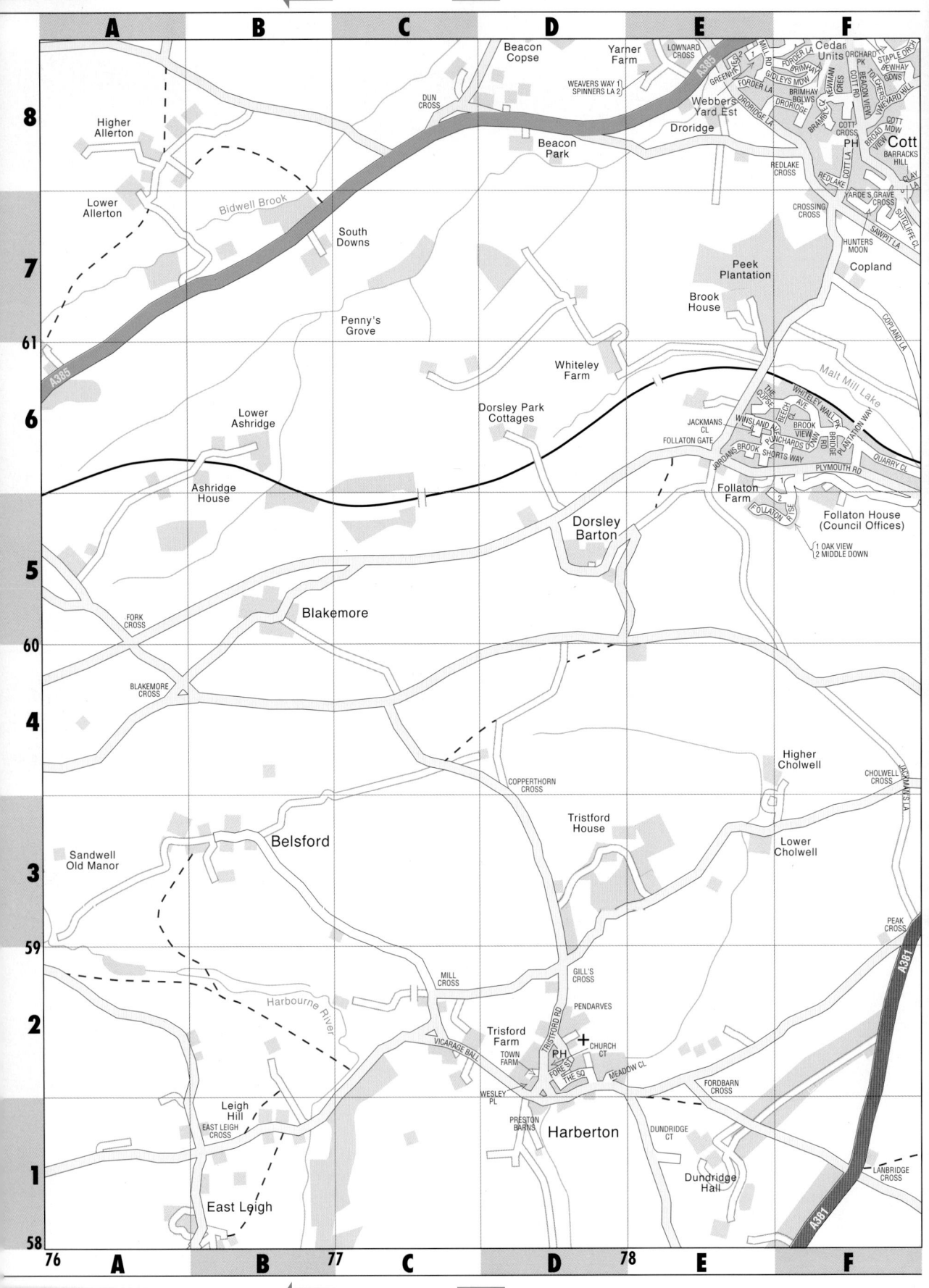

8
Higher
Allerton
Beacon
Copse
Yarner
Farm
Lownard
Cross
Cedar
Units
ORCHARD
PK
STAPLE ORCH
BEWHAY
GDNS
Dun
Cross
WEAVERS WAY 1
SPINNERS LA 2
Webbers
Yard Est
Droridge
GREENWAY
FORDER LA
GIDLEYS MDW
BRIMHAY
BGLWS
NEWMAN
CRES
COTT RD
BRAMB
BROAD MDW
COTT VIEW
COTT
MDW
Cott
BARRACKS
HILL

7
Lower
Allerton
Bidwell Brook
South
Downs
Beacon
Park
REDLAKE
CROSS
REDLAKE
YARDE S GRAVE
CROSS
CLAY
PH
CROSSING
CROSS
HUNTERS
MOON
Copland

61
Penny's
Grove
Peek
Plantation
Brook
House
SAWPIT LA
SUTLIFFE CL
COPLAND LA

6
A385
Lower
Ashridge
Whiteley
Farm
Dorsley Park
Cottages
JACKMANS
CL
FOLLATON GATE
WINSLAND AV
PINCHARDS D
SHORTS WAY
THE
CLOSE
WHITELEY WALL
BEECH
BROOK
VIEW
BRIDGE
PLANTATION WAY
Malt Mill Lake
QUARRY CL
PLYMOUTH RD

5
Ashridge
House
Dorsley
Barton
Follaton
Farm
JORDANS BROOK
FOLLATON
2
Follaton House
(Council Offices)
1 OAK VIEW
2 MIDDLE DOWN

60
Blakemore
FORK
CROSS

4
BLAKEMORE
CROSS
COPPERTHORN
CROSS
Higher
Cholwell
CHOLWELL
CROSS
Lower
Cholwell
JACKMANS LA

3
Sandwell
Old Manor
Belsford
Tristford
House
PEAK
CROSS

59
Harbourne River
MILL
CROSS
GILL'S
CROSS
PENDARVES
A361

2
VICARAGE BALL
Trisford
Farm
TOWN
FARM
PH
FORE ST
THE SQ
TRISTFORD RD
CHURCH
CT
MEADOW CL
FORDBARN
CROSS

Leigh
Hill
EAST LEIGH
CROSS
WESLEY
PL
PRESTON
BARNS
Harberton
DUNDRIDGE
CT

1
East Leigh
Dundridge
Hall
LANBRIDGE
CROSS

58

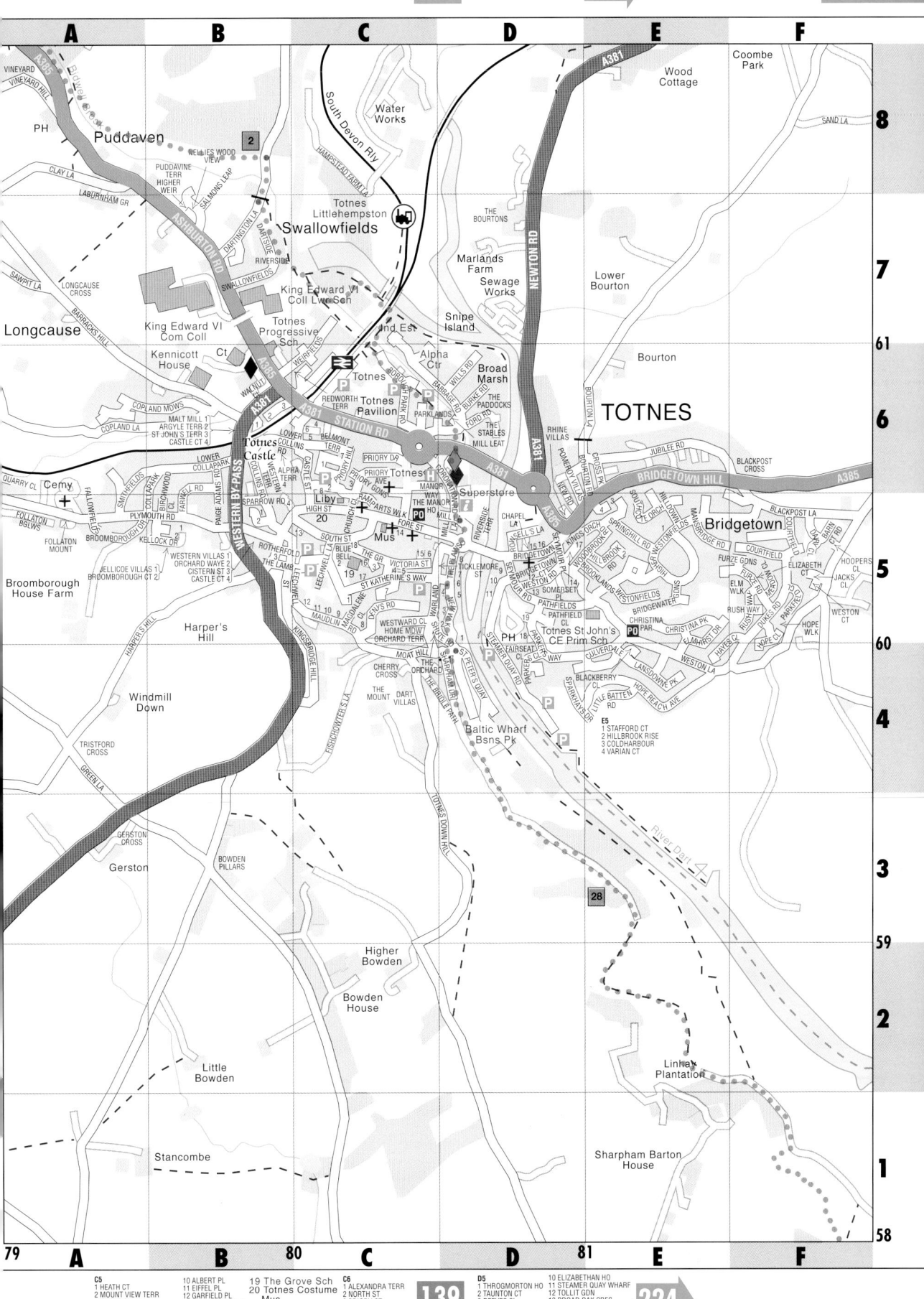

C5
1 HEATH CT
2 MOUNT VIEW TERR
3 GROVE CL
4 VICTORIA CT
5 ST KATHERINE S MEWS
6 BANK LA
7 THE CARRIONS
8 SUNNYMEAD TERR
9 SHAFTSBURY PL
10 ALBERT PL
11 EIFFEL PL
12 GARFIELD PL
13 GILL'S NURSERY
14 ATHERTON LA
15 TIMES MEWS
16 GROVE MEWS
17 MOORASHES
18 BLUEBALL HL

19 The Grove Sch
20 Totnes Costume Mus

C6
1 ALEXANDRA TERR
2 NORTH ST
3 PRIORY CT
4 QUEEN'S TERR
5 ANTRIM TERR
6 GLENARM TERR
7 PRIORY TERR
8 NORTH CASTLE MEWS

D5
1 THROGMORTON HO
2 TAUNTON CT
3 REEVES CL
4 WINDEATT SQ
5 THE MALTHOUSE
6 APPLE WHARF
7 THE CHAPEL
8 WATERSIDE HO
9 SEYMOUR CT
10 ELIZABETHAN HO
11 STEAMER QUAY WHARF
12 TOLLIT GDN
13 BROAD OAK CRES
14 BARING COTTS
15 DEVON PL
16 DEVON TERR
17 SOMERSET CT
18 MEADOW BROOK
19 MEADOWBROOK

E5
1 STAFFORD CT
2 HILLBROOK RISE
3 COLDHARBOUR
4 VARIAN CT

223
217

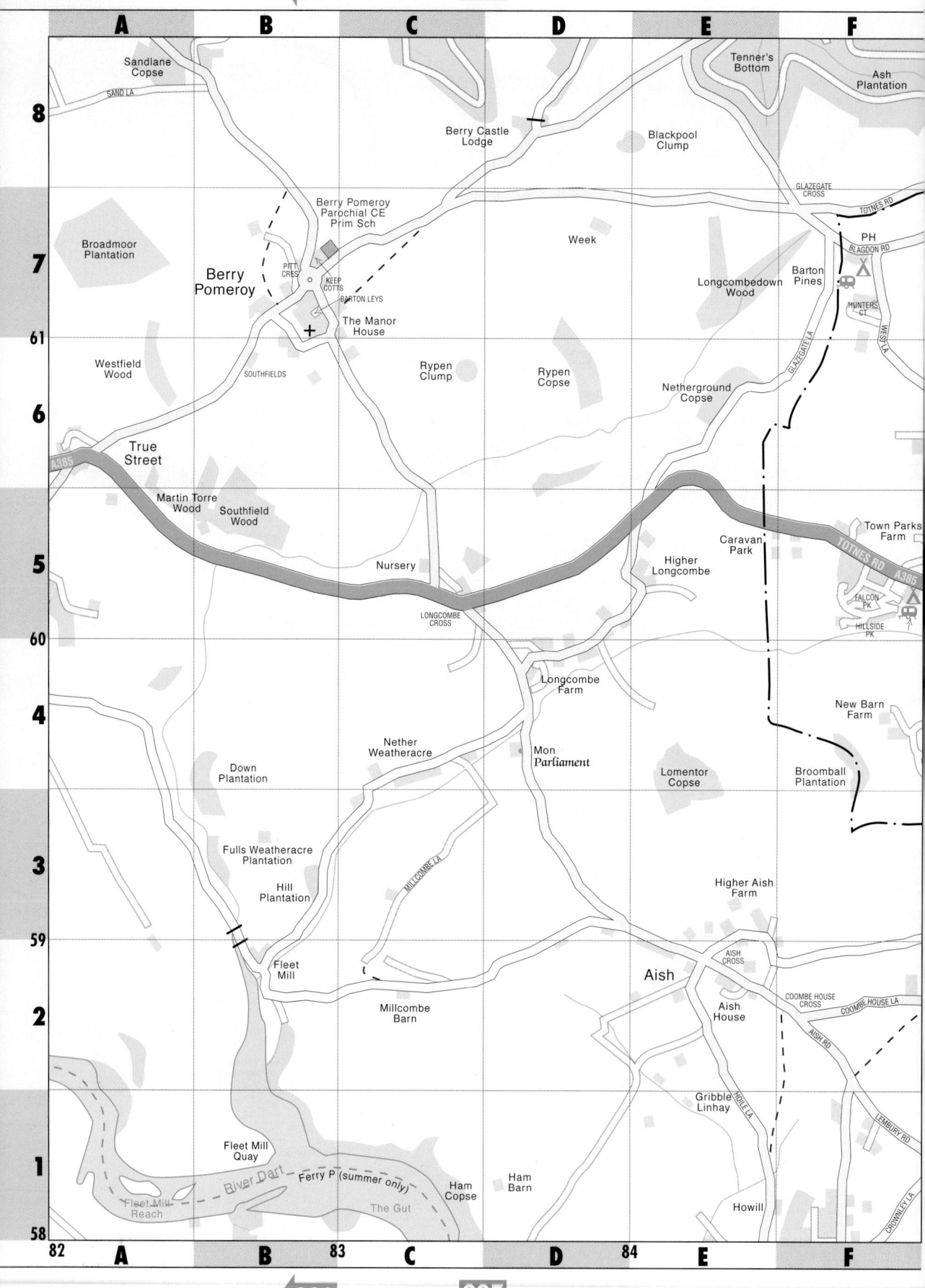
Sandlane Copse
SAND LA
Berry Castle Lodge
Blackpool Clump
Tenner's Bottom
Ash Plantation
GLAZEGATE CROSS
TOTNES RD
Berry Pomeroy Parochial CE Prim Sch
Broadmoor Plantation
Berry Pomeroy
PITT CRES
KEEP COTTS
BARTON LEYS
The Manor House
Week
PH
BLAGDON RD
Barton Pines
Longcombedown Wood
HUNTERS CT
WEST LA
GLAZEGATE LA
Westfield Wood
SOUTHFIELDS
Rypen Clump
Rypen Copse
Netherground Copse
True Street
A385
Martin Torre Wood
Southfield Wood
Nursery
Caravan Park
Town Parks Farm
Higher Longcombe
TOTNES RD
A385
FALCON PK
HILLSIDE PK
LONGCOMBE CROSS
Longcombe Farm
New Barn Farm
Nether Weatheracre
Mon Parliament
Down Plantation
Lomentor Copse
Broomball Plantation
Fulls Weatheracre Plantation
Hill Plantation
MILLCOMBE LA
Higher Aish Farm
Fleet Mill
Aish
AISH CROSS
COOMBE HOUSE CROSS
COOMBE HOUSE LA
Millcombe Barn
Aish House
AISH RD
Gribble Linhay
HOILE LA
LEMBURY RD
Fleet Mill Quay
River Dart
Ferry P (summer only)
Ham Copse
Ham Barn
Fleet Mill Reach
The Gut
Howill
CROWNLEY LA
A B C D E F
8 7 61 6 5 60 4 3 59 2 1 58
82 83 84

223
227

218
226
E8
1 BROOKMAN CT
2 TAVISTOW CT

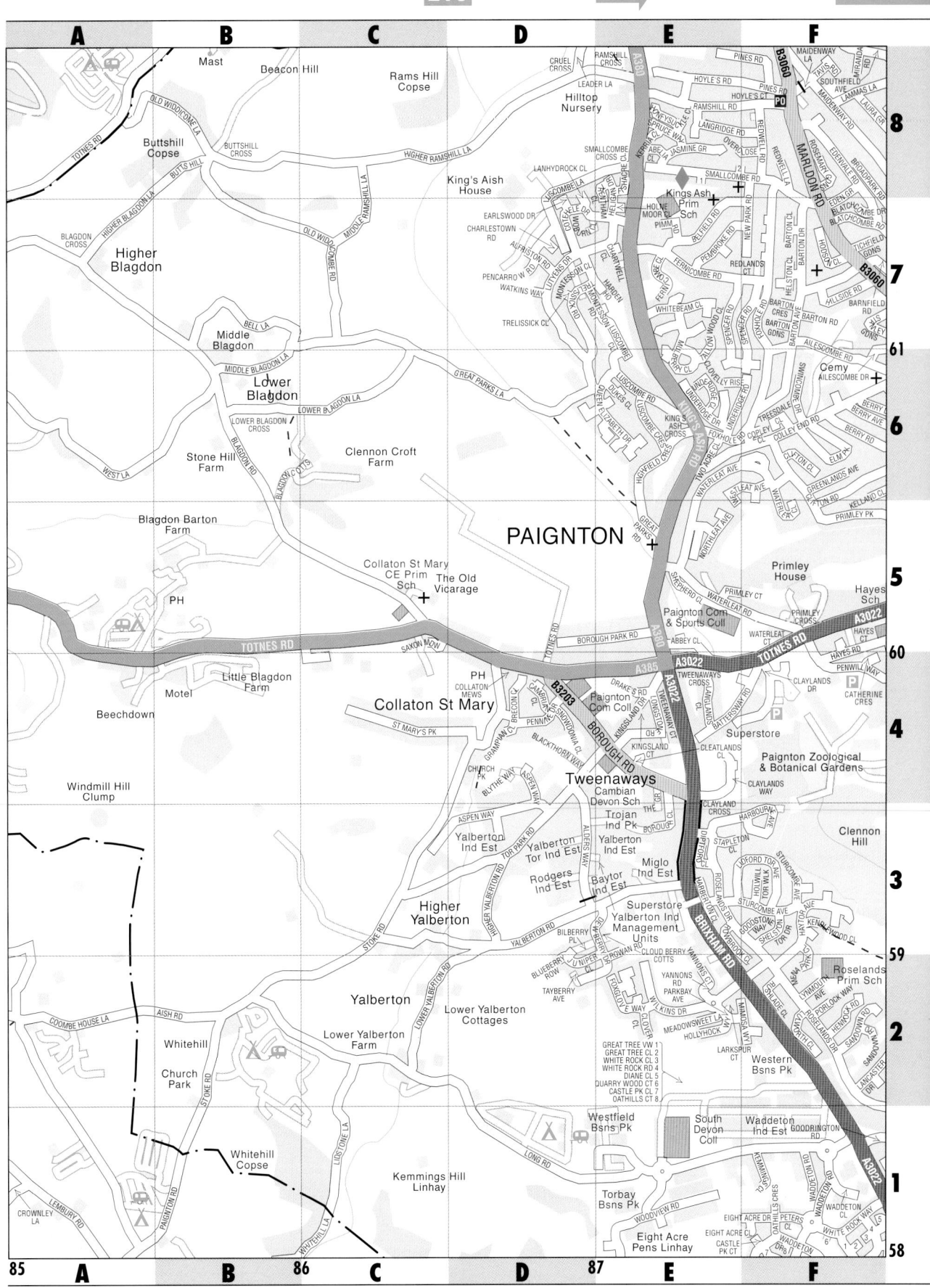
A
B
C
D
E
F
Mast
Beacon Hill
Rams Hill Copse
Hilltop Nursery
Buttshill Copse
BUTTSHILL CROSS
HIGHER RAMSHILL LA
OLD WIDDICOMBE LA
TOTNES RD
BUTTS HILL
BLAGDON CROSS
HIGHER BLAGDON LA
Higher Blagdon
MIDDLE RAMSHILL LA
OLD WIDDICOMBE RD
King's Aish House
Kings Ash Prim Sch
SMALLCOMBE CROSS
SMALLCOMBE RD
LANHYDROCK CL
LUSCOMBE LA
EARLSWOOD DR
CHARLESTOWN RD
PENCARROW RD
WATKINS WAY
TRELISSICK CL
PINES RD
HOYLE'S RD
HOYLE'S CT
RAMSHILL RD
LANGRIDGE RD
REDWELL RD
MAIDENWAY LA
MAIDENWAY RD
SOUTHFIELD AVE
LAMMAS LA
MARLDON RD
B3060
A380
PO
BARTON CL
BARTON DR
BARTON RD
FERNICOMBE RD
WHITEBEAM CL
SPENCER RD
FOXHOLE RD
REDLANDS CT
HELSTON CL
HOBSON CL
HILLSIDE RD
BARNFIELD RD
AILESCOMBE RD
AILESCOMBE DR
Cemy
BELL LA
Middle Blagdon
MIDDLE BLAGDON LA
Lower Blagdon
LOWER BLAGDON LA
LOWER BLAGDON CROSS
GREAT PARKS LA
Stone Hill Farm
Clennon Croft Farm
WEST LA
BLAGDON RD
BLAGDON COTTS
KING'S ASH RD
KING'S ASH CROSS
LUSCOMBE RD
QUEEN ELIZABETH DR
HIGHFIELD CRES
TWO ACRE CL
FOXHOLE RD
COLLEY END RD
BERRY RD
BERRY AVE
ELM PK
GREENLANDS AVE
PRIMLEY PK
KELLAND CL
WATERLEAT AVE
NORTHLEAT AVE
Blagdon Barton Farm
PAIGNTON
GREAT PARKS RD
Collaton St Mary CE Prim Sch
The Old Vicarage
Primley House
Hayes Sch
PRIMLEY CT
WATERLEAT RD
SHEPHERD CL
Paignton Com & Sports Coll
PRIMLEY CROSS
WATERLEAT CT
A3022
HAYES CT
HAYES RD
PENWILL WAY
CLAYLANDS DR
CATHERINE CRES
PH
TOTNES RD
SAXON MDW
TOTNES RD
BOROUGH PARK RD
ABBEY CL
A385
A380
TWEENAWAYS CROSS
Little Blagdon Farm
Motel
Beechdown
COLLATON MEWS
Collaton St Mary
ST MARY'S PK
B3203
BOROUGH RD
Paignton Com Coll
DRAKE'S RD
KINGSLAND DR
LONGSTONE RD
TWEENAWAY CT
KINGSLAND CT
BATTERSWAY RD
Superstore
CLEATLANDS CL
Paignton Zoological & Botanical Gardens
CLAYLANDS WAY
BLACKTHORN WAY
GRAMPIAN CL
CHURCH PK
BLYTHE WAY
ASPEN WAY
Windmill Hill Clump
Tweenaways
Cambian Devon Sch
Trojan Ind Pk
CLAYLAND CROSS
Clennon Hill
Yalberton Ind Est
Yalberton Tor Ind Est
Yalberton Ind Est
Miglo Ind Est
TOR PARK RD
ALDERS WAY
Rodgers Ind Est
Baytor Ind Est
STAPLETON CL
HARBOURN AVE
LIDFORD TOR AVE
STURCOMBE AVE
Higher Yalberton
HIGHER YALBERTON RD
Superstore
Yalberton Ind Management Units
BRIXHAM RD
STOKE RD
YALBERTON RD
BILBERRY PL
ROWAN RD
CLOUD BERRY COTTS
YANNONS RD
YANNONS CT
PARKBAY AVE
BLUEBERRY ROW
TAYBERRY AVE
JUNIPER CL
Roselands Prim Sch
LYNMOUTH AVE
PORLOCK WAY
Yalberton
LOWER YALBERTON RD
Lower Yalberton Cottages
Lower Yalberton Farm
COOMBE HOUSE LA
AISH RD
Whitehill
Church Park
STOKE RD
WILKINS DR
MEADOWSWEET LA
HOLLYHOCK WAY
MIMOSA WAY
LARKSPUR CT
Western Bsns Pk
GREAT TREE VW 1
GREAT TREE CL 2
WHITE ROCK CL 3
WHITE ROCK RD 4
DIANE CL 5
QUARRY WOOD CT 6
CASTLE PK CL 7
OATHILLS CT 8
Westfield Bsns Pk
South Devon Coll
Waddeton Ind Est
GOODRINGTON RD
Whitehill Copse
LONG RD
Kemmings Hill Linhay
LIDSTONE LA
Torbay Bsns Pk
WOODVIEW RD
Eight Acre Pens Linhay
EIGHT ACRE DR
EIGHT ACRE CL
CASTLE PK CT
WADDETON RD
WADDETON CL
WHITE ROCK WAY
PAIGNTON RD
WHITEHILL LA
CROWNLEY LA
LEMBURY RD
8
7
61
6
5
60
4
3
59
2
1
58
85
86
87

228
226

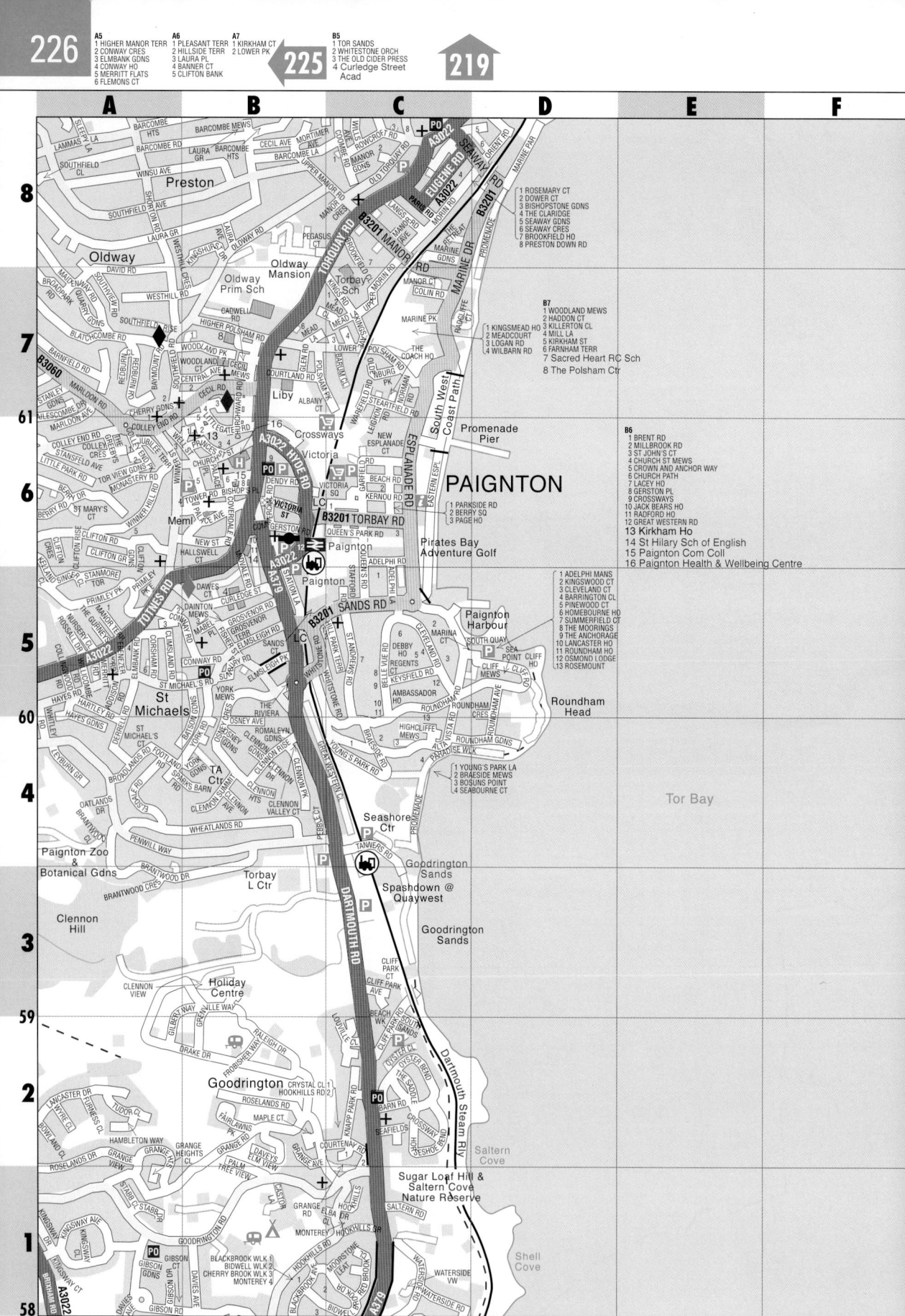

A5
1 HIGHER MANOR TERR
2 CONWAY CRES
3 ELMBANK GDNS
4 CONWAY HO
5 MERRITT FLATS
6 FLEMONS CT

A6
1 PLEASANT TERR
2 HILLSIDE TERR
3 LAURA PL
4 BANNER CT
5 CLIFTON BANK

A7
1 KIRKHAM CT
2 LOWER PK

B5
1 TOR SANDS
2 WHITESTONE ORCH
3 THE OLD CIDER PRESS
4 Curledge Street Acad

225

219

PAIGNTON

Preston

Oldway

Oldway Mansion

Oldway Prim Sch

Torbay's Sch

Liby

Crossways

Victoria

Meml

St Michaels

Paignton

Paignton Harbour

Promenade Pier

Pirates Bay Adventure Golf

Paignton Marina

South Quay

Roundham Head

Tor Bay

Paignton Zoo & Botanical Gdns

Torbay L Ctr

Clennon Hill

Holiday Centre

Seashore Ctr

Goodrington Sands

Spashdown @ Quaywest

Goodrington Sands

Goodrington

Grange Heights

Saltern Cove

Sugar Loaf Hill & Saltern Cove Nature Reserve

Dartmouth Steam Rly

Shell Cove

B7
1 WOODLAND MEWS
2 HADDON CT
3 KILLERTON CL
4 MILL LA
5 KIRKHAM ST
6 FARNHAM TERR
7 Sacred Heart RC Sch
8 The Polsham Ctr

1 ROSEMARY CT
2 DOWER CT
3 BISHOPSTONE GDNS
4 THE CLARIDGE
5 SEAWAY GDNS
6 SEAWAY CRES
7 BROOKFIELD HO
8 PRESTON DOWN RD

1 KINGSMEAD HO
2 MEADCOURT
3 LOGAN RD
4 WILBARN RD

B6
1 BRENT RD
2 MILLBROOK RD
3 ST JOHN'S CT
4 CHURCH ST MEWS
5 CROWN AND ANCHOR WAY
6 CHURCH PATH
7 LACEY HO
8 GERSTON PL
9 CROSSWAYS
10 JACK BEARS HO
11 RADFORD HO
12 GREAT WESTERN RD
13 Kirkham Ho
14 St Hilary Sch of English
15 Paignton Com Coll
16 Paignton Health & Wellbeing Centre

1 PARKSIDE RD
2 BERRY SQ
3 PAGE HO

1 ADELPHI MANS
2 KINGSWOOD CT
3 CLEVELAND CT
4 BARRINGTON CL
5 PINEWOOD CT
6 HOMEBOURNE HO
7 SUMMERFIELD CT
8 THE MOORINGS
9 THE ANCHORAGE
10 LANCASTER HO
11 ROUNDHAM HO
12 OSMOND LODGE
13 ROSEMOUNT

1 YOUNG'S PARK LA
2 BRAESIDE MEWS
3 BOSUNS POINT
4 SEABOURNE CT

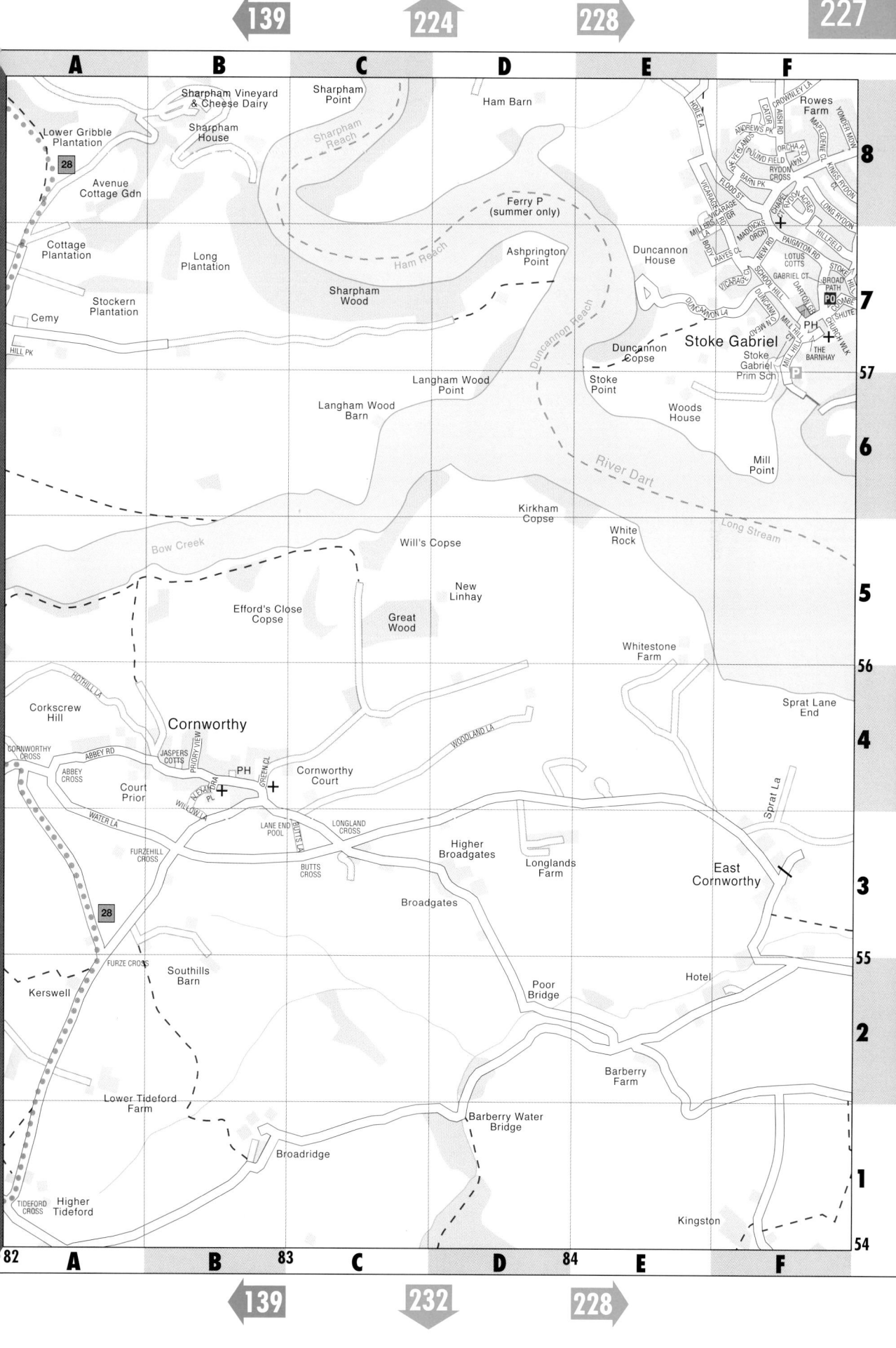

8
7
57
6
5
56
4
3
55
2
1
54

A B C D E F

Lower Gribble Plantation
28
Avenue Cottage Gdn
Cottage Plantation
Cemy
Stockern Plantation
HILL PK

Sharpham Vineyard & Cheese Dairy
Sharpham House
Long Plantation

Sharpham Point
Sharpham Reach
Sharpham Wood

Ham Barn
Ham Reach
Ferry P (summer only)
Ashprington Point

Duncannon House
Duncannon Copse
Stoke Gabriel
Stoke Gabriel Prim Sch
Woods House
Mill Point

HOLE LA
CROWNLEY LA
AISH RD
CALOR
ANDREWS PK
ST YELANDS
CROWNLEY PK
ORCHA
ROUND FIELD
BARN PK
RYDON CROSS
RYDON
VICARAGE
FLOOD ST
MADDICKS ORCH
MILL BRS
HAYES CL
NEW RD
VICARAGE
SCHOOL HILL
VICARAGE
GABRIEL CT
DUNCANNON
CHAPEL
RYDON ACRE
LOTUS COTTS
DARTMOUTH
PAIGNTON RD
HILLFIELD
STOKE HILL
MILL HILL
MILL TILL
PO
BROAD PATH
PH
CHUTE
CHURCH WALK
THE BARNHAY
P
Rowes Farm
YONDER MDW
MAPLETONE CL
KINGS RYDON
LONG RYDON
COOMBE

Duncannon La
Duncannon Reach
Langham Wood Point
Langham Wood Barn
Stoke Point

River Dart
Kirkham Copse
White Rock
Long Stream

Bow Creek
Will's Copse
New Linhay
Great Wood
Whitestone Farm
Efford's Close Copse

Corkscrew Hill
HOTHILL LA
Cornworthy
JASPERS COTTS
PRIORY VIEW
PH
GREEN CL
WOODLAND LA
Sprat Lane End
Sprat La

CORNWORTHY CROSS
ABBEY RD
ABBEY CROSS
Court Prior
WATER LA
ALEXANDRA PL
WILLOW LA
Cornworthy Court
LANE END POOL
BUTTS LA
LONGLAND CROSS
Higher Broadgates
Longlands Farm
East Cornworthy

FURZEHILL CROSS
28
BUTTS CROSS
Broadgates

FURZE CROSS
Southills Barn
Poor Bridge
Hotel

Kerswell
Lower Tideford Farm
Barberry Farm
Barberry Water Bridge
TIDEFORD CROSS
Higher Tideford
Broadridge
Kingston

82 83 84

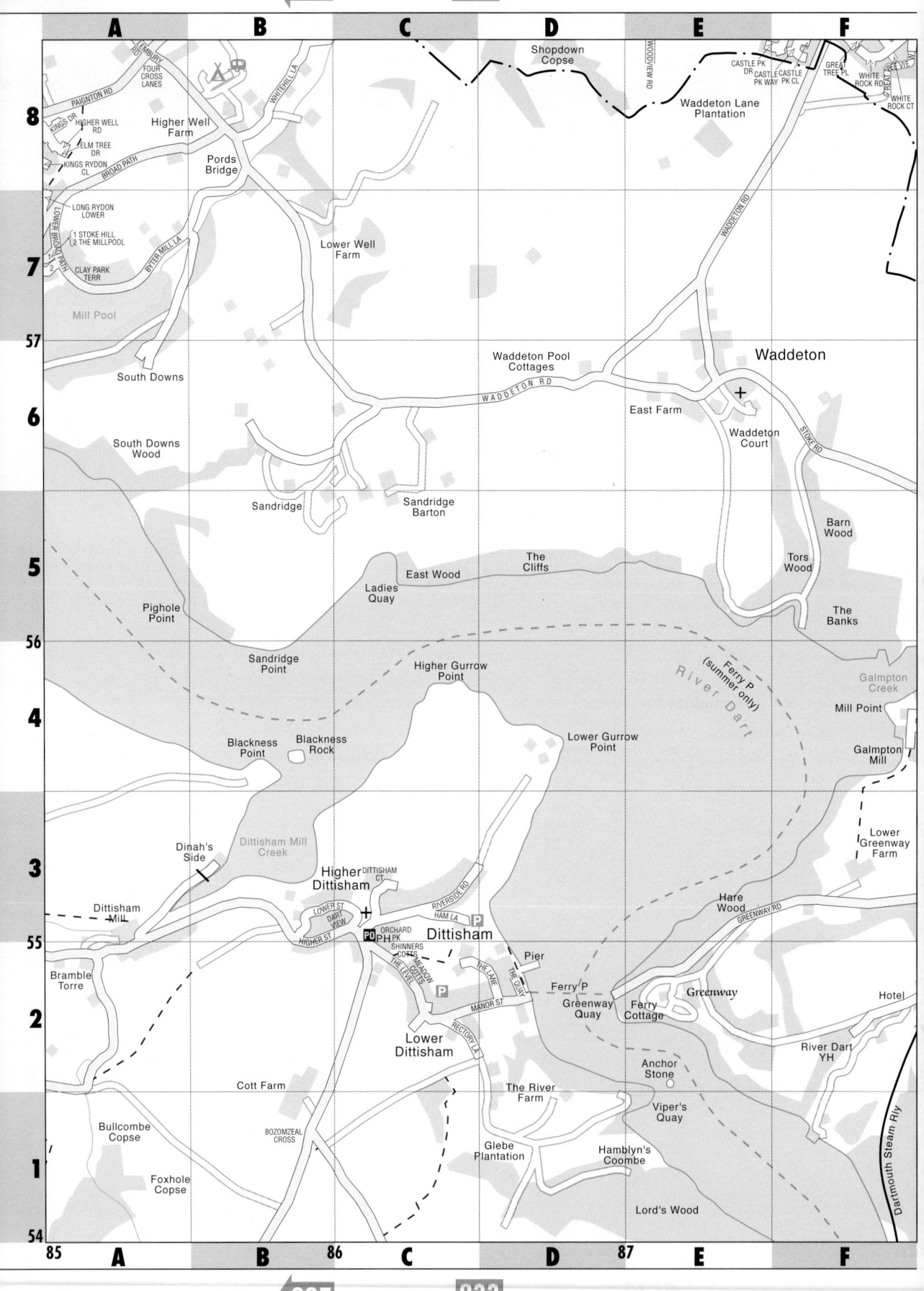

A   B   C   D   E   F

8
Four Cross Lanes
PEMBURY
PAIGNTON RD
KINGS DR
HIGHER WELL RD
ELM TREE DR
KINGS RYDON CL
Higher Well Farm
Higher Well Farm
BROAD PATH
WHITEHILL LA
Pords Bridge

Shopdown Copse
WOODVIEW RD
CASTLE PK DR
CASTLE PK WAY
CASTLE PK CL
GREAT TREE PL
SEE VIEW
WHITE ROCK RD
WHITE ROCK CT

Waddeton Lane Plantation

WADDETON RD

7
LONG RYDON LOWER
1 STOKE HILL
2 THE MILLPOOL
CLAY PARK TERR
LOWER BROAD PATH
BYTER MILL LA
Lower Well Farm

Mill Pool

57
South Downs

Waddeton Pool Cottages
WADDETON RD
East Farm
Waddeton
Waddeton Court

6
South Downs Wood
Sandridge
Sandridge Barton
STOKE RD

Barn Wood

5
Pighole Point
Ladies Quay
East Wood
The Cliffs
Tors Wood
The Banks

56
Sandridge Point
Higher Gurrow Point
River Dart
Ferry P (summer only)
Galmpton Creek
Mill Point
Galmpton Mill

4
Blackness Point
Blackness Rock
Lower Gurrow Point
Lower Greenway Farm

3
Dinah's Side
Dittisham Mill Creek
Higher Dittisham
DITTISHAM CT
LOWER ST
DART VIEW
RIVERSIDE RD
HAM LA
Hare Wood
GREENWAY RD

Dittisham Mill
HIGHER ST
PH PK
ORCHARD
SHINNERS COTTS
Dittisham
Pier

55
Bramble Torre
MEADOW COTTS
THE LEVEL
MANOR ST
RECTORY LA
THE LANE
THE QUAY
Ferry P
Greenway Quay
Ferry Cottage
Greenway
Hotel

2
Lower Dittisham
Cott Farm
The River Farm
Anchor Stone
River Dart YH

1
Bullcombe Copse
BOZOMZEAL CROSS
Viper's Quay
Glebe Plantation
Hamblyn's Coombe
Foxhole Copse
Lord's Wood
Dartmouth Steam Rly

54
85   A   B   86   C   D   87   E   F

226 230

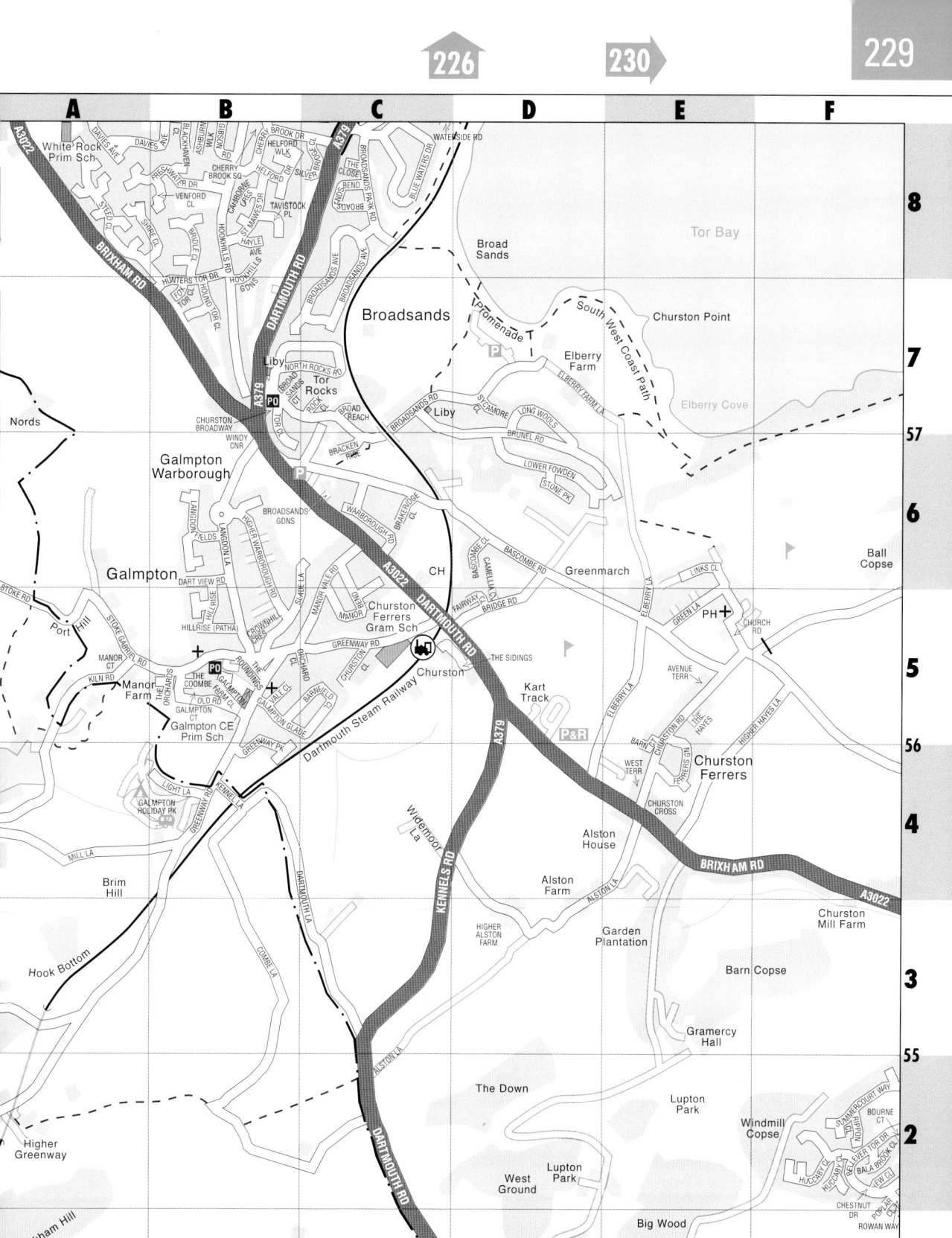
A
B
C
D
E
F
A3022
BRIXHAM RD
A379
DARTMOUTH RD
White Rock Prim Sch
DAVIES AVE
CHERRY BROOK DR
HELFORD WLK
CHERRY BROOK SQ
FRESHWATER DR
VENFORD CL
TAVISTOCK PL
HAYLE AVE
HOOKHILLS RD
HUNTERS TOR DR
HOUND TOR CL
WATERSIDE RD
BLUE WATERS DR
BROADSANDS PARK RD
BROADSANDS AVE
Tor Bay
Broad Sands
Broadsands
Promenade
South West Coast Path
Churston Point
Elberry Farm
ELBERRY FARM LA
Elberry Cove
Liby
NORTH ROCKS RD
Tor Rocks
BROAD REACH
BROADSANDS RD
SYCAMORE CL
LONG WOOLS
BRUNEL RD
LOWER FOWDEN
STONE PK
Nords
CHURSTON BROADWAY
WINDY CNR
TOR CL
BRACKEN RISE
Galmpton Warborough
BROADSANDS GDNS
LANGDON FIELDS
LANGDON LA
HIGHER WARBOROUGH RD
WARBOROUGH RD
BRAKERIDGE CL
BASCOMBE CL
BASCOMBE RD
CAMELLIA CL
Greenmarch
LINKS CL
Ball Copse
Galmpton
DART VIEW RD
HILLRISE
SLADE LA
MANOR VALE RD
CH
STOKE RD
Port Hill
STOKE GABRIEL RD
HILLRISE (PATH)
CROWNHILL CRES
MANOR BEND
Churston Ferrers Gram Sch
FAIRWAY
BRIDGE RD
GREEN LA
PH
CHURCH RD
ELBERRY LA
MANOR CT
KILN RD
Manor Farm
THE ORCHARDS
THE COOMBE
OLD RD
GALMPTON FARM CL
THE ROUNDINGS
VALE CL
ORCHARD RD
GREENWAY RD
CHURSTON CL
THE SIDINGS
Churston
AVENUE TERR
Kart Track
GALMPTON CT
Galmpton CE Prim Sch
GALMPTON GLADE
BARNFIELD CL
Dartmouth Steam Railway
P&R
CHURSTON RD
THE HAYES
HIGHER HAYES LA
BARN CL
WEST TERR
FERRERS GN
Churston Ferrers
GREENWAY PK
LIGHT LA
GALMPTON HOLIDAY PK
GREENWAY RD
KENNELS LA
CHURSTON CROSS
Widemoor La
KENNELS RD
Alston House
MILL LA
Brim Hill
DARTMOUTH LA
Alston Farm
ALSTON LA
Churston Mill Farm
HIGHER ALSTON FARM
Garden Plantation
Hook Bottom
COMBE LA
Barn Copse
Gramercy Hall
The Down
Lupton Park
Windmill Copse
SUMMERCOURT WAY
BOURNE CT
RIPPON CL
BELLEVER TOR DR
BALA BROOK CL
YEW CL
HUCCABY CL
CHESTNUT DR
POPLAR CL
ROWAN WAY
Higher Greenway
West Ground
Lupton Park
Big Wood
Oakham Hill
Guzzle Down
KINGSWEAR RD
GATTERY LA
8
7
57
6
5
56
4
3
55
2
1
54
88
89
90

234 230

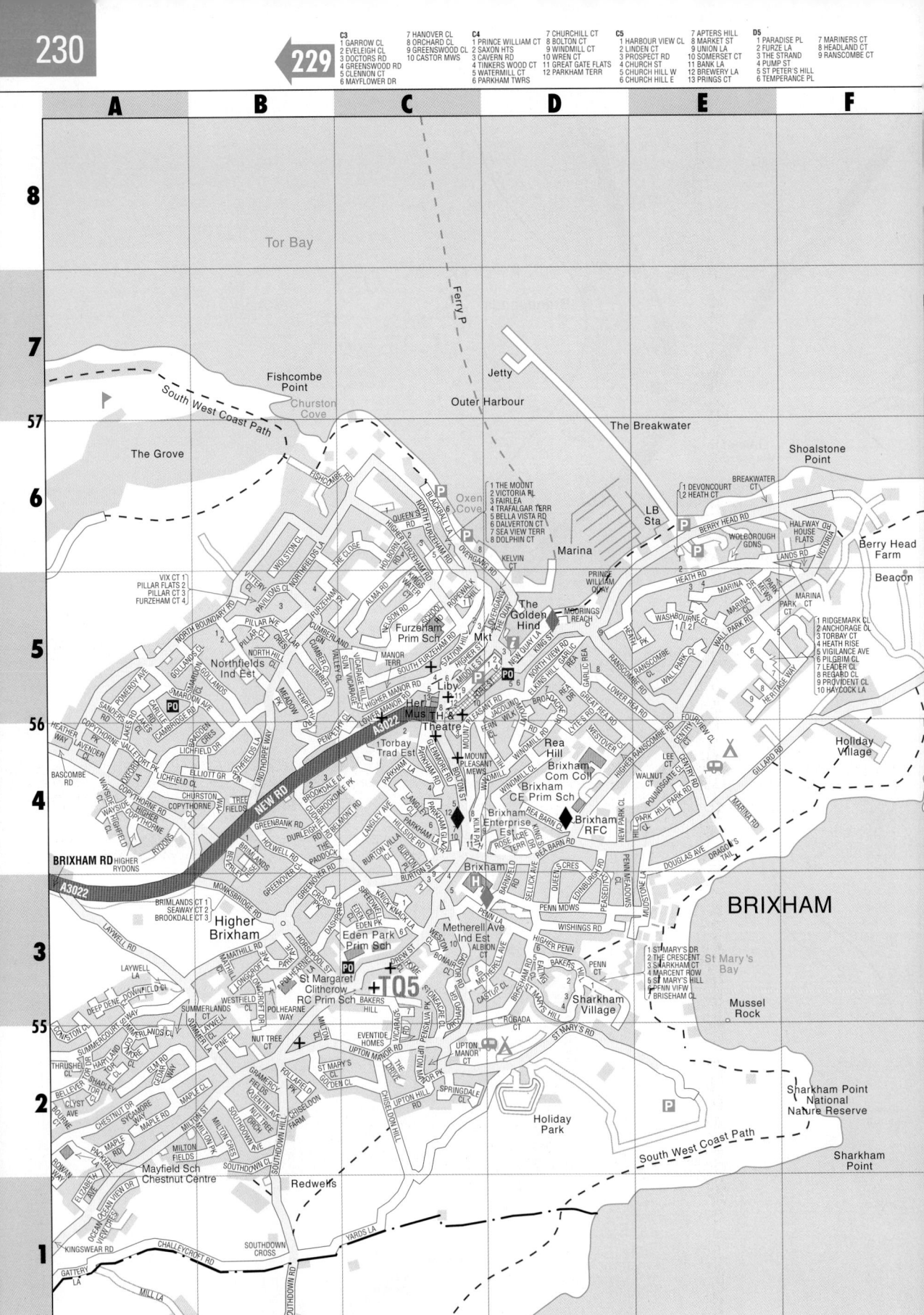

C3
1 GARROW CL
2 EVELEIGH CL
3 DOCTORS RD
4 GREENSWOOD RD
5 CLENNON CT
6 MAYFLOWER DR

7 HANOVER CL
8 ORCHARD CL
9 GREENSWOOD CL
10 CASTOR MWS

C4
1 PRINCE WILLIAM CT
2 SAXON HTS
3 CAVERN RD
4 TINKERS WOOD CT
5 WATERMILL CT
6 PARKHAM TWRS

7 CHURCHILL CT
8 BOLTON CT
9 WINDMILL CT
10 WREN CT
11 GREAT GATE FLATS
12 PARKHAM TERR

C5
1 HARBOUR VIEW CL
2 LINDEN CT
3 PROSPECT RD
4 CHURCH ST
5 CHURCH HILL W
6 CHURCH HILL E

7 APTERS HILL
8 MARKET ST
9 UNION LA
10 SOMERSET CT
11 BANK LA
12 BREWERY LA
13 PRINGS CT

D5
1 PARADISE PL
2 FURZE LA
3 THE STRAND
4 PUMP ST
5 ST PETER'S HILL
6 TEMPERANCE PL

7 MARINERS CT
8 HEADLAND CT
9 RANSCOMBE CT

229

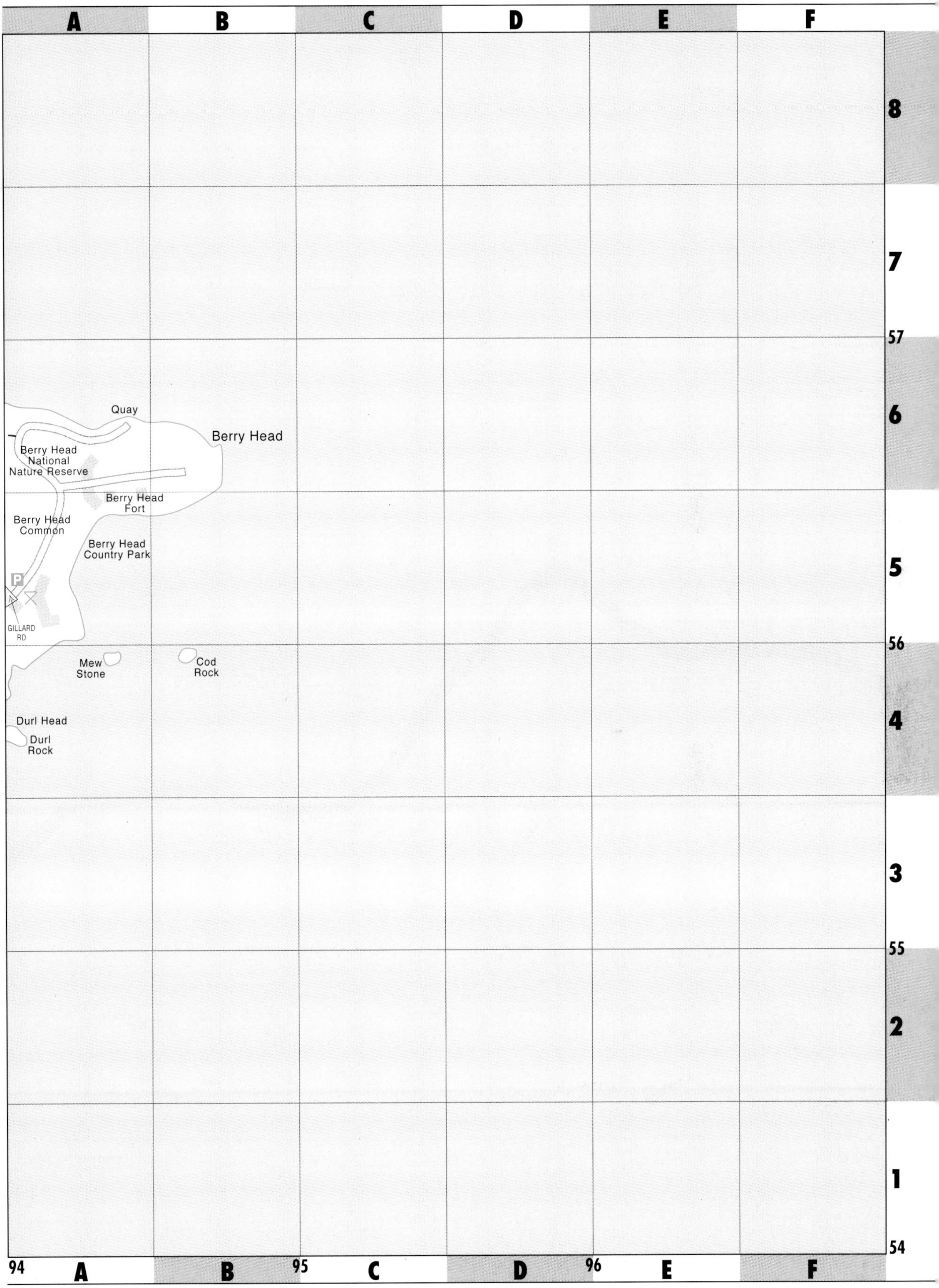

A B C D E F

8

7

57

6

Quay

Berry Head

Berry Head
National
Nature Reserve

Berry Head
Fort

Berry Head
Common

Berry Head
Country Park

P

GILLARD
RD

5

56

Mew
Stone

Cod
Rock

4

Durl Head
Durl
Rock

3

55

2

1

54

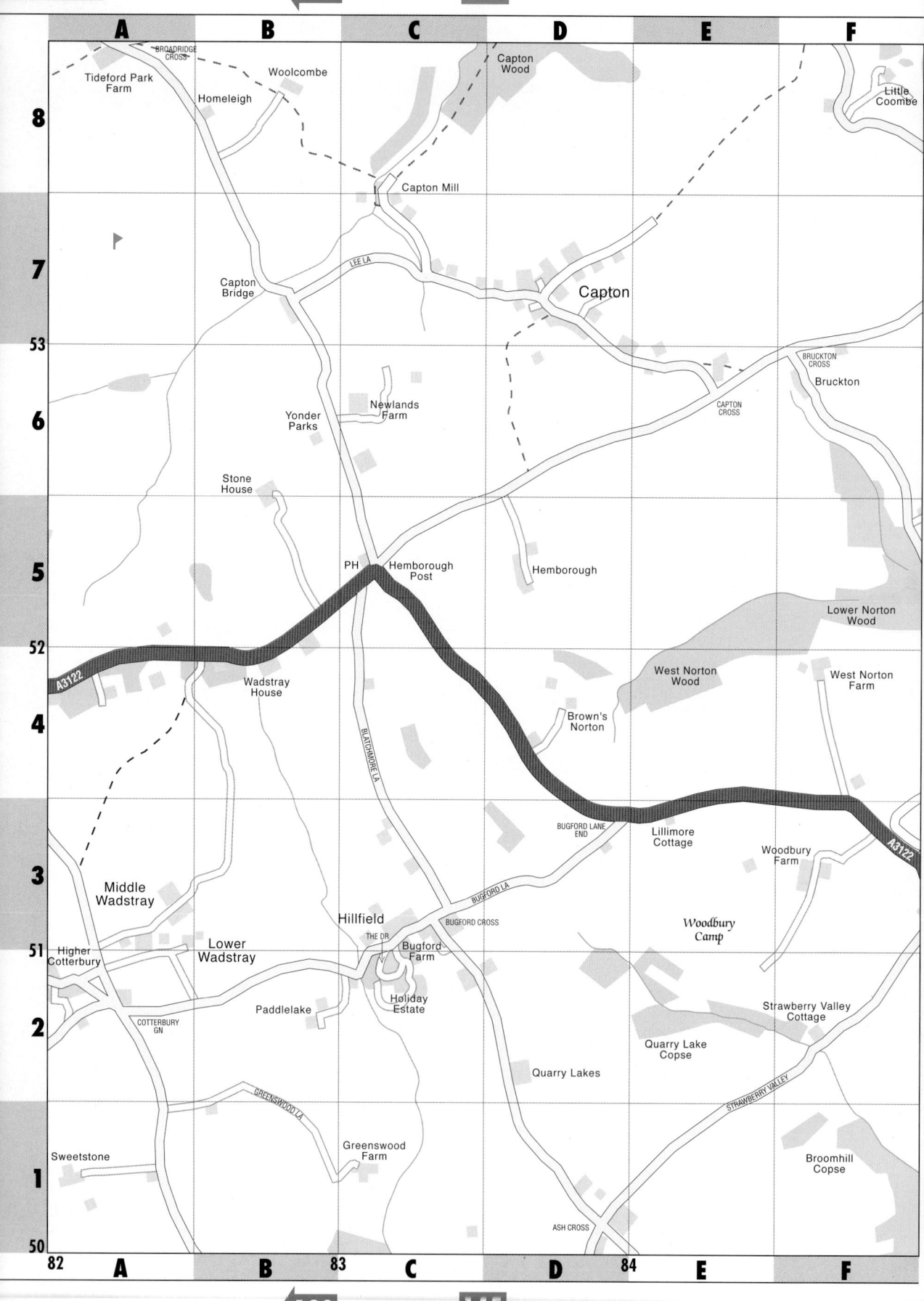

A B C D E F

8
7
53
6
5
52
4
3
51
2
1
50

Tideford Park Farm
BROADRIDGE CROSS
Woolcombe
Homeleigh
Capton Wood
Little Coombe

Capton Mill
Capton Bridge
LEE LA
Capton
BRUCKTON CROSS
Bruckton
Newlands Farm
Yonder Parks
CAPTON CROSS
Stone House
Lower Norton Wood
PH
Hemborough Post
Hemborough
West Norton Wood
West Norton Farm
A3122
Wadstray House
Brown's Norton
BLATCHMORE LA
Bugford Lane End
Lillimore Cottage
Woodbury Farm
A3122
Middle Wadstray
Hillfield
Bugford La
Bugford Cross
Woodbury Camp
Higher Cotterbury
Lower Wadstray
THE DR
Bugford Farm
Strawberry Valley Cottage
COTTERBURY GN
Paddlelake
Holiday Estate
Quarry Lake Copse
Sweetstone
GREENSWOOD LA
Greenswood Farm
Quarry Lakes
Strawberry Valley
Broomhill Copse
ASH CROSS

82 A B 83 C D 84 E F

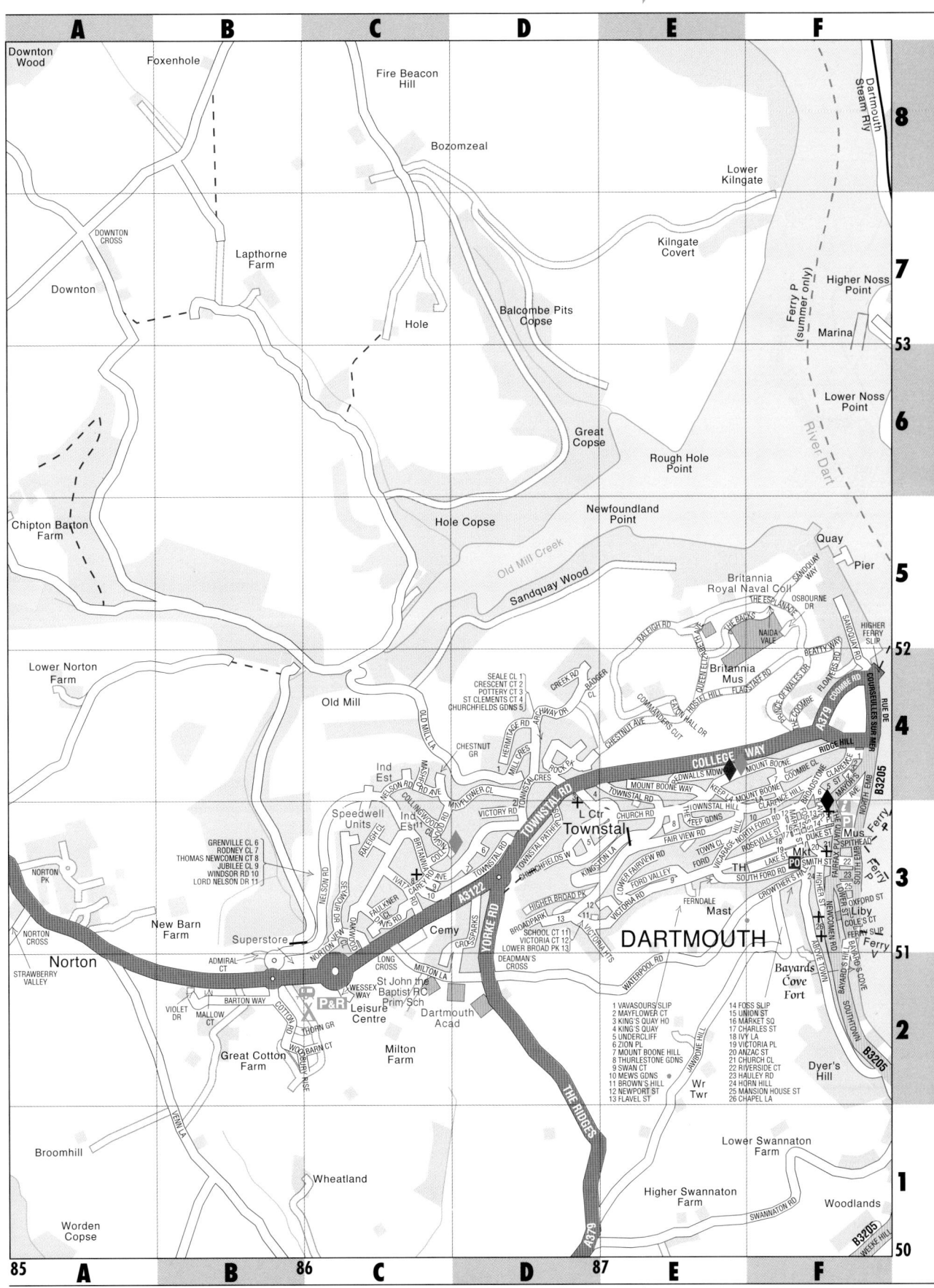

DARTMOUTH

Downton Wood
Foxenhole
Fire Beacon Hill
Bozomzeal
Lower Kilngate
Kilngate Covert
Downton Cross
Lapthorne Farm
Downton
Hole
Balcombe Pits Copse
Higher Noss Point
Ferry P (summer only)
Marina
Great Copse
Lower Noss Point
River Dart
Chipton Barton Farm
Hole Copse
Rough Hole Point
Newfoundland Point
Old Mill Creek
Sandquay Wood
Quay
Pier
Sandquay Way
Britannia Royal Naval Coll
Lower Norton Farm
THE ESPLANADE
Osbourne Dr
Dartmouth Steam Rly
Old Mill
SEALE CL 1
CRESCENT CT 2
POTTERY CT 3
ST CLEMENTS CT 4
CHURCHFIELDS GDNS 5
RALEIGH RD
THE BACKS
NAIDA VALE
Britannia Mus
HIGHER FERRY SLIP
CREEK RD
BADGER CL
HERMITAGE RD
MILL LA
CHESTNUT GR
CHESTNUT AVE
COMMANDERS CUT
RUE DE COURSEULLES SUR MER
COLLEGE WAY
REDWALLS MDW
Mount Boone
RIDGE HILL
A379 COOMBE RD
B3205
Ind Est
MILL CRES
POCK LA
MOUNT BOONE WAY
KEEP LA
MOUNT BOONE
CLARENCE
BROADSTONE
COOMBE CL
MAYFLOWER CL
TOWNSTAL CRES
TOWNSTAL HILL
CLARENCE ST
MAYOR'S AVE
Speedwell Units
NELSON RD AVE
VICTORY RD
L Ctr
CHURCH RD
TOWNSTAL HILL
DUKE ST
Mus
Ind Est
GRENVILLE CL 6
RODNEY CL 7
THOMAS NEWCOMEN CT 8
JUBILEE CL 9
WINDSOR RD 10
LORD NELSON DR 11
RALEIGH CH
BRITANNIA AVE
CLARENCE HILL
CARE'S COL
TOWNSTAL RD
CHURCH CL
Townstal
DEEP DEAN
TOWNE GDNS
FAIR VIEW RD
NORTH FORD RD
ROSEVILLE ST
TOWN CL
FORD
SOUTH FORD RD
SMITH ST
TH
PO
Mkt
Liby
OXFORD ST
COLE'S CT
FERRY
NELSON RD
FAULKNER CL
DAVIS RD
KINGSTON LA
LOWER FAIRVIEW RD
FORD VALLEY
CROWTHER'S
NEWCOMEN RD
SPITHEAD
LAKE ST
Norton Pk
CRO-SPARKS
HIGHER BROAD PK
VICTORIA RD
FERNDALE
Mast
HIGHER STREET
BAYARD'S COVE
New Barn Farm
YORKE RD
A3122
Cemy
BROADPARK
SCHOOL CT 11
VICTORIA CT 12
LOWER BROAD PK 13
WATERPOOL RD
DARTMOUTH
SOUTHTOWN
B3205
Norton Cross
Superstore
ADMIRAL CT
LONG CROSS
MILTON LA
DEADMAN'S CROSS
Bayards Cove Fort
Norton
COTTON RD
WESSEX WAY
St John the Baptist RC Prim Sch
Dartmouth Acad
JAWBONE HILL
Dyer's Hill
Strawberry Valley
VIOLET DR
MALLOW CT
BARTON WAY
THORN GR
WOODBARN CT
P&R
Leisure Centre
VENN LA
Milton Farm
Wr Twr
1 VAVASOURS SLIP
2 MAYFLOWER CT
3 KING'S QUAY HO
4 KING'S QUAY
5 UNDERCLIFF
6 ZION PL
7 MOUNT BOONE HILL
8 THURLESTONE GDNS
9 SWAN CT
10 MEWS GDNS
11 BROWN'S HILL
12 NEWPORT ST
13 FLAVEL ST
14 FOSS SLIP
15 UNION ST
16 MARKET SQ
17 CHARLES ST
18 IVY LA
19 VICTORIA PL
20 ANZAC ST
21 CHURCH CL
22 RIVERSIDE CT
23 HAULEY RD
24 HORN HILL
25 MANSION HOUSE ST
26 CHAPEL LA
Lower Swannaton Farm
Broomhill
THE RIDGES
Great Cotton Farm
Higher Swannaton Farm
Woodlands
SWANNATON RD
A379
B3205
WEEKE HILL
Worden Copse
Wheatland

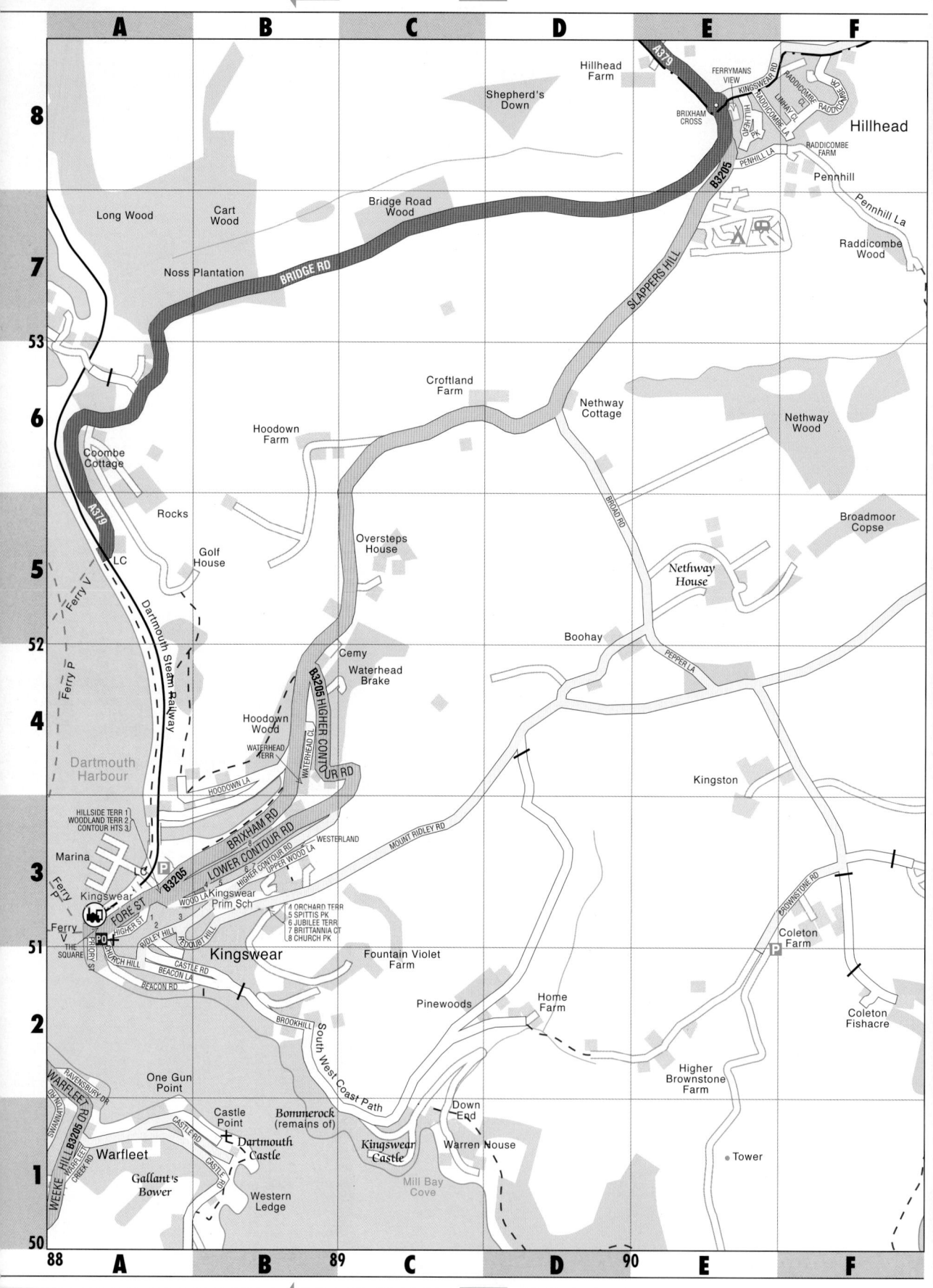
A
B
C
D
E
F
8
7
53
6
5
52
4
3
51
2
1
50
88
89
90
Hillhead Farm
Shepherd's Down
Hillhead
FERRYMANS VIEW
KINGSWEAR RD
RADDICOMBE CL
LINHAY CL
RADDICOMBE DR
BRIXHAM CROSS
HILLHEAD PK
RADDICOMBE LA
RADDICOMBE FARM
PENHILL LA
Pennhill
Pennhill La
Raddicombe Wood
A379
B3205
Long Wood
Cart Wood
Bridge Road Wood
Noss Plantation
BRIDGE RD
SLAPPERS HILL
Croftland Farm
Nethway Cottage
Nethway Wood
Hoodown Farm
Coombe Cottage
Rocks
Broadmoor Copse
BROAD RD
Oversteps House
Golf House
LC
Nethway House
Ferry V
Dartmouth Steam Railway
Boohay
Cemy
Waterhead Brake
PEPPER LA
Ferry P
B3205 HIGHER CONTOUR RD
Hoodown Wood
WATERHEAD TERR
WATERHEAD CL
Dartmouth Harbour
HOODOWN LA
Kingston
HILLSIDE TERR 1
WOODLAND TERR 2
CONTOUR HTS 3
BRIXHAM RD
LOWER CONTOUR RD
WESTERLAND
MOUNT RIDLEY RD
Marina
HIGHER CONTOUR RD
UPPER WOOD LA
WOOD LA
Kingswear Prim Sch
Kingswear
FORE ST
HIGHER ST
4 ORCHARD TERR
5 SPITTIS PK
6 JUBILEE TERR
7 BRITTANNIA CT
8 CHURCH PK
BROWNSTONE RD
Coleton Farm
Ferry V
THE SQUARE
PRIORY ST
RIDLEY HILL
REDOUBT HILL
CHURCH HILL
CASTLE RD
BEACON LA
BEACON RD
Fountain Violet Farm
Pinewoods
Home Farm
Coleton Fishacre
BROOKHILL
South West Coast Path
Higher Brownstone Farm
RAVENSBURY DR
WARFLEET RD
One Gun Point
Castle Point
Bommerock (remains of)
Down End
Dartmouth Castle
Kingswear Castle
Warren House
Tower
Warfleet
WARFLEET CREEK RD
WEEKE HILL
Gallant's Bower
Western Ledge
Mill Bay Cove

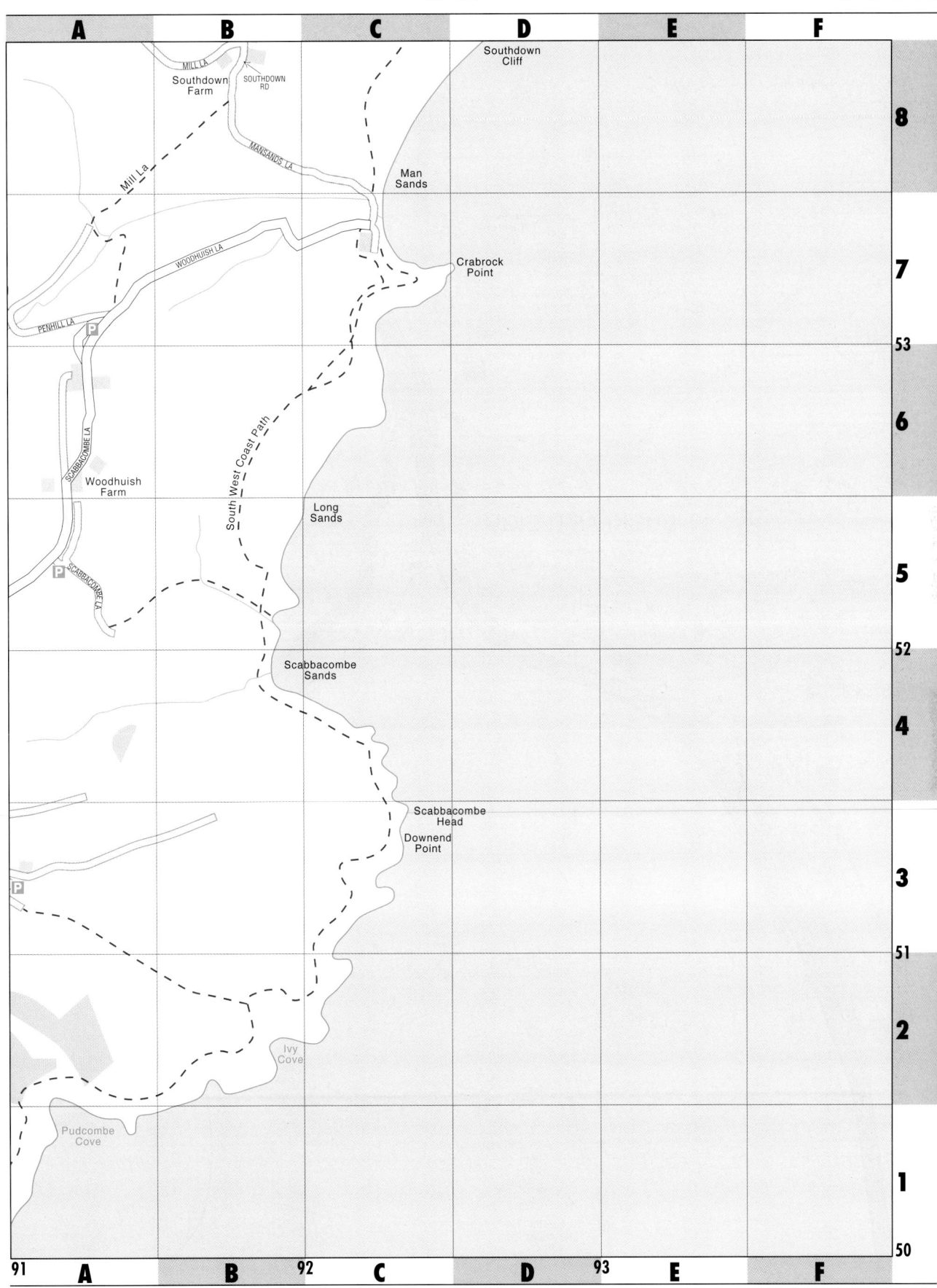

Southdown
Cliff

MILL LA

Southdown
Farm

SOUTHDOWN
RD

Mill La

MANSANDS LA

Man
Sands

WOODHUISH LA

Crabrock
Point

PENHILL LA

P

SCABBACOMBE LA

Woodhuish
Farm

South West Coast Path

Long
Sands

P SCABBACOMBE LA

Scabbacombe
Sands

P

Scabbacombe
Head

Downend
Point

Ivy
Cove

Pudcombe
Cove

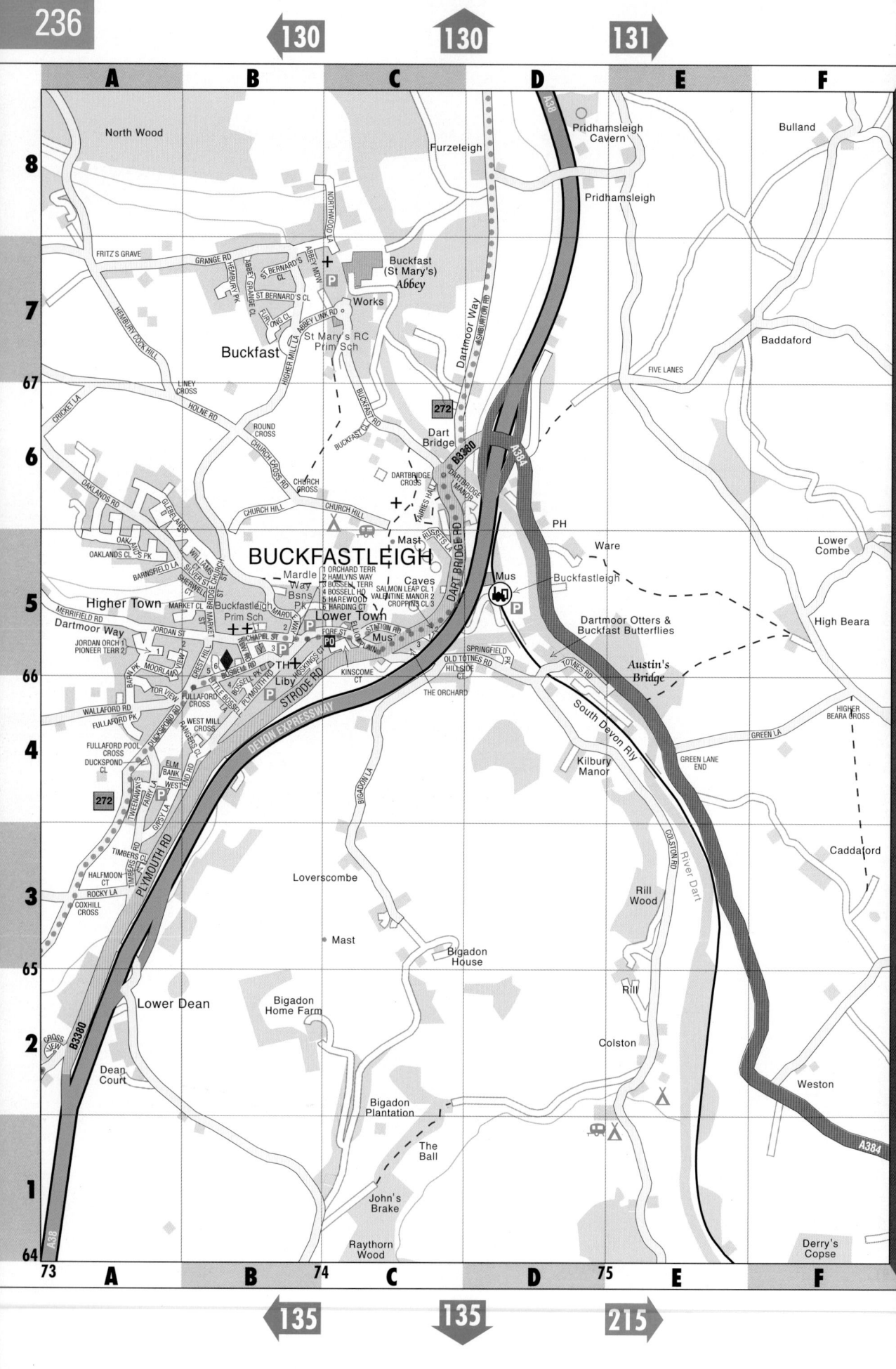

A   B   C   D   E   F

8

North Wood

Furzeleigh

Pridhamsleigh Cavern

Bulland

Pridhamsleigh

7

FRITZ'S GRAVE

GRANGE RD

NORTHWOOD LA

ST BERNARD'S CL

HEMBURY PK

ABBEY GRANGE CL

FURZ ONG CL

ST BERNARD'S

Buckfast (St Mary's) Abbey

Works

ABBEY MDW

Dartmoor Way

ASHBURTON RD

Baddaford

HEMBURY COCK HILL

HIGHER MILL LA

ABBEY LINK RD

Buckfast

St Mary's RC Prim Sch

Five Lanes

67

LINEY CROSS

HOLNE RD

BUCKFAST RD

272

Dart Bridge

CRICKET LA

ROUND CROSS

DARTBRIDGE RD

DART BRIDGE RD

6

OAKLANDS RD

GLEBE LANDS

CHURCH CROSS RD

BUCKFAST CK RD

CHURCH CROSS

DARTBRIDGE CROSS

B3380

A384

DARTBRIDGE MANOR

PH

Ware

Lower Combe

CHURCH HILL

CHURCH HILL

FAIRIES HALL

Mast

Buckfastleigh

OAKLANDS

BARNSFIELD LA

OAKLANDS CL S PK

WILLIAMS CL

SILVER ST

SHERWELL LA

BUCKFASTLEIGH

Caves

Mus

Dartmoor Otters & Buckfast Butterflies

Lower Combe

5

Higher Town

MARKET CL

Mardle Way

Buckfastleigh Prim Sch

MARDLE WAY

1 ORCHARD TERR
2 HAMLYNS WAY
3 BOSSEL'S TERR
4 BOSSELL HO
5 HAREWOOD
6 HARDING CT

SALMON LEAP CL 1
VALENTINE MANOR 2
CROPPINS CL 3

P

High Beara

MERRIFIELD RD

JORDAN ST

Lower Town

Dartmoor Way

JORDAN ORCH 1
PIONEER TERR 2

MOORLAN

CHAPEL ST

FORE ST

Mus

SPRINGFIELD

66

BARN PK

CREST HILL

LITTLE BOSSEL

BOSSELL RD

TH

PLYMOUTH RD

Liby

P

STRODE RD

KINGS CL

KINSCOME CT

OLD TOTNES RD

HILLSIDE

Austin's Bridge

TOR VIEW

FULLAFORD CROSS

WEST MILL CROSS

THE ORCHARD

TOTNES RD

South Devon Rly

HIGHER BEARA CROSS

WALLAFORD RD

DEVON EXPRESSWAY

COLSTON RD

GREEN LA

4

FULLAFORD PK

DUCKSPOND RD

WEST

ELM BANK

BIGADON LA

Kilbury Manor

GREEN LANE END

FULLAFORD POOL CROSS

DUCKSPOND CL

RANGERS

River Dart

TWEENAWAYS

272

TIMBERS CL

GIRTS LA

Loverscombe

Rill Wood

Caddaford

3

HALFMOON CT

ROCKY LA

PLYMOUTH RD

Mast

Bigadon House

Rill

COXHILL CROSS

65

Lower Dean

Bigadon Home Farm

Colston

2

CROSS VIEW

B3380

Dean Court

Bigadon Plantation

Weston

A38

The Ball

A384

1

John's Brake

Derry's Copse

Raythorn Wood

64

73   A   B   74   C   D   75   E   F

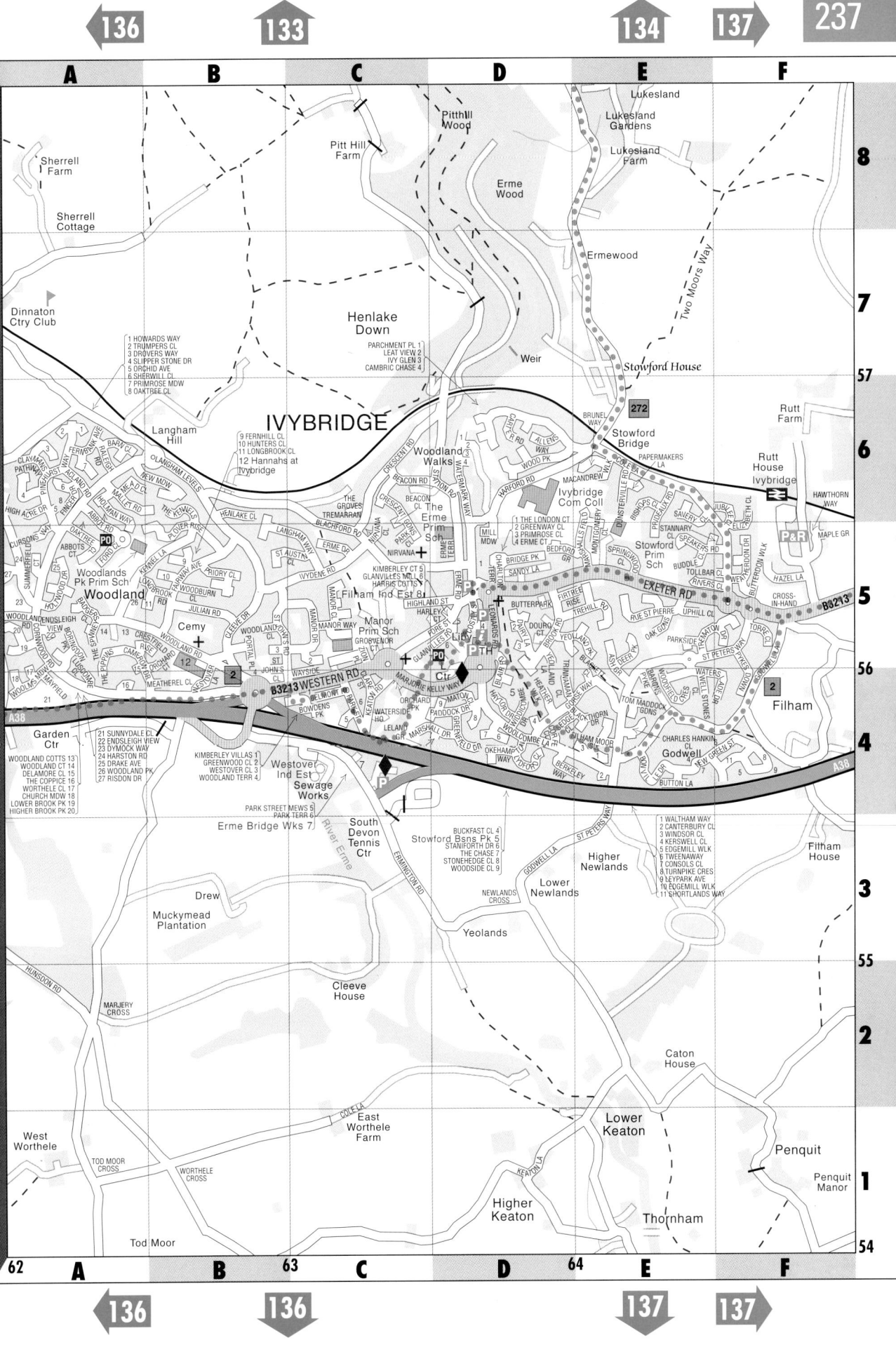

A   B   C   D   E   F

8
7
57
6
5
56
55
4
3
2
1
54

IVYBRIDGE

Sherrell Farm
Sherrell Cottage
Dinnaton Ctry Club
Pitt Hill Farm
Pitthill Wood
Erme Wood
Lukesland
Lukesland Gardens
Lukesland Farm
Ermewood
Two Moors Way
Stowford House
Henlake Down
Weir
PARCHMENT PL 1
LEAT VIEW 2
IVY GLEN 3
CAMBRIC CHASE 4

1 HOWARDS WAY
2 TRUMPERS CL
3 DROVERS WAY
4 SLIPPER STONE DR
5 ORCHID AVE
6 SHERWILL CL
7 PRIMROSE MDW
8 OAKTREE CL

Langham Hill
9 FERNHILL CL
10 HUNTERS CL
11 LONGBROOK CL
12 Hannahs at Ivybridge

Stowford Bridge
272
Brunel Way
Papermakers Rd
Rutt Farm
Rutt House Ivybridge
Hawthorn Way
Maple Gr

Woodland Walks
Ivybridge Com Coll
P&R
Hazel La

Woodlands Pk Prim Sch
Woodland
Cemy
The Groves Tremarran
Beacon Rd
The Erme Prim Sch
Nirvana
KIMBERLEY CT 5
GLANVILLES MILL 6
HARRIS COTTS 7
Filham Ind Est 8
Stowford Prim Sch
Tollbar Cl
Cross-in-Hand
B3213
EXETER RD

1 THE LONDON CT
2 GREENWAY CL
3 PRIMROSE CL
4 ERME CT

Manor Prim Sch
Grosvenor
PO
Liby
PTH
Ctr
Butterpark
Filham
2

B3213 WESTERN RD
Marjorie Kelly Way
Garden Ctr
A38

21 SUNNYDALE CT
22 ENDSLEIGH VIEW
23 DYMOCK WAY
24 HARSTON RD
25 DRAKE AVE
26 WOODLAND PK
27 RISDON DR

WOODLAND COTTS 13
WOODLAND CT 14
DELAMORE CL 15
THE COPPICE 16
WORTHELE CL 17
CHURCH MDW 18
LOWER BROOK PK 19
HIGHER BROOK PK 20

KIMBERLEY VILLAS 1
GREENWOOD CL 2
WESTOVER CL 3
WOODLAND TERR 4

Westover Ind Est
Sewage Works
PARK STREET MEWS 5
PARK TERR 6
Erme Bridge Wks 7
South Devon Tennis Ctr

BUCKFAST CL 4
Stowford Bsns Pk 5
STANIFORTH DR 6
THE CHASE 7
STONEHEDGE CL 8
WOODSIDE CL 9

Godwell
Charles Hankin
BUTTON LA

1 WALTHAM WAY
2 CANTERBURY CL
3 WINDSOR CL
4 KERSWELL CL
5 EDGEMILL WLK
6 TWEENAWAY
7 CONSOLS CL
8 TURNPIKE CRES
9 LEYPARK AVE
10 EDGEMILL WLK
11 SHORTLANDS WAY

Higher Newlands
Lower Newlands
NEWLANDS CROSS
Yeolands
Fitham House

Drew
Muckymead Plantation
Cleeve House
HUNSDON RD
MARJERY CROSS
River Erme
ERMINGTON RD
Caton House

West Worthele
TOD MOOR CROSS
WORTHELE CROSS
East Worthele Farm
COLE LA
KEATON LA
GODWELL LA
ST PETERS WAY

Lower Keaton
Penquit
Penquit Manor

Tod Moor
Higher Keaton
Thornham

62   A   B   63   C   D   64   E   F

125

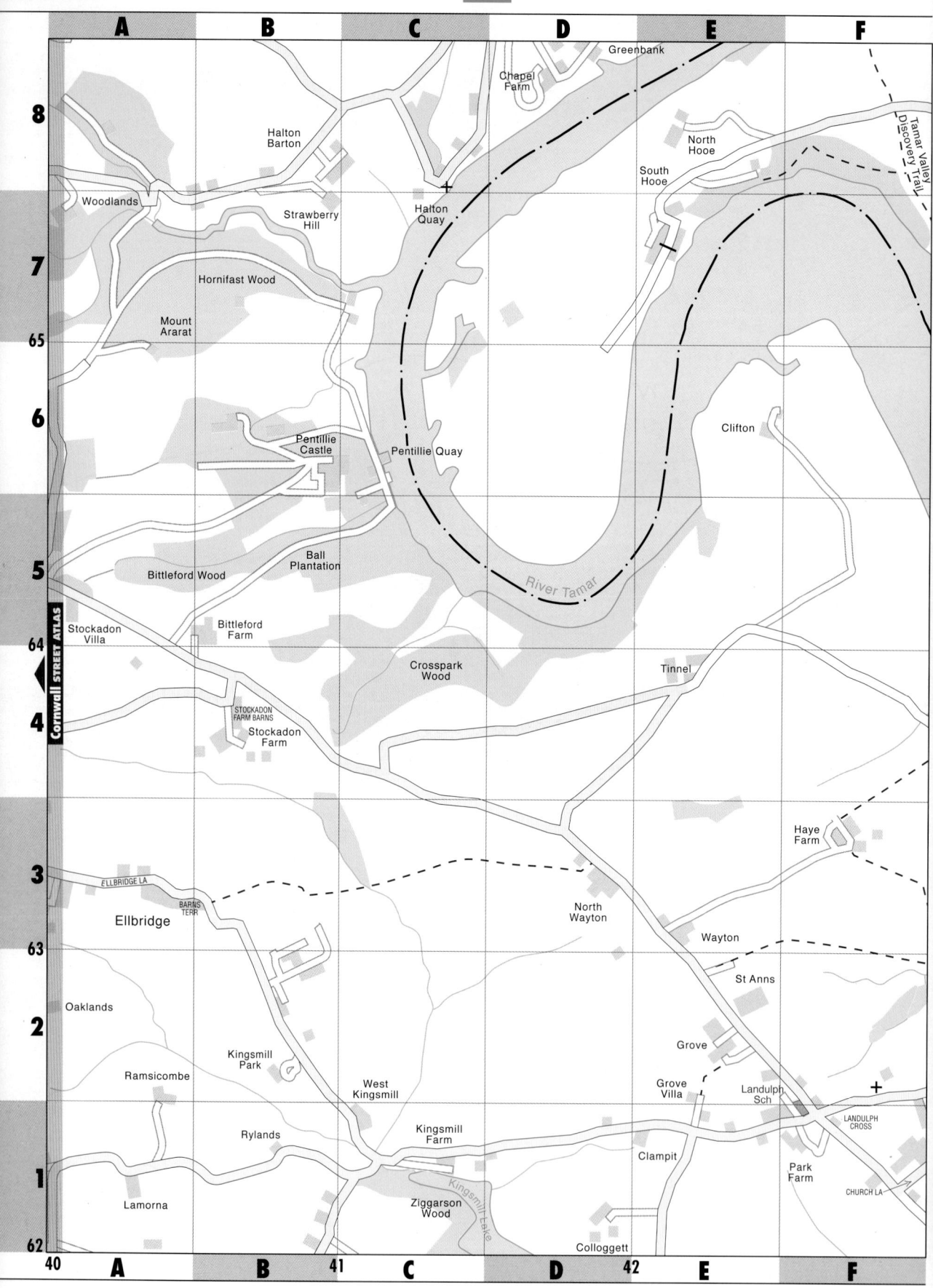
A
B
C
D
E
F
8
7
65
6
5
64
4
3
63
2
1
62
40
41
42
Greenbank
Chapel Farm
Halton Barton
North Hooe
South Hooe
Tamar Valley Discovery Trail
Woodlands
Strawberry Hill
Halton Quay
Hornifast Wood
Mount Ararat
Clifton
Pentillie Castle
Pentillie Quay
Ball Plantation
Bittleford Wood
River Tamar
Stockadon Villa
Bittleford Farm
Crosspark Wood
Tinnel
STOCKADON FARM BARNS
Stockadon Farm
Cornwall STREET ATLAS
Haye Farm
ELLBRIDGE LA
BARNS TERR
Ellbridge
North Wayton
Wayton
St Anns
Oaklands
Kingsmill Park
Grove
Ramsicombe
West Kingsmill
Grove Villa
Landulph Sch
Rylands
Kingsmill Farm
LANDULPH CROSS
Clampit
Park Farm
Kingsmill Lake
CHURCH LA
Lamorna
Ziggarson Wood
Colloggett

242

125
240

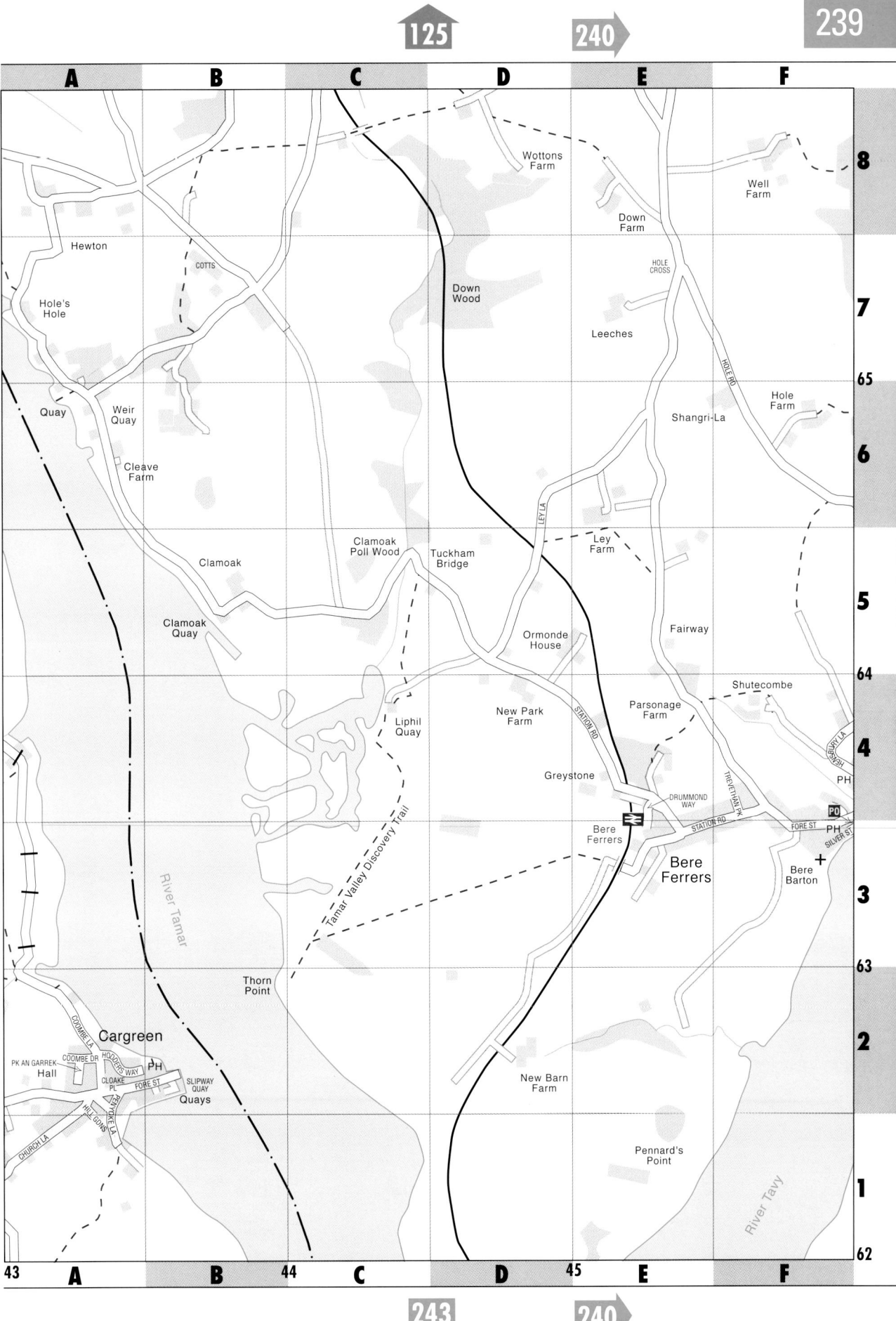
A
B
C
D
E
F
8
7
65
6
5
64
4
3
63
2
1
62
43
44
45
Wottons Farm
Well Farm
Down Farm
Hewton
COTTS
HOLE CROSS
Down Wood
Hole's Hole
Leeches
HOLE RD
Hole Farm
Quay
Weir Quay
Shangri-La
Cleave Farm
LEY LA
Clamoak Poll Wood
Tuckham Bridge
Ley Farm
Clamoak
Clamoak Quay
Ormonde House
Fairway
Shutecombe
New Park Farm
STATION RD
Parsonage Farm
Liphil Quay
HENSBURY LA
PH
Greystone
TREVETHAN PK
DRUMMOND WAY
PO
Tamar Valley Discovery Trail
Bere Ferrers
STATION RD
FORE ST
PH
SILVER ST
Bere Ferrers
Bere Barton
River Tamar
Thorn Point
COOMBE LA
Cargreen
PK AN GARREK
COOMBE DR
HODDERS WAY
PH
Hall
CLOAKE PL
FORE ST
SLIPWAY QUAY
Quays
PENYOKE LA
HILL GDNS
CHURCH LA
New Barn Farm
Pennard's Point
River Tavy

243
240

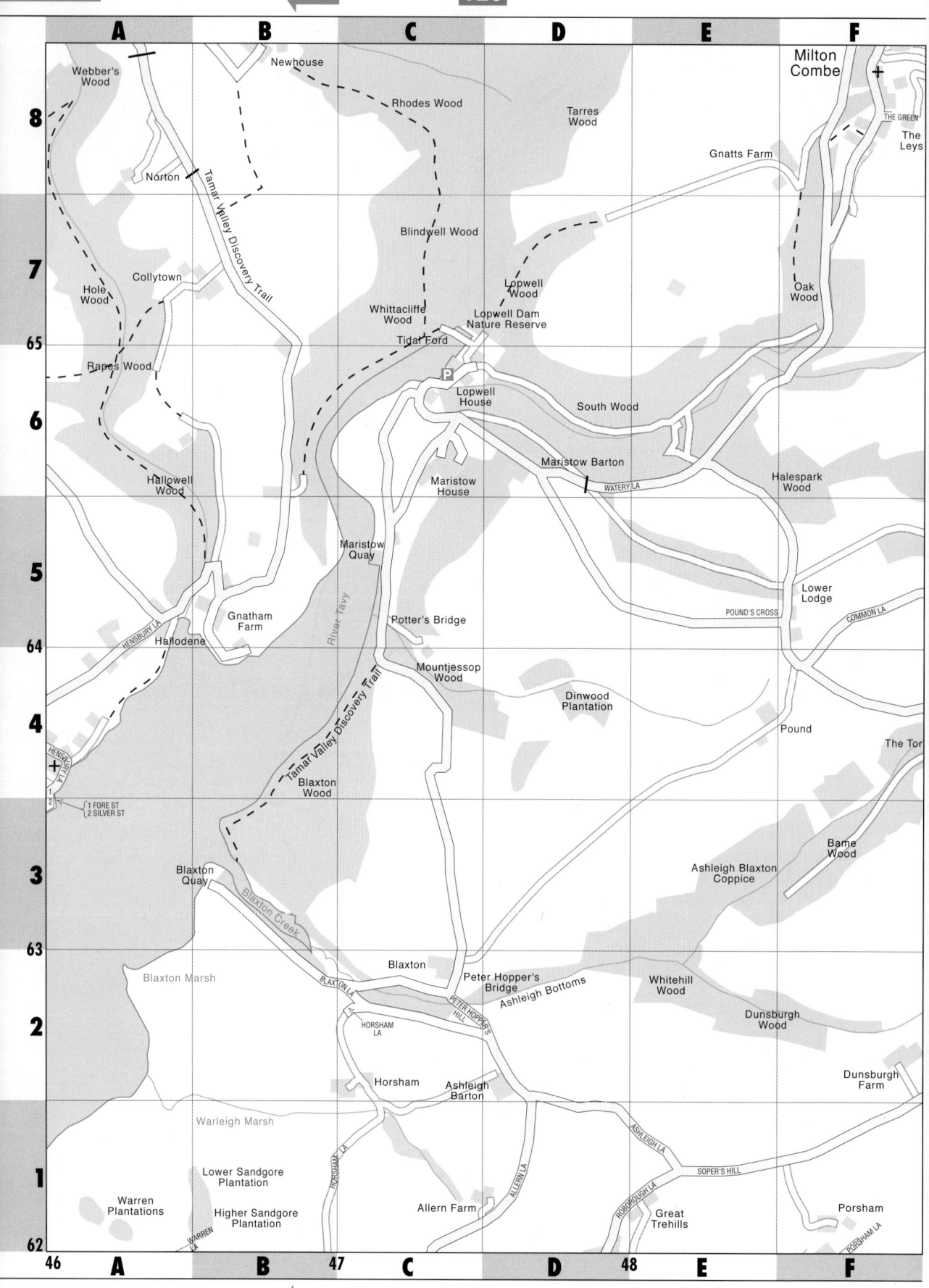

Milton
Combe

THE GREEN
The
Leys

Webber's
Wood

Newhouse

Rhodes Wood

Tarres
Wood

Gnatts Farm

Norton

Tamar Valley Discovery Trail

Blindwell Wood

Lopwell
Wood

Oak
Wood

Hole
Wood

Collytown

Whittacliffe
Wood

Lopwell Dam
Nature Reserve

Rapes Wood

Tidal Ford

Lopwell
House

South Wood

Hallowell
Wood

Maristow Barton

WATERY LA

Halespark
Wood

Maristow
House

Maristow
Quay

River Tavy

Potter's Bridge

POUND'S CROSS

Lower
Lodge

COMMON LA

HENSBURY LA

Hallodene

Gnatham
Farm

Mountjessop
Wood

Dinwood
Plantation

Pound

The Tor

HENSBURY LA

Tamar Valley Discovery Trail

Blaxton
Wood

1 FORE ST
2 SILVER ST

Bame
Wood

Blaxton
Quay

Ashleigh Blaxton
Coppice

Blaxton Creek

Blaxton

BLAXTON LA

Whitehill
Wood

Blaxton Marsh

Peter Hopper's
Bridge

Ashleigh Bottoms

Dunsburgh
Wood

PETER HOPPER'S HILL

Horsham
LA

HORSHAM LA

Warleigh Marsh

Horsham

Ashleigh
Barton

Dunsburgh
Farm

ASHLEIGH LA

SOPER'S HILL

Lower Sandgore
Plantation

HORSHAM LA

ALLERN LA

ROBOROUGH LA

Warren
Plantations

Higher Sandgore
Plantation

Allern Farm

Great
Trehills

Porsham

WARREN LA

PORSHAM LA

8

7

65

6

5

64

4

3

63

2

1

62

A B C D E F

Uphill

Morey House

Hotel

27

Dashel

Bickham

Bickham

Upper Road Plantation

Charity Bickham

Bulteel Bickham

Webbers

SOWTON RD

MOORLAND DR

YEOLAND DOWN

A386

Middlelodge Plantation

The Wilderness

Higher Park

Commonlane Plantation

COMMON LA

Middle Lodge

Henshears

Higher Lodge

DEVONPORT LEAT

Combe Park Farm

Lower Upperton

ROBOROUGH DOWN LA

Little Down

Welltown Bridge

Marrowpark Plantation

UPPERTON LA

North Broadley

Coppers

Haxter Lodge

Roborough Farm

Roborough Plantation

Leigh

BACK LA

Broadley

Broadley Ind Pk

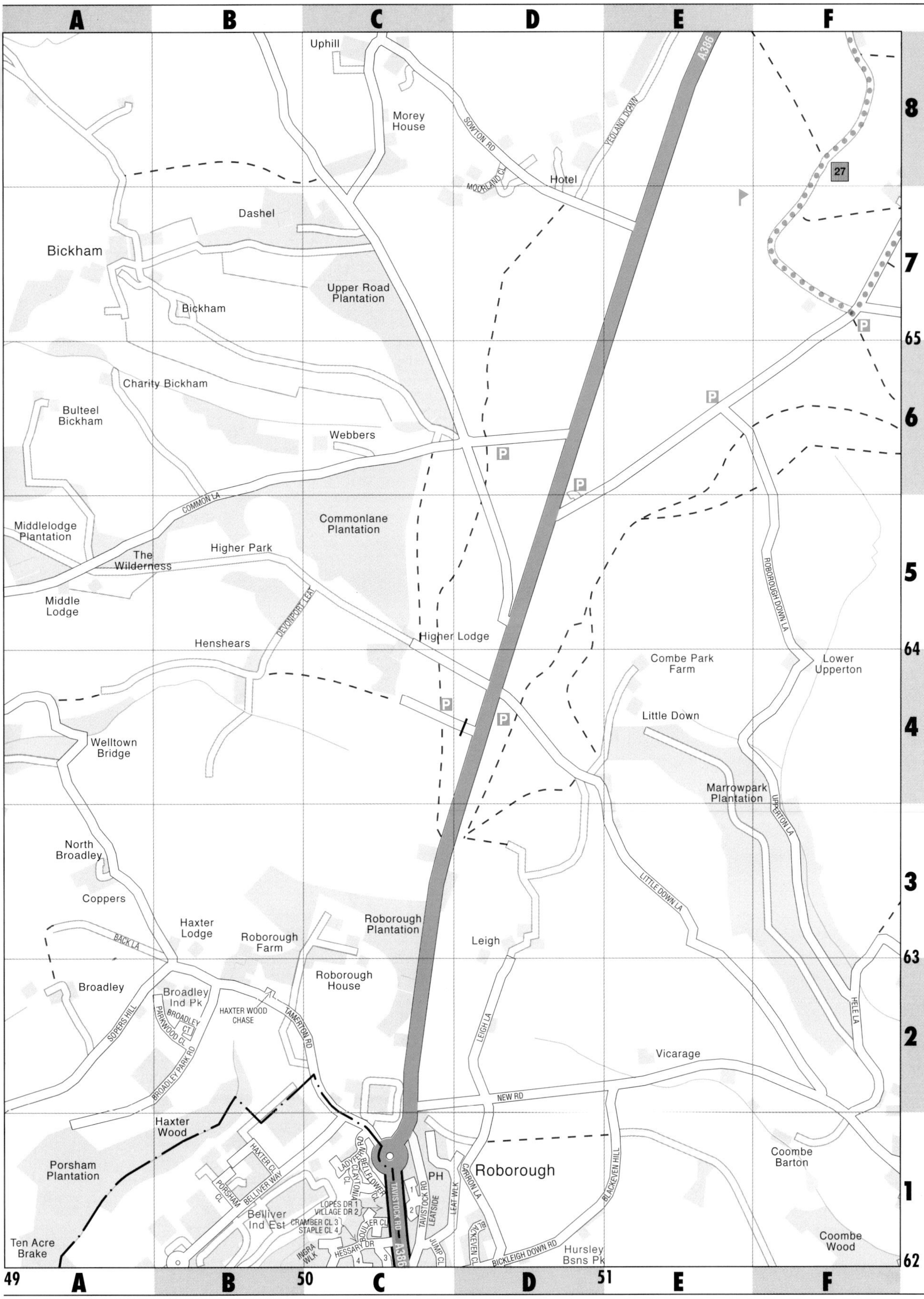

BROADLEY CL

Roborough House

Haxter Wood Chase

TAMERTON RD

LITTLE DOWN LA

Vicarage

LEIGH LA

Coombe Barton

HELE LA

SOPERS HILL

PARKWOOD RD

BROADLEY PARK RD

Haxter Wood

HAXTER CL

PORSHAM CL

BELLIVER WAY

NEW RD

BLACKEVEN HILL

Porsham Plantation

Belliver Ind Est

Roborough

PH

CARPON LA

Coombe Wood

Ten Acre Brake

LADYCROFT

BELLFLOWER CL

CLAYTON CL

LOPES DR 1

VILLAGE DR 2

CRAMBER CL 3

STAPLE CL 4

INGRA WLK

HESSARY DR

TAVISTOCK RD

TUFTON CL

LEATSIDE

JUMP CL

LEAT WLK

BLACKEVEN CL

BICKLEIGH DOWN RD

Hursley Bsns Pk

A386

P 27

49 A B 50 C D 51 E F

62

238
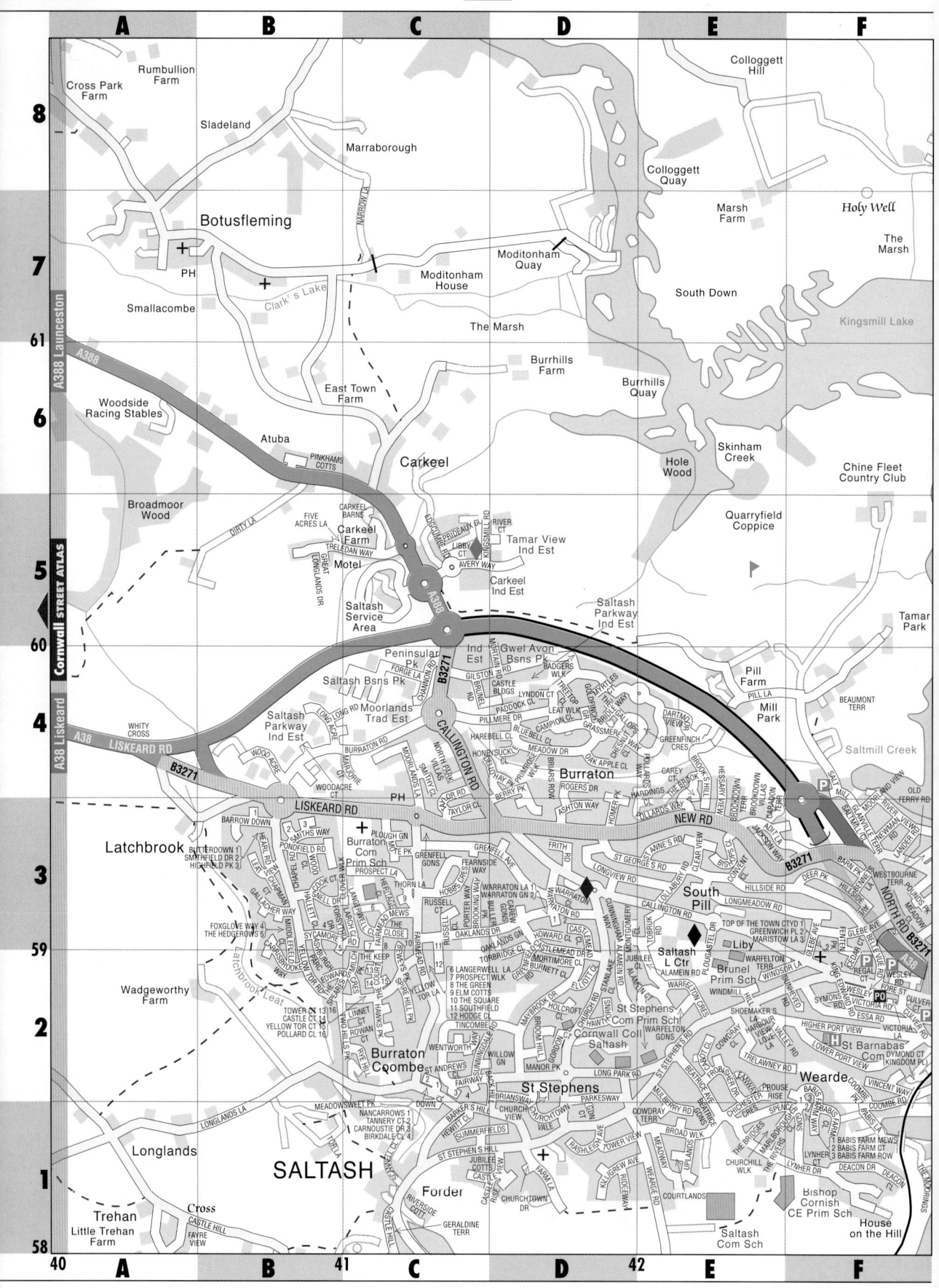
A
B
C
D
E
F
8
7
61
6
5
60
4
3
59
2
1
58
40
41
42
A38 Launceston
Cornwall STREET ATLAS
A38 Liskeard
Rumbullion Farm
Cross Park Farm
Sladeland
Marraborough
Colloggett Hill
Colloggett Quay
Marsh Farm
Holy Well
The Marsh
Botusfleming
PH
Smallacombe
Clark's Lake
Moditonham Quay
Moditonham House
South Down
Kingsmill Lake
The Marsh
Burrhills Farm
Burrhills Quay
East Town Farm
Woodside Racing Stables
Atuba
PINKHAMS COTTS
Carkeel
Hole Wood
Skinham Creek
Chine Fleet Country Club
Broadmoor Wood
DIRTY LA
FIVE ACRES LA
CARKEEL BARNS
Carkeel Farm
Motel
Tamar View Ind Est
Quarryfield Coppice
Carkeel Ind Est
Saltash Service Area
Saltash Parkway Ind Est
Tamar Park
A388
B3271
Peninsular Pk
Saltash Bsns Pk
Ind Est
Gwel Avon Bsns Pk
Pill Farm
Mill Park
Beaumont Terr
Moorlands Trad Est
Saltash Parkway Ind Est
WHITY CROSS
A38 LISKEARD RD
CALLINGTON RD
Burraton
Saltmill Creek
LISKEARD RD
NEW RD
PH
Latchbrook
Burraton Com Prim Sch
South Pill
Saltash L Ctr
Liby
Brunel Prim Sch
St Stephens Com Prim Sch
Cornwall Coll Saltash
Wadgeworthy Farm
Latchbrook Leat
Burraton Coombe
St Stephens
Wearde
St Barnabas Com
Longlands
LONGLANDS LA
SALTASH
Forder
Bishop Cornish CE Prim Sch
Trehan
Cross
Little Trehan Farm
CASTLE HILL
Saltash Com Sch
House on the Hill
246

A B C D E F

8

Warleigh House

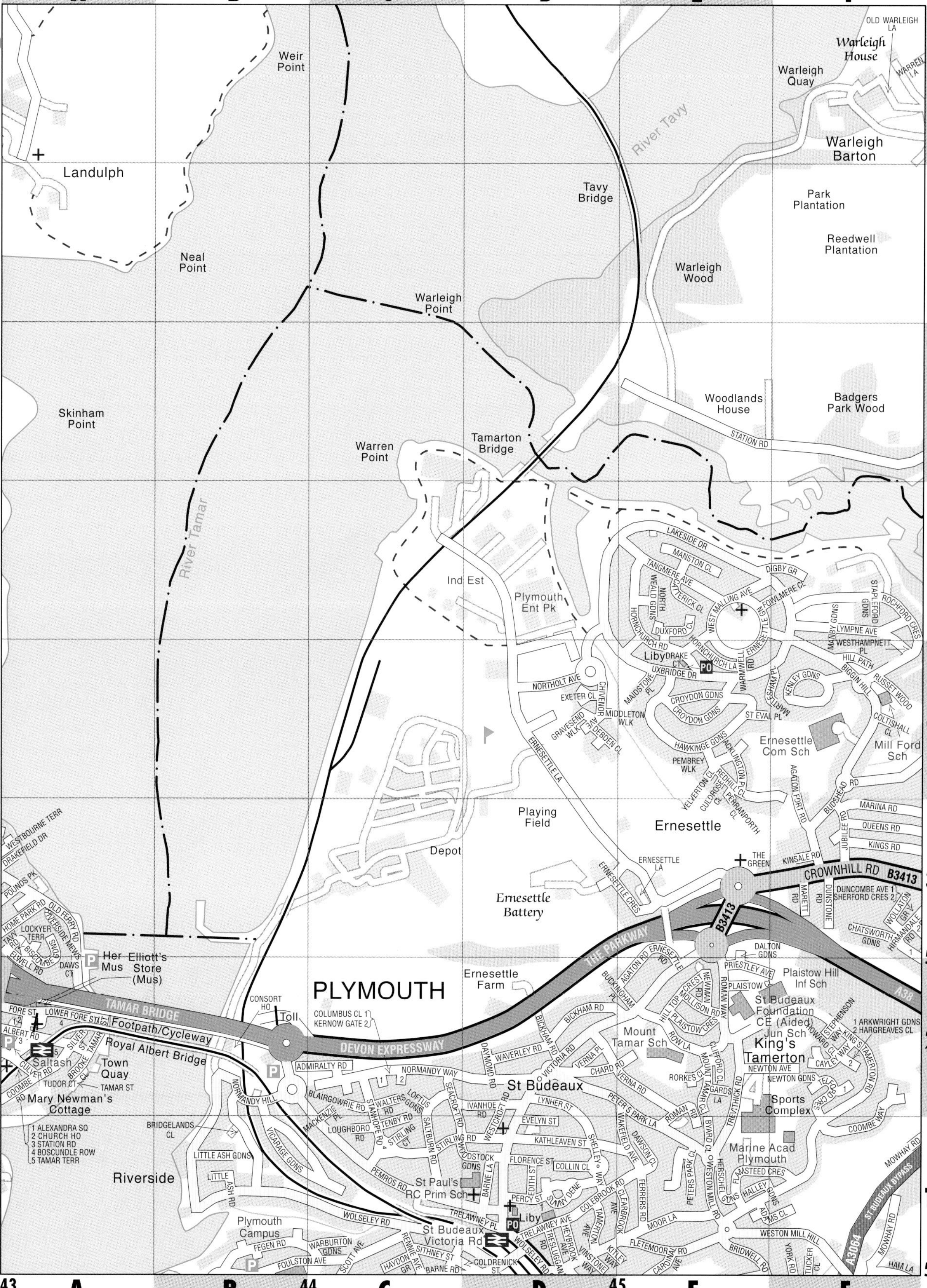

OLD WARLEIGH LA

Weir Point

Warleigh Quay

WARREN

Landulph

Warleigh Barton

Tavy Bridge

River Tavy

Park Plantation

7

Neal Point

Warleigh Wood

Reedwell Plantation

61

Warleigh Point

Woodlands House

Badgers Park Wood

6

Skinham Point

Warren Point

Tamarton Bridge

STATION RD

River Tamar

Ind Est

LAKESIDE DR

MANSTON CL

DIGBY GR

5

Plymouth Ent Pk

TANGMERE AVE
MANSTON CL
WEALD GDNS
NORTH
MAVERICK CL
WEST MALLING AVE
STAPLEFORD GDNS
ROCHFORD CRES
HORNCHURCH AVE
DUXFORD CL
HORNCHURCH LA
LYMPNE AVE
MANBY GDNS

60

Liby
DRAKE
PO
WESTHAMPNETT PL
HILL PATH
BIGGIN HILL
RUSSEL WOOD

NORTHOLT AVE
EXETER LA
CHIVENOR
UXBRIDGE DR
MAIDSTONE
CROYDON GDNS
KENLEY GDNS
ST EVAL PL
COLTISHALL CL

4

GRAVESEND WLK
DEBDEN CL
CROYDON GDNS
HAWKINGE GDNS
ERNESETTLE LA
MIDDLETON WLK
Mill Ford Sch

PEMBREY WLK
Ernesettle Com Sch
MARINA RD

Playing Field
YELVERTON CL
BUDSHEAD RD
QUEENS RD

Depot
Ernesettle
KINGS RD

Ernesettle Battery
ERNESETTLE CRES
ERNESETTLE LA
THE GREEN
KINSALE RD
CROWNHILL RD B3413

3

DUNCOMBE AVE
SHERFORD CRES
DUNSTONE
CHATSWORTH GDNS

B3413
THE PARKWAY
DALTON GDNS

59

PLYMOUTH

Ernesettle Farm
PRIESTLEY AVE
Plaistow Hill Inf Sch
A38

Her Mus
Elliott's Store (Mus)

TAMAR BRIDGE
CONSORT HO
Toll
COLUMBUS CL
KERNOW GATE
DEVON EXPRESSWAY
St Budeaux Foundation CE (Aided) Jun Sch
ARKWRIGHT GDNS
HARGREAVES CL

2

Royal Albert Bridge
Town Quay
ADMIRALTY RD
NORMANDY WAY
Mount Tamar Sch
King's Tamerton
NEWTON AVE

Saltash
NORMANDY HILL
St Budeaux
Sports Complex

Mary Newman's Cottage
BLAIRGOWRIE RD
WALTERS RD
SEATON
VICTORIA RD
VERNA RD
COOMBE WAY

1 ALEXANDRA SQ
2 CHURCH HO
3 STATION RD
4 BOSCUNDLE ROW
5 TAMAR TERR

BRIDGELANDS CL
MACKENZIE
LOUGHBORO RD
STIRLING
EVELYN ST
Marine Acad Plymouth

LITTLE ASH GDNS
LYNHER ST
KATHLEAVEN ST

Riverside
VICARAGE GDNS
PEMROS RD
COSTOCK
FLORENCE ST
COLLIN CL
PETER'S PARK LA

Plymouth Campus
WOLSELEY RD
St Paul's RC Prim Sch
EDITH ST
PERCY ST
WESTON MILL HILL

FEGEN RD
WARBURTON GDNS
TRELAWNEY
St Budeaux Victoria Rd
Liby
PO
BRIDWELL RD

1

HAYDON
SCOTT AVE
BARNE RD
COLDRENICK ST

58

D1
1 Victoria Road Prim Sch

243 240

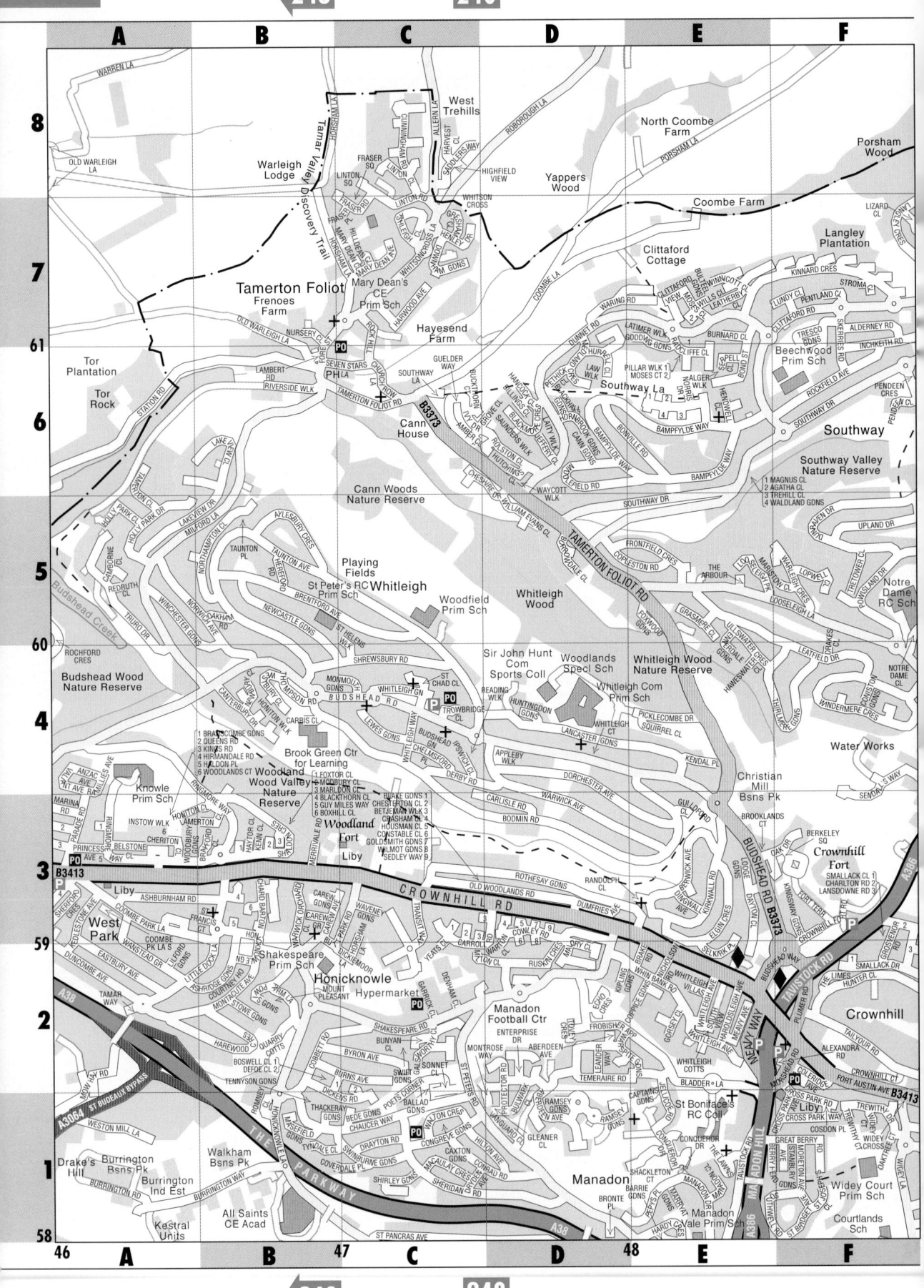
A B C D E F
8
7
61
6
5
60
4
3
59
2
1
58
46 47 48
West Trehills
North Coombe Farm
Porsham Wood
Warleigh Lodge
Tamar Valley Discovery Trail
Yappers Wood
Coombe Farm
Langley Plantation
Clittaford Cottage
Tamerton Foliot
Frenoes Farm
Mary Dean's CE Prim Sch
Hayesend Farm
Tor Plantation
Tor Rock
Southway La
Beechwood Prim Sch
Southway
Cann House
Southway Valley Nature Reserve
Cann Woods Nature Reserve
Playing Fields
St Peter's RC Prim Sch
Whitleigh
Woodfield Prim Sch
Whitleigh Wood
Notre Dame RC Sch
Budshead Creek
Budshead Wood Nature Reserve
Sir John Hunt Com Sports Coll
Woodlands Specl Sch
Whitleigh Wood Nature Reserve
Whitleigh Com Prim Sch
Water Works
Brook Green Ctr for Learning
Woodland Wood Valley Nature Reserve
Knowle Prim Sch
Christian Mill Bsns Pk
Woodland Fort
Liby
Crownhill Fort
West Park
Shakespeare Prim Sch
Honicknowle
Hypermarket
Manadon Football Ctr
Crownhill
St Boniface's RC Coll
Drake's Hill
Burrington Bsns Pk
Burrington Ind Est
Walkham Bsns Pk
Manadon
Widey Court Prim Sch
All Saints CE Acad
Kestral Units
Manadon Vale Prim Sch
Courtlands Sch
TAMERTON FOLIOT RD
B3373
BUDSHEAD RD
CROWNHILL RD
B3413
A386
A38
A3064 ST BUDEAUX BYPASS
THE PARKWAY
TAVISTOCK RD
MANADON HILL
MEAVY WAY
SOUTHWAY DR
BAMPFYLDE WAY
ST PANCRAS AVE
A B C D E F

243 248

241
132

A
B
C
D
E
F
8
7
6
5
4
3
2
1
61
60
59
58
49
50
51
Arnold's Hill Coppice
Porsham Coppice
Belliver Ind Est
BELLIVER WAY
INGRA WLK
STAPLE CL
A386
BICKLEIGH DOWN RD
Bickleigh Down
Rock Wood
SOLAR CRES
1 BLACKTHORN CL
2 BRACKEN CL
Pick Pie Plantation
1 ROCKWOOD RD
2 CHURCH PARK CT
3 CHURCHLANDS RD
Bickleigh Down Bsns Pk
ECO WAY
BEVERSTON WAY
CHEPSTOW AVE
TREAGO GDNS
BARBURY CRES
CALDICOT GDNS
TIVERTON CL
Hypermarket
HAZELWOOD DR
WOOLWELL CRES
Bickleigh Down CE Prim Sch
REDWING DR
KESTREL CL
MERVIN CL
SKYLARK RISE
PICK PIE DR
NEW WOOD
HEDGEROW CL
CHURCH PARK RD
VIOLET DR
CAMPION VIEW
CLOVER RISE
HIGHCLERE GDNS
FLEETWOOD GDNS
LANGLEY CRES
CROMER WLK
CROMER CL
BARDSEY CL
HARTLAND CL
WHITEHAVEN WY
LIZARD CL
LIZARD CHURCH WLK
CLITTAFORD RD
DENNIS CAMP RD
RIFLEMANS WALK
Ind Est
Liby
PRESTONBURY CL
HOLNE CHASE
HEDINGHAM GDNS
WARFDOUR WLK
WIDEWELL LA
Widewell
BOUNDARY PL
Widewell Prim Acad
LULWORTH DR
SAMUEL BASSETT AVE
HAM GDNS
RISHAM AVE
CROMWELL GATE
COPPER BEECH WAY
KIRKLAND CL
OAKLANDS CL
HAWTHORN CL
WOOLWELL RD
WOOLWELL DR
SYCAMORE DR
RIVERFORD CL
WARREN PK
THE HEATHERS
HOLMER DOWN
CORNER BRAKE
MEADOWLANDS
FOREST VIEW
VALLEY VIEW
WOODEND RD
1 CROFT PK
2 COPPICE WOOD DR
3 SILVER BIRCH CL
4 FORRESTERS DR
Woolwell
TRENDLEWOOD RD 1
ASHTREE CL 2
OAKWOOD CL 3
TRAMWAY RD
THISTLE CL
ROSEHIP CL
CANN WOOD VIEW
BOWERS PARK DR
SPRING PK
COPPERS PK
HONEYSUCKLE CL
CHURCHLANDS CL
Darklake
MULBERRY CL
BIRCH CL
ROWAN WAY
MAPLE WAY
PINEWOOD DR
LA ROCH DR
ACORN DR
West Wood
Darklake Wood
West Devon Way
LAUNCESTON CL
SOUTHWAY DR
SOUTHWAY LA
WIDEWELL RD
LITTLE ANCY CL
THE COURT
LONGSTONE AVE
GOODWIN AVE
PENDEEN CRES
Oakwood Prim Sch
FLAMBOROUGH WAY
FREWIN GDNS 1
TRENTHAM CL 2
CORINGDEAN CL 3
EASTCOTE CL 4
BUTLER CL
DAVENHAM CL
CORSHAM CL
TYLNEY CL
BROCKTON GDNS
BARNINGHAM GDNS
BARNDALE CRES
HAZEL CL
OLDLANDS CL
BURTON CL
ARNEY CRES
COLSTON CL
OLYMPIC WAY
P&R
BUENA VISTA DR
BUENA VISTA GDNS
BUENA VISTA WAY
APPLEDORE CL
ASHTON CL
GLENHOLT RD
GLENHOLT CL
HOLTWOOD RD
Glenholt
JASMINE GDNS
1 KINGFISHER CL
2 MAPLE CL
3 NELSON TERR
4 QUEENS CL
5 PRINCES RD
6 BAYTREE CL
7 BEECH CT
8 WILLOW WLK
Common Wood
VALLEY WLK
JULIAN WLK
GLENFIELD WAY
GLENFIELD CL
ELM RD
SYCAMORE WAY
LAUREL DR
UNITY CL
B3432
MORGAN RD
TAVISTOCK RD
WESTWOOD AVE
ST ANNE'S RD
GLENFIELD RD
OAK TREE PK
THE BIRCHES
ELMWOOD CL
WOODLANDS END
BLUE HAZE CL
DUNRAVEN DR
STOKESAY AVE
UPLAND DR
MOORLAND VIEW
SHARON WAY
POWISLAND DR
ROBOROUGH AVE
ROBOROUGH CL
Common Wood Cottage
DARKLAKE VIEW
DARKLAKE CL
FORGET ME NOT LA 1
RIVERFORD 2
Forresters Bsns Pk
Notre Dame RC Sch
Sports Ground
UPLAND DR
1 JODEL CL
2 LYSANDER LA
3 ALBACORE DR
4 CANBERRA RD
PLYMBRIDGE RD
JETSTREAM WY
RUNWAY RD
RADAR RD
PIPER ST
HAWKINS CL
CARADON CL
ALWIN PK
DELGANY DR
BEATTY CL
HONEYFORD CL
NOTRE DAME CL
GLADE CL
FRANKLYNS CL
LOOSELEIGH LA
LOOSELEIGH CL
BRYMON WY
PLYMBRIDGE LA
COLLEGE DEAN CL
ST MARKS CL
ST JOHNS
Plymouth Marjon Univ
SISNA PK RD
MOORVIEW CT
ESTOVER CL
Colwill Wood
Estover Ind Est
ESTOVER RD
Phoenix Bsns Pk
AIRBORNE DR
Plymouth Hosp
MARJON
A3860
HOWESON LA
DERRIFORD RD
CHALLOCK CL
FINDON GDNS
ROGATE WLK
DURRIS GDNS
DURRIS CL
COMBLEY DR
THORNBURY RD
Works
Superstore
LEATFIELD DR 1
ESTHWAITE LA 2
Derriford
MORLAIX DR
Derriford Bsns Pk
BREST WAY
DERRIFORD PK
ROSCOFF RISE
Derriford
RESEARCH WAY
DAVY RD
Plymouth Science Pk
DOCKRAY CL
KINVER CL
MARDON CL
ROTHBURY CL
Thornbury Prim Sch
RHEOLA GDNS
Estover
WENTWOOD PL
ARMSIDE CL
PENRITH WLK
PATTERDALE CL
PATTERDALE WLK
MILLER WAY
WENTWOOD GDNS
Peninsula Medical Sch
Derriford Health & L Ctr
Bircham Valley Nature Reserve
TA Ctr
ALPHA WAY
BREST RD
Seaton Bsns Pk
Plymouth Cross City Link
Fursdon
BLUNT'S LA
PENRITH GDNS
LABATT CL
RENDLESHAM GDNS
DOVER RD
LONG DOWN GDNS
BUSH PK
EARLS WOOD CL
PLYMBRIDGE RD
EARLS WOOD DR
COLWILL WLK
COLWILL RD
RAMAGE CL
WILLIAM PRANCE RD
Plymouth Medical & Tech Pk
CHARLTON RD
RICHMOND RD
COLBORNE RD
St Matthew's CE Prim Acad
PEREGRINE RD
SHAMROCK ST
BUTTERCUP RD
PARTRIDGE RD
BLUEBELL ST
SMALLACK DR
HUNTER CL
HOLLYHOCK WAY
STARLING DR
JACKDAW RD
SANDPIPER RD
PINTAIL WAY
WITHBURN GDNS
ASHDOWN CL 1
ASHDOWN WLK 2
LEYPARK CL
Sp Ctr
Tor Bridge High
Liby
Cann Bridge Sch
Tor Bridge Prim Sch
CHELSON GDNS
HURRABROOK GDNS
TOWERS CL
WEIR RD
Mainstone
PATTINSON CT
PATTINSON CL
PATTINSON DR
BRIARLEIGH CL
WEIR CL
CRESSBROOK WLK
CRESSBROOK DR
Mainstone Wood
CRESSBROOK CL
EDEN VALLEY GDNS 1
RAVENGLASS CL 2
AMBLESIDE PL 3
WASDALE CL
WASDALE GDNS
KESWICK CRES
TORVER CL
LEYPARK DR
LEYPARK WLK
NOVOROSSISK RD
Superstore
RUNNYMEDE CT
PLYMOUTH
CROWN GDNS 1
SANDON WLK 2
LYDCOT WLK 3
BROOKING CL 4
ALDERSLEY WLK 5
GRATTON PL 6
BRIDGWATER CL 7
CHARFIELD DR 8
FRESHFORD WLK 1
FRESHFORD CL 2
CHILDREY GDNS 3
CHILDREY WLK 4
DUNLEY WLK 5
COCKINGTON WLK 6
GOOSEWELL HILL 7
Bircham Farm
Poole Farm
LANGDALE GDNS
LANGDALE CL
HALLERTON CL
PARKFIELD DR
WOODLANDS LA
BEECHWOOD RISE
River Plym
TAILYOUR RD
FORT AUSTIN AVE
Bowden Battery
FORDER VALLEY RD
B3432
Leigham Prim Sch
COCKINGTON CL
BRADLEY CL
LUXMORE CL
BOWDEN PARK RD
WHITBY CRES
WINSBURY CT
DUCANE WLK
FORDER HTS
HINTON CT
AUSTIN CRES
Mast
MOAT PK
FORT AUSTIN AVE
BIRCHAM VIEW
ERLSTOKE CL
BAMPTON RD
SHELL CL
MILLWOOD DR
LEIGHAMMANOR DR
MAYFAIR CRES
KIMBERLY DR
COX'S WAY
CAMERON WAY
KINGSWEAR CRES
CARISBROOKE RD
St Edward's CE Prim Sch
B3413
THURLESTONE WLK
SHEEPSTOR RD
WALKHAMPTON WLK
BOLTON CL
MOTHECOMBE WLK
CHURCHSTOW WLK
GRAINGE RD
WHITBY RD
CADOVER CL
BICKLEIGH CL
MILES MITCHELL AVE
GEORGE DOWNING HO
SHIPLEY WLK
CHURCH HILL
LINKETTY LA E
BELLAMY CL
ST EDWARD GDNS
SHIRBURN RD
27

249
132

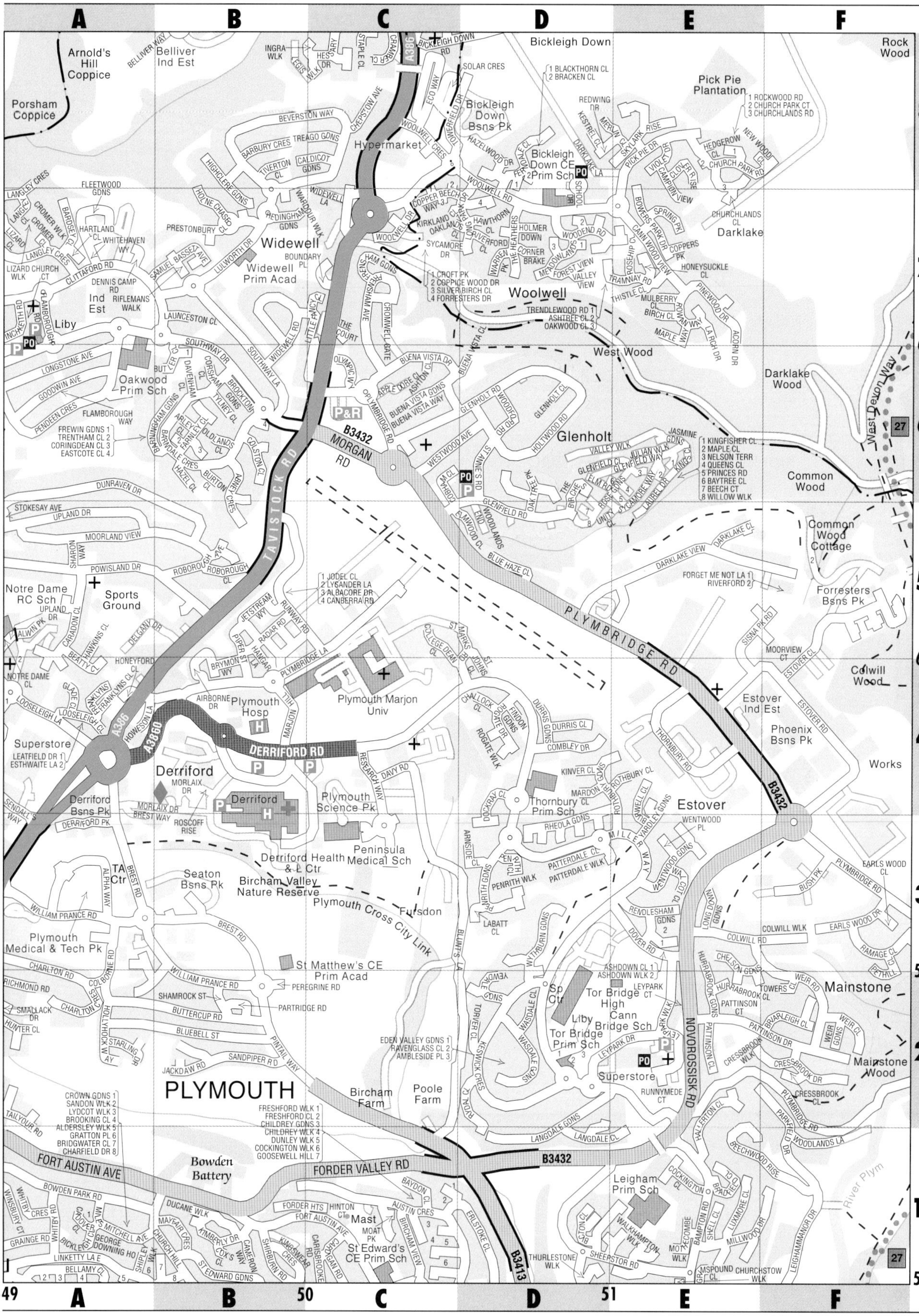

242

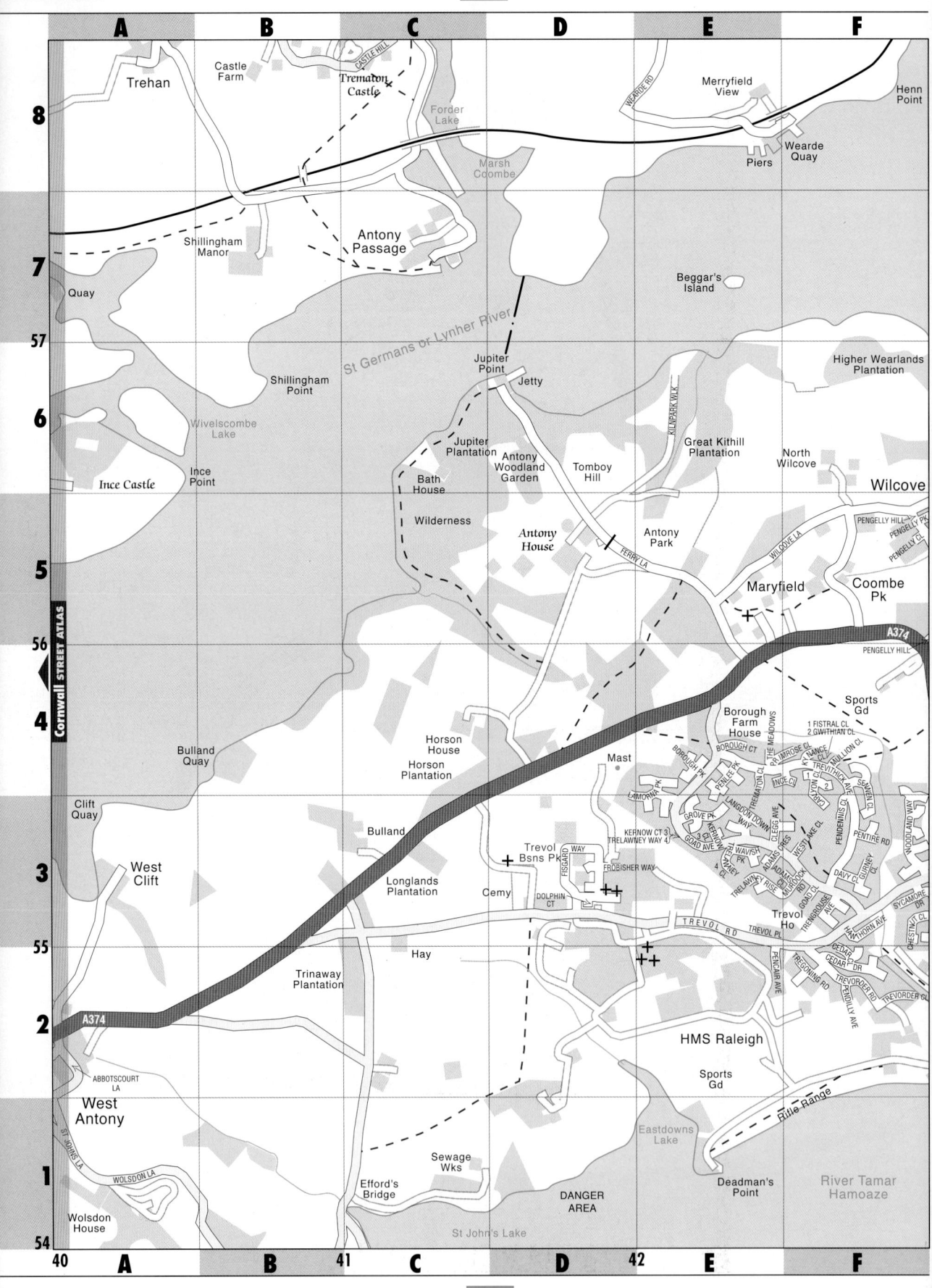
A B C D E F
8 7 57 6 5 56 4 3 55 2 1 54
40 41 42
Trehan
Castle Farm
Trematon Castle
Forder Lake
Merryfield View
Henn Point
Wearde Quay
Piers
Marsh Coombe
Antony Passage
Shillingham Manor
Beggar's Island
Quay
St Germans or Lynher River
Jupiter Point
Jetty
Higher Wearlands Plantation
Shillingham Point
Wivelscombe Lake
Jupiter Plantation
Antony Woodland Garden
Tomboy Hill
Great Kithill Plantation
North Wilcove
Wilcove
Ince Castle
Ince Point
Bath House
Wilderness
Antony House
Antony Park
Maryfield
Coombe Pk
A374
Sports Gd
Borough Farm House
Horson House
Horson Plantation
Bulland Quay
Mast
Clift Quay
Bulland
Trevol Bsns Pk
West Clift
Longlands Plantation
Cemy
Trevol Ho
Hay
Trinaway Plantation
HMS Raleigh
Sports Gd
Rifle Range
West Antony
Eastdowns Lake
Sewage Wks
Efford's Bridge
DANGER AREA
Deadman's Point
River Tamar Hamoaze
Wolsdon House
St John's Lake
Cornwall STREET ATLAS

F5
1 NEPEAN ST
2 ADELAIDE ST
3 BRUNEL TERR
4 EPWORTH TERR
5 SUSSEX TERR
6 RAILWAY COTTS

7 YORK TERR
8 ST MAWES TERR
9 SANCTUARY CL

243

248

F7
1 DELAWARE GDNS
2 CAROLINA GDNS
3 COOMBE VIEW
4 MAUNSELL CL
5 OVERDALE RD
6 WYATT AVE

253

248

F3
1 CLARENDON HO
2 GARFIELD TERR
3 TRAFALGAR PL
4 THE MEWS
5 NELSON GDNS
6 BEYROUT PL
7 ST MICHAEL'S CT

8 ST MICHAEL'S TERR
9 PORTLAND CT
10 MOLYNEAUX PL
11 CLARENDON LA
12 ACRE COTTS

F4
1 ST GEORGES CT
2 HORNBY ST
3 PHILLIMORE ST
4 FREMANTLE GDNS
5 FAIRFAX TERR
6 HARGOOD TERR
7 HARRISON ST

8 KEPPEL TERR
9 HEALY CT
10 BRUNSWICK PL

A5
1 MELVILLE PL
2 Wolseley Bsns Pk
3 AUCKLAND TO
4 HALEY BARTON
5 GREATLANDS PL

6 WADHAM TERR
7 CRANTOCK TERR
E5
1 Hyde Park
Infs & Jun Sch

E6
1 BRENT KNOLL RD
2 LUDLOW RD
3 SWAINDALE RD
4 TYTHING WLK
5 GLENHURST RD
6 VENN CL

E8
1 Manadon Vale
Prim Sch

F4
1 GROSVENOR COTTS
2 HILLSBOROUGH
3 PEARSON AVE
4 PENLEE PL
5 PENROSE VILLAS
6 CROZIER RD

7 MARINA TERR
8 KENSINGTON PL
9 SIDMOUTH CTS
10 COLERIDGE RD

F6
1 RESERVOIR LA
2 PEARN COTTS
3 BRANDRETH RD
4 GLENEAGLE AVE
5 GLENEAGLE VILLAS
6 HENDERS CNR

7 ROSEVEAN HO
8 ROSEVEAN CT
9 MANNAMEAD CT
10 FOSBROOKE CT

A7
1 RUFFORD CL
2 WYKEHAM DR
3 GLASTONBURY CL
4 KESTOR CL
5 SHARPITOR GDNS
6 TEMPLE WLK

D8
1 POLZEATH GDNS
2 MARAZION WY
3 POLPERRO PL

A38 B3250 THE PARKWAY A386 OUTLAND RD WOLSELEY RD B3396 A386 ALMA RD WESTERN APP COBOURG ST NORTH HILL TOTHILL RD EXETER ST UNION ST A374

PLYMOUTH

Pennycross Manadon Wood Hartley Peverell Kings Mannamead Mutley Ham North Prospect Ford Stoke Pennycomequick Mutley Central Park Home Park (Plymouth Argyle FC) Plymouth Life Ctr Royal Eye Infirmary Victoria Park Univ of Plymouth drakecircus Stonehouse Millbay Millbay Docks Barbican Sutton Harbour Aquarium Barracks

For full street detail of the highlighted area see pages 262 and 263.

A3
1 UNDERHILL VILLAS
2 OSBORNE VILLAS
3 EDGCUMBE CT
4 NELSON GDNS
5 COLLINGWOOD VILLAS
6 PAVILAND GRANGE
7 FITZROY TERR
8 BELMONT VILLAS

A4
1 WESLEY PL
2 MASTERMAN RD
3 DUCKWORTH ST
4 DUNDAS ST
5 BROMLEY PL
6 BROMLEY HO
7 LEESIDE CT
8 BELMONT CT
9 Stoke Damerel Bsns Ctr

A4
10 GOMERGET COTTG
11 SOMERSET PLACE LA
12 PARK PLACE LA

F4
1 HERMITAGE CT
2 WARLEIGH RD
3 ROCHESTER RD
4 CHESTER PL
5 ALEXANDRA PL
6 CONNAUGHT LA

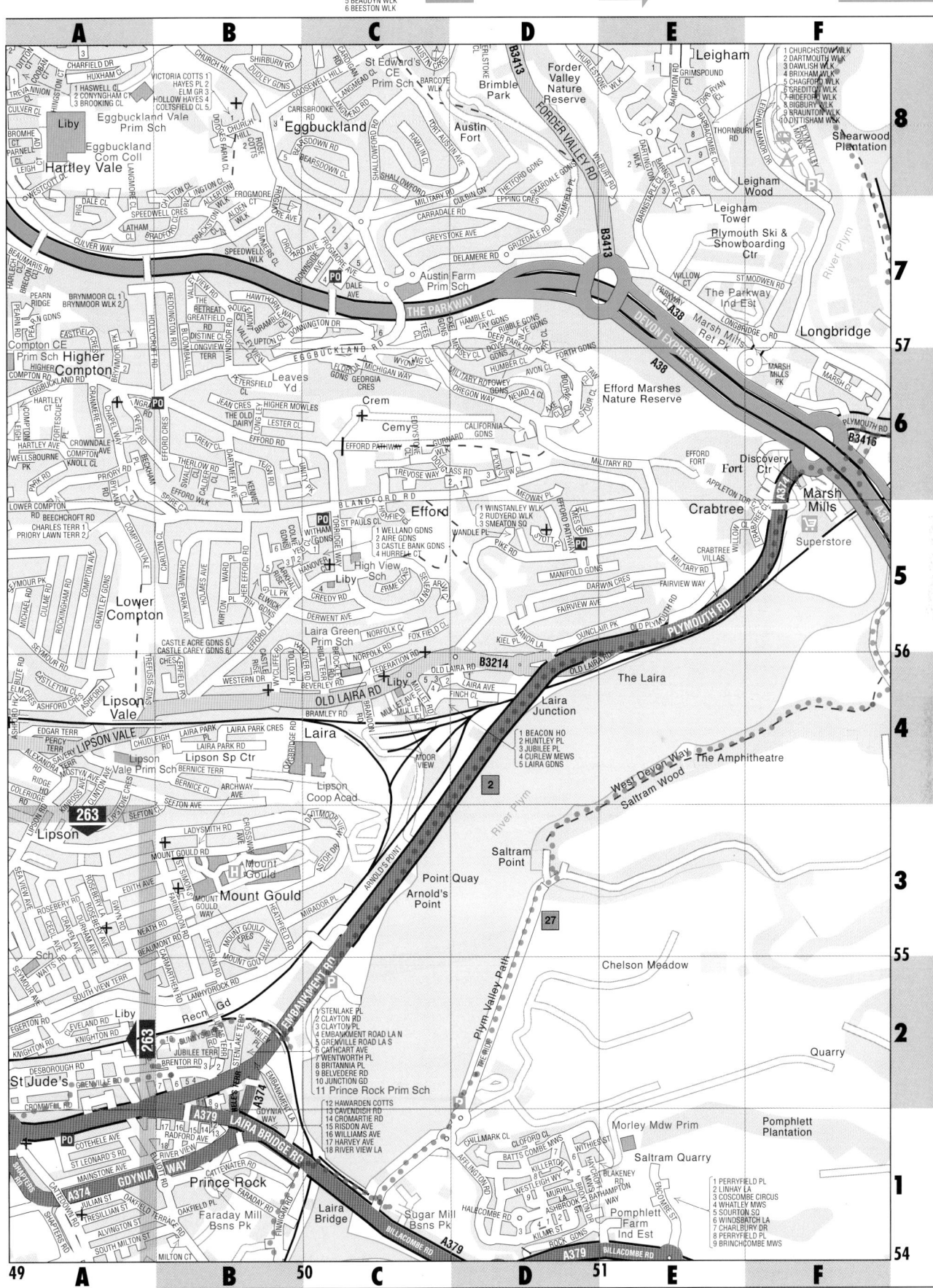

For full street detail of the highlighted area see page 263.

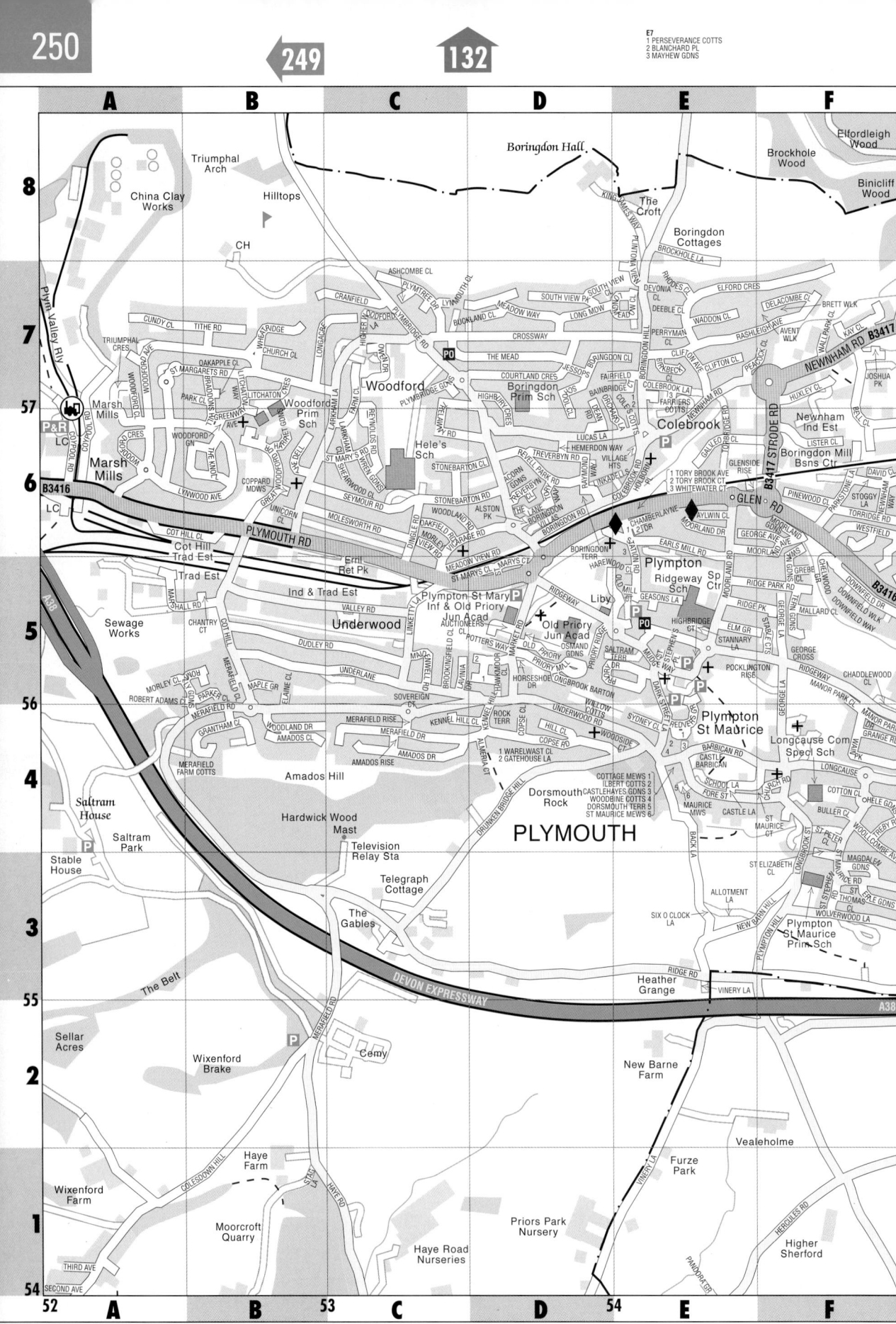

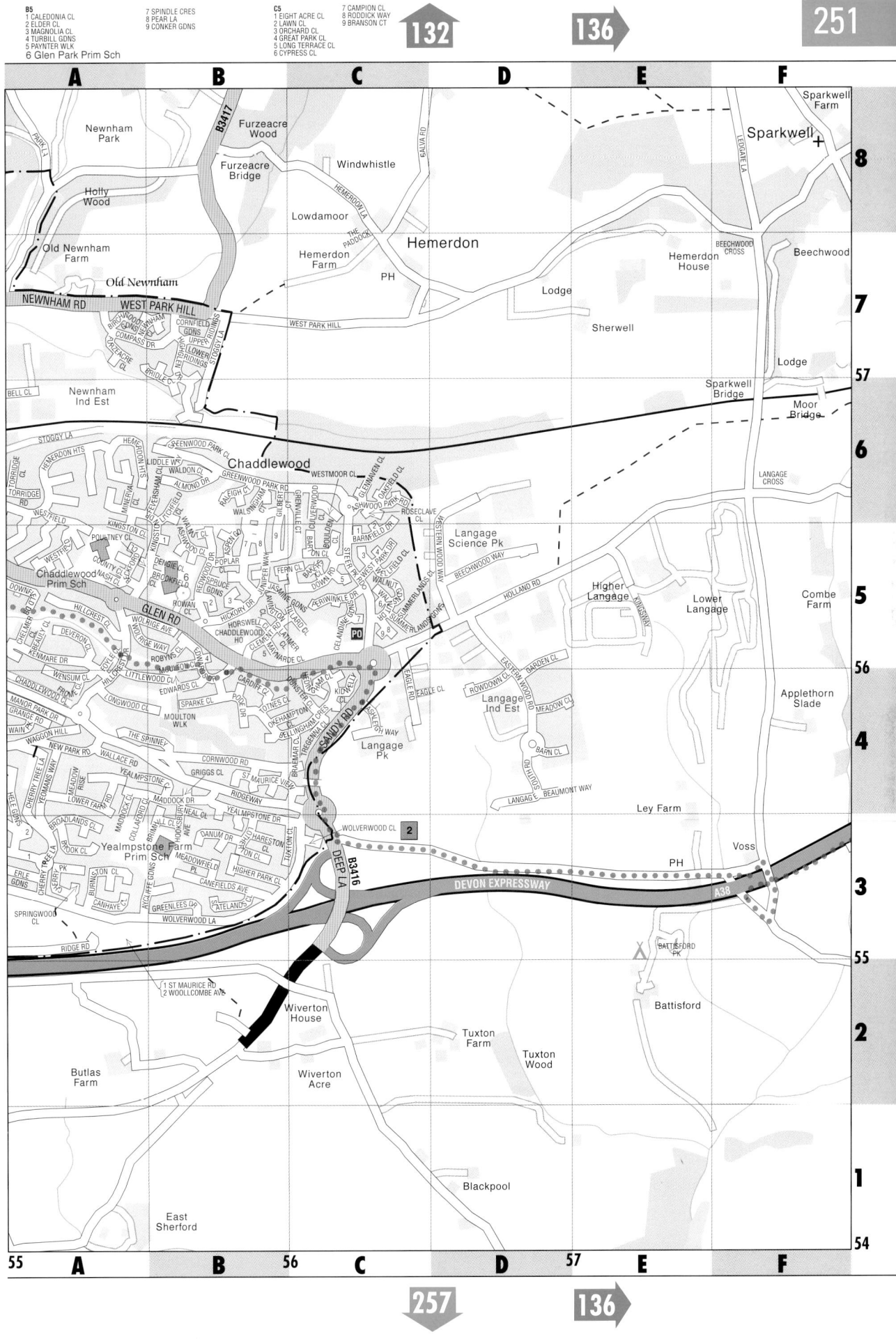

B5
1 CALEDONIA CL
2 ELDER CL
3 MAGNOLIA CL
4 TURBILL GDNS
5 PAYNTER WLK
6 Glen Park Prim Sch

7 SPINDLE CRES
8 PEAR LA
9 CONKER GDNS

C5
1 EIGHT ACRE CL
2 LAWN CL
3 ORCHARD CL
4 GREAT PARK CL
5 LONG TERRACE CL
6 CYPRESS CL

7 CAMPION CL
8 RODDICK WAY
9 BRANSON CT

A   B   C   D   E   F

Newnham Park
Sparkwell Farm
Sparkwell

Furzeacre Wood
Windwhistle
Beechwood

Holly Wood
Furzeacre Bridge
Lowdamoor
Hemerdon
Hemerdon House
Beechwood Cross

Old Newnham Farm
Hemerdon Farm
PH
Lodge
Sherwell
Lodge

Old Newnham
WEST PARK HILL
Sparkwell Bridge
Moor Bridge

NEWNHAM RD
WEST PARK HILL
Langage Cross

Bell Cl
Newnham Ind Est
Chaddlewood
Westmoor Cl
Langage Science Pk

Stoggy La
Greenwood Park Rd
Rosaclave
Langage

Chaddlewood Prim Sch
Glen Rd
Beechwood Way
Higher Langage
Lower Langage
Combe Farm

Hillcrest
Langage Ind Est
Applethorn Slade

Langage Pk
Holland Rd
Barn Cl

Cornwood Rd
Langage
Beaumont Way

Yealmpstone Farm Prim Sch
Ley Farm
Voss

Wolverwood Cl
DEEP LA
B3416
PH
Battisford Pk

Springwood Cl
Ridge Rd
DEVON EXPRESSWAY
A38
Battisford

1 ST MAURICE RD
2 WOOLLCOMBE AVE

Wiverton House
Tuxton Farm
Tuxton Wood

Butlas Farm
Wiverton Acre

Blackpool

East Sherford

55   A   B   56   C   D   57   E   F

246

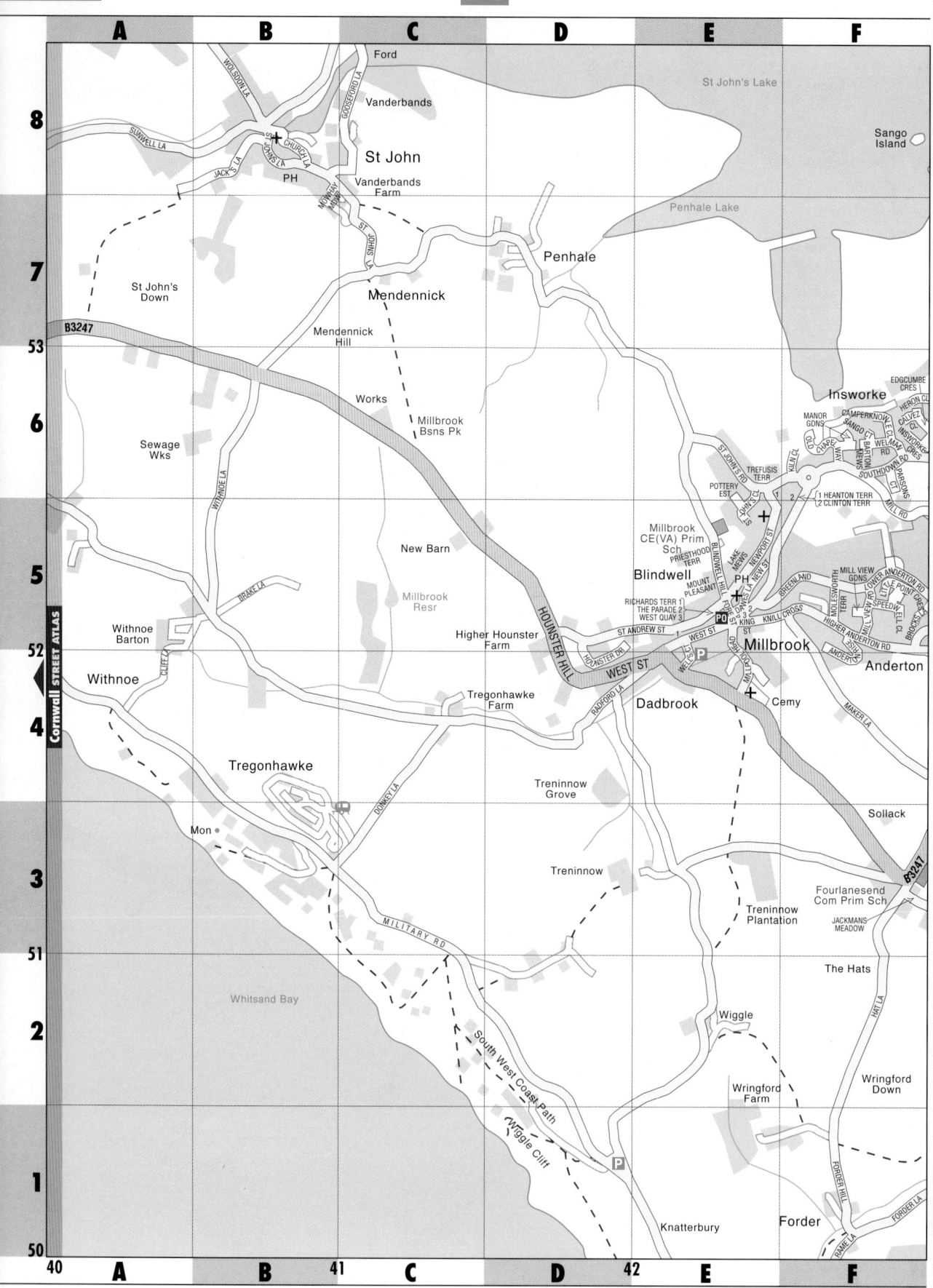

A
B
C
D
E
F
8
7
53
6
5
52
4
3
51
2
1
50
40
41
42
Ford
St John's Lake
Vanderbands
Sango Island
WOLSDON LA
GOOSEFORD LA
SUNWELL LA
CHURCH LA
ST JOHNS LA
JACK'S LA
St John
PH
Vanderbands Farm
MOWHAY MDW
ST JOHNS LA
Penhale Lake
Penhale
St John's Down
Mendennick
B3247
Mendennick Hill
Works
Millbrook Bsns Pk
Sewage Wks
WITHNOE LA
Insworke
EDGCUMBE CRES
HERON CL
MANOR GDNS
CAMPERKNOWLE CL
SANGO CT
CALVEZ CL
INSWORKE CRES
WELMAN RD
OLD CHAPEL WAY
BARTON MEWS
SOUTHDOWN RD
PARSONS CT
KILN CL
ST JOHN'S RD
TREFUSIS TERR
POTTERY EST
ST JOHN'S CL
1 HEANTON TERR
2 CLINTON TERR
MILL RD
New Barn
Millbrook CE(VA) Prim Sch
PRIESTHOOD TERR
BLINDWELL HILL
LAKE MEWS
NEWPORT ST
Blindwell
MOUNT PLEASANT
PH
MILL VIEW GDNS
LOWER ANDERTON RD
MOLESWORTH TERR
GREENLAND
Millbrook Resr
BRAKE LA
RICHARDS TERR 1
THE PARADE 2
WEST QUAY 3
PO
KING ST
KNILL CROSS
HIGHER ANDERTON RD
ST ANDREW ST
WEST ST
Millbrook
Withnoe Barton
Higher Hounster Farm
HOUNSTER HILL
HOUNSTER DR
WEST ST
WELLS CT
P
Anderton
Withnoe
CLIFF LA
Tregonhawke Farm
RADFORD LA
Dadbrook
Cemy
MAKER LA
Tregonhawke
Treninnow Grove
DONKEY LA
Sollack
Mon
Treninnow
B3247
Fourlanesend Com Prim Sch
JACKMANS MEADOW
MILITARY RD
Treninnow Plantation
The Hats
Whitsand Bay
Wiggle
HAT LA
South West Coast Path
Wringford Farm
Wringford Down
Wiggle Cliff
P
FORDER HILL
Knatterbury
Forder
FORDER LA
RAME LA
Cornwall STREET ATLAS

140

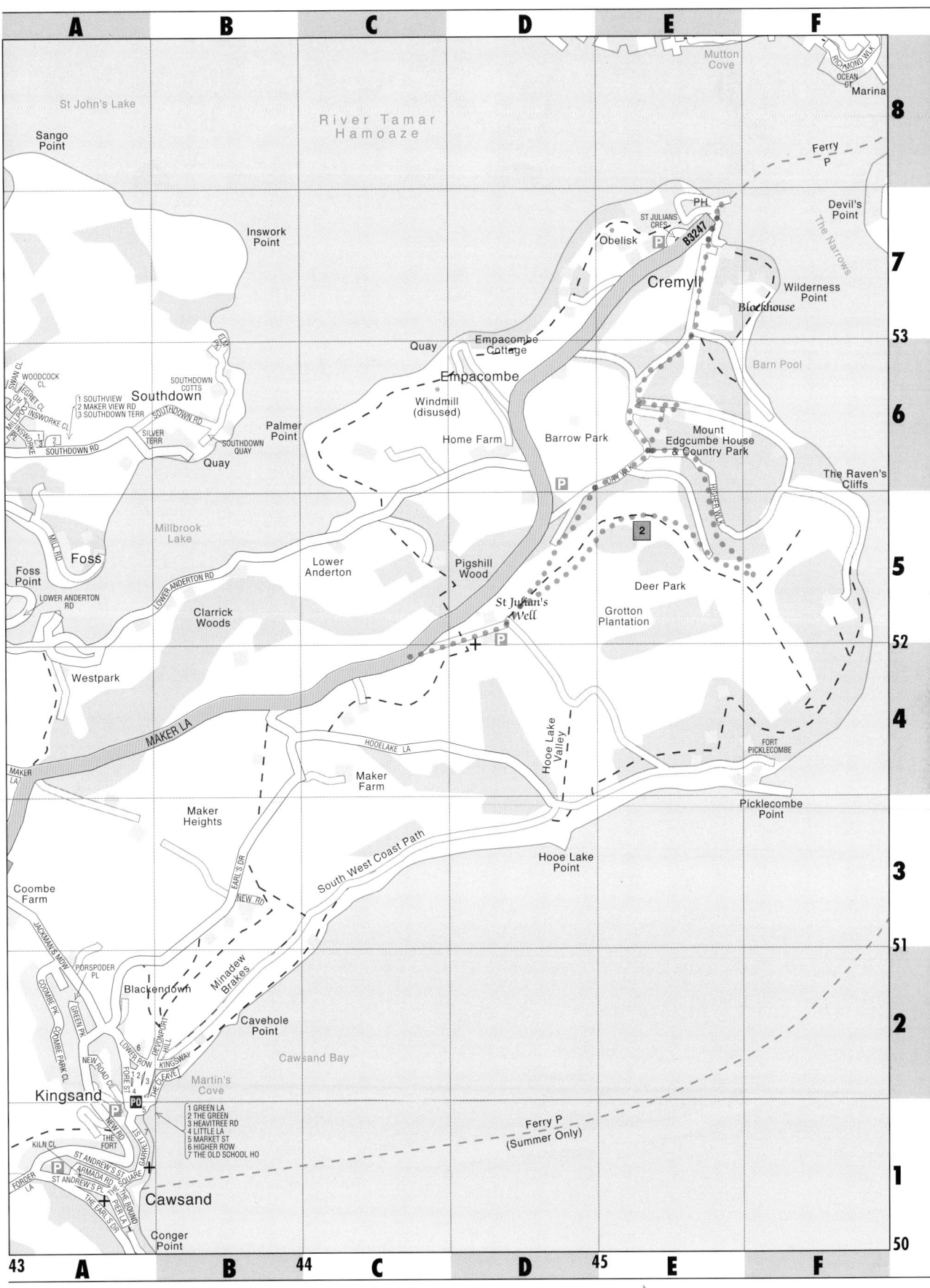
A
B
C
D
E
F
Mutton Cove
RICHMOND WLK
OCEAN CT
Marina
St John's Lake
River Tamar
Hamoaze
Sango Point
8
Ferry P
PH
Devil's Point
ST JULIANS CRES
Obelisk
B3247
The Narrows
Inswork Point
7
Cremyll
Wilderness Point
Blockhouse
53
Quay
Empacombe Cottage
Barn Pool
Empacombe
WOODCOCK CL
SWAN CL
EGRET CL
SOUTHDOWN COTTS
Southdown
1 SOUTHVIEW
2 MAKER VIEW RD
3 SOUTHDOWN TERR
INSWORKE CL
SOUTHDOWN RD
Windmill (disused)
6
Mount Edgcumbe House & Country Park
Palmer Point
Home Farm
Barrow Park
SILVER TERR
SOUTHDOWN QUAY
SOUTHDOWN RD
Quay
DRY WLK
HIGHER WLK
The Raven's Cliffs
Millbrook Lake
MILL RD
2
Foss
Lower Anderton
Pigshill Wood
5
Foss Point
LOWER ANDERTON RD
LOWER ANDERTON RD
Deer Park
Clarrick Woods
St Julian's Well
Grotton Plantation
52
Westpark
4
MAKER LA
HOOELAKE LA
Hooe Lake Valley
FORT PICKLECOMBE
MAKER LA
Maker Farm
Picklecombe Point
Maker Heights
Hooe Lake Point
South West Coast Path
3
Coombe Farm
EARL'S DR
NEW RD
51
JACKMAN'S MDW
PORSPODER PL
Minadew Brakes
Blackendown
COOMBE PK
GREEN PK
2
Cavehole Point
DEVONPORT HILL
LOWER ROW
KINGSWAY
Cawsand Bay
COOMBE PARK CL
NEW ROAD CL
FORE ST
THE CLEAVE
Martin's Cove
Kingsand
PO
1 GREEN LA
2 THE GREEN
3 HEAVITREE RD
4 LITTLE LA
5 MARKET ST
6 HIGHER ROW
7 THE OLD SCHOOL HO
NEW RD
THE FORT
Ferry P (Summer Only)
KILN CL
ST ANDREW'S ST
ARMADA RD
GARRETT ST
1
FORDER LA
ST ANDREW'S PL
THE SQUARE
THE BOUND
PIER LA
THE EARL'S DR
Cawsand
Conger Point
50
43
44
45

253

248

For full street detail of the highlighted area see pages 262 and 263.

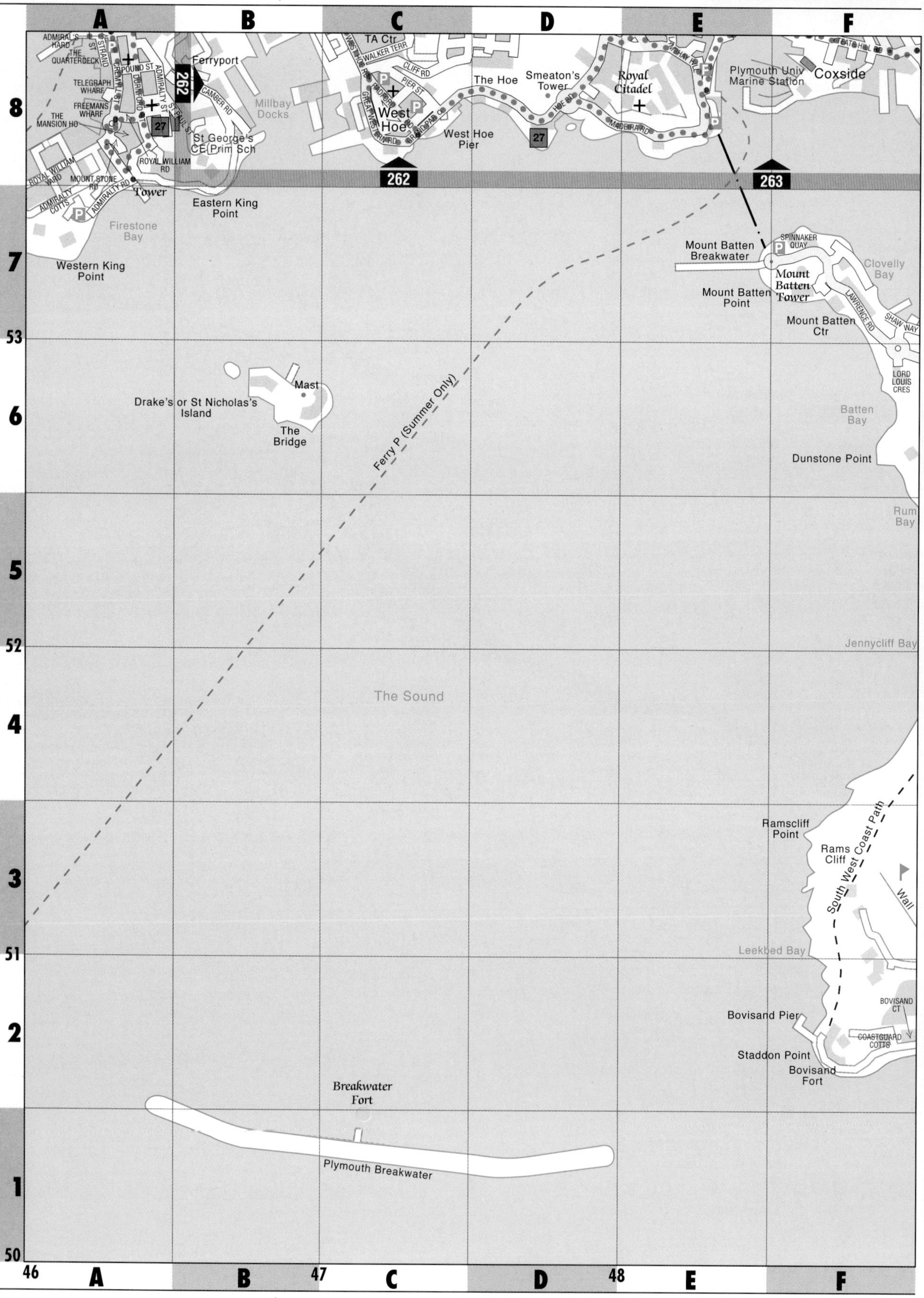

A   B   C   D   E   F

8

ADMIRAL'S HARD
THE QUARTERDECK
TELEGRAPH WHARF
POUND ST
DURNFORD ST
ADMIRALTY ST
ST PAUL ST
THE STRAND
Ferryport
CAMBER RD
262
TA Ctr
WALKER TERR
CLIFF RD
PIER ST
GREAT WESTERN RD
RADNOR PL
P
P
CRESCENT AVE
Smeaton's Tower
The Hoe
HOE RD
MADEIRA RD
Royal Citadel
LAMBHAY HILL
BATH HILL RD
Plymouth Univ Marine Station
Coxside
FREEMANS WHARF
THE MANSION HO
West Hoe
West Hoe Pier
27
262
263

ROYAL WILLIAM YARD
MOUNT STONE RD
ADMIRALTY COTTS
P
Tower
27
St George's CE Prim Sch
ST GEORGE'S RD
ROYAL WILLIAM RD
Eastern King Point

Firestone Bay

Western King Point

Mount Batten Breakwater
SPINNAKER QUAY
P
Mount Batten Tower
Clovelly Bay

7

Mount Batten Point
Mount Batten Ctr
LAWRENCE RD
SHAW WAY

53

Mast
Drake's or St Nicholas's Island
The Bridge

Batten Bay

LORD LOUIS CRES

6

Ferry P (Summer Only)

Dunstone Point

Rum Bay

5

Jennycliff Bay

52

4

The Sound

Ramscliff Point

3

Rams Cliff
South West Coast Path
Wall

51

Leekbed Bay

BOVISAND CT

2

Bovisand Pier
Staddon Point
COASTGUARD COTTS
Bovisand Fort

Breakwater Fort

Plymouth Breakwater

1

50

46   47   48

A   B   C   D   E   F

For full street detail of the highlighted area see page 263.

249

256

255

F5
1 CHALLGOOD CL
2 ORCHARDTON TERR

F7
1 THE DUKES RYDE
2 MAPLE CT
3 MAGNOLIA CT
4 HORN LANE FLATS
5 SELKIRK HO

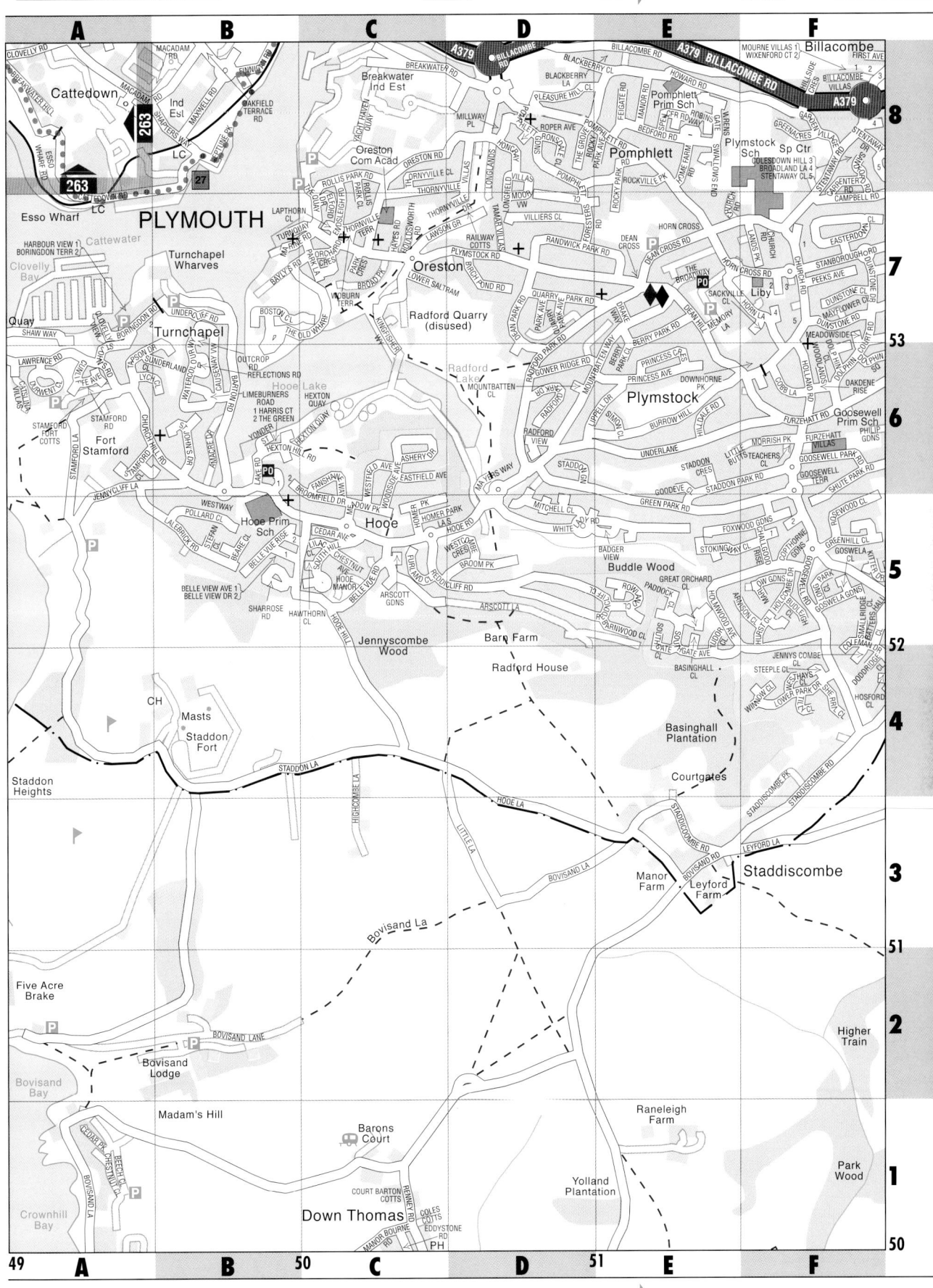

255
250

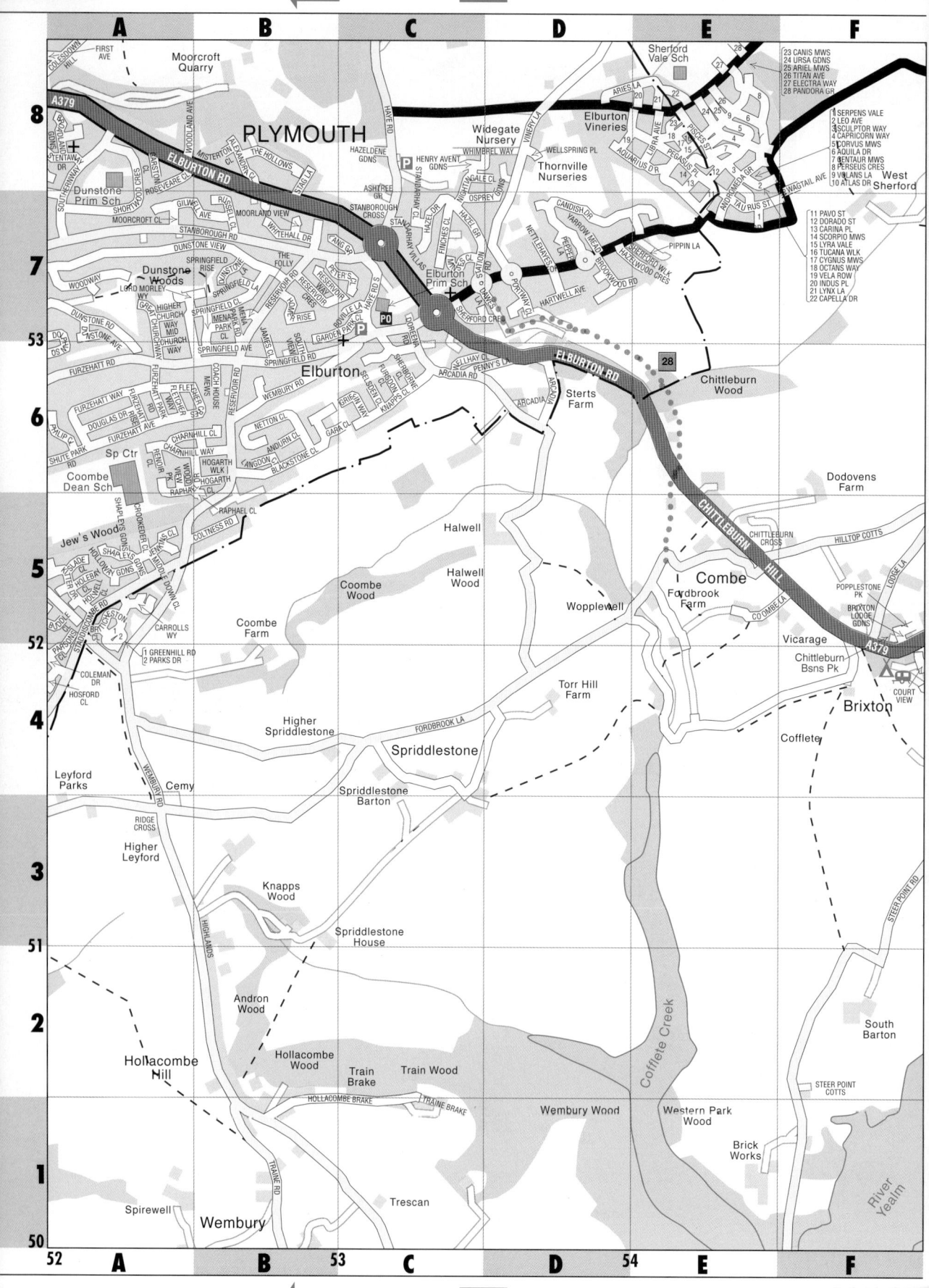
PLYMOUTH
ELBURTON RD
A379
Elburton
Dunstone Woods
Dunstone Prim Sch
Moorcroft Quarry
Widegate Nursery
Thornville Nurseries
Elburton Vineries
Sherford Vale Sch
West Sherford
Elburton Prim Sch
Sterts Farm
Chittleburn Wood
Sp Ctr
Coombe Dean Sch
Jew's Wood
Halwell
Halwell Wood
Coombe Wood
Coombe Farm
Wopplewell
Combe
Fordbrook Farm
CHITTLEBURN HILL
Dodovens Farm
Vicarage
Chittleburn Bsns Pk
Brixton
Cofflete
Torr Hill Farm
Higher Spriddlestone
Spriddlestone
Spriddlestone Barton
Leyford Parks
Cemy
Higher Leyford
Knapps Wood
Spriddlestone House
Andron Wood
Hollacombe Hill
Hollacombe Wood
Train Brake
Train Wood
Wembury Wood
Western Park Wood
Cofflete Creek
South Barton
Brick Works
River Yealm
Spirewell
Wembury
Trescan
23 CANIS MWS
24 URSA GDNS
25 ARIEL MWS
26 TITAN AVE
27 ELECTRA WAY
28 PANDORA GR
1 SERPENS VALE
2 LEO AVE
3 SCULPTOR WAY
4 CAPRICORN WAY
5 CORVUS MWS
6 AQUILA DR
7 CENTAUR MWS
8 PERSEUS CRES
9 VOLANS LA
10 ATLAS DR
11 PAVO ST
12 DORADO ST
13 CARINA PL
14 SCORPIO MWS
15 LYRA VALE
16 TUCANA WLK
17 CYGNUS MWS
18 OCTANS WAY
19 VELA ROW
20 INDUS PL
21 LYNX LA
22 CAPELLA DR
1 GREENHILL RD
2 PARKS DR

255
140

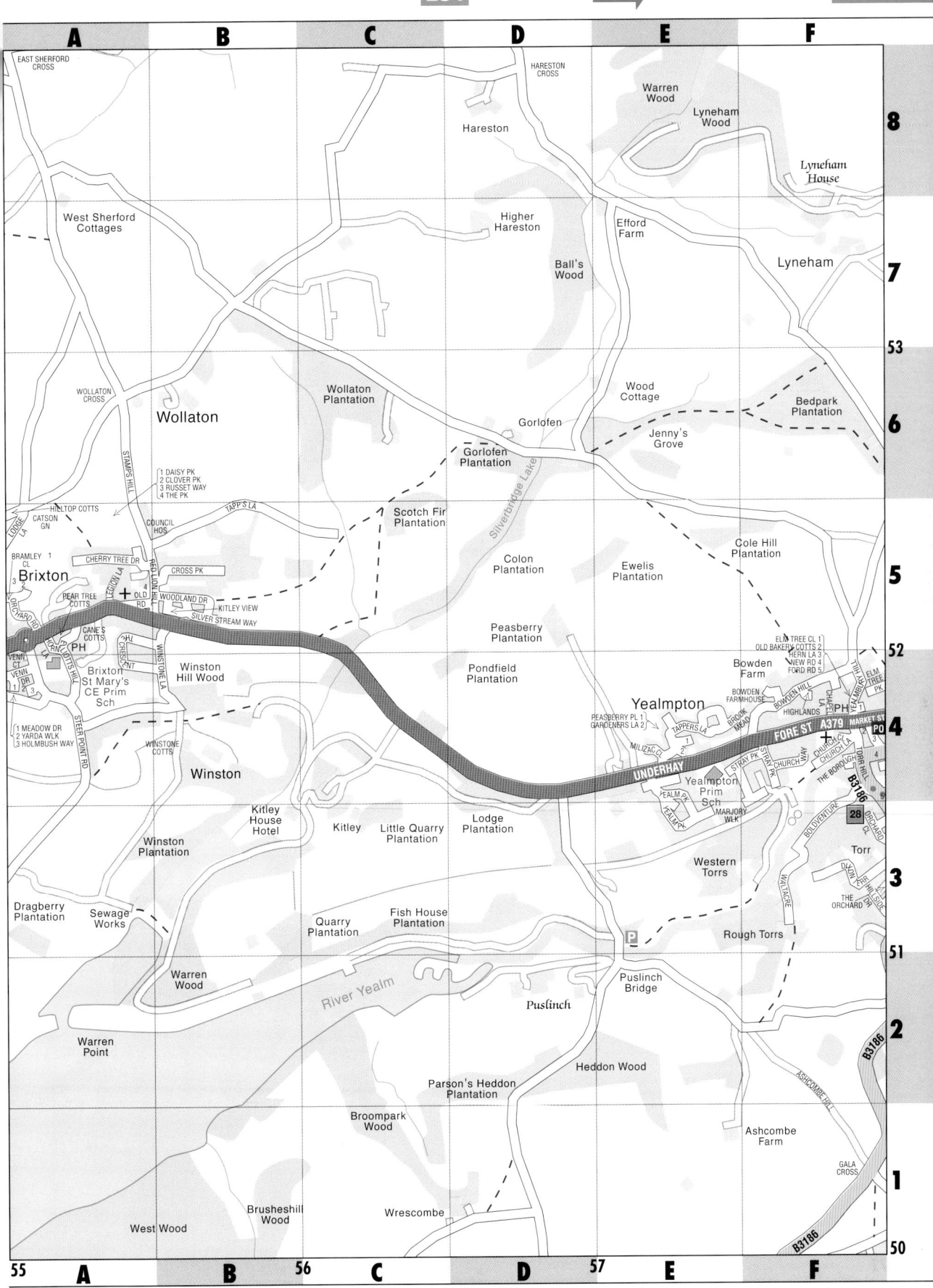

A　B　C　D　E　F

8

EAST SHERFORD CROSS

Hareston
HARESTON CROSS

Warren Wood
Lyneham Wood
Lyneham House

West Sherford Cottages

Higher Hareston

Efford Farm

7

Lyneham

Ball's Wood

53

Wollaton Cross

Wollaton

Wollaton Plantation

Gorlofen

Wood Cottage

Jenny's Grove

Bedpark Plantation

6

HILLTOP COTTS
CATSON GN
Gorlofen Plantation

Silverbridge Lake

Cole Hill Plantation

1 DAISY PK
2 CLOVER PK
3 RUSSET WAY
4 THE PK

Scotch Fir Plantation

Colon Plantation

Ewelis Plantation

5

BRAMLEY CL
Brixton
CHERRY TREE DR
CROSS PK

Peasberry Plantation

ELM TREE CL 1
OLD BAKERY COTTS 2
HERN LA 3
NEW RD 4
FORD RD 5

52

PEAR TREE COTTS
CANE'S COTTS
PH

Pondfield Plantation

Bowden Farm

Bowden Farmhouse

HIGHLANDS
BOWDEN HILL

VENN CT
VENN DR

Brixton St Mary's CE Prim Sch

Winston Hill Wood

Peasberry PL 1
GARDENERS LA 2
Yealmpton

TAPPERS LA
BROOK MEAD

PH

FORE ST A379
MARKET ST
PO

4

1 MEADOW DR
2 YARDA WLK
3 HOLMBUSH WAY

WINSTONE COTTS

MILIZAC CL

UNDERHAY

Yealmpton Prim Sch

STRAY PK
CHURCH WAY
CHURCH HILL
THE BOROUGH

B3186

28

Winston

Kitley House Hotel

Kitley

Little Quarry Plantation

Lodge Plantation

Western Torrs

Torr
THE ORCHARD

3

Winston Plantation

Rough Torrs

51

Dragberry Plantation

Sewage Works

Quarry Plantation

Fish House Plantation

P

Puslinch Bridge

B3186

Warren Wood

River Yealm

Puslinch

2

Warren Point

Heddon Wood

Ashcombe Farm

Parson's Heddon Plantation

GALA CROSS

1

Broompark Wood

Brusheshill Wood

West Wood

Wrescombe

B3186

50

55　A　B　56　C　D　57　E　F

143 143 144 144

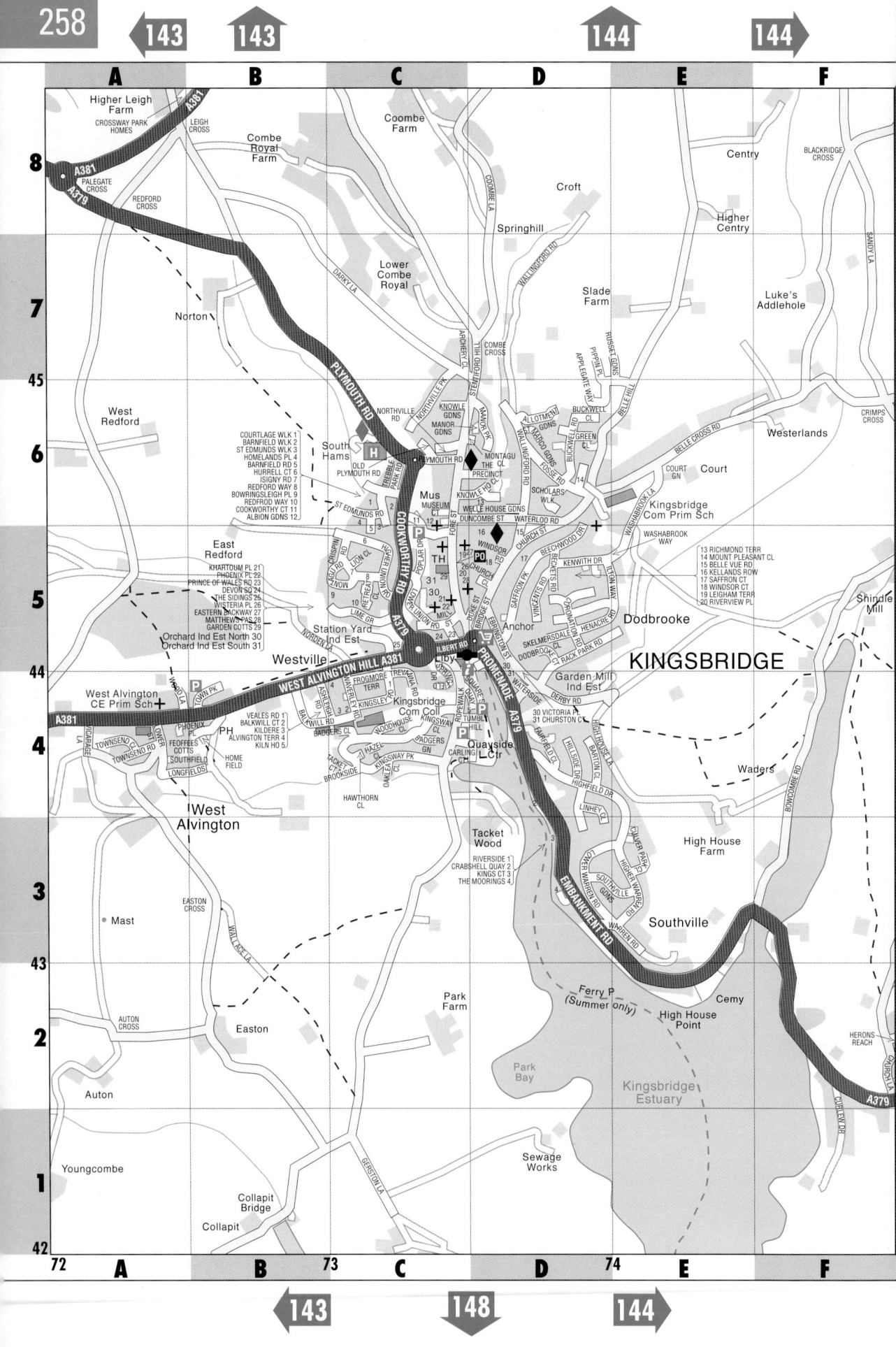

A
B
C
D
E
F
8
7
45
6
5
44
4
3
43
2
1
42
72
73
74
Higher Leigh Farm
CROSSWAY PARK HOMES
A381
LEIGH CROSS
Combe Royal Farm
Coombe Farm
Centry
BLACKRIDGE CROSS
PALEGATE CROSS
A379
REDFORD CROSS
COOMBE LA
Croft
Springhill
Higher Centry
SANDY LA
WALLINGFORD RD
DARKY LA
Lower Combe Royal
Slade Farm
Luke's Addlehole
Norton
ARCHERY CL
STENTIFORD HILL
COMBE CROSS
RUSSET GDNS
PIPPIN PL
APPLEGATE WAY
PLYMOUTH RD
BELLE HILL
West Redford
NORTHVILLE RD
NORTHVILLE PK
KNOWLE GDNS
MANOR PK
ALLOTMENT GDNS
BUCKWELL CL
CRIMPS CROSS
Westerlands
MANOR GDNS
GREEN CL
BELLE CROSS RD
COURTLAGE WLK 1
BARNFIELD WLK 2
ST EDMUNDS WLK 3
HOMELANDS PL 4
BARNFIELD RD 5
HURRELL CT 6
ISIGNY RD 7
REDFORD WAY 8
BOWRINGSLEIGH PL 9
REDFROD WAY 10
COOKWORTHY CT 11
ALBION GDNS 12
South Hams
H
OLD PLYMOUTH RD
TREBBLE PARK RD
MONTAGU CL
THE PRECINCT
MARCO GDNS
FOSSE RD
BUCKWELL RD
COURT GN
Court
KNOWLE HO CL
SCHOLARS WLK
WASHABROOK LA
Mus
MUSEUM CT
WELLE HOUSE GDNS
Kingsbridge Com Prim Sch
ST EDMUNDS RD
DUNCOMBE ST
WATERLOO RD
FORE ST
COOKWORTHY RD
P
WINDSOR RD
CHURCH ST
WASHABROOK WAY
East Redford
CRISPIN RD
LION CL
HIGHER UNION RD
POPLAR DR
PO
BEECHWOOD DR
13 RICHMOND TERR
14 MOUNT PLEASANT CL
15 BELLE VUE RD
16 KELLANDS ROW
17 SAFFRON CT
18 WINDSOR CT
19 LEIGHAM TERR
20 RIVERVIEW PL
TH
CHURCH CL
KENWITH DR
KHARTOUM PL 21
PHOENIX PL 22
PRINCE OF WALES RD 23
DEVON SQ 24
THE SIDINGS 25
WISTERIA PL 26
EASTERN BACKWAY 27
MATTHEWS PAS 28
GARDEN COTTS 29
Orchard Ind Est North 30
Orchard Ind Est South 31
RETREAT CL
SAFFRON PK
VINCENTS RD
BECKETS RD
CORONATION RD
TILTON WAY
Shindle Mill
LOWER UNION RD
MILL ST
DUKE ST
BRIDGE ST
EBRINGTON ST
Anchor
HENACRE RD
Dodbrooke
LIME GR
Station Yard Ind Est
NORDEN LA
SKELMERSDALE CL
DODBROOKE CL
RACK PARK RD
Westville
ILBERT RD
Liby
PROMENADE
KINGSBRIDGE
WEST ALVINGTON HILL A381
FROMORE TERR
TREVANNA RD
SPRINGFIELD DR
Garden Mill Ind Est
WATERSIDE
DERBY RD
West Alvington CE Prim Sch
WOOD LA
TOWN PK
ASHLEIGH RD
WAVERLEY RD
KINGSLEY RD
Kingsbridge Com Coll
SQUARE'S QUAY
ROPEWALK
30 VICTORIA PL
31 CHURSTON CT
VEALES RD 1
BALKWILL CT 2
KILDERE 3
ALVINGTON TERR 4
KILN HO 5
BALKWILL RD
WOODHOUSE CL
KINGSWAY CL
TUMBLY HILL
PHOENIX PL
PH
BADGERS CL
BADGERS GN
FAIRFIELD CL
HIGH HOUSE LA
BARTON CL
VICARAGE LA
TOWNSEND CL
TOWNSEND RD
FEOFFEES COTTS
SOUTHFIELD
LONGFIELDS
LOWER ST
HOME FIELD
HAZEL CL
KINGSWAY PK
CARLING CT
Quayside L Ctr
HILLSIDE DR
TACKET CT
BROOKSIDE
OAKLEA CL
Waders
HIGHFIELD DR
HAWTHORN CL
LINHEY CL
BOWCOMBE RD
West Alvington
Tacket Wood
High House Farm
CULVER PARK CL
RIVERSIDE 1
CRABSHELL QUAY 2
KINGS CT 3
THE MOORINGS 4
LOWER WARREN RD
HIGHER WARREN RD
SOUTHVILLE GDNS
EMBANKMENT RD
Mast
EASTON CROSS
Southville
WALLACE LA
WARREN RD
Ferry P (Summer only)
Cemy
Park Farm
High House Point
AUTON CROSS
Easton
HERONS REACH
Park Bay
CHURCH LA
Auton
Kingsbridge Estuary
CURLEW DR
Sewage Works
Youngcombe
GERSTON LA
Collapit Bridge
Collapit

143 148 144

147 148 148

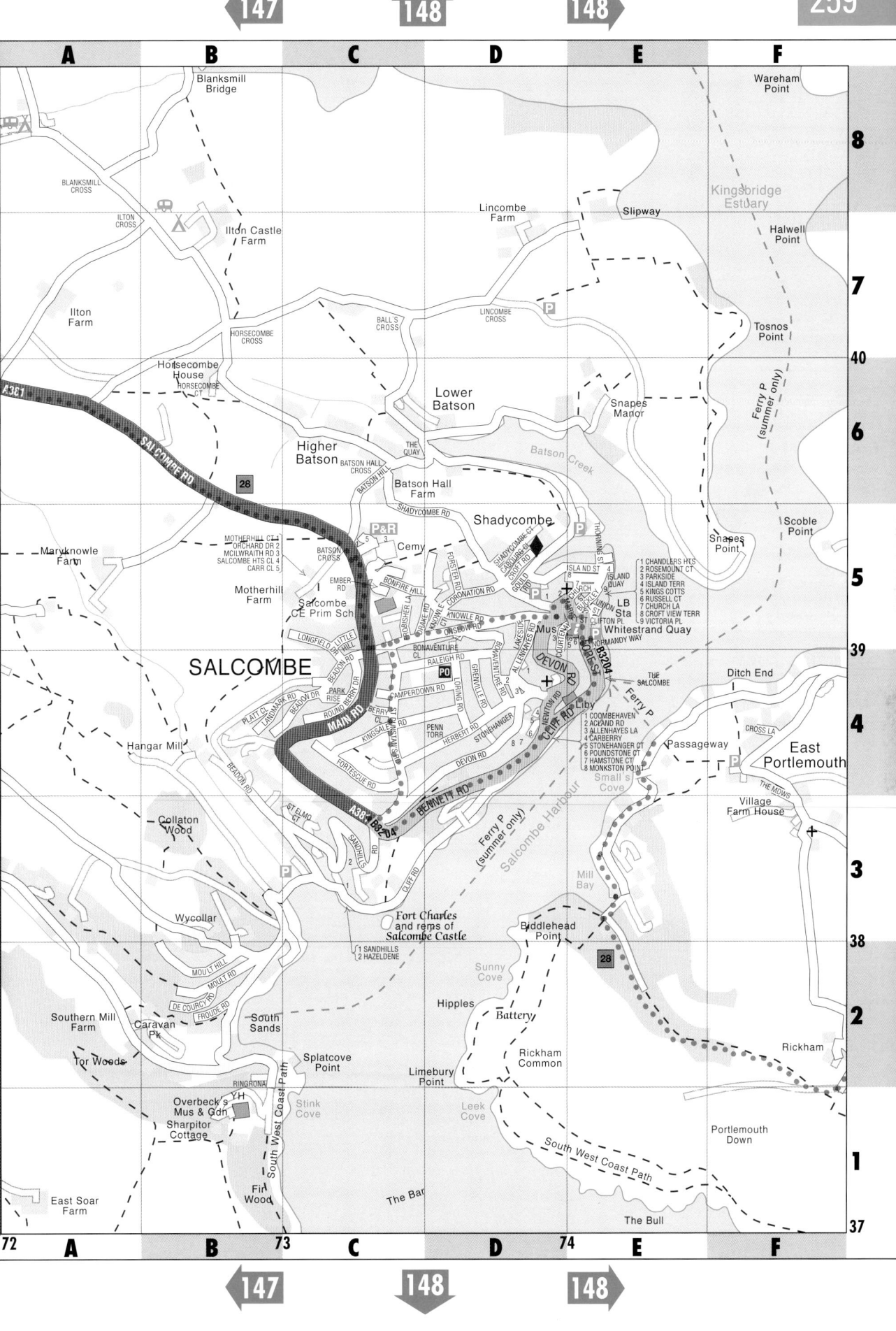

A B C D E F
8 7 40 6 5 39 4 3 38 2 1 37
72 73 74
Blanksmill Bridge
BLANKSMILL CROSS
ILTON CROSS
Ilton Castle Farm
Ilton Farm
HORSECOMBE CROSS
Horsecombe House
HORSECOMBE CT
A381
SALCOMBE RD
28
BALL'S CROSS
LINCOMBE CROSS
Lincombe Farm
Slipway
Kingsbridge Estuary
Wareham Point
Halwell Point
Tosnos Point
Ferry P (summer only)
Lower Batson
Snapes Manor
Higher Batson
BATSON HALL CROSS
THE QUAY
Batson Creek
Batson Hall Farm
BATSON HILL
SHADYCOMBE RD
Shadycombe
P&R
Cemy
MOTHERHILL CT 1
ORCHARD DR 2
MCILWRAITH RD 3
SALCOMBE HTS CL 4
CARR CL 5
Maryknowle Farm
BATSON CROSS
EMBER RD
Motherhill Farm
Salcombe CE Prim Sch
BONFIRE HILL
CORONATION RD
FORSTER RD
ISLAND ST
ISLAND QUAY
1 CHANDLERS HTS
2 ROSEMOUNT CT
3 PARKSIDE
4 ISLAND TERR
5 KINGS COTTS
6 RUSSELL CT
7 CHURCH LA
8 CROFT VIEW TERR
9 VICTORIA PL
LB Sta
Whitestrand Quay
Mus
NORMANDY WAY
Scoble Point
Snapes Point
SALCOMBE
LONGFIELD DR
LITTLE HILL
BONAVENTURE CL
RALEIGH RD
PO
DEVON RD
FORE ST
B3204
THE SALCOMBE
Ditch End
Ferry P
CAMPERDOWN RD
LORING RD
GRENVILLE RD
PARK RISE
BEADON DR
ROUND BERRY DR
MAIN RD
PLATT CL
LANDMARK RD
Liby
1 COOMBEHAVEN
2 ACLAND RD
3 ALLENHAYES LA
4 CARBERRY
5 STONEHANGER CT
6 POUNDSTONE CT
7 HAMSTONE CT
8 MONKSTON POINT
CROSS LA
Passageway
East Portlemouth
Hangar Mill
PENN TORR
HERBERT RD
STONEHANGER
CLIFF RD
NEWTON RD
KINGSALE RD
FORTESCUE RD
BEADON RD
Small's Cove
THE MDWS
Village Farm House
Collaton Wood
ST ELMO CT
A381 B3204
BENNETT RD
Salcombe Harbour
Ferry P (summer only)
SANDHILLS RD
Mill Bay
Wycollar
Fort Charles and rems of Salcombe Castle
1 SANDHILLS
2 HAZELDENE
Biddlehead Point
MOULT HILL
MOULT RD
DE COURCY RD
FROUDE RD
Sunny Cove
Hipples
Battery
Southern Mill Farm
Caravan Pk
South Sands
Tor Woods
Splatcove Point
Limebury Point
Rickham Common
Rickham
RINGRONA
Overbeck's Mus & Gdn
YH
Sharpitor Cottage
Stink Cove
Leek Cove
South West Coast Path
Portlemouth Down
Fir Wood
The Bar
East Soar Farm
The Bull

147 148 148

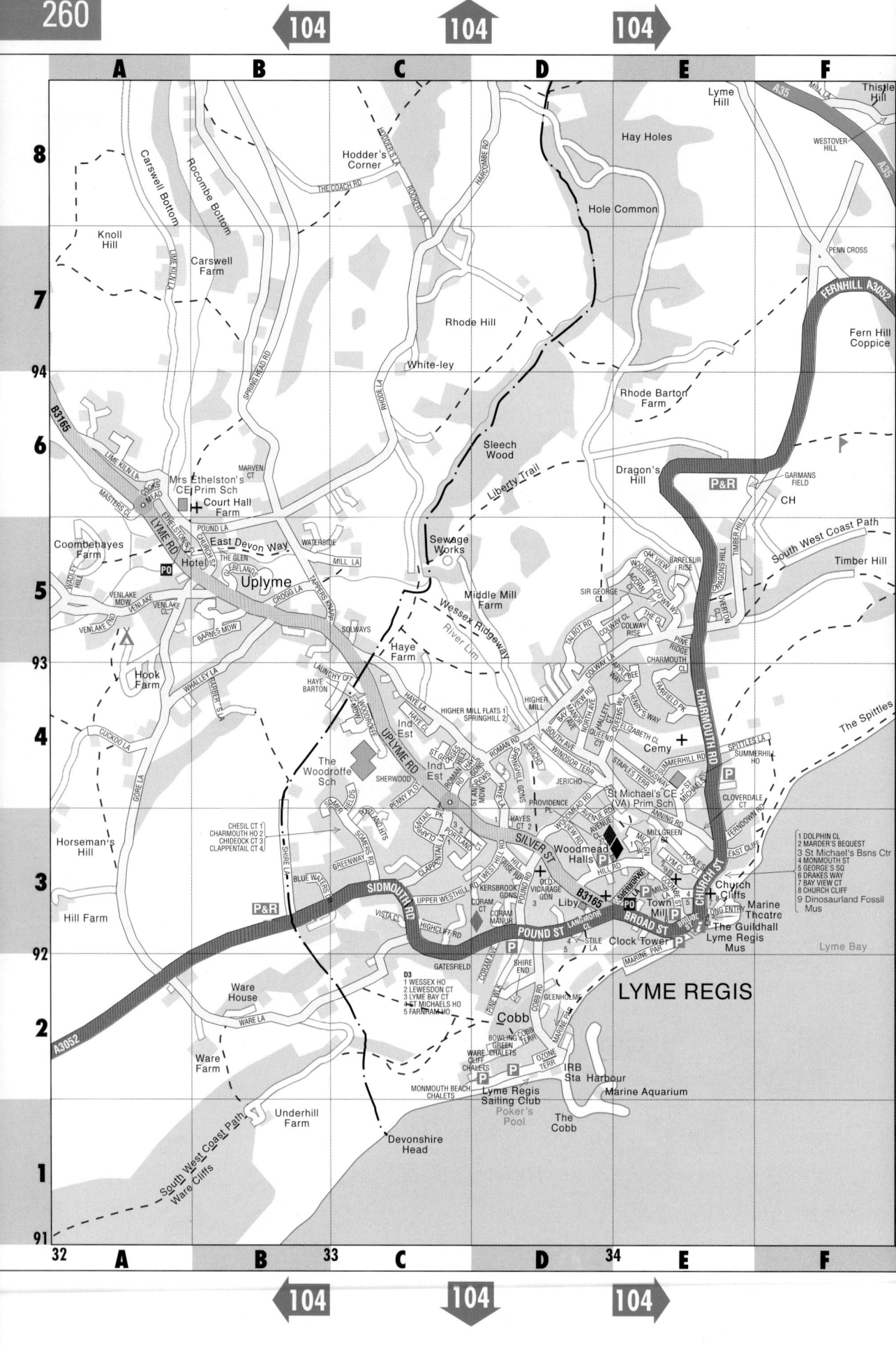

A B C D E F

8

7

94

6

5

93

4

3

92

2

1

91

LYME REGIS

Uplyme

Cobb

Lyme Bay

1 DOLPHIN CL
2 MARDER'S BEQUEST
3 St Michael's Bsns Ctr
4 MONMOUTH ST
5 GEORGE'S SQ
6 DRAKES WAY
7 BAY VIEW CT
8 CHURCH CLIFF
9 Dinosaurland Fossil Mus

CHESIL CT 1
CHARMOUTH HO 2
CHIDEOCK CT 3
CLAPPENTAIL CT 4

D3
1 WESSEX HO
2 LEWESDON CT
3 LYME BAY CT
4 ST MICHAELS HO
5 FARNHAM HO

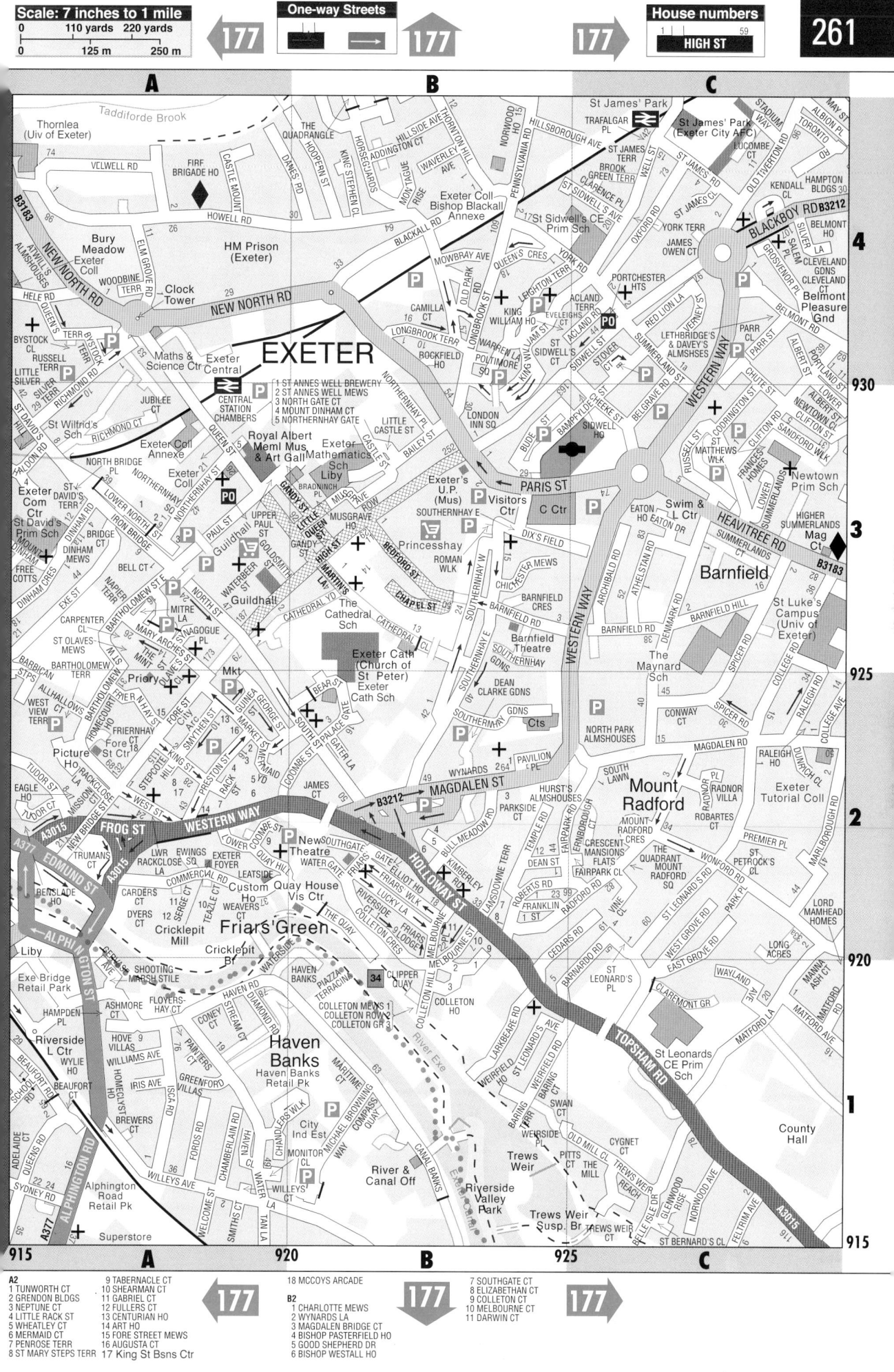

Scale: 7 inches to 1 mile

0   110 yards   220 yards

0   125 m   250 m

177   177   177

One-way Streets

House numbers
1 ————————————— 59
HIGH ST

261

A   B   C

Taddiforde Brook

Thornlea
(Univ of Exeter)

FIRE BRIGADE HO

VELWELL RD

CASTLE MOUNT

74

86

Bury Meadow
Exeter Coll

WOODBINE TERR

ELM GROVE RD

B3183

NEW NORTH RD

ATWILL'S ALMSHOUSES

HELE RD

QUEEN'S TERR

BYSTOCK CL

RUSSELL TERR

LITTLE SILVER

SILVER TERR

RICHMOND RD

ST DAVID'S HILL

HM Prison
(Exeter)

Clock Tower

HOWELL RD

THE QUADRANGLE

HOOPER ST

KING STEPHEN CL

HORSEGUARDS

ADDINGTON CT

HILLSIDE AVE

MONTAGUE RISE

NORTHERNHAY PL

BLACKALL RD

Exeter Coll Bishop Blackall Annexe

PENNSYLVANIA RD

MOWBRAY AVE

OLD PARK RD

CAMILLA TERR

LONGBROOK TERR

WAVERLEY AVE

HORNTON HILL

HILLSBOROUGH AVE

NORWOOD RD

QUEEN'S CRES

KING WILLIAM HO

WARREN LA

ROCKFIELD HO

POLTIMORE SQ

EXETER

Maths & Science Ctr

Exeter Central

CENTRAL STATION CHAMBERS

JUBILEE RD

RICHMOND CT

St Wilfrid's Sch

Exeter Coll Annexe

NORTH BRIDGE PL

Exeter Com Ctr

St David's Prim Sch

DINHAM CRES

DINHAM FREE COTTS

EXE LA

CARPENTER CL

ST OLAVES MEWS

BARTHOLOMEW TERR

BARBICAN STPS

ALLHALLOWS CT

WEST VIEW TERR

Picture Ho

BRACKCLOSE LA

EAGLE HO

TUDOR ST

A4015

EDMUND ST

Liby

Exe Bridge Retail Park

HAMPDEN PL

Riverside L Ctr

BEAUFORT RD

ADELAIDE CT

QUEENS RD

SYDNEY RD

A377

Royal Albert Meml Mus & Art Gall

Exeter Mathematics Sch Liby

Exeter Coll

NORTHERNHAY SQ

PAUL ST

Guildhall

GANDY ST

QUEEN ST

HIGH ST

UPPER PAUL ST

GOLDSMITH ST

WATERBEER ST

Guildhall

GUINEA ST

MARTIN'S LA

The Cathedral Sch

Exeter Cath
(Church of St Peter)

Exeter Cath Sch

BRADNINCH PL

MUSGRAVE ROW

MUSGRAVE HO

Princesshay

BEDFORD ST

CHAPEL ST

CATHEDRAL YD

CATHEDRAL CL

ROMAN WLK

1 ST ANNES WELL BREWERY
2 ST ANNES WELL MEWS
3 NORTH GATE CT
4 MOUNT DINHAM CT
5 NORTHERNHAY GATE

PARIS ST

LITTLE CASTLE ST

BAILEY ST

LONDON INN SQ

Exeter's U.P. (Mus)

Visitors Ctr

C Ctr

SOUTHERNHAY E

SOUTHERNHAY W

CHICHESTER MEWS

Barnfield CRES

Barnfield Theatre

SOUTHERNHAY GDNS

DEAN CLARKE GDNS

Cts

WESTERN WAY

TRAFALGAR PL

St James' Park

St James' Park
(Exeter City AFC)

BROOK GREEN TERR

CLARENCE PL

ST SIDWELL'S AVE

St Sidwell's CE Prim Sch

OXFORD RD

QUEEN'S RD

YORK RD

JAMES OWEN CT

PORTCHESTER HTS

ACLAND RD

ACLAND TERR

EVELEIGHS CT

KING WILLIAM HO

ST SIDWELL ST

SIDWELL HO

SUMMERLAND ST

BELGRAVE RD

RUSSELL ST

MATTHEWS WLK

FRANCES HOMES

EATON HO

EATON DR

DIX'S FIELD

Swim & L Ctr

ARCHIBALD RD

ATHELSTAN RD

DENMARK RD

Barnfield HILL

WESTERN WAY

STADIUM

MAY ST

ALBION PL

TORONTO RD

HAMPTON BLDGS

KENDALL CL

BELMONT HO

LUCOMBE CT

SILVER TERR

SALEM PL

GROSVENOR PL

BLACKBOY RD

B3212

CLEVELAND GDNS

CLEVELAND CT

Belmont Pleasure Gnd

PARR CL

PARR ST

CHUTE ST

CODRINGTON RD

CLIFTON RD

SANDFORD WLK

ALBERT ST

PORTLAND ST

LOWER ST

NEWTOWN CL

CLIFTON ST

Newtown Prim Sch

930

HEAVITREE RD

SUMMERLANDS

Higher Summerlands

Mag Ct

B3183

Barnfield

St Luke's Campus
(Univ of Exeter)

The Maynard Sch

SPICER RD

RALEIGH RD

COLLEGE AVE

CONWAY CT

MAGDALEN RD

RALEIGH HO

DENMARK RD

925

North Park Almshouses

Mount Radford

Exeter Tutorial Coll

RADNOR PL

RADNOR VILLA

ROBARTES RD

PREMIER PL

ST PETROCK'S CL

MARLBOROUGH RD

LORD MAMHEAD HOMES

MOUNT RADFORD CRES

MOUNT RADFORD SQ

The Quadrant

WONFORD RD

LONG ACRES

MANNA ASH CT

3

2

920

915

FROG ST

WESTERN WAY

B3212

MAGDALEN ST

WYNARDS

PAVILION PL

HURST'S ALMSHOUSES

PARKSIDE CT

TEMPLE RD

FAIRPARK RD

DEAN ST

FRANKLIN ST

SOUTH LAWN

FINBOROUGH RD

Crescent Mansions Flats

FAIRPARK CL

New Theatre

Exeter Foyer

LEATSIDE

Custom Quay House Vis Ctr

Cricklepit Mill

Friars' Green

Cricklepit Br

WATERSIDE

ALPHINGTON ST

BENSLADE HO

TRUMANS CT

A4015

EWINGS LA

RACKCLOSE LA

COMMERCIAL RD

CARDERS CT

DYERS CT

SERGE CT

TEALE CT

COLLETON CRES

FRIARS

HOLLOWAY ST

GATE ELLIOT HO

WATER GATE

SOUTHGATE

FRIARS WLK

LUCKY LA

FRIARS LODGE

RIVERSIDE RD

MELBOURNE ST

KIMBERLEY RD

LANDSDOWNE TERR

ROBERTS RD

RADFORD RD

VINE CL

ST LEONARD'S RD

WEST GROVE RD

EAST GROVE RD

BULL MEADOW RD

CEDARS RD

ST LEONARD'S PL

BARNARDO RD

COLLETON HILL

COLLETON HO

River Exe

CLIPPER QUAY

34

PIAZZA TERRACINA

COLLETON MEWS

COLLETON ROW

COLLETON GR

CLAREMONT GR

WAYLAND

MATFORD LA

MATFORD AVE

Haven Banks

Haven Banks Retail Pk

HOVE VILLAS

CONEY STREAM CT

DIAMOND RD

PAINTERS CT

WILLIAMS AVE

ISCA RD

GREENFORD VILLAS

IRIS AVE

FORDS RD

CHAMBERLAIN RD

HAVEN RD

WATER LA

City Ind Est

MICHAEL BROWNING WAY

COMPASS QUAY

MONITOR CL

WILLEYS AVE

River & Canal Off

CANAL BANKS

LARKBEARE RD

WEIRFIELD RD

ST LEONARD'S RD

BARING CRES

BARING TERR

SWAN CT

WEIRSIDE

OLD MILL CL

The MILL

Trews Weir

PITTS CT

TREWS WEIR REACH

CYGNET CT

St Leonards CE Prim Sch

Topsham RD

GLENWOOD RISE

NORWOOD AVE

BELLE ISLE DR

FELTRIM AVE

A4015

County Hall

Riverside Valley Park

Trews Weir Susp. Br

TREWS WEIR CT

ST BERNARD'S CL

Alphington Road Retail Pk

Superstore

WELCOME ST

SMITHS CT

TAN LA

BREWERS CT

ALPHINGTON RD

SCHOOL RD

915   A   920   B   925   C   915

177   177   177

A2
1 TUNWORTH CT
2 GRENDON BLDGS
3 NEPTUNE CT
4 LITTLE RACK ST
5 WHEATLEY CT
6 MERMAID CT
7 PENROSE TERR
8 ST MARY STEPS TERR
9 TABERNACLE CT
10 SHEARMAN CT
11 GABRIEL CT
12 FULLERS CT
13 CENTURIAN HO
14 ART HO
15 FORE STREET MEWS
16 AUGUSTA CT
17 King St Bsns Ctr

18 MCCOYS ARCADE

B2
1 CHARLOTTE MEWS
2 WYNARDS LA
3 MAGDALEN BRIDGE CT
4 BISHOP PASTERFIELD HO
5 GOOD SHEPHERD DR
6 BISHOP WESTALL HO

7 SOUTHGATE CT
8 ELIZABETHAN CT
9 COLLETON CT
10 MELBOURNE CT
11 DARWIN CT

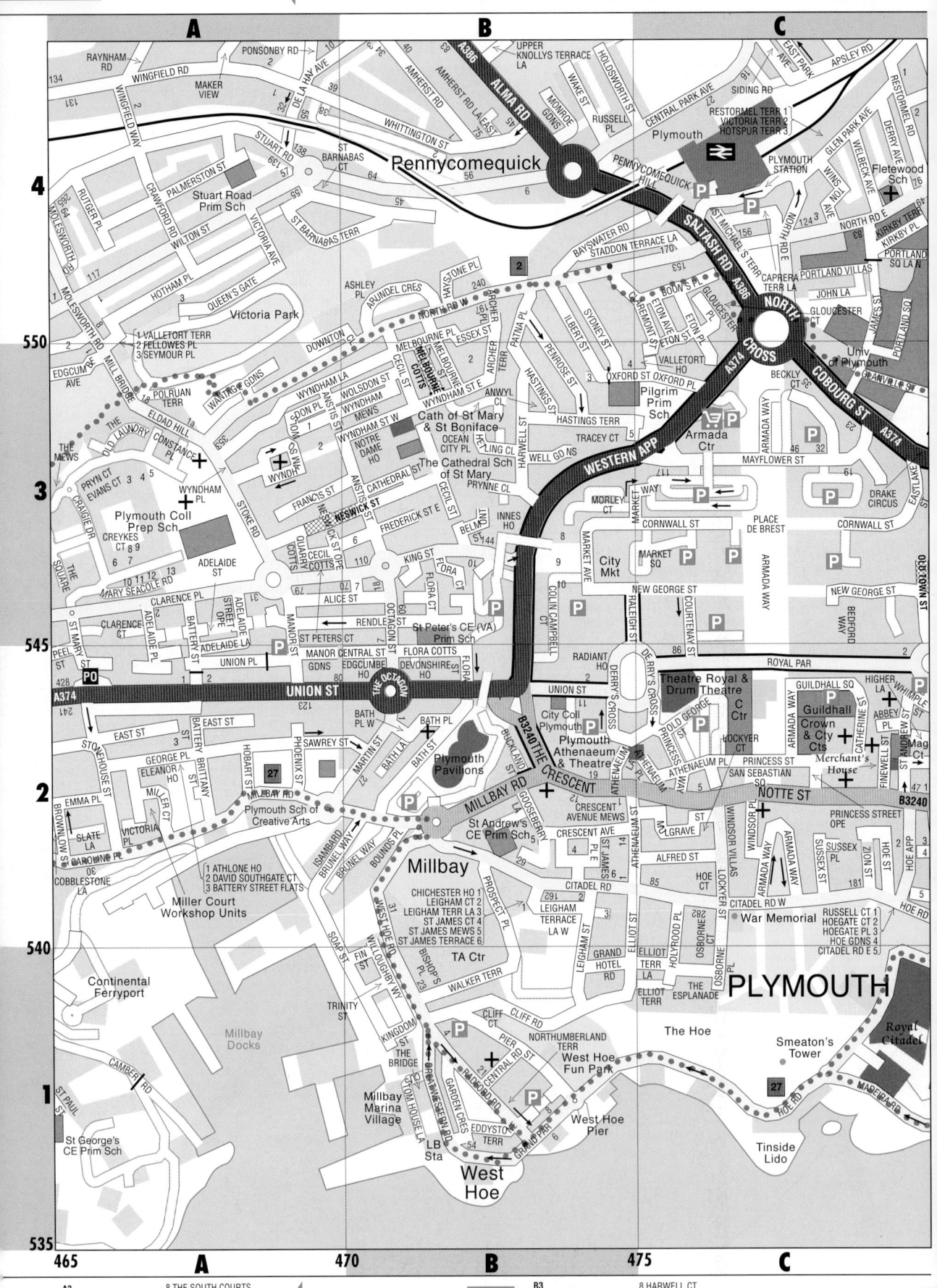

262

One-way Streets

House numbers
1 59
HIGH ST

248   248

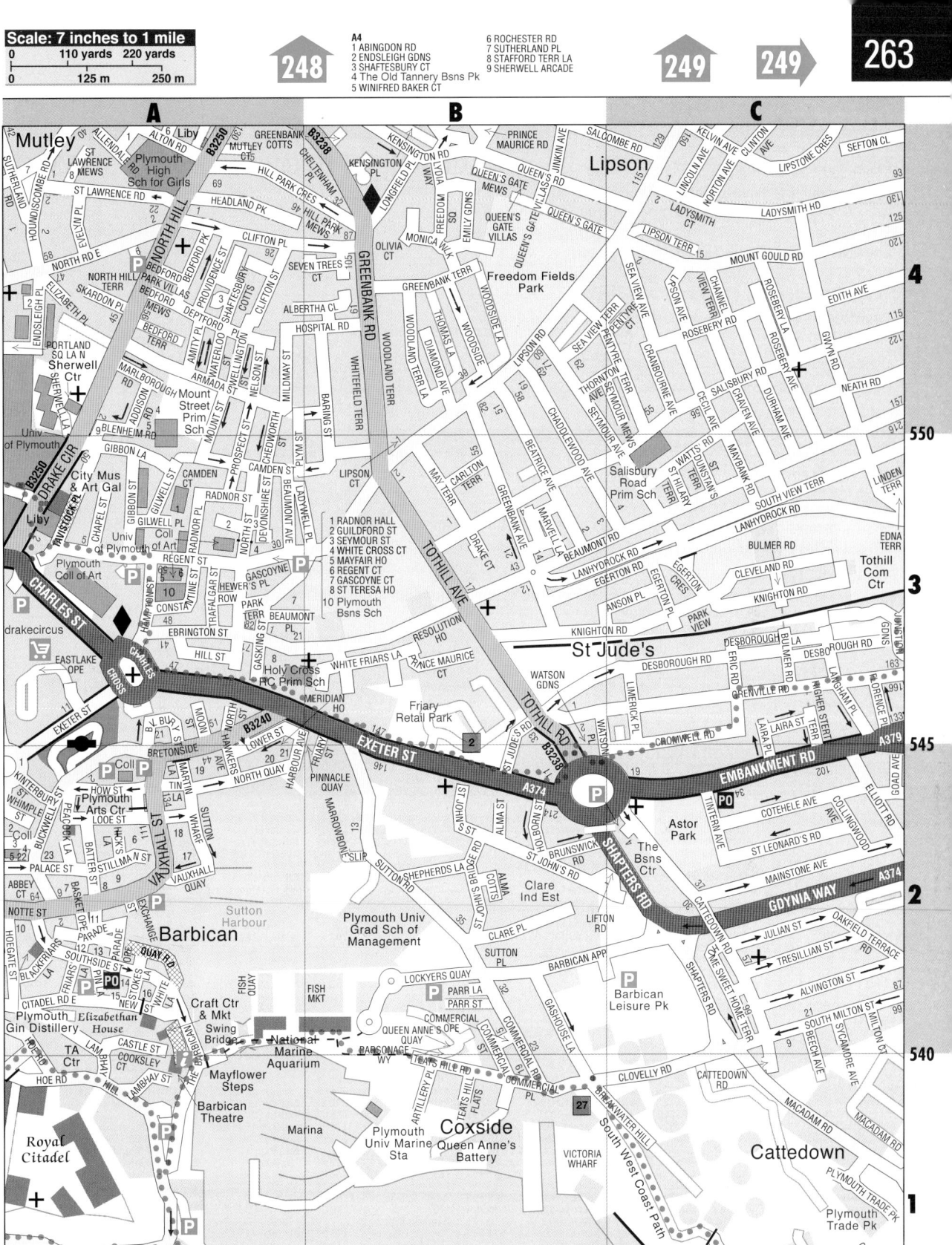

A4
1 ABINGDON RD
2 ENDSLEIGH GDNS
3 SHAFTESBURY CT
4 The Old Tannery Bsns Pk
5 WINIFRED BAKER CT

6 ROCHESTER RD
7 SUTHERLAND PL
8 STAFFORD TERR LA
9 SHERWELL ARCADE

A   B   C

Mutley

Lipson

Freedom Fields Park

St Jude's

Salisbury Road Prim Sch

Tothill Com Ctr

1 RADNOR HALL
2 GUILDFORD ST
3 SEYMOUR ST
4 WHITE CROSS CT
5 MAYFAIR HO
6 REGENT CT
7 GASCOYNE CT
8 ST TERESA HO
10 Plymouth Bsns Sch

City Mus & Art Gal

Univ of Plymouth

Plymouth Coll of Art

drakecircus

Friary Retail Park

EXETER ST

EMBANKMENT RD

Astor Park

Plymouth Arts Ctr

GDYNIA WAY

Barbican

Sutton Harbour

Plymouth Univ Grad Sch of Management

Clare Ind Est

Barbican Leisure Pk

Craft Ctr & Mkt
Swing Bridge

Fish Quay

Fish Mkt

Plymouth Elizabethan Gin Distillery House

National Marine Aquarium

Coxside

Cattedown

Mayflower Steps

Barbican Theatre

Marina

Plymouth Univ Marine Sta

Queen Anne's Battery

Victoria Wharf

Royal Citadel

South West Coast Path

Plymouth Trade Pk

Cattewater

Wallsend Ind Est

The Sound

480   A   485   B   490   C

254

A2
1 ST ANDREWS CROSS
2 ELIZABETH CT
3 HIGHER LA
4 EASTLAKE HO
5 LOWER LA
6 STILLMAN CT
7 WOOLSTER CT

8 BROCK HO
9 VAUXHALL CT
10 ELSPETH SITTERS HO
11 BARBICAN CT
12 CITADEL OPE
13 SOUTHSIDE OPE
14 MITRE CT
15 HANOVER CT

16 JOHN SPARKE HO
17 DOLPHIN HO
18 VAUXHALL STREET FLATS
19 DISCOVERY WHARF
20 BEAUFORT HO
21 SUTTON MEWS
22 PRIDEAUX CT
23 PALACE CT

255   255

Index

Place name May be abbreviated on the map → Church Rd
Location number Present when a number indicates the place's position in a crowded area of mapping → [6]
Locality, town or village Shown when more than one place has the same name → Beckenham
Postcode district District for the indexed place → BR2
Page and grid square Page number and grid reference for the standard mapping → 53 C6

Church Rd [6] Beckenham BR2..........53 C6

Cities, towns and villages are listed in CAPITAL LETTERS

Public and commercial buildings are highlighted in magenta **Places of interest** are highlighted in blue

Abbreviations used in the index

Abbr	Meaning	Abbr	Meaning	Abbr	Meaning	Abbr	Meaning	Abbr	Meaning
Acad	Academy	Comm	Common	Gd	Ground	L	Leisure	Prom	Promenade
App	Approach	Cott	Cottage	Gdn	Garden	La	Lane	Rd	Road
Arc	Arcade	Cres	Crescent	Gn	Green	Liby	Library	Recn	Recreation
Ave	Avenue	Cswy	Causeway	Gr	Grove	Mdw	Meadow	Ret	Retail
Bglw	Bungalow	Ct	Court	H	Hall	Meml	Memorial	Sh	Shopping
Bldg	Building	Ctr	Centre	Ho	House	Mkt	Market	Sq	Square
Bsns, Bus	Business	Ctry	Country	Hospl	Hospital	Mus	Museum	St	Street
Bvd	Boulevard	Cty	County	HQ	Headquarters	Orch	Orchard	Sta	Station
Cath	Cathedral	Dr	Drive	Hts	Heights	Pal	Palace	Terr	Terrace
Cir	Circus	Dro	Drove	Ind	Industrial	Par	Parade	TH	Town Hall
Cl	Close	Ed	Education	Inst	Institute	Pas	Passage	Univ	University
Cnr	Corner	Emb	Embankment	Int	International	Pk	Park	Wk, Wlk	Walk
Coll	College	Est	Estate	Intc	Interchange	Pl	Place	Wr	Water
Com	Community	Ex	Exhibition	Junc	Junction	Prec	Precinct	Yd	Yard

Index of towns, villages, streets, hospitals, industrial estates, railway stations, schools, shopping centres, universities and places of interest

3rd–Ald

3rd Ave [8] EX2 ....178 D5

A

Abbeville Cl EX2 .....177 E3
Abbey Cl
Axminster EX13 ......167 C4
Bovey Tracey TQ13 ....180 C7
Crapstone PL20 ......126 E2
Paignton TQ3 ....225 E5
Tatworth TA20.........88 D8
Teignmouth TQ14 .....210 C7
Abbey Cross TQ9.....227 A4
Abbey Ct
Exeter EX2 ....178 F5
Plymouth PL1 ....263 A2
Abbeydale EX10 .....188 A3
Abbeyfield Ho [7] TQ14..............210 C5
Abbeyford Ct EX20 ...170 C5
ABBEY GATE 167 C2
Abbey Gate La EX13 ..167 C2
Abbey Grange Cl TQ11...............236 B7
Abbey La EX13 ....167 B3
Abbey Link Rd TQ11 ..236 B7
Abbey Mdw
Buckfast TQ11........236 B7
Yelverton PL20 ....126 E2
Abbeymead Mews PL19...............171 C5
Abbey Mews
Tatworth TA20.........88 D8
Torquay TQ1 ....220 B8
Abbey Pl
Plymouth PL1 ....262 C2
Tavistock PL19 ....171 C5
Abbey Rd
Barnstaple EX31......154 E6
Bovey Tracey TQ13 ....180 D7
Cornworthy TQ9 ......227 A4
Dunkeswell EX14 ......67 C2
Dunkeswell EX15 ......67 C3
Exeter EX4 ....177 F7
Torquay TQ2 ....220 A5
Abbey Rise
Okehampton EX20 ....170 D6
Tavistock PL19 ....171 C5
Abbey Sch The TQ1...220 C8
Abbot Rd PL21.......237 A6
ABBOTSBURY.......207 B4
Abbotsbury Rd TQ12 .207 B4
Abbotsbury Sch TQ12..............207 D2
Abbotsbury Way PL2 247 F8
Abbots Cl
Lee Mill PL21 ....136 D6
Woolfardisworthy EX39 . 38 F8
Abbotscourt La PL11 .246 A2
Abbot's Cross EX36 ... 31 E6
Abbots Ct PL21 ......237 A5
Abbots Dr EX39 ....26 A4
Abbotsfield Cl PL19 ..126 A8
Abbotsfield Cres PL19..............126 A8
ABBOTSHAM........156 A2
Abbotsham Cross EX39...............25 C4
Abbotsham La EX19 ... 59 C3
Abbotsham Rd
Bideford EX39........156 E2
[20] Bideford EX39 .....157 A2
Abbotshill Pk TQ12...212 A6
Abbots Keep EX4 ....176 D6
ABBOTSKERSWELL..212 B6
Abbotskerswell Cross TQ12..............212 A7
Abbotskerswell Prim Sch TQ12..............212 B6
Abbots Mdw EX37..... 28 F4
Abbot's Rd EX4 ......177 E8
Abbotsridge Dr TQ12 206 F1
Abbot's Way PL20....128 C5
Abbotswood
East Ogwell TQ12 .....206 F1
Kingsteignton TQ12 ...207 F8
Abbott Cl EX11.......169 E4
ABBOTTS BICKINGTON........54 E8
Abbotts Hill EX33 ....152 D6
Abbotts Pk PL21 .....133 C2
Abbotts Rd PL3 ......248 E6
Abbrook Ave [9] TQ12..............123 E1
Abelia Cl TQ3........225 E8
Aberdeen Ave
Plymouth PL5 ....244 D1
Plymouth TQ12 ....244 D2
Aberfeldy [9] TQ1 ....220 C5
Abingdon Rd [1] PL4..263 A4
Abney Cres PL6......245 B6
Above Down TQ7 ....147 D7
Above Town TQ6.....233 F2
Aboveway EX3.......182 B3
Abscott La PL9.......255 C5
Abyssinia Ct [9] EX32 .155 B3
Abyssinia Terr [8] EX32..............155 B3
Acacia Cl
Bideford EX39........156 E1
Kingsteignton TQ12 ...207 F6
Acacia Mews EX6 ....181 B1
Acadia Rd TQ1.......220 E4
Acer Row EX7 ....204 E8
Ackland Cl
Bideford EX39........157 A1
Shebbear EX21........ 55 E4
Ackland Pk EX14......84 D2
Acklington Pl PL5....243 E4
Ackrells Hill
Littlehempston TQ9....216 F3
Uphempston TQ9 .....217 A3
Acland Cross EX32.... 17 B2
Acland Rd
Broadclyst EX5.......175 C6
Exeter EX4 ....261 C4
Ivybridge PL21.......237 A6
Landkey EX32......... 17 B2
Salcombe TQ8........259 D4
Aclands EX36........158 D3
Acland Terr EX4 .....261 C4
Acland Way EX16 ....161 A6
Acombe Cross TA3.... 68 B8
Acorn Dr PL6 ....245 E7
Acorn Gdns PL7......250 D6
Acorn Gr [1] EX32 ....155 C4
Acorn Way EX32 ...... 17 F4
Acre Cl EX39.......... 24 E2
Acre Cotts
Plymouth PL1 ....247 F3
Plymouth PL5 ....247 F3
Wellington TA21 ......160 E6
Acre La TQ1 ....220 E6
Acre Pl PL1..........247 F3
Acre Rd EX39 .... 24 E2
Acre The TQ13.......111 A6
Adams Cl
Plymouth PL5 ....243 F1
Torpoint PL11........246 F3
Adams Cres PL11 ....246 E3
Adams Ct EX39........25 D4
Adam's La PL9.......140 C8
Ada's Terr EX34........ 7 F8
Adcroft Rise EX13....103 D5
Adder La EX31 .... 16 B6
Addington Ct EX4 ....261 B4
Addiscombe La EX6..113 D5
Addison Cl EX4 ......176 E6
Addison Rd
Newton Abbot TQ12 ...207 E1
Paignton TQ4 ....226 A5
Plymouth PL4 ....263 A4
Addlehole TQ9.......144 D7
Adelaide Ct
Exeter EX2 ....261 A1
Exmouth EX8.........202 A5
Adelaide La PL1 .....262 A2
Adelaide Pl PL1......262 A3
Adelaide St
Plymouth PL1 ....262 A3
[2] Plymouth, Ford PL2 247 F5
Adelaide Street Ope PL1...............262 A3
Adelaide Terr [6] EX34...............150 B6
Adela Rd PL11 ....247 A3
Adelphi La TQ4 ......226 C5
Adelphi Mans TQ4 ...226 C5
Adelphi Rd TQ4 ......226 C6
Adit La PL12 ....242 E3
Adits The PL18.......125 D3
Adley La TQ13 ....111 B7
Admiral Ct TQ6 ......233 B2
Admirals Ct
[22] Exmouth EX8 ......202 A6
[5] Northam EX39 .....156 F7
Admiral's Hard PL1 ..254 A8
Admiral Swimming Ctr TQ5...............230 D4
Admirals Wlk
Exmouth EX8.........196 D2
Teignmouth TQ14 .....210 A8
Admiralty Cotts PL1..254 A7
Admiralty Ope S PL5 .247 E6
Admiralty Rd
Plymouth, Millbay PL1...............254 A8
Plymouth, St Budeaux PL5...............243 C2
Admiralty St Ope N PL5...............247 E6
Admiralty St
Plymouth, Keyham PL2...............247 E6
Plymouth, Millbay PL1 .254 A8
Admiral Way
Exeter EX1 ....178 D1
Exeter EX3 ....182 D8
Admiral Wy EX2 .....182 C8
Adrian Cl EX39.......157 A4
Adworthy La EX17..... 46 B2
Affeton Castle Cross EX17................ 60 F8
Affeton Hill EX17...... 60 F8
Affeton Moor Cross EX17................46 A2
Afflington Rd PL3....249 D1
AFTON 217 E2
Agatha Cl [2] TQ12....244 E6
Agaton Fort Rd PL5 ..243 F4
Agaton Rd PL5.......243 E3
Aggett Gr TQ13 ......180 F7
Aidan Ave EX32 ......155 C2
Ailescombe Dr TQ3 ..225 F6
Ailescombe Rd TQ3 ..225 F6
Ainslie Terr PL2......247 E7
Airborne Dr PL6 .....245 B4
Aire Gdns PL3 ....249 B5
Airfield Ind Est EX14 .. 67 B2
AISH
Paignton............224 E2
South Brent 134 F3
Aish Cross TQ9 ......224 E2
Aish La TQ10.........134 E3
Aish Lane End TQ10 ..134 F2
Aish Pk EX21 .... 55 E4
Aish Rd
Paignton TQ4 ....225 B2
Stoke Gabriel TQ9.....224 F2
Alamein Ct PL12 .....242 E2
Alamein Rd
Saltash PL12.........242 D2
Saltash PL12.........242 E2
Alandale Cl TQ14.....210 C6
Alandale Rd TQ14....210 C6
Alansway EX11 ......169 C3
A-La Ronde★ EX8....196 A3
Albacore Dr PL6 .....245 B5
Alba Ct EX1..........178 E7
Albany Cl EX8........196 E2
Albany Ct TQ3 ....226 B7
Albany Rd TQ3.......219 A1
Albany St
[10] Newton Abbot TQ12..............207 C3
Plymouth PL1 ....247 E2
ALBASTON.........125 C5
Albatross Rd EX2 ....178 D1
Albemarle Villas PL1 247 F3
Alberta Cres EX4.....177 F8
Alberta Ct [14] TQ14 ...210 C5
Albert Cl
[11] Crediton EX17 .....165 C5
Ottery St Mary EX11...169 C3
Albert Cotts TQ12....208 E3
Albert Ct
[7] Ilfracombe EX34 ...150 C6
[3] Torquay TQ1.......220 B5
Albertha Cl PL4......263 B4
Albert La [9] EX32 ....155 A5
Albert Pl
Exmouth EX8.........202 A6
[10] Totnes TQ9........223 C5
Albert Rd
Crediton EX17........165 C5
Plymouth PL2 ....247 F3
Saltash PL12.........243 A2
Torquay TQ1 ....220 B5
Albert St
[18] Dawlish EX7 ......204 D6
Exeter EX1 ....261 C4
Exeter EX2 ....177 D7
Albert Terr
Bovey Tracey TQ13 ....180 C7
Gunnislake PL18......125 C5
[14] Newton Abbot TQ12..............207 C3
Princetown PL20 .....128 B8
Albert Villas PL2.....247 E4
Albion Cl EX12.......191 F8
Albion Ct
Brixham TQ5.........230 C3
[6] Exmouth EX8 ......202 A7
Torpoint PL11........247 B3
Albion Dr PL2........248 B7
Albion Gdns TQ7.....258 C6
Albion Hill
Exmouth EX8.........202 B7
Newton Abbot TQ12 ...207 C2
Albion Pl
Exeter EX4 ....261 C4
Exmouth EX8.........202 A7
Albion Rd PL11 ......247 B3
Albion St
Exeter EX4 ....177 A5
Exmouth EX8.........202 A7
Teignmouth TQ14 .....210 A3
Albion Terr [9] EX8 ...202 A7
Alcester Cl PL2 ......247 E4
Alcester St PL2 ......247 F4
Aldborough Ct EX8...202 C6
Aldens Bsns Ct EX2 ..181 B8
Aldens Green EX2....181 B8
Aldens Rd EX2.......181 B8

Alden Wlk PL6 . . . . 249 B7
Alder Cl
Newton Abbot TQ12 . . . 212 F8
Teignmouth TQ14 . . . . . 210 B7
Alder Glade EX31 . . . . 154 C3
Alderney Rd PL6 . . . . . 244 F7
Alder Rd PL19 . . . . 171 C3
Aldersley Wlk PL6 . . . . 245 A1
Alderson Dr EX2 . . . . . 178 D5
Alders Way TQ4 . . . . . . 225 D3
Aldridge Mill Hill
EX16 . . . . 48 C6
Aldridge Pl EX1 . . . . . . 179 C8
Aldrin Rd EX4 . . . . 173 E2
Alexander Ct EX17 . . . 165 D4
Alexander Pk EX38 . . . 159 C5
Alexander Pl EX11 . . . 169 D4
Alexander Rd 23 EX7 . 204 D6
Alexander Wlk 4
EX2 . . . . 178 D5
Alexandra Cl
Crediton EX17 . . . . 165 A6
Plymouth PL9 . . . . 256 B8
Alexandra Ct 15
EX32 . . . . 155 A5
Alexandra Dr PL20 . . . 125 F1
Alexandra Ho TQ12 . . . 207 E2
Alexandra La TQ1 . . . . 220 B6
Alexandra Mews EX6 201 B8
Alexandra Pl
Cornworthy TQ9 . . . . . . 227 B4
5 Plymouth PL4 . . . . . . 248 E4
Alexandra Rd
Axminster EX13 . . . . . . 167 C5
Barnstaple EX32 . . . . . . 155 A5
Crediton EX17 . . . . 165 B6
1 Newton Abbot
TQ12 . . . . 207 C2
Plymouth PL3 . . . . 249 A4
Plymouth, Crownhill
PL6 . . . . 244 F2
Plymouth, Ford PL2 . . . . 247 F5
Plymouth, Mutley PL4 . . 248 F4
Torquay TQ1 . . . . 220 B6
Wellington TA21 . . . . . . 160 D6
Alexandra Sq PL12 . . . 243 A2
Alexandra Terr
Bideford EX39 . . . . 157 A3
Clyst Honiton EX5 . . . . . 175 E2
Exeter EX4 . . . . 177 E7
Exmouth EX8 . . . . 201 F6
Newton Abbot TQ12 . . . 207 C2
Plymouth PL2 . . . . 247 F5
South Molton EX36 . . . . 158 C5
1 Teignmouth TQ14 . . . 210 B4
Torpoint PL5 . . . . 247 B2
1 Totnes TQ9 . . . . 223 C6
Alexandra Way EX17 . 165 A6
Alexandria Ind Est
EX15 . . . . 163 D4
Alexandria Rd EX10 . . 188 A6
Alexandria Terr 6
EX16 . . . . 161 B4
Alexandria Trad Est
EX10 . . . . 188 A6
ALFARDISWORTHY . . . 53 B6
ALFINGTON 100 F8
Alfington Rd
Alfington EX11 . . . . 84 F1
Ottery St Mary EX11 . . . 169 F6
Alford Cl EX1 . . . . 178 C7
Alford Cres EX1 . . . . . . 178 B7
Alford Terr EX35 . . . . . 151 B5
Alfred Ct EX11 . . . . 169 B2
Alfred Pl PL2 . . . . 247 F5
Alfred Rd PL2 . . . . 247 F5
Alfred St PL1 . . . . 262 C2
Alfriston Rd TQ3 . . . . . 225 D7
Alger Wlk PL6 . . . . 244 E6
Al Hill PL20 . . . . 126 D1
Alice La 7 PL1 . . . . 262 B3
Alice Mews EX38 . . . . . 159 C5
Alice St PL1 . . . . 262 A3
Alison Rd TQ3 . . . . 219 A1
ALLALEIGH 139 E4
Allaleigh Cross TQ9 . . 139 F4
Allaleigh La TQ9 . . . . . 139 F4
Allaway EX10 . . . . 188 B6
Allen Bank EX32 . . . . . 155 A3
Allenby Rd PL2 . . . . . . 248 A6
Allen Cl EX16 . . . . 161 F5
Allendale Cl TA21 . . . . 160 A5
Allendale Rd PL4 . . . . . 263 A4
Allenhayes La TQ8 . . . 259 D4
Allenhayes Rd TQ8 . . . 259 D4
Allens Rd PL21 . . . . . . 237 D6
Allenstyle Cl EX31 . . . 153 B5
Allenstyle Dr EX31 . . . 153 B5
Allenstyle Gdns EX31 153 B5
Allenstyle Rd EX31 . . . 153 B5
Allenstyle View EX31 153 A5
Allenstyle Way EX31 . 153 B5
Aller Brake Rd TQ12 . . 212 F8
Aller Brook Nature
Reserve★ TQ12 . . . . . 207 E4
Aller Cl TQ12 . . . . 213 A6
ALLERCOMBE 168 A6
Allercombe Cross EX5 99 E5
Allercombe Hill EX5 . . 168 A6
Allercombe La EX5 . . . . 99 E5
Aller Cotts TQ12 . . . . . 212 F7
Aller Cross
Chillington TQ7 . . . . 145 A1
Kentisbeare EX15 . . . . . . 65 F1
Kingskerswell TQ12 . . . . 212 E6
South Molton EX36 . . . . . 29 F7
Allerdown Cross EX17 80 A7
Aller Gate EX17 . . . . 78 D5
Aller Gr EX5 . . . . 99 F7
Aller Grove Cotts EX5 . 99 F7
Aller Hill
Bishop's Nympton
EX36 . . . . 30 F4
Bishops Nympton EX36 . . 31 A4
Dawlish EX7 . . . . 204 B5
Aller La EX20 . . . . 94 F8
Allern La PL5 . . . . 240 D1
Aller Park Rd TQ12 . . . 212 F8
Aller Rd
Dolton EX19 . . . . 57 F7
Kingskerswell TQ12 . . . 212 F6
Allers View TA22 . . . . . . 33 D6
Allerton Wlk PL6 . . . . . 249 B7
Aller Vale Bldgs
TQ12 . . . . 212 F6
Allervale Cl EX2 . . . . . . 178 B4
Alleyn Ct EX12 . . . . 191 F7
Alleyn Gdns PL3 . . . . . 248 E8
Allhalland St 17
EX39 . . . . 157 A2
Allhallows Ct
Exeter EX4 . . . . 261 A2
1 Honiton EX14 . . . . . . 166 C6
Allhallows Mus★
EX14 . . . . 166 C6
All Hallows Rd TQ3 . . . 219 C2
Alliance Ct 16 EX14 . . . . 85 C2
Allington Mead EX4 . . 173 A3
Allington Terr EX17 . . . 78 F7
Allison La EX17 . . . . 95 D7
Allotment Dro TA20 . . . 69 F5
Allotment Gdns TQ7 . . 258 D6
ALL SAINTS 88 A4
All Saints Babbacombe
CE Prim Sch TQ1 . . . . 220 D6
All Saints CE Acad
PL5 . . . . 244 B1
All Saints CE Prim Sch
EX13 . . . . 88 A4
All Saints CE Sch
TA22 . . . . 33 D6
All Saints Cl EX9 . . . . 198 B6
All Saints Ct EX14 . . . . 166 A5
All Saints Marsh CE Prim
Sch TQ12 . . . . 207 D3
All Saints Mews 11
EX8 . . . . 202 A7
All Saints Pk PL18 . . . . 125 B5
All Saints' Rd EX10 . . . 188 A4
All Saints' Rd TQ1 . . . . 220 C7
Allshire La EX16 . . . . . . 32 F3
Alma Cotts PL4 . . . . . . 263 B2
Alma La EX10 . . . . 188 C4
Alma Rd
Brixham TQ5 . . . . 230 C5
Plymouth PL3 . . . . 248 C4
Alma St PL4 . . . . 263 B2
Alma Terr PL18 . . . . . . 125 D6
Alma Villa Rise EX5 . . . 99 A5
Almeria Ct PL7 . . . . . . 250 D4
Alminstone Cross
EX39 . . . . 39 A7
Almond Ct 3 EX31 . . . 154 C2
Almond Dr PL7 . . . . . . 251 B6
Almshouse Cross
TQ10 . . . . 135 E4
Almshouses 6 EX4 . . . 177 D8
Almshouses The 7
TQ13 . . . . 180 D8
Alpha Ctr TQ9 . . . . 223 C6
Alpha Pl 24 EX39 . . . . . 15 A1
Alpha St EX1 . . . . 177 F6
Alpha Terr TQ9 . . . . . . 223 B6
Alpha Way PL6 . . . . 245 A3
Alphin Brook Ct EX2 . 177 C1
Alphin Brook Rd EX2 177 C1
ALPHINGTON 181 B7
Alphington Prim Sch
EX2 . . . . 177 B1
Alphington Rd EX2 . . . 177 B3
Alphington Road Ret Pk
EX1 . . . . 261 A1
Alphington St EX2 . . . 261 A1
Alpine Rd TQ1 . . . . 220 B5
Alsa Brook Mdw
EX16 . . . . 161 C6
Alscott Gdns EX31 . . . . 27 A4
ALSTON 88 A5
Alston Cross
Ashburton TQ13 . . . . . . 131 B6
Slapton TQ7 . . . . 145 B5
Alstone Rd EX16 . . . . . 161 F3
Alston La TQ5 . . . . 229 D4
Alston Pk PL7 . . . . 250 D6
Alston Terr EX8 . . . . . . 201 F6
ALSWEAR 30 C1
Alswear New Rd
Alswear EX36 . . . . 30 C1
South Molton EX36 . . . . 158 E3
Alswear Old Rd
South Molton EX36 . . . . 158 C2
South Molton EX36 . . . . 158 D2
Altamira EX3 . . . . 182 F5
Altamira Cotts EX39 . . . 25 D2
Alta Vista Cl TQ14 . . . . 210 D7
Alta Vista Rd TQ4 . . . . 226 C4
Alton Pl PL4 . . . . 248 E4
Alton Rd PL4 . . . . 263 A4
Aluric Rise TQ12 . . . . . 207 F4
ALVERDISCOTT 26 F4
Alverdiscott Rd EX39 . . 26 B4
Alverdiscott Road Ind Est
EX39 . . . . 26 A4
Alver Gn EX39 . . . . 157 D1
Alvington St PL4 . . . . . 263 C2
Alvington Terr TQ7 . . . 258 C4
ALWINGTON 25 A2
Alwin Pk PL6 . . . . 245 A5
Alwyns Cl 3 TQ14 . . . . 210 C5
Alwyns Ct 5 TQ14 . . . . 210 C5
Amacre Dr PL9 . . . . . . 255 B6
Amados Cl PL7 . . . . . . 250 B4
Amados Dr PL7 . . . . . . 250 C4
Amados Rise PL7 . . . . 250 C4
Ambassador Dr EX1 . . 178 E7
Ambassador Ho TQ4 . 226 C5
Amber Cl TQ12 . . . . . . 244 C6
Amberley Cl TQ13 . . . . 130 E5
Amberley Gdns
TQ12 . . . . 207 D7
Amber Rise EX1 . . . . . . 175 B1
Amber Tor TQ13 . . . . . 121 F7
Ambleside Pl PL6 . . . . 245 D2
Ambrosia Cl EX17 . . . . . 60 C2
American Rd EX33 . . . . 15 A4
Amersham Ct EX2 . . . . 178 A4
Amethyst Dr TQ14 . . . . 204 B1
Amherst Rd PL3 . . . . . 262 B4
Amherst Rd La East
PL3 . . . . 262 B4
Amity Pl PL4 . . . . 263 A4
Amory Pl EX36 . . . . 158 C4
Amory Rd
Dulverton TA22 . . . . 33 D6
Tiverton EX16 . . . . 161 C2
Amyas Way EX39 . . . . . 157 A6
Amyatt's Terr EX10 . . . 188 B3
Anchorage Cl TQ5 . . . . 230 E5
Anchorage The TQ4 . . 226 C5
Anchor Bldgs TQ12 . . . 123 B2
Anchor Cotts TQ7 . . . . 147 B7
Anchor Mill EX31 . . . . 154 E8
Anchor Row EX3 . . . . . 182 D7
Anchor Sh Ctr TQ7 . . . 258 D5
Anchorwood View
EX31 . . . . 154 B4
Ander's La TA3 . . . . 68 E8
ANDERTON 252 F4
Anderton Cl PL19 . . . . 171 E1
Anderton Ct PL19 . . . . 171 E2
Anderton La PL19 . . . . 171 D2
Anderton Rise PL10 . . 252 F4
Andor Ave TQ12 . . . . . . 207 D7
Andrew Allan Rd
TA21 . . . . 160 B4
Andrew Cl EX10 . . . . . . 187 F8
Andrew Rd EX31 . . . . . 154 E3
Andrews Cl EX1 . . . . . . 174 F3
Andrew's Cl La EX17 . . 60 D7
Andrewshayes La
EX13 . . . . 87 A1
Andrew's Hill TA22 . . . . 33 D6
Andrew's Hill Cross
TA22 . . . . 33 C6
Andrews Pk TQ9 . . . . . 227 F8
Andromeda Gr PL9 . . . 256 E7
Andurn Cl PL9 . . . . 256 B6
Andurn Est PL9 . . . . . . 140 A8
Angel Hill EX16 . . . . . . 161 C4
Angelhill Cross EX36 . . 30 F2
Angel Mews 2 EX14 . . 166 C6
Angel The 4 EX14 . . . . 166 C6
Animal Sanctuary Rd
TA20 . . . . 69 D2
Anne Cl EX4 . . . . 173 E1
Anne Cres EX31 . . . . . . 154 E3
Annery Kiln Cotts
EX39 . . . . 26 A1
Anning Rd
Blackhorse EX1 . . . . 179 A8
Lyme Regis DT7 . . . . . . 260 E4
Ann's Pl PL3 . . . . 248 A4
Anson Ho 1 PL1 . . . . . 262 B3
Anson Pl
Plymouth, Devonport
PL2 . . . . 247 F4
Plymouth, St Jude's
PL4 . . . . 263 C3
Anson Rd EX8 . . . . 196 C2
Anstey Cres EX16 . . . . 161 F3
Anstey Gate TA22 . . . . . 32 B8
Ansteys Cl TQ1 . . . . . . 220 E5
Anstey's Cove Rd
TQ1 . . . . 220 E6
Ansteys Ct EX16 . . . . . . 46 E1
Anstey Way
Instow EX39 . . . . 15 B1
Instow EX39 . . . . 157 E8
Anstis Ct EX10 . . . . . . 188 A7
Anstis St PL1 . . . . 262 A3
Anthea Rd TQ3 . . . . . . 218 F1
Anthony Cottages
EX10 . . . . 100 F8
Anthony Rd EX1 . . . . . 177 F6
Anthony Way EX15 . . . . 65 F7
Antonine Cres EX4 . . . 176 E6
Antony Gdns PL2 . . . . . 248 C8
Antony House★
PL11 . . . . 246 D5
Antony Rd PL11 . . . . . . 247 B3
Antony Woodland Gdn★
PL11 . . . . 246 D6
Antrim Terr 5 TQ9 . . . 223 C6
Anvil Cnr EX22 . . . . 72 D7
Anvil Ct PL17 . . . . 115 B1
Anwyl Cl PL1 . . . . 262 B3
Anzac Ave PL5 . . . . 244 A4
Anzac St TQ6 . . . . 233 F3
Applebee Way DT7 . . . 260 E4
Appleby Wlk PL5 . . . . . 244 D4
Apple Cl EX8 . . . . 196 B3
APPLEDORE
Bideford 14 F1
Uffculme 51 A1
Appledore Cl
Cullompton EX15 . . . . . 163 B3
Plymouth PL6 . . . . 245 C6
Appledore Com Prim Sch
35 EX39 . . . . 15 A1
Appledore Hill EX20 . . 170 F8
Appledore Rd
Bideford EX39 . . . . 156 F8
Northam EX39 . . . . 157 A8
Apple Dr EX15 . . . . 162 D4
Apple Farm Grange
EX2 . . . . 178 E3
Applegarth Ave TQ12 206 E4
Applegarth Cl TQ12 . . 206 E4
Applegate Way TQ7 . . 258 D7
Applehayes EX8 . . . . . 202 C5
Applehayes La EX15 . . . 52 F2
Apple La EX2 . . . . 178 E4
Applemede EX5 . . . . 82 B6
Apple Orch EX38 . . . . . 159 B4
Appleton Tor Cl PL3 . . 249 F5
Appletree Cl
Barnstaple EX32 . . . . . . 155 D4
Uffculme EX15 . . . . 66 A7
Apple Tree Cl
Chudleigh Knighton
TQ12 . . . . 123 C4
Frogmore TQ7 . . . . 144 E1
Witheridge EX16 . . . . 46 E1
Appletree Gdns EX39 157 A4
Appletree Mews 5
EX39 . . . . 15 A1
Apple Way EX5 . . . . 99 C6
Apple Wharf 6 TQ9 . . 223 D5
APPLEY 51 B8
Appley Cross TA21 . . . . 51 B7
App's La EX39 . . . . 25 E2
April Cl EX8 . . . . 196 B3
Apsley Ho TQ1 . . . . 220 C3
Apsley Rd PL4 . . . . 248 D4
Apsley Terr
Braunton EX33 . . . . 152 F7
1 Ilfracombe EX34 . . . 150 C5
Apsley Villas 4 EX34 150 C5
Apters Hill 7 TQ5 . . . . 230 C5
Aquarius Dr PL9 . . . . . 256 D8
Aquila Dr PL9 . . . . 256 E8
Arbour Cl EX34 . . . . . . 150 B3
Arbour The PL6 . . . . . . 244 E5
Arcade Rd EX34 . . . . . . 150 B6
Arcade The EX20 . . . . . 170 B5
Arcadia PL9 . . . . 256 D6
Arcadia Rd PL9 . . . . . . 256 C6
Arch Cotts TQ12 . . . . . 207 D7
Archer Pl PL1 . . . . 262 B4
Archers Cl EX15 . . . . . . 163 B3
Archers Ct 8 PL8 . . . . 141 A7
Archer Terr PL1 . . . . . . 262 B3
Archery Cl TQ7 . . . . . . 258 C7
Arches The EX2 . . . . . . 177 A4
Archibald Rd EX1 . . . . 261 C3
Archipark EX32 . . . . 17 E1
Architect Way PL5 . . . . 247 B8
Arch St 5 TQ14 . . . . . . 210 A3
Arch The EX5 . . . . 184 B3
Archway Ave PL4 . . . . 249 B3
Archway Dr TQ6 . . . . . 233 D4
Arcot Gdns EX10 . . . . . 188 B6
Arcot Pk EX10 . . . . 188 B6
Arcot Rd EX10 . . . . 188 B6
Arden Cl EX9 . . . . 199 G2
Arden Dr TQ2 . . . . 219 D6
Arden Gr PL2 . . . . 248 C8
Arden Ho TQ7 . . . . 143 A1
Ardenney Ct EX8 . . . . . 202 C5
Ardwyn TA21 . . . . 160 D4
Arena Pk EX4 . . . . 174 B1
Argent Ct EX16 . . . . . . 161 D4
Argus Cl EX14 . . . . 166 E6
Argyle Mews EX4 . . . . 173 A1
Argyle Terr TQ9 . . . . . . 223 B6
Argyll Rd EX4 . . . . 173 B2
Ariel Mws PL9 . . . . 256 E8
Aries La PL9 . . . . 256 D8
Arimoor Gdns PL19 . . . 171 E5
Ark Royal Ave EX2 . . . 182 C8
Ark Royal Cl PL5 . . . . . 247 D8
Arkwright Gdns PL5 . . 243 F2
Arley Cl PL6 . . . . 245 B6
ARLINGCOTT
BECCOTT 10 D4
ARLINGTON 10 D3
Arlington Court★
EX31 . . . . 10 D3
Arlington Pl EX34 . . . . . . 8 A6
Arlington Rd
Plymouth PL4 . . . . 248 F4
Woolacombe EX34 . . . . . . 7 F6
Arlington Terr 5
EX33 . . . . 152 D5
Armada Cl EX12 . . . . . . 192 A7
Armada Cres
Paignton TQ3 . . . . 219 B2
Torquay TQ2 . . . . 219 C6
Armada Ct PL19 . . . . . . 171 B4
Armada Dr TQ14 . . . . . 210 A8
Armada Rd PL10 . . . . . 253 A1
Armada (Sh) Ctr PL1 262 C3
Armada St PL4 . . . . 263 A4
Armada Way
Plymouth PL1 . . . . 262 C2
Plymouth PL3 . . . . 262 C4
Westward Ho! EX39 . . . 156 B6
Armlet Row EX1 . . . . . 175 B1
Armourwood La EX5 . . 81 D5
Armstrong Ave EX4 . . 173 D2
Armytage Rd EX9 . . . . 198 A2
Arnison Cl PL9 . . . . 255 F5
Arnold Cres EX16 . . . . 161 B2
Arnold's Cl TQ7 . . . . . . 142 C6
Arnold's Point PL4 . . . 249 C3
Arnside Cl PL6 . . . . 245 D3
Arran Cl TQ2 . . . . 213 E2
Arscott Gdns PL9 . . . . 255 C5
Arscott La PL9 . . . . 255 D5
Arthington TQ1 . . . . . . 219 F7
Art Ho 14 EX1 . . . . 261 A2
Arthurs Cl EX8 . . . . 196 D2
Arthurs Lea EX39 . . . . 156 B2
Arthur Terr PL11 . . . . . 247 B2
Artillery Ave EX3 . . . . . 182 E7
Artillery Ct EX2 . . . . . . 177 F3
Artillery Pl PL4 . . . . . . 263 B1
Artizan's Dwellings
EX36 . . . . 158 D4
Arum Gr PL18 . . . . 125 B5
Arun Cl PL3 . . . . 249 C5
Arundel Cl EX2 . . . . . . 181 B8
Arundel Cres PL1 . . . . 262 B4
Arundell Cl PL16 . . . . . 105 E4
Arundell Gdns PL16 . . 105 E4
Arundell Pl TQ7 . . . . . . 143 E7
Arundell Rd EX20 . . . . . 77 C4
Arundells Cnr 3
EX17 . . . . 165 D5
Arundel Terr PL2 . . . . . 247 F4
Ascension Way TQ2 . . 213 F2
Ascerton Cl EX10 . . . . 188 B5
Ascerton Rd EX10 . . . . 188 B5
ASH 145 E8
Ashacre Cross TQ1 . . . 214 B6
Ash Bridge Cross
EX20 . . . . 95 D1
ASHBRITTLE 50 F8
Ashbrook St PL9 . . . . . 249 D1
Ashburgh Parc PL12 . 242 B3
Ashburn Cl TQ13 . . . . . 130 F4
Ashburn Gdns TQ13 . . 130 F5
Ashburnham Rd PL5 . 244 A3
Ashburn Wlk TQ4 . . . . 229 B8
ASHBURTON 130 E5
Ashburton &
Buckfastleigh District
Hospl TQ13 . . . . 131 A5
Ashburton Cl TQ13 . . . 180 C5
Ashburton Mus★
TQ13 . . . . 130 F4
Ashburton Prim Sch
TQ13 . . . . 130 F4
Ashburton Rd
Bovey Tracey TQ13 . . . . 180 C5
Buckfast TQ11 . . . . 236 D7
Newton Abbot TQ12 . . . 206 D4
Totnes TQ9 . . . . 223 B7
ASHBURY 92 E8
Ashbury Cross EX20 . . . 93 B5
Ashbury Station Cross
EX20 . . . . 92 C7
Ash Cl
Willand EX15 . . . . 162 C3
7 Yelverton PL20 . . . . . 126 F3
Ashclyst View EX5 . . . 175 D6
ASHCOMBE 124 D6
Ashcombe Cl PL7 . . . . 250 C7
Ashcombe Cross
EX7 . . . . 124 C6
Ashcombe Hill PL8 . . . 257 F2
Ashcombe Rd EX7 . . . 204 B8
Ashcroft Rd EX1 . . . . . 178 D6
Ash Cross
Bradninch EX5 . . . . 82 F7
Dartmouth TQ6 . . . . 232 D1
Halberton EX16 . . . . 65 A6
Oakford EX16 . . . . 48 D6
Petrockstow EX20 . . . . . . 56 F3
Ash Ct
Crediton EX17 . . . . 165 C6
Lee Mill PL21 . . . . 136 D6
Shillingford St George
EX2 . . . . 114 C6
ASHCULME 52 C1
Ashculme Hill EX15 . . . 52 C2
Ashdown Cl PL6 . . . . . 245 E3
Ashdown Cross EX22 . . 38 F3
Ashdown Wlk PL6 . . . . 245 E3
Ash Dr
Cullompton EX15 . . . . . 163 C5
South Molton EX36 . . . . 158 D5
Asheldon Ho TQ1 . . . . 220 E5
Asheldon Manor
TQ1 . . . . 220 D5
Asheldon Rd TQ1 . . . . 220 E5
Ashelford Cnr EX31 . . . 10 A3
Ashery Dr PL9 . . . . 255 C6
Ashes Rd
Dalwood EX13 . . . . 87 B1
Shute EX13 . . . . 103 B8
Ash Farm Cl EX1 . . . . . 174 F1
Ashfield Cl
Ashford EX31 . . . . 16 B6
Exmouth EX8 . . . . 196 E1
Ashfield La EX31 . . . . . . 16 B6
Ashfield Rd TQ2 . . . . . . 219 E5
Ashfield Terr EX39 . . . 157 A7
ASHFORD
Aveton Gifford 143 C7
Barnstaple 16 B6
Ashford Cl PL3 . . . . 249 A4
Ashford Cres PL3 . . . . 249 A4
Ashford Hill PL4 . . . . . 249 A4
Ashford Rd
Plymouth PL4 . . . . 248 F4
Topsham EX3 . . . . 182 E5
Wellington TA21 . . . . . . 160 D4
Ash Gr
Exmouth EX8 . . . . 196 B2
Ash Gr *continued*
Ivybridge PL21 . . . . 237 E5
Plymouth PL2 . . . . 247 F7
Seaton EX12 . . . . 192 A8
Ashgrove Rd TQ13 . . . 180 C4
Ash Hill
Oakford EX16 . . . . 48 D6
Petrockstow EX20 . . . . . . 56 F3
Ash Hill Cross EX16 . . . 48 D6
Ash Hill Ct EX12 . . . . . 191 C5
Ash Hill Rd TQ1 . . . . . . 220 A6
ASHILL 66 D6
Ashill TQ14 . . . . 209 A8
Ashill Ctyd EX15 . . . . . . 66 C6
Ash La
Iddesleigh EX19 . . . . 57 F1
Withypool TA24 . . . . 21 F6
Woolfardisworthy EX17 . 62 A2
Ashlake Rd EX6 . . . . . . 113 F7
Ashlar Row EX1 . . . . . . 175 B1
Ash Leigh EX2 . . . . 181 A8
Ashleigh CE (VC) Prim
Sch 20 EX32 . . . . 155 A5
Ashleigh Cl
Exeter EX4 . . . . 176 F6
Plymouth PL5 . . . . 244 C7
Teignmouth TQ14 . . . . . 210 B7
Torquay TQ2 . . . . 213 F3
Ashleigh Cres EX32 . . 155 B4
Ashleigh Ct TQ1 . . . . . 220 D3
Ashleigh Dr TQ14 . . . . 210 B7
Ashleigh La PL5 . . . . . 240 D1
Ashleigh Mount
TQ14 . . . . 210 B7
Ashleigh Mount Rd
EX4 . . . . 176 F6
Ashleigh Pk
Bampton EX16 . . . . 49 C8
Teignmouth TQ14 . . . . . 210 B7
Ashleigh Rd
Barnstaple EX32 . . . . . . 155 A5
Exmouth EX8 . . . . 202 C7
Honiton EX14 . . . . 166 B6
Kingsbridge TQ7 . . . . . . 258 B4
Ashleigh Rise TQ14 . . 210 B7
Ashleigh Way
Plymouth PL7 . . . . 251 C4
Teignmouth TQ14 . . . . . 210 B7
Ashley Back La EX16 . . 64 A5
Ashley Brake EX11 . . . 168 D4
Ashley Cl EX15 . . . . 66 B8
Ashley Cres EX10 . . . . 188 A7
Ashley Ho 2 EX8 . . . . 202 B6
Ashley Pl PL1 . . . . 262 B4
Ashley Priors La TQ1 214 C4
Ashley Rd
Okehampton EX20 . . . . 170 C5
Uffculme EX15 . . . . 66 A7
Ashley Rise EX16 . . . . . 161 B1
Ashley Terr
Bideford EX39 . . . . 156 F1
13 Ilfracombe EX34 . . . 150 B5
Ashley Way EX7 . . . . . . 204 F7
ASHMANSWORTHY . . . 39 A5
Ashmead Gr EX33 . . . . 152 C6
ASHMILL 90 F6
ASH MILL 31 C2
Ashmill Cross EX21 . . . 90 F6
Ashmill Ct TQ12 . . . . . 206 F4
Ash Mill Hill EX36 . . . . 31 B2
Ashmore Ct EX2 . . . . . 261 A1
Ashott La TA24 . . . . 13 F1
Ashplants Cl EX19 . . . . 58 F3
Ash Plants Cl EX39 . . . 156 D2
ASHPRINGTON 139 F8
Ashprington Cross
TQ9 . . . . 139 F8
Ash Rd
Braunton EX33 . . . . 152 F7
Kingsteignton TQ12 . . . 207 E6
ASHREIGNEY 58 F8
ASHRIDGE 26 D6
Ashridge Gdns
Kingsteignton TQ12 . . . 207 F6
Plymouth PL5 . . . . 244 B2
Ashridge La EX20 . . . . . 77 D6
Ashridge Moor Cross
EX20 . . . . 77 E6
ASH THOMAS 65 A5
Ashton Bsns Ctr EX2 . 177 B2
Ashton Cl PL6 . . . . 245 C6
Ashton Cres EX33 . . . . 152 C5
Ashton Ct 11 TQ12 . . . 123 F1
Ashton Ind Units EX2 177 B2
Ashton Rd EX2 . . . . 177 B2
Ashtons Cotts EX39 . . . 40 B7
Ashton Terr TQ1 . . . . . 220 E5
Ashton Way PL12 . . . . 242 D3
Ashtown Cross EX16 . . 34 A3
Ashtree Cl PL6 . . . . 245 D7
Ashtree Gr PL9 . . . . . . 256 C8
Ash Units EX17 . . . . . . 165 F5
Ash Vale PL16 . . . . 105 E4
ASHWATER 90 D6
Ashwater Prim Sch
EX21 . . . . 90 F6
Ash Way TQ12 . . . . 207 F1
ASHWELL 124 B1
Ashwell La TQ13 . . . . . 122 E6
Ashwickla TA22 . . . . 33 A8
Ashwood 5 TQ10 . . . . 134 F3
Ashwood Cl
Loddiswell TQ7 . . . . 143 E7
Plymouth PL7 . . . . 251 B5
Ashwood Ct TQ12 . . . . 207 E2

Ashwood Park Rd PL7 251 C6
Ashwood Pk TQ7 143 E7
Ashwood Rd EX2 177 B3
Aspen Cl
Exeter EX2 178 C4
3 Honiton EX14 85 C2
Newton Abbot TQ12 212 F8
Tavistock PL19 171 C3
Willand EX15 162 E5
Aspen Dr TQ12 212 F8
Aspen Gdns PL7 251 B5
Aspen Gr EX31 153 D4
Aspen Way
Paignton TQ4 225 D3
Tiverton EX16 161 E7
Aspin Cl TA21 160 F6
Aspin Rd TA21 160 F6
Astley Corte EX20 170 A5
Astor Dr PL4 249 C3
Aswell Orch TQ7 143 F7
Athelstan Cl EX13 167 D4
Athelstan Rd EX1 261 C3
Athenaeum La PL1 262 B2
Athenaeum Pl PL1 262 C2
Athenaeum St PL1 262 B2
ATHERINGTON 28 A2
Atherton La 14 TQ9 223 C5
Atherton Pl PL2 247 E4
Atherton Way EX16 64 D7
Athlone Ho PL1 262 A2
Atkinson Cl EX4 174 A1
Atlantic Acad EX39 24 B1
Atlantic Ct EX33 152 F3
Atlantic Highway EX39 156 E4
Atlantic Park Way EX39 25 C4
Atlantic Village Outlet Shopping EX39 25 D4
Atlantic Way EX39 156 D7
Atlas Dr PL9 256 E8
Attwyll Ave EX2 178 A5
Atway Cl 3 TQ13 180 C8
Atwill-Kingdom Almshouses EX1 177 E6
Atwill's Almshouses EX4 261 A4
Atworthy Cross EX22 38 D3
Aubyns Wood Ave EX16 161 B1
Aubyns Wood Cl EX16 161 B1
Aubyns Wood Rise EX16 161 B1
Auckland Rd 3 PL2 248 A5
Auctioneers Cl PL7 250 D5
Auction Pl EX13 167 D5
Auction Way EX39 38 F8
Audley 2 EX10 188 A4
Audley Ave TQ2 219 F8
Audley Rise TQ12 208 A1
Augusta Ct 16 EX1 261 A2
Augustine Cl EX12 191 F8
Aunay Cl EX22 164 D5
Aune Cl TQ10 135 B1
Aunemouth Cross TQ7 143 A3
AUNK 83 E3
Ausewell Cross TQ13 130 D7
Austen Cl EX4 178 C8
Austin Ave PL2 248 A6
Austin Cres PL6 245 C1
Austin Farm Prim Sch PL6 249 C7
Authers Hts EX16 161 B2
Auton Cross TQ7 258 A2
Autumn Field EX19 58 E3
Avalon Cl EX4 174 A2
Avanti Hall Sch EX4 173 A2
Aveland Rd TQ1 220 C7
Avent Wlk PL7 250 F7
Avenue Cl DT7 260 D3
Avenue Cottage Gdn* TQ9 227 A8
Avenue Ho EX17 165 C6
Avenue Mezidon-Canon EX14 166 D5
Avenue Rd
Bovey Tracey TQ13 180 C6
Ilfracombe EX34 150 B6
Kingskerswell TQ12 213 A5
Lyme Regis DT7 260 D3
Torquay TQ2 219 F5
Avenue Terr TQ5 229 E5
Avenue The
Chudleigh Knighton TQ13 123 D4
Exton EX3 183 C1
Newton Abbot TQ12 207 D4
4 Seaton EX12 192 A5
Tiverton EX16 161 E3
Avery Ct EX8 196 D2
Avery Hill TQ12 207 E8
Avery Way PL12 242 C5
Ave The 3 PL7 136 B6
AVETON GIFFORD 143 C6
Aveton Gifford CE Prim Sch TQ7 143 C6
Aviemore Ind Est EX31 154 D3
Avoca Ave TQ1 219 F6
Avocet Dr EX3 183 C2
Avocet Pl EX7 201 A2
Avocet Rd EX2 178 F6
Avon Cl
Plymouth PL3 249 D6
South Brent TQ10 135 A2
Avon Ct TQ7 142 F3
Avondale Ho 10 TQ10 134 F2
Avondale Rd
Exeter EX2 178 A5
Exmouth EX8 202 D8
Avondale Wlk 11 TQ10 134 F2
Avon Dam* TQ11 134 D8
Avon La EX39 156 D7
Avon Quillet TQ7 142 E3
Avon Rd
Bideford EX39 157 C1
Torquay TQ2 219 B7
Avon Valley Cotts TQ7 143 C6
AVONWICK 135 B1
Avonwick TQ1 220 C7
Avonwick Gn TQ10 135 B1
Avranches Ave EX17 165 A6
AWLISCOMBE 85 B4
Awliscombe CE Prim Sch EX14 85 B4
Axe Cl PL3 249 D6
Axe Cliff View 11 EX12 192 A5
Axeford TA20 88 E8
Axeford Mdws TA20 88 E8
Axe Valley Cl EX13 104 C7
Axe Valley Sports Ctr EX13 167 E6
Axeview Rd EX12 192 A7
AXMINSTER 167 C6
Axminster Community Prim Acad EX13 167 D6
Axminster Com Prim Sch EX13 167 E6
Axminster Hospl EX13 167 D6
Axminster Mus* EX13 167 D5
Axminster Rd
Charmouth DT6 104 F4
Honiton EX14 166 F5
Maidenhayne EX24 103 D6
Musbury EX13 103 D5
Offwell EX14 86 A3
Tatworth TA20 88 C7
Axminster Sta EX13 167 C5
AXMOUTH 192 E7
Axmouth Rd
Axmouth EX24 103 B2
Seaton EX12 192 C5
Axmouth to Lyme Regis National Nature Reserve* DT7 193 D4
Axtown La PL20 126 F2
Aycliffe Gdns PL7 251 A3
AYLESBEARE 99 D2
Aylesbury Cres PL5 244 B5
Aylescott Cross EX37 43 E3
Aylescott Hill EX34 9 A4
Aylescott La EX34 9 A4
Ayleston Cross PL21 137 D2
Ayleston Pk PL21 137 C2
Aylwin Cl PL7 250 E6
Ayres Cl EX39 157 C1
Ayreville Rd PL2 248 B7
Aysha Gdns EX39 156 D8
AYSHFORD 50 E2
Ayshford EX15 66 A7
Azalea Cl EX14 67 C1
Azes La EX32 155 A5

B

BABBACOMBE 220 D7
Babbacombe Bsns Pk TQ1 220 E7
Babbacombe Cl PL6 249 E8
Babbacombe Cliff TQ1 220 D7
Babbacombe Cliff Rly* TQ1 220 D8
Babbacombe Downs Rd TQ1 220 D8
Babbacombe Model Village* TQ1 220 C8
Babbacombe Rd TQ1 220 E6
Babbage Rd TQ9 223 D6
Babbages EX31 154 A4
Babbage Wy EX5 179 A7
Babblebrook Mews EX1 178 F8
Babeleigh Rd EX39 39 E7
Babeleigh Water EX39 39 E7
Baber Ct PL12 125 A2
Babis Farm Cl PL12 242 F1
Babis Farm Ct PL12 242 F1
Babis Farm Mews PL12 242 F2
Babis Farm Row PL12 242 F1
Babis Farm Way PL12 242 F2
Babis La PL12 242 F1
Babland Cross PL21 137 D2
Bableigh Cl EX39 40 B7
Bableigh Rd
Landkey EX32 17 B1
Swimbridge EX32 28 B8
Baby La TA22 33 E7
Babylon La EX5 82 B5
Backaborough La 6 EX39 156 F1
Backfield 7 EX39 15 A1
Back Hill PL12 242 D2
Back Hill Ind Est EX18 44 E1
Back La
Abbotsham EX39 156 A1
Bickleigh EX16 63 D2
Black Torrington EX21 74 A8
Bradninch EX5 82 E6
Chawleigh EX18 60 C8
Chittlehampton EX37 28 F4
Chulmleigh EX18 44 E1
Colaton Raleigh EX10 186 B3
Copplestone EX17 79 A4
Ermington PL21 136 F3
Frithelstock Stone EX38 40 F5
High Bickington EX38 43 C7
Lutton PL21 133 B2
Merton EX20 57 A7
Newton Poppleford EX10 186 E8
North Molton EX36 30 D8
Okehampton/North Tawton EX20 77 A1
Ottery St Mary EX10 100 A6
Ottery St Mary EX10 168 D8
Plymouth PL7 250 E4
Roborough PL6 241 A3
Sandford EX17 80 A5
Sidmouth EX10 187 C7
Sticklepath EX20 95 A5
Stockland EX14 87 A5
Whimple EX11 168 D8
Back Rd
Calstock PL18 125 D3
Moreleigh TQ9 139 A3
Newton Abbot TQ12 207 B3
Backshay Cl TQ7 143 C1
Backshay Pk TQ7 143 C1
Back's Hill
Crediton EX17 79 F7
Sandford EX17 80 A7
Back St
Bampton EX16 34 B1
16 Modbury PL21 137 B2
Woolfardisworthy EX39 38 F8
Backs The TQ6 233 E5
Backstone La EX16 47 B6
Backswood La EX16 64 B4
Backways La TA21 51 F6
Backwells Mead EX24 102 B6
Badgaver La EX34 3 B3
Badger Cl
Dartmouth TQ6 233 D4
10 Exeter EX2 178 D5
Honiton EX14 166 E7
Newton Poppleford EX10 186 D7
Paignton TQ3 218 F1
Badger La 1 TQ12 207 A5
Badgers Cl
Ivybridge PL21 237 A5
Kingsbridge TQ7 258 C4
Kingsteignton TQ12 207 D8
Badgers Gn TQ7 258 C4
Badgers Holt EX20 170 A5
Badger's Way TQ13 180 D7
Badgers Wlk PL12 242 D4
Badger View PL9 255 E5
Badger Way EX5 99 B6
Bad Homburg Way EX2 181 D8
Badlake Cl EX7 204 C7
Badlake Hill EX7 204 C7
Badlake La EX36 32 D6
Badlake Moor Cross TA22 32 D7
Badon Cl EX4 174 A2
BADWORTHY 134 D4
BAGLEY GREEN 160 A3
Bagley Rd TA21 160 A3
Bagmore Hill EX5 82 F8
Bagshot Ave EX2 177 D3
Bagton La TQ7 147 E8
Bailey La EX5 98 F7
Bailey Mws EX39 156 D1
Bailey's Knapp EX16 50 B4
Baileys Mdw TQ6 146 B7
Bailey St EX4 261 B3
Bailey Terr EX22 70 F5
Bainbridge Ave PL3 248 F7
Bainbridge Ct PL7 250 F7
Baker Cl EX10 188 A8
Bakers Cl PL7 251 C5
Bakers Cotts EX8 195 F5
Bakers Court La EX35 151 B5
Baker's Cross TA3 68 A7
Bakers Ct EX35 151 B5
Bakers Hill
Aveton Gifford TQ7 143 C6
Brixham TQ5 230 C3
Exeter EX2 176 C3
Baker's Hill
Newton Abbot TQ12 207 B3
Tiverton EX16 161 A4
Baker's La
Churchinford TA3 68 A7
Lower Tippacott EX35 6 A3
Wellington TA21 160 E6
Bakers Mead EX13 87 A1
Baker's Pk TQ13 130 A4
Bakers Pl PL1 247 F1
Baker St EX2 177 F5
Bakers Terr TQ7 143 C6
Bakers View TQ12 207 A3
Bakers Wy EX4 178 D8
Bakery La EX8 202 A7
Bakery Mdw EX16 62 B5
Bakery Way EX32 17 B2
BAKESDOWN 70 C3
Bakesdown La EX6 96 B3
Bala Brook Cl TQ5 229 F2
Bald Hill EX10 101 B2
Baldwin Ct EX20 170 D6
Balfour Cl EX14 166 E5
Balfour Gdns EX10 188 A6
Balfour Manor EX10 188 A5
Balfour Manor Ct EX10 187 F5
Balfour Mews EX10 188 A5
Balfours EX10 188 A6
Balfour Terr
Kilmington EX13 87 C1
Plymouth PL2 247 E4
Balkwill Ct TQ7 258 C4
Balkwill Rd TQ7 258 B4
Bal La PL19 117 E6
Balland La TQ13 131 A5
Balland Pk 5 TQ13 131 A5
Ballards Cres EX31 153 A4
Ballards Gr EX31 153 A4
Ballards Way EX31 153 A4
Balleroy Cl EX21 55 E4
Ball Hill
Cheriton Fitzpaine EX17 62 F2
Cheriton Fitzpaine EX17 63 A2
Ballhill La EX16 49 B8
Ball Hill La EX20 170 D5
Ball La EX24 101 F5
Ball Mdw EX20 170 D5
Balls Cnr EX37 44 A3
Balls Corner EX20 57 C8
Balls Corner Cross EX20 57 C8
Balls Cross EX36 20 B2
Ball's Cross TQ8 259 C7
Balls Farm Rd EX2 176 F2
Balls Hill EX37 44 A2
Balmoral Ave PL2 247 F5
Balmoral Cl TQ12 207 E2
Balmoral Cres EX20 170 D5
Balmoral Gdns EX3 182 F5
Balmoral Ho EX31 154 E7
Balmoral La 7 TQ10 134 F3
Balmoral Terr 12 EX34 150 B5
Balsdon Rd EX22 70 E1
Baltic Wharf Bsns Pk TQ9 223 D4
Bamfylde Cotts EX6 114 B4
Bampflyde Way PL6 244 D6
Bampfylde Cl
Poltimore EX4 174 F6
Tiverton EX16 161 F3
Bampfylde Cross EX36 19 D2
Bampfylde Rd TQ2 219 F5
Bampfylde St EX1, EX4 261 C3
BAMPTON 34 C1
Bampton Cl TQ3 218 D2
Bampton Down Rd EX16 49 F7
Bampton Rd PL6 245 E1
Bampton St EX16 161 D4
Bampton VA Prim Sch EX16 34 B1
Bamson La EX16 62 B6
Banbury Pk TQ2 219 C8
Banfield Rd EX31 154 F8
Banfield Way EX14 166 B4
Bankart La EX3 182 B7
Bank End EX39 157 B4
Bankhart La EX3 182 B7
Bank La
11 Brixham TQ5 230 C5
6 Totnes TQ9 223 C5
Bankland La EX20 77 D8
Banks Cl EX16 49 C1
Banksia Cl EX16 161 E7
Bankside EX8 196 C3
Bank Sq TA22 33 D6
Bank St
Newton Abbot TQ12 207 B3
12 Teignmouth TQ14 210 C4
Bank The 11 EX32 17 B2
Bannawell Ct 1 PL19 171 B6
Bannawell St PL19 171 B6
Banner Ct 4 TQ3 226 A6
BANTHAM 142 F2
Bantham Cross TQ7 143 D4
Baptist Chapel Ct EX17 165 C5
Baptist St PL17 125 D3
Bapton Cl EX8 196 B2
Bapton La EX8 196 B1
Barberry Cl EX4 178 A8
Barbers La EX13 104 C3
Barber's La
Uplyme DT7 260 B4
West Buckland TA21 52 F7
BARBICAN 263 A2
Barbican App PL4 263 B2
Barbican Cl EX32 155 A4
Barbican Ct
Exeter EX4 177 A5
11 Plymouth PL4 263 A2
Barbican La EX32 155 B4
Barbican L Pk PL4 263 C2
Barbican Pl 9 EX32 155 A4
Barbican Rd
Barnstaple EX32 155 A4
Plymouth PL7 250 E4
Barbican Stps EX4 261 A2
Barbican Terr EX32 155 A4
Barbican The PL1 263 A2
Barbican Theatre* PL1 263 A1
BARBROOK 151 B1
Barbrook Rd EX35 151 B3
Barbury Cres PL6 245 B8
Barchington Ave TQ2 213 F3
Barcombe Hts TQ3 226 B8
Barcombe La TQ3 226 B8
Barcombe Mews TQ3 226 B8
Barcombe Rd TQ3 226 A8
Barcote Wlk PL6 249 C8
Bardon Walk EX2 178 E3
Bardsey Cl PL6 245 A7
Barewell Cl TQ1 220 B8
Barewell Rd TQ1 220 B8
Barfield Cl EX19 57 F7
Barfield Rd EX19 57 F7
Barfleur Rise DT7 260 E5
Barham Ave TQ14 204 B1
Baring Cotts 14 TQ9 223 D5
Baring Cres EX1 177 E6
Baring Ct
Exeter EX2 261 B1
Lewtrenchard EX20 106 F5
Baring Flats EX1 177 E6
Baring St PL4 263 B4
Baring Terr EX1 261 B1
Barkerhancock Cl EX4 174 D1
Barker's Hill PL12 242 C1
Barkers Way EX20 77 C4
Barkingdon Workshops TQ9 215 D7
Barlands Way EX19 57 F7
Barle Cl EX2 178 D4
Barle Ct EX16 161 E7
Barle Ent Ctr TA22 33 D5
Barley Cl EX15 163 B2
Barleycorn Fields 6 EX32 17 B2
Barley Farm Rd EX4 176 E4
Barley La EX4 176 D5
Barley Lane Sch EX4 176 D4
Barley Market St PL19 171 C6
Barley Mount EX4 176 F5
Barley Rd EX5 99 B6
Barley Valley Nature Reserve* EX4 176 D6
Barley Wlk EX6 201 A8
Barline EX12 191 D5
Barlow Gdns PL2 248 B7
Barlow Rd EX31 155 A7
Barnacott Cross EX39 26 D8
Barnade View EX1 175 B1
Barnardo Rd EX2 261 C1
Barnards Farm EX12 191 D5
Barnards Hill La EX12 192 A7
Barn Cl
Barnstaple EX32 155 C3
Churchinford TA3 68 D7
Ivybridge PL21 237 A6
Plymouth PL7 251 D4
Shebbear EX21 55 E4
Whiddon Down EX20 95 F3
Barn Close La EX12 192 E5
Barnclose Rd TA22 21 E4
Barncroft EX22 39 C1
Barn Cross EX14 85 F8
Barn Ct
Churston Ferrers TQ5 229 E4
Dartmouth TQ6 233 C2
Barn Ct Rd TQ9 223 F5
Barndale Cres PL6 245 B6
BARNE BARTON 247 C8
Barne Cl PL5 247 C8
Barne Cross TQ13 112 A2
Barne La PL5 243 D1
Barne Rd PL5 247 C8
Barnes Cl
Honiton EX14 166 B4
Willand EX15 162 C5
Barnes Close Mead TA22 33 D6
Barnes Mdw DT7 260 B5
BARNFIELD 261 C3
Barnfield
Crediton EX17 165 C5
East Allington TQ9 144 D7
Barnfield Ave EX8 202 D7
Barnfield Cl
Braunton EX33 152 E5
Crediton EX17 165 C5
Galmpton TQ5 229 C5
Barnfield Cotts EX5 81 F3
Barnfield Cres EX1 261 B3
Barnfield Dr PL7 251 C5
Barnfield Hill EX1 261 C3
Barnfield Rd
Brixham TQ5 230 D3
Exeter EX1 261 B3
Kingsbridge TQ7 258 C6
Paignton TQ3 225 F7
Paignton TQ3 226 A7
Torquay TQ2 219 D2
Barnfield Terr TQ12 212 B6
Barnfield Theatre* EX1 261 B3
Barnfield Wlk TQ7 258 C6
Barnhay 6 EX16 34 B1
Barn Hayes EX10 187 F7
Barnhay The TQ9 227 F7
Barn Hill
Down St Mary EX17 78 F7
Morwenstow EX23 36 F1
Barnhill Rd TQ12 213 A4
Barningham Gdns PL6 245 B6
Barn La
Budleigh Salterton EX9 197 F2
Kingskerswell TQ12 212 F7
Stoke Rivers EX32 17 F6
Barn Meads Rd TA21 160 E4
Barn Orchard 21 EX5 99 A6
Barn Owl Cl TQ2 213 D3
Barnpark Cl TQ14 210 C6
Barn Park Cl TQ12 211 E2
Barn Park Gdns EX21 73 C2
Barnpark Rd TQ14 210 C5
Barn Park Rd
Fremington EX31 153 D5
Plymouth PL3 248 D6
Barnpark Terr TQ14 210 C6
Barn Pk
Ashwater EX21 90 E6
Buckfastleigh TQ11 236 A5
Coldeast TQ12 122 F1
Crediton EX17 165 C5
Saltash PL12 242 F3
Stoke Gabriel TQ9 227 F8
Wrafton EX33 152 E3
Barn Rd TQ4 226 C2
Barns Cl
Bradninch EX5 82 F6
Cove EX16 49 B6
Kingsteignton TQ12 207 E6
Barnsclose TA22 33 D6
Barns Close Ind Est TA22 33 D6
Barnsclose N TA22 33 D6
Barnsclose W TA22 33 D6
Barnsey Gdns TQ13 130 F5
Barnsfield La TQ11 236 A5
Barnshill Cl EX17 62 F1
Barnsley Cl 1 TQ14 210 C5
Barnsley Dr TQ14 210 C6
Barns Rd EX9 198 B1
BARNSTAPLE 155 C4
Barnstaple Cl
Chittlehampton EX37 28 F4
Plymouth PL6 249 E7
Barnstaple Cross
Burrington EX37 43 C3
Crediton EX17 79 E4
Barnstaple Heritage Ctr* EX31 154 F5
Barnstaple Hill EX32 17 D1
Barnstaple Rd
Filleigh EX32 29 F7
South Molton EX36 30 A6
South Molton EX36 158 A7
Barnstaple Ret Pk EX31 154 F4
Barnstaple St
Bideford EX39 157 B2
South Molton EX36 158 C4
Winkleigh EX19 58 F3
Barnstaple Sta EX31 154 F4
Barns Terr PL12 238 A3
Barnstone Ct EX2 181 A8
Barntown Gate EX19 58 E1
Barntown La EX19 58 D1
Barnwood Cl PL9 255 E5
Barometer World (Mus)* EX20 57 A7
Baron Ct EX31 154 B1
Barons Pyke PL21 237 E4
Barons Rd PL20 127 B3
Baron Way
Barnstaple EX31 154 B1
Newton Abbot TQ12 207 F4
Barossa Pl 10 PL5 247 B3
Barossa Rd PL11 247 B3
Barpark Cnr EX15 52 E3
Barrack La EX2 181 A6
Barrack Pl PL1 248 A1
Barrack Rd
Exeter EX2 177 E4
Ottery St Mary EX11 169 C3
Princetown PL20 128 B8
Yelverton PL20 119 A1
Barracks Hill TQ9 223 A7
Barracks Rd
Fremington EX31 153 E6
Modbury PL21 137 B3
Barrack St PL1 247 E2
Barradon Cl TQ2 214 A4
Barrel Cl EX11 169 C3
Barrington Ct TQ4 226 C5
Barrington Ho TQ1 220 E5
Barrington Mead EX10 188 B4
Barrington Rd TQ1 220 E5
Barrington St EX16 161 D4
Barrington Wy TA21 160 B4
Barris EX17 60 C3
Barrowdale Cl EX8 196 C3
Barrow Down PL12 242 B3
Barrow Rd EX14 84 C4
Barrow Way Cross EX20 110 D8
Bar's La EX9, EX10 199 B8
Bartholomew Rd PL2 248 B5
Bartholomew Street E EX4 261 A3
Bartholomew Street W EX4 261 A2
Bartholomew Terr EX4 261 A2

BARTON 213 F3
Barton Ave
Braunton EX33 152 D4
Paignton TQ3 225 F7
Plymouth PL2 247 E5
Barton Brake PL9 140 D8
Bartonbury Cross EX17 78 E6
Barton Cl
Cheriton Fitzpaine EX17 62 E1
Cranbrook EX5 99 C6
Exton EX3 183 C1
Filleigh EX32 29 C6
Georgeham EX33 8 B4
Kingsbridge TQ7 258 D4
North Tawton EX20 77 C4
Okehampton EX20 170 C5
Paignton TQ3 225 F7
Parkham EX39 39 E8
Plymouth PL7 251 C5
Stoke Canon EX5 81 F1
Wembury PL9 140 D8
Barton Cnr EX17 61 B2
Barton Cotts EX20 95 C1
Barton Cres
Dawlish EX7 204 C6
Paignton TQ3 225 F7
Barton Cross
East Anstey EX16 32 E5
Filleigh EX32 29 A6
Heasley Mill EX36 19 C2
Instow EX39 15 B2
Morchard Bishop EX17 61 C2
Poltimore EX5 174 B8
Sandford EX17 80 C6
Torquay TQ2 213 F4
Barton Ct
Ashwater EX21 90 E6
Exeter EX1 178 C7
Parkham EX39 39 E8
Sidmouth EX10 188 A3
Barton Dr
Newton Abbot TQ12 206 F3
Paignton TQ3 225 F7
BARTON GATE 11 E4
Barton Gate La 4 EX34 3 A3
Barton Gdns TQ3 225 F7
Barton Head Cross EX20 76 C4
Barton Hill
Berrynarbor EX34 2 E4
Daccombe TQ1, TQ12 214 A6
Dawlish EX7 204 D6
North Tawton EX20 77 C4
Barton Hill Acad TQ2 213 F2
Bartonhill Cross TQ9 215 F6
Barton Hill Rd TQ2 213 F2
Barton Hill Way TQ2 213 F2
Barton Ho EX39 26 A4
Barton La
Barton Town EX31 11 D3
Berrynarbor EX34 2 E4
Braunton EX33 152 D5
Brayford EX32 18 F4
Dawlish EX7 204 D6
Lapford EX17 60 A2
Shillingford Abbot EX2 114 C7
Staverton TQ9 216 A5
Witheridge EX16 46 E1
Barton Lane Cl EX33 152 D4
Barton Leys TQ9 224 B7
Barton Meadow Rd EX37 43 B7
Barton Mews
Exton EX3 183 C1
Millbrook PL10 252 F6
Parkham EX39 39 E8
Venn Ottery EX11 100 B2
Barton Orch EX10 100 D2
Barton Paddocks EX10 100 D2
Barton Rd
Barnstaple EX32 155 D4
Buckland Brewer EX39 40 B7
Exeter EX2 176 F4
Okehampton EX20 170 C5
Paignton TQ3 225 F7
Parkham EX39 39 E8
Plymouth PL9 255 B6
Tiverton EX16 161 D6
Torquay TQ1, TQ2 219 E7
West Down EX34 8 F5
Woolacombe EX34 7 F6
Barton Rise EX14 84 E2
Barton Road Ind Units TQ2 219 E8
Barton St EX20 77 C4
Barton Steep EX35 5 E4
Barton Terr EX7 204 D6
Barton The TA4 35 E8
Barton Tors EX39 157 C1
BARTON TOWN 11 D3
Barton View EX20 77 C4
Barton Villas EX7 204 C6
Barton Way TQ6 233 B2
Bartows Cswy EX16 161 D5
Bartows Mews EX16 161 D5
Bartridge Hill EX31 27 A5
Barum Arc EX32 155 A5
Barum Cl TQ3 226 C7
Barum Gate Bsns Pk EX32 155 D3
Barum Mews 5 EX32 155 A5
Barum Ware Way 13 EX31 154 A2
Barwick Cross EX19 58 B2
Bary Cl EX17 62 F1
Bary Hill Cross EX17 62 F1
Bary La EX17 62 F1
Bascombe Cl TQ5 229 D6
Bascombe Rd
Brixham TQ5 230 A4
Churston Ferrers TQ5 229 D6
Basepoint Bsns Ctr EX2 181 E8
Basinghall Cl PL9 255 E5
Basket Ope PL4 263 A2
Bason Cross
Bradford EX22 55 B2
Shebbear EX22 55 B2
Basset's Cross EX20 75 E5
Bassett Cl 1 EX33 152 D5
Bassetts Cl
Copplestone EX17 79 A5
Northam EX39 156 F8
Bassetts Farm Prim Sch EX8 196 E1
Bassetts Gdns EX8 196 D2
Bastard's La EX38 159 D6
Bastard's Park Cnr PL21 137 D3
Batavia Dr EX2 178 D1
Batcombe La EX5 81 F6
Bate Cl EX2 177 A1
Bateman's Cross EX13 88 E7
Bath Cl EX14 84 D2
Bath Ct EX39 156 C7
Bathern Cl 3 EX16 49 B8
Bathern Rd EX2 178 D4
Bath Hotel Rd EX39 156 C7
Bath La
Plymouth PL1 262 B2
Torquay TQ2 219 F5
Bath Meadow Dr TA22 33 E6
Bath Pl
Ilfracombe EX34 150 B6
Plymouth PL1 262 B2
Bath Place W PL1 262 B2
Bath Rd EX8 202 A6
Bath St PL1 262 B2
Bath Terr
6 Instow EX39 15 B1
19 Teignmouth TQ14 210 C4
Batson Cross TQ8 259 C5
Batson Gdns TQ4 226 B4
Batson Hall Cross TQ8 259 C6
Batson Hill TQ8 259 C5
BATSWORTHY 46 F6
Batsworthy Cross EX16 46 F7
Batsworthy Hill EX16 47 A7
Battens EX14 87 A7
Battens Cross EX16 65 C8
Batterbridge Hill PL19 117 E3
Batteridge Hill PL19 117 F2
Battershall Cl PL9 255 F5
Batter St PL4 263 A2
Battersway Rd TQ4 225 E4
Battery La PL19 171 C4
Battery St PL1 262 A2
Battery Street Flats PL1 262 A2
BATTISBOROUGH CROSS 141 E7
Battisford Pk PL7 251 E3
Battishorne Way EX14 166 B4
Battle Abbey Way 2 EX1 178 F8
Battledown Cross EX21 55 F4
Battleford La TQ9 217 C5
Battle Rd TQ12 180 F2
Battle St EX15 52 E1
Battleton TA22 33 D6
Batts Combe Mws PL3 249 D1
Batt's La EX11 169 D3
Batts Pk EX15 66 C6
Batworthy Mill Cross TQ13 111 A4
Bavent Cl EX5 173 F8
Baxter Cl EX2 178 D3
Baxworthy Cross EX39 23 A1
Bayard's Cove TQ6 233 F3
Bayards Cove Fort★ TQ6 233 F2
Bayard's Hill TQ6 233 F3
Bayclose La EX31 10 D6
Bay Ct 11 EX12 192 B4
Baydon Cl PL6 245 C1
Bay Fort Mans TQ1 220 A4
Bayley Pl EX1 179 B8
Bayly's Rd PL9 255 B7
Baymount Rd TQ3 226 A7
Baynes Cl TA21 160 E7
Bay Rd EX9 199 A7
Bayside La PL9 140 A8
Bayswater Rd PL1 262 B4
Baythorpe Lodge TQ2 219 E2
Baytor Ind Est TQ4 225 E3
Baytree Cl PL6 245 D6
Baytree Gdns PL2 248 A7
Bay Trees EX6 114 D4
Bay View TQ3 219 D1
Bay View Cl
Croyde EX33 7 E1
Stoke Fleming TQ6 146 B7
Bay View Ct
Lyme Regis DT7 260 E3
Northam EX39 156 F6
Bay View Dr TQ14 210 C6
Bay View Est TQ6 146 B7
Bay View Rd
Lyme Regis DT7 260 D4
Northam EX39 156 E6
Woolacombe EX34 7 F6
Baze La EX35 6 B4
Bazley Sq 3 EX1 178 E8
Beachdown TQ7 142 E3
Beach Mdw EX22 53 E1
Beach Rd
Croyde EX33 7 D2
Dawlish Warren EX7 201 B2
Heybrook Bay PL9 140 A7
Ilfracombe EX34 150 F6
Paignton TQ4 226 C6
Seaton EX12 192 B4
Torquay TQ1 220 D7
Westward Ho! EX39 156 D7
Woolacombe EX34 8 A6
Beach St 12 EX7 204 E6
Beach View Cres PL9 140 D7
Beach Wlk TQ4 226 C2
BEACON 85 F8
Beacon Ave EX4 178 A8
Beacon Castle EX34 150 A6
Beacon CE VA Prim Sch The 24 EX8 202 A6
Beacon Cl PL21 237 C6
Beacon Cotts TQ13 130 C8
Beacon Cross
Bradninch EX5 82 F7
Copplestone EX17 79 D6
North Tawton EX20 77 A2
Romansleigh EX36 45 C5
Talaton EX5 84 B1
Beacon Down Ave PL2 248 B7
Beacon Down Cnr EX6 98 D2
Beacondown Cross EX16 63 E8
Beacon Down Cross EX20 93 E5
Beacon Down Hill EX20 93 F5
Beacon Dr TQ12 206 E5
Beaconfield Rd PL2 248 B7
Beacon Heath EX4 174 C1
BEACON HILL 174 C3
Beacon Hill
Bradninch EX5 82 F7
16 Exmouth EX8 202 A6
Torquay TQ1 220 B3
Beacon Hill La EX14 87 A5
Beacon Ho PL3 249 D4
Beacon Hts EX33 152 E6
Beacon La
Broadhempston TQ9 131 E1
Chulmleigh EX18 45 C3
Cullompton EX15 65 A3
Exeter EX4 178 A8
Hennock TQ13 123 A7
Kingswear TQ6 234 A2
Wellington TA21 52 C4
Beaconpark La EX20 95 D3
Beacon Park Rd PL2 248 B7
Beacon Pk PL15 89 D2
Beacon Pl EX8 202 A6
Beacon Quay TQ1 220 B3
Beacon Rd
Bradninch EX5 82 F7
Ivybridge PL21 237 C6
Kingswear TQ6 234 A2
Beacon Rise 5 EX18 44 E1
Beaconsfield Cross EX22 72 E6
Beacon Terr
4 South Brent TQ10 134 F2
Torquay TQ1 220 B3
Beacon The EX8 202 A6
Beacon View
3 Bittaford PL21 137 C7
Dartington TQ9 222 F8
8 South Brent TQ10 134 F2
Beadle Ct 6 PL19 171 B4
Beadon Dr TQ8 259 C4
Beadon La
Bovey Tracey TQ13 123 A8
Chulmleigh EX18 45 B3
Hennock TQ13 112 F1
Beadon Rd TQ8 259 B4
BEAFORD 42 D1
Beaford Arts★ EX19 42 D1
Beaford Com Prim Sch EX19 42 D1
Beagle Rd PL1 247 F1
Bealey Court Cross EX18 45 E2
BEALSMILL 115 C3
Bealswood Cl PL18 125 D6
Bealswood Rd PL18 125 D6
Beanhay Cl 12 TQ12 122 F1
Beans Mdw EX20 170 A5
Beaple's Moor Cross EX36 47 A8
BEARA 9 A1
Beara Cotts TQ13 131 C1
Beara Cross
Bratton Fleming EX31 18 A8
Highampton EX21 74 A6
King's Nympton EX37 44 F6
Roborough EX38 42 E6
Beara Down Cross EX31 8 F1
Beara Head EX38 42 E6
Beara Hill EX32 19 A5
Beara Hill Head EX36 19 B6
Beara La
Bratton Fleming EX31 18 A8
Combe Martin EX34 3 C3
Beara Way EX38 159 D6
Beardown Rd EX20 170 E5
Beards Rd EX31 153 E5
BEARE 82 E3
Beare Bridge Rd EX20 170 C6
Beare Cl PL9 255 B5
Beare Copse La EX19 58 F2
Beare La
Beare EX5 82 E3
Bondleigh EX20 77 B7
Beare Lane Cross EX20 77 B7
Beare Sq EX5 82 E4
Bearne's La 8 TQ12 207 B3
Bearnes (V) Prim Sch 19 TQ12 207 C3
Bearsdown Cl PL6 249 C8
Bearsdown Rd PL6 249 C8
Bears Farm Cotts EX20 170 B7
Bears La EX9 197 E3
Bear St
Barnstaple EX32 155 A5
Exeter EX1 261 B2
BEASTON 131 D1
Beaston Cross TQ9 131 D1
Beatland Cross PL7 132 C5
Beatlands Rd EX10 188 B4
Beatrice Ave
Plymouth, Keyham PL2 247 E5
Plymouth, St Jude's PL4 263 B3
Saltash PL12 242 E2
Beatrice Gdns PL12 242 E1
Beattie Rd PL5 247 B8
Beatty Ave EX2 182 C8
Beatty Cl PL6 245 A4
Beatty Way TQ6 233 F4
Beauchamp Cres PL2 248 C7
Beauchamp Rd PL2 248 C7
Beaudyn Wlk 5 PL6 249 C7
Beaufort Cl
Plymouth PL5 247 C8
Sampford Peverell EX16 50 D1
Beaufort Ct EX2 261 A1
Beaufort Ho 20 PL4 263 A2
Beaufort Rd EX2 261 A1
Beaufort Wlk EX32 155 B6
Beauly Cl PL7 251 A5
Beaumaris Gdns PL3 248 F8
Beaumaris Rd PL3 248 F7
Beaumont Ave PL4 263 A3
Beaumont Cl
5 Coldeast TQ12 122 F1
Torquay TQ2 219 D6
Beaumont Pl PL4 263 A3
Beaumont Rd
Newton Abbot TQ12 207 C3
Plymouth PL4 263 B3
Beaumont St PL2 248 A5
Beaumont Terr PL12 242 F4
Beaumont Way PL7 251 D4
Beauvale Cl EX11 169 E4
Beavers Brook Cl TQ3 219 B2
Beavor La EX13 167 F6
BEAWORTHY 74 A2
Beaworthy Cl EX2 177 A3
Beccott Cross EX31 10 D4
Becket Rd TQ13 180 E7
Beckets Rd TQ7 258 D5
Beckford Cl PL7 251 A5
Beckford Cross EX13 87 C4
Beckham Pl PL3 249 A6
Beckhamstree Hill EX6 112 F2
Becklake Cl EX31 154 A2
Beckland Cross EX39 22 F4
Beckly Ct PL1 262 C3
Becky Falls★ TQ13 122 A7
Bede Gdns PL5 244 C1
Bedford Cl PL18 125 C6
Bedford Ct EX10 188 B3
Bedford Flats EX10 188 A3
Bedford Gr PL21 237 D5
Bedford Mews PL4 263 A4
Bedford Park Villas PL4 263 A4
Bedford Pk
10 Bere Alston PL20 125 E1
Plymouth PL4 263 A4
Bedford Pl
6 Bere Alston PL20 125 E1
12 Horrabridge PL20 126 F4
Bedford Rd
Horrabridge PL20 126 F4
Plymouth PL9 255 E8
Torquay TQ1 220 D8
Bedford Row 19 EX31 154 F5
Bedford Sq
Sidmouth EX10 188 B3
Tavistock PL19 171 C5
Bedford St
12 Barnstaple EX32 155 A5
Bere Alston PL20 125 E1
Exeter EX4 261 B3
Plymouth PL2 247 F5
Bedford Terr PL4 263 A4
Bedford Units PL18 125 C5
Bedford Villas 7 PL20 125 E1
Bedford Way PL1 262 C3
Bedlam La EX13 87 C6
Bedland's La EX9 197 F2
Beech Ave
Exeter EX4 173 D1
Plymouth PL4 263 C2
Beech Bank EX39 25 D4
Beech Cl
Barnstaple EX31 154 B2
Broadclyst EX5 175 D6
Honiton EX14 166 A4
Tavistock PL19 171 C2
Torpoint PL11 247 A3
Totnes TQ9 222 F6
Wembury PL9 255 A1
Willand EX15 162 D4
Beech Copse EX1 178 E2
Beech Cres PL20 128 A8
Beech Croft EX15 163 C5
Beechcroft Rd
Plymouth, Lower Compton PL3 249 A6
Plymouth, North Prospect PL2 248 B7
Beech Ct
Plymouth PL6 245 D5
2 Wellington TA21 160 D6
Beech Dr
Down St Mary EX17 78 E7
Ipplepen TQ12 211 E2
Beeches Cl EX5 184 B2
Beeches The
Okehampton EX20 76 E1
St Ann's Chapel PL18 125 A5
Woolfardisworthy EX39 38 F8
Beechfield Ave
Torquay TQ2 213 F2
Yelverton PL20 127 A3
Beechfield Cl EX31 153 D5
Beechfield Gr PL3 248 E6
Beechfield Pl TQ2 213 F2
Beechfield Rd EX31 153 D5
Beech Gr
Barnstaple EX31 154 F7
Braunton EX33 152 C7
South Molton EX36 158 D5
Wellington TA21 160 C6
Beech Grove Prim Sch TA21 160 C6
Beechgrove Terr EX31 154 F7
Beech Hill TA21 160 F5
Beech Hill Cross EX17 61 B3
Beech Hill Ho EX17 61 C3
Beeching Cl EX21 73 E3
Beech La EX13 88 E1
Beech Lea EX18 58 F8
Beechlea Ind Est EX19 58 F4
Beech Pk
Crediton EX17 80 B3
Crediton EX17 165 D6
Fremington EX31 153 E5
Holsworthy Beacon EX22 54 C3
West Hill EX11 168 D4
Beech Rd
Buckland St Mary TA20 69 D8
Cranbrook EX5 99 B6
Lee Mill PL21 136 C7
Stibb Cross EX38 40 D1
Tiverton EX16 64 C8
Tiverton EX16 161 F5
Beech Tree Cross TA22 33 C7
Beechtree Ct EX17 79 D7
Beech Tree Dr EX16 161 B5
Beechtree La EX10, EX12 101 F2
Beech Tree Mdw EX20 107 F8
Beech Trees La TQ12 211 C3
Beechway EX8 202 A8
Beech Wlk EX14 85 C1
Beechwood Ave
Barnstaple EX31 154 D4
Bovey Tracey TQ13 180 C4
Newton Abbot TQ12 207 E1
Plymouth PL4 248 D4
Beechwood Cl EX31 154 D4
Beechwood Cres EX7 201 A2
Beechwood Cross PL7 251 F7
Beechwood Ct TQ14 124 E1
Beechwood Dr TQ7 258 D5
Beechwood Pk 10 TQ7 143 E7
Beechwood Prim Sch PL6 244 F6
Beechwood Rd TQ13 123 E6
Beechwood Rise PL6 245 E1
Beechwood Terr PL4 248 D4
Beechwood Way PL7 251 D5
Bee Farm Mws EX36 158 C5
Beeley Orch EX16 161 C8
Beenleigh Cross TQ9 139 D6
BEER 191 E5
Beerash Cross EX16 63 B4
Beer CE Prim Sch EX12 191 C5
Beer Cross EX20 94 E6
Beere Cross EX36 32 A5
Beer Heights Light Rly★ EX12 191 C5
Beer Hill
Clawton EX22 72 B1
Seaton EX12 191 E6
Beerhill La EX20 76 F5
Beer La
Burlescombe EX16 51 B2
Dulverton TA22 33 B5
Puddington EX16 62 C6
Zeal Monachorum EX17 78 C7
Beer Quarry Caves★ EX12 191 A5
Beer Rd EX12 191 E6
Beers Cotts EX6 181 B2
Beers Hill EX17 79 A5
BEESANDS 149 E7
Beesands TQ7 149 E7
BEESON 149 D7
Beeson Cross TQ7 149 D7
Beeson Pool TQ7 149 C8
Beeston Wlk 6 PL6 249 C7
Beetham La TA20 69 E6
Beetland La EX35 151 D2
Beetor Cross TQ13 111 B3
Beggar's Bush TQ10 134 F2
Beggars La EX14 166 A5
Beggars Roost EX35 151 B2
Behind Hayes EX9 198 E7
Bekhams Tree Cross EX6 113 B2
Belair Rd PL2 248 C7
Belair Villas PL2 248 C7
Belcombe Dro TA20 69 E7
Belfield Ave TQ3 218 D3
Belfield Cl TQ3 218 D3
Belfield Rd TQ3 225 E7
Belfield Rise TQ3 218 D3
Belfield Way TQ3 218 D3
Belgrave Ct EX9 203 F8
Belgrave La PL4 248 F4
Belgrave Mews 5 TQ2 219 F5
Belgrave Rd
Exeter EX1 261 C3
Newton Abbot TQ12 207 F1
Plymouth PL4 248 F4
Torquay TQ2 219 F5
Belgrave Terr
6 Teignmouth TQ14 210 C5
Upton Pyne EX5 173 A8
Belladown Hill EX31 27 A6
Bellaire EX31 154 E7
Bellaire Dr EX31 154 E7
Bellamarsh La TQ13 123 C4
Bellamy Cl PL6 245 A1
Bellamys The EX20 76 C5
Bella Vista Rd TQ5 230 C6
Bell Cl PL7 250 F6
Bell Ct EX4 261 A3
Belle Acre Cl PL3 248 F6
Belle Ave EX17 165 B5
Belle Cross Rd TQ7 258 E6
Belle Ct EX17 165 B5
Belle Hill TQ7 258 E6
Belle Isle Dr EX2 261 C1
Belle Meadow Ct 22 EX32 154 F5
Belle Meadow Rd 10 EX32 155 A5
Belle Parade EX17 165 D5
BELLEVER 120 B4
Bellever Cl 2 PL20 128 B8
Bellever Tor Dr TQ5 229 F2
Belle View EX22 164 C4
Belle View Terr TA20 88 C8
Belle Vue
Axminster EX13 167 D6
Chawleigh EX18 60 A7
Holsworthy TA20 72 A6
Holsworthy TA20 164 C4
Belle Vue Ave
Lynton EX35 151 B5
Plymouth PL9 255 B5
Belle Vue Cl EX6 114 E4
Belle Vue Cotts EX22 164 C4
Bellevue Cross EX31 42 A8
Belle Vue Cross
Great Torrington EX38 41 F7
Great Torrington EX38 42 A8
Great Torrington EX38 159 F7
Belle Vue Dr PL9 255 B5
Belle Vue Rd
Exeter EX4 173 A2
Exmouth EX8 202 A8
Kingsbridge TQ7 258 D5
Paignton TQ4 226 C5
Plymouth PL9 255 C5
Saltash PL12 242 F2
Belle Vue Rise
Plymouth PL9 255 B5
Uffculme EX15 66 A8
Bellevue Sq PL11 247 B2
Belle Vue Terr
Bideford EX39 156 F2
Cullompton EX15 163 C4
Gunnislake PL18 125 D6
Kennford EX6 114 D4
Bellflower Cl PL6 241 C1
Bellingate EX17 79 A2
Bellingham Cres PL7 251 C4
Belliver Ind Est PL6 241 B1
Belliver Way PL6 241 B1
Bell La
Hennock TQ13 123 A7
Paignton TQ3 225 B7
Bell Mdw EX16 64 A2

Bellrock Cl TQ2......214 B3
Bells Cl EX18......60 A7
Bell St EX9......198 F7
Belmont EX32......155 A5
Belmont Ave
Combe Martin EX34......2 F4
Ilfracombe EX34......150 A5
Belmont Cl
4 Kingsteignton TQ12......123 F1
Tiverton EX16......161 D5
Belmont Ct 8 PL3......248 A4
Belmont Ho
Exeter EX4......261 C4
6 Seaton EX12......192 A5
Belmont Pl PL3......248 A4
Belmont Rd
Barnstaple EX32......155 B6
Brixham TQ5......230 C4
Exeter EX1......261 C4
Ilfracombe EX34......150 A5
Ivybridge PL21......237 C4
Tiverton EX16......161 D5
Torquay TQ1......220 C6
Belmont St PL1......262 B3
Belmont Terr
Exmouth EX8......196 C1
Totnes TQ9......223 C6
Belmont Villas 8 PL2......248 A3
Belmont Wy 8 EX16......161 D4
BELSFORD......222 B3
BELSTONE......94 D4
Belstone Cl PL5......244 A3
Belstone Cnr Cross EX20......76 E1
Belstone Cross EX20......94 E4
Bel Tor Cnr TQ13......129 F8
Beltor Cross TQ12......211 D1
Belvedere Cl EX3......182 E6
Belvedere Ct
5 Dawlish EX7......204 E6
3 Wellington TA21......160 D6
Belvedere Pk EX2......113 F5
Belvedere Rd
Exmouth EX8......202 A7
Ilfracombe EX34......150 B6
Newton Abbot TQ12......206 E5
Plymouth PL4......249 B2
Belvidere Meadows Nature Reserve* EX4......173 B3
Belvidere Rd EX4......173 B2
Belvoir Rd EX39......156 F2
Benbow St PL2......247 F4
Bench Tor Cl TQ2......219 B7
Bendarroch Rd EX11......168 D5
Bendibus Cross EX22......72 E2
Bendibus Hill EX21......72 E3
Bendle La EX36......30 E8
Bendle Lane Cross EX36......30 E8
Bendley Hill EX16......46 E1
Benedict Cl TQ14......210 C7
Benedicts Cl 19 TQ12......122 F1
Benedicts Rd TQ12......122 F1
Benedict Way 2 PL21......137 B2
Ben Jonson Cl TQ2......219 D6
Benlears Acre 13 TQ12......122 F1
Benley Cross EX18......45 D2
BENNACOTT......89 B3
Bennah Hill EX6......113 A3
Bennets La PL12......242 F3
Bennett Cl EX2......181 B8
Bennett Rd TQ8......259 D3
Bennetts Cl EX12......190 E4
Bennett's Cross TQ9......139 C8
Bennetts Hill EX10......187 F7
Bennett Sq EX4......178 A8
Bennett St PL1......247 E1
Benning Ct EX31......154 C6
Bens Cl TQ7......147 D7
Benson Cl EX16......46 E1
Benson Dr EX39......157 A6
BENTON......18 B7
Benton Cross EX32......18 B7
Benton La EX31......18 B7
Benton Rd EX32......18 B8
BENTWICHEN......19 C4
Ben Venue Cl TQ1......220 C5
Berachah Rd TQ1......220 B6
BERE ALSTON......125 E1
Bere Alston Prim Sch PL20......125 E1
Bere Alston Sta PL20......125 E2
Berea Rd TQ1......220 C6
BERE FERRERS......239 E3
Bere Ferrers Sta PL20......239 E3
Bere Hill EX7......204 B6
Beresford St PL2......248 A4
Berkeley Ave TQ2......213 C1
Berkeley Pl 6 EX34......150 B5
Berkeley Rise TQ2......213 C1
Berkeley Sq TQ12......244 F3
Berkeley Way PL21......237 D4
Berkshire Cl TQ12......211 F8
Berkshire Dr
Exeter EX4......176 E4
Plymouth PL2......247 F5
Bernadette Cl EX4......174 C1
Berner's Cross EX19......58 F4
Bernice Cl PL4......249 B4
Bernice Terr PL4......249 B4
Berretts Way TQ12......123 A1
Berrow Park Rd PL3......248 E6
Berry Ave TQ3......225 F6
Berryball Cl EX20......170 C6
Berrybrook Mdw EX6......182 B3
Berry Cl
Abbotskerswell TQ12......212 B6
Exmouth EX8......202 E8
Salcombe TQ8......259 C4
Berry Cottage La TA20......69 C4
Berry Cotts EX6......182 B3
Berry Cross
Dunsford EX6......112 E8
Langtree EX38......41 B1
Shebbear EX21......55 D5
Berrydown Cross EX34......2 F1
Berry Down Cross EX34......9 F6
Berry Dr TQ3......226 A6
Berry Head Country Pk* TQ5......231 A5
Berry Head Gdns PL6......244 E1
Berry Head National Nature Reserve* TQ5......231 A6
Berry Head Rd TQ5......230 E6
Berry Hill
Beer EX12......191 D5
Bishopsteignton TQ14......208 F8
Branscombe EX12......190 A4
North Tawton EX20......59 C1
Berry La
Axminster EX13......88 F3
Beer EX12......191 D6
Combe Martin EX34......2 F4
Dunsford EX6......112 E8
Gunn EX32......17 F4
Kingsteignton TQ12......207 E6
Berry Mdw TQ12......207 E6
BERRYNARBOR......2 E3
Berrynarbor Pk EX34......2 E3
Berrynarbor (VC) Prim Sch EX34......2 E3
Berry Park Cl PL9......255 E6
Berry Park Rd PL9......255 E7
Berry Pk PL12......242 D4
BERRY POMEROY......224 B7
Berry Pomeroy Castle* TQ9......217 D1
Berry Pomeroy Parochial CE Prim Sch TQ9......224 B7
Berry Rd
Barnstaple EX32......155 C4
Braunton EX33......152 E7
Paignton TQ3......225 F6
BERRYSBRIDGE......81 E4
Berry's Ground La EX31......4 C5
Berry's La PL7......133 A1
Berrys Meadow EX17......95 F7
Berry Sq TQ4......226 C6
Berrys Wood TQ12......206 F3
Berthon Rd PL5......247 C8
Berwick Ave PL5......244 E3
Besigheim Pl 10 TQ12......207 B3
Besigheim Way TQ12......207 F4
Besley Cl EX16......161 F3
Besley Ct EX2......177 B3
Besshill La EX31......10 F3
Best Pk EX5......99 A6
Bestridge Mdw EX32......28 E8
Bests La
Great Torrington EX38......41 D6
Great Torrington EX38......159 D5
Best's La EX38......159 D5
Betham Hill EX16......46 F2
Betham La EX18......59 B6
Bethany Gdns PL2......248 C8
Bethelcombe Cross TQ12......122 C1
Bethel Cross TQ12......122 C1
Bethel Terr 1 TQ1......220 B5
Betjeman Cl EX10......187 F8
Betjeman Wlk PL5......244 C3
Betjemen Dr EX8......196 C3
Betony Dr TQ12......206 C5
Betony Rise EX2......178 C3
Betton Way TQ13......111 F5
Betton Way Ind Est TQ13......111 E5
Bettys Mead
Exeter EX4......174 A1
Exeter EX4......178 A8
Beuvron Cl EX39......38 F8
Bevan Rd
Barnstaple EX32......155 A5
Exeter EX1......178 C7
Beverley Cl EX2......178 B4
Beverley Gdns 6 TQ13......131 A5
Beverley Rd PL3......249 C4
Beverley Rise TQ5......230 B4
Beverley Way TQ12......207 A2
Beverston Way PL6......245 B8
Bevil Cl EX39......157 A1
Bevin Sq EX17......79 A6
Beweys Pk PL12......242 C2
Bewhay Gdns TQ9......222 F8
Bewick Ave EX3......182 E6
Bewley Down Rd TA20......69 D3
Bewsley Hill EX17......79 B5
Bexley La 6 TQ2......219 F5
Beyrout Pl 6 PL1......247 F3
Bhutan Cl EX14......166 D5
Bias La 4 EX33......152 D6
Bibors Hill TA4......35 E4
Bicclescombe Ct EX34......150 B4
Bicclescombe Gdns EX34......150 B4
Bicclescombe Park Rd EX34......150 B4
Bickell Cross EX32......28 C6
Bickern Rd PL11......247 B3
BICKERTON......149 D5
Bickerton Top TQ7......149 C5
Bickfont Hill EX31......11 F4
Bickford La 2 TQ14......210 C4
Bickfords Gn 14 TQ12......122 F1
BICKHAM......241 A7
Bickham La EX16......47 E7
Bickham Park Rd PL3......248 D7
Bickham Rd PL5......243 D2
BICKINGCOTT......31 B7
Bickingcott Cross EX36......31 C7
Bickingcott Hill EX36......31 C8
BICKINGTON
Ashburton......131 D7
Barnstaple......154 B4
Bickington Lodge EX31......16 A3
Bickington Pk EX31......154 A3
Bickington Rd EX31......154 C3
BICKLEIGH
Plymouth......132 A5
Tiverton......64 A1
Bickleigh Castle* EX16......63 F1
Bickleigh Cl
Exeter EX4......174 D2
Plymouth PL6......245 A1
Bickleigh Down Bsns Pk PL6......245 D8
Bickleigh Down CE Prim Sch PL6......245 D7
Bickleigh Down Rd PL6......241 D1
Bickleigh Mill* EX16......63 F2
Bickleigh-on-Exe CE Prim Sch EX16......64 A2
BICKLETON......153 C3
Bickleton Cross EX31......153 A2
Bickley Mill Cross TQ12......212 C1
Bickley Rd TQ12......212 C2
Bickwell House La EX10......187 E5
Bickwell La EX10......187 F5
Bickwell Valley EX10......187 F4
Bickwill Cross EX36......46 D8
Bicton Cl PL6......245 D1
Bicton Coll EX9......186 C1
Bicton Gdns EX9......198 C8
Bicton Park Botanical Gdns* EX9......198 C8
Bicton Pk
Bicton EX9......186 B2
Bicton EX9......198 A8
Bicton Pl
Exeter EX1......177 F6
Exmouth EX8......202 A6
Bicton St
Barnstaple EX32......155 A5
Exmouth EX8......202 A6
Bicton Villas EX8......202 B6
Bidbrooke La EX36......32 A6
Biddacott Cross EX37......28 E4
Biddamoor La EX19......42 C2
Bidders Cl TQ6......146 B7
Bidders Ct EX36......158 C4
Bidders Wlk TQ6......146 B7
Biddiblack Way EX39......157 C2
Biddick Dr PL2......247 F6
Biddington Way EX14......166 A4
Biddlecombe Cross TQ13......124 A6
Biddypark La EX2......113 F6
Biddypark Lane Cross EX2......113 F6
BIDEFORD......156 E3
Bideford Arts Ctr* EX39......157 A2
Bideford Coll EX39......156 E1
Bideford Com Hospl EX39......156 F2
Bideford Wlk PL6......249 E8
Bidmead Cl EX8......202 E7
Bidna La EX39......157 B8
Bidwell Brook Dr TQ4......226 C1
Bidwell Brook Sch TQ9......215 F1
Bidwell Cross
Langford EX5......172 E8
Thorverton EX5......81 E6
Bidwell La
Brampford Speke EX5......81 C1
Thorverton EX5......81 F6
Bidwell Wlk TQ4......226 B1
Biera View TQ13......111 A6
Bigadon La TQ11......236 C4
BIGBURY......142 F5
Bigbury Ct TQ7......142 F5
BIGBURY-ON-SEA......142 E3
Bigbury Way TQ2......214 B2
Bigbury Wlk PL6......249 E8
Biggin Hill PL5......243 F4
BIG Sheep (Farm Pk) The* EX39......156 B1
Bilberry Pl TQ3......225 D2
Bilbie Cl EX15......163 B3
Bilbury St PL4......263 A3
BILLACOMBE......255 F8
Billacombe Rd PL9......249 E1
Billacombe Villas PL9......255 F8
Bill Douglas Centre for the History of Cinema & Popular Culture (Mus)* EX4......177 B8
Billhole La EX17......61 C6
Billings Cl PL6......244 D6
Billington Cl PL6......249 B7
Bilton Terr 7 EX39......157 A1
Biltor Rd TQ12......211 D1
Bilver Cross TQ12......217 C8
Bimbom La EX13......103 C8
Bindon Rd EX4......174 E2
Binford Cl EX1......178 B6
Bingfield Cl TQ1......220 C5
Bingham Cres EX32......155 B4
Bingwell Ho EX16......161 F3
Binhamy Rd EX23......70 A8
Binkham Hill PL20......127 A3
Binnamore Cross TQ10......134 E4
Binneford Cross EX17......96 F8
Binneford Hill EX17......62 B2
Bircham Valley Nature Reserve PL6......245 B3
Bircham View PL6......245 C1
Birchanger Cross TQ13......122 B2
Birch Cl PL6......245 E7
Birch Cross
Doddiscombsleigh EX6......113 D8
Yarcombe EX14......69 A4
Zeal Monachorum EX17......78 B8
Birch Ct EX2......178 A4
Birchenbeer Cnr EX17......61 C1
Birch End EX5......99 C5
Birchen La
Highampton EX20, EX21......74 E5
7 Tiverton EX16......161 C3
Birchen Tree Cross EX15......66 C4
Birches The PL6......245 D6
Birchfield Ave PL2......248 B6
Birch Gr EX11......168 D3
BIRCHILL......88 A5
Birchill Cross EX13......88 A6
Birch La
Barnstaple EX31......154 C2
Landkey EX32......17 D3
Morchard Bishop EX17......61 A2
Stoke Rivers EX32......17 F6
Stoke Rivers EX32......18 A6
Zeal Monachorum EX17......78 A8
Birchland Rd PL7......133 A1
Birchland Way PL7......136 A8
Birchlea TQ13......180 C4
Birchman's Cross EX17......78 E1
Birchpark La EX20......77 B4
Birch Pond Rd PL9......255 D7
Birch Rd
Landkey EX32......17 B2
Lympstone EX8......195 F5
Newton Abbot TQ12......207 F1
Wellington TA21......160 E5
Birch Way EX5......99 B6
Birch Wlk TQ2......219 C8
Birchwood Cl
Tavistock PL19......171 C3
Totnes TQ9......223 B5
Birchwood Gdns PL7......251 A7
Birchwood Rd
Buckland St Mary TA20......69 B8
Exmouth EX8......196 D2
Birchy Barton Hill EX1......178 B6
Birdcage La EX11......168 E8
Birdie Walk EX2......178 D1
Birdshaven TQ2......219 E5
Birdswell La EX34......2 D3
Birdwood Cres EX39......156 D1
Birkbeck Cl PL7......250 E7
Birkdale Cl PL12......242 C2
Birkett Cl EX2......178 C4
Birks Halls of Residence EX4......173 A1
Birlea Business Pk EX23......70 B8
BISCOMBE......67 F8
Biscombe Cross TA3......67 E8
Biscombe Gdns PL12......243 A2
BISH MILL......30 E4
Bishmill Gate EX36......30 E4
Bishop Cornish CE Prim Sch PL12......242 F1
Bishop Ct 2 EX24......103 A4
Bishop Pasterfield Ho 4 EX2......261 B2
Bishops Ave TQ14......208 F8
Bishops Cl
Ivybridge PL21......237 E6
Saltash PL12......242 E3
Starcross EX6......201 B8
Torquay TQ1......221 A4
Bishop's Clyst EX5......179 A3
Bishops Court Ind Est EX2......178 E4
Bishop's Court La EX5......179 C4
Bishops Ct TQ14......208 F8
Bishops Dr EX17......79 A6
Bishop's Hill TA21......51 B7
Bishops Mdw EX17......61 A2
Bishops Mead 3 TQ10......134 F3
BISHOPS NYMPTON......31 A2
Bishops Nympton EX36......31 C1
Bishop's Nympton Cross EX36......30 F1
Bishops Nympton Prim Sch EX36......30 F2
Bishop's Pl
Paignton TQ3......226 B6
Plymouth PL1......262 B1
Bishops Rise
Kentisbeare EX15......66 A3
Torquay TQ1......221 A4
BISHOP'S TAWTON......16 F1
Bishop's Tawton Prim Sch 12 EX32......16 E1
Bishop's Tawton Rd
Barnstaple EX32......155 B2
Bishop's Tawton EX32......16 E1
BISHOPSTEIGNTON......208 E7
Bishopsteignton Mus of Rural Life* TQ14......209 A8
Bishopsteignton Rd TQ14......209 D6
Bishopsteignton Sch TQ14......208 F8
Bishopstone Gdns TQ3......226 C8
Bishops Way 3 EX1......178 E3
BISHOPSWOOD......69 C7
Bishops Wy EX2......178 E3
Bishop Westall Ho 6 EX2......261 B2
Bishop Westall Rd EX2......178 A2
Bishop Wilfrid Rd TQ14......209 D8
Bitney La TQ12......212 C5
BITTADON......9 C4
Bittadon La EX31......9 C4
BITTAFORD......137 C8
Bittaford Terr 2 PL21......137 C7
Bittaford Wood 6 PL21......137 C7
Bittam's La TQ9......217 B4
Bittern Ind Units EX2......178 E5
Bittern Rd EX1......178 E6
Bittery Cross EX5......84 B2
Bittescombe La TA4......35 B6
Bitthams La PL18......125 C7
Bitton Ave TQ14......210 B5
Bitton Ct TQ14......210 A5
Bitton Park Rd 13 TQ14......210 B5
Blachford Cl PL21......133 C2
Blachford Rd PL21......237 C5
Blackabrook Ave
Princetown PL20......119 A1
Princetown PL20......128 A8
Blackacre Rd EX24......102 C6
Blackalder Terr PL7......132 F4
Blackaller La EX16......33 C1
Blackall Rd EX4......261 B4
Black-a-Tor Copse National Nature Reserve* EX20......108 E8
BLACKAWTON......139 F2
Blackawton Prim Sch TQ9......139 E2
Blackball La TQ5......230 C6
Blackberry Cl
Plymouth PL9......255 E8
Totnes TQ9......223 E4
Blackberry Ct TA21......160 D4
Blackberry La
Bigbury TQ7......142 E6
Plymouth PL9......255 E8
Blackberry Way 6 TQ12......123 F1
Blackbird Cres PL15......105 A2
BLACKBOROUGH......66 D4
Blackboy Rd EX1......177 E7
Blackbrook Ave TQ4......226 B1
Blackbrook Cl PL20......127 B4
Blackbrook Wlk TQ4......226 B1
Blackditch Cross EX17......60 B1
Blackditch La EX17......78 B8
BLACK DOG......61 E4
Black Dog Cross EX17......61 E4
Blackdown Bsns Pk TA21......160 E6
Blackdown Cross
Cornworthy TQ9......139 E4
Loddiswell TQ7......138 B2
Tedburn St Mary EX17......97 E8
Blackdown La
Halwell TQ9......139 D4
Tedburn St Mary EX4......98 C5
Blackdown Mdw TA21......160 F7
Blackdown Pk EX15......162 C5
Blackdown Rd TA21......160 B4
Blackdown View
2 Hemyock EX15......67 B8
Sampford Peverell EX16......50 C1
Blackenway La TQ12......213 B7
Blackerton Cross EX16......32 E3
Blackett Cl PL21......237 E4
Blackeven Cl PL6......241 D1
Blackeven Hill PL6......241 E1
Blackfriars La PL1......263 A2
Black Gate
Challacombe EX31......11 F4
Holemoor EX22......73 B8
Blackgate Cross EX39......26 C7
Blackhall Gdns PL6......244 D6
Black Hat La EX6......176 B3
Blackhaven Cl TQ4......229 B8
Blackhayes La EX14......68 F1
BLACKHORSE......179 B7
Black Horse Cnr EX18......59 C4
Blackhorse La EX5......179 B8
Black La
Hemyock EX15......52 D2
Holcombe Rogus TA21......50 E6
Peter Tavy PL19......118 E7
Blacklands Cl PL7......133 A1
Blackler's Land Cross TQ9......216 B5
Blackley La TQ13......113 D1
Black Lion Ct 9 EX14......166 C6
BLACKMOOR......52 E5
BLACKMOOR GATE......11 A6
Blackmoor Rd TA21......160 F4
Blackmoor's Path EX35......151 B5
Blackmore Ave EX39......156 D1
Blackmore Cres PL6......244 D6
Blackmore Ct EX8......196 E1
Blackmore Dr EX10......188 B4
Blackmore Mews EX2......178 C4
Blackmore Rd
Exeter EX5......99 A1
Tiverton EX16......161 F3
Blackmore Theatre* EX8......202 A6
BLACKPOOL......122 F1
Blackpool CE Prim Sch TQ12......122 F1
BLACKPOOL CORNER......88 D1
Blackpool Cross EX17......78 D4
Blackpool Gdns* TQ6......146 A7
Blackpool Hill TQ6......146 A6
Blackpool La EX36......29 E4
Blackpool Rd EX17......78 D4
Blackpool Valley Rd TQ6......146 A7
Blackpost Cross
Kingston TQ7......142 C7
Totnes TQ9......223 F6
Totnes, Littlehempston TQ9......217 A2
Blackpost La TQ9......223 F5
Blackridge Cross TQ7......258 F8
Blacksmith La TQ10......137 D8
Blacksmiths Cnr EX17......81 A6
Blackstone Cl PL9......256 B6
Blackstone Cross TQ12......211 D1
Blackstone Rd TQ12......211 D1
Blackswan Pl 11 EX7......204 D6
Black Swan Rd EX7......200 F2
Blackthorn Ave EX16......161 F6
Blackthorn Cl
Honiton EX14......166 C4
Launceston PL15......105 A2
Plymouth, Honicknowle PL5......244 B3
Plymouth, Woolwell PL6......245 D8
Sidmouth EX10......187 F8
Blackthorn Cres EX1......178 C6
Blackthorn Dr PL21......237 E4
Blackthorn La EX5......99 B6
Blackthorn Way TQ4......225 D4
BLACK TORRINGTON......74 A8
Black Torrington CE Prim Sch EX21......74 A8
Blackwalls La EX18......60 B7
Blackwater La EX13......88 F3
Blackwater Rd EX15......66 E8
BLACKWELL......35 B5
Blackwell Cross
Broadhempston TQ13......131 D3
Strete TQ6......145 E7
Blackwell La TQ13......131 D2
Bladder La PL5......244 E2
Bladon Cl
Newton Abbot TQ12......207 D1
Newton Abbot TQ12......212 D8
Blagaton Gate EX21......73 B1
Blagdon EX17......165 D5
Blagdon Cl EX17......165 D5
Blagdon Cotts TQ3......225 B6
Blagdon Cross
Ashwater EX21......90 C7
Paignton TQ3......225 A7
Blagdon Lodge Cross EX21......90 C8
Blagdon Rd TQ3......225 B6
Blagdon Rise EX17......165 D6
Blagrove Hill EX17......46 C3
Blairgowrie Rd PL5......243 C2
Blair Rd PL21......237 D5
Blake Cl TQ1......220 B8
Blake Gdns PL5......244 C3
Blakeland Rd EX31......153 D5
BLAKEMORE......222 B5
Blakemore Cross TQ9......222 A4
Blakeney Rd PL3......249 D1

Blakes Hill Rd
Landkey EX32 17 B2
Swimbridge EX32 17 D1
Blakeslee Dr
Exeter EX1 178 E1
Exeter EX3 182 E8
Blakewell Cl EX31 154 D1
Blakewell Cross EX37 28 E3
Blakewell Hill EX32 18 E2
Blakey Down La TQ3 218 F1
Blamphayne Cross EX24 102 D7
Blanchard Pl 2 PL7 250 E7
Blanchdown Dr PL18 125 C7
Blandford Rd PL3 249 C6
Blangy Cl EX20 77 C4
Blanksmill Cross TQ7 259 A8
Blatchborough Cross EX22 38 B1
Blatchcombe Dr TQ3 225 F7
Blatchcombe Rd TQ3 226 A7
Blatchford La EX20 92 F2
Blatchfords Ct EX20 170 B5
Blatchmore La TQ6 232 C4
Blaxton La PL5 240 C2
Bleachfield Rise EX13 167 E6
Blenheim Cl
Newton Abbot TQ12 207 A5
Torquay TQ1 220 E4
Willand EX15 162 D5
Blenheim Ct EX2 177 C1
Blenheim Ct EX15 162 D5
Blenheim Dr EX15 162 D4
Blenheim La EX20 76 C4
Blenheim Rd
Exeter EX2 177 B2
Plymouth PL4 263 A4
Blenheim Terr TQ13 180 C7
Bligh Cl TQ14 210 A8
Blights Hill EX16, TA22 33 F3
Blind Acres La EX33 15 A8
Blind La
Aylesbeare EX5 99 E2
Buckland St Mary TA20 69 A8
Exeter EX4 173 F5
Huxham EX5 174 B8
Stoke Canon EX4 174 A6
Umborne EX13 102 F8
BLINDWELL 252 E5
Blindwell Ave TQ12 207 F7
Blindwell Cres EX5 99 C6
Blindwell Farm Cotts TQ12 207 E7
Blindwell Hill PL10 252 E5
Blindwell La TA4 34 E6
Blindwylle Rd TQ2 219 E5
Blogishay La TQ13 130 F4
Bloomball Cl PL3 249 B6
Blossom Cl EX14 67 C1
Blossom Hill EX14 67 C1
Blue Anchor Cross EX14 84 B4
Blueball Cross EX14 84 D3
Blueball Hill 18 TQ9 223 C5
Blue Bell TQ9 223 C5
Bluebell Ave EX16 161 F6
Bluebell Cl
Saltash PL12 242 D4
Seaton EX12 192 B7
Bluebell Rd EX14 67 C1
Bluebell St PL6 245 B2
Bluebell Way
Launceston PL15 105 A2
Tavistock PL19 171 E4
Blueberry Downs EX9 199 I2
Blueberry Row TQ3 225 D2
Blue Cedar Ct EX8 202 B6
Bluecoat Cl EX36 158 B4
Bluecoat Villas EX38 159 C5
Blue Gate TA24 19 F8
Bluegate Hill PL21 137 A2
Bluehayes La
Clyst Honiton EX5 175 F3
Rockbeare EX5 99 A5
Blue Haze Cl PL6 245 D5
Blue Jay Way EX2 177 F6
Blue La EX17 96 A3
Blueridge Rd TQ13 180 C4
Bluett Rd TA21 160 D4
Blue Waters TQ13 180 C4
Blue Waters Dr
Lyme Regis DT7 260 B3
Paignton TQ4 229 C8
Blue Waters Ind Est TQ13 180 C5
Blundell's Ave EX16 161 F4
Blundells Prep Sch EX16 64 D8
Blundell's Rd
Tiverton EX16 161 E4
Tiverton, Cowleymoor EX15 64 D8
Blundell's Sch EX16 64 D7
Blunt's La PL6 245 C3
Blyth Ct EX39 156 B6
Blythe Way TQ3 225 D4
Blythwoods Cres 4 TQ1 220 B7
Boarden Barn EX8 202 B6
Boards Ct 16 EX39 157 B1
Boasley Cross EX20 92 E4
Boasley Cross Com Prim Sch EX20 92 E4
Bockland Cl EX15 163 A3
Boconnic La PL20 127 A3
BODLEY 4 C2
Bodley Cl EX1 178 B7
Bodley Cross EX31 4 D1
Bodley La EX31 4 C2
Bodmin Rd PL5 244 D3
Bodmin St EX22 164 C4
Body Hayes Cl TQ9 227 F7
Body's Ct PL18 125 C6
Bogmoor La EX5 99 D8
BOGTOWN 92 D8
Bogtown Cross EX20 92 D8
BOHETHERICK 125 B2
BOLBERRY 147 D6
Bolberry Cross TQ7 147 E6
Bolberry Rd TQ7 147 C6
Boldventure PL8 257 F3
Boldventure Cross EX21 91 E6
BOLHAM 161 C8
Bolham Halt Cotts EX16 161 C8
Bolham La EX16 161 D8
Bolham Prim Com Sch EX16 161 C8
Bolham Rd EX16 161 C7
BOLHAM WATER 67 E7
Bolt House Cl PL19 171 A5
Bolton Ct 8 TQ5 230 C4
Bolton St TQ5 230 C4
Bommertown Cross EX36 32 A4
Bonair Cl TQ5 230 C3
Bonaventure Cl TQ8 259 D5
Bonaventure Rd TQ8 259 D5
Bondhouse La EX6 98 E3
Bond La EX16 62 F5
BONDLEIGH 77 B7
Bondleigh Bridge Cross EX20 77 B7
Bondleigh Cross EX20 77 B7
Bondleigh Moor Cross EX20 76 F6
Bondleigh Wood Cross EX20 77 B7
Bonds Cross
Chulmleigh EX18 44 E1
Petrockstow EX20 56 C5
Bonds Farm Meadow EX37 28 B2
Bond's La EX5 184 B5
Bonds Mdw TQ13 180 C8
Bond St
Beaford EX19 42 D2
Cornwood PL21 133 C2
Plymouth PL6 244 E6
Bonehayne and Purlbridge Rd EX24 102 E5
Bone Mill Cross TQ12 131 F6
Bone St
Tetcott EX22 89 F7
Tetcott EX22 90 A7
Bonfire Cross EX10 101 C3
Bonfire Hill
Black Torrington EX21 74 A8
Salcombe TQ8 259 C5
Bonfire La EX5 184 C3
Bonhay Cl EX6 201 B8
Bonhay Rd
Exeter EX4 177 A6
Starcross EX6 201 B8
Boniford Cross EX14 87 A4
Bonners Cswy EX13 167 F7
Bonners Dr EX13 167 F6
Bonners Glen EX13 167 F6
Bonnicott La EX33 7 D1
Bonnington Gr EX1 177 F6
Bonny Cross
Clayhanger EX16 35 B1
Morebath EX16 34 B3
Bonville Cl EX1 178 B7
Bonville Cres EX16 64 D7
Bonville Dr PL21 237 E4
Bonville Rd PL6 244 E6
Boobery EX16 50 D1
Boode Cross EX33 152 F7
Boode Rd EX33 152 F7
Booklands EX32 18 B2
Boon's Pl PL1 262 C4
Booth Way EX8 196 B2
Borden Gate EX16 50 B8
Border Rd EX14 166 A5
Boringdon Ave PL5 247 D8
Boringdon Cl PL7 250 D7
Boringdon Hill PL7 250 E7
Boringdon Mill Bsns Ctr PL7 250 F6
Boringdon Pk PL21 237 A5
Boringdon Prim Sch PL7 250 D7
Boringdon Rd
Plymouth, Plympton PL7 250 D6
Plymouth, Turnchapel PL9 255 A7
Boringdon Terr
Plymouth, Plympton PL7 250 D6
Plymouth, Turnchapel PL9 255 A7
Boringdon Villas PL7 250 D6
BORNE 44 B1
Borne Cross EX37 44 B2
BOROUGH 70 E5
Borough Cl TQ4 225 E3
Borough Cross
Aveton Gifford TQ7 143 B7
Borough Cross *continued*
Bridgerule EX22 70 E5
Chilsworthy EX22 53 E2
Newton Tracey EX31 27 A3
Woolacombe EX34 1 B1
Borough Ct PL11 246 E4
Borough La TQ9 144 B6
Borough Park Rd
Paignton TQ3 225 E5
Totnes TQ9 223 C6
Borough Pk PL11 246 E4
Borough Rd
Combe Martin EX34 2 F4
Great Torrington EX38 159 C5
Paignton TQ4 225 E4
Torquay TQ1 214 B1
Borough The PL8 257 F4
Borough View EX38 159 E5
Borrowdale Cl PL6 244 D5
Boscastle Gdns PL2 248 C8
Boscawen Pl
Plymouth PL2 247 E4
10 Teignmouth TQ14 210 B5
Boscundle Row PL12 243 A2
Boshill Hill
Axmouth DT7 193 C8
Colyford DT7, EX12 103 D3
Bossell Ho TQ11 236 B4
Bossell Pk TQ11 236 B4
Bossell Rd TQ11 236 B5
Bossell Terr TQ11 236 B5
Boston Cl PL4 255 B7
Bosun Cl EX3 182 D7
Bosuns Point TQ4 226 C4
Boswell Cl PL5 244 B2
Boswell's La EX20 77 D4
Boswell's Lane End EX20 77 D4
Boswell Way EX12 191 F8
Bothy The DT7 193 E6
Bottle Bridge Hill TQ13 123 F7
Bottle Hill PL21 132 E1
Bottle Pk PL21 136 B6
Bottom La EX13 103 D6
Bottompark La TQ2 213 F3
Bottoms La EX33 8 B2
Bottom's La TQ12 213 E4
Bottreaux Mill Cross EX36 32 A5
BOTUSFLEMING 242 B7
Boucher Rd EX9 198 B1
Bouchers Hill EX20 77 C5
Boucher's La TA4 35 E4
Boucher Way EX9 198 B1
Bouchiers Cl EX20 77 C5
Boughmore La EX10 187 F3
Boughmore Rd EX10 187 F4
Boughthayes Est PL19 171 A5
Boulden Cl PL7 251 C5
Boulter Cl PL6 241 C1
Boundary Cl TQ12 212 F5
Boundary Dr EX23 70 A6
Boundary Pk
Bideford EX39 26 F4
Seaton EX12 192 A8
Boundary Pl PL6 245 C7
Boundary Rd
Dousland PL20 127 B3
Torquay TQ2 219 D5
Bounds Cross EX22 71 A4
Bounds Pl PL1 262 B2
Boundstone Cotts EX39 25 D2
Bound The PL10 253 A1
Boundy's Cross EX17 61 B8
Bounsells La EX20 57 A7
Bountice La
Berrynarbor EX34 2 D2
Berrynarbor EX34 9 D8
Bourchier Cl 13 EX16 34 B1
Bourchier Dr 12 EX16 34 B1
Bourne Bridge Cross EX36 46 A5
Bourne Cl PL3 249 D6
Bourne Ct TQ5 229 F2
Bourne Rd TQ12 213 A5
Bourn Rise EX4 174 D2
Bourton La
Littlehempston TQ9 216 F1
Totnes TQ9 223 E6
Bourton Rd TQ9 223 E6
Bourtons The TQ9 223 D7
Boutport St (Mermaid Wlk) 11 EX31 154 F6
Boutport St EX31 154 F5
Bovacott La EX22 73 C7
Bovemoor's La EX2 178 A4
Bove Park Rd TQ2 214 A4
Bovet St TA21 160 C6
Bovey Cross
Broadhempston TQ13 131 D3
Moretonhampstead TQ13 111 E3
Bovey Fir Cross EX12 190 F6
BOVEY HEATH 180 E4
Bovey Heathfield Nature Reserve★ TQ12 123 A3
Bovey La
Beer EX12 191 B7
Broadhempston TQ12, TQ13 131 D3
Bovey Rd TQ13 123 C4
BOVEY TRACEY 180 D7
Bovey Tracey Heritage Ctr★ TQ13 180 C7
Bovey Tracey Prim Sch TQ13 180 C8
Bovey Tracey Rd TQ13 122 E7
Boville La PL9 256 C7
Bovisand Ct PL9 254 F2
Bovisand Est PL9 140 A8
Bovisand La
Down Thomas PL9 255 B2
Staddiscombe PL9 255 D3
Bovisand Pk
Down Thomas PL9 255 A1
Heybrook Bay PL9 140 A8
Bovisand Rd PL9 255 E3
BOW
Ashprington 139 F7
Blackawton 145 B8
Copplestone 78 C4
Bow Beer Cross EX17 78 A1
Bowbeer La EX17 78 B1
Bowbridge Cross TQ9 145 B8
Bowcombe Rd
Kingsbridge TQ7 144 B2
Kingsbridge TQ7 258 F4
Bow Com Prim Sch EX17 78 C4
Bow Creek TQ9 139 F6
Bow Cross
Blackawton TQ9 145 B8
Staverton TQ9 216 C7
BOWD 100 F1
Bowd Ct EX10 100 E1
BOWDEN 145 F8
Bowden Cnr EX31 9 F3
Bowden Cotts 12 EX32 17 B2
Bowden Cross
Buckland Brewer EX39 40 B8
Drewsteignton EX6 96 E3
Kingsbridge TQ7 144 C3
Bowden Farmhouse PL8 257 F4
Bowden Gn EX39 25 E4
Bowden Hill
Ashburton TQ13 130 F4
Crediton EX17 165 D5
Newton Abbot TQ12 207 C2
Yealmpton PL8 257 F4
Bowden Hill Terr 1 EX17 165 D5
Bowden La TQ13 123 A7
Bowden Park Rd PL6 245 A1
Bowden Pillars TQ9 223 B3
Bowden Rd TQ12 211 E2
Bowdens Cl TQ13 180 C7
Bowdens La
Ideford TQ13 124 B4
Shillingford EX16 34 E3
Bowdens Pk PL21 237 C4
Bowdown Cross TQ10 135 C5
Bowe Ct EX1 177 E7
Bowen Ct 9 EX33 152 D5
Bowerhayes Cross EX14 67 C3
Bowerhayes La EX14 67 C3
Bowering Ct 1 EX32 155 B3
Bowerland Ave
Torquay TQ2 213 F4
Torquay TQ3 214 A4
Bowerland Cross EX20 93 D3
Bowerland Rd EX20 93 D4
Bowers Park Dr PL6 245 E7
Bowers Rd PL2 248 B5
Bowerthy La EX17 60 D4
Bowhay EX21 74 A8
Bowhay Cl EX21 74 A8
Bowhay La
Combe Martin EX34 3 A3
Exeter EX4 176 E4
Bowhays Wlk 2 PL6 249 C7
Bowhill EX5 83 A7
Bowhill Prim Sch EX4 176 F4
Bow La TQ13 111 F4
Bowland Cl TQ4 226 A2
Bowley Mdw EX5 82 F6
Bowling Gn TQ7 142 F4
Bowling Gn La EX14 166 C5
Bowling Gn View EX15 163 B1
Bowling Green Chalets DT7 260 D2
Bowling Green La
Combe Martin EX34 3 A3
Hatherleigh EX20 75 B7
Bowling Green Rd EX3 183 A4
Bowls Cross
Bigbury TQ7 142 F5
Stoke Canon EX4 82 C1
Bowmans Mdw EX20 75 C7
Bow Mill La EX17 78 B4
BOWOOD 25 B4
Bowpound Cross EX17 78 B7
Bow Rd TQ9 139 C7
Bowring Cl EX1 178 B7
Bowring Mead TQ13 111 F4
Bowring Pk TQ13 111 F4
Bowringsleigh Pl TQ7 258 C5
Bow Station Cross EX17 78 C2
Boxfield Rd EX13 167 D5
Boxhill Cl PL5 244 B3
Boxhill Gdns PL2 248 C8
Box's Cnr EX18 60 B6
Boyce Pl 3 EX16 161 B4
Boyds Dr TQ14 210 C5
Boyes Cl EX16 65 A7
Boyland Rd EX6 112 D8
Boyne Rd EX9 198 A2
BOYTON 89 E2
Boyton Com Prim Sch PL15 89 D3
Bozomzeal Cross TQ6 228 B1
Bracken Cl
10 Honiton EX14 85 C2
Newton Abbot TQ12 212 F8
Plymouth PL6 245 D8
Brackendale EX8 196 C4
Brackendown EX11 168 D2
Bracken Rise TQ4 229 C6
Bracken Way EX7 201 A2
Brackenwood EX8 196 C1
Bradaford Cross EX21 90 F6
Bradbury La EX32 29 D6
Bradden Cres TQ5 230 B4
Braddon Cnr EX16 81 D8
Braddons Cliffe TQ1 220 B4
Braddons Hill PL7 250 B7
Braddons Hill Road E TQ1 220 B4
Braddons Hill Road W TQ1 220 B4
Braddons St TQ1 220 B4
BRADFIELD 65 F4
Bradfield Cl PL6 245 E1
Bradfield Rd EX4 174 D1
BRADFORD 55 C2
Bradford Cl
Exmouth EX8 196 C3
Plymouth PL6 249 B7
Bradford Cross EX16 47 A3
Bradford Ct EX39 157 A6
Bradford Moor Hill EX16 47 A3
Bradford Prim Sch EX22 73 B8
Bradham Ct EX8 202 D8
Bradham La EX8 202 D8
BRADIFORD 154 D7
Bradiford EX31 154 E7
Bradley Barton Prim Sch TQ12 206 E3
Bradley Ct 6 TQ12 207 B3
Bradleyford Cnr TQ13 180 F6
Bradley La TQ12 207 A3
Bradley Lane Ind Est 1 TQ12 207 A3
Bradley Manor★ TQ12 206 F2
Bradley Park Rd TQ1 214 B1
Bradley Rd
Bovey Tracey TQ13 180 E7
Newton Abbot TQ12 207 A1
Plymouth PL4 248 F4
Bradman Way EX2 177 C2
BRADNINCH 82 F7
Bradninch Cross EX32 17 D4
Bradninch Pl EX4 261 B3
Bradridge Cross TQ9 138 D8
Bradridge Ct PL15 89 D4
BRADSTONE 115 D7
BRADWELL 8 D5
Bradwell EX34 150 A5
Bradwell Rd EX34 8 D5
BRADWORTHY 38 E1
Bradworthy Cross EX22 53 D7
Bradworthy Prim Acad EX22 38 E1
Brady Cl EX17 80 B5
Braemar Cl PL7 251 C4
Braeside Mews TQ4 226 C4
Braeside Rd
Paignton TQ4 226 C4
Torquay TQ2 214 A4
Braggs Hill PL15 89 E3
Braggs' Hill EX37 43 B7
Brag La PL7 132 C6
Brahms Way EX32 155 C5
Braid Dr EX16 64 E8
Brakefield TQ10 135 A2
Brake Ho TQ12 207 E2
Brake La PL10 252 B5
Brake Rd PL5 244 E2
Brakeridge Cl TQ5 229 C6
Brake Wood Cl EX31 153 D5
Bramble Acre EX2 191 F8
Bramble Cl
Budleigh Salterton EX9 198 C1
Dartington TQ9 222 F8
Plymouth PL3 249 B7
Sidmouth EX10 188 B8
Torquay TQ2 219 D5
Bramble Hill Ind Est EX14 166 B6
Bramble La
Brampford Speke EX5 81 C1
Crediton EX17 165 E6
Honiton EX14 166 B5
Bramble Mead EX5 99 D2
Brambleoak Cross TQ12 131 E3
Bramble Path 7 EX32 17 B2
Brambles The TA21 160 D4
Bramble Wlk
Barnstaple EX31 154 B3
1 Plymouth PL6 249 C7
Bramfield Pl PL6 249 D7
Bramleigh Rd PL18 125 C6
Bramley Ave EX1 178 C6
Bramley Cl
Brixton PL8 257 A5
Kenton EX6 194 E3
Tiverton EX16 161 D7
Wellington TA21 160 F7
Willand EX15 162 D4
Bramley Gdns EX5 99 E7
Bramley Mdw EX32 17 C2
Bramley Rd PL3 249 C4
Bramleys The EX14 166 E7
Bramley Way EX15 66 C6
Brampford Cross EX5 172 F7
BRAMPFORD SPEKE 81 E1
Brampford Speke CE Prim Sch EX5 81 E1
Brampton Down Cross EX16 49 F8
Branches Cross EX22 54 E3
Brancker Rd PL2 248 C6
Brand Cl EX14 166 C4
Brandiron Cross EX6 123 B7
Brandirons Cnr EX17 79 C5
Brandis Cnr
Little Torrington EX20 41 F1
North Tawton EX17 77 F1
Petrockstow EX20 56 C6
Rackenford EX16 47 F1
BRANDIS CORNER 73 B6
Brandis Cross EX20 95 E4
Brandise Cross EX17 79 C2
Brandise Hill EX20 56 F3
Brandis La EX20 95 E4
Brandis Pk TQ7 145 C3
Brandize Pk EX20 170 B3
Brandon Rd PL3 249 C4
Brand Rd EX14 166 C4
Brandreth Rd 3 PL3 248 F6
Brandy Wells EX37 44 E6
Branksome Cl TQ3 219 C2
Brannam Cres EX31 154 B2
Brannam Ct EX31 154 B2
Brannams Ct 13 EX32 155 A4
Brannams Sq 2 EX32 155 A4
BRANSCOMBE 190 D3
Branscombe Cl
Colyford EX24 103 A3
Exeter EX4 176 E5
Torquay TQ1 220 D6
Branscombe Cross EX10 101 F1
Branscombe Gdns PL5 244 A3
Branscombe La EX7 200 C3
Branscombe Prim Sch EX12 190 D4
Branscombe Rd EX16 161 F4
Branscombe:The Old Bakery, Manor Mill & Forge★ EX12 190 D4
Bransgrove Hill EX18 59 B5
Bransgrove La EX18 59 B5
Branson Ct 9 PL7 251 C5
Branson Pk PL19 126 D6
Brantwood Cl TQ4 226 A4
Brantwood Cres TQ4 226 A3
Brantwood Dr TQ4 226 A3
BRATTON CLOVELLY 92 A2
Bratton Cross EX31 17 E7
BRATTON FLEMING 18 A8
Bratton Fleming Com Prim Sch EX31 18 A8
Braundsworthy Cross EX21 73 E8
BRAUNTON 152 B6
Braunton Burrows Biosphere Reserve★ EX33 15 F5
Braunton & District Mus★ EX33 152 D6
Braunton Rd EX31 154 D7
Braunton Sch & Com Coll EX33 152 E4
Braunton Wlk PL6 249 E8
Bray Cl
Burlescombe EX16 51 B3
Tavistock PL19 171 A5
BRAYFORD 18 F5
Brayford Acad EX32 18 F5
Brayford Cl PL5 244 B3
BRAYFORDSHILL 18 E5
Brayhams Terr EX20 170 C6
Bray Hill EX32 18 F3
Brayley Hill EX32 18 E1
Bray Mill Cross EX37 29 D4
Bray Rd EX22 164 C6
Brays Cl EX17 165 C5
Braytown Cotts EX32 18 F5
Breach Hill TA21 51 F5
Breaka La EX19 57 E5
Breakneck Cross EX37 28 F5
Breakneck Hill
Chittlehampton EX37 28 F5
Teignmouth TQ14 124 F2
Breakwater Ct TQ5 230 E6
Breakwater Hill
Plymouth PL4 263 C1
Plymouth PL9 255 A8
Breakwater Ind Est PL9 255 C8
Breakwater Rd PL9 255 C8
Brean Down Cl PL3 248 E6

Brean Down Rd PL3 . . 248 E7
Brecon Cl
Bideford EX39 . . 157 D1
East-the-Water EX39 . . 26 A5
Paignton TQ4 . . 225 D4
Plymouth PL3 . . 249 A7
Breech Cotts TA21 . . 51 F5
Bremley Cross EX36 . . 31 F7
BRENDON
Bradworthy . . 54 B8
Holsworthy Beacon . . 54 C2
Lynton . . 6 A5
Brendon Cross EX39 . . 39 F6
Brendon Hill EX17 . . 79 C6
Brendon Rd TA21 . . 160 D7
Brendons Ave TQ2 . . 219 C3
Brendons The EX16 . . 50 D1
Brendon Two Gates TA24 . . 13 A6
Brennacott Pl EX39 . . 25 D4
Brennacott Rd EX39 . . 25 D4
Brent Cl EX5 . . 184 C3
Brentford Ave PL5 . . 244 B5
Brent Hill PL8 . . 136 D1
Brent Knoll Rd 1 PL3 . . 248 E6
Brent Mill TQ10 . . 135 A2
Brent Mill Ind Est TQ10 . . 134 F2
Brenton Rd EX6 . . 114 C5
Brentor Cl EX4 . . 176 F8
Brentor Rd
Mary Tavy PL19 . . 117 D6
Plymouth PL4 . . 249 B2
Brent Rd 1 TQ3 . . 226 B6
Brent Tor★ PL19 . . 117 B7
Brest Rd PL6 . . 245 A3
Brest Way PL6 . . 245 A3
Bretonside PL4 . . 263 A2
Breton Way EX8 . . 196 E1
Bretteville Cl
Chagford TQ13 . . 111 A6
Woodbury EX5 . . 184 C3
Brett Wlk PL7 . . 250 F7
Brewer Ave EX13 . . 167 E7
Brewer Rd EX32 . . 155 C4
Brewers Ct EX1 . . 261 A1
Brewers Hill EX39 . . 39 F8
Brewers La EX39 . . 39 F8
Brewery La
12 Brixham TQ5 . . 230 C5
Exeter EX2 . . 177 F5
Sidmouth EX10 . . 188 B5
Brewin Rd EX16 . . 161 C3
Briansway PL12 . . 242 D2
Briar Cl
Exmouth EX8 . . 202 D8
Honiton EX14 . . 166 C3
Briar Cres EX2 . . 177 F2
Briardale Rd PL2 . . 247 F6
Briarleigh Cl PL6 . . 245 F2
Briar Rd PL3 . . 248 F7
Briars Row PL12 . . 242 D4
Briar Tor PL20 . . 127 A3
Briary La TQ1 . . 220 B5
Briary Mews 13 TQ1 . . 220 D4
Brick Cross EX9 . . 198 C7
Brickfields Sp Ctr PL1 . . 247 F2
Brickhouse Dr EX16 . . 161 D6
Brickhouse Hill
Bolham EX16 . . 49 C1
Tiverton EX16 . . 161 D6
Brick Kiln Cl EX4 . . 174 C1
Brickyard La EX6 . . 201 A8
Brickyard Rd EX5 . . 168 A7
Bridespring Rd EX4 . . 173 F1
Bridespring Wlk EX4 . . 173 F1
BRIDESTOWE . . 107 F8
Bridestowe Prim Sch EX20 . . 107 F8
Bridewell Ct 9 EX16 . . 161 C3
Bridewell Ho 11 EX16 . . 161 C3
BRIDFORD . . 112 F5
Bridford Rd
Christow EX6 . . 113 A4
Exeter EX2 . . 177 C2
BRIDGE BALL . . 5 E3
Bridge Bldgs 18 EX31 . . 154 F5
Bridge Chambers 15 EX31 . . 154 F5
Bridge Cl EX5 . . 82 D3
Bridge Cotts
Chard Junction TA20 . . 88 D8
East Budleigh EX9 . . 198 B5
4 Exeter EX4 . . 177 D8
Lympstone EX8 . . 195 D5
Bridge Croft TQ13 . . 130 F5
Bridge Cross
Bishops Nympton EX36 . . 30 F4
Fortescue Cross EX37 . . 44 B4
Bridge Ct EX4 . . 261 A3
BRIDGE END
Aveton Gifford . . 143 C5
Newton Poppleford . . 187 A8
Bridge End EX36 . . 31 C5
Bridgefield EX11 . . 169 E4
Bridge Hill
Topsham EX3 . . 182 F5
Topsham EX3 . . 183 A5
Bridgehill Garth EX3 . . 182 F5
Bridge Ho 1 TQ12 . . 207 C3
Bridgehouse Cross EX15 . . 52 D1
Bridge La
Budlake EX5 . . 82 D3
7 Instow EX39 . . 15 B1
Bridgelands Cl PL5 . . 243 B1
Bridgeland St EX39 . . 157 A2
Bridgeman Pl EX1 . . 174 F2
Bridge Meadow Cl EX17 . . 60 C2
Bridge Mill La PL21 . . 133 C2
Bridgemoor Cross EX22 . . 71 B6
BRIDGEND . . 141 A7
Bridgend Hill PL8 . . 141 A7
Bridge Park La EX31 . . 9 E5
Bridge Pk
Ashwater EX21 . . 90 F6
Bridgerule EX22 . . 70 F5
Ermington PL21 . . 136 F2
Ivybridge PL21 . . 237 D5
Bridge Plats Way EX39 . . 156 E2
Bridge Rd
Budleigh Salterton EX9 . . 198 B2
Churston Ferrers TQ5 . . 229 D5
Exeter EX2, EX6 . . 182 A8
Exmouth EX8 . . 202 A8
Kingswear TQ5, TQ6 . . 234 B7
Teignmouth TQ14 . . 210 A3
Torquay TQ2 . . 219 F5
Totnes TQ9 . . 222 F6
BRIDGE-REEVE . . 59 B8
Bridge Reeve Cross EX18 . . 59 C8
Bridge Ret Pk TQ2 . . 219 E8
BRIDGERULE . . 70 F6
Bridgerule CE Prim Sch EX22 . . 70 F5
Bridgerule Ind Est EX22 . . 70 E4
Bridgerule Rd TA20 . . 71 C2
Bridgeside TQ9 . . 139 C7
Bridge St
Bideford EX39 . . 157 A1
Buckfastleigh TQ11 . . 236 B5
Dulverton TA22 . . 33 D6
Hatherleigh EX20 . . 75 C7
Ipplepen TQ12 . . 211 D2
Kingsbridge TQ7 . . 258 D5
Lyme Regis DT7 . . 260 E3
Sidbury EX10 . . 101 B2
Tiverton EX16 . . 161 C4
Uffculme EX15 . . 66 A7
Bridges The PL12 . . 242 E1
Bridge Terr
Ashprington TQ9 . . 139 F6
Bampton EX16 . . 34 B1
Bridge The PL1 . . 262 B1
BRIDGETOWN
Launceston . . 105 A8
Totnes . . 223 F5
Bridgetown TQ9 . . 223 D5
Bridgetown Ct TQ9 . . 223 D5
Bridgetown Hill TQ9 . . 223 E6
Bridge View EX5 . . 99 C6
Bridge View Cl 2 EX1 . . 178 E3
Bridge Vw PL5 . . 247 D8
Bridgewater Gdns TQ9 . . 223 E5
Bridgwater Cl PL6 . . 245 B1
Bridle Cl
Paignton TQ4 . . 229 B8
Plymouth PL7 . . 251 B7
Bridle Path The TQ9 . . 223 C4
Bridle Way PL12 . . 242 D4
Bridwell Ave
Uffculme EX15 . . 65 F7
Uffculme EX15 . . 162 F8
Bridwell Cl PL5 . . 247 E8
Bridwell Cres EX15 . . 65 F7
Bridwell Lane N PL5 . . 247 E8
Bridwell Rd PL5 . . 247 E8
BRIGHTLEY . . 94 B8
Brightley Cross EX20 . . 94 B8
Brightley Rd EX20 . . 170 C8
Bright View EX20 . . 170 A4
Brimacombe Rd EX39 . . 22 E3
Brim Brook Ct TQ2 . . 219 B8
Brimford Cross EX39 . . 38 A4
Brimhay TQ9 . . 222 F8
Brimhay Bglws TQ9 . . 222 F8
Brim Hill TQ1 . . 214 C5
Brimhill Cl PL7 . . 251 B3
Brimhill La PL19 . . 117 F6
Brimlands TQ5 . . 230 B4
Brimlands Ct TQ5 . . 230 B4
BRIMLEY . . 88 D3
Brimley Bsns Pk TQ13 . . 180 C5
Brimley Cnr TQ13 . . 123 F6
Brimley Cross
Bovey Tracey TQ13 . . 180 B5
Hemyock TA3 . . 52 F1
Brimley Ct
Bovey Tracey TQ13 . . 180 B5
Teignmouth TQ14 . . 210 C6
Brimley Dr TQ14 . . 210 C5
Brimley Gdns TQ13 . . 180 C5
Brimley Grange TQ13 . . 180 B5
Brimley Halt TQ13 . . 180 C5
Brimley Hill EX13 . . 88 D2
Brimley La TQ13 . . 180 A5
Brimley Pk TQ13 . . 180 C5
Brimley Rd
Axminster EX13 . . 88 D3
Bovey Tracey TQ13 . . 180 B5
Brimley Vale TQ13 . . 180 C6
Brimlicombe Mdw EX1 . . 175 A3
Brimpenny Rd EX8 . . 196 C1
Brimstone La
Rockwell Green TA21 . . 160 A2
Sampford Arundel TA21 . . 51 F6
Sampford Peverell EX16 . . 50 E2
Brinchcombe Mws 9 PL3 . . 249 D1
Brindifield La EX17 . . 62 A5
Brindiwell Cross EX17 . . 63 B3
Brindiwell Hill EX17 . . 63 B2
Brinkburn Ct EX10 . . 188 A3
Brinscombe Cross EX13 . . 103 E6
Brinscombe La
Arlington EX31 . . 10 F3
Membury EX13 . . 87 E6
BRINSWORTHY . . 19 F1
Brinsworthy Cross EX36 . . 19 F1
Briseham Cl TQ5 . . 230 D3
Briseham Rd TQ5 . . 230 D3
Brismar Wlk 3 PL6 . . 249 C7
Britannia Ave TQ6 . . 233 C3
Britannia Mus★ TQ6 . . 233 E4
Britannia Pl PL4 . . 249 B2
Britannia Row 5 EX34 . . 150 C6
Britannia Royal Naval Coll TQ6 . . 233 F5
Britannia Way EX39 . . 156 E7
BRITHEM BOTTOM . . 65 B5
Briticheston Cl PL9 . . 256 A5
Briton St 2 EX16 . . 34 C1
Briton Streetlane EX6 . . 112 F7
Brittannia Ct TQ6 . . 234 B3
Brittany Rd EX8 . . 196 C4
Britten Dr
Barnstaple EX32 . . 155 B5
Exeter EX2 . . 178 B5
Britton Cl EX16 . . 65 A7
Brittons Cl EX33 . . 152 E5
Brittons The EX33 . . 152 E5
Briwere Rd TQ1 . . 219 E7
BRIXHAM . . 230 E3
Brixham CE Prim Sch TQ5 . . 230 D4
Brixham Com Coll TQ5 . . 230 D4
Brixham Cross TQ5 . . 234 E8
Brixham Enterprise Est TQ5 . . 230 D4
Brixham Heritage Mus★ TQ5 . . 230 C5
Brixham Hospl TQ5 . . 230 C3
Brixham Rd
Brixham TQ5 . . 230 A3
Churston Ferrers TQ5 . . 229 E4
Kingswear TQ6 . . 234 B3
Paignton TQ4 . . 225 E3
Brixham Theatre★ TQ5 . . 230 C5
Brixham Wlk PL6 . . 249 E8
BRIXINGTON . . 196 D3
Brixington Dr EX8 . . 196 D1
Brixington La EX8 . . 196 C2
Brixington Prim Sch EX8 . . 196 C2
BRIXTON
South Hams PL8 . . 256 F4
South Hams PL8 . . 257 A5
Brixton Lodge Gdns PL8 . . 256 F5
Brixton St Mary's CE Prim Sch PL8 . . 257 A4
Broadacre Dr TQ5 . . 230 D5
Broad Cl
Crediton EX17 . . 165 A6
North Molton EX36 . . 30 E8
Broadclose Hill EX16 . . 46 F6
Broadclose Rd EX31 . . 154 D3
BROADCLYST . . 175 C6
Broadclyst Com Prim Sch EX5 . . 175 C7
Broadclyst Rd EX5 . . 99 D8
Broadclyst Sports Ctr EX5 . . 175 D5
Broad Croft EX13 . . 87 E8
Broad Down Cl TQ7 . . 147 F6
Broaddown Cross EX14 . . 86 A1
Broadfield Rd EX32 . . 155 B4
Broadfields Rd EX2 . . 178 C5
Broadgate
Barnstaple EX31 . . 154 E7
Exeter EX1 . . 261 A3
Broadgate Cl
Barnstaple EX31 . . 154 E7
Braunton EX33 . . 152 D6
Broadgate Cres TQ12 . . 212 F4
Broadgate La EX17 . . 61 B2
Broadgate Rd TQ12 . . 213 A4
Broadhayes Cross EX14 . . 86 E5
BROADHEMBURY . . 84 E7
Broadhembury CE Prim Sch EX14 . . 84 E7
Broadhembury Cross EX14 . . 84 E7
BROADHEMPSTON . . 131 F1
Broadhempston Prim Sch TQ9 . . 131 E1
Broad La
Appledore EX39 . . 14 F1
Braunton EX33 . . 152 A8
Hawkridge TA22 . . 21 D1
Tiverton EX16 . . 161 C3
Broadland Gdns PL9 . . 256 A8
Broadland La PL9 . . 255 F8
BROADLANDS . . 207 A4
Broadlands
Bideford EX39 . . 157 D1
Northam EX39 . . 156 F8
Teignmouth TQ14 . . 210 A3
Thorverton EX5 . . 81 E4
Broadlands Ave TQ12 . . 207 A3
Broadlands Cl PL7 . . 251 A3
Broadlands Ct
Bideford EX39 . . 157 D1
Newton Abbot TQ12 . . 207 A3
Broadlands Rd TQ4 . . 226 A4
Broad Lane Head TA22 . . 21 D1
Broadleaf Cl EX1 . . 178 E8
Broad Leaf Pk
Dawlish TQ14 . . 210 E7
Teignmouth EX7 . . 204 C1
Broadley Ct PL6 . . 241 B2
Broadley Dr TQ2 . . 219 C3
BROADLEY HILL . . 68 F2
Broadley Ind Pk PL6 . . 241 B2
Broadley Park Rd PL6 . . 241 B2
Broadmead
Exmouth EX8 . . 196 D2
Woodbury EX5 . . 184 B3
Broadmead Bglws EX32 . . 155 C2
Broadmead Cross EX16 . . 48 A5
Broadmeade Ct TQ12 . . 207 D2
Broadmead Gdns EX35 . . 151 B5
Broadmeadow Ave EX4 . . 176 F4
Broadmeadow Ind Est TQ14 . . 209 D7
Broadmeadow La TQ14 . . 209 D7
Broadmeadow Sports Ctr TQ14 . . 209 D7
Broadmeadow View TQ14 . . 209 D7
Broadmoor Cross EX37 . . 29 A2
Broadmoor La EX20 . . 170 A5
BROAD OAK . . 168 D3
Broadoak Cl EX11 . . 168 D3
Broad Oak Cres 13 TQ9 . . 223 D5
Broadoak Hill EX31 . . 4 C3
Broadoaks Cotts PL7 . . 132 E4
Broadpark
Bovey Tracey TQ13 . . 180 B5
Brampford Speke EX5 . . 81 E1
Dartmouth TQ6 . . 233 D3
Okehampton EX20 . . 170 D5
Broad Park Ave EX34 . . 150 A5
Broad Park Cl EX33 . . 7 E2
Broad Park Cres EX34 . . 150 A4
Broadpark La
Parracombe EX31 . . 4 C2
Parracombe EX31 . . 11 C8
Whiddon Down EX20 . . 95 D4
Broadpark Rd
Paignton TQ3 . . 226 A7
Torquay TQ2 . . 219 D2
Broad Park Rd
Bere Alston PL20 . . 125 E2
Exmouth EX8 . . 196 C1
Plymouth PL3 . . 248 D6
Broadparks Ave EX4 . . 174 E2
Broadparks Cl EX4 . . 174 E2
Broad Path
Stoke Gabriel TQ9 . . 228 A8
Uffculme EX15 . . 66 A8
Broad Pk
Ashburton TQ13 . . 130 F5
Plymouth PL9 . . 255 C7
Broad Rd
Kerswell EX15 . . 66 C1
Kingswear TQ6 . . 234 D5
Broad Reach TQ4 . . 229 C7
Broadridge Cl TQ12 . . 206 D4
Broadridge Cross TQ9 . . 232 A8
Broadridge La EX17 . . 61 A4
BROADSANDS . . 229 C7
Broadsands Ave TQ4 . . 229 C7
Broadsands Bend TQ4 . . 229 C8
Broadsands Ct TQ4 . . 229 B7
Broadsands Gdns TQ5 . . 229 C6
Broadsands Park Rd TQ4 . . 229 C8
Broadsands Rd TQ4 . . 229 C7
Broadshell Cross EX22 . . 71 D5
Broad St
Black Torrington EX21 . . 74 A8
Churchinford TA3 . . 68 A7
Ilfracombe EX34 . . 150 C6
Lifton PL16 . . 105 E4
Lyme Regis DT7 . . 260 E3
Broad St *continued*
11 Modbury PL21 . . 137 B2
Ottery St Mary EX11 . . 169 D3
South Molton EX36 . . 158 C4
Broadstone TQ6 . . 233 F4
Broadstone Park Rd TQ2 . . 219 D3
Broad View
Broadclyst EX5 . . 175 C6
Dartington TQ9 . . 222 F8
Broadway
Exeter EX2 . . 176 F3
Fremington EX31 . . 153 F5
Sidmouth EX10 . . 187 F5
Trusham TQ13 . . 113 D1
Woodbury EX5 . . 184 C2
Broadway Ave TQ12 . . 207 D7
Broadway Hill EX2 . . 176 E3
Broadway La EX33 . . 7 D3
Broadway Rd TQ12 . . 207 C7
Broadways Head EX14, TA20 . . 68 F6
Broadway The
Exmouth EX8 . . 202 E8
Plymouth PL9 . . 255 E7
Broad Wlk PL12 . . 242 E1
BROADWOODKELLY . . 76 D8
BROADWOODWIDGER . . 106 B8
Broadwoodwidger Prim Sch PL16 . . 91 A4
Broady Strap EX31 . . 153 F5
Brockenbarrow La EX31 . . 11 C4
BROCKFIELD . . 88 A8
Brock Ho 8 PL4 . . 263 A2
Brockhole La
Plymouth PL7 . . 250 E8
Tatworth EX13, TA20 . . 88 B7
Brockhurst Pk TQ3 . . 218 D2
Brockington's Rd EX5 . . 99 C8
Brockley Rd PL3 . . 249 C4
BROCKSCOMBE . . 92 A5
Brockscombe Cross EX21 . . 91 F5
Brocks Cross EX17 . . 79 A2
Brocks La
Heathfield TQ12 . . 123 C2
Millbrook PL10 . . 252 F5
Brockton Gdns PL6 . . 245 B6
Brodick Cl EX4 . . 173 D1
Bromhead Ct PL6 . . 249 A8
Bromley Ho 6 PL2 . . 248 A4
Bromley Pl 5 PL2 . . 248 A4
Bronescombe Ave TQ14 . . 209 A8
Bronshill Ho TQ1 . . 220 B6
Bronshill Mews TQ1 . . 220 B6
Bronshill Rd TQ1 . . 220 B6
Bronte Pl PL5 . . 244 D1
BROOK . . 171 B2
Brook Cl
Bovey Tracey TQ13 . . 180 C7
Exeter EX1 . . 178 B8
Holcombe EX7 . . 210 E8
Plymouth PL7 . . 251 A3
Sidford EX10 . . 101 B1
Brook Ct
Aveton Gifford TQ7 . . 143 C6
Barnstaple EX31 . . 154 B3
Brookdale EX11 . . 169 E4
Brookdale Ave EX34 . . 150 A5
Brookdale Cl TQ5 . . 230 B4
Brookdale Ct
Brixham TQ5 . . 230 B4
Exeter EX2 . . 178 A2
Brookdale Pk TQ5 . . 230 B4
Brookdale Terr
8 Barnstaple EX32 . . 155 B4
18 Dawlish EX7 . . 204 E6
Brookdown Terr PL12 . . 242 E3
Brookdown Villas PL12 . . 242 E3
Brooke Ave EX2 . . 177 F3
Brooke Cl
Saltash PL12 . . 243 A2
Sampford Courtenay EX20 . . 76 F3
Brookedor TQ12 . . 212 F5
Brookedor Gdns TQ12 . . 212 F5
Brooke Rd EX16 . . 46 E1
Brookesby Hall TQ1 . . 220 D3
Brookfield EX39 . . 25 E4
Brookfield Cl
6 Braunton EX33 . . 152 D5
Kingsteignton TQ12 . . 207 E7
Paignton TQ3 . . 226 C8
Plymouth PL7 . . 251 B5
Brookfield Cotts EX8 . . 195 D5
Brookfield Ct 1 TQ13 . . 123 F6
Brookfield Dr
7 Colyton EX24 . . 103 A4
Teignmouth TQ14 . . 210 C7
Brookfield Gdns EX2 . . 177 B1
Brookfield Ho TQ3 . . 226 C8
Brookfield Pl EX34 . . 150 B5
Brookfield Rd EX9 . . 198 B6
Brookfields Cl PL1 . . 247 F1
Brookfield St 8 EX39 . . 157 B1
Brook Green Ctr for Learning PL5 . . 244 B4
Brook Green Terr EX4 . . 261 C4
Brook Haven Cl TQ12 . . 212 F5
Brookhayes Cl EX8 . . 202 B8
Brookhill TQ6 . . 234 B2
Brookhill Gdns EX13 . . 167 E6
Brook Ho EX7 . . 204 C6
BROOKING . . 135 F3
Brooking Barn TQ9 . . 139 F8
Brooking Cl PL6 . . 249 A8
Brookingfield Cl PL7 . . 250 C5
Brooking Way PL12 . . 242 C3
Brook La
Calverleigh EX16 . . 48 F2
Colaton Raleigh EX9 . . 186 D2
Shaldon TQ14 . . 209 D5
3 Sidford EX10 . . 101 B1
Tavistock PL19 . . 171 B2
Washfield EX16 . . 48 F1
Brooklands
24 Dawlish EX7 . . 204 D6
Exeter EX2 . . 177 F2
Tavistock PL19 . . 171 D6
Totnes TQ9 . . 223 D5
Brooklands Cross EX10 . . 100 C1
Brooklands Ct PL6 . . 244 E3
Brooklands Farm Cl EX13 . . 103 D8
Brooklands La TQ2 . . 219 E4
Brooklands Orch
Kilmington EX13 . . 103 D8
Ottery St Mary EX11 . . 169 E4
Brooklands Rd
Exmouth EX8 . . 196 D1
Rockwell Green TA21 . . 160 B5
Brookland Terr EX11 . . 169 E3
Brook Lane Cotts TQ13 . . 121 B3
Brooklea La TQ7 . . 145 A1
Brookleigh Ave EX1 . . 178 B5
Brooklyn Ct EX1 . . 178 D6
Brooklyn Pk EX8 . . 196 C1
Brookman Ct 1 TQ3 . . 225 E8
Brook Mdw
Exmouth EX8 . . 196 C1
Newton Poppleford EX10 . . 186 F8
South Molton EX36 . . 158 D4
Brook Mead PL8 . . 257 E4
Brook Orch TQ12 . . 212 F4
Brook Rd
Budleigh Salterton EX9 . . 199 G2
Cullompton EX15 . . 163 B2
Dolton EX19 . . 57 F7
Ipplepen TQ12 . . 211 D2
Ivybridge PL21 . . 237 D5
Brooks Ave EX22 . . 164 B5
Brooks Hill EX15 . . 66 C8
Brookside
Barnstaple EX31 . . 154 A3
Broadhembury EX14 . . 84 C7
Kingsbridge TQ7 . . 258 C4
Pathfinder Village EX6 . . 98 C4
Sidmouth EX10 . . 188 A7
Brookside Cl
Heybrook Bay PL9 . . 140 A7
Kilmington EX13 . . 87 C1
Teignmouth TQ14 . . 210 A5
Brookside Cres EX4 . . 174 B2
Brookside Ind Units EX4 . . 174 D1
Brookside Units EX4 . . 98 D4
Brookside Villas 23 EX34 . . 3 A3
Brooks Pl TA21 . . 160 E6
Brook St
Bampton EX16 . . 34 B1
Dawlish EX7 . . 204 D6
Ottery St Mary EX11 . . 169 E3
Slapton TQ7 . . 145 C3
Tavistock PL19 . . 171 C6
16 Teignmouth TQ14 . . 210 C5
Brooks Warren 15 EX5 . . 99 A6
Brook Terr EX12 . . 192 D7
Brook The PL12 . . 242 E4
Brookvale Orch TQ14 . . 209 D4
Brook View TQ9 . . 222 F6
Brookway EX1 . . 178 C7
Brook Way
Exeter EX4 . . 174 E2
Kingsteignton TQ12 . . 123 F1
Brookwood Cl 4 TQ10 . . 134 F3
Brookwood Rd PL9 . . 256 D7
Broomball Cross TA22 . . 32 F5
Broomball La EX16 . . 32 E5
Broomborough Ct TQ9 . . 223 B5
Broomborough Dr TQ9 . . 223 A5
Broom Cl
Dawlish EX7 . . 204 F8
Exeter EX2 . . 178 A5
Broome Cl EX13 . . 167 E6
Broomfield Dr PL9 . . 255 C5
Broomham Cross EX37 . . 45 A7
BROOMHILL . . 133 F1
Broom Hill
Chagford TQ13 . . 111 A6
Saltash PL12 . . 242 D2
Broomhill Cross
Chilsworthy EX22 . . 53 B3
Copplestone EX17 . . 79 A4
Broomhill Rd EX16 . . 161 B4
Broomhill Sculpture Gdns★ EX31 . . 16 E7

Broomhill Villas EX32 . 18 E5
Broomhill Way TQ2 . . 213 E1
Broomhouse La EX36 . . 30 A2
Broomhouse Pk EX16 . 46 E1
Broom La EX13 . . . . 88 C5
Broom Pk
Dartington TQ9 . . . . 215 E1
Okehampton EX20 . . . . 170 E6
Plymouth PL9 . . . . 255 D5
[20] Rockbeare EX5 . . . . . 99 A6
Torquay TQ2 . . . . 213 F3
Broom's La TA3 . . . . 68 C7
Broomstreet La TA24 . . . 6 F4
Broughton Cl PL3 . . . . 248 F7
Brow Hill TQ12 . . . . 123 B2
Brown Down La
Churchinford TA20 . . . . . 68 F7
Churchinford TA20 . . . . . 69 A7
Browne Memorial
Almshouses PL19 . . . 171 A5
BROWNHEATH 52 C2
Brownhill La PL9 . . . . . 140 D8
Brownhills Rd TQ12 . . 207 A3
Brownie Cross PL7 . . . 132 C3
Browning Cl EX2 . . . . . 178 A4
Browning Rd PL2 . . . . 248 A5
Brownings End TQ12 206 F1
Brownings Mead
EX6 . . . . 112 F7
Brownings Wlk TQ12 206 F1
Brownlands Cl EX10 . . 188 C5
Brownlands Rd EX10 . 188 C5
Brownlees EX6 . . . . . . 182 A4
Brownlow St PL1 . . . . 262 A2
Brown's Bridge La
EX15 . . . . 65 B7
Browns Bridge Rd
TQ2 . . . . 213 D2
Brownscombe Cl
TQ3 . . . . 218 D2
Brown's Ct EX6 . . . . . . 114 C4
Brownsey La TA20 . . . . 69 C5
Brown's Hill TQ6 . . . . . 233 F3
Brown's Hill Head
EX37 . . . . 27 F2
BROWNSTON 137 F3
Brownston Cross
TQ10 . . . . 135 F5
Brownstone Cross
EX17 . . . . 61 C3
Brownstone Moor Cross
EX17 . . . . 61 D4
Brownstone Rd TQ6 . . 234 E3
Brownston St PL21 . . . 137 B2
Brownswell La
Holbeton PL7 . . . . 136 E1
Holbeton PL8 . . . . 142 B8
Broxfords Hill EX17 . . . 80 C7
Broxton Dr PL9 . . . . . . 249 E1
Bruckland La EX12,
EX13 . . . . 103 D3
Bruckton Cross TQ6 . . 232 F6
Brunel Ave
Plymouth PL2 . . . . 247 F5
Torquay TQ2 . . . . 214 B4
Brunel Cl
Exeter EX4 . . . . 177 A7
Teignmouth TQ14 . . . . . 210 C6
Brunel Ct [16] EX7 . . . . . 204 E6
Brunel Ind Est TQ12 . . 207 D3
Brunel Mews TQ2 . . . . 219 F4
Brunel Prim Sch
PL12 . . . . 242 E2
Brunel Rd
Cullompton EX15 . . . . . 163 E4
Newton Abbot TQ12 . . . 207 D3
Paignton TQ4 . . . . 229 D6
Saltash PL12 . . . . 242 C4
Starcross EX6 . . . . 201 A8
Brunel Terr [3] PL2 . . . . 247 F5
Brunel Vw EX6 . . . . 182 B5
Brunel Way
Ivybridge PL21 . . . . 237 E6
Plymouth PL1 . . . . 262 A2
Brunenburg Way
EX13 . . . . 167 D4
Brunswick Ho [2]
TQ12 . . . . 207 B4
Brunswick Pl
Dawlish EX7 . . . . 204 E6
[10] Plymouth PL2 . . . . . . 247 F4
Brunswick Rd PL4 . . . . 263 B2
Brunswick Sq [4] TQ1 219 F6
Brunswick St
Exeter EX4 . . . . 177 A5
Teignmouth TQ14 . . . . . 210 C4
Brunswick Terr TQ1 . . 219 F6
BRUSHFORD
Bondleigh 59 D2
Dulverton 33 D4
Brushford La
Chevithorne EX16 . . . . . . 49 F3
Chulmleigh EX18 . . . . . . 59 D2
Brushford New Rd
TA22 . . . . 33 E4
Brymon Wy PL6 . . . . . . 245 B4
Brynmoor Cl PL3 . . . . . 249 A7
Brynmoor Pk PL3 . . . . . 249 A6
Brynmoor Wlk PL3 . . . . 249 A6
Brynsworthy Ct [7]
EX31 . . . . 154 A2
Brynsworthy La EX31 154 A1
Brynsworthy Lawn [8]
EX31 . . . . 154 A2
Brynsworthy Pk EX31 154 B3
Bsns Ctr The PL4 . . . . 263 C2
Buchanan Cl EX14 . . . . 166 B4
Buckerall Cross EX14 . 84 F2
BUCKERELL 85 A3
Buckerell Ave EX2 . . . 177 E3
Buckeridge Ave
TQ14 . . . . 210 B6
Buckeridge Rd
Exmouth EX8 . . . . 202 E7
Teignmouth TQ14 . . . . . 210 B6
Buckeridge Twrs [2]
TQ14 . . . . 210 B6
BUCKFAST 236 B7
Buckfast Cl
Buckfast TQ11 . . . . 236 C6
Ivybridge PL21 . . . . 237 D4
Plymouth PL2 . . . . 248 A8
BUCKFASTLEIGH 236 C5
Buckfastleigh Prim Sch
TQ11 . . . . 236 B5
Buckfastleigh Sta★
TQ11 . . . . 236 D5
Buckfast Rd TQ11 . . . . 236 C6
Buckfast (St Mary's)
Abbey★ TQ11 . . . . 236 C7
Buckgrove Cotts EX38 . 42 B6
Buckham Cross EX36 . . 45 D7
Buckham Hill EX36 . . . . 45 D7
BUCKHORN 72 D2
Buckhouse La EX24 . . 102 C7
Buckingham Cl
Exmouth EX8 . . . . 202 E7
South Molton EX36 . . . . 158 C3
Buckingham Orch
TQ13 . . . . 123 C4
Buckingham Pl PL5 . . 243 E2
Buckingham Rd EX2 . 178 D3
BUCKLAND
Newton Abbot 207 E3
Thurlestone 143 B2
Buckland Abbey★
PL20 . . . . 126 C1
Buckland Brake
TQ12 . . . . 207 E2
BUCKLAND BREWER . . 40 C7
Buckland Brewer Com
Prim Sch EX39 . . . . 40 C7
Buckland Cl
Bideford EX39 . . . . 25 E4
Plymouth PL7 . . . . 250 D7
Buckland Cross
Braunton EX33 . . . . 152 C8
Slapton TQ7 . . . . 145 C6
BUCKLAND FILLEIGH . 56 A4
Buckland Hall TQ13 . . 130 D7
BUCKLAND IN THE
MOOR 130 C8
BUCKLAND
MONACHORUM 126 D3
Buckland Rd
Caddsdown EX39 . . . . . . 25 D4
Georgeham EX33 . . . . 8 B3
Netherton TQ12 . . . . . . 208 A4
Newton Abbot TQ12 . . . 207 F4
BUCKLAND ST MARY . 69 C8
Buckland St Mary CE
Prim Sch TA20 . . . . 69 D8
Buckland St PL1 . . . . . 262 B2
Buckland Terr PL20 . . 126 F2
BUCKLAND-TOUT-
SAINTS 144 C4
Buckland View
Bideford EX39 . . . . 156 F2
Buckland Brewer EX39 . . 40 B7
Newton Abbot TQ12 . . . 207 D4
Buckland Wlk EX6 . . . 181 F5
BUCKLEIGH 156 D6
Buckleigh Cross
EX39 . . . . 156 C6
Buckleigh Grange
EX39 . . . . 156 C6
Buckleigh Rd EX39 . . . 156 C5
Buckle Rise EX1 . . . . . 175 B1
Buckley Cross EX10 . . 101 C1
Buckley Rd EX10 . . . . . 101 C2
Buckley St TQ8 . . . . . . 259 E5
Bucknall Cl EX12 . . . . 190 D4
Bucknell Way EX36 . . 158 C7
Bucknill Cl EX6 . . . . . . 182 A4
Bucknole Cross EX14 102 A8
Bucknole Hill Rd
EX24 . . . . 102 A7
Bucks Cl TQ13 . . . . 180 D7
BUCK'S CROSS 24 A1
Buckshots Cross EX14 69 A4
Bucks La [4] TQ13 . . . . 180 D7
BUCK'S MILLS 24 B2
Buckthorn Ct TQ12 . . . 244 C6
Buckton La EX10 . . . . . 101 C1
Buckwell TA21 . . . . 160 E6
Buckwell Cl TQ7 . . . . . 258 D6
Buckwell Rd TQ7 . . . . . 258 D6
Buckwell St PL1, PL4 . 263 A2
Buctor Pk PL19 . . . . . . 126 A8
Budbrook La EX6 . . . . . 96 F3
Buddle Cl
Ivybridge PL21 . . . . 237 E5
Plymouth PL9 . . . . 256 A5
Tavistock PL19 . . . . 171 B6
Buddle La
Exeter EX4 . . . . 176 F5
Hatherleigh EX20 . . . . . . 75 C7
Bude Hill EX19 . . . . 59 A3
Bude Moor Cross
EX19 . . . . 76 D7
Bude Rd EX22 . . . . 164 B5
Bude St
Appledore EX39 . . . . 15 A1
Exeter EX4 . . . . 261 B3
Bude-Stratton Business
Pk EX23 . . . . 70 A8
Budge Mdws PL15 . . . 115 A4
Budgetts TA21 . . . . 52 F6
Budgett's Cross TA21 . 52 F6
BUDLAKE 82 E3
Budlake Cross EX24 . 101 F6
Budlake Old Post Office★
EX5 . . . . 82 D2
Budlake Rd EX2 . . . . . 177 C1
Budlake Units EX2 . . . 177 C1
Budleigh Cl
Plymouth PL9 . . . . 255 F5
Torquay TQ1 . . . . 220 D6
Budleigh Hill EX9 . . . . 198 B5
BUDLEIGH
SALTERTON 198 A2
Budshead Gn PL5 . . . . 244 C4
Budshead Rd PL5 . . . . 244 C4
Budshead Way PL5 . . . 244 E2
Budshead Wood Nature
Reserve★ PL5 . . . . . . 244 A4
Buena Vista Cl PL6 . . . 245 D6
Buena Vista Dr PL6 . . 245 C6
Buena Vista Gdns
PL6 . . . . 245 C6
Buena Vista Way
PL6 . . . . 245 C6
BUGFORD 10 C5
Bugford Cross TQ6 . . 232 C3
Bugford La TQ6 . . . . . . 232 D3
Bugford Lane End
TQ6 . . . . 232 D3
Bughead Cross TQ13 111 D4
Bughole La TA21 . . . . . . 51 E8
Bugle Pl TQ12 . . . . 206 C5
Building's Cross
EX17 . . . . 63 A4
Bulford TA21 . . . . 160 D5
Bulford La
Kennford EX6 . . . . 181 A2
Wellington TA21 . . . . . . 160 D5
Bulgis Pk EX36 . . . . . . 158 B5
Bulkamore Cross TQ10 . 135 E5
BULKWORTHY 39 F1
Bullaford Gate EX36 . . . 31 E4
Bulland Cross EX20 . . . 76 E4
Bulland La
Poughill EX17 . . . . 62 D3
Sampford Courtenay
EX20 . . . . 76 F4
Bullands Cl [4] TQ13 . . 180 C8
Bullaton Cross TQ13 . 112 E1
Bull Ct EX31 . . . . 154 F5
Bulleid Cl PL2 . . . . 247 F7
Bulleigh Barton Farm
Units TQ12 . . . . 218 B8
Bulleigh Cross TQ12 . 218 B8
Bulleigh Elms Cross
TQ12 . . . . 212 A1
Bullens Cl EX5 . . . . 81 E4
Bullen St EX5 . . . . 81 E5
Buller Cl
Cullompton EX15 . . . . . 163 C4
Plymouth PL7 . . . . 250 F4
Torpoint PL11 . . . . 247 A3
Buller Ct EX2 . . . . 177 A4
Buller Pk PL12 . . . . 242 D3
Buller Rd
[11] Barnstaple EX32 . . . 155 A5
Crediton EX17 . . . . 165 B6
Exeter EX4 . . . . 177 A5
Newton Abbot TQ12 . . . 207 D2
Torpoint PL11 . . . . 247 B3
Bullers Hill EX6 . . . . . . 113 F3
Bullfinch Cl EX15 . . . . 163 A2
Bullhead Cross EX19 . . 58 B2
Bull Hill
Barnstaple EX31 . . . . . . 154 F7
Bideford EX39 . . . . 157 A1
Bullhorn Cross TQ7 . . 142 F6
Bull Meadow Rd EX2 . 261 B2
Bullow View EX19 . . . . . 58 F2
Bull Ring TQ13 . . . . . . 130 F4
Bulls Ct [11] EX24 . . . . . 103 A4
Bull's La TA20 . . . . 88 C8
Bully Shoot Cross
EX24 . . . . 103 A3
Bulmer Rd PL4 . . . . 263 C3
Bulmoor Cross EX13 . 103 F5
Bulsworthy La PL15 . . 105 B2
Bulteel Gdns PL6 . . . . 244 E7
BULVERTON 187 F6
Bulverton Pk EX10 . . . 187 F6
Bulwark Cl TQ12 . . . . . 244 D2
Bulworthy Cross EX16 . 47 E5
Bulworthy Knap EX16 . 47 E5
Bumpston Cross
TQ11 . . . . 215 C7
Bungalows The
Axminster EX13 . . . . . . 167 C4
Dawlish Warren EX7 . . . 201 B2
[4] Tiverton EX16 . . . . . . 161 C3
Bunkers Farm TQ9 . . . 144 E7
Bunker Square EX2 . . 178 D2
Bun La [8] TQ14 . . . . . . 210 B4
Bunneford Cross EX15 64 E1
Bunn Rd EX8 . . . . 196 D4
Bunny Burrow's Track
Bury TA22 . . . . 33 F7
Bury TA22 . . . . 34 A7
Hartford TA4 . . . . 34 A8
Bunson Gate EX18 . . . . 45 A4
Bunting Cl
Newton Abbot TQ12 . . . 207 A1
Teignmouth TQ14 . . . . . 210 A5
Buntings The EX6 . . . . 181 F4
Bunts La EX12 . . . . 191 F7
Bunyan Cl PL5 . . . . 244 C2
Burch Cl EX8 . . . . 196 E2
Burches Cross EX16 . . . 48 A1
Burch Gdns EX7 . . . . . 200 E1
Burchills Cl TA21 . . . . . 160 A6
Burchill's Hill TA21 . . 160 B7
Burcombe Hill EX36 . . 158 E8
Burdon La EX21 . . . . 74 C7
BURFORD 23 C1
Burgage TA21 . . . . 160 D6
Burgh Island Cswy
TQ7 . . . . 142 E3
Burgmanns Hill EX8 . 195 D5
Burke Rd TQ9 . . . . 223 D6
Burland Cross EX31 . . . . 9 B4
Burland La EX33 . . . . 8 F1
Burlands The EX14 . . . . 84 D2
Burleigh La
Malborough TQ7 . . . . . . 147 E7
Plymouth PL3 . . . . 248 D7
Burleigh Lane End
TQ7 . . . . 147 E8
Burleigh Manor PL3 . . 248 D7
Burleigh Park Rd
PL3 . . . . 248 D6
Burleigh Rd TQ2 . . . . . 219 C7
BURLESCOMBE 51 B3
Burlescombe CE Prim
Sch EX16 . . . . 51 B3
BURLESTONE 145 D7
Burlington Cl EX32 . . . 155 B3
Burlington Gr EX32 . . 155 B2
Burnard Cl PL6 . . . . . . 244 E7
Burnards Cl [15] EX24 . . 103 A4
Burnards Field Rd
EX24 . . . . 103 A4
Burnbreach Cnr
EX24 . . . . 102 B2
Burnbridge Hill EX16 . . 63 D2
Burne Cross TQ12 . . . . 131 D6
Burnet Cl EX2 . . . . 178 C3
Burnet Rd TQ12 . . . . . . 206 C5
Burnett Cl PL12 . . . . . . 242 D2
Burnett Rd PL6 . . . . . . 248 F8
Burnham Cl EX12 . . . . . 192 A8
Burnham Ct TQ12 . . . . 207 E7
Burnham Park Rd
PL3 . . . . 248 D6
Burniston Cl PL7 . . . . . 251 A3
Burnistone Cl PL7 . . . 251 A3
Burn La
Lydford PL19 . . . . 107 C1
North Brentor PL19 . . . 117 C8
Burnley Cl TQ12 . . . . . 206 D4
Burnley Rd TQ12 . . . . . 206 D4
Burn River Rise TQ2 . . 219 B8
Burns Ave
Exeter EX2 . . . . 177 F3
Plymouth PL5 . . . . 244 C2
Burns Ct EX7 . . . . 204 E5
Burnside EX8 . . . . 196 B1
Burnside Rd EX34 . . . . 150 A3
Burns La [13] PL21 . . . . 137 B2
Burnsome La EX14,
EX15 . . . . 67 B5
Burnthouse Cross
EX14 . . . . 67 B5
Burnthouse Hill
TQ12 . . . . 212 E1
Burnthouse La EX2 . . . 177 F3
Burnt Mdws EX6 . . . . . 113 D5
Burnt Oak EX10 . . . . . . 101 B1
BURRATON
Ermington 136 D3
St Dominick 125 A2
Saltash 242 D4
Burraton Com Prim Sch
PL12 . . . . 242 C3
BURRATON
COOMBE 242 C2
Burraton Cross PL21 . 136 D4
Burraton Rd PL12 . . . . 242 C4
Burrator Arboretum★
PL20 . . . . 127 E3
Burrator Ave PL20 . . . 128 A8
Burrator Dr EX4 . . . . . . 176 E8
Burrator Rd PL20 . . . . 127 B3
BURRIDGE 16 E6
Burridge Ave TQ2 . . . . 219 D5
Burridge Cross EX18 . . 58 F8
Burridge La
Chawleigh EX17 . . . . 60 E7
Torquay TQ2 . . . . 220 A5
Burridge Moor Cross
EX18 . . . . 60 E6
Burridge Rd
Torquay TQ2 . . . . 219 D5
Upton Pyne EX5 . . . . . . 173 B8
BURRINGTON 43 F3
Burrington Bsns Pk
PL2 . . . . 244 A1
Burrington CE Prim Sch
EX37 . . . . 43 F3
Burrington Dr EX17 . . . 80 E4
Burrington Ind Est
PL5 . . . . 244 A1
Burrington Moor Cross
EX37 . . . . 43 C3
Burrington Rd PL5 . . . 244 A1
Burrington Way PL5 . . 244 B1
Burrough Fields EX5 . . 99 A6
Burrough Lawn
EX39 . . . . 157 A6
Burrough Rd EX39 . . . 157 A6
Burrough Way TA21 . . 160 D4
BURROW
Broadclyst 175 E8
Newton Poppleford 186 C8
Burrow Ct EX10 . . . . . . 186 D8
Burrow Cl EX10 . . . . . . 186 D8
Burrow Cnr
Butterleigh EX16 . . . . . . 64 C4
Dalwood EX13 . . . . 86 F2
Burrow Cross
Budlake EX5 . . . . 82 E1
Burrow EX5 . . . . 175 E7
Meshaw EX17 . . . . 46 A4
Monkokehampton EX19 . 76 A8
Burrow Ctyd EX16 . . . . . 64 C4
Burrowe The [2]
EX17 . . . . 165 C5
Burrow Farm Gdns★
EX13 . . . . 87 A2
Burrow Hill PL9 . . . . . 255 E6
Burrow Knap EX13 . . . . 87 A2
Burrow Knap Way
EX13 . . . . 86 F2
Burrow La
Ashbrittle TA21 . . . . 50 D8
Bow EX17 . . . . 78 A5
Newton Poppleford
EX10 . . . . 186 D8
Burrowplot Cross
EX17 . . . . 59 F2
Burrow Rd
Burrow EX5 . . . . 175 E8
[10] Ilfracombe EX34 . . . 150 B5
Seaton EX12 . . . . 192 B4
Burrows Cl EX33 . . . . . 152 C5
Burrows Close La
EX33 . . . . 15 A7
Burrowshot Cross
EX13 . . . . 104 B7
Burrows La EX39 . . . . . . 14 F1
Burrows Pk EX33 . . . . . 152 C5
Burrows Way EX39 . . . 156 F8
Burrow The [1] EX12 . . 192 B4
Burscombe La EX10 . . 101 A1
Burscott EX39 . . . . 23 D3
Bursdon Moor Cross
EX39 . . . . 37 E7
Bursledon Ct EX7 . . . . 204 F6
BURSTON 78 B5
Burston Cross EX17 . . . 78 B4
Burston La EX16 . . . . . . 34 A4
Burton Acad The
TQ2 . . . . 213 E2
Burton Art Gallery & Mus
The★ EX39 . . . . 157 A3
Burton Cl PL6 . . . . 245 B6
Burton Pl TQ5 . . . . 230 C4
Burton Rd EX39 . . . . . . 156 E1
Burton St TQ5 . . . . 230 C3
Burton Villa Cl TQ5 . . . 230 C4
Burvill St EX35 . . . . . . 151 B5
Burwell Cl PL6 . . . . 245 E4
Burwell La EX36 . . . . 30 F7
Burwood La EX38 . . . . 159 F5
Burwood Mews EX38 159 F4
Burwood Rd EX38 . . . . 159 E5
BURY 34 A6
Bury Cross
Lapford EX17 . . . . 60 D2
Petrockstow EX20 . . . . . . 56 F5
Bury Hill TA22 . . . . 33 F7
Bury Rd
Bury TA22 . . . . 34 A6
Dulverton TA22 . . . . 33 F6
Newton Abbot TQ12 . . . 207 B4
Bury The EX5 . . . . 81 E5
Buscombe La EX31 . . . . 11 E2
Bushayes Cnr EX3 . . . 183 C6
Bush Cnr EX18 . . . . 58 F8
Bush Cross EX18 . . . . . . 58 F8
Bushell Rd TQ12 . . . . . 207 A4
Bushes La EX12, DT7 . 193 B7
Bushmead Ave TQ12 . 213 A5
Bushmead Cl TQ2 . . . 213 A5
Bush Pk PL6 . . . . 245 F3
Busland La EX16 . . . . . . 63 D4
Bussel Cl EX4 . . . . 174 F3
Bussell's Moor Cross
EX36 . . . . 32 C4
Butcher Park Hill
PL19 . . . . 171 B7
Butcher's Moor La
EX19 . . . . 58 E4
Butchers Row EX31 . . 154 F5
Butcombe La EX17 . . . . 61 D1
Bute Rd PL4 . . . . 249 A4
Butlakes La EX24 . . . . 101 F6
Butland Ave TQ3 . . . . . 219 C1
Butland Mdw PL19 . . . 126 C3
Butland Rd TQ12 . . . . . 207 D8
Butlands Ind Est
TQ12 . . . . 211 F2
Butler Cl
Plymouth PL6 . . . . 245 B6
Tiverton EX16 . . . . 161 E3
Butler Way EX14 . . . . . . 86 A6
Buttercombe Cl
TQ12 . . . . 211 F8
Buttercombe La
Braunton EX33 . . . . 15 E8
Knowle EX31, EX34 . . . . . 8 F1
West Down EX34 . . . . 8 E5
Buttercup Cl EX12 . . . . 192 B8
Buttercup Mdw PL15 105 A2
Buttercup Rd
Plymouth PL6 . . . . 245 B2
Willand EX15 . . . . 162 E5
Buttercup Way TQ12 . 206 C5
Butterdon Wlk PL21 . . 237 F5
Butterdown PL12 . . . . 242 B3
Butterfly La TQ12 . . . . 209 C2
Butterlake TQ3 . . . . . . 218 D3
BUTTERLEIGH 64 C3
Butterleigh Dr EX16 . . 161 E3
Buttermere Ct EX4 . . . 176 F5
Buttermoor Cross
EX16 . . . . 48 D3
Butterpark PL21 . . . . . 237 D5
Buttery Cl EX14 . . . . . . 166 C4
Buttery Rd EX14 . . . . . 166 C4
Buttgarden St EX39 . . 157 A1
Buttle's Cross TA3 . . . . 68 C7
Buttle's La TA3 . . . . 68 B6
Button La
Bratton Fleming EX31 . . . 11 A1
Ivybridge PL21 . . . . 237 E4
Butt Park Rd PL5 . . . . . 244 B3
Butt Parks EX17 . . . . . . 165 D4
Butt Pk
Hennock TQ13 . . . . 123 B7
Stokenham TQ7 . . . . 145 B1
Butts Cl
Bridford EX6 . . . . 112 F5
Chawleigh EX18 . . . . 60 B7
Honiton EX14 . . . . 166 B4
Witheridge EX16 . . . . 46 E1
Butts Cross
Buckfastleigh TQ11 . . . . 135 B6
Cornworthy TQ9 . . . . . . 227 C3
Butts Ct EX2 . . . . 178 A5
Buttsford Terr PL21 . . 136 B6
Butts Hill
Kenton EX6 . . . . 194 D3
Paignton TQ3 . . . . 225 B8
Butt's Hill EX11 . . . . . . 169 E4
Buttshill Cross TQ3 . . 225 B8
Butts La
Christow EX6 . . . . 113 B3
Ideford TQ13 . . . . 124 B4
Kenton EX6 . . . . 194 D1
Starcross EX6 . . . . 200 D8
Buttsons Cl TQ7 . . . . . . 145 B1
Butts Park Ct PL8 . . . . 141 A7
Butts Path EX33 . . . . . . 152 D6
Butts Pk PL8 . . . . 141 A7
Butts Rd
Exeter EX2 . . . . 178 A5
Ottery St Mary EX11 . . . 169 E4
Butts The
Colyton EX24 . . . . 103 A4
Loddiswell TQ7 . . . . 143 E8
Newton Ferrers PL8 . . . 141 A7
Butts Way EX20 . . . . 77 C4
Buzzacott Cl EX34 . . . . . . 3 B2
Buzzacott La EX34 . . . . . 3 B2
Buzzard Rd PL19 . . . . . 171 D2
Buzzard Rise PL18 . . . 125 C5
Buzzard Way EX5 . . . . . 99 B6
Byard Cl PL5 . . . . 243 E1
Bycott La EX18 . . . . 45 B4
Bydown Cross EX32 . . . 28 D8
Bye Cross EX33 . . . . 8 B3
Byes Cl EX10 . . . . 188 C8
Byeside Rd EX10 . . . . . 188 C8
Byes La EX10 . . . . 188 D8
Bygones (Mus)★
TQ1 . . . . 220 C8
Byland Rd PL3 . . . . 249 A6
Byng Cl TQ12 . . . . 207 F4
Byron Ave PL5 . . . . 244 C2
Byron Cl EX31 . . . . 154 F7
Byron Rd
Exeter EX2 . . . . 178 C5
Torquay TQ1 . . . . 220 A8
Byron Way EX8 . . . . . . 196 C3
Bystock Cl EX4 . . . . 261 A4
Bystock Mews EX8 . . . 196 E3
Bystock Rd EX8 . . . . . . 196 D4
Bystock Terr EX4 . . . . 261 A4
Byter Mill La TQ9 . . . . 228 A7
Byways Cl EX31 . . . . . . 153 F5

C

Cabbage Hill TQ13 . . . 130 F4
Cabbage La EX14 . . . . . 85 A3
Cabot Cl PL12 . . . . 242 E2
Cabourg Cl TQ8 . . . . . . 259 D5
CADBURY 81 D7
Cadbury Cres EX1 . . . . 178 D7
Cadbury Cross EX17 . . . 81 C8
Cadbury Gdns EX9 . . . 198 B6
Caddecleave La
Kentisbury EX31 . . . . 3 E1
Kentisbury EX31 . . . . 10 E6
Caddiford Cross EX17 . 97 B6
Cadditon Cross EX20 . . 76 F7
Caddsdown Ind Pk
EX39 . . . . 25 D4
Caddy Pl EX2 . . . . 178 D2
Caddywell La EX38 . . . 159 E5
Caddywell Mdw
EX38 . . . . 159 E5
CADELEIGH 63 D3
Cades Gdns TA21 . . . . 160 E7
Cades Mead TA21 . . . . 160 F7
Cadewell Cres TQ2 . . . 213 D1
Cadewell La TQ2 . . . . . 219 C8
Cadewell Park Rd
TQ2 . . . . 213 C1
Cadewell Pk Rd TQ2 . 213 C1
Cadford La EX19 . . . . . . 59 B3
Cadhay Cl EX11 . . . . . . 169 B3
Cadhay House★
EX11 . . . . 169 B5
Cadhay La EX11 . . . . . . 169 B4
Cadlake La EX20 . . . . . . 77 A3
Cadleigh Cl PL21 . . . . . 136 D6

Cadleigh Court La EX16 63 D2
Cadleigh Cross PL21 136 D7
Cadleigh La PL21 136 D6
CADLEIGHPARK 136 D6
Cadover Bridge Rd PL20 132 D7
Cadover Cl PL6 245 A1
Cadway Cl EX11 169 B3
Cadwell Rd TQ3 226 B7
Caen Com Prim Sch 7 EX33 152 D6
Caen Field EX33 152 D6
Caen Field Sh Ctr 6 EX33 152 D6
Caen Gdns EX33 152 D6
Caen Ho 1 EX33 152 D6
Caen St EX33 152 D6
Caen View EX33 152 C5
Caernarvon Gdns PL2 248 B7
Caesars Ct EX20 170 D7
Caffyns Cross EX35 5 A4
Cairn Rd EX34 150 B4
Cairnside EX34 1 F3
Cairn Side EX34 150 B3
Cake Down La EX36 158 E4
Calder Cl PL3 249 B6
Caldicot Gdns PL6 245 C8
Caledonia Cl 1 PL7 251 B5
Calf St EX38 159 D5
California Cl EX4 173 D3
California Cross PL21 138 A3
California Gdns PL3 249 D6
Callard's La EX36 30 E1
Caller's La EX15 52 D1
Callington Rd
Gulworthy PL19 125 F7
Saltash PL12 242 E3
Tavistock PL19 171 A4
CALSTOCK 125 D3
Calstock Cl PL2 248 C8
Calstock Com Prim Sch PL12 125 D3
Calstock Rd PL18 125 D6
Calstock Sta PL18 125 D3
Calthorpe Rd EX4 177 F8
Calvados 18 EX32 155 A5
Calvados Cl 20 TQ13 123 E6
Calvados Pk TQ12 207 F7
CALVERLEIGH 48 E1
Calverleigh Cross EX16 48 C1
Calvesford Cl EX38 159 E6
Calvesford Cross EX38 159 E5
Calvesford Rd EX38 159 E6
Calvez Cl PL10 252 F6
Cambercombe Terr 5 EX34 150 D5
Camber Rd PL1 262 A1
Cambian Devon Sch TQ3 225 E4
Camborne Cl PL5 244 A5
Camborne Cres TQ4 229 B8
Cambrian Cl TQ4 225 D4
Cambric Chase PL21 237 D6
Cambridge Gr 3 EX34 150 C5
Cambridge Lane W 5 PL1 262 B3
Cambridge Rd
Brixham TQ5 230 A4
Plymouth PL2 247 F5
Torquay TQ1 214 B1
Cambridge St 4 EX4 177 A5
Cambridge Terr EX10 188 B4
Cambridge Wy EX15 163 A3
Camden Ct PL4 263 A3
Camden Rd TQ1 220 B5
Camden St PL4 263 A3
Came Cross EX14 84 C7
Camellia Cl
Churston Ferrers TQ5 229 D5
1 Tiverton EX16 161 F6
Camelot Cl EX4 174 A1
CAMELS HEAD 247 E7
Cameron Cl EX16 161 B3
Cameron Dr PL21 237 A5
Cameron Way PL6 245 B1
Camfield Dr EX16 161 F6
Camilla Ct EX4 261 B4
Camilla Terr PL2 248 D7
Camomile Way TQ12 206 D5
Campbellhays Hill EX16 47 A1
Campbell Rd PL9 255 F7
Camp Cross PL15 105 E7
Camperdown Rd TQ8 259 C4
Camperdown St PL2 247 F4
Camperdown Terr EX8 201 F6
Camperknowle Cl PL10 252 F6
Campian Way 11 EX14 85 C2
Campion Cl
Launceston PL15 105 A2
7 Plymouth PL7 251 C5
Saltash PL12 242 D4
Campion Ct
Torquay TQ1 214 B1
Campion Ct *continued*
Willand EX15 162 D5
Campion Dr EX32 155 E5
Campion Gdns EX2 178 C3
Campion Pl TQ12 206 C5
Campion Rise PL19 171 D6
Campion View PL6 245 E8
Camp Rd EX20 170 C2
Camps Cross EX17 80 E2
Canaan Way EX11 169 D3
Canada Hill
East Ogwell TQ12 206 F1
Ogwell TQ12 211 F8
Canada Hill Prim Sch TQ12 206 F1
Canal Banks EX2 177 D2
Canal Cl TA21 160 B8
Canal Hill EX16 161 F3
Canal Rd
Holsworthy EX22 164 D6
Tavistock PL19 171 B5
Canal Rise EX22 70 F5
Canberra Cl EX4 173 E2
Canberra Rd PL6 245 B5
Candar The EX34 150 B6
Candish Dr PL9 256 D7
Candys Cotts 1 TQ13 123 C4
Canefields Ave PL7 251 B3
Cane's Cotts PL8 257 A5
Canhaye Cl PL7 251 A3
Canis Mws PL9 256 E8
Canna Pk Dr EX21 74 C7
Cann Bridge Sch PL6 245 E2
Cann Gdns PL6 244 D6
Cannington La DT7 104 B3
Cannington Rd EX16 46 E1
Cannon Rd TQ12 123 B2
Cannon St PL1 247 D2
Canns Water EX39 39 C6
Cann Woods Nature Reserve★ PL6 244 C5
Cann Wood View PL6 245 E7
Canons Cl TQ14 208 F8
Canons Gate PL19 171 A3
Canons Way PL19 171 A3
Canonteign Falls★ EX6 113 B1
Canon Way EX2 181 B8
Canterbury Cl
Feniton EX14 84 D2
Ivybridge PL21 237 E4
Canterbury Dr PL5 244 B4
Canterbury Rd EX4 176 E7
Canterbury Way EX8 196 E4
Capel La EX8 202 F8
Capella Dr PL9 256 E8
Capern Cl EX33 152 E4
Capern Pk EX39 40 B7
Capern Rd EX39 156 F1
Capper Cl EX10 186 E8
Capra Cl TQ12 207 F4
Caprera Terr La PL3 262 C4
Capricorn Way PL9 256 E8
Capstone Cres EX34 150 C6
Capstone Ct EX34 150 D5
Capstone Pde EX34 150 B7
Capstone Pl 4 EX34 150 C6
Capstone Rd EX34 150 C6
Captain Brooks Cross EX39 39 B8
Captain's Cross EX16 63 C3
Captains Gdns PL5 244 E1
Captains Rd TQ12 207 D8
CAPTON 232 D7
Capton Cross TQ6 232 E6
Caradon Cl PL6 245 A5
Caradon Ct 2 PL20 126 F4
Caradon Terr PL12 242 E3
Carbeile Jun Sch PL11 247 A3
Carbeile Rd PL11 247 A2
Carberry TQ8 259 D4
Carberry Ave EX8 196 A1
Carbis Cl TQ12 244 B4
Carders Ct EX2 261 A2
Carder Way EX36 158 C5
Cardiff Cl PL7 251 B8
Cardigan Rd PL6 245 C1
Cardinal Ave PL5 247 D8
Cardu Cl EX15 65 F7
Carehouse Cross TQ7 145 B1
Careswell Ave PL2 247 F8
Carew Ave PL5 244 B3
Carew Gdns
Newton Abbot TQ12 207 F3
Plymouth PL5 244 B3
Saltash PL12 242 D3
Carew Gr PL5 244 B3
Carew Rd EX16 161 D6
Carew Terr PL11 247 B2
Carew Wharf PL11 247 C2
Carew Wharf Bsns Ctr PL11 247 C2
Carey Ct PL12 242 E3
Carey Rd TQ6 233 C3
CARGREEN 239 A2
Carhaix Way EX7 204 F8
Carina Pl PL9 256 E8
Carisbrooke Rd PL6 245 C1
CARKEEL 242 C6
Carkeel Barns PL12 242 C5
Carkeel Ind Est PL12 242 D5
Carlile Rd
Brixham TQ5 230 A5
Exeter EX2 178 A5
Carling Ct TQ7 258 C4
Carlisle Rd PL5 244 D3
Carlisle St 4 TQ12 207 C3
Carlton Cl
Paignton TQ3 219 C2
Plymouth PL3 249 B5
Carlton Ct TQ12 209 B2
Carlton Dr TQ3 219 C2
Carlton Hill EX8 202 A5
Carlton Mews TQ1 220 C6
Carlton Pl 20 TQ14 210 C4
Carlton Rd
Exeter EX2 178 B4
Torquay TQ1 220 C6
Carlton Terr
18 Barnstaple EX32 155 A4
6 Dawlish EX7 204 E6
Plymouth, Lipson PL4 263 B3
Plymouth, Weston Mill PL5 247 E8
Carlyle Ave EX32 155 A6
Carlyon Cl
Exeter EX1 178 A6
Torpoint PL11 246 F4
Carlyon Gdns EX1 178 A6
Carmarthen Rd PL4 249 B2
Carmel Gdns PL19 171 A5
Carnac Dr
Dawlish EX7 200 E1
Dawlish EX7 204 E8
Carnegie N EX39 156 F6
Carnegie S EX39 156 F6
Carnock Rd PL2 248 D8
Carnoustie Dr PL12 242 C2
Carolina Gdns PL2 247 F7
Caroline Ave EX2 178 D1
Caroline Cl
Exmouth EX8 196 D1
Kingskerswell TQ12 213 A3
Carousel Ct EX4 177 A4
Carpenter Cl
Exeter EX4 261 A3
Tiverton EX16 161 C3
Carpenter Dr TQ13 180 B6
Carpenter Rd PL9 255 F8
Carpenter's Cross EX18 60 A5
Carpenter's La EX18 60 A5
Carpenter Way PL19 171 B7
Carradale Rd PL6 249 C7
Carr Cl TQ8 259 C5
Carrick Mill EX3 182 E7
Carrington Terr 5 EX32 155 A6
Carrionpit La EX19 58 F3
Carrions The 7 TQ9 223 C5
Carrisbrooke Way PL12 242 B2
Carr La TQ7 145 C4
Carroll Rd PL5 244 C2
Carroll Rise EX22 53 E1
Carrolls Way PL9 256 A5
Carron La PL6 241 D1
Carscombe La EX16 48 E6
Carslake Cl EX10 188 C7
Carswells TQ12 212 F5
Carter Ave EX8 202 A8
Carter Cl EX36 158 C5
Carter Rd PL21 237 D6
Carters Cross EX13 87 A3
Cart Land Rise EX1 179 B8
Cartwright Cres TQ14 209 D8
Cary Ave TQ1 220 C7
Cary Castle TQ1 220 B8
Cary Parade TQ2 220 B4
Cary Park Rd TQ1 220 C7
Cary Pk TQ1 220 C7
Cary Rd
Paignton TQ3 219 A1
Torquay TQ2 220 A4
Caseberry La EX5 82 E6
Case Gdns EX12 192 B6
Cassiobury Way TQ2 213 E2
Castlands EX5 172 C7
CASTLE 88 D4
Castle Acre Gdns PL3 249 B5
Castle Bank Gdns PL3 249 B5
Castle Barbican PL7 250 E4
Castlebar Cl EX16 161 E3
Castle Bldgs PL12 242 D4
Castle Carey Gdns PL3 249 B5
Castle Cir TQ1 220 A5
Castle Circus Ct TQ1 220 A5
Castle Cotts
Exmouth EX8 203 A7
Tuckenhay TQ9 139 F6
Wellington TA21 52 D8
Woodbury EX5 184 C3
Castle Cross
Axminster EX13 88 D4
Bratton Clovelly EX20 92 C6
Membury EX13 87 E4
Castle Ct
Saltash PL12 242 C2
Torquay TQ1 220 C7
4 Totnes TQ9 223 B5
Totnes TQ9 223 B6
Castle Drogo★ EX6 96 C1
Castle Farm EX11 168 E4
Castleford Way EX20 170 B4
Castle Gate EX6 194 E3
Castle Ham Lodge EX20 170 B4
Castlehayes Gdns PL7 250 E4
Castle Hill
Axminster EX13 167 D6
Berrynarbor EX34 2 E3
Great Torrington EX38 159 D4
Ilfracombe EX34 150 C6
Lynton EX35 151 C5
Saltash PL12 242 B1
Saltash PL12 242 C1
Seaton EX12 192 A4
Upton TA4 34 E7
Castle Hill Ave EX34 150 C6
Castle Hill Gdns EX38 159 D5
Castle Hill Ind Pk EX13 167 C6
Castle Hill View 11 EX10 101 B1
Castle Hill Villas 14 EX34 150 C6
Castle Ho EX13 167 D6
Castle Hts EX35 151 C5
Castle La
Blackawton TQ9 139 E2
Budleigh Salterton EX9 197 C1
Exmouth EX8, EX9 203 B8
Okehampton EX20 170 A3
Paignton TQ3 218 C6
Plymouth PL7 250 E4
Torquay TQ1 220 B5
Woodbury EX5 184 D3
Castlemain TA20 69 D8
Castleman Wy EX15 163 E4
Castle Mdw EX39 40 B8
Castlemead Cl PL12 242 D3
Castlemead Dr PL12 242 D3
Castle Mill 15 EX32 17 B2
Castle Mount
Exeter EX2 177 B7
Exeter EX4 261 A4
Castle Park Ind Est EX32 155 E3
Castle Park Rd EX32 155 E3
Castle Pk EX15 67 B8
Castle Pk Cl
7 Paignton TQ3 225 F1
Paignton TQ4 228 F8
Castle Pk Ct TQ3 225 F1
Castle Pk Dr TQ4 228 F8
Castle Pk Way TQ4 228 F8
Castle Prim Sch The EX16 161 D4
Castle Quay EX31 154 F5
Castle Quay Ct 5 EX31 154 F5
Castle Rd
Dartmouth TQ6 234 B1
Kingswear TQ6 234 A2
Okehampton EX20 170 B4
Torquay TQ1 220 B5
Wellington TA21 52 D8
Castle Rise
Plymouth PL3 249 B4
Saltash PL12 242 D1
Castle Rock EX34 7 F7
Castle St
Axminster EX13 167 D6
Bampton EX16 34 B1
Barnstaple EX31 154 F5
Combe Martin EX34 3 A3
Exeter EX2 177 C6
Exeter EX4 261 B3
Great Torrington EX38 159 D5
Northam EX39 156 F6
Plymouth PL1 263 A2
Tiverton EX16 161 D4
Totnes TQ9 223 C6
Winkleigh EX19 58 F3
Castle Terr 5 EX34 150 C5
Castleton Cl PL3 249 A4
Castleton Tor TQ1 219 F7
Castle View
17 Colyton EX24 103 A4
Saltash PL12 242 D1
Castle Way TQ12 206 E4
Castlewood Ave TQ12 206 F4
Castle Wood La TA20 69 F1
Castor Cl TQ5 230 D3
Castor La TQ4 226 B1
Castor Mws 10 TQ5 230 A3
Castor Rd TQ5 230 C3
Castra Ave EX20 170 E7
Catalina Cl EX14 67 C1
Catalina Villas PL9 255 A6
Cater Rd EX32 155 B4
Cat & Fiddle Pk EX5 179 E3
Catharine Cl EX16 161 E5
Cathcart Ave PL4 249 B2
Cathedral Cl EX1 261 B3
Cathedral of St Mary's & St Boniface★ PL1 262 B3
Cathedral School of St Mary The PL1 262 B3
Cathedral St PL1 262 B3
Catherine Cres TQ4 225 F4
Catherines Cl 2 EX1 178 D1
Catherine St
Exeter EX1 261 B3
Plymouth PL1 262 C2
Cathole La DT7 104 B5
Catkill Cross EX36 46 C7
Cat La EX34 150 E5
Catmoor Cross EX13 88 A5
Catnip Cl EX13 167 E6
CATON 131 C6
Caton Cross TQ12 131 C6
Cator TQ9 227 F8
Catriage Hill EX32 18 C2
Catriage La EX32 18 C2
Catsborough Cross EX39 40 E6
Catshole La EX39 156 F1
Catsmoor Cross EX20 92 F1
Catson Gn PL8 257 A5
CATTEDOWN 263 C1
Cattedown Rd PL3 263 C1
Catterick Cl PL5 243 E5
Cattewater Rd PL4 249 B1
Cattledown Ind Est PL9 255 B8
Catt's La TA21 52 E6
Cauleston Cl EX8 196 A2
Caulfield Ct 7 TQ12 207 C3
Caumont Cl EX15 65 F7
Caunters Cl TQ12 211 D2
Causeway EX12 191 D5
Causeway Cl EX39 157 A7
Causeway Cross TQ12 211 E2
Causeway End EX14 84 D7
Causeway The TQ12 211 D2
CauseWy View PL4 255 B6
Causey Gdns EX1 174 F1
Causey La EX1 174 F1
CAUTE 55 D5
Cavalier Ct EX38 159 D5
Cavalier Rd TQ12 180 F3
Cavalry Chase EX20 170 D7
Cavalry Dr TQ12 180 F1
Cavell Way EX20 170 C6
Cavendish Cl EX7 204 C7
Cavendish Pl EX35 151 B5
Cavendish Rd
Exeter EX1 177 F6
Plymouth PL4 249 B1
Cavern Rd
11 Brixham TQ5 230 C4
Torquay TQ1 220 B5
Caversham Cl EX6 113 B4
Cavie Cres EX33 152 B6
Cavie Rd EX33 152 B6
Cawkett La TA22 33 A6
Cawley Ave EX13 167 F7
Cawley's La EX14 86 F6
CAWSAND 253 B1
Caxton Gdns PL5 244 C1
Caxton Row EX16 161 D6
Cayley Way PL5 243 F2
Cayman Cl TQ2 213 E3
Cecil Ave
Paignton TQ3 226 B8
Plymouth PL4 263 C4
Cecil Cotts PL1 262 A3
Cecilia Rd TQ3 219 B1
Cecil Mews TQ3 226 B7
Cecil Rd
Exeter EX2 177 A4
Paignton TQ3 226 B7
Cecil St PL1 262 B3
Cedar EX7 201 A2
Cedar Ave PL9 255 C5
Cedar Cl
Axminster EX13 167 D5
Exmouth EX8 196 D3
Honiton EX14 166 B5
Seaton EX12 192 A7
Teignmouth TQ14 210 D7
Torpoint PL11 246 F2
Cedar Court Rd TQ1 220 B7
Cedarcroft Rd PL2 248 B7
Cedar Ct
Rockbeare EX5 99 B6
Saltash PL12 242 F2
Wellington TA21 160 E5
Cedar Dr
Loddiswell TQ7 143 F7
Torpoint PL11 246 F2
Cedar Gdns EX13 167 D5
Cedar Gr EX31 154 B2
Cedar Ho 2 EX33 152 D6
Cedar Pk PL9 255 A1
Cedar Rd
Newton Abbot TQ12 212 F8
Paignton TQ3 219 C1
Tiverton EX16 161 F5
Cedars EX8 203 B6
Cedars Pk EX31 154 B4
Cedars Rd
Exeter EX2 261 B2
Torquay TQ1 220 D5
Cedars The EX14 166 E7
Cedar Units TQ9 222 F8
Cedar Way
Bideford EX39 25 D4
Brixham TQ5 230 A2
Celandine Cl EX12 192 B7
Celandine Gdns PL7 251 C5
Celandine Lawns EX15 162 D5
Celia Cres EX4 174 A2
Celtic Cl EX1 178 E8
Celtic Fields EX7 204 E7
Cembra Cl EX14 166 E5
Cemetery La EX5 82 F6
Cemetery Rd PL18 125 C5
Centaur Mws PL9 256 E8
Centenary Rd 6 PL5 247 E2
Centenary Way
Bovey Tracey TQ13 180 F7
Torquay TQ2 213 C2
Centery La
Bittadon EX31 9 C5
Parracombe EX31 4 D2
Central Ave
Exeter, Countess Wear EX2 182 D7
Exeter, Whipton EX4 174 B2
Holsworthy EX22 164 B4
Lee Mill PL21 136 C6
Paignton TQ3 226 B7
Central Park Ave PL4 262 C4
Central Pl 16 EX14 166 C6
Central Rd PL1 262 B1
Central St PL3 262 B3
Central Station Chambers EX4 261 A3
Centre Ct 8 PL21 137 C8
Centry Ct TQ5 230 E4
Centry Rd TQ5 230 E4
Centurian Cl EX1 178 D8
Centurian Ho 13 EX1 261 A2
Century Dr EX39 156 E6
Ceramic Terr 3 EX32 155 A4
Chackrell La EX16 50 F2
Chaddiford La EX31 154 D7
CHADDLEWOOD 251 B6
Chaddlewood Ave PL4 263 B3
Chaddlewood Cl
Plymouth PL7 250 F5
Plymouth PL7 251 A4
Chaddlewood Ho PL7 251 B5
Chaddlewood Prim Sch PL7 251 A5
Chad Rd PL9 140 A8
Chaffcombe Cross EX17 78 F5
Chaffcombe La EX17 79 A6
Chaffinch Dr EX15 163 B2
Chaffinch Rise EX5 99 B6
CHAGFORD 111 A6
Chagford CE Prim Sch TQ13 111 A7
Chagford Cross TQ13 111 E5
Chagford Wlk PL6 249 E8
Chains Rd EX16 50 D1
Chalcombe Rocks La TA4 34 E5
Chalfield Cl TQ2 213 F3
Chalk Pit Rd TA20 69 F7
Chalk St EX4 174 D2
CHALLABOROUGH 142 E3
Challabrook La TQ13 180 B6
CHALLACOMBE 11 F3
Challacombe Cotts PL20 120 F6
Challacombe Cross
Chagford TQ13 110 F2
Challacombe EX31 11 F3
Chulmleigh EX18 45 A2
Challacombe Hill EX34 8 A5
Challacombe Hill Rd EX34 7 F6
Challenger Cross EX13 87 E7
Challeycroft Rd TQ5 230 A1
Challgood Cl 1 PL9 255 F5
Challgood Rise PL9 255 F5
Challices Cotts EX18 59 E4
Challick La TA4 35 F6
Challock Cl PL6 245 D4
Challowell La
Braunton EX33 152 D8
Knowle EX33 8 D1
Chaloner's Rd EX33 152 D6
CHAMBERCOMBE 150 D5
Chambercombe La EX34 150 E4
Chambercombe Manor★ EX34 150 E4
Chambercombe Park Rd EX34 150 E5
Chambercombe Pk EX34 150 E5
Chambercombe Pk Terr EX34 150 E5
Chambercombe Rd EX34 150 D5
Chamberlain Ave EX8 202 E7
Chamberlain Rd
Exeter EX2 177 B4
Exeter EX2 261 A1
Chamberlayne Dr PL7 250 E6
Chambers Cl EX10 188 A8
Chambers La EX1 179 B8
Champernhayes La DT6 104 F7
Champernowne PL21 137 B3
Champernowne Cres 7 EX34 150 D5
Champford La TA21 160 D5
Champford Mews 2 TA21 160 D5
Champion Cross TA4 35 E3
Champion Way EX16 64 E8
Chancel Ct EX4 174 D1
Chancel La EX4 174 D1
Chancellor's Way EX4 174 A2
Chandlers Ct 9 EX39 15 B1
Chandlers Hts TQ8 259 D5
Chandlers' La EX10 188 B5
Chandlers Way EX34 150 B3
Chandlers Wlk EX2 261 A1
Channel Park Ave PL3 249 B5

Channel View
Ilfracombe EX34 150 D5
Woolacombe EX34 1 A2
Channel View Dr TQ7 147 B6
Channel View La EX7 204 C3
Channel View Terr PL4 263 C4
Channer Pl EX39 156 C6
Channings Dr EX1 179 B8
Channon Rd PL12 242 C4
Channons Ct 8 EX14 166 B6
Chanter Ct EX2 178 A2
Chanter's Hill EX32 155 B5
Chanters Rd EX39 157 A3
Chantry Ave EX39 157 A3
Chantry Cl TQ14 210 D7
Chantry Ct PL7 250 B5
Chantry Hill TQ7 145 D4
Chantry Mdw EX2 181 B8
Chantry Orch EX24 103 A5
Chantry The EX20 170 C5
Chapel Cl
Crediton EX17 79 C1
Gunnislake PL18 125 B5
Halberton EX16 65 A8
5 Horrabridge PL20 126 F4
Petrockstow EX20 56 F4
Chapel Cnr EX22 70 F5
Chapel Cotts PL7 132 F4
Chapel Cross
Dunkeswell EX14 67 C2
Iddesleigh EX19 57 E3
Petrockstow EX20 56 F8
Puddington EX16 62 B5
Thorverton EX5 81 D5
Thurlestone TQ7 143 A2
Chapel Ct
Chudleigh TQ12 123 F6
Exeter EX2 177 A4
Stoke Gabriel TQ9 227 F8
Swimbridge EX32 28 E8
Torquay TQ1 219 F7
Chapel Down La PL21 137 F3
Chapel Down Lane End PL21 137 E3
Chapeldown Rd PL11 247 A2
Chapel Downs Dr EX17 165 A6
Chapel Downs Rd EX17 165 A6
Chapel Fields 6 TQ10 134 F3
Chapel Hill
5 Budleigh Salterton EX9 198 A1
Cheriton Fitzpaine EX17 62 F1
Clyst St George EX3 183 C6
15 Exmouth EX8 202 A6
Longdown EX6 98 E2
5 Newton Abbot TQ12 207 B3
Uffculme EX15 65 A6
Uffculme EX15 66 A7
Whiddon Down EX20 95 E3
Chapel Hill Cross EX17 62 F1
Chapel Ho 4 EX39 156 F7
Chapel Knap EX13, EX24 102 F7
Chapel La
Chilsworthy EX22 53 E1
Colaton Raleigh EX9 186 C4
11 Coldeast TQ12 122 F1
Coldeast TQ13 180 D1
Combe Martin EX34 3 A3
Dartmouth TQ6 233 F3
Folly Gate EX20 93 F8
4 Horrabridge PL20 126 F4
2 Horrabridge PL20 126 F5
Loddiswell TQ7 143 E7
Lutton PL21 133 B2
Malborough TQ7 147 E6
Mary Tavy PL19 117 E6
Ottery St Mary EX11 169 E4
Patsford EX31 9 B2
Stoke Fleming TQ6 146 B7
Totnes TQ9 223 D5
Withypool TA24 21 C6
Yealmpton PL8 257 F4
Chapel Mdw PL20 126 C3
Chapel Park Cl EX39 157 C2
Chapel Pk EX17 96 A8
Chapel Rd
Brampford Speke EX5 81 E1
Bratton Clovelly EX20 92 A2
Exeter EX2 177 B1
Lympstone EX8 195 D5
Newton Abbot TQ12 207 D3
Parkham EX39 39 E8
Saltash PL12 242 B3
Sidmouth EX10 188 B3
Yealmpton PL8 136 A2
Chapel Row TQ7 142 C6
Chapelry The 5 TQ13 123 C4
Chapel St
Axmouth EX12 192 D7
4 Bere Alston PL20 125 E1
18 Bideford EX39 157 A2
Blackawton TQ9 139 E1
Braunton EX33 152 D5
Buckfastleigh TQ11 236 B5
Budleigh Salterton EX9 199 G2
Chapel St *continued*
Dolton EX19 57 F7
Dulverton TA22 33 D6
Ermington PL21 136 F4
Exeter EX4 261 B3
1 Exmouth EX8 202 A6
Georgeham EX33 8 A2
Gunnislake PL18 125 D6
Holsworthy EX22 164 C3
Honiton EX14 166 C6
Lifton PL16 105 E4
Morchard Bishop EX17 61 A2
Plymouth PL4 263 A3
Plymouth, Mount Wise PL1 247 E2
Sidbury EX10 101 B2
Sidmouth EX10 188 B3
Tavistock PL19 171 B5
19 Teignmouth TQ14 210 B4
Tiverton EX16 64 C7
Tiverton EX16 161 D4
Woolfardisworthy EX39 38 F7
Chapel The 7 TQ9 223 D5
CHAPELTON 27 F5
Chapelton Cross EX37 27 F5
Chapelton Sta EX37 28 A4
Chapeltown Cross EX5 63 C1
Chapel Way
Axminster EX13 167 E7
Plymouth PL3 249 A6
Chapman Ct PL12 242 B3
Chapmans Gn EX22 54 C4
Chapmans Ope PL1 247 D2
Chapple Cl EX6 201 B8
Chapplecroft Rd EX13 87 E5
Chapple Cross
Bovey Tracey TQ13 180 B5
Chagford TQ13 110 D8
Dolton EX19 57 E6
Chapple Cross Cross TQ13 110 D7
Chapple Hill EX16 62 C5
Chapple La EX20 76 E4
Chapple Rd
Bovey Tracey TQ13 180 A6
Witheridge EX16 46 E1
Charberry Rise DT6 104 F4
Chard Ave 4 EX5 99 E8
Chard Barton PL5 244 B3
CHARD JUNCTION 88 E7
Chard Rd
Axminster EX13 88 B4
Axminster EX13 167 E6
Exeter EX1 178 A6
Plymouth PL5 243 D2
Chard St
Axminster EX13 167 D6
Chardstock EX13 88 B7
CHARDSTOCK 88 B7
Chard Stock Cl EX1 178 D6
Chardstone Gr EX13 88 B7
Charfield Dr
Plymouth PL6 245 A1
Plymouth PL6 249 A8
Charford Cross TQ10 135 B1
Chariot Dr TQ12 207 F6
Chariot Way EX20 170 D7
Charlacott Cross EX31 27 B6
Charlbury Dr 7 PL3 249 D1
Charlemont Rd TQ14 210 B8
CHARLES 18 E3
Charles Ave EX39 157 A2
CHARLES BOTTOM 18 E2
Charles Cross
East Buckland EX32 18 E3
Plymouth PL4 263 A3
Charles Ct EX8 195 E5
Charles Dart Cres EX32 155 A6
Charles Darwin Rd PL1 247 F1
Charles Hankin Cl PL21 237 E4
Charles Hudson La 2 EX31 155 A7
Charles Rd
Honiton EX14 166 C6
Kingskerswell TQ12 213 A2
Charles St
14 Barnstaple EX32 154 F6
Dartmouth TQ6 233 F3
3 Exmouth EX8 202 A7
Plymouth PL4 263 A3
Charles Terr PL3 249 A6
Charlestown Rd TQ3 225 D7
Charleton CE Prim Sch TQ7 144 C1
Charleton Court Barns TQ7 144 C1
Charleton Way TQ7 144 C1
Charlotte Cl TQ2 219 F8
Charlotte Ct TQ1 214 B1
Charlotte Mews 1 EX2 261 B2
Charlottes Oak TQ12 123 E1
Charlotte St
Crediton EX17 165 D5
Plymouth PL2 247 E4
Charlton Cres PL6 245 A2
Charlton Ho EX7 204 F6
Charlton Rd PL6 245 A3
Charlton Terr PL21 237 D5
Charlwood Ct TQ1 220 C8
CHARMOUTH 104 F4
Charmouth Bypass EX13 104 F5
Charmouth Cl
Lyme Regis DT7 260 E4
Torquay TQ1 220 D6
Charmouth Ho DT7 260 C3
Charmouth Rd
Lyme Regis DT7 260 E4
Raymond's Hill EX13 104 C7
Charneymore Cross EX18 44 E1
Charnhill Cl PL9 256 A6
Charnhill Way PL9 256 A6
Charnley Ave EX4 176 E5
Charter Cl EX16 161 B4
Charter Rd EX13 167 C7
CHARTON 104 A1
Charton Cross DT7 104 A2
Chartwell Cl TQ3 225 E7
Chartwell Dr TQ12 207 A4
Charwell Mdw EX5 82 F6
Chase The
Exeter EX3 182 D6
Honiton EX14 166 D7
Ivybridge PL21 237 D4
CHASTY 164 C2
Chasty La EX22 164 C3
Chatham Cl EX8 202 D8
Chatsworth Gdns PL5 243 F3
Chatsworth Rd TQ1 220 B6
Chatto Rd TQ1 220 A7
Chatto Way TQ1 220 A7
Chatwell La PL21 137 B3
Chaucer Ave EX2 177 F3
Chaucer Grove EX4 177 F8
Chaucer Rd PL19 171 D5
Chaucer Rise 4 EX8 196 C3
Chaucer Way PL5 244 C1
Chaves Cl EX16 161 F3
CHAWLEIGH 60 B7
Chawleigh Cl PL18 125 C5
Chawleigh Hill EX18 59 F8
Chawleigh Week Cross EX18 59 E8
Chawleigh Week La EX18 59 D8
Chawleigh Week Mill Cross EX18 59 D8
Cheavestone Lea TQ9 139 E1
Checkridge La EX13 88 D2
Chedworth St PL4 263 A3
Cheeke St EX1 261 C3
Cheese La EX10 187 F4
Cheevor Pl TQ12 208 A3
Cheffers Mws EX3 182 D7
CHEGLINCH 8 F6
Cheglinch Cnr EX34 8 F5
Cheglinch La EX34 8 F6
CHELDON 60 D8
Cheldon Barton Moor La EX18 60 D8
Cheldon Cross
Chawleigh EX18 60 D8
Chulmleigh EX18 45 D2
CHELFHAM 17 D6
Chelfham Mill Sch EX32 17 C6
Chelmer Cl PL7 251 A5
Chelmsford Pl PL5 244 C4
Chelmsford Rd EX4 176 E6
Chelsea Pl 8 TQ14 210 B5
Chelsea Trad Ctr EX2 178 E5
Chelson Gdns PL6 245 E3
Chelson La EX10 101 E1
CHELSTON
Torquay 219 E4
Wellington 52 D8
Chelston Bsn Pk TA21 52 D8
CHELSTON HEATHFIELD 52 E7
Chelston Rd
Newton Abbot TQ12 207 B4
Torquay TQ2 219 E3
Chelston Terr TA21 52 D8
Cheltenham Cl EX4 176 E7
Cheltenham Pl PL4 263 B4
Chelwood Gr PL7 250 F5
Chene Ct 6 PL21 137 B2
Cheney's La EX14 166 E8
CHENSON 60 A4
Chepstow Ave PL6 245 C8
Chepstow Cl EX2 182 B8
Chequers Haigh PL8 140 F6
Chequer Tree Ct PL18 125 C5
Chercombe Bridge Rd
Newton Abbot TQ12 206 C3
Ogwell TQ12 211 B8
Chercombe Cl TQ12 206 E4
Chercombe Valley Rd TQ12 206 E4
CHERISTOW 22 D4
Cheriswood Ave EX8 196 D1
Cheriswood Cl EX8 196 D1
CHERITON 5 D3
CHERITON BISHOP 97 A4
Cheriton Bishop Com Prim Sch EX6 97 B4
Cheriton Cl PL5 244 A3
CHERITON CROSS 97 B3
Cheriton Cross
Cadbury EX5 81 C8
Chilton EX17 80 D7
CHERITON FITZPAINE 62 E1
Cheriton Fitzpaine Prim Sch EX17 62 F1
Cheriton Hill EX35 5 D3
Cheriton Mill Cross EX17 62 E2
Cheriton Rd EX35 151 D1
Cherry Arbour EX32 155 C3
CHERRYBRIDGE 5 A4
Cherrybridge Cross EX35 151 A2
Cherry Brook Dr TQ4 229 B8
Cherry Brook Sq TQ4 229 B8
Cherry Brook Wlk TQ4 226 B1
Cherry Cl
Cheriton Fitzpaine EX17 62 F1
Exmouth EX8 196 C3
5 Honiton EX14 85 C2
Tiverton EX16 161 D5
Willand EX15 162 D4
Cherry Cross TQ9 223 C4
Cherry Ct PL19 116 E3
Cherry Dr EX12 192 A5
Cherryford La EX31 4 C4
Cherry Gdns
Crediton EX17 165 C5
Exeter EX2 178 A4
Paignton TQ3 226 A7
Cherry Gr EX32 155 C2
Cherry Mdw EX17 62 F1
Cherry Park Cl TQ2 219 D2
Cherry Pk
Appledore EX39 14 F1
Plymouth PL7 251 A3
Cherry Tree Cl
Exeter EX4 173 A2
Rockbeare EX5 99 B6
Cherry Tree Dr
Brixton PL8 257 A5
3 Landkey EX32 17 B2
Cherry Tree Gdns EX16 161 E5
Cherry Tree La PL7 251 A4
Cherry Tree Rd EX13 167 E6
Cherrywood Cl TQ12 206 E4
Cheshire Dr PL6 244 D6
Cheshire Rd EX8 196 E2
Chesil Ct DT7 260 C3
Chesnut Cl PL12 242 D4
Chester Cl EX4 176 E7
Chester Ct EX8 201 F7
Chesterfield Rd PL3 249 B4
Chestermoor Cross EX20 92 D5
Chester Pl 4 PL4 248 E4
Chester Terr 17 EX32 155 A4
Chesterton Cl PL5 244 C3
Chestnut Ave
Cullompton EX15 163 C2
Dartmouth TQ6 233 E4
Exeter EX2 178 A3
Plymouth PL9 255 C5
Torquay TQ2 219 F4
Chestnut Cl
22 Bere Alston PL20 125 E1
Braunton EX33 152 E6
Cheriton Bishop EX6 97 B4
Crediton EX17 165 D6
Exmouth EX8 196 C3
Lamerton PL19 116 E4
Seaton EX12 192 A7
Tavistock PL19 171 D2
Torpoint PL11 246 F3
Wellington TA21 160 E5
Wembury PL9 255 A1
Chestnut Cres
7 Chudleigh TQ13 123 F6
Stoke Canon EX5 173 F8
Chestnut Ct EX2 181 B8
Chestnut Dr
Bideford EX39 25 D4
Brixham TQ5 230 A2
Kingsteignton TQ12 207 F6
Newton Abbot TQ12 208 A1
Willand EX15 162 C4
Chestnut Gr TQ6 233 C4
Chestnut Mews EX14 84 E2
Chestnut Pk TQ7 149 D7
Chestnut Rd
Plymouth PL3 248 D7
Tiverton EX16 161 F5
Chestnuts The EX5 99 D2
Chestnut Terr PL19 116 E3
Chestnut View EX13 87 D6
Chestnut Way
Honiton EX14 166 A4
Newton Poppleford EX10 186 F8
Chestnut Wlk EX7 204 C5
Chestnut Wy 11 TQ7 143 E7
Cheston Cross TQ10 134 E1
CHESTWOOD 155 B1
Chestwood Ave EX31 154 C3
Chestwood Cl EX31 154 D4
Chestwood Villas EX32 16 E1
CHETTISCOMBE 161 F8
CHEVITHORNE 49 D2
Cheyne Beach 2 EX34 150 C6
Cheynegate La EX4 174 C3
Cheyne Rise EX4 174 D2
Cheyney Cross EX36 30 B2
Cheyney La EX36 30 B2
Chibbet Hill TA24 21 B8
Chibbet Post TA24 21 C8
Chichacott Cross EX20 170 F7
Chichacott Rd EX20 170 D7
Chichester Cl
Barnstaple EX32 155 B2
Exmouth EX8 202 C8
Ilfracombe EX34 150 A4
11 Instow EX39 15 B1
Teignmouth TQ14 210 A8
Chichester Cres
Barnstaple EX32 155 B2
Saltash PL12 242 E1
Chichester Ct
Barnstaple EX32 155 C5
Horrabridge PL20 126 F4
Outer Hope TQ7 147 B7
Shirwell EX32 17 B8
Chichester Ho
Barnstaple EX31 155 B8
Exeter EX2 178 B5
Plymouth PL1 262 B2
Chichester Mews EX1 261 B3
Chichester Pk EX34 8 A6
Chichester Pl 7 EX16 64 D7
Chichester Rd EX32 155 B2
Chichester Way
East Budleigh EX9 198 B6
Newton Abbot TQ12 207 F3
Westward Ho! EX39 156 C6
Chicory Cl TQ12 206 D5
Chideock Ct DT7 260 C3
Chieftain Wy EX2 177 A4
Chilbridge La EX31 17 B8
Chilcombe Cross EX24 102 B7
Chilcombe La EX24 102 A6
Chilcote Cl TQ1 220 C8
Chilcott Cl 5 EX16 64 D7
Chilcott Cross TA22 33 A7
Chilcott La TA22 33 A7
Childrey Gdns PL6 245 C1
Childrey Wlk PL6 245 C1
CHILLA 73 E5
Chilla Chapel EX21 73 E4
Chilla Rd EX21 73 E3
CHILLATON 116 D8
Chillaton Cross TQ7 138 A1
Chillaton Ct PL16 106 E1
CHILLINGTON 145 A2
Chillmark Cl PL3 249 D1
Chill Park Brake EX1 175 D1
Chill Pits La EX13 88 B8
Chilpark EX31 153 D5
CHILSON 88 C6
CHILSON COMMON 88 D7
CHILSWORTHY
Gunnislake 125 B7
Holsworthy 53 E1
Chiltern Cl TQ2 219 D3
Chiltern Cross EX16 34 B2
CHILTON 80 E7
Chilton Ave TQ14 210 C6
Chilton Cl PL6 249 B7
Chilton Gate EX16 81 D8
Chilton La EX17 80 E7
Chilverton Cross EX17 59 F1
Chilverton Hill Gate EX17 59 F1
Chilverton La EX17 59 F1
Chineway Gdns EX11 169 F3
Chineway Head EX11 101 B6
Chineway Hill EX11 101 A6
Chineway Rd
Ottery St Mary EX11 100 F6
Ottery St Mary EX11 101 A6
Chingswell St 2 EX39 157 A2
Chinkwell Rise TQ2 219 B8
Chinon Ct EX16 64 D8
Chinon Pl EX16 161 A6
Chinston Cl EX14 85 B4
Chipmunk Wlk EX32 155 B6
Chipple Pk PL21 133 B2
CHIPSTABLE 35 E6
Chircombe La EX39 157 A4
Chiseldon Farm TQ5 230 B2
Chiseldon Hill TQ5 230 C2
Chiseldon Ho EX4 173 A1
Chitterley Bsns Ctr EX5 82 A7
Chittleburn Bsns Pk PL8 256 F6
Chittleburn Cross PL8 256 E5
Chittleburn Hill PL8 256 E5
CHITTLEHAMHOLT 44 B8
CHITTLEHAMPTON 28 F4
Chittlehampton CE Prim Sch EX37 28 F4
CHIVELSTONE 149 A6
Chivelstone Cross TQ7 149 A5
CHIVENOR 15 E5
Chivenor Airfield EX31 152 F1
Chivenor Ave PL5 243 D4
Chivenor Cross EX31 15 E5
Chiverstone La EX6 194 C4
Chiverstone Rd EX6 194 C4
Chockenhole La EX9 199 A8
Chockland Rd 12 TQ12 123 E1
Cholhouse La EX20 77 C7
Chollacott Cl PL19 171 C4
Chollacott La PL19 171 D3
Chollaton Cross EX22 39 E1
Cholwell Cross TQ9 222 F4
Chope Rd EX39 156 F6
Chopes Cl EX39 26 A4
Chough Cl
Launceston PL15 105 A2
Marhamchurch EX23 70 A8
Christ Cross EX5 82 C8
Christcross La EX5 82 D7
Christian Mill Bsns Pk PL6 244 E4
Christina Par TQ9 223 F5
Christina Pk TQ9 223 E5
Christone Cross TQ9 138 D7
CHRISTOW 113 A3
Christow Com Prim Sch EX6 113 B4
Christow Rd EX2 177 B2
Chrystel Cl EX10 100 D2
Chubb Dr PL3 248 B4
Chubb Rd EX39 26 A4
Chubby Croft Cl EX39 22 E3
Chubs Cross EX20 77 F5
Chubworthy Cross TA4 35 D5
CHUDLEIGH 123 F6
Chudleigh Ave EX39 157 B1
Chudleigh CE Com Prim Sch TQ13 123 E6
CHUDLEIGH KNIGHTON 123 C4
Chudleigh Knighton CE Prim Sch TQ13 123 C4
Chudleigh Rd
2 Bideford EX39 157 B1
Exeter EX2 181 B7
Kingsteignton TQ12 207 D8
Kingsteignton TQ13 123 E1
Plymouth PL4 249 A4
Chudleigh Terr 6 EX39 157 B1
Chudley Cl EX8 196 D1
Chuggaton Cross EX37 28 C5
Chuley Cross TQ13 130 F3
Chuley Hill TQ13 130 F4
Chuley Rd TQ13 130 F4
CHULMLEIGH 44 F1
Chulmleigh Community College EX18 44 E1
Chulmleigh Hill 10 EX18 44 E1
Chulmleigh Prim Sch EX18 44 E1
Chulmleigh Rd
Morchard Bishop EX17 61 A2
Winkleigh EX19 58 F3
Church Ave
Lamerton PL19 116 F3
Okehampton EX20 170 A5
Church Cl
Ashprington TQ9 139 F8
Aylesbeare EX5 99 D2
Bratton Fleming EX31 18 A8
Broadclyst EX5 175 C7
15 Chulmleigh EX18 44 E1
Dartmouth TQ6 233 F3
Dolton EX19 57 F6
Goodleigh EX32 17 B5
Kingsbridge TQ7 258 D5
Lapford EX17 60 D3
Plymouth PL7 250 B7
Puddington EX16 62 B5
Totnes TQ9 223 C5
Yealmpton PL8 257 F4
Church Cliff DT7 260 E3
Church Cross
Buckfastleigh TQ11 236 B6
Cheriton Fitzpaine EX17 62 E1
Exeter EX4 174 D3
Filleigh EX32 29 C6
Sandford EX17 80 A5
Church Cross Rd TQ11 236 B6
Church Ct
Harberton TQ9 222 D2
Kingsteignton TQ12 207 E6
14 Newton Abbot TQ12 207 B3
Plymouth PL6 245 A7
Church Dr TA21 52 F7
Church End Rd TQ12 212 F4
Church Farm TQ7 143 A1
Churchfield Rd 26 EX39 15 A1
Churchfields TA21 160 D7
Church Fields TA21 160 E6
Churchfields Dr TQ13 180 D7
Churchfields Gdns TQ6 233 D3
Churchfields W TQ6 233 D3
Church Flats EX6 201 B8
Churchford Rd EX33 8 D1
Church Gate EX36 30 E1
Church Gr EX32 155 B3
CHURCH GREEN 101 F7
Church Hill
Awliscombe EX14 85 B4
Beer EX12 191 D5
Blackawton TQ9 139 E1
Brendon EX35 5 F4
Buckfastleigh TQ11 236 C6
Calstock PL18 125 D3
Exeter EX4 174 E2
Fremington EX31 153 E5
Holbeton PL8 136 D1
Honiton EX14 166 D5

Church Hill *continued*
Ilfracombe EX34 150 A5
Kingswear TQ6 234 A2
Lynton EX35 151 C5
Marldon TQ3 218 D4
Milton Combe PL20 126 C1
Musbury EX13 103 D5
Otterton EX9 198 D7
Plymouth PL6 245 B1
Tavistock PL19 171 E2
Tedburn St Mary EX6 97 F5
Winkleigh EX19 58 F3
Church Hill Cl TQ9 139 E2
Church Hill Cross EX20 94 E7
Church Hill E 6 TQ5 230 C5
Church Hill La EX33 8 D1
Church Hill Rd PL9 255 A6
Church Hill W 5 TQ5 230 C5
Church Ho
Exeter EX2 177 A4
Saltash PL12 243 A2
Church House Cl 8 TQ13 123 C4
CHURCHILL
Axminster 87 F4
Barnstaple 10 B3
Churchill EX34 8 F4
Churchill Ave EX7 204 D5
Churchill Cl
Barnstaple EX32 155 B6
Kenton EX6 194 D3
Churchill Cotts PL21 137 D6
Churchill Cres EX36 158 C3
Churchill Ct
7 Brixham TQ5 230 C4
Lympstone EX8 195 E6
Churchill Dr
Crediton EX17 165 B6
Teignmouth TQ14 210 C6
Churchill Gdns EX17 78 C7
Churchill Hill EX31 10 C4
Churchill La
Axminster EX13 88 A5
Calverleigh EX16 48 C3
Chipstable TA4 35 C5
Churchill Rd
Bideford EX39 26 A4
Exeter EX2 176 F4
Exmouth EX8 196 D2
Tavistock PL19 171 D2
Tiverton EX16 161 A4
Churchill Rise EX13 167 E7
Churchills 11 EX15 67 B8
Churchills Nature Reserve★ TQ12 207 A5
Churchills Rise 16 EX15 67 B8
Churchills The TQ12 207 A4
Churchill Way
Appledore EX39 14 F1
Northam EX39 156 F6
Northam EX39 157 A7
Plymouth PL3 248 E6
Churchill Wlk PL12 242 E1
CHURCHINFORD 68 D7
Church La
Alfington EX11 84 F1
Aveton Gifford TQ7 143 C6
10 Barnstaple EX31 154 F5
Bideford EX39 25 E2
4 Bittaford PL21 137 C8
Bridford EX6 112 F5
Broadclyst EX5 175 C7
Calstock PL18 125 D3
Cargreen PL12 238 F1
Cargreen PL12 239 A1
Cheriton Bishop EX6 97 B4
Christow EX6 113 B3
Clyst St Mary EX5 179 B2
Crediton EX17 165 D5
Dulverton TA22 33 D6
East Budleigh EX9 198 B6
Exeter EX2 177 A4
Exeter, Heavitree EX2 177 F5
Exeter, Pinhoe EX4 174 D2
Feniton EX14 84 E2
Frithelstock Stone EX38 40 F5
Great Torrington EX38 159 C5
Hatherleigh EX20 75 C7
Holsworthy EX22 164 C4
Kingsbridge TQ7 258 F2
Langtree EX38 40 F2
Membury EX13 87 D5
Modbury PL21 137 B2
Newton St Cyres EX5 82 F8
North Tamerton EX22 89 D8
Parracombe EX31 4 D1
St John PL11 252 B8
Salcombe TQ8 259 E5
Sheldon EX14 66 F3
Shobrooke EX17 80 E4
Slapton TQ7 145 D3
Stokeinteignhead TQ12 209 B2
Swimbridge EX32 28 E8
Tavistock PL19 171 C5
Torquay TQ2 219 F5
Trusham TQ13 113 D1
Whitestone EX4 98 E4
Winkleigh EX19 58 F3
Yealmpton PL8 257 F4
Church Lake 8 EX32 17 B2
Churchlands EX17 78 C4
Churchlands Cl PL6 245 E7
Churchlands Rd PL6 245 E8
Church Lane Cross EX17 59 F2
Church Lane Head TQ13 121 B2
Church Lea PL19 171 E2
Church Mdw
High Bickington EX37 43 B7
Ivybridge PL21 237 A4
Landkey EX32 17 B2
Langtree EX38 40 F2
Church Mdws
Bratton Clovelly EX20 92 A2
Okehampton EX20 170 A5
Church Mead EX14 85 B1
Church Mews TQ12 207 E6
Church Park Cl TQ9 138 C7
Church Park Ct PL6 245 E8
Church Park Rd
1 Newton Ferrers PL8 141 A7
Plymouth PL6 245 E8
Yealmpton PL8 136 A2
Church Parks EX17 80 A5
Church Path
Ashburton TQ13 130 F4
Barnstaple EX31 154 F7
Exeter EX1 178 A5
Halberton EX16 65 A7
Ipplepen TQ12 211 C2
Kingsteignton TQ12 207 E6
Okehampton EX20 170 A5
6 Paignton TQ3 226 B6
Shute EX13 102 F8
Churchpath La EX31 10 D3
Church Path Rd EX2 176 F3
Church Pk
Bideford EX39 25 A3
Cornwood PL21 133 C2
Horrabridge PL20 126 F4
Kingston TQ7 142 C6
Kingswear TQ6 234 B3
2 Newton Ferrers PL8 141 A7
Paignton TQ4 225 D4
Church Pool EX34 8 F5
Church Quillet TQ9 139 E1
Church Rd
Bishopsteignton TQ14 209 A7
Brixham TQ5 229 E5
Churchinford TA3 68 C8
Churchstanton TA3 68 B8
Cockwood EX6 201 A6
Colaton Raleigh EX10 186 E3
Dartmouth TQ6 233 E3
East Ogwell TQ12 206 D1
Ermington PL21 136 F4
Exeter, Alphington EX2 177 B1
Exeter, St Thomas EX2 177 A4
Exmouth EX8 202 A7
Georgeham EX33 8 A2
Hennock TQ13 123 B7
Highampton EX21 74 C7
Ideford TQ13 124 B4
Ilfracombe EX34 150 A5
Kenton EX6 194 F5
Luton TQ13 124 C4
Lympstone EX8 195 E5
Newton Abbot TQ12 207 C2
Plymouth, Plympton PL7 250 F4
Plymouth, Plymstock PL9 255 F7
Saltash PL12 242 D2
Silverton EX5 82 B5
Stoke Fleming TQ6 146 B7
Torquay, Barton TQ2 214 A3
Torquay, St Marychurch TQ1 220 B8
Wembury PL9 140 D8
Whimple EX5 99 E7
Church Row La PL5 244 C6
Church St Mews 4 TQ3 226 B6
Church Side EX5 179 D7
Church St
Axminster EX13 167 D5
Axmouth EX12 192 D7
Bradninch EX5 83 A7
Braunton EX33 152 D7
4 Brixham TQ5 230 C5
Buckfastleigh TQ11 236 B5
Calstock PL18 125 D3
Chulmleigh EX18 58 E8
Colyton EX24 103 A5
Combe Martin EX34 3 A3
Crediton EX17 165 D5
Cullompton EX15 163 C3
Dawlish EX7 204 C6
Dolton EX19 57 F7
Exeter EX2 177 F5
Exmouth EX8 202 A6
Halwell TQ9 139 B4
3 Honiton EX14 166 C6
Ilfracombe EX34 150 B5
Kenton EX6 194 D3
Kingsbridge TQ7 258 D5
Kingsteignton TQ12 207 E6
Lyme Regis DT7 260 E3
Modbury PL21 137 B2
Morchard Bishop EX17 61 B2
Okehampton EX20 170 B5
Paignton TQ3 226 B6
Plymouth PL3 248 A4
Salcombe TQ8 259 E5
Sandford EX17 80 A5
Sidbury EX10 101 C2
Church St *continued*
8 Sidford EX10 101 B1
Sidmouth EX10 188 B3
14 South Brent TQ10 134 F3
South Molton EX36 158 C4
Starcross EX6 201 B8
Tiverton EX16 161 C4
Torquay TQ2 219 F5
Uplyme DT7 260 B5
Witheridge EX16 46 E1
Churchstanton Prim Sch TA3 68 B8
Church Steps Cotts EX5 184 B3
Church Stile EX6 182 B4
Church Stile La EX5 184 B3
CHURCHSTOW 143 E4
Churchstow Wlk
Plymouth PL6 245 E1
Plymouth PL6 249 E8
Church Terr
7 Bampton EX16 34 B1
Exeter EX2 177 F5
CHURCHTOWN
Bridgerule 71 A6
Parracombe 4 D2
Churchtown Cl PL21 133 C2
Churchtown Dr PL12 242 D1
Churchtown Vale PL12 242 D1
Church View
Bideford EX39 26 A1
5 Chudleigh TQ13 123 E6
Dawlish EX7 204 C6
Kingsteignton TQ12 207 E6
Ottery St Mary EX11 169 D3
St Dominick PL12 125 A2
Saltash PL12 242 D2
Sutcombe EX22 54 A6
Walkhampton PL20 127 B4
Church View Ho EX5 184 B3
Churchward Rd TQ3 226 B7
Churchwater La EX18 58 D8
Churchway TQ1 220 C7
Church Way
Newton Abbot TQ12 207 E1
Plymouth PL5 247 E8
Yealmpton PL8 257 F4
Church Ways EX20 95 B5
Church Wlk
Avonwick TQ10 135 B1
17 Bideford EX39 157 A1
Stoke Gabriel TQ9 227 F7
Wembury PL9 140 C8
Churchwood Ct TQ1 220 C5
Churchyard La EX17 61 C7
CHURSCOMBE 218 E2
Churscombe Gn TQ3 218 E2
Churscombe Pk TQ3 218 D2
Churscombe Rd TQ3 218 D2
Churston Broadway TQ4 229 B7
Churston Cl TQ5 229 C5
Churston Cross
Churston Ferrers TQ5 229 E4
West Putford EX22 39 B2
Churston Ct TQ7 258 D4
CHURSTON FERRERS 229 E4
Churston Ferrers Gram Sch TQ5 229 C5
Churston Rd TQ5 229 E5
Churston Rise EX12 191 F8
Churston Sta★ TQ5 229 C5
Churston Way TQ5 230 B4
Chute St EX1 261 C4
Cider Press Rd PL15 89 D2
Cider Way EX36 158 B4
Cinder Hill TA20 69 C5
Cinders La TQ6 146 B7
Cintra Terr EX39 157 A4
Cistern St TQ9 223 B5
Citadel Ope 12 PL1 263 A2
Citadel Rd PL1 262 B2
Citadel Road E PL1 263 A2
Citadel Road W PL1 262 C2
City Arc EX4 261 A2
City Bsns Pk PL3 248 A4
City Coll Plymouth (Camels Head Tech Ctr) PL5 247 E8
City Coll Plymouth (Deep Blue Sound) PL1 263 A2
City Coll Plymouth (Goschen Ctr) PL2 247 E5
City Coll Plymouth (Kings Road Ctr) PL1 248 A2
City Coll Plymouth (Learning Warehouse) PL1 262 B2
City Coll Plymouth (Marine Skills Ctr) PL1 247 F1
City Coll Plymouth (Prince's Trust Ctr) PL4 263 A2
City Ind Est EX2 261 B1
Claddon La TQ1, TQ2 214 A5
Clampet La 9 TQ14 210 C4
Clampits Stile TQ11 135 C6
Clampitt Cl TQ12 211 D1
Clampitt Rd TQ12 211 D2
Clampitts EX15 163 B2
Clanage Cross TQ14 124 C1
Clanage St TQ14 208 F8
Clannaborough Cross EX17 78 E5
CLAPHAM 114 B6
Claponmill Cross EX5 83 B2
Clappentail Ct DT7 260 C4
Clappentail La DT7 260 C3
Clappentail Pk DT7 260 C3
Clapperbrook La EX2 177 B1
Clapperbrook La E EX2 177 D2
Clapper Cross
Bondleigh EX20 77 B8
Zeal Monachorum EX17 78 B5
Clapper La EX14 166 C7
Clapps La EX11 169 D3
Clapp's La
Beer EX12 191 D5
Seaton EX12 192 B5
CLAPWORTHY 29 D3
Clapworthy Cross EX36 29 D2
Clara Pl EX3 182 E5
Claredale Rd EX8 202 B6
Clare Dr EX16 161 F6
Clare Ind Est PL4 263 B2
Claremont Ave TQ12 213 A4
Claremont Field EX11 169 D3
Claremont Gr
Exeter EX2 261 C1
Exmouth EX8 202 B7
Claremont La EX8 202 C7
Claremont Pl EX20 75 C7
Claremont St PL1 262 C4
Clarence Cotts 5 EX34 150 B6
Clarence Ct PL1 262 A3
Clarence Hill TQ6 233 F4
Clarence Ho TQ2 219 E6
Clarence Pl
15 Barnstaple EX32 155 B3
Exeter EX4 261 C4
Plymouth, Morice Town PL2 247 E4
Plymouth, Stonehouse PL1 262 A3
Clarence Rd
Budleigh Salterton EX9 198 A2
6 Exeter EX4 177 A5
Exmouth EX8 202 A7
Torpoint PL11 247 B3
Clarence St TQ6 233 F4
Clarendon TQ1 220 C3
Clarendon Cl TQ1 219 F6
Clarendon Ct TQ1 220 C4
Clarendon Gdns 3 EX31 154 C1
Clarendon Ho 1 PL1 247 F3
Clarendon La 11 PL3 247 F3
Clarendon Rd TQ12 211 D2
Clare Pl PL4 263 B2
Clare St PL21 237 C4
Claridge The TQ3 226 C8
Clarke Cl EX15 65 F7
Clarke Ctr The EX2 177 C2
Clarke Mead EX2 178 C4
Clarks Barn Rd TQ7 143 E7
Clarks La EX20 57 A6
Clatworthy La EX32 29 E7
Claude Dix Cl 1 EX31 155 A7
Claw Cross EX39 38 F5
Clawford Cross EX22 72 D3
Clawford Vineyard & Fisheries★ EX22 72 D3
Claw Hill EX16 62 F4
Claw Pk EX22 72 B2
CLAWTON 72 B2
Clawton Prim Sch EX22 72 B1
Clayfield Villas 6 EX32 155 B4
Clayford La TA22 33 C5
Clayford Rd TA22 33 C5
CLAYHANGER 35 C1
CLAYHIDON 52 E2
Clayhidon Crossway EX15 52 E2
Clay La
Chudleigh Knighton TQ13 123 C3
Colyton EX24 102 F4
Colyton EX24 103 A4
Copplestone EX17 79 A6
Dartington TQ9 223 A8
Lympstone EX8 195 E4
Teignmouth TQ14 210 B5
Uffculme EX15 66 A8
Clayland Cross TQ4 225 E4
Claylands Dr TQ4 225 F4
Claylands View EX14 166 B4
Claylands Way TQ3 225 E4
Claymans Pathway PL21 237 A6
Claypark Hill EX16 47 D5
Clay Park Terr TQ9 228 A7
Clay Pit Cl EX5 179 B3
CLAYPITS 34 C4
Claypits Covert Cross EX31 154 A2
Claypits Rd EX31 154 A3
Claypits Way TQ13 123 E2
Claytonia Cl PL6 241 C1
Clayton Pl PL4 249 B2
Clayton Rd
Exeter EX4 177 A7
Plymouth PL4 249 B2
CLEARBROOK 132 A8
Clearbrook Ave PL5 243 E1
Clear View PL12 242 E3
Cleatlands Cl TQ4 225 E4
CLEAVE 86 C3
Cleaveanger La EX17 60 B1
Cleave Cl
Barnstaple EX31 154 D4
Folly Gate EX20 75 F1
Tedburn St Mary EX6 97 F4
Cleave Cross EX14 86 C3
Cleave Hill
Dolton EX19 57 E6
Meshaw EX36 46 A6
Cleave La
Bishop's Tawton EX32 27 F7
Burrington EX37 44 A2
Chapelton EX32 28 A7
Wilmington EX14 86 C3
Cleave La End EX32 28 A7
Cleaveland Rise TQ12 206 F1
Cleave Lane End EX32 27 F7
Cleave Pk EX31 153 F5
Cleave Rd EX31 154 D4
Cleaves Cl EX5 81 E5
Cleave The PL10 253 B2
Cleavewood Dr EX39 157 D1
Cleeve Dr PL21 237 B5
Cleeve Gdns PL2 248 A8
Cleeve The EX15 66 E8
Clegg Ave PL11 246 E3
Cleland Ct TQ14 208 F8
Clematon Hill TQ7 142 E3
Clement Rd PL7 251 B5
Clement's La EX32 28 B8
Clennon Ave TQ4 226 B4
Clennon Ct
5 Brixham TQ5 230 C3
Torquay TQ2 214 A2
Clennon Dr TQ4 226 B4
Clennon Gdns TQ4 226 B4
Clennon Hts TQ4 226 B4
Clennon La TQ2 214 A2
Clennon Pk TQ4 226 B4
Clennon Rise TQ4 226 B4
Clennon Summit TQ4 226 B4
Clennon Valley Ct TQ4 226 B4
Clennon View TQ3 226 B3
Clerk Cl EX8 196 C2
Cleve Ct TQ1 220 E5
Clevedon Cl EX4 173 D1
Clevedon Ho EX10 188 C5
Clevedon Park Ave PL2 248 B6
Clevedon Pk EX10 188 C5
Cleveland EX17 78 F7
Cleveland Ct
Exeter EX1 261 C4
Paignton TQ4 226 C5
Cleveland Dr TQ7 142 E3
Cleveland Gdns EX1 261 C4
Cleveland Pl
8 Dawlish EX7 204 E6
Exmouth EX8 201 F6
Cleveland Rd
Paignton TQ4 226 C5
Plymouth PL4 263 C3
Torquay TQ2 219 F6
Clevelands Pk EX39 157 A6
Cleveland St 7 EX4 177 A5
Cleveland Terr EX39 156 C7
Cleve Rd EX4 176 F6
Cleverdon Cross EX22 53 F8
Cleverhayes La EX14 86 B4
Cleve Terr TQ1 220 E5
Cliff Bastin Cl EX2 178 C4
Cliff Castle 4 EX12 192 A4
Cliff Ct PL1 262 B1
Cliffden Cl TQ14 210 C5
Cliff Ho TQ4 226 D5
Cliff La PL10 252 A4
Cliff Mews TQ4 226 D5
CLIFFORD 38 C8
Clifford Ave TQ12 123 E1
Clifford Cl
13 Chudleigh TQ13 123 E6
Exeter EX1 178 B7
Kingsteignton TQ12 207 E7
Plymouth PL5 243 E2
Teignmouth TQ14 210 A3
Clifford Cross EX6 112 C8
Clifford Dr TQ12 180 F2
Clifford Gdns EX17 165 D5
Clifford Mews TA21 160 E6
Clifford Rd EX4 177 F8
Clifford Rd Ind Est EX4 177 F8
Clifford St
Chudleigh TQ13 123 C4
14 Chudleigh TQ13 123 E6
Kingsteignton TQ12 207 E7
Clifford Terr TA21 160 E6
Cliff Park Ave TQ4 226 C3
Cliff Park Ct TQ4 226 C3
Cliff Park Rd TQ4 226 C2
Cliff Rd
Budleigh Salterton EX9 199 G2
Paignton TQ4 226 D5
Plymouth PL1 262 B1
Salcombe TQ8 259 C3
Sidmouth EX10 188 C3
Teignmouth TQ14 210 D7
Torquay TQ2 219 F2
Wembury PL9 140 D7
Cliffside EX34 7 F6
Cliffside Rd TQ1 220 C8
Cliff Terr EX9 199 G2
Cliff View Terr PL18 125 D6
CLIFTON 10 C4
Clifton Ave PL7 250 E7
Clifton Bank 5 TQ3 226 A6
Clifton Cl
Paignton TQ3 225 F6
Plymouth PL7 250 E7
Clifton Cres TQ3 226 A6
Clifton Ct
Croyde EX33 7 E3
Exeter EX1 177 E7
3 Ilfracombe EX34 150 B5
Clifton Gdns TQ3 226 A6
Clifton Gr TQ3 226 A6
Clifton Hill EX1 177 E7
Clifton Hill Sp Ctr EX1 177 E7
Clifton Ho 17 TQ14 210 C5
Clifton La EX31 10 B4
Clifton Pl
Dawlish EX7 204 C6
16 Ilfracombe EX34 150 B5
Plymouth PL4 263 A4
Salcombe TQ8 259 E5
Clifton Rd
Exeter EX1 261 C3
Paignton TQ3 226 A6
Clifton Rise TQ3 226 A6
Clifton St
Barnstaple EX31 154 F4
Bideford EX39 157 B1
Exeter EX1 177 E6
Plymouth PL4 263 A4
Clifton Terr
Barnstaple EX31 154 E4
11 Northam EX39 157 A7
12 South Brent TQ10 134 F3
Torquay TQ1 220 B4
Climsland Rd TQ4 226 A5
Clinket La EX33 8 D1
Clinton Ave
Exeter EX4 177 E8
Plymouth PL4 249 A4
Clinton CE Prim Sch The EX20 57 A6
Clinton Cl EX9 197 F2
Clinton Gdns EX20 57 A7
Clinton Rd EX32 155 B3
Clinton Rise EX12 191 E6
Clinton Sq EX8 201 F6
Clinton St EX4 177 A5
Clinton Terr
11 Barnstaple EX32 155 B3
Budleigh Salterton EX9 198 A2
Great Torrington EX38 159 B5
Merton EX20 57 A7
Millbrook PL10 252 F6
Clipper Quay EX2 261 B1
Clipper Wharf EX8 201 E6
Cliston Ave EX8 196 E2
Cliston Cross TQ9 139 C2
Cliston La EX20 76 E4
Clittaford Rd PL6 244 F7
Clittaford Road Ind Est PL5 245 A7
Clittaford View PL6 244 E7
Cliveden Rd EX39 26 A4
Cloake Pl PL12 239 A2
Cloakham Dr EX13 167 E7
Clobells 3 TQ10 134 F2
Cloepark La EX17 60 B6
Cloford Cl PL3 249 D1
Cloggshill Cross EX31 27 B1
Cloister Rd EX4 177 F7
Clonway 1 PL20 126 F3
Clooneavin Path EX35 151 C5
Close The
Barnstaple EX32 155 C5
14 Bere Alston PL20 125 E1
Brixham TQ5 230 C6
Holcombe EX7 210 F8
Paignton TQ4 229 C8
Rewe EX5 82 A2
Saltash PL12 242 C3
Seaton EX12 192 A5
Tiverton EX16 161 F6
Closewool Gr EX36 158 B5
Cloud Berry Cotts TQ3 225 E3
Cloutman's La EX33 7 E2
CLOVELLY 23 E3
Clovelly Apts 17 EX34 150 B5
Clovelly Cl EX39 156 E1
Clovelly Court Gdns★ EX39 23 D4
Clovelly Cross EX39 23 D2
Clovelly Gardens N EX39 156 E1
Clovelly Gardens S 2 EX39 156 F1
Clovelly Prim Sch EX39 23 D3
Clovelly Rd
Bideford EX39 25 D4
Plymouth PL4 263 C1
Clovelly Rise
Dawlish EX7 204 D5
Paignton TQ3 225 E6
Clovelly Road Ind Est EX39 25 D4
Clovelly View PL9 255 A7
Clover Ave EX4 176 E8
Clover Cl TQ3 225 E2
Cloverdale Ct DT7 260 E3

Clo–Coo 275

Clover Dr
Cullompton EX15 ... 163 B2
Dawlish EX7 ... 204 E8
Clover Pk PL8 ... 257 A5
Clover Rise PL6 ... 245 E8
Clover Way EX32 ... 155 E4
Clover Wlk PL12 ... 242 C3
Clover Wy TQ12 ... 206 D5
Clowance Cl PL1 ... 247 F1
Clowance La PL1 ... 247 E1
Clowance St PL1 ... 247 F1
Cluden Rd EX39 ... 156 F6
Cludens Cl EX2 ... 181 B8
Clumpit La EX6 ... 194 A1
Clydesdale Ct EX5 ... 173 A1
Clydesdale Rd EX4 ... 173 A1
Clyde St PL2 ... 247 F5
Clyst Ave
Brixham TQ5 ... 230 A2
Clyst Honiton EX5 ... 175 E2
Clyst Ct EX5 ... 179 F2
Clyst Halt Ave EX2 ... 178 E3
Clyst Hayes Gdns
EX9 ... 197 E1
Clyst Heath EX2 ... 178 D3
Clyst Heath Com Prim
Sch EX2 ... 178 D3
CLYST HONITON ... 179 D8
CLYST HYDON ... 83 D4
Clyst Hydon Prim Sch
EX15 ... 83 D4
Clyst Rd
Exeter EX3 ... 178 F2
Topsham EX3 ... 182 F7
CLYST ST GEORGE ... 183 C6
CLYST ST
LAWRENCE ... 83 C3
CLYST ST MARY ... 179 B3
Clyst St Mary Prim Sch
EX5 ... 179 A2
Clyst Units EX2 ... 177 D1
Clyst Vale Com Coll
EX5 ... 175 D5
Clyst Valley Rd EX5 ... 179 B2
Clyst View EX1 ... 178 D7
Clyst William Cross
EX15 ... 84 B5
Coach Dr EX39 ... 25 F4
Coach Ho La TQ2 ... 219 E4
Coach Ho The
Grenofen PL19 ... 126 D6
Paignton TQ3 ... 226 C7
Coach House Mews
PL9 ... 256 B6
Coach House Mws 15
TQ13 ... 123 E6
Coach Pl TQ12 ... 207 C2
Coach Rd
Newton Abbot TQ12 ... 207 B1
Noss Mayo PL8 ... 140 F6
Silverton EX5 ... 82 B6
Coach Rd The DT7 ... 260 C8
Coaker Rd EX1 ... 174 F2
Coarsewell Cross
PL21 ... 138 A5
Coastguard Cotts
Challaborough TQ7 ... 142 D4
Dawlish EX7 ... 204 F6
Down Thomas PL9 ... 254 F2
Inner Hope TQ7 ... 147 B6
Stoke EX39 ... 22 B3
Torquay TQ1 ... 220 D2
Coastguard Hill EX9 ... 199 H2
Coastguard Rd EX9 ... 198 B1
Coast Rd EX34 ... 2 E4
Coates Rd
East-the-Water EX39 ... 26 B4
Exeter EX2 ... 178 B5
COBB ... 260 D2
Cobbacombe Cross
EX16 ... 49 D6
COBBATON ... 28 D5
Cobbaton Combat
Collection (Mus)★
EX37 ... 28 D5
Cobbaton Cross EX37 ... 28 D6
Cobbett Rd PL5 ... 244 B2
Cobb La PL9 ... 255 F6
Cobblestone La PL1 ... 248 A1
Cobb Rd DT7 ... 260 D2
Cobb Terr DT7 ... 260 D2
Cobb The★ DT7 ... 260 D1
Cob Castle TA21 ... 52 D8
Cobden La EX5 ... 99 D7
Cobham Cl PL6 ... 245 C6
Coblands Cross EX5 ... 82 A7
Cobley Ct EX1 ... 178 D8
Cobley La
Bideford EX39 ... 26 C6
Lapford EX17 ... 60 E4
West Worlington EX17 ... 60 F6
Cob Mdw EX20 ... 75 C7
Cobourg St PL1 ... 262 C3
COBURG ... 123 E5
Coburg Cl TA21 ... 52 F7
Coburg Cres 23 TQ13 ... 123 E6
Coburg Pl
Cullompton EX15 ... 163 C6
Torquay TQ2 ... 220 B4
Coburg Rd EX10 ... 188 A3
Coburg Terr
8 Ilfracombe EX34 ... 150 C6
Sidmouth EX10 ... 188 A3
Cockeram's Rd EX5 ... 99 C8
Cockhaven Cl TQ14 ... 208 F7
Cockhaven Mead
TQ14 ... 208 F7
Cockhaven Rd TQ14 ... 208 F7
COCKINGFORD ... 121 B2
COCKINGTON ... 219 C4
Cockington Cl PL6 ... 245 E1
Cockington Com Prim
Sch 8 TQ2 ... 219 F5
Cockington Ctry Pk★
TQ2 ... 219 B4
Cockington La
Paignton TQ3 ... 219 C1
Torquay TQ2 ... 219 D4
Cockington Rd TQ3 ... 219 A3
Cockington Wlk PL6 ... 245 C1
Cockland Hill TA21 ... 51 C8
Cockland La EX16 ... 48 F3
Cockles La 2 EX17 ... 165 D5
Cockles Rise EX17 ... 165 D5
Cockpit Hill EX15 ... 163 C3
Cockrams Butt Cross
EX37 ... 29 B1
Cockram's La EX37 ... 43 F7
Cockrattle La EX17 ... 61 B3
Cockspark La EX14 ... 84 F8
Cocks Pk TQ7 ... 142 D7
Cocktree Throat EX20 ... 95 C8
COCKWOOD ... 201 B5
Cockwood Prim Sch
EX6 ... 201 B6
Codden Cross EX32 ... 28 A8
Codden Hill Cross
EX32 ... 27 E8
Coddiford Cross EX17 ... 62 E2
Coddiford Hill EX17 ... 62 E1
Coddiford La EX17 ... 62 F2
Codrington St EX1 ... 261 C3
Coffins La EX6 ... 181 F4
COFFINSWELL ... 213 B6
Coffinswell La TQ12 ... 213 A4
Coffintree Cross EX17 ... 80 F6
Coffintree Hill EX17 ... 80 F7
COFTON ... 200 F5
Cofton Hill EX6 ... 201 A5
Cofton La
Cockwood EX6 ... 200 F5
Westwood EX6 ... 201 A6
Cofton Rd EX2 ... 177 D1
Cohort Cl EX20 ... 170 D7
Coil Cross EX31 ... 10 B6
Coker Ave TQ2 ... 214 A4
Cokers Elm EX14 ... 87 A7
Cokers Elm Cross
EX14 ... 87 A7
Colands Ct EX2 ... 181 A8
Colaton La EX5 ... 81 E5
COLATON RALEIGH ... 186 D3
Colaton Terr EX10 ... 187 F4
Colborne Rd PL6 ... 245 A2
Colcombe La
Dalwood EX13 ... 86 F1
Shute EX13 ... 102 F8
Colcombe Rd EX24 ... 103 A5
COLDEAST ... 180 D1
Cold East Cross
TQ13 ... 121 E1
COLDHARBOUR ... 66 A7
Coldharbour
Bideford EX39 ... 157 A2
3 Totnes TQ9 ... 223 E5
Uffculme EX15 ... 66 A7
Coldharbour Cross
Chilsworthy EX22 ... 53 E1
Loddiswell PL21 ... 138 B3
Coldharbour Mill (Mus)★
EX15 ... 66 A7
Coldharbour Rd
EX16 ... 161 A3
Coldrenick St PL5 ... 243 D1
COLDRIDGE ... 59 F2
Coldwell La EX12 ... 192 D6
Coldwell Lane Terr
EX12 ... 192 D7
Colebred Cl EX11 ... 169 E4
COLEBROOK
Cullompton ... 65 A1
Plymouth ... 250 E6
COLEBROOKE ... 79 A3
Colebrooke La EX15 ... 65 A1
Colebrook La PL7 ... 250 E7
Colebrook Rd
Plymouth, Plympton
PL7 ... 250 E6
Plymouth, St Budeaux
PL5 ... 243 D1
COLEFORD ... 79 A3
Coleford Hill EX16 ... 48 B6
Cole La
Ivybridge PL21 ... 237 E6
Ivybridge, Higher Keaton
PL21 ... 237 C1
Coleman Ave TQ14 ... 210 A5
Coleman Cl EX16 ... 64 D8
Coleman Dr PL9 ... 255 F4
Colemans Cross
PL15 ... 105 B5
Coleman's Cross
EX24 ... 102 D6
Cole Moore Mdw
PL19 ... 171 B6
Coleridge Ave PL6 ... 244 F2
Coleridge Barns TQ7 ... 145 A2
Coleridge Cl EX8 ... 196 C4
Coleridge Ct TQ2 ... 214 A2
Coleridge La TQ7 ... 145 A2
Coleridge Rd
Exeter EX2 ... 176 F4
Ottery St Mary EX11 ... 169 F4
10 Plymouth PL2 ... 248 F4
Plymouth PL4 ... 249 A4
8 Tiverton EX16 ... 64 D7
Cole's Cnr EX18 ... 59 C8
Coles Cotts PL9 ... 255 C1
Cole's Cotts PL7 ... 250 E6
Cole's Cross TQ9 ... 144 F5
Coles Ct EX18 ... 58 E8
Cole's Ct TQ6 ... 233 F3
Colesdown Hill PL9 ... 250 B1
Cole's La TQ12 ... 212 F5
Coles Mead EX16 ... 161 F4
Coles Mews EX2 ... 177 A4
Coles Mill Cl EX22 ... 164 C4
Coles's La EX13 ... 104 B8
Colesworthy Cross
TQ12 ... 180 B2
Coleton Fishacre★
TQ6 ... 234 F2
Colhayne La
Dalwood EX13 ... 86 F1
Shute EX13 ... 102 F8
Colin Campbell Ct
10 Plymouth PL1 ... 262 B3
Plymouth PL3 ... 262 B3
Colin Rd TQ3 ... 226 C7
Collabear Cnr EX31 ... 27 D8
Collabridge Hill
Dunsford EX6 ... 97 D1
Dunsford EX6 ... 112 E8
Collabridge La EX6 ... 112 E8
Collabridge Rd EX6 ... 112 E8
Collacombe Cross
PL19 ... 116 D4
Collacott Cl EX22 ... 38 E1
Collacott Cross
EX38 ... 40 F2
Collacotts La EX19 ... 59 B2
Collaford Cl PL7 ... 251 A4
Collaford Farm Bsns
Units PL7 ... 136 A6
Collapark TQ9 ... 223 B6
Collard La PL7 ... 132 D4
Collaton Cross
Halwell TQ9 ... 139 D4
Malborough TQ7 ... 147 F6
Yealmpton PL8 ... 141 B8
Collaton Ct TQ2 ... 219 C8
Collaton Ho 7 TQ1 ... 220 D4
Collaton La PL19 ... 117 F2
Collaton Mews TQ4 ... 225 D4
Collaton Rd
Malborough TQ7 ... 147 F6
Torquay TQ2 ... 219 C8
COLLATON ST
MARY ... 225 C4
Collaton St Mary CE Prim
Sch TQ3 ... 225 C5
Collatons Wlk EX17 ... 78 C4
Coll Ct EX15 ... 66 A7
College TQ13 ... 180 E8
College Ave
Exeter EX2 ... 261 C2
Plymouth PL3 ... 248 E5
Tavistock PL19 ... 117 C1
Tavistock PL19 ... 171 D6
College Cl EX39 ... 156 C6
College Ct
Barnstaple EX31 ... 154 D3
1 Torquay TQ1 ... 219 F6
College Dean Cl PL6 ... 245 C5
College Gn
Bideford EX39 ... 156 F2
Uffculme EX15 ... 66 A7
College La
Clyst Hydon EX5, EX15 ... 83 B5
Ide EX2 ... 176 C2
Plymouth PL4 ... 248 F4
College Park Pl PL3 ... 248 E5
College Rd
Cullompton EX15 ... 163 C4
Exeter EX1 ... 261 C3
Newton Abbot TQ12 ... 207 C2
Plymouth PL2 ... 247 E5
Shebbear EX21 ... 55 F4
College Road Prim Sch
PL2 ... 247 E5
College The
Exeter EX2 ... 176 D2
Ottery St Mary EX11 ... 169 D4
College View
Plymouth PL3 ... 248 E4
Tiverton EX16 ... 161 C6
College Way
Dartmouth TQ6 ... 233 E4
Exeter EX1 ... 178 E7
Colleton Cl EX8 ... 202 C8
Colleton Cres EX2 ... 261 B2
Colleton Ct 9 EX2 ... 261 B2
Colleton Gate EX18 ... 44 C1
Colleton Gr EX2 ... 261 B1
Colleton Hill EX2 ... 261 B1
Colleton Ho EX2 ... 261 B1
Colleton Mews EX2 ... 261 B1
COLLETON MILLS ... 44 C2
Colleton Row EX2 ... 261 B1
Colleton Way EX8 ... 202 C8
Collett Way TQ12 ... 207 E3
Colleybrook Cl 1
TQ12 ... 123 E1
Colley Cres TQ3 ... 226 A6
Colley End Pk TQ3 ... 226 A6
Colley End Rd TQ3 ... 226 A6
Colley Farm La TA20 ... 69 B8
Colley La EX7, TQ13 ... 124 D5
Colley Lane Cross
TQ13 ... 124 D4
Colley Park Rd EX33 ... 152 D5
Colliepriest View
EX16 ... 161 B1
Colliers Cl 5 PL9 ... 140 D8
Collier's Mews 1
EX20 ... 170 B6
Collin Cl PL5 ... 243 D1
Collingsdown Cross
EX39 ... 39 F4
Collingwood Ave
PL4 ... 263 C2
Collingwood Cl
Dartmouth TQ6 ... 233 C3
Torquay TQ1 ... 220 C2
Collingwood Rd
Dartmouth TQ6 ... 233 C3
Paignton TQ4 ... 226 A5
Plymouth PL1 ... 248 A3
Collingwood Villas 5
PL1 ... 248 A3
Collins Pk EX9 ... 198 B6
Collins Rd
Exeter EX4 ... 173 E2
Totnes TQ9 ... 223 B6
COLLIPRIEST ... 161 C2
Collipriest Ho EX16 ... 161 C2
Collipriest La EX16 ... 161 C1
Collipriest Rd EX16 ... 161 C2
COLLITON ... 84 C7
Colliton Cross EX14 ... 84 C6
Colliver Cross EX9 ... 198 E5
Collyland La EX17 ... 62 C3
Colmer Cross PL21 ... 138 A4
Colmer Ho PL21 ... 138 A4
Colne Gdns PL3 ... 249 B5
Colombelles Cl EX31 ... 153 E5
Colscott Cross EX22 ... 39 C1
Colston Cl PL6 ... 245 B6
Colston Cross EX13 ... 88 B4
Colston La EX16 ... 47 E1
Colston Rd
Buckfastleigh TQ11 ... 236 E3
Rattery TQ9 ... 215 A3
Coltishall Cl PL5 ... 243 F4
Coltness Rd PL9 ... 256 B5
Coltsfield Cl PL6 ... 249 B8
COLUMBJOHN ... 82 C2
Columbjohn Cross
EX5 ... 82 B2
Columbus Cl PL5 ... 243 C2
Colvin Cl EX8 ... 202 D7
Colway Cl DT7 ... 260 D5
Colway Cross TQ14 ... 124 B1
Colway La
Chudleigh TQ13 ... 123 F6
Lyme Regis DT7 ... 260 D4
Colway Rise DT7 ... 260 E5
Colwill Rd PL6 ... 245 E3
Colwill Wlk
Bideford EX39 ... 156 D1
Plymouth PL6 ... 245 F3
Colwyn Ct TQ1 ... 220 E5
Colwyn Rd PL11 ... 247 A3
COLYFORD ... 103 B3
Colyford Comm Nature
Reserve★ EX24 ... 103 B3
Colyford Rd EX12 ... 192 B7
Coly Rd
Colyton EX24 ... 103 A4
Honiton EX14 ... 166 C4
COLYTON ... 103 A5
Colyton Bsns Pk
EX24 ... 103 A5
Colyton Cross EX14 ... 86 C2
Colyton Gram Sch
EX24 ... 103 A3
Colyton Hill EX13,
EX24 ... 103 B6
Colyton Prim Sch 26
EX24 ... 103 A4
Colyton Rd
Colyton EX13, EX24 ... 103 A6
Northleigh EX24 ... 102 C6
Colyton Sports Ctr
EX24 ... 103 A3
Coly Vale EX24 ... 103 A4
Combas La EX33 ... 7 E2
COMBE
Brixton ... 256 E5
Buckfastleigh ... 130 A2
Combe Beacon La
TA20 ... 69 F7
Combe Cl EX13 ... 167 D5
Combe Cross
Ashburton TQ13 ... 131 C5
Aveton Gifford PL21 ... 143 A8
Ivybridge PL21 ... 137 B6
Kingsbridge TQ7 ... 258 D7
Loddiswell TQ7 ... 138 C1
Shillingford EX16 ... 34 D4
Strete TQ6 ... 145 E7
Combe Farm Barns
TQ7 ... 143 A7
COMBE FISHACRE ... 217 E7
Combefishacre Cross
TQ12 ... 217 D8
Combefishacre La TQ9,
TQ12 ... 217 D6
Combe Hayes EX10 ... 188 B8
Combehead Droveway
EX13 ... 86 E3
Combehead La EX13 ... 86 F3
Combe Hill EX15 ... 52 C2
Combe Hill Cross
TQ12 ... 123 F2
Combe Hill Dro TA20 ... 69 F5
COMBEINTEIGNHEAD
... 208 E4
Combe La
Dulverton TA22 ... 33 D6
East Anstey TA22 ... 32 F6
Galmpton TQ5 ... 229 B3
Combe La continued
Northleigh EX24 ... 102 B7
North Tawton EX17 ... 77 F1
Spreyton EX17 ... 95 F8
Torquay TQ2 ... 214 A1
Whitestaunton TA20 ... 69 E5
Combeland La TA22 ... 34 A5
COMBE MARTIN ... 3 B3
Combe Martin Mus★
EX34 ... 2 F4
Combe Martin Prim Sch
EX34 ... 2 F4
Combe Martin Wildlife &
Dinosaur Pk★ EX34 ... 3 C2
Combe Moor La EX17 ... 77 F1
COMBE PAFFORD ... 214 A1
Combe Pafford Sch
TQ2 ... 214 B3
Combepark Cross
TQ9 ... 217 A1
Combe Pk
Ilfracombe EX34 ... 150 D5
Torquay TQ3 ... 214 A1
COMBE RALEIGH ... 85 D5
Combe Rd
Axmouth EX12, DT7 ... 193 B6
Torquay TQ2 ... 214 B2
Comber's Cross EX31 ... 27 E6
COMBE ST NICHOLAS ... 69 F6
Combesdown Cross
EX22 ... 72 C6
Combeshead Cross
Cornwood PL21 ... 133 F1
Diptford TQ9 ... 138 E6
Heasley Mill EX36 ... 19 C2
Combeshead La
Dunchideock EX2 ... 114 A7
West Anstey EX36 ... 32 A7
Combe Wood Rd TA20 ... 69 F5
Combley Dr PL6 ... 245 D4
COMBPYNE ... 103 F3
Combpyne La DT7,
EX13 ... 193 E8
Combpyne Rd EX13 ... 103 D5
Combrew La EX31 ... 16 A3
Combsland Cross
EX36 ... 31 B4
Combsland New Cross
EX36 ... 31 B4
Comburg Cl EX8 ... 196 E3
Come Park La EX35 ... 151 E2
Comer Cl EX1 ... 174 F3
Comer's Cross TA24 ... 21 E6
Comer's Gate TA24 ... 21 E6
Comers La EX34 ... 3 B3
Comfrey Ave TQ12 ... 206 B5
Comilla Cl EX8 ... 196 C3
Commanders Cut
TQ6 ... 233 E4
Commercial Ope PL4 ... 263 B2
Commercial Pl PL4 ... 263 B1
Commercial Point EX34 ... 1 F1
Commercial Rd
Barnstaple EX31 ... 154 F5
Calstock PL18 ... 125 D3
Crediton EX17 ... 165 E5
9 Dawlish EX7 ... 204 E6
Exeter EX2 ... 261 A2
Horrabridge PL20 ... 126 F4
Paignton TQ4 ... 226 B6
Plymouth PL4 ... 263 B2
Uffculme EX15 ... 66 A7
Commercial St
Gunnislake PL18 ... 125 D6
Plymouth PL4 ... 263 B2
Commin's Rd EX1 ... 177 F7
Commodore Cl EX39 ... 156 E7
Common Head EX37 ... 43 C3
Common Hill EX12 ... 191 D4
Common La
Beer EX12 ... 191 D5
Huish Champflower TA4 ... 35 D7
Kingskerswell TQ12 ... 212 E2
Milton Combe PL6 ... 241 B5
Commonmarsh La
EX17 ... 165 E5
Common Moor La
EX38 ... 56 A7
Common Moors La
EX36 ... 158 A6
Commons Hill
Christow EX6 ... 112 F3
Christow EX6 ... 113 A4
Commons La TQ14 ... 210 A2
Commons Mews
EX39 ... 156 E7
Commons Old Rd
TQ14 ... 210 A2
Common The EX8 ... 197 A4
Company Rd EX31 ... 153 E6
Compass Dr PL7 ... 251 A7
Compass Quay EX2 ... 261 B1
Compass South TQ1 ... 221 A3
COMPTON ... 218 D6
Compton Ave PL3 ... 249 A5
Compton Castle★
TQ3 ... 218 C6
Compton CE Prim Sch
PL3 ... 249 A6
Compton Ho TQ1 ... 220 C7
Compton Knoll Cl
PL3 ... 249 A6
Compton Leigh PL3 ... 249 A6
Compton Park Rd
PL3 ... 248 F5
Compton Pl TQ1 ... 214 B1
Comptonpool Cross
TQ3 ... 218 C8
Compton Rd TQ7 ... 144 C1
Compton Vale PL3 ... 249 A5
Concorde Dr EX32 ... 155 C5
Concorde Rd EX8 ... 196 F1
Condor Dr TQ2 ... 213 D2
Conduit Sq 11 TQ13 ... 123 E6
Coney Ave EX32 ... 155 B3
Coney Ct EX2 ... 261 A1
Coneypark La EX34 ... 3 A3
Congella Rd TQ1 ... 220 C6
Congram's Cl 7
EX32 ... 155 B3
Congreve Gdns PL5 ... 244 C1
Conifer Cl EX15 ... 163 C5
Conifer Mews EX2 ... 178 D3
Conifers The
Bovey Tracey TQ13 ... 180 C4
Torquay TQ2 ... 214 B3
Conigar Cl EX15 ... 67 B8
Conigar La EX15 ... 67 A7
Coniger Cross EX8 ... 196 B7
Coniston Cl TQ5 ... 230 A2
Coniston Gdns PL6 ... 244 F4
Coniston Rd TQ12 ... 211 F8
Conker Gdns 9 PL7 ... 251 B5
Connaught Ave PL4 ... 248 F4
Connaught Cl EX10 ... 188 A4
Connaught La 6 PL4 ... 248 E4
Connaught Rd EX10 ... 188 A4
Conniford La TQ12 ... 211 D1
Connybear Cross
TQ12 ... 213 B8
Connybear La TQ12 ... 213 C7
Conqueror Dr PL5 ... 244 E1
Conrad Ave EX4 ... 178 B8
Conrad Rd PL5 ... 244 D1
Consols Cl PL21 ... 237 E4
Consort Cl PL3 ... 248 E7
Consort Ho PL5 ... 243 B2
Constable Cl PL5 ... 244 D3
Constance Pl PL1 ... 262 A3
Constantine Cl EX12 ... 191 F8
Constantine St PL4 ... 263 A3
Constitution Hill
EX32 ... 155 B4
Contour Hts TQ6 ... 234 A3
Convent Cl
Barnstaple EX32 ... 155 C2
Saltash PL12 ... 242 E3
Convent Fields EX10 ... 187 F4
Convent Lodge 3
TQ14 ... 210 B6
Convent Rd EX10 ... 187 F4
Conway Cres 2 TQ4 ... 226 A5
Conway Ct EX1 ... 261 C2
Conway Gdns PL2 ... 248 B7
Conway Ho 4 TQ3 ... 226 A5
Conway Rd TQ4 ... 226 B5
Conybeare Cl EX4 ... 178 B7
Conybeare Dr EX39 ... 156 E6
Conyngham Ct PL6 ... 249 A8
Cooban Ct PL6 ... 249 A8
COOKBURY ... 73 A8
COOKBURY WICK ... 72 F8
Cook Ct PL12 ... 242 B3
Cooke Dr TQ12 ... 211 E2
Cooks Cl
12 Ashburton TQ13 ... 131 A5
Kingsteignton TQ12 ... 207 F7
Cooks Cross EX36 ... 158 C3
Cooks Farm EX5 ... 184 C6
Cooks La EX13 ... 104 B7
Cooksley Ct PL1 ... 263 A1
Cooks Mead DT7 ... 260 A6
Cookson's Rd EX6 ... 201 A8
Cookworthy Ct TQ7 ... 258 C6
Cookworthy Forest Ctr★
EX21 ... 73 A4
Cookworthy Mus of Rural
Life★ TQ7 ... 258 C6
Cookworthy Rd
Kingsbridge TQ7 ... 258 C5
Plymouth PL2 ... 247 F6
COOMBE
Tipton St John ... 100 E2
Tiverton ... 50 A4
Coombe Ave TQ14 ... 210 A5
Coombe Ball Hill
East Worlington EX17 ... 61 C8
Witheridge EX16 ... 46 D1
Coombe Cl
Bovey Tracey TQ13 ... 180 E7
Dartmouth TQ6 ... 233 F4
Goodleigh EX32 ... 17 B5
Honiton EX14 ... 166 C4
Coombe Cross
Bovey Tracey TQ13 ... 180 E7
Christow EX6 ... 113 B2
Goodleigh EX32 ... 17 B4
Great Torrington EX38 ... 159 F8
Coombe Dean Sch
PL9 ... 256 A6
Coombe Dean Sp Ctr
PL9 ... 256 A6
Coombe Down La
PL8 ... 140 F6
Coombe Dr PL12 ... 239 A2
Coombefield La
EX13 ... 167 D5
Coombehaven TQ8 ... 259 D4
Coombe Hill EX16 ... 47 F1
Coombe House Cross
TQ9 ... 224 F2
Coombe House La
TQ9 ... 225 A2

Coombe La
Axminster EX13 ....167 D5
Bickleigh EX16 ....63 C3
Bovey Tracey TQ13 ....180 F8
Cadbury EX5.........81 C7
Cargreen PL12 ....239 A2
Cheriton Fitzpaine EX16,
  EX17............63 B3
Chulmleigh EX18......44 E4
Combe PL8 ....256 E5
Harford EX6 ....97 F7
Kingsbridge TQ7 .....258 D8
Okehampton EX20 ....170 E6
Plymouth PL5 ....244 D7
Puddington EX16 ......62 B6
Silverton EX5 ....82 B7
Silverton EX6 ....82 B7
Teignmouth TQ14 .....210 A7
COOMBELAKE.......169 B6
Coombe Mdw TQ13 ...180 E7
Coombe Mdws TQ7 ...144 F1
Coombe Orch EX12 ...192 E6
Coombe Park Cl
  PL10.............253 A2
Coombepark La EX23 .70 B7
Coombe Park La PL5 244 A3
Coombe Park Rd
  TQ14.............210 A6
Coombe Pk
  Kingsand PL10 .....253 A2
  Saltash PL12 ....242 F2
Coombe Pk La S
  TQ12.............244 A3
Coombe Rd
  Dartmouth TQ6 .....233 F4
  Paignton TQ3 ......219 C1
  Saltash PL12 ....243 A2
  Shaldon TQ14 ......209 C5
Coombesend Rd
  TQ12.............207 F7
Coombesend Road E
  TQ12.............208 A7
Coombeshead Acad
  TQ12.............207 A4
Coombeshead Rd
  TQ12.............206 F4
Coombe Shute TQ9 ...227 F7
Coombe St
  Exeter EX1 ....261 B2
  Lyme Regis DT7 ....260 E3
Coombes The [1].....154 A2
Coombe Terr EX12 ...192 E6
Coombe The
  Dartmouth TQ6 .....233 F4
  Galmpton TQ5 .....229 B5
Coombe Vale EX10 ...100 D2
Coombe Vale Rd
  TQ14.............210 A5
Coombe Valley Nature
  Reserve★ TQ14 ...124 E1
Coombe View
  Plymouth PL2 ......247 F7
  Teignmouth TQ14 ...124 E1
Coombe Way
  Bishopsteignton
  TQ14.............209 B8
  Plymouth PL5 ......243 F1
Coopers Cross EX37...44 E6
Cooper's Cross
  Chawleigh EX18 .....60 C6
  Lydford EX20 ......107 A3
Coopers Dr EX31 ....154 B2
Coopers Hill EX19....58 F3
Cooper St [1] EX39 ...157 A2
Coot Hide EX16 ......50 D1
Copland La TQ9.......223 A6
Copland Mdws TQ9 ..223 B6
Copleston Rd PL6 ....244 E5
Copley Cl TQ3 ....225 H6
Copley Dr EX31 .....154 D3
Coppard Mdws PL7 ..250 B6
Copper Beech Way
  PL6..............245 C7
Copper Castle EX14 ..166 E6
Copper Cl EX39 ......38 F8
Copperfield TQ7 .....144 F1
Copperfield Cl EX8...196 E1
Copperfields PL20 ...126 E5
Copper Pl PL1 ......262 A3
Coppers Pk PL6 .....245 E7
Copperthorn Cross
  TQ9..............222 D4
Copper Tree Cross
  TQ9..............216 C5
Copperwood Cl
  TQ13.............130 F4
Copp Hill La EX9 ....198 A2
Coppice Cl
  Barnstaple EX32....155 E3
  Fremington EX31 ...153 F6
  Raymond's Hill EX13..104 B7
Coppice Gate EX32...155 C3
Coppice Gdns PL5 ...244 E2
Coppice La EX17 .....80 A7
Coppice The
  Dawlish EX7 ....204 D4
  Ivybridge PL21 .....237 A4
Coppice Wood Dr
  PL6..............245 C7
Coppledown Gdns
  EX9..............197 F2
COPPLESTONE.......79 B6
Copplestone Dr EX4..173 A1
Copplestone La EX9..186 C4

Copplestone Prim Sch
  EX17.............79 B5
Copplestone Rd EX9 .198 A1
Copplestone Sta EX17 79 A6
Copp Path EX7.......204 C5
Copp's Cl EX39......157 A3
Copse Cl PL7........250 D4
Copse Hill La EX20 ...77 B7
Copse Rd PL7........250 D4
Copse The
  Barnstaple EX31....154 B3
  Chillington TQ7 ....145 A1
  Exeter EX2 ....182 C7
  Exmouth EX8 ......196 E2
  Newton Poppleford
  Okehampton EX20 ..170 D6
  Totnes TQ9 ....222 E6
Copsey La TQ12 .....211 B6
Copstone EX39 ......39 E7
Copstone Hill EX1....61 D5
Copthorne Gdns PL9 .255 F5
Copydown La EX5 .....82 A6
Copythorne Cl TQ5...230 A4
Copythorne Pk TQ5 ..230 A4
Copythorne Rd TQ5 ..230 A4
Coral Ave EX39 .....156 D7
Coram Ave DT7 .....260 D2
Coram Ct DT7........260 D3
Coram Manor DT7 ...260 D3
Corams La TA21 .....160 B6
Cordery Rd EX2 .....176 F3
Cordwents View EX16..65 A7
Corea Terr PL1 ......248 A2
Core Fields EX10.....188 B8
Core Hill Rd EX10 ....100 F1
Coreway EX10 ....188 B8
Coreway Cl EX10.....188 B8
CORFCOTT GREEN...71 F2
Corfe Ave PL3 ....248 F8
Corfe Cl PL21 ....237 D4
Corfe Cres TQ2 .....213 F1
Corilhead Rd EX33 ...152 D8
Coringdean Cl PL6 ...245 B6
Coriolis Way N EX1...178 D7
Cormelles Ct [13] EX34.. 3 A3
Cormorant Cl
  Marhamchurch EX23..70 A8
  Seaton EX12 ....192 B5
  Torquay TQ2 ....213 D3
Cornacre Cl TQ2 ....219 C7
Cornacre Rd TQ2 ....219 C7
Cornborough Rd
  EX39..............156 B6
Corn Cl EX5..........99 B6
Corndon Cross TQ13 .110 F4
Corner Brake PL6.....245 D7
Corner Cl TA21 ......160 D4
Corner Cotts EX16 ...65 A7
Corner La
  Combe Martin EX34...3 B3
  Halberton EX16 .....65 A7
Cornermoor Cross
  EX16..............47 C1
Cornerstone Ct PL11..247 B3
Cornfield Gdns PL7 ..251 B7
Cornfield Gn TQ2 ....214 B2
Cornfield Way EX20 ..77 C4
Cornflower Cl
  Barnstaple EX31....154 B3
  Willand EX15 ....162 E5
Cornflower Cres
  PL15..............105 A2
Cornflower Hill EX4 ..176 D8
Cornflower Way [1]
  PL19..............171 A6
Cornflower Wy TQ12 .206 D5
Cornham Farm La
  TA24..............12 C2
Cornhill
  Hemyock EX15 ......67 B8
  [5] Wellington TA21...160 D6
Cornlands EX16......50 D1
Cornmarket St EX38..159 D5
Corn Mill Ct EX34 ...150 E6
Corn Mill Cres EX2...177 A1
Corn Park Rd TQ12...212 A6
Corn Pk TQ10.......134 F2
Cornridge View EX20..93 C2
Corntown Cross
  PL21..............133 C1
Cornwall Beach PL1..247 D2
Cornwall Coll Saltash
  PL12..............242 D2
Cornwall St
  Bere Alston PL20 ...125 E1
  [5] Exeter EX4......177 A5
  Plymouth PL1 ......262 C3
  Plymouth, Morice Town
  PL1..............247 D2
CORNWOOD........133 C2
Cornwood CE Prim Sch
  PL21..............133 C2
Cornwood Rd
  Ivybridge PL21 .....237 A5
  Plymouth PL7 ......251 B4
CORNWORTHY.......227 A4
Cornworthy Cl PL2...248 A7
Cornworthy Cross
  TQ9..............227 A4
Coronation Ave EX7..204 D5
Coronation Cres EX15 66 A7
Coronation Pl
  Plymouth PL5 ......247 E8
  Shebbear EX21.....55 E4
Coronation Rd
  Bideford EX39......156 F1

Coronation Rd *continued*
  Exeter EX2 ....178 A4
  Kingsbridge TQ7 ...258 D5
  Kingsteignton TQ12 .207 E7
  [1] Newton Abbot
  TQ12.............207 B3
  Salcombe TQ8 .....259 D5
  [1] Teignmouth TQ14..210 A3
  Totnes TQ9 ....223 D6
Coronation St EX32 ..154 F6
Coronation Terr
  Abbotsham EX39 ...156 A2
  [11] Ilfracombe EX34..150 C6
  Starcross EX6......201 B8
Coronation Villas
  EX18..............59 C4
Corondale Rd PL2....248 B7
Coronet Cl EX2 ......178 D3
Corporation Cres [14]
  EX32..............155 B3
Corporation Rd PL2..248 D7
Corporation St [12]
  EX32..............155 B3
Corporation Terr [13]
  EX32..............155 B3
Corry Ho TQ1 ....220 E5
Corscombe La EX20 ..94 E6
Corsham Cl PL6......245 B6
Corsham Rd TQ4 ....226 A5
Corstone Cross EX19 .76 D7
Corvid Cl
  Barnstaple EX31....16 A3
  [2] Roundswell EX31..154 A1
Corvus Mws PL9 ....256 E8
Cory Ct PL9.........140 E8
CORYTON
  Axminster...........87 D1
  Lewtrenchard.......106 F2
Coryton Cl EX7......204 E6
Coryton La EX13 ....87 C1
Coscombe Circus [3]
  PL3..............249 D1
Cosdon Pl PL6.......244 F1
Cosgates Feet or County
  Gate EX35 ....6 D5
Cossick Cross TQ13 ..112 B5
Costly St PL21.......237 D5
Cosway St EX16 .....161 D5
Cotehele Ave
  Plymouth, Keyham
  PL2..............247 F5
  Plymouth, Prince Rock
  PL4..............263 C2
Cotehele Dr TQ3 ....225 D7
Cotehele House★
  PL12..............125 C3
Cotehele Quay Mus★
  PL12..............125 C3
Cotehele View PL18..125 D3
Coteland La EX32 ....18 F1
Coteland Lane End
  EX32..............18 F1
Cotfield Cl EX14 ....166 D7
Cotfield St EX2 .....177 C3
COTFORD..........101 C3
Cotford Cl EX10.....101 C3
Cotford Rd EX10 ....101 C3
Cot Green Cross EX14. 85 B5
Cothay La
  Chittlehampton EX37..29 C1
  Satterleigh EX37....44 C8
Cothay Manor & Gdns★
  TA21..............51 C8
Cot Hill PL7.........250 B5
Cot Hill Cl PL7.......250 A6
Cot Hill Trad Est PL7..250 B6
Cot La EX5...........82 D5
Cotlands EX10.......187 F3
Cotleigh Cross EX14..86 C5
Cotleigh Crossing
  EX14..............68 C1
Cotley La EX5........113 C8
Cot Manor [6] EX32...155 B3
COTMATON.........187 F4
Cotmaton Rd EX10 ..187 F3
Cotmore Cl
  Brixham TQ5 ......230 A2
  Chillington TQ7 ....145 A1
Cotmore Way TQ7 ...145 A1
Cotsford Cl EX5......179 B2
Cotswold Cl TQ2 ....219 D3
COTT...............222 F8
Cottage Cl EX33......8 D1
Cottage Cross
  Ashburton TQ13 ...131 B5
  Cheriton Bishop EX6..97 B4
Cottage Homes
  EX36..............158 D4
Cottage La TA22 .....33 D6
Cottage Mews PL7...250 E4
Cottages The TQ7 ...142 F2
Cott Cross
  Ash Mill EX36 ......31 C2
  Chawleigh EX18 ....59 E6
  Dartington TQ9 ....222 F8
  Membury EX13 .....87 C7
Cotte Cl EX12 ....190 B5
Cotterbury Gn TQ9 ..232 A2
Cotterell Rd EX5 ....175 E2
Cotters Cl EX15......66 A3
Cottey Brook EX16 ..161 B4
Cottey Cres EX4.....174 A2
COTTEYLANDS.......161 A3
Cottey Mdw TQ12 ...207 E6
Cott Hill EX31.......10 D1
Cottingham Cres
  EX39..............156 F3
Cottington Ct EX10..188 A4

Cottington Mead
  Sidmouth, Lower Woolbrook
  EX10..............188 B6
  Sidmouth, Weston Town
  EX10..............188 A4
Cottisbourne TQ13 ..111 A6
Cott La
  Croyde EX33 ....7 E1
  Petrockstow EX20 ..56 F4
  Totnes TQ9 ....222 F8
Cottlass La PL21 ....137 A2
Cottles La EX5 ......184 D4
Cottles View EX20....77 C4
Cott Mdw TQ9 ......222 F8
Cotton Cl PL7.......250 F4
Cotton La
  Cheriton Fitzpaine
  EX17.............63 A3
  Tiverton EX16......63 B5
Cotton Rd TQ6......233 B2
Cott Pk EX5.........184 C2
Cott Rd TQ9 ....222 F8
Cotts PL20..........239 B7
Cottshayne La EX24..102 E5
COTTWOOD.........43 D1
Couches La EX5......184 C2
Couchill Dr EX12....191 F8
Couchill La EX10....191 F8
Coulsdon Rd EX10 ...188 B6
Coulson Cross EX20..76 B8
Coulsworthy Crook
  EX34..............3 D2
  [2] Coulsworthy La EX34..3 E2
Council Chambers [2]
  EX9..............198 A1
Council Hos
  Brixton PL8........257 B5
  Clyst St Mary EX5 ...179 F3
Council Hos The EX5 179 E7
Council Houses The
  TQ7..............149 D7
Countessmead EX6 .161 F8
Countess Pl EX16 ...161 E5
COUNTESS WEAR ...178 B1
Countess Wear Com Sch
  EX2..............182 B8
Countess Wear Ho
  EX2..............182 A8
Countess Wear Rd
  EX2..............182 A8
Counties Cres EX6 ..201 B7
COUNTISBURY.......5 E6
Countisbury Hill
  EX35..............151 E5
Country Cousins
  EX34..............150 B4
Country Ho [4] EX10 .101 B1
County Cl PL7........251 A5
Couper Mdws EX2 ..178 D3
Coursebeer La EX20..95 E5
COURSHAY.........88 E3
Court Baron Cross
  EX14..............84 E3
Court Barton TQ7 ...147 D8
Court Barton Cl EX5..81 B4
Court Barton Cotts
  Coffinswell TQ12....213 C6
  Down Thomas PL9...255 C1
Court Barton Hill
  EX12..............191 D6
Court Barton La EX5 .172 A8
Court Barton Mews
  PL19..............116 F4
Court Dr
  Cullompton EX15 ..163 C5
  Wellington TA21 ...160 D5
Courtenay EX14......166 A5
Courtenay Cl
  [23] Colyton EX24...103 A4
  Starcross EX6......195 A1
Courtenay Cotts EX16. 48 F2
Courtenay Dr [24]
  EX24..............103 A4
Courtenay Gdns
  Exeter EX2 ....181 A8
  Newton Abbot TQ12 .207 C2
Courtenay Manor
  TQ1..............220 C4
Courtenay Park Rd
  TQ12.............207 D3
Courtenay Pk TQ10..135 A3
Courtenay Pl TQ14 ..210 C4
Courtenay Rd
  Exeter EX2 ....177 B3
  Newton Abbot TQ12 .207 C2
  Okehampton EX20 ..170 C4
  Paignton TQ4 .....226 C2
  Tavistock PL19 ....171 B6
Courtenay St
  Newton Abbot TQ12 .207 B3
  Plymouth PL1 .....262 C3
  Salcombe TQ8 .....259 D5
Courtenay Terr EX6 ..201 B8
Court Farm Barns
  TQ12.............212 B6
Courtfield Cl EX11 ...168 D5
Court Field La TA20..69 E5
Courtfield Rd PL3....248 F5
Court Fields Com Sch
  TA21..............160 C5
Court Gate Cl TQ12..211 C1
Court Gn TQ7 ....258 E6
Court Grange TQ12 ..212 B6
Courtis Gdns EX17 ..165 D5
Court La
  Morebath EX16......34 D4

Court La *continued*
  Seaton EX12 ....192 A6
  Thurlestone TQ7 ...143 A2
Courtlage Wlk TQ7 ..258 C6
Courtland Cres PL7 ..250 D7
Courtland Cross
  TQ12.............211 A4
Courtland Rd
  Paignton TQ3 ......226 B7
  Torquay TQ2 ....219 B7
  Wellington TA21 ...160 D6
Courtlands
  Saltash PL12 ......242 E1
  Tiverton EX16 .....161 E7
Courtlands Cl PL19...171 B6
Courtlands Cross
  EX8..............196 A3
Courtlands La EX8 ..195 F3
Courtlands Rd
  Newton Abbot TQ12 .207 D2
  Tavistock PL19 ....171 B6
Courtlands Sch PL6..244 F1
Court Moors La TA21..51 E5
Courtney Ho PL5....244 B2
Courtney Rd EX16 ..161 E5
Court Orch EX5......81 A1
Court Pk TQ7 ....143 A2
Court Pk Rd TQ7 ....143 A1
Court Rd
  Abbotskerswell TQ12 .212 B6
  Newton Ferrers PL8 .140 F7
  Torquay TQ2 ......219 C5
Court Royal EX5 .....99 B6
Court St TQ13 ....111 F4
Court Terr TA21 .....160 C5
Court The
  Dunsford EX6......112 F8
  Plymouth PL6 .....245 C7
  Saltash PL12 ......242 C2
Court View PL8 .....256 F4
Court Way EX14......50 D1
Court Wlk EX19 .....58 F3
Court Wood PL6 ....140 E7
Courtyard Cotts
  PL21..............136 C3
Cousens Cl EX7 .....204 F8
Cousin's Cross TQ7 ..149 A6
COVE..............49 B6
Cove Hill EX16 ......49 C6
Cove Mdw PL11.....247 A6
Coventry Cl EX14....84 C2
Coventry Farm Est
  TQ2..............213 B2
Coventry Rd EX4 ....176 F6
Coverdale Pl PL5 ....244 C1
Coverdale Rd
  Exeter EX2 ....177 B3
  Paignton TQ3 .....226 B6
Covert Cl EX13......167 E7
Coverts Cl [14] EX31..154 A2
Cow Down Rd TA20 ..88 B8
Cowdray Cl PL12....242 E2
Cowdray Terr PL12...242 E1
Cowflop Cross EX18..43 A1
Cowick Cl EX2 ......177 A2
Cowick Hill EX2......176 F3
Cowick La
  Exeter EX2 ....176 F3
  Exeter EX4 ....176 F3
Cowick Rd EX2 .....177 A4
Cowick St EX4 ......177 A4
Cow La EX34........150 B6
COWLEY............49 B6
Cowley Bridge Rd Bsns
  Pk EX4............173 A1
Cowley Hill EX5 .....172 F4
COWLEYMOOR......161 D5
Cowley Moor Rd
  EX16..............161 E6
Cowley Pl EX5.......172 F5
Cowley Rd PL5.......244 D3
Cowley Wood Head
  EX31..............4 A2
Cowley Wood Hill EX31. 4 A2
Cownhayne La EX24..103 B4
Cowpark Terr [1]
  EX39..............156 F7
Cowper Ave EX2 ....177 F3
Cowsen La
  Sourton EX20 ......92 F2
  Sourton EX20 ......93 A2
Cowslip Ave PL19 ...171 A5
Cowslip Cres TQ12 ..206 C5
Cowslip Mdw EX4 ...204 E8
Coxhill Cross TQ11...236 A3
Coxley La EX13, EX24. 102 F7
Coxmoor Cross EX17. 78 A1
Coxmoor La EX17....78 A2
COXPARK...........125 A7
Cox Rd TA21 ....160 C4
Cox's Cl PL6 ....245 B1
COXSIDE...........263 B3
Coxs La EX33 ....8 C3
Coxs Mdw EX22.....89 F7
Cox Tor Cl [6] PL20 ..126 F3
Cox Tor Rd PL19 ....171 E5
Coypool Rd PL7......250 A6
Coysh Sq EX3.......182 E5
Crabadon Cross TQ9 .138 F5
Crabbers Cross TQ10 135 D4
Crabb La EX2........177 A2
Crabbs Cl PL15......90 C1
Crabshell Quay TQ7 .258 D4
CRABTREE..........249 E5
Crabtree Cl
  Cranbrook EX5......99 B6
  Plymouth PL3 .....249 F5
Crabtree Villas PL3 ..249 E5

Crackaway La EX34 ...9 A4
Crackington Ave EX4 174 D1
Crackston Cl PL6 ....249 B7
CRADDOCK.........66 C7
Craddock Cl EX22...164 C6
Cradlemans Cross
  EX32..............155 E1
Craig Ct EX10 ......188 C4
Craigie Dr PL1.......262 A3
Craigmore Ave PL2 ..247 F5
Cramber Cl
  Roborough PL6.....245 C8
  [5] Tavistock PL19...171 B4
Crammer Ash Cross
  EX15..............84 C8
Crammers Cross
  TQ13.............123 F5
Crampit La
  Westleigh EX39 ....26 A7
  Westleigh EX39 ....157 E5
Cramp La EX36 .....31 E6
Cranapool Cross EX22. 54 E3
Cranbourne Ave PL4 .263 C4
CRANBROOK EX5 ...99 A6
Cranbrook Education
  Campus EX5........99 B7
Cranbrook Rd EX2 ..178 A5
Crandford Cl EX20 ..107 F8
Crandons Cross EX14. 87 B6
Cranesbill Way TQ12 206 D5
Cranes La EX9 ......198 B6
Cranfield PL7........250 C7
CRANFORD.........39 A8
Cranford EX10 ......188 B5
Cranford Ave EX8 ...202 D6
Cranford Cl EX8.....202 D6
Cranford Cross
  Great Torrington EX38 .42 C8
  Woolfardisworthy EX39..39 A8
Cranford Ho EX8....202 D6
Cranford Rd TQ3....219 A1
Cranford View EX8...202 D6
Cranishaies La EX5...8 B7
Cranleigh [4] EX32 ..154 F6
Cranleigh Terr [2] EX34. 3 A3
Cranley Gdns TQ13...111 A6
Cranmere Ct EX2 ...181 C8
Cranmere Rd
  Okehampton EX20 ..170 E6
  Plymouth PL3 .....249 A6
Cranmore View
  EX16..............161 B1
Crannaford La EX5...99 B3
Crannafords Ind Pk
  TQ13.............111 B7
Crantock Terr [7]
  PL2..............248 A5
Craon Gdns EX20 ...170 D6
CRAPSTONE.........126 E2
Crapstone Rd PL19...126 E2
Crapstone Terr PL20 .126 E2
Crashaw Cl PL5......244 D3
Craven Ave PL4......263 C4
Crawford Gdns EX2 .177 A3
Crawford Rd PL1.....262 A4
CRAWLEY...........69 C2
Crawley Cutting TA20 69 C3
CRC Units EX1......177 D1
Creacombe Barton Cross
  EX16..............46 F6
Creacombe Cross
  PL8..............141 E8
Creacombemoor Cross
  EX16..............47 A6
Creacombe Parsonage
  Cross EX16........47 A5
Crealy Great Adventure
  Pk★ EX5..........99 A1
Creamery Cl PL8....136 A2
Crease La
  Millhill PL19.......116 F1
  Tavistock PL19 ....117 A1
  Tavistock PL19 ....171 A4
Creber Dr PL21......137 E8
Crebor Rd PL19......171 B7
CREDITON..........165 D4
Crediton Cross EX17 .62 D8
Crediton Hospl EX17 165 A6
Crediton La EX6 ....97 C5
Crediton Lane End
  EX6..............97 C4
Crediton Rd EX20 ...170 C5
Crediton Sta EX17 ..165 E3
Crediton Wlk PL6 ...249 E8
Creedy Bridge EX17..165 F7
Creedy Cross EX17...62 D2
Creedy Rd
  Crediton EX17......165 D5
  Plymouth PL3 .....249 C5
Creedy View EX5....80 F2
Creedy Vw EX17 ....80 B5
Creek Cl TQ7 ....144 E1
Creek Cross TQ13 ..131 B5
Creek End TQ7......148 F5
Creek Rd
  Camels Head PL2...247 E5
  Dartmouth TQ6.....233 D4
Creely Cl EX2........181 C8
Crelake Cl PL19......171 C4
Crelake Ind Est [1]
  PL19..............171 B4
Crelake Pk PL19.....171 C4
CREMYLL...........253 E7
Cremyll Rd PL11.....247 B2
Cremyll St PL1......254 A8
Crescent Ave
  Barnstaple EX31....154 D3
  Plymouth PL1 .....262 B2

Crescent Avenue Mews PL1 262 B2
Crescent Ct TQ6 233 D4
Crescent Gdns PL21 237 C6
Crescent Mansions Flats EX2 261 C2
Crescent Rd PL21 237 C6
Crescent The
  Brixham TQ5 230 D3
  Brixton PL8 257 A5
  Crapstone PL20 126 E3
  Exmouth EX8 202 E8
  Gunnislake PL18 125 D6
  Kilmington EX13 87 C1
  Langtree EX38 40 E2
  Lifton PL16 105 E4
  Pathfinder Village EX6 98 B4
  Plymouth PL1 262 B2
Cresents Gdns PL21 237 C6
Cressbrook Cl PL6 245 F2
Cressbrook Dr PL6 245 F2
Cressbrook Wlk PL6 245 E2
Cresswell Cl TQ12 213 A5
Crestfield Rise PL21 237 A5
Crestfields TQ6 145 E5
Crest Hill TQ11 236 B5
Cresthill Rd PL2 248 B7
Crestway TQ6 145 E5
Crewkerne Rd EX13 104 C7
Crewkerne Turning EX13 88 C6
Creykes Ct PL1 262 A3
Cricket Cl EX18 44 F1
Cricketers Gn TQ2 219 E8
Cricketers The EX13 167 D7
Cricketfield Cl TQ13 123 F6
Cricket Field Ct EX9 198 A1
Cricket Field La EX9 198 A1
Cricketfield Rd TQ1, TQ2 219 F7
Cricket Field Rd 9 TQ12 207 C3
Cricket La TQ11 236 A6
Cricket Pk EX23 70 A6
Cricklepit Mill★ EX2 261 A2
Cridlake EX13 167 E5
Crier St EX14 166 A6
CRIMP 37 D2
Crimps Cross TQ7 258 F6
Crispin Rd TQ7 258 C5
Critchards EX5 184 C2
Criterion Pl 14 EX8 202 A6
Crocadon Mdws TQ9 139 B4
Crockaton Cotts TQ13 130 F5
Crocken Tor Rd EX20 170 D5
CROCKERNWELL 96 F3
Crockernwell Ct EX6 96 F3
Crockers Cl EX31 154 A2
Crocker's Row PL18 125 D6
Crockers Way PL15 90 C1
Crockwells Cl EX6 182 B3
Crockwells Rd EX6 182 B3
Croft Chase EX4 176 E4
Croft Cl TQ12 206 D1
Croft Cotts TQ12 211 D2
Croft Ct TQ2 220 A5
Croft Hill TQ2 220 A5
Croft Ho EX22 164 C4
Croft La
  Brushford TA22 33 C4
  Charleton TQ7 144 C1
  Skilgate TA4 34 E6
  Spreyton EX17 96 A6
Croft Mdw TQ12 211 D2
Croft Orch TQ12 211 D2
Croft Pk PL6 245 C7
Croft Rd
  East Ogwell TQ12 206 D1
  Holsworthy EX22 164 C4
  Ipplepen TQ12 211 D2
  Salcombe TQ8 259 D5
  Torquay TQ2 220 A5
Croft's Est EX17 80 A5
Croftside 5 EX34 150 B5
Crofts Lea EX34 2 E3
Crofts Lea Pk EX34 150 D5
Croftswood EX34 150 D5
Croftswood Gdns EX34 150 D4
Croft The EX20 95 A4
Croft View Terr TQ8 259 E5
Crogg La DT7 260 B5
Croker's Mdw TQ13 180 C8
Crokers Way TQ12 211 D2
Cromartie Point Flats TQ2 219 E2
Cromartie Rd PL4 249 B1
Cromer Cl PL6 245 A7
Cromer Wlk PL6 245 A7
Cromlech Ho EX38 159 B5
Cromwell Cl EX38 159 F6
Cromwell Cotts TQ12 131 F7
Cromwell Ct EX1 178 A5
Cromwell Gate PL6 245 C7
Cromwell Pk
  Modbury PL21 137 B3
  Tiverton EX16 64 D6
Cromwell Rd PL4 263 C3
Cromwells Mdw EX17 165 E6
Cromwells Way TQ13 180 C8
Cromwell Terr 7 EX2 178 D5
Crook Copse 6 EX1 178 F8
Crookeder Cl PL9 256 A5
Crooked Oaks EX36 30 C1
Crooke La EX20 77 E3
Crooklake Hill EX5 98 E8
Crookmans Cl EX32 155 A7
Crookmans Cnr EX32 155 C5
Croppins Cl TQ11 236 C5
Cropp La PL5 247 E4
Croscombe La EX35 4 E4
CROSS 7 F2
Cross Cl EX31 153 D5
Crosscut Way EX14 166 C5
Cross Farm 5 EX33 152 D6
Cross Farm Ct 6 EX32 16 E1
Cross Furzes TQ11 129 F1
Crossgate EX18 59 C7
Cross Gate EX32 18 F6
Crossgates PL7 132 C6
Cross Gn PL15 105 E7
Crossgrange Trad Est TQ12 180 F3
Cross Hill
  Combeinteignhead TQ12 208 D3
  Crediton EX17 79 E5
  East Buckland EX32 18 D1
  East Village EX17 80 C8
  Plymouth PL2 247 E4
Cross Hill Cross EX17 80 C8
Crosshill La EX6 97 A5
Crossing Cross TQ9 222 F7
Crossingfields Dr EX8 196 A1
Crossings Cl PL19 117 E6
Cross-in-Hand PL21 237 F5
Cross La
  Berrynarbor EX34 2 E3
  Brendon EX35 6 A4
  East Portlemouth TQ8 259 F4
Crossland La EX14 68 C2
CROSSLANDS 160 C8
Crosslands
  Barnstaple EX31 154 C4
  Thurlestone TQ7 143 A1
  Wellington TA21 160 B8
Cross Lane Cross EX36 19 D1
Cross Lanes
  Ashprington TQ9 139 F8
  Ashwater EX21 90 F6
  Launcells EX23 70 D8
  South Pool TQ7 148 F6
Crossley Cl TQ12 207 E7
Crossley Moor Rd TQ12 207 E7
Cross Mdw EX17 96 A7
Cross Mdws EX31 154 A2
Crossmead EX35 151 B5
Crossmoor Cross
  Rackenford EX16 47 E1
  Templeton EX16 47 E1
Cross Moor La EX36 31 E2
Crosspark Ave TQ2 219 C8
Cross Park Ave PL6 244 F1
Crosspark Cl EX31 154 E7
Crosspark Cres EX31 17 A7
Crosspark Cross
  Bradworthy EX22 38 E1
  Holsworthy EX22 164 E5
Crosspark Hill EX16 48 C8
Cross Park Rd
  Plymouth PL6 244 F1
  3 Wembury PL9 140 D8
CROSSPARKS 164 F5
Crossparks
  Dartmouth TQ6 233 D3
  Tiverton EX16 64 F6
Cross Parks
  Cullompton EX15 163 A2
  High Bickington EX37 43 C7
Cross Park Way PL6 244 F1
Cross Pk
  Berrynarbor EX34 2 E3
  Brixham TQ5 230 B3
  Brixton PL8 257 B5
  Buckland Monachorum PL20 126 D3
  Combeinteignhead TQ12 208 D4
  Ilfracombe EX34 150 B6
  South Zeal EX20 95 A4
  Thurlestone TQ7 143 C3
  Totnes TQ9 223 E6
CROSS ROADS 106 F5
Cross Side Hill EX36 31 F2
Cross St
  Barnstaple EX31 154 F5
  Combe Martin EX34 2 F4
  Lynton EX35 151 B5
  Moretonhampstead TQ13 111 F5
  Northam EX39 157 A7
  Seaton EX12 192 A5
Cross Terr PL18 125 C5
Cross The
  Kilmington EX13 87 D1
  St Dominick PL12 125 A2
Crosstown EX23 36 E2
Cross Tree EX9 198 E7
Cross Tree Ctr 3 EX33 152 D6
Cross View
  Buckfastleigh TQ11 236 A2
  Exeter EX2 177 B1
Cross View Terr EX2 176 E2
Crosswater EX23 36 F1
Crossway
  Paignton TQ4 226 C2
Crossway *continued*
  Plymouth PL7 250 D7
Crossway Ave PL4 249 B3
Crossway Cross EX20 94 E6
Crossway Hill EX17 61 F2
Crossway Park Homes TQ7 258 A8
Crossways
  Cornwood PL21 133 C2
  Milton Damerel EX22 54 E5
  9 Paignton TQ4 226 B6
  Ringmore TQ7 142 E4
  South Chard EX13 88 D7
  Tatworth TA20 88 D8
  4 Wembury PL9 140 D8
  Whitestone EX4 98 E4
Crossways Ct EX34 7 F7
Crossways Sh Ctr TQ3 226 B6
Croucher Cl EX1 174 F2
Crowbeare Mdw EX38 159 E6
Crowborough La EX33 8 A2
Crowborough Rd EX33 8 A2
Crow Bridge EX15 163 B3
Crowbridge Pk EX15 163 B2
CROWDEN 74 D2
Crowden Cres EX16 161 F3
Crowden Cross EX20 74 D2
Crowden Rd EX20 74 E2
Crowder Cross TQ10 135 A2
Crowder Mdw TQ10 135 A2
Crowder Pk TQ10 135 A2
Crowder's Cross EX14 84 C3
Crowdhole Cross EX16 46 F4
Crowdhole Hill EX16 46 F4
Crow Gn EX15 163 B3
Crow La EX16 47 C3
Crown and Anchor Way 5 TQ3 226 B6
Crowndale Ave PL3 249 A6
Crowndale Rd PL19 126 A6
Crown Gdns PL6 245 A1
CROWNHILL 244 F2
Crown Hill
  Halberton EX16 64 F7
  West Buckland TA21 52 F7
Crownhill Cross PL21 137 B3
Crownhill Ct PL6 244 F2
Crown Hill Ct TQ2 219 E6
Crownhill Fort★ PL6 244 F3
Crownhill Fort Rd PL6 244 F3
Crownhill La EX5 81 C5
Crown Hill Pk TQ2 219 E6
Crownhill Rd PL5 244 C3
Crown Hill Rise TQ2 219 E6
Crown Hill Terr 9 EX17 165 C5
Crownley La
  Stoke Gabriel TQ3 225 A1
  Stoke Gabriel TQ9 227 F8
Crown Mews TA21 52 F7
Crown Sq 6 TQ14 210 A3
Crown Way EX2 178 D3
Crow Pk PL3 248 F5
Crowther's Hill TQ6 233 F3
Crow View EX32 155 C5
CROYDE 7 E2
CROYDE BAY 7 D2
Croyden Cross EX22 55 A4
Croyde Rd EX33 7 D1
Croyde Sands Bglws EX33 7 D2
Croydon Gdns PL5 243 E4
Croylands Ct EX8 202 C6
Croyle Cross EX15 66 A4
Crozier Rd 6 PL4 248 F4
Cruel Cross TQ3 225 D8
Cruffen Cross EX33 8 B1
Cruffen La EX33 8 B1
Cruwys Morchard Hill EX16 63 A7
Cruwy's Morchard Mill La EX16 63 A7
Cruwys Morchar Hill EX16 62 F2
Crystal Cl TQ4 226 C2
Cuckoo Down La EX14 166 E4
Cuckoo Hill EX17 61 C3
Cuckoo La DT7 260 A4
Cuckoo's La EX32 28 B5
Cuddeford Cnr EX4 98 C6
Cuddenhay La EX17 46 A2
Cuddyford Cross TQ13 130 F5
Cudemoor Cross EX38 41 A1
Cudhill Rd TQ5 230 B4
CUDLIPPTOWN 118 A6
Cudmore Pk EX16 64 D6
Cuffe Rd PL3 248 C4
Culbin Gn PL6 249 D7
Culdrose Cl PL5 243 E4
Cullaford Cross EX17 95 E8
CULLOMPTON 163 A3
Cullompton Com Coll EX15 163 C2
Cullompton Hill EX5 83 A7
Cullompton Rd
  Awliscombe EX14 85 C4
  Honiton EX14 166 A7
Culmbridge La EX15 67 C7
Culmbridge Rd EX15 67 C8
Culm Cl
  Bideford EX39 157 C2
  Exeter EX2 178 D4
Culm Cl *continued*
  Torquay TQ2 219 B8
Culm Cross EX20 77 A4
CULM DAVY 52 A2
Culme Cl EX14 67 C1
Culme Rd PL3 249 A5
Culme Way EX14 67 C1
Culm Gr EX2 178 D4
Culm Haven EX15 66 A7
Culm Lea EX15 163 E3
CULMSTOCK 66 E8
Culmstock Prim Sch EX15 51 E1
Culmstock Rd EX15 67 B8
Culm Valley Sports Ctr EX15 163 C2
Culm Valley Way EX15 65 F7
Culver Cl
  Bradninch EX5 83 A6
  Plymouth PL6 249 A8
  Tiverton EX16 161 F3
Culver Ct PL12 242 F2
Culverdale TQ9 223 E4
Culver Gdns EX10 188 B4
CULVERHILL 116 C3
Culver Ho 12 TQ13 123 E6
Culver La
  8 Chudleigh TQ13 123 F6
  Rattery TQ10 135 E3
Culverlake La EX13 88 G3
Culverland Cl EX4 177 D8
Culverland Rd EX4 177 D8
Culver Park Cl TQ7 258 E3
Culver Rd PL12 242 F2
Culvert Rd EX5 81 F1
Culver Way PL6 249 A7
Culverwood Cl PL7 251 C6
Culvery Cl EX5 184 C3
Culvery Cross EX17 165 C2
Culvery Gn TQ2 219 B8
Cumber Cl
  Brixham TQ5 230 B5
  Malborough TQ7 147 F6
Cumber Dr TQ5 230 B5
Cumberland Cl EX8 202 D8
Cumberland Dr EX2 178 D4
Cumberland Gn TQ5 230 B5
Cumberland Rd PL1 247 F1
Cumberland St PL1 247 E2
Cumberland Way
  Exeter EX1 178 E7
  Exeter EX4 178 B8
Cumbernauld TQ1 220 D4
Cummings Cross TQ12 180 C1
Cummings Ct TQ12 180 C1
Cummins Cnr EX6 97 E5
Cummins La EX14 87 B6
Cundy Cl PL7 250 A7
Cunliffe Ave PL9 255 A6
Cunningham Ave EX13 167 F7
Cunningham Rd
  Exmouth EX8 196 D2
  Plymouth PL5 244 C8
Cunningham's La EX10 187 F3
Cunningham Way PL12 242 D3
Cuppiers Piece Cross EX19 43 A1
Curie Mews EX2 177 E4
Curium Ct 9 EX12 192 B4
Curledge St TQ4 226 B5
Curledge Street Acad 4 TQ4 226 B5
Curlew Cl
  Okehampton EX20 170 A6
  Torquay TQ2 213 C3
Curlew Dr
  Kingsbridge TQ7 258 F1
  Torquay TQ2 213 C2
Curlew Mews PL3 249 C4
Curlew Rd EX23 70 A8
Curlew Way
  Dawlish EX7 200 F2
  Dawlish Warren EX7 201 A2
  Exeter EX4 173 C2
Currington Mdw EX31 154 A3
Curriton Hill EX17 61 C5
Curriton La EX17 61 B6
Curscombe Cross EX14 84 F4
Curscombe La EX14 84 F4
Cursons Way PL21 237 A5
Curtis Cross EX22 54 B3
CURTISKNOWLE 138 D4
Curtis Rd EX31 154 F8
Curtis St PL1 247 E1
Curve Acre EX33 152 E5
Curwood Cres 2 EX16 161 C3
Cussacombe EX36 20 D1
Cussacombe Gate EX36 20 E1
Custance Ho 8 EX14 166 C6
Custom House Hill 4 TQ14 210 B4
Custom House La PL1 262 B1
Custom La EX16 64 B4
Cuthays La EX13 88 B1
Cuthbert Cl TQ1 214 A1
Cuthbert Mayne Sch TQ1 214 A1
Cutland Cross EX18 44 D4
Cutliffe La EX39 22 D3
Cutterburrow La EX33 152 C5
Cutteridge La EX4 176 A6
Cut Tongue La TA20 69 F7
Cutwell Cross TQ10 134 E1
Cuxton Mdws PL20 126 C3
Cygnet Ct EX2 261 C1
Cygnet Units EX2 178 E5
Cygnus Mws PL9 256 E8
Cypress Cl
  12 Honiton EX14 85 C2
  6 Plymouth PL7 251 C5
  Torquay TQ2 220 A5
Cypress Dr EX4 176 F7
Cyprus Gdns EX8 202 B6
Cyprus Rd EX8 202 B6
Cyprus Terr EX32 155 B3

D

Dabby La EX6 97 B4
Daccabridge Rd TQ12 212 F4
DACCOMBE 213 E5
Daccombe Cross TQ12 213 E5
Daccombe Hill TQ2, TQ12 213 E4
Daccombe Mill La TQ12 213 B4
DADBROOK 252 E4
Daddon Cl EX39 25 C4
Daddon Hill EX39 156 E6
Daddyhole Rd TQ1 220 D3
Daggeridge Plain EX16 63 B4
Daggers Copse TQ12 206 F3
Dagmar Rd EX8 202 A6
Dagmar St TQ14 210 A3
Dagra La TQ12, TQ14 209 B4
Daimonds La TQ14 210 B5
DAINTON 212 A2
Dainton Elms Cross TQ12 211 F2
Dainton Mews TQ4 226 B5
Dairs Orch TA20 88 C8
Dairy Cl
  Exminster EX6 182 B3
  Totnes TQ9 223 F5
Dairy Gr EX4 174 E2
Dairy Hill TQ2 219 C7
Dairy La PL21 237 D5
Daison Cotts TQ1 220 A7
Daison Cres TQ1 220 B8
Daisy La TQ12 206 C5
Daisy Links EX4 176 D8
Daisy Pk PL8 257 A5
Dakota Way EX1 175 F1
Dalbury Ct TQ12 207 C4
Dalditch La EX9 197 D3
Dale Ave PL6 249 C7
Dale Gdns PL4 248 D4
Dale Rd PL4 248 D4
Daleside Ct TQ1 220 E4
Daleside Rd EX4 173 E1
Daleswood Rd PL19 171 A4
Dalton Gdns PL5 243 E3
Dalverton Ct TQ5 230 C6
DALWOOD 87 B3
Dalwood La EX13 87 B3
Damerel Cl PL1 247 F2
Damson Cl EX15 162 D4
Damson Cres
  Wellington TA21 160 E4
  Wellington TA21 160 F7
Damson Row TA21 160 F7
Danby Heights Cl TQ1 220 E4
Danby Terr EX8 202 A7
Dandy La EX4 174 D5
Dane Ct EX39 157 A6
Daneheath Bsns Pk TQ12 180 F3
Danes Cl EX14 68 C2
Danes Cross EX5 82 C2
Daneshay EX39 157 A7
Danes Hill EX4, EX5 82 C2
Daneshill Cross EX13 87 B3
Danes Mead EX15 163 C6
Danes' Rd EX4 261 B4
Danesway EX4 174 E2
Daniel's Grave EX16 62 D4
Daniel's La
  Broadhempston TQ9 131 E1
  West Charleton TQ7 144 C1
Danisco Pack Westward
  Burlescombe EX16 51 C3
  Tiverton EX16 51 C3
Danum Dr PL7 251 B3
Danvers Rd TQ2 213 F2
Daphne Cl TQ1 220 D5
D'arcy Ct TQ12 207 C4
Dares Field EX13 87 C1
Dares Orch EX24 103 A3
Darke Ave EX31 153 B4
Darke La PL19 117 B8
Darkey La
  Lifton PL16 105 E4
  Okehampton EX20 170 A5
Dark La
  Ashbrittle TA21 50 E8
  Barnstaple EX31 154 F7
  Budleigh Salterton EX9 197 F1
  Hockworthy EX16 50 B8
  Modbury PL21 137 B3
  Northlew EX20 74 D2
  Sidmouth EX10 187 F6
Dark La *continued*
  Thorverton EX5 81 E5
Darklake Cl PL6 245 E5
Darklake La PL6 245 D8
Darklake View PL6 245 E5
Dark Street La PL7 250 E4
Darky La
  Chulmleigh EX18 59 E8
  Kingsbridge TQ7 258 C7
Darlick Cnr EX36 20 C4
Darlick Corner EX36 20 C4
Darnell Cl EX10 188 B6
DARRACCOTT 37 A4
Darracombe Cres TQ12 206 E5
DARRACOTT 8 B2
Darracott
  Great Torrington EX38 41 E7
  Great Torrington EX38 159 E7
  Huntshaw EX39 26 F1
Darracott Cross EX38 41 E8
Darracott Hill EX39 37 B4
Darran Cl TQ12 207 F7
Darran Rd TQ12 207 F7
Dart Ave TQ2 219 C7
Dartbridge Cross TQ11 236 C6
Dartbridge Manor TQ11 236 C6
Dart Bridge Rd TQ11 236 C5
Dart Bsns Ctr TQ9 215 F1
Dart Cl
  Braunton EX31 15 E5
  Plymouth PL3 249 D7
  St Giles on t H PL15 90 C1
Dart Hill EX16 46 D2
DARTINGTON 215 E1
Dartington CE Prim Sch TQ9 215 F1
Dartington Cider Press Sh Ctr★ TQ9 215 F1
Dartington Cl EX38 159 E6
Dartington Crystal (Glass Factory)★ EX38 159 C5
Dartington Fields EX38 159 E6
Dartington Hall★ TQ9 216 B2
Dartington La TQ9 223 B7
Dartington Wlk
  Exminster EX6 181 F5
  Plymouth PL6 249 E8
DARTMEET 129 D8
Dartmeet★ PL20 129 D8
Dartmeet Ave PL3 249 B6
Dartmoor Cotts PL7 132 D4
Dartmoor Ct TQ13 180 C7
Dartmoor Expedition Ctr, Rowden★ TQ13 120 F3
Dartmoor Otters & Buckfast Butterflies★ TQ11 236 D5
Dartmoor Prison Mus★ PL20 119 A1
Dartmoor Rly★ EX20 170 B3
Dartmoor View
  2 Chulmleigh EX18 44 E1
  Okehampton EX20 170 F5
  Plymouth PL4 249 C3
  Saltash PL12 242 E4
  Woolfardisworthy EX17 61 E4
Dartmoor Visitor Ctr (Princetown)★ PL20 128 A8
Dartmoor Zoological Pk★ PL7 133 A1
DARTMOUTH 233 E3
Dartmouth Acad TQ6 233 D2
Dartmouth Castle★ TQ6 234 B1
Dartmouth Hill TQ6 146 B7
Dartmouth & Kingswear Hospl TQ6 233 F3
Dartmouth La TQ5 229 C4
Dartmouth L Ctr TQ6 233 E3
Dartmouth Mus★ TQ6 233 F3
Dartmouth Rd
  Brixham TQ5 229 C2
  East Allington TQ9 144 E7
  Paignton TQ4, TQ5 226 C3
  Stoke Fleming TQ6 146 B8
Dartmouth Steam Rly★
  Churston TQ5 229 C5
  Kingswear TQ6 234 A4
  Paignton TQ4 226 C2
Dartmouth Wlk PL6 249 E8
Darton Gr TQ9 227 F7
Dart Pk EX36 158 D4
Dartridge La EX18 44 D1
Dartside TQ9 223 B7
Dart View TQ6 228 C3
Dart View Rd TQ5 229 B6
Dart Villas TQ9 223 C4
Darwin Cres
  Barton TQ2 213 F3
  Plymouth PL3 249 D5
Darwin Ct 11 EX2 261 B2
Dashley Cnr TQ9 131 D2
Dashpers TQ5 230 B3
Dathan Cl PL19 171 C5
Daucus Cl PL19 171 B4
Davenham Cl PL6 245 B6
Daveycourt La EX20 95 F3

Davey's Cross PL21 .. 137 B7
Daveys Elm Vw TQ4 .. 226 B2
David Cl
Braunton EX33 .. 152 D5
Plymouth PL7 .. 250 F6
David Rd TQ3 .. 226 A7
David's Cl EX10 .. 101 B2
David's Hill EX33 .. 8 A2
Davids La PL21 .. 137 B7
David Southgate Ct PL1 .. 262 A2
Davies Ave TQ4 .. 229 A8
Davies Cl EX5 .. 82 B6
Davis Ave TQ2 .. 219 D6
Davis Rd TQ6 .. 233 C3
Davy Cl PL11 .. 246 F3
Davy Rd PL6 .. 245 C4
Dawes Cl TQ12 .. 211 F8
Dawes Ct TQ4 .. 226 B5
Dawes La
Millbrook PL10 .. 252 E5
Plymouth PL9 .. 256 D7
DAWLISH .. 204 F6
Dawlish Bsns Pk EX7 200 F2
Dawlish Com Coll EX7 .. 204 F7
Dawlish Com Hospl EX7 .. 204 D6
Dawlish L Ctr EX7 .. 204 F8
Dawlish Mus* EX7 .. 204 D6
Dawlish Park Terr EX8 .. 195 F4
Dawlish Rd
Exeter EX2 .. 181 C8
Exminster EX3 .. 182 B3
Teignmouth TQ14 .. 210 C6
Dawlish Sta EX7 .. 204 E6
DAWLISH WARREN .. 201 A1
Dawlish Warren National Nature Reserve* EX7 .. 201 D3
Dawlish Warren Rd EX6 .. 201 B4
Dawlish Warren Sta EX7 .. 201 B2
Dawlish Wlk PL6 .. 249 E8
Dawn Cl EX1 .. 178 A6
Daws Ct PL12 .. 243 A2
Daws Mdw TQ12 .. 207 E6
Dawson Cl PL5 .. 243 E1
Daymond Dr TQ13 .. 180 F7
Daymond Rd PL5 .. 243 D2
Days-Pottles La EX6, EX2 .. 181 D4
Dayton Cl PL6 .. 244 E3
Deacon Cl EX2 .. 181 B8
Deacon Dr PL12 .. 242 F1
Deacons Gn PL19 .. 171 A3
Deadhorse La EX13 .. 103 C5
Dead La EX15 .. 65 F2
Deadman's Cross TQ6 .. 233 D2
Dead Road Cross EX15 .. 65 F2
Deaf Acad The EX8 .. 202 B5
DEAN
Combe Martin .. 3 E2
Lynton .. 5 A5
West Down .. 8 E5
Dean Clarke Gdns EX4 .. 261 B2
Dean Cross
Combe Martin EX31 .. 3 E1
Gunn EX32 .. 17 E4
Lynton EX35 .. 5 A5
Plymouth PL9 .. 255 E7
South Brent TQ10 .. 135 C5
West Down EX34 .. 8 E5
Dean Cross Rd PL9 .. 255 E7
Deane Cl EX33 .. 8 D1
Deane La TQ12 .. 209 D2
Deane Rd TQ12 .. 209 B2
Deanes The EX16 .. 161 B3
Deane Way TA20 .. 88 D8
Dean Hill PL9 .. 255 E7
Dean Hill Rd EX15 .. 162 B3
Dean La
Combe Martin EX31 .. 3 E1
Lynton EX35 .. 5 A5
West Down EX34 .. 8 F5
Dean Lane End TQ10 .. 135 D5
Dean Park Rd PL9 .. 255 D7
DEAN PRIOR .. 135 C6
Dean Rd PL7 .. 250 D6
Deans Cl
Bishopsteignton TQ14 .. 208 F8
Northam EX39 .. 156 F7
Deans La EX36 .. 158 D5
Deans Mead EX10 .. 188 A5
Deans Pk EX36 .. 158 D5
Dean St
Crediton EX17 .. 165 D5
Exeter EX2 .. 261 B2
Dean Steep EX35 .. 5 A4
Dean Wood La
Dean EX31 .. 3 F2
Dean EX31 .. 10 F8
Deave La
Throwleigh EX20 .. 95 C1
Wonson EX20 .. 110 D8
De Bathe Cross EX20 .. 77 C3
Debden Cl PL5 .. 243 D4
De Brionne Hts EX20 .. 170 C5
Deckport Cross
Hatherleigh EX20 .. 75 D7
Winkleigh EX19 .. 75 F8
De Courcy Rd TQ8 .. 259 B2
Decoy Com Prim Sch
Newton Abbot TQ12 .. 207 D1
Newton Abbot TQ12 .. 212 D8
Decoy Ctry Pk* TQ12 .. 207 C1
Decoy Ind Est TQ12 .. 212 D8
Decoy Rd TQ12 .. 207 D1
Deeble Cl PL7 .. 250 E7
Deep Cut Cross EX14 .. 67 C2
Deep Dene Cl TQ5 .. 230 A3
Deepdene Pk EX2 .. 177 E4
Deep La
Bratton Fleming EX32 .. 17 F7
Combe Martin EX34 .. 10 C7
Crediton EX17 .. 165 C6
High Bickington EX37 .. 43 D7
Kentisbury EX31 .. 3 C1
Plymouth PL7 .. 251 C3
Deeplane Head EX22 164 C5
Deepway EX10 .. 101 B2
Deepway Ct EX6 .. 182 A4
Deepway Gdns EX6 .. 181 F4
Deepway La
Branscombe EX12 .. 190 D4
Exeter EX2 .. 181 D4
Exminster EX6 .. 182 A4
Deepways EX9 .. 197 F2
Deerhill La EX36 .. 158 C6
Deerhill Rd EX36 .. 158 B5
Deer La EX22 .. 89 D8
Deer Leap PL19 .. 171 D4
Deer Park Ave TQ14 .. 210 A6
Deer Park Cl
Tavistock PL19 .. 171 C5
Teignmouth TQ14 .. 210 A6
Deer Park Cres PL19 .. 171 C5
Deer Park Dr
Plymouth PL3 .. 249 D7
Teignmouth TQ14 .. 210 A6
Deer Park Est TQ6 .. 146 B8
Deer Park La
Daccombe TQ12 .. 213 E7
Tavistock PL19 .. 171 C5
Deer Park Rd
Barnstaple EX32 .. 155 C2
Newton Abbot TQ12 .. 207 D1
Stoke Fleming TQ6 .. 146 B8
Tavistock PL19 .. 171 C5
Deer Pk
Chudleigh Knighton TQ12 .. 123 C6
Ivybridge PL21 .. 237 E5
Saltash PL12 .. 242 F3
Deers Leap Cl TQ3 .. 219 B2
Deer Valley Rd EX22 .. 164 C4
Deer Wood View 4 EX32 .. 16 E1
De Ferrers Dr PL8 .. 141 A7
Defoe Cl PL5 .. 244 C1
De Havilland Rd EX1 .. 175 F1
Delacombe Cl PL7 .. 250 F7
De la Hay Ave PL3 .. 262 A4
Delamere Rd PL6 .. 249 D7
Delamore Cl PL21 .. 237 A5
De La Rue Way EX4 .. 174 D1
Delaware Com Prim Sch PL18 .. 125 C5
Delaware Cotts PL18 125 C6
Delaware Ct PL18 .. 125 C5
Delaware Gdns PL2 .. 247 F7
Delaware Rd PL18 .. 125 C6
Delderfield Gdns EX8 .. 202 C6
Delgany Dr PL6 .. 245 A5
Delia Gdns EX5 .. 99 C5
Delius Cres EX2 .. 178 C5
Dell Court TQ12 .. 207 C3
Dellohay Pk PL12 .. 242 D4
Dell The
Plymouth PL7 .. 250 B6
Tavistock PL19 .. 171 B6
Delve's Grave Cross EX38 .. 41 F8
Demouville Gdns EX17 80 B5
Denarius Rd 8 EX1 .. 178 E8
Denbow Cross EX5 .. 99 A2
Den Brook Cl TQ1 .. 220 D6
DENBURY .. 211 B6
Denbury Cross TQ12 .. 211 D3
Denbury Ct EX2 .. 181 D8
Denbury Down Cross TQ12 .. 131 F3
Denbury Down La
Denbury TQ12 .. 131 F3
Denbury TQ12 .. 211 A7
Denbury Prim Sch TQ12 .. 211 A6
Denbury Rd TQ12 .. 211 E6
Denby Ho TQ4 .. 226 C5
Den Cres TQ14 .. 210 C4
Dencroft La EX14 .. 87 A5
Dendles Wood National Nature Reserve* PL21 .. 133 D4
Dendy Rd TQ4 .. 226 B6
Dene Cl EX8 .. 196 D1
Deneridge Cross EX17 .. 60 F6
Deneridge Hill
Lapford EX17 .. 60 F6
Morchard Bishop EX17 .. 61 A5
Dene's Cl 2 EX32 .. 17 B2
Denes Rd EX32 .. 17 B2
Dengie Cl PL7 .. 251 B5
Denham Cl PL5 .. 244 C2
Dening Ct EX8 .. 202 B8
Denise Cl EX2 .. 181 B8
Denmark Rd
Exeter EX1, EX2 .. 261 C3
Exmouth EX8 .. 202 D8
Denners Way EX15 .. 66 A7
Dennesdene Cl EX8 .. 196 B3
Dennington Cross EX32 .. 28 D8
Dennington Hill EX32 .. 28 D8
Dennington La
Churchinford EX14 .. 68 F6
Dulverton TA22 .. 33 B4
Dennis Camp Rd PL6 245 A7
Dennis Cl PL5 .. 247 C7
Dennis Cross EX19 .. 57 F7
Dennis's Down Cross EX6 .. 96 C5
Dennysmead Ct EX4 .. 173 A1
Den Prom TQ14 .. 210 C4
Den Rd TQ14 .. 210 C4
Densdon Gate EX16 .. 46 E6
Densdon Rd EX36 .. 46 E6
Densham La EX17 .. 61 F4
Den The TQ14 .. 210 C4
Denver Cl EX3 .. 182 E6
Denver Rd EX3 .. 182 E6
Denys Rd
Torquay TQ1 .. 220 C5
Totnes TQ9 .. 223 C5
DEPTFORD .. 43 B5
Deptford Pl PL4 .. 263 A4
Deptford Villas 2 EX31 .. 154 C3
DERBY .. 155 B6
Derby Rd
Barnstaple EX32 .. 155 B6
Kingsbridge TQ7 .. 258 D4
Plymouth PL5 .. 244 C4
Derick Rd EX16 .. 161 B5
Derncleugh Gdns EX7 .. 210 F8
Derrell Rd TQ4 .. 226 A4
DERRIFORD .. 245 B4
Derriford Bsns Pk PL6 .. 245 A4
Derriford Health & L Ctr PL6 .. 245 B3
Derriford Hospl PL6 .. 245 B4
Derriford Pk PL6 .. 245 A3
Derriford Rd PL6 .. 245 B4
DERRITON .. 164 A3
Derriton Mill Cross EX22 .. 164 B3
Derriton Rd EX22 .. 71 E6
Derry Ave PL4 .. 262 C4
Derry's Cross PL1 .. 262 B2
Derwent Ave PL3 .. 249 C5
Derwent Rd TQ1 .. 220 B7
Derworthy Cross EX22 .. 54 D6
Derworthy La EX22 .. 54 D6
Desborough La PL4 .. 263 C3
Desborough Rd PL4 .. 263 C3
De Tracey Pk TQ13 .. 180 D7
Deveron Cl PL7 .. 251 A5
Devon Bsns Pk EX15 .. 163 D4
Devon Cliffs Holiday Pk EX8 .. 203 B5
Devoncourt TQ5 .. 230 E6
Devondale Ct EX7 .. 201 B2
Devon East Bsns Ctr EX14 .. 85 C3
Devon Expressway
Ashburton TQ13 .. 131 B6
Buckfastleigh TQ11 .. 236 B4
Exeter EX6 .. 181 C3
Lee Mill PL21 .. 136 C6
Plymouth PL5 .. 243 C2
Plymouth PL7 .. 250 C3
Devon Guild of Craftsmen The* TQ13 .. 180 D7
Devon Heath 2 TQ13 .. 123 C4
Devon Ho TQ13 .. 180 E8
Devon House Dr TQ13 .. 180 E8
Devonia Cl PL7 .. 250 E7
Devon Oaks PL19 .. 126 E5
Devon Pl 15 TQ9 .. 223 D5
DEVONPORT .. 247 D4
Devonport High Sch for Boys PL1 .. 248 A2
Devonport High Sch for Girls PL2 .. 248 C6
Devonport Hill
Kingsand PL10 .. 253 A2
Plymouth PL1 .. 247 F1
Devonport Leat PL6 .. 241 B5
Devonport Rd PL3 .. 247 F3
Devonport Sta PL1 .. 247 F3
Devon Railway Ctr* EX16 .. 63 F2
Devon Rd
Exeter EX4 .. 177 F8
Salcombe TQ8 .. 259 D4
Devonshire Ct
14 Honiton EX14 .. 85 C2
Torpoint PL11 .. 247 B3
Devonshire Gdns EX20 .. 77 C4
Devonshire Ho
Plymouth PL1 .. 262 B2
2 Tavistock PL19 .. 171 B5
Torquay TQ1 .. 220 C8
Devonshire Pk EX39 .. 157 A1
Devonshire Pl EX4 .. 177 D8
Devonshire Rd EX14 .. 85 C2
Devonshire Rise EX16 .. 161 E3
Devonshire St PL4 .. 263 A3
Devonshire Way 4 EX14 .. 166 A4
Devon Sq
Kingsbridge TQ7 .. 258 C5
Newton Abbot TQ12 .. 207 C3
Devons' Rd TQ1 .. 220 C7
Devon Terr
Plymouth PL3 .. 248 E5
16 Totnes TQ9 .. 223 D5
Devon Tors PL20 .. 127 A3
Devon Tors Rd 9 PL20 .. 126 F3
Devon Units
Exeter EX2 .. 177 C1
Great Torrington EX38 .. 159 F6
Devon View EX7 .. 201 B2
Dewberry Dr
Barnstaple EX31 .. 154 B3
Paignton TQ3 .. 225 E2
Deyman's Hill EX16 .. 161 D3
Dial Ho The EX9 .. 198 A1
Dial St EX19 .. 58 F3
Diamond Ave PL4 .. 263 B4
Diamond La TQ10 .. 134 D5
Diamond Rd EX2 .. 261 A1
Diamond St 21 EX32 .. 154 F5
Diana Cl PL16 .. 106 A8
Diane Cl
Exmouth EX8 .. 196 D4
5 Paignton TQ3 .. 225 F1
Dibbon's La EX34 .. 1 D2
Dickens Dr EX2 .. 177 F3
Dickens Rd PL5 .. 244 B1
Dickers Terr TQ12 .. 207 E7
Dickiemoor La PL5 .. 244 C2
Dickna St PL15 .. 90 C1
Dick Pym Cl EX2 .. 178 C4
Dick's Hill EX36 .. 46 E8
Dickshill La EX38 .. 159 D5
DIDDYWELL .. 157 B8
Diddywell Cl EX39 .. 157 A8
Diddywell Rd
Appledore EX39 .. 14 F1
10 Northam EX39 .. 156 F7
Northam EX39 .. 157 A8
Northam EX39 .. 157 B8
DIDWORTHY .. 134 E5
Didworthy Bglws TQ10 .. 134 E5
Didworthy Pk TQ10 .. 134 E5
Dieppe Cl PL1 .. 247 F2
DIGBY .. 178 D3
Digby Dr EX2 .. 178 D3
Digby Gr PL5 .. 243 F5
Digby Rd EX2 .. 178 C3
Digby & Sowton Sta EX2 .. 178 E4
Diggerland Devon* EX15 .. 162 C2
Diggories La 5 EX14 166 B6
Dillons PL8 .. 141 A7
Dillybridge Hill EX6 .. 97 D4
Dinan Way EX8 .. 196 E3
Dinan Way Trad Est EX8 .. 196 F1
Dince Hill Cl EX5 .. 99 E7
Dingle Cl PL17 .. 115 B1
Dingle Ct PL18 .. 125 C5
Dingle Rd
Plymouth, North Prospect PL2 .. 248 A6
Plymouth, Plympton PL7 .. 250 C6
Dingles Fairground Museum* PL16 .. 106 A5
Dingwall Ave PL5 .. 244 E3
Dinham Cres EX4 .. 261 A3
Dinham Mews EX4 .. 261 A3
Dinham Rd EX4 .. 261 A3
Dinneford St EX5 .. 81 E5
Dinnis Cl EX6 .. 97 F4
Dinosaurland Fossil Mus* DT7 .. 260 E3
DINWORTHY .. 38 D2
Dipford Gate EX16 .. 48 C3
Dipford La EX16 .. 48 C4
Dipper Dr PL19 .. 171 D2
DIPPERTOWN .. 106 D3
DIPTFORD .. 138 C7
Diptford Cl TQ4 .. 225 E3
Diptford Cross TQ9 .. 138 C7
Diptford Parochial CE Prim Sch TQ9 .. 138 C7
Dirty La PL12 .. 242 B5
Discover Wistlandpound* EX31 .. 11 A5
Discovery Rd PL1 .. 247 F1
Discovery Wharf 19 PL4 .. 263 A2
Distine Cl PL3 .. 249 B7
Ditch End Cross EX32 .. 18 C7
Ditchett Cross EX16 .. 46 E6
Dittiscombe Cross TQ9 .. 145 A6
DITTISHAM .. 228 C3
Dittisham Ct TQ6 .. 228 C3
Dittisham Wlk PL6 .. 249 E8
Ditton Ct PL6 .. 249 A8
Divett Dr 6 TQ12 .. 122 F1
Dixon Cl TQ3 .. 218 E1
Dixon Dr EX5 .. 179 B3
Dixon Pl PL2 .. 247 F4
Dixon Terr PL8 .. 257 F3
Dix's Field EX1 .. 261 B3
Doatshayne Cl EX13 .. 103 D5
Doatshayne La
Musbury EX13 .. 103 D6
Musbury, Maidenhayne EX13 .. 103 D5
Dobbin Arch TQ12 .. 212 F4
Dobbsmoor Cross EX18 .. 44 F3
Dobles Cl EX22 .. 164 C5
Dobles La EX22 .. 164 C6
Dobles Lane Ind Est EX22 .. 164 C6
Dobles Terr EX22 .. 164 D5
Dobree Pk TA21 .. 160 A4
DOCCOMBE .. 112 C5
Doccombe Cross TQ13 .. 112 B5
Dockeys La TQ7 .. 145 D1
Dockray Cl PL6 .. 245 D4
Dock Rd EX8 .. 201 F6
Dockworthy Cross EX18 .. 60 C8
Dockyard Sta PL2 .. 247 E4
Docton Mill Gdns* EX39 .. 22 B1
Doctors Cnr EX16 .. 61 D7
Doctors Rd 3 TQ5 .. 230 C3
Doctors Wlk EX2 .. 176 E2
DODBROOKE .. 258 E5
Dodbrooke Ct TQ7 .. 258 D5
DODDISCOMBSLEIGH .. 113 C5
Doddiscombsleigh Prim Sch EX6 .. 113 D5
Doddridge Cl PL9 .. 255 F4
DODSCOTT .. 42 C6
Dodscott Cross EX38 .. 42 B7
Doe Ct EX38 .. 159 D5
Dog Down Cross EX16 50 A8
Doggie La
Higher Slade EX34 .. 8 E8
Ilfracombe EX34 .. 1 E2
DOG VILLAGE .. 175 D5
Doidges Farm Cl PL6 249 B8
Dokkum Rd EX17 .. 165 D4
Dolbeare Rd 14 TQ13 131 A5
Dole Park Cross East EX37 .. 43 D5
Dolepark Cross West EX37 .. 43 C5
Dolepark La EX37 .. 43 D5
Dolphin Cl
Lyme Regis DT7 .. 260 E3
Plymouth PL9 .. 255 F6
Dolphin Court Rd
Paignton TQ3 .. 218 F1
Plymouth PL9 .. 255 F6
Dolphin Cres TQ3 .. 218 F1
Dolphin Ct
Brixham TQ5 .. 230 C6
Cullompton EX15 .. 163 C3
13 Honiton EX14 .. 166 C6
Northam EX39 .. 156 E7
22 Teignmouth TQ14 .. 210 C4
Torpoint PL11 .. 246 D3
Dolphin Ho 17 PL4 .. 263 A2
Dolphin Rd EX2 .. 191 D5
Dolphin Sq
Bovey Tracey TQ13 .. 180 C7
Plymouth PL9 .. 255 F6
Dolphin St EX24 .. 103 A5
DOLTON .. 57 F7
Dolton CE Prim Sch EX19 .. 57 E7
Dolvin Rd PL19 .. 171 C5
Domehayes EX20 .. 170 B5
Dommett Cl EX13 .. 167 E7
Donkey La
Millbrook PL10 .. 252 C4
Ugborough PL21 .. 137 D6
Donkey Sanctuary The* EX10 .. 189 B7
Donn Gdns EX39 .. 157 C2
Donnington Dr PL3 .. 249 C7
Doomsford La EX37 .. 44 B5
Doone Way EX34 .. 150 B4
Dorado St PL9 .. 256 E8
Dorchester Ave PL5 .. 244 D4
Dorchester Gr TQ2 .. 213 F1
Dorchester Way EX8 .. 196 D4
Doreena Rd PL9 .. 256 C7
Doriam Cl EX4 .. 173 C2
Dormy Ave PL3 .. 248 F5
Dornafield Cl TQ12 .. 211 D2
Dornafield Cross
Abbotskerswell TQ12 .. 211 E5
Ipplepen TQ12 .. 211 D3
Dornafield Drive E TQ12 .. 211 E2
Dornafield Drive W TQ12 .. 211 D2
Dornafield La TQ12 .. 211 E4
Dornafield Rd TQ12 .. 211 D3
Dornaford Cross EX20 .. 76 C2
Dorridge Gate EX37 .. 28 D3
Dorset Ave EX4 .. 176 E4
Dorset Pk PL15 .. 89 D2
DORSLEY BARTON .. 222 D5
Dorsmouth Terr PL7 .. 250 E4
Dosson Gr TQ1 .. 219 E7
Dotheridge La EX39 .. 25 A1
Dots Cl EX21 .. 90 E6
Dotton Cl EX1 .. 178 D6
Dotton La EX10 .. 186 E6
Double White Rise PL18 .. 125 B5
Doughy La TQ12 .. 211 A7
Douglas Ave
Brixham TQ5 .. 230 E4
Exmouth EX8 .. 202 C6
Douglas Dr PL9 .. 256 A6
Douglas Ho 14 TQ14 .. 210 B5
Douglass Rd PL3 .. 249 C6
Douro Ct PL21 .. 237 D5
DOUSLAND .. 127 C3
Dousland Ho PL20 .. 127 B3
Dousland Rd PL20 .. 127 A3
Dousland Terr PL20 .. 127 B3
Dove Cl
Cullompton EX15 .. 163 A2
Honiton EX14 .. 166 B4
Dovedale Cl EX34 .. 150 E5
Dovedale Rd PL2 .. 248 A7
Dove Gdns PL3 .. 249 D7
Dove La
Cranbrook EX5 .. 99 B6
Sidmouth EX10 .. 188 B3
Dover Rd PL6 .. 245 E3
Dover's Hill EX17 .. 80 E8
Dove Way EX2 .. 176 D3
Dowell St EX14 .. 166 B6
Dower Ct TQ3 .. 226 C8
Dower Ho The TQ10 .. 135 C4
Dower Rd TQ1 .. 220 A7
DOWLAND .. 57 F5
Downash La EX13 .. 88 E3
Downaway La TQ12 .. 213 E5
Down Cl
Newton Poppleford EX10 .. 186 D7
Saltash PL12 .. 242 C2
Down Cross EX16 .. 47 A2
Down End EX17 .. 165 F5
Downes Cl EX17 .. 165 E4
Downeshead La EX17 .. 165 E5
Downfield Cl TQ5 .. 230 A3
Downfield Dr PL7 .. 250 F5
Downfield Way PL7 .. 250 F5
Downfield Wlk PL7 .. 250 F5
Downgate Gdns PL2 .. 248 D8
Downham Gdns PL5 .. 244 C7
Downhayne Brake Rd EX24 .. 102 E6
Downhayne Hill EX17 .. 62 B1
Downhayne Rd EX24 .. 102 F6
Down Hill
Morchard Bishop EX17 .. 78 F8
Rackenford EX16 .. 47 A3
Downhorne Pk PL9 .. 255 F6
Down La
Braunton EX33 .. 152 E6
Doddiscombsleigh EX6 113 D5
Dunsford EX6 .. 112 D8
East Buckland EX32 .. 18 C3
Georgeham EX33 .. 8 A4
Georgeham, North Buckland EX33 .. 8 B3
Kentisbury EX31 .. 10 F6
Knowle EX33 .. 8 F2
Molland EX36 .. 31 E7
Rackenford EX16 .. 47 A3
Winkleigh EX19 .. 58 D4
Downland Cross
Clovelly EX39 .. 23 E1
Clovelly EX39 .. 23 E2
Downlands Cross EX15 .. 66 E2
Downlands La TA3 .. 52 F1
Downlea PL19 .. 171 D4
Downmoor Cross EX38 .. 55 B8
Down Park Dr PL19 .. 171 D4
Down Rd
Instow EX39 .. 15 B1
Plymouth PL7 .. 251 C5
Tavistock PL19 .. 171 D4
DOWN ST MARY .. 78 E7
Downside Ave PL6 .. 249 C7
Downside Cl DT6 .. 104 F4
Downs The TQ7 .. 143 A2
DOWNSTOW .. 134 F5
Downstow Cross TQ10 .. 134 F5
Downs View EX22 .. 54 D6
Down The PL20 .. 125 F1
DOWN THOMAS .. 255 C1
Downton Cl PL1 .. 262 A4
Downton Cross TQ6 .. 233 A7
Down View Rd TQ12 .. 211 A6
Dowrich Cross EX17 .. 80 A7
Dracaena Ave EX31 .. 154 C4
Draco Dr PL2 .. 247 F6
Dragdown Hill EX17 .. 95 F7
Dragon Hill EX38 .. 40 F2
Dragons Hill DT7 .. 260 E5
Dragon's Mead EX13 167 C4
Dragon's Tail TQ5 .. 230 E4
Dragoon Cl TQ12 .. 180 E3
Drake Ave
5 Exeter EX2 .. 178 D5
Ivybridge PL21 .. 237 A5
Teignmouth TQ14 .. 210 A8
Torquay TQ2 .. 219 C6
Drake Cir PL1, PL4 .. 263 A3
Drake Circus PL3 .. 262 C3
Drakecircus Sh Ctr PL1 .. 263 A3
Drake Cl EX39 .. 156 B6
Drake Ct
Plymouth, Ernesettle PL5 .. 243 E4
Plymouth, St Jude's PL4 .. 263 B3
Drake Dr TQ4 .. 226 B2

Drakefield Dr PL12 ... 243 A3
Drake Gdns PL19 ... 171 C4
Drake La TQ13 ... 180 E7
DRAKELAND CORNER ... 132 E1
Drake Mdws [5] TA3 ... 68 D7
Drake Prim Sch PL2 ... 247 E6
Drake Rd
Bovey Tracey TQ13 ... 180 E7
Cullompton EX15 ... 163 C4
Newton Abbot TQ12 ... 207 F3
Salcombe TQ8 ... 259 C5
Tavistock PL19 ... 171 C6
Drake's Ave
Exmouth EX8 ... 202 D8
Sidmouth EX10 ... 188 C8
Drake's CE Prim Sch EX9 ... 198 B6
Drakes Cl PL6 ... 244 F4
Drakes Cres TA20 ... 88 D8
Drakes Ct TQ1 ... 220 B8
Drakes Farm EX2 ... 176 E2
Drakes Gdns EX8 ... 202 D8
Drakes Mdw
Cheriton Fitzpaine EX17 ... 62 F1
Yarcombe EX14 ... 69 A3
Drakes Pk TA21 ... 160 D7
Drake's Pk [3] PL20 ... 125 E1
Drakes Pk N TA21 ... 160 D7
Drakes Rd EX4 ... 177 A4
Drake's Rd TQ4 ... 225 E4
Drakes Way DT7 ... 260 E3
Drake Villas
Tavistock PL19 ... 171 A4
Tavistock PL19 ... 171 B4
Drakewalls Gdns PL18 ... 125 C5
Drakewalls Pl PL18 ... 125 C5
Drake Way PL9 ... 255 E7
DRAKEWELLS ... 125 C6
Drapers Cl EX34 ... 3 B3
Draper Terr [3] PL19 ... 171 B5
Drax Gdns PL6 ... 248 E8
Draycott Cl EX2 ... 178 A4
Dray Ct [21] EX8 ... 202 A6
Draydon La
Dulverton TA22 ... 21 F2
Dulverton TA22 ... 33 B8
Drayford Rd EX16 ... 46 E1
Drayton Rd PL5 ... 244 C1
Drayway Cross EX16 ... 63 D1
Drayway La
Bickleigh EX16 ... 63 E1
Cadbury EX16 ... 81 E8
Drew's Cl EX6 ... 201 A8
Drews Field La TQ3 ... 218 D7
Drewsmead TQ13 ... 122 C3
Drew St TQ5 ... 230 C3
DREWSTEIGNTON ... 96 D2
Drewsteignton County Prim Sch TQ13 ... 96 D1
Drewston Cross TQ13 ... 111 C6
Drewstone Cross EX36 ... 30 E6
Dreys Ct EX1 ... 177 E6
Dreyton Cross TQ9 ... 139 F3
Drift La EX14 ... 66 F3
Drift Lane Cross EX14 ... 66 F3
Drift The TA20 ... 88 E8
Drive The
Bishopsteignton TQ14 ... 208 E8
Brixham TQ5 ... 230 C2
Dawlish EX7 ... 204 E6
East Budleigh EX9 ... 198 D8
Exeter EX5 ... 99 B3
Hillfield TQ6 ... 232 C2
Holbeton PL8 ... 136 D1
Kingskerswell TQ12 ... 213 A4
Plymouth PL3 ... 248 E7
Droridge TQ9 ... 222 F8
Droridge La TQ9 ... 222 E8
Drovers Way
Ivybridge PL21 ... 237 A6
Seaton EX12 ... 192 B8
Drove Way TA3 ... 68 C8
Druid Cross TQ13 ... 130 E5
Druid Rd TQ13 ... 130 E6
Drum Bridge TQ12 ... 180 F1
Drummond Cl PL2 ... 247 F7
Drummond Pl PL1 ... 247 F3
Drummond Way PL20 ... 239 E3
Drum Theatre* PL1 ... 262 C2
Drum Way TQ12 ... 180 F2
Drunken Bridge Hill PL7 ... 250 D4
Drupe Farm Ct EX10 ... 186 D3
Drybridge Cross TQ10 ... 135 C5
Dryburgh Cres PL2 ... 248 A8
Dryden Ave PL5 ... 244 C1
Dryden Cl EX8 ... 196 C4
Dryden Cotts EX5 ... 99 D2
Dryden Rd EX2 ... 177 F4
Dryfield EX6 ... 182 B4
Dry La
Christow EX6 ... 113 B4
Okehampton EX20 ... 93 D5
Drymump Hill EX36 ... 45 F7
Dry Wlk PL10 ... 253 E6
Dualstone Cross EX22 ... 71 C3
Dubbs Cross EX21 ... 90 E3
Ducane Wlk PL6 ... 245 B1
Duchy Ave TQ3 ... 219 B2
Duchy Coll PL17 ... 115 B1
Duchy Cotts PL17 ... 115 B1
Duchy Ct EX8 ... 196 E1
Duchy Dr TQ3 ... 219 B2
Duchy Gdns TQ3 ... 219 A3
Duchy Pk TQ3 ... 219 A2
Duchy Rd EX14 ... 166 A4
Duchy Sch The EX5 ... 82 F6
Duckham La EX17 ... 60 C5
Duck La EX20 ... 76 C5
Duckpool Rd EX31 ... 15 E5
Ducks Field EX36 ... 158 E4
Ducksmoor Cross EX16 ... 63 E8
Ducks Orchard Rd EX6 ... 182 B3
Duckspond Cl TQ11 ... 236 A4
Duckspond Rd TQ11 ... 236 A4
Duckworth Rd EX2 ... 177 A4
Duckworth St [3] PL2 ... 248 A4
Ducky Row PL17 ... 125 A4
Dudley Gdns PL6 ... 249 B8
Dudley Rd PL7 ... 250 B5
Dudley Way EX39 ... 156 B6
Dudmoor La EX31 ... 10 B4
DUERDON ... 38 E6
Duerdon Cross EX39 ... 38 E6
Duke of Cornwall Cl EX8 ... 196 E1
Dukes Cl
Otterton EX9 ... 198 E7
Paignton TQ3 ... 225 E6
Dukes Cres EX8 ... 196 E1
Dukes Dr PL19 ... 125 E4
Duke's Dr PL17 ... 115 C4
Dukes Mead EX15 ... 163 C2
Dukes Orch EX5 ... 82 F6
Dukes Rd TQ9 ... 223 F5
Duke's Rd EX9 ... 197 F2
Dukes Ryde The [1] PL9 ... 255 F7
Duke St
Cullompton EX15 ... 163 C2
Dartmouth TQ6 ... 233 F3
Kingsbridge TQ7 ... 258 D5
Plymouth PL1 ... 247 E2
South Molton EX36 ... 158 C4
Tavistock PL19 ... 171 C6
Dukes Way EX13 ... 167 C4
Dukes Wlk [4] EX1 ... 178 D1
Dulcis Cross EX13 ... 87 C2
DULFORD ... 84 B8
Dulford Bsns Pk EX15 ... 66 A1
Dulford Cross EX15 ... 66 B1
Dulings Mdw EX17 ... 79 B5
Duloe Gdns PL2 ... 248 C8
DULVERTON ... 33 E6
Dulverton La TA4 ... 35 D7
Dulverton Mid & Com Sch TA22 ... 33 D6
Dumfries Ave PL5 ... 244 D3
Dumpdon La EX14 ... 85 F6
Dumpdon View EX14 ... 86 A6
DUMPINGHILL ... 55 F3
Duncan Ho TQ1 ... 220 C4
Duncannon La TQ9 ... 227 E7
Duncannon Mead TQ9 ... 227 F7
Duncan St PL1 ... 247 E1
DUNCHIDEOCK ... 114 A6
Dunclair Pk PL3 ... 249 D5
Duncombe Ave PL5 ... 244 A2
Duncombe Cross TQ7 ... 144 C2
Duncombe St TQ7 ... 258 D6
Dun Cross TQ9 ... 222 C8
Dundas St [4] PL2 ... 248 A4
Dundonald St PL2 ... 247 F4
Dundridge Ct TQ9 ... 222 E1
Dunes The [12] EX39 ... 15 B1
Dune View
Braunton EX33 ... 152 B7
Westward Ho! EX39 ... 156 D7
Dune View Rd EX33 ... 152 B6
Dunheved Rd PL12 ... 242 F2
DUNKESWELL ... 67 C2
Dunkeswell Airfield EX14 ... 67 B2
Dunkeswell Bsns Pk EX14 ... 67 B2
Dunkeswell Cl PL2 ... 247 F8
Dunkeswell Meml Mus* EX14 ... 67 B2
Dunkirk EX11 ... 169 C4
Dunley Cross TQ13 ... 123 B4
Dunley La TQ13 ... 123 B5
Dunley Wlk PL6 ... 245 C1
Dunlin Cl EX7 ... 200 F2
Dunlin Dr
Yelland EX31 ... 15 C3
Yelland EX31 ... 153 A5
Dunlins Wlk EX3 ... 182 E6
Dunmere Rd TQ1 ... 220 B6
Dunmore Ct TQ14 ... 210 B2
Dunmore Dr TQ14 ... 210 B2
Dunnet Rd PL6 ... 244 D7
Dunning Ct EX14 ... 166 B6
Dunning Gn [1] EX31 ... 154 C3
Dunning Rd TQ14 ... 210 A7
Dunning Wlk TQ14 ... 210 A6
Dunn La EX39 ... 25 E2
Dunns Cl EX33 ... 152 F4
Dunn's Hill TA21 ... 51 A6
Dunraven [20] EX32 ... 155 A4
Dunraven Dr PL6 ... 245 A6
Dunrich Cl EX2 ... 261 C2
Dunscombe La
Sidmouth EX10 ... 189 B7
Trow EX10 ... 189 B7
Dunsdon Cross EX22 ... 53 C3
Dunsdon Farm National Nature Reserve* EX22 ... 53 B2
DUNSFORD ... 112 F8
Dunsford Cl EX8 ... 202 D6
Dunsford Com Prim Sch EX6 ... 112 F8
Dunsford Gdns EX4 ... 176 E3
Dunsford Hill EX5 ... 81 E3
Dunsford Rd EX2 ... 176 E3
Dunsford Way [1] EX16 ... 161 C3
Dunsgreen La EX15 ... 67 D8
Dunsland Cross EX22 ... 73 A6
Dunsley Hill EX16, EX36 ... 32 D5
Dunster Cl PL7 ... 251 C4
Dunsterville Rd PL21 ... 237 E6
Dunster Wlk EX6 ... 181 F5
DUNSTONE
Chillington ... 149 B7
Widecombe in the Moor ... 121 B2
Yealmpton ... 136 B2
Dunstone Ave PL9 ... 256 A7
Dunstone Cl
Paignton TQ3 ... 218 E1
Plymouth PL9 ... 255 F7
Dunstone Cross TQ7 ... 149 C7
Dunstone Ct TQ3 ... 218 E1
Dunstone Dr PL9 ... 255 F7
Dunstone La PL9 ... 256 B7
Dunstone Park Rd TQ3 ... 218 E1
Dunstone Prim Sch PL9 ... 256 A8
Dunstone Rd
Plymouth, Plymstock PL9 ... 255 F7
Plymouth, St Budeaux PL5 ... 243 F3
Dunstone Rise TQ3 ... 218 E1
Dunstone View PL9 ... 256 A7
DUNTERTON ... 115 D6
Duntz Hill PL16 ... 105 E4
Dunvegan Cl EX4 ... 177 A8
Dunwell Cross PL21 ... 137 D5
Dural Cross EX22 ... 38 B3
Durant House EX20 ... 77 C4
Durban Rd PL3 ... 248 D5
Durbin Cl EX14 ... 166 D5
Durdon Cross EX20 ... 75 A1
Dure La EX36 ... 30 E8
Durham Ave PL4 ... 263 C4
Durham Cl
Exeter EX1 ... 178 C7
Exmouth EX8 ... 196 D4
Paignton TQ3 ... 219 B1
Durham Way EX14 ... 166 A4
Durleigh Rd TQ5 ... 230 B4
Durlestone Cross TQ7 ... 149 B8
Durleymoor Cross EX16 ... 50 F4
Durley Rd EX12 ... 191 F7
Durnford St PL1 ... 248 A1
Durnford Street Ope PL1 ... 248 A1
Durrant Cl
Northam EX39 ... 157 A5
Plymouth PL1 ... 247 E3
Durrant La
Northam EX39 ... 156 F5
Northam EX39 ... 157 A5
Durris Cl PL6 ... 245 D4
Durris Gdns PL6 ... 245 D4
Dursley Way EX39 ... 156 E2
Durwent Cl PL9 ... 255 A6
DURYARD ... 173 A1
Duryard Halls of Residence EX4 ... 173 A2
Duryardwood La EX5 ... 172 E5
Dutchbarn La EX3 ... 182 D7
DUTSON ... 105 A4
Dux Cross EX22 ... 71 B6
Duxford Cl PL5 ... 243 E5
Dyehouse Cnr TA22 ... 34 A6
Dyehouse Cross TA22 ... 33 F5
Dyehouse La TA22 ... 34 A5
Dyers Cl
Braunton EX33 ... 152 D6
West Buckland TA21 ... 52 F7
Dyers Ct EX2 ... 261 A2
Dyke Hill Terr TA20 ... 88 D8
Dymock Way PL21 ... 237 A5
Dymond Ct (Kingdom Pl) PL12 ... 242 F2
Dymond Rd EX39 ... 156 F1
Dynevor Cl PL3 ... 248 F7

E

Eager Way EX6 ... 181 F5
Eagle Cl
Kingsteignton TQ12 ... 123 E1
Plymouth PL7 ... 251 C4
Eagle Cotts EX4 ... 177 A5
Eagle Cres TQ12 ... 207 A5
Eagle Ct TQ2 ... 219 E8
Eagle Ho EX4 ... 261 A2
Eagle Hurst Ct [5] EX10 ... 188 A4
Eagle Hurst Lodge [4] EX10 ... 188 A4
Eagle Pl TQ13 ... 111 F5
Eagle Rd PL7 ... 251 C4
Eaglescott Airfield EX37 ... 43 C3
Eagles Nest EX2 ... 176 D4
Eagle Way EX2 ... 178 F5
Eaglewood Cl TQ2 ... 213 C2
Ealing Cl TQ5 ... 230 D3
Earl Richard's Road N EX2 ... 177 E3
Earl Richard's Road S EX2 ... 177 F2
Earl's Acre PL3 ... 248 C4
Earls Ct TQ1 ... 219 F6
Earl's Dr PL10 ... 253 B3
Earl's Dr The
Cawsand PL10 ... 253 A1
Rame PL10 ... 140 I2
Earls Mill Rd PL7 ... 250 E6
Earls Wood Cl PL6 ... 245 F3
Earlswood Dr TQ3 ... 225 D7
Earls Wood Dr PL6 ... 245 F3
EASTACOMBE ... 27 C8
Eastacombe Cross
Barnstaple EX31 ... 16 B1
Northlew EX20 ... 74 E2
Eastacombe La EX31 ... 15 E6
Eastacombe Rise EX31 ... 15 E6
EASTACOTT ... 28 E2
Eastacott Cross EX37 ... 28 E2
Eastacott La EX34 ... 8 B6
EAST ALLINGTON ... 144 E7
East Allington Prim Sch TQ9 ... 144 D7
EAST ANSTEY ... 32 E5
East Anstey Prim Sch EX16 ... 32 E5
EAST ASH ... 95 D2
East Ash Cross
Bradworthy EX22 ... 38 F3
Whiddon Down EX20 ... 95 D2
East Ave EX1 ... 177 E6
East Ball Hill EX39 ... 22 E3
Eastbourne Terr EX39 ... 156 D7
Eastbrook Ho [7] TQ14 ... 210 B6
EAST BUCKLAND ... 18 D2
East Buckland Cross EX32 ... 18 D2
EAST BUDLEIGH ... 198 B6
East Budleigh Rd
Budleigh Salterton EX9 ... 198 B3
East Budleigh EX9 ... 198 C6
Eastbury Ave PL5 ... 244 A2
EAST BUTTERLEIGH ... 64 E3
East Butterleigh Cross EX15 ... 64 E3
East Challacombe La EX34 ... 3 B4
EAST CHARLETON ... 144 D1
Eastchurch La EX6 ... 96 D6
East Cl EX16 ... 46 E1
East Cliff DT7 ... 260 E3
East Cliff Cl EX7 ... 204 E7
East Cliff Gdns EX7 ... 204 E7
East Cliff Rd EX7 ... 204 E7
Eastcliff Wlk TQ14 ... 210 D5
East Cliff Wlk TQ14 ... 210 D7
East Coombe Cross EX17 ... 81 A6
Eastcoombe La EX17 ... 81 A6
Eastcote Cl PL6 ... 245 B6
EASTCOTT ... 37 D3
Eastcott Cross EX23 ... 37 D2
East Courts The [5] PL1 ... 262 A3
East Dartmoor Woods & Heaths National Nature Reserve* TQ13 ... 122 B5
East Devon Bsns Pk EX14 ... 86 C3
EASTDON ... 201 B4
Eastdown EX39 ... 22 F3
EAST DOWN ... 10 C4
Eastdown Cross TQ9 ... 145 D8
East Down Cross
Combe Martin EX34 ... 9 F6
Okehampton EX20 ... 93 D8
East Dr EX8 ... 196 A1
Eastella Rd PL20 ... 127 A2
East End EX17 ... 62 D3
East End Terr [16] TQ13 ... 131 A5
Easterbrook La EX6 ... 96 D8
Easter Close Cross EX31 ... 3 D1
Easter Ct EX31 ... 154 B2
Easterdown Cl PL9 ... 255 F7
Easterfield La TQ1 ... 214 C2
Easter Ground La EX34 ... 8 F5
Easter Hill EX37 ... 28 B2
Easter Hill La EX6 ... 201 A7
Easter La
Berrynarbor EX34 ... 2 E3
Lower Tippacott EX35 ... 6 B4
Easter Lane Cross TQ13 ... 121 B2
Easterley Terr EX31 ... 154 C3
Easterly Pk EX33 ... 152 F5
Eastern Ave
Barnstaple EX32 ... 155 C4
Exeter EX2 ... 182 C7
Eastern Backway TQ7 ... 258 D5
Eastern Down La EX33 ... 8 C3
Eastern Espl TQ4 ... 226 C6
Eastern Rd
Ashburton TQ13 ... 131 A5
Zeal Monachorum EX17 ... 78 C7
Easterntown PL8 ... 136 D1
EASTERN TOWN ... 188 B3
Eastern Wood Rd PL7 ... 251 D4
Easter Rd EX36 ... 19 A2
Easter St EX32 ... 16 E1
East Farm TQ7 ... 144 D1
Eastfield EX11 ... 168 D4
Eastfield Ave PL9 ... 255 C6
Eastfield Cres PL3 ... 249 A6
Eastfield Gdns EX11 ... 168 D4
Eastfield Orch
Uffculme EX15 ... 66 A8
West Hill EX11 ... 168 D4
East Grove Rd EX2 ... 261 C2
Easthay La TA20 ... 88 F4
East Hill EX33 ... 152 E6
East Horner La EX13 ... 87 B5
EAST ILKERTON ... 5 B3
EASTINGTON ... 60 E4
Eastington Cross EX17 ... 60 E4
Eastington Hill EX17 ... 60 E3
East John Wlk EX1 ... 177 E6
EAST KNOWSTONE ... 32 B2
Eastlake Ho [4] PL1 ... 263 A2
Eastlake Ope PL3 ... 263 A3
Eastlake St PL4 ... 262 C3
Eastlands EX15 ... 67 B8
EASTLEIGH ... 26 C6
EAST LEIGH
Haberton ... 222 B1
Zeal Monachorum ... 77 F8
Eastleigh Cl EX13 ... 103 D8
East Leigh Cross
Harberton TQ9 ... 222 B1
Zeal Monachorum EX17 ... 77 F8
East Lyn La EX35 ... 151 F2
East Mead EX15 ... 67 B8
East Meadow EX31 ... 27 B8
East Meadow Rd EX33 ... 152 B7
East Mere Cross EX16 ... 50 B2
EAST MIDDLETON ... 4 B1
East Moore Cross TQ9 ... 135 E1
East Nymph La EX17 ... 95 E6
EAST OGWELL ... 206 E1
EASTON ... 111 B7
Easton Cross
Hittisleigh EX6 ... 96 C5
West Alvington TQ7 ... 258 B3
Easton La EX16 ... 50 D1
Easton Moor Cross EX31 ... 27 C1
Easton Rd EX6 ... 96 C4
East Pafford Ave TQ2 ... 214 B3
Eastpark TQ7 ... 149 B8
East Park Ave PL4 ... 262 C4
East Park Cl EX19 ... 58 F3
East Park Rd EX32 ... 155 D4
East Pitton Barns PL7 ... 136 A5
East Pk EX39 ... 38 F8
EAST PORTLEMOUTH ... 259 F4
EAST PRAWLE ... 149 A3
East Pugsley Cross EX37 ... 29 B2
EAST PUTFORD ... 39 C3
East Ridge View EX39 ... 157 B1
East Rowley La EX36 ... 45 D6
East Sherford Cross PL8 ... 257 A8
East St
Ashburton TQ13 ... 130 F5
Bishop's Tawton EX32 ... 16 E1
Black Torrington EX21 ... 74 A8
Bovey Tracey TQ13 ... 180 D8
Braunton EX33 ... 152 D6
Chittlehampton EX37 ... 28 F4
Chulmleigh EX18 ... 44 E1
Crediton EX17 ... 165 D5
Denbury TQ12 ... 211 A7
Great Torrington EX38 ... 159 D5
Ipplepen TQ12 ... 211 E2
Newton Abbot TQ12 ... 207 C3
North Molton EX36 ... 19 E1
North Molton EX36 ... 30 E8
Okehampton EX20 ... 170 C5
Plymouth PL1 ... 262 A2
Sheepwash EX21 ... 56 C1
Sidmouth EX10 ... 188 B3
South Molton EX36 ... 158 D4
Torquay TQ2 ... 219 F6
Uffculme EX15 ... 66 A7
EAST STOWFORD ... 28 F5
East Tapps La EX16 ... 33 B2
East Terr
Budleigh Salterton EX9 ... 199 H2
Exeter EX1 ... 178 A6
EAST-THE-WATER ... 157 C2
East-the-Water Com Prim Sch EX39 ... 157 C1
EAST TOWN ... 165 E6
East Town La EX6 ... 194 D3
East View Cotts [5] EX14 ... 166 C6
East View Pl EX16 ... 161 E4
East View Terr EX39 ... 157 A1
EAST VILLAGE ... 80 C8
East Village Cross EX17 ... 80 C8
East Way PL21 ... 136 D6
Eastwell La TQ12 ... 217 C7
Eastwick Barton EX16 ... 62 B8
East Wonford Hill EX2 ... 178 B5
Eastwood EX35 ... 151 B4
Eastwood Cres TQ12 ... 206 E5
Eastwood La EX6 ... 96 C7
EAST WORLINGTON ... 61 B8
East Worlington Cross EX17 ... 61 B8
East Worlington Prim Sch EX17 ... 61 B8
EAST YOULSTONE ... 37 F2
East Youlstone Cross EX23 ... 37 F2
Easy Bridge Cross EX13 ... 102 F7
Easy La TQ13 ... 123 B7
Eaton Ct TQ14 ... 210 B7
Eaton Dr EX1 ... 261 C3
Eaton Hall Dr TQ6 ... 233 E4
Eaton Ho EX1 ... 261 C3
Eaton Pl TQ4 ... 226 B5
Ebberley Lawn EX32 ... 155 A5
Ebberly Arms EX38 ... 42 F6
Ebberly Cross EX19 ... 42 E5
Ebberly Ct [14] EX32 ... 155 A5
EBBERLY HILL ... 42 F6
Ebdon Ct EX10 ... 101 B2
Ebdon Way TQ1 ... 219 F6
Ebenezer Rd TQ3 ... 226 A5
EBFORD ... 183 C4
Ebford La EX3 ... 183 D4
Ebrington Rd EX2 ... 177 B3
Ebrington St
Kingsbridge TQ7 ... 258 D5
Plymouth PL4 ... 263 A3
Echo Cres PL5 ... 244 D2
Eco Way PL6 ... 245 C8
Eddy's La [10] EX32 ... 155 B3
Eddystone Cl
Heybrook Bay PL9 ... 140 A7
Plymouth PL3 ... 249 C6
Eddystone Rd
Down Thomas PL9 ... 255 C1
Thurlestone TQ7 ... 143 A1
Eddystone Rise TQ7 ... 147 D7
Eddystone Terr PL1 ... 262 B1
Eden Cl TQ5 ... 230 C3
Eden Gr TQ3 ... 225 F7
Eden Park Prim Sch TQ5 ... 230 C3
Eden Pk TQ5 ... 230 C3
Edenside PL3 ... 248 F6
Edenvale Rd TQ3 ... 225 F8
Eden Valley Gdns PL6 ... 245 D2
Eden Way EX10 ... 186 E3
Edford St EX2 ... 177 C6
Edgar Terr PL4 ... 249 A4
Edgbaston Mead EX2 ... 178 C4
Edgcumbe Ave PL1 ... 262 A3
Edgcumbe Cl PL18 ... 125 D6
Edgcumbe Cres PL10 ... 252 F6
Edgcumbe Ct [3] PL3 ... 248 A3
Edgcumbe Dr PL19 ... 171 B6
Edgcumbe Ho PL1 ... 262 B2
Edgcumbe Park Rd PL3 ... 248 D6
Edgcumbe Rd
St Dominick PL12 ... 125 A2
Saltash PL12 ... 242 C5
Edgcumbe St PL1 ... 248 A1
Edgcumbe Terr
[13] Bere Alston PL20 ... 125 E1
Milton Abbot PL19 ... 116 A6
Edgecombe Way PL18 ... 125 B5
Edgecumbe Rd PL19 ... 116 A6
Edgeland Cross TQ12 ... 217 D8
Edgelands La TQ12 ... 211 C1
Edgeley Rd TQ2 ... 214 A2
Edgemill Wlk PL21 ... 237 E4
Edgemount Ho [5] TQ1 ... 220 B5
Edgerley Cross EX17 ... 60 C1
Edgerton Park Rd EX4 ... 177 D8
Edgeworthy Hill EX16 ... 62 C8
Edgiford Cross EX18 ... 45 B1
Edgiford La EX18 ... 45 A1
EDGINSWELL ... 213 B1
Edginswell Cl TQ2 ... 213 C1
Edginswell La TQ2, TQ12 ... 213 A1
Edinburgh Cres EX8 ... 195 E6
Edinburgh Dr EX4 ... 176 E6
Edinburgh Rd TQ5 ... 230 D3
Edinburgh St PL1 ... 247 E1
EDISTONE ... 37 C8
Edith Ave PL4 ... 263 C4
Edith St PL5 ... 243 D1
Edmonton Cl EX4 ... 178 A8
Edmund St EX2, EX4 ... 261 A2
Edmunds Way
[1] Exeter EX1 ... 178 D1
Exeter EX3 ... 182 D8
Edna Terr PL4 ... 263 C3
Edward Cl TQ7 ... 143 A1
Edward Dr EX11 ... 169 B3
Edwards Cl PL7 ... 251 B4
Edwards Cres PL12 ... 242 C2

Edwards Ct EX2 ... 178 D4
Edwards Dr
Plymouth PL7 ... 251 B5
Westward Ho! EX39 ... 156 E7
Edwards Rd PL15 ... 90 C1
Edwin Rd EX2 ... 177 B3
Effingham Cres PL3 ... 248 D7
EFFORD ... 249 C5
Efford Barns EX17 ... 81 B4
Efford Cres PL3 ... 249 B6
Efford Fort PL3 ... 249 E6
Efford La PL3 ... 249 B5
Efford Marshes Nature Reserve★ PL3 ... 249 E6
Efford Pathway PL3 ... 249 C6
Efford Rd PL3 ... 249 B6
Efford Wlk PL3 ... 249 B6
Egerton Cres PL4 ... 263 C3
Egerton Pl PL4 ... 263 C3
Egerton Rd
Plymouth PL4 ... 263 C3
Torquay TQ1 ... 220 C6
EGGBUCKLAND ... 249 C8
Eggbuckland Com Coll PL6 ... 249 A8
Eggbuckland Rd
Plymouth PL3 ... 249 A6
Plymouth PL3 ... 249 C7
Eggbuckland Vale Prim Sch PL6 ... 249 A8
Eggesford Cross EX17 60 A3
Eggesford Ctry Est EX18 ... 59 E6
Eggesford Fourways EX18 ... 59 E5
Eggesford Garden & Country Ctr★ EX18 ... 59 E6
Eggesford Rd
Winkleigh EX19 ... 58 F3
Winkleigh EX19 ... 59 A2
Eggesford Sta EX18 ... 59 E6
Egg Moor La EX13 ... 88 A7
Egham Ave EX2 ... 177 D3
Egremont Cross EX14 ... 84 C6
Egremont Rd EX8 ... 202 A7
Egret Cl
Dawlish EX7 ... 200 F2
Millbrook PL10 ... 253 A6
Egypt La 9 EX18 ... 44 E1
Eiffel Pl 11 TQ9 ... 223 C5
Eight Acre Cl
Paignton TQ3 ... 225 F1
1 Plymouth PL7 ... 251 C5
Eight Acre Dr TQ3 ... 225 F1
Eight Acre La TA21 ... 160 E5
Eight Trees TQ9 ... 216 A5
Elaine Cl
Exeter EX4 ... 174 A2
Plymouth PL7 ... 250 B5
Elba Cl TQ4 ... 226 C1
Elberry Farm La TQ4 ... 229 D7
Elberry La TQ5 ... 229 E5
Elbow La PL19 ... 171 C6
ELBURTON ... 256 B6
Elburton Prim Sch PL9 ... 256 C7
Elburton Rd PL9 ... 256 B8
Elbury Cl EX4 ... 175 E6
Eldad Hill PL1 ... 262 A3
Elderberry Way EX15 162 E5
Elder Cl 2 PL7 ... 251 B5
Elder Gr EX17 ... 165 E6
Eldertree Gdns EX4 ... 177 A7
Eldridge Ho EX13 ... 167 F7
Eleanor Ho PL1 ... 262 A2
Electra Way PL9 ... 256 E8
Elford Cres PL7 ... 250 E7
Elford Dr PL9 ... 255 C7
Elford Pk PL20 ... 127 A2
Elgar Cl
Barnstaple EX32 ... 155 C5
Exeter EX2 ... 178 C5
Elgin Cres PL5 ... 244 E3
Elim Cl EX10 ... 188 B5
Elim Ct PL3 ... 248 E5
Elim Terr PL3 ... 248 E5
Elim Villas EX10 ... 188 B5
Eliot St PL5 ... 247 E8
Elizabethan EX39 ... 156 B7
Elizabethan Ct 8 EX2 ... 261 B2
Elizabethan Ho 10 TQ9 ... 223 D5
Elizabethan Wy TQ14 204 B1
Elizabeth Ave
Brixham TQ5 ... 230 A1
Exeter EX4 ... 177 E8
Elizabeth Cl
Barnstaple EX31 ... 154 D2
Ivybridge PL21 ... 237 F5
Lyme Regis DT7 ... 260 E4
Rockwell Green TA21 ... 160 A4
2 Whimple EX5 ... 99 E8
Elizabeth Ct
2 Plymouth PL1 ... 263 A2
Torquay TQ2 ... 219 F5
Totnes TQ9 ... 223 F5
Elizabeth Dr EX31 ... 154 D3
Elizabeth Gdns EX1 ... 178 C7
Elizabeth House Mus & Arts Gall★ PL4 ... 263 A2
Elizabeth Lea Cl EX22 ... 38 E1
Elizabeth Penton Way EX16 ... 34 B1
Elizabeth Pl PL4 ... 263 A4
Elizabeth Rd
Exmouth EX8 ... 196 C2
Seaton EX12 ... 192 A7
Elizabeth Sq 4 TQ12 207 F2
Elizabeth Way EX12 ... 192 A6
Elkins Hill TQ5 ... 230 D5
ELLACOMBE ... 220 C6
Ellacombe Acad 7 TQ1 ... 220 B6
Ellacombe Church Rd TQ1 ... 220 C6
Ellacombe Rd TQ1 ... 220 B6
Ellacott Rd EX2 ... 181 C6
Ellards Cl EX2 ... 177 E3
Ellbridge La PL12 ... 238 A3
Ellen Tinkham Sch EX1 ... 178 E7
Ellen Tinkham Sch Further Ed Coll EX1 178 B7
Elleralie Ho TQ14 ... 210 B3
Ellerhayes EX5 ... 82 D4
Ellersdown La TA22 ... 33 E4
Ellerslie Rd EX31 ... 154 B4
Ellesmere TQ1 ... 220 C4
Ellesmere Rd TQ1 ... 220 E5
Elley Cross EX17 ... 79 B2
Ellimore Rd TQ13 ... 122 C8
Elliot Cl
Barnstaple EX32 ... 155 C4
Ottery St Mary EX11 ... 169 C3
Elliot Ho EX2 ... 261 B2
Elliot Plain TQ11 ... 236 C5
Elliots Hill TQ13 ... 130 C8
Elliot Sq PL11 ... 247 B3
Elliot St PL1 ... 262 B1
Elliott Cl
Exeter EX4 ... 173 E2
Saltash PL12 ... 242 D2
Elliott Ct TQ12 ... 211 C2
Elliot Terr PL1 ... 262 C1
Elliot Terrace La PL1 262 C1
Elliott Gdns EX1 ... 174 F2
Elliott Gr TQ5 ... 230 B4
Elliott Rd PL4 ... 249 B1
Elliotts Hill PL8 ... 257 A4
Elliott's Hill EX17 ... 61 C3
Elliott's Store★ PL12 243 A2
Elliott Way EX2 ... 178 D5
Ellis Dr TQ13 ... 111 A6
Ellis Yard EX34 ... 150 B5
Ellmead Cross EX20 ... 93 F7
Ellwood Ct TQ1 ... 220 B6
Ellwood Rd EX8 ... 196 D2
Elm Bank TQ11 ... 236 A4
Elmbank Gdns 3 TQ4 ... 226 A5
Elmbank Rd TQ4 ... 226 A5
Elmbridge Gdns EX4 ... 177 A8
Elm Cl
Broadclyst EX5 ... 175 C6
Stibb Cross EX38 ... 40 D2
Tavistock PL19 ... 171 C3
Elm Cotts
Barnstaple EX31 ... 16 A3
Saltash PL12 ... 242 C3
Elm Cres PL3, PL4 ... 249 A4
Elm Croft PL2 ... 248 B7
Elmcroft La TQ12 ... 212 E6
Elm Ct EX6 ... 201 B8
Elmdale Rd EX39 ... 157 A3
Elmdon Cl EX4 ... 173 D1
Elm Dr TQ12 ... 207 F7
Elm Farm La EX24 ... 103 A3
Elmfield Cres EX8 ... 196 B2
Elmfield Mdw EX20 ... 74 E1
Elmfield Rd
Barnstaple EX31 ... 16 A3
Seaton EX12 ... 192 A7
Elmfield Terr EX39 ... 157 A7
Elmfield Way TQ12 ... 207 E6
Elm Gr
Bideford EX39 ... 156 F2
Exmouth EX8 ... 201 F6
Plymouth, Eggbuckland PL6 ... 249 B8
Plymouth, Plympton PL7 ... 250 E5
Teignmouth TQ14 ... 210 B8
Elm Grove Ave EX3 ... 182 F5
Elm Grove Cl EX7 ... 204 E7
Elm Grove Dr EX7 ... 204 E7
Elm Grove Gdns EX3 ... 182 F5
Elm Grove Rd
Dawlish EX7 ... 204 E7
Exeter EX4 ... 261 A4
Topsham EX3 ... 182 F5
Elmhirst Dr TQ9 ... 223 E5
Elmhurst Ct 3 TQ14 ... 210 B5
Elm La EX8 ... 202 F7
Elmlea Ave EX31 ... 153 E5
El Monte Cl 6 TQ14 ... 210 B6
Elm Orch EX12 ... 192 D7
Elmoreswell Ave EX1 ... 179 A8
Elmore Way
Tiverton EX16 ... 64 C8
Tiverton EX16 ... 161 E5
Elm Pk
Millbrook PL10 ... 253 B6
Paignton TQ3 ... 225 F6
Elm Pk Way EX1 ... 179 B8
Elm Rd
Brixham TQ5 ... 230 A2
Exmouth EX8 ... 202 C7
8 Newton Abbot TQ12 ... 207 C3
Plymouth, Glenholt PL6 ... 245 D6
Elm Rd *continued*
Plymouth, Mannamead PL4 ... 248 F4
ELMSCOTT ... 37 B8
Elmscroft Terr 7 EX39 ... 157 A2
Elmside
Budleigh Salterton EX9 ... 198 A1
Exeter EX4 ... 177 E7
Willand EX15 ... 65 D5
Willand EX15 ... 162 D3
Elmside Cl EX4 ... 177 E7
Elmsleigh EX32 ... 27 E8
Elmsleigh Pk TQ4 ... 226 B5
Elmsleigh Rd TQ4 ... 226 B5
Elms Mdw EX19 ... 58 F2
Elms Rd TA21 ... 160 F5
Elms The
Colyford EX24 ... 103 A3
Holsworthy EX22 ... 164 C4
Plymouth PL3 ... 248 A3
Elm Terr
Honiton EX14 ... 166 D6
1 Plymouth PL3 ... 248 F5
Tiverton EX16 ... 161 B4
Elm Tree Cl
Torquay TQ2 ... 213 C2
Yealmpton PL8 ... 257 F4
Elm Tree Dr TQ9 ... 228 A8
Elm Tree Pk PL8 ... 136 A2
Elm Units EX2 ... 177 D1
Elm Villas EX24 ... 103 A3
Elm Way EX10 ... 101 A1
Elm Wlk TQ9 ... 223 F5
Elmwood Ave TQ12 ... 206 E4
Elmwood Cl PL6 ... 245 D5
Elmwood Cres EX7 ... 204 E7
Elmwood Gdns EX24 ... 103 A3
Elmwood Pk TQ7 ... 143 E7
Elphinstone Rd PL2 ... 248 C7
Elsdale Rd TQ4 ... 226 A4
Elsdon EX11 ... 168 E4
Elsdon La EX11 ... 168 E4
Elsdon's La DT6 ... 104 D7
Elsie Pl EX1 ... 178 D6
Elspeth Sitters Ho 10 PL4 ... 263 A2
Elston Cross
Churchstow TQ7 ... 143 D4
Copplestone EX17 ... 79 C6
ELSTONE ... 44 D3
Elstone Cross EX18 ... 44 C3
Elston La EX17 ... 79 B5
Elston Mdw EX17 ... 165 A5
Elton Cl EX16 ... 161 B5
Elton Rd EX4 ... 177 E8
Elvestone EX9 ... 198 B1
Elvis Rd EX8 ... 202 D7
ELWELL ... 18 C2
Elwell Cross EX32 ... 18 B2
Elwell Rd PL12 ... 243 A2
Elwick Gdns PL3 ... 249 B5
Elworthy Cross EX16 ... 47 C2
Elworthy Dr TA21 ... 160 D4
Elworthy Hill EX16 ... 47 D2
Elwyn Rd EX8 ... 202 C6
Ely Cl
Exeter EX4 ... 176 D6
Feniton EX14 ... 84 D2
Elysian Ct EX36 ... 158 D5
Elysian Fields EX10 ... 188 B5
Embankment La PL4 ... 249 B2
Embankment Rd
Kingsbridge TQ7 ... 258 D3
Plymouth PL4 ... 249 B2
Embankment Road Lane N PL4 ... 249 B2
Embankment The TQ14 ... 209 D5
Embercombe Cross EX32 ... 18 F1
Ember Rd TQ8 ... 259 C5
Embleford Cres TQ13 ... 111 F5
Emblett Dr TQ12 ... 206 E4
Emblett Hill View TQ12 ... 206 F1
Embridge Cross TQ6 ... 145 F7
Embridge Hill TQ6 ... 146 A7
Embury Cl TQ12 ... 213 A4
Emily Gdns PL4 ... 263 B4
Emma Gr PL19 ... 171 B7
Emmanuel Cl 1 EX4 ... 177 A5
Emmanuel Rd 2 EX4 ... 177 A5
Emma Pl PL1 ... 248 A1
Emma Place Ope PL1 ... 248 A1
Emmasfield EX8 ... 202 D7
Emmetts Pk 9 TQ13 131 A5
EMPACOMBE ... 253 D6
Emperor Way EX1 ... 178 E7
Empire Ct 2 TQ1 ... 220 A7
Empire Rd TQ1 ... 220 A7
Empsons Cl EX7 ... 204 C6
Empsons Hill EX7 ... 204 C6
Encombe St PL3 ... 249 E1
Endeavour Ave EX2 ... 182 C8
Endeavour Ct PL1 ... 248 A3
Endfield Cl EX1 ... 178 B6
Endsleigh Cres EX5 ... 179 B7
Endsleigh Dr PL15, PL19 ... 115 D5
Endsleigh Gdns★ PL19 ... 115 F5
Endsleigh Gdns 2 PL4 ... 263 A4
Endsleigh Park Rd PL3 ... 248 D6
Endsleigh Pk EX23 ... 70 A6
Endsleigh Pl PL4 ... 263 A4
Endsleigh Rd PL9 ... 255 C7
Endsleigh View PL21 237 A5
Energic Terr EX15 ... 163 C4
Enfield Cl EX17 ... 165 A5
Enfield Cotts TQ1 ... 220 D7
Enfield Rd TQ1 ... 220 C7
Engineers Way EX8 ... 202 E7
England's Cl 13 EX10 101 B1
Eningdale Rd PL19 ... 171 A4
Ennaton Cross PL21 ... 137 E7
Ennerdale Gdns PL6 ... 244 E5
Ennerdale Way EX4 ... 176 F6
Ennisfarne Rd EX39 ... 156 B7
Ensign Ct EX39 ... 156 E7
Ensis Cross EX31 ... 27 D5
Enterprise Ave EX16 ... 64 E8
Enterprise Rd
Roundswell EX31 ... 16 B2
Roundswell EX31 ... 154 B1
Entrance Cross EX37 ... 44 B7
Epping Cres PL6 ... 249 D7
Epworth Terr 4 PL2 ... 247 F5
Erica Dr TQ2 ... 213 F3
Eric Rd
Calstock PL18 ... 125 E3
Plymouth PL4 ... 263 C3
Erith Ave PL2 ... 247 E7
Erle Gdns PL7 ... 250 F3
Erlstoke Cl PL6 ... 245 D1
Erme Bridge Wks PL21 ... 237 C4
Erme Ct PL21 ... 237 D5
Erme Dr PL21 ... 237 C5
Erme Gdns PL3 ... 249 C5
Erme Pk PL21 ... 136 F3
Erme Prim Sch The PL21 ... 237 D5
Erme Rd PL21 ... 237 D5
Ermeside Cotts PL21 ... 136 F4
Erme Terr PL21 ... 237 D5
ERMINGTON ... 136 F4
Ermington Prim Sch PL21 ... 136 F4
Ermington Rd
Ivybridge PL21 ... 237 C3
Ivybridge PL7 ... 136 F6
Ermington Terr PL4 ... 248 E4
Ermington Workshops PL21 ... 137 A4
Ernborough Ct EX2 ... 261 C2
ERNESETTLE ... 243 E3
Ernesettle Com Sch PL5 ... 243 F4
Ernesettle Cres PL5 ... 243 E3
Ernesettle Gn PL5 ... 243 E4
Ernesettle La PL5 ... 243 D4
Ernesettle Lane Ind Est PL5 ... 243 C5
Ernesettle Rd PL5 ... 243 E3
Ernsborough Gdns EX14 ... 166 B5
Erril Ret Pk PL7 ... 250 C5
Escot★ EX11 ... 84 C1
Escot Cotts EX5 ... 184 B2
Eskil Pl EX38 ... 159 C6
Esmonde Gdns PL5 ... 247 B8
Esplanade
Exmouth EX8 ... 202 A5
Seaton EX12 ... 192 B4
Teignmouth TQ14 ... 210 C4
Esplanade Rd TQ4 ... 226 C6
Esplanade The
Dartmouth TQ6 ... 233 F5
Plymouth PL1 ... 262 C1
Sidmouth EX10 ... 188 B3
Woolacombe EX34 ... 7 F7
Essa Rd PL12 ... 242 F2
Essex Cl EX4 ... 176 E4
Essex St PL1 ... 262 B4
Essington Cl EX8 ... 196 B3
Essington Ct EX20 ... 77 C4
Essington La EX20 ... 77 D4
Essington Rd EX20 ... 77 C4
Esso Wharf Rd PL4 ... 263 C1
Esthwaite La PL6 ... 245 A4
ESTOVER ... 245 E4
Estover Cl PL6 ... 245 F5
Estover Ind Est PL6 ... 245 E4
Estover Rd PL6 ... 245 F4
Estuary Ave EX39 ... 157 B8
Estuary Bsns Pk EX31 ... 15 C3
Estuary Ct TQ14 ... 209 D7
Estuaryview TQ12 ... 207 F6
Estuary View
Budleigh Salterton EX9 ... 198 B1
Northam EX39 ... 157 A8
Yelland EX31 ... 15 C2
Estuary Vw EX8 ... 196 A3
Estuary Wy PL5 ... 243 C1
Esworthy Cross EX16 ... 32 F1
Ethelston's Cl DT7 ... 260 A5
Ethelwynne Brown Cl EX39 ... 157 B2
Eton Ave PL1 ... 262 C4
Eton Cl EX39 ... 156 F3
Etonhurst Cl EX2 ... 178 D3
Eton Pl PL1 ... 262 C4
Eton St PL1 ... 262 C4
Eton Terr 3 PL1 ... 262 B3
Eton Wlk EX4 ... 176 E4
Eugene Rd TQ3 ... 226 C8
Eureka Terr
Bovey Tracey TQ13 ... 180 D8
Eureka Terr *continued*
1 Honiton EX14 ... 166 C5
Europa Pk EX34 ... 8 B6
Evans Ct PL1 ... 262 A3
Evans Field EX9 ... 197 F2
Evans Pl PL2 ... 248 B5
Eveleigh Cl
2 Brixham TQ5 ... 230 C3
West Clyst EX4 ... 174 E3
Eveleighs Ct EX4 ... 261 B4
Evelyn Pl PL4 ... 263 A4
Evelyn St PL5 ... 243 D1
Evenden Ct PL11 ... 247 A3
Eventide Homes TQ5 ... 230 C2
Everest Dr EX12 ... 192 A7
Everett Pl EX16 ... 161 E6
Evergreen Cl EX8 ... 196 D3
Evett Cl EX8 ... 202 E8
Evran Dr EX8 ... 196 E3
Ewings Sq EX2 ... 261 A2
Ewin's Ash EX14 ... 85 C8
EWORTHY ... 91 E6
Eworthy Cross EX21 ... 91 E6
EXBOURNE ... 76 C4
Exbourne CE Prim Sch EX20 ... 76 C4
Exbourne Cross EX20 ... 76 C4
Excalibur Cl EX4 ... 174 A1
Excelsior Mews 2 TQ1 ... 220 B7
Exchange St PL4 ... 263 A2
EXEBRIDGE ... 33 F3
Exebridge Ind Est TA22 ... 33 F3
Exe Bridge Retail Ctr EX4 ... 261 A1
Exe Cl EX31 ... 15 E5
Execliff EX8 ... 202 A5
Exe Dene EX3 ... 182 E5
Exe Gdns PL3 ... 249 C7
Exe Hill TQ2 ... 219 B8
Exe St
Exeter EX4 ... 261 A3
Topsham EX3 ... 182 F5
EXETER ... 261 B4
Exeter Acad EX4 ... 173 D1
Exeter Airport Bsns Pk EX5 ... 99 A4
Exeter Arena Athletics Stadium EX4 ... 174 B1
Exeter Bsns Ctr EX2 ... 177 C2
Exeter Bsns Pk EX1 ... 178 E6
Exeter Cath (Church of St Peter) EX1 ... 261 B3
Exeter Cathedral Sch
Exeter EX2 ... 261 B2
Exeter EX4 ... 261 A3
Exeter Central Sta EX4 ... 261 A4
Exeter Cl
Feniton EX14 ... 84 D2
Plymouth PL5 ... 243 D4
Exeter Coll EX4 ... 261 A3
Exeter Coll Annexe EX4 ... 261 A3
Exeter Coll Bishop Blackall Annexe EX4 ... 261 B4
Exeter College Construction Training Centre (Falcon House) EX2 ... 178 E4
Exeter Coll Maths & Science Ctr
Exeter EX2 ... 177 B7
Exeter EX4 ... 261 A4
Exeter Coll Tech Centre EX2 ... 178 E7
Exeter Community Hospl (Whipton) EX1 ... 178 C7
Exeter Cross
Coldeast TQ12 ... 123 A1
Sidmouth EX10 ... 188 B6
Exeter Foyer EX2 ... 261 A2
Exeter Gate EX36 ... 158 C3
Exeter Hill
Cullompton EX15 ... 163 B2
Kenton EX6 ... 194 D3
Shobrooke EX17 ... 80 F5
Tiverton EX16 ... 161 E2
Exeter Hill Cross EX17 ... 80 F4
Exeter Hospl, Nuffield Health (private) EX2 ... 177 E4
Exeter International Airport EX5 ... 99 A4
Exeter Mathematics Sch EX1 ... 261 B3
Exeter Racecourse★ EX6 ... 114 C2
Exeter Rd
Braunton EX33 ... 152 E4
Chudleigh TQ13 ... 123 F7
Crediton EX17 ... 165 D4
Cullompton EX15 ... 163 B2
Dawlish EX7 ... 200 E3
Doccombe TQ13 ... 112 A5
Exmouth EX8 ... 196 A2
Exmouth EX8 ... 202 A7
Honiton EX14 ... 166 A5
Ivybridge PL21 ... 237 E5
Kennford EX6 ... 181 A2
Kingsteignton TQ12 ... 207 D8
Moretonhampstead TQ13 ... 111 F4
Newton Abbot TQ12 ... 207 B5
Exeter Rd *continued*
Newton Poppleford EX10 ... 186 C8
Okehampton EX20 ... 170 D5
Ottery St Mary EX11 ... 169 A3
Rockwell Green TA21 ... 160 B4
Rockwell Green TA21 ... 160 B5
Silverton EX5 ... 82 B5
South Brent TQ10 ... 135 A3
South Molton EX36 ... 29 E3
Teignmouth TQ14 ... 210 B6
Tiverton EX16 ... 64 B4
Topsham EX2, EX3 ... 182 D6
West Hill EX11 ... 168 E7
Whiddon Down EX20 ... 95 F3
Whimple EX5 ... 168 B8
Winkleigh EX19 ... 58 F2
Exeter Road Bsns Pk 8 TQ12 ... 123 E1
Exeter Road Com Prim Sch EX8 ... 202 A7
Exeter Road Ind Est EX20 ... 170 E6
Exeter St David's Sta EX4 ... 177 A7
Exeter Sch EX2 ... 177 E5
Exeter St
North Tawton EX20 ... 77 C4
Plymouth, Barbican PL4 ... 263 A3
Plymouth, St Jude's PL4 ... 263 B2
Teignmouth TQ14 ... 210 B5
Exeter's Underground Passage Mus★ EX4 ... 261 B3
Exeter Trad Ctr EX2 ... 181 E8
Exeter Tutorial Coll EX4 ... 261 C2
Exe Units EX2 ... 177 D1
Exe Vale Rd EX2 ... 178 A1
Exe Vale Terr 6 EX16 ... 161 C3
Exe Valley Fishery★ TA22 ... 33 F3
Exe Valley L Ctr EX16 ... 161 C5
Exe Valley Way EX5 ... 81 F2
Exe View EX6 ... 182 A4
Exe View Cotts EX4 ... 176 F8
Exe View Rd EX8 ... 196 C6
Exhibition Rd EX17 ... 165 E6
Exhibition Way EX4 ... 178 D8
EXMINSTER ... 182 B4
Exminster Com Prim Sch EX6 ... 182 A4
Exminster Hill
Exminster EX6 ... 182 B2
Powderham EX6 ... 194 B8
Exminster Marshes (RSPB Reserve)★ EX6 ... 182 D3
Exmoor Cl EX16 ... 161 E6
Exmoor Gdns TA22 ... 33 D6
Exmoor La EX16 ... 49 C1
Exmoor National Park Visitor Ctr★ EX35 ... 151 C6
Exmoor View EX36 ... 158 C5
Exmoor Way EX15 ... 163 A3
Exmoor Zoo★ EX31 ... 11 B3
EXMOUTH ... 202 B7
Exmouth Archery Club EX8 ... 197 B4
Exmouth Com Coll EX8 ... 202 B8
Exmouth Ct
Exmouth EX8 ... 202 B6
Plymouth PL1 ... 247 F3
Exmouth Hospl EX8 ... 202 B7
Exmouth Model Rly★ EX8 ... 203 B5
Exmouth Mus★ EX8 ... 202 A7
Exmouth Nature Reserve★ EX8 ... 195 E2
Exmouth Rd
Aylesbeare EX5 ... 185 D8
Budleigh Salterton EX9 ... 197 E1
Clyst St Mary EX5 ... 179 A1
Exton EX3 ... 183 C3
Lympstone EX8 ... 195 F5
Lympstone EX8 ... 195 F7
Newton Poppleford EX10 ... 186 D5
Plymouth PL1 ... 247 F3
Exmouth Sports Ctr EX8 ... 201 F7
Exmouth Sta EX8 ... 201 F7
Exmouth Tennis & L Ctr EX8 ... 202 B8
Exonia Pk EX2 ... 176 D3
Explorer Ct PL2 ... 248 B5
Explorer Wlk TQ2 ... 213 F3
EXTON ... 183 D2
Exton La EX3 ... 183 C2
Exton Rd EX2 ... 177 C3
Exton Sta EX3 ... 183 C1
EXWICK ... 176 E7
Exwick Ct EX4 ... 176 F8
Exwick Heights Prim Sch EX4 ... 176 E7
Exwick Hill EX4 ... 176 F8
Exwick Ho EX4 ... 176 F8
Exwick La EX4 ... 176 D7
Exwick Rd EX4 ... 176 F7
Exwick Villas EX4 ... 176 F7
Eyewell Gn EX12 ... 192 A6
Eymore Dr EX11 ... 168 C3
Eyrecourt Rd EX12 ... 192 A4

F

Factory Cotts TQ9...139 C7
Factory Cross TQ13...110 F6
Factory La TA20...88 D8
Factory Ope 1 EX39...15 A1
Factory Row
South Molton EX36...158 E4
Torquay TQ2...220 A5
Fairacre Ave EX32...155 C2
Fairby Cl EX16...161 D6
Fairend La TA20...69 D8
Fairfax Gdns EX2...177 B2
Fairfax Pl TQ6...233 F3
Fairfax Rd
Cullompton EX15...163 C4
Heathfield TQ12...180 F3
Fairfax Terr 5 PL2...247 F4
Fairfax Way
Great Torrington EX38...159 F5
Ottery St Mary EX11...169 F5
Fairfield
Bratton Fleming EX31...18 A8
Ilfracombe EX34...150 C5
Plymouth PL7...250 E7
Sampford Peverell EX16 50 D1
South Brent TQ10...135 A2
Fairfield Ave
Exeter EX4...178 C8
Plymouth PL2...248 C7
Fairfield Cl
Axminster EX13...167 D5
Bovey Tracey TQ13...180 C7
Exmouth EX8...202 B6
Kingsbridge TQ7...258 D4
Fairfield Gdns EX14...166 C5
Fairfield Gn TA3...68 D7
Fairfield Pk DT7...260 E4
Fairfield Rd
Crediton EX17...165 C6
Exeter EX2...181 B8
Exmouth EX8...202 B5
Kingskerswell TQ12...213 A3
Torquay TQ2...219 F8
Fairfield Terr
Exeter EX2...177 A4
Newton Abbot TQ12...207 C3
Fairfield Way TQ7...145 A1
Fairhazel Dr EX4...176 F7
Fairholme Rd EX34...7 F6
Fairies Hall TQ11...236 C6
Fair Isle Cl TQ2...213 E2
Fairlands Ave EX6...113 B3
Fairlawn Ct EX10...188 B5
Fairlawns Pk TQ4...226 B2
Fairlea TQ5...230 C6
Fairlea Cl EX7...200 F1
Fairlea Cres EX39...156 F6
Fairlea Ct EX9...197 E1
Fairlea Gdns EX39...156 E6
Fairlea Rd EX7...200 F1
Fairleigh EX10...186 E8
Fairlinch Cross EX33...152 B8
Fairlynch Cl EX33...152 B7
Fairlynch Gr EX33...152 C7
Fairlynch La EX33...152 B7
Fairlynch Mus★ EX9...199 H2
Fairmead EX10...187 F8
Fairmead Ct TQ2...213 F2
Fairmead Mews PL12...242 C3
Fairmead Rd PL12...242 C2
FAIRMILE...169 B7
Fair Oak Cl EX5...99 A4
Fair Oak Ct EX5...99 A4
Fair Oak Rd EX5...99 A4
Fair Oaks TQ14...210 A6
Fairpark Cl EX2...261 C2
Fairpark Rd EX2...261 B2
Fairplace Terr EX20...170 B5
Fairseat Cl TQ9...223 D4
Fair View
Barnstaple EX31...154 E6
Bradworthy EX22...53 E8
Colyford EX24...103 A3
Fairview Ave
Clyst St Mary EX5...179 D2
Plymouth PL3...249 D5
Fair View La EX24...103 A3
Fairview Pk TQ13...180 C5
Fairview Rd TQ12...211 A7
Fair View Rd
Dartmouth TQ6...233 E3
Honiton EX14...166 C5
Fairview Terr EX1...174 F1
Fairview Way PL3...249 E5
Fairwater Cl TQ12...207 F7
Fairwaters TQ12...207 E8
Fairway
Appledore EX39...14 F1
Saltash PL12...242 C2
Tiverton EX16...64 E8
Fairway Ave PL21...237 B5
Fairway Cl
Braunton EX33...152 B6
Churston Ferrers TQ5...229 D5
Fairway Gdns 3 PL7...136 A8
Fairways Cl EX37...43 B6
Fairways Dr EX37...43 B6
Fairways The EX39...156 D7
Fairways View EX37...43 C6
Fairway The
Braunton EX33...152 B6
Exeter EX4...173 E1
Newton Ferrers PL8...140 F7
FAIRY CROSS...25 A3
Fairy La TQ11...236 A4
Falcon Ct EX36...158 C4
Falcon Pk TQ4...224 F5
Falcon Rd
Exeter EX2...178 E4
Mount Wise PL1...247 F1
Falcon Units TQ12...207 A3
Falcon Way 7 EX16...161 E6
FALKEDON...96 A6
Falkedon Cross EX17...96 A6
Falkland Cl EX4...173 E2
Falkland Dr TQ12...207 F8
Falkland Rd TQ2...219 F5
Falkland Way TQ14...210 A6
Fallapit Turn TQ9...144 C8
Falloway Cl TQ2...214 A2
Fallow Cl EX36...158 B5
Fallowfield Cl TQ12...207 F3
Fallowfields TQ9...223 A5
Fallow Fields EX32...155 C2
Falmouth Cl TQ2...219 B8
Fancy Cross PL21...137 A2
Fanny's Cross EX36...46 E7
Fanny's La EX17...80 B5
Fannys Lane Cross EX17...80 B5
Fanshawe Way PL9...255 C6
Faraday Ho EX1...177 E6
Faraday Mill Bsns Pk PL4...249 B1
Faraday Rd PL4...249 B1
Faringdon Rd PL4...249 B3
Farleigh TQ12...206 B5
Farleigh Back Rd EX16...63 C2
Farleigh Cross TQ9...139 A4
Farleigh Front Rd EX16...63 C2
Farleigh Mdws EX16...161 A6
Farley Gr EX1...174 F2
Farley Hill TQ13...123 D8
Farley La EX35...5 E3
Farley's Grave EX20...77 E7
Farm Cl
Exeter EX2...178 C4
Kingskerswell TQ12...212 F6
Plymouth PL7...250 C7
Roundswell EX31...154 A1
Farmer Frank's La EX19...58 F2
Farm Hill EX4...176 E8
Farmhouse Ave EX1...178 F8
Farm House Rise EX6...181 F4
Farm La
Plymouth PL5...244 B2
Saltash PL12...242 D1
Farm Mdw EX3...182 D8
Farm Rd
Bideford EX39...25 D4
Rousdon DT7...193 E6
Farm The EX5...99 D8
Farm Way EX14...84 D2
Farmyard La TQ3...218 E6
Farnham Ho 5 DT7...260 D3
Farnham Terr 6 TQ3...226 B7
Farnley Cl PL6...245 B6
Farpark Hill La
Beara EX31...9 A1
Halsinger EX33...8 F1
Farrant Ct EX10...188 A6
Farrant's Hill EX6...113 B8
Farriel La EX34...8 F5
Farriers Cotts PL7...250 E7
Farriers The PL19...116 E4
FARRINGDON...99 B1
Farringdon Cross
Chilton EX17...80 E7
Exeter EX5...99 A1
Farringdon Ct EX5...99 B2
Farringdon Hill EX17...80 F7
Farringdon Ho EX5...99 B2
Farthing Cross TQ3...218 C3
Farthing Down TA21...51 E7
Farthing La TQ3...218 C2
Farthing Lake Cross EX32...29 A7
Farthingland Cross EX20...76 B5
Farthings La EX10...186 E7
Farthings Lodge Bsns Ctr EX15...83 F6
Farthing's Pitts TA21 160 C4
Far View Rd EX20...170 C5
FARWAY...102 A6
Farway CE Prim Sch EX24...101 F7
Farway Common Rd EX14, EX24...101 E7
Farwell Rd TQ9...223 B6
Farwood Cross EX24...102 C6
Fatacott Cross EX39...22 F5
Fatherford Rd EX20...170 D5
Faulkner Cl TQ6...233 C3
Fawns Cl PL21...136 F4
Fay Rd EX7...204 E6
Fayre View PL12...242 B1
Fearnside Way PL12...242 C3
Featherbed La
Clayhanger EX16...35 C1
Exmouth EX8...196 B2
Monkton EX14...86 D6
Offwell EX14...86 B2
Featherstone Rd EX8 196 A2
Federation Rd PL3...249 C4
Fegen Rd PL5...243 B1
Felixwell Ct EX4...176 F5
Fell Cl PL8...141 B8
Fellowes Ct 7 PL1...262 A3
Fellowes Pl PL1...248 A2
Feltrim Ave EX2...261 C1
FENITON...84 E2
Feniton CE Prim Sch EX14...84 E2
Feniton Gdns EX14...84 D2
Feniton Sta EX14...84 D2
Fenten Pk PL12...242 F3
Feoffe Cotts EX31...154 F7
Feoffees Cotts TQ7...258 A4
Ferguson Cl EX11...169 B3
Ferguson Rise
West Clyst EX4...174 F3
West Clyst EX4...175 A4
Fernbank Ave PL21...237 A6
Fern Cl
Brixham TQ5...230 D4
Okehampton EX20...170 C6
Plymouth PL7...251 C5
Ferncombe Cl 3 TQ12...123 F1
Ferncombe Dr 2 TQ12...123 F1
Ferndale TQ6...233 E3
Ferndale Ave PL2...247 E7
Ferndale Cl
8 Honiton EX14...85 C2
Plymouth PL6...245 D8
Ferndale Gdns EX2...177 A4
Ferndale Mews TQ2...219 B7
Ferndale Rd
Exeter EX2...177 A4
Plymouth PL2...247 F7
Teignmouth TQ14...210 B6
Torquay TQ2...219 B7
Ferndown Cl EX39...156 E2
Ferndown Rd DT7...260 E3
Ferne Animal Sanctuary★ TA20...69 D2
Fernery The 6 EX34...150 D5
Fernham La EX32...18 D7
Fernhill DT7...260 F7
Fernhill Cl PL21...237 B5
Fernhill Cross TQ7...143 E8
Fernhill Hts DT6...104 F4
Fernicombe Cl TQ3...225 E7
Fernicombe Rd TQ3...225 E7
Fernleigh Cl EX20...77 C4
Fernleigh Rd PL3...248 F5
Fern Mdw
Okehampton EX20...170 C6
Tavistock PL19...171 D6
Fernpark Cl
Exeter EX2...177 E2
Exeter EX2...177 E3
Fern Pk EX34...150 B5
Fern Rd TQ12...207 F1
Fern Way EX34...150 B4
Fernworthy Cl
Copplestone EX17...79 B5
Torquay TQ2...219 A7
Fernworthy Forest Trail★ TQ13...110 D2
Fernworthy Gdns EX17...79 B5
Fernworthy Pk EX17...79 B5
Ferrers Gn TQ5...229 E4
Ferrers Rd PL5...243 E1
Ferry La PL11...246 D5
Ferryman's Reach TQ14...210 B3
Ferrymans View TQ5 234 E8
Ferryman Way EX3...182 D7
Ferry Rd
Plymouth PL1...247 E3
Topsham EX3...182 E5
Topsham EX3...182 F4
Ferry Slip TQ6...233 F3
Ferry St PL11...247 C3
Feversham Cl PL7...251 B6
Fiddlecott La EX17...60 B6
Field Cl
Braunton EX33...152 C5
Paignton TQ3...219 B2
Field End
Axminster EX13...167 E5
Bideford EX39...156 E2
Fieldings The EX37...28 F4
Field La
Ashford EX31...16 B6
Braunton EX33...152 C5
Field Rd EX1...175 B1
FILHAM...237 F4
Filham Ind Est PL21...237 D5
Filham Moor Cl PL21 237 E4
Fillablack Way EX39...157 C2
Fillace La 11 PL20...126 F4
Fillace Pk PL20...126 F4
FILLEIGH...29 C7
Filleigh Com Prim Sch EX32...29 C6
Filleigh Mill New Rd EX32...29 D7
Filleigh Moor Cross EX17...60 D5
Filleighmoor Gate EX21...56 C3
Filmer Way EX2...177 B3
Fincer Dr PL21...237 A6
Finch Cl
Plymouth PL3...249 D4
Shillingford Abbot EX2...181 B7
Finches Cl PL9...256 C7
Finch Foundary★ EX20...95 A5
Findon Gdns PL6...245 D4
Finewell St PL1...262 C2
Fingle Bridge★ TQ13 111 E8
Fingle Cl EX4...176 E8
Fingle Glen EX6...98 B4
Finisterre Ave EX7...204 E8
Finnigan Rd PL4...249 B1
Finnimore Ind Est EX11...169 C3
Finning Ave EX4...174 D1
Fin St PL1...262 B1
Firbank Rd EX7...200 F1
Fir Cl
Honiton EX14...166 B5
Willand EX15...162 D5
Firconia Terr EX21...73 B4
Fircroft Rd PL2...248 B7
Firebeacon Cross EX39...37 C7
Fire Beacon Cross
Bishop's Tawton EX31...27 D7
Chittlehampton EX37...29 B2
Fire Beacon Hill Nature Reserve★ EX10...100 F1
Firebeacon La
Bolham EX16...49 C3
Chittlehampton EX37...29 B2
Fire Beacon La EX10...100 E1
Fire Brigade Hos EX4...261 A4
Firestone Cross EX20...95 C3
Fire Stone Cross EX20 95 C4
Firestone La TQ12...212 A8
Fir La EX17...62 F3
Firlands TQ14...210 B7
Firlands Rd TQ2...214 A2
Firleigh Rd 7 TQ12...123 E1
Firs Cross TQ9...144 C7
Firs Gr EX32...155 B5
Firs Pk EX2...176 C3
First Ave
Axminster EX13...167 F7
Dawlish EX7...204 D5
Exeter, Countess Wear EX2...182 D7
Exeter, Heavitree EX1...177 F6
Plymouth, Billacombe PL9...255 F8
Plymouth, Stoke PL1...248 A2
Teignmouth TQ14...210 A5
Torquay TQ1...220 A8
First Dr TQ14...210 B5
First Field La EX33...152 C5
Firs The
4 Barnstaple EX32...155 B5
Kennford EX6...114 D4
Wilmington EX14...86 D2
First Raleigh EX39...156 E3
Fir Terr EX36...158 D4
Fir Tree Cl EX8...196 E2
Firtree Rise PL21...237 D5
Firway Cross EX16...34 C3
Fir Wlk TQ2...219 C8
Fisgard Way PL11...246 D3
Fishacre Cl TQ3...225 E8
Fishacre Cross TQ9...216 F6
Fishchowter's La TQ9...223 C4
Fishcombe Rd TQ5...230 B6
Fisherman's Path TQ13...111 B8
Fisher Rd
Newton Abbot TQ12...207 B3
Plymouth PL2...248 A5
Fisher's Hill TA21...51 D7
Fishers Mead TA22...33 D6
Fisher St TQ4...226 B5
Fishers Way EX16...65 A7
Fisherton Cross EX37...28 C2
Fishingclose Cross EX20...76 F6
Fishleigh Cross EX20...75 C8
Fishleigh Rd EX31...154 B2
Fish Mkt PL4...263 B2
Fish Quay PL4...263 A2
Fistral Cl PL11...246 F4
Fitzford Cotts PL19...171 B4
Fitzroy Rd
Exeter EX1...178 E6
Plymouth PL1...248 A3
Fitzroy Terr 7 PL1...248 A3
Five Acres TQ13...180 C4
Five Acres La PL12...242 B5
Five Barrow La EX13...104 A4
Five Barrows Cross EX36...19 D7
Five Bridges EX15...163 C6
Five Bridges Cross EX15...67 C7
Five Cross TQ12...122 C1
Five Crosses
Modbury PL21...137 A2
Rackenford EX16...47 C1
Five Crossway EX36...46 D8
Five Cross Way
Brayford EX31...18 F8
Plymtree EX15...83 E8
West Buckland TA21...52 F6
Five Cross Ways TA22...32 F7
Five Elms Cross EX5...80 E1
Five Elms La EX5...80 E1
Five Hos TA21...160 B8
Five Lane End EX38...159 A1
Five Lanes
Buckfastleigh TQ13...236 E7
Dawlish EX7...200 A3
Hennock TQ13...123 B7
4 Kingsteignton TQ12 123 E1
Marldon TQ3...218 E3
Five Lanes Cross EX22 54 D8
Five Lanes Rd TQ3...218 D2
Five Mile Hill EX6...98 C4
Five Mile Hill Cross EX6...98 C4
Five Oaks TQ11...130 C2
Five Oaks Cross
Brampford Speke EX5...81 C1
Burrington EX37...43 D4
Five Turnings EX34...3 A4
Five Wyches Cross TQ13...180 B7
Flagstaff Rd TQ6...233 F4
Flamborough Rd PL6...245 A7
Flamborough Way PL6...245 A6
Flamsteed Cres PL5...243 E1
Flavel Pl TQ6...233 F3
Flavel St TQ6...233 F3
Flaxmeadow La EX13 167 E6
Flayes Almshouses 2 EX4...178 C8
Flay Field EX1...179 B8
Fleet Court EX12...192 B5
Fleet St
Plymouth PL2...247 E6
Torquay TQ1, TQ2...220 B4
Fleet Walk Sh Ctr TQ2...220 B4
Fleetwood Gdns PL6...245 A7
Fleming Ave EX10...188 C8
Fleming Way EX2...177 E4
Flemons Ct 6 TQ4...226 A5
Fletcher Cl TQ2...219 E7
Fletcher Cres PL9...256 B6
Fletcher Ind Est EX39...25 E4
Fletcher Way PL9...256 A6
Flete★ PL21...136 E2
Flete Ave TQ12...207 F2
Flete Cl TQ12...207 F2
Flete Ho PL21...136 E2
Fletemoor Rd PL5...243 E1
Flete View Terr 10 PL21...137 C8
Fletewood Sch PL4...262 C4
Flexapark EX34...3 A3
Flexton The EX11...169 D4
Flightway EX14...67 B3
Flightway Bsns Pk EX14...67 B3
FLITTON BARTON...19 B1
Floaters Rd TQ6...233 F4
Flood's La EX15...163 B3
Flood St TQ9...227 F8
Flora Cl EX8...196 D1
Flora Cotts PL1...262 B2
Flora Ct PL1...262 B3
Flora St PL1...262 B2
Florence Cotts TQ7...145 D1
Florence Pl
Newton Abbot TQ12...207 D1
Plymouth PL4...263 C3
Florence St PL5...243 D1
Florence Way EX1...178 D6
Florida Dr EX4...173 D2
Florida Gdns PL3...249 C6
Florida Rd TQ1...220 C6
Flower La EX5...184 C3
Flowerpot La EX4...177 A5
Flowers Mdw 9 TQ12...122 F1
Flower St EX5...184 C3
Flow La TQ14...208 F7
Floyd Cl PL2...247 F7
Floyers-Hay Ct EX2...261 A1
Floyte La EX6...98 B5
Fluder Cres TQ12...213 B3
Fluder Hill TQ12...213 B3
Fluder La TQ12...213 F5
Fluder Rise TQ12...213 B3
FLUXTON...100 C3
Foldhay Cross EX17...78 A6
Foldhay La EX17...78 A6
Foliot Ave PL2...248 A6
Foliot Rd PL2...248 A6
Follafield Pk TQ5...230 B2
Follaton Bglws TQ9...223 A5
Follaton Gate TQ9...222 E6
Follaton Mount TQ9...223 A5
Follaton Rise TQ9...222 E5
Follett Cl TA21...160 D8
Follett Rd
Tiverton EX16...64 D7
Topsham EX3...182 E5
Folley La EX4...98 D4
Folly Cross TQ10...134 E1
Folly Ct TQ13...180 D4
Folly Farm Cl EX33...152 C6
FOLLY GATE...93 E8
Folly Gate Cross EX20...93 F8
Folly Goyle Cross EX19...43 B3
Folly Hill TQ7...142 E3
Folly La
Buckland St Mary TA20...69 D8
South Molton EX36...30 D4
Folly The PL9...256 B7
Football La TQ12...207 E8
Footland La
Daccombe TQ12...213 F5
Ipplepen TQ12...217 F5
Footland Rd TQ4...226 A4
Footpark La EX6...96 D2
Forbes Cl TQ12...180 F2
Forcefield Rd EX15...163 B2
Forces Cross TQ9...139 E3
Forches Ave EX32...155 C4
Forches Cnr EX17...165 C6
Forches Cross
Burrington EX37...43 F4
Crediton EX17...165 C6
Langtree EX38...40 F1
Newton Abbot TQ12...206 D7
Newton Abbot TQ12...206 E7
Forches Cross Com Prim Sch EX32...155 C4
Forches Cross Rd TQ12...206 C7
Forches Green Flats 4 EX32...155 B4
Forches Head EX5...175 F8
Forches Hill TQ12...209 B2
Forches Row EX1...179 A8
FORD
Bideford...25 B3
Chillington...149 A7
Holbeton...136 D1
Holcombe Rogus...50 F5
Plymouth...248 A5
Ford TQ6...233 E3
FORDA...93 B1
Fordbarn Cross TQ9...222 E2
Fordbrook La PL9...256 C4
Ford Cl PL21...237 A5
Ford Cres EX22...53 E8
Ford Cross
Ash Mill EX36...31 D1
Chawleigh EX18...59 E7
Chulmleigh EX18...44 D2
Ford TQ7...149 A7
Hittisleigh EX6...96 D4
Kentisbury EX31...10 D5
Molland EX36...31 F7
Monkton EX14...86 A5
Oakford EX16...48 D5
Shirwell EX31...17 C8
South Zeal EX20...95 A4
Staverton TQ9...216 E5
Tedburn St Mary EX17...97 D8
Ford Down La EX36...158 A3
Forde Abbey & Gardens★ TA20...88 F8
Forde Cl
Abbotskerswell TQ12...212 A7
Newton Abbot TQ12...207 D3
Forde Cross EX17...80 F8
Forde Gdns TQ12...207 D1
Forde La EX38...26 E2
Fordens La EX7...204 C3
Forde Pk TQ12...207 D2
FORDER
Cawsand...252 F1
Saltash...242 C1
Forder Cross
Bishopsteignton TQ14...208 D7
Blackawton TQ9...145 C8
Chagford EX20...110 D8
Ugborough PL21...137 E7
Forder Rd TQ12...207 D3
FORDER GREEN...131 C2
Forder Hill PL10...252 F1
Forder Hts PL6...245 B1
Forder La
Bishopsteignton TQ14...208 E8
Bovey Tracey TQ13...122 E7
Cawsand PL10...252 F1
Dartington TQ9...222 E8
South Brent TQ10...135 B4
Ugborough PL21...137 D7
Forder Mdw TQ13...111 F5
Forder Valley Nature Reserve★ PL6...249 D8
Forder Valley Rd PL6...249 D8
Ford Farm Ct EX6...194 D3
Ford Hill
Bow EX17...78 F4
Cheriton Bishop EX6, EX17...97 C6
Hartland EX39...22 E3
Kentisbury EX31...10 D5
Plymouth PL2...248 A5
Thorverton EX5...81 E6
Fordishaies La EX5, EX15...82 F8
Ford La
Cheriton Fitzpaine EX16...63 B6
Clifton EX31...10 B5
Hittisleigh EX6...96 D4
South Molton EX36...30 A6
South Molton EX36...158 A8
West Hill EX11...168 E3
Whitestone EX4...98 E4
Fordland Bottom Rd EX2, EX6...176 B2
FORDLANDS...156 F5
Fordlands Cres EX39 156 F4
Fordlands Rd TQ13...111 F5
Ford Lane Cross EX6...96 D4
Fordmill Cross EX16...34 D1
Fordmoor Cross EX16 48 C8
Ford Moor Cross EX18...59 E7
Ford Orch EX16...50 D1
FORD PARK...248 D4
Ford Park La PL4...248 E4
Ford Park Rd PL4...248 D4

282 For–Gar

Ford Pk
6 Chudleigh Knighton TQ13 . . . . 123 C4
Plymouth PL4 . . . . 248 E4
Ford Plain EX5 . . . . 81 E5
Ford Prim Sch
Plymouth PL2 . . . . 247 F5
Plymouth PL2 . . . . 248 A5
Ford Rd
Abbotskerswell TQ12 . . 212 B7
Bampton EX16 . . . . 34 C1
Tiverton EX16 . . . . 64 D7
Totnes TQ9 . . . . 223 D6
Wembury PL9 . . . . 140 D8
Yealmpton PL8 . . . . 136 A2
Ford Rise EX39 . . . . 25 F4
Fords Rd EX2 . . . . 261 A1
Ford St
Moretonhampstead TQ13 . . . . 111 F5
Tavistock PL19 . . . . 171 B5
Wellington TA21 . . . . 160 F4
FORD STREET 52 D5
FORDTON 165 E3
Fordton Cross EX17 . . 165 E2
Fordton Ind Est EX17 165 E3
Fordton Plain EX17 . . 165 E3
Fordton Terr EX17 . . . 165 D3
Ford Valley TQ6 . . . . 233 E3
Ford Way Arrow EX1 . 175 B1
Fordworth Cotts TQ7 149 D5
Foredown La TQ12 . . . 212 E4
Foredown Rd TQ12 . . . 211 E2
Foreland Ho EX34 . . . 150 A4
Foreland View EX34 . . 150 B3
Fore St Hill 11 EX18 . . . 44 E1
Fore St
Aveton Gifford TQ7 . . . 143 C6
9 Bampton EX16 . . . . 34 B1
Beer EX12 . . . . 191 D5
Bere Alston PL20 . . . . 125 E1
Bere Ferrers PL20 . . . . 239 F3
Bishopsteignton TQ14 . . 208 F8
Bovey Tracey TQ13 . . . . 180 D7
Bradninch EX5 . . . . 82 F6
Bridestowe EX20 . . . . 107 F8
Brixham TQ5 . . . . 230 C5
Buckfastleigh TQ11 . . . . 236 C5
Budleigh Salterton EX9 . . . . 199 G2
Calstock PL18 . . . . 125 D3
Cargreen PL12 . . . . 239 A2
Chudleigh TQ13 . . . . 123 E6
Cornwood PL21 . . . . 133 C2
Cullompton EX15 . . . . 163 C3
Culmstock EX15 . . . . 66 E8
Dartmouth TQ6 . . . . 234 A3
Dolton EX19 . . . . 57 F7
Dulverton TA22 . . . . 33 D6
Exbourne EX20 . . . . 76 C5
Exeter EX4 . . . . 261 A2
Exeter, Heavitree EX1 . . 177 F5
Exmouth EX8 . . . . 202 A6
Great Torrington EX38 . 159 D5
Gunnislake PL18 . . . . 125 D6
Gunnislake, Albaston PL18 . . . . 125 C5
Harberton TQ9 . . . . 222 D2
Hartland EX39 . . . . 22 E3
7 Hemyock EX15 . . . . 67 B8
Holbeton PL8 . . . . 136 D1
Holbeton PL8 . . . . 142 A8
Holcombe Rogus TA21 . . 50 F5
Holemoor EX22 . . . . 73 C8
Holsworthy EX22 . . . . 164 C4
Ide EX2 . . . . 176 E2
Ideford TQ13 . . . . 124 B4
Ilfracombe EX34 . . . . 150 C6
Ipplepen TQ12 . . . . 211 D2
Ivybridge PL21 . . . . 237 D5
Kentisbeare EX15 . . . . 66 A3
Kenton EX6 . . . . 194 D3
Kingsand PL10 . . . . 253 A2
Kingsbridge TQ7 . . . . 258 C6
Kingskerswell TQ12 . . . 212 F4
Kingskerswell TQ12 . . . 213 A4
Kingsteignton TQ12 . . . 207 E7
Langtree EX38 . . . . 40 E2
Lifton PL16 . . . . 105 E4
Loddiswell TQ7 . . . . 143 E7
Luton TQ13 . . . . 124 C3
Millbrook PL10 . . . . 252 E5
Milton Abbot PL19 . . . . 116 A6
Morchard Bishop EX17 . . 61 A2
Moretonhampstead TQ13 . . . . 111 F5
Northam EX39 . . . . 156 F6
North Molton EX36 . . . . 30 D8
North Tawton EX20 . . . . 77 B4
Okehampton EX20 . . . . 170 B5
Otterton EX9 . . . . 198 E7
Plymouth, Devonport PL1 . . . . 247 F2
Plymouth, Plympton PL7 . . . . 250 E4
Plymouth, Tamerton Foliot PL5 . . . . 244 B6
Salcombe TQ8 . . . . 259 E4
Saltash PL12 . . . . 242 F2
Seaton EX12 . . . . 192 B5
Shaldon TQ14 . . . . 210 A3
Shebbear EX22 . . . . 55 D1
Sidbury EX10 . . . . 101 B2
Sidmouth EX10 . . . . 188 B3
Silverton EX5 . . . . 82 B5
Fore St *continued*
13 South Brent TQ10 . . . 134 F3
South Tawton EX20 . . . . 95 B5
Tatworth TA20 . . . . 88 D8
19 Teignmouth TQ14 . . . 210 B5
8 Teignmouth TQ14 . . . 210 C4
Tiverton EX16 . . . . 161 D4
Topsham EX3 . . . . 182 F5
Torpoint PL11 . . . . 247 B3
4 Torquay TQ2 . . . . 220 B8
Torquay, Barton TQ2 . . 214 A2
Totnes TQ9 . . . . 223 C5
Uffculme EX15 . . . . 66 A7
Ugborough PL21 . . . . 137 D6
Wellington TA21 . . . . 160 D6
Winkleigh EX19 . . . . 58 F3
Witheridge EX16 . . . . 46 E1
Yealmpton PL8 . . . . 257 F4
Forest Ave PL2 . . . . 248 C7
Foresters Rd
Holsworthy EX22 . . . . 164 C5
Plymouth PL9 . . . . 255 D7
Forester's Terr TQ14 210 B4
Forest Hill
Bideford EX39 . . . . 25 F4
Budleigh Salterton EX9 198 B1
Forest Hos EX21 . . . . 73 B4
Forest Rd
Stover TQ13 . . . . 123 B1
Torquay TQ1 . . . . 220 A7
Fore Street Ctr EX4 . . 261 A2
Fore Street Hill EX9 . 199 H2
Fore Street Mews 15 EX4 . . . . 261 A2
Forest Ridge Rd TQ3 . 218 F1
Forestry Hos PL20 . . . 120 B4
Forest View PL6 . . . . 245 D7
Foretown EX15 . . . . 83 D3
Forge Cl EX9 . . . . 197 F2
Forge End EX19 . . . . 58 F2
Forge La
Butterleigh EX15 . . . . 64 D3
Saltash PL12 . . . . 242 C4
Forge Pl
Bovey Tracey TQ13 . . . 180 C7
Uffculme EX15 . . . . 162 F7
Forge Rd EX15 . . . . 162 F7
Forges Hill EX15 . . . . 64 F3
Forget Me Not La PL6 . . . . 245 F5
Forge Way EX15 . . . . 163 C3
Forgeway Cl TQ2 . . . . 219 D4
Fork Cross TQ9 . . . . 222 A5
Forresters Bsns Pk PL6 . . . . 245 F5
Forresters Dr PL6 . . . 245 D7
Forrest Units EX2 . . . 177 D1
Forster Rd TQ8 . . . . 259 D5
Forsythia Dr PL12 . . . 242 C3
Fort Austin Ave PL6 . 245 C1
FORTESCUE 188 D7
Fortescue Bglws EX34 . . 8 C6
Fortescue Cl EX33 . . . 152 E5
FORTESCUE CROSS . . 44 C4
Fortescue Cross EX5 . . 81 E2
Fortescue Pl PL3 . . . . 249 A6
Fortescue Rd
Barnstaple EX32 . . . . 155 B2
Exeter EX2 . . . . 177 B3
Ilfracombe EX34 . . . . 150 B6
Paignton TQ3 . . . . 219 C1
Salcombe TQ8 . . . . 259 C4
Sidmouth EX10 . . . . 188 D7
Fortescue Terr PL19 . 171 A6
Fortessque Ct PL19 . . 116 E3
Fortfield EX12 . . . . 192 B5
Fortfield Gdns EX10 . 188 A3
Fortfield Terr EX10 . . 188 A3
Forth Gdns PL3 . . . . 249 D6
Fort Hill Dr EX32 . . . 155 B5
Fortibus Rd EX3 . . . . 182 B7
Fortmead Cl EX32 . . . 155 A5
Forton Rd EX8 . . . . 196 C1
Fort Picklecombe PL10 . . . . 253 F4
Fort Rd EX20 . . . . 170 D6
Fort St EX32 . . . . 155 A5
Fort Terr
13 Barnstaple EX32 . . . 155 A5
5 Bideford EX39 . . . . 157 B1
Plymouth PL6 . . . . 244 F3
Fort The PL10 . . . . 253 A1
Fortune Way TQ1 . . . 220 B7
Forum La EX20 . . . . 170 E7
Forward Gn EX5 . . . . 82 E7
Fosbrooke Ct 10 PL3 . 248 F6
Fosketh Hill EX39 . . . 156 C6
Fosketh Terr EX39 . . . 156 C6
FOSS 253 A5
Fossa Ct EX20 . . . . 170 D6
Fosse Rd TQ7 . . . . 258 D6
Fosse Way EX13 . . . . 88 C7
Fosseway Cl EX13 . . . 167 D5
Fosse Way Ct 2 EX12 . . . . 192 B4
Foss Slip TQ6 . . . . 233 F3
Foss St TQ6 . . . . 233 F3
Fosterlea EX15 . . . . 163 B3
Fosters Mdw PL18 . . . 125 A6
Foulston Ave PL5 . . . 247 B8
Foundary Mews PL19 . . . . 171 D6
Foundry Ct 1 TQ13 . . 123 E6
Foundry La PL8 . . . . 140 F6
Foundry Mews PL19 . . 171 D6
Fountain Ct TQ13 . . . 180 D7
Fountain Fields EX37 . . 43 B7
Fountain Hill EX9 . . . 203 F8
Fountain Ho TQ1 . . . . 220 C4
Fountains Cres PL2 . . 248 C8
Fouracre Cl EX4 . . . . 174 A1
Four Acres EX39 . . . . 156 D2
Four Acres Cl EX14 . . . 86 B2
Fouracre Way TQ12 . . 207 F8
Four Cross
Axminster EX13 . . . . 167 B7
Ilsington TQ12 . . . . 122 C2
Kingston TQ7 . . . . 142 C7
Wilmington EX14 . . . . 86 C4
Four Cross Elms EX24 . . . . 103 A4
Fourcross Hill EX13 . . 167 B7
Four Cross Lanes TQ9 . . . . 228 A8
Four Cross Way EX32 . . 11 C1
Four Crossways EX18 . 44 E1
Four Cross Ways
Cheriton Bishop EX6 . . . 97 A4
North Tawton EX20 . . . . 77 D4
Willand EX15 . . . . 162 D5
Winkleigh EX19 . . . . 58 D2
Four Elms
Holcombe Rogus TA21 . . 51 A6
Sidmouth EX10 . . . . 187 C8
Four Elms Hill EX10 . . 187 B8
Four Firs EX5 . . . . 185 A1
Four Lanes EX15 . . . . 84 B8
Fourlanesend Com Prim Sch PL10 . . . . 252 F3
Four Mills La EX17 . . . 165 D4
Four Oak EX32 . . . . 17 B2
Four Oak Cross EX32 . . 17 B2
Four Oaks Cl 1 EX32 . . 17 B2
Four Oaks Rd EX6 . . . . 97 F4
Four Seasons Village EX19 . . . . 58 E3
Fourth Ave TQ14 . . . . 210 A6
Fourview Cl TQ5 . . . . 230 E5
Four Ways Cotts EX18 . 59 E4
Fourways Cross EX15 . 67 C8
Four Ways Dr 3 EX18 . 44 E1
Four White Gates Cross EX37 . . . . 29 B4
Fowelscombe Gate PL21 . . . . 137 F6
Fowey Ave TQ2 . . . . 219 B8
Fowey Cl EX1 . . . . 177 F7
Fowey Gdns PL3 . . . . 249 D6
Fowey Rd EX31 . . . . 15 E5
Fowler Cl EX6 . . . . 182 A4
Fowley Cross EX20 . . . 93 D5
Fowlmere Cl PL5 . . . . 243 E5
Foxbeare Rd EX34 . . . 150 E5
Fox Cl
Okehampton EX20 . . . . 170 D6
Rockwell Green TA21 . . 160 A6
Foxdown Hill
Wellington TA21 . . . . 52 B6
Wellington TA21 . . . . 160 C4
Foxdown Ho TA21 . . . 160 C4
Foxdown Terr TA21 . . 160 D4
Foxes' Cross EX38 . . . . 26 E1
Foxes Lair EX20 . . . . 170 A6
Fox Field Cl PL3 . . . . 249 C5
Foxglove Chase EX15 . . . . 162 D5
Foxglove Cl
Barnstaple EX32 . . . . 155 E4
Dunkeswell EX14 . . . . 67 C1
Launceston PL15 . . . . 105 A2
Newton Abbot TQ12 . . . 206 C5
9 Tiverton EX16 . . . . 161 F6
Fox Glove End PL19 . . 126 D2
Foxglove La 2 PL19 . . 171 A6
Foxglove Rd EX12 . . . . 192 B7
Foxglove Rise EX4 . . . 176 D8
Foxglove Way
Paignton TQ3 . . . . 225 E2
Saltash PL12 . . . . 242 B3
FOXHAYES 176 F7
Foxhayes Rd EX4 . . . . 176 F6
Fox Hill EX39 . . . . 156 F6
Foxhill La TQ12 . . . . 211 A2
Foxhole Hill EX6 . . . . 113 B4
Foxhole La EX39 . . . . 156 F6
Foxhole Rd
Paignton TQ3 . . . . 225 F7
Torquay TQ2 . . . . 219 D5
Foxholes Hill EX8 . . . 202 D4
Foxhollows TQ12 . . . . 208 A2
Fox & Hounds Cross EX20 . . . . 108 A5
Foxlands Wlk TQ1 . . . 220 C8
Foxley Cres TQ12 . . . . 206 F3
Fox Rd EX4 . . . . 174 B2
Fox's Cnr EX10 . . . . 187 F2
Fox's Cross EX17 . . . . 63 B1
Foxtor Cl PL5 . . . . 244 B3
Fox Tor Cl TQ4 . . . . 229 B7
Foxtor Rd EX4 . . . . 176 E8
Foxwell La TQ12 . . . . 207 A4
Foxwood Gdns
Plymouth, Plymstock PL9 . . . . 255 F5
Plymouth, Southway PL6 . . . . 244 E5
Foxworthy Rd TQ13 . . 111 F1
Foyle Cl PL7 . . . . 251 A5
Frances Homes EX1 . . 261 C3
Francis Cl EX4 . . . . 176 F4
Francis Court Cotts EX5 . . . . 82 D2
Francis Cres 4 EX16 . . 64 D7
Francis Ct
3 Crediton EX17 . . . . 165 C5
Exeter EX2 . . . . 177 E5
Francis Dr EX39 . . . . 156 C6
Francis St PL1 . . . . 262 A3
Francis Way EX24 . . . . 103 B3
Franeth Cl TQ12 . . . . 207 D8
Frankford La
Pathfinder Village EX6 . . 82 A6
Tedburn St Mary EX6 . . . 97 F5
Frankfort Gate 9 PL1 . . . . 262 B3
Franklea Cl EX11 . . . . 169 D3
Franklin St EX2 . . . . 261 B2
Franklyn Ave EX33 . . . 152 E6
Franklyn Cl EX2 . . . . 176 F3
Franklyn Dr EX2 . . . . 176 F3
Franklyn Hospl EX2 . . 176 F3
Franklyns' PL6 . . . . 245 A4
Franklyns Cl PL6 . . . . 245 A4
Frankmarsh Pk EX32 155 B6
Frankmarsh Rd EX32 155 B6
Frankmills Hill TQ13 . 113 A1
Frank Webber Rd TA21 . . . . 160 A5
Fraser Dr TQ14 . . . . 210 A6
Fraser Pl PL5 . . . . 244 C7
Fraser Rd
Exmouth EX8 . . . . 196 D2
Plymouth PL5 . . . . 244 C7
Fraser Sq PL5 . . . . 244 C7
Frederick Street E PL1 . . . . 262 B3
Frederick Street W 6 PL1 . . . . 262 B3
Frederick Terr 6 EX7 . . . . 204 D6
Fredington Gr PL2 . . . 248 B6
Free Cotts EX4 . . . . 261 A3
Freedom Sq PL4 . . . . 263 B4
Freelands Cl EX8 . . . . 202 D8
Freemans Wharf PL1 254 A8
Freestone Rd TQ12 . . 207 D8
Fremantle Gdns 4 PL2 . . . . 247 F4
Fremantle Pl PL2 . . . . 247 F4
FREMINGTON 153 E6
Fremington Com Prim Sch EX31 . . . . 153 D5
Fremington Nature Reserve★ EX31 . . . . 153 E6
Fremington Quay EX31 . . . . 153 F7
Fremington Rd EX12 . 191 F7
French Cl EX5 . . . . 82 B6
French Furze Rd TQ9 139 E2
French St 7 TQ14 . . . 210 C4
Frenchstone Cross EX36 . . . . 30 B2
Frensham Ave PL6 . . . 245 C7
Frensham Gdns PL6 . . 245 C7
Freshford Cl PL6 . . . . 245 C1
Freshford Wlk PL6 . . . 245 C1
Freshwater Dr TQ4 . . . 229 B8
Frewin Gdns PL6 . . . . 245 B6
Frewins EX9 . . . . 197 F2
Friars' Gate EX2 . . . . 261 B2
FRIARS' GREEN 261 A2
Friar's Hele Cross EX20 . . . . 57 B2
Friars' La PL1 . . . . 263 A2
Friars Lodge EX2 . . . . 261 B2
Friars Wlk PL19 . . . . 171 E2
Friars' Wlk EX2 . . . . 261 B2
Friary Pk PL4 . . . . 263 B3
Friary St PL4 . . . . 263 B3
Friendship Ct PL19 . . . 117 E6
Friernhay Ct EX4 . . . . 261 A2
Friernhay St EX4 . . . . 261 A2
FRITHELSTOCK 41 A6
FRITHELSTOCK STONE 40 F5
Frith Rd PL12 . . . . 242 D3
FRITTISCOMBE 145 B2
Fritz's Grave TQ11 . . . 236 A7
Frobisher App PL5 . . . 244 D2
Frobisher Cl TQ14 . . . 210 A8
Frobisher Dr PL12 . . . 242 E2
Frobisher Gn TQ2 . . . . 219 C6
Frobisher La TQ8 . . . . 259 C5
Frobisher Rd
Exmouth EX8 . . . . 196 C2
Newton Abbot TQ12 . . . 207 F4
Frobisher Way
Paignton TQ4 . . . . 226 B2
Tavistock PL19 . . . . 171 B5
Torpoint PL11 . . . . 246 D3
Frogbury Cross EX17 . . 59 F1
Froggy Mill Cross EX6 97 C5
Frog La
Braunton EX33 . . . . 152 D7
Clyst St Mary EX5 . . . . 179 A3
Holcombe Rogus TA21 . . 50 F5
South Molton EX36 . . . . 158 B5
FROGMORE 144 E1
Frogmore Ave PL6 . . . 249 B7
Frogmore Cross EX5 . . 82 B5
Frogmore Ct PL6 . . . . 249 B7
Frogmore Farm TQ9 . . 139 F7
Frogmore Rd EX9 . . . . 198 C6
Frogmore Terr TQ7 . . 258 C4
Frogs La TA21 . . . . 52 F7
Frog St
Bampton EX16 . . . . 34 B1
Exeter EX1, EX2 . . . . 261 A2
Woolacombe EX34 . . . . 7 F6
Frogstreet Hill EX33 . . . 8 A2
Frogwell Cross TA4 . . . 34 D6
Frogwell La TA22 . . . . 34 B6
Frome Cl PL7 . . . . 251 A4
Frontfield Cres PL6 . . 244 E5
FROST 61 A1
Frost Cross
Bovey Tracey TQ13 . . . . 123 B6
Morchard Bishop EX17 . . 61 B1
Frost's Cnr EX19 . . . . 42 D1
Froude Ave TQ2 . . . . 214 B3
Froude Rd TQ8 . . . . 259 B2
Fry's La 5 EX10 . . . . 101 B1
Fry St EX22 . . . . 164 C4
Fuge Cross TQ6 . . . . 145 E6
Fuidge Cross EX17 . . . . 96 A5
Fuidge La EX17 . . . . 96 A5
Fulda Cres EX17 . . . . 165 D4
Fulford Cl
Bideford EX39 . . . . 157 D1
Tedburn St Mary EX6 . . . 97 F4
Fulford Dr EX15 . . . . 163 B2
Fulford Gdns EX20 . . . . 77 C4
Fulford Rd
Cheriton Bishop EX6 . . . . 97 D1
Dunsford EX6 . . . . 112 F8
Exeter EX1 . . . . 177 F7
Fulford Way EX5 . . . . 184 C2
Fullaford Cross TQ11 . . . . 236 B4
Fullaford Hill EX31 . . . . 18 E8
Fullaford Pk TQ11 . . . . 236 A4
Fullaford Pool Cross TQ11 . . . . 236 A4
Fullers Ct 12 EX2 . . . . 261 A2
Fullers Pl TQ12 . . . . 123 E5
Fullerton Rd PL2 . . . . 248 A5
Fullingcott Cross EX39 . . . . 153 A2
Fulton Cl TQ12 . . . . 211 D2
Fulton Ho 2 EX12 . . . . 192 A5
Furland Cl PL9 . . . . 255 C5
FURLEY 87 D7
Furley Cross EX13 . . . . 87 D6
Furlong Cl TQ11 . . . . 236 B7
Furlong Cotts EX16 . . . 51 A4
Furneaux Ave PL2 . . . . 248 B5
Furneaux Rd PL2 . . . . 248 B6
Furness Cl TQ4 . . . . 226 A2
Furrough Cross TQ1 . 220 C8
Furrough Ct TQ1 . . . . 220 C8
Fursdon Cl PL9 . . . . 256 C6
Fursdon Cross
East Allington TQ7 . . . . 144 E4
Hittisleigh EX6 . . . . 96 C5
Fursdon House★ EX5 . . . . 81 E7
Fursdon La EX6, EX17 . . 96 B5
Furse Pk PL5 . . . . 247 C7
Fursham Cross EX6 . . . 96 B4
Furzeacre Cl PL7 . . . . 251 A7
Furzebeam Row EX38 . . . . 159 B5
Furzebeam Terr 14 EX39 . . . . 157 B1
Furzebrake Cl TQ2 . . . 213 C2
Furzebrook EX11 . . . . 169 E4
Furze Cap 3 TQ12 . . . 123 E1
Furze Cross
Bridgerule EX22 . . . . 71 A5
Chittlehampton EX37 . . . 29 A5
Cornworthy TQ9 . . . . 227 A2
Kingsbridge TQ7 . . . . 144 D3
Furze Ct EX4 . . . . 176 E3
Furzedown Cross
Copplestone EX17 . . . . 79 A5
Taw Green EX20 . . . . 95 A6
Furzedown Rd TQ12 . . . . 213 A5
Furze Gdns
Shop EX23 . . . . 37 A1
Totnes TQ9 . . . . 223 F5
Furzegood TQ3 . . . . 218 D3
Furzeham Ct TQ5 . . . . 230 B5
Furzeham Pk TQ5 . . . . 230 B5
Furzeham Prim Sch TQ5 . . . . 230 C5
Furzehatt Ave PL9 . . . 256 A6
Furzehatt Park Rd PL9 . . . . 256 A6
Furzehatt Rd PL9 . . . . 255 F6
Furzehatt Rise PL9 . . . 256 A6
Furzehatt Way PL9 . . . 256 A6
Furzehill EX10 . . . . 101 B2
Furzehill Cross TQ9 . . 227 B3
Furzehill Rd
Heybrook Bay PL9 . . . . 140 A7
Plymouth PL4 . . . . 248 F4
Torquay TQ1 . . . . 220 A6
Furze Hill Rd EX34 . . . 150 B4
Furze La 2 TQ5 . . . . 230 D5
Furzeland Hill EX17 . . . 79 C6
Furzeleigh Cross TQ13 . . . . 122 F6
Furzeleigh La TQ13 . . . . 180 D8
Furzendown Rd TQ7 . . . . 147 F6
Furzepark Cross
Bittaford PL21 . . . . 137 C7
Dolton EX19 . . . . 58 A5
Furzepark La
Hartland EX39 . . . . 22 E3
Kentisbury EX31 . . . . 10 E6
Zeal Monachorum EX17 . 78 C6
Furze Park Rd EX31 . . . 18 A8
Furze Pk EX34 . . . . 2 F3
Furze Pk La EX31 . . . . 9 B2
Furze Rd
Totnes TQ9 . . . . 223 F5
Woodbury EX5 . . . . 184 C3
FYLDON 19 D4
Fyldon Hill EX36 . . . . 19 D5

G

Gabber La PL9 . . . . 140 B8
Gable Pk TQ1 . . . . 220 C6
Gables Lea EX15 . . . . 162 C4
Gables Rd EX15 . . . . 162 C4
Gables The
Combe Martin EX34 . . . . 2 F4
Exmouth EX8 . . . . 202 D6
Rousdon DT7 . . . . 193 F7
Teignmouth TQ14 . . . . 210 A5
Wellington TA21 . . . . 160 C6
Willand EX15 . . . . 162 C4
Gabriel Ct
11 Exeter EX2 . . . . 261 A2
Stoke Gabriel TQ9 . . . . 227 F7
Gabriels Wharf EX2 . . 177 C3
Gabwell Hill TQ1, TQ12 . . . . 214 C7
Gabwell La TQ12 . . . . 214 C7
Gaddacombe Cross EX20 . . . . 91 D1
Gainsborough Cl TQ1 . . . . 220 E4
Gainsborough Dr EX39 . . . . 156 B6
Gainsborough Ho
Exeter EX1 . . . . 177 E6
Tavistock PL19 . . . . 171 B6
Gains Cross EX22 . . . . 53 C3
Gala Cross PL8 . . . . 257 F1
Galahad Cl EX4 . . . . 174 A1
Galbraith Rd EX20 . . . 170 F6
Gale Rd TQ13 . . . . 131 B5
Gales Crest 3 TQ13 . . 123 C4
Gales Hill 18 TQ14 . . . 209 F6
Gale Wy EX16 . . . . 161 B5
Galileo Cl PL7 . . . . 250 E6
Gallacher Way PL12 . . 242 B3
Galleon Way EX39 . . . 156 E7
Gallery Cl 4 EX14 . . . 166 B6
Galloping La EX39 . . . . 39 B8
Gallops The PL12 . . . . 242 D4
Galloway Dr TQ14 . . . 124 E1
Gallows Cross TQ12 . . 207 C8
Gallows Gate TQ3 . . . . 218 F6
Gallows Park Cross TQ13 . . . . 131 B5
GALMPTON
Malborough 147 C7
Paignton 229 A6
Galmpton CE Prim Sch TQ5 . . . . 229 B5
Galmpton Cross TQ7 . 147 D7
Galmpton Ct TQ5 . . . . 229 B5
Galmpton Farm Cl TQ5 . . . . 229 B5
Galmpton Glade TQ5 229 B5
Galmpton Rise EX4 . . . 173 E1
GALMPTON WARBOROUGH 229 B6
Galpin St PL21 . . . . 137 C2
Galsworthy Cl PL5 . . . 244 C2
Galsworthy Sq EX4 . . . 178 C8
Galva Rd
Hemerdon PL7 . . . . 251 C8
Sparkwell PL7 . . . . 132 E1
Gamberlake EX13 . . . . 167 C4
Gamberlake Cross EX13 . . . . 167 C4
Gamblyn Cross TA4 . . . 34 F5
Gamlin Cl TA21 . . . . 160 D8
GAMMATON 26 C4
GAMMATON MOOR . . . 26 D3
Gammaton Moor Cross EX39 . . . . 26 D3
Gammaton Rd EX39 . . . 26 B4
Gammons Hill EX13 . . . 87 D1
Gammon Walk 23 EX31 . . . . 154 F5
Ganders Pk TQ2 . . . . 213 A2
Gandy St EX4 . . . . 261 A3
Ganges Rd PL2 . . . . 248 A5
Ganna Park Rd PL3 . . . 248 D6
Gappah Cross TQ13 . . 123 E4
Gappah La TQ13 . . . . 123 E4
Gara Cl PL9 . . . . 256 B6
Gara Lodge TQ12 . . . . 212 F4
Gard Cl TQ2 . . . . 214 A3
Garden Cl
Braunton EX33 . . . . 152 B6
Exeter EX2 . . . . 178 C4
Holbeton PL8 . . . . 142 A8
Plymouth PL7 . . . . 251 D5
Rattery TQ10 . . . . 135 D4
Garden Cotts TQ7 . . . 258 C5
Garden Cres PL1 . . . . 262 B1
Garden Ct EX9 . . . . 198 A1
Gardeners La PL8 . . . . 257 E4
Garden Gn EX32 . . . . 155 C2
Garden House The★ PL20 . . . . 126 D3
Gardenia Dr
Bolham EX16 . . . . 49 C1
Tiverton EX16 . . . . 161 E7
Garden La PL19 . . . . 171 B5
Garden Mill Ind Est TQ7 . . . . 258 D4
Garden Park Cl PL9 . . 256 C7
Garden Pk TQ10 . . . . 135 D4
Garden Rd TQ1 . . . . 220 B6
Garden Spot La TQ13 123 F6
Garden St PL2 . . . . 247 E4
Gardens The
6 Chudleigh TQ13 . . . . 123 E6
Dulverton TA22 . . . . 33 D7
Holemoor EX22 . . . . 73 B7

Gardens The *continued*
Rousdon DT7 193 E5
1 Wellington TA21 160 D5
Garden Terr
Cullompton EX15 163 C4
Wellington TA21 160 B7
Garden Village PL9 255 F8
Gardiner Cl EX5 82 A1
Gards La PL5 243 E2
Gareth Cres EX4 173 F2
Garfield Pl 12 TQ9 223 C5
Garfield Rd TQ4 226 C6
Garfield Terr PL1,
PL3 248 A3
Garland Cl EX4 176 E8
Garland Cross EX37 45 B5
GARLANDHAYES 52 F2
Garlandhayes La EX15 52 E2
Garland Meadow
EX1 179 B8
Garland's La EX16 64 A5
Garlic Rea TQ5 230 D5
Garliford La EX36 30 F4
Garners Cl TQ12 206 D1
Garners La TQ12 206 D1
Garratt Cl EX8 196 C3
Garratt Rd EX5 179 B3
Garrett Cl EX12 192 B6
Garrett St PL10 253 A1
Garrick Cl PL5 244 C2
Garrison Cl PL1 247 E1
Garrow Cl 1 TQ5 230 C3
Garston Ave TQ12 207 B4
Garston Cl PL9 256 A8
Garth Rd TQ2 214 A2
Gascon Cl TQ12 211 F8
Gascoyne Ct PL4 263 A3
Gascoyne Pl PL4 263 A3
Gashay La EX13 88 H3
Gashouse La PL4 263 B2
Gasking St PL4 263 A3
Gas La EX38 159 D5
Gatcombe Ash EX12 102 E2
Gatcombe La
Beer EX12 191 C8
Seaton EX12 102 E2
Gatcombe Mws 2
EX31 154 C1
Gate Cl EX13 88 E3
Gate Cross EX24 102 F6
Gatedown La
Salcombe Regis
EX10 101 E1
Sidmouth EX10 189 D8
Gate Field Rd EX39 156 E2
Gatehouse ACE Academy
EX7 204 E8
Gatehouse Cl
Cullompton EX15 163 B3
Dawlish EX7 204 E7
Gatehouse Hill EX7 204 E7
Gatehouse La 2
PL7 250 D5
Gatehouse Rise EX7 204 E7
Gate Reach EX2 177 E2
Gater La EX1 261 B2
Gatesfield DT7 260 C2
Gate Tree Cl TQ12 207 F7
GATHERLEY 105 D1
Gattery La TQ5 229 F1
Gavel The EX36 158 D4
Gaverick Ct TQ12 123 B1
Gawton Way PL19 171 B7
Gay Cl TA21 160 E6
Gaydon St EX32 155 A5
Gays Cross EX17 79 C7
Gays La EX17 79 C7
Gay St TA21 160 E6
Gaze Hill TQ12 206 F5
Gdn Ct PL12 242 D1
Gdynia Way
Plymouth PL3 249 B2
Plymouth PL4 263 C2
Geasons La PL7 250 E5
Gees La PL21 137 C2
Gemini Rd PL9 256 E7
Generals Cl EX6 201 A7
Generals La EX6 201 B7
Genesis La 3 EX34 3 A3
Geneva Cl EX2 177 E4
Geneva Ct
Bideford EX39 156 F1
Exeter EX2 177 E4
Geneva Pl EX39 156 F1
Gennys Cl PL18 125 B6
Gentian Cl TQ3 218 D2
George Ave PL7 250 F6
George Cross PL7 250 F5
George Downing Ho
PL6 245 A1
GEORGEHAM 8 B2
Georgeham CE Prim(VC)
Sch EX33 8 A2
Georgeham Cross
EX33 152 D7
Georgeham Rd
Croyde EX33 7 F2
Woolacombe EX34 8 B5
George Hill EX17 165 B6
Georgehill Cross
EX17 165 A6
George La
Kilmington EX13 87 C1
Plymouth PL7 250 F5
GEORGE NYMPTON 30 A1
George Nympton Cross
George Nympton EX36 30 A2
George Nympton EX37 29 F1
George Nympton Rd
EX36 158 C2
George Pl PL1 262 A2
George Rd TQ3 219 B1
Georges Cl EX1 178 B6
George Shopping Mews
EX36 158 C4
George Sq PL1 247 F1
George's Sq DT7 260 E3
George St
Axminster EX13 167 D6
12 Barnstaple EX32 154 F6
Exeter EX1 261 A2
1 Exmouth EX8 202 A7
Honiton EX14 166 C6
Newton Abbot TQ12 207 B3
Okehampton EX20 170 B5
Plymouth PL1 247 F1
11 Teignmouth TQ14 210 C4
Wellington TA21 160 D6
George Teign Rd
EX6 113 D2
Georgia Cres PL3 249 C6
Georgian Ct TQ1 220 E6
Georgian Ho The
EX6 201 B8
Gerald Dinnis Units
EX2 177 D1
Geraldine Terr PL12 242 C1
Gerbera Ho EX4 176 E8
Gerbera Way EX15 163 D3
Gerbestone La TA21 52 E6
GERMANSWEEK 91 D5
Gerrydown Rd EX19 58 D3
Gerston Cross TQ9 223 A3
Gerston La TQ7 258 C1
Gerston Pl 8 TQ3 226 B6
Gerston Rd TQ4 226 B6
Gervase Ave EX2 261 A1
Gerway Cl EX11 169 D2
Gerway La EX11 169 E2
Gestridge Cross
TQ12 207 D7
Gestridge Rd TQ12 207 D7
Giant's Grave TA20 69 D7
Giant's Grave Rd TA20 69 D7
Gibb Hill PL21 133 B2
Gibbon La PL4 263 A3
Gibbon St PL4 263 A3
Gibbs Plantation
EX31 153 C5
Giblands Cross EX20 170 D5
Giblands Pk EX20 170 D5
Gibraltar Rd EX8 195 E6
Gibson Cl EX8 196 E1
Gibson Ct TQ4 226 A1
Gibson Dr TQ4 226 A1
Gibson Gdns TQ4 226 A1
Gibson Rd TQ4 226 A1
Gidcott Cross EX22 55 A4
GIDLEIGH 110 D7
Gidley Arms Cross
EX36 46 A5
Gidley Cross EX36 46 B4
Gidleys Mdw TQ9 222 F8
Gidley's Meadow Ind Est
EX6 113 B4
Gidley's Turn EX6 113 C4
Gifford Cl EX39 22 E3
Gifford Pl PL3 248 D4
Gifford Terrace Rd
PL3 248 E5
Gilbert Ave
Exeter EX2 178 C4
Teignmouth TQ14 210 A7
Gilbert Cl TQ2 219 D6
Gilbert Ct PL7 251 B6
Gilbert Gr 6 EX34 150 C6
Gilbert La PL2 248 C5
Gilbert Rd TQ12 207 E3
Gilbert Way TQ4 226 A3
Gilbrook Cl EX5 184 B2
Gilchrist Way EX10 188 C5
Gillard Rd
Brixham TQ5 230 F4
Brixham TQ5 231 A5
Gillards Cl TA21 160 B4
Gillards Mead TA3 68 D7
Gillard Way PL21 136 D6
Gilley Cl TQ13 180 F7
Gill Pk PL3 249 B5
Gillscott Cross EX17 60 B1
Gill's Cross TQ9 222 D2
Gill's Nursery 13 TQ9 223 C5
Gilly's Wlk PL18 125 C5
Gilpin Cl EX7 204 F8
GILSCOTT 24 E2
Gilston Rd PL12 242 D4
Gilwell Ave PL9 256 B7
Gilwell Pl PL4 263 A3
Gilwell St PL4 263 A3
Gimbletts Ct 14 EX22 164 C4
Gingaford Cross
TQ10 135 A5
Gipsies Cnr EX17 79 F6
Gipsies La EX17 79 F6
Gipsy Cnr
Bovey Tracey TQ13 122 D5
Budlake EX5 82 E1
Whiddon EX31 9 C1
Gipsy Cross EX14 67 A5
Gipsy Dro TA20 69 F4
Gipsy Hill La EX1 178 F8
Gipsy Hill Mews EX1 178 F7
Gipsy La
Bideford EX39 25 B4
Bittadon EX31 9 F3
Buckfastleigh TQ11 236 A4
Gipsy La *continued*
Exeter EX1 178 F8
Exmouth EX8 202 B8
Ilfracombe EX34 150 D5
Ivybridge PL21 136 D7
Muddiford EX31 9 F2
Sampford Arundel TA21 51 D5
Girt La EX34 3 B4
Gissage Hill EX17 78 B7
Gissage View 7
EX14 166 B6
Gissons EX6 182 B4
Gissons La EX6 114 D4
GITTISHAM 85 B1
Gittisham Cl EX1 178 D6
Gittisham Farm Cross
EX14 85 A1
Gittshayne Cross
EX24 102 F5
Glade Cl PL6 245 A4
Glades The EX16 161 E3
Glade The PL20 126 E2
Glade Wlk EX5 179 E2
Gladstone Pl 11
TQ12 207 C3
Gladstone Rd EX1 177 E6
Gladstone Terr
8 Teignmouth TQ14 210 C5
Wellington TA21 160 E6
Glanville Ave 1
PL19 171 B5
Glanville Rd
Offwell EX14 102 A8
Tavistock PL19 171 B6
Glanvilles Mill PL21 237 D5
Glanvilles Rd PL21 237 D5
Glanville St PL1, PL4 262 C3
Glanville Terr PL12 242 F3
Glanvill's Cl EX6 98 C4
Glanvill Way EX14 166 B4
Glascott Cl EX20 75 B6
Glasshouse La EX2 182 B7
Glastonbury Cl
Exeter EX4 174 A2
3 Plymouth PL2 248 A7
Glave Saunders Ave
EX2 178 C4
Glazebrook Ct TQ10 134 E2
Glazegate Cross TQ3 224 F7
Glazegate La TQ3, TQ4,
TQ9 224 E6
Glazon Way EX39 157 A8
Gleaner Cl TQ12 244 D1
Glebe Ave PL12 242 F3
Glebe Cl
Exmouth EX8 202 F7
Hatherleigh EX20 75 C7
Lympstone EX8 195 E6
Newton Abbot TQ12 206 F3
Otterton EX9 198 E7
Upton Pyne EX5 172 F7
Glebe Cotts EX5 99 B1
Glebe Ct EX39 156 F6
Glebefield EX33 8 A2
Glebe Field TQ7 143 A2
Glebefields EX39 156 F6
Glebe Hos EX39 156 A1
Glebe Houses
Abbotsham EX39 25 C5
Abbotsham EX39 156 A1
Glebeland
Churchstow TQ7 143 E4
Down St Mary EX17 78 E7
Glebe Land TQ7 143 C6
Glebeland Ct TQ2 219 A8
Glebelands
Buckfastleigh TQ11 236 A6
Cheriton Bishop EX6 97 B4
12 Chudleigh TQ13 123 F6
Exminster EX6 182 A4
Holsworthy EX22 164 B4
Holsworthy TA20 71 F6
Lympstone EX8 195 E6
Newton Poppleford
EX10 186 F8
Puddington EX16 62 B5
Sidmouth EX10 188 A4
Uplyme DT7 260 B5
Wrafton EX33 152 E4
Glebelands Rd EX16 64 D7
Glebelands The TQ13 111 F4
Glebeland Villas EX36 31 A2
Glebeland Way TQ2 219 B8
Glebe Mdw EX22 164 B4
Glebe The
Bratton Fleming EX31 18 B8
Ipplepen TQ12 211 C2
Poughill EX17 62 D3
Thorverton EX5 81 E4
Glenarm Terr 6 TQ9 223 C6
Glenavon Rd PL3 248 E5
Glenburn Cl PL3 248 E6
Glenburnie Ho EX39 157 A3
Glenburnie Rd EX39 157 A3
Glencarnock Cl TQ1 219 E7
Glen Cl
Clyst St Mary EX5 179 E2
Sidmouth EX10 188 A3
Glencoe EX2 177 E5
Glendale Rd EX20 170 A6
Glendale Terr EX39 157 A3
Glendaragh Rd 12
TQ14 210 C5
Glendenning Acad
TQ12 207 F3
Glendon Cross EX20 170 F8
Glendorgal Pk PL18 125 C5
Glendower Rd PL3 248 D5
Gleneagle Ave 4
PL3 248 F6
Gleneagle Rd PL3 248 F6
Gleneagle Villas 5
PL3 248 F6
Glen Farm Cres
EX14 166 D5
Glenfield Cl PL6 245 D6
Glenfield Rd
Bideford EX39 157 A4
Plymouth PL6 245 D5
Glenfield Way PL6 245 E6
Glengarth Cl EX39 157 A5
Glen Gdns EX39 156 F4
Glenholme DT7 260 D2
GLENHOLT 245 D6
Glenholt Cl PL6 245 D6
Glenholt Rd PL6 245 D6
Glenhurst Rd 5 PL3 248 E6
Glen Isla EX10 188 B3
Glen Lyn 21 EX32 155 A4
Glen Lyn Gorge★
EX35 151 C5
Glen Lyn Pk TQ13 180 D5
Glenmore Ave PL2 247 F5
Glenmore Rd
Brixham TQ5 230 C4
Exeter EX2 178 A5
Glennaven Cl PL7 251 C6
Glenorchy Ct 5 EX8 202 A7
Glen Park Ave PL4 262 C4
Glen Park Prim Sch 6
PL7 251 B5
Glen Rd
Paignton TQ3 226 B7
Plymouth, Mannamead
PL3 248 F5
Plymouth, Plympton
PL7 250 F6
Sidmouth EX10 188 A3
Glenside Cl 5 TQ14 210 B6
Glenside Ct TQ1 220 E5
Glenside Rise PL7 250 E6
Glen The
Beer EX12 191 E6
3 Newton Abbot
TQ12 207 F2
Okehampton EX20 170 B4
Uplyme DT7 260 B5
Glenthorne Cl TQ1 220 D4
Glenthorne Rd EX4 173 A1
Glentor Rd PL3 248 E7
Glentorr Rd EX39 157 A3
Glenview EX14 166 D5
Glenwater Cl EX12 192 D6
Glen Wlk EX4 173 D2
Glenwood Dr EX31 154 A1
Glenwood Rd PL3 248 E6
Glenwood Rise
EX2 261 C1
Globe Ct EX15 163 C3
Globefield EX3 182 F5
Globe Hill EX5 184 B3
Globe La EX3 182 F4
Globe Ley EX3 182 F5
Gloster Rd EX32 155 A4
Gloucester Cl
Honiton EX14 166 A5
Torquay TQ2 213 F1
Gloucester Cres
EX14 166 A5
Gloucester Ct PL1 262 C4
Gloucester Pl PL1 262 C4
Gloucester Rd
Exeter EX4 176 E7
Exmouth EX8 196 E3
Newton Abbot TQ12 207 C3
9 Teignmouth TQ14 210 B5
Glove Ct EX38 159 C5
Glovers Cl 11 EX22 164 C4
Gloyn Pk EX22 53 E1
Glynsmead TA20 88 C8
Gnaton Cotts PL8 141 C8
Gnome Reserve & Wild
Flower Gdn★ EX22 39 B2
Goad Ave
Plymouth PL4 263 C2
Torpoint PL11 246 E3
Goad Cl PL11 246 F3
Goaman Pk EX39 22 E3
Goaman Rd EX39 26 A4
Go Ape! (Haldon)★
EX6 114 A3
Goats Hill Rd EX39 157 A6
Goblin Hill EX17 79 C4
Goblin La EX15 163 C4
Godborough View
EX39 156 D2
Godding Gdns PL6 244 E6
Godford Cross EX14 85 B5
Godfrey Ave TQ3 219 B2
Godfrey Cl EX11 169 C3
Godfreys Gdns EX17 78 C4
Godhams La TA4 35 A7
Godolphin Cl EX5 81 A1
Godolphin Ho PL19 171 C5
Godwell La
Ivybridge PL21 237 D3
Ivybridge PL21 237 F5
Ivybridge PL7 136 F6
Gogwell La
Cove EX16 49 B5
Tiverton EX16 161 F1
Goldburn Cross EX20 76 B1
Golden Bay Ct EX39 156 C7
Golden Cl TQ5 230 B2
Golden Hind (Mus Ship)
The★ TQ5 230 D5
Golden Inn Cross
EX21 74 C7
Golden Joy EX17 165 D6
Golden La EX14 66 F2
Golden Lane Cross
EX14 66 E2
Golden Lion Ct TQ13 130 F4
Golden Park Ave
TQ2 213 F4
Golden Pk Ave TQ3 214 A4
Golden Square EX14 86 E6
Golden Terr 20 EX7 204 D6
Goldfinch Cl
Kingsteignton TQ12 207 C8
Launceston PL15 105 A2
Goldfinch Gdns PL19 171 D2
Goldfinch Gr
Cullompton EX15 163 A2
Saltash PL12 242 D4
Golds Cross EX6 97 E4
Goldscross Hill EX6 97 D4
Golds La EX6 97 E5
Goldsmith Gdns PL5 244 D3
Goldsmiths La EX13 88 A4
Goldsmith St
Exeter EX4 261 A3
Exeter, Heavitree EX1 177 F6
Goldsmoor Cross
EX16 50 E3
Gold St
Ottery St Mary EX11 169 D4
Tiverton EX16 161 D4
GOLDWORTHY 24 F1
Golf Links Rd
South Brent TQ10 134 D1
Westward Ho! EX39 156 D7
Yelverton PL19 126 F1
Golland La EX37 44 B2
Gollands TQ5 230 B5
Gollands Cl TQ5 230 A5
Gollands La
Copplestone EX17 79 B8
Morchard Bishop EX17 61 B1
Golvers Hill Cl TQ12 207 E7
Golvers Hill Rd TQ12 207 E7
Goodacre Cross PL16 91 B1
Goodeve Cl PL9 255 E6
Goodgates Cl EX33 152 C6
Goodgates Cres
EX33 152 B6
Goodgates Gr EX33 152 B6
Goodgates Pk EX33 152 C6
Goodgates Rd EX33 152 B6
Goodiford Cross EX15 65 F3
Gooding Rise EX16 161 B4
GOODLEIGH 17 C5
Goodleigh CE Prim Sch
EX32 17 B5
Goodleigh Cross
EX32 155 F7
Goodleigh La EX19 58 E3
Goodleigh Rd
6 Barnstaple EX32 155 B5
Barnstaple EX32 155 D5
Goodleigh View 4
EX32 155 C5
Goodridge Cl EX7 204 E8
GOODRINGTON 226 B2
Goodrington Rd
Paignton TQ3 225 F1
Paignton TQ4 226 B1
Goodrington Sands Halt★
TQ4 226 C4
Goodshelter Cross
TQ8 148 E5
Good Shepherd Dr 5
EX2 261 B2
GOODSTONE 131 C6
Goodstone Cross
TQ12 131 C6
Goodstone Way TQ4 225 F3
Goodwells Head EX32 18 C3
Goodwin Ave PL6 245 A6
Goodwin Cres PL2 248 A6
Goodwood Park Rd
EX39 157 A5
Gooseberry La PL1 262 B2
Gooseford Cross EX20 95 D2
Gooseford La PL11 252 C8
Goose Gn EX38 159 E5
GOOSEHAM 37 B3
GOOSEMOOR 186 B7
Goose Moor La EX6 114 B4
GOOSEWELL 2 D4
Goosewell Hill
Plymouth PL6 245 C1
Plymouth PL6 249 C8
Goosewell Park Rd
PL9 255 F6
Goosewell Prim Sch
PL9 255 F6
Goosewell Rd PL9 255 F5
Goosewell Terr PL9 255 F6
Gora La EX34 8 A6
Gorbut Gdns PL19 171 D4
Gordon Ct
6 Plymouth PL1 262 A3
Saltash PL12 242 D2
Gordon Rd
Exeter EX1 177 E7
Topsham EX3 182 E6
Gordon's Pl EX1 177 F5
Gordon Terr
Beer EX12 191 D5
Plymouth PL4 248 E4
Gore La
Exmouth EX8 202 E4
Kilmington EX13 103 C8
Gore La *continued*
Uplyme DT7 260 A4
Gorfin Cl EX8 202 E8
Gorhuish Cross EX20 75 C1
Gorlegg TA21 51 E5
Gornhay Cross EX16 64 D8
Gornhay Orch EX16 64 D8
Gorrans Down EX39 22 F1
Gorse Ho EX4 176 E8
Gorse La EX8 196 D4
Gorse Way
Ivybridge PL21 237 E4
Sidmouth EX10 187 F4
Gorsey Cl PL5 244 E2
Gorvin Cross EX39 38 B6
Gorway TQ14 210 C6
Gorwell Rd EX32 155 C5
Gorwood Rd EX39 40 B7
Gorwyn La EX6 97 C4
Gosceline Wlk EX14 166 C4
GOSFORD 169 D7
Gosford La EX11 169 C7
Gosford Rd EX11 169 D7
Goshawk Units EX2 178 F6
Goshen Rd TQ2 219 E4
Goshen St PL5 247 E5
Goslings The TQ7 145 A1
Gosling Wlk EX12 192 A8
Goss Mdw EX17 78 C4
Gostwick Cl EX20 77 C4
Goswela Cl PL9 255 F5
Goswela Gdns PL9 255 F5
Gothic Rd TQ12 207 B2
Gould Cl EX32 155 B4
Gould Pl TQ12 207 F4
Gould Rd
Barnstaple EX32 155 C4
Exeter EX1 178 E8
Salcombe TQ8 259 D5
Gourders La TQ12 212 F2
Goutsford Gate PL21 136 F2
Govers Mdw EX24 103 A4
GOVETON 144 C5
Govetts EX5 184 C3
Gower Ridge Rd
PL9 255 D6
Gowman's Terr EX20 77 B4
Goyleacre La EX13 87 D6
Goyle Acre La EX13 87 D4
Grace Gdns TQ14 209 E8
Grace Parade EX2 177 B2
Grace Road Central
EX2 177 C2
Grace Road S EX2 177 D1
Grace Road W EX2 177 B2
Graddon Cross
Black Torrington EX21 73 F6
Okehampton EX20 93 E4
Grafton Ct TQ1 220 B4
Grafton Hts 8 TQ1 220 C5
Grafton Pl 12 TQ12 207 B3
Grafton Rd
Exeter EX4 173 B1
Plymouth PL4 248 E4
Torquay TQ1 220 B4
Grafton Terr TQ1 220 B4
Graham Cl EX16 161 D5
Graham Rd TQ3 219 A1
Graham Way EX39 156 C6
Grainger Cl EX2 178 C5
Grainge Rd PL6 245 A1
Grambrel Rise 4
EX1 178 F8
Gramercy Fields TQ5 230 B2
Grammar La EX10 189 D7
Grampian Cl TQ4 225 D4
Granary La EX9 198 C1
Granby Ct PL1 247 E2
Granby Gn PL1 247 E2
Granby Pl PL1 247 E2
Granby St PL1 247 E2
Granby Way PL1 247 E2
Grand Hotel Rd PL1 262 B1
Grandison Ave TQ14 209 A8
Grandisson Ct EX2 178 A2
Grandisson Dr EX11 169 F3
Grandisson St TQ12 123 D6
Grand Par PL1 262 B1
Grand View Rd
(Cliff Rd) TQ7 147 B7
Grand Western Canal Ctry
Pk Nature Reserve★
EX16 64 F7
Grand Western Canal
(Ctry Pk Nature
Reserve)★ EX16 50 F2
Grange Ave
Barnstaple EX31 154 C2
Exmouth EX8 202 B8
Paignton TQ4 226 B2
Grange Bglws EX39 157 B1
Grange Cl
Bratton Fleming EX32 18 A8
Ipplepen TQ12 211 C3
Lympstone EX8 195 F5
Newton Abbot TQ12 207 D1
Wellington TA21 52 C7
Wellington TA21 160 E5
Grange Cotts EX5 99 C6
Grange Cross EX14 84 D7
Grange Ct
4 Barnstaple EX32 155 A6
Teignmouth TQ14 210 A5
Grange Dr TQ14 210 B6

Grange Heights Cl TQ4 226 A1
Grange Hill EX32 18 B8
Grange Hill Ind Est EX31 18 B8
Grange Hts TQ4 226 A2
Grange La EX20 57 A7
GRANGE PK 208 D8
Grange Pk TQ12 212 A6
Grange Rd
Abbotskerswell TQ12 212 B6
Bideford EX39 157 B1
Buckfast TQ11 236 B7
Paignton TQ4 226 B2
Plymouth PL7 251 A4
Torquay TQ1 220 C5
Yelverton PL20 126 F3
Grange The
Braunton EX33 152 E5
Dousland PL20 127 B3
Grange View TQ4 226 A2
Grant Ct EX39 156 D1
Grantham Cl PL7 250 B4
Grantland Hill EX16, EX17 63 A4
Grantlands EX15 66 A7
Grantley Gdns PL3 249 A5
Grant's Hill EX16, TA22 33 F2
Granville Ave EX32 154 F6
Granville Pl EX15 162 C5
Granville Rd EX34 150 B6
Grapple Cl EX31 153 E6
Gras Lawn EX2 177 E4
Grasmere Cl
Plymouth PL6 244 E5
Torquay TQ2 214 B2
Grasmere Ct EX4 176 F5
Grassendale Ave PL2 247 F7
Grass La PL2 248 C6
Grasslands Dr EX1 178 F8
Grassmere Way PL12 242 D4
Grasspark Hill EX32 18 E3
Grass Rd TQ13 131 A3
Grassy La PL8 136 C4
Grattan La EX31 16 B6
Grattans Way EX17 78 C4
GRATTON 54 F5
Gratton Cl TQ6 146 B8
Gratton Cross
Shebbear EX22 55 A5
Yelverton PL20 127 A2
Gratton Ct EX31 154 C2
Gratton Dr TQ7 145 A1
Gratton La
Bittadon EX31 9 C5
Chulmleigh EX18 59 D3
Combe Martin EX31 3 F2
Lower Tippacott EX35 6 A4
Parracombe EX31 4 C2
Yelverton PL20 127 A2
Gratton Pk 10 EX5 99 A6
Gratton Pl PL6 245 A1
Grattons Dr EX35 151 B5
Grattons La TQ9 216 E2
Gratton Way EX31 154 C2
Gravel La EX12 192 B7
Gravel Pit Cross EX36 20 A6
Gravel Wlk EX15 163 C3
Gravesend Gdns PL11 247 B3
Gravesend Wlk PL5 243 D4
Graybridge Rd PL20 126 F4
Gray Cres PL5 247 C8
Graynfylde Dr EX39 157 B2
Grays Cotts TQ1 220 D7
Grays Ct TQ13 112 B3
Gray's Hill EX15 52 D1
Gray's La EX15 52 D1
Grays Mdw TQ13 111 F5
Great Ambrook Ave TQ12 217 A7
Great Berry Rd PL6 244 F1
Great Bridge TQ13 130 F5
Great Burrow Rise EX39 156 F8
Great Churchway PL9 256 A7
Great Cl EX15 51 E1
Great Fellingfield PL19 117 E6
Great Field Gdns EX33 152 C5
Great Field La EX37 45 A6
Greatfield Rd PL3 249 B7
Great Furlong TQ14 208 E8
Great Gate Flats 13 TQ5 230 C4
GREAT HAYNE 63 A2
Great Headland Cres TQ3 219 D1
Great Headland Rd TQ3 219 C1
Great Hele La EX36 158 D2
Great Hill 3 TQ13 123 E6
Great Hill Cross TQ1 213 F5
Great Hill Rd TQ2 213 F4
Great Hill View EX4 173 E2
Great La TQ7 147 E6
Greatlands Cres PL2 248 A6
Greatlands Pl 5 PL2 248 A5
Great Lightleigh La EX18 44 F5
Great Links Tor Rd EX20 170 E5
Great Longlands Dr PL12 242 B5
Great Mdw TA22 33 D6
Great Mead EX6 112 F7
Great Meadow 3 EX5 99 A6
Great Mis Tor Cl 5 PL20 126 F3
Greatoak Cross TQ12 212 C5
Great Oak Cross EX5 81 D2
Great Oak Gdns PL16 105 F4
Great Oak Mdw EX22 164 C5
Great Orchard Cl PL9 255 E5
Great Park Cl
Bishopsteignton TQ14 208 F7
4 Plymouth PL7 251 C5
Greatpark La TQ3 225 D6
Great Parks Rd TQ3 225 E5
Great Pitford La EX18 58 D6
Great Pk TQ7 147 E6
Great Rea Rd TQ5 230 D5
Great Ringaton La EX36 32 B6
Great Tor Cl TQ3 218 F1
GREAT TORRINGTON 159 D6
Great Torrington Bluecoat CE Prim Sch EX38 159 E5
Great Torrington Com Sch & Sports Coll EX38 159 E5
Great Tree Cl TQ4 225 F1
Great Tree Pk TQ13 96 A1
Great Tree Pl TQ4 228 F8
Great Tree View TQ4 228 F8
Great Tree Vw TQ4 225 F1
Greatweek Cross TQ13 111 B6
GREAT WEEKE 111 B6
Great Western Cl TQ4 226 C4
Great Western Ind Est EX32 155 B3
Great Western Rd
12 Paignton TQ4 226 B6
Plymouth PL1 262 B1
Great Western Way EX16 161 D3
Great Woodford Dr PL7 250 B6
Greatwood Terr EX3 182 F5
Grebe Cl PL7 250 F5
Grebe Row EX7 200 E2
Grebe Way TQ12 207 C8
Grecian Way EX2 178 C4
Greebys The TQ3 226 A6
Greenacre
Braunton EX33 152 C6
Cranbrook EX5 99 C6
Green Acre EX16 65 B7
Greenacre Cl
Bradworthy EX22 53 E8
Northam EX39 157 A7
North Tawton EX20 77 C4
Greenacres
Exeter EX4 173 A3
Plymouth PL9 255 F8
Torquay TQ1 220 E5
Greenacres Cl EX14 84 D1
Greenaway EX17 61 A2
Greenaway Ho EX22 164 C3
Greenaway La TQ12 213 B6
Greenaway Rd TQ12 207 A4
Greenaway Villas 4 TQ12 207 B4
Greenawell Cl TQ13 111 D2
Greenbank EX38 159 F6
Green Bank EX10 186 E8
Greenbank Ave
Kingsteignton TQ12 207 D8
Plymouth PL4 263 B3
Greenbank Cl EX38 159 F6
Greenbank Cottages PL4 263 B4
Greenbank Rd
Barnstaple EX32 155 C4
Brixham TQ5 230 B4
Plymouth PL4 263 B4
Greenbanks TQ7 145 C3
Green Banks Cl TQ7 145 C3
Greenbank Terr
Plymouth PL4 263 B4
Yelverton PL20 127 A3
Green Cl
Cornworthy TQ9 227 B4
Exmouth EX8 202 C8
Kingsbridge TQ7 258 D6
Greenclose Ct 3 EX24 103 A4
Green Close La EX31 10 B5
Greenclose Rd EX34 150 B6
Greendale Bsns Pk EX5 184 D8
Greendale Cross EX5 183 F7
Greendale La
Exeter EX5 99 A1
Woodbury Salterton EX5 184 A8
Greendale Rd PL2 248 A7
Greendown Cross EX20 74 C2
Green End La EX15 83 F5
Greenfield Cl EX39 156 F2
Greenfield Dr
Ivybridge PL21 237 D4
7 South Brent TQ10 134 F2
Greenfield Rd
Paignton TQ3 219 A1
Saltash PL12 242 D2
Greenfield Terr TA20 88 D8
Greenfinch Cres PL12 242 E4
Greenford Villas EX2 261 A1
Green Gables EX10 188 A4
GREEN GATE 50 B2
Green Gate EX16 50 B2
Green Gdns EX39 156 E6
GREENHAM 51 B7
Greenham Bsns Pk TA21 51 C5
Greenhaven EX9 197 F2
Greenhayes
Charmouth DT6 104 F4
Dartington TQ9 222 E8
Greenhays Foot EX13 88 B6
Greenhead EX10 101 B2
Green Hedges EX19 58 E8
GREENHILL 207 E5
Greenhill
East Allington TQ9 144 D7
Kingsteignton TQ12 207 E6
Green Hill
Lamerton PL19 116 E3
Poughill EX16, EX17 62 D3
Sampford Courtenay EX20 76 F3
Tavistock PL19 171 D5
Greenhill Ave
Exmouth EX8 202 C7
Lympstone EX8 195 E5
Greenhill Cl PL9 255 F5
Greenhill Cross
East Knowstone EX36 32 B2
Knowle EX33 8 E1
Poughill EX17 62 D3
Sampford Chapple EX20 77 A3
Greenhill Gdns TQ12 212 F4
Greenhill Ind Units TQ12 207 E6
Greenhill La TQ12 211 B6
Greenhill Rd
Kingskerswell TQ12 212 F4
Kingsteignton TQ12 207 E6
Plymouth PL9 256 A5
Greenhill Terr TQ9 144 D7
Greenhill Way TQ12 207 E6
Greenhouse Gdns EX15 163 D3
Greenings Rd EX39 40 C7
Green Knap La TA20 69 F2
Green La
23 Appledore EX39 15 A1
Axmouth EX12 193 C8
Axmouth EX12, DT7 193 B8
1 Barnstaple EX31 154 F5
Beaford EX19 42 D1
Bittaford TQ10 137 E8
Blackawton TQ9 139 B1
Braunton EX33 15 D7
Braunton EX33 152 E6
Buckfastleigh TQ11 236 F4
Chard Junction TA20 88 D7
Chardstock EX13 88 B7
Cheriton Bishop EX6 97 C2
Churchstanton EX15 68 B8
Churston Ferrers TQ5 229 E5
Colyford EX24 103 A3
East Allington TQ9 144 D8
Exeter EX4 176 E5
Exton EX3 183 B2
Feniton EX14 84 E2
Hatherleigh EX20 75 D7
Ilsington TQ13 122 C4
Kemacott EX31 4 C4
Kingsand PL10 253 A2
Merton EX20 57 A7
Molland EX36 31 B8
North Molton EX36 19 F1
Rackenford EX16 47 C5
Raymond's Hill EX13 104 C7
Rewe EX5 82 A2
Rousdon DT7 193 F8
Sampford Arundel TA21 51 F4
Sidbury EX10 101 D2
Southleigh EX24 102 D3
Spreyton EX17 96 A7
Swimbridge EX32 28 B8
Tavistock PL19 171 E5
Totnes TQ9 223 A4
Venn Ottery EX10 100 B2
West Sandford EX17 79 F6
Whitstone EX23 70 E1
Yelverton PL20 126 F1
Greenlake Cross EX39 22 D1
Greenland PL10 252 F5
Greenland Head Cross
Churchstow TQ7 143 E6
Pennymoor EX16 62 E6
Greenlands Ave TQ3 225 F6
Greenlands Est PL19 171 D5
Greenlane Cross EX36 31 C8
Green Lane End
Blackawton TQ9 139 B1
Buckfastleigh TQ11 236 E4
Green Lanes Sh Ctr EX31 154 F5
Greenlees Dr PL7 251 B3
Greenmeadow Dr EX31 155 A7
Green Mews EX9 198 A1
Green Mount EX10 188 C6
Greenover Cl TQ5 230 B3
Greenover Rd TQ5 230 B3
Greenpark Ave EX1 178 D7
Green Park Ave PL4 248 D4
Greenpark Rd EX8 196 D2
Green Park Rd
Paignton TQ3 218 F1
Plymouth PL9 255 E5
Green Park Way TQ7 145 A1
Green Park Wlk TQ3 218 F1
Green Pk PL10 253 A2
Greenslade Cross EX20 77 A3
Greenslade Rd
Blackawton TQ9 139 E1
Totnes TQ9 145 B8
Witheridge EX16 46 E1
Greenslinch La EX5 82 D6
Greensway Rd PL19 171 A4
Greenswood Cl 9 TQ5 230 C3
Greenswood La TQ6 232 B1
Greenswood Rd 4 TQ5 230 C3
Green The
Ashburton TQ13 130 F4
Bridgerule EX22 70 F5
Brushford TA22 33 E4
Denbury TQ12 211 A6
Down St Mary EX17 78 E7
East Ogwell TQ12 206 E1
Exeter EX1 178 D1
Exeter EX3 182 D8
Exmouth EX8 202 F8
6 Horrabridge PL20 126 F5
Ide EX2 176 D1
Kingsand PL10 253 A2
Meavy PL20 127 C2
Milton Combe PL20 240 F8
Otterton EX9 198 E7
Plymouth, Ernesettle PL5 243 E3
Plymouth, Hooe PL9 255 B6
Saltash PL12 242 C3
Teignmouth TQ14 210 A3
Whimple EX5 99 E8
Green Tree La EX5 175 D6
Greenville Way EX15 163 C4
Greenway
Crediton EX17 80 A3
Crediton EX17 165 B5
Exeter EX2 176 F3
Greenway★ TQ5 228 E2
Greenway
Halberton EX16 65 A8
Lyme Regis DT7 260 C3
Seaton EX12 191 F7
Woodbury EX5 184 C3
Greenway Ave PL7 250 B6
Greenway Cl
3 Horrabridge PL20 126 F5
Ivybridge PL21 237 D5
Torquay TQ2 214 A1
Greenway Dr EX39 156 E8
Greenway Gdns
Budleigh Salterton EX9 198 A2
Tiverton EX16 161 C4
Torquay TQ2 214 A2
Greenway La
Ashcombe EX7 124 F5
Awliscombe EX14 85 B5
Beacon EX14 85 D8
Budleigh Salterton EX9 198 A2
Sidmouth EX10 187 E8
Torquay TQ1 220 B8
Greenway Pk TQ5 229 B4
Greenway Rd
Galmpton TQ5 229 B4
Paignton TQ5 228 E3
Rockwell Green TA21 160 A5
Torquay, Chelston TQ2 219 E4
Torquay, St Marychurch TQ1 220 B8
Greenways EX34 150 A5
Greenwich Pl PL12 242 F3
Greenwood Cl
Aveton Gifford TQ7 143 C6
Ivybridge PL21 237 C5
Greenwood Ct EX39 156 D1
Greenwood Dr EX2 178 D5
Greenwood Park Cl PL7 251 B6
Greenwood Park Rd PL7 251 B6
Greenwoods The EX39 22 E3
Gregory Cl
Bow EX17 78 C4
Tiverton EX16 161 F4
Gregorys Cres TA21 160 D7
Gregory's Ct TQ13 110 F6
Gregory's Mdw PL15 105 A2
Gregory Terr EX39 22 E3
Grenadier Rd EX1 178 E7
Grenadine Cl TQ2 213 E3
Grendon Almshouses EX1 177 E6
Grendon Bldgs 2 EX1 261 A2
Grendon Ct TQ14 210 A5
Grendon La EX16 46 E4
Grendon Rd EX1 177 E6
Grenfell Ave PL12 242 D3
Grenfell Gdns PL12 242 C3
Grenofan Cross PL19 126 D6
GRENOFEN 126 D6
Grenofen Cl PL19 126 D6
Grenville Ave
Exeter EX4 178 D8
Teignmouth TQ14 210 A7
Grenville Ave *continued*
Torquay TQ2 219 D6
Grenville Cl
Dartmouth TQ6 233 D3
Newton Abbot TQ12 207 E3
South Molton EX36 158 C4
Stokenham TQ7 145 B2
Grenville Ct PL7 251 C6
Grenville Dr PL19 171 B3
Grenville Estate Cres
Bideford EX39 25 E4
Bideford EX39 156 E1
Grenville Est The EX39 25 E4
Grenville Ho EX31 155 A8
Grenville Pk PL20 127 A2
Grenville Rd
Exmouth EX8 196 C2
Plymouth PL4 263 C3
Salcombe TQ8 259 D4
Grenville Road Lane S PL4 249 B2
Grenville St 16 EX39 157 A2
Grenville Terr
4 Bideford EX39 157 B1
Northam EX39 157 A7
Grenville Way TQ4 226 B3
Gresham Cl PL5 244 C7
Greycoat La TQ12 206 F7
Greyfriars Rd EX4 177 F8
Greyhill Cross TQ7 138 A1
Greysand Cres 31 EX39 15 A1
Greysholt Cross EX32 28 B8
Greystoke Ave PL6 249 D7
Greystone Cross EX6 96 E2
Greystone Way TQ1 220 C7
Greystone Wlk EX15 163 A3
Gribble Cl EX32 155 C4
Gribbleford Cross EX20 75 A4
Gribble La EX5 99 D6
Gribblemead EX24 103 A4
Grieg Dr EX32 155 C5
Griffin Way PL9 256 C6
Griggs Cl
Northam EX39 157 A6
Plymouth PL7 251 B4
Griggs Gdn EX31 153 D5
Grigg's La EX10 188 D7
Grimspound★ TQ13 121 A7
Grimspound Cl PL6 249 E8
Grimstone Terr PL20 126 E2
Grinacombe Cross PL16 91 B2
GRINACOMBE MOOR 91 B2
Grinacombe Moor cross PL16 91 B2
Grindhill Cross EX20 92 D5
Grindle Way EX5 179 B2
Grizedale Rd PL6 249 D7
Gronau Cl EX14 166 C4
Grooms Orch TA21 160 C5
Gropers La
Ipplepen TQ3, TQ12 218 C8
North Whilborough TQ12 212 B1
Gropy La
Ash Mill EX36 31 D1
South Molton EX36 46 D8
Grosvenor Ave TQ2 213 C1
Grosvenor Cl TQ2 213 C1
Grosvenor Cotts 1 PL4 248 F4
Grosvenor Ct
3 Barnstaple EX32 155 A5
Ivybridge PL21 237 C5
Grosvenor Pl EX1 261 C4
Grosvenor Rd
Paignton TQ4 226 B5
Plymouth PL6 244 F2
Grosvenor St 2 EX32 155 A5
Grosvenor Terr
4 Barnstaple EX32 155 A5
Paignton TQ4 226 B5
4 Teignmouth TQ14 210 B6
Groundhead Rd EX14 86 F6
Grove Ave 12 TQ14 210 B5
Grove Cl
Plymouth TQ12 244 D6
3 Totnes TQ9 223 C5
Grove Cres 6 TQ14 210 B5
Grove Cross EX22 39 D3
Grove Ct
Dawlish EX7 204 F6
Teignmouth TQ14 210 C6
Grove Hill
12 Colyton EX24 103 A4
Topsham EX3 182 F5
Grove Ho EX3 182 F5
Grove La
Copplestone EX17 79 B7
West Anstey EX36 32 D6
Grove Mdw EX20 94 F5
Grove Mews 16 TQ9 223 C5
Grove Pk
Tavistock PL19 171 D5
Torpoint PL11 246 E3
Grove Sch The 19 TQ9 223 C5
Groves The PL21 237 C6
Grove Terr 11 TQ14 210 B5
Grove The
5 Bittaford PL21 137 C8
Blackawton TQ9 139 E1
Exeter EX4 174 E2
Paignton TQ4 225 E4
Grove The *continued*
Plymouth, Plymstock PL9 255 D8
Plymouth, Stoke PL3 248 A4
Sidmouth EX10 188 B4
Totnes TQ9 223 C5
Woolacombe EX34 7 F6
Guardian Rd EX1 178 E6
Gubbin's La EX33 152 D5
Guelder Way TQ12 244 C6
Guernsey Ave EX4 174 E2
Guernsey Cnr EX24 102 F4
Guestland Rd TQ1 220 C7
Guildford Cl
Exeter EX4 176 E6
Plymouth PL5 244 E3
Guildford St PL4 263 A3
Guildhall Sh Ctr EX4 261 A3
Guildhall Sq PL1 262 C2
Guinea St EX1 261 A2
Guinevere Way EX4 174 A1
Guinness La EX4 176 E8
Gulland Cross TQ12 212 B4
Gullet Cross TQ7 148 F6
Gulliford Cl EX8 195 F6
Gulliford Cotts EX8 195 F6
Gulliver La EX20 77 D7
Gullyhole Hill EX36 31 F7
Gully La EX14 86 C5
Gully Shoot EX24 103 A3
Gulway Mead TA20 88 D8
GULWORTHY 125 E8
Gulworthy Cotts PL19 125 E7
Gulworthy Cross PL19 125 E7
Gulworthy Prim Sch PL19 125 E7
Gun La
Heasley Mill EX36 19 D4
North Heasley EX36 19 D4
Plymouth PL5 247 E2
GUNN 17 F4
Gunn Cross EX32 17 F3
GUNNISLAKE 125 D6
Gunnislake Prim Sch PL18 125 C6
Gunnislake Rural Workshops PL18 125 C6
Gunnislake Sta PL18 125 C5
Gunsdown Villas EX36 158 D5
Gunstone Cross EX17 79 E2
Gunstone Mill Cross EX17 79 E1
Gunswell La EX36 158 B5
Gurnard Wlk PL3 249 C6
Gurney Cl PL11 246 F3
Gurneys The TQ3 226 A5
GUSCOTT 26 E2
Guscott La EX38 26 E2
Gussiford La EX8 202 B6
Guy Miles Way PL5 244 B3
Guys Rd EX4 176 F6
Gwel Avon Bsns Pk PL12 242 D4
Gwithian Cl PL11 246 F4
Gwyn Rd PL4 263 C4
Gwythers EX36 158 D4
Gypsy La
Simonsbath TA24 13 E1
Simonsbath TA24 20 E8

H

Hacche La
South Molton EX36 30 B6
South Molton EX36 158 C6
South Molton EX36 158 C8
Haccombe Cl EX4 176 E5
Haccombe Cross TQ12 213 E6
Haccombe Path TQ12 208 A2
Haccombe View TQ12 207 F6
Hacker Cl EX10 186 F7
Hackney La
Kingsteignton TQ12 207 F6
Newton Abbot TQ12 208 B4
Hackney Marshes Nature Reserve★ TQ12 207 E6
Hackpen Cross Way EX15 66 E6
Hackworthy Cnr EX4 98 F5
Hackworthy Cross EX6 97 E5
Hackworthy Cross La EX6 97 E5
Hackworthy La
Nadderwater EX4 98 F5
Tedburn St Mary EX6 97 D4
HADDACOTT 26 E3
Haddacott Cross EX38 26 F3
Haddeo Dr EX2 178 D4
Haddington Rd PL2 247 F4
Haddon Cnr EX13 103 C8
Haddon Ct 2 TQ3 226 B7
Haddon Hill TA4 34 D7
Haddon La TA4 34 C7
Haddon Rd EX13 103 B8
Hadfield Ct 4 TQ13 123 C4
Hadrian Dr EX4 176 F6
Hadrians Way EX8 196 D1
HALBERTON 65 B8
Halberton Prim Sch EX16 65 A7

Halcyon Ct PL2 ......248 A6
Halcyon Rd
Newton Abbot TQ12 ...207 B3
Plymouth PL2 ....248 A6
Haldene Terr 6
EX32 ....154 F6
Haldon Ave TQ14 .....210 C6
Haldon Belvedere*
EX6 ....113 F5
Haldon Cl
2 Newton Abbot
TQ12 ....207 F2
Topsham EX3 ....182 E6
Torquay TQ1 ....220 E4
Haldon Ct EX8 ....196 B2
Haldon Dr EX6 ....114 A4
Haldon La TQ13 ......124 B4
Haldon Lodge EX6 ...114 B5
Haldon Pl PL5 ....244 A3
Haldon Plain EX6 ....114 B3
Haldon Rd
Exeter EX4 ....177 A6
Torquay TQ1 ....220 D4
Haldon Ridge EX6 ....114 C2
Haldon Rise 1 TQ12 .207 F2
Haldon Terr 14 EX7 ..204 D6
Haldon View TQ13 ...123 F6
Haldon View Terr
EX2 ....177 F5
Haldron's Almshouses
EX16 ....161 C4
Halecombe Rd PL3 ...249 D1
Hale La
Honiton EX14 ....85 F3
Honiton EX14 ....166 E6
Haley Barton 4 PL2 ..248 A5
Haley Cl EX8 ....196 C2
Half Farthing La EX20 .77 C7
Halfmoon Ct TQ11 ...236 A3
Half Moon The EX13 ...87 E8
HALF MOON
VILLAGE 172 C7
HALFORD 122 F1
Halford Cross TQ12 ..122 E1
Halfpenny Cross EX16 .49 B7
Halfpenny Ct PL1 ....248 A2
Halsfbury Cross EX37 .43 E4
Halfway House Flats
TQ5 ....230 F6
Halfyard Ct TA21 ....160 F4
Hallamore La PL21 ...133 B2
Hall Cross PL21 .....133 E2
Hallerton Cl PL6 ....245 E2
Hallett Cl PL12 .....242 B3
Hallett Ct DT7 ......260 D4
Halletts Way EX13 ...167 E6
Halley Gdns PL5 .....243 E1
Hall Hill EX35 ....6 B5
Hall La
Holcombe EX7 ....210 E8
Morchard Bishop EX17 ..60 F2
HALLSANDS 149 E5
HALLSANNERY 25 F3
Halls Cross EX31 ......10 E4
Hall's La TQ12 ....212 F4
Hall's Mill La EX31 ..154 E8
HALLSPILL 26 B2
Hallswell Ct TQ4 .....226 B6
Halmpstone Cross
EX32 ....28 C7
Halsbury Rd EX16 ....161 F4
Halscombe La
Ide EX2 ....176 C1
Sidbury EX10 ....101 F8
Halsdon Ave EX8 .....196 A1
Halsdon Cross EX22 ...54 C1
Halsdon La EX8 ......196 A2
Halsdon Rd EX8 ......202 A7
Halsdon Terr EX38 ...159 C5
Halsdon Wildlife
Reserve* EX19 ....57 D6
Halsegate Cross EX20 .77 D3
Halse Hill EX9 ....197 F1
Halse La
North Tawton EX20 .....77 D4
West Worlington EX17 ..61 B6
Halses Cl EX4 ....176 D8
Halsewood Gate EX15 .64 E2
Halsey Lake Cross
EX31 ....10 D1
HALSFORDWOOD 98 F4
Halsfordwood La
EX4 ....98 F4
Halshanger Cross
TQ13 ....130 F8
HALSINGER 8 E1
Halsteads Rd TQ2 ....214 A2
Halswell Cross EX36 ..29 D2
Halt The EX2 ....177 B1
HALWELL 139 B4
Halwell Bsns Pk TQ9 .139 C3
Halwell Cross
Denbury TQ12 ....211 A5
Halwell TQ9 ....139 C4
Halwell Ho TQ7 .....148 E7
HALWILL 73 C2
Halwill Com Prim Sch
EX21 ....73 E2
HALWILL JUNCTION 73 E2
Halwill Mdw EX21 .....73 D3
Halyards EX3 ....182 E5
HAM
Axminster 86 F4
Plymouth 248 A8
Wellington 52 D8
Hambeer La
Exeter EX2 ....176 E3
Exeter EX4 ....176 F2
Hamberhayne Cross
EX24 ....102 D6
Hamble Cl PL3 ......249 D7
Hamblecombe La
TQ13 ....124 A4
Hambleton Ho 4
TQ14 ....210 C5
Hambleton Way TQ4 .226 A2
Ham Butts TQ7 ......143 F7
Ham Cl PL2 ....248 B8
Ham Cross EX13 ....86 F4
Ham Dr PL2 ....248 B8
Hameldown Bsns Pk
EX20 ....170 E6
Hameldown Cl TQ2 ..219 B7
Hameldown Rd EX20 .170 E5
Hameldown Way
TQ12 ....207 D4
Hamelin Way TQ2,
TQ3 ....219 A8
Ham Farm La TA20 ....69 F8
Ham Gn PL2 ....248 A7
Ham Green Ct PL2 ...248 A7
Ham Green La PL2 ...248 A7
Ham Hill
Ashreigney EX18 ......43 E1
Ashreigney EX18 ......58 E8
Street Ash TA20 ......69 F8
Tracebridge EX16 .....51 A8
Ham Ho PL2 ....248 A8
Hamilton Ave EX2 ...177 F2
Hamilton Cl
Bideford EX39 ....25 E4
14 Sidford EX10 .....101 B1
Hamilton Ct 4 EX8 ..202 B6
Hamilton Dr
Exeter EX2 ....178 D5
Newton Abbot TQ12 ..207 B5
Hamilton Gdns PL4 ..248 D4
Hamilton Gr EX6 ....201 B7
Hamilton La EX8 ....202 C7
Hamilton Rd
Exmouth EX8 ....202 D7
Topsham EX3 ....182 E6
Hamiltons The TQ14 .210 A3
Ham La
Colyton EX24 ....103 A4
Combe St Nicholas TA20 .69 F8
Dittisham TQ6 ......228 C3
Plymouth PL2 ....248 A8
Shaldon TQ14 ....209 D4
Sidmouth EX10 ......188 B3
South Molton EX36 ..158 E4
Hamley La TA20 ......69 E8
Hamlin Gdns EX1 ....178 A7
Hamlin Ho EX1 ......178 A7
Hamlin La EX1 ......178 A7
Hamlintoo La EX17 ...95 E7
Hamlyns La EX4 .....176 F8
Hamlyns Way TQ11 ..236 B5
Hammett Rd EX15 ...163 B3
Hammetts La
Barnstaple EX32 .....155 B1
Bishop's Tawton EX32 ..16 E1
Hammond Croft Way
EX2 ....181 B8
Hamoaze Ave PL5 ...247 D8
Hamoaze Pl PL1 ....247 D2
Hamoaze Rd PL11 ...247 B2
Hampden Pl EX2 ....261 A1
Ham Pl 10 EX16 ....161 C3
Hampshire Cl EX4 ...176 E4
Hampson Cross EX17 ..78 A4
Hampson La EX17 .....78 A4
Hampstead Farm La
Littlehempston TQ9 ..216 C1
Littlehempston TQ9 ..223 C8
HAMPTON 103 C7
Hampton Ave TQ1 ....220 C8
Hampton Bldgs EX4 ..261 C4
Hampton Ct EX13 ....103 C6
Hampton La
Torquay TQ1 ....220 C8
Whitford EX13 ......103 C6
Hampton Pk EX39 ....156 E4
Hampton Rd
Newton Abbot TQ12 ..207 C3
Whitford EX13 ......103 C7
Hampton St PL4 .....263 A3
Ham Rd
Dalwood EX13 ....87 A3
Wellington TA21 ......52 D8
Hamslade Cross EX16 .48 D8
Hamslade Hill EX16 ...48 D8
Hams The EX2 ....176 D1
Hamstone Ct TQ8 ....259 D4
Hamway La TA20 ......69 F8
Hancock Cl PL6 .....244 D6
Hand and Pen La EX5 ..99 E6
HAND & PEN 99 E6
Hand & Pen Cotts EX5 .99 E6
Handy Cross EX39 .....25 E4
Hangar La PL6 ......245 B5
Hanger La EX14 ....84 F8
Hanging La EX35 ....5 A3
Hangman Path EX34 ....2 F4
Hangman's Cross
PL21 ....138 A2
Hangman's Hill EX16 ..48 D7
Hangman's Hill Cross
EX16 ....48 E7
Hankford Cross EX22 ..39 E2
Hannaburrow La
Braunton EX33 ....14 F8
Saunton EX33 ....14 F8
HANNAFORD 28 C8
Hannaford Cross EX32 .28 C8
Hannaford La EX32 ....28 D8
Hannaford Rd
Lifton PL16 ....105 E3
Noss Mayo PL8 ......140 F5
Hannahs at Ivybridge
PL21 ....237 B5
Hannaton Cross EX32 .28 D8
Hanniford Gdns EX1 .175 A3
Hann Rd EX16 ....64 E8
Hanover Cl
7 Brixham TQ5 ......230 C3
Exeter EX1 ....177 F6
Plymouth PL3 ....249 B5
Hanover Ct
Dulverton TA22 ....33 D7
Exeter EX2 ....181 C8
15 Plymouth PL1 ....263 A2
Hanover Gdns EX15 ..163 C5
Hanover Ho TQ1 .....220 D3
Hanover Rd
Exeter EX1 ....177 F6
Plymouth PL3 ....249 C4
Hansetown Rd TA4 ....34 F8
Hansford Cross
Ashreigney EX18 ......44 A1
Burrington EX37 ......44 B2
Hansford Ct EX14 ...166 C5
Hansford Way EX11 ..169 C3
Hanson Pk
Bideford EX39 ......156 F4
Bideford EX39 ......157 A4
Happaway Cl TQ2 ....214 A2
Happaway Rd
Torquay TQ2 ....213 F2
Torquay TQ2 ....214 A2
HARBERTON 222 D1
Harberton Cl TQ4 ...225 E3
HARBERTONFORD 139 C6
Harbertonford CE Prim
Sch TQ9 ....139 C7
Harbour Ave
Plymouth PL4 ....263 A2
Plymouth, Camels Head
PL5 ....247 E8
Harbour Ct
Exmouth EX8 ....201 F6
6 Seaton EX12 ......192 B4
Harbourne Ave TQ4 ..225 F3
HARBOURNEFORD 135 B5
Harbourneford Cross
TQ10 ....135 B4
Harbour Rd EX12 ....192 B4
Harbourside 3 EX34 .150 C6
Harbour St PL11 ....247 B3
Harbour The
Lynmouth EX35 ......151 C6
Seaton EX12 ....192 C5
Harbour View
Plymouth PL9 ....255 A7
Saltash PL12 ....242 E2
Harbour View Cl 1
TQ5 ....230 C5
Harbour View Rd
PL5 ....247 E8
HARCOMBE
Chudleigh 124 A8
Sidford 101 D1
HARCOMBE
BOTTOM 104 D6
Harcombe Cross
Raymond's Hill EX13 .104 C6
Sidbury EX10 ....101 C1
Harcombe Fields
EX10 ....188 D8
Harcombe La EX10 ...188 D8
Harcombe Lane E
EX10 ....188 E8
Harcombe Rd
Raymond's Hill DT7 .104 D6
Uplyme DT7 ....260 D8
Hardaway Head 7
EX32 ....155 A5
Harden Ho TQ3 ......225 E7
Harding Cres EX16 ..161 E5
Harding Ct TQ11 ....236 B5
Hardings Cl PL12 ...242 E3
HARDISWORTHY 37 A7
Hardisworthy Cross
EX39 ....37 B7
Hardway Rd TA22 ......21 D2
Hardwick Farm PL7 ..250 C3
Hardy Cl
Exeter EX2 ....182 C8
Torquay TQ1 ....220 C2
Hardy Cres PL5 .....244 E1
Hardy Rd EX2 ....178 D5
Hardys Ct EX10 .....186 D4
Harebell Cl PL12 ...242 D4
Harebell Copse EX4 .176 D8
Harebell Dr EX15 ...162 E5
Haredon Cross PL21 .137 D6
Harefield Cl EX4 ...177 A8
Harefield Cotts EX8 .195 D5
Harefield Dr
Lympstone EX8 ......195 F5
Stoke Fleming TQ6 ..146 B7
Harefield Rd EX8 ...195 F6
Harefoot Cross TQ13 .121 D3
Hare La EX4 ....98 D4
Harepath Hill EX12 ..192 A8
Harepath Ind Est
EX12 ....192 A8
Harepath Rd EX12 ...192 A7
Harepathstead Rd EX5 .83 B1
Harepie Cross EX31 ..27 D6
Hares Cl TQ13 ......111 A6
Haresdown Cross
EX36 ....47 C7
Hares Gn EX36 ......158 C4
Hares La TQ13 ......130 F4
Hareston Cl PL7 ....251 B3
Hareston Cross PL8 ..257 D8
Harestone Cross EX13 .88 B7
Hare Tor Cl EX20 ...170 E5
HAREWOOD 125 E4
Harewood TQ11 .....236 B5
Harewood Cl PL7 ...250 E5
Harewood Cres PL5 ..244 B2
Harewood Rd PL18 ..125 D3
HARFORD
Cornwood 133 F2
Tedburn St Mary 97 F7
Harford Cross EX32 ..17 C2
Harford La EX6, EX17 ..97 F7
Harford Rd
Ivybridge PL21 .....237 D6
Landkey EX32 ....17 B2
Harford Way 14 EX32 ..17 B2
Hargood Terr 6 PL2 .247 F4
Hargreaves Cl PL5 ..243 F2
Harker La EX6 ......114 B2
Harlech Cl PL3 .....249 A7
Harlequins Sh Ctr
EX4 ....261 A3
HARLESTON 145 A4
Harleston Cross TQ7 .144 F4
Harley Ct PL21 .....237 D5
Harlington Ct TQ12 .207 C4
Harlseywood EX39 ...156 E2
Harlyn Drive PL2 ...248 D8
Harman Wlk EX32 ....155 C5
Harnorlen Rd PL2 ...248 D7
Harold Cl EX11 .....169 B3
Haroldsleigh Ave
PL5 ....244 E2
Harper's Hill
Northlew EX20 ....74 E2
Totnes TQ9 ....223 A5
HARPFORD 100 C1
Harpins Ct TQ12 ....213 A6
Harpitt Cl EX15 ....162 C3
Harp La EX5 ....99 E2
Harp's Corner Cross
EX36 ....46 C6
Harpson Hill EX36 ....31 F1
Harpson La
Bishops Nympton
EX36 ....31 F1
South Molton EX36 ....46 F8
Harracott Cross EX31 .27 E6
Harraton Cross PL21 .137 D1
Harrier Pl TQ12 ....207 A5
Harriers Cl EX12 ...192 A6
Harrier Way EX2 ....178 E4
Harriet Gdns PL7 ...250 B6
Harringcourt Rd EX4 .174 E2
Harrington Dr EX4 ..174 E2
Harrington Gdns EX4 .174 E1
Harrington La EX4 ..174 D2
Harris Cl EX16 ....51 A4
Harris Cotts
Blackawton TQ9 .....139 E1
Ivybridge PL21 .....237 C5
Harris Cross EX39 ....38 D8
Harris Ct PL9 ......255 B6
Harrison St 7 PL2 ..247 F4
Harrisons Way EX5 ..173 F8
Harris Pl EX1 ......174 F3
Harris Way PL21 ....136 B6
HARROWBARROW 125 A4
Harrowbarrow Sch
PL17 ....125 A4
Harrowbeer La PL20 .126 F3
Harrowby Cl EX16 ...161 F4
Harston Rd PL21 ....237 A5
HARTFORD 34 C8
Hartford Rd TA4 ......34 B8
HARTLAND 22 E3
Hartland Abbey & Gdns*
EX39 ....22 C3
Hartland Cl PL6 ....245 A7
Hartland Cross EX17 ..79 C4
Hartland Prim Sch
EX39 ....22 E3
Hartland Quay Mus*
EX39 ....22 A3
Hartland Tor Cl TQ5 .230 A2
Hartland View Rd EX34 .8 C6
HARTLEY 248 E7
Hartley Ave PL3 ....249 A6
Hartley Ct PL3 .....249 A6
Hartley Park Gdns
PL3 ....248 F6
Hartley Rd
Exmouth EX8 ....202 A6
Paignton TQ4 ....226 A5
Plymouth PL3 ......248 E6
Hartleys The EX8 ...202 A6
HARTLEY VALE 249 A8
Hart Manor EX33 ....152 E3
Hartnoll Cross EX16 ..64 E8
Harton Cross EX39 ....22 E3
Harton Way EX39 .....22 E3
Harton Way Ind Pk
EX39 ....22 E3
Hartopp Rd EX8 .....202 A8
Hartop Rd TQ1 .....214 B1
Harts Cl
1 Exeter EX1 ....178 E8
Teignmouth TQ14 ....210 A6
Harts La EX1 ....178 E8
Hart's La EX1 ......178 D8
Hart's Path TA4 ......35 E7
Hart St 9 EX39 .....157 A2
Hart Way
Oareford TA24 ....6 F3
Oareford TA24 ....13 F8
Hartwell Ave PL9 ...256 D7
Harvest Cl
Plymouth TQ12 .....244 C8
4 Roundswell EX31 ..154 A1
Harvest La
Bideford EX39 ......156 D2
Exeter EX3 ....182 D7
Harvey Ave PL4 ....249 B1
Harveys Cl
11 Chudleigh Knighton
TQ13 ....123 C4
Sampford Courtenay
EX20 ....76 F4
Harvey St PL11 .....247 B3
Harveys Walk TQ7 ...143 F7
Harveys Wk 13 TQ7 ..143 E7
Harwell Ct 8 PL1 ...262 B3
Harwell La TQ10 ....135 A3
Harwell St PL1 .....262 B3
Harwood Ave PL5 ....244 C7
Harwood Cl EX8 ....196 D1
Haskins Cross EX14 ..84 C5
Hask La EX6 ....96 D3
Haslam Ct TQ1 .....220 A7
Haslam Rd TQ1 .....220 A7
Hastings St PL1 ...262 B3
Hastings Terr PL1 ..262 B3
Haswell Cl PL6 ....249 A8
HATCH 143 E5
Hatcher Cl EX14 ...166 C3
Hatcher St 10 EX7 ..204 D6
Hatchland Rd
Poltimore EX4 ......174 F6
Poltimore EX4 ......175 A6
Hatchmoor Common La
EX38 ....159 F6
Hatchmoor Est EX38 .159 E5
Hatchmoor Ind Est
EX20 ....75 B6
Hatchmoor Lane Ind Est
EX38 ....159 F6
Hatchmoor Rd EX38 ..159 F5
Hatfield TQ1 ......220 B6
Hatfield Rd TQ1 ...220 B6
Hatherdown Hill
TQ13 ....123 B6
HATHERLEIGH 75 C6
Hatherleigh Com Prim
Sch EX20 ....75 C7
Hatherleigh La TQ13 .122 D7
Hatherleigh Rd
Exeter EX2 ....177 A2
Okehampton EX20 .....93 F7
Winkleigh EX19 ....58 E2
Hatherton La EX20 ....76 E2
Hat La PL10 ....252 F2
Hatris La EX32 ....18 D2
Hatshill Cl PL6 ....132 A2
Hatshill Farm Cl PL6 .132 A5
Hatswell Rd EX2 ...181 E7
Hatway Hill EX10 ...101 C3
Hauley Rd TQ6 .....233 F3
Havelock Rd TQ1 ...214 B1
Havelock Terr
Lutton PL21 ....133 B2
Plymouth PL2 ......247 F3
Haven Banks EX2 ...261 B1
Haven Banks Ret Pk
EX1 ....261 A1
Haven Cl EX2 ......261 A1
Haven Ct 5 EX12 ...192 B4
Haven Rd EX2 .....261 A1
Haven The TQ14 ...208 F7
Havenview Rd EX12 .192 A5
Have's Hill EX17 .....61 C8
Hawarden Cotts PL4 .249 B1
Hawcombe La EX33 .....8 E1
Haweswater Cl PL6 .244 E4
Hawk Ave TQ12 .....207 A5
HAWKCHURCH 88 E3
Hawkchurch CE Prim Sch
EX13 ....88 E3
Hawkchurch Cross
EX13 ....88 E2
Hawkchurch Rd EX13 ..88 E3
Hawkerland Rd EX10 .186 C4
Hawkers Ave PL4 ...263 A2
Hawkers Dr EX23 ......37 A1
Hawkers La PL3 ....248 E5
Hawkesdown Cl
EX12 ....192 D7
Hawkinge Gdns PL5 ..243 E4
Hawkins Ave TQ2 ...219 C7
Hawkins Cl PL6 ....245 A5
Hawkins La EX11 ...168 E3
Hawkin's La TA4 .....35 E7
Hawkins Pl EX15 ...163 C4
Hawkins Rd
Exeter EX1 ....174 F3
Newton Abbot TQ12 .207 F3
West Clyst EX4 ....175 A4
Hawkins Way EX17 ..165 E5
Hawkins Wlk EX20 ..170 D5
Hawkmoor Cl PL7 ...250 D5
Hawkmoor Cotts
TQ13 ....122 E7
Hawkmoor Hill EX13,
DT6 ....88 H2
Hawkmoor Pk TQ13 ..122 E7
HAWKRIDGE 21 D1
Hawkridge Cross
Hawkridge TA22 ......21 D1
Umberleigh EX37 .....28 C4
Hawkridge Loop Rd
TA22 ....21 D2
Hawkridge Rd EX31 ...15 E5
Hawksdown View
EX12 ....192 A7
Hawks Dr 8 EX16 ...161 E6
Hawks Pk PL12 .....242 C2
Hawks Way EX32 ......17 F4
Hawkweed Cl TQ12 ..206 D5
Hawkwell Cross EX16 .32 F4
Hawkwell La
Brushford TA22 ....33 A4
East Anstey EX36 .....32 F4
Hawley Cl EX32 ....155 C5
Hawley Cross EX13 ....86 F3
Hawley Manor EX32 ..155 C5
Hawson Cross TQ11 ..130 B3
Hawthorn Ave
Ilfracombe EX34 ....150 D5
Torpoint PL11 .....246 F3
Hawthorn Cl
Cullompton EX15 ...163 B2
Honiton EX14 ......166 B5
Kingsbridge TQ7 ...258 C4
Plymouth, Hooe PL9 .255 C5
Plymouth, Woolwell
PL6 ....245 D7
Hawthorn Dr
Sidmouth EX10 .....187 F8
Wembury PL9 ....140 D7
Hawthorne Cl
Newton Abbot TQ12 .212 F8
West Hill EX11 ....168 D4
Hawthorne Rd
10 Tiverton EX16 ...161 F6
Wellington TA21 ...160 F5
Hawthorn Gr
Exmouth EX8 ....196 E1
Plymouth PL2 ......248 C7
Hawthorn Park Cl
TQ2 ....219 D3
Hawthorn Park Rd
PL9 ....140 D7
Hawthorn Pk
Bideford EX39 .....156 E1
Lydford EX20 ......107 F4
Hawthorn Rd
Barnstaple EX32 ...155 E4
Crediton EX17 .....165 C5
Exeter EX2 ....177 F3
Tavistock PL19 ....171 C2
Hawthorns PL12 ....242 D2
Hawthorn Way
Exeter EX2 ....181 A8
Ivybridge PL21 ....237 F5
Plymouth PL3 ......249 B7
Haxter Cl PL6 .....241 B1
Haxter Wood Chase
PL6 ....241 B2
Haxton Down La EX31 .18 B8
Haxton La EX31 ......18 A8
Haycock La TQ5 ....230 E5
Haycroft Ho 3 EX39 .157 A1
Haycroft Mws PL3 ..249 D1
Haycross Hill EX21 ..55 D4
Haydn Cl EX32 .....155 C5
Haydon Cross EX16 ...48 C4
Haydon Gr PL5 .....243 C1
Haydon Rd EX16 ....161 B5
Haydons Pk EX14 ...166 C5
Haye Barton DT7 ...260 C4
Haye Cl DT7 ....260 C4
Haye Gdns DT7 .....260 C4
Haye La
Colyford DT7, EX13 .103 D3
Lyme Regis DT7 ....260 D4
Haye Rd PL7, PL9 ..250 C1
Haye Road S PL9 ...256 C7
Hayes Barton* EX9 ..197 E7
Hayes Barton Ct EX4 .177 A5
Hayes Cl
Budleigh Salterton
EX9 ....198 A2
Otterton EX9 ......198 E7
Totnes TQ9 ....223 E4
Hayes Copse EX32 ....17 B2
Hayes Cross EX21 ....55 E3
Hayes Ct
Lyme Regis DT7 ....260 D3
Paignton TQ4 ......225 F5
Hayes End EX11 ....168 C4
Hayes Gdns TQ4 ....226 A4
Hayes La
Ashreigney EX18 ....58 D8
East Budleigh EX9 ..198 A6
Otterton EX9 ......198 E7
Hayes Pl PL6 ......249 B8
Hayes Rd
Paignton TQ3, TQ4 .226 A5
Plymouth PL9 ......255 C7
Hayes Sch TQ4 .....225 F5
Hayes Square 24 EX5 ..99 A6
Hayes The TQ5 .....229 E5
Hayeswood La EX9 ..198 A6
Hayfield Rd EX20 ....76 C5
Hay La TQ7 ....147 E6
Hayle Ave TQ4 .....229 B8
Hayley Pk TQ12 ....212 F3
Hayman's Cl EX15 ..163 B2
Haymans Gn EX15 ..163 B2
Haymans Orch EX5 ..184 C3
Hayne Barton Cotts
EX15 ....163 E6
Hayne Cl
Exeter EX4 ....178 A7
Tipton St John EX10 .100 D2
Hayne Cross
Ashill EX15 ....66 F5
Bishops Nympton EX36 .31 A4
Cheriton Fitzpaine EX17 .63 A2

Hayne Cross *continued*
Lewtrenchard EX20 106 B5
Lustleigh TQ13 121 F7
Morebath EX16 34 B4
Plymtree EX15 83 F6
Zeal Monachorum EX17 78 B6
Hayne Ct
Bolham EX16 49 C1
Tiverton EX16 161 E7
Hayne Hill EX10 100 D2
Hayne Ho EX16 49 B2
Hayne La
Bolham EX16 49 B2
Butterleigh EX15 64 C2
Honiton EX14 85 C2
Silverton EX5 82 C4
Wilmington EX14 86 D3
Hayne Pk
Barnstaple EX32 155 B4
Tipton St John EX10 100 D2
Haynes La EX6 176 A2
Hayne Town Cross
EX37 44 B8
Hayridge Mws EX14 84 E2
Hayrish Cross EX20 95 B7
Haystone Pl PL1 262 B4
Haytor Ave TQ4 225 F3
Haytor Cl
Plymouth PL5 244 B3
Teignmouth TQ14 209 D8
Haytor Ct TQ13 122 A4
Haytor Dr
Exeter EX4 176 E7
Ivybridge PL21 237 D4
Newton Abbot TQ12 208 A3
Haytor Gr TQ12 208 A3
Haytor Pk TQ12 207 E7
Haytor Rd
Bovey Tracey TQ13 122 C5
Torquay TQ1 220 B7
Haytor Rocks★ TQ13 121 F3
Haytor Terr 17 TQ12 207 B3
Haytor Vale TQ13 122 B4
Haytor View
Chudleigh Knighton
TQ12 123 C5
Heathfield TQ12 123 B3
Haytor View Com Prim Sch TQ12 207 F3
HAYTOWN 39 E1
Haytown Pottery★
EX22 39 E1
Haywain Cl TQ2 213 B1
Haywards Prim Sch 5
EX17 165 D5
Hay Webb Cl EX1 174 F3
Hazel Ave
Braunton EX33 15 D8
Braunton EX33 152 E7
Hazel Cl
Kingsbridge TQ7 258 C4
Newton Abbot TQ12 208 A1
Newton Poppleford
EX10 186 F8
Plymouth PL6 245 B6
Seaton EX12 192 A7
Teignmouth TQ14 210 C8
Hazel-Crest TQ13 123 B7
Hazeldene TQ8 259 C3
Hazeldene Cl PL21 136 B6
Hazeldene Gdns
Exmouth EX8 196 A1
Plymouth PL9 256 C8
Hazeldown Rd TQ14 210 B7
Hazeldown Sch TQ14 210 B8
Hazel Dr PL9 256 C7
Hazel Gr
4 Barnstaple EX31 154 C2
Plymouth PL9 256 C7
Rockbeare EX5 99 C5
Yelverton PL20 127 A3
Hazel La PL21 237 F5
Hazelmead Rd EX5 179 E2
Hazel Mws EX36 158 D5
Hazel Rd
Exeter EX2 177 F2
Tavistock PL19 171 C2
Hazelwood 6 TQ1 220 D5
Hazelwood Cl EX14 166 C4
Hazelwood Cres PL9 256 D7
Hazelwood Dr
Dawlish Warren EX7 201 A2
Plymouth PL6 245 D8
Hazelwood Pk EX7 201 B2
Headborough Rd
TQ13 130 F5
Headgate EX36 20 B1
Head Hill EX18, EX37 44 C5
Headingley Cl EX2 178 C4
Headland Cl EX1 178 C7
Headland Cres EX1 178 C7
Headland Cross EX17 96 A6
Headland Ct
8 Brixham TQ5 230 D5
Woolacombe EX34 7 F8
Headland Gr TQ3 219 C1
Headland La EX17 96 A5
Headland Park Rd
TQ3 219 C1
Headland Pk PL4 263 A4
Headland Rd TQ2 219 E2
Headlands The TQ2 219 E2
Headlands View Ave
EX34 1 B1
Headless Cross TQ13 112 B6
HEADON 72 C5
Headon Cross EX22 72 C5
Headon Gdns EX2 178 A1
Headson Cross EX20 91 E1
Headstock Rd TA20 88 E7
Headway Cl TQ14 209 D7
Headway Cross Rd
TQ14 209 D8
Headway Rise TQ14 209 D8
Head Weir Rd EX15 163 C5
HEALE 4 A3
Heale Down La EX31 4 A3
Heal Park Cres EX31 153 D5
Heal's Field EX13 167 F7
Healy Ct 9 PL2 247 F4
Healy Pl PL2 247 F4
Heanton Cl EX33 152 E6
Heanton Ct TQ1 220 C4
Heanton Hill EX33 152 F4
Heanton Hill La EX31 15 E6
Heanton Lea EX31 15 E6
HEANTON PUNCHARDON 15 E6
Heanton St EX33 152 D5
Heanton Terr PL10 252 E6
Heard Ave EX8 202 E8
Heard Cl EX39 22 E3
Hearl Rd PL12 242 B3
Hearson Cross EX32 28 B8
Heasley Cross EX36 19 C3
Heasley La EX36 19 D3
HEASLEY MILL 19 D3
Heasley Mill Cross
EX36 19 D3
HEATH 175 D6
Heathayne Cross
EX24 102 F5
Heathbrook Mews
EX4 174 C2
Heath Cl
Heathfield TQ12 123 B2
15 Honiton EX14 85 C2
Heathcoat Prim Sch
EX16 161 B3
Heathcoat Sq EX16 161 C4
Heathcoat Way EX16 161 F5
Heath Comm EX13 87 E6
Heath Cross
Cheriton Fitzpaine
EX16 63 A5
Spreyton EX17 96 A8
Tedburn St Mary EX4 98 C5
Heath Ct
Brixham TQ5 230 E6
1 Totnes TQ9 223 C5
Heather Cl
Exeter EX1 178 B6
9 Honiton EX14 85 C2
Newton Abbot TQ12 206 F4
Okehampton EX20 170 B5
Seaton EX12 192 B7
Tavistock PL19 171 D4
Teignmouth TQ14 210 B7
8 Tiverton EX16 161 F6
Heatherdale EX8 202 C6
Heatherdene TQ13 180 C7
Heather Est TQ12 180 F3
Heatherfield EX6 98 C4
Heather Grange
EX11 168 D4
Heather Pk TQ10 135 A3
Heathers The
Okehampton EX20 170 D6
Plymouth PL6 245 D7
Heather Terr PL20 128 A8
Heatherton Park Ho
TA4 52 E8
Heather Way TQ5 230 A4
Heather Wlk PL21 237 D4
HEATHFIELD 180 F2
Heathfield Cl TQ13 180 C5
Heathfield Cross
Axmouth DT7 193 D8
Cornwood PL21 133 B3
Heathfield TQ12 123 B2
Modbury PL21 137 E2
Poltimore EX4 174 C7
Woodbury Salterton
EX5 184 A7
Heathfield Ind Est
TQ12 180 F3
Heathfieldlake Hill
Chudleigh TQ12 123 F7
Chudleigh TQ13 123 F7
Heathfield Mdw
TQ13 180 D5
Heathfield Pk PL20 127 A3
Heathfield Rd
Bideford EX39 157 C1
Cornwood PL21 133 C2
Denbury TQ12 211 A6
Plymouth PL4 249 B3
Heathfield Terr
Bovey Tracey TQ13 180 C6
Denbury TQ12 211 A6
Heath Hill TQ12 123 B2
Heath La
Cheriton Fitzpaine
EX16 63 A6
Hollocombe EX19 58 F5
Tedburn St Mary EX4,
EX6 98 C4
Heathlands Ct TQ14 210 A8
Heathlands Rise
TQ14 210 A8
Heathland View EX38 40 D1
Heathpark Ind Est
EX14 166 A5
Heathpark Way 13
EX14 85 C2
Heath Pk
Brixham TQ5 230 E5
Newton Abbot TQ12 208 A1
Heath Rd
Brixham TQ5 230 E5
Dunsford EX6 112 F7
Exeter EX2 178 B5
Spreyton EX17 95 F8
Heath Rise TQ5 230 E5
HEATHSTOCK 87 A6
Heath Terr PL18 125 C5
Heatree Cl TQ14 210 B8
Heatree Cross TQ13 121 D7
Heaviside Cl TQ2 214 B3
HEAVITREE 178 B6
Heavitree Gallows
EX1 178 C5
Heavitree Pk EX1 178 A5
Heavitree Rd
Exeter EX1 177 E6
Kingsand PL10 253 A2
Hebditch Cl TQ13 180 E7
Heberton Cl EX5 99 E8
Heckpen View EX15 66 D6
Hectors Cl EX19 57 F7
Heddeswell Cross
TQ7 143 E2
HEDDON 29 B7
Heddon Cross
Heddon EX32 29 A7
Milton Damerel EX22 54 C5
Hederman Cl EX5 82 B5
Hedge Cross EX20 107 C4
Hedge Field Cl EX14 85 C2
Hedgend Rd EX14 86 B5
Hedgerow Cl
Crediton EX17 165 E6
Plymouth PL6 245 E8
Hedgerows The PL12 242 B3
Hedingham Cl PL7 251 C4
Hedingham Gdns
PL6 245 B7
Heggadon Cl EX5 83 A7
Heiffers La EX16 47 A5
Heights The PL19 171 A6
Heirland Cross TQ7 143 D3
HELE
Bradninch 82 F5
Ilfracombe 150 F6
Torquay 219 F8
Hele Almshouses
PL9 140 E8
Hele Barton Cross
EX17 61 D6
Helebridge Rd EX23 70 A6
Hele Cl
Barnstaple EX31 154 A3
Bickleigh PL6 132 A5
Torquay TQ2 213 F1
Hele Corn Mill★
EX34 150 E5
Hele Cross
Ashburton TQ13 130 E5
Bradworthy EX22 38 E4
Cornwood PL21 133 D4
King's Nympton EX37 44 D7
St Giles on t H PL15 90 B3
Torquay TQ2 213 F1
Hele Gdns PL7 251 A4
Hele Hill EX17 61 C5
Hele La
Barnstaple EX31 154 A3
Bickington EX31 154 A3
Frithelstock Stone EX38 40 F5
Roborough PL6 241 F2
Shaugh Prior PL6, PL7 132 A6
Hele Lane Hill EX17 61 D6
Hele Manor La EX16 33 E3
Helena Pl 7 EX8 202 A6
Helens Mead Cl TQ2 214 A4
Helens Mead Rd TQ2 214 A4
Hele Park TQ12 206 C5
Hele Rd
Bradninch EX5 82 F6
Exeter EX4 261 A4
Kingsteignton TQ12 123 E1
Torquay TQ2 213 F1
Torquay TQ2 219 E8
Hele Rise EX31 154 A3
Hele Sq EX5 82 F5
Hele's Sch PL7 250 C6
Hele's Terr PL4 249 B2
Helford Dr TQ4 229 B8
Helford Wlk TQ4 229 B8
Heligan Dr TQ3 225 E8
Hellevoetsluis Way
TQ3 218 F4
Hellier Cl EX14 166 A4
Hellinghayes La EX16 46 C3
Hellings Gdns EX5 175 C7
Hellings Parks La
EX5 175 E4
Helmdon Rise TQ2 219 B8
Helmers Way TQ7 145 A1
Helston Cl TQ3 225 F7
HELTOR 112 D6
Heltor Bsns Pk TQ12 180 F4
Hembury Cock Hill
TQ11 236 A7
Hembury Cotts TQ9 131 E1
Hembury Cross
Holbeton PL8 141 F8
Stibb Cross EX38 40 C4
Hembury Fort★ EX14 84 F6
Hembury Fort Cross
EX14 84 E5
Hembury Pk TQ11 236 B7
HEMERDON 251 D7
Hemerdon Hts PL7 251 A6
Hemerdon La PL7 251 C8
Hemerdon Way PL7 250 D6
Hems Brook Ct TQ2 219 B8
HEMSFORD 216 F4
Hems La TQ9 216 D7
Hemsworthy Gate
TQ13 121 E3
HEMYOCK 67 C8
Hemyock Castle★
EX15 67 B8
Hemyock Prim Sch
EX15 67 B8
Hemyock Rd EX15 66 E8
Henacre Rd TQ7 258 D5
Henacroft Cross EX19 58 B3
Henbury Cl TQ1 220 B6
Henceford Cross EX17 62 A6
Henderbarrow Cross
EX21 73 E1
Henders Cnr 6 PL3 248 F6
Henderson Pl PL2 247 F6
Hendon Cross EX16 50 B8
Hendwell Cl PL6 244 E6
Heneaton Sq EX2 182 B8
HENFORD 90 C5
Henlake Cl PL21 237 B6
Henley Cl EX13 88 B7
Henley Dr PL5 244 C7
Henley Ho TQ7 143 A1
Henley Rd EX8 202 C7
Hennapyn Rd TQ2 219 E3
HENNOCK 123 B7
Hennock Com Prim Sch
TQ13 123 B7
Hennock Ct EX2 181 D8
Hennock Rd TQ4 225 F2
Hennock Rd Central
EX2 177 C1
Hennock Road E EX2 177 D1
Hennock Road N
EX2 177 C2
Henrietta Pl 7 EX8 202 A7
Henrietta Rd 8 EX8 202 A7
Henry Avent Gdns
PL9 256 C8
Henry Cl PL21 136 B6
Henry Gdns EX11 169 C3
Henry Lewis Cl 7 EX5 99 E8
Henry's Run 9 EX5 99 A6
Henry's Way DT7 260 E4
Hensbury La PL20 239 F4
Hensford Mews EX7 200 C3
Hensford Rd EX7 200 C2
Hensleigh Dr EX2 177 E5
Hensleigh Rd EX16 63 F7
Henson Ct EX20 77 C4
Hensons Dr EX16 51 A3
Hen St EX5 83 A7
Henstill La EX17 79 F7
HENSTRIDGE 3 A1
Henty Ave EX7 204 F7
Henty Cl EX7 204 F8
Heppenstall Rd EX32 155 B6
Heraldry Way EX2 178 D4
Herbert Ho TA22 33 D6
Herbert Pl PL2 247 E4
Herbert Rd
Exeter EX1 177 F7
Salcombe TQ8 259 D4
Torquay TQ2 219 D4
Herbert St PL2 247 E4
Hercules Rd
Plymouth PL9 256 D8
Sherford PL7 250 F1
Herdicott Cross EX22 71 F2
Hereford Cl EX8 196 D4
Hereford Rd
Exeter EX4 176 D6
Plymouth PL5 244 B5
Heritage Cl PL12 242 C3
Heritage Ct 15 EX14 166 C6
Heritage Pk PL19 171 D6
Heritage Rd EX1 178 D6
Heritage Way
Brixham TQ5 230 E5
Sidford EX10 188 B8
Hermes Ave EX16 161 E3
Hermitage Ct 1 PL4 248 E4
Hermitage Rd
Dartmouth TQ6 233 D4
Ilfracombe EX34 150 B6
Plymouth PL3 248 E5
Hermitage The 1
EX34 150 B5
Hermosa Gdns 5
TQ14 210 B5
Hermosa Rd TQ14 210 B5
Hernaford Cross TQ9 139 B6
Hernaford Rd TQ9 139 C6
Hern La PL8 257 F4
Heron Cl PL10 252 F6
Heron Cres EX12 192 C5
Heron Ct
Barnstaple EX32 155 E4
Exmouth EX8 202 C6
Heron Ind Units EX2 178 E5
Heron Rd
Drakewalls PL18 125 C5
Exeter, Middle Moor
EX2 176 D3
Exeter, Sowton EX2 178 E5
Honiton EX14 166 B4
Herons Brook EX20 170 A6
Herons Reach
Charleton TQ7 258 F2
Herons Reach *continued*
West Charleton TQ7 144 C1
Heron Way
Cullompton EX15 163 B2
Kingsteignton TQ12 207 C8
Torquay TQ2 213 C3
Herschel Gdns PL5 243 E1
Herschell Rd EX4 177 E8
Hertland Wlk PL2 248 A7
Hescane Pk EX6 97 B4
Hesketh Cres TQ1 220 D3
Hesketh Mews TQ1 220 D3
Hesketh Rd TQ1 220 D3
Hessary Dr PL6 241 C1
Hessary Terr PL20 128 A8
Hessary View
Princetown PL20 120 B8
Saltash PL12 242 E4
Tavistock PL19 171 B6
Hestow Rd TQ12 123 F1
Hetling Cl PL1 262 B3
Hewer's Row PL4 263 A3
Hewetson Wy EX39 156 D1
Hewett Cl TQ12 208 A3
Hewitt Cl PL12 242 C1
Hexdown Barns TQ7 142 F3
Hexham Pl PL2 248 A8
Hexton Hill Rd PL9 255 B6
Hexton Quay PL9 255 C6
HEXWORTHY 129 B7
Hexworthy Ave EX4 176 E8
Heybrook Ave PL5 243 D1
HEYBROOK BAY 140 B8
Heybrook Dr PL9 140 A7
Heydon's La EX10 188 A4
Heyridge Mdw EX15 163 B1
Heyswood Ave EX32 155 C2
Heywood Cl
Hartland EX39 22 E3
Torquay TQ2 219 E7
Heywood Cross EX18 59 D5
Heywood Dr EX6 201 A8
Heywood Est TQ12 207 D6
Heywood Rd EX39 156 F5
Heywoods Cl 11
TQ14 210 C5
Heywoods Rd TQ14 210 C5
Hibernia Terr PL5 247 E8
Hickory Cl EX14 166 E5
Hickory Dr PL7 251 B5
Hick's La PL4 263 A2
Hide Market Rd
EX15 162 C5
Hides Rd EX10 188 C8
Hidewood La EX15 52 F1
Hiern Dr EX32 155 A2
Hierns La EX34 150 C6
High Acre Dr PL21 237 A6
HIGHAMPTON 74 C7
Highampton Com Prim Sch EX21 74 C7
Highampton Cross
EX21 74 C7
Highaton Head Cross
EX36 32 C4
High Bank
Exeter EX4 178 B8
West Hill EX10 100 A4
West Hill EX11 168 D3
Highbank Cl PL19 171 A4
Highbarrow Cross
EX22 54 A4
HIGH BICKINGTON 43 B7
High Bickington CE Prim Sch EX37 43 B7
High Bolham EX16 33 C1
HIGH BRAY 18 F5
High Bray EX32 18 F5
Highbridge Ct PL7 250 E5
HIGH BULLEN 42 B7
High Bullen EX5 82 B6
High Bullen Cross
EX36 19 E1
High Bullen La EX35 5 B3
Highbury Cres PL7 250 D7
Highbury Hill EX39 157 A8
Highbury Pk EX8 196 A1
Highbury Rd
Barnstaple EX32 155 C3
Torquay TQ1 220 B6
High Cl TQ13 180 E7
Highclere Gdns PL6 245 B8
Highcliff Ct EX7 204 E6
Highcliffe Cl
Lympstone EX8 195 D4
Seaton EX12 191 F6
Highcliffe Cres EX12 191 F6
Highcliffe Ct EX8 195 D4
Highcliffe Mews TQ4 226 C4
Highcliff Rd DT7 260 C3
Highclyffe Ct EX12 191 F6
Highcombe La PL9 255 C4
High Cott EX36 19 C2
High Creek Cross
EX10 188 F8
Highcroft EX4 173 A1
Highcroft Ct EX4 173 A1
Highcroft Pk TQ12 123 E7
High Cross
Bampton EX16 34 A1
14 Combe Martin EX34 3 A3
High Cross Ho★ TQ9 216 A1
Highcross Rd EX4 177 C8
Highdown Cross
EX39 23 A4
Higher Aboveway
EX6 182 B3
Higher Aller La TQ13 122 E6
Higher Alston Farm
TQ5 229 D3
Higher Anderton Rd
PL10 252 F5
HIGHER ASHTON 113 D3
Higher Audley Ave
Torquay TQ2 219 F8
Torquay TQ2 220 A8
Higher Axmouth Cotts
EX12 192 F6
Higher Barley Mount
EX4 176 E5
HIGHER BATSON 259 C6
Higher Beara Cross
TQ11 236 F4
Higher Bedlands EX9 197 F2
Higher Beetham TA20 69 D7
Higher Bibbery TQ13 180 E7
Higher Birch Dr 1
EX1 178 E3
HIGHER BLAGDON 225 A7
Higher Blagdon La
TQ3 225 A7
Higher Borough TQ7 149 A4
Higher Brand La
EX14 166 C4
Higher Brimley Rd
8 Teignmouth TQ14 209 F8
Teignmouth TQ14 210 C5
HIGHER BRIXHAM 230 B3
Higher Broad Oak Rd
EX11 168 D2
Higher Broad Pk
TQ6 233 D3
Higher Brook Mdw 1
EX10 101 B1
Higher Brook Pk
PL21 237 A5
Higher Brownston Cross
PL21 138 A4
Higher Buckeridge Rd
TQ14 210 B7
Higher Budleigh Mdw
TQ12 206 F3
Higher Bulkamore Cross
TQ10 135 E5
Higher Bull Ring
EX15 163 C3
Higher Bulworthy Cross
EX16 47 E4
Higher Bulworthy La
EX16 47 E4
HIGHER BURROWTON 99 A8
Higher Buzzacott La
EX34 3 B3
Higher Cadewell La
TQ2 219 C8
Higher Cheglinch La
EX34 8 F6
HIGHER CHERITON 84 E3
Higher Church St 6
EX32 155 A4
Higher Churchway
PL9 256 A7
Higher Clevelands
Northam EX39 156 F6
Northam EX39 157 A6
HIGHER CLOVELLY 23 D2
Higher Collaton Cross
TQ7 147 F6
Higher Colleybrook
TQ13 124 B4
Higher Combe La
TA24 21 E8
Higher Combe Rd
TA22 33 C8
Higher Commons
TQ3 214 D8
HIGHER COMPTON 249 A6
Higher Compton Barton
TQ3 218 E6
Higher Compton Rd
PL3 248 F6
Higher Contour Rd
TQ6 234 B3
Higher Coombe Dr
6 Teignmouth TQ14 209 E8
Teignmouth TQ14 210 A7
Higher Coombses
TA20 88 D8
Higher Copythorne
TQ5 230 A4
Higher Cotteylands
EX16 161 B3
Higher Cross EX15 51 C1
Higher Cross Rd
EX31 154 B4
Higher Davis Cl EX32 17 F6
HIGHER DEAN 135 C7
Higher Dean TQ11 135 C7
Higher Dean La EX34 3 B3
Higher Doats Hayne La
EX13 103 D5
Higher Down EX6 194 D3
Higher Down Pk EX14 85 C2
Higher Downs Rd
TQ1 220 C8
Higher Dr EX7 204 F8
Higher East St EX36 30 D8
Higher Edginswell La
TQ2 219 B8
Higher Efford Rd
PL3 249 B5
Higher Elmwood
EX31 154 C3
Higher Elstone Cross
EX18 44 D3

Higher Erith Rd TQ1...220 D4
Higher Exeter Rd TQ14...124 E2
Higher Exwick Hill EX4...176 E7
Higher Ferry Slip TQ6...233 F4
Higher Forches Cross EX17...60 D4
Higher Fortescue EX10...188 D7
Higher French Pk TQ12...206 F3
Higher Furlong Rd EX5...99 C6
Higher Furzeham Rd TQ5...230 C6
HIGHER GABWELL...214 B7
Higher Gn TQ10...135 A2
Higher Green Cross TQ7...145 C4
Higher Greenhead EX10...101 A2
Higher Greenway La
Sidmouth EX10...187 D8
Sidmouth EX10...187 E7
Higher Gunstone EX39...157 A2
Higher Hayes La TQ5 229 F5
Higher Hendham Barns TQ7...138 E1
Higher Hewish La EX31. 9 D4
Higher Hill View EX10...188 A5
Higher Ho EX38...42 B5
Higher Holcombe Cl TQ14...210 C7
Higher Holcombe Dr TQ14...210 C8
Higher Holcombe Rd
Holcombe EX7...204 B3
Teignmouth TQ14...210 C8
Higher Hoopern La EX4...173 C1
Higher Island TQ9...139 E2
HIGHER KEATON...237 D1
Higher Kelly PL18...125 D3
Higher King's Ave EX4...177 D8
Higher Kingsdown Rd TQ14...209 D7
Higher Kinsman's Dale TQ13...111 F5
Higher La
Axmouth EX12...192 E7
Axmouth EX12...193 A6
Plymouth PL1...262 C2
Sampford Courtenay EX20...76 D5
Higher Lane Cl EX12 .192 D7
Higher Ley EX17...60 B3
Higher Lincombe Rd TQ1...220 E3
Higher Longford Cvn Site PL19...117 F1
Higher Loughborough EX16...161 B5
Higher Manor Rd TQ5...230 C5
Higher Manor Terr 1 TQ3...226 A5
Higher Marley Rd EX8...196 D4
Higher Maudlin St 7 EX32...155 A6
Higher Maunders Hill
Otterton EX9...198 E5
Otterton EX9...198 E7
Higher Mdw EX5...99 A5
Higher Mdws
Beer EX12...191 D5
High Bickington EX37...43 B7
Higher Mead EX15...67 B8
HIGHER METCOMBE...168 D1
Higher Mill DT7...260 D4
Higher Mill Flats DT7...260 D4
Higher Millhayes EX15 52 B1
Higher Mill La
Buckfast TQ11...236 B7
Cullompton EX15...163 C3
Higher Mogworthy Cross EX16...47 D4
Higher Moor TQ10...135 B1
Highermoor Cross EX22...53 B1
Higher Moor Sq 4 EX16...161 F6
Higher Mowles PL3..249 B6
HIGHER MUDDIFORD..9 D1
Higher Newclose La EX31...16 B6
Higher Park Cl PL7...251 B3
Higher Park Rd EX33 152 E5
Higher Penn TQ5...230 D3
Higher Pk TQ7...149 A3
Higher Polsham Rd TQ3...226 B7
Higher Port View PL12...242 F2
HIGHER PRESTACOTT...90 F7
Higher Preston Cross TQ12...123 D1
Higher Queens Terr TQ1...220 B5
Higher Rake La TQ7..143 F6
Higher Raleigh Rd EX31...155 A7
Higher Ramshill La TQ3...225 C8
Higher Ranscombe Rd TQ5...230 D4
Higher Rd
Crediton EX17...165 B6
Fremington EX31...153 E5
Woodbury Salterton EX5...184 B7
Higher Redgate EX16...161 D5
Higher Ridgeway EX11...169 E4
Higher Ringmore Rd TQ14...209 D4
Higher Roborough 8 TQ13...131 A5
Higher Rocombe TQ3...214 B5
HIGHER ROSCOMBE BARTON...214 A6
Higher Row PL10...253 A2
Higher Rydons TQ5..230 A4
Higher Sackery TQ12 208 D4
Higher Shapter Cl EX3...182 F4
Higher Shapter St EX3...182 F4
Higher Shippon EX6...97 B4
HIGHER SLADE...1 E3
Higher Slade Rd EX34...150 A2
Higher Spring Gdns EX11...169 E3
Higher St
Brixham TQ5...230 C5
Cullompton EX15...163 C4
Dartmouth TQ6...233 F3
Dittisham TQ6...228 B2
Hatherleigh EX20...75 C7
Kingswear TQ6...234 A3
Higher Stert Terr PL4...263 C3
Higher Stockley Mead EX20...170 F6
Higher Summerlands EX1...261 C3
HIGHER TALE...84 A4
Higher Tamar Terr PL18...125 D7
Higher Thorn Cl EX33...152 D5
HIGHER TOWN...236 A5
Higher Town
Malborough TQ7...147 E6
Sampford Peverell EX16 50 C1
Higher Tuckers Pk EX22...38 E1
Higher Union La TQ2 220 A5
Higher Union Rd TQ7...258 C5
Higher Venn Cross EX32...17 A1
Higher Warberry Rd TQ1...220 D5
Higher Warborough Rd TQ5...229 B6
HIGHER WARCOMBE...1 B2
Higher Warcombe Cross TQ7...144 A5
Higher Warren Rd TQ7...258 E3
Higher Way EX10...187 A8
HIGHER WEAR...178 A1
Higher Wear Rd EX2 .182 C7
Higher Weaver Cross EX15...83 E7
Higher Weir TQ9...223 B7
Higher Wellbrook St EX16...161 B4
Higher Well Rd TQ9..228 A8
Higher Westlake Rd
4 Barnstaple EX31...154 A2
Barnstaple EX31...154 B2
Higher Westonfields TQ9...223 E5
Higher Wlk PL10...253 E5
Higher Woodfield Rd TQ1...220 D3
Higher Woodford La PL7...250 C7
Higher Woodway Cl TQ14...210 C7
Higher Woodway Rd TQ14...210 B8
HIGHER WOOLBROOK...187 F7
Higher Woolbrook Pk EX10...187 F7
HIGHER YALBERTON...225 C3
Higher Yalberton Rd TQ4...225 D3
Higher Yannon Dr TQ14...210 A6
Highfield
Honiton EX14...166 B5
Lapford EX17...60 D3
Northam EX39...156 F6
Sidmouth EX10...188 A5
Topsham EX3...182 F7
Highfield Cl
Barnstaple EX32...155 B4
Brixham TQ5...230 A4
High Bickington EX37...43 B7
Plymouth PL3...249 C5
Highfield Cres TQ3...225 E6
Highfield Ct 3 EX8..202 B6
Highfield Dr
Kingsbridge TQ7...258 D4
2 Wembury PL9...140 D8
Highfield Gdns EX34...3 A3
Highfield La EX8...202 B6
Highfield Pk PL12...242 B3
Highfield Rd
Dunkeswell EX14...67 C1
Ilfracombe EX34...150 C5
Highfield Terr
Beer EX12...191 D5
2 Bishop's Tawton EX32...16 E1
4 Bittaford PL21...137 C7
8 Ilfracombe EX34...150 C5
Highfield View TQ12 .244 C8
High Gate EX16...62 F6
Highglen Dr PL7...251 B7
Highgow Cl EX31...154 A2
Highgrove EX31...154 D1
Highgrove Pk TQ14..210 C7
High House Cl EX7...204 E7
High House La
Kingsbridge TQ7...144 B2
Kingsbridge TQ7...258 D4
Highland Cl TQ2...219 C6
Highland Pk EX15...66 A7
Highland Rd TQ2...219 C5
Highlands
Ottery St Mary EX11...169 D3
Wembury PL9...256 B3
Yealmpton PL8...257 F4
Highlands Pk 9 TQ13...123 E6
Highland St PL21...237 D5
Highland Terr
6 Tiverton EX16...161 D4
Uffculme EX15...66 A7
Highland View EX20..170 C3
High Mdw EX10...188 B7
High Mdws EX4...176 E5
High Park Cl EX39...25 D4
High Path TA21...160 C7
High Rd PL9...140 C8
Highridge Cross EX37 . 45 B7
High School for Girls PL4...263 A4
High St
Bampton EX16...34 B1
Barnstaple EX31...154 F5
Bideford EX39...157 A2
Budleigh Salterton EX9...199 G2
Chagford TQ13...111 A6
Clovelly EX39...23 D3
Combe Martin EX34...3 A3
Crediton EX17...165 C5
Cullompton EX15...163 C3
Dawlish EX7...204 E6
Dulverton TA22...33 D6
East Budleigh EX9...198 B6
Exbourne EX20...76 C4
Exeter EX4...261 B3
Exmouth EX8...202 A6
Great Torrington EX38 .159 D5
Halberton EX16...65 A7
Hatherleigh EX20...75 C7
Hemyock EX15...67 B8
High Bickington EX37...43 B7
4 Holsworthy EX22...164 C4
Honiton EX14...166 C6
Ide EX2...114 B8
Ide EX2...176 D1
Ilfracombe EX34...150 B6
Kentisbeare EX15...66 A3
Kenton EX6...194 D3
Newton Poppleford EX10...186 E8
North Tawton EX20...77 C4
Okehampton EX20...170 B5
Plymouth, Stonehouse PL1...248 A2
Sidford EX10...188 B8
Sidmouth EX10...188 B4
Silverton EX5...82 B6
Stoke Canon EX5...81 F1
Stoke Canon EX5...173 F8
Swimbridge EX32...28 E8
Topsham EX3...182 E6
Totnes TQ9...223 C5
Uffculme EX15...66 A7
Wellington TA21...160 E6
Winkleigh EX19...58 F3
Highstead Cross EX22 73 C8
Highstone Gr EX8...195 F5
High Street Prim Sch PL1...248 A2
High Street & Waterloo Street Flats PL1...248 A1
High Trees EX7...204 E7
High View
Bideford EX39...156 E1
Feniton EX14...84 E2
Sheepwash EX21...56 C1
High View Gdns EX8..202 B7
High View Prim Sch PL3...249 D6
High View Sch PL3...249 C5
High View Terr EX39 .156 C6
High Wall EX31...154 E4
High Way EX16...48 D8
Highwaymans Gr EX20 93 B1
HIGHWEEK...206 F5
Highweek Com Prim Sch TQ12...207 A3
Highweek Cross EX21. 73 E8
Highweek Rd TQ12...207 A4
Highweek St TQ12...207 B3
Highweek Village
Newton Abbot TQ12...206 F5
Newton Abbot TQ12...207 A5
Highweek Way TQ12 .207 B3
Highwell Rd EX12...192 A5
Highwood Grange TQ12...207 B2
Highworthy Cross EX21...55 E3
Hilary Cl EX13...167 E6
Hilary Gdns EX13...167 E6
Hill Barton Bsns Pk
Clyst St Mary EX5...179 F2
Exeter EX5...99 A1
Hill Barton Cl EX1...178 C7
Hill Barton La EX1...178 C7
Hill Barton Rd EX2...178 C7
Hillbrook Rd TQ9...223 E5
Hillbrook Rise 2 TQ9...223 E5
Hill Budge Terr 8 EX17...165 C5
Hill Cl
Exeter EX4...173 D1
Plymouth PL7...250 D4
Hillcliffe Terr 30 EX39 15 A1
Hill Cres EX14...166 D6
Hillcrest
Cullompton EX15...163 C4
Ilsington TQ13...122 C3
Oakford EX16...48 D5
Ottery St Mary EX11...169 D3
Hill Crest
Exminster EX6...182 A4
Kilmington EX13...87 C1
Plymouth PL3...248 E5
South Tawton EX20...95 B5
Tiverton EX16...161 D5
Hillcrest Cl
Plymouth PL7...251 A5
9 Wembury PL9...140 D8
Hillcrest Dr PL7...251 A4
Hillcrest Gdns EX8...196 E1
Hillcrest Pk EX4...173 C2
Hillcrest Rd
Barnstaple EX32...155 B2
Bideford EX39...26 A4
Silverton EX5...82 C6
Hillcroft Terr 5 EX39...157 A2
Hill Cross
Cobbaton EX32...28 B5
Kingsbridge TQ7...144 B5
Hilldale Rd PL9...255 E6
Hilldean Cl PL5...244 C7
Hilldown TQ9...223 E5
Hilldown Cross EX17..78 D2
Hilldown La EX17...78 D2
Hilldown Rd EX17...78 C3
Hill Dr EX8...196 B3
Hilldrop Terr TQ1...220 B5
Hiller La TQ12...208 B2
HILLERTON...78 C1
Hillerton Cross EX17 . 78 B1
Hillesdon Rd TQ1...220 B4
HILLFIELD...232 C3
Hillfield
South Zeal EX20...95 A4
Stoke Gabriel TQ9...227 F7
Hill Garden Cl 10 EX39...157 A2
Hill Gdns PL12...239 A2
HILLHEAD...234 F8
Hillhead
Colyton EX24...103 A4
Halberton EX16...65 A7
Noss Mayo PL8...140 F6
Hill Head EX37...28 F4
Hillhead Bglws 13 EX24...103 A4
Hillhead Cross PL21..137 D7
Hill Head Cross
Chittlehampton EX37...28 F4
King's Nympton EX37...44 C5
Hillhead Pk TQ5...234 E8
Hillhead Terr EX13...167 D5
Hillhouse EX14...69 A3
Hilliers EX19...57 F7
Hillingdown Cross TQ7...143 D1
Hillington EX34...150 A4
Hill La
Chipstable TA4...35 C6
Exeter EX1...178 B7
Plymouth PL3...248 F7
Waterrow TA4...35 E5
Whitestone EX4...98 E4
Hillmans Rd TQ12...207 D2
HILLMOOR...66 E8
Hillmoor Cross EX21...73 F7
Hillmorhayes EX6...96 D1
Hillpark EX39...40 C7
Hill Park Cl TQ5...230 E4
Hill Park Cres PL4...263 A4
Hill Park Mews PL4..263 B4
Hill Park Rd
Brixham TQ5...230 E4
Newton Abbot TQ12...206 F4
Torquay TQ1...220 A7
Hill Park Terr TQ4...226 C5
Hill Path PL5...243 F5
Hill Pk
Ashprington TQ9...139 F8
Kellaton TQ7...149 C6
Hill Rd
Bondleigh EX20...77 C7
Hill Rd *continued*
Lyme Regis DT7...260 D3
Newton Abbot TQ12...207 B2
Hillrise TQ5...229 B5
Hill Rise EX1...178 C7
Hillrise (Patha) TQ5..229 B5
Hill Rise Rd DT7...260 D3
Hillsborough
2 Plymouth PL4...248 F4
Torquay TQ1...220 B4
Hillsborough Ave EX4...261 B4
Hillsborough Cross EX22...71 C7
Hillsborough Nature Reserve* EX34...150 E6
Hillsborough Park Rd EX34...150 E5
Hillsborough Rd
Ilfracombe EX34...2 A4
Ilfracombe EX34...150 D5
Hillsborough Terr 15 EX34...150 C6
Hillsborough Terr Mews
16 EX34...150 C6
Hillsdunne Rd PL3...248 E6
HILLSIDE...135 A3
Hillside
Bittaford PL21...137 C8
Branscombe EX12...190 B5
14 Colyton EX24...103 A4
George Nympton EX36..30 A2
Honiton EX14...85 E5
Newton Poppleford EX10...186 D8
Northleigh EX24...102 B6
Payhembury EX14...84 C4
Rawridge EX14...68 C1
Sidbury EX10...101 B2
South Brent TQ10...135 A3
Southleigh EX24...102 C4
Talaton EX5...84 B1
Hill Side PL7...133 B2
Hillside Ave
Exeter EX4...261 B4
Plymouth PL4...248 D4
Saltash PL12...242 F3
Hillside Cl
Buckland Monachorum PL20...126 C3
South Brent TQ10...135 A3
Teignmouth TQ14...124 E1
Hillside Cotts
Abbotskerswell TQ12...212 A6
Noss Mayo PL8...140 F6
Hillside Cres PL9...255 F8
Hillside Cross EX21...72 F4
Hill Side Cross EX36...45 F5
Hillside Ct TQ11...236 C5
Hillside Dr
Kingsbridge TQ7...258 D4
Okehampton EX20...170 E6
Yealmpton PL8...257 F3
Hillside Ind Units EX32...155 F1
Hillside Pk TQ4...224 F5
Hillside Rd
Brixham TQ5...230 C4
Ilfracombe EX34...150 E5
Paignton TQ3...225 F7
Saltash PL12...242 E3
Sidmouth EX10...188 C4
Hillside Terr
4 Bideford EX39...157 A2
Kingswear TQ6...234 A3
2 Paignton TQ3...226 A6
Hillside Way PL8...136 A2
Hill's La EX14...86 C5
Hill St PL4...263 A3
Hills The EX10...188 B5
Hills View
Barnstaple EX32...155 A5
Braunton EX33...152 D6
Hill The EX13...87 C1
Hilltop TQ7...142 F6
Hill Top EX31...153 E6
Hilltop Cotts
Brixton PL8...257 A5
Combe PL8...256 F5
Fremington EX31...153 E5
Hill Top Crest PL5...243 E2
Hilltop Mdw TQ12...207 B2
Hilltop Rd EX39...156 E4
Hilltown Cross
Chittlehampton EX37...29 B2
Okehampton EX20...93 E5
Rackenford EX16...47 D2
Hilltown Hill EX36...31 C5
Hilltown La
Chawleigh EX18...59 F5
Northlew EX20...74 E2
Hill View
Buckland Monachorum PL20...126 C3
Ottery St Mary EX11...169 D3
Sidmouth EX10...188 B5
Hill View Terr 4 TQ1...220 A7
Hillway La
Newton Poppleford EX10...187 A7
Newton Poppleford EX10...187 B6
Hillyfield Rd EX1...178 C7
Hilly Gardens Rd TQ1...214 B1
Hilly Head TA21...160 B5
Hillymead EX12...192 B6
Hilton Ave PL5...244 D1
Hilton Cres TQ3...219 C1
Hilton Dr TQ3...219 C1
Hilton Park Homes EX33...152 C5
Hilton Rd
Marhamchurch EX23...70 A6
Monkleigh EX39...40 F7
Newton Abbot TQ12...207 C3
Hil Top Rd 4 EX1...178 E8
Hinam Cross TA22...33 B7
Hindharton La EX39...22 E3
Hind St
Bovey Tracey TQ13...180 D8
Ottery St Mary EX11...169 D3
Hingston Ct PL6...249 A8
Hingston Post TQ9...144 E8
Hingston Rd TQ1...220 C7
Hingston Rise TQ7...142 F5
Hinham La
Dulverton TA22...33 A8
Dulverton TA22...33 B7
Hinton Ct PL6...245 C1
Hirmandale Rd PL5..243 F3
HISCOTT...27 C5
Hitchcocks Bsns Pk EX15...162 F7
HITTISLEIGH...96 D5
Hittisleigh Cross EX6..96 D5
Hittisleigh Mill La EX6 96 D5
Hittsford La EX36...32 A1
Hobart St PL1...262 A2
Hobbacott La
Marhamchurch EX23...70 A6
Marhamchurch EX23...70 B7
Hobbacott Rise EX23..70 A6
Hobbs Cl TA21...160 A3
Hobbs Cres PL12...242 C3
Hobb's Hill EX33...7 E2
Hobbs La EX32...18 E2
Hobbs Way EX17...78 B4
Hobby Dr The EX39...23 E3
Hobby House La EX36 . 30 C1
Hobbymoor Cross EX17...60 A1
Hockey Fields TQ6...146 A7
HOCKHOLLER...52 E8
HOCKHOLLER GREEN. 52 E8
Hockings Gn EX1...178 B6
Hockmoor Head TQ11...130 C2
Hockmoor Hill TQ11..130 C2
Hockmore Dr TQ12...207 F4
HOCKWORTHY...50 D6
Hodder's La DT7...260 C8
Hodders Way PL12...239 A2
Hodge Cl PL12...242 C2
Hodges Wlk EX38...159 E5
Hodson Cl TQ3...225 F7
Hoe App PL1...262 C2
Hoe Ct PL1...262 C2
Hoegate Ct PL1...262 C2
Hoegate Pl PL1...262 C2
Hoegate St PL1...263 A2
Hoe Gdns PL1...262 C2
Hoe Rd PL1...262 C1
Hoe St PL1...262 C2
Hoe The PL1...262 C1
Hofheim Dr EX16...161 A6
Hogarth Cl PL9...256 B6
Hogarth Ho 2 PL19...171 B6
Hogarth Wlk PL9...256 B6
HOGGS PARK...54 A1
Hoile La TQ9...224 E1
Hoker Rd EX2...178 A5
Holbeam Cl TQ12...206 E4
Holbeam La
Bickington TQ12...131 F6
Newton Abbot TQ12...206 A4
HOLBETON...136 D1
Holbeton Sch PL8...136 D1
Holborn Pl PL7...250 E6
Holborn Rd TQ5...230 C6
Holborn St PL4...263 B2
Holbrook Terr TQ7...145 B1
HOLCOMBE
Lyme Regis...104 B4
Teignmouth...204 D3
Holcombe Barton Cnr EX6...98 D2
Holcombe Cross EX7 210 F8
Holcombe Down Cross TQ14...124 F2
Holcombe Down Rd EX7, TQ14...204 A4
Holcombe Dr
Holcombe EX7...210 F8
Plymouth PL9...255 F5
Holcombe La
Ottery St Mary EX11...100 F7
Uplyme DT7...104 B4
Holcombe Rd EX7, TQ14...210 E8
HOLCOMBE ROGUS...50 F5
Holcombe Village TQ14...210 E8
Holcroft Cl PL12...242 D2
Holden Cross EX6...113 E2
Holdridge La EX36...30 D8
Holdstone Way EX34...3 B2
Holdsworth St PL4...262 B4
Hole Ball Cross EX21..92 A8
Holebay Cl PL9...256 A5
Holebrook Cross EX20 76 C4

Holebrook La EX20....76 C5
Hole Cleave Rd EX33... 8 A1
Hole Cross
　Halwill EX21........73 F1
　Hittisleigh EX6.......96 E4
　Yelverton PL20......239 E7
Hole Ct EX20........75 C7
Hole Hill
　Branscombe EX12....190 C5
　Exbourne EX20......76 C4
　Witheridge EX16....46 F2
Hole La
　Chulmleigh EX18.....45 B3
　Combe Martin EX31...10 B6
　Croyde EX33.........7 F1
　North Tawton EX20...77 E6
HOLEMOOR.........73 B8
Holemoor Cross EX22..73 C8
Holemore Cross EX14..68 C5
Hole Rd PL20........239 F7
Hole's La
　Broadhempston TQ9..131 C1
　Staverton TQ9......216 B8
Holestone La EX9....187 A1
HOLEWATER.........19 A6
Holewater Cross EX32 19 A6
Holewater Hill EX32...19 A6
Holewell La EX14.....96 E4
Hole Well La TA20....69 F8
HOLLACOMBE........72 D6
Hollacombe Brake
　PL9...............256 C1
Hollacombe Cross
　Holsworthy EX22.....72 D6
　Yeoford EX17.......79 D3
HOLLACOMBE HILL..256 A2
Hollacombe La TQ3...219 D1
Hollam Cross TA22....33 E7
Hollam Dr TA22......33 D6
Hollam La TA22......33 D7
Hollamoor View
　EX31..............154 B3
Hollam Way TQ12....207 F8
Holland Cl EX31......154 A4
Holland Copse EX6...98 C4
Holland Dr
　West Clyst EX1.....175 A1
　West Clyst EX4.....174 F3
Holland Pk EX2......178 C1
Holland Rd
　Exeter EX1.........176 F4
　Exmouth EX8.......196 D1
　Plymouth, Chaddlewood
　　PL7.............251 D5
　Plymouth, Peverell PL3 248 E6
　Plymouth, Plymstock
　　PL9.............255 C4
Holland's La TA4.....35 E8
Hollands Park Ave
　EX34..............3 A3
Hollands Rd 4 TQ14 210 C4
Holland St 6 EX31...154 F5
Holland's Wash Dro
　TA20..............69 F5
Hollerday Dr EX35....151 B6
Holley Cl EX6........182 A4
Holley Pk EX20......170 D6
Holleys St TA20......88 D8
HOLLICOMBE........219 D1
Hollies The EX31.....154 B3
Hollingarth Way EX15. 67 B8
Hollington Ho 15
　TQ1..............220 D4
Hollis Cl EX11.......169 E4
HOLLOCOMBE.......58 E6
Hollocombe Cnr EX18 58 E6
Hollocombe Moor Gate
　EX18..............58 D7
Hollocombe Moor Head
　EX18..............58 D7
HOLLOCOMBE TOWN. 58 E6
Holloway Gdns PL9 256 A5
Holloway St EX2.....261 B2
Holloway The TA21...51 E7
Hollowcombe Cross
　PL21..............136 B3
Hollowcombe Head
　TQ7..............149 D5
Hollow Hayes PL6....249 B8
Hollow Head Cross
　EX10..............100 F2
Hollow La EX1.......178 E7
Hollow Pits Ct EX2...181 B8
Hollows The
　Exmouth EX8.......202 B7
　Plymouth PL9......256 B8
Hollow Tree Cross
　EX18..............60 A7
Hollowtree Ct 5
　EX32..............155 B3
Hollowtree Rd EX32..155 B3
Holly Ball La
　Whimple EX10......100 A8
　Whimple EX5.......99 F8
Hollyberry Rd PL7...136 B7
Holly Cl
　Broadclyst EX5.....175 C7
　2 Chudleigh TQ13...123 F6
　Halwill Junction EX21..73 D3
　Honiton EX14......166 C4
　Tiverton EX16......161 E5
Hollycombe Cross
　EX20..............95 C4
Hollycombe La TQ9 216 E7
Hollycroft Rd PL3....249 A7

Holly Ct PL6........249 E7
Hollyford La EX17.....62 C2
Hollyhead Cross
　EX12..............191 C7
Hollyhead Rd EX12...191 B8
Holly Ho 2 EX34.....150 B6
Hollyhock Cres TQ12 206 C4
Hollyhock Way TQ4...225 E2
Hollymount Cl EX8...196 C3
Holly Park Cl PL5....244 A5
Holly Park Dr PL5....244 A5
Holly Rd
　Exeter EX2.........177 F3
　Tiverton EX16......161 E5
Holly Villas TQ9......139 F8
Hollywater Cl TQ1...220 D5
Holly Water Rd EX17..62 E1
Holly Way EX15......163 C5
Holly Wlk
　Cullompton EX16....64 F2
　Exmouth EX8......196 D3
Hollywood Terr 2
　PL1..............262 A3
HOLMACOTT........26 E7
Holmacott Cross EX39.26 E7
Holman Cl EX7.......204 E6
Holman Ct PL2......248 C8
Holman Hill TQ12....212 A2
Holmans Bldgs PL1...247 D2
Holmans Mdw PL15..105 B1
Holman Way
　Ivybridge PL21......237 A6
　Topsham EX3.......182 F5
Holmbush Way PL8..257 A4
Holm Cross EX17.....59 F2
Holmdale EX10......188 B4
Holmead Cross EX16 48 B3
Holme Ct 3 TQ1.....220 D4
Holmer Down PL6...245 D7
Holmes Ave PL3.....249 B5
Holmes Field EX20...95 A5
Holmes Rd TQ12....180 F2
Holm Hill EX17......59 E2
Holmleigh Rd TQ7...145 D1
Holmsleigh Cross
　EX14..............166 D6
HOLMSLEIGH GREEN. 86 C5
Holmwood Ave PL9..255 E5
HOLNE............130 A4
Holne Chase PL6....245 E6
Holne Cross TQ13....130 B5
Holne Ct EX4........176 E8
Holne Moor Cl TQ3...225 E7
Holne Rd TQ11......236 B6
Holne Rise EX2......178 B4
Holne Turn
　Ashburton TQ13....130 B5
　Holne TQ13........130 B5
Holset Cross TQ8....148 D5
Holsome La TQ9.....138 D7
Holstock Cross EX20..74 D3
HOLSWORTHY......164 D5
HOLSWORTHY
　BEACON.........54 C3
Holsworthy CE Prim Sch
　EX22..............164 C5
Holsworthy Com Coll
　EX22..............164 C5
Holsworthy Hospl
　EX22..............164 D6
Holsworthy Ind Est
　EX22..............164 C5
Holsworthy L Ctr
　EX22..............164 C5
Holsworthy Mus★
　EX22..............164 C4
Holsworthy Rd
　Hatherleigh EX20....75 B6
　Okehampton EX20...93 D5
Holt The
　19 Appledore EX39....15 A1
　Honiton EX14......166 F4
Holtwood Dr PL21...237 A5
Holtwood Rd PL6....245 D6
Holway TA20........88 D8
Holwell Cl PL9......256 A5
Holwell La EX16......64 B5
Holwell Rd TQ5......230 B4
Holwill Dr EX38......159 D5
Holwill Tor Wlk TQ4..225 F3
HOLY CITY.........87 F7
Holy Cross RC Prim Sch
　PL4..............263 A3
Holyford La EX24.....102 F3
Holyford Woods Nature
　Reserve★ EX12....102 A3
Holy Moor Cross EX36 32 C1
Holy Moor La EX36....32 C1
Holyoake St TA21....160 C7
Holyrood Pl PL1......262 C2
Holyshute Cross
　EX14..............166 D6
Holyshute Gdns
　EX14..............166 D6
Holywell CE Prim Sch
　EX31..............27 D8
Holywell Cross EX36...19 F2
HOLYWELL LAKE....51 E7
Holywell Pk EX21....73 D3
Homebaye Ho 3
　EX12..............192 B4
Homebourne Ho
　TQ4..............226 C6
Home Cl
　Brixham TQ5.......230 C3
　Chillington TQ7.....145 A1
　Cranbrook EX5......99 B6

Homeclose La EX13,
　TA20..............88 A8
Homeclyst Ho EX5....99 B6
Homecombe Ho TQ1 220 C8
Homecourt Ho EX4..261 A2
Homedown Cross
　EX37..............28 F4
Home Farm EX6.....114 E1
Home Farm Cl
　Croyde EX33.........7 E2
　Kingston TQ7......142 C6
Home Farm Cross
　EX15..............65 F4
Home Farm Ct TQ12 209 B2
Home Farm N DT7...193 E6
Home Farm Rd
　Fremington EX31....153 D5
　Plymouth PL9......255 E8
Home Farm S DT7...193 E6
Homefield
　Thurlestone TQ7....143 A1
　Wellington TA21....160 E4
Homefield Cl EX11...169 E3
Homefield Cotts TQ7 143 A1
Homefield Rd EX1...177 F6
Home Gate EX6......98 A3
Home La EX34.........1 C3
Homelace Ho EX14..166 C7
Homelands PL7......247 D2
Homelands Prim Sch 1
　TQ1..............220 B8
Home Mdw TQ9.....223 C8
Homemeadows Ho
　EX10..............188 B5
Home Orch
　Sampford Peverell
　　EX16............50 D1
　Tiverton EX16.....50 D1
Homepalms Ho 3
　TQ1..............219 F6
Home Park Ave PL3.248 C6
Home Park (Plymouth
　Argyle FC) PL2.....248 C5
Home Park Rd PL12 243 A3
Home Pk
　Ashburton TQ13....130 F5
　Plymouth PL2......247 F4
Home Pk
　Plymouth PL9......255 C5
Homer Cl EX31......18 A8
Homer Cres EX33....152 B7
Homer Ct EX33......152 B7
Homer Dr EX33......152 B7
Homer La EX12......191 F8
Homer Park Lane S
　PL9..............255 C5
Homer Pk
　Plymouth PL9......255 C5
　Saltash PL12.......242 D3
Homer Rd EX33......152 B7
Homer Rise EX33....256 B7
Homers Cl TQ12.....207 D6
Homers Cres TQ12...207 D6
Homershill Cross
　PL21..............137 B6
Homers La TQ12.....207 D6
Homesleigh Rd EX14..86 A5
Homestead Rd TQ1..220 A8
Homestead Terr TQ1 220 A8
Home Sweet Home Terr
　PL4..............263 A2
Hometeign Ho TQ12 207 D4
Hometor Ho EX8....202 A8
Homeyards The
　TQ14..............210 A3
Homing Down Cross
　EX20..............75 A1
Honcray PL9........255 D8
Hone Cross EX16.....34 F5
Honest Heart Cross
　EX15..............66 A3
Honestone St EX39..157 A1
Honeybeetle Cross
　EX37..............29 A5
HONEYCHURCH.....76 E5
Honeychurch La EX20. 76 E5
Honeychurch Moor Cross
　EX20..............76 F6
Honey Cl EX39......157 D2
Honeycroft Cross
　EX22..............54 A4
Honey Ditches Dr
　EX12..............191 F8
Honey Farm Cl 9
　EX36..............158 C5
Honeyford Cl PL6....245 A4
Honey La
　Daccombe TQ1,
　　TQ12............213 F5
　Exeter EX1.........174 F2
　Woodbury Salterton
　　EX5.............184 D7
Honeylands Childrens Ctr
　(Royal Devon & Exeter
　Hospl) EX4........178 B7
Honeylands Dr EX4..178 A7
Honeylands Way
　EX4..............178 A7
Honey Mdws EX22..164 C4
Honeymead TA24....13 D2
Honeymoor La EX16...48 E7
Honey Park Rd EX9...198 B2
Honey St EX39......157 A7
Honeysuckle Cl
　2 Barnstaple EX31...154 B3
　Paignton TQ3......225 E8
　Plymouth PL6......245 E7
　Tiverton EX16......161 F6
Honeysuckle Ct EX4..176 D8

Honeysuckle Dr
　Dawlish EX7.......204 D8
　Honiton EX14......85 C2
　Tavistock PL19....171 A6
Honeysuckle Gdns
　PL15..............105 A2
Honeywell TQ12.....207 E6
Honeywell Cl EX32...155 B2
Honeywell La TQ13...122 C3
Honeywell Rd TQ12..207 E6
Honeywins Cross
　EX36..............19 C2
HONICKNOWLE.....244 B2
Honicknowle PL5....244 B2
Honicknowle Gn PL5 244 B2
Honicknowle La PL5 244 B1
Honicombe Cnr PL17 125 B5
Honicombe Pk PL17. 125 B5
HONITON..........166 D4
Honiton Bottom Rd
　Honiton EX14......166 C3
　Honiton EX14......166 C4
Honiton Bsns Pk
　EX14..............166 B6
Honiton Cl PL5......244 B3
Honiton Com Coll
　EX14..............166 C6
Honiton Cross EX36...29 F3
Honiton Hospl EX14. 166 C5
Honiton La EX13.....29 E3
Honiton L Ctr EX14..166 C7
Honiton Prim Sch
　EX14..............166 C6
Honiton Rd
　Blackhorse EX5.....179 C7
　Cullompton EX15...163 E3
　Exeter EX1.........178 C5
Honiton Sta EX14...166 C5
Honiton Wlk PL5....244 B4
Honors Farm EX5...173 F8
Hooda Cl EX32.......17 E1
Hood Dr EX2.........182 C8
Hoodown La TQ6....234 B4
HOOE............255 C5
Hooe Hill PL9.......255 C5
Hooe La PL9.........255 D3
Hooelake La PL10....253 C4
Hooe Manor PL9.....255 C5
Hooe Prim Sch PL9.. 255 B5
Hooe Rd PL9........255 C5
HOOK...........88 B8
Hook Cross EX13....87 D7
Hook Dr EX2........178 D2
Hooker Cl EX9.......197 F2
Hookhill La EX17.....62 A3
Hookhills Dr TQ4....226 C1
Hookhills Gdns TQ4. 226 B1
Hookhills Gr TQ4....226 C1
Hookhills Rd TQ4....226 B1
Hookmoor Cross
　PL21..............137 E7
Hooksbury Ave PL7. 251 B3
Hooks Cross TQ12...131 C2
Hookway EX17........80 D1
Hookway Cross EX5...80 D1
Hookway Hill
　Lynton/Lynmouth EX35.. 6 F3
　Oareford TA24......6 F3
Hookway La EX16.....63 B5
Hookwell Down La
　EX36..............30 A8
HOO MEAVY.......132 A8
Hoop Cross EX15.....83 B4
Hooper Cl EX20......75 B7
Hooperhayne Rd
　EX24..............102 E5
Hoopern Ave EX4...173 D1
Hoopern La EX4.....177 C8
Hoopern St EX4.....261 B4
Hoopern Terr 4 EX4 204 D6
Hoopers Cl TQ9.....223 F5
Hoopers Cross EX16..34 D3
Hoopers La PL18....125 C6
Hooperton Cross EX6. 96 E3
Hooperton La EX6....96 E3
HOOPS...........24 D2
Hope By−Pass TQ7.. 147 B7
Hope Cl TQ9........223 F5
Hope Close PL2......248 A7
Hope Rd EX2........178 A5
Hope Reach Ave TQ9 223 E4
Hope's Cl TQ14......210 A6
Hopes Cove La TQ1.220 F5
Hope Wlk TQ9......223 F5
Hopkins Ct 3 TQ12 207 C3
Hopkins La TQ12....207 C3
Hopperstyle EX31....154 B3
Hopton Cl PL6.......248 F8
Hopton Dr EX38.....159 F5
HOPWORTHY.......71 C5
Horace Rd TQ2......213 F2
Hore Down Gate EX34. 9 B6
Hore's Cross PL21...137 D7
Horestone Cross EX16. 47 F4
Hornapark Cl PL16..105 E3
Hornbeam Cl
　Honiton EX14......166 A4
　Tiverton EX16......161 F5
Hornbeam Gdns EX5. 83 A7
Hornbeam Hollow 1
　EX31..............154 C2
Hornbeam Rd EX1...178 C6
Hornbrook Gdns PL6 244 D6
Hornby St 2 PL2....247 F4
Hornchurch La PL5. 243 E4
Hornchurch Rd PL5.. 243 E5

Horn Cross
　Kentisbeare EX15....65 F2
　Plymouth PL9.......255 F7
Horn Cross Rd PL9... 255 F7
HORNDON.........118 A7
Horndon Terr EX5...184 C2
Hornebrook Ave 9
　EX34..............150 B5
Horne Park Ave 14
　EX34..............150 B5
Horne Park Rd EX34. 150 B5
Horne Rd EX34......150 B5
Horner Tongue TQ9. 138 F5
Horner Turn Cross
　TQ9..............139 A5
Horn Hill
　Dartmouth TQ6.....233 F3
　Poltimore EX4.....174 E4
Horn La
　Brixton PL8.........257 A5
　Plymouth PL9......255 F7
Horn Lane Flats 4
　PL9..............255 F7
Horn Rd EX15.......65 E2
HORNS CROSS......24 E2
Hornshayes Knap Cross
　EX14..............86 F7
Hornshayne Rd EX24 102 E5
Horns Pk TQ14......208 E7
HORRABRIDGE.....126 F5
Horrabridge Com Prim
　Sch PL20.........126 F4
Horridge La EX18....59 A8
Horry Mill La
　Hollocombe EX18....58 F6
　Hollocombe EX18....59 A6
Horsdon Rd EX16...161 E4
Horsdon Terr EX16...161 F4
HORSEBRIDGE.....116 A1
HORSEBROOK.....135 B1
Horsecombe Cross
　TQ8..............259 B6
Horseguards EX4....261 B4
Horsehill Cross EX17..60 F7
Horse Hill Cross EX22. 38 F1
Horse La TQ14......210 B3
Horsepond Mdw
　EX36..............158 C5
Horsepool St TQ5...230 B3
Horse Rd EX23......36 F1
Horseshoe Bend TQ4 226 C2
Horseshoe Cl 19
　TQ13..............123 E6
Horseshoe Dr
　Newton Abbot TQ12..207 A5
　Plymouth PL7......250 D5
Horseway TA20......69 E6
Horsewell Rd EX5....99 B6
Horsham La
　Plymouth, Honicknowle
　　PL5.............244 C2
　Plymouth, Tamerton Foliot
　　PL5.............244 C7
Horslears EX13......167 C4
Horslett Hill EX22....89 E8
Horswell Cl PL7.....251 B5
Horton Cross EX22...38 C3
Horwell Rd EX5.....99 B6
HORWOOD........26 C7
Horwood Cross EX39. 26 D7
Horwood & Newton
　Tracey Com Prim Sch
　EX31..............27 A6
Horwood Sq 11 EX31 154 F5
Hosegood Way TQ12 207 D7
Hosford Cl PL9......256 A4
Hoskings Ct TQ11...236 B5
Hospital Hill EX7....204 D6
Hospital La
　17 Ashburton TQ13...131 A5
　Exeter EX1.........178 C4
Hospital Rd PL4....263 B4
Hostel Hill TQ6......233 E4
Hostle Park Gdns 12
　EX34..............150 C6
Hostle Park Rd EX34 150 C6
Hostle Pk EX34......150 C6
Hotham Pl PL1......262 A4
Hothill La
　Ashprington TQ9....139 F6
　Cornworthy TQ9....227 A5
Hotspur Terr PL1....262 C4
HOUGHTON.......206 C6
Houghton Gr EX4...174 F4
Houghton La EX10...187 A5
Houldsworth Rd PL9 255 C7
Houndbeare La EX5.. 99 E4
Houndhead Cross
　TQ9..............216 D8
Houndiscombe Rd
　PL4..............262 C4
Houndspool★ EX7.. 200 A3
Hound Tor Cl TQ4...229 B7
Hounster Dr PL10...252 D4
Hounster Hill PL10...252 D4
Housman Cl PL5....244 D3
Hove Villas EX5......261 A4
Howard Ave EX32...155 B4
Howard Cl
　Exeter EX4.........176 F8
　Okehampton EX20..170 D6
　Plymouth PL5......243 F7
　Saltash PL12.......242 D3
Howard Cross EX6...96 D7
Howard Ct TQ14....210 A7

Howard La
　Hittisleigh EX6......96 D7
　Morchard Bishop EX23.. 70 B8
Howard Rd
　Plymouth PL9......255 E8
　Wellington TA21....160 D7
Howards Cl EX36....158 C2
Howards Way
　Ivybridge PL21.....237 A6
　Newton Abbot TQ12...207 F4
Howarth Cl EX10....188 A8
Howden Ind Est EX16 161 B3
Howden La EX16....161 B3
Howden Rd
　Tiverton EX16......64 B7
　Tiverton EX16......161 C3
Howell Rd EX4......261 A4
Howeson Ct 10 PL1. 262 A3
Howeson La PL6....245 A4
HOWLEY..........69 C4
Howley Pk La EX32...18 D2
How St PL4.........263 A2
Howton La TQ12....206 B5
Howton Rd
　Newton Abbot TQ12..206 C6
　Newton Abbot TQ12..206 C7
Hoxton Rd TQ1.....220 B5
Hoyles Cl TA21.....160 E4
Hoyle's Ct TQ3......225 F8
Hoyles Rd TA21.....160 E4
Hoyle's Rd TQ3......225 E8
Hubbastone Rd EX39 157 C8
HUCCABY.........129 C7
Huccaby Cl TQ5.....229 F2
HUCCOMBE........149 C7
Huckham Barn Cross
　TQ7..............149 C7
Huckham La EX31...10 F3
Huckland Cross EX20. 76 E4
HUDDISFORD......38 C6
Huddisford Cross
　EX39..............38 D7
Hudley Mill Hill EX32. 18 C8
Hudson Cross EX22..53 B4
Hue La EX33.........8 F1
Hughball Cross EX19. 76 A8
Hughes Ave EX32...155 B3
Hughes Gdns EX39 156 D2
Hugh Squier Ave
　EX36..............158 D5
HUISH..........57 B6
HUISH
　CHAMPFLOWER....35 E7
Huish Cleeve TA4...35 E7
Huish Cross TQ13...123 C6
Huishlane End EX6...97 F5
Hukeley Head Cross
　EX16..............34 D3
HULHAM..........196 B3
Hulham Rd
　Exmouth EX8.......196 B1
　Exmouth EX8.......196 B2
Hulham Vale EX8...196 C2
Hulk La EX5.........81 F4
HUMBER.........124 C2
Humber Cl PL3......249 D6
Humber La
　TQ14..............124 C1,
　　...............124 C2
Hume Ave EX35.....151 A5
Huish Cross TQ13... 123 C6
Hummingbird Cl EX14 174 E1
Humphrey's Cross
　TQ13..............130 C4
Humphreys Rd TQ1. 160 E7
Humphries Pk EX8.. 196 D1
Humpy The EX7.....204 C8
Hungerford Rd PL2.. 248 B5
Hungry Fox Est EX5. 175 E3
Huniver's La EX17...165 C4
Hunivers Pl EX17...165 C4
Hunsdon Ct TQ1....220 C4
Hunsdon Rd
　Ivybridge PL21.....237 A6
　Lee Mill PL21.......136 D6
　Torquay TQ1......220 C4
Hunstone Cross EX36 19 B2
Huntacott Way TQ2. 219 B8
Hunter Cl PL6.......244 F2
Hunter La EX34......7 F6
Hunters Cl PL21.....237 B5
Hunters Ct TQ3.....224 F7
Hunters Gate EX20. 170 D6
Hunter's Hill EX15...51 E1
Hunters Moon TQ9. 222 F7
Hunters's Oak PL20. 126 A2
Hunters Tor Dr TQ4. 229 B7
Hunter's Way EX15...51 E1
Hunterswell Rd
　TQ12..............207 A3
Hunterswood EX38. 159 F5
Hunthay Bsns Pk
　EX13..............167 A6
Hunthay La EX13....167 B6
Huntingdon Gdns
　PL5..............244 C6
Huntley Cl EX13.....167 F7
Huntley La EX13.....88 A8
Huntley Pl PL3......249 C4
Hunton Cl EX8......195 F5
Hunts Cross PL21...137 B1
HUNTSHAM.......50 A7
Huntsham Rd EX1...178 D7
HUNTSHAW........26 E7
Huntshaw La EX31...27 B1
Huntshaw Moor Cross
　EX38..............26 F2
HUNTSHAW WATER. 26 E2
Hurdwick Rd PL19...171 A5
Hurrabrook Cl PL6...245 E2

Hurrabrook Gdns PL6 245 E2
Hurrell Cl PL6 244 D6
Hurrell Ct
Kingsbridge TQ7 258 C5
Plymouth PL3 249 C5
Hurrell Rd TQ7 258 C5
Hursley Bsns Pk PL6 241 D1
Hurst Ave EX2 178 B4
Hurst Cl PL9 255 F5
Hurstone Nature Reserve★ TA4 35 F3
Hurst's Almshouses EX2 261 C2
Husseys Cross EX14 86 F6
Hussey's La EX14 86 F6
Hutcherleigh Cross TQ9 139 B1
Hutcherleigh Turn TQ9 139 D1
Hutchings Cl PL6 244 D6
Hutchings Dr
Clyst Honiton EX1 179 B8
Clyst Honiton EX1 179 C8
Hutchings Mead EX1 178 F8
Hutchings Way TQ14 209 D8
Hutgate Rd EX14 86 A4
Hutton Rd TQ3 219 A1
Huxford La EX37 44 F7
HUXHAM 174 B8
Huxham Cl PL6 249 A8
Huxham's Cross TQ9 215 E3
Huxham's Cross Est TQ9 215 E3
HUXHILL 26 D2
Huxley Cl PL7 250 F7
Huxley Vale TQ12 212 F3
Huxnor Cross TQ12 212 F2
Huxnor Rd TQ12 212 F3
Huxtable Hill TQ2 219 E4
Huxtable La EX32 18 C2
Huxton Cross TQ7 143 D3
Huxton Fork TQ7 143 D3
Hyacinth Terr TA21 160 C5
Hyde Park Infs & Jun Sch 1 PL3 248 E5
Hyde Park Rd PL3 248 E5
Hyde Rd TQ4 226 B6
Hyfield Gdns TQ1 220 B4
Hyfield Pl 4 EX39 157 A1
Hylands Cl EX11 168 D3
Hylton Gdns EX4 176 F6
Hyne Town TQ6 145 E5
Hynetown Est TQ6 145 E5
Hynetown Rd TQ6 145 E5
Hyperion TQ2 219 E2

I

Ian Hay Cl EX39 157 C1
Ibex Ct EX39 15 A1
Ice House La EX10 187 F7
Icy Pk TQ7 143 C6
IDDESLEIGH 57 F3
Iddesleigh Cross EX19 57 E3
Iddesleigh Rd EX4 177 E8
Iddesleigh Terr 10 EX7 204 E6
IDE 176 D1
IDEFORD 124 A4
Ide La EX2 177 A1
Ide Prim Sch EX2 176 E1
Idestone Brook Cross EX2 113 F7
Idestone Cross EX2 114 A7
Idestone La EX2 114 A8
Ide Village Rd EX2 176 E2
Idewell Rd TQ2 214 B2
Idston Cross TQ7 143 D7
Ikea Way EX1 178 D2
Ilbert Cotts PL7 250 E4
Ilbert Rd
Kingsbridge TQ7 258 C5
Thurlestone TQ7 143 A1
Ilbert St PL1 262 B4
Ilex Cl
Exeter EX4 174 B2
Shillingford St George EX2 114 C6
ILFRACOMBE 150 B6
Ilfracombe Acad EX34 150 C5
Ilfracombe Academy EX34 150 C5
Ilfracombe Aquarium★ EX34 150 D6
Ilfracombe CE Jun Sch EX34 150 C5
Ilfracombe & District Tyrrell Hosp EX34 150 B5
Ilfracombe Inf Sch 18 EX34 150 B5
Ilfracombe Mus★ EX34 150 B6
Ilfracombe Rd
Braunton EX33 152 D7
West Down EX34 8 F5
Ilfracombe Swimming Pool EX34 150 D5
Ilkerton Hill EX35 151 A1
Ilsham CE Prim Sch TQ1 220 E5
Ilsham Cl TQ1 220 F5
Ilsham Cres TQ1 220 F4
Ilsham Ho TQ1 220 E5
Ilsham Marine Dr TQ1 221 A4
Ilsham Mws TQ1 220 D5
Ilsham Rd TQ1 220 F5
ILSINGTON 122 C3
Ilsington CE Prim Sch TQ13 122 C3
Ilton Cross TQ7 259 A7
Ilton Way TQ7 258 D5
Immenstadt Dr TA21 160 D4
Imperial Bldgs TQ12 207 D8
Imperial Ct
Lynton EX35 151 C5
Torquay TQ1 220 C7
Imperial Mews 12 TQ12 207 C3
Imperial Rd EX8 201 F6
Imperial St EX4 176 F5
Impham Cl PL19 171 B7
Improvement Pl 5 TA21 160 D5
Ince Cl PL11 246 F4
Inchcoulter EX8 202 C5
Inchkeith Rd PL6 244 F7
Incledon Hill EX33 8 A3
Indicombe La EX32 18 B2
Indio Rd TQ13 180 C6
Indus Pl PL9 256 E8
Inglebrook Hts EX39 156 E7
Ingleside EX13 167 E6
Ingleside Ct EX9 198 A1
Ingrams Pl EX5 99 C6
Ingra Rd PL3 249 A6
Ingra Tor Cl 2 PL20 126 F3
Ingra Wlk PL6 245 B8
INLEIGH GREEN 58 C2
Innerbrook Rd TQ2 219 E5
INNER HOPE 147 C6
Inner Relief Rd 11 EX31 154 F6
Inner Ting Tong EX9 197 C3
Inner Westland 2 EX5 99 A6
Innes Ho PL1 262 B3
Instaple Cross EX22 53 D6
INSTOW 15 B1
Instow Com Prim Sch EX39 15 C2
Instow Ho 4 EX39 15 B1
Instow Signal Box (Mus)★ EX39 15 B1
Instow Wlk PL5 244 A3
Inswell Ct PL19 171 A6
INSWORKE 252 F6
Insworke Cl PL10 253 A6
Insworke Cres PL10 252 F6
Insworke Pl PL10 253 A6
International Ho TQ12 180 F2
Inverdene PL3 248 D5
Inverteign Com Nursery & Prim Sch TQ14 209 D8
Inverteign Dr TQ14 210 A5
Inverteign Hts TQ14 209 D8
INWARDLEIGH 75 E2
Inwardleigh Cross EX20 75 D2
Iolanthe Dr EX4 174 A2
Iona Ave EX8 196 A2
IPPLEPEN 211 C2
Ipplepen Bsns Pk TQ12 217 D8
Ipplepen Cross TQ12 211 C6
Ipplepen Prim Sch TQ12 211 D1
Ipplepen Rd TQ3 218 C4
Ipswich Cl PL5 244 C4
Irene Way EX16 161 F6
Iris Ave
Exeter EX2 177 B4
Exeter EX2 261 A1
Irishcombe Gate EX36 46 B5
Irishcombe La EX36 46 C4
Iron Bridge EX4 261 A3
Iron Bridge Cross EX20 77 B3
Iron Letters Cross EX34 2 B1
Iron Mine La PL20 127 B3
Iron Post TA22 33 B5
Iron Shovel La EX36 31 A3
Irsha St EX39 15 A1
Irving Cl EX33 152 B6
Isaac Cl EX9 198 E7
Isaac Gr TQ2 213 F3
Isaacs Rd TQ2 214 A2
Isabella Rd EX16 161 D5
Isambard Brunel Way PL3 262 A2
Isambard Ct TQ2 214 B3
Isambard Kingdom Brunel Prim Sch TA21 160 E7
Isambard Par EX4 177 A7
ISCA Coll of Media Arts EX2 177 E2
Isca Ct EX2 177 D1
Isca Rd
Exeter EX2 261 A1
Exmouth EX8 202 C5
Isigny Rd TQ7 258 C5
Isis Cl EX14 166 E7
Island Lodge Camping & Cvn Site TQ7 144 B6
Island Quay TQ8 259 E5
Island St TQ8 259 E5
Island Terr TQ8 259 E5
Island View TQ7 143 A2
Isleworth Rd EX4 176 F5
Iter Cnr EX17 78 C4
Iter Cross EX17 78 C4
Iter Ct EX17 78 C4
Iter Pk EX17 78 C4
Itton Cross EX20 77 D2
Itton Moor La
North Tawton EX17 77 F2
Spreyton EX17 95 E8
Spreyton EX20 77 F1
Itton Rd EX17 77 E2
Ivanhoe Rd PL5 243 D2
Ivatt Rd TQ6 233 C3
Iveagh Ct EX4 176 F8
IVYBRIDGE 237 C6
Ivybridge Com Coll PL21 237 D6
Ivybridge La PL20 120 B8
Ivybridge L Ctr PL21 237 D4
Ivybridge Rd
Ermington PL7 136 F4
Tavistock PL19 126 A4
Ivybridge Sta PL21 237 F6
Ivy Cl
Exeter EX2 178 A4
Sidmouth EX10 188 B7
Ivycombe Hill
South Allington TQ7 149 B5
South Allington TQ7 149 B4
Ivy Cotts PL18 125 C6
Ivy Cross TA21 51 D7
Ivy Ct 28 EX39 15 A1
Ivydale EX8 196 D3
Ivydale Rd PL4 248 F4
Ivydene Rd PL21 237 C5
Ivy Dr TQ12 244 C6
Ivy Glen PL21 237 D6
Ivy Ho TA21 160 C6
Ivyhouse Cross PL16 91 A4
Ivy La
Dartmouth TQ6 233 F3
15 Teignmouth TQ14 210 B4
Ivy Tree Hill TQ12 209 A2

J

Jack Backs Cross EX17 79 F7
Jack Bears Ho 10 TQ4 226 B6
Jackdaw Rd PL6 245 B2
Jackets La EX39 156 F7
Jacketts EX9 198 E7
Jacketts Cotts EX9 198 F7
Jackey's La EX17 78 C5
JACK-IN-THE-GREEN 99 B6
Jack Leslie Way PL2 248 C6
Jackmans Cl TQ9 222 E6
Jackman's La TQ9 222 F4
Jackman's Mdw PL10 253 A3
Jackmans Meadow PL10 252 F3
Jackmoor Cross
Brampford Speke EX5 81 C1
Newton St Cyres EX5 81 B1
Jack Sadler Wy EX3 178 E1
Jacks Cl TQ9 223 F5
Jack's La
St John PL11 252 B8
Torquay TQ2 213 F3
Jackson Cl PL5 247 F8
Jackson Mdw EX8 195 E5
Jackson Pl PL2 247 F4
Jackson Way PL12 242 E3
Jacks Wy EX5 179 F2
Jacobs Field EX39 39 E8
Jacob's Pool EX20 170 B5
JACOBSTOWE 76 A4
Jacolind Wlk TQ5 230 D5
Jago Ave PL11 247 B3
James Ave TQ3 218 E1
James Cl PL9 256 B6
James Ct EX4 261 B2
James La EX14 69 C2
James Lane Cross EX13 69 C2
James Owen Ct EX4 261 C4
James Rd PL19 171 E2
James St
Plymouth PL4 262 C4
Plymouth, Mount Wise PL1 247 E1
James's Week EX18 59 E8
James's Week La EX18 59 E8
Jane Way's Grave EX17 61 B1
Jardine Pk EX2 177 C1
Jarmins Pit Cross EX15 66 A4
Jarvis Cl EX8 202 E7
Jasmine Cl EX16 161 F6
Jasmine Gdns
Plymouth, Chaddlewood PL7 251 B5
Plymouth, Glenholt PL6 245 E6
Jasmine Gr TQ3 225 E8
Jaspers Cotts TQ9 227 B4
Jawbone Hill TQ6 233 E2
Jays Cross PL15 105 B6
Jean Cres PL3 249 B6
Jedburgh Cres PL2 248 A8
Jeffery Cl
Hartland EX39 22 E3
Plymouth PL6 244 D6
Jefford Ho EX4 173 A1
Jeffries Rd TA21 160 F5
Jeffs Way EX13 167 E6
Jellicoe Rd
Newton Abbot TQ12 207 F3
Plymouth PL5 244 E1
Jellicoe Villas TQ9 223 B5
Jenker's Hill EX33 8 B2
Jenkins Cl PL9 256 A5
Jenner Rd EX16 161 B6
Jennifer Cl EX2 177 E3
Jennings Gdns EX1 179 B8
Jenns Cross EX22 53 D7
Jennycliff La PL9 255 A6
Jennys Combe Cl PL9 255 F4
Jenny's Portion EX5 82 A6
Jenwood Rd EX14 67 B1
Jephson Rd PL4 249 B3
Jericho DT7 260 D4
Jericho St EX5 81 E5
Jerrard Cl EX14 166 C5
Jerrard Cres EX14 166 C5
Jersey Rd EX4 174 E2
Jesmond Rd EX1 177 E7
Jessops PL7 250 D7
Jesu St EX11 169 D3
Jetstream Wy PL6 245 B5
Jetty Marsh Nature Reserve★ TQ12 207 C5
Jetty Marsh Rd TQ12 207 B5
Jewell Cres EX32 155 C6
Jewell Meadow EX39 39 E8
JEWEL'S CROSS 70 E6
J.H.Taylor Dr EX39 157 A7
Jimmy's La EX18 45 F6
Jingles La EX32 155 A4
Jinkin Ave PL4 263 B4
Joan Spry Cl EX16 46 E1
Jobble's La EX24 102 E4
Jocelyn Mead EX17 165 B6
Jocelyn Rd EX9 198 A2
Jockey Hill EX17 165 C6
Jodel Cl PL6 245 B5
Joeys Field EX36 30 F3
John Acres La TQ12 123 D3
John Cole Cl TA21 160 D7
John Gay Cl EX32 155 C4
John Gay Rd EX32 155 C4
John Greenway Cl EX16 161 D3
John Grinter Way TA21 160 D4
John Hannam Ho EX1 261 C3
John Howe Cl EX38 159 D5
John La PL4 262 C4
John Levers Way EX4 176 F5
John Nash Dr EX7 204 C4
John Smale Rd EX31 154 C4
Johnson Cl 2 PL20 125 E1
Johnson Pk PL18 125 D3
John Sparke Ho 16 PL1 263 A2
John St
Plymouth PL1 247 E3
Tiverton EX16 161 C4
John's Terr 7 EX16 161 B4
Johnstone Dr EX16 161 B5
Johnstone La EX36 30 D4
Jones's Hill EX33 7 E2
Jonida Cl TQ1 220 A7
JORDAN 121 A2
Jordan Cl EX32 155 C3
Jordan Cross TQ13 121 A2
Jordan Dr TQ14 209 D8
Jordan La PL20 126 F5
Jordan Mdw 15 TQ13 131 A5
Jordan Orch TQ11 236 A5
Jordans Brook TQ9 222 E6
Jordan St TQ11 236 A5
Joseph Locke Wy EX17 165 E4
Jose's Cross EX37 44 F8
Jose's La EX31 4 B5
Joslin Ct TQ12 207 D8
Joslin Rd EX14 166 B5
Joy St EX31 154 F5
Jubilee Cl
Dartmouth TQ6 233 C3
Exminster EX6 182 B4
Great Torrington EX38 159 E6
Holcombe TQ14 204 B1
2 Ilfracombe EX34 150 B5
Ivybridge PL21 237 F6
Okehampton EX20 170 B5
Saltash PL12 242 D2
Jubilee Cotts PL12 242 C1
Jubilee Ct
Ashwater EX21 90 E6
Exeter EX4 261 A3
Torquay TQ1 220 B5
8 Wellington TA21 160 D5
Jubilee Dr
Exmouth EX8 196 C3
8 Hemyock EX15 67 B8
Jubilee Gdns
Cullompton EX15 163 C2
North Molton EX36 30 D8
Sidmouth EX10 188 C8
Jubilee Gr EX8 195 F5
Jubilee Lodge EX12 192 B5
Jubilee Pl PL3 249 C4
Jubilee Rd
Appledore EX39 14 F1
Bradninch EX5 82 F6
Exeter EX1 177 E7
Malborough TQ7 147 F6
Jubilee Rd *continued*
Newton Abbot TQ12 207 B2
Plymouth PL5 243 F3
Totnes TQ9 223 E6
Jubilee Sq 21 EX39 157 A2
Jubilee St TQ7 143 C6
Jubilee Terr
1 Bittaford PL21 137 C7
Copplestone EX17 79 B5
Kingswear TQ6 234 B3
Paignton TQ3 226 A6
Plymouth PL4 249 B2
Julian Cotts PL21 136 D6
Julian Rd PL21 237 B5
Julian St PL4 263 C2
Julian Wlk PL6 245 E6
Jump Cl PL6 241 C1
Junction Gdns PL4 263 C3
Junction Rd EX17 78 C4
Juniper Cl
Exeter EX4 174 B2
3 Honiton EX14 166 A4
Paignton TQ3 225 D2
3 Tiverton EX16 161 F6
Juniper Ct EX31 154 C3
Juniper Dr
Dawlish EX7 200 E1
Dawlish EX7 204 E8
Junipers (Hosp) The EX2 177 F4
Juniper Way PL7 251 B5
Junket St EX37 43 B7
Jupes Cl EX6 182 B3
Juries La EX38 159 D6
Jurston Cross TQ13 110 F4
Jurston Ct TA21 160 F5
Jurston Fields TA21 160 F5
Jurston La TA21 160 E6
Jury Hill TA22 33 E6
Jury Pk EX36 158 B4
Jury Rd TA22 33 E6
Jurys Cnr TQ12 213 A4
Jurys Corner Cl TQ12 213 A4
Justment Cross EX17 77 F2
Jutland Way 5 EX1 178 D1

K

Kabale Cl EX16 161 A6
Kala Fair EX39 156 E7
Karen Cl EX39 157 D1
Katherines La EX11 169 E4
Kathleaven St PL5 243 D1
Kathleen Grange EX39 157 D1
Kay Cl
Exmouth EX8 202 C8
Plymouth PL7 250 F7
Keals Croft EX35 151 B5
Keaton Barns PL8 141 E6
Keaton La
Ivybridge PL21 237 D1
Ivybridge PL7 136 F6
Keaton Rd PL21 237 C4
Keats Cl
Exmouth EX8 196 C4
Teignmouth TQ14 124 E1
Keats Mill La TA20 69 C7
Keat St PL2 247 E4
Kedlestone Ave PL5 244 A3
Keep Cotts TQ4 224 B7
Keepers Cross EX16 49 A2
Keeper's Ct EX11 169 B7
Keep Gdns The TQ6 233 E3
Keephill Bglws EX22 164 E1
Keep La TQ6 233 E4
Keep The PL12 242 C2
KELLACOT 105 F7
Kellacott Cross PL16 105 F7
Kelland Cl TQ3 226 A5
Kelland Cnr EX6 98 A1
Kelland Cross EX17 60 C2
Kelland Hill EX17 60 C2
Kellands La EX20 170 E6
Kellands Row TQ7 258 D5
KELLATON 149 B6
Kellaton Cross
East Allington TQ9 144 E7
Kellaton TQ7 149 C6
Kellett Cl 10 TQ13 131 A5
Kellock Dr TQ9 223 B5
KELLY 115 F8
Kelly Cl
Plymouth PL5 247 C7
Torquay TQ1 220 C2
Kelly Coll Preparatory Coll PL19 117 D3
Kelly Coll Prep Coll PL19 171 E8
Kelly Coll Prep Sch PL19 171 D7
Kelly Cross TQ13 122 D8
Kelly La EX16 62 E8
Kelvin Ave PL4 263 C4
Kelvin Ct
Brixham TQ5 230 D5
Torquay TQ1 214 C1
Kelway Rd TA21 160 E7
KEMACOTT 4 C4
Kemmings Cl TQ4 225 F1
Kempe Cl PL2 247 F6
Kempland La EX18 45 B2
Kempley Rd EX20 170 B5
Kemps Field 23 EX5 99 A6
Kemp's La EX12 192 D7
Kemps Way TA22 33 D6
Kempton Terr PL11 247 B2
Kemyell Pl PL2 247 E4
Kenbury Cres EX6 201 B6
Kenbury Dr EX2 181 C8
Kendall Cl EX4 261 C4
Kendall Gr TQ13 180 F7
Kendall Ho EX14 166 C5
Kendal Pl PL5 244 E4
Kendlewood Cl TQ4 225 F3
Kenilworth TQ1 220 D3
Kenilworth Rd PL2 248 B7
Kenley Gdns PL5 243 F4
Kenmare Dr PL7 251 A5
Kenmay Mws EX3 182 D7
KENN 114 E4
Kennacott Cross EX22 72 B1
Kennaway Rd EX11 169 F4
Kenn CE Prim Sch EX6 181 B1
Kenn Cl PL5 244 B3
Kennedy Way
Dunkeswell EX14 67 C2
Tiverton EX16 161 C5
Kennel Bridge Cross EX20 92 E8
Kennel Hill PL7 250 D4
Kennel Hill Cl PL7 250 C4
Kennel La
Galmpton TQ5 229 B4
Georgeham EX33 8 A2
Ivybridge PL21 237 B5
Kennels Rd TQ5 229 C4
Kennels The PL21 237 B6
Kennerland Cross EX39 38 E8
KENNERLEIGH 61 F2
Kennerley Ave EX4 178 B8
Kennet Cl PL3 249 B6
Kenneth Ct TQ2 219 C8
KENNFORD 181 B2
Kennford Rd EX2 177 B3
Kennicott House TQ9 223 B6
Kenniford Cross EX5 183 D8
Kenn La
Exeter EX6 181 F1
Exminster EX6 182 A2
Powderham EX6 194 B6
Kennydown La EX18 59 B7
Kensall Cross EX36 20 B1
Kensey Cl TQ1 220 E6
Kensey Valley Mdw PL15 105 A3
Kensham Ave EX5 83 A6
Kensham Cl EX5 82 F6
Kensington Cl 1 EX31 154 C1
Kensington Pl 8 PL4 248 F4
Kensington Rd PL4 263 B4
Kenson Hill EX5 82 B5
Kent Cl EX2 178 A4
KENTISBEARE 66 A3
Kentisbeare CE Prim Sch EX15 66 A3
KENTISBURY 10 E6
KENTISBURY FORD 10 E5
Kentisbury Prim Sch EX31 10 E6
Kentisknowle TQ1 220 E5
KENTON 194 E3
Kenton Brook Ct TQ2 219 B8
Kenton Hill EX6 194 E3
Kenton Mews EX6 194 D3
Kenton Pl EX2 177 C2
Kenton Prim Sch EX6 194 D3
Kenton Vineyard★ EX6 194 A2
Kent Rd
Plymouth PL2 247 F5
Tatworth TA20 88 D8
Kent's Bglws TA20 88 D8
Kents Cavern★ TQ1 220 E5
Kents Cavern Rd TQ1 220 D5
Kents Cl
Tatworth TA20 88 C8
Uffculme EX15 66 A7
Kent's Cotts TA20 88 D8
Kents La
Tatworth TA20 88 D8
Torquay TQ1 220 E5
Kent's Orch TA20 88 D8
Kents Rd TQ1 220 E5
Kenwith Dr TQ7 258 D5
Kenwith Rd EX39 156 F4
Kenwith Terr EX39 156 F3
Kenwith Valley Nature Reserve★ EX39 156 F3
Kenwith View EX39 156 D2
Kenwyn Rd TQ1 220 C6
Kenyon Ct EX3 182 F5
Kenyon St TA21 160 F5
Keppel Pl PL2 247 F4
Keppel St PL2 247 F4
Keppel Terr 8 PL2 247 F4
KERNBOROUGH 149 B8
Kernou Rd TQ4 226 C6
Kernow Cl PL11 246 E3
Kernow Ct PL11 246 E3
Kernow Gate PL5 243 C2
Kernstone Cross EX39 22 B2
Kerria Cl TQ3 225 E8
Kerries Ct TQ10 135 A2

Kerries La TQ10 135 A2
Kerries Rd TQ10 135 A2
Ker St Ope PL1 247 E2
KERSBROOK 198 B3
Kersbrook Gdns DT7 260 D3
Kersbrook La EX9 198 A3
KERSCOTT 28 F8
Kerscott EX32 28 F8
Kerscott Hill EX32 28 F8
Kerse Cross
Thurlestone TQ7 143 B2
Thurlestone, South Milton TQ7 143 C2
Kerse La TQ7 143 B2
Kerslake's Ct 10 EX14 166 C6
Ker St PL1 247 E1
KERSWELL 66 C1
Kerswell Cl PL21 237 E4
Kerswell Cross TQ13 124 A7
Kerswell La
Kingskerswell TQ12 213 A5
Molland EX36 31 C8
Kerswill Cross TQ9 135 D1
Kerswill Rd EX4 176 F4
Kestell Rd EX10 188 C4
Kestor Cl
Okehampton EX20 170 D5
4 Plymouth PL2 248 A7
Kestor Dr
Exeter EX4 176 E8
Paignton TQ3 219 A1
Kestral Bsns Pk EX2 178 F5
Kestral Units PL5 244 A1
Kestrel Cl
Kingsteignton TQ12 207 C8
Okehampton EX20 170 B6
Plymouth PL6 245 D8
6 Tiverton EX16 161 E6
Kestrel Ct TQ1 220 C8
Kestrel Pk PL19 171 D2
Kestrel Way
Barnstaple EX32 155 E5
Dawlish EX7 200 F2
Exeter EX2 178 E5
Keswick Cres PL6 245 D2
Keverel Rd EX8 196 A1
Kew Ct EX2 178 C3
Keyberry Cl TQ12 207 D1
Keyberry Mill TQ12 207 D1
Keyberry Pk TQ12 207 D1
Keyberry Rd TQ12 207 D1
Keyes Cl PL1 247 F2
KEYHAM 247 E5
Keyham Barton RC Prim Sch PL2 247 E6
Keyham Ct PL2 247 E6
Keyham Rd PL2 247 E4
Keyham St PL5 247 E8
Keyham Sta PL2 247 E6
Keymelford Cross EX17 79 C2
Keysfield Rd TQ4 226 C5
Khartoum Pl TQ7 258 C5
Khyber Cl PL11 247 A3
Kiddicott EX17 165 B5
Kidland La
Bishops Nympton EX36 31 E1
South Molton EX36 46 E8
Kidwelly Cl PL7 251 C4
Kiel Pl PL3 249 D5
Kieran Ct 1 TQ1 220 A6
Kigbeare Cross EX20 93 B5
Kilbarran Rise EX4 177 A8
Kildere TQ7 258 C4
Kilgannon Gdns EX1 174 F3
Killatree Cross EX22 71 E7
Killerton Cl 3 TQ3 226 B7
Killerton House★ EX5 82 D3
Killerton La PL9 249 D1
Killerton Wlk EX6 181 F5
Killigrew Ave PL12 242 D1
KILLINGTON 4 C3
Killington Cross EX31 4 D2
Kilmar St PL9 249 D1
KILMINGTON 103 D8
Kilmington Prim Sch EX13 103 D8
Kilmorie TQ1 220 F3
Kilmorie Cl TQ1 220 F3
Kiln Cl
Bovey Tracey TQ13 180 C5
Cawsand PL10 253 A1
Millbrook PL10 252 F6
Plymouth PL5 247 C8
Kiln Close La 5 EX39 15 B1
Kiln Cross TQ3 218 D3
Kilnford Rd TQ12 207 F7
Kiln Ho TQ7 258 C4
Kiln La
1 Barnstaple EX32 155 A4
Branscombe EX12 190 B4
Combe Martin EX34 3 B2
Stokenham TQ7 145 B1
Kiln Orch TQ12 206 F3
Kiln Path TQ5 230 C4
Kiln Rd
Bovey Tracey TQ13 180 C5
Galmpton TQ5 229 A5
Marldon TQ3 218 C3
Kilnwood Pk EX31 154 A3
Kilworthy TQ1 220 B8
Kilworthy Hill PL19 171 C6
Kilworthy Pk PL19 171 C6
Kilworthy Rd PL19 171 C6
Kimber Cross EX20 74 E2
Kimberlands EX20 74 E2
Kimberley Ct PL21 237 D5
Kimberley Pk EX39 157 A4
Kimberley Rd EX2 261 B2
Kimberley Terr EX39 157 A8
Kimberley Villas PL21 237 C4
Kimberly Dr PL6 245 B1
Kimbland Cross EX32 18 C5
Kincraig EX8 202 C6
Kinevor Cl EX34 7 F8
King Alfred Cres EX39 157 A6
King Alfred Way EX10 186 E8
King Arthur's Rd EX4 174 A1
King Ave EX2 182 C8
King Charles I Bsns Pk TQ12 180 E4
King Charles Way EX10 188 B8
Kingdom Ave EX36 158 B5
Kingdom Fields EX31 18 B8
Kingdom Mews EX4 177 A7
Kingdom's Cnr EX16 63 C4
Kingdom St PL3 262 B1
Kingdon Ent Pk EX39 25 D4
Kingdons Ct EX36 158 D5
Kingdon Wy EX22 164 C6
King Edward Rd
Axminster EX13 167 C5
Saltash PL12 242 F2
King Edward St
13 Barnstaple EX32 154 F6
Exeter EX4 173 A1
King Edward Studios EX4 173 A1
King Edward VI Coll Lower Sch TQ9 223 B7
King Edward VI Com Coll (Kennicott Sixth Form) TQ9 223 B6
Kingfisher Ave EX2 176 D4
Kingfisher Cl
Newton St Cyres EX17 81 A1
Plymouth PL6 245 E6
Tavistock PL19 171 D2
Torquay TQ2 213 D2
Kingfisher Ct EX4 174 D1
Kingfisher Dr
Barnstaple EX32 155 E4
Exeter EX4 173 D2
Okehampton/North Tawton EX20 170 A6
Kingfisher Gdns EX15 163 B2
Kingfisher Gn EX2 176 D3
Kingfisher Way
Exeter EX2 178 E5
Kingsteignton TQ12 207 C8
Plymouth PL9 255 C7
KINGFORD 43 E6
King Henry's Rd EX2 177 E3
King James Way PL7 250 E8
King Pl EX15 162 F7
Kingsacre EX33 152 C6
Kingsacre Prim Sch EX33 152 C6
King St Bsns Pk 17 EX1 261 A2
Kingsale Rd TQ8 259 C4
KINGSAND 253 A2
King's Ash Cross TQ3 225 E6
King's Ash Prim Sch TQ3 225 E7
King's Ash Rd TQ3 225 E6
Kings Ave
Ottery St Mary EX11 169 F4
Paignton TQ3 226 C7
KINGSBRIDGE 258 E5
Kingsbridge TQ1 220 B8
Kingsbridge Com Coll TQ7 258 C4
Kingsbridge Com Prim Sch TQ7 258 E6
Kingsbridgefork Cross TQ9 144 E5
Kingsbridge Hill TQ9 223 C4
Kingsbridge La TQ13 130 F4
Kingsbridge Rd TQ10 137 E8
Kings Cl PL6 245 E6
King's Cl EX32 155 C2
Kings Cl Field TQ9 131 E1
King's Cnr TA22 33 D6
Kings Coombe Dr 13 TQ12 123 F1
KINGSCOTT 42 B5
Kingscott Hill EX38 42 B4
Kings Cotts
13 Newton Abbot TQ12 207 C3
Salcombe TQ8 259 E5
King's Cres EX16 161 E4
King's Cross TQ13 122 E6
Kings Ct
7 Honiton EX14 166 C6
Kingsbridge TQ7 258 D3
Kingsteignton TQ12 207 E6
Plymouth PL1 248 A3
7 Seaton EX12 192 B4
Kingsdale 18 TQ1 220 D4
KINGSDON 103 B5
Kingsdon Hill EX24 103 B5
Kingsdown Cl
Dawlish EX7 204 E7
Teignmouth TQ14 209 D7
Kingsdown Cres EX7 204 E7
Kingsdown Rd TQ14 209 D7
Kings Dr TQ9 228 A8
King's Dr TQ5 230 D4
King's Dr The TQ2 219 F4
Kings Farm La EX19 58 F3
Kingsgate EX4 177 D8
Kingsgate Bsns Ctr 5 EX14 166 A4
Kingsgate Cl TQ2 214 B4
King's Gdns EX14 166 C6
Kingsholme EX24 103 B3
Kingshurst Dr TQ3 226 B8
KINGSKERSWELL 213 B4
Kingskerswell CE Prim Sch TQ12 213 A5
Kingskerswell Cross TQ2 213 C3
Kingskerswell Rd
Newton Abbot TQ12 212 D7
Torquay TQ2 213 D3
Kings La EX10 188 B3
King's La
Bishop's Tawton EX32 27 F7
Lynton EX31 4 B5
Kingslade La EX10 187 B2
Kingslake Ct EX8 202 A8
Kingslake Rise EX8 202 A8
Kingsland Ct TQ4 225 E4
Kingsland Dr TQ4 225 E4
Kingsland Gardens Cl PL3 248 E6
Kingsleigh Manor 5 TQ1 220 C5
Kingsley Ave
10 Appledore EX39 15 A1
9 Barnstaple EX32 154 F6
Exeter EX4 178 B8
Ilfracombe EX34 150 B3
Torpoint PL11 247 B2
Torquay TQ2 213 F3
Kingsley Cl PL21 136 D6
Kingsley Ct EX39 156 C6
Kingsley Ho EX31 155 A8
Kingsley Pk EX39 156 E7
Kingsley Rd
Bideford EX39 157 A3
Kingsbridge TQ7 258 C4
Plymouth PL4 248 E4
Westward Ho! EX39 156 C6
Kingsley Sch EX39 156 E2
Kingsley St EX39 157 A2
Kingsley Terr
9 Bideford EX39 157 A1
8 Combe Martin EX34 3 A3
Kings Mdw TQ12 212 F4
Kingsmead Dr EX38 159 E6
Kingsmead Ho TQ3 226 C7
Kings Meadow Dr EX19 58 F3
King's Mews EX14 166 C5
Kingsmill Ind Est EX15 163 E5
Kingsmill Rd PL12 242 C5
King's Mill Rd EX15 163 E5
Kingsmoor Cross EX21 73 E7
KING'S NYMPTON 44 E6
King's Nympton County Prim Sch EX37 44 E6
King's Nympton Sta EX37 44 C3
Kings Orch TQ9 223 E5
Kings Pk EX18 44 E1
King's Quay TQ6 233 F4
King's Quay Ho TQ6 233 F4
Kings Rd
Barnstaple EX32 155 B6
Paignton TQ3 226 C7
Plymouth, Devonport PL1 247 F2
Plymouth, West Park PL5 243 F3
King's Rd
Dunchideock EX6 113 F5
Dunchideock EX6 114 A5
Exeter EX4 177 E8
Honiton EX14 166 D6
Plymouth PL1 248 A2
Kings Rydon Cl
Stoke Gabriel TQ9 227 F8
Stoke Gabriel TQ9 228 A8
Kings Sch PL3 248 E6
King's Sch The EX11 169 B3
King St
12 Bideford EX39 157 A2
Brixham TQ5 230 D5
Colyton EX24 103 A5
Combe Martin EX34 3 A3
17 Dawlish EX7 204 D6
Exeter EX1, EX4 261 A2
8 Exmouth EX8 202 A6
Gunnislake PL18 125 D6
Honiton EX14 85 E3
Honiton EX14 166 C6
Millbrook PL10 252 E5
Newton Abbot TQ12 207 C3
Plymouth PL1 262 B3
Silverton EX5 82 B6
South Molton EX36 158 C4
Tavistock PL19 171 B6
Tiverton EX16 161 C3
Torpoint PL11 247 C3
KING'S TAMERTON 243 F2
King's Tamerton Rd PL5 243 F2
KINGSTEIGNTON 207 C8
Kingsteignton Rd
Chudleigh Knighton TQ12 123 D4
Newton Abbot TQ12 207 C4
Kingsteignton Sch TQ12 207 C8
King Stephen Cl EX4 261 B4
King's Terr EX14 166 C6
KINGSTON
Bigbury 142 C6
Colaton Raleigh 186 A4
Stoke Climsland 115 C2
Kingston Ave 5 EX34 3 A3
Kingston Cl
Kingskerswell TQ12 213 A5
Plymouth PL7 251 A5
Kingston Dr PL7 251 B5
Kingston Gate Cross TQ9 216 A6
Kingston La TQ6 233 E3
Kingston Rd
Exmouth EX8 202 C7
Stoke Climsland PL17 115 C1
Kingston Workshops TQ9 216 A7
Kings Tor PL20 127 B4
Kingswater Ct TQ5 230 C5
Kingsway
Exeter EX2 177 F5
Kingsand PL10 253 B2
Langage PL7 251 E5
Lyme Regis DT7 260 E4
South Molton EX36 158 C3
Teignmouth TQ14 209 D7
Kings Way EX20 106 E5
Kingsway Ave TQ4 226 A1
Kingsway Cl
Kingsbridge TQ7 258 C4
Paignton TQ4 226 A1
Kingsway Ct TQ4 226 A1
Kingsway Dr TQ4 226 A1
Kingsway Gdns PL6 244 F3
Kingsway Pk TQ7 258 C4
KINGSWEAR 234 B2
Kingswear Cres PL6 245 B1
Kingswear Prim Sch TQ6 234 B3
Kingswear Rd
Brixham TQ5 230 A1
Brixham TQ5 234 E8
Kingswear Sta★ TQ6 234 A3
Kingswood Cl EX4 176 E8
Kingswood Ct TQ4 226 C5
Kingswood Ct TQ10 134 F2
Kingswood Mdw EX22 164 D5
Kingswood Park Ave PL3 248 D6
Kingswood Rd PL18 125 D6
King William Ho EX4 261 B4
King William St EX4 261 B4
Kinlacey Ct TQ1 220 C4
Kinnard Cres PL6 244 F7
Kinnerton Ct EX4 176 F8
Kinnerton Way EX4 176 E8
Kinross Ave PL4 249 A4
Kinsale Rd PL5 243 F3
Kinscome Ct TQ11 236 C5
Kinsford Gate Cross TA24 19 D7
Kinsford Hill TA24 19 E7
Kinterbury Rd PL5 247 B8
Kinterbury St PL1 263 A2
Kinterbury Terr PL5 247 B8
Kintyre Cl TQ2 213 E2
Kinver Cl PL6 245 D4
Kipling Cl EX8 196 C3
Kipling Ct EX39 156 C6
Kipling Dr EX2 177 F4
Kipling Fields EX39 156 D6
Kipling Gdns PL5 244 D2
Kipling Ho EX31 155 A8
Kipling Terr EX39 156 C6
Kipscombe Cross EX35 6 A6
Kipscombe Hill EX31 11 D2
Kirby Cl EX13 167 D5
Kirkby Pl PL4 262 C4
Kirkby Terr PL4 262 C4
Kirkdale Gdns PL2 248 B7
Kirkella Rd PL20 127 A2
Kirkham Ct 1 TQ3 226 A7
Kirkham House★ 13 TQ3 226 B6
Kirkham St 5 TQ3 226 B7
Kirkland Cl PL6 245 C7
Kirkstall Cl PL2 248 A8
Kirkstead Cl TQ2 219 E8
Kirkwall Rd PL5 244 E3
Kirton Dr EX17 165 D4
Kirton La EX16 47 E4
Kirton Pl PL3 249 B5
Kirtons Rd TQ12 214 B7
Kismeldon Cross EX22 39 B3
Kissing Gate Cross EX16 48 D5
KITBRIDGE 88 A6
Kitchadon Gate EX18 59 D4
Kitchadon Rd EX18 59 D3
Kitcott Cross EX36 45 F6
Kitcott Hill EX36 45 F6
Kit Hill Cres PL5 247 C8
Kitley View PL8 257 B5
Kitley Way PL5 243 D1
Kitridge La TA24 21 B7
Kits Cl 11 TQ13 123 F6
Kitter Dr PL9 256 A5
Kitterford Cross PL21 137 F7
Kittersley Dr 10 TQ12 122 F1
Kittiwake Dr TQ2 213 C2
Kitts TA21 160 D4
Kitts Cross EX10 187 A7
Kitts La EX10 187 B6
Kitt's La EX5 81 F2
Kitwell St EX15 66 A7
Kivell Cl EX22 164 B6
Klondyke Rd EX20 170 C3
Knackershole La EX17 61 B2
Knacker's Hole La TA3 68 D6
Knap Cross PL21 136 C4
KNAP DOWN 3 B4
Knap Down La EX34 3 B4
Knapp Copse Nature Reserve★ EX11 101 D6
Knapp Hill EX10 188 A5
Knapp Park Rd TQ4 226 C2
Knapps Cl PL9 256 C6
Knapp's La EX10 100 D1
Knaves Ash Cross TQ9 217 A5
Kneela Hill EX21 74 A8
Kneele Gdns PL3 248 E8
Kneller Cl EX34 150 C4
Knick Knack La TQ5 230 C3
Knightacott Cross EX31 11 C2
Knighthayes Wlk EX6 181 F5
Knightley Rd EX2 177 E3
KNIGHTON 140 D8
Knighton Cross TQ12 131 F8
Knighton Hill Bsns Ctr PL9 140 E8
Knighton Rd
Plymouth PL4 263 C3
Wembury PL9 140 D8
Knighton Terr 4 PL20 126 F5
Knights Cres EX2 178 D3
Knights Field Rise EX39 157 A8
Knightshayes Court★ EX16 49 C2
Knight's La EX13 88 A4
Knights Mead TQ13 123 C4
Knights Pl EX4 174 A1
Knights Rd TA21 52 D8
Knightstone Down La EX17 61 C2
Knightstone La
Ottery St Mary EX11 169 F3
Ottery St Mary, Wiggaton EX11 169 F1
Knightstone Rd EX11 169 F1
Knightswood EX15 163 C2
Knill Cross PL10 252 E5
Knill Cross Cotts PL10 252 E5
Knobcrook EX38 56 C6
Knockworthy Cross EX38 26 F1
Knoll Knap EX13 103 E4
Knoll The PL7 250 B6
KNOTTY CORNER 25 B4
Knowland Cl PL1 247 F3
KNOWLE
Braunton 8 D1
Budleigh Salterton 197 E2
Copplestone 79 C4
Knowle Ave PL2 247 E6
Knowle Bsns Units EX2 181 D8
Knowle Cl
Ashburton TQ13 130 E4
Cullompton EX15 163 A3
Honiton EX14 166 C6
Landkey EX32 17 B2
Knowle Cnr EX9 197 D1
Knowle Cross
Copplestone EX17 79 C4
Hennock TQ13 123 C8
Whimple EX5 99 E8
Knowle Cross La EX5 99 E8
Knowle Ct TQ8 259 D5
Knowle Dr
Exeter EX4 176 F7
Sidmouth EX10 188 A4
Knowle Fork TQ7 148 F4
Knowle Gdns
Combe Martin EX34 3 A3
Kingsbridge TQ7 258 C6
Sidmouth EX10 187 F4
Knowle Grange 1 EX10 188 A4
Knowle Hill EX9 197 C2
Knowle House Cl TQ7 258 D6
Knowle Ind Est EX33 8 D1
Knowle La
Butterleigh EX15 64 F1
Copplestone EX17 79 C4
Drewsteignton EX6 96 D1
Knowle Mews EX9 197 E2
Knowle Prim Sch PL5 244 A4
Knowle Rd
Knowle EX9 197 E1
Lustleigh TQ13 122 C8
Lustleigh TQ13 122 D7
Salcombe TQ8 259 D5
Knowles Cross TQ13 130 E4
Knowles Dr 22 EX24 103 A4
KNOWLES HILL 207 B4
Knowles Hill Rd TQ12 207 B4
Knowle Terr PL20 127 B4
Knowle The TQ12 207 F6
Knowle View EX20 170 D6
Knowle Village EX9 197 E2
KNOWSTONE 32 A2
Knowstone Cross EX16 47 D6
Knowstone Moor Cross EX36 47 B8
Kola Dr EX4 174 D1
Kyl Cober Parc PL17 115 C1
Kynance Cl PL11 246 F4
Kynock Ind Est EX39 25 F4

L

Labatt Cl PL6 245 D3
Labbett's Cross EX18 60 C6
Labdon La EX18 59 C7
Laburnham Gr TQ9 223 A7
Laburnum PL19 171 C6
Laburnum Cl
Exmouth EX8 196 D3
1 Honiton EX14 85 C2
Laburnum Cotts 7 TA21 160 D5
Laburnum Ct TQ12 212 B6
Laburnum Dr
Barnstaple EX32 155 E3
6 Wembury PL9 140 D8
Laburnum Rd
Exeter EX2 177 F3
Newton Abbot TQ12 207 E1
Wellington TA21 160 E5
Laburnum Row 5 TQ2 219 F6
Laburnum St TQ2 219 F5
Laburnum Terr TQ12 212 B7
Laburnum Villas PL19 117 E6
Laburnum Way
East Allington TQ9 144 E7
Okehampton EX20 170 C5
Lace Cres EX16 161 B6
Lace Wlk EX14 166 C6
Lacey Ho 7 TQ3 226 B6
Lackaborough Ct EX2 181 A8
Lacy Rd TQ3 219 A1
Ladford Mill Cross EX21 55 C6
Ladies Mile EX31 4 A4
Ladies' Mile EX32 155 A3
Ladram Rd EX9 199 A8
Ladybird La PL20 127 A3
Ladyfern Rd PL6 241 C1
Lady Harriet Acland's Dr
Bury TA22 33 F5
Bury TA22 34 A6
Lady Harriet Acland's Dr TA22 34 A8
Ladymead EX10 187 F8
Lady Meadow Terr TQ13 121 B2
Lady Modifords CE(VA) Prim Sch PL20 127 B4
Lady Park Rd TQ2 219 D3
Lady Seawards CE Prim Sch EX3 183 C6
Ladysmith Ct PL4 263 C4
Ladysmith Inf Sch EX1 177 F7
Ladysmith Jun Sch EX1 177 F7
Ladysmith Rd
Exeter EX1 177 F7
Plymouth PL4 249 B3
Lady St TA22 33 D7
Lady Victoria's Dr TA22 33 E6
Ladywell EX31 154 F7
Ladywell Mdws EX37 44 E1
Ladywell Path EX35 151 A5
Ladywell Pl PL4 263 B3
Lafrowda Cott EX4 177 C8
Lagge Hill Cross EX17 80 F8
Lag Hill EX17 62 F1
Lagoon View EX31 153 A4
LAIRA 249 C4
Laira Ave PL3 249 D4
Laira Bridge Rd PL4 249 B1
Laira Gdns PL3 249 C4
Laira Green Prim Sch PL3 249 C4
Laira Park Cres PL4 249 B4
Laira Park Pl PL4 249 B4
Laira Park Rd PL4 249 B4
Laira Pl PL4 263 C2
Laira St PL4 263 C3
Laity Wlk PL6 244 D6
LAKE
Barnstaple 154 E2
Yelverton 127 B3
Lake Ave
5 Teignmouth TQ14 209 E8
Teignmouth TQ14 210 A7
Lake Cl EX14 166 D5
Lake Cross TQ9 131 D2
Lake Ind Est EX21 55 E4
Lake La
Ashreigney EX18 58 F7
Dousland PL20 127 B3
Newton St Cyres EX5 80 F2
Northlew EX20 74 D2
Stockleigh Pomeroy EX17 81 A7
Lakeland TQ12 212 B6
Lakelands Cl EX16 46 E1

Lakelands Dr EX4 ... 176 F6
Lake Mews PL10 ... 252 E5
Lakenham Cotts
EX39 ... 156 E7
Lakenham Hill EX39 ... 156 F7
Lake Rd PL9 ... 255 B6
Lakerise EX7 ... 201 A2
Lake Rural Workshops
EX21 ... 55 E4
Lakes Cl TQ5 ... 230 A5
Lakes Cross EX20 ... 57 A8
Lakes Ct EX10 ... 188 B3
Lakes Down EX5 ... 172 F7
Lakeside
Salcombe TQ8 ... 259 D5
Tavistock PL19 ... 171 B6
Lakeside Ave EX2 ... 182 B8
Lakeside Cl TQ13 ... 180 C4
Lakeside Dr PL5 ... 243 E5
Lakeside Village
TQ12 ... 123 C6
Lakes La EX4 ... 98 F4
Lakes Rd TQ5 ... 230 A4
Lake St TQ6 ... 233 F3
Lakeview EX7 ... 201 A2
Lake View EX17 ... 165 E6
Lake View Cl PL5 ... 244 B6
Lakeview Dr PL5 ... 244 B5
Lakewater Cross
TQ9 ... 131 E1
Lalebrick Rd PL9 ... 255 B5
Lamacraft Cl EX7 ... 204 F8
Lamacraft Dr EX4 ... 178 A7
Lama Cross EX18 ... 59 C4
Lamaton Pk EX36 ... 158 D3
Lambert Cl EX7 ... 204 F8
Lambert Cross EX20 ... 75 A3
Lambert La EX6 ... 96 F3
Lambert Rd PL5 ... 244 B6
Lambert's La TQ14 ... 209 D4
Lambhay Hill PL1 ... 263 A1
Lambhay St PL1 ... 263 A1
Lamb Park Cl 10
TQ12 ... 123 F1
Lambpark Ct TA3 ... 68 C6
Lamb Pk
Chagford TQ13 ... 111 A6
Drewsteignton EX6 ... 96 D1
Ilfracombe EX34 ... 150 A4
Lambs Cl TQ7 ... 143 A2
Lambscombe Cross
EX36 ... 31 A8
Lambscombe Hill
EX36 ... 31 A8
Lamb The TQ9 ... 223 B5
Lamejohns Field
EX17 ... 165 D6
Lamerhooe Cross
PL19 ... 116 A1
Lamerhooe Dr PL19 ... 116 A1
LAMERTON ... 116 F3
Lamerton CE Prim Sch
PL19 ... 116 E3
Lamerton Cl PL5 ... 244 B3
Lamerton Cross EX20 ... 75 F2
Lammacott Cross
EX17 ... 78 E5
Lammacott La EX17 ... 78 E6
Lammas La TQ3 ... 226 A8
Lamorna Pk PL11 ... 246 E4
Lampard Com Sch The
EX32 ... 155 C3
Lamplighters 14
EX14 ... 166 C6
Lamplough Rd EX8 ... 196 A3
LANA
Holsworthy ... 53 C2
Tetcott ... 89 F7
Lana Cotts EX22 ... 89 F7
Lana Cross EX22 ... 55 C1
Lanbridge Cross TQ9 222 F1
Lancaster Cl
Cullompton EX15 ... 163 C5
Exeter EX2 ... 178 B5
Lancaster Dr TQ4 ... 226 A2
Lancaster Gdns PL5 ... 244 D4
Lancaster Ho TQ4 ... 226 C5
Lancelot Rd EX4 ... 174 A2
Lancercombe EX10 ... 100 D3
Lancercombe La
EX10 ... 100 D3
Lancer Ct TA21 ... 160 D6
Lanchitt Cross EX36 ... 19 B2
Lancin La TA20 ... 69 E2
Lancock St TA21 ... 160 A5
Landacre La TA24 ... 21 A7
Landboat Cotts EX17 ... 62 F1
Landboat View EX17 ... 62 F1
Landcroft La
Sheldon EX15 ... 66 F4
Sheldon EX15 ... 67 A4
LANDCROSS ... 26 A2
Lander Rd PL12 ... 242 F3
Landhayes Rd EX4 ... 176 F5
LANDKEY ... 17 B2
LANDKEY NEWLAND ... 17 B1
Landkey Prim Sch 13
EX32 ... 17 B2
Landkey Rd
Barnstaple EX32 ... 155 C2
Barnstaple EX32 ... 155 D2
Barnstaple EX32 ... 155 E2
Landlord's Hill TA21 ... 51 E7
Landmark Rd TQ8 ... 259 B4
Landmark Theatre*
EX34 ... 150 B6
Landpath TQ7 ... 143 A2
Land Pk 1 EX18 ... 44 E1
Landrace Cl TQ12 ... 211 F8
Landrake Cl PL5 ... 247 C8
Landscore EX17 ... 165 B5
Landscore Cl
Crediton EX17 ... 165 B5
Teignmouth TQ14 ... 210 B5
Landscore Prim Sch
EX17 ... 165 A5
Landscore Rd
3 Exeter EX4 ... 177 A5
Teignmouth TQ14 ... 210 B5
LANDSCOVE ... 131 B1
Landscove CE Prim Sch
TQ13 ... 131 B1
Landsend La EX17 ... 78 E3
Lands Pk PL9 ... 255 F7
Lands Rd
Brixham TQ5 ... 230 F6
Exeter EX4 ... 174 D1
LANDULPH ... 243 A7
Landulph Cross PL12 238 F1
Landulph Gdns PL5 ... 247 C8
Landulph Sch PL12 ... 238 F1
Landunvez Pl EX5 ... 82 F6
Lane Cross EX22 ... 53 F7
LANE END ... 73 D3
Lane End Cl 1 EX39 ... 15 B1
Lane End Cross
Broadhembury EX14 ... 84 E8
Broadhempston TQ13 ... 131 D3
Halwill EX21 ... 73 D3
Horsebridge PL19 ... 116 B2
Ipplepen TQ12 ... 211 D2
Lane End Pk EX32 ... 155 D4
Lane End Pool TQ9 ... 227 B3
Lane End Rd EX39 ... 15 B1
Lane Field Rd EX39 ... 156 D2
Lanehead EX2 ... 191 D5
Lane Head Cl EX33 ... 7 E2
Lanehead Rd EX12 ... 191 D5
Lane The
Dittisham TQ6 ... 228 D2
Lutton PL21 ... 133 B2
Plymouth PL7 ... 250 D6
LANGAFORD ... 73 B2
Langaford La EX21 ... 73 B2
Langage Cross PL7 ... 251 F6
Langage Ind Est PL7 251 D4
Langage Pk PL7 ... 251 C4
Langage Science Pk
PL7 ... 251 D5
Langage South Rd
PL7 ... 251 D4
Langaller Cl TQ13 ... 180 B5
Langaller Hill TA22 ... 33 D4
Langaller La
Bovey Tracey TQ13 ... 122 E3
Bovey Tracey TQ13 ... 180 B4
Langarra Pk EX15 ... 162 B4
Langarron Pk EX32 ... 155 B5
Langaton Gdns EX1 ... 174 F1
Langaton La EX1 ... 175 A1
LANGBROOK ... 136 D3
Langbrook Cross
PL21 ... 136 E3
Langdale Cl PL6 ... 245 D1
Langdale Gdns PL6 ... 245 D1
Langdon Cross PL21 ... 137 F1
Langdon Ct PL9 ... 256 B6
Langdon Down Way
PL11 ... 246 E3
Langdon Fields TQ5 ... 229 B6
Langdon Hospl EX7 ... 200 E2
Langdon La
Dawlish EX7 ... 204 C8
Galmpton TQ4, TQ5 ... 229 B6
Langdon Rd
Bradworthy EX22 ... 38 E1
Dawlish EX7 ... 204 D8
Paignton TQ3 ... 219 C1
Langdons Way TA20 ... 88 C8
Langdon Way EX5 ... 179 B3
LANGDOWN ... 95 D7
Langerwehe Way
EX8 ... 201 F6
Langerwell Cl PL12 ... 242 C3
Langerwell La PL12 ... 242 C3
LANGFORD
Brampford Speke ... 172 E8
Plymtree ... 83 C5
Langford Ave EX14 ... 166 D6
Langford Cres TQ2 ... 213 F3
Langford Cross EX17 ... 78 C4
Langford Gate PL21 ... 137 F8
Langford Gn EX15 ... 83 D5
Langford Rd
Honiton EX14 ... 166 D7
Langford EX5 ... 172 E7
Lang Gdns PL18 ... 125 D3
Lang Gr
Plymouth PL9 ... 256 C7
Tavistock PL19 ... 171 D5
Langham Cross EX19 ... 57 D6
Langham La EX17 ... 61 F2
Langham Levels
PL21 ... 237 B6
Langham Pl PL4 ... 263 C3
Langham Way PL21 ... 237 C5
Langhill Rd PL3 ... 248 D5
Langland Hill EX17 ... 61 A4
Langland La EX11 ... 169 B7
Langlands Bsns Pk
EX15 ... 65 F6
Langlands Cl TQ4 ... 225 E4
Langlands Cross EX14 87 A6
Langlands Rd EX15 ... 163 A3
LANGLEIGH ... 150 A4
Langleigh La EX34 ... 150 A4
Langleigh Pk EX34 ... 150 A4
Langleigh Rd EX34 ... 150 A5
Langley EX18 ... 44 E1
Langley Ave TQ5 ... 230 C4
Langley Cl
Brixham TQ5 ... 230 C4
Plymouth PL6 ... 245 A7
Langley Cres PL6 ... 244 F7
Langley Cross EX37 ... 27 F3
Langley Gdns 6 EX18 ... 44 E1
Langley La EX18 ... 44 E1
Langman Ct 17 PL20 ... 125 E1
Langmans Cross TQ7 143 A2
Langmead
Westleigh EX39 ... 26 B7
Westleigh EX39 ... 157 E5
Langmead Cl PL6 ... 249 C8
Langmead Dr EX39 ... 157 E1
Langmead Rd PL6 ... 249 C8
Langmoor Cl DT7 ... 260 D3
Langmoor La EX13 ... 88 D2
Langmore Cl PL6 ... 249 A7
Langport La EX7 ... 200 D3
Langridge Cross EX37 ... 27 F1
LANGRIDGEFORD ... 27 F1
Langridge Rd TQ3 ... 225 E8
Langsfield EX33 ... 7 D1
Langsford Rd PL19 ... 117 E3
Langs Rd TQ3 ... 226 C8
Langston Cross
Kingston TQ7 ... 142 D7
Whiddon Down EX20 ... 95 D1
Langstone Cl
Heathfield TQ12 ... 180 F2
Torquay TQ1 ... 220 D6
Langstone Cross
TQ13 ... 121 E8
Langstone Dr EX8 ... 196 C1
Langstone Hill
Lustleigh TQ13 ... 121 E8
Moretonhampstead
TQ13 ... 111 E1
Langstone Rd PL2 ... 248 C7
Langstone Terr PL2 ... 248 C7
Langton Rd 8 PL20 ... 126 F3
LANGTREE ... 40 F2
LANGTREE COMMON ... 41 A3
Langtree Com Prim Sch
EX38 ... 40 F2
Langtreemoor La
EX38 ... 40 E2
Lang Way TQ12 ... 211 E2
Langwells Ct TQ9 ... 139 E1
Langworthys Barn
TQ7 ... 143 E2
Lanherne EX7 ... 204 E6
Lanherne Fst Sch 26
EX7 ... 204 D6
Lanhydrock Cl TQ3 ... 225 D8
Lanhydrock Rd PL4 ... 249 B2
Lannacombe Gn TQ7 149 C5
Lanscore La EX14 ... 101 A8
Lansdowne EX2 ... 178 B4
Lansdowne La 2
TQ2 ... 219 F5
Lansdowne Pk
Northam EX39 ... 156 F8
Totnes TQ9 ... 223 E4
Lansdowne Rd
Budleigh Salterton
EX9 ... 197 D1
Plymouth PL6 ... 244 F2
1 Torquay TQ2 ... 219 F5
Lansdowne Terr
Bideford EX39 ... 156 F1
Exeter EX2 ... 261 B2
Lansdown Terr 2
EX32 ... 155 A6
Lanteglos Cl 5 PL21 ... 137 C7
LAPFORD ... 60 C3
Lapford Com Prim Sch
EX17 ... 60 D3
LAPFORD CROSS ... 60 C2
Lapford Cross EX17 ... 60 C2
Lapford Sta EX17 ... 60 C2
Laps Cottage TA20 ... 69 C5
Lapthorn Cl PL9 ... 255 C7
Lapthorne Ind Est
TQ12 ... 211 F3
Lapwing Cl
Cullompton EX15 ... 163 A3
Dawlish EX7 ... 200 F2
Dawlish Warren EX7 ... 201 A2
Lapwing Gr EX31 ... 15 C3
Larch Cl
Exmouth EX8 ... 196 D3
Saltash PL12 ... 242 C3
Seaton EX12 ... 192 A8
Teignmouth TQ14 ... 210 B6
Larch Dr PL6 ... 245 E7
Larch Gr
Plympton PL7 ... 132 B1
Sparkwell PL7 ... 132 C1
Larch Rd
Dawlish EX7 ... 204 E8
Exeter EX2 ... 176 F3
Larch Wlk TQ2 ... 219 C8
Larcombe End TQ9 ... 135 F1
LARKBEARE ... 100 B8
Larkbeare Ave EX5 ... 100 B8
Larkbeare Cross EX5 100 B8
Larkbeare Rd EX2 ... 261 B1
Lark Cl EX4 ... 173 D1
Larkey La EX16 ... 63 D4
Larkhall Rise PL3 ... 249 B5
Larkham Cl PL7 ... 250 C6
Larkham La PL7 ... 250 C6
Lark Hill PL2 ... 248 A6
Larkin Cl TQ13 ... 180 F7
Lark Rise
5 Barnstaple EX31 ... 154 A2
Newton Poppleford
EX10 ... 186 E8
Larks Cl TQ14 ... 209 D4
Larkshayes Cross
EX13 ... 86 E3
Larkshayes Droveway
EX13 ... 86 F3
Larkshayes Knap EX13 86 F3
Larksmead Cl TQ12 ... 207 A1
Larksmead Way
TQ12 ... 207 A1
Larkspur Ct TQ3 ... 225 E2
Larkspur Dr TQ12 ... 206 E5
Larkspur Gdns EX32 ... 155 E4
Larks Rise EX15 ... 163 A2
Larkstone Cres 3
EX34 ... 150 D5
Larkstone Gdns
EX34 ... 150 D5
Larkstone La EX34 ... 150 D6
Larkstone Terr EX34 ... 150 D6
Larks Way EX32 ... 17 F4
Lashbrook EX5 ... 84 B2
Lashingcott Cross
EX31 ... 27 B3
Lashingcott Lane End
EX31 ... 27 B2
Laskeys Heath 1
TQ12 ... 122 F1
Laskeys La EX10 ... 188 C4
Latches Wlk EX13 ... 167 D6
Latchgate Cross EX36 ... 31 F7
Latchgate Hill EX36 ... 31 F7
Latch La EX38 ... 40 E2
Latchmount Gdns
EX13 ... 167 D6
Latham Cl PL6 ... 249 A7
Latham Ct EX39 ... 156 F2
Latimer Cl PL7 ... 251 B5
Latimer Rd EX4 ... 178 A8
Latimer Wlk PL6 ... 244 E7
Lauderdale 2 EX32 ... 155 B4
Lauderdale Dr EX32 ... 155 B4
Lauder La EX31 ... 154 C1
LAUNCESTON ... 105 B2
Launceston Cl PL6 ... 245 B7
Launceston Head EX5 83 C1
Launceston Rd
Bridestowe EX20 ... 107 E8
Tavistock PL19 ... 171 A5
Laundry Cotts EX5 ... 98 F8
Laura Ave TQ3 ... 226 B8
Laura Gr TQ3 ... 226 A8
Laura Pl 3 TQ3 ... 226 A6
Laurel Ave EX39 ... 156 E1
Laurel Bank EX14 ... 85 B4
Laurel Ct PL2 ... 248 A7
Laurel Dene PL2 ... 248 A7
Laurel Dr PL6 ... 245 E5
Laurel La TQ14 ... 209 D5
Laurel Rd
Exeter EX2 ... 177 F3
1 Honiton EX14 ... 166 A4
Plymouth PL2 ... 248 A7
Laurel Rise EX8 ... 202 D8
Laurels The
Barnstaple EX31 ... 154 B2
Dunkeswell EX14 ... 67 C3
Gunnislake PL18 ... 125 B5
Sidmouth EX10 ... 188 A5
Torquay TQ1 ... 220 D8
Laureston Rd TQ12 ... 207 C2
Laurie Ave TQ12 ... 206 F4
Lauriston Cl TQ2 ... 220 A5
Lavender Cl TQ5 ... 230 A4
Lavender Rd EX4 ... 176 E8
Lavender Wy EX32 ... 155 C4
Lavington Cl PL7 ... 251 B5
Lavinia Dr PL7 ... 250 C5
LAWHITTON ... 105 B1
Lawhitton Down
PL15 ... 105 A1
Law Memorial Ho 5
EX32 ... 16 E1
Lawn Cl
2 Plymouth PL7 ... 251 C5
Torquay TQ2 ... 213 F4
Lawn Dr
Chudleigh TQ13 ... 123 E6
14 Chudleigh TQ13 ... 123 F6
Lawn Gdns 16 TQ13 ... 123 E6
Lawn Hill 3 EX7 ... 204 E6
Lawn Rd EX8 ... 202 A7
Lawns End TQ14 ... 208 E8
Lawns The
Barnstaple EX32 ... 155 D2
Plymouth PL5 ... 244 E1
Torpoint PL11 ... 247 A4
Lawn Terr 25 EX7 ... 204 D6
Lawn The
3 Budleigh Salterton
EX9 ... 198 A1
Tavistock PL19 ... 171 D6
1 Wellington TA21 ... 160 D6
Lawn Vista EX10 ... 188 B5
Lawrence Ave EX4 ... 177 A4
Lawrence Cl EX14 ... 84 D7
Lawrence Pl TQ2 ... 220 B4
Lawrence Rd PL9 ... 255 A6
Lawrence Wlk EX6 ... 181 F5
Lawson Gr PL9 ... 255 C7
Law Wlk PL6 ... 244 D6
Laxton Ave EX1 ... 178 C6
Layne Cl EX6 ... 113 B4
Layne Fields EX6 ... 113 B4
Laywell Cl TQ5 ... 230 B2
Laywell La TQ5 ... 230 A3
Laywell Rd TQ5 ... 230 A3
Lazenby Rd EX16 ... 161 F3
Leach Ave TQ13 ... 180 B6
Leaches La EX18 ... 60 B7
Leachway La EX2 ... 113 F7
Leachway Lane Cross
EX2 ... 113 F7
Lea Combe EX13 ... 167 D5
Leadengate Cl EX33 ... 7 E1
Leadengate Fields
EX33 ... 7 D1
Leader Cl TQ5 ... 230 E5
Leader La
Marldon TQ3 ... 218 D1
Marldon TQ3 ... 218 D2
Paignton TQ3 ... 225 D8
Leaholes Ave EX20 ... 170 C5
Lea La EX9 ... 198 F7
Lealands TQ13 ... 180 C6
Lea Mount TQ14 ... 209 A8
Lea Mount Cl EX7 ... 204 D5
Lea Mount Dr EX7 ... 204 D5
Lea Mount Rd EX7 ... 204 E5
Leander Ct 18 TQ14 ... 210 B4
Leander Way PL5 ... 244 D2
Leanway PL12 ... 242 E2
Lea Rd
Otterton EX9 ... 198 E7
Tiverton EX16 ... 161 F6
Torquay TQ2 ... 214 B3
Lear La EX13 ... 167 C4
Lear Pk EX15 ... 83 F5
Lears La TQ13 ... 123 F6
Leary Cross EX32 ... 29 B8
Lease Cotts EX5 ... 82 D4
Lease Hill EX5 ... 82 E4
Lea Side EX6 ... 112 E8
Leas Rd EX9 ... 198 A1
Leas The EX34 ... 150 A3
Leat Cl
Dousland PL20 ... 127 B3
Kingsteignton TQ12 ... 207 E7
Lea Terr EX39 ... 15 A1
Leatfield Dr
Plymouth PL6 ... 244 F4
Plymouth PL6 ... 245 A4
Lea The TQ14 ... 209 C7
Leatherby Cl PL6 ... 244 E7
Leather Tor Cl 4
PL20 ... 126 F3
Leat Mdw
3 Coldeast TQ12 ... 122 F1
Tiverton EX16 ... 161 B5
Leat Rd PL16 ... 105 F3
Leatside
Exeter EX2 ... 261 A2
Roborough PL6 ... 241 C1
Leatside Ho TQ12 ... 207 A3
Leat St
Tiverton EX16 ... 161 B5
Tiverton EX16 ... 161 C4
Leat View
Ivybridge PL21 ... 237 D6
Saltash PL12 ... 242 B3
Leatway Gdns EX15 ... 163 B3
Leat Wlk
Plymouth PL3 ... 248 E6
Roborough PL6 ... 241 D1
Saltash PL12 ... 242 D4
Lea Vale Rd TQ12 ... 207 A3
Leaveacre EX17 ... 79 D6
Leaves Yd PL3 ... 249 B7
Lea View EX15 ... 162 D5
Leaway Cotts EX16 ... 161 E4
Leaze Rd TQ12 ... 207 D8
Lebanon Cl EX4 ... 173 E1
Leburnick Cross
PL15 ... 115 B8
Ledgate La PL7 ... 251 F8
Ledsgrove TQ12 ... 211 E2
LEDSTONE ... 144 B5
Ledstone Cross TQ7 ... 144 B5
LEE ... 1 C3
Lee Ave EX39 ... 25 F1
Lee Ball Cross EX31 ... 11 E3
Lee Ball Hill EX31 ... 11 D3
Leechwell La TQ9 ... 223 C5
Leechwell St TQ9 ... 223 B5
Lee Cl EX14 ... 166 B6
Lee Cliff Pk EX7 ... 201 B1
Lee Cross
Broadhempston TQ9 ... 131 E1
Great Torrington EX37 ... 42 F7
North Molton EX36 ... 30 B8
Woolacombe EX34 ... 1 C1
Leecross Gate EX17 ... 61 A7
Leecross La EX5 ... 81 F8
Lee Ct TQ5 ... 230 E4
LEEFORD ... 6 B5
Leeford La EX35 ... 6 B5
Leeford Rd TA4 ... 35 B7
Lee La
Bishops Nympton
EX36 ... 31 F6
Dartmouth TQ6 ... 232 C7
Dunsford EX6 ... 112 E7
Molland EX36 ... 32 A5
Lee Lane End TQ7 ... 148 F8
LEE MILL ... 136 C7
Lee Mill Hosp PL7 ... 136 C7
Lee Mill Ind Est PL21 136 C6
LEE MOOR ... 132 F5
Lee Moor La PL7 ... 132 E4
Lee Pk TA21 ... 52 F7
Lee Pl EX34 ... 150 C6
Lee Rd EX35 ... 151 B5
Leeside Ct 7 PL2 ... 248 A4
Lees Mdw EX5 ... 84 A2
Lee Terr 2 TQ13 ... 123 E6
Leeward Ct EX8 ... 201 E6
Leeward La TQ2 ... 213 E3
Leeze Pk EX20 ... 170 B4
Leggetts La DT7 ... 193 C7
Legion Hall La PL18 ... 125 C5
Legion La PL8 ... 257 A5
Legion Way EX2 ... 177 B2
Legis Wlk PL6 ... 245 B8
Leg O Mutton Corner
PL19 ... 126 F2
Leicester Mead EX4 ... 176 E7
LEIGHAM ... 249 E8
Leigham Ct
7 Dawlish EX7 ... 204 E6
Plymouth PL1 ... 262 B2
Leighammanor Dr
PL6 ... 245 F1
Leigham Manor Dr
PL6 ... 249 F8
Leigham Prim Sch
PL6 ... 245 E1
Leigham St PL1 ... 262 B1
Leigham Terr TQ7 ... 258 C5
Leigham Terrace La
PL1 ... 262 B2
Leigham Terrace Lane W
PL1 ... 262 B2
Leighan Bsns Units
EX2 ... 181 D8
Leigh Cl PL21 ... 137 C8
Leighcott Cross EX17 ... 62 A2
Leighcott La EX17 ... 62 A2
Leigh Cross
Ashill EX15 ... 66 F6
Bittaford PL21 ... 137 D8
Bridford EX6 ... 113 B6
Chulmleigh EX18 ... 59 C8
Hennock TQ13 ... 123 C7
Kingsbridge TQ7 ... 258 A8
Modbury PL21 ... 137 F3
South Brent TQ10 ... 135 A4
Zeal Monachorum EX17 ... 77 F7
Leigh Ct PL6 ... 249 A8
Leighdene Cl EX2 ... 177 E4
Leigh Dene Cl EX2 ... 177 E4
Leigh La
Bittaford PL21 ... 137 C8
Chawleigh EX17 ... 60 C6
Combe Martin EX34 ... 3 C2
Moorhaven Village
TQ10 ... 137 C8
Roborough PL6 ... 241 D2
Leighmoor Cross
PL21 ... 137 F3
Leighon Rd TQ3 ... 226 C7
Leigh Rd
Bideford EX39 ... 156 E1
Chulmleigh EX18 ... 44 D1
Combe Martin EX34 ... 3 B2
Leighton Rd PL3 ... 248 F8
Leighton Terr EX4 ... 261 B4
Leighty Water EX38 ... 42 A6
Leigh Villas EX18 ... 44 E1
Leland Gr PL21 ... 237 D4
Le Locle Cl EX10 ... 187 F8
Le Marchant Cl EX14 ... 67 B1
Lembury Rd TQ9 ... 225 A1
Le Molay-Littry Way
TQ13 ... 180 E7
Lemon Ct 18 TQ12 ... 207 C3
Lemonford La TQ12 ... 131 D7
Lemonford Mills
TQ12 ... 131 D6
Lemon Pl TQ12 ... 207 C3
Lemon Rd TQ12 ... 207 C3
Lenards Rd EX39 ... 156 F6
Lenda La TQ12 ... 122 C2
Lendon Way EX19 ... 58 F2
Lennard Rd 6 EX17 ... 165 C5
Lennards Ct EX10 ... 188 B3
Lennox Ave EX10 ... 188 B4
Lentney Cl PL9 ... 140 A8
Lenton La EX37 ... 44 C6
Lenwood Ctry Club
EX39 ... 156 E5
Lenwood Pk EX39 ... 156 E4
Lenwood Rd EX39 ... 156 E5
Leo Ave PL9 ... 256 E8
Leofric Rd EX16 ... 161 D6
Leonard Moor Cross
EX15 ... 65 F8
Leonards Cl TQ7 ... 143 A1
Leonards Rd PL21 ... 237 D5
Lerwell Beech Tree Cross
EX37 ... 29 A5
Leslie Rd EX8 ... 202 A8
Lester Cl PL3 ... 249 B6
Lestock Cl EX8 ... 202 F7
Lethaby Rd EX32 ... 155 B6
Lethbridge Rd EX2 ... 178 B4
Lethbridge's & Davey's
Almshouses EX1 ... 261 C4
Letheren's La EX20 ... 77 B5
Letherens Mdw EX20 ... 77 C5
Lettaford Cross TQ13 111 B3
LEUSDON ... 130 A8
Level The TQ6 ... 228 C2
Lever Cl EX39 ... 156 F8
Leverlake Cl EX16 ... 161 F6
Leverlake La
Chettiscombe EX16 ... 49 C1
Tiverton EX16 ... 161 F7

Lewdon Cross EX6 97 A5
LEWDOWN 106 E5
Lewesdon Ct 2 DT7 260 D3
Lewes Gdns PL5 244 C4
Lewhaven Cl EX20 106 E5
Lewis Ave EX16 161 E4
Lewis Cres EX2 178 D3
Lewis Ct 4 EX34 150 B5
Leworthy Cross
Holsworthy EX22 71 D4
Woolfardisworthy EX39 39 B6
Leworthy Dr EX4 174 E3
Leworthy Hill EX31 11 D1
Leworthy Post EX32 11 C1
Lewsley Cross EX13 87 E4
Lewsley La EX13 87 E4
Lewthorn Cross
TQ13 122 B3
LEWTRENCHARD 106 F4
Lew Trenchard CE Prim
Sch EX20 106 F5
Lexhayne La EX13 103 A7
Leyburn Gr TQ4 226 A4
Ley Cl TQ12 180 B1
Ley Cres TQ12 180 B1
Ley Cross
Ashreigney EX18 58 F8
Aveton Gifford PL21 143 A8
Ermington PL21 136 D4
Holsworthy Beacon
EX22 54 F3
North Molton EX36 30 F8
Widecombe in the Moor
TQ13 121 C6
Leyfield Wlk EX7 204 E7
Leyford Cl PL9 140 D8
Leyford La PL9 255 F3
Ley La
Bere Ferrers PL20 239 D6
Kentisbury EX31 10 D6
Kingsteignton TQ12 207 D8
Ley La Cross TQ12 207 D8
Leyland Cross EX22 53 E8
Ley Meadow Dr EX31 154 A3
Leypark Ave PL21 237 E4
Leypark Cl EX1 178 C7
Leypark Cres EX1 178 C7
Leypark Ct PL6 245 E2
Leypark Dr PL6 245 E2
Leypark Rd EX1 178 C7
Leypark Wlk PL6 245 E2
Ley's Cross EX17 62 E2
Ley's La EX31 4 C1
Leys Rd TQ2 219 D5
Leyton Ct EX15 163 C3
Leywood EX14 86 D7
Libby Ct PL12 242 C5
Liberator Way EX14 67 C1
Liberty Rd EX31 154 B2
Liberty Stile EX39 22 C2
Liberty Way EX2 178 E1
Libra Ave PL9 256 E8
Libra Gdns EX34 2 F4
Libra Sch The EX36 19 E3
Lichfield Ave TQ2 214 A1
Lichfield Cl TQ5 230 A4
Lichfield Dr TQ5 230 A4
Lichfield Rd EX4 176 D6
Lichgate Rd EX2 181 C8
Lidburn Hill EX6 97 E5
LIDDATON 106 F1
Liddle Way PL7 251 B6
Lidford Tor Ave TQ4 225 F3
Lidstone La TQ3 225 C1
Lidyates La DT7, EX13 103 F3
Lifeboat La
4 Shaldon TQ14 209 F5
Shaldon TQ14 210 B3
Liffey Rise EX4 176 E8
LIFTON 105 E4
Lifton Com Prim Sch
PL16 105 E4
LIFTONDOWN 105 C4
Liftondown Cross
PL16 105 C4
Lifton La EX19 59 B3
Lighthouse Cross
EX39 23 B3
Light La TQ5 229 B4
Lightleigh Cross EX18 44 F5
Lilac Cl PL9 255 C5
Lilac Haven EX14 166 C5
Lilac Rd
Exeter EX2 177 F3
Tiverton EX16 161 F5
Lilac Terr 2 EX16 161 D4
Lilac Way 3 EX32 155 C4
Lilford Gdns TQ12 244 A2
Lilian Cl EX17 78 B4
Lillage La EX9 198 A6
Lillebonne Cl TA21 160 F6
Lillebonne Wy TA21 160 D7
Lilley Wlk EX14 166 D5
Lillicrap Ct EX20 170 B5
Lillybrook La EX6 98 A5
Lillycombe La TA3,
EX15 67 E8
Lilly La EX5 172 A8
Lilybridge EX39 157 A7
Lily Cl EX39 157 A7
Lilylake Cross EX24 102 F7
Lily Mount EX4 176 D8
Lilypond La EX5 99 F8
Limberland Ave TQ9 215 E1
Lime Ave TQ2 219 F5
Limeburners Rd PL4 255 B6
Lime Cl
Broadclyst EX5 175 C6
Tiverton EX16 161 F5
Lime Cres EX15 162 C4
Lime Gr
Bideford EX39 156 F2
Bideford EX39 157 A2
Exminster EX6 182 A5
Exmouth EX8 196 C3
Kingsbridge TQ7 258 C5
Limegrove Rd EX4 176 F5
Limehayes Rd EX20 170 C5
Limekiln La EX31 16 A6
Lime Kiln La
Exeter EX2 178 A1
Uplyme DT7 260 A6
Uplyme DT7 260 A7
Lime Kiln Rd EX16 161 F3
Limekilns Cl EX36 158 B3
Lime Rd EX16 161 F5
Limerick Pl PL4 263 C3
Limers Cross
Chittlehampton EX37 29 A4
Wolverstone EX14 85 C7
Limer's Hill EX38 159 B5
Limers La
Merton EX20 57 A7
Northam EX39 156 F5
Northam EX39 157 A5
Wolverstone EX14 85 C7
Limer's La EX36 158 B2
Limer's Lane Cross
EX36 158 B2
Limes Cotts EX6 182 A4
Limes Ct EX6 182 B4
Limes La PL19 171 A6
Lime St
Moretonhampstead
TQ13 111 F5
Sheepwash EX21 56 C1
Limes The PL6 244 F2
Limestone Dr EX4 174 C2
Lime Tree Cl EX2 178 C3
Limetree Cross EX16 64 D6
Limetree Gr EX33 152 C6
Lime Tree Mead 1
EX16 64 D7
Limetree Rd PL3 248 D7
Lime Tree Wlk TQ12 207 E1
Lime Way EX12 192 A7
Lime Wy EX36 158 C6
Linacre La TQ12 213 C6
Linacre Rd TQ2 213 F4
Lincoln Ave PL4 263 C4
Lincoln Cl
Exmouth EX8 196 E4
Feniton EX14 84 D2
Lincoln Gn TQ2 214 A1
Lincoln Rd EX4 176 E6
LINCOMBE 1 D3
Lincombe Cross
Diptford TQ9 138 D8
Salcombe TQ8 259 D7
Lincombe Dr TQ1 220 E3
Lincombe Hill Rd
TQ1 220 E4
Linda Cl EX1 178 B5
Linden Cl
Barnstaple EX31 154 C3
Braunton EX33 152 D6
Exmouth EX8 196 D2
Great Torrington EX38 159 C5
Linden Ct 2 TQ5 230 C5
Linden Gdns EX31 154 C3
Linden Hill
Rockwell Green
TA21 160 A6
Wellington TA21 160 A6
Linden Rd
Cullompton EX15 163 C4
Dawlish EX7 204 D5
Linden Terr
Newton Abbot TQ12 207 A3
Plymouth PL4 263 C3
Lindfield Cl TQ2 219 F8
Lindisfarne Way TQ2 213 E2
Lindridge Cl 5 TQ12 123 E1
Lindridge Hill
Kingsteignton TQ12 123 F1
Kingsteignton TQ12 124 A2
Lindridge La 6 TQ12 123 E1
Lindridge Pk TQ14 124 B2
Lindridge Rd
Ashwell TQ14 124 B1
Torquay TQ1 220 C8
Lindsay Rd TQ3 219 A2
Lindthorpe Way TQ5 230 B4
Linett Cl TQ12 207 C8
Liney Cross TQ11 236 A6
Linfield Gdns EX4 176 F4
Linhay Bsns Pk TQ13 131 A5
Linhay Cl
Brixham TQ5 234 F8
Honiton EX14 166 B3
Millmoor EX15 51 E1
Linhay Dr
Fremington EX31 153 F6
Kingsteignton TQ12 207 F6
Linhay La PL9 249 D1
Linhay Pk EX17 80 A5
Linhay Rd EX5 99 C6
Linhey Cl TQ7 258 D4
Linkadells PL7 250 D6
Linketty La PL7 250 C5
Linketty Lane E PL6 245 A1
Linketty Lane W PL6 248 F8
Linkhay TA20 88 D8
Linkhay Cl TA20 88 D8
Link House Cl EX39 156 C7
Link Rd EX20 170 C6
Links Cl
Churston Ferrers
TQ5 229 E6
Exmouth EX8 202 C8
Links Ct TQ7 143 A1
Links Rd EX9 203 E8
Links The
Northam EX39 156 E7
Torquay TQ1 214 C1
Linnet Cl EX4 173 D2
Linnet Ct PL12 242 C2
Linnet Dene EX15 163 A2
Linscott Cres EX31 153 A4
Linseed Dr EX13 167 E6
Linton Cl PL5 244 C8
Linton La EX39 37 B5
Linton Rd
Exeter EX1 178 D6
Plymouth PL5 244 C7
Linton Sq PL5 244 C8
Lion Cl TQ7 258 C5
Lion Ho EX8 202 A5
Lion's Close Hill
EX24 103 A5
Lions Mill EX31 154 E7
Lions Rest Eco Pk
EX6 182 D3
Lion's Rump EX32,
EX36 18 F1
Lippell Dr PL9 255 E6
Lipscomb Ave EX8 202 E7
LIPSON 263 C4
Lipson Ave PL4 263 C4
Lipson Cooperative Acad
PL4 249 C4
Lipson Ct PL4 263 B3
Lipson Rd PL4 263 B4
Lipson Sp Ctr PL4 249 B4
Lipson Terr PL4 263 C4
LIPSON VALE 249 A4
Lipson Vale PL4 249 A4
Lipson Vale Prim Sch
PL7 249 A4
Lipstone Cres PL4 263 C4
Lisa Cl EX2 178 A4
Lisburne Cres 16
TQ1 220 D4
Lisburne Pl 10 TQ1 220 D4
Lisburne Sq TQ1 220 D4
Liscawn Terr PL11 247 B3
Liscombe Cl PL18 125 D7
Lisham's Drain EX24 103 A5
Lishaperhill Cross
EX22 53 B2
Liskeard Rd PL12 242 B3
Lisson Gr PL4 248 F4
Lister Cl
Exeter EX2 177 E4
Plymouth PL7 250 F6
Lister Way TQ9 144 E7
Litchardon Cross EX31 26 F8
Litchaton Cres PL7 250 B7
Litchaton Cross
East Buckland EX32 18 F1
North Molton EX36 30 A8
Litchaton Hill
East Buckland EX36 18 F1
North Molton EX36 30 A8
Litchaton Way PL7 250 B7
Litchdon La EX32 154 F4
Litchdon St EX32 155 A4
Litchfield Cl PL7 251 B6
Litelbury Rd EX16 64 D7
Littabourne EX31 154 F7
Little Ash Gdns PL5 243 B1
Little Ash Rd PL5 243 B1
Little Barley EX4 176 F5
Little Barton 7
TQ12 123 F1
Little Batten Rd TQ9 223 E4
Little Bewden TQ13 130 A4
Little Bickington
Courtyard EX38 43 C7
Little Bickington La
EX38 43 C7
Little Bicton Ct 18
EX8 202 A6
Little Bicton Pl EX8 202 A6
Littleborough Cross
EX17 62 A5
Little Bossell La
TQ11 236 B4
Little Bray Cross EX32 18 C8
Littlebray La EX32 18 E6
Little Bridge Bsns Pk
EX5 179 D1
Little Bridge Cross
EX22 70 F5
Littlebridge Mdw
EX22 70 F5
Little Buddies Pre-school
10 PL7 251 B5
Little Butts PL9 255 E6
Little Castle St EX4 261 B3
Little Chockenhole La
EX9 187 A1
Little Cl
Kingsteignton TQ12 207 E8
Ottery St Mary EX11 169 D3
LITTLE COMFORT 115 A7
Little Court EX39 26 A4
Little Cross TQ13 130 A4
Little Dock La PL5 244 B2
Littledown Cl EX8 202 F7
Littledown La EX10 186 D7
Little Down La
East Budleigh EX9 198 A5
Roborough PL6 241 E3
Little Down Orch
EX10 186 D7
Little Esworthy La
EX16 48 A1
Little Fancy Cl PL6 245 C7
Littlefield TQ14 208 E8
Little Field
Bideford EX39 156 D2
Cranbrook EX5 99 C6
Littlefield Cl
Barnstaple EX32 155 D4
Torquay TQ2 213 D1
Little Field Ct PL19 171 E5
Littlefields EX12 192 A7
Littleford Cross EX22 53 E8
Little Gate TQ7 143 F7
Littlegate Rd TQ3 226 B6
Little Gornhay La
Chevithorne EX16 49 D1
Tiverton EX15 64 D8
5 Tiverton EX16 161 F6
LITTLEHAM
Bideford 25 D2
Exmouth 202 F7
Littleham CE Prim Sch
EX8 202 F7
Littleham Church Path
Budleigh Salterton
EX9 203 E8
Exmouth EX9 203 C8
Littleham Cross
Bideford EX39 25 C2
Exmouth EX8 202 D7
Littleham Rd
Exmouth EX8 202 D7
Exmouth EX8 202 E7
Littleham Trad Est
EX8 202 E7
Little Hayes 12 TQ12 123 F1
Little Hayes La EX18 58 D8
Little Heath Cross
EX16 63 A6
Little Helstonbench Cross
TQ13 123 B6
LITTLEHEMPSTON 216 F2
Littlehempston Cross
TQ9 216 F2
LITTLE HILL TA20 69 C8
Little Hill
Buckland St Mary
TA20 69 D7
Salcombe TQ8 259 C5
Little Hill Cl TQ12 123 F1
Little John's Cross Hill
EX2 176 E3
Little John's Wlk
TQ13 122 F6
Littlejoy Rd TQ12 206 C4
LITTLE KNOWLE 197 F1
Little Knowle EX9 197 F1
Little Knowle Ct EX9 197 F1
Little La
Beer EX12 191 D4
Bishop's Nympton EX36 30 F3
Bishop's Nympton EX36 31 A3
Kingsand PL10 253 A2
Staddiscombe PL9 255 D3
Little Liverton Bsns Pk
TQ12 122 F1
Little Marsh Rd EX20 170 E6
Little Mdw
Clyst Honiton EX1 175 B1
Exmouth EX8 196 E3
Pyworthy EX22 71 D5
Little Mdws EX18 59 C4
Little Mead EX5 99 B6
Littlemead La EX8 196 B3
Little Meadow Way
EX39 156 E2
Littlemoor Cl EX31 153 A4
Little Normans EX15 83 F6
Little Park Rd TQ3 226 A6
Little Point Cres
PL10 252 F5
Little Princes TQ1 220 C3
Little Queen St EX4 261 B3
Little Rackenford La
EX16 47 E5
Little Rack St 4 EX1 261 A2
Little Raddon Cross
EX17 80 F6
Little Roborough
TQ13 130 F5
LITTLE SILVER 63 D4
Little Silver
Exeter EX4 261 A4
Tiverton EX16 161 D3
Little Silver La
Exeter EX2 181 D5
Wellington TA21 160 D2
Little Toms EX15 65 A2
Littleton Pl PL2 247 F4
LITTLE TORRINGTON 41 D3
Little Torrington
EX38 159 B1
LITTLETOWN 166 B4
Littletown Prim Sch
EX14 166 C4
Littletown Rd EX14 166 B4
Littletown Villas
EX14 166 C4
Littleway EX2 176 F3
Little Week Cl EX7 200 F1
Little Week Gdns
EX7 200 F1
Little Week La EX7 200 F1
Little Week Rd EX7 200 F1
Little Wiveliscombe La
TA4 35 D6
Littlewood Cl PL7 251 A4
Little Wood Cl EX5 99 A5
Littleworth Cl EX1 179 B8
Livarot Wlk EX36 158 B4
Livaton Cross EX20 95 D4
LIVERMEAD 219 E2
Livermead Hill TQ2 219 E2
Livermore Rd EX14 166 C5
Liverpool Hill EX4 176 E7
LIVERTON 180 A1
Liverton Bsns Pk EX8 196 F1
Liverton Cl EX8 202 E8
Liverton Ct TQ12 180 A1
Liverton Hill EX8 197 B1
Livery Dole Almshouses
EX2 177 E5
Living Coasts (Zoo)★
TQ1 220 B3
Livingshayes Rd EX5 82 C6
Livingstone Ave PL8 141 B8
Livingstone Rd TQ14 210 C6
Livonia Rd EX10 188 B6
Lixton Pk PL21 137 F1
Lizard Cl PL6 244 F7
Lizard Wlk PL6 245 A7
Llantillio Dr PL2 248 B8
Lloyd Ave TQ2 219 D7
Lloyd Maunder Rd
EX15 162 C5
Lloyds Cres EX1 178 C8
Lloyds Ct EX1 178 C8
Loatmead Cross EX22 38 B3
LOBB 152 A8
Lobbthorn Stile EX33 8 B1
LOBHILLCROSS 107 A5
Locarno Ave TQ3 219 D1
Locarno Rd EX4 176 F4
Lock Cl EX10 188 A8
Lockeridge Rd PL20 125 E1
Lockfield Ct EX2 177 B1
Lockington Ave PL3 248 F7
Lock La EX31 10 E4
Lock Lane Cross EX31 10 F3
Locks Cl
Braunton EX33 152 D5
Torquay TQ1 220 D7
Locksey's La EX12 190 D6
Locksey's La EX12 190 D8
Lock's Gate Cross
TQ13 129 F8
Locks Hill TQ1 220 D7
Locksley Cl
Exeter EX2 182 A8
Torquay TQ1 220 B7
Locksley Grange
TQ1 220 A7
Locks Wlk PL1 247 E1
Lockyear Pl TQ13 180 F7
Lockyer Ave EX10 188 C8
Lockyer Cres EX16 161 A6
Lockyer Ct PL1 262 C2
Lockyer Mews PL19 171 C6
Lockyer Rd PL3 248 E5
Lockyers Quay PL4 263 B2
Lockyer St PL1 262 C2
Lockyer Terr PL12 243 A3
LODDISWELL 143 F7
Loddiswell Butts TQ7 143 E8
Loddiswell Prim Sch
TQ7 143 F7
Lodgecastle Ham
EX20 170 B4
Lodge Cl TA21 160 D6
Lodge Cnr EX31 27 D8
Lodge Cross
Chulmleigh EX18 45 A1
Longdown EX6 98 E1
Lodge Gdns PL6 244 E3
Lodge Hill
Exeter EX4 177 A8
Okehampton EX20 170 B5
Lodge La
Axminster EX13 88 B2
Bratton Fleming EX31 18 E8
Brixton PL8 256 F5
Shute EX13 103 A8
Tudhay EX13 88 C3
Lodge Rd EX16 161 E4
Lodge The
Crediton EX17 165 A6
1 Ilfracombe EX34 150 D5
Lodge Trad Est EX5 175 E3
Lofoten Cl PL1 247 E2
Loftus Gdns PL5 243 C2
Logan Rd TQ3 226 C7
Logan Way EX15 67 B8
Lolesbury Cross PL8 136 A1
Lollabury Rd PL12 242 E3
Lombard Cl EX39 25 D4
London Cl 5 EX20 170 B5
London Ct The PL21 237 D5
London Inn Sq EX1 261 B3
London Rd
Whimple EX11 168 A8
Whimple EX5 99 D6
Longacre PL7 250 B7
Long Acre PL12 242 B4
Long Acres EX2 261 C2
Long Barton 5
TQ12 123 F1
Long Barton Ave
EX20 170 D6
LONGBRIDGE 249 F7
Longbridge Cl PL6 249 F6
Long Bridge Cross
EX13 87 B8
Longbridge Meadow Trad
Est EX15 163 D4
Longbridge Rd
Plymouth, Laira PL3 249 C4
Plymouth, Longbridge
PL6 249 E7
Longbridge Wharf 13
EX39 157 A1
Longbrook TQ7 145 A1
Longbrook Barton
PL7 250 D5
Longbrook Cl PL21 237 B5
Longbrook La EX8 195 F4
Longbrook Rd PL21 237 B5
Longbrook St
Exeter EX4 261 B4
Plymouth PL7 250 F4
Longbrook Terr EX4 261 B4
LONGCAUSE 223 A7
Longcause PL7 250 F4
Longcause Com Specl
Sch PL7 250 F4
Longcause Cross
TQ9 223 A7
Longcombe Cross
TQ9 224 C5
Long Copp EX9 198 A2
Longcroft Ave TQ5 230 B3
Longcroft Dr TQ5 230 B3
Long Cross
Dartmouth TQ6 233 C3
South Pool TQ7 148 F7
Longcross Cotts
PL19 116 D6
Long Cswy EX8 202 B6
Longdogs Cl EX11 169 E3
Longdogs La EX11 169 E3
LONGDOWN 98 E2
Long Down Gdns
PL6 245 E3
Longdown Rd EX2,
EX6 176 B3
Long Drag EX15 65 E3
Longdrag Hill EX16 161 A4
Long Entry DT7 260 E3
Longfield
11 Appledore EX39 15 A1
Lutton PL21 133 B1
Longfield Ave TQ12 207 F8
Longfield Cl
Braunton EX33 152 E5
Lutton PL21 133 B2
Longfield Dr TQ8 259 C5
Longfield Est EX6 201 A8
Longfield Pl PL4 263 B4
Longfields TQ7 258 A4
Longfield Terr 7
EX34 150 C5
Longfield Villas PL9 255 D8
Longford Cross TQ12 207 E8
Longford Down Head
PL21 137 F6
Longford Field EX8 195 A1
Longford La TQ12 207 E8
Longford Pk TQ12 207 E8
Longforth Rd TA21 160 D6
Long-Go La EX14 84 E8
Long Hill EX12 191 D5
Long Holcombe Cross
EX36 20 A6
Long La
Appledore EX39 14 F1
Ashford EX31 16 B6
Blackmoor Gate EX31 11 A6
Bradiford EX31 154 A8
Calverleigh EX16 48 D2
Combe Martin EX31,
EX34 3 D1
Dawlish EX7 200 B1
Exmouth EX8 202 C6
Georgeham EX33 8 B1
Newton Abbot TQ12 208 B1
Northam EX39 157 A8
Shaldon TQ14 209 C4
Tiverton EX16 161 A7
Wolverstone EX14 85 B8
Longland Cl EX32 17 B5
Longland Cross TQ9 227 C3
Longland La EX33 8 A2
LONGLANDS 242 A1
Longlands
Dawlish EX7 204 D6
Plymouth PL9 255 D8
Longlands Cross
Ashwater EX21 90 E6
Corfcott Green EX22 71 F2
Longlands Dr PL9 140 A8
Longlands La PL12 242 B1
Longlands Way EX14 85 C2
Long Ley PL3 249 B6
Long Mdw
Plymouth PL7 250 D7
South Brent TQ10 134 F2
Long Mdw Rd EX5 99 C6
Longmead
Hemyock EX15 67 B8
Huish Champflower TA4 35 E8
Lynton EX35 151 A5
Longmead Cl TA21 160 B8
Longmead Cotts
TA21 160 B8
Longmead La EX20 76 F4
Longmeadow
Budlake EX5 82 E1
Tiverton EX16 161 D5
Long Meadow EX5 184 C3

Longmeadow Cl PL7 . 250 E7
Long Meadow Dr
EX32 . 155 B6
Longmeadow Rd
Lympstone EX8 . 195 F5
Saltash PL12 . 242 E3
Longmeadows EX17 . 165 D6
Longmead Rd TQ3 . 218 F1
Longmead Wlk TQ3 . 218 F1
Long Moor
Cullompton EX15 . 163 F6
Willand EX15 . 162 E1
Long Orch PL20 . 125 E1
Long Park Cl PL9 . 255 F5
Long Park Dr PL6 . 245 D7
Longpark Hill TQ1 . 214 C6
Long Park Rd PL12 . 242 D2
Long Pk
Ashburton TQ13 . 131 A5
Cranbrook EX5 . 99 C6
Modbury PL21 . 137 B3
Woodbury EX5 . 184 C3
Longpot La EX31 . 17 D8
Long Pot La EX31 . 10 D1
Long Ragg Ct EX13 . 167 D5
Long Range Pk EX10 . 100 A7
Long Rd
Paignton TQ4 . 225 D1
Saltash PL12 . 242 B4
Long Rowden PL3 . 248 E6
Long Rydon TQ9 . 227 F8
Long Rydon Lower
TQ9 . 228 A7
Longstem Dr TQ9 . 215 E1
Longstone Ave PL6 . 245 A6
Longstone Cross 1
TQ13 . 131 A5
Longstone Rd TQ4 . 225 E4
Long Terrace Cl 5
PL7 . 251 C5
Longthorn Rd TQ13 . 124 B4
Longview Rd PL12 . 242 D3
Longview Terr PL3 . 249 B7
Long Walk Dr EX32 . 29 C6
Longwood Cl PL7 . 251 A4
Longwood La TA21 . 51 C4
Longwool Mdw EX23 . 70 A6
Longwool Run EX15 . 163 A3
Long Wools TQ4 . 229 D7
Lonsdale Rd
Exeter EX1 . 178 B5
Newton Abbot TQ12 . 207 D2
Lonse Gdns TQ12 . 212 F5
Loo Cross TQ7 . 144 F1
Looe Rd EX4 . 177 A7
Looe St PL4 . 263 A2
Lookout Cotts EX31 . 16 B6
Loom End
Tiverton EX16 . 64 A8
Tiverton EX16 . 161 B6
Looseall La TA22 . 33 D8
Loosebeare Cross
EX17 . 78 B8
Loosebeare La EX17 . 78 B8
Loosedon Cross EX19 . 58 B4
Looseland Cross EX16 47 D1
Looseleigh Cl PL6 . 245 A4
Looseleigh La PL6 . 244 F5
Looseleigh Pk PL6 . 244 E5
Lopes Cres EX20 . 170 C5
Lopes Dr PL6 . 241 C1
Lopes Rd
Dousland PL20 . 127 B3
Plymouth PL2 . 248 B6
Lopwell Cl PL6 . 244 F5
Lopwell Dam Nature
Reserve PL6 . 240 C7
Loram Way EX2 . 181 C8
Lord Louis Cres PL9 . 254 F6
Lord Mamhead Homes
EX2 . 177 E4
Lord Nelson Dr TQ6 . 233 C3
Lords Mdw 5 EX16 . 49 B8
Lords Meadow Ind Est
EX17 . 165 E5
Lords Meadow La 5
EX16 . 34 B1
Lords Meadow L Ctr
EX17 . 165 E5
Lords Pl TQ1 . 220 B6
Lords Way EX2 . 178 C4
Loretto Gdns EX13 . 167 E5
Loretto Rd EX13 . 167 E5
Loring Rd TQ8 . 259 D4
Lorrie Dr TQ14 . 210 B6
Lorrimore Ave PL2 . 247 F5
Lotherton Cl PL7 . 251 B3
Lotus Cotts TQ9 . 227 F7
Loughboro Rd PL5 . 243 C1
Loughwood La EX13 . 87 B2
Louisa Gate TA22 . 33 F7
Louisa Pl EX8 . 202 A5
Louisa Terr EX8 . 202 A5
Louise Terr
Great Torrington EX38 . 41 D6
Great Torrington EX38 . 159 C5
Louis Way EX14 . 67 C1
Loup Ct EX13 . 167 F5
Louvigny Cl EX14 . 84 E2
Louville Cl TQ4 . 226 C2
Lovacott Cross EX31 . 153 F1
Lovacott Gr EX31 . 26 F6
Lovacott School Cross
EX31 . 27 A6
LOVATON . 127 C1
Love La
Ashburton TQ13 . 130 F4
Bickington TQ12 . 131 D7
Love La *continued*
Bideford EX39 . 156 E1
Colyton EX24 . 103 A4
Marldon TQ3 . 218 D4
Marldon TQ3 . 218 E4
Saltash PL12 . 242 E2
Lovelace Cres EX8 . 202 D8
Lovelace Gdns EX2 . 181 B8
Loveland Cross EX20 . 74 C1
Love Lane Cl TQ3 . 218 D4
Lovell Cl EX8 . 196 C3
Lovell Rd PL3 . 248 F6
Loventor Cres TQ3 . 218 D2
Loventor La TQ3, TQ9 . 217 F3
Loveridge Dr EX2 . 181 C6
Loveridge La TA20 . 88 D8
Lovering Cl EX8 . 196 C3
Loverings Ct 3 EX31 154 F5
Low Brook EX5 . 99 C5
Lowena La
West Hill EX10 . 100 A5
West Hill EX10 . 168 D5
West Hill EX11 . 168 D5
Lower Albert St EX1 . 261 C3
Lower Aller La TQ13 . 122 E6
Lower Almshouses 2
EX31 . 154 F6
Lower Anderton Rd
PL10 . 252 F5
Lower Argyll Rd EX4 . 173 A2
LOWER ASHTON . 113 C3
Lower Audley Rd
TQ2 . 219 F8
Lower Ave EX1 . 177 F6
Lower Barton 6 EX5 . 99 A6
LOWER BATSON . 259 D6
Lower Bitcford Cross
EX39 . 38 B6
LOWER BLAGDON . 225 B6
Lower Blagdon Cross
TQ3 . 225 B6
Lower Blagdon La
TQ3 . 225 C6
Lower Brand La
EX14 . 166 C4
LOWER BRIMLEY . 180 A5
Lower Brimley Cl 2
TQ14 . 210 C5
Lower Brimley Rd
Teignmouth TQ14 . 210 B6
Teignmouth TQ14 . 210 C5
Lower Broad Oak Rd
EX11 . 168 E4
Lower Broad Path
TQ9 . 228 A7
Lower Broad Pk
Dartmouth TQ6 . 233 D3
West Down EX34 . 8 F5
Lower Brookfield Cotts
TQ13 . 122 C8
Lower Brookfield Terr
TQ13 . 122 C8
Lower Brook Mdw 2
EX10 . 101 B1
Lower Brook Pk
PL21 . 237 A5
Lower Brook St 13
TQ14 . 210 C5
Lower Budleigh EX9 . 198 B5
Lower Budleigh Mdw
TQ12 . 206 F3
Lower Bulkamore Cross
TQ10 . 135 E5
Lower Bull Ring
EX15 . 163 C3
Lower Bulworthy Gate
EX16 . 47 D4
Lower Bulworthy La
EX16 . 47 D4
Lower Burston EX17 . 78 B5
Lower Burwood Rd
EX38 . 159 E5
Lower Cannon Rd
TQ12 . 123 B2
LOWER CHERITON . 84 E4
Lower Church St
5 Barnstaple EX32 . 155 A4
Colyton EX24 . 103 A5
Lower Cl EX16 . 65 A7
Lower Claypark EX34 . 7 F7
Lower Cleave
Braunton EX33 . 152 C7
Northam EX39 . 157 B5
Lower Cloister Wlk
EX6 . 181 F5
Lower Cobbaton EX37 28 D5
Lower Collapark
TQ9 . 223 B6
Lower Collins Rd
TQ9 . 223 B6
LOWER COMPTON . 249 A5
Lower Compton Rd
PL3 . 248 F5
Lower Congella Rd
TQ1 . 220 C6
Lower Contour Rd
TQ6 . 234 B3
Lower Cookworthy Cross
PL16 . 106 A6
Lower Coombe La
EX16 . 63 D4
Lower Coombe Rd
TQ12 . 207 F7
Lower Coombe St
EX1 . 261 A2
Lower Coombses
TA20 . 88 D8
Lower Coppice EX1 . 175 A2
Lower Cotteylands
EX16 . 161 B3
Lower Court Rd PL8 . 140 F7
Lower Crooked Mdw
EX20 . 170 C5
Lower Cross EX15 . 51 C1
Lower Cross Rd EX31 154 B4
Lowerdale Turn TQ9 . 144 B8
Lower Dawlish Water Rd
EX7 . 204 A7
LOWER DEAN . 236 A2
Lower Dean Cross EX31 3 F2
Lower Dean La EX34 . 3 B3
Lowerdown TQ13 . 122 D5
Lower Dr EX7 . 204 F8
Lower Duck St EX6 . 182 B3
Lower Dunscombe La
TQ13 . 124 A5
Lower Ellacombe Church
Rd TQ1 . 220 C6
Lower Erith Rd TQ1 . 220 D4
Lower Fairview Rd
TQ6 . 233 E3
Lower Farm Rd PL7 . 251 A4
Lower Farthings
EX10 . 186 F8
Lower Fern Rd
Newton Abbot TQ12 . 212 F8
Newton Abbot TQ2 . 213 A8
Lower Forches Cross
EX17 . 60 D4
Lower Fore St
3 Exmouth EX8 . 202 A6
Saltash PL12 . 243 A2
Lower Fowden TQ4 . 229 D6
Lower Foxmoor Rd
TA21 . 160 B5
Lower French Pk
TQ12 . 206 F3
Lower Furlong Cl EX5 . 99 C6
Lower Fyldon Cross
EX36 . 19 D4
LOWER GABWELL . 214 B8
Lower Gaydon St 1
EX32 . 155 A5
Lower Green TQ10 . 135 A2
Lower Green Cross
TQ7 . 145 C4
Lower Green Way
EX14 . 85 C2
Lower Greystone EX34 . 1 C3
Lower Griggs EX10 . 188 D7
Lower Gunstone
EX39 . 157 A2
Lower Harrington La
EX4 . 174 E1
Lower Haske Cross
EX17 . 165 F7
Lower Hill Barton Rd
EX1 . 178 C6
Lowerhill Head Rd
EX5 . 179 B2
LOWER HOLDITCH . 88 D5
Lower Holditch La
EX13 . 88 D5
Lower Hollicombe Cotts
TQ3 . 219 D1
LOWER KEATON . 237 E1
Lower Kelly PL18 . 125 D3
Lower King's Ave
EX4 . 177 D8
Lower Kingsdown Rd
TQ14 . 209 D7
Lower Kinsman's Dale
TQ13 . 111 F5
Lower La
Chulmleigh EX18 . 59 C8
Dalwood EX13 . 87 B2
Ebford EX3 . 183 C4
5 Plymouth PL1 . 263 A2
Sampford Courtenay
EX20 . 76 D5
Lower Ladram La
Otterton EX9 . 198 F7
Otterton EX9 . 199 A7
Lower Lodfin EX16 . 34 B2
Lower Loughborough
EX16 . 161 B5
LOWER LOVACOTT . 27 A6
Lower Lowton La
EX6 . 112 E6
LOWER LOXHORE . 17 D8
Lower Manor Rd
TQ5 . 230 C5
Lower Marlpits Hill
EX14 . 166 D4
Lower Mead EX13 . 167 E6
Lower Meadow Rise
EX7 . 204 C6
Lower Meddon St 8
EX39 . 157 A1
LOWER MILCOTT . 173 A4
Lower Millhayes EX15 67 C8
Lower Mill La EX15 . 163 C3
Lower Moor EX32 . 155 D4
Lower Moor Way
EX15 . 64 D8
LOWER NETHERON . 208 C4
Lower Northcote Rd
EX14 . 166 E7
Lower North St EX4 . 261 A3
Lower Park EX37 . 28 D2
Lower Park Dr PL9 . 255 F4
Lower Park Rd EX33 . 152 E5
Lower Penns Rd TQ3 219 C1
Lower Pk 2 TQ3 . 226 A7
Lower Polsham Rd
TQ3 . 226 C7
Lower Port View
PL12 . 242 F2
Lower Preston TQ12 . 123 D1
Lower Preston Cross
TQ9 . 138 E2
Lower Rackclose La
EX1 . 261 A2
Lower Raleigh Rd
Barnstaple EX31 . 155 A7
Barnstaple EX32 . 154 F6
Lower Ray EX5 . 99 B6
Lower Rd EX5 . 184 B7
Lower Rea Rd TQ5 . 230 D5
LOWER RIDGE . 86 F4
Lower Ridings PL7 . 251 B7
Lower Row PL10 . 253 A2
Lower St German's Rd
EX4 . 177 C8
Lower Saltram PL9 . 255 C7
Lower Shapter St
EX3 . 182 F4
Lower Shirburn Rd
TQ1 . 220 A7
Lowerside PL2 . 248 A8
LOWER SLADE . 150 B2
Lower Sladesmoor Cres
PL15 . 90 B1
Lower St
Chagford TQ13 . 111 A6
Dartmouth TQ6 . 233 F3
Dittisham TQ6 . 228 B3
Plymouth PL4 . 263 A3
West Alvington TQ7 . 258 A4
Lower Summerlands
EX1 . 261 C3
LOWER TALE . 84 A5
Lower Tamar Terr
PL18 . 125 D7
Lower Terr EX22 . 38 E1
Lower Three Acres
Cranbrook EX5 . 99 C6
Rockbeare EX5 . 99 C6
Lower Thurlow Rd
TQ1 . 220 A6
Lower Tidderson Cross
EX16 . 47 E4
LOWER TIPPACOTT . 6 A4
LOWER TOWN
Ashburton . 130 A7
Buckfastleigh . 236 C5
Halberton . 65 A7
Lower Town
Halberton EX16 . 65 A7
Malborough TQ7 . 147 E6
Sampford Peverell EX16 50 D1
Stoke Climsland PL17 . 115 C1
Winkleigh EX19 . 58 F2
Woolfardisworthy EX39 . 38 F7
Lowertown Cotts
EX20 . 107 A3
Lower Trindle Cl 24
TQ12 . 123 E6
Lower Union La TQ2 . 220 B5
Lower Union Rd TQ7 . 258 C5
LOWER WADSTRAY . 232 B2
Lower Warberry Rd
Torquay TQ1 . 220 B5
Torquay TQ1 . 220 C4
Lower Warcombe Cross
TQ7 . 144 A6
Lower Warren Rd
TQ7 . 258 D3
Lower Way EX10 . 187 A8
LOWER WEAR . 182 B7
Lower Wear Rd EX2 . 182 B8
Lower Westaway Ct
EX31 . 27 A6
LOWER WESTFORD . 160 A6
Lower Westlake Rd
EX31 . 154 A2
Lower Wheathill
EX10 . 188 B8
Lower Winsham Rd
EX33 . 8 D1
Lower Woodfield Rd
TQ1 . 220 C4
Lower Woodhayes Ct
EX5 . 99 E7
LOWER
WOOLBROOK . 188 A6
Lower Yalberton Rd
TQ4 . 225 C2
Lowery Cross PL20 . 127 C4
Loweswater Ho EX4 . 176 F6
Lowley Brook Ct TQ2 219 B8
Lowman Cross EX16 . 50 B2
Lowman Gn EX16 . 161 D4
Lowman Units EX16 . 64 D8
Lowman Way EX15 . 64 D8
Lowmoor Ind Est
TA21 . 160 B8
Lownard Cross TQ9 . 222 E8
Low Rd PL9 . 140 D8
Lowton Cross EX20 . 77 C7
Lowton La EX6 . 112 E6
Lowtrow Cross TA4 . 35 A8
LOXBEARE . 48 C3
Loxbury Rd TQ2 . 219 D4
Loxbury Rise TQ2 . 219 D5
Loxdown Rd EX39 . 41 A7
LOXHORE . 10 D1
LOXHORE COTT . 10 D1
Loxhore Cross EX31 . 17 D7
Lucas Ave EX4 . 177 D8
Lucas La PL7 . 250 D6
Lucas Terr PL4 . 249 B2
Lucas Wy EX15 . 162 F7
Luccombe Oak EX5 . 99 B6
Lucerne 1 TQ1 . 220 D4
Lucius St TQ2 . 219 F5
Luckhams La TQ7 . 147 E6
Lucky La EX2 . 261 B2
Lucombe Ct EX4 . 261 C4
Lucombe Oaks EX5 . 179 B6
LUDBROOK . 137 C5
Ludbrook Gate PL21 . 137 C5
Ludlow Rd 2 PL3 . 248 E6
Ludwell La EX2 . 178 A3
Ludwell Rise EX1 . 178 B4
LUFFINCOTT . 89 F5
Lugsmoor La EX10 . 189 E7
Lugworthy Cross EX21 91 B5
Lukes Cl TA21 . 160 D8
Lukesland Gardens★
PL21 . 237 E8
Luke St EX16 . 34 B1
Lulworth Cl TQ4 . 225 F2
Lulworth Dr PL6 . 245 B7
Lumley Cl EX6 . 194 E3
Lummaton Cross
TQ2 . 214 A2
Lummaton Pl TQ2 . 214 B1
Lundy Cl
Barnstaple EX32 . 155 C5
Plymouth PL6 . 244 F7
Lundy View EX39 . 156 E6
LUPPITT . 67 E1
Luppitt Rd EX14 . 86 A5
Lurley Cross EX16 . 48 E2
Luscombe Ave PL19 . 171 B7
Luscombe Cl
Ipplepen TQ12 . 211 D1
Ivybridge PL21 . 237 A4
Paignton TQ3 . 225 E7
Luscombe Cres TQ3 . 225 E6
Luscombe Cross
TQ9 . 139 D8
Luscombe Hill
Dawlish EX7 . 204 A6
Teignmouth EX7 . 124 E3
Luscombe La TQ3 . 225 D8
Luscombe Rd TQ3 . 225 E6
Luscombe Terr 12
EX7 . 204 D6
LUSON . 136 C1
Luson Cross PL8 . 136 C1
LUSTLEIGH . 122 C8
Lustleigh Cl EX2 . 181 C8
Lusways Ct EX10 . 188 C4
Lutehouse La EX19 . 58 E3
LUTON
Payhembury . 84 B5
Teignmouth . 124 C3
LUTSFORD . 37 D6
Lutsford Cross EX39 . 37 D6
Luttrell St PL21 . 137 D6
LUTTON
Cornwood . 133 B2
South Brent . 134 F4
Lutyens Dr TQ3 . 225 D7
Lutyens Fold PL19 . 116 A6
Luxmoore Way EX20 . 170 D6
Luxmore Cl PL6 . 245 E1
LUXTON . 68 D6
Luxton Cl EX21 . 73 E3
Luxton Ct EX15 . 163 C3
Luxton La EX20 . 77 B8
Luxton Moor La EX20 . 59 A1
Luxton Rd TQ12 . 211 F8
Luxtons Pk EX11 . 169 C3
Lych Cl PL9 . 255 A6
Lychgate Pk EX17 . 79 A5
Lydacott Cross EX31 . 153 F3
LYDCOTT . 18 F7
Lydcot Wlk PL6 . 245 A1
Lyddicleave EX31 . 154 A3
Lyddon Cl TA21 . 160 D4
LYDFORD . 107 F4
Lydford Castle & Saxon
Town★ EX20 . 107 E3
Lydford Cl PL21 . 237 D4
Lydford Gorge★
EX20 . 107 E3
Lydford Ho TQ12 . 207 D4
Lydford Park Rd PL3 . 248 D5
Lydford Prim Sch
EX20 . 107 F4
Lydgates Rd EX12 . 192 A6
Lyd Gdns PL19 . 171 D5
Lydia Cl EX10 . 186 D8
Lydiate La EX35 . 5 A5
Lydia Way PL4 . 263 B4
Lydon La TA4 . 35 D5
Lydwell Park Rd TQ1 . 220 E5
Lydwell Rd TQ1 . 220 D6
Lye La EX14 . 87 A8
Lym Cl DT7 . 260 E3
Lyme Bay Ct 3 DT7 . 260 D3
Lyme Bay Rd TQ14 . 210 C7
Lymeborne Ave EX1 . 178 A6
Lymebourne Ave
EX10 . 188 B6
Lymebourne Ho
EX10 . 188 B6
Lymebourne La EX10 188 B6
Lymebourne Pk EX10 188 B6
Lyme Cl EX13 . 167 D5
Lyme Mews 10 EX12 . 192 B4
Lyme Rd
Axminster EX13 . 167 E5
Uplyme DT7 . 104 B5
LYME REGIS . 260 E2
Lyme Regis Ind Est
DT7 . 260 C4
Lyme Regis Mus★
DT7 . 260 E3
Lyme St EX13 . 167 D6
Lyme View Cl TQ1 . 220 D7
Lyme View Rd TQ1 . 220 D7
Lymington Rd TQ1 . 220 A6
Lympne Ave PL5 . 243 F5
LYMPSTONE . 195 E5
Lympstone CE Prim Sch
EX8 . 195 E5
Lympstone Commando
Sta EX8 . 195 C8
Lympstone Ct EX34 . 150 B6
Lympstone Village Sta
EX8 . 195 D5
Lynbridge Ct 5 PL19 171 B5
Lynbridge Hill EX35 . 151 B3
Lynbridge Rd EX35 . 151 C4
Lynbro Rd EX31 . 154 F7
Lynch Cl
Axminster EX13 . 167 D7
Thorverton EX5 . 81 E5
Lynch Head EX10 . 100 C1
Lynch Rd EX5 . 81 D5
Lyncombe Cl EX4 . 173 E1
Lyncombe Cres TQ1 . 220 E3
Lyncombe La EX35 . 12 D8
Lyncourt TQ1 . 220 D3
Lyn Cross EX35 . 151 D2
Lyndale Rd TQ12 . 207 D8
Lyndhurst Ave TQ12 . 213 A5
Lyndhurst Cl
Kingskerswell TQ12 . 213 A6
Plymouth PL2 . 248 C6
Lyndhurst Rd
Exeter EX2 . 177 E5
Exmouth EX8 . 202 A8
Plymouth PL2 . 248 C6
Lyndon Ct PL12 . 242 D4
Lyndons The EX2 . 177 E5
Lyndrick Rd PL3 . 248 E7
Lyndridge Ct 3
EX20 . 170 A5
LYNEHAM . 257 F7
Lyneham Cross TQ13 123 D6
Lyn & Exmoor Mus★
EX35 . 151 C5
Lyn Gr TQ12 . 212 F6
Lyngrove Ct TQ12 . 212 F6
Lynhayes EX13 . 87 C1
Lynher Ct PL12 . 242 F1
Lynher Dr PL12 . 242 F1
Lynher St PL5 . 243 D2
Lyn Hill
Lynton EX35 . 5 C5
West Lyn EX35 . 151 C3
Lynhurst Ave EX31 . 154 C4
Lyn La EX35 . 151 D3
LYNMOUTH . 151 D5
Lynmouth Ave TQ4 . 225 F2
Lynmouth Cl PL7 . 250 C7
Lynmouth Hill EX35 . 151 C5
Lynmouth St EX35 . 151 C6
Lynn Terr EX38 . 159 C5
LYNTON . 151 B4
Lynton & Barnstaple Rly★
EX31 . 4 D3
Lynton CE Prim Sch
EX35 . 151 C5
Lynton Cross EX34 . 9 B6
Lynton & Lynmouth Cliff
Rlwy★ EX35 . 151 C6
Lynton Rd EX34 . 3 B3
Lynway EX35 . 151 C4
Lynway Ct TQ1 . 220 B6
Lynwood TQ12 . 206 F1
Lynwood Ave
Exeter EX4 . 177 A5
Plymouth PL7 . 250 B6
Lynx La PL9 . 256 E8
Lyra Vale PL9 . 256 E8
Lysander La PL6 . 245 B5
Lyster Ct 9 PL1 . 262 A3
Lyte Hill La TQ2 . 213 F3
Lyte La TQ7 . 144 C1
Lyte's Rd TQ5 . 230 D4
Lythe-Land Cross
EX16 . 63 A6
Lytton Ho TQ2 . 220 A4

M

Mabel Pl TQ4 . 226 B5
Mabry Way EX12 . 192 C5
Macadam Rd
Plymouth PL4 . 263 C1
Plymouth PL9 . 255 B8
Macandrew Wlk
PL21 . 237 E6
Macaulay Cres PL5 . 244 C1
Macauley Cl EX14 . 166 E6
Macey St PL11 . 247 C3
Macey's Terr EX20 . 170 B6
Macford Court EX13 . 167 F8
Machine Cross TA22 . 33 F6
Mackenzie Pl PL5 . 243 C2
Mackenzie Way
EX16 . 161 F4
MACKHAM . 67 D4
Mackrell's Almshouses
TQ12 . 207 A2
Maclins Cl EX36 . 158 C4
Macwood Dr EX12 . 192 A6
Madagascar Cl EX8 . 202 E8
Maddacombe Cross
TQ12 . 212 C4

Maddacombe Rd
TQ12 . . . .**212** D4
Madden Rd PL1 . . . . . .**247** F2
Maddick Rd EX1 . . . . .**174** F3
Maddock Cl PL7 . . . . .**251** A4
Maddock Dr PL7 . . . . .**251** B4
Maddocks Cross EX22 .**38** D2
Madeira Ct EX8 . . . . . .**202** B5
Madeira Pl TQ2 . . . . . .**220** A5
Madeira Rd PL1 . . . . . .**263** A1
Madeira Villas
Exmouth EX8 . . . .**202** A7
[1] Horrabridge PL20 . .**126** F5
Madeira Wlk EX9 . . . . .**199** H2
MADFORD **67** D6
Madford Cross EX15 . . .**67** C6
Madge Ct [3] PL19 . . . .**171** B6
Madge La PL19 . . . . . .**171** B6
Madgeon La TA20 . . . . .**69** B8
Madges Cross
Aylesbeare EX5 . . . .**99** E2
Rockbeare EX5 . . . .**99** E5
Madicks Orch TQ9 . . . .**227** F8
Madison Ave EX1 . . . . .**178** A6
Madison Cl EX5 . . . . . .**173** F8
Madison Wharf EX8 . . .**201** E6
Madrepore Rd TQ1. . . .**220** B4
Maer Bay Ct EX8 . . . . .**202** B5
Maer La EX8 . . . .**202** E5
Maer Nature Reserve
The★ EX8 . . . .**202** B5
Maer Rd EX8 . . . .**202** C5
Maer Top Way EX31 . .**155** A7
Maer Vale EX8 . . . .**202** C6
Magdala Rd EX31 . . . .**154** A3
Magdalen Bridge Ct [3]
EX2 . . . .**261** B2
Magdalen Court Sch
EX2 . . . .**177** E5
Magdalene Cl TQ9 . . . .**223** C5
Magdalene Lawn [9]
EX32 . . . .**155** E4
Magdalene Rd TQ1 . . .**220** A6
Magdalene Way
EX36 . . . .**158** B4
Magdalen Gdns
Exeter EX2 . . . .**177** E5
Plymouth PL7 . . . .**250** F3
Magdalen Rd EX2 . . . .**261** C2
Magdalen St EX1, EX2 **261** B2
Magnolia Ave
Exeter EX2 . . . .**178** A4
Exmouth EX8 . . . .**202** E8
Magnolia Cl
Barnstaple EX32 . . . . . .**155** E4
[3] Plymouth PL7 . . . . .**251** B5
Magnolia Ct
Bolham EX16 . . . .**49** C1
[5] Exmouth EX8 . . . . .**202** B6
[3] Plymouth PL9 . . . .**255** F7
Tiverton EX16 . . . .**161** E7
Magnolia Ho [10] EX8. .**202** A6
Magnolia Way EX20 . .**170** E5
Magnolia Wlk [2]
EX8 . . . .**202** A6
Magnus Cl [1] TQ12 . . .**244** E6
Magpie Cres EX2 . . . . .**176** D4
Magpie Hill TQ13 . . . .**130** C4
Maida Vale Terr PL4 . .**248** C1
MAIDENCOMBE **214** D6
Maidencombe Cross
TQ1 . . . .**214** C6
Maidencombe Ho
TQ1 . . . .**214** C4
MAIDENHAYNE **103** D6
Maidenhayne La
EX13 . . . .**103** D6
Maidenhead Cross
EX16 . . . .**51** C2
Maiden St [17] EX31 . . .**154** F5
Maidenway La TQ3 . . .**225** F8
Maidenway Rd TQ3 . . .**225** F8
Maidenwell Rd PL7 . . .**250** C5
Maidstone Pl PL5 . . . .**243** E4
Main Ave TQ1 . . . .**220** A8
Maine Cl EX39 . . . .**156** D2
Maine Gdns PL2 . . . . . .**247** F7
Main Rd
Exeter EX4 . . . .**174** E2
Exminster EX3 . . . .**182** A4
Salcombe TQ8 . . . .**259** C4
Main St TQ9 . . . .**139** E1
MAINSTONE **245** F2
Mainstone Ave PL4. . .**263** C2
Maire Rd EX36 . . . .**46** E5
Maisy Mws EX3 . . . . . .**182** D8
Maitland Dr PL3 . . . . .**248** B8
Major Cross EX16 . . . . .**64** A2
Majorfield Rd EX3 . . . .**182** F5
Major's Mdw EX20 . . .**170** C5
Major Terr [3] EX12. . .**192** A5
Maker Cl PL10 . . . .**253** B4
Maker Rd PL11. . . . . . .**247** A2
Maker View
Plymouth PL3 . . . .**248** B4
Plymouth PL3 . . . .**248** B4
Maker View Rd PL10 .**253** B4
MALBOROUGH **147** E6
Malborough Gn TQ7 . .**147** E6
Malborough Pk TQ7. . .**147** E6
Malborough with South
Huish CE Prim Sch
TQ7 . . . .**147** E6
Malden Cl EX10 . . . . . .**188** B7

Malden La EX10. . . . . . .**188** B8
Malden Rd EX10 . . . . . .**188** C8
Malderek Ave TQ3 . . . .**219** C1
Mallands Mdw TQ12 . .**212** A7
Mallard Cl
Plymouth PL7 . . . .**250** F5
Torquay TQ2 . . . .**213** D3
Mallard Rd EX2 . . . . . .**178** E5
Mallet Rd PL21. . . . . . .**237** A6
Malletts La EX32 . . . . .**155** A5
Mallingbrook Cross
EX18 . . . .**44** E1
Mallison Cl EX4 . . . . . .**176** F8
Mallock Rd TQ2 . . . . . .**219** E5
Mallocks Cl EX10 . . . . .**100** D2
Mallow Ct
Dartmouth TQ6 . . . . . .**233** B2
Willand EX15 . . . .**162** D5
Mallow Pl TQ12 . . . . . .**206** C4
Malmesbury Cl PL2 . .**248** B8
MALMSMEAD **6** C4
Malmsmead Bridge
EX35 . . . .**6** D4
Malory Cl PL5 . . . .**244** D2
Malson La EX16. . . . . . .**47** B4
Malston Cross TQ7 . . .**144** D4
Malt Field EX8 . . . .**195** F5
Malthouse The
Bridgend PL8 . . . .**141** A7
[5] Totnes TQ9 . . . . . .**223** D5
Malting Ct [4] EX7 . . . .**204** E6
Maltings The
[21] Appledore EX39. . . .**15** A1
Black Torrington EX21. . .**74** A8
Crediton EX17 . . . .**165** D5
Exeter EX2 . . . .**177** F5
South Allington TQ7 . . .**149** B5
Malt Mill TQ9 . . . .**223** B6
Malvern Cl EX2 . . . . . .**178** A4
Malvernleigh TQ1. . . .**220** B8
Malvern Rd EX10. . . . .**188** B6
Malvern Way EX39 . . .**156** D2
Mambury Cross EX22. .**39** D3
Mamhead Bsns Units
EX2 . . . .**181** D8
Mamhead Rd
Exeter EX2 . . . .**178** C4
Kenton EX6 . . . .**194** C2
Kenton EX6. . . . .**200** B8
Mamhead Sensory Trail★
EX6 . . . .**124** E7
Mamhead View EX8. . .**201** E6
MANADON **244** D1
Manadon Cl PL5 . . . . .**244** E1
Manadon Dr PL5 . . . . .**244** E1
Manadon Football Ctr
PL2 . . . .**244** D2
Manadon Hill PL5,
PL6 . . . .**244** E1
Manadon Vale Prim Sch
[1] Plymouth PL5 . . . . .**248** E8
Plymouth PL12 . . . .**244** E1
MANATON **121** F8
Manaton Cl EX2 . . . . .**181** C8
Manaton Ct EX2 . . . . .**181** C8
Manaton Tor Rd TQ3 .**218** F1
Manby Gdns PL5. . . . .**243** F5
Manchester Rd EX8 . .**201** F6
Manchester St EX8 . . .**201** F6
Mandarin Way TQ12. .**207** C8
Mandrake Cl EX2 . . . .**177** A1
Mandrake Rd EX2 . . . .**177** A1
Manifold Gdns PL3. . .**249** D5
Manitoba Gdns EX15 .**163** B3
Manley Cl [1] EX5. . . . .**99** E8
Manley La EX16 . . . . . .**64** E7
Manley Mdw EX4 . . . .**174** F4
Manleys La EX14 . . . . .**67** B2
Manna Ash Ct EX2 . . .**261** C1
Mannacott La EX31 . .**4** C4
Mannacott Lane Head
EX31 . . . .**4** C4
MANNAMEAD **248** F5
Mannamead Ave PL3 **248** F5
Mannamead Ct [9]
PL3 . . . .**248** F6
Mannamead Rd PL3. .**248** F6
Manning Ave EX15 . . .**163** A2
Mannings Mdw
TQ13 . . . .**180** D7
Mannings Way EX31. .**154** F7
Manor Ave
Lyme Regis DT7 . . . . . .**260** D4
Paignton TQ3 . . . .**226** C8
Manor Bend TQ5. . . . .**229** C5
MANOR BOURNE **140** A8
Manor Bourne Rd
Down Thomas PL9. . . . .**255** C1
Heybrook Bay PL9. . . . .**140** A8
Manor Cl
Abbotskerswell
TQ12 . . . .**212** A7
Awliscombe EX14 . . . . . .**85** C3
Barnstaple EX31. . . . . .**154** C3
Dawlish EX7 . . . .**204** D6
Fremington EX31 . . . . .**153** E6
Ivybridge EX21 . . . .**237** C5
Kentisbeare EX15. . . . . .**66** A3
Kingskerswell TQ12 . . .**213** A3
[1] Seaton EX12 . . . . .**192** A5
Sidmouth EX10 . . . . . .**188** A5
Tavistock PL19 . . . .**171** A6
Uffculme EX15 . . . .**66** B8
Wrafton EX33 . . . .**152** E4
Manor Cotts
[16] Newton Abbot
TQ12 . . . .**207** B3
Rackenford EX16 . . . . . .**47** C6

Manor Court Barns
TQ7 . . . .**147** F8
Manor Cres
Honiton EX14 . . . .**166** C4
Paignton TQ3 . . . .**226** C8
Manor Ct
Barnstaple EX32. . . . . .**155** F1
[5] Dawlish EX7 . . . . .**204** D6
Galmpton TQ5 . . . .**229** A5
Kingskerswell TQ12 . . .**213** A3
Landkey EX32 . . . .**17** B2
Paignton TQ3 . . . .**226** C7
Seaton EX12 . . . .**192** A5
[9] South Brent TQ10. .**134** F3
Stoke Fleming TQ6 . . . .**146** B7
Torquay TQ2 . . . .**219** F6
Manor Dr
Chagford TQ13 . . . .**110** F6
Clyst St Mary EX5 . . . . .**179** B1
Ivybridge PL21 . . . .**237** C5
Kingskerswell TQ12 . . .**213** A3
Manor Est
Horrabridge PL19. . . . .**126** E4
Horrabridge PL20. . . . .**126** E4
Manor Farm PL20. . . .**127** B3
Manor Farm Cl TA20 . .**88** C8
Manor Farm Mews
EX5 . . . .**99** E4
Manor Gdn TQ1. . . . . .**220** E3
Manor Gdns
Abbotskerswell TQ12 . .**212** B6
Exbourne EX20 . . . .**76** C5
Halwill Junction EX21. . .**73** E2
Horrabridge PL20. . . . .**126** E4
Kingskerswell TQ12 . . .**213** A3
Millbrook PL10 . . . .**252** F6
Paignton TQ3 . . . .**226** C8
Plymouth PL1 . . . .**262** B2
Seaton EX12 . . . .**192** B5
Manorglade Ct [1]
TQ1 . . . .**220** D5
Manor Gn EX14 . . . . . .**68** C2
Manor Ho
Lympstone EX8 . . . . . .**195** D5
Torquay TQ1 . . . .**220** B3
Manor Ho The TQ9 . . .**223** C6
Manor La PL3 . . . .**249** D5
Manor Mead TQ12 . . .**131** D7
Manor Mill Rd EX33 . . .**8** D1
Manor Park Cl PL7 . . .**250** F5
Manor Park Dr PL7. . .**251** A4
Manor Pavilion Theatre★
EX10 . . . .**188** A3
Manor Pk
Ashwater EX21. . . . .**90** E6
Barnstaple EX31. . . . . .**154** C3
Bradworthy EX22 . . . . . .**53** E8
Clyst St Mary EX5 . . . . .**179** A2
Dousland PL20 . . . .**127** B3
Kingsbridge TQ7 . . . . .**258** D6
Saltash PL12. . . . .**242** D2
Woolfardisworthy EX39 .**38** F8
Manor Prim Sch
PL21 . . . .**237** C5
Manor Rd
Abbotskerswell TQ12 . .**212** B7
Bishopsteignton TQ14. .**208** F8
Chagford TQ13 . . . .**110** F6
Exeter EX4 . . . .**177** A5
Landkey EX32 . . . .**17** A2
Landkey EX32 . . . .**17** B2
Landkey EX32 . . . .**155** F1
Newton Abbot TQ12 . . .**206** F3
Newton Abbot TQ12 . . .**207** A3
Paignton TQ3 . . . .**226** C8
Seaton EX12 . . . .**192** A5
Sidmouth EX10 . . . . . .**188** A3
Tavistock PL19 . . . .**171** B6
Torquay TQ1 . . . .**220** C8
Manor St
Dittisham TQ6 . . . .**228** D2
Plymouth PL1 . . . .**262** A3
Manor Terr
Brixham TQ5 . . . .**230** C5
Paignton TQ3 . . . .**226** A5
Manor Vale Rd TQ5 . .**229** C5
Manor View TQ12 . . . .**207** A3
Manor Way
Ivybridge PL21 . . . .**237** C5
Tavistock PL19 . . . .**171** B6
Totnes TQ9 . . . .**223** C6
Manot Gdns [3] EX7 . .**204** E6
Mansands La TQ5 . . . .**235** B8
Mansbridge Rd TQ9 . .**223** E5
Manscombe Cl TQ2 . .**219** D3
Manscombe Rd TQ2. .**219** D3
Mansfield Rd EX4 . . . .**177** E8
Mansfield Terr EX9 . . .**198** B2
Mansion Ho EX4 . . . . .**161** F5
Mansion Ho The PL1 .**254** A8
Mansion House St
TQ6 . . . .**233** F3
Mansion Terr [6] EX34 . .**3** A3
Mansion The PL21 . . .**137** C8
Manston Cl PL5. . . . . .**243** E5
Manston Ct TQ1 . . . . .**220** C4
Manstone Ave EX10 . .**188** A7
Manstone Cl EX10. . . .**188** B7
Manstone La EX10. . . .**188** B7
Manstone Mead
EX10 . . . .**188** B8
Manstone Workshops [3]
EX10 . . . .**188** B7
Manston Rd EX1 . . . . .**177** E5
Manston Terr EX2. . . .**177** E5
Manstree Cross EX2. .**114** A6

Manstree Rd EX2 . . . .**114** B6
Manstree Terr EX2. . . .**114** C6
Manteo Way EX39. . . .**157** C2
Mantle Gdns PL5. . . . .**247** D8
Mantle St TA21 . . . . . .**160** C5
Maple Ave
Bovey Tracey TQ13 . . . .**180** C4
Torpoint PL11 . . . .**247** A3
Maple Cl
Brixham TQ5 . . . .**230** A2
[10] Chudleigh Knighton
TQ13 . . . .**123** C4
[7] Honiton EX14 . . . . .**85** C2
Kingsteignton TQ12 . . .**207** E6
Plymouth PL6 . . . .**245** E6
Seaton EX12 . . . .**192** A4
Tavistock PL19 . . . .**171** C3
Willand EX15 . . . .**162** C4
Maple Ct
Cheriton Bishop EX6. . .**97** B3
Paignton TQ4 . . . .**226** B2
[2] Plymouth PL9 . . . .**255** F7
Mapledene Cl TQ9 . . .**227** F8
Maple Dr EX8 . . . .**196** D3
Maple Gr
Barnstaple EX31. . . . . .**154** C3
Ivybridge PL21 . . . .**237** F5
Plymouth, Mutley PL4. .**248** D4
Plymouth, Plympton
PL7 . . . .**250** B5
Maple Rd
Brixham TQ5 . . . .**230** A2
Broadclyst EX5 . . . .**175** D6
Exeter EX4 . . . .**177** A5
Maples Ct [7] EX2 . . . .**154** F6
Mapleton Cl TQ12. . . .**206** F4
Maple Way PL6 . . . . . .**245** E7
Maple Wlk TQ2 . . . . . .**219** C8
Mapstone Hill
Lustleigh TQ13 . . . .**112** B1
Lustleigh TQ13 . . . .**122** C8
Marazion Wy [2] PL2. .**248** D8
Marber Cross TQ7 . . . .**149** A8
Marcent Row TQ5. . . .**230** D3
Marchant's Cross
PL20 . . . .**127** C1
Marchant's Way
PL20 . . . .**127** C2
March Ct EX20 . . . .**170** B5
Marchweeke La EX16 .**61** A6
Marcombe Rd TQ2 . . .**219** E5
Marcom Cl EX8 . . . . . .**196** D3
Marcus Rd
Dunkeswell EX14 . . . . . .**67** B2
Exmouth EX8 . . . .**196** D1
Marder's Bequest
DT7 . . . .**260** E3
Mardle Way TQ11 . . . .**236** B5
Mardle Way Bsns Pk
TQ11. . . . .**236** B5
Mardon Cl PL6 . . . . . .**245** D4
Mardon Cross EX6 . . .**112** C2
Mardon Hill EX4 . . . . .**173** B1
Mare Hill EX17 . . . .**61** C5
Mare La
Beer EX12 . . . .**191** B5
Middle Marwood EX31 . . .**9** B1
Marepark Cross TQ7 .**144** D3
Marepark Gate EX20 . .**77** C7
Marett Rd PL5 . . . .**243** F3
Margaret Cl
East Ogwell TQ12 . . . . .**206** B1
Kingsteignton TQ12 . . .**207** E2
Margaret Ct [7] EX4 . .**178** C8
Margaret Gdns
TQ12 . . . .**207** F2
Margaret Pk PL3 . . . . .**248** E8
Margaret Rd
East Ogwell TQ12 . . . . .**206** B1
Exeter EX4 . . . .**173** E1
Kingsteignton TQ12 . . .**207** E2
Margaret St [4] EX8. . .**202** A6
Margrove Terr [10]
EX32 . . . .**154** F6
Marguerite Cl TQ12 . .**206** F4
Marguerite Rd EX16. .**161** F6
Marguerite Way
TQ12 . . . .**213** A4
MARHAMCHURCH **70** A6
Marhamchurch CE Prim
Sch EX23 . . . .**70** A6
MARIANSLEIGH **30** D1
Mariansleigh Cross
EX36 . . . .**30** E1
Marina Cl TQ5 . . . .**230** E5
Marina Ct
Brixham TQ5 . . . .**230** F6
Exmouth EX8 . . . .**202** B5
Paignton TQ4 . . . .**226** C5
[23] Teignmouth TQ14 .**210** C4
Marina Dr TQ5 . . . .**230** E5
Marina Rd
Brixham TQ5 . . . .**230** E4
Plymouth PL5 . . . .**243** F3
Marina Terr [7] PL4. . .**248** F4
Marina Way PL6 . . . . . .**64** D7
Marine Acad Plymouth
PL5 . . . .**243** E1
Marine Aquarium★
DT7 . . . .**260** D2
Marine Cres [6] EX12 .**192** A4
Marine Ct
Budleigh Salterton
EX9 . . . .**199** H2
Instow EX39 . . . .**15** B1
Torpoint PL11 . . . .**247** B2

Marine Dr
Bigbury-on-ST QT7 . . .**142** E3
Heybrook Bay PL9. . . . .**140** A7
Paignton TQ3 . . . .**226** C7
Topsham EX3 . . . .**182** E7
Torpoint PL11 . . . .**247** B2
Woolacombe EX33, EX34 . .**7** F5
Marine Gdns TQ3 . . . .**226** C8
Marine House at Beer★
EX23 . . . .**191** D5
Marine Mount TQ1 . . .**221** A3
Marine Par
Appledore EX39 . . . . . .**15** A1
Budleigh Salterton
EX9 . . . .**199** H2
Dawlish EX7 . . . .**204** E5
Instow EX39 . . . .**15** B1
Lyme Regis DT7 . . . . . .**260** D2
Paignton TQ3 . . . .**226** D8
Teignmouth TQ14 . . . .**210** B3
Marine Pk TQ3. . . . . . .**226** C7
Marine Pl
Ilfracombe EX34. . . . . .**150** B6
Seaton EX12 . . . .**192** A4
Marine Rd PL9 . . . .**255** B7
Mariners Cl EX33 . . . .**152** C5
Mariners Ct
[7] Brixham TQ5 . . . . .**230** D5
[13] Dawlish EX7. . . . .**204** E6
Mariners Way TQ3 . . .**218** F1
Mariner's Way [33]
EX39 . . . .**15** A1
Marine Terr [17] TQ14 .**210** B4
Marine Theatre★
DT7 . . . .**260** E3
Marine Way
Exmouth EX8 . . . .**201** F7
Plymouth PL2 . . . .**247** F5
Marino The EX10 . . . . .**187** F3
Marions Way EX4 . . . .**196** D2
Marion View TQ1 . . . .**220** C4
Maristow Ave
Exeter EX4 . . . .**196** B2
Plymouth PL2 . . . .**247** F5
Maristow Cl PL6 . . . . .**244** F5
Maristow La PL12 . . . .**242** F3
Marist Way EX32 . . . . .**155** C2
Maritime Sq PL1 . . . . .**247** F1
Marjery Cross PL21 . .**237** A2
Marjon Hill PL6 . . . . . .**245** B4
Marjorie Ct PL12. . . . .**242** C4
Marjorie Kelly Way
PL21. . . . .**237** D4
Marjory Wlk PL8 . . . . .**257** E3
Markadon Cotts EX39 .**22** B4
Markers EX15. . . . .**66** A7
Marker's Cottage★
EX5. . . . .**175** D7
Markers Pk EX14 . . . . .**84** C4
Markers Rd EX15. . . . . .**66** A7
Marker Way EX14 . . . .**166** C4
Market Ave PL1 . . . . . .**262** B3
Market Cl
Ashburton TQ13 . . . . . .**130** F4
[4] Bampton EX16 . . . .**34** B1
Brushford TA22. . . . . . .**33** E4
Buckfastleigh TQ11. . . .**236** B5
Plymouth PL1 . . . .**248** A1
Market Field EX38 . . . .**40** C2
Market Forum the (Sh
Ctr) TQ1. . . . .**220** B5
Market Mws EX3 . . . .**182** D7
Market Pl
Bideford EX39. . . . .**157** A2
Burlescombe EX16 . . . . .**51** B4
Colyton EX24 . . . .**103** A5
Sidmouth EX10 . . . . . .**188** B3
Willand EX15 . . . .**162** C5
Market Rd
Plymouth PL7 . . . .**250** D5
Tavistock PL19 . . . .**171** C5
Market Sq
Axminster EX13 . . . . . .**167** D6
Dartmouth TQ6 . . . . . .**233** F3
[3] Ilfracombe EX34 . .**150** B6
Plymouth PL1 . . . .**262** C3
Market St
[3] Appledore EX39 . . .**15** A1
[4] Barnstaple EX31. . .**154** F5
[8] Brixham TQ5 . . . . .**230** C5
Buckfastleigh TQ11. . . .**236** B5
Crediton EX17. . . . .**165** C5
Dartmouth TQ6 . . . . . .**233** F3
Exeter EX1, EX4 . . . . . .**261** A2
Exmouth EX8 . . . .**202** A6
Hatherleigh EX20 . . . . .**75** C7
Ilfracombe EX34. . . . . .**150** B6
Kingsand PL10 . . . .**253** A1
Lynton EX35 . . . .**151** C5
Newton Abbot TQ12 . . .**207** B3
North Tawton EX20 . . . .**77** C4
Okehampton EX20 . . . .**170** B5
Plymouth PL1 . . . .**248** A1
Salcombe TQ8 . . . .**259** C5
South Molton EX36 . . . .**158** C4
Tavistock PL19 . . . .**171** C5
Torquay TQ1 . . . .**220** B5
Yealmpton PL8 . . . .**257** F4
Market Terr EX16 . . . .**161** C4
Market Way
[7] Chudleigh TQ13 . . .**123** E6
Plymouth PL1 . . . .**262** C4
Market Wlk [7] TQ12. .**207** B3
Market Wlk EX16. . . . .**161** D4
Markham Cross EX2. .**114** B8
Markham La
Exeter EX2 . . . .**181** C2
Ide EX2 . . . .**114** C8

Mark's Cross EX6 . . . .**176** B2
Mark Twain Ho [1]
EX4 . . . .**178** C8
Marland Cross PL8. . .**136** B1
Marland Prim EX39 . .**156** B6
Marland Sch EX38 . . . .**56** B8
Marland Terr EX39 . . .**156** F1
Marlborough Ave
TQ1 . . . .**220** D5
Marlborough Cl
Exmouth EX8. . . . .**196** E2
Ilfracombe EX34 . . . . . .**150** B5
Musbury EX13. . . . .**103** D5
Saltash PL12 . . . .**242** F1
Marlborough Cross
EX5 . . . .**179** D6
Marlborough Ct
Bideford EX39. . . . .**157** A3
Exeter, Alphington EX21 .**181** C8
Exeter, Heavitree EX2. .**177** E5
Marlborough Dr [9]
TQ2 . . . .**178** D5
Marlborough Pk [7]
EX34 . . . .**150** B5
Marlborough Pl
TQ12 . . . .**207** A4
Marlborough Prim Sch
PL1 . . . .**247** E2
Marlborough Rd
Exeter EX2 . . . .**261** C2
Ilfracombe EX34. . . . . . .**2** A3
Ilfracombe EX34. . . . . .**150** C5
Musbury EX13. . . . .**103** D5
Plymouth PL4 . . . .**263** A4
Marlborough Row
PL1 . . . .**247** E2
Marlborough St PL1. .**247** E2
Marlborough Terr
TQ13 . . . .**180** C7
Marlborough Way
EX34 . . . .**150** C4
Marlcombe Cross
EX14 . . . .**85** A6
MARLDON **218** C3
Marldon Ave TQ3 . . . .**226** A6
Marldon CE Prim Sch
TQ3 . . . .**218** D3
Marldon Cl PL5 . . . . . .**244** B3
Marldon Cross TQ3 . .**218** C2
Marldon Cross Hill
TQ3 . . . .**218** B3
Marldon Gr TQ3. . . . . .**218** D3
Marldon La TQ3. . . . . .**218** B4
Marldon Rd
Dainton TQ12 . . . .**212** A1
Ipplepen TQ12 . . . .**211** F2
Paignton TQ3 . . . .**225** F8
Torquay TQ2 . . . .**219** B7
Marldon Way TQ3. . . .**218** E2
Marlen Ct EX39 . . . . . .**25** F4
Marles Cl EX14. . . . . . .**85** B4
Marles The EX8 . . . . . .**196** C5
Marley Cl EX16 . . . . . .**161** D6
Marley Dr EX8 . . . .**196** D5
Marley Head TQ10 . . .**135** C3
Marley Rd EX8 . . . .**196** C3
Marlow Cres PL16. . . .**106** D1
Marlow Ct EX39. . . . . .**156** D7
Marlowe Cl TQ2. . . . . .**219** D7
Marlow Gdns PL9 . . . .**255** F5
Marlpit Cl PL12 . . . . . .**191** F7
Marlpit Cross EX14 . . .**87** A6
Marlpit La EX12 . . . . . .**192** A5
Marlpits La EX14. . . . .**166** C5
Marl Pk
Harbertonford TQ9. . . .**139** C7
Holne TQ11. . . . .**130** A3
Marmora Terr EX12 . .**191** D5
Marnham Rd TQ1 . . . .**220** B7
Marpool Cres EX8. . . .**202** C8
Marpool Hill EX8. . . . .**202** B7
Marpool Prim Sch
EX8. . . . .**202** C8
Marridge Cross PL21 .**137** F5
Marriott Way TQ13. . .**180** B6
Marrowbone Slip
PL4 . . . .**263** B2
Marryat Gdns PL5. . . .**244** E1
MARSH **69** B5
Marshall Cl
Tavistock PL19 . . . .**171** D2
Tiverton EX16 . . . .**161** F3
Marshall Dr PL21 . . . .**237** D4
Marshall Rd
Plymouth PL7 . . . .**250** A4
Tavistock PL19 . . . .**171** D2
Marshalls Field PL21 .**237** E5
Marshalls Mead EX19 .**42** D1
Marsh Barton La
EX5. . . . .**172** D8
Marsh Barton Rd
EX2. . . . .**177** B3
Marsh Barton Trad Est
EX2. . . . .**177** C2
Marshbridge Cross
TA22. . . . .**33** C2
Marsh Cl PL6 . . . .**249** F6
Marshclose Hill TA22. .**21** E2
Marsh Cotts [14] EX39 . .**15** E2
Marsh Cross EX15. . . . .**83** E4
Marsh Dro EX13. . . . . .**87** B2
Marsh End EX17 . . . . .**165** F5
MARSH GREEN **99** E5
Marsh Green La EX5. . .**99** E5
Marsh Green Road E
EX2. . . . .**177** C2
Marsh Green Road N
EX2. . . . .**177** C2

- **Marsh Green Road W** EX2 ... 177 C2
- **Marsh Hill**
  - Cheriton Fitzpaine EX16 ... 63 A4
  - Dulverton TA22 ... 33 C8
  - Lynton EX35 ... 151 C5
- **Mars Hill Way** EX35 ... 151 C5
- **Marsh La**
  - Bow EX17 ... 78 B5
  - Calstock PL18 ... 125 D3
  - Cheriton Fitzpaine EX16 ... 63 A4
  - Chudleigh TQ13 ... 123 F8
  - Chudleigh TQ13 ... 124 A8
  - Clyst St George EX3 ... 183 B6
  - Crediton EX17 ... 165 E5
  - Instow EX39 ... 15 B1
  - Newton St Cyres EX5 ... 98 F8
  - North Molton EX36 ... 30 E6
  - Seaton EX12 ... 192 B7
  - South Molton EX36 ... 158 F7
  - Stockland EX14 ... 87 A7
  - West Charleton TQ7 ... 144 C1
- **Marsh La Cross** TQ13 ... 123 F8
- Marsh Mill Ct EX5 ... 172 D7
- **MARSH MILLS** ... 249 F6
- **Marsh Mills** PL6 ... 249 F7
- **Marsh Mills Pk** PL6 ... 249 F6
- Marsh Mills Ret Pk PL6 ... 249 E7
- Marsh Mills Sta★ PL7 ... 250 A7
- **Marsh Path** TQ13 ... 180 C7
- **Marsh Rd**
  - Crediton EX17 ... 165 E5
  - Newton Abbot TQ12 ... 207 C3
  - Seaton EX12 ... 192 B5
- **Marshrow La** EX3 ... 182 C1
- **Marston Cl** EX7 ... 204 F7
- **MARTINHOE** ... 4 C5
- **Martinhoe Cross** EX31 ... 4 E3
- **Martinique Gr** TQ2 ... 213 F3
- **Martin La** PL4 ... 263 A2
- **Martin Rd** EX32 ... 155 B5
- **Martins Bldgs** 4 TA21 ... 160 D5
- **Martins Cl**
  - Great Torrington EX38 ... 159 F5
  - Okehampton/North Tawton EX20 ... 75 C7
  - Wellington TA21 ... 160 D5
- Martins Gate - City Coll PL4 ... 263 A2
- **Martins La** EX16 ... 161 D4
- **Martin's La** EX1, EX4 ... 261 B3
- **Martins Rd** EX8 ... 196 E2
- **Martin St** PL1 ... 262 B2
- **Martlesham Pl** PL5 ... 243 F4
- **Mart The** EX20 ... 170 B5
- **Marvell La** PL3 ... 263 B3
- **Marven Ct** DT7 ... 260 B6
- **Marwell Cross** TQ7 ... 142 E6
- **MARWOOD** ... 16 C8
- **Marwood Cross** EX5 ... 99 B3
- **Marwood Ct** EX38 ... 159 D5
- Marwood Hill Gdns★ EX31 ... 16 C8
- **Marwood La** EX5 ... 99 C3
- **Marwood Pl** EX14 ... 166 D6
- Marwood Sch EX31 ... 9 D1
- **Marwood's Cross** TQ10 ... 134 D1
- **Mary Arches St** EX4 ... 261 A3
- **Mary Cross** PL21 ... 137 C3
- **Mary Dean Ave** PL5 ... 244 C7
- **Mary Dean Cl** PL5 ... 244 C7
- Mary Dean's CE Prim Sch PL5 ... 244 C7
- **Maryfield Ave** EX4 ... 177 D8
- **Mary La** 10 EX16 ... 34 B1
- **Maryland Gdns** PL2 ... 247 F7
- Mary Newman's Cottage★ PL12 ... 243 A2
- **Marypole Rd** EX4 ... 173 F1
- **Marypole Wlk** EX4 ... 173 F1
- **Mary Rose Ho**
  - 9 Hemyock EX15 ... 67 B8
  - Torquay TQ1 ... 220 D7
- **Mary Seacole Rd** PL1 ... 262 A3
- **Mary St** TQ13 ... 180 D8
- **MARYSTOW** ... 106 D1
- **MARY TAVY** ... 117 E6
- Mary Tavy & Brentor Com Prim Sch PL19 ... 117 E6
- **Marythorne Rd** 15 PL20 ... 125 E1
- **Masefield Ave**
  - Barnstaple EX31 ... 154 F7
  - 5 Barnstaple EX32 ... 155 A7
- **Masefield Gdns** PL5 ... 244 B1
- **Masefield Rd** EX4 ... 178 C8
- **Masey Rd** EX8 ... 202 D8
- **Mashford Ave** TQ6 ... 233 C4
- **Masons Row** PL18 ... 125 C6
- **Masons Yard** PL8 ... 136 D1
- **Massey Rd** EX16 ... 161 E6
- **Masterman Rd** PL2 ... 247 F4
- **Masters Cl** DT7 ... 260 A6
- **Masterson St** EX2 ... 177 F3
- **Matford Ave** EX2 ... 177 E4
- **Matford Bsns Pk** EX2 ... 181 C8
- **Matford La** EX2 ... 261 C1
- **Matford Mews** EX2 ... 181 D7
- **Matford Park Rd** EX2 ... 181 D8
- **Matford Rd** EX2 ... 177 E4
- **Matford Wy** EX2 ... 181 D7
- **Mathew Ho** 2 TQ1 ... 219 F6
- **Mathews Cl** EX14 ... 166 B4
- **Mathill Cl** TQ5 ... 230 B3
- **Mathill Rd** TQ5 ... 230 B3
- **Maton Cl** PL21 ... 237 D4
- **Matthews Cross** EX15 ... 66 B1
- **Matthews Ct** EX4 ... 174 D2
- **Matthew's Ct** EX15 ... 163 C3
- **Matthews Pas** TQ7 ... 258 C5
- **Mattiscombe Cross** TQ7 ... 145 B1
- **Mattys Cross** EX14 ... 68 A3
- **Maudlin Dr** TQ14 ... 210 B8
- **Maudlin Rd** TQ9 ... 223 C5
- **Maudlins La** PL19 ... 171 A5
- **Maudlins Pk** PL19 ... 171 A5
- **Maunder's Hill** EX9 ... 198 E7
- **MAUNDOWN** ... 35 F7
- **Maundown Rd** TA4 ... 35 F7
- **Maunsell Cl** PL2 ... 247 F7
- **Maurice Mws** PL7 ... 250 E4
- **Mavisdale** PL2 ... 247 F6
- **Mawes Ct** PL18 ... 125 A5
- **Maxstoke Ct** 4 TQ1 ... 220 D5
- **Maxwell Rd** PL4 ... 255 B8
- **Maybank Rd** PL4 ... 263 C3
- **Maybrook Dr** PL12 ... 242 D2
- **May Ct** EX39 ... 157 D1
- **Mayers Way** PL9 ... 255 D6
- **Mayfair** EX16 ... 64 E8
- **Mayfair Cres** PL6 ... 245 B1
- **Mayfair Ho** PL4 ... 263 A3
- **Mayfair Rd** TQ12 ... 211 D2
- **Mayfield** PL21 ... 237 A4
- **Mayfield Cres** TQ12 ... 206 F3
- **Mayfield Dr** EX8 ... 202 D6
- **Mayfield Rd**
  - Exeter, Pinhoe EX4 ... 174 E1
  - Exeter, Wonford EX2 ... 178 A5
- **Mayfield Sch** TQ2 ... 214 B3
- Mayfield Sch Chestnut Centre TQ5 ... 230 A2
- **Mayfield Way** 1 EX5 ... 99 A6
- **Mayfield Wy** 11 EX5 ... 99 A6
- **Mayflower Ave**
  - Exeter EX4 ... 173 D2
  - Newton Abbot TQ12 ... 207 F2
- **Mayflower Cl**
  - 18 Bere Alston PL20 ... 125 E1
  - Chittlehampton EX37 ... 28 F4
  - Dartmouth TQ6 ... 233 D4
  - Dawlish EX7 ... 204 E6
  - Plymouth PL9 ... 255 F7
- Mayflower Com Acad PL2 ... 248 A7
- **Mayflower Ct** TQ6 ... 233 F4
- **Mayflower Dr**
  - 6 Brixham TQ5 ... 230 C3
  - Plymouth PL2 ... 248 B5
- **Mayflower St** PL1 ... 262 C3
- **Mayhew Gdns** 3 PL7 ... 250 E7
- **Maynarde Cl** PL7 ... 251 B5
- **Maynard Pk** PL20 ... 125 E1
- Maynard Sch The EX1 ... 261 C3
- **Mayne Cl** EX20 ... 75 B7
- **Mayor's Ave** TQ6 ... 233 F4
- **May St** EX4 ... 261 C4
- **May Terr**
  - Plymouth PL4 ... 263 B3
  - Sidmouth EX10 ... 188 B4
- **Maytree Cl** EX21 ... 73 D3
- **Mazard Tree Hill**
  - Ash Mill EX36 ... 31 C1
  - South Molton EX36 ... 46 C8
- **Mazzard Cl** 9 EX32 ... 17 B2
- **McCoys Arcade** 18 EX1 ... 261 A2
- **McDonald Ct** 12 PL1 ... 262 A3
- **Mcilwraith Rd** TQ8 ... 259 C5
- **Mckay Ave** TQ1 ... 219 F6
- **MEAD** ... 37 A4
- **Mead Cl**
  - Cullompton EX15 ... 163 B2
  - Ivybridge PL21 ... 237 A6
  - Paignton TQ3 ... 226 C7
- **Mead Cnr** EX39 ... 37 A4
- **Meadcombe Rd** TQ7 ... 143 A1
- **Mead Cotts** EX8 ... 202 F7
- **Meadcourt** TQ3 ... 226 C7
- **Mead Cross**
  - Ashburton TQ13 ... 131 B6
  - 13 Rockbeare EX5 ... 99 A6
- **Mead Dr** TQ7 ... 143 A1
- **Meadfoot** TQ7 ... 143 A1
- **Meadfoot Cl** TQ1 ... 220 F4
- **Meadfoot Ct** TQ1 ... 220 C3
- **Meadfoot Grange** TQ1 ... 220 C3
- **Meadfoot La** TQ1 ... 220 C3
- **Meadfoot Rd** TQ1 ... 220 C3
- **Meadfoot Sea Rd** TQ1 ... 220 D3
- **Meadfoot Terr** 2 PL4 ... 248 F5
- **Meadhurst Ct** EX10 ... 188 A3
- **Mead La**
  - Paignton TQ3 ... 226 C7
  - Thurlestone TQ7 ... 143 A1
- **Meadow Acre Rd** EX14 ... 85 C2
- **Meadow Ave** EX12 ... 192 A6
- **Meadow Bank** EX13 ... 87 D1
- **Meadowbrook** 19 TQ9 ... 223 D5
- **Meadow Brook**
  - Barnstaple EX31 ... 154 B2
- **Meadow Brook** *continued*
  - Tavistock PL19 ... 171 A4
  - 18 Totnes TQ9 ... 223 D5
- **Meadowbrook Cl** EX4 ... 176 E8
- Meadow Bsns Pk EX17 ... 165 F5
- **Meadow Cl**
  - Bratton Fleming EX31 ... 18 A8
  - Budleigh Salterton EX9 ... 197 F1
  - Clyst St Mary EX5 ... 179 E3
  - Harberton TQ9 ... 222 D2
  - Ilfracombe EX34 ... 150 B4
  - Kingskerswell TQ12 ... 212 F6
  - Landkey EX32 ... 17 C1
  - Lympstone EX8 ... 195 F5
  - 7 Newton Ferrers PL8 ... 141 A7
  - Ottery St Mary EX11 ... 169 E4
  - Plymouth PL7 ... 251 D4
  - Saltash PL12 ... 242 F3
  - Totnes TQ9 ... 223 F5
- **Meadow Cotts** TQ6 ... 228 C2
- **Meadow Court Barns** TQ7 ... 145 B1
- **Meadow Cres** EX8 ... 203 A6
- **Meadowcroft Dr** TQ12 ... 123 E1
- **Meadow Dr**
  - Brixton PL8 ... 257 A4
  - Newton Poppleford EX10 ... 186 F8
  - Saltash PL12 ... 242 D4
- **Meadowfield Pl** PL7 ... 251 B3
- **Meadow Gdns** EX17 ... 165 D5
- **Meadow Halt** TQ12 ... 207 A1
- **Meadow La**
  - Croyde EX33 ... 7 E2
  - Cullompton EX15 ... 163 C2
  - Instow EX39 ... 15 B1
- **Meadowlands**
  - Newton St Cyres EX5 ... 98 F8
  - Plymouth PL6 ... 245 D7
- Meadowlands L Pool 7 PL19 ... 171 B5
- **Meadow Lea** EX5 ... 82 B6
- **Meadow Park Dr** EX37 ... 43 F3
- **Meadow Pk**
  - Barnstaple EX31 ... 154 B2
  - Bideford EX39 ... 25 D4
  - Brixham TQ5 ... 230 B5
  - Dawlish EX7 ... 204 C7
  - Marldon TQ3 ... 218 D3
  - Molland EX36 ... 31 E7
  - Plymouth PL9 ... 255 C5
  - Shebbear EX21 ... 55 E4
  - South Molton EX36 ... 158 C3
  - Willand EX15 ... 162 C4
- **Meadow Rd**
  - Barnstaple EX31 ... 154 E7
  - Budleigh Salterton EX9 ... 197 F1
  - Budleigh Salterton EX9 ... 203 F8
  - Seaton EX12 ... 192 A5
  - Torquay TQ2 ... 219 E3
- **Meadow Rise**
  - Dawlish EX7 ... 204 C7
  - Mile End TQ12 ... 206 D5
  - Northam EX39 ... 157 A6
  - Plymouth PL7 ... 251 A4
  - Spreyton EX17 ... 96 A7
  - Teignmouth TQ14 ... 124 E1
  - Torquay TQ1 ... 220 F5
- **Meadows Cres** EX14 ... 166 C5
- **Meadows Edge** EX6 ... 97 B4
- **Meadowside**
  - Ashford EX31 ... 16 B6
  - Chillington TQ7 ... 145 A1
  - Plymouth PL9 ... 255 F7
  - Rockwell Green TA21 ... 160 B5
- **Meadow Side**
  - Burrow EX10 ... 186 E8
  - Newton Abbot TQ12 ... 207 A3
- **Meadowside Rd** EX17 ... 80 B5
- **Meadow St** EX8 ... 202 A7
- **Meadows The**
  - Beer EX12 ... 191 D5
  - East Portlemouth TQ8 ... 259 F4
  - Kingsteignton TQ12 ... 207 F6
  - Okehampton/North Tawton EX20 ... 74 E2
  - St Dominick PL12 ... 125 A2
  - Torpoint PL11 ... 246 E4
  - Yeoford EX17 ... 79 C2
- **Meadowstone Cl** EX38 ... 40 F5
- **Meadowsweet La**
  - 3 Barnstaple EX31 ... 154 B3
  - Paignton TQ4 ... 225 E2
- **Meadowsweet Pk** PL12 ... 242 C2
- **Meadow Vale** EX20 ... 57 A7
- **Meadow View**
  - 2 Bampton EX16 ... 34 B1
  - Bishops Nympton EX36 ... 30 F2
  - Bishopsteignton TQ14 ... 208 C7
  - East Ogwell TQ12 ... 206 F1
  - Hartland EX39 ... 22 E3
  - Holsworthy EX22 ... 164 C6
  - Lympstone EX8 ... 195 F5
  - Rackenford EX16 ... 47 D5
  - Uffculme EX15 ... 66 A7
- **Meadow View Cl**
  - Sidmouth EX10 ... 188 C5
  - Woodbury EX5 ... 184 B2
- **Meadowview Rd** EX8 ... 196 E2
- **Meadow View Rd** PL7 ... 250 D5
- **Meadowville Ct** EX39 ... 157 A3
- **Meadowville Rd** EX39 ... 157 A3
- **Meadow Way**
  - Colaton Raleigh EX10 ... 186 D3
  - Exeter EX2 ... 177 F5
  - Gunn EX32 ... 17 F4
  - Plymouth PL7 ... 250 D7
- **Mead Park Cl** EX31 ... 16 A3
- **Mead Pk** EX31 ... 16 A3
- **Mead Rd** TQ2 ... 219 D2
- **Meads Cl** EX15 ... 67 B1
- **Mead The**
  - Plymouth PL7 ... 250 D7
  - Silverton EX5 ... 82 B5
- **Mead View Rd** EX14 ... 166 C5
- **Meadville** TQ1 ... 220 D3
- **Meadway**
  - Newton Abbot TQ12 ... 212 D8
  - Saltash PL12 ... 242 E1
  - Sidmouth EX10 ... 188 B6
- **Mead Way** EX12 ... 192 A6
- **MEADWELL** ... 116 A8
- **Meadwood** TQ1 ... 220 D3
- **Mear Top** EX31 ... 154 F7
- **Measbury Moor Cross** EX18 ... 45 C5
- **Meatherel Cl** PL21 ... 237 B4
- **MEAVY** ... 127 C2
- **Meavy Ave**
  - Plymouth PL5 ... 244 E2
  - Torquay TQ2 ... 219 B7
- **Meavy Bourne** PL20 ... 127 A2
- Meavy CE Prim Sch PL20 ... 127 C2
- **Meavy La** PL20 ... 127 A2
- **Meavy Villas** PL20 ... 127 A2
- **Meavy Way**
  - Plymouth PL5 ... 244 E2
  - Tavistock PL19 ... 171 D5
- **Medard Ho** 17 EX32 ... 155 A5
- **MEDDON** ... 37 F4
- **Meddon Cross**
  - Edistone EX39 ... 37 F5
  - Welcombe EX39 ... 37 F4
- Meddon Green Nature Reserve★ EX39 ... 37 F4
- **Meddon St**
  - 5 Bideford EX39 ... 156 F1
  - Bideford EX39 ... 157 A1
- **Mede The**
  - Exeter EX4 ... 178 B8
  - Topsham EX3 ... 182 E5
- **Medland Cres** PL6 ... 244 D6
- **Medland Cross** EX6 ... 97 C6
- **Medland La** EX6 ... 97 B6
- **Medley Ct** EX4 ... 176 E8
- **Medway Pl** PL3 ... 249 D6
- **Medway Rd** TQ2 ... 214 B2
- **Meerhay La** DT6 ... 104 F6
- **Meetford Cross** EX6 ... 97 F7
- **MEETH** ... 57 C3
- **MEETHE** ... 29 D1
- **Meethe Gate Cross** EX36 ... 29 D2
- **Meethe Hill** EX36 ... 29 D1
- **Meeting La** EX8 ... 195 E6
- **Meeting St**
  - Appledore EX39 ... 15 A1
  - Exmouth EX8 ... 202 A6
- **Melbourne Cotts** PL1 ... 262 B3
- **Melbourne Ct**
  - 10 Exeter EX2 ... 261 B2
  - Torquay TQ1 ... 220 A6
- **Melbourne Gn** 2 PL1 ... 262 B3
- **Melbourne Pl**
  - Exeter EX2 ... 261 B2
  - Plymouth PL1 ... 262 B4
- **Melbourne St**
  - Exeter EX2 ... 261 B2
  - Plymouth PL1 ... 262 B3
  - Tiverton EX16 ... 161 B4
- **Melbury Rd** EX39 ... 39 E8
- **Melcot Cl** TQ12 ... 207 E7
- **MELDON** ... 93 D3
- **Meldon La** EX20 ... 93 E3
- Meldon Quarry Sta★ EX20 ... 93 E3
- **Meldon Rd** TQ13 ... 111 A6
- **Meldrum Cl** EX7 ... 204 E6
- **Melhuish Cl** EX16 ... 46 E1
- **Mellons Cl** TQ12 ... 206 D4
- **Mellons Wlk** TQ12 ... 206 D4
- **Mellowmead** TQ13 ... 121 F7
- **Mellows Mdw** TQ12 ... 206 F3
- **Melrose Ave**
  - Exeter EX1 ... 178 D6
  - Plymouth PL2 ... 248 C8
- **Melrose Cl** EX16 ... 161 D4
- **Melville La** TQ1 ... 220 B4
- **Melville Pl** 1 PL2 ... 248 A5
- **Melville Rd** PL2 ... 248 A5
- **Melville St** TQ1 ... 220 B4
- **Melville Terrace La** PL2 ... 248 A5
- **MEMBLAND** ... 141 B7
- **Membland Ct** PL8 ... 141 C6
- **MEMBURY** ... 87 D6
- **Membury Cl** EX1 ... 178 D6
- Membury Prim Sch EX13 ... 87 D6
- **Membury Rd**
  - Axminster EX13 ... 87 E3
  - Axminster EX13 ... 167 B8
  - Wambrook TA20 ... 69 D2
- **Memory Cross** TQ13 ... 215 E8
- **Memory La** PL9 ... 255 E7
- **Mena Park Cl**
  - Paignton TQ4 ... 225 F2
  - Plymouth PL9 ... 256 B7
- **Mena Park Rd** PL9 ... 256 B7
- **MENDENNICK** ... 252 C7
- **Mendip Rd** TQ2 ... 219 D3
- **Menors Pl** EX22 ... 164 C5
- **Merafield Cl** PL7 ... 250 B5
- **Merafield Dr** PL7 ... 250 C4
- **Merafield Farm Cotts** PL7 ... 250 B4
- **Merafield Rd** PL7 ... 250 B4
- **Merafield Rise** PL7 ... 250 C4
- **Mercer Ct** EX2 ... 178 A2
- **Mercers Dr** EX16 ... 161 E6
- **Merchant Row** EX3 ... 182 C7
- **Merchants Cnr** EX17 ... 61 C1
- **Merchant's Gdn** TQ7 ... 143 A1
- Merchant's House (Mus)★ PL1 ... 262 C2
- **Meredith Rd** PL2 ... 248 C6
- **Mere La** 15 TQ14 ... 210 C5
- **Meresyke** EX8 ... 202 C6
- **Merewood Cl** EX31 ... 16 C7
- **Meriden** TQ14 ... 210 C7
- **Meridian Ho** PL4 ... 263 A3
- **Meridian Pl** EX34 ... 150 B6
- **Merivale** PL20 ... 126 F2
- **Merivale Cl** TQ14 ... 210 C7
- **Merley Rd** EX39 ... 156 B7
- **Merlin Bsns Pk** EX5 ... 99 A4
- **Merlin Cl** PL6 ... 245 E8
- **Merlin Cres** EX4 ... 174 A1
- **Merlin Way** TQ2 ... 213 D2
- **Mermaid Ct** 6 EX1 ... 261 A2
- **Mermaid Yd** EX1 ... 261 A2
- **MERRIFIELD** ... 70 F4
- **Merrifield Cross**
  - Bridgerule EX22 ... 70 E4
  - Slapton TQ7 ... 145 C6
- **Merrifield Rd** TQ11 ... 130 C1
- **Merrion Ave** EX8 ... 202 D6
- **Merritt Flats** 5 TQ3 ... 226 A5
- **Merritt Rd** TQ3 ... 226 A5
- **MERRIVALE** ... 118 A2
- **Merrivale Cl** TQ2 ... 214 B4
- **Merrivale Rd**
  - Exeter EX4 ... 176 F4
  - Okehampton EX20 ... 170 E6
  - Plymouth, Ham PL2 ... 248 B7
  - Plymouth, Honicknowle PL5 ... 244 B3
- **Merrivale View Rd** PL20 ... 127 B3
- **Merrow Down Dr** EX12 ... 191 F8
- **Merrydale Cres** EX31 ... 27 D6
- **Merryfield La** EX6 ... 95 F2
- **Merryfield Rd** EX39 ... 157 C1
- **Merryland Cl** TQ3 ... 219 B2
- **Merryland Gdns** TQ3 ... 219 B2
- **Merrylees Dr** EX32 ... 155 C3
- **Merrymeet**
  - Tedburn St Mary EX17 ... 97 F8
  - Whitestone EX4 ... 82 F4
  - Whitestone EX4 ... 98 E4
- **Merryside Villas** EX16 ... 61 E8
- **Merrythorn Rd** EX31 ... 153 D5
- **Merryweather Way** EX36 ... 158 B4
- **Merrywood** TQ12 ... 206 F1
- **Mersey Cl** PL3 ... 249 D6
- **MERTON** ... 57 A7
- **MESHAW** ... 45 F6
- **Meshaw Cross Rds** EX36 ... 46 A5
- **Meshaw Moor Cross** EX36 ... 46 A5
- **Meshaw Rectory Cross** EX36 ... 46 A5
- **METCOMBE** ... 100 B2
- **Metcombe Cross** EX31 ... 9 C2
- **Metcombe La** EX31 ... 9 B1
- **Metcombe Rise** EX11 ... 100 C2
- **Metcombe Vale** EX11 ... 100 C2
- **Meteor Wlk** 2 EX32 ... 155 B5
- **METHERELL** ... 125 A4
- **Metherell Ave** TQ5 ... 230 D3
- **Metherell Avenue Ind Est** TQ5 ... 230 C3
- **Metherell Cross** EX21 ... 91 F8
- **Metherell Rd** EX39 ... 156 F1
- **Metley Cross** TQ12 ... 131 E5
- **Mettaford Cross** EX39 ... 22 F3
- **Metticombe La**
  - Barbrook EX35 ... 5 C4
  - Barbrook EX35 ... 151 B1
- **Mews Ct** 19 EX7 ... 204 E6
- **Mews Gdns** TQ6 ... 233 F3
- **Mews The**
  - 1 Bittaford PL21 ... 137 C8
  - Dawlish EX7 ... 204 E6
  - Exmouth EX8 ... 196 F3
  - Plymouth, Devonport PL1 ... 248 A3
  - Plymouth, Stonehouse PL1 ... 262 A3
  - 7 Teignmouth TQ14 ... 210 B4
- **Mewstone Ave** PL9 ... 140 D8
- **Meyer Cl** TA21 ... 160 F6
- **Meyrick Rd** TQ1 ... 220 C7
- **Michael Browning Way** EX2 ... 261 B1
- **Michael Foot Ave** PL1 ... 247 E1
- **Michael Rd** PL3 ... 249 A5
- **MICHELCOMBE** ... 129 F4
- **Michelcombe La** TQ13 ... 130 A4
- **Michigan Way**
  - Exeter EX4 ... 173 C2
  - Plymouth PL3 ... 249 C6
- **Mid Churchway** PL9 ... 256 A7
- Mid Devon Bsns Pk EX15 ... 162 D6
- **Middle Blagdon La** TQ3 ... 225 B6
- **Middleborough La** EX33 ... 7 D3
- **Middle Budleigh Mdw** TQ12 ... 206 F3
- **Middle Combe Dr** EX31 ... 154 A3
- **Middlecombe La** PL8 ... 140 F6
- **MIDDLECOTT** ... 73 B8
- **Middlecott Cross**
  - Holemoor EX22 ... 73 B8
  - Virginstow EX21 ... 90 E4
- **Middlecott Hill** EX32 ... 18 D3
- **Middlecott La** EX17 ... 60 F2
- **Middle Down** TQ9 ... 222 F5
- **Middle Down Cl** PL9 ... 256 A5
- **Middlefield Rd** PL6 ... 244 D6
- **Middlefield Cl** PL12 ... 242 B2
- **MIDDLE GREEN** ... 160 D3
- **Middle Green** TQ10 ... 135 A2
- **Middle Green Rd** TA21 ... 160 E3
- **Middle La** EX33 ... 8 E1
- **Middle Leigh** PL8 ... 140 F7
- **Middle Lincombe Rd** TQ1 ... 220 D3
- **MIDDLE LUXTON** ... 68 C5
- **MIDDLE MARWOOD** ... 9 B1
- **Middlemead Rd** EX16 ... 161 D5
- **Middle Mill La** EX15 ... 163 C3
- **MIDDLEMOOR** ... 171 F2
- **MIDDLE MOOR** ... 178 D4
- **Middlemoor Cross** EX37 ... 43 C3
- Middlemoor Police Training Coll EX2 ... 178 D5
- **Middle Park Terr** TQ7 ... 143 B1
- **Middle Ramshill La** TQ3 ... 225 C7
- **Middle Rd** PL9 ... 140 D8
- **MIDDLE ROCOMBE** ... 213 F7
- **Middle St**
  - Brixham TQ5 ... 230 C5
  - East Budleigh EX9 ... 198 B6
  - Teignmouth TQ14 ... 210 A3
- **Middleton Rd** EX39 ... 156 F3
- **Middleton Wlk** PL5 ... 243 D4
- **Middletown La** EX9 ... 198 B6
- **MIDDLE WADSTRAY** ... 232 A3
- **Middle Warberry Rd** TQ1 ... 220 D5
- **Middle Westerland Cross** TQ3 ... 218 D1
- **Middlewood** EX6 ... 201 A5
- **MIDDLE WOOLBROOK** ... 188 A8
- **Midella Rd** PL20 ... 127 A2
- **Midvale Rd** TQ4 ... 226 B5
- **Midway**
  - Exmouth EX8 ... 202 E8
  - Kingskerswell TQ12 ... 212 F6
- **Midway Cl** EX2 ... 177 A1
- **Midway Terr** EX2 ... 177 A1
- **Miers Cl** PL5 ... 247 C8
- **Miglo Ind Est** TQ4 ... 225 E3
- **Mignonette Wlk** EX39 ... 157 A3
- **MILBER** ... 207 F1
- **Milber La**
  - Coffinswell TQ12 ... 213 B6
  - Newton Abbot TQ12 ... 208 A1
- Milber Trad Est TQ12 ... 208 A1
- **Milbury Cl** EX6 ... 182 B5
- **Milbury Farm Mdw** EX6 ... 182 A5
- **Milbury La** EX6 ... 182 B4
- **Milch Pk** PL12 ... 242 C2
- **Mildmay Cl** EX4 ... 176 F7
- **Mildmay St** PL4 ... 263 A4
- **Mildren Wy** PL1 ... 247 E2
- **MILE END** ... 206 E5
- **Mile End Rd** TQ12 ... 206 E5
- **Mile Gdns** EX4 ... 173 F2
- **Milehouse Rd** PL2 ... 248 A5
- **Mile La** EX4 ... 174 A1
- **Miles Mitchell Ave** PL6 ... 245 A1
- **Milestone Cotts** EX6 ... 182 B3
- **Milestone Cross** TQ13 ... 123 F8
- **Milestone La** TQ13 ... 123 F8
- **MILFORD** ... 22 B1
- **Milford Ave** EX10 ... 188 B4
- **Milford Cl** TQ14 ... 210 A5
- **Milford Cotts** EX6 ... 181 B2
- **Milford Cross** EX39 ... 22 B1
- **Milford La** PL5 ... 244 B5
- **Milford Rd** EX10 ... 188 B4
- **Military Rd**
  - Millbrook PL10 ... 252 C3
  - Plymouth PL3 ... 249 C6
  - Rame PL10 ... 140 I2

Milizac Cl PL8 257 E4
Milkaway La EX33 7 E1
Milk Hill EX5 81 D7
Milky Way Adventure Pk★ EX39 23 E1
Milland Cross EX20 75 B1
Millards Hill 10 EX39 15 B1
Mill Ave EX17 79 A6
Millbarn Cross EX16 61 F8
MILLBAY 262 B2
Millbay Rd PL1 262 A2
Mill Bottom La
Stokeinteignhead TQ12 209 A3
Stokeinteignhead TQ14 209 A2
Mill Bridge PL1 262 A3
MILLBROOK
Axminster 167 E6
North Molton 19 F1
Torpoint 252 E5
Millbrook Bsns Ctr PL11 252 C6
Millbrook CE(VA) Prim Sch PL10 252 E5
Millbrook Cross EX13 167 E6
Millbrook Dale EX13 167 E6
Millbrook La EX2 177 F2
Millbrook Park Rd TQ2 219 E5
Millbrook Rd 2 TQ3 226 B6
Mill Cl
Lee Mill PL21 136 D6
Newton Abbot TQ12 206 F4
Millcombe Cnr TQ9 139 E1
Millcombe La TQ9 224 C3
Mill Cotts
Okehampton EX20 170 B5
Stoke Canon EX5 173 F7
Mill Cres TQ6 233 D4
Millcroft EX11 169 D3
Mill Cross
Bickington TQ12 131 F7
Halwill EX21 73 C1
Harberton TQ9 222 C2
Rattery TQ10 135 D4
Milldale Cres EX14 166 B5
Mill Dr EX2 177 F1
Mill End 1 TQ12 123 F1
Millenium St PL2 248 C8
Millen La TQ12 209 C2
Millennium Way
Cullompton EX15 163 C5
Westward Ho! EX39 156 E7
Miller Cl EX2 178 C4
Miller Court Workshop Units PL1 262 A2
Miller Cres EX32 155 A5
Miller Ct PL1 262 A2
Miller Gr EX4 174 F4
Millers Brook EX33 7 E2
Millers La TQ9 227 E7
Millers Way
Honiton EX14 166 B5
Tedburn St Mary EX6 97 F4
Miller Way
Exminster EX6 181 F5
Plymouth PL6 245 E3
Milletts Cl EX6 182 A4
Millfields Trust Bsns Units 11 PL1 262 A3
Millford Rd EX10 188 B4
Mill Ford Sch PL5 243 F4
Mill Gn DT7 260 E3
Millgreen Ct DT7 260 E3
Millgreen La EX13 87 D1
Millham La TA22 33 D6
MILLHAYES
Hemyock 52 C1
Honiton 86 F6
Millhayes Cross EX14 86 F6
Millhayes Rd EX14 86 F6
Mill Head EX34 150 C6
Millhead Rd
Honiton EX14 85 D3
Honiton EX14 166 B5
MILLHILL 116 F1
Mill Hill
Barnstaple EX31 16 A3
Fremington EX31 153 F5
Stoke Gabriel TQ9 227 F7
Witheridge EX16 61 F7
Mill Hill Cotts PL19 116 F1
Mill Hill Ct TQ9 227 F7
Mill Hill La
Millhill PL19 116 F1
Tavistock PL19 117 A1
Tavistock PL19 171 A6
Millhouse Pk PL11 247 A2
Millin Wy EX7 201 A2
Mill La
Alfington EX11 84 F1
Ashill EX15 66 D6
Aveton Gifford TQ7 143 C6
Axminster EX13 88 F3
Barnstaple EX31 154 E6
Barton Town EX31 11 E3
Beaford EX20 42 C1
Berrynarbor EX34 2 D4
Bow EX17 78 B4
Branscombe EX12 190 D4
Brayford EX32 18 F6
Brixham TQ5 230 A1
Burrington EX37 44 A2

Mill La *continued*
Charmouth DT6 104 F6
Cheriton Fitzpaine EX17 62 E2
Clyst Honiton EX1 175 C1
East Buckland EX32 18 E2
East Ogwell TQ12 206 D1
Exebridge EX16 33 F3
Exeter, Alphington EX2 177 B1
Exeter, Higher Wear EX2 177 F1
Exton EX3 183 D2
Frithelstock Stone EX39 40 E6
Galmpton TQ5 229 A4
George Nympton EX36 30 A1
Loddiswell TQ7 138 C7
Lower Loxhore EX31 17 F8
Lyme Regis DT7 260 E3
Meshaw EX36 45 F7
Millhayes EX14 86 F6
Newton Poppleford EX10 186 F6
North Tawton EX20 77 B4
North Whilborough TQ12 212 D2
Offwell EX14 86 B1
4 Paignton TQ3 226 B7
Sandford EX17 80 B5
Stockland EX13 87 B7
Stoke Fleming TQ6 146 A7
Teignmouth TQ14 209 D7
Torpoint PL11 247 A2
Torquay TQ2 219 F5
Totnes TQ9 223 D5
Uplyme DT7 260 C5
Wambrook TA20 69 F2
Whitestaunton TA20 69 E5
Woolacombe EX34 7 F6
Wootton Fitzpaine EX13 104 F7
Wrafton EX33 152 F4
Mill Lane Cotts EX20 77 B4
Mill Leat
14 Hemyock EX15 67 B8
Totnes TQ9 223 D6
Mill Leat Cotts EX17 78 B4
Mill-Leat Gdns EX32 17 B2
Millmans Rd TQ3 218 D3
Mill Mdw
Ashburton TQ13 130 F5
10 Combe Martin EX34 3 A3
Harbertonford TQ9 139 C7
Ivybridge PL21 237 D5
MILLMOOR 51 E1
Millmoor EX15 66 E8
Millmoor Cross EX37 44 B2
Millmoor La EX10 186 F8
Millmoor Vale EX10 186 F8
Mill-on-the-Mole Mobile Home Pk EX36 158 E4
Mill Park Ind Est EX5 184 E8
Mill Path TQ13 130 F4
Mill Pk 2 TQ12 123 E1
Millpool Head PL10 252 E4
Millpool Rd PL10 253 A6
Millpool The TQ9 228 A7
Mill Rd
Barnstaple EX31 154 E5
Beaford EX19 57 C8
Bradworthy EX22 38 E1
Exeter EX2 177 F1
Fremington EX31 153 E5
High Bickington EX37 43 B7
Landkey EX32 17 B1
Lustleigh TQ13 122 C7
Millbrook PL10 253 A5
Okehampton EX20 170 B4
Totnes TQ9 222 E8
Mill Rise EX14 85 F8
Mills St Comm EX38 159 B4
Mills Dr TA21 160 F7
Millsome La
Bondleigh EX18 77 C8
North Tawton EX18 59 D1
Mills Rd PL1 247 F2
Mill St
Bideford EX39 157 A2
Chagford TQ13 110 F6
Crediton EX17 165 D5
Great Torrington EX38 159 C4
Honiton EX14 166 B5
Kingsbridge TQ7 258 C5
Ottery St Mary EX11 169 C3
Plymouth PL1 247 E2
Sidmouth EX10 188 B4
South Molton EX36 158 D4
Uffculme EX15 66 B7
Mill Steep
Molland EX36 31 C8
Twitchen EX36 20 C1
Mill Stile EX33 152 C5
Millstream EX2 177 F2
Mill Stream Ct EX11 169 D3
Mill Stream Gdns
Halberton EX16 65 A7
Wellington TA21 160 B7
Millstream Mdw 4 TQ13 123 F6
Mills Way EX31 154 F6
Mill The EX2 261 C1
MILLTOWN 9 D1
Milltown Hill EX36 45 F7
Milltown La EX10 188 C6
Mill View 13 TQ13 123 F6
Mill View Gdns PL10 252 F5
Mill View Rd PL10 252 F5
Mill Water Sch EX9 186 B2
Millway
Bradninch EX5 82 F6

Millway *continued*
18 Chudleigh TQ13 123 E6
Wambrook TA20 69 F2
Millway Gdns EX5 82 F6
Millway Pl PL9 255 D8
Millwey Ave EX13 167 F7
Millwey Ct EX13 167 F7
MILLWEY RISE 167 F7
Millwey Rise Ind Est EX13 167 F7
Millwood TQ13 180 C4
Millwood Bsns Pk TQ12 207 E3
Millwood Dr PL6 245 E1
Millwood Terr EX37 28 C2
Milne Pl PL1 247 F3
Milsfords La EX5 81 E5
MILTON ABBOT 116 B6
Milton Abbot Sch PL19 116 B5
Milton Cl
Brixham TQ5 230 B2
Exmouth EX8 196 C4
Plymouth PL5 244 D2
MILTON COMBE 240 F8
Milton Cres
Brixham TQ5 230 B2
Tavistock PL19 171 D5
Milton Ct
2 Newton Abbot TQ12 207 C2
Plymouth, Cattedown PL4 263 C2
Plymouth, Prince Rock PL4 249 B1
MILTON DAMEREL 54 D5
Milton Fields TQ5 230 A2
MILTON GREEN 116 B5
MILTON HILL 124 E5
Milton La TQ6 233 C2
Milton Pk TQ5 230 B2
Milton Pl EX39 156 F1
Milton Rd
Exeter EX2 177 F3
Newton Abbot TQ12 207 B4
Milton St TQ5 230 A2
Miltons Yard EX13 167 D5
Milverton Rd TA21 160 B8
Mimosa Cl 2 EX16 161 F6
Mimosa Ct EX9 198 C1
Mimosa Wy TQ4 225 F2
Minacre La TQ12 212 E1
Mincent Cl TQ2 214 A3
Mincent Hill TQ2 214 A3
Minchin La EX5 99 D2
Minchin Orch EX5 99 E2
Mincinglake Rd EX4 173 F1
Minden Rd 4 TQ14 210 B5
Minehead La TA22 33 F7
Miners Cl 11 TQ13 131 A5
Minerva Bsns Pk TQ12 207 E3
Minerva Cl PL7 251 A6
Minerva Way
Newton Abbot TQ12 207 E3
Okehampton EX20 170 E7
Mines Rd EX39 157 C1
Miniature Pony Ctr The★ TQ13 111 B3
Minifie Rd EX14 166 B6
Minniemoor Cross EX31 4 B1
Minniemoor La EX31 4 C1
Minses Cl PL9 256 C7
Minster Rd EX6 182 B5
Mint Park Rd EX33 152 B7
Mint The EX4 261 A3
Mirador Pl PL4 249 C3
Miranda Rd TQ3 225 F8
Mire La
Sidmouth EX10 189 B7
Trow EX10 189 B7
Mirey La EX5 184 C3
Misdon Cotts EX20 75 F1
Mission Ct EX1 261 A2
Misterton Cl PL9 256 B8
Mistletoe View 15 TQ12 123 F6
Mitchell Cl PL9 255 D5
Mitchell Gdns 13 EX13 167 D5
Mitchell Ho EX4 177 D8
Mitchell's Pool TA21 160 E6
Mitchell St
Wellington TA21 52 B8
Wellington TA21 160 C7
Mitre Cl
Bishopsteignton TQ14 208 E8
Tavistock PL19 171 A3
Mitre Ct 14 PL1 263 A2
Mitre La EX4 261 A3
Mizzen Rd PL1 247 F1
Moat Hill TQ9 223 C4
Moat Pk PL6 245 C1
Mockham Down Gate EX32 18 C7
Mockham La EX32 18 D6
MODBURY 137 C2
Modbury Cl PL5 244 B3
Modbury Cross PL21 136 E2
Modbury Ct 5 PL21 137 B2
Modbury Prim Sch PL21 137 B2
Model Terr 2 EX39 157 A1
Modred Cl EX4 174 A1
Modyford Wlk PL20 126 C3
MOGWORTHY 47 D4

Mogworthy La EX16 47 D3
Mohun's Cl PL19 171 C4
Mohun's Pk PL19 171 C3
Mole Bridge La EX36 158 E4
Mole Ridge Way EX36 158 C5
Moles Cotts EX6 182 A4
Moles Cross TQ3 218 E7
Moles La
Kingskerswell TQ12 212 E1
Paignton TQ3 218 E8
Molesworth Rd
Plymouth, Plympton PL7 250 C6
Plymouth, Stoke PL1, PL3 248 A3
Molesworth Terr PL10 252 F5
Molesworth Wy EX22 164 A4
Molford Ct EX36 158 B3
MOLLAND 31 E7
Molland Cross
Brayford EX36 19 B4
Chulmleigh EX18 45 E3
Molland Hill EX32, EX36 19 A5
Mollison Rd PL5 243 E2
Moll Tall's Cross PL7 136 A8
Molyneaux Pl 10 PL1 247 F3
Molyneux Dr EX17 165 E4
Monastery Rd TQ3 226 A6
Mondeville Way
Northam EX39 156 F6
8 Northam EX39 156 F7
Money Acre Cross EX24 101 E7
Money Acre Rd
Church Green EX24 101 F7
Farway EX24 101 E7
Money Pit La EX13 69 D1
Monica Wlk PL4 263 B4
Monitor Cl
Exeter EX2 261 A1
South Molton EX36 158 B5
MONKERTON 178 E8
Monkerton Com Prim Sch EX1 178 E8
Monkerton Ct 2 EX1 178 E8
Monkerton Dr EX1 178 E8
Monkey La EX10 186 E6
Monkey Puzzle Dr EX20 170 E5
MONKLEIGH 40 F7
Monkleigh Mill La EX39 40 D8
Monkleigh Prim Sch EX39 40 F7
MONKOKEHAMPTON 76 B8
Monkokehampton Cross EX19 76 A8
Monksbridge Rd TQ5 230 B3
Monks Cl
Bideford EX39 26 A4
Crediton EX17 165 B6
Monks Hill PL15 115 A4
Monksmead PL19 171 A4
Monks Orch TQ12 212 A6
Monk's Rd EX4 177 F7
Monkstone Gdns EX13 167 E5
Monkston Point TQ8 259 D4
Monks Way TQ13 180 C6
Monkswell Rd EX4 177 E8
MONKTON 86 A5
Monkton Rd
Honiton EX14 166 E7
Monkton EX14 86 A5
MONKTON WYLD 104 D7
Monkton Wyld Camping Site DT6 104 C7
Monkton Wyld Cross DT6 104 C7
Monkton Wyld La DT6 104 E7
Monmouth Ave EX3 182 F4
Monmouth Beach Chalets DT7 260 C2
Monmouth Gdns PL5 244 C4
Monmouth Hill EX3 182 F4
Monmouth St
Lyme Regis DT7 260 E3
Topsham EX3 182 F4
Monmouth Way EX14 166 D5
Monroe Gdns PL4 262 B4
Monro Mead 7 TQ12 122 F1
Monshall EX19 57 E3
Mons Terr 11 TQ10 134 F3
Montacute Ave PL5 244 B2
Montagu Cl
3 Exeter EX1 178 D1
Kingsbridge TQ7 258 C6
Montague Gdns EX9 197 E1
Montague Pl EX39 156 F1
Montague Rise EX4 261 B4
Montague Terr PL7 132 F4
Montagu Rd TQ7 258 C5
Monterey TQ4 226 C1
Monterey Cl TQ2 219 E3
Monterey Gdns EX4 173 E1
Monterey Pk TQ12 207 F1
Montery Pl 3 EX32 155 B3
Montesson Cl TQ3 225 D7
Montesson Rd TQ3 225 D7
Montgomery Cl
Ivybridge PL21 237 E5
Saltash PL12 242 D3

Montgomery Dr PL19 171 A6
Montgomery Prim Sch
Exeter EX4 176 F5
11 Exeter EX4 177 A5
Montgomery Rd 6 EX2 178 D5
Mont Le Grand EX1 177 E6
Montpelier Ct
Exeter EX4 177 A7
Paignton TQ3 219 B1
Montpelier La 13 EX34 150 C6
Montpelier Prim Sch PL2 248 B6
Montpelier Rd
Ilfracombe EX34 150 C6
Plymouth PL2 248 C7
Montpellier Ct 1 EX8 202 B6
Montpellier Rd
Exmouth EX8 202 A6
Torquay TQ1 220 B4
Montrose Way TQ12 244 D2
Montserrat Rise TQ2 213 E3
Monument Cl TA21 160 E4
Monument Rd TA21 160 E3
Monument St PL1 247 E1
Monument View TA21 52 D8
Moonhayes Cross EX14 68 C4
Moon Hill Cl EX2 181 C8
Moon La 4 PL21 137 B2
Moonridge EX2 182 C7
Moon's Cross EX20 95 B5
Moon St PL4 263 A3
Moorashes 17 TQ9 223 C5
Moor Cl TQ14 210 C7
Moorcourt Cl EX10 187 F3
Moorcox Cross EX13 86 E2
Moor Cres PL20 128 A8
Moorcroft Cl
Okehampton EX20 170 E5
Plymouth PL9 256 A7
Moorcroft Ct EX20 170 E5
MOOR CROSS 133 C1
Moor Cross EX22 71 C3
Moor Ct EX10 187 F3
Moore Cl TQ12 212 F8
Moore Ct EX17 165 C5
Mooredge La EX5 82 E1
Mooremeadow EX1 179 B8
Moor Farm Cotts TQ8 148 F4
Moorfield PL16 105 E4
Moorfield Ave 4 PL6 249 C7
Moorfield Cl EX8 202 C8
Moorfield Gdn TA24 21 C6
Moorfield Rd
Exmouth EX8 202 C8
St Giles on t H PL15 90 C1
Moorfields
6 Bittaford PL21 137 C8
19 Colyton EX24 103 A4
Moorfoot Cross TQ12 131 E3
Moor Gate EX20 170 C1
Moorhaven EX9 197 F2
Moorhaven Cl TQ1 219 E7
MOORHAVEN VILLAGE 137 C8
MOORHAYES 161 E6
Moorhayes TQ13 180 D7
Moorhayes Bglws EX16 161 E5
Moorhayes Cross EX15 67 B6
Moorhayes Ct EX5 84 A1
Moorhayne Cross EX15 66 A2
Moorhen Cl TQ12 207 C7
Moorhouse La TA4 35 A8
Moorings Reach TQ5 230 D5
Moorings The
Braunton EX33 152 D6
Exmouth EX8 202 C5
Exmouth, The Point EX8 201 E6
Kingsbridge TQ7 258 D3
Paignton TQ4 226 C5
Saltash PL12 242 F1
Moor La
Bittadon EX31 9 C5
Bovey Tracey TQ13 180 C5
Braunton EX33 152 A5
Broadclyst EX5 175 C8
Brushford TA22 33 F4
Budlake EX5 82 E1
Budleigh Salterton EX9 197 F2
Churchinford TA3 68 D7
Croyde EX33 7 D2
Exeter EX2 178 F5
Hatherleigh EX20 75 D7
Molland EX36 31 E7
Nethercott EX33 8 C2
Plymouth PL5 243 E1
Poltimore EX4 174 F7
Shobrooke EX17 80 E4
Staverton TQ9 216 B5
Torquay TQ2 214 B3
Venn Ottery EX10 100 C1
Woodbury EX5 184 B5
Yarnscombe EX31 27 E2
Zeal Monachorum EX17 78 B8
MOORLAKE 79 F2
Moorland Ave
Denbury TQ12 211 A7

Moorland Ave *continued*
Plymouth PL7 250 F6
Moorland Cl
7 Bittaford PL21 137 C8
Yelverton PL20 241 D8
Moorland Ct PL20 126 F2
Moorland Dr PL7 250 E6
Moorland Gate
Heathfield TQ12 123 B2
Roborough EX19 43 B3
Moorland Gdns PL7 250 F6
Moorland Pk TQ13 180 D5
Moorland Rd PL7 250 E5
Moorland Rise EX36 158 C4
Moorlands
Chagford TQ13 110 F6
Tiverton EX16 161 E6
West Hill EX11 168 D5
Moorlands Cl TQ12 207 F2
Moorlands La PL12 242 C4
Moorlands Rd EX9 197 E1
Moorlands Trad Est PL12 242 C4
Moorland Terr EX38 159 B5
Moorland View
Buckfastleigh TQ11 236 A5
Lapford EX17 60 D3
Newton Abbot TQ12 208 A2
Plymouth, Derriford PL6 245 A5
Plymouth, Plymstock PL9 256 B7
Princetown PL20 128 A8
Saltash PL12 242 F4
South Molton EX36 46 D8
Moorland Way
Exeter EX4 176 F8
Gunnislake PL18 125 C5
Moor Lane Cl TQ2 214 A3
Moor Lane Cross N EX36 31 E8
Moor Lea EX33 152 F5
Moormead EX9 197 F1
Moorpark
Bittaford PL21 137 C8
Exmouth EX8 202 C6
Moor Park Cl EX33 7 D2
Moor Park Rd TQ12 212 F6
Moor Pk
Chagford TQ13 111 A6
Honiton EX14 166 B3
Kingskerswell TQ12 212 F6
Moor Rd
Ipplepen TQ12 211 E3
Staverton TQ9 216 B5
Moorsend TQ12 206 E4
Moor's End TQ12 207 D8
Moorshead Cross
Buckfastleigh TQ11 135 B6
Yealmpton PL21 136 D2
Moorside
Malborough TQ7 147 E6
Mary Tavy PL19 117 E6
Moors Pk TQ14 208 F7
Moorstone Leat TQ4 226 C1
MOORTOWN
Great Torrington 41 F7
Tavistock 127 A8
Tetcott 89 F7
Moortown EX18 59 F8
Moortown Cross
Chulmleigh EX18 59 F8
Rackenford EX36 47 B8
Moorview
Broadhempston TQ13 131 B1
Marldon TQ3 218 D2
Payhembury EX14 84 D3
Moor View
Bovey Tracey TQ13 180 C5
Chudleigh TQ13 123 E6
Hatherleigh EX20 75 B6
Mary Tavy PL19 117 E6
Northlew EX20 74 E2
North Tawton EX20 77 C4
Pennymoor EX16 62 E6
Plymouth PL9 255 D7
Plymouth, Keyham PL2 247 F5
Plymouth, Laira PL3 249 C4
Torpoint PL11 247 B3
Moorview Cl EX4 173 D1
Moor View Cl EX10 187 F7
Moorview Cres TQ3 218 D2
Moorview Ct PL6 245 F5
Moorview Dr TQ14 209 D8
Moor View Dr TQ14 210 A6
Moorview End TQ3 218 D2
Moor View Terr
9 Bittaford PL21 137 C8
Plymouth PL4 248 E4
Yelverton PL20 127 A2
Moory Mdw EX34 2 F4
Moothill Cross TQ9 216 A6
MORCHARD BISHOP 61 A2
Morchard Bishop CE Prim Sch EX17 61 B2
MORCHARD ROAD 78 F7
Morchard Road Sta EX17 78 F8
MOREBATH 34 B3
Morecombe Cross EX21 73 A4
MORELEIGH 139 A3
Moreton Ave
Bideford EX39 156 E1
Plymouth PL6 244 F1
Moreton Dr EX39 156 E2

MORETONHAMPSTEAD 111 E4
Moretonhampstead Hospl TQ13 111 F5
Moretonhampstead Motor Museum★ TQ13 111 E4
Moretonhampstead Prim Sch TQ13 111 F5
Moretonhampstead Rd
Bovey Tracey TQ13 122 F6
Lustleigh TQ13 112 C1
Lustleigh TQ13 122 D8
Moreton Park Rd EX39 156 E1
Moreton Terr EX6 112 F5
Morgan Ave TQ2 220 A5
Morgan Ct EX8 202 A6
Morganhayes Cross EX24 102 D4
Morgans Quay TQ14 210 B3
Morgan Sweet EX5 99 B6
Morice Sq PL1 247 E2
Morice St PL1 247 E2
Morice Terr EX22 54 A6
MORICE TOWN 247 D3
Morice Town Prim Sch PL2 247 E4
Morin Rd TQ3 226 C8
Morlaix Cl EX7 204 E8
Morlaix Dr PL6 245 B4
Morleigh Cross TQ9 139 A3
Morleigh Gn TQ9 139 A3
Morleigh Green Cross TQ9 139 A4
Morleigh Rd TQ9 139 C6
MORLEY 206 B3
Morley Cl PL7 250 A5
Morley Ct PL1 262 B3
Morley Dr PL20 126 D2
Morley Rd EX4 177 E8
Morley View Rd PL7 250 C6
Mornacott Cross EX36 31 A4
Mornacott Rd EX36 31 A4
Morningside
Dawlish EX7 204 C4
Torquay TQ1 220 E5
Mornington Pk TA21 160 E5
Morrell's Cross EX16 34 B4
Morrell's La EX16 50 B6
Morris Cl EX20 75 B7
Morrish Pk PL9 255 F6
Morshead Rd PL6 244 F2
Mortain Rd PL12 242 D4
MORTEHOE 7 F8
Mortehoe Her Ctr★ EX34 7 F8
Mortehoe Station Rd EX34 1 B1
Mortimer Ave TQ3 226 B8
Mortimer Ct EX2 178 A2
Mortimer Ho EX1 177 E6
Mortimers Cross EX15 66 B4
Mortimore Cl PL12 242 D2
Morton Cres EX8 201 F6
Morton Crescent Mews EX8 201 F6
Morton Dr EX38 159 D5
Morton Rd EX8 201 F6
Morton Way EX13 167 D4
Morven Dr EX8 196 A2
Morwell Gdns PL2 248 A6
MORWELLHAM 125 E4
Morwellham Cl PL5 247 C8
Morwellham Quay★ PL19 125 E4
Morwenna Park Rd EX39 156 F7
Morwenna Rd EX23 37 A1
Morwenna Terr 2 EX39 156 F7
MORWENSTOW 36 E2
Moses Cl PL6 244 E7
Moses Ct PL6 244 E7
Mosshayne La EX1, EX5 175 B2
Mossop Cl EX11 169 D3
Mostyn Ave PL4 249 A4
Motehole Rd TQ12 211 D2
Mote Pk PL12 242 C3
MOTHECOMBE 142 A6
Mothecombe Wlk PL6 245 E1
Motherhill Ct TQ8 259 C5
Motton Rd EX16 161 B6
Mott's Cross EX15 84 A7
Motts La EX15 84 A7
Moult Hill TQ8 259 B2
Moulton Cl PL7 251 B5
Moulton Wlk PL7 251 B4
Moult Rd TQ8 259 B2
Mounson Hill EX6 97 C5
Mountain Cl EX8 202 F8
Mountain Hill EX8 197 A1
Mountbatten Cl
Exmouth EX8 196 D2
Plymouth PL9 255 D6
Mount Batten Ctr★ PL9 254 F7
Mountbatten Dr EX1 178 C1
Mountbatten Rd EX16 161 C5
Mountbatten Way PL9 255 E6
Mount Batton Dr EX2 182 C8
Mount Boone TQ6 233 F4
Mount Boone Hill TQ6 233 F4
Mount Boone La TQ6 233 F4
Mount Boone Way TQ6 233 E4
Mount Cl EX14 166 B5
Mount Dinham
Exeter EX4 177 A6
Exeter EX4 261 A3
Mount Dinham Ct EX4 261 A4
Mount Edgcumbe Ho & Country Pk★ PL10 253 E6
Mounter's Hill TA20 69 E2
Mount Ford PL19 171 A5
Mountford Dr
Bovey Tracey TQ13 123 A5
Bovey Tracey TQ13 180 F7
MOUNT GOULD 249 B3
Mount Gould Ave PL4 249 B2
Mount Gould Cres PL4 249 B3
Mount Gould Hospl PL4 249 B3
Mount Gould Rd PL4 249 B3
Mount Gould Way PL4 249 B3
Mount Hermon Rd TQ1 220 B6
Mounthill Cotts TQ12 122 F1
Mounthill Cross EX24 103 B5
Mounthill La EX13 103 E5
Mount House Sch PL19 171 E7
Mounticombe Cross EX18 45 C1
Mounticombe La EX18 45 C1
MOUNT LANE 90 B6
MOUNT PLEASANT 86 B3
Mount Pleasant
Bideford, East-t-W EX39 157 C3
Bideford, Littleham EX39 25 D2
3 Bishop's Tawton EX32 16 E1
10 Crediton EX17 165 C5
Millbrook PL10 252 E5
Moretonhampstead TQ13 111 F4
Plymouth PL5 244 B2
Mount Pleasant Ave EX8 196 B3
Mount Pleasant Cl
Kingsbridge TQ7 258 D6
Kingskerswell TQ12 213 A3
Mount Pleasant Ct EX8 196 B2
Mount Pleasant La 7 TQ14 210 A3
Mount Pleasant Mews TQ5 230 C4
Mount Pleasant Rd
Brixham TQ5 230 C4
Dawlish Warren EX7 201 B1
Exeter EX4 177 E8
Kingskerswell TQ12 213 A3
Newton Abbot TQ12 207 C2
2 Torquay TQ1 220 B6
MOUNT RADFORD 261 C2
Mount Radford Cres EX2 261 C2
Mount Radford Sq EX2 261 C2
Mount Raleigh Ave EX39 156 F4
Mount Raleigh Dr EX39 156 E3
Mount Rd TQ5 230 D5
Mount Ridley Rd TQ6 234 C3
Mount Rise EX6 114 E4
Mount Sandford Gn EX32 155 D2
Mount Sandford Rd
Barnstaple EX32 155 D1
Landkey EX32 155 E2
Mount St
Plymouth, Mount Wise PL1 247 E1
Plymouth, Mutley PL4 263 A4
MOUNTS THE 144 C7
Mount Stone Rd PL1 254 A8
Mount Street Prim Sch PL4 263 A4
Mount Stuart Hospl (Private) TQ1 219 F7
Mount Tamar Cl PL5 243 E2
Mount Tamar Sch PL5 243 E2
Mount Tavy Rd PL19 171 E6
Mount The
32 Appledore EX39 15 A1
Brixham TQ5 230 C6
Teignmouth TQ14 210 B6
Torquay TQ2 213 F4
Totnes TQ9 223 C4
Mount View
18 Colyton EX24 103 A4
Feniton EX14 84 E2
2 Ilfracombe EX34 150 D5
Mount View Cotts EX32 155 F2
Mount View Home Pk EX32 155 E2
Mount View Terr 2 TQ9 223 C5
Mount Wear Sq EX2 182 C8
MOUNT WISE 247 F1
Mount Wise Com Prim Sch PL1 247 E1
Mount Wise Cres PL5 247 F1
Mount Wise Ct PL1 247 F1
Mourne Villas PL9 255 F8
Mousebeare La EX16 48 E2
Mouseberry Cross EX17 46 A4
Mouseberry La TQ13 124 B4
Mousehole Cross EX14 84 D5
Mouse Hole La EX14 84 C4
MOUTH MILL 23 B5
Mowbars Hayes EX13 87 A3
Mowbray Ave EX4 261 B4
Mowbray Ct EX2 178 A5
Mowhay Mdw PL11 252 B8
Mowhay Rd PL5 244 A2
Mowhay The 15 EX22 164 C4
Mowlish La EX6 200 B7
Mowstead Pk EX33 152 B7
Mowstead Rd EX33 152 B7
Moxeys Cl EX17 62 E1
Moyses La EX20 170 B4
Moyses Mdw EX20 170 A4
Mrs Ethelston's CE Prim Sch DT7 260 A5
Mucky Duck EX20 107 E2
Mucky La EX19 57 D6
Mudbank La
Exmouth EX8 202 A8
Lympstone EX8 195 F1
MUDDIFORD 9 E1
Muddix Mews EX39 156 F6
MUDDLEBRIDGE 16 A3
Muddlebridge Cl EX31 16 A3
Muddle Brook EX31 16 A3
Muddy La
East Buckland EX32 18 E2
Ottery St Mary EX11 101 B7
Popham EX36 19 A3
Mudford Gate EX16 62 E7
Mudgate Cross EX36 20 D3
Mudge La TQ12 217 E6
Mudge's La EX17 78 D3
Mudges Terr PL18 125 D6
Mudge Way PL7 250 E5
Mudhouse Cross EX19 58 B7
Mudstone La TQ5 230 E3
Mulberry Cl
Exeter EX1 178 B6
Paignton TQ3 225 E6
Plymouth PL6 245 E7
Willand EX15 162 D4
Mulberry Gr PL19 171 C2
Mulberry Rd PL12 242 E1
Mulberry Rise EX12 192 A8
Mulberry St 3 TQ14 210 B4
Mulberry Way EX31 154 B2
Mulgrave St PL1 262 C2
Mullacott Cross EX34 1 E1
Mullacott Cross Ind Est EX34 1 F1
Mullet Ave PL3 249 C4
Mullet Cl PL3 249 C4
Mullet Rd PL3 249 C4
Mulligan Dr EX2 178 D2
Mullion Cl PL11 246 F4
Munro Ave PL8 141 B8
Munro Ho EX31 155 B8
Muralto Ho PL19 171 A4
MURCHINGTON 110 E7
Murchington Cross TQ13 110 E7
Murch Rise EX1 179 B8
Murdock Rd PL11 246 F3
Murhill La PL9 249 D1
Murley Cl EX17 165 A6
Murley Cres TQ14 208 E8
Murley Grange TQ14 208 E8
Murrayfield Cl PL2 248 C7
MUSBURY 103 D5
Musbury Castle★ EX13 103 E5
Musbury Prim Sch EX13 103 D5
Musbury Rd EX13 167 C4
MUSEHILL 106 F6
Museum Ct TQ7 258 C6
Museum Rd TQ1 220 C4
Musgrave Ho EX4 261 B3
Musgrave Row EX4 261 B3
Musgraves TA22 33 E6
Mushroom Rd EX5 99 A1
Musket Rd TQ12 180 F2
Mus of Barnstaple & North Devon★ EX32 154 F4
Mus of Dartmoor Life★ EX20 170 B5
MUTLEY 248 E4
Mutley Ct PL4 263 A4
Mutley Plain PL4 248 E4
Mutley Plain La PL4 248 E4
Mutley Rd PL3 248 E5
Muttersmoor Rd EX10 187 E5
MUTTERTON 83 D8
Mutton La
Exeter EX2 181 C8
Torrington EX38 159 C3
Muxbeare La
Willand EX15 65 E7
Willand EX15 162 D7
Muxey La
Great Torrington EX38 41 D5
Great Torrington EX38 159 D3
Muxworthy La EX32 19 A8
Mylor Cl PL2 248 D8
Myra Ct 27 EX39 15 A1
Myrtleberry La EX35 151 F3
Myrtlebury Way EX1 178 D6
Myrtle Cl
Exeter EX2 177 B1
Yelverton PL20 127 B3
Myrtle Farm View EX33 7 E2
Myrtle Gdns EX39 157 A2
Myrtle Gr
Bideford EX39 156 F2
Bideford EX39 157 A2
Myrtle Hill TQ14 210 C5
Myrtle La TA21 51 E7
Myrtle Rd EX4 176 E4
Myrtle Row
25 Exmouth EX8 202 A6
4 Torquay TQ1 220 B5
Myrtles Ct PL12 242 D4
Myrtle St 17 EX39 15 A1
Myrtleville Cres PL2 248 A6

N

Nadder Bottom EX4 176 B8
Nadder La
Nadderwater EX4 176 B8
South Molton EX36 158 B4
Nadder Mdw EX36 158 B4
Nadder Park Rd EX4 176 D5
NADDERWATER 176 B7
Nadrid Cross EX36 30 A8
Nadrid East Cross EX36 30 A8
Nags Head Rd EX14 85 B2
Naida Vale TQ6 233 F5
Naish's La EX13 87 B3
Nancarrows PL12 242 C2
Napier St PL1 247 F3
Napier Terr
Exeter EX4 261 A3
Plymouth PL4 248 E4
Nap La EX18 44 C1
Naps La EX10 186 C5
Nap View EX14 85 B4
NARFORD'S 69 F1
Narfords La TA20 69 F1
Narracott La
Hollocombe EX18 58 E7
South Molton EX36 158 A2
Narratons Rd EX20 93 E6
Narrow La
Botusfleming PL12 242 C7
Knowle EX17 79 C4
Tiverton EX16 161 C2
Narrowmoor Cross TQ7 144 D4
Narthmoor Hill TA22 33 B7
Naseby Dr TQ12 180 F2
Nash Cl
Exmouth EX8 202 E7
Plymouth PL7 251 A5
Nash Dr TA21 160 F6
Nash Gdns EX7 204 D4
Nash La DT6 88 H2
Nasmith Cl EX8 196 D1
NATCOTT 22 F2
Natcott La EX39 22 F2
National Marine Aquarium★ PL4 263 A2
Nats La
Cornwood PL21 133 D1
Sparkwell PL21 136 C8
Natsley La EX32 18 F8
Natson La EX6 97 C6
Natson Mill La EX17 78 B4
Nattadon Rd TQ13 111 A6
Natty Cross EX38 43 A5
Nautilus EX39 156 C7
Neadon La EX6 112 F5
Neal Cl PL7 251 B4
Neath Rd PL4 263 C4
Needlewood Cl EX11 168 C3
Needs Dr EX39 156 E1
Neet Way EX22 164 C6
Neilgate Cnr TQ13 131 A3
Nellies Wood View TQ9 223 B7
Nelson Ave PL1 247 F3
Nelson Cl
Staverton TQ9 216 A5
Teignmouth TQ14 210 A6
Topsham EX3 182 E5
Torquay TQ1 220 D2
Nelson Dr
Exmouth EX8 202 E8
Westward Ho! EX39 156 C7
Nelson Gdns 5 PL1 247 F3
Nelson Mews EX39 156 C7
Nelson Pl TQ12 207 B5
Nelson Rd
Brixham TQ5 230 C5
Dartmouth TQ6 233 C3
Exeter EX4 177 A5
Westward Ho! EX39 156 C7
Nelson St PL4 263 A4
Nelson Terr
Plymouth PL6 245 E6
Westward Ho! EX39 156 C7
Nelson Way 1 EX2 178 D5
NEOPARDY 79 D1
Neopardy Cross EX17 79 D1
Nepean St 1 PL2 247 F5
Neptune Ct 3 EX1 261 A2
Neptune Pk PL9 255 B8
Ness Dr TQ14 210 B2
Ness View Rd TQ14 210 C8
Neswick St PL1 262 B3
Neswick Street Ope PL1 262 A3
NETHERCOTT 8 C2
Nethercott Cross
Ashwater EX21 90 C7
Oakford EX16 48 C8
Nethercott Hill EX16 48 C7
Nethercott La
Oakford EX16 48 C7
Spreyton EX17, EX20 95 F6
Nethercott Rd EX33 8 C2
NETHEREXE 81 F2
Netherham Cross EX33 8 A2
Netherhams Hill EX33 8 A2
Netherleigh Rd TQ1 220 B7
Nether Mdw TQ3 218 D3
NETHERTON 208 C3
Netherton Cross EX34 3 A4
Netherton Est PL20 126 D3
Netherton Hill EX6 96 D1
Netherton La EX34 3 A4
Netley Rd TQ12 207 B4
NETTACOTT 81 C2
Nettacott Cross EX5 81 B2
Nettle Cl TQ12 206 C5
Nettleford Hill EX16 46 F5
Nettlehayes PL9 256 D7
Netton Cl PL9 256 D6
Nevada Cl PL3 249 D6
Nevada Ct 10 EX12 192 A5
Neville Rd
Newton Abbot TQ12 207 A4
Okehampton EX20 170 C5
Newacott Cross EX22 70 E5
New Barn Cross EX5 172 A7
New Barn Hill PL7 250 F3
New Barnstaple Rd EX34 150 E3
Newberry Cl EX34 2 E4
Newberry Cotts EX33 8 A2
Newberry Hill EX34 2 F4
Newberry La EX34 2 F4
Newberry Rd
Combe Martin EX34 2 F4
Georgeham EX33 8 A2
Newberry's Patch TA3 68 D7
Newbery Cl
Axminster EX13 167 E6
Colyton EX24 103 A4
Newbery Comm Ctr EX5 99 A4
Newberys EX13 87 A3
New Bldgs
3 Bampton EX16 34 C1
8 Barnstaple EX32 155 A6
Chittlehampton EX37 28 F3
Doddiscombsleigh EX6 113 D5
3 Exeter EX4 177 D8
Fremington EX31 153 E5
Thurlestone TQ7 143 C2
Newbridge Cl EX39 157 B4
Newbridge Cross
Bishop's Tawton EX32 27 F7
Cowley EX5 172 D6
New Bridge Cross EX31 27 E7
Newbridge Cswy EX31, EX32 27 E7
Newbridge Hill
Cowley EX5 172 E6
Gunnislake PL18 125 D6
Holne TQ13 130 A6
Witheridge EX16 46 D1
New Bridge St EX4 261 A2
NEWBUILDINGS 79 D6
Newbuildings Cross EX17 79 D6
Newbuilding's Hill EX17 63 A3
Newbury Cl PL5 244 B4
Newbury Dr TQ13 180 E7
Newcastle Gdns PL5 244 B5
Newcombe Cl EX20 170 D5
Newcombes 5 EX17 165 C5
Newcombe St EX1 178 A6
Newcombe Street Gdns EX1 178 A6
Newcombe Terr EX1 177 F6
Newcomen Rd TQ6 233 F3
Newcot Cross EX15 67 D5
NEWCOTT 68 F3
New Cotts EX8 202 F7
Newcourt Dr EX2 178 D1
Newcourt Rd
Silverton EX5 82 B5
Topsham EX3 182 E7
Newcourt Sta EX1 178 E1
Newcourt Wy EX2 178 D2
New Cross
Avonwick TQ10 135 C2
Kingsteignton TQ12 123 E1
Newcross Pk 10 TQ12 123 E1
New Cut
Beer EX12 191 D5
Crediton EX17 165 B5
New England Hill PL7 136 B5
New England Rd PL7 136 B5
New Esplanade Ct TQ4 226 C6
New Est EX5 81 A2
New Exeter St TQ13 123 E6
Newfoundland Cl EX4 173 E2
Newfoundland Rd TQ14 209 D6
Newfoundland Way 13 TQ12 207 B3
Newgate Cross TA22 33 D7
New George St PL1 262 C3
New Green St PL21 237 E4
Newground La
Parracombe EX31 4 D2
Parracombe EX31 11 D8
NEWHAVEN 24 F1
Newhay Cl EX7 204 C6
Newhay Cross TQ12 211 C1
Newhayes TQ12 211 C1
Newhayes Cl EX2 177 A2
Newhouse Hill
Bickington TQ12 131 E7
Witheridge EX16 46 E2
Newhouse La
Chipstable TA4 35 E6
Hittisleigh EX6 96 D5
New House Plain TA4 35 F7
New Houses TQ7 149 A5
New Inn Cross 5 EX5 99 E8
New Inn Ct
Cullompton EX15 163 C3
6 Holsworthy EX22 164 C4
New La
Bampton EX16 33 F2
Braunton EX33 15 D8
Broadhempston TQ9 131 E1
Knowle EX33 8 D1
Ottery St Mary EX11 169 E4
Staverton TQ9 215 F5
Tatworth TA20 88 C8
Newland EX32 17 C1
Newland Cotts EX32 17 C1
Newland Cross
King's Nympton EX37 44 C8
North Tawton EX20 77 B3
Rackenford EX16 47 B2
Newland La TA24 13 F1
Newland Pk Rd EX32 17 B1
Newlands
Dawlish EX7 204 E7
Honiton EX14 166 C6
Newlands Ave EX8 202 D8
Newlands Cl
Exeter EX2 177 A2
Landkey EX32 17 C2
Sidmouth EX10 188 B8
Newlands Cross PL21 237 D3
Newlands Dr TQ13 180 C4
Newlands Pk
Aylesbeare EX5 99 E1
Seaton EX12 192 A6
Newlands Rd EX10 188 B8
Newlane End TQ9 215 F5
New London PL20 128 B8
Newman Cres TQ9 222 F8
Newman Ct EX4 176 E5
Newman Rd
Exeter EX4 176 F5
Plymouth PL5 243 E2
Saltash PL12 242 F3
New Market Rd
Holsworthy EX22 164 D7
Holsworthy TA20 72 A8
New Mdw PL21 237 B6
New Mill La EX35 5 A4
New Mills Ind Est PL21 137 B2
Newnham Cross EX37 44 B4
Newnham Ind Est PL7 250 F6
Newnham La EX18, EX37 44 C4
Newnham Rd PL7 250 F7
Newnham Way PL7 250 F6
New North Rd
Exeter EX4 261 A4
Exmouth EX8 202 A7
New Orchard 9 TQ10 134 F2
New Park TQ13 180 C4
New Park Cl TQ5 230 D4
New Park Cres TQ12 207 D8
New Park Rd
Kingsteignton TQ12 207 D8
Lee Mill PL7, PL21 136 B6
Paignton TQ3 225 F7
Plymouth PL7 251 A4
New Passage Hill PL1 247 E3
New Path EX17 97 C7
New Pk
Bridford EX6 112 F5
East Anstey EX16 32 E4
Horrabridge PL20 126 F4
NEWPORT 155 B3
Newport Com Sch Prim Acad EX32 155 B3
Newport Rd
Barnstaple EX32 155 A3
Exeter EX2 182 C7
Newport St
Dartmouth TQ6 233 F3
Millbrook PL10 252 E5

Newport St *continued*
Plymouth PL1 ... 248 A1
Tiverton EX16 ... 161 D4
Newport Terr
Barnstaple EX32 ... 155 A3
7 Bideford EX39 ... 157 B1
New Quay La TQ5 ... 230 D5
New Quay St
Appledore EX39 ... 15 A1
Teignmouth TQ14 ... 210 B4
New Rd
Allercombe EX5 ... 168 B5
Barnstaple EX32 ... 155 A4
Beer EX12 ... 191 D6
Bere Alston PL20 ... 125 E2
Bickleigh PL6, PL7 ... 132 A5
Bideford EX39 ... 157 A1
Bishop's Tawton EX32 ... 16 E1
Brixham TQ5 ... 230 B4
Buckfastleigh TQ11 ... 236 B5
Cawsand PL10 ... 253 A1
Chard Junction TA20 ... 88 F8
Clyst St Lawrence EX5 ... 83 B3
Great Torrington EX38 ... 159 D4
Instow EX39 ... 15 C1
Kingsand PL10 ... 253 B2
Lifton PL16 ... 105 F4
Loddiswell TQ7 ... 143 F7
Lutton PL21 ... 133 B2
Merton EX20 ... 57 A6
Modbury PL21 ... 137 B2
Morchard Bishop EX17 ... 61 B2
Oare EX35 ... 6 D4
Okehampton EX20 ... 93 F5
Okehampton EX20 ... 170 A3
Roborough PL6 ... 241 D2
Saltash PL12 ... 242 E3
South Molton EX36 ... 158 D4
Starcross EX6 ... 201 A8
Stoke Fleming TQ6 ... 146 B7
Stoke Gabriel TQ9 ... 227 F7
Teignmouth TQ14 ... 210 C7
Totnes TQ9 ... 223 D6
Upottery EX14 ... 68 B1
Waterrow TA21 ... 35 F4
Wilmington EX14 ... 86 D2
Yealmpton PL8 ... 136 A2
New Road Cl PL10 ... 253 A2
New Road Cross
Milton Damerel EX22 ... 54 D3
Okehampton EX20 ... 93 F5
South Molton EX36 ... 46 D6
Wilmington EX14 ... 86 D1
New Road Est EX20 ... 93 F8
New Road Gate EX35 ... 6 D5
New Row 8 EX39 ... 157 A2
New Sch Exeter The EX6 ... 182 A5
New Sidmouth Rd EX24 ... 102 F4
New St
6 Appledore EX39 ... 15 A1
13 Bideford EX39 ... 157 A2
Chagford TQ13 ... 111 A6
14 Chulmleigh EX18 ... 44 E1
Cullompton EX15 ... 163 B3
Exmouth EX8 ... 202 A7
Great Torrington EX38 ... 159 C5
Honiton EX14 ... 166 C6
Millbrook PL10 ... 252 E5
Moretonhampstead TQ13 ... 111 F5
Ottery St Mary EX11 ... 169 E4
Paignton TQ3 ... 226 B6
Plymouth PL1 ... 263 A2
Sidmouth EX10 ... 188 B3
NEWTAKE ... 208 A1
Newtake Rd PL19 ... 171 E2
Newtake Rise TQ12 ... 207 F2
Newte's Hill EX16 ... 64 D5
New Theatre (Cygnet)★ EX1 ... 261 B2
NEWTON ABBOT ... 207 A2
Newton Abbot Coll
Newton Abbot TQ12 ... 207 A4
Newton Abbot TQ12 ... 207 B4
Newton Abbot Com Hosp TQ12 ... 207 B5
Newton Abbot Hospl TQ12 ... 207 C3
Newton Abbot L Ctr TQ12 ... 207 A4
Newton Abbot Racecourse★ TQ12 ... 207 D5
Newton Abbot Sta TQ12 ... 207 D3
Newton Abbot Town & GWR Mus★ TQ12 ... 207 C3
Newton Ave PL5 ... 243 E2
Newton Cl 3 PL8 ... 141 A7
Newton Cross
Blackawton TQ9 ... 145 B7
Denbury TQ12 ... 211 B6
Hartland EX39 ... 22 C2
Zeal Monachorum EX17 ... 77 F7
Newton Ct
10 Bampton EX16 ... 34 B1
Newton Ferrers PL8 ... 140 F7
Newton Down PL16 ... 106 B4
NEWTON FERRERS ... 140 F7
Newton Ferrers CE Prim Sch PL8 ... 141 A7
Newton Gdns PL5 ... 243 F2
Newton Hall TQ12 ... 207 C2
Newton Hill
Daccombe TQ12 ... 213 F6
Newton Ferrers PL8 ... 140 F7
Newton Ho EX5 ... 80 F1
Newton La EX17 ... 77 F7
NEWTON POPPLEFORD ... 186 E7
Newton Poppleford Prim Sch EX10 ... 186 F8
Newton Rd
Bideford EX39 ... 157 A3
Bishopsteignton TQ14 ... 208 D7
Bovey Tracey TQ13 ... 180 C6
Heathfield TQ12 ... 123 A2
Heathfield TQ13 ... 180 E3
Kingskerswell TQ12 ... 212 F6
Kingskerswell TQ12 ... 213 A5
Kingsteignton TQ12 ... 207 D5
Littlehempston TQ9 ... 216 F1
Salcombe TQ8 ... 259 D4
Torquay TQ2 ... 213 B2
Torquay TQ2 ... 213 D1
Totnes TQ9 ... 223 D7
Newton Road Ret Pk TQ12 ... 207 D6
NEWTON ST CYRES ... 172 A8
Newton St Cyres Prim Sch EX5 ... 172 A8
Newton St Cyres Sta EX5 ... 81 A1
NEWTON ST PETROCK ... 55 B7
Newton St Petrock Cross EX38 ... 40 B1
Newton School EX38 ... 55 C7
Newtons Orch EX13 ... 87 C1
Newton Sq 8 EX16 ... 34 B1
Newton's Row PL7 ... 136 A8
NEWTON TRACEY ... 27 A5
NEWTOWN
Buckland St Mary ... 69 D7
Exeter ... 177 E6
South Molton ... 31 A4
Newtown
Cornwood PL21 ... 133 C2
Sidmouth EX10 ... 188 B4
NEW TOWN ... 188 B4
Newtown Cl EX1 ... 261 C3
Newtown Cross EX36 ... 31 A4
Newtown La EX36 ... 31 A3
Newtown Prim Sch EX1 ... 261 C3
Newtown Rd TA20 ... 69 D8
New Valley Rd EX4 ... 176 F7
New Village Cross EX17 ... 59 F2
New Way EX5 ... 184 C6
New Way Est EX14 ... 67 B2
New Wlk TQ9 ... 223 D5
New Wood Cl PL6 ... 245 E8
New Zealand Ho PL3 ... 248 B4
Nexus Way EX20 ... 170 E6
Nibbys Cross EX15 ... 66 B5
Nicholas Cl TA22 ... 33 E4
Nicholas Mdw PL17 ... 125 B4
Nicholas Rd EX1 ... 178 A6
Nicholas Way EX8 ... 202 E7
Nicholls Pl TQ13 ... 180 F7
Nichols Nymett Cross EX20 ... 77 F4
Nichols Nymett La EX20 ... 77 F5
Nichols Nymett Moors Cross EX20 ... 77 F5
Nicholson Rd
Plymouth PL5 ... 244 E2
Torquay TQ2 ... 213 D1
Nichols Way 4 EX1 ... 177 E7
Nick Reed's La EX15 ... 52 D1
Nightcott La TA22 ... 33 C4
Nightingale Cl
Plymouth PL9 ... 256 C8
Torquay TQ2 ... 213 E2
Nightingale Hospital Exeter EX1 ... 178 F6
Nightingale Lawns EX15 ... 163 A2
Nightingale Wlk EX2 ... 176 D3
Nile Rd EX2 ... 182 C8
Nilgala Cl EX39 ... 156 E4
Nine Acre La EX12 ... 190 C8
Nine Ash Cross EX16 ... 49 D6
Nine Milestone Cross PL21 ... 137 D7
Nine Oaks EX5 ... 99 C1
Nine Oaks Est PL20 ... 127 C3
Nirvana PL21 ... 237 C5
Nirvana Cl PL21 ... 237 C5
Noctule Ave 3 TQ12 ... 207 A5
Noelle Dr TQ12 ... 207 A4
Noland Pk TQ10 ... 135 A2
Nomandsland Cross EX16 ... 62 B8
No Mans Chapple EX5 ... 81 D3
Nomansland EX17 ... 80 D5
No Man's Land
Georgeham EX33 ... 8 B1
Whiddon EX31 ... 9 C1
Nook The PL19 ... 171 D6
No Place Hill TQ9 ... 131 E1
Norah Bellot Ct 2 EX31 ... 154 F5
Norbury Ct 3 PL1 ... 262 A3
Norden La TQ7 ... 258 B5
Nordon Cross TQ12 ... 131 F3
Norfolk Cl PL3 ... 249 C5
Norfolk Rd PL3 ... 249 C4
Norfolk Terr 25 EX32 ... 155 A4
Norleigh Cross EX20 ... 75 C3
NORLEY ... 74 E3
Norley Rd EX33 ... 8 D1
Norman Cl
Axminster EX13 ... 167 D5
Exmouth EX8 ... 196 D2
Newton Abbot TQ12 ... 206 E5
Norman Cres EX9 ... 198 A2
Norman Ct EX2 ... 177 C1
Norman Dr EX15 ... 163 C5
Normandy Cl EX8 ... 196 E1
Normandy Hill PL5 ... 243 B2
Normandy Ho 19 EX32 ... 155 A5
Normandy Rd EX1 ... 177 F6
Normandy Way
Plymouth PL5 ... 243 C2
Salcombe TQ8 ... 259 E5
South Molton EX36 ... 158 B4
Norman Lockyer Observatory★ EX10 ... 188 D5
Norman Mews EX2 ... 178 D4
Norman Pl EX2 ... 178 D4
Norman Rd TQ3 ... 226 C7
Normans Cleave EX35 ... 151 B5
Norman Terr EX39 ... 157 A7
Norns La TQ6 ... 145 F6
Norris Dr TQ12 ... 244 E6
NORRIS GREEN ... 125 B4
Norse Pl EX1 ... 178 E8
Norsworthy's Grave EX17 ... 97 E8
NORTHAM ... 157 A6
Northam Burrows Ctry Pk★ EX39 ... 14 E1
Northam Ho EX39 ... 156 F6
Northampton Cl PL5 ... 244 B5
Northam Rd EX39 ... 156 F3
Northams Mdw EX20 ... 170 A4
North Ave
Bideford EX39 ... 157 D1
Exeter EX1 ... 177 E6
Lyme Regis DT7 ... 260 D4
NORTHAY
Axminster ... 88 G3
Chard ... 69 E6
Northay Cross EX13 ... 88 H3
Northay La
Axminster EX13 ... 88 G3
Northay TA20 ... 69 E6
North Barton Cl EX32 ... 18 B2
Northbeer Cross EX17 ... 96 A8
Northbeer La EX17 ... 95 F8
North Beer La PL15 ... 89 C3
North Boundary Rd TQ5 ... 230 B5
NORTH BOVEY ... 111 E2
North Bovey Rd TQ13 ... 111 E4
NORTH BRENTOR ... 117 C8
North Bridge Pl EX4 ... 261 A3
Northbrook Cl EX4 ... 174 A1
Northbrook La EX31 ... 10 F5
Northbrook Swimming Pool EX4 ... 174 B1
NORTH BUCKLAND ... 8 C3
North Buckland Hill EX33 ... 8 C3
North Castle Mews 8 TQ9 ... 223 C6
Northclose Rd EX18 ... 59 D2
North Combe Cross EX16 ... 48 A3
Northcombe La TA22 ... 33 E7
North Combe Rd EX14 ... 86 C2
North Coombe La EX16 ... 47 A3
Northcote Cross EX37 ... 43 E4
Northcote Hill EX14 ... 166 F7
Northcote La
Honiton EX14 ... 166 B6
Pennymoor EX16 ... 62 F8
Northcote Rd EX14 ... 166 E7
NORTHCOTT ... 90 A3
Northcott Gdns EX39 ... 157 A7
Northcott Terr 8 EX22 ... 164 C4
North Courts The 4 PL1 ... 262 A3
North Cross PL1 ... 262 C4
Northdene EX39 ... 156 E4
North Devon Cottage Rd EX16 ... 161 B5
North Devon District Hospl EX31 ... 155 A8
North Devon Farm Pk★ EX32 ... 17 D1
North Devon L Ctr EX31 ... 154 F4
North Devon Link Rd
Ash Mill EX36 ... 31 D2
Bolham EX16 ... 49 C1
Filleigh EX32 ... 29 C8
Knowstone EX16 ... 46 F8
Loxbeare EX16 ... 48 C3
Rackenford EX36 ... 47 D7
Sampford Peverell EX16 ... 50 C1
South Molton EX36 ... 30 D4
South Molton EX36 ... 158 C8
Swimbridge EX32 ... 17 C2
Swimbridge EX32 ... 28 F8
Tiverton EX16 ... 49 F1
Tiverton EX16 ... 64 D8
Tiverton EX16 ... 161 E7
North Devon Maritime Mus★ EX39 ... 15 A1
North Dimson Cotts PL18 ... 125 C6
North Down Cres PL2 ... 247 F6
North Down Cross EX17 ... 79 B1
Northdown Dr EX39 ... 156 F3
North Down Gdns PL2 ... 247 F6
Northdown La EX36 ... 45 F6
Northdown Rd
Bideford EX39 ... 156 F2
Cadbury EX5 ... 81 F7
North Down Rd
Braunton EX33 ... 152 E6
Plymouth PL2 ... 248 B6
North East St EX39 ... 157 A7
North Emb TQ6 ... 233 F4
NORTH END ... 51 E3
North End Cl TQ12 ... 211 C2
Northernhay 17 TQ12 ... 207 C3
Northernhay Gate 5 EX4 ... 261 A3
Northernhay Pl EX4 ... 261 B3
Northernhay Sq EX4 ... 261 A3
Northernhay St EX4 ... 261 A3
Northern La
Branscombe EX12 ... 190 B5
Sidmouth EX10 ... 189 E8
Northesk St PL2 ... 248 A4
Northfield EX13 ... 103 D5
Northfield La EX31 ... 154 F7
Northfield Pk EX31 ... 154 F7
Northfield Rd
Bideford EX39 ... 157 C1
Georgeham EX33 ... 8 B2
Ilfracombe EX34 ... 150 B6
Okehampton EX20 ... 170 B5
Northfields Ind Est TQ5 ... 230 B5
Northfields La
Brixham TQ5 ... 230 B4
Brixham TQ5 ... 230 B5
Northfield Terr 1 EX34 ... 150 B6
North Ford Rd TQ6 ... 233 F3
North Furzeham Rd TQ5 ... 230 C6
North Garron 3 EX32 ... 155 B5
Northgate EX39 ... 22 D3
North Gate Ct EX4 ... 261 A3
Northgate La EX14 ... 86 A3
North Gn 3 EX32 ... 155 B4
North Grange EX2 ... 178 D3
Northground La EX10 ... 101 D1
North Hayne Cross EX36 ... 31 B4
NORTH HEASLEY ... 19 D4
North Heasley Cross EX36 ... 19 C4
North Hill Cl TQ5 ... 230 B5
North Hill La
Morchard Bishop EX17 ... 61 B3
Stockland EX14 ... 86 F8
North Hill Terr PL4 ... 263 A4
NORTH HUISH ... 138 B7
North Huish Cross TQ10 ... 138 B8
North Jaycroft EX15 ... 162 D5
North La
Ashford EX31 ... 16 A6
Barnstaple, Bickington EX31 ... 154 A4
Challacombe EX31, TA24 ... 12 B4
Cheriton EX35 ... 5 D3
Cheriton EX35 ... 151 F7
Middle Marwood EX31 ... 9 B3
Whiddon EX31 ... 9 D2
Northland Cnr EX31 ... 11 D2
Northland Cross EX36 ... 19 A1
North Lawn Ct EX1 ... 177 F6
Northleat Ave TQ3 ... 225 E5
NORTHLEIGH ... 102 B7
Northleigh Cross
Chelfham EX32 ... 17 C6
Northleigh EX24 ... 102 B7
Northleigh Hill EX32 ... 17 C5
Northleigh Hill Rd
Honiton EX14 ... 166 E3
Offwell EX14 ... 86 A1
Northleigh Rd EX24 ... 102 D6
NORTHLEW ... 74 E1
Northlew & Ashbury Parochial CE Prim Sch EX20 ... 74 E2
Northlew Rd EX20 ... 93 D6
North Lodge Cl EX7 ... 204 C5
NORTH MOLTON ... 30 D8
North Molton Cross EX36 ... 30 D8
North Molton Sch EX36 ... 30 D8
NORTHMOOR ... 38 C3
North Moor Cross EX22 ... 38 C3
Northmoor Rd TA22 ... 33 D7
North Morte Rd EX34 ... 7 F8
NORTHMOSTOWN ... 187 B7
Northmostown Ct EX10 ... 187 A7
Northolt Ave PL5 ... 243 D4
North Park Almshouses EX2 ... 261 C2
North Park Cnr TQ9 ... 139 C6
North Park Rd
Exeter EX4 ... 173 B1
Tedburn St Mary EX6 ... 97 F4
North Park Villas PL12 ... 242 C4
NORTH PROSPECT ... 248 A6
North Prospect Rd PL2 ... 248 A6
North Quay PL4 ... 263 A2
NORTH RADWORTHY ... 19 F5
North Rd
Barnstaple EX31 ... 155 A7
Bideford EX39 ... 157 A2
Bradworthy EX22 ... 38 E1
Hartland EX39 ... 22 D3
High Bickington EX37 ... 43 B7
Holsworthy EX22 ... 164 D5
Lee Mill PL21 ... 136 C7
Lifton PL16 ... 105 F4
Okehampton EX20 ... 170 C7
Saltash PL12 ... 242 F3
Saltash PL5 ... 242 F3
South Molton EX36 ... 158 C5
Torpoint PL11 ... 247 B3
Yelverton PL20 ... 126 F3
Northridge Cross EX5 ... 98 E7
Northridge La EX5 ... 98 E7
North Road E PL4 ... 262 C4
North Road Ind Est EX20 ... 170 C6
North Road W PL1 ... 262 B4
North Rocks Rd TQ4 ... 229 C7
Northside TA21 ... 160 B5
North St
Ashburton TQ13 ... 130 F5
Axminster EX13 ... 167 D6
Braunton EX33 ... 152 D6
Chagford TQ13 ... 111 A6
Crediton EX17 ... 165 C5
Denbury TQ12 ... 211 A7
Dolton EX19 ... 57 F7
Exeter EX4 ... 261 A3
Exeter, Heavitree EX1 ... 177 F6
Exmouth EX8 ... 202 A7
Hartland EX39 ... 22 D3
Ipplepen TQ12 ... 211 D2
Northam EX39 ... 157 A7
North Tawton EX20 ... 77 C4
Okehampton EX20 ... 170 B5
Ottery St Mary EX11 ... 169 E4
Plymouth PL4 ... 263 A3
Sheepwash EX21 ... 56 C1
South Molton EX36 ... 158 C5
Tavistock PL19 ... 171 C5
Topsham EX3 ... 182 F4
2 Totnes TQ9 ... 223 C6
Wellington TA21 ... 160 D6
Witheridge EX16 ... 46 E1
Witheridge EX16 ... 47 A1
NORTH STAR ... 198 F8
NORTH TAMERTON ... 89 C8
NORTH TAWTON ... 77 C5
North Tawton Com Prim Sch EX20 ... 77 C4
North Terr EX31 ... 154 A4
North Thorne La EX31 ... 11 A4
NORTH TOWN ... 56 E4
Northumberland Pl TQ14 ... 210 B4
Northumberland St PL5 ... 247 E8
Northumberland Terr PL1 ... 262 B1
North Upton Barns TQ7 ... 143 B3
North View EX21 ... 55 E4
North View Ave EX39 ... 156 F3
North View Hill EX39 ... 156 F3
Northview Rd EX9 ... 203 F8
North View Rd TQ5 ... 230 D5
North Villas 2 EX20 ... 170 B6
Northville Pk TQ7 ... 258 C6
Northville Rd TQ7 ... 258 C6
North Walk Hill EX35 ... 151 C6
NORTHWAY ... 24 D2
Northways La PL21 ... 137 D7
North Weald Gdns PL5 ... 243 E5
NORTH WHILBOROUGH ... 212 E2
North Wlk
Barnstaple EX31 ... 154 F5
Lynton EX35 ... 151 B6
Northwood Cross EX17 ... 61 B3
Northwood La
Buckfast TQ11 ... 236 C8
Buckland Brewer EX39 ... 40 C7
Morchard Bishop EX17 ... 61 B3
Northwoods TQ13 ... 180 C4
North Wyke Cotts EX20 ... 77 B1
NORTON
Dartmouth ... 233 A2
Hartland ... 22 E4
Norton Ave PL4 ... 263 C4
Norton Cross TQ6 ... 233 A3
Norton Pk TQ6 ... 233 A3
Norton Pl EX8 ... 202 E8
Nortons Cross EX5 ... 81 A2
Norton View TQ6 ... 233 C3
Nortonwood La EX17 ... 81 A2
Norwich Ave PL5 ... 244 B5
Norwich Cl EX8 ... 196 D4
Norwich Rd EX4 ... 176 F6
Norwood Ave EX2 ... 261 C1
Norwood Ho EX4 ... 261 B4
Norwood Rd EX16 ... 161 D6
NOSS MAYO ... 140 F6
Notley Gdns PL2 ... 248 A8
Notre Dame Cl PL6 ... 244 F5
Notre Dame Ho PL1 ... 262 B3
Notre Dame RC Sch PL6 ... 244 F5
Notte St PL1 ... 262 C2
Nottiston Cross EX31 ... 16 A1
Novorossisk Rd PL6 ... 245 E2
Nower Rd EX13 ... 87 C3
N St Mdw EX33 ... 152 D6
Nuffield Health Exeter Hospl (private) EX2 ... 177 E4
Nuffield Health Plymouth Hospl (private) PL6 ... 245 B4
Nurseries Cl
Exton EX3 ... 183 C1
Topsham EX3 ... 182 E6
Nursery Cl
Exmouth EX8 ... 202 C8
Paignton TQ3 ... 226 A5
Plymouth PL5 ... 244 B7
St Giles in the Wood EX38 ... 42 B6
Nursery End EX31 ... 154 F7
Nursery Gdns 7 EX1 ... 178 F8
Nursery Mews EX8 ... 202 C8
Nursery Rd TQ12 ... 207 E7
Nursey Cl EX16 ... 49 B2
Nutaberry Hill EX39 ... 157 B1
Nutaberry Yd EX39 ... 157 B1
Nutbrook EX8 ... 196 B1
Nut Bush Cnr TQ2 ... 219 B7
Nut Bush La
Torquay TQ2 ... 219 B7
Torquay TQ2 ... 219 C6
Nutcombe Hill EX34 ... 3 C2
Nuthatch Cl
Drakewalls PL18 ... 125 C5
Torquay TQ2 ... 213 E2
Nuthatch Dr TQ2 ... 213 E2
Nuttaberry EX39 ... 25 F4
Nuttaberry Bglws EX39 ... 25 F4
Nut Tree Ct TQ5 ... 230 B2
Nut Tree Orch TQ5 ... 230 B2
Nutt's La
Combe Martin EX31 ... 3 C2
Combe Martin EX34 ... 10 C8
Nutwell Rd EX8 ... 195 E7
Nymet Ave EX17 ... 78 C4
Nymet Bridge Cross EX17 ... 60 B4
NYMET ROWLAND ... 60 B3
NYMET TRACEY ... 78 C3
Nymet Villas EX37 ... 44 E6
Nymetwood Cross EX6 ... 96 D8
Nymphayes La EX17 ... 78 C8
Nynehead Rd TA21 ... 160 F8

O

Oakapple Cl PL7 ... 250 B7
Oak Apple Cl PL12 ... 242 D4
Oakbank TQ13 ... 180 C4
Oakbeer Orchard 4 EX5 ... 99 A6
Oak Cl
Bickington EX31 ... 154 A3
Dulford EX15 ... 84 B8
Exeter EX4 ... 174 E1
Exminster EX6 ... 182 A4
Kingsteignton TQ12 ... 207 F6
Ottery St Mary EX11 ... 169 D3
Shillingford Abbot EX2 ... 181 A6
Silverton EX5 ... 82 C6
Tiverton EX16 ... 161 D5
Oak Cottage Cross EX22 ... 72 E2
Oak Cres EX15 ... 162 C4
Oakcroft Rd PL2 ... 248 B6
Oak Cross
Bondleigh EX18 ... 77 D8
Inwardleigh EX20 ... 75 C1
Oak Ct
Holsworthy EX22 ... 164 C5
Lee Mill PL21 ... 136 D6
Oakdale Ave EX32 ... 17 E1
Oakdene Ct EX6 ... 114 F1
Oakdene Rise PL9 ... 255 F6
Oak Dr
Cullompton EX15 ... 163 C5
Plymouth PL6 ... 244 F3
Oak End Ct TQ3 ... 218 D2
Oaken Ground TA21 ... 160 B5
Oaken Hill
Great Torrington EX31 ... 42 E8
Yarnscombe EX31 ... 27 D1
Oakery Cres PL20 ... 128 B8
Oakey Orch PL17 ... 125 A4
Oakfield Cl PL7 ... 251 C6
Oakfield Pk TA21 ... 160 E4
Oakfield Pl PL4 ... 249 B1
Oakfield Rd
Exeter EX4 ... 177 A5
Hatherleigh EX20 ... 75 C7
Plymouth PL7 ... 250 C6
Oakfields EX16 ... 161 D6
Oakfield St EX1 ... 177 F5
Oakfield Terr EX39 ... 157 A7
Oakfield Terrace Rd PL4 ... 249 B1
OAKFORD ... 48 C8
Oakford TQ12 ... 207 D7
OAKFORDBRIDGE ... 48 D8
Oakford Cl EX36 ... 30 D8

Oakford Cross
Kingsteignton TQ12 207 D7
North Molton EX36 30 C8
Oakford Villas EX36 30 D8
Oak Gdns
Ivybridge PL21 237 E5
Uffculme EX15 65 F7
Oakham Rd PL5 244 B5
Oakhayes Rd EX5 184 B3
Oakhays EX36 158 D4
Oak Hill
Budleigh Salterton EX9 198 C6
Dawlish EX7 204 C5
East Budleigh EX9 198 B6
Oak Hill Cross Rd
Dawlish EX7 204 C4
Teignmouth TQ14 210 D8
Oak Hill Rd TQ1 219 F6
Oakhill Rise 3 EX31 154 C3
Oak La
East Anstey TA22 32 E6
Stockleigh Pomeroy EX17 81 A4
Whitstone EX22 70 E1
Oakland Ave EX31 154 D4
Oakland Dr EX7 204 D5
Oakland Park S EX31 154 B4
Oakland Pk EX31 154 D3
Oakland Rd TQ12 207 F2
Oaklands
Bideford EX39 25 D4
Petrockstowe EX20 56 F4
Tavistock PL19 171 D2
Oaklands Cl
Buckfastleigh TQ11 236 A5
Plymouth PL6 245 C7
Seaton EX12 192 A8
Oaklands Ct EX31 154 D4
Oaklands Dr
Okehampton EX20 170 B6
Saltash PL12 242 C3
Oaklands Gdns EX31 154 D4
Oaklands Gn PL12 242 D3
Oaklands Pk
Buckfastleigh TQ11 236 A5
Okehampton EX20 170 A5
Oaklands Rd TQ11 236 A6
Oakland Wlk EX7 204 D5
Oak Lawn TQ12 207 C2
Oaklawn Ct TQ1 219 F7
Oaklawn Terr TQ1 219 F7
Oaklea
Honiton EX14 166 B6
Tiverton EX16 161 D6
Oaklea Cl TQ7 258 C4
Oaklea Cres EX31 153 D5
Oakleaf Cl EX21 73 E2
Oakleaf Way EX32 17 F4
Oaklea Pk TQ12 123 A1
Oakleigh EX15 66 F3
Oakleigh Rd
Barnstaple EX32 155 A4
Exmouth EX8 202 B7
Oakley Cl
Exeter EX1 174 E1
Teignmouth TQ14 210 B7
Oakley Wlk EX5 179 E3
Oak Mdw EX36 158 B4
Oak Park Ave TQ2 219 D8
Oak Park Cl TQ2 219 D8
Oakpark Cross PL21 137 E6
Oakpark La EX7 124 E6
Oak Park Rd TQ12 206 F4
Oak Park Villas EX7 204 E7
Oak Pl TQ12 207 D3
Oak Rd
Aylesbeare EX11 168 A2
Exeter EX4 176 F4
Okehampton EX20 170 C6
Tavistock PL19 171 C2
West Hill EX11 168 C2
Oakridge TQ1 220 C3
Oak Ridge
Exeter EX2 181 A8
Lifton PL16 105 E4
Oaks The
Bovey Tracey TQ13 180 E7
4 Hemyock EX15 67 B8
Mary Tavy PL19 117 E6
Newton Abbot TQ12 212 F8
Yeoford EX17 79 C1
Oaktree Cl
Broadclyst EX5 175 D6
Exmouth EX8 196 B3
Ivybridge PL21 237 A5
Oak Tree Cl EX14 68 C2
Oaktree Ct PL6 244 F1
Oak Tree Dr
Barnstaple EX32 155 E4
Newton Abbot TQ12 212 F8
Oaktree Fishery★ EX36 31 F4
Oak Tree Gdns
Ilfracombe EX34 150 B5
West Hill EX11 168 D4
Oak Tree Gr 8 TQ14 210 A3
Oak Tree La PL19 171 C3
Oak Tree Pk
Plymouth PL6 245 D6
Sticklepath EX20 95 A5
Oak Tree Pl EX2 181 C8
Oaktree Rd EX36 158 B4
Oak Tree Villas EX10 186 F8
Oak Units EX17 165 F5
Oak View
Honiton EX14 166 A3
Lyme Regis DT7 260 E5
Oak View *continued*
Totnes TQ9 222 F6
Oak View Cl TQ2 213 B1
Oakwell Cl EX38 159 E5
Oakwell La EX37 44 E8
Oakwood Cl
Barnstaple EX31 154 C2
Dartmouth TQ6 233 C3
Plymouth PL6 245 D7
Oakwood Ct EX36 158 D4
Oakwood Dr PL21 137 B3
Oakwood Pk TQ7 143 E7
Oakwood Prim Sch PL6 245 A6
Oakwood Rise EX8 196 E3
Oakwood Specialist Coll EX7 204 E7
Oakymead Pk TQ12 207 D6
OARE 6 E4
OAREFORD 6 F3
Oates Rd PL2 248 B5
Oathills Cres TQ3 225 F1
Oathills Ct 8 TQ3 225 F1
Oatlands Ave EX32 155 A1
Oatlands Dr TQ4 226 A4
Oberon Rd EX1 178 E7
Observer Cl EX36 158 B5
Occombe Cross TQ3 218 F3
Occombe Farm & Scadson Woods Nature Reserve★ TQ3 219 A3
Occombe Valley Rd TQ3 219 A2
Occombe Valley Woods Nature Reserve★ TQ3 218 F2
Ocean City Pl PL3 262 B3
Ocean Ct PL1 253 F8
Ocean Pk EX39 156 B7
Ocean St PL2 247 E6
Ocean View Cres TQ5 230 A1
Ocean View Dr TQ5 230 A1
Ochil Cl EX39 26 A4
Ockington Cl EX20 170 D5
Ockment Ct EX20 170 B5
Octagon St PL1 262 B3
Octagon The PL1 262 B2
Octans Way PL9 256 E8
Octon Gr TQ1 219 E7
Odam Cross EX36 45 E7
Odam La EX18 45 E6
Odam Moor Cross EX36 45 E5
Oddicombe Beach Hill TQ1 220 D8
Odette Ave TA21 160 A3
ODHAM 74 B5
Odhams Wharf EX3 183 B5
Odle Hill TQ12 212 A6
Odlehill Gr TQ12 212 A6
Odun Pl 34 EX39 15 A1
Odun Rd 22 EX39 15 A1
Odun Terr 36 EX39 15 A1
OFFWELL 86 B2
Offwell CE Prim Sch EX14 86 B2
Offwell Turn EX14 102 B8
Ogwell Cross TQ12 207 A1
Ogwell End Dr TQ12 206 F2
Ogwell Gn TQ12 206 E1
Ogwell Green TQ12 211 E8
Ogwell Mill Rd TQ12 206 E3
Ogwell Rd
East Ogwell TQ12 206 F1
Ogwell TQ12 211 E8
Oilmill Cross EX5 179 C2
Oilmill La
Clyst St George EX5 183 D8
Clyst St Mary EX5 179 C1
Oil Mill La EX6 184 A7
Okefield Ave EX17 165 C6
Okefield Rd
Crediton EX17 80 A3
Crediton EX17 165 C6
Okefield Ridge EX17 165 C6
OKEHAMPTON 170 A6
Okehampton Bsns Ctr EX20 170 F5
Okehampton Castle★ EX20 170 A3
Okehampton Cl PL7 251 B4
Okehampton Coll EX20 170 B4
Okehampton Com Hospl EX20 170 C6
Okehampton Pl 8 EX4 177 A5
Okehampton Prim Sch EX20 170 B5
Okehampton Rd EX4 177 A5
Okehampton St EX4 177 A5
Okehampton Sta EX20 170 C3
Okehampton Way PL21 237 D4
OKEMOOR PARK 170 E5
Oketor Cl EX20 170 D5
Oke Tor Cl TQ3 219 A2
Okewill Cross EX31 10 A2
Okewood Ct EX8 202 B5
Olands Rd TA21 160 D6
OLCHARD 123 F3
Olchard La TQ12, TQ13 124 A4
Old Abbey Ct EX2 177 E2
Oldaway La EX5 172 C7
Oldaway Tongue TQ7 143 E1
Old Bakery Cl EX4 176 F7
Old Bakery Cotts
Bickington EX31 154 A4
Yealmpton PL8 257 F4
Old Bakery The EX8 202 B8
Old Barn Cl
Stoke Canon EX5 173 F8
Winkleigh EX19 58 E2
Oldbarn Cross TQ12 212 A7
Oldbarn La EX16 33 E1
Old Barnstaple Rd
Bideford, East-t-W EX39 157 C2
Braunton EX31 15 F7
Ilfracombe EX34 150 D2
Old Beer Rd EX12 191 E6
Old Bell Hill EX16 47 D5
Oldberry La TA22 33 D6
Old Berrynarbor Rd EX34 150 F5
Old Bideford Cl EX31 154 B2
Old Bideford Rd EX31 154 C2
Old Blundell's★ EX16 161 D3
OLDBOROUGH 61 B1
Oldborough Cross EX17 61 B1
Oldborough La EX17 61 B1
Old Bridge Rd EX15 83 F6
Old Bridwell EX15 65 F7
Old Butterleigh Rd EX5 82 B6
Old Bystock Dr EX8 196 E3
Old Canal Cl EX23 70 A6
Old Chapel Gdns EX19 58 F3
Old Chapel Rd PL7 133 B2
Old Chapel Way PL10 252 F6
Old Chappel La PL7 132 F4
Old Chard Rd EX14 86 C6
Old Cider Press The 3 TQ4 226 B5
Old Cider Works La TQ12 212 A7
Old Cider Works The TQ12 212 A7
Old Coach Rd EX5 175 C6
Old Coal Yard The EX10 186 F8
Old Coastguard Cotts PL9 140 E7
Old Coastguard Sta EX12 192 D5
Old Coast Rd EX34 2 E4
Old Cooperage The EX2 177 F5
Old Court EX31 154 C4
Old Ct Mws 4 TA21 160 D6
Old Dairy The PL3 249 B6
Old Dawlish Rd EX6 181 C2
Old Ebford La EX3 183 C4
Olde Ct EX22 164 C3
Oldenburg Pk TQ3 226 C7
Old English Ind Est PL20 127 B3
Old Exeter Rd
Bishop's Tawton EX32 16 E1
Chudleigh TQ13 123 F8
Chudleigh TQ13, EX6 114 A2
Newton Abbot TQ12 207 B4
Tavistock PL19 171 D7
Old Exeter St TQ13 123 E6
Old Farm Bglws 2 EX10 188 B7
Old Farm Rd PL5 247 C8
Old Farm Way EX7 204 D4
Old Ferry Rd
Saltash PL12 242 F3
Saltash PL12 243 A3
Oldfields EX8 202 C6
Old Fire Sta The TQ13 110 F6
Old Fore St EX10 188 B3
Old Foundry The PL19 171 D6
Old Frogmore Rd TQ7 144 E1
Old Garden Pasture 22 EX5 99 A6
Old Gatehouse Rd EX7 204 E7
Old George St PL1 262 C2
Old Greystone Hill PL15, PL19 115 D6
Oldham Rd EX20 75 B7
Old Hayes 8 EX10 188 A4
Old Hazard Cotts TQ9 135 F2
Old Hill
Bickington TQ12 131 D7
Cullompton EX15 163 D2
Old Home Farm
Rousdon DT7 193 E6
Rousdon EX12 193 E6
Oldhouse La TQ7 142 E7
Old Ide Cl EX2 176 E2
Old Ide La EX2 176 E2
Old Inn Mews EX38 159 D5
Old Jaycroft
Willand EX15 162 D4
Willand EX15 162 E4
Old Laira Rd PL3 249 C4
Old Lake La EX35 5 A4
Oldlands Cl PL6 245 B6
Old Launceston Rd PL19 171 B6
Old Laundry The PL1 262 A3
Old Liverton Rd
Coldeast TQ12 122 F1
6 Coldeast TQ12 123 A1
Coldeast TQ12 180 D1
Old Lyme Hill DT6 104 F4
Old Lyme Rd DT6 104 F4
Old Main Rd TA20 69 C3
Old Manor Cl TQ13 130 E5
Old Manor Ct 21 EX7 204 D6
Old Manor Gdns EX24 103 B3
Old Market Cl EX2 177 B3
Old Market Dr EX39 38 F8
Old Market Field EX16 46 E1
Old Market Field Ind Est EX16 46 E1
Old Market Pl EX22 164 C3
Old Matford La EX6, EX2 181 E6
Old Mill Cl
Exeter EX2 261 C1
Tiverton EX16 161 C3
Old Mill Ct PL7 250 E5
Old Mill Ind Est EX5 173 E7
Old Mill La TQ6 233 C4
Old Mill Rd
Livermead TQ2 219 E2
Torquay TQ2 219 E4
Torquay TQ2 219 E5
Old Mill The
Culmstock EX15 66 E8
Harbertonford TQ9 139 B8
Old Mine La PL18 125 B6
Old Mkt The 15 EX15 67 B8
Old Newton Rd
Bovey Tracey TQ13 180 E4
Heathfield TQ12 123 A3
Kingskerswell TQ12 212 E5
Old Nursery Dr EX4 178 B8
Old Orchard TQ13 180 D7
Old Orchard Cl EX23 70 A6
Old Orchard The EX20 74 E2
Old Paignton Rd
Torquay TQ2 219 D2
Torquay TQ2 219 D3
Old Park Ave EX1 174 F3
Old Park Rd
Exeter EX4 261 B4
Plymouth PL3 248 D6
Old Pavilion Cl EX2 178 C4
Old Pinn La EX1 174 E1
Old Plymouth Rd
Kingsbridge TQ7 258 C6
Plymouth PL3 249 E5
Old Post Office Mews 19 EX39 157 A2
Old Printworks The TQ1 220 B4
Old Priory PL7 250 D5
Old Priory Jun Acad PL7 250 D5
Old Quarry Dr EX6 182 A5
Old Quarry Rd PL20 126 D3
Old Quay La 8 EX39 15 B1
Old Quay St TQ14 210 B4
Old Rd
Brixton PL8 257 A5
Galmpton TQ5 229 B5
Harbertonford TQ9 139 C7
Lutton PL21 133 B2
Okehampton EX20 170 A4
Stoke Fleming TQ6 146 B7
Tiverton EX16 161 E4
Old Rectory Cl EX39 15 C2
Old Rectory Cross TQ13 110 C7
Old Rectory Gdns
Morchard Bishop EX17 61 B2
Thurlestone TQ7 143 A2
Old Rectory La
Ashwater EX21 90 E6
Bratton Fleming EX31 18 A8
Oldridge Rd EX4 98 B6
Oldridge View EX6 97 F5
Old Rydon Cl EX2 178 E2
Old Rydon La EX2 178 D1
Old Rydon Ley EX2 178 D2
Old Saddlery The 18 EX14 166 C6
Old Sawmills Ind Est The EX10 186 C4
Old Sawmills The EX37 28 B1
Old School Cl EX16 161 B4
Old School Ct
6 Hemyock EX15 67 B8
6 Honiton EX14 166 C6
Topsham EX3 182 F5
Old School Ho The
Cawsand PL10 253 A1
North Tawton EX20 77 C4
Old School La EX31 153 E5
Old School Rd
Barnstaple EX32 155 C2
Plymouth PL5 247 C8
Old School The 5 EX16 161 D4
Old Show Field Way EX14 166 A6
Oldshute La TA22 33 C7
Old Sidmouth Rd EX24 103 A4
Old Smithy Cotts EX39 37 B4
Old Stables The
14 Bideford EX39 157 A1
Clyst St Mary EX5 179 A1
Old Station Rd
Barnstaple EX32 155 B4
Horrabridge PL20 126 F4
Old Station The PL20 126 E4
Old Station Yard 17 TQ10 134 F3
Old Sticklepath Hill EX31 154 E3
Old Stone Cl EX39 156 B6
Oldstone Cross TQ9 139 F2
Old's View EX4 177 A7
Old Tannery Bsns Pk The 4 PL4 263 A4
Old Tannery The EX32 28 D8
Old Taunton Rd
Dalwood EX13 86 F1
Dalwood EX13 87 A1
Old Teignmouth Rd EX7 204 D4
Old Tinhay PL16 105 F4
Old Tiverton Rd
Bampton EX16 34 C1
Bampton EX16 49 C8
Crediton EX17 165 E6
Exeter EX4 177 D8
Old Torquay Rd TQ3 226 C8
Old Torrington Rd EX31 154 D2
Old Torwood Rd TQ1 220 D4
Old Totnes Rd
Ashburton TQ13 130 F4
Buckfastleigh TQ11 236 C5
Cockington TQ2 219 C4
Newton Abbot TQ12 207 A1
Old Town EX39 157 A1
Old Town Hill TQ12, TQ13 122 C2
Old Town Park Nature Reserve★ EX20 170 A3
Old Town St
Dawlish EX7 204 D6
Plymouth PL1 262 C3
Old Tram Dr 1 EX31 154 A3
Old Turnpike Rd PL7 136 A6
Old Vicarage Cl EX2 176 D1
Old Vicarage Gdn DT7 260 D3
Old Vicarage Rd EX2 177 A4
Old Vicarage The
Sidmouth EX10 187 F3
Wellington TA21 160 E6
Old Walls Hill
Teignmouth TQ14 124 D1
Teignmouth TQ14 209 F8
Old Warleigh La PL5 244 B7
OLDWAY 226 A8
Oldway TQ13 123 E6
Old Way
Chipstable TA4 35 D6
Chudleigh TQ13 123 E6
Oldway Cl TQ12 123 E6
Oldway Ho TA21 160 F4
Oldway Mansion★ TQ3 226 B8
Oldway Pk TA21 160 F4
Oldway Prim Sch TQ3 226 B7
Oldway Rd
East Anstey TA22 32 F5
Paignton TQ3 226 B8
Wellington TA21 160 E4
OLDWAYS END 32 E3
Old Weighbridge The 19 EX8 202 A6
Old Wharf The PL9 255 C7
Old Widdicombe Rd TQ3 225 C7
Old Widdicombe La TQ3 225 B8
Old Woodlands Rd PL5 244 D3
Old Woods Hill TQ2 219 E7
Old Woods Trad Est TQ2 219 E8
Old Workhouse Dr EX36 158 C5
Olga Terr EX8 195 F5
Olive Gdns EX7 201 B2
Olive Gr EX7 201 B2
Oliver Rd EX32 155 B5
Olivia Ct PL4 263 B4
Ollan Gwella PL18 125 A6
Olympian Wy EX15 163 A4
Olympic Wy PL6 245 C6
Olympus Bsns Pk TQ12 207 C4
Omaha Dr EX2 178 D1
Omaha Way EX31 153 E6
Omega Ctr The EX2 178 E5
One End St 4 EX39 15 A1
One Fir EX15 83 C4
OneSchool Plymouth Campus
Plymouth PL5 243 B1
Plymouth PL5 247 B8
Onslow Rd
Plymouth PL2 248 C7
Salcombe TQ8 259 D5
Ora Cl EX33 7 E2
Ora La EX33 7 E2
Orange Gr TQ2 214 A2
Orange Moor Cross EX18 44 F3
Orangery The EX6 181 F5
Ora Stone Pk EX33 7 E1
Orbec Ave TQ12 207 F7
Orchard Ave PL6 249 B7
Orchard Cl
Ashprington TQ9 139 F7
Barnstaple EX31 154 C3
Beesands TQ7 149 D7
Braunton EX33 152 C6
8 Brixham TQ5 230 C3
10 Chudleigh TQ13 123 F6
Coldridge EX17 59 C4
Colyford EX24 103 B3
9 Combe Martin EX34 3 A3
Dawlish EX7 204 D6
Denbury TQ12 211 A6
East Budleigh EX9 198 B6
East Ogwell TQ12 206 D1
Exeter EX1 174 F1
Exmouth EX8 196 B1
Exmouth, Littleham EX8 203 A6
Frogmore TQ7 144 E1
Galmpton TQ5 229 C5
Kingsteignton TQ12 207 F7
Kingsteignton, Sandygate TQ12 123 E2
Langford EX5 109 F7
Lympstone EX8 195 E5
Newton Poppleford EX10 186 D8
Okehampton EX20 170 B4
Ottery St Mary EX11 169 E3
3 Plymouth PL7 251 C5
Rockwell Green TA21 160 A5
St Giles on t H PL15 90 C1
Sandford EX17 80 A5
Shaldon TQ14 209 D5
Sidford EX10 188 C8
Sidmouth EX10 187 F3
Talaton EX5 84 A2
Tavistock PL19 126 A8
Uffculme EX15 66 A7
Upton Pyne EX5 173 A7
Whitford EX13 103 B6
Wilmington EX14 86 C2
Woodbury EX5 184 C3
Yealmpton PL8 257 F3
Orchard Cotts
Holbeton PL8 136 D1
Lamerton PL19 116 F3
Newton Tracey EX31 27 A6
Orchard Cres PL9 255 C7
Orchard Cross EX17 60 D3
Orchard Ct
1 Crediton EX17 165 C5
Exeter EX1 178 E6
Ivybridge PL21 237 B5
Lamerton PL19 116 E3
22 Newton Abbot TQ12 207 B3
Newton St Cyres EX5 81 A1
North Tawton EX20 77 C4
3 Whimple EX5 99 E8
Orchard Dr
Ipplepen TQ12 211 D2
Kingskerswell TQ12 212 F4
Otterton EX9 198 E7
Salcombe TQ8 259 C5
Orchard Farm EX14 85 A3
Orchard Gate EX19 57 F7
Orchard Gdns
Bideford EX39 157 A4
Broadclyst EX5 175 D6
15 Dawlish EX7 204 D6
Exeter EX4 176 F4
10 Teignmouth TQ14 210 C4
West Buckland TA21 52 F7
Orchard Gr
Brixham TQ5 230 C3
Croyde EX33 7 E1
Mile End TQ12 206 D4
ORCHARD HILL 157 A4
Orchard Hill
Bideford EX39 157 A4
Exeter EX2 176 F3
Talaton EX14 84 B2
Yealmpton PL8 136 B3
Orchard Ho
8 Chudleigh TQ13 123 E6
1 Teignmouth TQ14 210 C4
Torquay TQ1 220 C5
Orchard Ind Est's North & South TQ7 258 C5
Orchard La
Plymouth PL7 250 E6
Silverton EX5 82 B6
Starcross EX6 201 A4
Orchard Leigh EX16 161 C3
Orchard Manor Sch EX7 204 C5
Orchard Mdw TQ13 111 A6
Orchardon La EX33 8 B1
Orchard Pk
Dartington TQ9 222 F8
Dittisham TQ6 228 C3
Ivybridge PL21 237 C4
Orchard Pl 3 TQ1 220 A7
Orchard Rd
Ashburton TQ13 130 F4
Barnstaple EX32 155 B3
Brixton PL8 257 A5
Knowle EX33 8 D1
Plymouth PL2 248 B7
4 Torquay, Ellacombe TQ1 220 B6
Torquay, Hele TQ2 213 F1
Wrafton EX33 152 E3
Orchard Rise EX39 157 A4

Orchardside EX10 188 B7
Orchard Side EX10 101 C3
Orchards The
Galmpton TQ5 229 B5
Landkey EX32 17 B2
Lower Lovacott EX31 27 A6
Swimbridge EX32 28 E8
Orchard Terr
Abbotskerswell TQ12 212 B7
Barnstaple EX32 155 B2
3 Bovey Tracey TQ13 180 D8
Buckfastleigh TQ11 236 B5
Chagford TQ13 111 A6
Crediton EX17 165 B5
Kingskerswell TQ12 212 F5
Kingswear TQ6 234 B3
Totnes TQ9 223 C5
Tuckenhay TQ9 139 F6
Orchard The
Abbotskerswell TQ12 212 B6
Avonwick TQ10 135 B1
Barnstaple EX31 154 A3
Bishopsteignton TQ14 208 F8
Buckfastleigh TQ11 236 C5
Dunsford EX6 112 F7
Gunnislake PL18 125 D6
Holcombe EX7 210 E8
Holywell Lake TA21 51 E7
Honiton EX14 166 F8
Kilmington EX13 87 D1
Modbury PL21 137 C2
Seaton EX12 192 A5
Tipton St John EX10 100 D2
Totnes TQ9 223 C5
Whiddon Down EX20 95 C1
Yealmpton PL8 257 F3
Orchardton Terr 2
PL9 255 F5
Orchard Vale Com Sch
EX32 155 E4
Orchard View
Frogmore TQ7 144 E1
Halberton EX16 65 B7
Orchard Vw EX31 154 A3
Orchard Way
1 Bovey Tracey
TQ13 180 D8
Chillington TQ7 145 A1
Cullompton EX15 163 B2
Honiton EX14 166 D6
Kenton EX6 194 D3
Lapford EX17 60 D3
Stoke Gabriel TQ9 227 F8
Tiverton EX16 161 B3
Topsham EX3 182 E5
Uffculme EX15 66 A7
Willand EX15 162 D4
Orchard Waye TQ9 223 B5
Orchard Wy TQ2 213 B1
Orch Cres 5 EX1 178 E3
Orchid Ave
Ivybridge PL21 237 A6
Kingsteignton TQ12 207 E7
Orchid Cl
Barnstaple EX31 154 F8
7 Tiverton EX16 161 F6
Orchid Ho EX4 176 E8
Orchid Meadow
TQ13 124 A8
Orchid Vale 14 TQ12 123 F1
Orchid Wy TQ2 213 F2
Orch The EX14 84 E2
Orcombe Ct EX8 202 D8
Orcombe Gdns EX8 202 C5
Ordnance St PL1 247 E2
Ordulf Rd PL19 171 A5
Oregon Way PL3 249 D6
ORESTON 255 C7
Oreston Com Acad
PL9 255 C7
Orestone Cross TQ2 213 D3
Orestone Dr TQ1 214 C6
Orestone La TQ2,
TQ12 213 E3
Oreston Rd PL9 255 C8
Orient Rd TQ3 226 D8
Oriole Dr EX4 173 D1
Orion Dr PL9 256 F8
Orkney Cl TQ2 213 E2
Orkney Mews EX16 161 D6
Orleigh Ave TQ12 207 B5
Orleigh Cl EX39 40 C7
Orleigh Cross TQ12 207 B5
Orleigh Ct EX39 25 C1
Orleigh Mill Wlk EX39 25 D1
Orleigh Pk TQ12 207 B5
Orley Rd TQ12 211 B2
Ormonde Ct EX36 158 D4
Orpington Ct EX16 65 B7
Orstone Cross EX32 18 E3
Orway Ash Cross EX15 66 B2
Orway Cross EX15 66 C1
Orwell Garth EX4 178 C8
Osbern Rd TQ3 219 A2
Osborn Cl TQ12 211 D2
Osborne Cl EX39 156 D2
Osborne Ct PL1 262 C2
Osborne Gdns 4
EX31 154 C1
Osborne La EX39 156 D2
Osborne Pl PL1 262 C1
Osborne Rd
Ilfracombe EX34 150 A5
Plymouth PL3 248 A3
Osborne St TQ12 207 D3
Osborne Villas 2
PL3 248 A3
Osbourne Dr TQ6 233 F5
Osbourne Terr EX31 154 F4
Osmand Gdns PL7 250 D5
Osmond Lodge TQ4 226 C5
Osmond's La 12 TQ14 210 B4
Osney Ave TQ4 226 B4
Osney Cres TQ4 226 B4
Osney Gdns TQ4 226 B4
Osprey Ave
4 Newton Abbot
TQ12 207 A5
Seaton EX12 192 B5
Osprey Dr TQ2 213 D3
Osprey Gdns PL9 256 C7
Osprey Gr EX7 200 F2
Osprey Ho TQ1 220 D7
Osprey Rd EX2 178 F6
OSSABOROUGH 8 B6
Ossaborough La EX34 8 C6
Oswald Browning Way 4
EX31 155 A7
Otterbourne Ct EX9 198 B1
Otter Cl
Okehampton EX20 170 D6
Tipton St John EX10 100 D3
Torquay TQ2 219 C7
West Hill EX11 168 D4
Otter Ct
Bickington TQ12 131 F8
Budleigh Salterton
EX9 198 C1
Exeter EX2 181 C8
Otter Estuary Reserve*
EX9 198 D1
Otterhead Lake Nature
Reserve* TA3 68 E8
Otter Rd TQ2 219 C7
Otter Reach EX10 186 F8
Otters The EX16 49 B2
OTTERTON 198 F7
Otterton CE Prim Sch
EX9 198 E7
Otterton Mews EX13 167 F7
Otterton Mill* EX9 198 D7
Otter Vale Cl EX14 68 C1
Ottervale Rd EX9 198 C1
Otter Valley Pk EX14 166 F8
Otter Way EX32 155 D4
OTTERY 116 E2
Ottery Cotts PL19 116 E2
Ottery La EX10 101 A1
Ottery Moor La
Honiton EX14 85 D3
Honiton EX14 166 A6
Ottery Park Ind Est
PL19 116 E2
OTTERY ST MARY 169 E3
Ottery St Mary Hospl
EX11 169 C3
Ottery St Mary L Ctr
EX11 169 B3
Ottery St Mary Prim Sch
EX11 169 E3
Ottery St EX9 198 F8
Our Lady & St Patrick's
RC Prim Sch TQ14 210 A6
Our Lady's RC Prim Sch
EX32 155 B5
Outcrop Rd PL9 255 B7
Outer Down PL19 116 E3
OUTER HOPE 147 C7
Outer Ting Tong EX9 197 B3
Outland Rd PL2 248 C7
Oval Gn EX2 178 C3
Overbeck's Mus & Gdn*
TQ8 259 B1
Overbrook EX7 204 D6
Overcliff Ct EX7 204 E7
Overclose TQ3 225 F8
Overcott La EX36 46 D8
Overdale Cl TQ2 213 F4
Overdale Rd PL2 248 A7
Overgang TQ5 230 D5
Overgang Rd TQ5 230 C6
Overland Ct EX4 174 E2
Overlangs TQ7 142 C6
Overseas Est TQ6 146 B6
Overton Cl DT7 260 E5
Overton Gdns 3 PL3 248 F5
Owen Dr PL7 250 C7
Owen St TA21 160 C6
Owlaborough La
EX36 32 B2
Owlacombe Cross
TQ12 131 A7
Oxenham Cross EX20 95 C5
Oxenham Gn TQ2 219 D6
Oxenpark Gate EX6 112 F5
Oxenpark La
Ilfracombe, Goosewell
EX34 2 C3
Ilfracombe, Two Pots
EX34 2 C2
Morchard Bishop EX17 61 C1
Stockleigh Pomeroy
EX17 80 F7
Oxford Ave PL3 248 E5
Oxford Cl EX8 196 E4
Oxford Cross EX33 8 A3
Oxford Ct TQ2 213 F1
Oxford Gdns PL3 248 E5
Oxford Gr EX34 150 B6
Oxford La TQ5 230 A4
Oxford Pk EX34 150 B5
Oxford Pl PL1 262 C3
Oxford Rd EX4 261 C4
Oxford St
Dartmouth TQ6 233 F3
Exeter EX2 177 A4
Plymouth PL1 262 B3
Oxford Terr
Crediton EX17 165 D5
4 Plymouth PL1 262 B3
Sandford EX17 80 A5
Oxham Cross EX36 45 D8
Oxman La EC36 45 D7
Ox Hill La EX24 102 F4
Oxlea Cl TQ1 220 E4
Oxlea Rd TQ1 220 E4
Oxman's Cotts EX39 157 E6
Oxmead EX5 99 D3
Oxmon's La EX39 157 A7
Oxton Ho EX6 114 E1
Oyster Bend TQ4 226 C2
Oystercatcher Ct 9
TQ14 210 A3
Oyster Cl TQ4 226 C2
Ozone Terr DT7 260 D2

P

Paccombe Pool La
EX10 189 C7
Pacehayne La
Dalwood EX13 87 A1
Shute EX13 103 A8
Packer Rd EX16 161 A6
Packhall La TQ5 230 A2
Packhorse Cl EX10 188 D8
Packington St PL2 248 A4
Packs Cl TQ9 139 C7
Packsheep Down
EX6 112 F3
Padacre Rd TQ2 214 A4
Paddock Cl
Plymouth PL9 255 E5
Saltash PL12 242 D4
Seaton EX12 191 F7
Paddock Dr PL21 237 D4
Paddocks The
Abbotskerswell TQ12 212 B7
Dolton EX19 57 F7
Honiton EX14 166 A2
Membury EX13 87 D6
Totnes TQ9 223 D6
Wellington TA21 160 E5
Whimple EX5 99 E7
Paddock The
Brixham TQ5 230 B4
Dawlish EX7 204 E7
Dulverton TA22 33 D6
Hemerdon PL7 251 C7
Torquay TQ1 214 B1
Paddons Coombe 9
TQ12 123 F1
Paddons La TQ14 210 A7
Paddons Row PL19 171 C6
Pafford Ave TQ2 214 B2
Pafford Cl TQ2 214 A2
Page Ho TQ4 226 C6
Page's Cross EX16 62 F7
Paige Adams' Rd
TQ9 223 B6
Paiges Farm PL9 255 C1
Paiges La 7 EX31 154 F5
PAIGNTON 226 D6
Paignton Com Coll
Paignton TQ4 225 D4
15 Paignton TQ4 226 B6
Paignton Com & Sports
Coll TQ3 225 E5
Paignton Health &
Wellbeing Centre 16
TQ3 226 B6
Paignton Hospl TQ3 226 B6
Paignton Rd TQ9 228 A8
Paignton Sta TQ4 226 B6
Paignton Zoological &
Botanical Gdns*
TQ4 225 F4
Pail Pk EX33 8 D1
Painsford Cross TQ9 139 D7
Painter's Cross EX13 102 F7
Painters Ct EX2 261 A1
Painton Water EX39 37 D8
Paisey La EX17 78 C5
Paizen La
Beer EX12 190 F6
Beer EX12 191 B6
Palace Ave TQ3 226 B6
Palace Cotts 10 EX8 202 A7
Palace Ct 23 PL1 263 A2
Palace Gate EX1 261 B2
Palace Gdns 22 TQ13 123 E6
Palace La PL21 137 B7
Palace Mdw TQ13 123 E6
Palace Pl TQ3 226 B6
Palace St PL1 263 A2
Palatine Cl TQ1 220 B5
Pale Gate Cl EX14 166 D7
Palegate Cross TQ7 258 A8
Palermo 12 TQ1 220 D4
Palermo Rd TQ1 220 C7
Palfrey's La EX16 49 C5
Palk Cl TQ14 209 D5
Palk St TQ2 220 B4
Palm Cl EX8 196 D3
Palm Cross 1 PL21 137 B2
Palm Ct
Dawlish Warren EX7 201 A2
Dawlish Warren EX7 201 B2
Palmer Cl EX4 175 A4
Palmer Ct EX9 198 A1
Palmers Cl EX33 152 D5
Palmers Ct EX38 159 E5
Palmer's La EX5 99 E5
Palmers Mead TA21 160 D8
Palmerston Dr EX4 176 E7
Palmerston Park Wood
Nature Reserve
EX16 161 B2
Palmerston Pk EX16 161 B2
Palmerston St PL1 262 A4
Palm Ho EX4 176 E8
Palm Rd TQ2 220 A5
Palm Rise TQ2 213 A3
Palms The 2 TQ1 220 D4
Palm Tree View TQ3 226 B1
Palstone La TQ10 135 A2
Pamela Rd EX1 177 F7
Pancheon Cl 10 EX31 154 A2
PANCRASWEEK 71 B8
Pandora Gr PL9 256 E8
Pankhurst Cl EX8 202 E7
Panney The EX4 178 A7
Pannier Mkt
Great Torrington
EX38 159 D5
Tavistock PL19 171 C5
Pannier Mws 16
EX39 157 A1
Panorama TQ2 219 E2
Panson Cross PL15 90 B3
Papaver Cl EX31 153 E6
Papermakers La
PL21 237 E6
Parade
Chudleigh TQ13 123 E6
Exmouth EX8 202 A7
Plymouth PL1 263 A2
Parade Bsns Pk 4
PL19 171 B4
Parade Ope PL1 263 A2
Parade Rd PL5 244 A3
Parade The
Chardstock EX13 88 A7
Millbrook PL10 252 E5
Milton Abbot PL19 116 A6
Paradise Glen TQ14 210 B6
Paradise Lawn EX36 158 D4
Paradise Pk EX22 70 E1
Paradise Pl
1 Brixham TQ5 230 D5
Plymouth PL1 248 A2
Paradise Rd
Plymouth PL1 248 A2
Teignmouth TQ14 210 C6
Paradise Wlk TQ4 226 C4
Paragon EX34 150 B6
Paramore Way EX36 158 C4
Parchment Pl PL21 237 D6
Par Dr EX16 64 E8
Parehayne La EX24 102 E7
Parely Hill TQ13 110 F6
Paris Rd TQ3 226 C8
Paris St EX1 261 B3
Park an Garrek PL12 239 A1
Park Ave
Barnstaple EX31 154 C4
Bideford EX39 157 A3
Brixham TQ5 230 B3
Plymouth, Devonport
PL1 247 E3
Plymouth, Plymstock
PL9 255 D7
Westward Ho! EX39 156 C7
Parkbay Ave TQ4 225 E2
Park Bglws EX16 51 B3
Park Cl
Clyst Hydon EX15 83 D4
Fremington EX31 153 E5
Holsworthy EX22 164 C6
Ivybridge PL21 237 C5
Plymouth PL7 250 B7
Silverton EX5 82 C5
Tiverton EX16 161 D5
Woodbury EX5 184 C2
Park Com Sch The
EX32 155 A3
Park Cotts
Bigbury TQ7 142 F5
Ugborough PL21 137 D6
Park Cres
Combe Martin EX34 3 A3
Plymouth PL9 255 C7
Park Cross EX17 62 C3
Park Ct
Brixham TQ5 230 E5
Chillaton PL16 106 D1
Honiton EX14 85 C2
Ilfracombe EX34 150 B4
Park Dr EX8 202 E7
Parkelands TQ13 180 C7
Parker Cl
Plymouth PL7 250 B5
Wellington TA21 160 E6
Parker Rd
Bigbury-on-S TQ7 142 E3
Plymouth PL2 248 B6
Parkers Cl TQ9 223 D4
Parkers Cross La
EX1 174 F2
Parker's Gn PL18 125 C6
Parkers Hollow EX31 154 B3
Parker's Rd EX6 201 A8
Parkers Way TQ9 223 D4
Parkes Rd EX38 159 F5
Parkesway PL12 242 D2
Parkfield TQ7 143 A2
Parkfield Cl
Marldon TQ3 218 D3
Parkfield Cl *continued*
Totnes TQ9 223 F5
Parkfield Cross TQ13 131 A3
Parkfield Dr PL6 245 F1
Parkfield Rd
Topsham EX3 182 F5
Torquay TQ1 219 F7
Park Field Terr EX12 190 D4
Parkfield Way EX3 182 F5
Parkfield Wlk TQ7 143 A2
Park Five Bsns Ctr
EX2 178 E4
Park Gate EX37 28 D2
Park Gdns EX35 151 B5
Park Grove EX22 164 C6
Park Hall TQ1 220 B3
PARKHAM 39 E8
PARKHAM ASH 39 C7
Parkham Cross EX39 24 F1
Parkham Glade TQ5 230 C4
Parkham La TQ5 230 C4
Parkham Prim Sch
EX39 39 E8
Parkham Rd TQ5 230 C4
Parkham Terr 12
TQ5 230 C4
Parkham Twrs 6
TQ5 230 C4
Parkhayes EX5 184 C7
Park Hill
Dainton TQ12 212 A2
Ipplepen TQ12 211 F2
Teignmouth TQ14 210 B5
Tiverton EX16 161 C5
Parkhill Cotts PL21 136 F4
Parkhill Ho TQ12 211 F3
Parkhill Rd TQ1 220 C3
Park Hill Rd EX34 150 B5
Park Hills Ind Units
EX34 3 A3
Parkhouse La
Stoodleigh EX16 48 E4
Stoodleigh EX16 48 F4
Parkhouse Rd EX2 176 F3
Parkhurst Rd TQ1,
TQ2 219 F7
Park La
Barnstaple EX32 155 A3
8 Bere Alston PL20 125 E1
Bideford EX39 157 A3
Blackawton TQ9 139 E1
Budleigh Salterton EX9 197 F1
Chittlehampton EX37 43 F8
Combe Martin EX34 2 F3
Combe Martin EX34 3 A3
Combe St Nicholas TA20 69 F6
Crediton EX17 165 B4
Exeter EX4 174 E2
Exmouth EX8 202 A8
Filleigh EX32 29 D7
Iddesleigh EX19 57 F3
Madford EX14 67 C4
Morchard Bishop EX17 61 A2
Otterton EX9 198 E6
Pennymoor EX16 62 D6
Plymouth PL9 255 C7
Sparkwell PL7 132 C1
Stowford EX31 11 B3
Torquay TQ1 220 B3
Wellington TA21 160 C1
Whitford EX13 103 B6
Parkland Dr EX2 178 C5
Parklands
Barnstaple EX31 154 C3
12 Hemyock EX15 67 B8
Okehampton EX20 170 B3
9 Seaton EX12 192 A5
South Molton EX36 158 B3
Totnes TQ9 223 C6
Parklands Cl EX36 158 B3
Parklands Rd TA21 160 D7
Parklands Way TQ13 180 C4
Park Lane Cotts EX32 29 D7
Park Lodge EX9 197 F1
Park Meadow Cl EX17 60 D3
Park Mews TQ5 230 E5
Park Mill Cross EX17 59 F3
Park Mill La EX18 59 F8
Park Pl
Exeter, Heavitree
EX1 177 F6
Exeter, Mount Radford
EX2 261 C2
Winkleigh EX19 58 F3
Park Place La 12 PL3 248 A4
Park Rd
Beer EX12 191 C5
Crediton EX17 165 D4
Dartington TQ9 216 B2
Dawlish EX7 204 D6
Exeter EX1 177 E7
Exmouth EX8 202 A8
Hatherleigh EX20 75 C7
Kingskerswell TQ12 212 F5
Lapford EX17 60 D3
Lifton PL16 105 E3
Plymouth PL3 249 A6
St Dominick PL12 125 A2
Silverton EX5 82 C5
Tiverton EX16 161 D5
Torpoint PL11 247 B3
Torquay TQ1 214 B1
Park Rise
Dawlish EX7 204 D7
Salcombe TQ8 259 C4
Park Row EX20 170 B5
Park School TQ9 216 C3
Parks Dr PL9 256 A5
Parkside
Ivybridge PL21 237 E5
Plymouth PL2 247 F5
Salcombe TQ8 259 D5
Parkside Cres EX1 174 F3
Parkside Ct EX2 261 B2
Parkside Dr EX8 196 E3
Parkside Rd
Exeter EX1 174 F3
Paignton TQ4 226 C6
Parkside Villas TQ1 220 C7
Park St
Crediton EX17 165 D5
Ivybridge PL21 237 C4
Lynton EX35 151 B5
Plymouth PL3 248 A4
Tiverton EX16 161 D5
Willand EX15 65 D6
Willand EX15 162 C5
Parkstone La PL7 250 F6
Park Street Mews
PL21 237 C4
Park Street Ope PL3 248 A4
Parks Villas EX33 152 D5
Park Terr
23 Barnstaple EX32 155 A4
Ivybridge PL21 237 C4
Plymouth PL4 263 A3
Tiverton EX16 161 D5
Park The PL8 257 A5
Parkview EX17 80 A5
Park View
Axminster EX13 88 A3
Beaford EX19 42 D1
Kenton EX6 194 F3
Lifton PL16 105 E4
Newton Abbot TQ12 212 F8
Plymouth PL4 263 C3
Pyworthy EX22 71 D5
Shute EX13 103 A7
Park View Cl 21 EX34 3 A3
Park View Cotts EX38 42 B6
Park View Rd EX32 155 A6
Park View Terr
Kingston TQ7 142 C6
Okehampton EX20 170 C3
Westward Ho! EX39 156 C7
Park Villas EX32 27 E8
Parkway
Exeter EX2 176 F3
Ilfracombe EX34 150 B3
Park Way
Exmouth EX8 202 C8
Woodbury EX5 184 C2
Parkway Ct PL6 249 E7
Parkway Ind Est The
PL6 249 E7
Parkway Rd TQ13 123 E6
Parkway The PL3, PL5,
PL6 244 B1
Parkwood Cl PL6 241 B2
Parkwood Ct PL19 171 D6
Parkwood Rd PL19 171 D6
Park Wood Rise
PL16 105 E4
Parkyns Cross EX19 43 B4
Parliament Ct 9
EX34 150 C6
Parliament St EX17 165 C5
Parlour Mdw EX8 202 F7
Parlour Mead EX15 163 A3
Parminter Cl EX8 202 E7
PARNACOTT 71 D8
Parnell Cl PL6 249 A8
PARRACOMBE 4 C2
Parracombe CE Prim Sch
Parracombe EX31 4 C1
Parracombe EX31 11 D7
Parracombe La EX31 4 D2
Parracombe Lane Head
EX31 4 D2
Parr Cl EX1 261 C4
Parricks La EX13 88 D3
Parr La PL4 263 B2
Parrocks La TA20 88 C8
Parr's La TQ13 123 E6
Parr St
Exeter EX1 261 C4
Plymouth PL4 263 B2
Parrys Farm Cl EX8 196 C2
Parsonage Cross
Chulmleigh EX18 44 F2
Dartington TQ9 215 F2
Germansweek EX21 91 D5
Staverton TQ9 216 E3
West Putford EX22 39 B2
Woodbury EX5 184 C3
Parsonage Ct PL16 105 E4
Parsonage Hill EX36 31 A3
Parsonage La
Awliscombe EX14 85 C1
George Nympton EX36 29 F2
Hittisleigh EX6 96 C6
Honiton EX14 166 D5
Kentisbury EX31 10 E5
Moreleigh TQ9 139 A3
Silverton EX5 82 B6
South Molton EX36 158 C5
Staverton TQ9 216 E4
Ugborough PL21 137 D6
Parsonage Lane Cross
EX32 18 B2
Parsonage Lane End
PL21 137 D6
Parsonage Rd PL8 141 A7
Parsonage St EX5 83 A7
Parsonage Way
Plymouth PL4 263 B2

Parsonage Way *continued*
Woodbury EX5 ... 184 C4
Parson Cl EX8 ... 196 C2
Parsons Cl
13 Holsworthy EX22 ... 164 C4
Newton Poppleford
EX10 ... 186 D8
Plymouth PL9 ... 256 A4
Parson's Cl EX15 ... 66 A3
Parsons Ct PL10 ... 252 F6
Parsons Hill
Bridford TQ13 ... 112 C4
Heltor EX6 ... 112 D6
Parsons La
Branscombe EX12 ... 190 E4
Rockbeare EX5 ... 99 B5
Parson St TQ14 ... 210 B5
Parthia Pl EX8 ... 196 E1
Partridge Cross EX16 ... 63 A8
Partridge Hill EX36 ... 45 D7
Partridge La
Hittisleigh EX6 ... 96 C4
Tiverton EX16 ... 63 A8
Partridge Rd
Exmouth EX8 ... 196 C2
Plymouth PL6 ... 245 B2
Partwayes PL19 ... 116 E3
Pasley St PL2 ... 247 E4
Pasley Street E PL2 ... 247 F4
Passaford La
Colaton Raleigh
EX10 ... 187 A4
Hatherleigh EX20 ... 75 C6
Passage Rd PL8 ... 140 F6
Passmore Rd EX5 ... 82 F6
Pasture Cross TQ9 ... 144 F8
Pastures The EX20 ... 92 A2
PATCHACOTT ... 74 B1
Patchacott Cross
Bratton Clovelly EX21 ... 92 A8
Northlew EX21 ... 74 B1
Patchel Cross EX20 ... 56 F3
Patches Rd EX16 ... 161 B4
PATCHOLE ... 10 D5
Paternoster La TQ12 ... 211 C2
Paternoster Row
8 Barnstaple EX31 ... 154 F5
Ottery St Mary EX11 ... 169 D4
Pathdown La EX33 ... 7 F2
Pathfield EX38 ... 159 F5
Pathfield Cl
Barnstaple EX31 ... 154 A3
Totnes TQ9 ... 223 D5
Path Field Cl EX32 ... 18 B2
Pathfield Lawn EX31 ... 154 E6
Pathfields
Croyde EX33 ... 7 E2
Totnes TQ9 ... 223 D5
Uffculme EX15 ... 66 A7
Pathfields Bsns Pk
EX36 ... 158 D6
Pathfield Sch
Barnstaple EX31 ... 154 E6
Barnstaple EX31 ... 154 F5
PATHFINDER
VILLAGE ... 98 C4
Path The 29 EX39 ... 15 A1
Pathwhorlands EX10 ... 188 A6
Patna Pl PL1 ... 262 B4
Pato Point PL11 ... 247 A5
Patricia Cl EX4 ... 173 C2
Pattard Cross EX39 ... 22 D4
Patterdale Cl PL6 ... 245 D3
Patterdale Wlk PL6 ... 245 D3
Patterson's Cross
EX11 ... 169 D8
Patteson Cl EX11 ... 100 F8
Patteson Dr EX11 ... 169 F4
Pattinson Cl PL6 ... 245 E2
Pattinson Ct PL6 ... 245 E2
Pattinson Dr PL6 ... 245 F2
Paullet EX16 ... 50 C1
Paul St EX4 ... 261 A3
Pauntley Gdn EX10 ... 187 F3
Pavey Run EX11 ... 169 C3
Paviland Grange 6
PL1 ... 248 A3
Pavilion Pl EX2 ... 261 B2
Pavilions Cl TQ5 ... 230 B5
Pavilion Sh Ctr TQ2 ... 220 B3
Pavilion View EX39 ... 156 C7
Pavington Cross EX37 ... 43 E3
Pavor Rd TQ2 ... 214 B2
Pavo St PL9 ... 256 E8
Paws Rd EX37 ... 43 B7
Paxford House Sq
EX11 ... 169 D4
PAYHEMBURY ... 84 C4
Payhembury CE Prim Sch
EX14 ... 84 C4
Payne Ct EX4 ... 178 B8
Payne's Cotts EX14 ... 85 C3
Paynsford Mews
TQ12 ... 207 B4
Paynsford Rd 1
TQ12 ... 207 B4
Paynter Wlk 5 PL7 ... 251 B5
PAYTON ... 51 F7
Payton Rd
Holywell Lake TA21 ... 51 F7
Rockwell Green TA21 ... 160 A5
Peacegate Cross EX20 ... 76 E4
Peacehay La TA21 ... 51 E4
Peacock Ave PL11 ... 247 A3
Peacock Cl PL7 ... 250 F7
Peacock La PL4 ... 263 A3
Peacock Pl EX6 ... 201 A8
Peacocks Cl TA21 ... 52 F7
Peadhill La EX16 ... 49 D2
Peak Cnr EX16 ... 62 E7
Peak Cross TQ9 ... 222 F3
Peakfield Cross Ways
EX5 ... 82 E6
Peak Hill Llamas★
EX10 ... 187 C2
Peak Hill Rd EX10 ... 187 E3
Peak Tor Ave TQ1 ... 220 C2
Pear Dr EX15 ... 162 D4
Peard Rd EX16 ... 64 D6
Peards Down Cl
EX32 ... 155 D4
Pear La 8 PL7 ... 251 D5
Pearl Assurance Ho 2
TQ12 ... 207 C3
Pearmain Cl EX15 ... 162 D4
Pearn Cotts 2 PL3 ... 248 F6
Pearn Gdns PL3 ... 249 A7
Pearn Rd PL3 ... 249 A7
Pearn Ridge PL3 ... 249 A7
Pearse Cl EX20 ... 75 B7
Pearson Ave 3 PL4 ... 248 F4
Pearson Cl EX22 ... 164 C5
Pearson Rd PL4 ... 248 F4
Pear Tree Cl
Kenton EX6 ... 194 E3
Westleigh EX16 ... 51 A4
Pear Tree Cotts PL8 ... 257 A5
Peartree Cross
Ashburton TQ13 ... 130 E4
Denbury TQ12 ... 211 A7
Pear Tree Way 5
EX32 ... 17 B2
Peasberry Pl PL8 ... 257 E4
Peaseditch TQ5 ... 230 D3
Peasland Rd TQ2 ... 214 A4
Peaslands Rd
Sidmouth EX10 ... 188 A5
Sidmouth EX10 ... 188 B5
Peaspark Cross TQ7 ... 144 D3
Peazen Flats EX12 ... 191 C6
Pebblebed Cl EX3 ... 182 D7
Pebble Cl EX39 ... 156 D7
Pebble Ct TQ4 ... 226 B4
Pebbleridge Rd EX39 ... 156 C8
Pebblestone Pl EX12 ... 192 A5
Pecorama Pleasure
Gdns★ EX12 ... 191 C5
Pedlerspool La EX17 ... 165 E7
Pedley La EX17 ... 61 B6
Peek La PL21 ... 137 C8
Peek Mead DT7 ... 193 F7
Peek Moor Cross
EX22 ... 90 B4
Peeks Ave PL9 ... 255 F7
Peel Row 3 EX4 ... 178 C8
Peel St PL1 ... 248 A1
Peep La 4 EX17 ... 165 D5
Pegasus Ct
Exeter EX1 ... 177 F6
Paignton TQ3 ... 226 B8
Pegasus Pl PL9 ... 256 E8
Pegwell La TQ14 ... 209 B3
Pelican Cl EX39 ... 156 B6
Pellew Ho 6 TQ14 ... 210 B4
Pellew Pl PL2 ... 247 F4
Pellew Way TQ14 ... 210 A7
Pellinore Rd EX4 ... 174 A1
Pembrey Wlk PL5 ... 243 E4
Pembroke La PL1 ... 247 E1
Pembroke Lodge 15
EX34 ... 150 B5
Pembroke Pk TQ3 ... 218 E3
Pembroke Rd
Paignton TQ3 ... 225 E7
Torquay TQ1 ... 220 B5
Pembroke St PL1 ... 247 E1
Pemros Rd PL5 ... 243 C1
Pencair Ave PL11 ... 246 E2
Pencarrow Rd TQ3 ... 225 D7
Pencarwick Ho EX8 ... 202 A5
Pencepool Cotts EX15 ... 83 F6
Pencepool Orch EX15 ... 83 F6
Pencombe Rocks EX31 ... 4 C1
Pencorse Rd TQ2 ... 219 F8
Pencreber Rd 3
PL20 ... 126 F4
Pencross View 1
EX15 ... 67 B8
Pendarves TQ9 ... 222 D2
Pendeen Cl PL6 ... 244 F6
Pendeen Cres PL6 ... 245 A6
Pendeen Pk TQ7 ... 145 A1
Pendennis Cl
Plymouth PL3 ... 248 F8
Torpoint PL11 ... 246 F3
Pendennis Rd TQ2 ... 219 F8
Pendilly Ave PL11 ... 246 F2
Pendragon Rd EX4 ... 174 A2
Penfield Gdns 1
EX7 ... 204 D6
Penfound Rd EX23 ... 70 A3
Pengelly Cl
Greenhill TQ12 ... 207 F7
Torpoint PL11 ... 246 F5
Pengelly Hill
Torpoint PL11 ... 246 F4
Torpoint PL11 ... 247 A5
Pengelly Pk PL11 ... 246 F5
Pengelly Way TQ2 ... 213 F3
Pengilly Way EX39 ... 22 E3
PENHALE ... 252 D7
Penhale Dr EX22 ... 164 B5
Penhaven Ct EX39 ... 39 E8
Penhayes Cl EX6 ... 194 E3
Penhayes Rd EX6 ... 194 E3
PENHILL ... 16 A4
Penhill Chalets TQ6 ... 146 B7
Penhill Cross EX6 ... 113 F5
Penhill La
Brixham TQ5 ... 234 E8
Hillhead TQ5 ... 235 A7
Penhill View EX31 ... 16 A3
Peninsula Medical Sch
Exeter EX2 ... 177 F5
Plymouth PL6 ... 245 C3
Peninsular Pk PL12 ... 242 C4
Penlee EX9 ... 199 G2
Penlee Cotts PL10 ... 140 I2
Penlee Gdns PL3 ... 248 A4
Penlee Pk PL11 ... 246 E4
Penlee Pl 4 PL4 ... 248 F4
Penlee Rd PL3 ... 248 A4
Penlee Way PL3 ... 248 A4
Penleonard Cl EX2 ... 177 E5
PENN ... 104 E6
Pennant Ho EX8 ... 201 E6
Pennant Way PL21 ... 136 D6
Pennball Cross TQ9 ... 217 B3
Penn Court TQ5 ... 230 D3
Penn Cross DT6 ... 260 F7
Penn Ho TQ12 ... 207 E2
Pennine Dr TQ4 ... 225 D4
Pennington Cl EX17 ... 79 A5
PENNINN ... 207 E1
Penn Inn Cl TQ12 ... 207 E2
Penn Kernow PL15 ... 105 A2
Penn La TQ5 ... 230 D3
Penn Mdws TQ5 ... 230 D3
Penn Meadows Cl
TQ5 ... 230 D3
Pennsland La TQ13 ... 130 F7
Penns Way TQ12 ... 207 F6
PENNSYLVANIA ... 173 C1
Pennsylvania Cl EX4 ... 177 D8
Pennsylvania Cres
EX4 ... 177 C8
Pennsylvania Pk EX4 ... 173 D1
Pennsylvania Rd
Exeter EX4 ... 173 C3
Torquay TQ1 ... 220 B5
Penn Torr TQ8 ... 259 D4
Penn View TQ5 ... 230 D3
Pennyacre Rd TQ14 ... 210 C6
Penny Cl
Exminster EX6 ... 182 A4
Wellington TA21 ... 160 D7
Pennycombe La EX6 ... 114 E4
PENNYCOMEQUICK ... 262 B4
Pennycomequick Hill
PL4 ... 262 B4
PENNYCROSS ... 248 C8
Pennycross Cl PL2 ... 248 D8
Pennycross Park Rd
PL2 ... 248 C7
Pennycross Prim Sch
PL2 ... 248 C8
Penny Hill EX33 ... 7 E2
PENNYMOOR ... 62 D6
Penny Plot DT7 ... 260 C4
Penny's Hill TQ1 ... 219 F7
Penny's La PL9 ... 256 D6
Penny's Terr EX13 ... 167 D5
Penny Thorn Cross
EX14 ... 85 E7
Pennywell Cl TQ13 ... 131 B1
Pennywell Farm &
Wildlife Ctr★ TQ11 ... 135 E6
Penpethy Cl TQ5 ... 230 B4
Penpethy Rd TQ5 ... 230 B5
PENQUIT ... 237 F1
Penrith Cl PL6 ... 245 D3
Penrith Gdns PL6 ... 245 D3
Penrith Wlk PL6 ... 245 D3
Penrose Almshouses 4
EX32 ... 155 A4
Penrose St PL1 ... 262 B3
Penroses Terr 9
EX22 ... 164 C4
Penrose Terr 7 EX1 ... 261 A2
Penrose Villas 5
PL4 ... 248 F4
Penryn Pl 4 TQ14 ... 210 A3
Penry Rd EX3 ... 182 B7
Penscombe Cross
PL15 ... 115 A6
Penshill La EX36 ... 31 C2
Penshurst Rd TQ12 ... 207 B1
Pensilva Pk TQ5 ... 230 C2
Pens La EX15 ... 67 B7
Penson Cross EX20 ... 59 B1
Penson La EX20 ... 77 B8
PENSTONE ... 79 B3
Penstone Barns EX5 ... 82 E4
Penswell Cross TQ10 ... 135 E4
Pentamar St PL2 ... 247 E4
Pentgrove Ct EX8 ... 202 D7
Pentice La EX34 ... 3 A3
Pentillie Cl 20 PL20 ... 125 E1
Pentillie Cres PL4 ... 248 D4
Pentillie Rd
Bere Alston PL20 ... 125 E1
Plymouth PL4 ... 248 E4
Pentillie View 21
PL20 ... 125 E1
Pentire Rd PL11 ... 246 F3
Pentland Cl PL6 ... 244 F7
Penton Cl EX17 ... 165 D6
Penton La EX17 ... 165 D5
Penton Rise EX17 ... 165 D6
Pentridge Ave TQ2 ... 219 C2
Pentyre Ct PL4 ... 263 C4
Pentyre Terr PL4 ... 263 C4
Penwill Way TQ4 ... 226 A4
Pen-y-dre EX15 ... 163 C4
Peoples Park Rd
EX17 ... 165 C6
PEPPERCOMBE ... 24 E2
Peppercombe Ave
EX1 ... 178 D7
Pepperdon Common
TQ13 ... 112 B4
Pepperdon Hall La
TQ13 ... 112 B3
Pepper La
Kingswear TQ6 ... 234 E4
Plymouth PL9 ... 256 D7
Pepper's Cnr EX9 ... 198 F7
Pepper St PL19 ... 171 C6
Peppery La TQ14 ... 209 D5
Pepys Pl PL5 ... 244 E1
Perceval Rd EX4 ... 174 A2
Perches Cl PL8 ... 141 B7
Percy Cross EX14 ... 67 B2
Percy Rd EX2 ... 177 B3
Percy St PL5 ... 243 D1
Percy Terr PL4 ... 249 A4
Peregrine Cl TQ2 ... 213 D3
Peregrine Rd PL6 ... 245 B2
Perinville Cl TQ1 ... 220 E6
Perinville Rd TQ1 ... 220 D7
Periwinkle Dr
Barnstaple EX31 ... 154 B3
Plymouth PL7 ... 251 C5
Perkins Cross EX5 ... 99 C1
PERKIN'S VILLAGE ... 99 C2
Perranporth Cl PL5 ... 243 E4
Perreyman Sq 7
EX16 ... 161 D4
Perriam's Pl EX9 ... 199 G2
Perridge Cl EX2 ... 176 E3
Perridge Cross EX6 ... 98 E1
Perridge La
Longdown EX6 ... 98 E1
Sidbury EX10 ... 101 F8
Perriman's Row EX8 ... 202 A7
Perrin Way EX4 ... 174 D1
Perriton Cross EX5 ... 99 E8
Perros Cl TQ14 ... 209 D8
Perry Cl PL19 ... 171 B6
Perry Cross TQ12 ... 206 D7
Perryfield Pl
8 Plymouth PL3 ... 249 D1
Pomphlett PL9 ... 249 D1
Perry Hill EX17 ... 80 E8
Perry La
Doddiscombsleigh
EX6 ... 113 D5
Newton Abbot TQ12 ... 206 D6
Perryman Cl PL7 ... 250 E7
Perryman's Hill EX17 ... 79 F7
Perry New Rd TA22 ... 33 F4
Perry Rd EX4 ... 177 B8
Perrys Gdns EX11 ... 168 D4
Perry St TA20 ... 88 D8
PERRY STREET ... 88 E8
Perseus Cres PL9 ... 256 E8
Perseverance Cotts 1
PL7 ... 250 E7
Perth Cl EX4 ... 173 E2
Peryam Cres EX2 ... 178 A4
Peryn Rd PL19 ... 171 A5
Peterborough Rd
EX4 ... 176 E7
Peterclose Rd EX16 ... 161 F3
Peter Hopper's Hill
PL5 ... 240 C2
Peters Cl TQ3 ... 225 F1
Peter's Cl PL9 ... 256 C7
Peters Cres TQ3 ... 218 D3
Petersfield EX1 ... 174 F2
Peters Field PL8 ... 141 A7
Petersfield Cl PL3 ... 249 B6
PETER'S FINGER ... 105 B7
Peters Park Cl PL5 ... 243 E1
Peter's Park La PL5 ... 243 E1
Peter St EX5 ... 82 F7
Peter's Well Hill EX17 ... 61 E5
PETER TAVY ... 117 F4
Petertavy Cross PL19 ... 117 E3
Petherton EX16 ... 65 A7
Pethick Cl PL6 ... 244 D6
Pethill Cl PL6 ... 245 F2
Pethybridge TQ13 ... 122 B8
Petitor Mews TQ1 ... 214 B1
Petitor Rd TQ1 ... 214 C1
Petit Well La TQ1 ... 214 B1
Petrel Cl TQ2 ... 213 C3
Petre Street EX13 ... 167 E7
PETROC
Barnstaple EX31 ... 154 E3
Tiverton EX16 ... 161 C6
Petroc (Brannams)
EX31 ... 154 C2
Petroc Ct PL18 ... 125 A6
Petroc Dr TQ12 ... 207 C4
PETROCKSTOW ... 56 F4
Petticoat La EX13 ... 167 A6
PETTON ... 35 A3
Petton Cross EX16 ... 35 A3
PEVERELL ... 248 D6
Peverell Park Rd
PL3 ... 248 D6
Peverell Terr PL3 ... 248 D5
Pew Tor Cl
Tavistock PL19 ... 171 E5
3 Yelverton PL20 ... 126 F3
Phear Ave EX8 ... 202 B7
Phelps Rd PL1 ... 247 E2
PHILHAM ... 22 D1
Philham Cross EX39 ... 22 D1
Philham La EX39 ... 22 D1
Philham Water EX39 ... 22 D1
Philip Ave EX31 ... 154 D2
Philip Cl PL9 ... 256 A6
Philip Gdns PL9 ... 255 F6
Philip Ho EX1 ... 178 E6
Philip Rd EX4 ... 177 F8
Philips La 2 EX33 ... 152 D5
Phillimore St 3 PL2 ... 247 F4
Phillipps Ave EX8 ... 196 B1
Phillips Ct EX13 ... 167 D5
Phillips Path 12 TQ7 ... 143 E7
Phillips Sq EX14 ... 166 B6
Philpott La PL19 ... 171 B2
Phobe Cl PL18 ... 125 B5
Phoenix Bsns Pk PL6 ... 245 F4
Phoenix Cl 9 PL20 ... 126 F4
Phoenix La EX16 ... 161 D3
Phoenix Pl
Kingsbridge TQ7 ... 258 C5
West Alvington TQ7 ... 258 B4
Phoenix Rd EX13 ... 161 D3
Phoenix St PL1 ... 262 A2
Piazza Terracina EX2 ... 261 B1
Picket Head Hill
TQ14 ... 210 A2
Picklecombe Dr
TQ12 ... 244 E4
Pick Pie Dr PL6 ... 245 E8
Picton Pl TA22 ... 33 D6
Pidgeley Rd EX7 ... 204 F8
Pidgeon's La EX13 ... 104 B7
Pidgley Rd EX7 ... 200 E1
Pidland La EX16 ... 47 F1
Pidsley Cres EX3 ... 182 D7
Pidsley Hill EX17 ... 79 F7
Pidsley La EX17 ... 79 F8
Piece Hill EX6 ... 97 E4
Piend La EX17 ... 62 B1
Pier Head EX8 ... 201 E6
Pier La PL10 ... 253 A1
Piermont Pl EX7 ... 204 E6
Pier St PL1 ... 262 B1
Piggy La EX39 ... 156 F7
Pig La EX13 ... 167 D6
Pigs Leg Cross EX20 ... 108 A8
Pigspark Cross TQ13 ... 131 A5
Pike Rd PL3 ... 249 D5
Pikes Hill EX6 ... 97 E3
Pike's Mead EX20 ... 170 B4
Pilchers Field PL20 ... 126 E3
Pilcock La
Alswear EX36 ... 30 B1
Alswear EX37 ... 45 B8
Pilemoor La EX16 ... 48 E3
Pilemore Cross EX16 ... 48 E4
Piley La TA21 ... 51 D8
Pilgrim Cl
Brixham TQ5 ... 230 E5
Plymouth PL2 ... 248 B6
Pilgrim Ct 11 PL20 ... 125 E1
Pilgrim Dr PL20 ... 125 E1
Pilgrim Prim Sch
PL1 ... 262 B3
Pilland Way EX31 ... 154 D6
Pillar Ave TQ5 ... 230 B5
Pillar Cl TQ5 ... 230 B5
Pillar Cres TQ5 ... 230 B5
Pillar Ct TQ5 ... 230 B5
Pillar Flats TQ5 ... 230 B5
Pillar Wlk PL6 ... 244 E7
Pillavins La EX36 ... 158 F6
Pill Gdns EX33 ... 152 D5
PILLHEAD ... 157 F2
Pill Ho EX32 ... 155 A2
Pilliven Cross EX16 ... 46 F2
Pilliven La EX16 ... 47 A2
Pill La
Barnstaple EX32 ... 155 A2
Saltash PL12 ... 242 E4
Pill Lawn EX32 ... 155 A2
Pillmere Dr PL12 ... 242 D4
Pillory Hill PL8 ... 140 F6
Pill Rd EX39 ... 157 A2
Pill View EX31 ... 153 E6
Pilmuir Ave TQ2 ... 219 E5
PILTON ... 154 E6
Pilton Bluecoat CE Acad
Jun Sch EX31 ... 154 E6
Pilton Com Coll EX31 ... 154 E7
Pilton Cswy EX32 ... 154 F6
Pilton Inf Sch EX31 ... 154 F6
Pilton La EX1 ... 178 D8
Pilton Lawn
Barnstaple EX31 ... 154 F6
7 Barnstaple EX32 ... 155 A7
Pilton Quay EX31 ... 154 F6
Pilton Row EX1 ... 175 A3
Pilton St EX31 ... 154 F6
Pimlico TQ1 ... 220 B5
Pimm Rd TQ3 ... 225 E7
Pinaster Cl EX14 ... 166 E5
Pinbridge Mews EX4 ... 174 D1
Pinbrook Ind Est
EX4 ... 174 D1
Pinbrook Mews EX4 ... 174 C2
Pinbrook Rd EX4 ... 174 D1
Pinbrook Units EX4 ... 174 D1
Pinces Cotts EX2 ... 177 A3
Pinces Gdns EX2 ... 177 A3
Pinces Rd EX2 ... 177 A3
Pinch Hill EX23 ... 70 A7
Pincombe Cnr EX36 ... 31 B3
Pincombe Rd EX39 ... 25 C4
Pinder Ct PL19 ... 171 B5
Pine Ave EX4 ... 176 F7
Pine Cl
Brixham TQ5 ... 230 B2
Pine Cl *continued*
Ilfracombe EX34 ... 150 E4
Teignmouth TQ14 ... 210 D7
Tiverton EX16 ... 161 B4
Pine Ct TQ1 ... 220 D5
Pinefields Cl EX11 ... 168 E3
Pine Gdns
Honiton EX14 ... 166 D6
Plymouth PL2 ... 248 E6
Pine Gr EX14 ... 166 D6
Pinehurst Way PL21 ... 237 A6
Pine Park Rd EX14 ... 166 D5
Pine Ridge DT7 ... 260 E5
Pineridge Cl EX4 ... 176 F4
Pines Cl
Hartland EX39 ... 22 E3
Westward Ho! EX39 ... 156 B6
Pines Rd
Exmouth EX8 ... 196 D3
Paignton TQ3 ... 225 F8
Pines The
Exeter EX4 ... 176 F7
Honiton EX14 ... 166 D5
Pine Tree Cl EX7 ... 201 B2
Pine View PL18 ... 125 D6
Pine View Ave TQ1 ... 220 C6
Pine View Cl
Exmouth EX8 ... 196 F2
Halwill Junction EX21 ... 73 E3
Pine View Gdns TQ1 ... 220 C6
Pine View Rd TQ1 ... 220 C6
Pine Wlk DT7 ... 260 D2
Pinewood Cl
Dawlish EX7 ... 205 A8
Plymouth PL7 ... 250 F6
Pinewood Ct TQ4 ... 226 C5
Pinewood Dr PL6 ... 245 E7
Pinewood La EX4 ... 174 B2
Pinewood Rd TQ12 ... 207 E2
PINHAY ... 104 B2
Pinhay Hollow DT7 ... 104 B2
Pinhey's Cross TQ9 ... 144 F5
PINHOE ... 174 F2
Pinhoe CE Prim Sch
EX4 ... 174 E1
Pinhoe Sta EX1 ... 174 E1
Pinhoe Trad Est EX4 ... 174 D1
Pinkhams Cotts PL12 ... 242 B6
Pinksmoor La TA21 ... 51 E7
Pinkworthy Cross
EX16 ... 48 C8
Pinkworthy Hill EX16 ... 48 B7
Pin La PL1 ... 263 A2
Pinnacle Quay PL4 ... 263 B2
Pinnacle The TQ12 ... 207 A1
Pinnbridge Ct 7
EX1 ... 178 E8
Pinncourt La EX1 ... 174 F2
Pinnex Moor Rd
EX16 ... 161 E6
Pinn Hill EX1 ... 174 F2
Pinn La
Exeter EX1 ... 178 F7
Exeter EX1 ... 178 F8
Otterton EX10 ... 187 B2
Pinn Lane Cnr EX10 ... 187 A1
Pinn Valley Rd EX1 ... 174 F1
Pinslow Cross PL15 ... 105 B8
Pins Pk EX22 ... 164 C5
Pintail La EX3 ... 182 E6
Pintail Way PL6 ... 245 B2
Pinwill Cres PL21 ... 137 A4
Pinwood La EX4 ... 174 B1
Pinwood Meadow Dr
EX4 ... 174 B2
Pioneer Cotts EX12 ... 191 D5
Pioneer Terr TQ11 ... 236 A5
Pipehouse La TQ13 ... 123 C4
Pipers Cross TQ7 ... 142 C7
Pipers Pl EX14 ... 68 C2
Piper St PL6 ... 245 B5
Pipistrelle Rd TQ12 ... 207 A5
Pipistrelle Way TQ12 ... 207 C8
Pippin Cl EX1 ... 178 C6
Pippin La PL9 ... 256 E7
Pippin Pl TQ7 ... 258 D7
Pippins EX12 ... 191 D5
Pippins Field EX15 ... 66 A7
Pippins The PL21 ... 237 A5
Piran Cl PL18 ... 125 A6
Pirates Bay Adventure
Golf★ TQ4 ... 226 C6
Pisces St PL9 ... 256 E8
Piscombe La EX9 ... 198 F7
Pissleton La
Crediton EX17 ... 61 A1
Morchard Bishop EX17 ... 60 F1
Pitcairn Cres TQ2 ... 213 E3
Pitchingstone Cross
TQ7 ... 147 C7
Pitcombe La TA4 ... 35 B5
Pitfield Cl EX15 ... 162 D3
Pitham La EX11 ... 169 F7
Pit Hill EX34 ... 2 D4
Pitland Cnr PL19 ... 117 B4
Pitland La TQ12 ... 213 E6
Pitlands La EX15 ... 67 A8
Pitley Cross TQ13 ... 131 A5
Pitley Hill TQ13 ... 131 B5
Pitley Rd TQ13 ... 131 B5
Pitman's La PL21 ... 133 C2
Pitsham La TA4 ... 34 E6
Pits La PL10 ... 140 H2
Pitson La EX10 ... 187 A5
Pitt Ave 12 EX39 ... 15 A1

Pitt Cres TQ4 224 B7
Pitt Cross EX39 22 C4
Pitt Ct
8 Appledore EX39 15 A1
Loddiswell TQ7 143 F7
Pitt Hill
Appledore EX39 157 B8
Crediton EX17 79 F3
Kenton EX6 194 D3
Shebbear EX21 55 D4
Pitt Hill Rd TQ12 206 F4
Pitt Ho TQ13 123 D5
Pitt La
Bideford EX39 157 A2
Bow EX17 78 B5
Butterleigh EX16 64 C4
Cadbury EX5 81 C8
Chevithorne EX16 49 D2
Dawlish EX7 204 B7
Huish Champflower TA4 35 E8
North Molton EX36 30 F8
Thorverton EX5 81 F7
Waterrow TA4 35 F5
Pitton Cross EX6 96 E5
Pitt Pk 12 EX5 99 A6
Pitts Cleave Ind Est PL19 117 D3
Pitts Cnr EX16 63 D4
Pitts Ct EX2 261 C1
Pixey Plain EX36 31 B3
Pixie Dell EX33 152 B7
Pixie La EX33 152 C6
Pixie Wlk EX11 169 B3
Pixon La PL19 171 B4
Pixon Trad Ctr 2 PL19 171 B4
Pixton Cross EX19 58 B2
Pixton Way TA22 33 E6
Place Cross
Ashburton TQ13 131 A6
Okehampton EX20 93 E5
Place de Brest PL1 262 C3
Place La TQ13 131 A5
Plainfield La EX16 63 C7
PLAINMOOR 220 B7
Plainmoor Rd 3 TQ1 220 B7
Plainmoor (Torquay United FC) TQ1 220 B7
Plains The TQ9 223 D5
Plaistow Cl PL5 243 E2
Plaistow Cres PL5 243 E2
Plaistow Hill Inf Sch PL5 243 E2
Plantagenet Dr EX15 163 C6
Plantagenet Wlk EX2 178 D4
Plantation Cl TQ12 207 F1
Plantation Terr EX7 204 E6
Plantation Way
Torquay TQ2 213 C1
Torquay TQ2 213 C2
Totnes TQ9 222 F6
Plant World (Gdns)★ TQ12 213 C7
Plassey Cl EX4 173 D2
Plaston Gn EX6 112 D5
Platt Cl TQ8 259 B4
Plat The TQ6 145 E5
Platway La TQ14 209 D5
Play Cross TQ13 130 A4
Playmoor Cotts EX1 174 E1
Playmoor Dr EX1 174 F1
PLEAMORE CROSS 160 A2
Pleasant Terr 1 TQ3 226 A6
Pleasure Hill Cl PL9 255 D8
Plintona View PL7 250 E7
Ploudal Rd EX15 163 B2
Plougastel Dr PL12 242 E3
Plough Gn PL12 242 C3
Ploughman Way PL8 136 A2
Plover Cl EX3 182 E6
Plover Rise PL21 237 B5
Plumbpk Ave EX8 202 E7
Plume of Feathers Cl EX11 169 E4
Plumer Rd PL6 244 F2
Plumper's Cross EX38 41 A7
Plumtree Dr EX2 178 B4
Plumtree La EX5 99 E7
Plum Way EX15 162 D4
Plymbridge Gdns PL7 250 C7
Plymbridge La PL6 245 B4
Plymbridge Rd
Plymouth, Eggbuckland PL6 245 C1
Plymouth, Estover PL6 245 E5
Plymouth, Mainstone PL6 245 F2
Plymouth, Plympton PL7 250 C7
Plym Cl TQ2 219 B7
Plym Cres PL19 171 D5
PLYMOUTH 262 C1
Plymouth Arts Ctr★ PL4 263 A2
Plymouth Athenaeum & Theatre★ PL1 262 B2
Plymouth Business Sch PL4 263 A3
Plymouth City Mus & Art Gal★ PL4 263 A3
Plymouth Coll Inf Sch 4 PL3 248 F5
Plymouth Coll of Art PL4 263 A3
Plymouth Coll Prep Sch PL1 262 A3
Plymouth Coll (Senior Sch) PL4 248 E4
Plymouth Discovery Ctr★ PL3 249 F6
Plymouth Ent Pk PL5 243 D5
Plymouth Gin Distillery★ PL4 263 A2
Plymouth Hill PL20 128 A8
Plymouth Hospl, Nuffield Health (private) PL6 245 B4
Plymouth Life Ctr PL2 248 C5
Plymouth Lipson Vale Prim Sch PL4 249 A4
Plymouth Marjon Univ PL6 245 C4
Plymouth Medical & Tech Pk PL6 245 A3
Plymouth Pavilions PL1 262 B2
Plymouth Rd
Buckfastleigh TQ11 236 B4
Buckfastleigh, Lower Dean TQ11 236 A3
Chudleigh Knighton TQ12 123 D4
Kingsbridge TQ7 258 C6
Plymouth PL7 250 B6
South Brent TQ10 134 F2
Tavistock PL19 171 B4
Totnes TQ9 223 B5
Plymouth Road Ind Est PL19 171 C3
Plymouth Sch of Creative Arts PL1 262 A2
Plymouth Science Pk PL6 245 C4
Plymouth Ski & Snowboard Ctr★ PL6 249 E7
Plymouth Sta PL4 262 C4
Plymouth Trade Pk PL4 263 C1
Plymouth Univ Marine Sta PL3 263 A3
Plymouth Univ Marine Stn PL1 263 B1
PLYMPTON 250 E5
Plympton Cross TQ7 147 F5
Plympton Hill PL7 250 F3
Plympton St Mary Inf & Old Priory Jun Acad PL7 250 D5
PLYMPTON ST MAURICE 250 E4
Plympton St Maurice Prim Sch PL7 250 F3
Plym St PL4 263 A3
PLYMSTOCK 255 E6
Plymstock Rd PL9 255 D7
Plymstock Sch PL9 255 F8
Plymstock Sp Ctr PL9 255 F8
PLYMTREE 83 E5
Plymtree CE Prim Sch EX15 83 F5
Plymtree Dr PL7 250 C7
Plym Valley Mdws PL6 249 F8
Plym Valley Rly★ PL7 250 A7
Plymview Cl PL3 249 D6
Poadmarsh Cross EX36 31 D1
Poadmarsh Hill
Ash Mill EX36 31 D1
Bishops Nympton EX36 30 F1
Rose Ash EX16 46 D8
Pocklington Rise PL7 250 E5
Pocombe Hill EX2 176 D3
Pode Dr PL7 251 B4
Pod La EX13 87 F4
Poets Corner TQ12 244 C1
Point In View Cotts EX8 196 B3
Point Terr EX8 201 E6
POINT THE 201 E7
POLEHAYS 74 B1
Polehouse La EX2 176 E1
Pole Rue TA20 69 F6
Pole Rue La TA20 69 F6
Poles Hill EX31 154 E7
Poleshill La EX31 154 D7
Polhearne La TQ5 230 B3
Polhearne Way TQ5 230 B3
Pollard Cl
Plymouth PL9 255 B5
Saltash PL12 242 B2
Pollardscl EX4 174 D1
Pollard's La TA21 52 F7
Pollards Pl EX39 157 C2
Pollards The EX32 155 C3
Pollards Way
Saltash PL12 242 E3
Saltash PL12 242 E4
Pollyblank Rd 2 TQ12 207 B3
Pollybrook EX5 184 C2
Polmer Mews EX9 199 G2
Polperro Pl 3 PL2 248 D8
Polruan Terr PL1 262 A3
Polsham Pk TQ3 226 B7
Polsloe Bridge Sta EX4 178 A7
POLSLOE PARK 177 E7
POLSLOE PRIORY 177 F8
Polsloe Rd EX1 177 E6
Polson Hill EX17 61 A2
POLTIMORE 174 F6
Poltimore Cl EX36 158 D4
Poltimore Cross EX4 174 E6
Poltimore Ct EX4 174 F7
Poltimore Dr 6 EX1 178 E8
Poltimore House★ EX4 174 F5
Poltimore Lawn EX32 155 B6
Poltimore Rd
Farway EX24 101 F7
Offwell EX14, EX24 102 A8
South Molton EX36 158 D4
Poltimore Sq EX4 261 B4
Poltimore Way EX4 175 A4
Polwhele Rd 14 EX16 64 D7
Polywell EX39 14 F1
Polzeath Gdns 1 PL2 248 D8
Pomarine Cl EX23 70 A8
Pomeroy Ave TQ5 230 A5
Pomeroy Pl 8 TQ12 122 F1
Pomeroy Rd
Newton Abbot TQ12 207 B3
Tiverton EX16 64 E8
Pomeroy Villas TQ9 223 D6
POMPHLETT 255 E8
Pomphlett Cl PL9 255 D8
Pomphlett Farm Ind Est PL9 249 E1
Pomphlett Gdns PL9 255 D8
Pomphlett Prim Sch PL9 255 E8
Pomphlett Rd PL9 255 E8
Pondfield Rd PL12 242 B3
Pond Hill EX16 65 A7
Pond La TA21 51 D3
Ponsford Cross EX15 65 A2
Ponsford La EX15 65 A2
Ponsonby Rd
Plymouth PL3 248 B4
Plymouth PL3 262 A4
PONSWORTHY 130 A8
Pooks La TQ13 130 F5
Pool Anthony Dr EX16 64 E8
Pool Cross EX20 107 F8
POOLE 160 F8
Poole Cross TQ12 211 A1
Poole Gate EX4 177 B8
Poole Hill TA22 33 B5
Poole Ind Est TA21 160 F8
Poole La EX34 8 B7
Poole Park Rd PL5 247 C8
Poole's Ct DT7 260 E3
Pooley Cross TQ7 143 E4
Pool Hill
Ashbrittle TA21 35 E1
Bridestowe EX20 107 F8
Pool La
Burrington EX37 44 A4
Chittlehampton EX37 29 A1
Woolacombe EX34 1 B1
Poolmill Cross TQ13 112 E1
Pool Pk TQ10 135 A3
Pools Weir TQ12 214 B8
Popes Cl EX17 165 C6
Popes La EX24 103 A3
Pope'S La EX20 59 B1
Pope's La
Lapford EX17 60 C3
Rockwell Green TA21 160 B4
POPHAM 19 A3
Popham Cl EX16 161 F4
Popham Cross EX36 19 A3
Popham Flats TA21 160 D6
Popham La EX36 19 A3
Popham Rd TA21 160 F7
Pop La EX13, TA20 88 B8
Poplar Cl
Brixham TQ5 229 F2
Exeter EX2 177 A3
Exmouth EX8 196 D3
Newton Abbot TQ12 213 A8
Plymouth PL7 251 B5
Poplar Dr TQ7 258 C5
Poplar Mount EX13 167 D6
Poplar Row EX9 199 H2
Poplars Dr TQ3 218 D2
Poplars The
7 Chudleigh Knighton TQ13 123 C4
Exeter EX4 174 E2
Poplars Wlk EX5 179 E2
Poplar Terr
High Bickington EX37 43 C7
Ipplepen TQ12 211 D2
Poplar Tree Cnr EX12 192 A8
Poplar Tree Dr EX12 192 A7
Poppin Ct EX3 182 E8
Popplestone Pk PL8 256 F5
Poppy Cl
Exeter EX4 176 D8
Mile End TQ12 206 D5
Tavistock PL19 171 A5
Popular EX7 201 A2
Porch EX13 88 A3
Porch Cotts 18 EX10 101 B1
Porcher Dr EX5 179 B3
Pork Hill PL19 117 F1
Porlock Way TQ4 225 F2
Porsham Cl PL6 241 B1
Porsham La PL5 244 E8
Porspoder Pl PL10 253 A2
Portal Pl PL21 237 B5
Portbridge Cross TQ9 215 F8
Portchester Hts EX4 261 C4
Port Cross
Bishops Nympton EX36 31 B4
Kentisbury EX31 10 F5
Porteous Cl PL1 247 F3
Porter's La EX8 195 E8
Porter Way PL12 242 C3
Portford Cross EX31 27 E3
Portford La TQ10 135 A2
PORTGATE 106 C4
Portgate Cross EX36 30 B8
Port Hill EX31 10 F5
PORTINGTON 116 C3
Port La
Bishops Nympton EX36 31 C4
Bury TA22 34 A5
Chillington TQ7 145 A1
Wotter PL7 132 C4
Portland Ave
Exmouth EX8 202 B6
Teignmouth TQ14 210 C7
Portland Bldgs 6 EX32 155 A6
Portland Ct
19 Barnstaple EX32 155 A4
Lyme Regis DT7 260 C3
9 Plymouth PL1 247 F3
Torquay TQ1 220 D7
Portland La
Kilmington EX13 103 C8
Kilmington EX24 103 C8
Meavy PL20 127 D2
Portland Pk EX34 150 C6
Portland Rd
Plymouth PL1 247 F3
Torquay TQ1 220 D7
Portland Sq PL4 262 C4
Portland Sq La N PL3 262 C4
Portland Square Lane N PL4 263 A4
Portland St
Barnstaple EX32 155 B3
Exeter EX1 177 E6
Ilfracombe EX34 150 C6
Portland Villas PL4 262 C4
Port Lane Cl TQ7 144 F1
Portledge Pl EX39 25 A3
Portlemore Cl TQ7 147 E6
Portlemore Gdns TQ7 147 E6
Portmarsh La EX32 155 A4
Port Mer Cl EX8 196 E3
Port Rd EX6 200 D4
Portsmouth Arms Cross EX18 60 B7
Portsmouth Arms Sta EX37 43 F6
Portugal Way EX20 170 D5
Portway EX15 66 C7
Portway Cl PL9 256 D7
Portway Gdns EX15 162 C3
POSBURY 97 F8
Possession Cross EX37 28 E7
Post Box Cross
Bondleigh EX20 76 F6
Cheriton Fitzpaine EX17 63 B3
POSTBRIDGE 120 A6
Postbury Pl EX1 178 D7
Post Cl TA21 160 E4
Post Coach Wy 19 EX5 99 A6
Post Cross EX15 65 F2
Post Cross Bsns Pk EX15 65 F2
Post Hill EX16 64 E8
Post La
Cotleigh EX14 86 C7
Malmsmead EX35 6 C4
Skilgate TA4 34 E7
Post Office La
Cheriton Fitzpaine EX17 62 F1
Tatworth TA20 88 C8
Westleigh EX16 51 A4
Potacre St EX38 159 D5
Potems' Cross EX37 27 F1
Potshop Cross EX17 79 D2
Potters Cl EX11 168 D5
Potter's Cross TA4 35 C7
Potters Hill TQ1 220 B5
Potters La TA20 69 E6
Potters Stile EX14 67 B1
Potters Way PL7 250 D5
Potterswell EX31 154 B3
Potters Yd TQ12 180 B1
Pottery Cl
Bovey Tracey TQ13 180 C5
Honiton EX14 166 D6
Pottery Ct TQ6 233 D4
Pottery Est PL10 252 E6
Pottery La EX31 153 A4
Pottery Mews TQ3 218 D3
Pottery Rd
Bovey Tracey TQ13 180 C5
Kingsteignton TQ12 207 D6
Plymouth PL1 247 D3
Pottery Units TQ12 207 D4
POTTINGTON 154 D6
Pottington Bsns Pk EX31 154 C6
Pottington Dr EX31 154 E6
Pottington Ind Est EX31 154 D5
Pottington Rd EX31 154 E6
Pottles Cl EX6 182 B3
POUGHILL 62 D3
Poultney Cl PL7 251 A5
Pouncel La 16 EX5 99 A6
Pouncers Cross EX18 60 E6
Pound Cl
Burrington EX37 43 F3
Exmouth EX8 196 C1
Sidbury EX10 101 B2
Topsham EX3 182 E6
Pound Cnr
Clyst Honiton EX5 179 E7
Whitestone EX4 98 C5
Pound Cross EX5 99 B5
Pound Down Cnr EX4 98 D5
Pound Field TQ9 227 F8
Poundfield Cl EX31 153 F5
Pound Gate EX6 112 F5
Pound Hill
Axmouth EX12 192 D7
Holcombe Rogus TA21 51 A5
Poundhouse Cross TQ6 146 B8
Pound La
Bridford EX6 113 A5
Buckland St Mary TA20 69 D8
Colaton Raleigh EX10 186 C5
15 Combe Martin EX34 3 A3
Exmouth EX8 196 C1
High Bickington EX37 43 C8
Kentisbury EX31 10 F5
Kingskerswell TQ12 212 F4
Nadderwater EX4 98 F4
Parracombe EX31 4 C2
Parracombe EX31 11 C8
Raymond's Hill DT6 104 D8
Shaldon TQ14 209 C5
Stoke Climsland PL17 115 C1
5 Teignmouth TQ14 210 C4
Topsham EX3 182 E6
Uplyme DT7 260 B5
Upottery EX14 68 C1
Woodbury EX5 184 C3
Yarcombe EX14 69 B2
Pound La End EX37 28 C3
Pound Lane End EX37 43 D8
Pound Lane Trad Est EX8 196 C1
Pound Mdw
Great Torrington EX38 42 B7
Hatherleigh EX20 75 C7
Parkham EX39 39 E8
Pound Pk EX20 170 D6
Pound Pl
Bovey Tracey TQ13 180 D8
19 Newton Abbot TQ12 207 B3
Pound Rd
Axminster EX13 88 F2
Crapstone PL20 126 E3
Lyme Regis DT7 260 D3
Poundsclose TA22 33 E4
Pound's Cross PL6 240 E5
POUNDSGATE 130 A7
Poundsgate Cl TQ5 230 E4
Pounds Hill EX17 165 D6
Poundshill Cross EX17 165 D6
Poundsland EX5 175 C6
Pounds Park Rd
1 Bere Alston PL20 125 E1
Plymouth PL3 248 D7
Pounds Pk PL12 242 F3
Pound Sq EX15 163 C2
Pound St
Exmouth EX8 202 A6
Lyme Regis DT7 260 D3
Moretonhampstead TQ13 111 F4
Plymouth PL1 254 A8
Poundstone Ct TQ8 259 D4
Pound Terr 3 TA21 160 D5
Pound Wall EX4 175 C6
Poundwell Ho 8 PL21 137 B2
Poundwell Mdws 7 PL21 137 B2
Poundwell St 9 PL21 137 B2
Powderham Castle★ EX6 194 F4
Powderham Cl
Newton Abbot TQ12 207 B2
Topsham EX3 182 E6
Powderham Cres EX4 177 D8
Powderham Ct
20 Newton Abbot TQ12 207 B3
21 Teignmouth TQ14 210 C4
Powderham Rd
Exeter EX2 177 A4
Newton Abbot TQ12 207 B2
Plymouth PL3 248 F7
Torquay TQ2 213 F1
Powderham Terr
Newton Abbot TQ12 207 B2
3 Shaldon TQ14 209 F5
Teignmouth TQ14 210 C4
Powderham Wlk EX6 181 F5
Powell Cl EX12 192 A6
Powells Way EX14 67 C1
Powis Gdns PL5 244 B2
Powisland Dr PL6 245 A5
Powlers Piece Pk EX22 39 C5
Powlesland La EX17 95 E6
Powlesland Rd EX4 177 B1
Powys Ho EX10 188 A4
Poyers EX33 152 E4
Pratt's La TQ7 143 B7
Precinct The TQ7 258 D6
Premier Pl EX2 261 C2
Prescot Rd EX4 176 E5
PRESCOTT 51 C1
Prescott Rd EX15 51 D1
Prestbury Ct EX4 176 D8
Prestbury Pk 4 TQ2 219 F5
PRESTON 226 B8
Preston Barns TQ9 222 D1
Prestonbury Cl PL6 245 B7
Preston Cross
Loddiswell TQ7 138 E3
West Alvington TQ7 143 E2
Preston Down Ave TQ3 219 B2
Preston Down Rd TQ3 219 C1
Preston Fork TQ9 138 E2
Preston Gate EX31 10 E6
Preston La EX17 80 D7
Preston Prim Sch TQ2 219 D2
Preston St EX1 261 A2
Prestor EX13 167 E5
Pretoria Rd EX1 177 F7
Pretoria Terr EX34 150 A3
Pretty Oak Main TA20 69 F6
Pretty Top
Little Torrington EX20 41 F1
Petrockstow EX20 56 F8
Prices Ave TA21 160 D7
Prickly Ball Farm & Hedgehog Hospl★ TQ12 211 F7
Priddis Cl EX8 196 C3
Priddles La TA20 69 F8
Prideaux Cl PL12 242 C5
Prideaux Cres EX16 161 D6
Prideaux Ct 22 PL1 263 A2
Prideaux La TQ6 145 F6
Prideaux Mdw EX38 159 F5
Prideaux Rd PL21 237 E6
Pridham La PL2 248 D7
Pridhams Way EX6 182 A4
PRIESTACOTT 55 C1
Priest Hill EX15 66 A3
Priesthood Terr PL10 252 E5
Priestley Ave
Exeter EX4 178 B8
Plymouth PL5 243 E2
Prigg Mdw TQ13 130 F4
Primley Cross TQ3 225 F5
Primley Ct TQ3 225 E5
Primley Gdns EX10 188 C7
Primley Mead EX10 188 C7
Primley Paddock EX10 188 B7
Primley Park E TQ3 226 A5
Primley Pk TQ3 225 F5
Primley Rd EX10 188 B7
Primrose Ave EX32 155 E4
Primrose Cl
Chillington TQ7 144 F1
Ivybridge PL21 237 D5
Kingsteignton TQ12 207 E7
6 Tiverton EX16 161 F6
Torpoint PL11 246 E4
Primrose Dr
Mile End TQ12 206 D5
Newton Abbot TQ12 206 D5
Primrose Gdns PL19 171 E4
Primrose La
Northam EX39 157 B8
Wrangaton TQ10 134 E1
Primrose Lawn EX4 176 D8
Primrose Mdw PL21 237 A6
Primrose Pk EX16 49 C8
Primrose Way
Crediton EX17 165 E6
Kingskerswell TQ12 212 F6
Seaton EX12 192 B7
Primrose Wlk PL12 242 D4
Prince Charles Cl EX8 196 E1
Prince Charles Ct TQ2 214 A3
Prince Charles Rd EX4 177 F8
Prince Charles Way EX12 192 A8
Prince Maurice Ct PL4 263 B3
Prince Maurice Rd
Plymouth PL3 263 B4
Plymouth PL4 248 F4
Prince of Wales Dr
Dartmouth TQ6 233 F4
Exmouth EX8 196 E1
Prince of Wales Rd
Crediton EX17 165 C6
Exeter EX4 177 B8
Kingsbridge TQ7 258 C5
PRINCE ROCK 249 B1
Prince Rock Prim Sch PL4 249 B2
Prince Rupert Way TQ12 123 B2
Princes Ct 6 TQ1 220 B6

Princes Point TQ1 ... 220 C3
Princes Rd
Plymouth PL6 ... 245 E6
Torquay TQ1 ... 220 B5
Princes Road E TQ1 ... 220 C5
Princes Road W TQ1 ... 220 B5
Princess Alexandra Ct 9 EX4 ... 177 A5
Princess Ave
Ilfracombe EX34 ... 150 C5
Plymouth, Plymstock PL9 ... 255 E6
Plymouth, West Park PL5 ... 244 A3
Princess Cotts TQ12 ... 213 C6
Princess Cres PL9 ... 255 E6
Princess Elizabeth Terr EX20 ... 107 F8
Princesshay Sh Ctr EX1 ... 261 B3
Prince's Sq EX2 ... 177 A3
Princess Rd
Kingskerswell TQ12 ... 213 A4
Kingsteignton TQ12 ... 207 D8
13 Kingsteignton TQ13 123 E1
Princess St
Barnstaple EX32 ... 155 A6
Plymouth PL1 ... 262 C2
Princess Street Ope PL1 ... 262 C2
Princes St
16 Dawlish EX7 ... 204 D6
23 Exmouth EX8 ... 202 A6
Paignton TQ3 ... 226 B6
Plymouth PL1 ... 247 E2
Torquay TQ1 ... 220 D7
Princess Theatre* TQ2 ... 220 B3
Prince's Street E EX2 177 A3
Prince's Street N EX2 ... 177 A4
Prince's Street S EX2 177 A3
Prince's Street W EX2 ... 177 A4
Princess Way PL1 ... 262 C2
Prince St TQ12 ... 207 C3
PRINCETOWN ... 128 B8
Princetown Com Prim Sch PL20 ... 128 A8
Princetown Rd PL20 ... 127 B3
Prince William Ct 1 TQ5 ... 230 C4
Prince William Quay TQ5 ... 230 D5
Prings Ct 13 TQ5 ... 230 C5
Priorton Hill EX17 ... 80 B7
Priorton La EX17 ... 80 B7
Priory
Bovey Tracey TQ13 ... 180 C8
Wellington TA21 ... 160 E6
Priory Ave
Kingskerswell TQ12 ... 213 A5
Totnes TQ9 ... 223 C6
Priory Cl
Barnstaple EX31 ... 154 F7
East Budleigh EX9 ... 198 B7
Ivybridge PL21 ... 237 B5
Tavistock PL19 ... 171 D3
Priory Ct
3 Totnes TQ9 ... 223 C6
Wellington TA21 ... 160 E7
Priory Dr
Plymouth PL7 ... 250 D5
Totnes TQ9 ... 223 C6
Priory Gdns
Barnstaple EX31 ... 154 F7
1 Dawlish EX7 ... 204 E6
Tavistock PL19 ... 171 D3
Totnes TQ9 ... 223 C6
Wellington TA21 ... 160 E6
Priory Gn EX4 ... 178 A7
Priory Hill
2 Dawlish EX7 ... 204 E6
Totnes TQ9 ... 223 C6
Priory La EX6 ... 113 B4
Priory Lawn Terr PL3 ... 249 A6
Priory Mill PL7 ... 250 D5
Priory Park Rd 13 EX7 ... 204 D6
Priory RC Prim Sch 3 TQ1 ... 220 B8
Priory Rd
Abbotskerswell TQ12 ... 212 C7
Barnstaple EX31 ... 154 F7
Dawlish EX7 ... 204 E6
Exeter EX4 ... 177 E8
Plymouth PL3 ... 249 A6
Tiverton EX16 ... 161 F6
Torquay TQ1 ... 220 B8
Priory Ridge PL7 ... 250 D5
Priory St TQ6 ... 234 A2
Priory Terr 7 TQ9 ... 223 C6
Priory The
Abbotskerswell TQ12 ... 212 C7
3 Modbury PL21 ... 137 B2
Priory View
Cornworthy TQ9 ... 227 B4
Exeter EX1 ... 178 E4
Priory Wall Cross EX15 ... 66 B2
Prisam La EX20 ... 75 E2
Prisam Lane Cross EX20 ... 75 F2
Priscott Way TQ12 ... 207 E6
Prispen Dr EX5 ... 82 B6
Prispen Ho EX5 ... 82 B6
Prispen View EX5 ... 82 B6
PRISTACOTT ... 27 C5
PRIXFORD ... 16 C7
Prixford EX31 ... 16 C7
Promenade
Ilfracombe EX34 ... 150 B6
Kingsbridge TQ7 ... 258 D5
Paignton TQ3 ... 226 D8
Paignton, Goodrington TQ4 ... 226 C4
Teignmouth TQ14 ... 210 C4
Prospect EX7 ... 204 E6
Prospect Cnr EX31 ... 27 A7
Prospect Cotts EX35 ... 151 B5
Prospect Cres EX15 ... 66 A7
Prospect Gdns 2 EX4 ... 177 E7
Prospect Hill
Okehampton EX20 ... 170 B4
Slapton TQ7 ... 145 C4
Prospect La PL12 ... 242 C3
Prospect Pk EX4 ... 177 D8
Prospect Pl
Barnstaple EX32 ... 155 B3
Exeter EX4 ... 177 A4
Ottery St Mary EX11 ... 169 D3
Plymouth PL1 ... 262 B2
5 Tiverton EX16 ... 161 B4
Prospect Rd 3 TQ5 ... 230 C5
Prospect Row PL1 ... 247 E1
Prospect St PL4 ... 263 A3
Prospect Terr
Gunnislake PL18 ... 125 D6
Gunnislake, St Ann's Chapel PL18 ... 125 B5
Newton Abbot TQ12 ... 207 C3
Prospect Way EX17 ... 60 D3
Prospect Wlk PL12 ... 242 C3
Protector Rd TQ12 ... 244 D2
Prouse Ave TQ13 ... 111 A6
Prouse Cres PL2 ... 248 C8
Prouse Rise PL12 ... 242 E2
Providence Pl
Calstock PL18 ... 125 D3
Lyme Regis DT7 ... 260 D3
Plymouth PL1 ... 248 A3
Providence Row 15 EX39 ... 157 A2
Providence St PL4 ... 263 A4
Provident Cl TQ5 ... 230 E5
Prowse La
East Village EX17 ... 80 C8
Lapford EX17 ... 60 D3
Prowses EX15 ... 67 B8
Prowse's La EX16 ... 63 E1
Prustacott Rd EX23 ... 70 E8
Pryn Ct PL1 ... 262 A3
Prynne Cl PL1 ... 262 B3
Puckridge Rd EX4 ... 174 D2
PUDDAVEN ... 223 A8
Puddavine Terr TQ9 ... 223 A8
PUDDINGTON ... 62 B5
PUDDINGTON BOTTOM ... 62 B4
Pudleylake Rd
Axminster EX13 ... 167 B1
Musbury EX13 ... 103 E6
Puffin Cl TQ2 ... 213 C2
Puffin Ct EX39 ... 156 C6
Puffin Way EX2 ... 176 D3
Pugsley Rd 9 EX16 ... 64 D7
Pulchrass St 11 EX32 155 A4
Pullen's Row EX16 ... 46 E1
Pulleys Cl TQ7 ... 143 C6
Pulling Rd EX4 ... 174 D2
Pullins Terr 10 TQ13 ... 123 E6
Pulpit Wlk EX2 ... 181 C7
Pump Field Cl EX15 ... 67 C1
Pump La
Abbotsham EX39 ... 156 A2
Lympstone EX8 ... 195 D4
Pump St
4 Brixham TQ5 ... 230 D5
Newton St Cyres EX5 ... 172 A8
Punchards Down TQ9 ... 222 F6
Purbeck Ave TQ2 ... 219 D2
Purcell Cl EX2 ... 178 C5
Purcombe Cross TQ13 ... 131 D3
Purlbridge Cross EX24 ... 102 D6
Purzebrook Cl EX13 ... 167 D5
Purzebrook Cotts EX13 ... 167 D5
PUSEHILL ... 156 B5
Pusehill Rd EX39 ... 156 B5
PUTSBOROUGH ... 7 F3
Putsborough Cl EX33 ... 8 A2
Putsborough Rd EX33 ... 7 F3
Putshole La EX38 ... 40 E1
Putson Cross EX16 ... 64 E8
Putts Cnr EX10 ... 101 C7
Pye Cnr
Brampford Speke EX5 ... 81 D1
Cullompton EX15 ... 163 C3
Kennford EX6 ... 181 B2
Pye La TA20 ... 88 E8
Pykes Down PL21 ... 237 F4
Pyles Thorne TA21 ... 160 F4
Pyles Thorne Cl TA21 ... 160 E5
Pyles Thorne Rd TA21 ... 160 E4
Pym St
Plymouth PL1 ... 247 F3
Plymouth PL5 ... 247 F4
Pym St *continued*
Tavistock PL19 ... 171 C6
Pyne Gdns EX5 ... 173 A7
Pyne Meadow Cross EX18 ... 44 D3
Pynes Cl
Cheriton Fitzpaine EX17 ... 62 E1
East Budleigh EX9 ... 198 B6
Pynes Hill EX2 ... 178 C2
Pynes Hill Bsns Pk EX2 ... 178 C3
Pynes La EX39 ... 156 E1
Pynes Wlk EX39 ... 25 E4
Pynsent Ct 4 TQ13 ... 123 E6
Pyramids Swimming & L Ctr The EX1 ... 261 C3
Pytte Gdns EX3 ... 183 C7
Pytte Ho EX3 ... 183 C7
PYWORTHY ... 71 D5
Pyworthy CE Prim Sch EX22 ... 71 D5

Q

Quadrangle The EX4 ... 177 C8
Quadrant The EX2 ... 261 C2
Quagmire La EX22 ... 164 C7
Quaker Lane PL3 ... 248 E5
Quantock Rd TA21 ... 160 D7
Quantocks EX33 ... 152 B6
Quantocks Rd TQ2 ... 219 C3
Quant Pk PL19 ... 171 C6
Quarries La EX37 ... 43 C7
Quarries The EX4 ... 176 D4
Quarry Cl
Bideford EX39 ... 156 E2
Totnes TQ9 ... 222 F6
Totnes TQ9 ... 223 A6
Quarry Cotts
Beer EX12 ... 191 B5
Plymouth PL1 ... 262 A3
Plymouth, Honicknowle PL5 ... 244 B2
Quarry Ct EX16 ... 161 D4
Quarryfields EX20 ... 170 C6
Quarry Foot Cross EX17 ... 79 C4
Quarry Gdns TQ3 ... 226 A7
Quarry Hts EX4 ... 174 C2
Quarry La
Beer EX12 ... 191 B5
Down St Mary EX17 ... 78 F6
Exeter EX1 ... 178 E4
Exeter EX2 ... 178 C4
Gunnislake PL18 ... 125 C6
Silverton EX5 ... 82 B5
Thorverton EX5 ... 81 D4
Quarryman Cl 4 EX16 ... 49 B8
Quarry Park Ave PL9 ... 255 D7
Quarry Park Rd
Exeter EX2 ... 178 C4
Plymouth, Peverell PL3 ... 248 D5
Plymouth, Plymstock PL9 ... 255 D7
Quarry Rd EX37 ... 43 B7
Quarry St PL11 ... 247 C3
Quarry Wood Ct 6 TQ3 ... 225 F1
Quarterdeck The PL1 ... 254 A8
Quarter Mile La EX5 ... 99 D3
Quartley Hill EX16 ... 34 E4
Quartz Row EX4 ... 174 C2
Quayfield Rd EX34 ... 150 C6
Quay Hill EX1, EX2 ... 261 A2
Quay House Visitor Ctr* EX2 ... 261 B2
Quay La
Instow EX39 ... 15 B1
Lympstone EX8 ... 195 D4
Quay Rd
Newton Abbot TQ12 ... 207 D3
Plymouth PL1 ... 263 A2
Teignmouth TQ14 ... 210 B4
Quayside 6 PL19 ... 171 B5
Quayside L Ctr TQ7 ... 258 D4
Quay Terr TQ12 ... 207 D3
Quay The
Appledore EX39 ... 15 A1
Ashprington TQ9 ... 139 F7
Bideford EX39 ... 157 A2
Brixham TQ5 ... 230 D5
Dartmouth TQ6 ... 233 F3
Dittisham TQ6 ... 228 D2
Exeter EX2 ... 261 B2
Ilfracombe EX34 ... 150 C6
Plymouth PL9 ... 255 C7
Salcombe TQ8 ... 259 C6
Quay View EX31 ... 153 E6
Quay View Sch PL18 ... 125 D3
Queen Annes 14 EX39 ... 157 A2
Queen Annes Copse TQ12 ... 206 F1
Queen Anne's Ct 14 EX31 ... 154 F5
Queen Anne's Mews 13 EX31 ... 154 F5
Queen Anne's Quay PL4 ... 263 B2
QUEEN DART ... 47 C3
Queen Dart Cross EX16 ... 47 B4
Queen Dart Hill EX16 ... 47 B3
Queen Elizabeth Ave TQ6 ... 233 E4
Queen Elizabeth Ct EX39 ... 156 C6
Queen Elizabeth Dr
Crediton EX17 ... 165 A6
Paignton TQ3 ... 225 E6
Queen Elizabeth's Sch, Barnfield Campus EX17 ... 165 B5
Queen Elizabeth's Sch, Western Road Campus EX17 ... 165 B6
Queen La 8 EX7 ... 204 D6
Queen's Ave EX34 ... 150 C5
Queens Cl
Kingsteignton TQ12 ... 207 F8
Plymouth PL6 ... 245 E6
Westward Ho! EX39 ... 156 C7
Queen's Cres
Brixham TQ5 ... 230 D3
Exeter EX4 ... 261 B4
Queens Ct 25 EX24 ... 103 A4
Queen's Ct 12 EX8 ... 202 A6
Queen's Dr EX8 ... 202 C5
Queen's Dr The EX4 ... 177 B8
Queen's Gate
Plymouth, Lipson PL4 ... 263 B4
Plymouth, Stoke PL3 ... 262 A4
Queen's Gate Mews PL4 ... 263 B4
Queen's Gate Villas PL4 ... 263 B4
Queenshays EX20 ... 95 A5
Queen's Ho 6 EX32 ... 155 A5
Queensland Dr EX4 ... 173 E2
Queen's Park Rd TQ4 226 C6
Queens Pk EX17 ... 80 D4
Queen's Pk EX22 ... 55 C1
Queen Sq EX15 ... 163 C3
Queens Rd
Exeter EX2 ... 261 A1
Plymouth PL5 ... 243 F3
Wellington TA21 ... 160 E4
Queen's Rd
Brixham TQ5 ... 230 C6
Budleigh Salterton EX9 197 F2
Moretonhampstead TQ13 ... 111 F5
Paignton TQ4 ... 226 C6
Plymouth PL4 ... 263 B4
Queen's Sq
Broadclyst EX5 ... 175 C7
8 Colyton EX24 ... 103 A4
Queen St
Barnstaple EX31 ... 154 F5
Barnstaple EX32 ... 155 A5
Bideford EX39 ... 157 A2
Budleigh Salterton EX9 ... 199 G2
9 Colyton EX24 ... 103 A4
Dawlish EX7 ... 204 D6
Exeter EX4 ... 261 A3
11 Exmouth EX8 ... 202 A6
17 Honiton EX14 ... 166 C6
Lynton EX35 ... 151 C5
Newton Abbot TQ12 ... 207 D3
Northlew EX20 ... 74 E2
Plymouth PL1 ... 247 D2
Seaton EX12 ... 192 A5
South Molton EX36 ... 158 C4
13 Teignmouth TQ14 ... 210 B4
Tiverton EX16 ... 161 C3
Torquay TQ1 ... 220 B5
Winkleigh EX19 ... 58 F3
Queen's Terr
Exeter EX4 ... 261 A4
Great Torrington EX38 ... 159 B5
Stoke Canon EX5 ... 81 F1
4 Totnes TQ9 ... 223 C6
Queensway
Newton Abbot TQ12 ... 207 E2
Tiverton EX16 ... 161 F5
Torquay TQ2 ... 219 D6
Queensway Cl TQ2 ... 219 E7
Queensway Cres TQ2 219 E7
Queensway Ho TQ12 ... 207 E2
Queensway RC Prim Sch TQ2 ... 219 D7
Queens Wlk DT7 ... 260 E4
Quentin Ave TQ5 ... 230 B2
Quern Rise EX1 ... 175 B1
Questant La EX10 ... 188 C6
Quicks Wlk EX38 ... 159 F5
Quilletts The TQ7 ... 147 E6
Quince Cross
South Molton EX36 ... 46 B8
Spreyton EX17 ... 96 C7
Quince Hill EX36 ... 31 A1
Quince Honey Farm* EX36 ... 158 C5
Quinnel Ho 7 TQ14 ... 210 B5
Quinta Cl TQ1 ... 220 C6
Quinta Ct TQ1 ... 220 C7
Quinta Rd TQ1 ... 220 D6
Quintet Cl EX1 ... 178 C5
Quirk Hill EX16 ... 63 D7
QUODITCH ... 91 A8
Quoditch Cross EX21 ... 73 B1
Quoitgate Cross EX22 ... 38 D3

R

Raceworld Karting* EX5 ... 184 D8
Rackclose La EX4 ... 261 A2
RACKENFORD ... 47 D5
Rackenford CE Prim Sch EX16 ... 47 D5
Rackenford Cross EX16 ... 47 D5
Rackenford Rd
Tiverton EX16 ... 161 A6
Witheridge EX16 ... 46 E1
Rackfield
Rockwell Green TA21 ... 160 A5
5 Tiverton EX16 ... 161 C3
Rackfield Cotts EX4 ... 176 F8
Rackfield Ct EX32 ... 154 F6
Rackfield Dr EX15 ... 67 C8
Rackleigh La EX17 ... 46 A2
Rackmead EX37 ... 28 F4
Rack Park Cl EX38 ... 159 C5
Rack Park Rd TQ7 ... 258 D5
Rack St EX1 ... 261 A2
Radar Rd PL6 ... 245 B5
Radcliffe Cl PL6 ... 244 E6
Radcliffe Ct TQ3 ... 226 C7
Raddenstile Ct EX8 ... 202 B6
Raddenstile La EX8 ... 202 B6
Raddick La PL20 ... 127 F5
Raddicombe Cl TQ5 ... 234 F8
Raddicombe Dr TQ5 ... 234 F8
Raddicombe Farm TQ5 ... 234 F8
Raddicombe La TQ5 ... 234 F8
RADDINGTON ... 35 B4
RADDON ... 81 D4
Raddon Cross EX17 ... 81 A5
Raddon Down Cross EX17 ... 79 D4
Raddon Hill EX17 ... 81 A6
Raddon Top EX17 ... 81 A6
Radford Ave PL4 ... 249 B1
Radford Grange EX7 ... 204 A7
Radford Ho 11 TQ4 ... 226 B6
Radford La PL10 ... 252 D4
Radford Park Dr PL9 ... 255 D6
Radford Park Rd PL9 255 D6
Radford Rd
Exeter EX2 ... 261 C2
Plymouth PL1 ... 262 B1
Radfords Orch TQ9 ... 131 E1
Radfordsturf EX5 ... 99 C6
Radfords Turf
Cranbrook EX5 ... 99 C6
Rockbeare EX5 ... 99 C6
Radford View PL9 ... 255 D6
Radford Way EX20 ... 170 E6
Radiant Ho PL1 ... 262 B2
Radish La EX12 ... 102 A2
Radley Cross EX36 ... 30 D2
Radnidge La EX16 ... 32 D4
Radnor Hall PL4 ... 263 A3
Radnor Pl
Exeter EX2 ... 261 C2
Plymouth PL4 ... 263 A3
Radnor St PL4 ... 263 A3
Radnor Villa EX2 ... 261 C2
Radsbury La EX35 ... 5 B3
Radshall Pk EX39 ... 156 F4
Radway EX10 ... 188 B4
Radway Ct TQ14 ... 209 A8
Radway Gdns TQ14 ... 209 A8
Radway Hill TQ14 ... 209 A8
Radway La EX9 ... 187 A1
Radway St TQ14 ... 209 A8
Ragged Field La EX34 ... 8 E5
Ragged La EX37 ... 44 B1
Ragg La EX9 ... 199 G2
Rag La
Aylesbeare EX5 ... 99 D4
Colebrooke EX17 ... 79 A2
Yarcombe EX14 ... 69 A2
Raglan Ct PL1 ... 247 F2
Raglan Gdns PL1 ... 247 F2
Raglan Rd PL1 ... 247 F2
Raglans EX2 ... 181 C8
Railway Cotts
Holsworthy EX22 ... 164 C3
10 Holsworthy EX22 ... 164 C4
6 Plymouth, Ford PL2 247 F5
Plymouth, Plymstock PL9 ... 255 D7
Tavistock PL19 ... 171 B6
Railway Terr
3 Bideford EX39 ... 157 B1
Broadclyst EX5 ... 175 E3
Rainbow Ct TQ2 ... 219 E7
Rainbow La
Biscombe TA3 ... 67 F8
Biscombe TA3 ... 68 A7
Rainsbury Hill TA4 ... 34 F8
Raisey La TA20 ... 69 F7
Rake Cnr TQ7 ... 143 F6
Rakeham Cotts EX38 ... 41 B6
Rakeham Hill EX38 ... 41 B6
Rakelane Cross TQ7 ... 143 F6
RALEIGH ... 155 A7
Raleigh Ave TQ2 ... 219 D6
Raleigh Cl
Dartmouth TQ6 ... 233 C3
Sidmouth EX10 ... 188 B7
South Molton EX36 ... 158 C4
Torquay TQ2 ... 219 D6
Raleigh Cotts 3 EX31 ... 155 A7
Raleigh Ct
Budleigh Salterton EX9 ... 198 B2
Plymouth PL7 ... 251 B6
Torquay TQ2 ... 219 D6
Raleigh Dr
Cullompton EX15 ... 163 C4
Raleigh Dr *continued*
Paignton TQ4 ... 226 B2
RALEIGH HILL ... 156 E4
Raleigh Hill
Bideford, Raleigh Hill EX39 ... 156 E4
Bideford, Silford EX39 ... 156 D5
Raleigh Ho
Exeter EX2 ... 261 C2
Ottery St Mary EX11 ... 169 D3
1 Sidmouth EX10 ... 188 B7
Raleigh Hts EX31 ... 154 F7
Raleigh Lawn EX31 ... 154 F7
Raleigh Mdw EX31 ... 155 A7
Raleigh Mead EX36 ... 158 C4
Raleigh Pk EX36 ... 158 C4
Raleigh Rd
Budleigh Salterton EX9 ... 198 B2
Dartmouth TQ6 ... 233 E4
Exeter EX1 ... 261 C2
Exmouth EX8 ... 202 A6
Ivybridge PL21 ... 237 A6
Newton Abbot TQ12 ... 207 F3
Ottery St Mary EX11 ... 169 E4
Salcombe TQ8 ... 259 D4
Teignmouth TQ14 ... 210 A8
Raleigh St PL1 ... 262 B3
Raleigh View EX39 ... 157 A3
Raleigh Works EX31 ... 154 E4
Raligh Mead EX36 ... 158 C4
Ralph Cl EX33 ... 152 B6
Ralph Rd EX33 ... 152 B6
Ralph's Ct PL19 ... 171 B5
Ramage Cl PL6 ... 245 F3
RAME ... 140 H2
Ramehead Cotts PL10 ... 140 H1
Ramehead La PL10 ... 140 H2
Rame La
Cawsand PL10 ... 252 F1
Rame PL10 ... 140 H2
Ramillies Ave PL5 ... 244 A4
Ramparts Wlk TQ9 ... 223 C5
Ramsden La EX14 ... 86 A3
Ramsey Gdns PL5 ... 244 D1
Ramsey La
Runnington TA21 ... 51 F8
Sampford Courtenay EX20 ... 76 F3
Ramshill Cross TQ3 ... 225 E8
Ramshill Rd TQ3 ... 225 E8
Ramsley EX20 ... 95 B4
Ramsons Ct EX31 ... 154 F8
Rance Dr EX8 ... 196 E3
Randell's Green EX8 ... 202 E6
Randolph Cl PL5 ... 244 E3
Randolph Ct TQ12 ... 207 A4
Randwick Park Rd PL9 ... 255 D7
Ranelagh Rd EX20 ... 170 A5
Rangers Cl TQ11 ... 236 B4
Ranjan Pl EX1 ... 174 F2
Ranscombe Cl TQ5 ... 230 E5
Ranscombe Ct 9 TQ5 ... 230 D5
Ranscombe Hill TQ12 ... 123 E8
Ranscombe Rd TQ5 ... 230 D5
Ransum Way PL19 ... 171 B4
Raphael Cl PL9 ... 256 B5
Raphael Dr PL9 ... 256 A6
Rapscott Cross EX36 ... 18 F1
Rapscott Hill EX36 ... 18 F1
Rashleigh Ave
Plymouth PL7 ... 250 F7
Saltash PL12 ... 242 D1
Rashleigh La EX18 ... 59 D7
Ratcliffe Sch EX7 ... 204 C4
Rathlin TQ1 ... 220 C7
Rathmore Rd TQ2 ... 219 F4
Ratshole Gate EX24 ... 102 E5
RATSLOE ... 174 D8
Ratsloe Cross EX4 ... 174 D8
Rattenbury Cotts EX12 ... 191 C6
Rattenbury Cross EX19 ... 76 A8
RATTERY ... 135 D4
Rattle St TQ13 ... 113 D1
Ravelin Gdns 5 EX32 ... 155 B5
Ravelin Manor Rd EX32 ... 155 B5
Raven Cl
Drakewalls PL18 ... 125 C5
Exeter EX4 ... 173 C1
Ravenglass Cl PL6 ... 245 D2
Ravensbourne La TQ6 ... 146 B7
Ravensbury Dr TQ6 ... 234 A2
Rawlin Cl PL6 ... 249 C8
Rawlyn Rd TQ2 ... 219 E4
Rawnsley La EX34 ... 7 F6
RAWRIDGE ... 68 C1
Rawridge Rd TA3 ... 68 C2
Rayer Rd 13 EX16 ... 64 D7
RAYMOND'S HILL ... 104 C7
Raymond Way PL7 ... 250 D6
Rayners EX6 ... 181 A1
Raynham Rd
Plymouth PL3 ... 248 B4
Plymouth PL3 ... 262 A4
Rea Barn Cl TQ5 ... 230 D4
Rea Barn Rd TQ5 ... 230 D4

Read Cl EX8 196 C1
Reading Wlk PL5 244 C4
Rea Dr TQ5 230 D5
Recreation Rd PL2 248 C7
Recreation Road Ind Est PL2 248 C7
Recreation Way PL7 132 F4
Rectory Cl
Filleigh EX32 29 B6
9 Whimple EX5 99 E8
Willand EX15 162 D4
Wrafton EX33 152 F4
Rectory Close Cross EX33 152 F3
Rectory Cross TQ10 138 A7
Rectory Dr EX2 181 B8
Rectory Hill
Berrynarbor EX34 2 D3
Cheriton Fitzpaine EX17 62 E1
Sampford Courtenay EX20 76 E3
Rectory La
Dittisham TQ6 228 C2
Meshaw EX16 46 A6
Parkham EX39 39 E8
Stoke Fleming TQ6 146 B7
Yelland EX39 15 C2
Rectory Pk EX39 156 F2
Rectory Rd
Ashbrittle TA21 50 F8
Bridestowe EX20 107 F8
Buckland St Mary TA20 69 D8
Combe Martin EX34 3 A3
Combe Martin EX34 10 A8
Dolton EX19 57 F7
East Ogwell TQ12 211 E8
Morchard Bishop EX17 61 A2
Plymouth PL1 248 A2
Rectory Rise EX20 56 F4
Recycling Way PL7 136 A6
Redavon Rise TQ2 219 B8
RED BALL 51 C4
Red Brook Cl TQ4 226 C1
Redburn Cl TQ3 226 A7
Redburn Rd TQ3 226 A7
Redcliff Ct EX9 199 G2
Redcliffe Rd TQ1 214 C1
Redcliffes The EX20 106 E5
RED COW VILLAGE 177 A8
Redcroft Heights TQ6 146 B7
Red Cross
Colyton EX24 102 F6
Raymond's Hill EX13 104 C7
Silverton EX5 82 C5
Red Cross Hill EX17 165 E6
Reddacleave Kiln Cross TQ11 135 A6
Reddaway Dr EX6 182 A4
Reddenhill Rd TQ1 220 C7
Red Devon Ct 10 PL21 137 B2
Reddicliff Cl PL9 255 E5
Reddicliffe Mws EX20 106 E5
Reddicliffes The EX20 106 E5
Reddicliff Rd PL9 255 D5
Reddington Rd PL3 249 B7
Redford Cross TQ7 258 A8
Redford Way TQ7 258 C5
Red Gate
King's Nympton EX37 44 E8
Winkleigh EX19 58 D2
Redgate Cl TQ1 220 D6
Redgate La EX16 50 C5
Redhill Cl PL5 243 E4
Redhill Cotts EX11 169 F6
REDHILLS 176 E5
Redhills
Budleigh Salterton EX9 199 G2
Exeter EX4 176 E6
Redhills Cl EX4 176 E6
Redhills Com Prim Sch EX4 176 F5
Red Ho The EX17 165 B5
Red House Cl 9 TQ13 123 C4
Red La
Churchinford TA3 68 C7
Hatherleigh EX20 75 C7
Hemyock EX15 52 E3
Raymond's Hill EX13 104 C6
Redlake TQ9 222 F8
Redlake Cross TQ9 222 F8
Redlake Trad Est PL21 137 B7
Redland Cross EX18 58 F7
Redlands EX16 161 F4
Redlands Cl EX4 178 A8
Redlands Ct TQ3 225 F7
Redlands Rd EX31 153 F5
Redlands The EX10 188 A3
REDLANE 68 C7
Redlane Cross DT7 104 C6
Redlap Cross TQ6 146 C8
Redlap La TQ6 146 B7
Redlap Rd TQ6 146 C8
Red Lion Hill PL8 257 B5
Red Lion La EX1, EX4 261 C4
Red Lion Pl 2 EX7 204 D6
Red Lion Yard EX20 170 B5
REDMONSFORD 38 C2
Redmoor Cl PL19 171 A7
Redoubt Hill TQ6 234 B3
RED POST 70 E8
Redpost Cross
North Tawton EX20 76 F5
Sampford Courtenay EX20 76 E5
Red Post Cross
Burrington EX37 43 F4
Totnes TQ9 217 C4
Red Rock EX5 81 E2
Red Rock Rd EX5 81 D1
Redruth Cl PL5 244 A5
Redside Terr EX5 172 E5
Redstart Cl TQ12 206 F1
Redvers Cl EX17 165 E4
Redvers Gr PL7 250 E4
Redvers Ho 7 EX17 165 C5
Redvers Rd EX4 177 A5
Redvers Way 5 EX16 161 E6
Redwalls Mdw TQ6 233 E4
Redwell La TQ3 225 F8
Redwell Rd TQ3 225 F8
Redwing Dr PL6 245 D8
Redwood Cl
Bovey Tracey TQ13 180 C4
Exmouth EX8 196 D3
10 Hemyock EX15 67 B8
4 Honiton EX14 85 C2
Redwood Dr
Loddiswell TQ7 143 E7
Plymouth PL7 251 B5
Redwood Rd EX10 188 C5
Redwoods TQ13 180 C5
Redworth Terr TQ9 223 C6
Redyeates Cross EX17 63 A2
Reed Mdw EX20 75 C7
Reeds Barn EX13 88 F1
Reed's Cross
Ashill EX15 66 C6
Bittadon EX31 9 E4
Reedsdown Cross EX17 79 F6
Reeds Pl EX15 163 C3
Reed Vale TQ14 210 A5
Reed Walk EX2 182 C7
REEDY 113 A8
Reedy Hill EX6 112 F8
Reeveacre Cross TQ9 216 D5
Reeves Cl 3 TQ9 223 D5
Reeves Rd The TQ2 219 D5
Reeves Way TQ7 143 D4
Reflections Rd PL4 255 B6
Reform St 3 EX31 154 F6
Regal Ct
Exeter EX1 178 E2
Saltash PL12 242 F2
Regard Cl TQ5 230 E5
Regency Cres EX8 202 C6
Regency Ct 8 EX34 150 B5
Regency Dr EX1 178 D1
Regency Gate EX10 188 C5
Regent Cl
Barnstaple EX31 154 C2
Fremington EX31 153 F5
Torquay TQ2 219 E8
Regent Ct PL4 263 A3
Regent Pl EX34 150 B6
Regents Ct TQ4 226 C5
Regents Gate EX8 202 B6
Regents Gdns 6 TQ14 210 C4
Regent's Pk EX1 177 E6
Regent Sq EX1 177 F5
Regent St
Dawlish EX7 204 D6
Exeter EX2 177 A3
Plymouth PL4 263 A3
18 Teignmouth TQ14 210 C4
Regis Ct EX10 188 C4
Reigate Rd PL9 255 E8
Reme Dr EX14 85 C2
Rena Hobson Ct EX16 161 F3
Renaissance Gdns PL2 248 C7
Rendells Mdw TQ13 180 E7
Rendlesham Gdns PL6 245 E3
Rendle St PL1 262 B3
Rennes Dr EX4 173 C1
Rennes Ho EX1 178 B7
Renney Rd
Down Thomas PL9 255 C1
Heybrook Bay PL9 140 B8
Rennie Ave PL5 243 C1
Rennie Rd 2 EX16 64 D7
Renoir Cl PL9 256 A6
Renown St PL2 247 E6
Rensey La EX17 60 C4
Renslade Ho EX4 261 A2
Renton La TQ7 142 E7
Research Way PL6 245 C4
Reservoir Cres PL9 256 B7
Reservoir Cross PL16 91 A4
Reservoir La 1 PL3 248 F6
Reservoir Rd
Plymouth, Hartley PL3 248 F6
Plymouth, Plymstock PL9 256 B7
Reservoir Way PL9 256 B7
Resolution Ho PL4 263 B3
Resolution Rd EX1 178 D1
Rest Hill TQ12 131 D7
Restland La EX20 94 F7
Restormel Rd PL4 262 C4
Restormel Terr PL4 262 C4
Retail Park Cl EX2 177 B3
Retreat Cl TQ7 258 C5
Retreat Dr The EX3 182 D6
Retreat Rd EX3 182 E6
Retreat The
Exmouth EX8 202 D7
Paignton TQ3 226 C8
Plymouth PL3 249 B7
Tiverton EX16 161 D4
Topsham EX3 182 D6
Revell Park Rd PL7 250 D6
Revel Rd PL3 249 A6
Revelstoke Rd
Noss Mayo PL8 140 F6
Noss Mayo PL8 141 A6
Revill Ind Units EX5 99 A4
REW
Ashburton 130 F6
Malborough 147 F5
Rew Cross
Ashburton TQ13 130 F5
Newton St Cyres EX5 81 A2
Rewdown Cross TQ13 130 F6
REWE 82 A2
Rewe Barton EX5 82 A2
Rewe Cross EX5 82 A2
Rewe Ct EX5 82 B3
Rewe La EX5 99 D6
Rewes Cross EX5 82 F2
Rewlea Cotts TQ13 130 F5
Rewlea Cross TQ13 130 F6
Rew Rd
Ashburton TQ13 130 F5
2 Ashburton TQ13 131 A5
Rew's Cl EX34 2 F4
Rews Cross EX36 19 C2
Rews Mdw EX1 174 F1
Rews Park Dr EX1 174 F1
REXON 106 B7
Rexona Cl EX2 177 A2
Rexon Cross PL16 106 B7
Reynell Ave TQ12 207 F3
Reynell Rd
East Ogwell TQ12 211 F8
Newton Abbot TQ12 211 F8
Reynolds Cl EX4 174 D1
Reynolds Gr PL5 247 C8
Reynolds Rd PL7 250 C6
REZARE 115 C4
Rheola Gdns PL6 245 D3
Rhine Villas TQ9 223 D5
Rhodanthe Rd TQ3 219 B1
Rhode Island Dr EX1 178 E1
Rhode La DT7 260 C6
Rhodes Cl PL7 250 E7
Rhododendron Ave
Barnstaple EX31 154 D3
Dunkeswell EX14 67 B1
RHS Gardens Rosemoor★ EX38 159 D2
Rhude Cross EX22 53 D2
Rhydda Bank Cross EX31 4 A5
Rhyll Gate Cross TA22 32 E7
Ribble Gdns PL3 249 D7
Ribston Ave EX1 178 C6
Ribston Cl EX1 178 C6
Rices Mews EX2 177 A4
Richard Cl
Bideford EX39 25 E4
Okehampton/North Tawton EX20 170 D5
Ottery St Mary EX11 169 B3
Richard Ford Ct EX2 177 F5
Richards Cl
Dawlish EX7 204 D5
Exmouth EX8 196 D2
Wellington TA21 160 C8
Richardson Dr PL8 141 B8
Richards Row PL3 248 F7
Richards Terr PL10 252 E5
Richina Dr EX20 77 B4
Richmond Ave EX34 150 A5
Richmond Cl
Sampford Peverell EX16 50 D1
Torquay TQ1 221 A4
Richmond Ct
14 Dawlish EX7 204 E6
Exeter EX1 261 A3
Richmond Gn EX39 14 F1
Richmond Hill TQ12 213 A5
Richmond Pk EX39 156 F7
Richmond Pl
15 Dawlish EX7 204 E6
Ivybridge PL21 136 C7
Shaldon TQ14 209 D5
Richmond Rd
Appledore EX39 15 A1
Exeter EX4 261 A3
Exmouth EX8 202 D7
Ilfracombe EX34 150 A4
Plymouth PL6 245 A2
Richmond St EX32 155 A5
Richmond Terr
9 Appledore EX39 15 A1
Buckland Monachorum PL20 126 C3
Kingsbridge TQ7 258 D6
Richmond Villas EX34 150 A5
Richmond Walk Ind Est PL1 247 F1
Richmond Wlk
10 Barnstaple EX32 155 A6
Plymouth PL1 247 F1
RICKARD'S DOWN 156 A3
Rickards Gn EX39 156 B2
Rickards Row EX39 40 B7
Rickham Cross TQ8 148 D4
Riddell Ave EX32 154 F6
Riddistone Cross EX20 77 A8
Riddistone La EX20 77 A8
RIDDLECOMBE 58 D8
Ride The
Beaworthy EX21 55 F4
Plymouth PL7, PL9 249 D2
Ridge Cross
Chillington TQ7 149 B8
Plymouth PL9 256 A3
Wilmington EX14 86 E4
Ridge Gr PL15 105 A3
Ridge Hill
Berrynarbor EX34 2 E3
Combe Martin EX34 3 A2
Dartmouth TQ6 233 F4
Ridge Ho PL4 249 A4
Ridge La
Chudleigh TQ13 124 B7
Cornworthy TQ9 139 F4
Paignton TQ3 218 F8
Tiverton EX16 63 F8
Wilmington EX14 86 C3
Ridge Lane Cross TQ9 139 E4
Ridgeleigh Ct 11 EX14 166 C6
Ridgemark Cl TQ5 230 E5
Ridge Park Ave PL4 248 D4
Ridge Park Rd PL7 250 F5
Ridge Pk PL7 250 E5
Ridge Rd
Combeinteignhead TQ12 208 D2
Maidencombe TQ1, TQ12 214 B7
Modbury PL21 137 B4
Molland EX36 20 F1
Molland TA22 21 A1
Molland TA22 32 C8
Plymouth PL7 250 E3
Stokeinteignhead TQ12 209 A1
Ugborough PL21 137 D7
West Anstey TA22 32 D7
Ridges The TQ6 233 D1
Ridgeway
Exeter EX4 173 A3
Honiton EX14 166 B4
Ottery St Mary EX11 169 E4
Plymouth, Plympton PL7 250 D5
Saltash PL12 242 D1
Sidbury EX10 101 B2
Ridge Way EX6 194 E2
Ridgeway Ave EX39 156 E7
Ridgeway Cl
Newton Abbot TQ12 207 F1
Sidbury EX10 101 B2
Westward Ho! EX39 156 D7
Ridgeway Ct EX39 156 D7
Ridgeway Dr EX39 156 D7
Ridgeway Gdns EX11 169 E4
Ridgeway Gn EX37 43 B7
Ridgeway Hts 17 TQ1 220 D4
Ridgeway La
Awliscombe EX14 85 A5
Coffinswell TQ12 213 D6
Ridgeway Mead EX10 187 F7
Ridgeway Rd
Newton Abbot TQ12 207 F1
Torquay TQ1 220 E4
Ridgeway Sch PL7 250 E5
Ridgeway's Cross EX17 79 E6
Ridgeway Sp Ctr PL7 250 E5
Ridgewood Cross EX15 67 D8
Ridgewood La EX15 67 D8
Ridgey Cross TQ13 130 B4
Ridgway Cross EX36 20 E1
Ridgway Ct EX13 167 D5
Ridgway La EX24 102 F4
Riding Cross EX37 29 A4
Ridings The EX3 183 C4
Ridley Hill TQ6 234 A3
Rifford Rd EX2 178 B4
Riflemans Walk PL6 245 B7
Rifton La EX16 48 B4
Riga Terr PL3 249 C4
Rigdale Cl PL6 249 A7
Riggles Cross EX14 68 A3
Rillage La TQ2 219 F6
Rill Cnr EX5 99 D3
Rill La EX9 199 H2
Ringdown La EX15 52 F2
Ring Hill EX20 95 C5
Ringhill Cross EX20 95 D5
RINGMORE
Bigbury-on-Sea 142 E4
Teignmouth 209 D4
Ringmore Cl TQ14 209 D5
Ringmore Dr TQ7 142 E3
Ringmore Rd
Shaldon TQ14 209 D5
Teignmouth TQ14 210 A3
Ringmore Way PL5 244 B3
Ringrona TQ8 259 B2
Ringslade Cl TQ12 206 F5
Ringslade Rd TQ12 206 F5
Ringswell Ave EX1 178 C6
Ringswell Cross TQ9 216 E6
Ringswell Pk 11 EX2 178 D5
Riphay Corner EX16 33 E3
Riphay Cross TA22 33 E3
Ripon Cl EX4 176 E6
Rippon Cl
Brixham TQ5 229 F2
17 Tiverton EX16 64 D7
Riscombe Hill EX5 98 F8
Risdon Ave PL4 249 B1
Risdon Dr PL21 237 A5
Rising Sun EX13 87 A3
Ritson La TQ9 139 D3
Rivenford La EX5, EX17 81 C3
Riverbank Cotts EX39 157 B4
River Cl
Newton Abbot TQ12 207 F6
Stoke Canon EX5 173 F8
River Ct
3 Okehampton EX20 170 B6
Saltash PL12 242 D5
Sidbury EX10 101 B2
Tavistock PL19 171 D6
Riverdale
Harbertonford TQ9 139 C7
Seaton EX12 192 B7
Riverdale Cl EX12 192 B7
Riverdale Orch EX12 192 B7
River Dart Ctry Pk★ TQ13 130 D5
River Dr EX15 163 D3
Riverford PL6 245 F5
Riverford Cl PL6 245 D7
River Front EX3 183 C2
Riveria Ct TQ1 220 C4
River Mdws EX2 177 C3
Rivermead EX15 163 C2
Rivermead Ave EX8 196 A3
Rivermead Ct EX8 196 A3
Rivermead Rd EX2 177 D3
River Pk PL21 137 A4
River Pk 14 PL20 126 F4
River Plate Rd EX2 178 D1
Rivers Cl PL21 237 E5
Riversdale Ave EX34 150 A6
RIVERSIDE
Plymouth 243 A1
Wellington 160 B6
Riverside
Chillaton PL16 116 D8
Dawlish Warren EX7 201 A2
Hemyock EX15 67 C8
Kingsbridge TQ7 258 D4
Teignmouth TQ14 210 A3
Totnes TQ9 223 B7
Wellington TA21 160 B6
Wellington TA21 160 B7
Riverside Apartments EX36 158 E4
Riverside Bsns Pk PL1 247 E3
Riverside Cl
Bideford EX39 157 B4
Honiton EX14 166 B6
1 Horrabridge PL20 126 F4
Riverside Com Prim Sch PL5 247 C8
Riverside Cott PL12 242 C1
Riverside Cross EX17 62 A3
Riverside Ct
12 Barnstaple EX31 154 F5
Bideford EX39 157 B4
Dartmouth TQ6 233 F3
Exeter EX2 261 B2
Newton Abbot TQ12 207 D4
Riverside L Ctr EX4 261 A1
Riverside Mdw EX3 182 D7
Riverside Mews PL12 243 A3
Riverside Pl
Plymouth PL1 247 D2
Plymouth PL5 247 D2
Riverside Rd
Barnstaple EX31 154 C6
Dittisham TQ6 228 C3
Lynmouth EX35 151 C6
Sidmouth EX10 188 B3
Topsham EX3 182 E6
Riverside Road E PL8 140 F6
Riverside Road W PL8 140 F6
Riverside Terr TQ9 223 D5
Riverside Units EX31 154 C6
Riverside Valley Pk★ EX2 177 E2
Riverside View EX11 169 D3
Riverside Way
Newton Abbot TQ13 130 F7
Seaton EX12 192 C5
Riverside Wlk
Plymouth PL5 244 B6
Yealmpton PL8 136 A2
Riverside Workshops EX12 192 C5
Riversmeet EX39 15 A1
Rivers The PL12 242 E1
Rivers Wlk EX2 182 C7
River Tamar Way EX22 164 C6
Riverton Rd EX31 154 D2
Rivervale Cl TQ13 110 F6
River Valley Rd 13 TQ13 123 C4
River View
Barnstaple EX32 155 C2
Exebridge TA22 33 F3
Gunnislake PL18 125 B5
River View *continued*
Plymouth PL4 249 B1
Saltash PL12 242 F3
River View Cl
12 Chudleigh Knighton TQ13 123 C4
20 Colyton EX24 103 A4
River View Commercial Ctr EX31 154 D6
Riverview Dr EX4 176 F8
River View Dr 21 EX24 103 A4
River View La PL4 249 B1
Riverview Pl TQ7 258 C5
River View Terr EX6 182 B3
Riviera Int Con Ctr★ TQ2 219 F4
Riviera Terr
Dawlish EX7 204 F7
Exminster EX6 182 B3
Riviera The
Paignton TQ4 226 B5
Torquay TQ1 220 B3
Riviera Way TQ2 213 D1
Rixafer Rd TQ13 124 B4
Rixdale Rd TQ13 124 C4
Rixey La EX17 61 B2
Rixeypark Cnr TQ13 123 D3
RIXLADE 25 B5
Roach Hill EX36 31 F7
Roachill Cross EX36 32 C1
Roach La EX5 82 C6
Road Down Cross EX6 96 F7
Road End Cross EX14 87 A8
Roadford Lake Nature Reserve★ EX21 91 D4
ROAD GREEN 103 A5
Road Pk TQ13 123 B7
Roadway Cnr EX34 8 A5
Robartes Ct EX2 261 C2
Robers Rd TQ12 207 D8
Robert Adams Cl PL7 250 B5
Robert Davey Rd EX2 178 D1
Roberts Ave PL11 247 B3
Roberts Cl
Cullompton EX15 163 B2
Torquay TQ2 214 B2
Roberts Field EX36 30 D8
Roberts Rd
Exeter EX2 261 B2
Plymouth PL5 247 D8
Roberts Way TQ12 206 F4
Robert Way EX10 186 F8
Robin Cl EX15 163 B2
Robin Dr PL15 105 A2
Robin La EX5 99 B6
Robins Cross EX16 63 A6
Robins Field TQ7 144 F1
Robins Hill EX39 156 E4
Robins Park Ind Est TQ7 143 E8
Robins Way PL9 255 E8
Robin Wlk 9 EX16 161 E6
ROBOROUGH
Great Torrington 42 F3
Plymouth 241 D1
Roborough Ave PL6 245 B5
Roborough Cl PL6 245 B5
ROBOROUGH DOWN 126 F3
Roborough Down La PL6 241 F5
Roborough Gdns 3 TQ13 131 A5
Roborough La
Ashburton TQ13 130 F5
Plymouth PL5 244 D8
Roborough Rd EX31 155 A8
Roborough Terr TQ13 130 F5
Robyns Cl PL7 251 B5
Roche Gdn EX2 182 A8
Rochester Rd
3 Plymouth PL4 248 E4
6 Plymouth PL4 263 A4
Rochford Cres
Plymouth PL5 243 F5
Plymouth TQ12 244 A5
ROCK 87 D5
Rock Ave
Barnstaple EX32 155 A3
Lynton EX35 151 B5
ROCKBEARE 99 C6
Rockbeare CE Prim Sch EX5 99 B5
Rockbeare Hill EX5 168 A5
Rock Cl TQ4 229 C7
Rockcliffe Ct 1 EX34 150 C6
Rock Cotts TQ7 142 C6
Rock Cross EX17 97 B7
Rockdale Rd PL8 136 A2
Rock End Ave TQ1 220 C2
Rockerhayne Cross EX24 102 D7
Rockey La
Newton Poppleford EX10 187 A6
Northlew EX20 74 E2
Rockfield Ave PL6 244 F6
Rockfield Cl TQ14 210 D7
Rockfield Cotts TA21 51 F7
Rockfield Ho EX4 261 B4
Rockfield Rd EX34 7 F7
ROCKFORD 5 F4
Rock Gdns
Barnstaple EX32 155 A3

Rock Gdns *continued*
Plymouth PL9 ... 249 D1
Rock Gdns The★ TQ13 ... 123 E5
Rock Head EX37 ... 28 C2
Rock Hill
Aveton Gifford TQ7 ... 143 C6
Berrynarbor EX34 ... 2 D3
Braunton EX33 ... 152 D6
Chulmleigh EX18 ... 59 E8
Georgeham EX33 ... 8 A2
Plymouth PL5 ... 244 C7
Umberleigh EX37 ... 28 C2
West Down EX34 ... 8 F4
Rock House La TQ1 ... 214 C5
Rockingham Rd PL3 ... 249 A5
Rock La
Cheriton Bishop EX17 ... 97 B7
Chudleigh TQ13 ... 123 F8
16 Combe Martin EX34 ... 3 A3
Offwell EX14 ... 86 C1
Rocklands TQ13 ... 123 E5
Rockley La EX32 ... 11 F1
Rock Lodge Pk EX35 ... 151 B5
Rockmount Terr 6 EX39 ... 157 A2
Rockpark Cross TQ13 ... 131 A5
Rock Park Terr 24 EX32 ... 155 A4
Rock Pk
4 Ashburton TQ13 ... 131 A5
Dartmouth TQ6 ... 233 D4
Rock Rd
Chudleigh TQ13 ... 123 E5
Torquay TQ2 ... 220 B4
Rockshead Hill EX32 ... 18 F3
Rockside EX4 ... 177 A6
Rocks The EX39 ... 156 B6
Rockstone The EX7 ... 205 A7
Rock Terr PL7 ... 250 D4
Rock The EX31 ... 154 F7
Rock View EX16 ... 65 B7
Rock Villas PL16 ... 105 F4
Rockville Pk PL9 ... 255 E8
Rock Walk Hts TQ1 ... 220 A4
Rockwell Gate TA21 ... 160 B5
Rockwell Gn TA21 ... 160 B5
ROCKWELL GREEN ... 160 B5
Rockwell Green CE Prim Sch TA21 ... 160 B5
Rockwood Rd PL6 ... 245 E8
Rocky Hill PL19 ... 171 B5
Rocky La
Abbotsham EX39 ... 156 A3
Arlington EX31 ... 10 C3
Buckfastleigh TQ11 ... 236 A3
Combe Martin EX34 ... 3 A4
Lydcott EX32 ... 18 F7
Modbury PL21 ... 137 E2
4 Teignmouth TQ14 ... 209 E8
Teignmouth TQ14 ... 210 A6
Rocky Park Ave PL9 ... 255 E8
Rocky Park Rd PL9 ... 255 E8
Rocombe Cl TQ2 ... 213 F4
Rocombe Cross
Daccombe TQ12 ... 213 F6
Raymond's Hill EX13 ... 104 C6
Rocombe Hill TQ12 ... 213 F7
Rodda Cl PL18 ... 125 D7
Roddick Way 8 PL7 ... 251 C5
Rodgements Cross EX18 ... 59 E8
Rodgemonts Cross EX18 ... 59 F8
Rodgemont's La EX18 ... 59 F8
Rodgers Ind Est TQ4 ... 225 D3
Rodney Cl
Dartmouth TQ6 ... 233 D3
Exmouth EX8 ... 203 A7
Rodney St PL5 ... 247 D8
Rods La PL19 ... 117 E6
Rodsworthy La EX36 ... 31 C1
Rodway Cross EX14 ... 87 A6
Roe Cl EX36 ... 158 B5
Roeselare Ave PL11 ... 247 A3
Roeselare Cl PL11 ... 247 A3
Rogada Ct TQ5 ... 230 D3
Rogate Dr PL6 ... 245 D4
Rogate Wlk PL6 ... 245 D4
Rogers Cl EX16 ... 161 E6
Rogers Cres EX39 ... 157 D2
Rogers Dr PL12 ... 242 D4
Roland Bailey Gdns PL19 ... 171 A6
Rolle Barton EX9 ... 198 D7
Rolle Cotts EX9 ... 197 E2
Rolle Ct EX38 ... 159 C5
Rolle Rd
Budleigh Salterton EX9 ... 199 G2
Exmouth EX8 ... 202 A6
Great Torrington EX38 ... 159 A5
Rolle's Quay EX31 ... 154 F5
Rolle St
Barnstaple EX31 ... 154 F6
Exmouth EX8 ... 202 A6
Rolles Terr EX39 ... 40 C7
Rollestone Cres EX4 ... 173 E2
Rolle The EX9 ... 199 G2
Rolle Villas EX8 ... 202 A6
Rollis Park Cl PL9 ... 255 C8
Rollis Park Rd PL9 ... 255 C8
Rollstone La EX17 ... 81 C1
Rolston Cl PL6 ... 244 D6
Romaleyn Gdns TQ4 ... 226 B4
Roman Rd
Feniton EX5 ... 84 C2
Roman Rd *continued*
Kilmington EX13 ... 87 C1
Kingsteignton TQ13 ... 123 E2
Lyme Regis DT7 ... 260 D4
Plymouth PL5 ... 243 E2
ROMANSLEIGH ... 45 C7
Romansleigh Cross EX36 ... 45 C7
Romansleigh Ridge EX18 ... 45 C5
Romans Way EX16 ... 161 F6
Roman Way
Honiton EX14 ... 166 E7
Plymouth PL5 ... 243 E2
Seaton EX12 ... 192 A6
Roman Wlk EX4 ... 261 B3
Roman Wy 8 EX5 ... 99 A6
Romilly Gdns PL7 ... 250 B5
Romney Cl PL5 ... 244 B1
Romsey Dr EX2 ... 177 E5
Ronald Gdns EX3 ... 182 D7
Ronald Terr PL2 ... 247 F5
Ronchetti Wy EX2 ... 177 F3
Roncombe Cnr EX24 ... 101 E5
Roncombe Gate EX24 ... 101 E5
Roncombe Hill EX10 ... 101 E5
Ronsdale Cl PL9 ... 255 D8
Rookabear Ave EX31 ... 154 A1
Rookbear La EX31 ... 9 E2
Rookery Cvn Pk EX20 ... 77 F5
Rookery Hill EX16 ... 48 C8
Rookery La DT7 ... 260 C8
Rookery Terr TA21 ... 160 C5
Rook La PL21 ... 133 C3
Rooklands 18 TQ12 ... 207 B3
Rooklands Ave TQ2 ... 219 E6
Rook Lane End PL21 ... 133 C3
Rooksbridge View 3 EX31 ... 154 A1
Rooks Cl EX31 ... 154 B3
Rooks Cross EX31 ... 27 D3
Rooks Farm Rd EX31 ... 153 A4
Rooks Nest EX31 ... 153 E5
Rooks Way EX16 ... 161 E6
Rookswood Ct 1 EX31 ... 154 A1
Rookswood La EX5 ... 99 C5
Rookwood Cl EX14 ... 166 B5
Rookwood Ho EX14 ... 166 B6
Room Hill Rd TA24 ... 21 D7
Roope Cl PL5 ... 247 C7
Rooty Cross EX31 ... 27 A7
Roper Ave PL9 ... 255 D8
Roperidge Cross PL21 ... 137 F6
Ropers Ct EX9 ... 198 E7
Roper's La EX9 ... 198 E7
Ropery Rd EX34 ... 150 C6
Ropewalk
Bideford EX39 ... 157 A2
Kingsbridge TQ7 ... 144 A2
Kingsbridge TQ7 ... 258 C4
Ropewalk Hill TQ5 ... 230 C5
Ropewalk Ho EX8 ... 201 E6
Rope Wlk
2 Teignmouth TQ14 ... 210 B5
Wellington TA21 ... 160 C4
Rorkes Cl PL5 ... 243 E2
Roscoff Cl EX38 ... 159 E5
Roscoff Rd EX7 ... 204 E8
Roscoff Rise PL6 ... 245 B4
Rosea Bridge La EX34 ... 3 A4
Rose Acre Terr TQ5 ... 230 D4
Rose And Crown Hill EX17 ... 80 A5
Rose Ave EX1 ... 178 D6
Rosebank Cres EX4 ... 173 E1
Rosebarn Ave EX4 ... 173 D1
Rosebarn La EX4 ... 173 E1
Rosebery Ave PL4 ... 263 C4
Rosebery La PL4 ... 263 C4
Rosebery Rd
Exeter EX4 ... 177 E8
Exmouth EX8 ... 202 A7
Plymouth PL4 ... 263 C4
Rose Cl
Rockwell Green TA21 ... 160 A3
Tiverton EX16 ... 161 F6
Roseclave Cl PL7 ... 251 C6
Rose Cotts
Beer EX12 ... 191 D5
9 Bishop's Tawton EX32 ... 16 E1
Frogmore TQ7 ... 144 E3
Plymouth PL6 ... 249 B8
Rosedale Ave PL2 ... 248 D7
Rose Dene TQ2 ... 213 F2
ROSEDOWN ... 22 F3
Rosedown Ave PL2 ... 248 A7
Rose Duryard EX4 ... 173 A1
Rose Gdns
Ipplepen TQ12 ... 211 E2
Plymouth PL6 ... 245 E6
Rose Hill
Kingskerswell TQ12 ... 212 F4
Wembury PL9 ... 140 D7
Rosehill Cl TQ1 ... 220 C5
Rose Hill Cl TQ12 ... 212 F4
Rosehill Gdns TQ12 ... 212 F4
Rosehill Rd TQ1 ... 220 C5
Rose Hill Terr PL17 ... 125 D3
Rosehip Cl PL6 ... 245 E7
Rose Ho TQ1 ... 220 D7
Rose La EX32 ... 155 C3
Roseland Ave EX1 ... 178 A6
Roseland Cres EX1 ... 178 A6
Roseland Cross EX22 ... 54 C8
Roseland Dr EX1 ... 178 A5
Roselands EX10 ... 188 A4
Roselands Cotts EX24 ... 103 A5
Roselands Dr TQ4 ... 225 F2
Roselands Prim Sch TQ4 ... 225 F2
Roseland Sq TQ12 ... 207 E7
Roselands Rd TQ4 ... 226 B2
Roselyn Terr EX31 ... 154 E6
Rosemary Ave TQ12 ... 206 F4
Rosemary Cl PL7 ... 132 D4
Rosemary Ct TQ3 ... 226 C8
Rosemary Gdns TQ3 ... 225 F8
Rosemary La
Colyton EX24 ... 103 A5
Dulverton TA22 ... 33 D6
Holne TQ11 ... 130 A3
Musbury EX13 ... 103 D5
ROSEMARY LANE ... 52 D1
Rosemarylane Cross EX15 ... 52 D1
Rosemary St EX4 ... 176 F5
Rosemont 9 TQ1 ... 220 D4
Rosemont Ct EX2 ... 177 B1
Rosemoor Rd EX38 ... 159 E5
Rose Moor Rd EX38 ... 159 E5
Rosemount
Bideford EX39 ... 156 E4
Paignton TQ4 ... 226 C5
Rosemount Cl EX14 ... 166 B5
Rosemount Ct TQ8 ... 259 D5
Rosemount La EX14 ... 166 B5
Rosery Rd TQ2 ... 219 E5
Rosevean Ct 8 PL3 ... 248 F6
Rosevean Gdns PL3 ... 248 F6
Rosevean Ho 7 PL3 ... 248 F6
Roseveare Cl PL9 ... 256 A8
Roseville St TQ6 ... 233 F3
Rosewarne Ave TQ12 ... 207 F2
Roseway EX8 ... 202 F8
Rosewell Cl EX14 ... 166 D7
Rosewood Cl PL9 ... 255 F5
Rosewood Cres EX5 ... 179 E2
Rosewood Gr EX31 ... 154 C3
Rosewood Terr 5 EX4 ... 177 D8
Roslyn Gdns EX39 ... 156 B7
Rospeath Cres PL2 ... 248 D8
Rossall Dr TQ3 ... 226 A5
Ross Cl EX1 ... 174 F1
Rosse Rd EX16 ... 161 D6
Rosshayne La EX14 ... 68 F2
Rosslyn Park Rd PL3 ... 248 D5
Ross Pk TQ12 ... 211 E3
Ross St PL2 ... 247 E4
Rosyl Ave EX7 ... 204 C3
Rothbury Cl PL6 ... 245 E4
Rothbury Gdns PL6 ... 245 D4
Rotherfold TQ9 ... 223 B5
Rothesay Gdns PL5 ... 244 D3
Rougemont
Shaldon TQ14 ... 209 F4
Shaldon TQ14 ... 210 B2
Rougemont Ave TQ2 ... 213 D1
Rougemont Cl PL3 ... 249 B7
Rougemont Ct EX6 ... 181 F4
Rougemont Dr EX1 ... 175 B1
Rougemont Terr EX13 ... 167 D5
Roundball Cl EX14 ... 166 C4
Roundball La EX14 ... 166 B2
Round Berry Dr TQ8 ... 259 C4
Round Cross TQ11 ... 236 B6
Roundham Ave TQ4 ... 226 D5
Roundham Cres TQ4 ... 226 D5
Roundham Gdns TQ4 ... 226 D4
Roundham Ho TQ4 ... 226 C5
Roundhead Rd TQ12 ... 180 F3
Roundhill EX16 ... 161 B3
Roundhill Cl EX4 ... 173 A3
Roundhill Rd TQ2 ... 219 D2
Roundhouse La EX8 ... 196 B2
Roundings The TQ5 ... 229 B5
Roundmoors Cl TQ12 ... 213 A3
Roundsleys La PL19 ... 117 E6
ROUNDSWELL ... 154 B2
Roundswell Com Prim Acad 3 EX31 ... 154 A3
Roundtable Meet EX4 ... 174 B1
Roundway The TQ12 ... 212 F6
ROUSDON ... 193 F7
Rousdown Rd TQ2 ... 219 E4
Rowan Cl
East Ogwell TQ12 ... 206 F1
Great Torrington EX38 ... 159 F6
2 Honiton EX14 ... 85 C2
Plymouth PL7 ... 251 B5
Tavistock PL19 ... 171 C3
Tiverton EX16 ... 161 F5
Rowancroft (Exeter Univ) EX2 ... 177 F6
Rowan Ct PL12 ... 242 C2
Rowan Dr EX12 ... 192 A8
Rowan Lea EX15 ... 162 C3
Rowan Pk 2 EX31 ... 154 C2
Rowan Rd TQ3 ... 225 E3
Rowans The PL16 ... 105 E4
Rowan Tree Rd TQ12 ... 207 E1
Rowan Way
Brixham TQ5 ... 229 F1
Brixham TQ5 ... 230 A2
Exeter EX4 ... 176 F7
Plymouth PL6 ... 245 E7
Rowan Wood Rd PL19 ... 117 D3
Rowbrook Cl TQ4 ... 225 E3
Rowcliffe Cotts TA21 ... 50 F8
Rowcroft Cl EX14 ... 166 B5
Rowcroft Rd TQ3 ... 226 C8
Rowden Cross
Salcombe TQ7 ... 148 A8
Teignmouth TQ14 ... 124 C1
Widecombe in the Moor TQ13 ... 121 A3
Rowden Ct PL8 ... 141 A6
Rowdens Ho The TQ14 ... 210 D6
Rowdens Rd TQ2 ... 219 F5
Rowden St PL3 ... 248 E5
Rowdens The TQ14 ... 210 C6
Rowdon Brook EX6 ... 112 F5
Rowdown Cl PL7 ... 251 D4
Rowe Cl
Bideford EX39 ... 25 E4
Rockwell Green TA21 ... 160 A4
Rowell Cross EX20 ... 107 F4
Rowells Mead 4 TQ12 ... 122 F1
Rowena EX39 ... 156 C6
Rowes Orchard EX15 ... 162 C3
Rowe St PL11 ... 247 B3
Rowhorne Rd EX4 ... 176 C8
Row La
Dulverton TA22 ... 33 A8
Hawkridge TA22 ... 21 E1
Hawkridge TA22 ... 32 F8
Plymouth PL5 ... 243 E2
Rowland Cl PL9 ... 255 E5
Rowley Cross EX31 ... 4 D1
Rowley Gate EX31 ... 11 B6
Rowley Rd TQ1 ... 214 C1
Rowlstone Cl EX8 ... 196 C3
Rowse Gdns PL18 ... 125 D3
Rowsell's La TQ9 ... 223 D5
Rows La
Bampton EX16 ... 34 A1
22 Combe Martin EX34 ... 3 A3
Row The EX36 ... 30 A2
Row Tor Cl EX20 ... 170 D5
Rowtry Cross EX20 ... 76 F5
Royal Albert Meml Mus & Art Gall★ EX4 ... 261 A3
Royal Ave The EX8 ... 201 F7
Royal Charter Pk 7 EX18 ... 44 E1
Royal Citadel★ PL1 ... 263 A1
Royal Cl EX2 ... 181 B7
Royal Clarence Appts 4 EX12 ... 192 B4
Royal Clarence Apts 4 EX34 ... 150 B6
Royal Cres EX2 ... 178 D3
Royal Ct
Princetown PL20 ... 128 A8
Torquay TQ1 ... 220 D7
Royal Devon & Exeter Hospl (Heavitree) EX1 ... 177 E6
Royal Devon & Exeter Hospl (Wonford) EX2 ... 177 F4
Royal Eye Infmy PL4 ... 248 E4
Royal London Ct EX10 ... 188 B3
Royal Navy Ave
Plymouth PL2 ... 247 F6
Plymouth PL5 ... 247 F6
Royal Oak Cl EX15 ... 67 B2
Royal Oak Cotts EX20 ... 107 F8
Royal Oak Cross EX14 ... 86 E6
Royal Observer Wy EX12 ... 192 B5
Royal Par PL1 ... 262 C2
Royal Pines TQ1 ... 220 E3
Royal Way EX6 ... 201 B8
Royal William Rd PL1 ... 254 A8
Royal William Yard PL1 ... 254 A8
Royston Ct 4 EX1 ... 178 C8
Royston Rd
Bideford EX39 ... 156 F1
Churchinford TA3 ... 68 D7
ROYSTON WATER ... 68 F8
Rozel TQ1 ... 220 D3
Rubby Cross EX6 ... 97 E5
Ruby Cl
Holsworthy TA20 ... 72 A6
Holsworthy TA20 ... 164 C3
Ruby Red Row EX3 ... 182 D8
Ruckamore Rd TQ2 ... 219 E5
Ruckham La EX16 ... 62 F6
Rudds Bldgs 4 EX16 ... 161 B4
Rudyard Way EX39 ... 156 B6
Rudyerd Wlk PL3 ... 249 D6
Rudy La TA22 ... 33 E6
Rue de Courseulles sur Mer TQ6 ... 233 F4
Rue St Pierre PL21 ... 237 E5
Rufford Cl 1 PL2 ... 248 A7
Rugby Rd EX4 ... 177 A4
Ruggaton La EX34 ... 2 D2
Rule Cross EX23 ... 37 B2
Rull Cross EX16 ... 48 C5
Rull Hill
Oakford EX16 ... 48 C5
West Worlington EX17 ... 61 B8
Rull La EX15 ... 163 B6
Rumbelow Rd EX16 ... 161 E6
RUMSAM ... 155 B1
Rumsam Cl EX32 ... 155 B2
Rumsam Gdns EX32 ... 155 C2
Rumsam Mdws EX32 ... 155 B2
Rumsam Rd EX32 ... 155 B2
Runaway La PL21 ... 137 A2
Rundle Rd TQ12 ... 207 C4
RUNDLESTONE ... 118 F2
Runnacleave Rd EX34 ... 150 B6
RUNNINGTON ... 51 F8
Runnon Moor La EX20 ... 75 B7
Runnymede Ct PL6 ... 245 E2
Runway Rd PL6 ... 245 B5
Rupert Price Way TQ12 ... 123 B2
Rupertswood EX34 ... 150 C6
Rus Cotts EX17 ... 165 A5
Rushcott Cl EX31 ... 153 A4
Rushcott Cross
Newton Tracey EX31 ... 27 B7
Stonyland EX31 ... 27 B8
RUSHFORD ... 116 E3
Rushforth Pl EX4 ... 176 E8
Rushlade Cl TQ4 ... 225 F2
Rush Meadow Rd EX5 ... 99 B6
Rush Park Terr PL18 ... 125 C7
Rush Way TQ9 ... 223 F5
Ruskin Cres PL5 ... 244 D2
Rusper Cl EX15 ... 83 F6
Russel Cl EX32 ... 17 C1
Russel La EX15 ... 65 A1
Russell Ave PL3 ... 248 F7
Russell Cl
East Budleigh EX9 ... 198 B6
Gunnislake PL18 ... 125 D7
Plymouth PL9 ... 256 B7
Saltash PL12 ... 242 C3
Russell Court Gdns PL19 ... 171 B6
Russell Ct
Plymouth PL1 ... 262 C2
Salcombe TQ8 ... 259 E5
Saltash PL12 ... 242 C3
Tavistock PL19 ... 171 B6
Russell Dr EX9 ... 198 B6
Russell Pl PL1 ... 262 B4
Russell St
Exeter EX1 ... 261 C3
Sidmouth EX10 ... 188 B3
Tavistock PL19 ... 171 C5
Russell Terr EX4 ... 261 A4
Russell Way EX2 ... 178 D2
Russell Wlk EX2 ... 178 C3
Russet Ave EX1 ... 178 C6
Russet Cl
Uffculme EX15 ... 66 A7
Wellington TA21 ... 160 E7
Russet Gdns TQ7 ... 258 E7
Russets La TQ11 ... 236 C5
Russet Way PL8 ... 257 A5
Russet Wood PL5 ... 243 F4
Russon's La EX37 ... 44 B7
Ruston Hill EX17 ... 61 A6
Rutger Pl PL1 ... 262 A4
Rutherford St EX2 ... 178 A4
Ruthven Cl PL6 ... 248 F8
Rutland Rd PL4 ... 248 F4
Rutley Field EX4 ... 174 F3
Rutt's Cross EX14 ... 84 E2
Ruxhill La EX31 ... 10 D5
Ryall's Cnr
Beaford EX20 ... 42 A1
Merton EX20 ... 57 A8
Ryall's Corner EX19 ... 57 A8
Ryalls Ct EX12 ... 192 A5
Rydal Cl PL6 ... 245 D2
Rydal Mews EX4 ... 176 F5
Ryde Cl TQ2 ... 214 A2
Ryder Cl 16 EX16 ... 64 D7
Ryder Rd PL2 ... 247 F4
RYDON ... 207 E8
Rydon Acres
Kingsteignton TQ12 ... 207 E8
Stoke Gabriel TQ9 ... 227 F8
Rydon Ave TQ12 ... 207 E8
Rydonball Cross TQ12 ... 211 F7
Rydon Cross
Denbury TQ12 ... 211 D6
Stoke Gabriel TQ9 ... 227 F8
Rydon Est TQ12 ... 207 E8
Rydon Ind Est TQ12 ... 207 D6
Rydon La
Abbotskerswell TQ12 ... 212 C6
Exeter EX2 ... 178 C3
Exton EX3, EX5 ... 183 E2
Holsworthy EX22 ... 71 E7
Payhembury EX14 ... 84 B4
Rydon Lane Ret Pk EX2 ... 178 C3
Rydon Orch EX9 ... 198 F8
Rydon Prim Sch TQ12 ... 207 E8
Rydon Rd
Holsworthy EX22 ... 164 B5
Kingsteignton TQ12 ... 207 E8
Rydons TQ5 ... 230 A4
Rye Hill PL12 ... 242 C2
Rye La TQ7 ... 144 B5
Ryeland Cl PL9 ... 140 D8
Ryelands Farm Ind Est TA21 ... 160 B3
Rye Park Cl EX19 ... 42 D1
Rye Pk
Beaford EX19 ... 42 D1
Monkton EX14 ... 86 C5
Ryll Cl EX8 ... 202 B7
Ryll Court Dr EX8 ... 202 B7
Ryll Gr EX8 ... 202 B7

S

Sabre Cl TQ12 ... 180 E3
Sabre Wlk 1 EX32 ... 155 B5
Sackery TQ12 ... 208 D4
Sackville Cl PL9 ... 255 F7
Sacred Heart RC Sch 7 TQ3 ... 226 D7
Saddleback Cl TQ12 ... 211 F8
Saddlers Cl EX6 ... 96 F3
Saddlers Way
Okehampton EX20 ... 170 D6
Plymouth TQ12 ... 244 C8
Saddle The TQ4 ... 226 C2
Sadler Cl EX8 ... 202 E8
Sadler Gn TQ13 ... 180 C6
Saffron Ct TQ7 ... 258 D5
Saffron Pk TQ7 ... 258 D5
Sage Gr EX16 ... 161 F4
Sage Park Rd EX33 ... 152 B7
Sages Lea EX5 ... 184 C6
Sailmakers Ct EX8 ... 201 E6
St Agnes La TQ2 ... 219 E3
St Albans Cl EX4 ... 176 E6
St Albans La TQ1 ... 220 C7
St Albans Pk PL20 ... 127 A2
St Albans Rd TQ1 ... 220 C7
St Andrew St N EX16 ... 161 C3
St Andrew St S EX16 ... 161 C3
St Andrew's CE Prim Sch
Buckland Monachorum PL20 ... 126 C3
Chardstock EX13 ... 88 A7
Plymouth PL1 ... 262 B2
St Andrews Cl
Ashburton TQ13 ... 130 F4
12 Bere Alston PL20 ... 125 E1
Cullompton EX15 ... 163 C3
Saltash PL12 ... 242 C2
Sutcombe EX22 ... 54 A6
St Andrew's Cl
Calstock PL18 ... 125 D3
Feniton EX14 ... 84 D2
Kennford EX6 ... 114 E4
Yarnscombe EX31 ... 27 E2
St Andrew's Cross 1 PL1 ... 263 A2
St Andrews Ct
3 Tiverton EX16 ... 161 E6
Torquay TQ2 ... 219 C8
St Andrews Dr EX13 ... 167 F7
St Andrew's Est EX15 ... 163 B4
St Andrews Ho EX8 ... 201 F6
St Andrews Mdw DT7 ... 260 D4
St Andrews Orch EX24 ... 103 A5
St Andrew's Pl PL10 ... 253 A1
St Andrews Prim Sch EX15 ... 163 B3
St Andrews Rd
Cullompton EX15 ... 163 C3
Fremington EX31 ... 153 D6
Paignton TQ4 ... 226 C5
Tavistock PL19 ... 171 D2
St Andrew's Rd
Cowley EX4 ... 172 F2
Exmouth EX8 ... 201 F6
St Andrew's Sq EX24 ... 103 A5
St Andrew's St PL10 ... 253 A1
St Andrew St
Millbrook PL10 ... 252 E5
Plymouth PL1 ... 262 C2
ST ANDREW'S WOOD ... 84 A8
St Annes EX6 ... 194 D3
St Annes Cl EX22 ... 70 E1
St Annes Ct TQ12 ... 207 B3
St Annes Pl EX5 ... 82 B5
St Anne's Rd
Exeter EX1 ... 177 E7
Plymouth PL6 ... 245 D6
Saltash PL12 ... 242 E3
Torquay TQ1 ... 220 D7
St Annes Well Brewery EX4 ... 261 A3
St Annes Well Mews EX4 ... 261 A3
ST ANN'S CHAPEL
Gunnislake ... 125 B6
Kingston ... 142 F6
St Anthony's Cl EX11 ... 169 E4
St Ash TA20 ... 69 F7
St Aubyn Ave PL2 ... 247 F5
St Aubyn Rd PL1 ... 247 E3
St Aubyns Pk EX16 ... 161 F3
St Aubyn St PL1 ... 247 E2
St Aubyn's Villas EX16 ... 161 F3
St Aubyn Terr PL7 ... 132 F4
St Augustines Cl TQ2 ... 214 A3
St Austin Cl PL21 ... 237 B5
St Barnabas Com Hospl PL12 ... 242 F2
St Barnabas Ct PL1 ... 262 A4
St Barnabas Terr PL1 ... 262 A4
St Bartholomews Rd TQ12 ... 211 F8
St Bartholomew Way TQ12 ... 206 D1

St Bernard's Cl
Buckfast TQ11 236 B7
Exeter EX2 261 C1
St Boniface Cl PL2 248 C7
St Boniface Dr PL2 248 C7
St Boniface Rd EX17 165 A5
St Boniface's RC Coll PL5 244 E1
ST BRANNOCKS 152 C7
St Brannock's Hill EX33 152 D7
St Brannock's Park Rd EX34 150 B4
St Brannock's Rd EX34 150 B4
St Brannock's Well Cl EX33 152 D7
St Briac Way EX8 196 E3
St Bridget Ave PL6 244 F1
ST BUDEAUX 243 D2
St Budeaux Bypass
Plymouth PL5 243 F1
Plymouth PL5 247 F8
Plymouth TQ12 244 A1
St Budeaux Cl EX11 169 E3
St Budeaux Ferry Rd Sta PL5 247 D8
St Budeaux Foundation CE (Aided) Jun Sch PL5 243 F2
St Budeaux Orch EX11 169 E3
St Budeaux Victoria Rd Sta PL5 243 D1
St Catherines CE Prim Sch TQ12 180 F1
St Catherines Pk 6 PL8 141 A7
St Catherine's Rd TQ1 220 B8
St Chad Cl PL5 244 C4
St Christopher's Prep Sch TQ9 216 C5
St Clares Cl EX12 192 B5
St Clements Ct TQ6 233 D4
St Columba Cl TQ12 207 E8
St Columbia Cl TQ12 207 E8
St Cyres Rd EX14 166 B6
St Davids 11 EX39 157 A1
ST DAVID'S 177 B8
St Davids Cl EX13 167 F7
St David's Dr EX13 167 F7
St David's Hill EX4 177 A7
St David's Pl EX4 177 A7
St David's Prim Sch EX4 261 A3
St Davids Rd TQ14 210 C8
St David's Rd PL19 171 E5
St David's Terr EX4 261 A3
ST DOMINICK 125 A3
St Dominick CE Prim Sch PL12 125 A2
St Dominic Pk PL17 125 A4
St Dominic's Cl TQ1 220 B8
St Dunstan's Rd TQ8 259 C4
St Dunstan's Terr PL4 263 C3
ST DYMPNA'S 192 A8
St Edmunds Rd TQ7 258 C6
St Edmund's Rd TQ1 220 B7
St Edmunds wlk TQ7 258 C6
St Edward Gdns PL6 245 B1
St Edward's CE Prim Sch PL6 245 C1
St Efride's Rd TQ2 219 F5
Ste Honorine Du Fay Cl EX32 28 E8
St Elizabeth Cl PL7 250 F3
St Elmo 3 EX12 192 A4
St Elmo Ct TQ8 259 C3
St Erth Rd PL2 248 D7
St Eval Pl PL5 243 E4
St Francis Ct PL5 244 B3
St Gabriel's Ave PL3 248 D5
St Georges Ave EX13 167 F7
St George's Ave PL2 248 C7
St George's CE Prim Sch PL1 262 A1
St George's CE (VA) Inf Sch EX39 156 F8
St Georges Cl 15 PL21 137 B2
St Georges Cres TQ1 220 C7
St Georges Ct 1 PL2 247 F4
St Georges Hill DT7 260 C4
St Georges La EX7 204 C3
St Georges Rd PL12 242 D3
St George's Rd
Barnstaple EX32 155 A6
Saltash PL12 242 E3
Torquay TQ1 220 C7
St George's Terr
1 Barnstaple EX32 155 A6
Plymouth PL2 247 F4
Shillingford St George EX2 114 C6
St George's View EX15 163 B4
St George's Way EX16 161 C3
ST GEORGE'S WELL 163 C5
St George's Well Ave EX15 163 B4
St Germans Rd EX4 173 C1
St German's Rd EX4 177 C8
ST GILES IN THE WOOD 42 B6
ST GILES ON THE HEATH 90 B1
St Giles on the Heath Com Sch PL15 90 C1
St Gregorys Ct EX12 192 A6
St Helens EX39 156 A2
St Helen's CE (VA) Prim Sch EX39 156 A1
St Helen's Cl EX33 7 E2
St Helen's Cl EX10 187 F3
St Helens Wlk PL5 244 C5
St Hilary Sch of English 14 TQ4 226 B6
St Hilary Terr PL4 263 C3
SAINT HILL 66 D3
St Hill Cl EX2 177 A2
St Ida's Cl EX2 176 D1
St Ives Ct 5 TQ1 220 A6
ST JAMES' 177 D8
St James CE Prim Sch EX20 170 D6
St James Cl
Exeter EX4 261 C4
Landkey EX32 17 C1
Parkham EX39 39 E8
St James Ct
Exeter EX4 177 E8
Plymouth PL1 262 B2
Torpoint PL11 247 B3
St James' Ho 16 TQ14 210 B5
St James Mews
Plymouth PL1 262 B2
18 Teignmouth TQ14 210 B5
St James' Park (Exeter City AFC) EX4 261 C4
St James' Park Sta EX4 261 C4
St James Pl TQ1 220 D7
St James' Place E PL1 262 B2
St James' Place W PL1 262 B2
St Jame's Prec 15 TQ14 210 B5
St James Rd
Torpoint PL11 247 B2
Torquay TQ1 220 A7
St James' Rd EX4 261 C4
St James Sch EX4 174 B1
St James's Pl EX34 150 C6
St James St EX20 170 B5
St James Terr
Exeter EX4 261 C4
Plymouth PL1 262 B2
St James Way 4 EX16 161 E6
St Joeseph's RC Prim Sch TQ12 207 A4
ST JOHN 252 C8
St John Cl 8 TQ13 180 C7
St Johns PL19 171 C5
St Johns Ave PL19 171 C5
St John's Bridge Rd PL4 263 B2
St John's CE Prim Sch
Totnes TQ9 223 E5
Wellington TA21 160 E6
Wellington TA21 160 E7
ST JOHN'S CHAPEL 27 B8
St Johns Cl
16 Colyton EX24 103 A4
Plymouth PL6 245 D4
11 Tiverton EX16 161 E6
Wellington TA21 160 E6
St John's Cl
Bishopsteignton TQ14 208 F7
Bovey Tracey TQ13 180 C6
Honiton EX14 166 C6
Ivybridge PL21 237 B5
Millbrook PL10 252 E5
Skilgate TA4 34 E6
St John's Cotts TQ13 180 C6
St Johns Ct
Bradworthy EX22 53 E8
Tavistock PL19 171 C4
St John's Ct 3 TQ3 226 B6
St John's Dr
Bradworthy EX22 53 E8
Plymouth PL9 255 B6
St Johns Farm Mews EX8 196 F3
St Johns La PL11 252 B8
St John's La
Barnstaple EX32 155 C3
Bovey Tracey TQ13 180 C7
St John's Pl TQ1 220 B4
St John's RC Prim Sch EX16 161 B4
St John's Rd
Exeter EX1 177 E7
Exmouth EX8 196 E2
Horrabridge PL20 126 F4
Ivybridge PL21 237 B5
Millbrook PL10 252 F5
Plymouth PL4 263 B2
Plymouth, Turnchapel PL9 255 A6
St John's Sch EX10 187 F5
St Johns St TQ12 207 D4
St John's St PL4 263 B2
St John's Terr TQ9 223 B6
St John's Villas EX2 177 F5
St John the Baptist RC Prim Sch TQ6 233 C2
St Joseph's Cl
Plymouth PL6 244 F1
Rumsam EX32 155 C2
St Joseph's RC Prim Sch
Exmouth EX8 202 B7
Plymouth PL1 247 E2
ST JUDE'S 263 B3
St Jude's Rd PL4 263 B2
St Julians Cres PL10 253 E7
St Katharine's Rd TQ2 219 E6
St Katherine's Cl EX31 153 A5
St Katherine's Mews 5 TQ9 223 C5
St Katherines Rd EX4 178 A8
St Katherine's Way TQ9 223 C5
St Keverne Pl PL2 248 D8
St Keyes Cl 10 EX32 17 B2
St Kitts Cl TQ2 213 F2
St Lawrence Cl 12 EX16 64 D7
St Lawrence Cres EX1 178 D6
St Lawrence Dr EX17 165 B5
St Lawrence La TQ13 130 F4
St Lawrence Mews PL4 263 A4
St Lawrence Rd PL4 263 A4
St Lawrence's Gn EX17 165 B5
St Leonard's Ave EX2 261 B1
St Leonard's CE Prim Sch EX2 261 C1
St Leonard's Cl 16 TQ12 207 B3
St Leonard's Pl EX2 261 C2
St Leonards Rd EX14 166 A5
St Leonard's Rd
Exeter EX2 261 C2
Newton Abbot TQ12 207 B3
Plymouth PL4 263 C2
St Leo Pl PL2 247 E4
St Levan Rd PL2 247 F5
ST LOYE'S 178 A3
St Loye's Ct EX2 178 A4
St Loyes Gdns EX2 178 A5
St Loyes Rd EX2 178 A5
St Loye's Terr EX2 178 A4
Saint Luke's Campus EX1 177 E6
St Luke's Cl TQ12 207 F1
St Lukes Dr TQ14 210 A6
St Lukes Pk TQ1 220 A4
St Luke's Pk TQ2 220 A4
St Luke's Rd
Kingskerswell TQ12 212 E8
Torquay TQ2 220 A4
St Luke's Road N TQ2 220 B4
St Luke's Road S TQ2 220 A4
St Luke's Science & Sports Coll EX1 178 D8
St Malo Cl EX8 196 E3
St Marco Gdns TQ7 258 D6
St Margaret Clitherow RC Prim Sch TQ5 230 B3
St Margaret's Acad 2 TQ1 220 B8
St Margaret's Ave TQ1 220 B7
St Margaret's CE (Aided) Jun Sch EX39 156 F7
St Margarets Cl EX15 67 B8
St Margaret's Cl TQ1 220 B8
St Margarets Ct EX3 182 E5
St Margaret's Ct 7 EX39 156 F7
St Margarets Gdn 1 EX31 154 F6
St Margarets La TA20 88 C8
St Margarets Rd PL7 250 B7
St Margaret's Rd TQ1 220 B8
St Margaret's Sch EX2 177 E5
St Margarets Terr EX3 182 F5
St Margaret's View EX8 203 A7
St Marks 20 EX7 204 E6
St Marks Ave EX1 177 F7
St Mark's CE Prim Sch EX23 37 B2
St Marks Dr TQ1 220 D3
St Marks Rd PL6 245 D5
St Mark's Rd
Honiton EX14 166 A4
Torquay TQ1 220 D3
St Martin's Ave PL3 248 D7
St Martin's CE Prim Sch
Cranbrook EX5 99 A6
Whimple EX5 99 A6
St Martins Cl EX10 188 B6
St Martin's Cl EX17 78 C4
St Martins Ct TQ2 213 F1
St Martin's La EX17 165 B6
St Martin's Mews TQ1 220 C8
St Martins Rd EX23 70 A8
St Marwenne Cl EX23 70 A6
ST MARYCHURCH 214 C1
St Marychurch CE Prim Sch TQ1 214 B1
St Marychurch Rd
Newton Abbot TQ12 207 F1
St Marychurch TQ1 214 C1
Torquay, Plainmoor TQ1 220 B6
St Mary Church Rd TQ2 213 F5
St Maryhaye PL19 171 A5
St Mary Magdalen Cl TQ14 208 F7
St Mary's CE Prim Sch EX39 157 A4
St Marys Cl
Abbotskerswell TQ12 212 A6
17 Chudleigh TQ13 123 E6
Plymouth PL7 250 D5
St Mary's Cl
Axminster EX13 167 F5
Brixham TQ5 230 B2
Great Torrington EX38 159 B4
St Mary's Cotts EX7 200 F4
St Marys Ct PL7 250 D5
St Mary's Ct
4 Newton Abbot TQ12 207 B3
Paignton TQ3 226 A6
Torquay TQ1 214 B1
St Marys Dr EX38 43 C7
St Mary's Dr TQ5 230 D3
St Mary's Flats 6 EX39 157 A1
St Marys Hill TQ5 230 D3
St Mary's Hill TQ5 230 D3
St Mary's La DT7 104 B6
St Marys Pk EX11 169 F3
St Mary's Pk TQ4 225 C4
St Marys Pl TQ12 211 D2
St Mary's RC Prim Sch
Axminster EX13 167 E5
Buckfast TQ11 236 C7
St Mary's Rd
Barnstaple EX32 155 A6
Brixham TQ5 230 D2
Croyde EX33 7 E2
Newton Abbot TQ12 207 B2
Plymouth PL7 250 C6
Teignmouth TQ14 210 A7
St Mary St PL1 262 A2
St Mary Steps Terr 8 EX1 261 A2
St Marys View
Silverton EX5 82 B5
West Hill EX11 168 E5
St Matthew's CE Prim and Nursery Acad PL6 245 C3
St Matthews Cl EX1 177 E6
St Matthew's Rd TQ2 219 D4
St Matthews Wlk EX1 261 C3
St Matthias Church Rd TQ1 220 E5
St Maurice Ct PL7 250 F4
St Maurice Mews PL7 250 E4
St Maurice Rd PL7 250 F3
St Maurice View PL7 251 B4
St Mawes Dr TQ4 229 B8
St Mawes Terr 8 PL2 247 F5
St Michael Ave PL2 247 F5
ST MICHAELS 226 A5
St Michaels DT7 260 E4
St Michael's TQ2 219 E6
St Michael's Bsns Ctr DT7 260 E3
St Michael's CE Prim Sch
Exeter EX1 177 F6
Kingsteignton TQ12 207 E7
St Michael's CE (VA) Prim Sch DT7 260 E4
St Michaels Cl
Lawhitton PL15 105 D1
Otterton EX9 198 E7
St Michael's Cl
Clyst Honiton EX5 179 D8
Exeter EX2 177 B1
Plymouth PL1 247 E1
Torquay TQ1 219 E6
St Michael's Ct
Paignton TQ4 226 A4
7 Plymouth PL1 247 F3
St Michael's Hill EX5 179 D8
St Michaels Ho 4 DT7 260 D3
St Michaels Rd
Kingsteignton TQ12 207 D6
Teignmouth TQ14 210 C7
St Michael's Rd
Newton Abbot TQ12 207 D1
Paignton TQ4 226 B5
Torquay TQ1 219 E7
St Michaels Terr 5 TQ10 134 F2
St Michael's Terr
Plymouth PL4 262 C4
8 Plymouth, Devonport PL1 247 F3
2 Torquay TQ1 220 B5
St Michaels View EX21 55 E4
St Michaels Wy 14 EX5 99 A6
St Modwen Rd PL6 249 F7
St Nazaire App PL1 247 F2
St Nazaire Cl PL1 247 E2
St Nicholas CE Prim Sch 1 EX10 188 A7
St Nicholas Cl 5 EX1 178 F8
St Nicholas Priory★ EX4 261 A2
St Nicholas RC Prim Sch EX1 178 C6
St Nicholas Rise EX14 85 D5
St Olave's Cl EX4 261 A3
St Olaves Mews EX4 261 A3
St Oswins TQ1 220 B8
St Pancras Ave PL2 248 D8
St Patrick's Cl TQ14 210 A6
St Pauls Cl
Bovey Tracey TQ13 180 D7
Exeter EX2 177 F3
Plymouth PL3 249 C5
Torquay TQ1 220 B7
St Paul's Cres TQ1 220 B7
St Paul's Ct 16 TQ12 207 C3
St Pauls Dr EX22 164 B5
St Paul's Rd
Honiton EX14 166 A5
15 Newton Abbot TQ12 207 C3
Paignton TQ3 219 D1
Torquay TQ1 220 B7
St Paul's Roman Catholic Primary Sch PL5 243 D1
St Paul's Sq EX16 161 C3
St Paul St
Plymouth PL1 254 A8
Tiverton EX16 161 C4
St Peter Cl PL7 250 F4
St Peters EX22 38 E1
St Peter's CE (Aided) Prim Sch EX9 197 F2
St Peter's CE (Aided) Sch EX1 178 D5
St Peter's CE Sch EX2 178 C5
St Peter's CE (VA) Jun Sch PL19 171 D5
St Peter's CE (VA) Prim Sch PL1 262 B3
St Peters Cl
Shirwell EX31 17 B8
Torquay TQ2 219 D6
West Buckland EX32 18 B2
St Peter's Cl TQ13 180 E8
St Peters Ct
Plymouth PL1 262 A3
Sidmouth EX10 188 B3
St Peter's Hill 5 TQ5 230 D5
St Peters Mount EX4 176 D7
St Peter's Quay TQ9 223 D4
St Peter's RC Prim Sch PL5 244 B5
St Peters Rd
Fremington EX31 153 D5
Holsworthy EX22 164 B5
Plymouth PL5 244 C2
St Peter's Rd EX14 166 A5
St Peter's School EX8 196 A6
St Peter St EX16 161 C4
St Peters Terr 2 EX34 150 C5
St Peter's Terr 9 EX31 154 F5
St Peters Way PL21 237 E3
St Peters Well La EX22 53 E8
St Petrock's Cl EX2 261 C2
St Phillips Ct EX4 176 F4
St Ronans 2 TQ1 220 D5
St Rumon's CE Inf Sch PL19 171 C6
St Saviours Ho 20 EX8 202 A6
St Saviours Rd EX11 169 D3
St Saviour's Way EX17 165 B5
St Scholastica's Abbey TQ14 210 D7
St Sevan Way EX8 196 E3
St Sidwell's Ave EX4 261 C4
St Sidwell's CE Prim Sch EX4 261 C4
St Sidwell's Ct EX4 261 B4
St Simon's La PL4 249 B3
St Stephen Rd PL7 250 F3
ST STEPHENS 242 D2
St Stephens Com Prim Sch PL12 242 E2
St Stephen's Hill PL12 242 C1
St Stephen's Pl PL7 250 E5
St Stephen's Rd PL12 242 E2
St Stephen St PL1 247 F1
St Swithin's EX17 80 A5
St Teresa Ho PL4 263 A3
St Teresa's Cl EX39 156 F7
St Teresa's Ct 9 EX39 156 F7
St Therese's Ct PL1 247 F2
ST THOMAS 177 A3
St Thomas Cl
Bovey Tracey TQ13 180 E7
Plymouth PL7 250 F3
St Thomas Ct
Exeter EX4 177 A4
2 Tiverton EX16 161 E6
StThomas Prim Sch EX2 177 A4
StThomas Sh Ctr EX4 177 A4
StThomas Sta EX4 177 A4
St Vincent Ho TQ1 220 C3
St Vincents Cl TQ1 219 F6
St Vincent's Rd TQ1 219 F7
St Vincent St PL2 247 E4
St Werburgh Cl PL9 140 D7
St Wilfrid's Sch EX4 261 A3
Salamanca St PL11 247 B3
SALCOMBE 259 B4
Salcombe CE Prim Sch TQ8 259 C5
Salcombe Ct EX10 188 C4
Salcombe Hill Cl EX10 188 B4
Salcombe Hill Rd EX10 188 C4
Salcombe Hts Cl TQ8 259 C5
Salcombe Lawn EX10 188 B4
Salcombe Maritime & Local History Mus★ TQ8 259 E5
Salcombe Rd
Malborough TQ7, TQ8 147 F6
Plymouth PL4 263 C4
Sidmouth EX10 188 B4
SALCOMBE REGIS 188 F6
Salcombe The TQ8 259 E4
Salcombe to Kingsbridge Nature Reserve★ TQ7 148 C7
Salem Almshouses 7 EX32 155 A4
Salem Pl EX4 261 C4
Salem St 8 EX32 155 A4
Salisbury Ave
Feniton EX14 84 D2
Torquay TQ2 213 F1
Salisbury Cl EX14 84 D2
Salisbury Ope PL3 248 B5
Salisbury Rd
Exeter EX4 177 E8
Exmouth EX8 202 A7
Newton Abbot TQ12 207 D4
Plymouth PL4 263 C4
Salisbury Road Prim Sch PL4 263 C3
Salisbury Terr
Kilmington EX13 87 C1
9 Teignmouth TQ14 210 C5
Sallicombe Rd EX24 101 F6
SALMONHUTCH 165 B2
Salmonhutch Cotts EX17 165 B3
Salmon Leap Cl TQ11 236 C5
Salmonpool La EX2 177 E3
Salmons Leap TQ9 223 B7
Salston Barton EX11 169 C2
Salston Ride
Ottery St Mary EX10 100 C5
Ottery St Mary EX11 169 B2
SALTASH 242 B1
Saltash Bsns Pk PL12 242 C4
Saltash Com Sch PL12 242 E1
Saltash Her Mus★ Pl12 243 A2
Saltash Ind Est PL12 242 C4
Saltash L Ctr PL12 242 E2
Saltash Parkway Ind Est PL12 242 B4
Saltash Rd
Plymouth PL3 262 C4
Plymouth, Keyham PL2 247 E6
Saltash Sta PL12 243 A2
Saltburn Rd PL5 243 C1
Salterne Mdws EX9 198 A2
Saltern Rd TQ4 226 C1
Salterns Terr EX39 157 B2
Salter's Bldgs 4 EX16 161 D4
Salter's Cross EX10 187 D6
Salters Ct EX2 178 A4
Salter's La EX24 103 A4
Salters Mdw EX10 188 B5
Salter's Rd EX2 178 A4
Salterton Ct EX8 202 F8
Salterton Rd
Budleigh Salterton EX8, EX9 197 B1
Exmouth EX8 202 C7
Salterton Workshops 1 EX9 198 A1
Salting Hill EX9 199 I2
Saltings The
Seaton EX12 192 B7
Shaldon TQ14 209 D5
Saltmer Cl EX34 150 A2
Salt Mill PL12 242 F4
Saltmill Cl PL12 242 F3
Saltram House★ PL7 250 A4
Saltram Terr
Lee Moor PL7 132 F4
Plymouth PL7 250 E5
SALTRENS 25 F1
Saltrens EX39 40 F8
Saltways La EX10 100 F1
Salt Wood La EX34 2 F3
Salty La TQ14 209 D5
Salutary Mount EX1 177 F5
Salway Cl EX15 163 B3
Salway Gdns EX13 167 F5
Samara Bsns Pk TQ12 180 F3
SAMPFORD ARUNDEL 51 E5

Sampford Arundel Prim Sch TA21 51 E5
SAMPFORD CHAPPLE 76 E3
SAMPFORD COURTENAY 76 F4
Sampford Courtenay Sta EX20 77 A2
Sampford Cross EX20 76 F3
Sampford Gdns PL20 127 A5
SAMPFORD MOOR 51 E5
SAMPFORD PEVERELL 50 E1
Sampford Peverell CE Prim Sch EX16 50 C1
SAMPFORD SPINEY 127 B7
Sampford Terr 7 PL20 126 F5
Sampson Cross EX37 44 E8
Sampson's Hill EX2 114 C6
Sampsons La EX1 177 E7
Sampsons Plantation EX31 153 C5
Sams Cl EX39 25 C4
Samuel Bassett Ave PL6 245 B7
Sanctuary Cl
Bishop's Tawton EX32 16 E1
9 Keyham PL2 247 F5
Sanctuary La
Hatherleigh EX20 75 C7
Woodbury Salterton EX5 185 B7
Woodbury Salterton EX6 184 F8
Sanctuary Rd EX22 164 C4
Sandaway La EX34 2 F4
Sandclose La EX36 31 D7
Sand Down La EX5 172 A8
Sanderling Cl 16 EX32 155 A4
Sanders Cl EX5 175 D6
Sanders Cross EX22 54 C8
Sandersfield EX15 83 F6
Sanders La 8 EX32 16 E1
Sanders' La EX22 164 C5
Sanders Lea EX17 62 F1
Sanders Plantation TA4 35 C7
Sanderspool Cross TQ10 135 A2
Sanders Rd
Bow EX17 78 C4
Brixham TQ5 230 A5
Exeter EX4 174 E1
Sanders Way EX15 66 C6
SANDFORD 80 A5
Sandford Ash La EX17 79 A7
Sandford Cl EX32 155 D1
Sandford Cross EX20 77 E4
Sandford La EX20 77 F3
Sandford Orleigh TQ12 207 B5
Sandford Rd PL9 255 F8
Sandfords EX6 181 B1
Sandford Sch EX17 80 A5
Sandfords Gdns EX38 159 B4
Sandford View TQ12 207 B4
Sandford Wlk EX1 261 C3
Sandgate La EX11 100 D4
Sand Grove EX2 178 D2
Sandheap Cross TQ7 143 C2
Sand Hill PL18 125 D6
Sandhill Cross TQ13 111 E5
Sand Hill Pk PL18 125 C6
Sandhills TQ8 259 C3
Sandhills Rd TQ8 259 C3
Sandhill St EX11 169 E4
Sandhole Cross EX39 37 A8
Sandick Cross EX32 17 F2
Sand La
Calstock PL18 125 D3
Littlehempston TQ9 223 F8
Totnes TQ9 224 A8
Sandoe Way EX4 174 E3
Sandon Wlk PL6 245 A1
Sandown Rd TQ4 225 F2
Sandpark La EX31 10 D5
Sandpark Rd EX18 59 D2
Sandpath Rd TQ12 207 E6
Sandpiper Ct
Exeter EX4 174 D1
Woolacombe EX34 8 A6
Sandpiper Dr EX3 183 C2
Sandpiper Gn EX2 176 D3
Sandpiper Rd
Marhamchurch EX23 70 A8
Plymouth PL6 245 B2
Sandpiper Way TQ2 213 C2
Sandpit Hill EX24 101 E6
Sand Pit Hill La EX24 102 F4
Sandquay Rd TQ6 233 F5
Sandquay Way TQ6 233 F5
Sandringham Dr TQ3 219 B2
Sandringham Gdn EX31 154 C1
Sandringham Gdns TQ3 219 C1
Sandringham Rd TQ12 207 E3
Sands Ct
Paignton TQ4 226 B5
Seaton EX12 191 F7
Sands Gate Cross TQ13 95 F1
Sands Rd
Paignton TQ4 226 C5
Sands Rd *continued*
Slapton TQ7 145 D3
Sands Sch TQ13 130 F4
Sandstone Cl 6 EX1 178 E3
Sanduck Cross TQ13 112 A2
Sandy Cross EX9 198 A8
SANDYGATE 123 E1
Sandygate TQ13 123 E1
SANDY GATE 178 F3
Sandygate Bsns Pk TQ12 123 E1
Sandygate Mill TQ12 123 E1
Sandy La
Brampford Speke EX5 81 E1
Braunton EX33 15 A6
Broadclyst EX5 175 D5
Chittlehampton EX37 29 A5
Croyde EX33 7 E2
Dawlish EX7 204 F7
Huxham EX4 174 D8
Ivybridge PL21 237 D5
Kingsbridge TQ7, TQ9 144 B5
Staverton TQ9 216 A6
Woolacombe EX34 1 A1
Sandylane Cross EX38 41 A2
Sandy Lane Ct EX34 7 F6
Sandy Lane End TQ9 144 B6
Sandymere Rd EX39 156 F7
Sandymoor Cross EX21 72 E1
SANDY PARK 111 B8
Sandypark La EX32 18 E3
Sandy Rd PL7 251 C4
Sandy's La EX14 68 C2
Sandy View 4 EX1 178 E3
Sandy Way
Croyde EX33 7 E1
Michelcombe TQ11 129 F3
Sandyway Cross EX36 20 D4
Sandyways Cross TQ13 111 C7
Sanford Mws TA21 160 F5
Sanford Pl EX2 177 A4
Sanford Rd TQ2 219 E5
Sanford Rise TA21 160 F5
Sango Ct PL10 252 F6
Sango Rd PL11 247 A2
Sannerville Way EX6 182 B5
San Remo Terr EX7 204 F7
San Sebastian Sq PL1 262 C2
Sanson Cl EX5 173 F8
Sarah Cl PL20 125 E1
Sargent Cl EX1 178 C6
Sargents Mdw EX23 37 A1
Sarlsdown Rd EX8 202 D7
Sarum Cl PL3 248 F7
SATTERLEIGH 29 C1
Satterleigh Cross EX37 29 C1
Saturday's La TQ12 212 F1
Saundercroft Rd EX5 99 B7
Saunders Way
Cullompton EX15 163 E4
West Charleton TQ7 144 C1
Saunders Wlk PL6 244 D6
SAUNTON 14 F8
Saunton Beach Villas EX33 14 E8
Saunton Cl EX33 152 C6
Saunton Rd EX33 152 B6
Savage Rd PL5 247 D7
Savery Cl PL21 237 E6
Savery Terr PL4 249 A4
Savile Rd EX4 176 F5
Savoy Hill EX4 174 A2
Savoy St EX3 182 D7
Sawmill La EX9 197 F7
Sawmills Way 3 EX14 166 C5
Sawpit La TQ9 222 F7
Sawrey St PL1 262 A2
Sawyer Dr TQ14 124 E1
Sawyers Cl TQ13 111 F4
SAWYER'S HILL 52 E7
Sawyers Mill EX16 34 E2
Saxe St 20 TQ14 210 B5
Saxon Ave EX4 174 F2
Saxon Cl EX17 165 D4
Saxon Hts 2 TQ5 230 C4
Saxon Mdw TQ3 225 C5
Saxon Rd
Exeter EX1 177 F6
Tavistock PL19 171 A6
Saxons Croft EX32 155 C3
Saxon Way EX15 163 C6
Saxon Wy TQ12 207 F7
Scabbacombe La TQ6 235 A6
Scadsbury La EX20 75 A4
Scalders La PL21 137 C2
Scalwell La EX12 192 A7
Scalwell Mead EX12 192 A7
Scalwell Pk EX12 192 A7
Scannell Cl PL12 242 C1
Scarborough Pl TQ2 219 F5
Scarborough Rd
Torquay TQ1 220 A5
Torquay TQ2 219 F5
Scarhill Cross EX20 95 D4
Scarsdale EX8 202 C5
Scattor View EX6 112 F5
Scholars Wlk TQ7 258 D6
School Cl
Bampton EX16 34 B1
Chulmleigh EX18 60 A7
Fremington EX31 153 E5
Plymouth PL7 250 D7
School Cl *continued*
Shobrooke EX17 80 E4
Tavistock PL19 171 D5
School Cotts TQ12 207 A8
School Ct TQ6 233 D3
School Dr PL6 245 D7
Schoolhayes EX20 106 F5
School Hill
Cockwood EX6 201 B6
7 Dawlish EX7 204 D6
Lympstone EX8 195 E5
Stoke Gabriel TQ9 227 F7
Whimple EX5 99 E8
School House EX13 88 F5
School La
7 Bishop's Tawton EX32 16 E1
Blackawton TQ9 139 E1
Broadclyst EX5 175 C7
Chilsworthy EX22 53 E1
5 Colyton EX24 103 A4
Cornwood PL21 133 C2
Exeter EX2 178 A1
Exmouth EX8 196 C1
Great Torrington EX38 159 C6
Hartland EX39 22 E3
Heathfield TQ13 180 F3
Honiton EX14 166 C6
Newton Poppleford EX10 186 F8
Plymouth PL7 250 E4
Rousdon DT7 193 F7
Stover TQ12 123 B3
Taleford EX10 100 D8
Taleford EX11 169 C7
Tatworth TA20 88 C8
Tedburn St Mary EX6 97 F4
3 Teignmouth TQ14 210 A3
Thorverton EX5 81 E4
West Hill EX11 168 E5
School Rd
Brixham TQ5 230 C5
Ermington PL21 136 F4
Exeter EX2 177 A4
Kingskerswell TQ12 212 F4
Lydford EX20 107 F4
Newton Abbot TQ12 207 C3
Silverton EX5 82 B5
Stoke Fleming TQ6 146 A7
Stokeinteignhead TQ14 209 B1
Tavistock PL19 171 D2
Teigngrace TQ12 206 F8
School St 9 EX10 101 B1
School Way EX20 170 B5
Schooners Ct EX8 201 E6
Schumacher Coll TQ9 215 F2
Scobhill Rd EX35 5 E3
Scoldens Cl 14 PL21 137 B2
Sconner Rd PL11 247 A3
Scoresby Cl TQ2 214 B3
Score View EX34 150 C3
Scorpio Mws PL9 256 E8
SCORRITON 130 A3
Scotchmead EX5 99 D3
Scott Ave
18 Appledore EX39 15 A1
Exeter EX2 177 F3
Plymouth PL5 247 C8
Scott Bsns Pk PL2 248 A6
SCOTT CL TQ12 207 C3
Scott Dr EX8 196 B2
Scottleigh TQ2 219 F3
Scott Rd PL2 248 A6
Scotts 1 EX16 49 B8
Scott's Cl TQ7 143 E4
Scott's Hill TA4 35 E8
Scott's La
Raymond's Hill EX13 104 C7
Wellington TA21 160 E6
Scouse Cross EX13 88 E2
Scouse La EX13 88 E2
Scrapton La TA20 69 F5
Scratchface La
Bideford EX39 25 D4
Bideford, Littleham EX39 25 F2
Buckland Brewer EX39 40 B6
Stockleigh Pomeroy EX17 81 B6
Scratch Face La EX2 176 C2
Scratton Path TQ12 211 F8
Screechers Hill TQ13 130 F5
Sculptor Way PL9 256 E8
Scurfield Cl EX33 152 D7
Seabee Wlk EX1 178 E1
Sea Birds Pk EX33 7 E1
Seabourne Ct TQ4 226 C4
Seabrook Ave EX2 182 C7
Seabrook Mews EX2 182 C7
Seachange EX9 198 B1
Seacliff TQ2 220 B4
Seacroft Rd PL5 243 C2
Seafield Ave EX8 196 A2
Seafield La EX10 188 A3
Seafield Rd
Seaton EX12 192 A5
Sidmouth EX10 188 A4
Seafields TQ4 226 C2
Seaforth Lodge EX12 191 F6
Sea Haven EX12 192 B4
Sea Hill
Beer EX12 191 E5
Seaton EX12 192 A4
Sea King Cl EX31 16 A3
Seaking Rd EX31 153 E6
Sea Lawn Terr EX7 204 F7
Seale Cl TQ6 233 D4
Seale Hayne TQ12 206 B6
Sealey Ct EX19 42 F4
Seapoint 18 TQ14 210 B4
Sea Point TQ4 226 D5
Searle St EX17 165 C5
Searle Terr EX39 157 A7
Seashore Ctr★ TQ4 226 C4
Seaside Hill EX34 2 F4
Seasons The 5 EX4 178 C8
SEATON 192 B5
Seaton EX12 192 B5
Seaton Ave PL4 248 E4
Seaton Bsns Pk PL6 245 B3
Seaton Burn EX10 187 F4
Seaton Cl TQ1 220 D7
Seaton Down Cl EX12 191 F8
Seaton Down Hill EX12 191 F8
Seaton Down Rd EX12 192 A5
Seaton Hospl EX12 192 A6
Seaton La PL4 248 E4
Seaton Marshes Nature Reserve★ EX12 192 C6
Seaton Orch PL7 136 A8
Seaton Pl PL2 247 F5
Seaton Prim Sch EX12 192 A6
Seaton Rd
Colyford EX24 103 A3
Farway EX10, EX24 101 E5
Musbury EX13 103 D5
Seaton EX24 192 B8
Seaton Tramway★ EX12 192 C7
Seaton Way PL20 126 D2
Sea Trout Mews TQ9 216 A5
Seaview TQ7 149 A3
Sea View
Gunnislake PL18 125 B5
Ilfracombe EX34 150 D4
Sea View Ave PL4 263 C4
Seaview Cres TQ3 219 C1
Sea View Dr 7 PL9 140 D8
Sea View Gdns TQ7 147 B7
Seaview Rd DT7 104 B4
Sea View Rd
Northam EX39 156 F7
Thurlestone TQ7 143 A2
Sea View Terr
Beer EX12 191 D5
Brixham TQ5 230 C6
Plymouth PL4 263 B4
Sidmouth EX10 188 A5
Thurlestone TQ7 143 A2
Seaward Cl EX12 190 E4
Seaway Cl TQ2 219 E3
Seaway Cres TQ3 226 D8
Seaway Ct TQ5 230 B4
Seaway Gdns TQ3 226 D8
Seaway La
Tipton St John EX10 100 D2
Torquay TQ2 219 E3
Seaway Rd TQ3 226 D8
Seckerleigh Cross EX16 64 E5
Seckington Cross EX19 58 E4
Secmaton Gdns EX7 200 E1
Secmaton La EX7 200 E1
Secmaton Rise
Dawlish EX7 200 E1
Dawlish EX7 204 F8
Second Ave
Axminster EX13 167 F7
Dawlish EX7 204 C5
Exeter, Countess Wear EX2 182 D7
Exeter, Heavitree EX1 177 F6
Plymouth, Billacombe PL9 250 A1
Plymouth, Devonport PL1 248 A2
Plymouth, Weston Mill PL2 247 E7
Teignmouth TQ14 210 A5
Torquay TQ1 220 A8
Second Dr TQ14 210 B5
Second Field La EX33 152 C6
SECTOR 88 B1
Sector Hill EX13 88 B1
Sector La EX13 167 F5
Sedemuda Cl EX10 188 A8
Sedemuda Rd EX10 187 F8
Sedge Cl PL21 237 D4
Sedgeclaire Cl EX1 174 F1
Sedgewell Cross EX21 55 F4
Sedley Way PL5 244 D3
Sefton Ave PL4 249 B3
Sefton Cl PL4 263 C4
Sefton Ct
22 Dawlish EX7 204 E6
Torquay TQ1 220 D7
Segrave Rd PL2 248 B6
Selcombe Cross TQ9 144 E4
Seldon Cres EX1 174 F3
Seldons Cl PL21 137 D6
Selkirk Ho 5 PL9 255 F7
Selkirk Pl PL5 244 E2
Sellbed Cross TA24 21 A8
Sellbed Rd TA22 21 A8
Sellers Cl EX24 103 B3
Seller's Grave EX24 103 A4
Seller's Wood Hill EX12 190 E6
Sellick Ave TQ5 230 D3
Selsden Cl PL9 256 C6
Senate Ct EX8 196 E1
Senate Way EX8 196 E1
Sendall's Way PL6 244 F4
Sennen Cl PL11 246 F4
Sennen Pl PL2 247 E5
Sentry Cnr EX39 157 C1
Sentry Cross EX31 18 A8
Sentry La
Bishop's Tawton EX32 16 F1
Bishop's Tawton EX32 28 A8
Huntsham EX16 49 E6
Sentrys Orch EX6 182 B3
Sercombes Gdns EX6 201 B8
Serge Ct EX2 261 A2
Serpell Cl PL6 244 E6
Serpens Vale PL9 256 E7
Serstone Cross EX17 78 C5
Sessland La
North Tawton EX17 77 E1
Spreyton EX17 95 D8
Sestertius Rd EX1 178 E8
Sett Cl TQ13 180 D7
Seven Acre Cross EX36 31 E6
Seven Acre La
Braunton EX33 152 E5
Bridford EX6 112 F5
Seven Acres EX5 99 A5
Seven Acres Pk EX33 152 E5
Seven Ash Cross EX34 3 C1
Seven Brethren Bank EX31 154 F4
Seven Brethren Ind Est EX31 154 F3
Seven Crosses EX16 63 F6
Seven Crosses Rd EX16 161 A3
Seven Hills Ho TQ2 220 A5
Seven Stars La PL5 244 C6
Seven Stones Cross TQ7 142 E8
Seventh St 15 EX32 154 F6
Seven Trees Ct PL4 263 B4
Severn Pl PL3 249 C5
Severn Rd TQ2 219 B7
Sewell Ct PL3 248 E5
Sexton's Cross EX6 113 E6
Seymore Cl EX8 196 B2
Seymour Ave PL4 263 B4
Seymour Bglws EX34 1 A1
Seymour Ct
Exmouth EX8 196 B2
9 Totnes TQ9 223 D5
Seymour Dr
Dartmouth TQ6 233 C3
Plymouth PL3 248 F5
Torquay TQ2 214 B4
Seymour Mews PL4 263 C4
Seymour Pk PL3 249 A5
Seymour Pl
Plymouth PL1 262 A4
Totnes TQ9 223 D5
Seymour Rd
Exmouth EX8 196 B2
Newton Abbot TQ12 207 C4
Plymouth, Mannamead PL3 248 F5
Plymouth, Plympton PL7 250 C6
Seymour St
Plymouth PL4 263 A3
Wellington TA21 160 C6
Seymour Terr EX16 161 C4
Seymour Villas EX34 1 A1
Shackel Cross TA3 67 E8
Shackhayes EX34 3 A4
Shackleton Cl EX8 196 B2
Shackleton Ct PL5 244 E1
Shackleton Wlk TQ14 210 A8
Shadrack Cross TQ9 217 B3
Shadrick Way EX22 164 C6
SHADYCOMBE 259 D5
Shadycombe Ct TQ8 259 D5
Shadycombe Rd TQ8 259 D5
Shady La TQ6 146 B7
Shady Nook Pk TQ12 207 E7
Shaftesbury Cl 21 EX7 204 E6
Shaftesbury Cotts PL4 263 A4
Shaftesbury Ct 3 PL4 263 A4
Shaftesbury Rd
Exeter EX2 177 A4
6 Ilfracombe EX34 150 C5
Shaftesbury Theatre★ EX7 204 D6
Shaftsborough La EX34 1 C1
Shaftsbury Pl 9 TQ9 223 C5
Shaggs Flood La TA20 69 E2
Shakespeare Cl
Tiverton EX16 161 D6
Torquay TQ2 219 D6
Shakespeare Prim Sch PL5 244 B2
Shakespeare Rd
Exeter EX2 177 F3
Plymouth PL5 244 C2
Shakespeare Way EX8 196 C4
SHALDON 210 AB
Shaldon Bridge TQ14 210 A4
Shaldon Cres PL5 244 B3
Shaldon Prim Sch TQ14 210 A3
Shaldon Rd
Combeinteignhead TQ12 208 F5
Newton Abbot TQ12 207 F2
Shaldon Wildlife Trust★ TQ14 210 B2
Shale Row
Blackhorse EX1 179 A8
Clyst Honiton EX1 175 B1
Shales Rd EX4 174 C1
Shalford Terr EX13 103 B6
Shallowford Cl PL6 249 C8
Shallowford Rd PL6 249 C8
Shambles Dr EX17 79 A6
Shamble Way EX35 151 E2
Shameface La TQ13 123 B7
Shamel's End EX16 64 E7
Shamrock Cl EX39 156 E7
Shamrock St PL6 245 B2
Shamwickshire Cl EX39 157 C1
Shand Pk
Axminster EX13 167 C5
Axminster EX13 167 D5
Shapcott La EX36 32 C2
Shapcott Wood Hill EX36 31 F2
Shapland Pl EX16 161 C2
Shapleys Gdns PL9 256 A5
Shapley Tor Cl TQ5 230 A2
Shapley Way TQ12 180 C1
Shapter Ct EX8 202 F7
Shapters Rd PL4 263 C2
Shapters Way
Plymouth PL4 255 B8
Plymouth PL9 255 B8
Shaptor Cross TQ13 122 F8
Shaptor View TQ13 180 B5
Shareford Way EX5 99 B6
Sharkham Ct TQ5 230 D3
Sharkham Point National Nature Reserve★ TQ5 230 F2
Sharland La EX17 78 F8
Sharland's La EX33 152 C6
Sharlands Rd EX23 70 A6
Sharlands View EX1 175 B1
Sharon Way PL6 245 A5
Sharper La TQ14 209 C3
Sharpham Dr TQ9 223 D4
Sharpham Vineyard & Cheese Dairy★ TQ9 227 B8
Sharp Hill EX20 170 B4
Sharpitor Cl TQ3 218 F1
Sharpitor Gdns 5 PL2 248 A7
Sharpitor Row PL20 127 B4
Sharp Rock EX34 7 F7
Sharps Cl TQ12 123 B2
Sharps Crest TQ12 123 B2
Sharps Ct
Exmouth EX8 201 E6
Exmouth EX8 201 F6
Sharrose Rd PL9 255 B5
SHAUGH PRIOR 132 C6
Shaugh Prior Prim Sch PL7 132 C6
Shaw Way PL9 255 A7
Sheafhayne Cross EX14 69 B4
Shearford Cl EX32 155 A8
Shearman Ct 10 EX2 261 A2
Shearwater Dr TQ2 213 D3
Shearwater Way EX12 192 B5
Shearwood Cl PL7 250 C6
SHEBBEAR 55 D4
Shebbear Coll EX21 55 E4
Shebbear Com Sch EX21 55 E4
Shebbear Cross EX38 41 A2
Shedden Hill Rd TQ2 220 A4
Sheepspine La EX13 88 F5
SHEEPSTOR 127 E2
Sheepstor Rd PL6 245 D1
SHEEPWASH 56 C1
Sheepwash Cross EX36 31 C6
Sheepwash Hill EX36 31 C6
Sheirs Orch EX9 197 F8
SHELDON 66 F3
Sheldon Cross EX14 66 F2
Sheldon La EX6 113 B5
Sheldon's La TA22 33 A7
Shelduck Way EX7 200 E2
Shell Cl PL6 245 E1
Shell Close EX7 204 D4
Shelley Ave
Tavistock PL19 171 D5
Torquay TQ1 220 B8
Shelley Cl EX2 177 A2
Shelley Ct EX8 201 E6
Shelley Way PL5 243 D1
Shell La EX16 47 F1
Shells La EX24 103 A3
Shell's La TA20 69 D3
Shelly Ct EX20 95 B4
Shelly Rd
Exmouth EX8 201 E6
South Zeal EX20 95 B4
Shelly Reach
Exmouth EX8 201 E6
Exmouth EX8 201 F6

Shelston Tor Dr TQ4 225 F3
Shelton Pl EX1 177 F6
Shepherd Cl TQ3 225 E5
Shepherd's Hl EX2 178 A1
Shepherds La
Colaton Raleigh EX10 186 E4
Plymouth PL4 263 B2
Teignmouth TQ14 124 E1
Teignmouth TQ14 209 D8
Shepherd's La EX15 52 F1
Shepherds Mdw
Abbotsham EX39 156 A2
Beaford EX19 42 D1
Sheplegh Ct TQ9 145 B8
Sheppard Rd EX4 173 D2
Sheppard's Knap EX13 87 A2
Sheppard's Row EX8 202 A7
Sheppaton La EX18, EX19, EX37 43 B2
SHERBERTON 129 A8
Sherborne Cl PL9 256 C6
Sherborne La DT7 260 E3
Sherborne Rd TQ12 207 B3
Sherbrook Cl EX9 203 F8
Sherbrook Hill EX9 203 F8
Shercroft Cl EX5 175 E2
Sherdon Bridge EX36 20 D5
SHERFORD 144 F3
Sherford Cres
Plymouth, Elburton PL9 256 C7
Plymouth, West Park PL5 244 A3
Sherford Cross TQ7 145 A3
Sherford Down Cross TQ7 144 D3
Sherford Down Rd TQ7 144 E3
Sherford Rd PL9 256 D7
Sherford Vale Sch PL9 256 E8
Sherford Wlk PL9 256 E7
Sheridan Rd
Exeter EX4 178 C8
Plymouth PL5 244 C1
Sherman Ho EX11 169 E3
Sherracombe Cross EX36 19 C6
Sherracombe La EX36 19 C6
Sherratt's Oak EX31 155 B7
Sherrell Pk PL20 125 E1
Sherril Cl PL9 255 F4
Sherwell Arcade 9 PL3 263 A4
Sherwell Cl
Dawlish Warren EX7 201 A2
Staverton TQ9 216 A5
Sherwell Ct TQ11 236 B5
Sherwell Hill TQ2 219 E5
Sherwell La
Plymouth PL4 263 A4
Torquay TQ2 219 E5
Sherwell Park Rd TQ2 219 E5
Sherwell Rise S TQ2 219 D5
Sherwell Valley Prim Sch TQ2 219 C7
Sherwell Valley Rd TQ2 219 D6
Sherwill Cl PL21 237 A6
Sherwill La TQ9 216 A5
Sherwood DT7 260 C4
Sherwood Cl EX2 177 F5
Sherwood Cross EX14 84 D2
Sherwood Dr EX8 196 E3
Sherwood Gn EX38 42 E7
Shetland Cl TQ2 213 E2
Shewte Cross TQ13 122 D5
Shields The EX34 150 C4
Shieling Rd EX31 16 A3
Shillands
Tiverton EX16 161 B4
Tiverton EX16 161 B5
Shillingate Cl EX7 204 C4
SHILLINGFORD 34 E2
SHILLINGFORD ABBOT 181 A6
Shillingford La EX6 181 A3
Shillingford Rd
Alphington EX2 181 B8
Exeter EX2 181 A7
SHILLINGFORD ST GEORGE 114 C7
Shilstone Cross EX32 28 C5
Shilstone La TQ13 113 C1
Shilston Gate PL21 137 D4
Shindle Pk TQ7 144 F1
Shinners Cotts TQ6 228 C2
SHIPHAY 219 C7
Shiphay Ave TQ2 219 D7
Shiphay La TQ2 219 D7
Shiphay Learning Acad TQ2 219 C8
Shiphay Manor Dr TQ2 219 D7
Shiphay Park Rd TQ2 219 D8
Ship La EX5 179 D8
Shipley Cl TQ10 135 A3
Shipley Rd EX14 166 E6
Shipley Wlk PL6 245 A1
Shipney La TQ13 124 A7
Shippens Mead EX8 202 E7
Shirburn Rd
Plymouth PL6 249 B8
Torquay TQ1 220 A7
Shire Cl
Honiton EX14 166 A5
Paignton TQ4 229 B8
Shire Ct EX22 70 E1
Shire End DT7 260 D2
Shire La DT7 260 B3
Shirley Cl EX8 196 D4
Shirley Cnr EX17 79 B5
Shirley Ct 8 TQ1 220 D4
Shirley Gdns PL5 244 C1
Shirley Towers TQ1 220 C3
Shirmart Pk EX33 8 E1
SHIRWELL 17 B8
Shirwell Com Prim Sch EX31 17 B8
Shirwell Cross
Barnstaple EX31 16 E6
Shirwell EX31 17 B8
Shirwell Rd EX31 17 A7
Shoalgate Cross EX20 94 F8
Shobbrook Hill TQ12 206 E4
SHOBROOKE 80 E4
Shobrooke Cross EX17 80 D4
Shobrook La EX17 78 F7
Shoemaker's La PL12 242 E2
Shooting La EX18 60 B7
Shooting Marsh Stile EX2 261 A1
Shoot La EX32 17 D6
Shoots Barn Cross EX14 84 D3
Shoot's La EX14 67 A3
SHOP
Kilkhampton 37 A1
Milton Damerel 54 F6
Shop Cotts PL7 132 F4
SHORE BOTTOM 86 F6
Shore Head EX14 86 F5
Shoreland Cross EX18 44 F5
Shorelands Rd EX31 154 D3
Shorelands Way EX31 154 D3
Shoreland Way EX39 156 E7
Shorelark Wy EX23 70 A8
Shoresgate Cross EX19 76 F8
Shoreside TQ14 210 A3
Shorland Cl EX7 204 F8
Shorneywell TQ7 145 A1
SHORTACOMBE 108 A5
Shortacombe Cnr EX31 10 A5
Shortacombe Dr EX33 152 B7
Shorta Cross TQ7 143 C7
Short Cl EX39 156 D2
Short Cotts PL11 247 A3
Short Cross TQ9 139 B3
Shorter Cross TQ9 135 D2
Short Furlong EX12 191 D5
Short La
Combe Martin EX34 2 F1
Halwill TQ9 139 B3
Shaldon TQ14 209 C4
Shortlands
Pyworthy EX22 71 D5
Yettington EX9 197 F8
Shortlands La EX15 163 B3
Shortlands Rd EX15 163 B3
Shortlands Way PL21 237 E4
SHORT MOOR 86 E7
Shortmoor Cross EX14 86 E6
SHORTON 219 A1
Shorton Rd TQ3 226 A8
Shorton Valley Rd TQ3 219 A1
Short Park Rd PL3 248 D5
Shortridge Cl
Honiton EX14 166 C4
Witheridge EX16 46 E1
Shortridge Mead 1 EX16 161 B4
Shorts Way TQ9 222 E6
Shortwood Cl EX9 197 F2
Shortwood Cres PL9 256 A7
Shortwood La EX9 197 D5
Shovelpiece La EX32 19 A7
Shrewsbury Ave
Torquay TQ2 213 F1
Torquay TQ2 214 A1
Shrewsbury Rd PL5 244 C4
Shrinkhill La EX16 161 D3
Shrubbery Cl EX32 155 C3
Shrubbery La EX14 86 E6
Shrubbery The
Axminster EX13 167 D5
Exbourne EX20 76 C5
SHUTE
Kilmington 103 A8
Newton St Cyres 81 A3
Shute TQ7 147 E6
Shute Barton★ EX13 103 B8
Shute Com Prim Sch EX13 103 B8
Shute Cross
Newton St Cyres EX17 81 B2
South Brent TQ10 134 E1
Shute Ct TQ14 209 A8
Shute Hill
Bishopsteignton TQ14 209 A8
Malborough TQ7 147 E6
Teignmouth TQ14 210 C5
Shute Hill Cres 10 TQ14 210 C5
Shute Ho EX13 103 B7
Shute La
Cheston TQ10 134 E1
Combe Martin EX34 3 A4
Denbury TQ12 211 A6
Huish Champflower TA4 35 C8
Moretonhampstead TQ13 111 F5
Winkleigh EX19 58 F2
Shuteleigh TA21 160 E5
Shute Meadow St 2 EX8 202 A7
Shute Park Rd PL9 255 F6
Shute Pk TQ7 147 E6
Shute Rd
Kilmington EX13 87 C1
Shute EX13 103 A7
Totnes TQ9 223 D5
Shute Row TA21 160 E5
Shutes Mead EX11 169 E4
Shute Wood EX18 58 F6
Shutscombe Hill EX32 18 E5
Shuttern Cl EX5 172 A8
Shutterton Ind Est EX7 200 F1
Shutterton La EX7 201 A3
Shutter Water Rd
Westwood EX15 83 C1
Whimple EX5 99 C8
Sicklemans Cl TQ7 144 C1
SID 188 C5
Sidborough Hill EX17 61 B1
SIDBURY 101 B2
Sidbury CE Prim Sch EX10 101 C2
Sidbury Cl EX1 178 D7
Sidcliffe EX10 188 C6
Siddalls Gdns EX16 161 E5
Siddals Gdns EX16 161 E4
Sideling Cl EX2 114 A6
Sideling Fields EX16 161 F2
Side Wood La EX36 32 A1
SIDFORD 101 B1
Sidford Cross 7 EX10 101 B1
Sidford Rd EX10 188 B7
Sidgard Rd EX10 188 C6
Sidholme Cotts EX10 188 B5
Siding Cross TQ10 137 E8
Siding Rd PL3 262 C4
Sidings The
Braunton EX33 152 D6
Churston Ferrers TQ5 229 D5
Halwill Junction EX21 73 E2
Kingsbridge TQ7 258 C5
Sid La EX10 188 C5
Sidlands EX10 188 A4
Sidleigh EX10 188 C5
Sidmount Gdns EX10 188 A5
Sidmouth CE Prim Sch
Sidmouth EX10 188 B4
Sidmouth EX10 188 B7
Sidmouth Coll EX10 188 C7
Sidmouth Cotts 9 PL4 248 F4
Sidmouth Hospital EX10 188 B4
Sidmouth Junc Cross EX14 84 D2
Sidmouth Mus★ EX10 188 B3
Sidmouth Rd
Bradninch EX5 83 B5
Clyst St Mary EX1 178 F3
Clyst St Mary EX2, EX5 179 A3
Clyst St Mary EX5 179 E2
Colyton EX24 102 F5
Colyton EX24 103 A4
Exeter EX2 178 D5
Exeter EX5 99 A1
Hele EX5 82 F5
Honiton EX14 166 A3
Lyme Regis DT7 260 C3
Ottery St Mary EX11 169 E2
Sidmouth Sp Ctr EX10 188 C7
SIDMOUTH VICTORIA 188 C3
Sidney Ct 3 EX7 204 D6
Sid Park Rd EX10 188 B5
Sid Rd EX10 188 C5
Sid Vale Cl 10 EX10 101 B1
Sidvale Ct 12 EX10 101 B1
Sidvale Mews 16 EX10 101 B1
Sidwell Ho EX1 261 C3
Sidwell St EX4 261 C4
SIGFORD 131 B8
Sigford Cross TQ13 122 B2
Sigford Rd EX2 181 D8
Signal Ct EX33 152 D5
Signals The EX14 84 D2
Signal Terr EX31 154 F4
Sign of the Owl Cross TQ10 137 E8
Signpost La EX17 80 A7
Silbury Place EX17 165 C5
Silbury Terr EX17 165 C5
Silcombe Cross EX36 30 F3
Silcombe Hill EX36 30 E4
Silent Woman Pk PL19 117 F1
SILFORD 156 D4
Silford Cross EX39 156 D5
Silford Rd EX39 156 E5
Silk Dr EX14 166 B6
Silvan Dr EX33 152 E7
Silverberry Cl EX1 178 C7
Silver Birch Cl
Exeter EX2 178 A3
Plymouth PL6 245 C7
Silver Birch Ct 5 EX31 154 C2
Silver Birch Vw EX32 155 B6
Silver Bridge Cl TQ4 229 C8
Silverdale
Exmouth EX8 196 E3
Silverton EX5 82 B6
Silverdale Cl TA22 33 E4
Silver Head Hill TQ9 216 F1
Silverhill Bldgs TQ12 212 D8
Silverhills Rd TQ12 212 D8
Silveridge La TQ7 144 A8
Silver La
Exeter EX4 261 C4
Rockbeare EX5 99 C5
Silver Lea EX13 87 C1
Silver Pk EX15 66 A3
Silver St
3 Appledore EX39 15 A1
Axminster EX13 167 D5
11 Bampton EX16 34 B1
Barnstaple EX32 154 F5
8 Barnstaple EX32 155 A5
Bere Ferrers PL20 240 A3
Berrynarbor EX34 2 E3
Bideford EX39 157 A1
Braunton EX33 152 D7
Buckfastleigh TQ11 236 B5
Colyton EX24 103 A5
Culmstock EX15 66 D8
Honiton EX14 166 C6
Ipplepen TQ12 211 C1
Kentisbeare EX15 66 A3
Kilmington EX13 87 C1
Lydford EX20 107 F3
Lyme Regis DT7 260 D3
Ottery St Mary EX11 169 D4
Saltash PL12 243 A2
Thorverton EX5 81 E4
Tiverton EX16 161 D4
West Buckland TA21 52 F7
Willand EX15 162 D4
Silvers The EX3 178 F2
Silver Stream Way PL8 257 B5
SILVER STREET 52 F8
Silver Terr
Exeter EX4 261 A3
Millbrook PL10 253 A6
SILVERTON 82 B5
Silverton CE Prim Sch EX5 82 B6
Silverton Rd EX2 181 D8
Silverton Rise EX14 84 E2
Silverway EX17 80 E4
Silverwell Pk PL21 137 C2
Silverwood Ave TQ12 207 E1
Silverwood Hts EX31 155 B6
Silworthy Cross EX22 38 F5
Simcoe Pl EX15 67 B8
Simcoe Way EX14 67 B1
Simey Cl EX4 176 F7
Simmonds Pl EX15 163 E4
Simmons Cl EX20 170 C5
Simmons Pk EX20 170 B4
Simmons Way EX20 170 C5
Simms Hill TQ12, TQ13 122 C2
Simon Cl PL9 255 E6
Simon Ct 5 TQ1 220 B6
SIMONSBATH 13 B2
SIMONSBURROW 52 C3
Simons Cross EX13 87 E4
Sims Terr PL18 125 D6
Sinai Hill EX35 151 C5
Singer Cl TQ3 226 A5
Singmore Rd TQ3 218 E2
Sing's La EX33 152 D5
Sink Well La TQ13 113 D1
Sion Cl EX14 166 B6
Sir Alex Wlk EX3 182 E5
Sir George Cl DT7 260 E5
Sir John Hunt Com Sports Coll PL5 244 D4
Sir Leonard Rogers Cl PL2 248 F6
Sir Robert's Path EX31 4 D5
Siskin Chase EX15 163 A2
Sisna Pk Rd PL6 245 F5
SITCOTT 90 C2
Sithney St PL5 243 C1
Sivell Mews EX2 177 F5
Sivell Pl EX2 177 F5
Six Acre Cross EX35 5 A4
Six Acre La EX35 5 A5
Six Acres EX6 98 C4
Six Mile Hill
Dunsford EX6 113 A8
Tedburn St Mary EX6 97 F5
Tedburn St Mary EX6 98 A5
Six O Clock La PL7 250 E3
Skardale Gdns PL6 249 D8
Skardon Pl PL4 263 A4
Skelmersdale Cl TQ7 258 D5
Skern Cl EX39 156 F8
Skern Way EX39 156 F8
Skerries Rd PL6 244 F7
SKILGATE 34 E6
Skinnard La PL18 125 C5
Skinner Cl 2 EX16 161 B4
Skirhead La EX34 3 B3
Skitt La
Lydford EX20 107 F3
Skitt La *continued*
Lydford PL19 108 A3
Skye Cl TQ2 213 E2
Skylark Cl TQ12 207 C8
Skylark Rise
Plymouth PL6 245 E8
Tavistock PL19 171 D1
Skylark Spinney 3 EX31 154 A2
Skyways Bsns Pk EX5 99 A4
Slade EX39 156 E2
Slade Cl
Ottery St Mary EX11 169 F4
Plymouth PL9 256 A5
Slade Cross
Kingsbridge TQ7 144 B6
Lustleigh TQ13 122 D8
North Tawton EX20 77 D5
Slade La
Abbotskerswell TQ12 212 B5
Abbotskerswell TQ12 212 B6
Combe Martin EX31 3 E1
Galmpton TQ5 229 B5
Hawkridge TA22 21 D1
Morchard Bishop EX17 61 A1
Sidmouth EX10 189 C7
West Anstey EX36 32 B6
Slade Lane Cross EX34 3 E1
Slade Rd
Ilfracombe EX34 150 A3
Ottery St Mary EX11 169 F3
Slade Valley Rd EX34 150 A3
Sladnor Park Rd TQ1 214 C5
Sladnor Pk TQ1 214 C5
Slanns Mdw TQ12 207 D6
Slappers Hill TQ4, TQ5 234 E7
SLAPTON 145 C4
Slapton Ley National Nature Reserve★ TQ7 145 D2
Slate La PL1 262 A2
Slatelands Cl PL7 251 B3
Slattenslade La EX31 4 D5
Sleap Hill EX9 198 C7
Sleepy Hollow EX2 182 C7
Sleepy La TQ3 219 A1
SLERRA 23 D3
Slerra EX39 23 D3
Sletchcott Cross EX37 44 E8
Slew Hill EX34 2 C2
Slewhill Cross EX20 95 B5
Slewton Cres EX5 99 E8
Slip Ct 12 EX31 154 A2
Slipperstone TQ9 139 A7
Slipperstone Cross TQ9 216 C7
Slipper Stone Dr PL21 237 A6
Slipperstone La TQ9 216 C7
Slipway Quay PL12 239 B2
Slittercombe La EX6 194 E3
Sloe Gdns
Clyst Honiton EX1 175 B1
Clyst Honiton EX1 179 B8
Sloe La 4 EX32 17 B2
SLONCOMBE 111 E5
Slough La
Bishops Nympton EX36 30 F3
Upottery EX14 68 C5
Sluggett Pl EX4 174 E3
Smallack Cl PL6 244 F2
Smallack Dr
Plymouth PL6 244 F2
Plymouth PL6 245 A2
Smallacombe Dross TQ10 135 D6
Smallacombe Hill EX16, EX36 32 D4
Smallacombe La EX36 31 F8
Smallacombe Rd EX16 161 B4
Smallacott Hill EX6 97 D3
Smallcombe Cross TQ3 225 E8
Smallcombe Rd TQ3 225 E8
Smalldon La TQ1, TQ2 214 B3
Small La
Broadclyst EX5 175 D7
Burlescombe EX16 51 B2
Rattery TQ10 135 D3
Smallpark La TQ13 131 E1
Smallridge Cl PL9 255 F5
Smallridge Rd EX13 87 F4
Smallwell La
Ashprington TQ9 139 E7
Marldon TQ3 218 C3
Smardon Ave TQ5 230 A5
Smardon Cl TQ5 230 A5
Smaridge Row TQ13 180 B6
SMEATHARPE 68 B5
Smeathy La EX15 52 F3
Smeaton Sq PL3 249 D6
Smeaton's Twr★ PL1 262 C1
Smiter's Pit La EX13 87 A1
SMITHALEIGH 136 A6
Smithay Mdws EX6 113 B4
Smithfield Dr PL12 242 B3
Smith Field Rd EX2 181 A8
Smithfields TQ9 223 A6
Smith Hill TQ14 208 F8
SMITHINCOTT 66 A6
Smiths Ct EX2 261 A1
Smith's La
Calverleigh EX16 48 E4
Hollocombe EX18 58 E6
Smith St TQ6 233 F3
Smiths Way PL12 242 B3
Smithy Cl PL12 242 C4
Smithys Way EX16 50 D1
Smockpark La PL9 140 B8
Smokey Cross TQ13 122 B3
Smoky House La EX32 155 B8
Smugglers' La EX7 210 F8
Smythen Cross EX34 9 E6
Smythen St EX1, EX4 261 A2
Smythes Cross EX15 67 F7
Snell Dr PL12 242 B3
Snodbrook Cross EX10 101 C1
Snowberry Cl TQ1 219 F7
Snowdonia Cl TQ4 225 D4
Snowdrop Cl 2 EX14 166 A4
Snowdrop Cres PL15 105 A2
Snowdrop Mews EX4 176 D8
Snows EX17 80 B5
Snydles La EX37 44 B6
Soap St PL1 262 A2
SOAR 147 E4
Soby Mws TQ13 180 C5
Sog's La EX10 100 C2
Solar Cres
Exeter EX4 176 F4
Plymouth PL6 245 D8
SOLDON CROSS 53 E5
Solidus Rd 9 EX1 178 E8
Solland Cross EX20 76 D4
Solland La EX20 76 D4
Soloman Dr EX39 157 A1
Solsbro Rd TQ2 219 E4
Solways DT7 260 C5
Somer Fields DT7 260 B3
Somerlea EX15 162 D5
Somerset Ave EX4 176 E4
Somerset Cotts 10 PL3 248 A4
Somerset Ct
10 Brixham TQ5 230 C5
17 Totnes TQ9 223 D5
Somerset Pl
20 Barnstaple EX31 154 F5
Plymouth PL3 248 A4
11 Teignmouth TQ14 210 B4
Totnes TQ9 223 D5
Somerset Place La 11 PL3 248 A4
Somerslea EX21 73 E2
Somers Rd DT7 260 C3
Somerthing La EX33 7 E1
Somerville Cl
Exmouth EX8 196 D1
Willand EX15 162 C5
Somerville Cres EX2 182 C8
Somerville Pk EX15 162 C4
Somerville Rd EX15 162 C5
Sommers' Cres EX34 150 C6
Sonnet Cl TQ12 244 C1
Soper Rd TQ14 210 A7
Sopers Hill PL6 241 A2
Soper's Hill PL5 240 E1
Soper Wlk TQ14 210 A7
Sophia Way TQ12 207 A2
SORLEY 143 F5
Sorley Green Cross TQ7 143 F5
Sorley La TQ7 143 F5
Sorrell Ct TQ12 207 D7
Sorrel Pl TQ12 206 D5
Sorrento 10 TQ1 220 C5
Sortridge Cl PL19 171 B7
Sortridge Pk PL19 126 E5
SOURTON 93 B1
Sourton Sq 5 PL3 249 D1
SOUTH ALLINGTON 149 B5
South Ave
Bideford EX39 157 D1
Exeter EX1 177 E6
Lyme Regis DT7 260 D4
Southay Cross TA20 69 D4
Southay La TA20 69 C4
Southbank TQ12 207 C4
South Bank Dr EX39 156 F2
SOUTH BRENT 134 F3
South Brent Prim Sch TQ10 135 A3
South Brent Rd TQ7 143 E7
Southbrook Cl 2 TQ13 180 C8
Southbrook La
Bovey Tracey TQ13 180 B8
1 Bovey Tracey TQ13 180 C8
Otterton EX10 187 B1
Rockbeare EX5 99 C7
Southbrook Mdw
Cranbrook EX5 99 C6
Rockbeare EX5 99 C6
Southbrook Rd
Bovey Tracey TQ13 180 C8
Exeter EX2 178 A2
Southbrook Sch EX2 178 A2
South Burrow Rd 11 EX34 150 B5
SOUTH CHARD 88 C8
South Church La EX20 170 A4
Southcombe Cross
Hittisleigh EX6 96 F4
Widecombe in the Moor TQ13 121 B3
Southcombe Hill EX6 96 F4
Southcombe St TQ13 111 A6

SOUTH COMMON 88 A4
South Common La EX13 88 A5
Southcoombe Terr EX12 192 E7
Southcote La EX14 86 C4
Southcote Orch TQ9 223 E5
SOUTHCOTT 157 D4
Southcott Cross
Chawleigh EX18 60 A6
Langtree EX38 40 F3
Okehampton EX20 93 C5
Southcott Rd EX39 156 F4
South Courts The 8 PL1 262 A3
South Dartmoor Com Coll 13 TQ13 131 A5
South Dartmoor Com Coll Sixth Form Ctr TQ13 131 A6
South Dean Cnr EX31 4 A5
South Dean La EX31 4 A5
South Devon Coll TQ4 225 E1
South Devon Coll Brunel Ctr TQ12 207 E3
South Devon Highway TQ2 213 B2
South Devon Rly★
Buckfastleigh TQ11 236 E4
Staverton TQ9 215 D4
Totnes TQ9 223 C8
South Devon Steiner Sch TQ9 215 C3
SOUTHDOWN 253 B6
SOUTH DOWN 68 C6
Southdown Ave TQ5 230 B2
Southdown Cl
Beer EX12 191 D5
Brixham TQ5 230 B2
Southdown Cotts PL10 253 B6
Southdown Cross
Brixham TQ5 230 B1
Burlescombe EX16 51 B2
South Molton EX36 46 A5
South Down Cross EX19 76 C7
South Down Farm TQ7 147 E5
Southdown Hill
Brixham TQ5 230 B2
Copplestone EX17 79 D7
Meshaw EX36 45 F6
Southdown Ho 5 TQ13 180 D8
Southdown La EX37 43 D3
South Down La EX36 31 E6
Southdown Quay PL10 253 B6
Southdown Rd
Beer EX12 191 D5
Brixham TQ5 230 B1
Millbrook PL10 253 A6
South Down Rd PL2 248 B6
South Downs Rd EX7 204 D4
Southdown Terr PL10 253 A6
South Dr EX38 159 B5
Southella Rd PL20 127 A2
South Emb TQ6 233 F3
South End Cl 7 EX33 152 D5
SOUTHERLY 108 A7
Southern Cl
Plymouth PL2 247 F7
Torquay TQ2 214 A4
Southernhay
Newton Abbot TQ12 207 C2
Winkleigh EX19 58 F3
Southernhay E EX1 261 B3
Southernhay Gdns EX1 261 B2
Southern Rd EX8 202 A8
Southerns Cross EX13 103 D5
Southern Terr PL4 248 F4
Southernway PL9 256 A8
Southern Wood EX8 196 E2
SOUTHERTON 100 B1
Southey Cres TQ12 213 A3
Southey Dr TQ12 213 A3
Southey La
Kingskerswell TQ12 213 A3
Sampford Courtenay EX20 76 F3
South Farm Rd EX9 198 C3
Southfield
Saltash PL12 242 C3
11 Torquay TQ1 220 D4
West Alvington TQ7 258 A4
Southfield Ave
Paignton TQ3 225 F8
Paignton TQ3 226 A8
Southfield Cl TQ3 226 A8
Southfield Dr EX17 165 B6
Southfield Rd
Bideford EX39 157 C1
Paignton TQ3 226 A7
Southfield Rise TQ3 226 A7
Southfields
Bridgerule EX22 70 F5
Totnes TQ9 224 B6
Southfield Way
Tiverton EX16 64 A7
Tiverton EX16 161 B4
Southford La
Staverton TQ9 215 F4
Staverton TQ9 216 A4
South Ford Rd TQ6 233 F3
South Furzeham Rd TQ5 230 C5
Southgate EX2 261 B2
Southgate Ave PL9 255 E4
Southgate Cl PL9 255 E4
Southgate Ct 7 EX2 261 B2
South Gn 5 EX32 155 B4
South Grange EX2 178 D3
South Hams Bsns Pk TQ7 143 C4
South Hams Hospl TQ7 258 C6
South Hayes Copse EX32 17 B2
South Hayes Mdw EX5 99 A5
South Hayne Cross EX36 31 B4
South Hele Cross EX16 35 C1
South Hill
Plymouth, Hooe PL9 255 C5
Plymouth, Stoke PL1 248 A3
South Hill Cotts EX22 38 C1
South Hill Rd TQ1 220 C4
SOUTH HOLE 37 A7
Southholme Terr EX39 157 B2
SOUTH HUISH 147 D7
SOUTH KNIGHTON 131 F7
South La
Braunton EX33 15 E8
Challacombe EX31 11 F3
Hartland EX39 22 E2
Lynton EX35 5 F5
Southland Park Cres 8 PL9 140 D8
Southland Park Rd PL9 140 D8
Southlands
8 Braunton EX33 152 D5
Exeter EX1 177 E6
Exeter EX2 177 E5
Wrafton EX33 152 E4
Southlands Dr EX38 40 F2
Southlands Rd TQ2 220 A5
South Lawn
Exeter EX2 261 C2
Sidmouth EX10 188 C8
South Lawn Terr EX1 177 F6
Southlea EX39 156 E6
South Lea EX33 152 E5
South Lea Cl EX33 152 E5
South Lee Cross EX36 30 B7
SOUTHLEIGH 102 C4
Southleigh Hill Cross EX24 102 B3
Southleigh Rd EX24 102 E5
South Ley Cross EX31 3 D1
Southley Rd EX36 158 C4
Southmead Prim Sch EX33 152 E4
SOUTH MILTON 143 D1
South Milton St PL4 263 C2
SOUTH MOLTON 158 D3
South Molton Com Coll EX36 158 C3
South Molton Com Prim Sch EX36 158 C5
South Molton & District Mus★ EX36 158 C4
South Molton Hospl EX36 158 C4
South Molton Rd
Bampton EX16 33 F1
Bampton EX16 34 B1
Chulmleigh EX37 44 C3
Oakfordbridge EX16 48 F8
South Molton St EX18 44 E1
South Molton United CE Jun Sch EX36 158 C5
South Molton United CE Prim Sch
South Molton EX36 30 A4
South Molton EX36 158 B3
South Moor La EX17 59 E1
Southmoor Rise PL21 137 E8
South Par EX9 199 H2
South Parks Rd TQ2 213 F2
SOUTH PILL 242 E3
South Pk
Barnstaple EX32 155 B3
Braunton EX33 152 F5
Woolfardisworthy EX39 38 F7
SOUTH POOL 148 F7
Southport Ave EX4 176 E5
South Quay TQ4 226 C5
SOUTH RADWORTHY 19 F3
South Rd
16 Appledore EX39 15 A1
Newton Abbot TQ12 207 B2
South Sands TQ4 226 C2
Southside EX17 59 F2
Southside Ope 13 PL1 263 A2
Southside St PL1 263 A2
South Sq 10 EX24 103 A4
South St
Axminster EX13 167 D5
Barnstaple EX32 155 B2
Braunton EX33 152 D5
Colyton EX24 103 A4
Denbury TQ12 211 A6
South St *continued*
Dolton EX19 57 F7
Exeter EX1 261 B2
Exmouth EX8 202 A6
Great Torrington EX38 159 C5
Hatherleigh EX20 75 C7
Holcombe Rogus TA21 50 F5
Sheepwash EX21 56 C1
Sheepwash EX21 74 C8
South Molton EX36 158 C4
Torquay TQ2 219 F6
Totnes TQ9 223 C5
Wellington TA21 160 E5
Winkleigh EX19 58 F3
Woolacombe EX34 7 F6
SOUTH TAWTON 95 B5
South Tawton Prim Sch EX20 95 B4
Southtown
Dartmouth TQ6 233 F2
Kenton EX6 194 F3
Southview PL10 253 A6
South View
Abbotskerswell TQ12 212 B6
Barnstaple EX31 154 D7
Bideford EX39 156 F2
Bishop's Tawton EX32 16 E1
Bovey Tracey TQ13 180 D7
Bratton Fleming EX31 18 A8
Braunton EX33 152 D4
5 Hemyock EX15 67 B8
10 Horrabridge PL20 126 F4
Ilfracombe EX34 1 E3
Lydford EX20 107 F4
Mary Tavy PL19 117 E6
Plymouth, Crownhill PL5 244 E2
Plymouth, Elburton PL9 256 B6
Prixford EX31 16 C7
Tiverton EX16 161 D4
Westleigh EX16 51 A3
South View Cl
Braunton EX33 152 D4
Plymouth PL7 250 D7
Willand EX15 162 D5
South View Est EX15 162 D5
South View Pasture EX5 99 A5
South View Pk PL7 250 D7
Southview Rd TQ3 226 A7
South View Rd EX15 162 D5
South View Terr
Exeter EX4 177 D8
Exminster EX6 182 B4
Plymouth PL4 263 C3
Sidmouth EX10 188 A5
SOUTHVILLE 258 E3
Southville Gdns TQ7 258 D3
SOUTHWAY 244 F6
Southway
Sidmouth EX10 188 C4
Tedburn St Mary EX6 97 F4
Southway Ave TQ2 213 F1
Southway Dr PL6 244 E6
Southway La
Plymouth TQ12 244 C6
Plymouth, Southway PL6 245 B6
Plymouth, Tamerton Foliot PL6 244 C6
Southway Valley Nature Reserve★ PL6 244 F6
Southwell Rd PL6 244 E1
SOUTH WONFORD 54 E3
Southwood Cross EX5 99 C4
Southwood Ct TQ1 220 C5
Southwood Dr EX39 157 A3
Southwood Mdws EX39 40 C7
South Yeo Cross
Northlew EX20 74 F2
Poughill EX17 62 E3
South Yeo Hill EX17 62 E3
SOUTH ZEAL 95 B3
Sovereign Cl EX8 196 E1
Sovereign Ct
Exeter EX1 178 D3
Plymouth PL7 250 C5
Sovereign Rd TQ12 206 E3
Sowden La
Barnstaple EX32 155 B5
Lympstone EX8 195 E4
Sowden Pk EX32 155 C4
SOWTON 179 B6
Sowton Ind Est EX2 178 E5
Sowton La EX5 179 B6
Sowton Rd PL20 241 D8
SOWTONTOWN 117 F3
Space Pl EX2 177 C1
Spa Ct TQ1 220 C4
Spanishlake Cross EX6 113 C6
Spanish Lane End TQ9 139 A5
Sparhanger Cross EX35 5 B3
Sparhanger La EX35 5 B3
Sparkatown La PL20 127 B3
Sparke Cl PL7 251 B4
Sparkhays Dr TQ9 223 D4
Sparks Barn Rd TQ4 226 B4
SPARKWELL 251 F8
Sparkwell All Saints Prim Sch PL7 136 A8
Sparkwell La TQ9 215 F8
Sparrow Dr EX5 99 B6
Sparrow La TA24 21 C7
Sparrow Pk TQ7 147 F6
Sparrow Rd TQ9 223 B5
Speakers Rd PL21 237 E5
Speares The PL12 242 B2
Spearfield Cl EX36 158 D4
Spears La TA21 35 F4
Speckled Wood Ct 16 EX31 154 A2
Speedwell Cl
Barnstaple EX32 155 E3
Bideford EX39 25 E4
Brixham TQ5 230 C3
Millbrook PL10 252 F5
Newton Abbot TQ12 206 D5
Speedwell Cres PL6 249 B7
Speedwell Units TQ6 233 C3
Speedwell Wlk PL6 249 B7
Spekes Cross EX18 59 C4
Spence Combe Cross EX17 79 D4
Spence Cross EX14 84 D4
Spence La DT6 104 F7
Spencer Cl EX8 196 E2
Spencer Ct EX11 169 D3
Spencer Dr EX16 161 F3
Spencer Gdns PL12 242 F1
Spencer Rd
Newton Abbot TQ12 207 C2
Paignton TQ3 225 E7
Plymouth PL9 255 E8
Spenser Ave EX2 177 F3
Speranza Gr 17 TQ14 210 B5
Spestos La EX17 78 C1
Spicer Cl EX15 163 B2
Spicer Rd EX1 261 C3
Spicers Rd TQ13, EX6 114 A1
Spider's La EX8 196 C3
Spindlebury EX15 163 A2
Spindle Cres 7 PL7 251 B5
Spindlewood Cl EX14 166 C3
Spinnaker Quay PL9 254 F7
Spinners La TQ9 222 E8
Spinners Sq TQ12 123 E5
Spinney Cl
Exeter EX2 178 C4
15 Roundswell EX31 154 A2
Spinney The
Ivybridge PL21 237 A5
Plymouth PL7 251 A4
Uffculme EX15 66 A8
Spinning Bath Gdns EX17 165 C4
Spinning La EX13 104 B8
Spire Ct PL3 249 B5
Spire Hill Pk PL12 242 C2
Spirelake EX36 30 F2
Spirelake Cross EX17 79 C8
Spirelake Hill EX17 79 C8
Spires Coll The TQ1 220 C7
Spire's Cross EX20 77 A3
Spitfire Ave
Clyst Honiton EX1 175 F1
Clyst Honiton EX1 179 E8
Spitfire Wlk EX32 155 C5
Spithead TQ6 233 F3
Spitlar Cross EX20 95 C6
Spittis Pk TQ6 234 B3
Spittle Cross EX18 44 D4
Spittles La DT7 260 E4
Spitup La EX10 187 E7
Splashdown@quaywest★ TQ4 226 C3
Splatford Dr EX15 163 C5
Splatts Cross EX19 76 C7
Splitwell Cross EX17 62 B2
Sportsmans Cl PL15 115 A4
Spotter Cl EX36 158 B5
Spreacombe Gdns EX33 8 C4
SPREYTON 95 F7
Spreyton Cross EX17 96 A7
Spreyton Sch
Spreyton EX17 95 F7
Spreyton EX17 96 A7
SPRIDDLESTONE 256 C4
Springbourne Dr EX15 163 B1
Spring Cl
Newton Abbot TQ12 206 E4
Northam EX39 156 E6
Springdale Cl TQ5 230 C2
Springfield
Dunkeswell EX14 67 C2
13 Horrabridge PL20 126 F4
Membury EX13 87 D6
Winkleigh EX19 58 E3
Spring Field EX39 22 D3
Springfield Ave
Barnstaple EX32 155 B3
Plymouth PL9 256 B6
Springfield Cl PL9 256 B7
Springfield Cres
Fremington EX31 153 F6
Northam EX39 156 F7
Springfield Dr
Kingsbridge TQ7 258 C5
Plymouth PL3 248 A4
9 Tiverton EX16 161 B4
Springfield Gdns EX7 200 F1
Springfield La PL9 256 B7
Springfield Pk
Bridestowe EX20 107 F8
Buckfastleigh TQ11 236 D5
Springfield Rd
Barnstaple EX31 154 B3
Exeter EX4 177 D8
Exmouth EX8 196 B1
Springfield Rd *continued*
Honiton EX14 166 F5
Ilfracombe EX34 150 B6
Offwell EX14 86 A3
Plymouth PL9 256 B6
1 South Brent TQ10 134 F3
Torquay TQ1 220 B7
Wellington TA21 160 C7
Woolacombe EX34 8 A6
Springfield Rise PL9 256 B7
Springfields EX24 103 A3
Springfield Terr
1 Bideford EX39 157 B1
12 Combe Martin EX34 3 A3
3 Northam EX39 156 F7
Tatworth TA20 88 D8
Westward Ho! EX39 156 C7
Spring Flower Ave 2 EX32 155 C4
Spring Gdns EX11 169 E3
Springhead Cross EX12 193 A6
Springhead La EX13 87 C1
Spring Head Rd DT7 260 B6
Springhill
Lyme Regis DT7 260 D4
Plymouth PL2 248 C8
Spring Hill PL19 171 B5
Springhill Down Hill EX16 47 D4
Springhill Gdns DT7 260 D4
Springhill Gn PL2 248 C8
Springhill Rd TQ9 223 E5
Spring Mdw EX8 195 E5
Spring Pk PL6 245 E7
Spring Rd PL9 140 B8
Springwood Cl
Ivybridge PL21 237 E5
Plymouth PL7 251 A3
Spruce Cl
Exeter EX4 174 B2
Exmouth EX8 196 D3
Spruce Gdns PL7 251 B5
Spruce Pk EX17 165 C4
Spruce Way TQ3 225 E8
Spry La
Lifton PL16 105 F4
Lifton PL16 106 A4
Sprys Shop Cross EX22 72 D2
SPRYTOWN 106 B4
Sprytown Cross PL16 106 B4
Sprywood Cross EX21 56 A1
Spur Cross EX39 22 E3
Spurfield Cotts EX6 182 A4
Spurge Rd TQ12 206 C5
Spurway Gdns EX34 3 B3
Spurway Hill EX16 48 A7
Spurway Hill Cross EX16 48 A8
Spurway Rd EX16 161 F3
Square's Quay TQ7 258 C4
Square The
Ashreigney EX18 58 E8
Barnstaple EX32 154 F5
Beer EX12 191 D5
16 Bere Alston PL20 125 E1
11 Bishop's Tawton EX32 16 E1
Bradworthy EX22 38 E1
Bradworthy EX22 53 E8
Braunton EX33 152 D6
Bridestowe EX20 107 F8
Cawsand PL10 253 A1
Chagford TQ13 111 A6
Chittlehampton EX37 28 F4
12 Chulmleigh EX18 44 E1
Ermington PL21 136 F4
Exeter, Exwick EX4 176 F8
3 Exeter, Middle Moor EX2 178 D5
Fremington EX31 153 E5
Gunnislake PL18 125 D6
Gunnislake, St Ann's Chapel PL18 125 B5
Hartland EX39 22 D3
5 Holsworthy EX22 164 C4
Inner Hope TQ7 147 B6
Kingswear TQ6 234 A3
Lutton PL21 133 B2
Merton EX19 57 A7
Moretonhampstead TQ13 111 F5
6 Northam EX39 156 F7
North Molton EX36 30 D8
North Tawton EX20 77 C4
Petrockstowe EX20 56 F4
Plymouth, Stonehouse PL1 248 A2
Rockbeare EX5 99 C5
Saltash PL12 242 C3
Sandford EX17 80 A5
Sandford EX17 80 B5
8 Seaton EX12 192 A5
Shebbear EX21 55 D4
Sheepwash EX21 56 C1
South Molton EX36 158 C4
Uffculme EX15 66 A7
Ugborough PL21 137 D6
8 Whimple EX5 99 E8
Witheridge EX16 46 E1
Squires Cl EX32 155 B2
Squires Cotts 1 PL20 128 B8
Squires' La EX21 55 D6
Squire's La EX12 192 C5
Squires' La EX21 55 D6
Squirrel Cl PL5 244 E4
Squirrel Ct TA21 160 D5
Stabb Cl TQ4 226 A1
Stabb Dr TQ4 226 A1
Stabdon La EX19, EX20 59 C1
Stable Cotts PL7 250 F5
Stable Ct TQ7 147 F6
Stable Ctyd DT7 193 E6
Stable La TQ1 214 B1
Stables The TQ9 223 D6
Stadbury Cross EX14 86 B5
Stadbury La EX14 86 C5
Staddens Lea La TQ2 219 C6
STADDISCOMBE 255 F3
Staddiscombe Pk PL9 255 F4
Staddiscombe Rd PL9 255 F4
Staddle Stone Rd EX1 178 F8
STADDON 72 C6
Staddon Cl
Braunton EX33 152 C6
Exeter EX4 178 B7
Plympton PL7 132 C2
Staddon Court Cotts PL9 140 B8
Staddon Cres PL9 255 E6
Staddon Cross EX22 72 C6
Staddon Gate EX20 77 D5
Staddon Gdns TQ2 214 B2
Staddon Gn PL9 255 D6
Staddonhill Rd TA24 21 F8
Staddon La PL9 255 B4
Staddon Moor Cross EX20 77 D5
Staddon Park Rd PL9 255 E6
Staddon Rd
Appledore EX39 15 A1
Holsworthy EX22 164 F3
Tedburn St Mary EX6 97 E2
Whimble EX22 164 F2
Staddons View TQ13 180 C8
Staddon Terrace La PL1 262 B4
Stadium Dr TQ12 213 A2
Stadium Way EX4 261 C4
Stadway Mdw EX10 187 E5
Staffick Cl EX6 194 E3
Stafford Cl EX6 113 B4
Stafford Cross EX24 102 D2
Stafford Ct 1 TQ9 223 E5
Stafford Hill EX14 84 F8
Stafford La EX24 103 A3
Stafford Moor Fishery★ EX19 58 B6
Stafford Rd
Dolton EX19 57 F7
Exeter EX4 176 F5
Paignton TQ4 226 C5
Stafford Terr La 8 PL3 263 A4
Stafford Way EX19 57 F7
Stag Cnr EX15 162 E1
Staggers La EX33 152 E3
Stag La
Plymouth, Elburton PL9 256 B8
Plymouth, Plympton PL9 250 B1
Stag Mill Cross EX16 50 B3
Stag's Head EX32 29 D6
Stags Wood Dr EX21 73 E2
Stakes Hill TQ7 143 A5
Stakes Rd TQ7 143 A6
Stallards EX33 152 C7
Stamford Cl PL9 255 A6
Stamford Fort Cotts PL9 255 A6
Stamford La PL9 255 A6
Stamford Rd PL9 255 A6
Stammery Hill EX13 88 C1
Stamps Hill PL8 257 A6
Stamps The PL17 125 A5
Stanborough Cross PL9 256 C7
Stanborough Ct TQ9 139 A3
Stanborough Rd PL9 256 B7
Stanbridge Pk EX39 156 D2
Stanbury Ave PL6 244 F1
Stanbury Cl PL15 90 C1
Stanbury Copse EX34 150 A4
Stanbury Cross
Holsworthy EX22 164 D6
Morwenstow EX23 36 F1
Stanbury Ct EX17 165 C5
Stanbury Rd
Knowle EX33 8 D1
Torquay TQ2 219 C7
Stanbury Row EX2 181 B6
Stanburys Orch EX6 96 F3
Stancombe Cross TQ7 144 E4
Standard Ct PL19 117 E6
Standarhay Cl PL9 256 C7
Standarhay Villas PL9 256 C7
Standle TA21 160 C3
Stanfield TQ1 220 E5
Stanford Rd EX2 178 C5
Stang La EX34 8 F5
Stangray Ave PL4 248 D4
Stanhope Cl EX22 164 C5
Stanhope Dr EX10 188 B6

Stanhope Rd PL5 243 C1
Stanhope Sq 7 EX22 164 C4
Stanhope Terr EX39 157 A3
Staniforth Dr PL21 237 D4
Stanley Cotts EX24 103 A3
Stanley Ct
  Parkham EX39 39 E8
  Torquay TQ1 220 C8
Stanley Gdns TQ3 226 A7
Stanley Mews EX9 198 A1
Stanley Pl PL4 249 B2
Stanley Rd TQ1 220 C8
Stanley Sq EX3 182 F4
Stanley St 10 TQ14 210 B4
Stanley Wlk EX8 196 D4
Stanmore Rise EX7 204 E7
Stanmore Tor TQ3 226 A5
Stannary Bridge Rd PL19 171 D6
Stannary Cl PL21 237 E5
Stannary Ct EX20 170 D5
Stannary La PL7 250 E5
Stannary Pl TQ13 111 A6
Stansfeld Ave TQ3 226 A6
Stansfield Ctr The EX2 178 E4
Stantaway Pk TQ1 219 F7
Stanton Ct TQ7 138 A1
Stantor La TQ3 218 F5
Stant Way TA20 69 F6
Stantyway Cross EX9 198 F6
Stantyway Ct EX9 198 E7
Stantyway Rd EX9 198 F5
Stanwell Dr EX39 156 C6
Stanwell Hill
  Bideford EX39 25 C4
  Westward Ho! EX39 156 C6
Stanwey EX1 178 A5
Staplake La EX6 201 A7
Staplake Rd
  Starcross EX6 195 B1
  12 Starcross EX6 201 A8
Staplake Rise EX6 195 A1
Staplanke Rd EX6 194 F1
Stapleback Cross EX19 57 E5
Staple Back La EX19 57 E5
Staple Cl PL6 241 C1
Staple Cross EX19 57 F5
Stapledon Cotts EX22 72 E7
Stapledon La TQ13 130 F5
Stapleford Dr TQ14 210 B7
Stapleford Gdns PL5 243 F5
Staplegate EX16 50 A3
Staplehill Rd
  Coldeast TQ12 122 F1
  Newton Abbot TQ12 206 B8
Staple Orch TQ9 222 F8
Staples Mdw TA20 88 D8
Staples Mews 4 EX8 202 A7
Staples Terr DT7 260 E4
Stapleton Cl TQ4 225 E3
Stapleton Way EX2 181 E7
STAPLEY 68 A8
Star Barton La EX5 172 D4
Starcombe La EX10 101 D4
STARCROSS 201 A8
Star Cross EX13 87 E6
Starcross Prim Sch EX6 201 A8
Starcross Sta EX6 201 B8
Starkey Cl 10 EX16 64 D7
Starling Dr PL6 245 A2
Starlings Roost EX15 163 A2
Starpitten Gr TQ2 214 B3
Starpitten Lane W TQ2 214 A2
Star Pk PL18 125 D6
Starre Cl EX12 192 A7
START 145 B4
Start Ave
  Chillington TQ7 145 A1
  Teignmouth TQ14 210 C7
Start Bay Pk TQ6 145 F6
Start Cross TQ12 211 B7
Starved Oak Cross EX5 81 D1
Station App
  Crediton EX17 165 E3
  South Brent TQ10 134 F3
Station App Rd TQ12 123 B3
Station Cl
  Braunton EX33 152 D5
  12 Holsworthy EX22 164 C4
Station Cotts
  Bittaford TQ10 137 E8
  Brandis Corner EX22 73 A5
Station Cross
  Bittaford TQ10 137 E8
  Crediton EX17 165 E4
Station Ct TQ13 180 C7
Station Fields EX21 73 E2
Station High Rd EX21 73 E3
Station Hill
  Barnstaple EX32 18 A4
  Bideford EX39 157 B1
  Bratton Fleming EX31 11 A1
  Bratton Fleming EX31 18 A8
  Brixham TQ5 230 C5
  Chudleigh TQ12 123 E5
  Great Torrington EX38 159 A6
  Lynton EX35 151 B4
  Swimbridge EX32 17 E1
Station La
  Calstock PL18 125 D3
  Paignton TQ4 226 B5
Station Rd
  Bampton EX16 34 B1
  Barnstaple EX31 154 F4
  Bere Alston PL20 125 E2
  Bere Ferrers PL20 239 E3
  Bickleigh PL6 132 A5
  Bovey Tracey TQ13 180 C7
  Bow EX17 78 B3
  Bratton Fleming EX31 18 A8
  Braunton EX33 152 D5
  Bridestowe EX20 107 F7
  Broadclyst EX5 175 E3
  Buckfastleigh TQ11 236 C5
  Budleigh Salterton EX9 198 A1
  Burlescombe EX16 51 B3
  Chard Junction TA20 88 D8
  Chulmleigh EX18 44 C3
  Colyton EX24 103 A5
  Crediton EX17 79 A6
  Cullompton EX15 163 C4
  17 Dawlish EX7 204 E6
  Exeter EX4 176 F8
  Exeter, Pinhoe EX1 174 E1
  Exeter, St David's EX4 177 A8
  Exminster EX6 182 D3
  Exton EX3 183 C1
  Feniton EX14 84 D2
  Gunnislake PL18 125 C6
  Halwill Junction EX21 73 E2
  Hele EX5 82 F5
  Hemyock EX15 67 B8
  Holsworthy EX22 164 C4
  Horrabridge PL20 126 F4
  Ide EX2 176 D1
  Ilfracombe EX34 150 A4
  Ivybridge PL21 237 D6
  Lifton PL16 105 F4
  Loddiswell TQ7 143 F7
  Lydford EX20 108 A6
  Mary Tavy PL19 117 E6
  Meeth EX20 57 C2
  Moretonhampstead TQ13 111 F4
  Newton Abbot TQ12 207 D3
  Newton Poppleford EX10 186 F8
  Newton Poppleford EX10 187 A8
  Newton St Cyres EX17 81 A1
  Newton St Cyres EX5 81 A1
  North Brentor PL19 117 C8
  Northlew EX20 74 E1
  Okehampton EX20 170 B4
  Plymouth, Elburton PL9 256 C7
  Plymouth, Keyham PL2 247 E5
  Plymouth, Plympton PL7 250 E5
  Plymouth, Tamerton Foliot PL5 244 A6
  Princetown PL20 128 A8
  Saltash PL12 243 A2
  Sidmouth EX10 188 A4
  8 South Brent TQ10 134 F3
  South Molton EX36 158 D5
  3 Teignmouth TQ14 210 C4
  Tiverton EX16 161 D4
  Topsham EX3 182 F5
  Totnes TQ9 223 C6
  Wellington TA21 160 C7
  Whimple EX5 99 E8
  Willand EX15 162 C5
  Woolacombe EX34 8 A6
  Yelverton PL20 127 A2
  Yeoford EX17 79 C1
Station Road Ind Est EX15 67 B8
Station View PL19 117 C8
Station Yard EX13 167 C5
Station Yard Bsns Pk TQ14 210 C5
Station Yard Ind Est TQ7 258 C5
STAVERTON 216 B5
Staverton Cotts TQ13 130 F4
Staverton Sta* TQ9 215 E4
Stawley County Prim Sch TA21 51 B8
Steamer Quay Rd TQ9 223 D4
Steamer Quay Wharf 11 TQ9 223 D5
Steartfield Rd TQ3, TQ4 226 C7
Steddaford Ct EX20 95 A5
Stedhams Cl TA21 160 D7
Steed Cl TQ4 229 A8
Steel Cl EX14 166 D6
Steeperton Cl EX20 170 D5
Steep Head EX36 19 B1
Steep Hill TQ1 214 D6
Steep La
  Hartford TA22 34 C8
  Landkey EX32 17 D2
Steeple Cl PL9 255 F4
Steeple Dr EX2 181 B8
Steeple Mdw EX37 44 E6
Steer Park Rd PL7 251 C5
Steer Point Cotts PL8 256 F2
Steer Point Rd
  Brixton PL8 257 A4
  Combe PL8 256 F3
Stefan Cl PL9 255 B5
Stella Maris Ct EX39 157 A2
Stella Rd TQ3 219 A1
Stemson Ave EX4 174 D1
Stenlake Pl PL4 249 B2
Stenlake Terr PL4 249 B2
Stentaway Cl PL9 255 F8
Stentaway Dr PL9 256 A8
Stentaway La EX33 7 E2
Stentaway Rd PL9 255 F8
Stentiford Hill TQ7 258 D7
Stentiford Hill Rd TQ1 220 B5
Stentiford La TQ13 122 D4
Stepcote Hill EX1 261 A2
Stephens Way EX1 179 B8
Steppes Mdw TQ12 207 A2
Steppingstone Cross EX33 8 D1
Stepps Cross EX12 192 E7
Stepps Rd EX12, DT7 193 B5
Steps Cl EX1 174 F1
Steps Cross TQ2 214 B3
Steps La TQ2 214 B3
Stepstone La EX33 8 D1
Sterlings Wy EX20 170 D6
Steven's Cross EX10 188 D8
Steven's Cross Cl EX10 188 E8
Stevens La EX10 188 A7
STEVENSTONE 42 A6
Stevenstone Ct EX38 42 A6
Stevenstone Rd EX8 202 D7
Stewart Cl EX8 196 E1
Stewart Ct EX13 167 F7
Stewart Gdns EX7 204 E7
Stewart Ho EX7 204 E7
Stewarts Rd EX22 70 C1
STIBB CROSS 40 C1
Stibb La PL21 136 D7
STICKLEPATH
  Barnstaple 154 E4
  Okehampton 95 A5
Stickle Path EX16 35 C1
Sticklepath Com Sch EX31 154 C3
Sticklepath Ct EX31 154 E3
Sticklepath Hill EX31 154 E4
Sticklepath Terr EX31 154 F4
Sticksend La TQ13 124 A8
Stidson Cross TQ10 135 B3
Stidston La TQ10 135 A3
Stile Ct EX15 163 B2
Stile Orch TQ7 143 F7
Stillman Ct 6 PL4 263 A2
Stillman St PL4 263 A2
Stiniel Cross TQ13 111 A4
Stintway La EX10 187 E5
Stirling Ct PL5 243 C1
Stirling Rd PL5 243 C1
Stitchill Rd TQ1 220 C4
Stitworthy Cross EX39 23 C1
Stoat Pk EX32 155 D4
Stoats Cl EX36 158 C2
Stoats Mews EX20 77 C4
Stockadon Farm Barns PL12 238 B4
Stockadon La EX17 63 A1
Stockbridge La 16 TQ10 134 F3
Stocker Rd EX4 173 B1
Stockeydown La EX17 79 E2
Stockham Hill TA22 33 E8
Stockham La TA20 88 C7
Stock Hill EX35 151 A1
Stock La EX12 192 A5
STOCKLAND 87 A7
Stockland CE Prim Acad EX14 87 A7
Stockland Cross EX15 66 A3
Stockland Head Cross EX15 84 B7
Stockland Hill EX14 86 E6
Stockland La EX33 8 D2
Stockland Rd TA20 69 D2
Stockleigh Cross
  Cheriton Fitzpaine EX17 62 C1
  Stockleigh Pomeroy EX17 80 F6
STOCKLEIGH ENGLISH 62 D1
Stockleigh La EX21 74 F7
STOCKLEIGH POMEROY 81 A6
STOCKLEY HAMLET 94 D6
Stockman La TA20 88 C7
Stockmeadow Gdns TQ14 209 A7
Stock Pk EX20 170 E6
Stock Rd EX35 5 B3
Stockstyle La EX13 88 A8
Stockton Ave EX7 204 E6
Stockton Hill EX7 204 D6
Stockton La 9 EX7 204 D6
Stockton Rd EX7 204 D6
STOCKWELL 82 D5
Stockwell Cross EX5 82 D5
Stoford Lane TA21 52 F7
STOFORD WATER 66 B3
Stoggy La
  Frogmore & Sherford TQ7 144 C3
  Plymouth PL7 250 F6
  Plymouth PL7 251 A6
  Plymouth PL7 251 B7
STOKE
  Ashburton 129 F5
STOKE *continued*
  Hartland 22 B3
  Plymouth 248 A3
STOKE CANON 173 E8
Stoke Canon CE Prim Sch EX5 173 F8
STOKE CLIMSLAND 115 C1
Stoke Climsland Sch PL17 115 B1
Stoke Cross PL8 141 B5
Stoke Damerel Bsns Ctr 9 PL3 248 A4
Stoke Damerel Com Coll PL3 248 B4
Stoke Damerel Prim Sch PL1 248 A3
STOKE FLEMING 146 B7
Stoke Fleming Com Prim Sch TQ6 146 A7
STOKE GABRIEL 227 F7
Stoke Gabriel Prim Sch TQ9 227 F7
Stoke Gabriel Rd TQ5 229 A5
STOKE HILL 173 E1
Stoke Hill
  Exeter EX4 173 E2
  Stoke Canon EX5 173 F6
  Stoke Climsland PL17 115 B1
  Stoke Gabriel TQ9 227 F6
Stoke Hill Cres EX4 173 E1
Stoke Hill Inf Sch EX4 173 E1
Stoke Hill Jun Sch EX4 173 E1
Stoke Hill La PL20 126 E2
Stoke House Gdns TQ6 146 B7
STOKEINTEIGNHEAD 209 B1
Stokeinteignhead Sch TQ12 209 B1
Stokelake TQ13 123 D5
Stoke Lyne EX8 196 C1
Stoke Meadow Cl EX4 173 E2
Stoke Mill La EX32 17 F6
STOKENHAM 145 C1
Stokenham Area Prim Sch TQ7 145 B1
Stokenham Cross TQ7 145 B1
STOKE POST 174 A5
Stoke Rd
  Higher Gabwell TQ1, TQ12 214 C7
  Noss Mayo PL8 141 A6
  Paignton TQ3 225 B1
  Paignton, Higher Yalberton TQ4 225 C3
  Paignton, Waddeton TQ5 228 F6
  Plymouth PL1 262 A3
  Stoke Canon EX4, EX5 173 D5
  Stokeinteignhead TQ14 209 B1
STOKE RIVERS 17 F6
Stokesay Ave PL6 245 A5
Stokes Cl TQ13 180 F7
Stokes La
  Plymouth PL1 263 A2
  Tiverton EX16 161 D4
Stokes Mead EX5 184 D3
Stoke Valley Rd EX4 173 D2
Stokewood La EX32 17 F6
Stokingway Cl PL9 255 E5
Stoneacre Cl TQ5 230 C3
Stone Ash La EX17 61 C3
Stonebarrow La EX13 88 F2
Stone Barton EX5 99 B6
Stonebarton Cl PL7 250 C6
Stonebarton Rd PL7 250 C6
Stonebarto Rd EX1 179 A8
Stoneborough Cnr EX9 198 B1
Stoneborough Ct EX9 198 B1
Stoneborough La EX9 198 B1
Stone Cl EX14 166 B4
STONECOMBE 10 C6
Stonecombe Hill EX31 10 C6
Stone Cross
  Chagford TQ13 96 A1
  Lifton PL16 105 E5
  Meeth EX20 57 C4
  Molland EX36 31 F7
  North Tawton EX20 77 E4
  West Buckland EX32 18 A4
  Widecombe in the Moor TQ13 121 B1
Stone Ct TQ2 213 D1
Stonehall Flats PL1 248 A1
Stonehanger TQ8 259 D4
Stonehanger Ct TQ8 259 D4
Stonehedge Cl PL21 237 D4
STONEHOUSE 248 A1
Stonehouse Bridge PL1 248 A1
Stonehouse St PL1 262 A2
Stone La
  Bickleigh EX5 82 A8
  Cadbury EX5 81 F7
  Chulmleigh EX17 60 A8
  Drewsteignton TQ13 96 A1
  Lympstone EX8 195 E5
Stoneland Cl EX5 99 B6
Stoneland Cross EX16 47 F4
Stoneland La EX16 47 F5
Stonelands EX6 96 F3
Stonelands Bridge EX7 204 C6
Stonelands Mews EX7 204 C6
Stonelands Pk EX7 204 C6
Stonelands Terr EX7 204 C6
Stone Lane Gdns* TQ13 96 A1
Stone Lane Ret Pk EX2 177 B3
Stoneleigh
  Sidmouth EX10 189 C7
  Wellington TA21 160 B8
Stoneleigh Cl TQ12 206 F4
Stoneleigh Dr TQ2 219 D3
Stoneleigh Gdns EX15 163 B3
Stoneman's Hill TQ12 212 B7
Stonemans La EX38 159 C5
Stonemoor Cross EX38 56 B7
Stone Moor Cross EX18 45 C1
Stonemoor La EX36 31 F7
Stonepark TQ13 130 F4
Stonepark Cres TQ13 130 F4
Stone Pk TQ4 229 D6
Stoneridge La TA4 35 D5
Stones Cl
  8 Kingsteignton TQ12 123 F1
  Modbury PL21 137 C2
Stones Gallop
  Cranbrook EX5 99 C6
  Rockbeare EX5 99 C6
Stone's Hill EX17 80 A7
Stoneshill Cross EX17 80 A7
Stonewall La EX17 165 C6
Stone Wlk EX1 174 F3
Stoneybrook Rise EX20 75 C7
Stoneycliffe Pl PL20 128 B8
STONEYCOMBE 212 D3
STONEYFORD
  Cullompton 163 E4
  Newton Poppleford 186 A6
Stoneyford Pk EX9 198 B1
Stoneyhill TQ12 212 B3
Stoneyhouse La EX14 86 D1
Stoney La
  Axminster EX13 167 E6
  Bradninch EX5 82 F7
  Honiton EX14 166 D2
Stoneylands EX5 99 C5
Stoney Lane Cross EX16 50 B3
Stoney Lane Hill EX16 48 C2
Stoney Park La EX20 170 A4
Stoneywell 3 EX39 15 B1
Stoning Cross EX20 75 C7
Stonley Ct 13 PL1 262 A3
Stonybridge Cross EX36 30 B8
Stonybridge Hill EX36 30 B8
Stony Cnr EX34 3 D3
STONY CROSS 26 F4
Stony Hill Cross EX36 31 A3
Stony La
  Gunnislake PL18 125 D6
  Landkey EX32 17 B1
  Lympstone EX8 195 F8
  Parracombe EX31 4 D1
  Swimbridge EX32 28 B8
  Winsham EX33 8 E2
  Woodbury Salterton EX5 184 C6
STONYLAND 27 B8
Stony Lane End EX32 17 B1
Stonyville Pl 3 PL20 128 B8
STOODLEIGH 48 E5
Stoodleigh Cross
  Calverleigh EX16 48 B4
  West Buckland EX32 18 B2
Stoodleigh Moor Cross EX16 48 D6
Stooke Bridge Rd EX15 83 C1
Stooks Cl EX5 81 E1
Stoop EX39 23 D3
Stoop Cross TQ9 131 E1
Stooper's Hill TA20 69 F6
Stopford Pl PL1 247 F3
STOPGATE 68 F4
Stopgate Cross
  Yarcombe EX14 68 F4
  Zeal Monachorum EX17 78 C8
STORMSDOWN 131 B7
Stormsdown Cotts TQ12 131 B7
Storridge La EX13 88 B6
Storrs Cl TQ13 180 C8
Stott Cl PL3 249 D6
Stour Cl PL3 249 D6
STOURSCOMBE 105 A2
Stourscombe Wood PL15 105 A2
Stout Cross EX14 68 F5
Stovar Long La
  Beer EX12 191 D6
  Beer EX2 191 E6
Stover Ct EX4 261 C4
Stover Ctry Pk* TQ12 123 B2
Stover Sch TQ12 123 B1
Stowbrook EX10 187 F8
Stowe Gdns PL5 244 B2
Stowe La EX20 76 C4
Stowell La TA20 88 D8
Stowe The EX23 37 A1
STOWFORD
  Bradworthy 53 B8
  Challacombe 11 B4
  Chittlehampton 28 E5
  Colaton Raleigh 186 A3
  Halwill Junction 91 D8
  Lewdown 106 D5
  Sidmouth 187 E8
Stowford Bsns Pk PL21 237 D4
Stowford Cl PL20 127 B3
Stowford Cross
  Bradworthy EX22 53 C8
  Chittlehampton EX37 29 A5
  Cobbaton EX37 28 E5
  Halwill EX21 91 D8
  South Molton EX36 19 B2
  Stowford EX31 11 C3
  West Putford EX22 39 E2
Stowford Gate EX10 187 E8
Stowford Hill EX17 61 A7
Stowford Hts EX12 191 F8
Stowford Prim Sch PL21 237 E5
Stowford Rise EX10 187 F8
Straightway Head EX5 100 A7
Strand
  Exmouth EX8 202 A6
  Shaldon TQ14 210 A3
  Topsham EX3 182 F4
  Torquay TQ1 220 B4
Strand Cl EX31 16 B6
Strand Ct
  1 Bideford EX39 157 A2
  Topsham EX3 182 F4
Strand Hill EX7 204 E6
Strand La EX31 16 B6
Strand St PL1 254 A8
Strand The
  Barnstaple EX32 154 F5
  Bideford EX39 157 A2
  3 Brixham TQ5 230 D5
  Culmstock EX15 66 E8
  Dawlish EX7 204 E6
  18 Ilfracombe EX34 150 C6
  Lympstone EX8 195 D5
  Ringmore TQ14 209 C5
  Starcross EX6 201 B7
  Topsham EX3 182 F4
Strand View EX3 182 F4
Strashleigh View PL21 136 D6
Stratford Ave EX4 178 C8
Strathculm Rd EX5 82 F5
Strathmore Ct EX39 25 E4
Stratton Dr EX3 182 E6
Stratton Wlk PL2 248 D8
Strawberry Ave EX2 181 C8
Strawberry Fields EX20 77 C4
Strawberry Hill EX8 195 F5
Strawberry La
  5 Exeter EX3 182 C8
  Holcombe EX7 204 C3
  Ottery St Mary EX10 100 C5
  Ottery St Mary EX11 169 C2
Strawberry Terr TQ12 207 E8
Strawberry Valley
  Dartmouth TQ6 233 A3
  Hillfield TQ6 232 E1
Straypark Cnr EX35 5 E4
Stray Pk PL8 257 F4
Streamcombe La TA22 33 B5
Stream Ct EX2 261 A1
Streamers Mdws EX14 166 C5
Streams La EX31 9 B2
Streatham Dr EX4 177 B8
Streatham Rise EX4 177 A8
STREET 190 B4
STREET ASH 69 F8
Street Ash La TA20 69 F8
Street The
  Kilmington EX13 87 C1
  Musbury EX13 103 D5
STRETE 145 E5
Strete Ralegh EX5 168 A8
Strode Rd
  Buckfastleigh TQ11 236 B4
  Plymouth PL7 250 F6
Stroma Cl PL6 244 F7
Strongs Hill Cross EX21 73 F1
Stroud Park Rd PL2 248 C7
STROXWORTHY 39 A6
Stroxworthy Cross EX39 38 F6
Stuart Cres EX15 163 C6
Stuart Ct EX7 204 D4
Stuart Rd
  Exeter EX1 177 F6
  Plymouth PL2 248 C3
  Plymouth, Pennycomequick PL3 262 A4
Stuart Road Prim Sch PL1 262 A4
Stuart Way EX5 99 A1
Stubbing Cross EX24 102 C5
Stubbins Cross TQ12 211 D7
Stubborn Cross EX16 62 C7
Stuckeridge Cross EX16 48 D8

Stucley Rd EX39 156 E1
Studd Dr EX32 29 C7
Studhayes Cross EX13 87 C1
Studhayes La EX13 87 B2
Studhayes Rd EX13 87 B2
Studley Ho 4 EX14 166 C5
Studley Rd TQ1 220 A7
Stumpy Cross
Shobrooke EX17 80 F4
Silverton EX5 82 B4
Stumpypost Cross TQ7 144 B6
Sturcombe Ave TQ4 225 F3
Sturdee Rd PL2 248 A5
Sturges Rd EX8 202 D8
Sturt Cotts EX17 78 E7
Sturtlebury La TQ7 143 F5
Style Cl EX32 155 B2
Subway App EX15 162 C4
Suddon's Cross EX24 102 B6
Suddon's La EX24 102 B6
Sugar Ho Hill EX3 182 D8
Sugar Loaf Hill & Saltern Cove Nature Reserve* TQ4 226 C1
Sugar Mill Bsns Pk PL9 249 C1
Sullivan Rd EX2 178 C5
Summer Cl
Exeter EX4 178 B8
Exmouth EX8 202 E8
13 Hemyock EX15 67 B8
Summercourt Way TQ5 230 A2
Summerfield
Sidmouth EX10 188 B8
Woodbury EX5 184 C4
Summer Field EX19 58 E4
Summerfield Ave TA21 52 D8
Summerfield Ct
Ivybridge PL21 237 A5
Paignton TQ4 226 C5
Summerfield Rd TQ2 219 E8
Summerfields PL12 242 D1
Summerfield Way TA21 52 D8
Summer Green PL19 116 E3
Summerhayes EX7 204 D4
Summerhill Cl 18 TQ12 122 F1
Summerhill Cres 17 TQ12 122 F1
Summerhill Cross TQ13 130 E4
Summerhill Ho DT7 260 E4
Summerhill Rd
16 Coldeast TQ12 122 F1
Lyme Regis DT7 260 E4
Summer House Hill Path EX35 151 D3
Summering Cl EX20 170 E6
Summering Wlk
Okehampton EX20 170 D6
Okehampton EX20 170 E6
Summer La
Alfington EX11 100 F8
Bovey Tracey TQ13 123 C2
Brixham TQ5 230 B2
Exeter EX4 174 B1
Exmouth EX8 196 B4
Northlew EX20 74 F2
Summerland EX14 166 C5
Summerland Ave EX7 204 D7
Summerland Cl EX7 204 D6
Summerland Cotts
Alfington EX11 100 F8
5 Newton Abbot TQ12 207 C3
Summerland Ct 6 TQ12 207 C3
Summerland Pl
12 Barnstaple EX32 155 A4
10 South Molton EX36 158 C4
Summerlands TQ12 123 A1
Summerlands Cl
Brixham TQ5 230 A2
Plymouth PL7 251 C5
Summerlands Ct
Brixham TQ5 230 A2
15 Coldeast TQ12 122 F1
Exeter EX1 261 C3
Summerlands Gdns PL7 251 C5
Summerland St
Barnstaple EX32 155 A5
Exeter EX1, EX4 261 C4
Summerland Terr 1 EX34 3 A3
Summer Mdw
Lympstone EX8 195 E5
Rockbeare EX5 99 A6
Summermoor La EX37 28 E6
Summersby Cl EX12 192 A6
Summers Cl PL6 249 B7
Summers' La EX17 79 D1
Summers Moor Cross EX19 58 F1
Summerville Cross EX39 37 F6
Summerway EX4 178 C8
Summerwell La EX16 62 D4
Summer Well La EX34 9 A5
Sumner Rd 7 PL21 137 C7
Sunbury Hill TQ1 220 A6
Sunbury Rd TQ4 226 B5
Sunbury Terr 4 TQ1 220 A6
Suncrest Cl TQ2 213 F3
Suncrest Pk TQ2 213 F3
Sun Ct 9 TQ12 207 B3
Sunderland Cl PL9 255 A6
Sunflower Rd EX32 155 A5
Sunhill Ave EX3 182 F6
Sunhill La EX3 182 F6
Sunleigh TQ2 219 E2
Sunningbrook Rd EX16 161 E5
Sunningdale EX39 157 A3
Sunningdale Rd PL12 242 C2
Sunnybank
Kenton EX6 194 E3
Newton Abbot TQ12 207 B5
Sunny Bank EX32 155 B4
Sunny Cl TQ12 207 F3
Sunny Ct 1 EX16 161 D4
Sunnydale
Beesands TQ7 149 E8
8 Bittaford PL21 137 C8
Sunnydale Cl PL21 237 A4
Sunny Dene PL5 243 D1
Sunnyfield EX5 175 C7
Sunny Gdns TQ1 220 A6
Sunny Hill
Ottery St Mary EX11 169 E4
Torquay TQ1 220 C5
Sunnyhill Mews TQ1 220 C5
Sunny Hollow TQ12 211 D8
Sunnylands Cross EX13 87 A2
Sunnylands Way EX7 210 F8
Sunnymead EX17 79 B5
Sunnymead Terr 8 TQ9 223 C5
Sunnymoor Cl EX1 174 F2
Sunnyside
Awliscombe EX14 85 C4
9 Bideford EX39 157 B1
3 Braunton EX33 152 D5
Burlescombe EX16 51 C2
Combe Martin EX34 3 A3
Cullompton EX15 163 C2
St Giles in t W EX38 42 B5
Thurlestone TQ7 143 C1
Woolfardisworthy EX39 38 F8
Sunnyside Cotts 18 EX34 3 A3
Sunnyside La EX31 4 D1
Sunnyside Rd
Kingskerswell TQ12 213 A4
Plymouth PL4 249 B2
Woolacombe EX34 7 F6
Sunnyside Terr EX35 151 B5
Sunny View EX19 58 F3
Sun Ray EX34 2 F4
Sunset Heights EX21 55 E4
Sunset Ho 1 EX12 192 A4
Sunset Hts EX32 155 A5
Sunshine Terr PL19 171 D6
Sun Valley Cl TQ5 230 C5
Sunway Cl PL19 171 A6
Sunwell La PL11 252 A8
Sunwine Pl EX8 202 B6
Surbiton Cres EX4 176 F4
Sussex Cl
Exeter EX4 176 E4
Torquay TQ2 214 A3
Sussex Pl PL1 262 C2
Sussex Rd PL2 247 F5
Sussex St PL1 262 C2
Sussex Terr 5 PL2 247 F5
Sutcliffe Cl TQ9 222 F7
SUTCOMBE 54 A6
Sutcombe Com Prim Sch EX22 54 A6
SUTCOMBEMILL 54 A6
Suter Dr 10 EX16 161 E6
Sutherland Cl TQ12 212 F8
Sutherland Dr TQ2 214 B2
Sutherland Pl 7 PL3 263 A4
Sutherland Rd
Plymouth PL4 263 A4
Torquay TQ1 220 C5
SUTTON 143 D1
Sutton Cl
Dawlish EX7 204 D7
Torquay TQ2 213 F4
Sutton Cross
Moretonhampstead TQ13 111 E5
Thurlestone TQ7 143 D1
Sutton Ct PL1 247 F1
Sutton Mews 21 PL4 263 A2
Sutton Pl PL4 263 B2
Sutton Rd
Exmouth EX8 202 E7
Plymouth PL4 263 B2
Suttons Cross EX14 86 D1
Sutton Wharf PL4 263 A2
Swaddicott Cross EX21 56 C2
Swain Cl EX13 167 D4
Swaindale Rd 3 PL3 248 E6
Swains TA21 160 D4
Swains Ct EX3 182 E5
Swains La TA21 160 D4
Swains Rd EX9 198 B1
Swale Cl
Plymouth PL3 249 B6
Torquay TQ2 214 A3
Swallerton Gate TQ13 121 D6
Swallow Cl EX32 155 E4
Swallow Ct EX4 176 F8
Swallow Ct EX16 50 F1
Swallow Ct EX12 192 C4
Swallow Dr EX2 176 D3
Swallow Field EX31 154 A2
Swallowfield Rd EX2 178 B2
Swallowfield Rise TQ2 213 C2
SWALLOWFIELDS 223 C7
Swallowfields TQ9 223 B7
Swallows Acre EX7 204 E7
Swallows End PL9 255 E8
Swallowtree Cross EX6 96 C7
Swallow Units EX2 177 D1
Swallow Way EX15 163 B2
Swallow Wy EX15 163 A3
Swanaford Rd EX6 112 F7
Swan Ave 1 EX16 161 E6
Swanborough Rd TQ12 208 A2
Swan Cl PL10 253 A6
Swan Ct
Dartmouth TQ6 233 E3
Exeter EX2 261 B1
Swan Gdns PL7 250 F5
Swan Hill Rd EX24 103 A3
Swan Maisonettes 10 EX2 177 A5
Swannaton La
Crediton EX17 79 E8
Morchard Bishop EX17 61 E1
Swannaton Rd TQ6 233 F1
Swannywell Hill EX17 78 F8
Swan Rd
Seaton EX12 192 B5
Starcross EX6 201 A8
Swan St TQ1 220 B4
Swanswood Gdns EX39 156 D7
Swan Units EX2 178 E5
Swan Yd
Exeter EX4 177 A5
12 Honiton EX14 166 C6
Swaynes Mews TQ1 220 C6
Sweb Entrance 3 TQ3 214 B2
Swedwell La TQ2 214 A4
Swedwell Rd TQ2 214 A4
Sweetbriar Cl EX7 204 C3
Sweetbriar La EX7 204 C3
Sweetbrier La EX1 178 B6
Sweet Coppin EX5 99 B6
Swiddacombe La EX36 32 C7
Swift Gdns PL5 244 C2
Swift Ind Est TQ12 207 D6
Swift Rd EX7 200 F2
SWIMBRIDGE 17 D1
Swimbridge CE Prim Sch EX32 17 D1
SWIMBRIDGE NEWLAND 17 C2
Swinburne Gdns PL5 244 C1
Swincombe Dr TQ3 225 F6
Swincombe La EX31 11 F4
Swingate Cross EX22 90 B8
Swing Gate EX6 194 A4
Swing Gate Cross EX37 29 A2
Swiss Cl EX8 196 B3
Sword Cl EX31 153 E6
Swordfish Ave EX1 179 E8
Sybil Mead EX1 178 F8
SYCAMORE 87 F8
Sycamore Ave
Dawlish Warren EX7 201 A2
Plymouth PL4 263 C2
Tavistock PL19 171 C2
Sycamore Cl
Broadclyst EX5 175 D6
Exeter EX1 178 B5
Exmouth EX8 196 E2
Honiton EX14 166 A4
13 Instow EX39 15 B1
Paignton TQ4 229 D7
Willand EX15 162 C4
Sycamore Dr
Plymouth PL6 245 C7
South Molton EX36 158 D5
Torpoint PL11 247 A3
Sycamore Rd
Saltash PL12 242 B3
Tiverton EX16 161 E5
Sycamore Way
Brixham TQ5 230 A2
6 Chudleigh TQ13 123 F6
Plymouth PL6 245 E6
Sydenham TQ1 220 D4
Sydenham Cross PL19 116 A2
SYDENHAM DAMEREL 116 B2
Sydenham Ho 3 EX4 177 E7
Sydenham La EX16 47 E6
Sydney Cl PL7 250 E4
Sydney Rd
Exeter EX2 177 A4
Torpoint PL11 247 B3
Sydney St PL1 262 B4
Sylvan Ave EX4 173 D1
Sylvan Cl EX8 196 A2
Sylvan Ct
Exmouth EX8 196 A2
Plymouth PL1 248 A3
Sylvania Dr EX4 173 E2
Sylvan Rd
Exeter EX4 173 D1
Wellington TA21 160 E5
Symons Cl TQ13 180 F7
Symons Rd PL12 242 F2
Synagogue Pl EX4 261 A3
Syncock's Cross EX39 157 F3

T

Tabernacle Ct 9 EX1 261 A2
Tackbear Rd EX22, EX23 70 D4
Tacket Ct TQ7 258 C4
Taddiford Rd EX4 177 A7
Taddiport EX38 159 B4
Taddyforde Court Mans EX4 177 A8
Taddyforde Ct EX4 177 A8
Taddyforde Est EX4 177 A8
Tadworthy Rd EX39 156 E7
Tail Cnr EX17 79 D7
Tailyour Rd PL6 244 F2
Tala Hill PL15 89 D2
TALATON 84 A2
Talaton Rd
Feniton EX14 84 C2
Whimple EX5 99 E8
Talbot Gdns PL5 247 D7
Talbot Rd DT7 260 D5
Tale Common Head Cross EX14 84 B4
TALEFORD 169 C6
Taleford Cl
Ottery St Mary EX11 169 C7
Taleford EX10 100 D8
Taleford Villas EX11 169 C7
Talewater Cross EX5 84 C2
Tallow Wood Cl TQ3 225 E6
Tamar Ave
Plymouth PL2 247 E5
Tavistock PL19 171 D5
Torquay TQ2 219 B7
Tamar Bridge PL5 243 A2
Tamar Bsns Units EX22 164 C6
Tamar Cl PL20 125 E1
Tamar Cotts PL19 116 A1
Tamar Ho PL1 247 E1
Tamarind EX15 162 C4
Tamarisk Cl EX4 174 B2
Tamar Rd EX31 15 E5
Tamar's Dr EX15 162 C4
Tamarside Sp Complex PL5 243 F2
Tamar St
Plymouth PL1 247 E3
Plymouth PL5 247 C3
Saltash PL12 243 A2
Torpoint PL11 247 C3
Tamar Terr
Calstock PL17 125 D3
Horsebridge PL19 116 A1
Saltash PL12 243 A2
Tamar Valley Donkey Pk* PL18 125 A5
Tamar View
Milton Abbot PL19 116 A6
St Dominick PL12 125 A2
Tamar View Ind Est PL12 242 D5
Tamar Villas PL9 255 D7
Tamar Way
Gunnislake PL18 125 D6
Plymouth TQ12 244 A2
Tamar Wharf PL1 247 D3
Tamerton Ave PL5 243 D1
Tamerton Cl PL5 244 A6
TAMERTON FOLIOT 244 B7
Tamerton Foliot Rd PL6 244 D5
Tamerton Hill EX22 89 D8
Tamerton Rd PL6 241 B2
Tamworth Cl TQ12 211 F8
Tangmere Ave PL5 243 E5
Tan La EX2 177 B3
Tanners Cl EX15 163 B2
Tanner's Hill TA4 35 E7
Tanners Mews EX15 162 E5
Tanners Rd
Landkey EX32 17 C2
Paignton TQ4 226 C4
Tannery Cl EX36 158 B4
Tannery Flats 4 EX17 165 C5
Tanpits Cross TQ7 145 A1
Tanpits La TQ7 145 A1
Tanpits Mdw TQ7 145 A1
Tanworth Ho TQ7 143 A1
Tanyard La TQ12 217 F6
Tanyards Ct 7 EX12 192 A5
Tape La EX14 85 B3
Tapeley Park & Gdns* EX39 157 F7
Tapfield Cross TQ7 142 F4
Tapley Gdns TQ14 209 A8
Tappers Cl EX3 182 F5
Tappers Knapp DT7 260 B5
Tappers La PL8 257 E4
Tappers Mdw EX20 170 D5
Tapp's La PL8 257 B5
Taps Cl EX6 182 B4
Tapson Dr PL9 255 A6
Tarbet Ave EX1 177 F7
Tarka Cl EX20 170 D6
Tarka La EX34 8 C6
Tarka Meade EX17 79 A6
Tarka Way
5 Braunton EX33 152 D4
Crediton EX17 165 E4
Tarn Wearfield Flats EX10 188 B3
Tarraway Rd TQ3 219 D1
Tarr Post TA22 21 C1
Tarr's Ave TQ12 207 E7
Tarrs End TQ12 207 E7
Tarrs La TQ12 207 E7
Tarr Steps* TA22 21 E3
Tarr Stps Woodland National Nature Reserve* TA22 21 D3
TATWORTH 88 C8
Tatworth Prim Sch TA20 88 C8
Tatworth St TA20 88 C8
Taunton Ave PL5 244 B5
Taunton Cl EX2 177 A3
Taunton Cross EX13 87 A1
Taunton Ct 2 TQ9 223 D5
Taunton Pl PL5 244 B5
Taunton Rd TA21 160 E7
Taurus St PL9 256 E7
Tavern Gdns EX39 26 B1
Tavern Mews EX38 159 D5
Tavis Rd TQ3 225 F8
Tavistock Coll PL19 171 A3
Tavistock Com Prim Sch PL19 171 B4
Tavistock Cross PL20 125 F2
TAVISTOCK GENERAL 171 E5
Tavistock Hospl PL19 171 B5
Tavistock Mus* PL19 171 C5
Tavistock Pl
Paignton TQ4 229 B8
Plymouth PL4 263 A3
Tavistock Rd
Exeter EX4 177 A7
Launceston PL15 105 A2
Okehampton EX20 93 E4
Plymouth PL6 245 B5
Plymouth, Manadon PL5 244 E1
Princetown PL20 128 A8
Yelverton PL20 126 F3
Tavistockretail Pk PL19 171 C3
Tavistock Viaduct Wlk Nature Reserve* PL19 171 A5
Tavistow Ct 2 TQ3 225 E8
Tavy Ave TQ2 219 B8
Tavy Pl PL4 248 F4
Tavy Rd
Saltash PL12 243 A3
Tavistock PL19 171 D5
Taw Bridge Cross EX20 77 B4
Taw Cl PL3 249 D6
Taw Cres EX31 15 E5
Tawcroft Way EX31 154 D2
Taw Ct 14 EX32 155 A4
TAW GREEN 95 B7
Tawgreen Cross EX18 59 C1
Taw Green Cross EX20 95 B7
Tawgreen La EX18 59 C1
Tawgreen Rd EX20 59 C1
Taw Meadow Cres EX31 153 F6
Taw Mill Bsns Pk EX32 155 C4
Taw Mills La EX18 59 C1
Tawmoor Cross EX20 95 C7
Tawny Cl EX36 158 C5
Tawny Rd 2 TQ12 207 A5
Taw Rd EX31 15 E5
TAWSTOCK 27 D8
Tawton La EX20 95 B4
Taw Trade Pk EX31 154 E6
Taw Vale EX32 154 F4
Taw Vale Ave EX20 77 B4
Taw Vale Cl EX20 77 B4
Taw View
1 Bishop's Tawton EX32 16 E1
Fremington EX31 153 F6
Umberleigh EX37 28 D3
Taw Wharf EX31 154 E5
Tayberry Ave TQ3 225 D2
Tay Gdns PL3 249 D7
Taylor Cl
Dawlish EX7 204 D5
Ottery St Mary EX11 169 B4
Saltash PL12 242 C3
Taylor Cres
Exmouth EX8 202 E7
Westward Ho! EX39 156 C6
Taylor Rd PL12 242 C4
Taylor's Cross EX17 62 E3
Taylors Ct
Bolham EX16 49 C1
Tiverton EX16 161 E7
Taylors Field EX20 77 C4
Taylor's Hill EX16, EX17 62 E4
Taylor's La EX37 43 D6
Taylors Newtake 2 TQ12 122 F1
Taylor Sq PL19 171 B6
TDC Units EX22 164 C6
Teachers Cl PL9 255 F6
Teal Cl
Kingsteignton TQ12 207 C8
Torquay TQ2 213 C2
Teal Pl EX7 200 F2
Teats Hill Flats PL4 263 B1
Teats Hill Rd PL4 263 B1
Teazle Ct EX2 261 A2
Technical Coll TQ12 207 C4
Tedburn Rd EX4 176 B5
TEDBURN ST MARY 97 F5
Tedburn St Mary Sch EX6 97 F5
Tedburrow La EX15 67 A8
Tedders Cl 3 EX15 67 B8
Tedstone Ho EX8 196 A6
Tedstone La EX8 196 A7
Ted's Way EX20 170 B5
Teeds The EX5 184 B2
Tees Cl PL3 249 C7
Teignbridge Bsns Ctr TQ12 180 F3
Teign Cl TQ14 208 E8
TEIGNCOMBE 110 D6
Teigncombe Ct EX6 113 B4
Teign Ct
Bishopsteignton TQ14 208 F8
Bishopsteignton TQ14 209 A8
Stokeinteignhead TQ12 209 B1
Teign Fort Dr TQ12 207 F7
TEIGNGRACE 206 F8
Teignharvey Rd TQ12 209 A3
Teignholt Cross EX6 96 D7
Teign La
Chudleigh TQ13 123 D7
Trusham TQ13 113 D1
TEIGNMOUTH 210 D4
Teignmouth Com Sch
Teignmouth TQ14 209 F8
Teignmouth TQ14 210 B5
Teignmouth Hill EX7 204 E5
Teignmouth Hospl TQ14 210 A5
Teignmouth Rd
Bishopsteignton TQ14 209 B7
Holcombe EX7, TQ14 210 E7
Kingsteignton TQ12, TQ14 208 B6
Maidencombe TQ1 214 C6
Shaldon TQ1, TQ14 210 A1
Torquay TQ1 220 A8
Teignmouth & Shaldon Mus* TQ14 210 C4
Teignmouth Sta TQ14 210 C5
Teign Rd
Newton Abbot TQ12 207 D4
Plymouth PL3 249 B6
Teign Sch TQ12 207 D8
Teign St TQ14 210 B4
Teign Terr EX6 113 B5
Teign View TQ13 123 C4
Teign View Pl 14 TQ14 210 B4
Teignview Rd TQ14 208 F8
Teign Village TQ13 123 B7
Tekoa Units EX2 177 C1
Telegraph Cross PL21 136 D4
Telegraph Hill EX6 114 D2
Telegraph La
Allercombe EX5 99 F5
Allercombe EX5, EX11 168 B6
Telegraph View TQ12 180 B1
Telegraph Wharf PL1 254 A8
Telford Cres PL5 243 F2
Telford Rd EX4 177 A7
Temeraire Rd PL5 244 D2
Temperance Pl 6 TQ5 230 D5
Temperance St TQ2 220 A5
Templar Way TQ12 123 C1
Temple Cres EX16 161 F4
Temple Gdns EX10 188 B5
Temple Mews EX10 188 B5
Temple Rd EX2 261 B2
Templer Pl TQ13 180 D5
Templer Rd TQ3 219 A3
Templers Cl TQ12 207 D4
Templers Rd TQ12 207 D4
Templer's Way 11 TQ12 123 E1
Temple St EX10 188 B5
TEMPLETON 48 A1
Templeton Cross EX16 48 A1
Templeton La EX16 47 F1
Templetown Ct EX8 201 F6
Temple Wlk 6 PL2 248 A7
Tenacott Hts EX39 26 A4
Ten Acre Gate EX13 87 E7
Tenby Rd PL5 243 C1
Tencery Orch EX14 67 C2
Teneriffe 7 TQ1 220 C5
Tennacott La EX39 26 B4
Tennyson Ave EX2 177 F3
Tennyson Cl TQ1 220 A8
Tennyson Gdns PL5 244 B1
Tennyson Way EX8 196 C4
Tern Gdns PL7 250 F5
Terrace The
Braunton EX33 152 D6
Harrowbarrow PL17 125 A5

Terrace The *continued*
Loddiswell TQ7 143 E7
Torquay TQ1 220 B4
Terra Nova Gn PL2 248 B5
Terris Cross EX20 76 A6
Terr The
Dawlish EX7 124 F3
Dawlish EX7 204 A5
TETCOTT 89 F7
Tewkesbury Cl PL2 248 A8
Tews La
Barnstaple, Bickington EX31 154 A3
Barnstaple, Roundswell EX31 154 A2
Tewsley Cl EX31 154 A3
Thackeray Cl EX11 169 E5
Thackeray Gdns PL5 244 B1
Thackeray Rd EX4 178 C8
Thames Gdns PL3 249 D5
Thanckes Cl PL11 247 A3
Thanckes Dr PL11 247 A4
Thatcher Ave TQ1 221 A3
Thatcher Dr TQ14 210 C8
Thatcher Hts TQ1 220 F3
Thatcher's La EX5 81 E6
Thatcher's Lane End EX5 81 E5
Thatches The PL21 137 E2
Theatre La 16 EX31 154 F5
Theatre Ope PL1 247 F1
Theatre Royal Plymouth★ PL1 262 C2
Thelbridge Cross EX17 61 D6
Thelbridge Hill EX17 61 C7
Thelma Hulbert Gall★ EX14 166 C7
Therlow Rd PL3 249 B6
Thetford Gdns PL6 249 D8
Third Ave
Dawlish EX7 204 D5
8 Exeter EX2 178 D5
Exeter, Countess Wear EX2 182 C7
Exeter, Heavitree EX1 177 F6
Plymouth, Billacombe PL9 250 A1
Plymouth, Camels Head PL2 247 E7
Plymouth, Stoke PL1 248 A2
Teignmouth TQ14 210 A5
Torquay TQ1 220 A8
Third Dr TQ14 210 B5
Thirlmere Gdns PL6 244 F4
Thistle Cl
Mile End TQ12 206 D5
Plymouth PL6 245 E7
Thomas Bassett Dr EX24 103 A3
Thomas Cl EX8 196 C4
Thomas Fox Rd TA21 160 B8
Thomas La
Exeter EX4 177 A8
Plymouth PL3 263 B4
Thomas Newcomen Ct TQ6 233 C3
Thomas Pl TA21 160 D7
Thomas's Cross EX6 112 F8
Thompson Rd
Exeter EX1 178 A7
Plymouth TQ12 244 B4
THORN 110 E5
Thornberry Ave EX1 178 B6
THORNBURY 55 A3
Thornbury Cross
Sampford Courtenay EX20 76 E4
Thornbury EX22 55 A3
Thornbury Mill EX22 55 A4
Thornbury Park Ave PL3 248 D6
Thornbury Primary Sch PL6 245 D4
Thornbury Rd PL6 245 E4
Thorn Cl
Exeter EX1 178 B6
Newton Abbot TQ12 206 E4
Thorncliff Cl TQ1 220 E5
Thorn Cnr EX18 77 E8
Thorn Cotts
Combeinteignhead TQ12 208 E3
Woodbury EX5 184 C3
Thorn Cross
Bovey Tracey TQ13 180 C5
Chagford TQ13 110 E5
Slapton TQ7 145 C6
Thorndale Cts EX4 176 D8
THORNDON CROSS 93 A4
Thorndon Cross EX22 71 E5
Thorne Cotts EX11 169 B3
Thorne Cross EX6 96 E4
Thorne Cross Way TA21 50 D8
Thorne Farm Way EX11 169 C3
Thorne La
Bow EX17 78 D3
Spreyton EX17 96 D8
Thorne Manor & Remains of Chapel★ EX22 71 C8
THORNE MOOR 105 E8
Thorne Moor Cross EX6 96 E4
Thornemoor La EX17 78 D2
Thorne Park Rd TQ2 219 D5
Thorne Pk EX34 8 F5
THORNE ST MARGARET 51 D8
Thornes Cross EX16 64 E5
Thornes Mdw EX2 114 A6
Thornes Terr EX36 158 C4
Thorney Cross EX21 90 E7
Thornfield Cl
Exmouth EX8 196 A2
Seaton EX12 192 A7
Thorn Gr TQ6 233 C2
THORNHAM 237 E1
Thornham Chapel Cross EX17 46 B1
Thornham La EX17 46 B1
Thornhedges Cross EX17 80 B5
Thornhedges La EX17 80 B5
Thorn Hill EX16 63 B6
THORNHILLHEAD 40 B3
Thornhillhead EX39 40 B3
Thornhill Rd PL3 248 E6
Thornhill Way PL3 248 E6
Thorning St TQ8 259 E5
Thorn La
Membury EX13 87 D7
Saltash PL12 242 C3
Thornlea Ave EX31 153 D5
Thornlea (Univ of Exeter) EX4 261 A4
Thornley Dr TQ14 210 A5
Thorn Moor Cross PL15 105 E7
Thorn Orch TQ12 211 E2
Thornpark Cross EX32 18 C6
Thornpark Rise EX1 178 B6
Thorn Pk PL3 248 F5
Thorns Cross TQ13 111 C4
Thornton Ave PL4 263 B4
Thornton Cl
Bideford EX39 156 E2
Budleigh Salterton EX9 199 G2
Thornton Hill EX4 261 B4
Thorntree Bsns Units EX8 196 F1
Thorntree Cl TQ12 206 F4
Thorn Villas TQ12 208 E3
Thornville Terr PL9 255 C7
Thorny Park La EX31 10 D3
Thornyville Cl PL9 255 C8
Thornyville Dr PL9 255 D8
Thornyville Villas PL9 255 C8
Thorpe Ave EX8 196 B3
THORVERTON 81 D5
Thorverton CE Prim Sch EX5 81 E4
Three Acre Cl EX13 167 E6
Three Ash Cross EX14 87 B5
Three Close La EX33 8 E2
Three Cnrs TQ12 207 F8
Three Corner Cross EX36 45 C5
Three Corner Field EX5 99 A5
Three Corner Pl EX2 181 C8
Three Corners Cross EX14 85 A6
Three Crossways
4 Chulmleigh EX18 44 E1
Zeal Monachorum EX17 78 A6
Three Cross Ways EX19 58 D2
Three Elms Cross EX15 83 D3
Three Firs EX15 83 D4
Threefoot Stool EX6 98 A3
Three Gate Cross
Cheriton Bishop EX17 97 B6
Yeoford EX17 79 D2
Three Gates Cross
Dulverton TA22 33 C6
Huntsham EX16 49 E6
Yarnscombe EX31 27 D1
Three Gates Hill EX16 49 E6
Three Hammers Cross EX17 61 A6
THREE HORSE SHOES 172 E5
Three Horse Shoes EX5 172 E5
Three Lane End EX22 38 E1
Three Limbed Oak EX5 81 D3
Three Mariners Cross EX14 86 C6
Three Sycamores Cross EX24 102 F6
Three Tree La TQ14 124 C2
Three Ways EX31 18 A8
Threshers EX17 165 A5
Threwstones Cl EX16 161 E5
Thriverton Cross EX22 39 B1
Throgmorton Ho 1 TQ9 223 D5
Throwcombe Cross EX16 48 A6
Throwcombe La
Oakford EX16 48 A6
Rackenford EX36 47 F6
Thrushel Cl TQ5 230 A2
THRUSHELTON 106 E6
Thuborough Cross EX22 54 A4
Thurlescombe Cross EX16 64 E6
THURLESTONE 143 A2
Thurlestone, All Saints CE Prim Sch TQ7 143 A2
Thurlestone Beach Ho TQ7 143 A1
Thurlestone Gdns TQ6 233 E3
Thurlestone Rd 3 TQ12 207 B4
Thurlestone Rock TQ7 147 B8
Thurlestone Wlk PL6 249 D8
Thurlow Cl EX17 165 A5
Thurlow Hill TQ1 220 A6
Thurlow Pk TQ1 220 A6
Thurlow Rd
Exeter EX4 177 E7
Torquay TQ1 220 A6
Thursby Wlk EX4 174 D1
Tichfield Gdns TQ3 225 F7
Tick La EX6 113 E5
Ticklemore St TQ9 223 D5
Tidcombe Cl 11 EX16 64 D7
Tidcombe La EX16 64 D7
Tidcombe Prim Sch EX16 64 D7
Tidcombe Wlk 18 EX16 64 D7
Tidderson Cross EX16 47 F4
Tidderson La EX16 47 E3
Tiddy Brook Rd
Tavistock PL19 171 E2
Whitchurch PL19 171 E2
Tiddy Cl PL19 171 B3
Tideford Cross TQ9 227 A1
Tidlake La EX36 45 C8
Tidwell Bsns Units EX8 196 F1
Tidwell Cl EX9 198 A2
Tidwell La EX9 198 B5
Tidwell Rd EX9 198 A2
Tiger Moth Rd
Clyst Honiton EX1 175 E1
Clyst Honiton EX5 179 E8
Tigers Wy EX13 167 E5
TIGLEY 135 F3
Tigley Cross TQ9 135 F3
Tilery EX14 69 A3
Tillage Way EX5 179 B3
Tillard Cl PL7 251 C5
Tillerton Steep EX6 97 C6
TILLWORTH 88 D3
Tilly Cl PL9 255 F4
Timber Hill DT7 260 E5
Timbers Cl TQ11 236 A3
Timbers Rd TQ11 236 A3
Timber Terr TQ12 212 F4
Times Mews 15 TQ9 223 C5
Timewell Hill EX16 34 C4
Timridge La EX6 113 E6
Tincombe PL12 242 C2
TINHAY 105 F4
Tinhay Cross PL16 105 F4
Tinhay Mill Ind Est PL16 105 F4
Tinker's Cross EX18 59 A5
Tinkers Wood Ct 4 TQ5 230 C4
Tinkley La TQ13 123 C8
Tin La PL4 263 A2
Tinners La TQ13 111 A6
Tinpit Hill EX5 98 F7
Tinside Lido PL1 262 C1
Tintagel Cl
Exeter EX4 174 A2
Torquay TQ2 219 F8
Tintagel Cres PL2 248 C8
Tintern Ave PL4 263 C2
Tip Hill EX11 169 D3
Tipleyhill Cross TQ12 122 D2
Tipleyhill La TQ12, TQ13 122 D3
Tippacott La EX35 6 A4
Tipple Cross PL15 105 B6
Tipton Cross EX11 168 B2
TIPTON ST JOHN 100 D2
Tipton St John CE VA Prim Sch EX10 100 C2
Tipton Vale EX11 100 C3
Titan Ave PL9 256 E8
TITCHBERRY 22 C6
Titchen's La
Calverleigh EX16 48 B1
Tiverton EX16 63 B8
Titching Park La EX34 9 B5
Titham Hill EX16 47 C6
Tithebarn Copse EX1 178 F8
Tithe Barn Cross EX15 51 D2
Tithebarn La
Blackhorse EX1 179 A8
1 Exeter EX1 178 F8
Tithebarn Way EX1 179 B8
Tithe Hill TQ7 143 E4
Tithe Rd PL7 250 B7
TITSON 70 C4
Titterton Cross EX20 77 D7
TIVERTON 161 D3
Tiverton Bsns Pk EX16 64 D8
Tiverton Castle★ EX16 161 C4
Tiverton Cl PL6 245 B8
Tiverton & District Hospl EX16 161 C5
Tiverton High Sch EX16 161 C5
Tiverton Mus of Mid Devon Life★ EX16 161 C3
Tiverton Parkway Sta EX16 65 E8
Tiverton Rd
1 Bampton EX16 34 C1
Bampton EX16 49 B8
Cullompton EX15 163 B3
Silverton EX5 82 B6
Tiverton Way EX16 161 F5
Toadpit La
West Hill EX11 168 E5
West Hill EX11 168 E6
Tobruk Rd PL12 242 E3
Toby Cross PL21 137 D6
Toby La EX5 184 E5
Tod Moor Cross PL21 237 A1
Tokesen Dr EX4 174 C1
Tolchers TQ9 222 F8
Tolcis Cross EX13 87 D3
Tollards Rd EX2 178 B2
Tollbar Cl PL21 237 F5
Tollbar Cross EX31 17 B8
Toll Bar Cross EX18 44 E3
Tolleys EX17 165 E5
Tollit Gdn 12 TQ9 223 D5
Tollox Pl PL3 249 B4
Tolman Cres EX12 192 B6
Tombstone La
Calverleigh EX16 48 C1
Tiverton EX16 63 D8
Tomhead Cross EX4 98 B6
Tom Maddock Gdns PL21 237 E4
Tomouth Cres 14 EX39 15 A1
Tomouth Rd EX39 15 A1
Tomouth Sq 15 EX39 15 A1
Tomouth Terr 13 EX39 15 A1
Tom Sanders Cl EX34 3 A3
Tomsclose La EX18 59 C2
Tom's Field EX33 7 E2
Tom's La EX39 25 A3
TONE 160 A8
TONEDALE 160 B7
Tonedale Bsns Pk TA21 160 B7
Tonedale Ind Est TA21 160 B8
Tone Hill TA21 160 B8
Tongue End Cross EX20 94 E5
Tongue Gate EX36 45 E7
Tongue Gate Hill EX36 45 E7
Tongue La PL21 137 F2
Tongue Lake La EX37 44 E5
Tonyfield Wood Cross EX17 60 B4
Top Cliff TQ14 209 D5
Topcliff Rd TQ14 209 D5
Top of the Town Ctyd PL12 242 F2
TOPSHAM 182 F5
Topsham Mus★ EX3 182 F4
Topsham Rd
Exeter EX2 178 A1
Exeter EX3 182 B8
Exeter EX3 182 C7
Topsham Sch The EX3 182 E5
Topsham Sta EX3 182 F5
TOR 133 D3
Torbay Bsns Pk TQ4 225 E1
Torbay Ct TQ5 230 E5
Torbay Hospl TQ2 219 D8
Torbay Hospl Annexe TQ2 213 D1
Torbay L Ctr TQ4 226 B3
Torbay Rd
Paignton TQ4 226 C6
Torquay TQ2 219 F3
Torbay Sch TQ3 226 C7
Torbay Trad Est TQ5 230 C4
Torbridge Cl PL12 242 D2
Tor Bridge High (Sec) PL6 245 D2
Tor Bridge Prim Sch PL6 245 D2
Torbridge Rd
7 Horrabridge PL20 126 F4
Plymouth PL7 250 E6
TORBRYAN 211 A2
Torbryan Cl PL6 249 E8
Torbryan Hill TQ12 211 A3
Torches Cnr EX19 42 D1
Tor Church Rd TQ2 220 A5
Tor Cl
Exeter EX4 174 A1
Paignton TQ4 229 B7
Plymouth, Hartley PL3 248 E7
Tor Cres PL3 248 E7
TORCROSS 145 D1
Tor Dale 3 TQ1 220 A6
Tor Down EX20 94 D5
Tordown Farm & Nature Trail★ EX32 17 F2
Tordown Gn EX32 17 F2
Tor Gdns TQ12 206 D1
Tor Haven TQ2 220 B4
Tor Hill Rd
Torquay TQ2 219 F5
Torquay TQ2 220 A5
Tor La PL12 242 B1
Torland Rd PL3 248 E7
Torlands Ct PL20 126 E2
Tor Lane End TQ9 144 C7
Tor Mare Ct TQ2 219 E4
Toronto Ho EX4 177 E8
Toronto Rd EX4 261 C4
Tor Park Rd
Paignton TQ4 225 D3
Torquay TQ2 219 F6
Torpeek Cross PL21 137 C7
TORPOINT 247 C3
Torpoint Com Coll PL11 247 A4
Torpoint Inf Sch PL11 247 B3
TORQUAY 220 B2
Torquay Acad TQ2 219 F8
Torquay Boys' Grammar Sch TQ2 219 D7
Torquay Girls' Grammar Sch TQ1 219 D7
Torquay Mus★ TQ1 220 C4
Torquay Rd
Kingskerswell TQ12 213 A3
Newton Abbot TQ12 207 C3
Newton Abbot, Milber TQ12 212 E8
Paignton TQ3 226 C8
Teignmouth TQ14 210 A3
Torquay Sta TQ2 219 F4
Torr Bridge Pk PL8 136 A2
Tor Rd PL3 248 E7
TORRE 219 F5
Torre Abbey★ TQ2 219 F4
Torre CE Prim Sch 1 TQ1 219 E7
Torre Cl PL21 237 F5
Torre Sta TQ2 219 E6
Torres Vedras Dr TA21 160 F7
Torr Farm Cotts PL8 136 A2
Torr Hill PL8 257 F4
Torridge Ave TQ2 219 B7
Torridge Cl
12 Bideford EX39 157 B1
Plymouth PL7 251 A6
Torridge Hill EX39 157 A1
Torridge Ho 15 EX39 157 B1
Torridge Mount EX39 157 B1
Torridge Pl 13 EX39 157 B1
Torridge Pool EX39 157 A7
Torridge Rd
Appledore EX39 15 A1
Braunton EX31 15 E5
Plymouth PL7 250 F6
Torridge St EX39 157 B1
Torridge View EX38 159 B5
Torridge View Bglws EX38 159 B5
Torridge Way
Holsworthy EX22 164 C6
Plymouth PL3 249 C5
Torrington Com Hospl EX38 159 D5
Torrington Cross EX37 29 C4
Torrington Heritage Mus★ EX38 159 C5
Torrington La EX39 157 B1
Torrington Pl EX6 194 D3
Torrington Pool EX38 159 C5
Torrington Rd EX19 58 E3
Torrington St 10 EX39 157 B1
Torr La
East Allington TQ9 144 B7
Plymouth PL3 248 E7
Yealmpton PL8 136 A2
Tor Royal La PL20 128 B8
Torr Quarry Ind Est TQ9 144 B7
Torr Rd PL3 248 E7
TORRS PARK 150 A5
Torrs Pk EX34 150 A5
Torrs Walk Ave EX34 150 A6
Torr View Ave PL3 248 D7
Tor Sands 1 TQ4 226 B5
Tors Pk EX35 151 D5
Tor Square Ho 6 TQ2 219 F6
Tors Rd
Lynmouth EX35 151 D5
Okehampton EX20 170 B3
Tors The TQ12 212 F4
Tors View EX39 156 B6
Tor Vale TQ1 219 F6
Torver Cl PL6 245 D2
Tor View
Buckfastleigh TQ11 236 A4
8 Horrabridge PL20 126 F4
Princetown PL20 119 A1
Tor View Ave TQ12 207 F2
Torview Flats 6 TQ13 180 D8
Tor View Gdns TQ3 226 A6
Torville Pk EX39 156 D7
Torwood Cl TQ1 220 C3
Torwood Ct TQ1 220 D4
Torwood Gables TQ1 220 C3
Torwood Gardens Rd TQ1 220 C4
Torwood Ho 4 TQ1 220 D4
Torwood Mount 6 TQ1 220 D4
Torwood St TQ1 220 C4
Torwood Villas TQ1 220 C4
Tory Brook Ave PL7 250 E6
Tory Brook Ct PL7 250 E6
Tory Way PL7 250 D6
TOSBERRY 37 E8
Tosberry Cross EX39 37 E8
Tothill Ave PL4 263 B3
Tothill Ct 2 TQ14 210 A3
Tothill Rd PL4 263 B3
TOTNES 223 E6
Totnes Castle★ TQ9 223 B6
Totnes Cl PL7 251 B4
Totnes Costume Mus★ 20 TQ9 223 C5
Totnes Cross TQ9 139 C3
Totnes Down Hill TQ9 223 D3
Totnes Elizabethan Ho Mus★ TQ9 223 C5
Totnes Hospl TQ9 223 C6
Totnes Littlehempston Sta★ TQ9 223 C7
Totnes Pavilion TQ9 223 C6
Totnes Progressive Sch TQ9 223 B7
Totnes Rd
Buckfastleigh TQ11 236 D5
Ermington PL7 136 F3
Ipplepen TQ12 211 F5
Marldon TQ3 218 C1
Paignton TQ3 225 D5
Paignton TQ3, TQ4 225 F5
10 South Brent TQ10 134 F3
Strete TQ6 145 F5
Torquay TQ2 219 C4
Totnes Sta TQ9 223 C6
Tottons Ct EX2 181 A8
Touts Ct EX36 158 D4
Tovey Cres PL5 244 D2
Towell La EX19 42 D2
Tower Cross EX14 86 A3
Tower Ct
Dunchideock EX6 114 A5
Saltash PL12 242 C2
Towerfield EX3 182 E7
Towerfield Dr PL6 245 C8
Tower Gdns EX17 165 C6
Tower Hill
Buckland Brewer EX39 40 B7
Cheriton Fitzpaine EX17 62 E1
Holcombe Rogus TA21 50 D5
Tower Hill Cross EX17 62 E1
Towerhill La TQ13 124 B4
Tower Hill Rd PL15 90 D1
Tower La
2 Bittaford PL21 137 C8
Buckland St Mary TA20 69 D8
Moorhaven Village PL21 137 C8
Tower Moor EX37 28 F6
Tower Pk EX36 158 C3
Tower Rd
Honiton EX14 166 F4
Offwell EX14 86 A3
Paignton TQ3 226 B6
Towers Cl PL6 245 F2
Tower St
5 Bideford EX39 157 A1
13 Exmouth EX8 202 A6
Northam EX39 156 F7
Tower View
Broadclyst EX5 175 C5
Saltash PL12 242 D1
Tower Way EX14 67 B1
Tower Wlk EX2 181 C8
Town Cl TQ6 233 E3
Town Ct EX13 87 A3
Town End EX5 175 D7
Town End Cross EX20 76 C5
Town Farm TQ9 222 D2
Town Farm Bldgs EX14 85 B1
Town Farm Cl
6 Honiton EX14 166 B6
6 Horrabridge PL20 126 F4
Town Farm Cotts TQ9 139 E1
Town Farm Ct
Braunton EX33 152 C6
Ideford TQ13 124 B4
Shirwell EX31 17 B8
Town Farm La TQ13 124 B4
Townfield EX6 182 A4
Townhall Pl 8 TQ13 180 D8
Town Hall Pl 4 TQ13 180 D8
Town Hill
Broadclyst EX5 175 C7
Culmstock EX15 66 E8
Ermington PL21 136 F3
Staverton TQ9 216 A5
West Anstey EX36 32 C6
Town La
Barton Town EX31 11 E3
Rackenford EX16 47 D4
Woodbury EX5 184 C3
TOWNLAKE 116 A1
Townland Rise EX20 56 F4
Townlands
Bradninch EX5 82 F6
Willand EX15 162 D3
Townliving Cross EX36 30 E1
Town Living Cross EX20 76 B5
Town Marsh TA22 33 D7
Town Mdw
Bridestowe EX20 107 F8
Ilsington TQ13 122 C3
Little Torrington EX38 41 D3
Town Mdws EX39 38 E8

Town Mill Gdns PL19 171 C6
Town Mills EX7 204 C6
Town Mill The★ DT7 260 E3
Town Moor Cross EX17 46 B1
Town Moor Hill EX17 46 B1
Town Pk
Crediton EX17 80 A3
Crediton EX17 165 B5
Great Torrington EX38 41 D6
Great Torrington EX38 159 C5
Loddiswell TQ7 143 E7
West Alvington TQ7 258 B4
Town Rd TQ7 148 F3
Townsend EX12 191 C6
Townsend Ave EX12 192 A6
Townsend Cl TQ7 258 A4
Townsend Cross
Malborough TQ7 147 E6
Winkleigh EX19 58 E2
Town's End Cross TQ7 145 C3
Townsend Farm La EX16 34 E6
Townsend Hill
Ipplepen TQ12 211 C3
Winkleigh EX19 58 E2
Townsend Rd
Seaton EX12 192 A5
West Alvington TQ7 258 A4
Townsend Terr TQ9 144 E7
Townshend Ave PL2 247 E5
Town's La TQ7 143 E7
TOWNSTAL 233 D3
Townstal Cres TQ6 233 D4
Townstal Hill TQ6 233 E3
Townstal Ind Est TQ6 233 C3
Townstal Pathfields TQ6 233 D3
Townstal Rd TQ6 233 D3
Town Tree Hill 19 EX7 204 D6
Town Wlk EX32 155 B4
TRACEBRIDGE 51 A8
Tracey Ct PL1 262 B3
Tracey Gn EX16 46 E1
Tracey Rd EX14 166 A7
Traceys Ave EX12 191 F8
Tracey Vale TQ13 180 C6
Tracey View 2 EX14 166 B6
Trackfordmoor Cross TA22 33 B3
Trafalgar Arc 20 EX34 3 A3
Trafalgar Cl
Newton Abbot TQ12 207 B5
Plymouth PL5 247 D8
Trafalgar Ct
Topsham EX3 182 E5
Uffculme EX15 66 A7
Trafalgar Dr EX38 99 A5
Trafalgar Gdns EX32 155 A3
Trafalgar Lawn EX32 155 A3
Trafalgar Pl
4 Bideford EX39 156 F1
Exeter EX4 261 C4
3 Plymouth PL1 247 F3
Trafalgar Place La PL1 247 F3
Trafalgar Rd
Exeter EX3 182 C8
Lympstone EX8 195 E6
Trafalgar St PL4 263 A3
Trafalgar Terr TQ5 230 C6
Trafalgar Way EX13 167 C5
Trafalgar Way The EX13 87 E1
Trafford Mews EX2 178 C3
Trago Mills Sh & L Pk TQ12 123 A1
Traine Brake PL9 256 C1
Traine Rd
Wembury PL9 140 D8
Wembury PL9 256 B1
Traine Terr PL21 137 C2
Traine Villas PL21 137 C3
Tramway Rd PL6 245 E7
Tramways TQ1 220 B7
Transit Way PL5 244 C3
Travellers Rest Cross EX37 28 D6
Traverses Cl EX8 196 B1
Traylane EX37 28 B1
Trayne Hts EX32 155 A8
Treable La EX6 96 B3
Treacle Hill TQ12 207 E7
Treago Gdns PL6 245 C8
Treasbeare La EX5 99 A5
Trebbleparke Rd TQ7 258 C6
TREBURLEY 115 A4
Treburley Cl PL15 115 A4
Treburley Ind Est PL15 115 A4
Treby Rd PL7 250 F4
TRECOMBE 115 D4
Trecott Cross EX20 76 F3
Tree Beech Rural Ent Pk EX32 17 F4
Tree Cl EX32 17 F4
Treefield EX31 18 A8
Treefields TQ5 230 B4
Treefield Wlk EX32 155 D4
Trees Ct EX3 182 F5
Treesdale Cl TQ3 225 F6
Tree Surfers★ PL19 125 D7
Treetop Cl PL12 242 D4
Trefusis Gdns PL3 249 A4
Trefusis Pl EX8 202 A5
Trefusis Terr
Exmouth EX8 202 A5
Merton EX20 57 A7
Millbrook PL10 252 E6
Trefusis Way EX9 198 B6
Tregenna Cl PL7 251 C4
TREGONHAWKE 252 B4
Tregoning Rd PL11 246 F2
TREHAN 242 A1
Trehill Cl 3 TQ12 244 E6
Trehill Ho EX6 114 D3
Trehill La PL10 140 H2
Trehill Rd PL21 237 E5
TREKENNER 115 A5
Trekenner Com Prim Sch PL15 115 A5
Trelawney Ave PL5 243 D1
Trelawney Cl PL11 246 E3
Trelawney Ct EX39 157 A7
Trelawney Pl PL5 243 D1
Trelawney Rd
Plymouth PL3 248 D5
Saltash PL12 242 E2
Trelawney Rise PL11 246 E3
Trelawney Way PL11 246 E3
Trelawny Rd
Plymouth PL7 250 C6
Tavistock PL19 171 C6
Treledan Way PL12 242 C5
Trelissick Cl TQ3 225 D7
Trelissick Rd TQ3 225 D7
Trelivan Cl EX8 196 E3
Trelorrin Gdns PL3 248 E5
Treloweth Cl PL2 248 D8
Tremaine Cl EX14 166 D6
Tremarran PL21 237 C6
Trematon Ave TQ1 220 A5
Trematon Cl PL11 246 E4
Trematon Dr PL21 237 E5
Trematon Terr PL4 248 E4
Tremayne Rise PL19 171 B5
Tremere Ct 22 EX32 155 A4
Tremlett Gr
Dartington TQ9 215 E1
Ipplepen TQ12 211 D2
Tremlett Meadow EX5 99 B6
Tremletts Cl EX6 97 F5
Trenance Dr PL19 116 E3
Trenavin Cl EX17 165 B6
Trenchfirs Cnr TQ9 139 E2
Trenchford Resr Woodland Wlk★ TQ13 112 E1
Trendle Gdns PL19 171 E7
Trendlewood Rd PL6 245 D7
Trenemans TQ7 143 B1
Trengrouse Ave PL11 246 F3
Treniffle La PL15 105 B2
Treninnow & Wiggle Chalets PL10 252 C2
Trennaway Cross EX6 96 C1
Trenode Ave EX34 2 F4
Trentbridge Sq EX2 178 C4
Trent Cl
Bideford EX39 26 A4
Plymouth PL3 249 B6
Trentham Cl
Paignton TQ3 225 E8
Plymouth PL6 245 B6
TRENTISHOE 4 A5
Trentishoe Hill EX31 4 A5
Trentishoe La EX31 4 A5
Trentworthy Cross EX22 38 B2
Tresco Gdns TQ12 244 F7
Trescote Way EX20 92 F1
Tresillian Cotts EX3 182 F3
Tresillian Gdns
Exeter EX4 177 E8
Topsham EX3 182 F4
Tresillian St PL4 263 C2
Tresluggan Rd PL5 243 D1
Treston Cl EX7 204 E7
Trethewey Gdns PL7 132 D4
Tretower Cl PL6 244 F5
Trevanna Rd TQ7 258 C4
Trevannion Cl PL6 249 A8
Trevelyan Rd EX12 192 C4
Trevendon PL17 115 B1
Treveneague Gdns PL2 248 D8
Trevenn Dr TQ12 213 A3
Treveor Gdns PL21 137 B3
Treverbyn Cl PL7 250 D6
Treverbyn Rd PL7 250 D6
Trevessa Cl PL2 248 D8
Trevethan Pk PL20 239 F4
Trevithick Ave PL11 246 F4
Trevithick Rd PL5 243 E2
Trevol Bsns Pk PL11 246 D3
Trevol Pl PL11 246 E3
Trevol Rd PL11 246 E3
Trevone Gdns PL2 248 D8
Trevorder Cl PL11 246 F2
Trevorder Rd PL11 246 F2
Trevose Way PL3 249 C6
Trevoya Pk PL15 89 D2
Trewithy Ct PL6 244 F1
Trewithy Dr PL6 244 F1
Trews Weir Ct EX2 261 C1
Trews Weir Reach EX2 261 C1
TREWYN 164 B5
Trewyn Pk EX22 164 B5
Trewyn Rd EX22 164 B6
Triangle Pl 15 TQ14 210 C4
Triangle The
4 Sidmouth EX10 188 A3
Triangle The *continued*
18 Teignmouth TQ14 210 C4
Tribune Dr TQ12 207 F6
Trickey Cl EX16 161 F5
Trick's Terr EX19 42 D1
Tricorn Cl TQ2 213 C1
Tridley Foot Cross EX17 61 F4
Tridley Foot Hill EX17 61 F3
Trigger's Hill EX19 42 D3
Trill Cross EX13 103 E6
Trill La
Axminster EX13 167 C2
Musbury EX13 103 E6
TRIMSTONE 8 E6
Trimstone Cnr EX34 8 F5
Trimstone Cross EX34 8 E6
Trimstone La
West Down EX34 8 E5
Woolacombe EX34 8 D6
Trinfield Ave EX8 196 B1
TRINITY 82 F8
Trinity CE VA Prim Sch EX2 182 C8
Trinity Cl
19 Bere Alston PL20 125 E1
1 Teignmouth TQ14 210 B6
Wellington TA21 160 C5
Trinity Cotts EX5 82 F8
Trinity Cross EX5 83 A8
Trinity Ct
Sidmouth EX10 188 B3
Westward Ho! EX39 156 B6
Trinity Gdns EX34 150 A5
Trinity Hill TQ1 220 C3
Trinity Hill Nature Reserve★ EX13 104 A6
Trinity Hill Rd
Axminster EX13 167 F1
Raymond's Hill EX13 104 B7
Uplyme EX13 104 B5
Trinity Mews TQ14 210 B7
Trinity Pl 15 EX32 155 A4
Trinity Rd EX8 201 E6
Trinity Row TA21 160 C5
Trinity Sch TQ14 210 B7
Trinity Sq EX13 167 D6
Trinity St
Barnstaple EX32 155 A4
Plymouth PL1 262 B1
Trinity Way PL19 171 A4
Trinnaman Cl PL21 237 D4
Trinnicks Orch PL21 137 D6
Tristan Cl EX4 174 A2
Tristford Cross TQ9 223 A4
Tristford Rd TQ9 222 D2
Trittencott Cross EX36 46 A8
Triumphal Cres PL7 250 A6
Triumph Pl TQ14 204 B1
Troarn Way 21 TQ13 123 E6
Trobridge Cross EX17 165 D2
Trojan Ind Pk TQ4 225 E3
Trood La EX2 181 D6
Trough La
Bovey Tracey TQ13 123 A6
Hennock TQ13 123 A6
Trouville 16 EX32 155 A5
TROW 189 A7
Trowbridge Cl PL5 244 C4
Trowell La TA4 35 E4
Trow Hill
Sidmouth EX10 188 D8
Trow EX10 189 A8
Truckham La EX34 3 D2
TRUE STREET 224 A6
Trumans Ct EX4 261 A2
Trumlands Rd TQ1 214 B1
Trumpers Cl PL21 237 A6
Trumpeter Pl EX7 200 E2
Trumps Cross EX16 50 E3
Trumps Ct EX10 188 B3
Trumps Orch EX15 163 A4
Truro Ave TQ2 214 A1
Truro Dr
Exeter EX4 176 F7
Exmouth EX8 196 D4
Plymouth PL5 244 A5
TRUSHAM 113 D1
Trusham Cross TQ13 113 D1
Trusham Hill
Trusham TQ12 123 C8
Trusham TQ13 113 D1
Trusham Rd EX2 177 C2
Tub Cnr EX5 99 C7
Tucana Wlk PL9 256 E8
TUCKENHAY 139 F7
Tucker Cl PL5 247 F8
Tucker Ct EX14 166 C6
TUCKERMARSH 125 E2
Tuckers Brook 12 PL21 137 B2
Tuckers Cl EX17 165 A5
Tucker's Hill PL21 133 C1
Tucker's Hill Head PL21 133 C2
Tuckers Maltings★ TQ12 207 D4
Tuckers Mdw EX17 165 A5
Tucker's Moor Cross EX16 32 F3
Tuckers Pk
Bradworthy EX22 38 E1
Buckland Brewer EX39 40 B7
Tuckfield Cl EX2 178 A4
Tucking Mill La EX36 158 E3
Tuckmill Cross EX14 84 C4
Tuckwell Gr EX1 175 A2
TUDHAY 88 C3
Tudor Cl
Lifton PL16 105 E4
11 Newton Abbot TQ12 207 B3
Northam EX39 156 F6
Paignton TQ4 226 A2
Plymouth PL9 255 E5
Tudor Ct
Exeter EX4 261 A2
Saltash PL12 243 A2
Tudor Dr EX31 154 D2
Tudor Gr EX15 163 C5
Tudor Rd TQ12 207 B3
Tudor St EX4 261 A2
Tuffery Ct EX4 177 F8
Tugela Terr EX5 179 A3
Tully Gdns EX10 188 B7
Tuly St EX31 154 F5
Tumbles The EX20 76 C5
Tumbling Field La EX16 161 D3
Tumbling Fields EX16 161 D3
Tumbling Weir Way EX11 169 C3
Tumbly Hill TQ7 258 D4
Tunnaford Cross TQ13 110 E4
Tunnel La EX14 166 F8
Tuns La EX5 82 B5
Tunworth Ct 1 EX1 261 A2
Tuplins TQ12 207 E8
Turbill Gdns 4 PL7 251 B5
Turbury Cross EX14 85 A8
TURFMOOR 87 D4
Turkey La EX5 99 E5
Turk's Head La EX14 166 A6
Turlake Ho EX5 172 F5
Turlake Mews EX5 172 F5
TURNCHAPEL 255 B7
Turner Ave EX8 202 C7
Turner Cl
Clyst Honiton EX1 179 B8
Newton Poppleford EX10 186 F7
Turner Rise EX16 161 B2
Turners Cres EX39 22 E3
Turner's La DT6 88 H2
Turning Ways EX17 61 A2
Turnlake Rd TQ13 111 A6
Turnpike
Gunnislake/Calstock PL18 125 B5
Halberton EX16 65 C8
Honiton EX14 166 D6
Sampford Peverell EX16 50 C1
Turnpike Cl
Clovelly EX39 23 D3
Whiddon Down EX20 95 F3
Turnpike Cres PL21 237 E4
Turnpike Cross EX34 8 C6
Turnpike Rd EX20 95 F3
Turnquay PL9 255 C7
Turnstone Ave EX12 192 C5
Turnstone Cl EX7 201 A2
Turnstone La EX31 15 C3
Turnstone Rd EX2 177 F2
Turpins Plot EX20 170 D5
Turret Gr PL4 248 F4
Tute's La EX34 3 B4
TUTWELL 115 E2
Tuxton Cl PL7 251 C3
Tweed Cl EX14 166 C4
Tweenaway PL21 237 E4
Tweenaway Ct TQ4 225 E4
TWEENAWAYS 225 E4
Tweenaways TQ11 236 A4
Tweenaways Cross TQ4 225 E4
Tween Moor Cross EX17 60 F6
Tweenways TQ12 207 D7
Twelve Acre Post TA22 33 A4
Twelve Milestone Hill EX17 79 D7
Twelve Oaks Cross EX18 58 E6
Twickenham Rd TQ12 208 A1
Twickenham St PL2 248 C8
Twinaway La EX2 114 B8
Twindle Beer TQ13 123 E6
Twiscombe Cnr EX4 98 D5
Twiscombe La EX4 98 C6
Twisted Oak EX6 97 D5
Twistgates La EX14 68 D4
TWITCHEN 20 D1
Twitchen Ball Cnr EX36 20 C3
Twitchen Cross
Great Torrington EX38 26 F2
West Down EX34 8 E6
Twitchen Gate EX31 11 F3
Twitchen La
Arlington EX31 10 F4
Burrington EX37 43 F3
Stowford EX31 11 A3
Two Acre Cl TQ3 225 E6
Twoacre Ct EX2 181 A8
TWO BRIDGES 119 C1
Two Bridges Rd
Princetown PL20 128 B8
Sidford EX10 101 B1
Two Crosses
Dunsford EX6 113 A8
Two Crosses *continued*
Yealmpton PL8 136 A1
Two Gate Cross EX37 44 A4
Two Gates Cross EX16 47 E5
Two Hills Pk PL12 242 C2
Two Mile Oak Cross TQ12 211 F5
Two Moors Prim Sch EX16 161 E5
Two Moors Way PL20 128 D7
Two Post Cross
Pennymoor EX16 62 E7
Taw Green EX17 95 D7
Two Post La EX17 95 D7
TWO POTS 2 B1
Two Rivers Ind Est EX31 154 E6
Two Stone La EX6 114 C5
Two Trees Rd EX31 153 D5
Twyford Pl
Tiverton EX16 161 D4
Wellington TA21 160 D5
Tyes Orch EX15 83 F5
Tylers Mdw EX38 159 E5
Tylney Cl PL6 245 B6
Tylor Pl TA21 160 D5
Tyndale Cl PL5 244 B1
Tyrrell Mead EX10 188 B7
Tyrrell Rd EX16 161 B4
TYTHECOTT 40 B4
Tytheing Cl EX5 172 A8
TYTHERLEIGH 88 C6
Tything Wlk 4 PL3 248 E6

U

UFFCULME 66 A8
Uffculme Ct EX15 66 A7
Uffculme Prim Sch EX15 66 A7
Uffculme Rd
Culmstock EX15 66 D8
Uffculme EX15 66 A7
Willand EX15 162 E6
Uffculme Sch EX15 66 A7
UGBOROUGH 137 E6
Ugborough Prim Sch PL21 137 D6
Ugborough Rd PL21 137 C7
Ugbrooke House & Pk★ TQ13 123 F5
Uggaton Cross EX14 84 D5
ULLCOMBE 68 D4
Ullcombe La EX14 68 C4
Ullswater Cres PL6 244 E4
Ullswater Ct EX4 176 F5
Umber Cl EX34 2 F4
UMBERLEIGH 28 D2
Umberleigh Com Prim Sch EX37 28 D2
Umberleigh Sta EX37 28 C2
Umberside 19 EX34 3 A3
UMBORNE 102 F8
Undercliff TQ6 233 F4
Undercliff Rd PL9 255 B7
Underdown
Clovelly EX39 23 D3
Kennford EX6 114 A4
Underdown La EX20 76 D4
Underfleet EX12 192 B6
Underfleet The EX12 192 B5
Underhay PL8 257 E4
Underhay Cl EX7 204 F8
Underheath 5 TQ1 220 D5
Underhill EX8 195 E5
Underhill Cl EX8 195 E4
Underhill Cres EX8 195 E4
Underhill Pk EX16 161 C5
Underhill Rd
Plymouth PL3 248 A4
Torquay TQ2 219 E3
Underhill Terr EX3 182 F5
Underhill Villas 1 PL3 248 A3
Underidge Cl TQ3 225 E6
Underidge Dr TQ3 225 E6
Underidge Rd TQ3 225 E6
Under La
Bovey Tracey TQ13 180 A5
Holsworthy EX22 164 C3
Sidbury EX10 101 C1
Underlane
Boyton PL15 89 D3
Marhamchurch EX23 70 A6
Plymouth, Plympton PL7 250 C5
Plymouth, Plymstock PL9 255 E6
Underleat Cl 3 TQ13 123 F6
Underleys EX12 191 C5
Under Minnow Rd EX31 154 E7
Under Rd
Bridgerule EX22 70 F5
Gunnislake PL18 125 D6
Undertown PL21 137 D6
Under Way TQ12 213 A6
Underways PL20 125 E1
UNDERWOOD 250 C5
Underwood Cl EX7 204 D4
Underwood Cotts EX15 83 C4
Underwood Rd PL7 250 D4
Unicorn Cl PL7 250 B6
Unicorn St EX2 178 D4
Union Cl EX39 156 F1
Union Hill EX17 78 E7
Union La 9 TQ5 230 C5
Union Mine Rd PL19 117 D3
Union Pl PL1 262 A2
Union Rd
Crediton EX17 165 C5
Exeter EX4 177 D8
Union Sq Sh Ctr TQ1 220 B5
Union St
Dartmouth TQ6 233 F3
Dulverton TA22 33 D6
Exeter EX2 177 A4
5 Exmouth EX8 202 A6
Newton Abbot TQ12 207 C3
Plymouth PL1 262 A2
Salcombe TQ8 259 E5
Torquay TQ1, TQ2 220 A5
Union Terr
Barnstaple EX32 155 A4
Barnstaple, Bickington EX31 154 A4
Crediton EX17 165 C5
Unity Cl PL6 245 D5
Unity Park PL3 249 C6
Univ of Exeter EX4 177 B8
Univ of Exeter (St Luke's Campus) EX1 261 C3
Univ of Exeter (Streatham Campus) EX4 173 B1
Univ of Plymouth
Exeter EX2 177 E2
Plymouth PL4 263 A3
UPCOTT
Dolton 57 F4
Holsworthy 72 E7
Upcott Ave EX31 154 C6
Upcott Cross
Cobbaton EX32 28 C5
Halwill EX21 91 D8
Holsworthy EX22 72 D7
Iddesleigh EX19 57 F4
St Giles on t H PL15 90 E1
Welcombe EX39 37 C5
West Buckland EX32 18 C3
Upcott Gate EX18 59 B3
Upcott Hill
Barnstaple EX31 154 D8
Bideford EX39 25 F4
Okehampton EX20 170 A6
Upcott La
Thorverton EX5 81 E6
West Buckland EX32 18 C3
Upcott Mead Rd EX16 161 B4
Upcott Valley EX20 170 A6
UP EXE 82 A5
Upexe La EX5 82 B5
UPHAM 63 A3
Upham Cross EX17 63 A3
Upham La EX5 99 C1
Uphay La EX13 167 B8
UPHEMPSTON 217 A3
Uphill Cl PL21 237 E5
Upland Chase EX14 166 B3
Upland Dr PL6 245 A5
Upland Gdns PL9 140 D8
Uplands
Saltash PL12 242 E1
Tavistock PL19 171 A4
Uplands Dr EX4 174 A1
Uplands Rd TQ3 219 A2
Uplands Terr
Holsworthy EX22 164 C3
Holsworthy TA20 72 A6
UPLOWMAN 50 B2
Uplowman CE Prim Sch EX16 50 B2
Uplowman Rd
Chevithorne EX16 49 F1
Tiverton EX16 64 E8
Uplowman Rd N EX16 64 E8
UPLYME 260 B5
Uplyme Rd DT7 260 C4
Uplyme Road Ind Est DT7 260 C4
UPOTTERY 68 C2
Upottery Prim Sch EX14 68 C2
UPPACOTT 27 D7
Uppacott Cnr EX31 27 D8
Uppacott Cross
Meshaw EX36 45 F8
Moretonhampstead TQ13 111 D7
Uppaton La PL21 133 D1
Upper Barton 5 EX5 99 A6
Upper Braddons Hill Rd TQ1 220 C4
Upper Church St 9 EX8 202 A6
Upper Churston Rise EX12 191 E8
Upper Claypark EX34 7 F7
Upper Cloister Wlk EX6 181 F5
Upper Cockington La TQ2 219 C7
Upper Cockington La (Path) TQ2 219 D3
Upper Crooked Mdw EX20 170 C5
Upper Headland Park Rd TQ3 219 C1
Upper Hermosa Rd 1 TQ14 210 B5

Upper Highfield EX10 ... 188 A5
Upper Knollys Terrace La PL3 ... 248 C4
Upper Longlands EX7 ... 204 D7
Upper Manor Rd TQ3 226 B8
Upper Mead EX13 ... 167 F6
Upper Morin Rd TQ3 . 226 C7
Upper Paul St EX4 ... 261 A3
Upper Penns Rd TQ3 . 219 C1
Upper Richardson
Blackhorse EX1 ... 179 A8
Exeter EX1 ... 178 F8
Upper Ridings PL7 ... 251 B7
Upper Seaway La EX10 ... 100 E2
Upper Stoneborough La EX9 ... 198 A1
Upperton La PL6 ... 241 F3
Upperton Rd
Cheriton Bishop EX6 ... 97 D1
Dunsford EX6 ... 112 E8
Upper Torrs EX34 ... 1 E4
Upper Westhill Rd DT7 ... 260 C3
Upper West Terr EX9 ... 198 A1
Upper Wood La TQ6 .. 234 B3
UPPINCOTT ... 81 A5
Uppincott Hill EX5 ... 63 C1
Uppincott La
Bickleigh EX5 ... 63 C1
Cadbury EX5 ... 81 C8
Upright Villas 4 EX33 ... 152 D5
UPTON
Payhembury ... 84 D5
Skilgate ... 34 F8
Torquay ... 220 A6
Upton Cl PL3 ... 249 B7
Upton Cross
Payhembury EX14 ... 84 D5
Thurlestone TQ7 ... 143 D2
Upton Ct 2 TQ1 ... 220 A6
Upton Farm La TA4 ... 34 E8
UPTON HELLIONS ... 80 C6
Upton Hill TQ1 ... 220 A6
Upton Hill Rd TQ5 ... 230 C2
Upton Manor Ct TQ5 . 230 C2
Upton Manor Pk TQ5 230 C2
Upton Manor Rd TQ5 ... 230 C2
UPTON PYNE ... 173 A8
Upton Pyne Cross EX5 ... 172 E4
Upton Pyne Hill
Upton Pyne EX17 ... 81 D1
Upton Pyne EX5 ... 172 F6
Upton Rd
11 Bideford EX39 ... 157 B1
Torquay TQ1 ... 219 F6
Upton St James CE Prim Sch 5 TQ1 ... 220 A7
Ursa Gdns PL9 ... 256 E8
Usticke La EX34 ... 3 B3
UTC Plymouth PL5 ... 247 E3
UTON ... 165 B1
Uton Steep Cross EX17 ... 165 B1
Uxbridge Dr PL5 ... 243 E4

V

Vaagso Cl PL1 ... 247 E2
Vachell Cres EX2 ... 178 D5
Vale Cl
Barnstaple EX32 ... 155 A6
Galmpton TQ5 ... 229 B5
Vale Ct 17 EX10 ... 101 B1
VALE DOWN ... 108 A5
Vale Dr EX2 ... 177 E3
Vale La EX13 ... 167 D6
Valentine Manor TQ11 ... 236 C5
Valentines TA22 ... 33 E6
Vale Rd
Exmouth EX8 ... 202 D7
Kingskerswell TQ12 ... 213 A5
Newton Abbot TQ12 ... 207 D1
Valerian Pl TQ12 ... 206 D5
Vales Rd EX9 ... 198 B1
Valiant Ave PL5 ... 244 A4
Valiant Soldier Mus The* TQ11 ... 236 C5
Valletort Flats PL1 ... 248 A2
Valletort Ho PL1 ... 262 C3
Valletort La PL1 ... 248 A3
Valletort Pk TQ5 ... 230 A4
Valletort Pl PL1 ... 248 A2
Valletort Rd PL1, PL3 . 248 A3
Valletort Terr PL1 ... 262 A4
Valley Cl
Barnstaple EX32 ... 155 B5
Teignmouth TQ14 ... 124 E1
Valley Dr PL9 ... 140 D8
Valley La 7 EX34 ... 3 A3
Valley of Rocks The* EX35 ... 5 A6
Valley Park Cl EX4 ... 173 D2
Valley Path TQ12 ... 206 E4
Valley Rd
Clyst St Mary EX5 ... 179 E3
Exeter EX4 ... 176 F7
Valley Rd *continued*
Plymouth PL7 ... 250 B5
Saltash PL12 ... 242 E2
Valleyside TQ7 ... 143 A2
Valley View
Axminster EX13 ... 167 E5
Bideford EX39 ... 156 D2
Chagford TQ13 ... 111 A6
Farway EX24 ... 101 F6
Landkey EX32 ... 17 C1
Millmoor EX15 ... 51 E1
Morebath EX16 ... 34 B3
Plymouth PL6 ... 245 D7
Seaton EX12 ... 192 A6
Shebbear EX21 ... 55 E4
Valley View Cl
Plymouth PL3 ... 249 B6
Seaton EX12 ... 192 B6
Torquay TQ1 ... 219 F7
Valley View Rd PL3 ... 249 B7
Valley Way EX8 ... 196 E3
Valley Wlk PL6 ... 245 E6
Van Buren Pl EX2 ... 178 D3
Vanehill Rd TQ1 ... 220 C3
Vanguard Cl PL5 ... 244 D1
Van Post EX16 ... 49 D6
Vanpost Hill EX16 ... 49 D5
Vansittart Dr EX8 ... 196 C3
Vansittart Rd TQ2 ... 219 F6
Vapron Rd PL3 ... 248 F6
Varco Sq EX2 ... 178 C4
Varian Ct 4 TQ9 ... 223 E5
Varley Ct EX16 ... 161 E6
Varve Cl 2 EX31 ... 154 A3
Vauban Pl PL2 ... 247 F4
Vaughan Cl PL2 ... 248 C7
Vaughan Par TQ2 ... 220 B4
Vaughan Rd
Exeter EX1 ... 178 B6
Torquay TQ2 ... 220 B3
Vaughan Rise EX1 ... 178 B6
Vauxhall Ct 9 PL4 ... 263 A2
Vauxhall Quay PL4 ... 263 A2
Vauxhall St PL4 ... 263 A2
Vauxhall Street Flats 18 PL4 ... 263 A2
Vavasours Slip TQ6 .. 233 F4
Veale Cl EX20 ... 75 B6
Vealenia Terr TQ13 .. 130 F4
Veales Rd TQ7 ... 258 C4
Veasypark PL9 ... 140 D8
Veille La TQ2 ... 219 C8
Veitch Cl EX2 ... 177 E4
Veitch Gdns EX2 ... 181 B8
Vela Row PL9 ... 256 D8
VELATOR ... 152 C4
Velator Cl EX33 ... 152 D4
Velator Dr EX33 ... 152 D4
Velator Lane Ave EX33 ... 152 D5
Velator Rd EX33 ... 152 D4
Vellacott La EX34 ... 3 C3
Vellaford Cross EX20 .. 75 E7
Velland Ave TQ2 ... 213 F4
Vellator Way EX33 ... 152 D4
Vellow Moor La EX19 .. 58 F1
VELLY ... 23 B3
Velwell Rd EX4 ... 261 A4
Venborough Cl EX12 . 191 F8
Venbridge Hill EX6 ... 97 B4
Venford Cl TQ4 ... 229 B8
Venford Hill
East Anstey TA22 ... 32 E8
Hawkridge TA22 ... 21 D1
Venford Villas EX36 ... 30 D4
Venhay Cross EX36 ... 46 D6
Venlake DT7 ... 260 A5
Venlake Cl DT7 ... 260 A5
Venlake End DT7 ... 260 A5
Venlake Mdw DT7 ... 260 A5
Venlock Cl EX32 ... 155 D4
Venmore Orch EX5 ... 184 B2
VENN ... 143 D5
Venn Bridge TQ10 ... 137 E8
Venn Cl
Instow EX39 ... 15 C2
6 Plymouth PL3 ... 248 E6
Stoke Fleming TQ6 ... 146 B7
Venn Cotts EX39 ... 15 C2
Venn Cres PL3 ... 248 E6
Venn Cross
Barnstaple EX32 ... 155 D1
Broadhempston TQ12 .. 131 D4
East Allington TQ9 ... 144 E5
Stoke Fleming TQ6 ... 146 B8
Ugborough PL21 ... 137 E7
Waterrow TA4 ... 35 D3
West Putford EX22 ... 39 D3
Venn Ct
Brixton PL8 ... 257 A4
Plymouth PL3 ... 248 E6
Venn Dr PL8 ... 257 A4
Venn Gdns PL3 ... 248 E7
Venn Gr PL3 ... 248 E6
VENNGREEN ... 54 D6
Venn Hill
Copplestone EX17 ... 79 B8
Milton Abbot PL19 ... 116 A6
Venn La
Cheriton Fitzpaine EX17 ... 63 A1
Dartmouth TQ6 ... 233 B1
Plymouth PL2, PL3 ... 248 C6
Stoke Fleming TQ6 ... 146 A8
Venn Lane End EX32 .. 17 B1
Venn Orch TQ12 ... 207 D7
VENN OTTERY ... 100 B2
Venn Ottery Rd EX10 . 186 E8
Venn Pk TQ6 ... 146 B8
Venn Rd
Barnstaple EX32 ... 155 C1
Landkey EX32 ... 28 A8
Venn Way
Plymouth PL3 ... 248 E7
Stoke Fleming TQ6 ... 146 B7
Venny Bridge EX4 ... 174 D1
VENNY TEDBURN ... 98 A8
VENTERDON ... 115 B2
Ventiford Cotts TQ12 123 C2
VENTION ... 7 F3
Vention La EX33 ... 7 E3
Vention Rd EX33 ... 7 E3
VENTON
Drewsteignton ... 95 F1
Ivybridge ... 136 B7
Venton Cross
Highampton EX21 ... 74 E6
Tigley TQ9 ... 135 F3
Venton Ct TQ9 ... 144 F5
Venton Dr
Westward Ho! EX39 ... 25 D8
Westward Ho! EX39 ... 156 D7
Venture Ct TQ12 ... 207 A3
Verbena Terr TQ14 ... 209 D5
Verden Cl PL3 ... 248 E5
Vermont Gdns PL2 ... 247 F7
Verna Pl PL5 ... 243 D2
Verna Rd PL5 ... 243 E2
Verney St EX1 ... 261 C4
Vernhill Cross PL7 ... 132 E3
Vernon Cl TQ1 ... 220 C2
Vernon Cres EX2 ... 182 C8
Vernon Ct TQ1 ... 220 A4
Vernon Rd EX8 ... 196 D2
Vernons La 25 EX39 ... 15 A1
Verona Ct 3 EX32 ... 155 A6
Verwill La EX34 ... 3 D3
Veryan Cl EX7 ... 200 E1
Vestry Dr EX2 ... 181 B8
Vetch Pl TQ12 ... 206 D5
Veysey Cl EX2 ... 177 E2
Viaduct View EX22 ... 164 C4
Vial's Cnr EX16 ... 48 D5
VICARAGE ... 190 F4
Vicarage Ball TQ9 ... 222 C2
Vicarage Cl
Brixham TQ5 ... 230 C5
Hartland EX39 ... 22 D3
Stoke Gabriel TQ9 ... 227 F7
Vicarage Gdns
Dawlish EX7 ... 204 C6
Milton Abbot PL19 ... 116 A6
Plymouth PL5 ... 243 B1
Vicarage Gr TQ9 ... 227 F8
Vicarage Hill
Brixham TQ5 ... 230 C5
Cornwood PL21 ... 133 D3
Dartmouth TQ6 ... 233 E3
Dulverton TA22 ... 33 D6
Holbeton PL8 ... 136 D1
Kingsteignton TQ12 ... 207 F7
Marldon TQ3 ... 218 E3
Torquay TQ2 ... 219 D4
Vicarage La
Exeter EX4 ... 174 E2
Longdown EX6 ... 98 E1
South Tawton EX20 ... 95 B5
Strete TQ6 ... 145 F6
West Alvington TQ7 ... 258 A4
Vicarage Lawn EX32 . 155 A5
Vicarage Rd
Abbotskerswell TQ12 .. 212 B6
Blackawton TQ9 ... 139 E1
Brixham TQ5 ... 230 C2
Cockwood EX6 ... 201 B6
East Budleigh EX9 ... 198 B6
Landkey EX32 ... 17 B2
Marldon TQ3 ... 218 E2
Okehampton EX20 ... 170 A5
Plymouth PL7 ... 250 C6
Sidmouth EX10 ... 188 B4
South Brent TQ10 ... 134 F3
Stoke Gabriel TQ9 ... 227 F8
Torpoint PL11 ... 247 B2
Torquay TQ2 ... 219 D4
Vicarage St
Barnstaple EX32 ... 154 F5
Colyton EX24 ... 103 A5
Vicary Cl TQ12 ... 207 A3
Vickers Ground EX39 156 F8
Vickery Cl
Cullompton EX15 ... 163 B3
West Clyst EX4 ... 174 F3
Vicks Mdw EX20 ... 75 C7
Victor Cl EX1 ... 178 A5
Victoria Ave PL1 ... 262 A4
Victoria Cl
7 Barnstaple EX32 ... 155 B4
5 Exeter EX1 ... 178 E8
Kenton EX6 ... 194 D3
Willand EX15 ... 162 D4
Victoria Cotts
2 Holsworthy EX22 ... 164 C4
Lee Mill PL21 ... 136 D6
North Tawton EX20 ... 77 C4
Plymouth PL6 ... 249 B8
Victoria Cres EX17 ... 165 D6
Victoria Ct
Dartmouth TQ6 ... 233 D3
4 Totnes TQ9 ... 223 C5
Victoria Gdns
1 Bideford EX39 ... 157 A1
Exmouth EX8 ... 196 A3
Victoria Gr EX39 ... 157 A1
Victoria Hill 1 EX22 . 164 C4
Victoria Hts TQ6 ... 233 D3
Victoria La PL12 ... 242 F2
Victoria Lawn EX32 .. 155 B4
Victoria Par TQ1 ... 220 B3
Victoria Park Rd
Exeter EX2 ... 177 E5
Torquay TQ1 ... 220 B7
Victoria Pl
Axminster EX13 ... 167 D6
Brixham TQ5 ... 230 C6
Budleigh Salterton EX9 ... 199 G2
Chardstock EX13 ... 88 A7
Dartmouth TQ6 ... 233 F3
6 Exmouth EX8 ... 202 A6
Kingsbridge TQ7 ... 258 D5
Newton Abbot TQ12 ... 207 C3
Plymouth PL1 ... 262 A2
Plymouth, Devonport PL2 ... 247 F4
Salcombe TQ8 ... 259 E5
Victoria Rd
Barnstaple EX32 ... 155 A4
Black Torrington EX21 ... 74 A8
Brixham TQ5 ... 230 F6
Dartmouth TQ6 ... 233 E3
1 Exeter EX4 ... 177 D8
Exmouth EX8 ... 201 F6
Hatherleigh EX20 ... 75 C7
Ilfracombe EX34 ... 150 B5
Plymouth PL5 ... 243 D2
Saltash PL12 ... 242 F2
Sidmouth EX10 ... 188 B4
Topsham EX3 ... 182 F5
Torquay TQ1 ... 220 B6
Victoria Road Prim Sch 1 PL5 ... 243 D1
Victoria Sh Ctr TQ4 ... 226 C6
Victoria Sq
3 Holsworthy EX22 ... 164 C4
Paignton TQ4 ... 226 C6
Victoria St
Barnstaple EX32 ... 155 B4
Exeter EX4 ... 177 D8
Holsworthy EX22 ... 164 C4
Okehampton EX20 ... 170 C5
Paignton TQ4 ... 226 B6
Torpoint PL11 ... 247 B3
Totnes TQ9 ... 223 C5
Wellington TA21 ... 160 D6
Victoria Terr
Barnstaple EX32 ... 155 A4
15 Bideford EX39 ... 157 A1
2 Bovey Tracey TQ13 .. 180 D8
Cullompton EX15 ... 163 C3
Honiton EX14 ... 166 B6
Kingsteignton TQ12 ... 207 E7
Ottery St Mary EX11 ... 169 C3
Plymouth PL4 ... 262 C4
Tiverton EX16 ... 161 B4
Victoria Way EX8 ... 201 F6
Victor La EX1 ... 178 A5
Victor St EX1 ... 178 A5
Victory Cl TQ12 ... 207 B5
Victory Dr EX2 ... 182 C8
Victory Rd
Dartmouth TQ6 ... 233 D3
North Tamerton EX22 ... 89 D8
Victory St PL2 ... 247 E6
Victory Way EX38 ... 159 C6
Vieux Cl EX9 ... 198 E7
View Rd DT7 ... 260 D3
Vigilance Ave TQ5 ... 230 E5
Vigo Bridge Rd PL19 . 171 C6
Vigo Mews PL19 ... 171 C6
Viking Gr EX1 ... 178 E8
Villa Capri TQ1 ... 220 D2
Villa Cl EX32 ... 155 B2
Village Cl EX8 ... 202 F7
Village Cross
Coldridge EX17 ... 59 F2
Loddiswell TQ7 ... 143 E7
Morchard Bishop EX17 .. 61 B2
Village Cross Rd TQ7 143 E7
Village Dr PL6 ... 241 C1
Village Farm Cl EX23 .. 70 A6
Village Hill
Upton TA4 ... 34 F7
Upton TA4 ... 35 A8
Village Hts PL7 ... 250 E6
Village La EX14 ... 86 B1
Village Rd
Christow EX6 ... 113 B3
Marldon TQ3 ... 218 D3
Woodbury Salterton EX5 ... 184 C6
Village St 10 EX32 ... 16 E1
Village The
Buckland Monachorum PL20 ... 126 C3
Milton Abbot PL19 ... 116 A6
North Bovey TQ13 ... 111 D3
St Giles in the Wood EX38 ... 42 B6
Village Way PL19 ... 117 F4
Villa Pardiso 4 TQ1 .. 220 C5
Villa Rd EX38 ... 159 C5
Villas The TQ12 ... 123 E1
Villiers Ave TQ12 ... 207 F2
Villiers Cl PL9 ... 255 D7
Vincents Rd TQ7 ... 258 D5
Vincent Way PL12 ... 242 F2
Vine Cl EX2 ... 261 C2
Vine Cres PL2 ... 248 B6
Vinegar Hill EX39 ... 157 B2
Vine Gdns PL2 ... 248 B6
Vine Passage EX14 ... 166 C6
Vine Rd TQ2 ... 219 F6
Vinery La PL7, PL9 ... 250 E1
Vinery The TQ1 ... 220 B4
Vine St EX19 ... 58 F2
Vineton Pl EX14 ... 84 E2
Vineyard TQ9 ... 223 A8
Vineyard Hill TQ9 ... 223 A8
Vineyard La
Axminster EX13 ... 87 F2
Axminster EX13 ... 167 B7
Vineyards The EX22 .. 164 C5
Vineyard Terr TQ9 ... 144 D7
Vineycroft La EX10 ... 188 F7
Viney Cross EX14 ... 86 B6
Viney La
Monkton EX14 ... 86 C7
Upottery EX14 ... 68 C1
Viney Lane Cross EX14 ... 86 B5
Vinivers Cross TQ8 ... 148 F4
Vinnicombes Rd EX5 173 F8
Vinstone Way PL5 ... 243 D1
Violet Dr
Dartmouth TQ6 ... 233 B2
Newton Abbot TQ12 ... 206 C5
Plymouth PL6 ... 245 E8
Violet La PL19 ... 171 E6
Virginia Cl EX39 ... 157 A1
Virginia Gdns PL2 ... 247 F7
Virginia Lodge 14 TQ1 ... 220 D4
VIRGINSTOW ... 90 D3
Vision Hill Rd EX9 ... 198 B2
Visitors Hill EX16 ... 63 D4
Vittery Cl TQ5 ... 230 B5
Vivid App PL5 ... 247 D2
Vix Ct TQ5 ... 230 B5
Vixen Tor Cl
Okehampton EX20 ... 170 E5
Yelverton PL20 ... 126 F3
Vixen Way PL5 ... 247 F7
Vognacott Cross EX22 . 53 F3
Volans La PL9 ... 256 E8
Voley Cl EX1 ... 178 D7
Voley La EX31 ... 4 A3
Voscombe Cross EX31 . 26 F7
Voulsdon Cross EX20 .. 92 A4
VOXMOOR ... 160 F1
Voysey Hill EX17 ... 62 F1
Vranch House Sch EX4 ... 178 B7
Vuefield Hill EX2 ... 176 E3
Vulscombe Cross EX16 ... 63 A6
Vulscombe La EX16 ... 63 B6
Vyvyan Ct EX1 ... 178 A5

W

WADBROOK ... 88 C4
Wadbrook Cross EX13 88 C4
Waddens Cross EX24 102 D4
Wadderly Hill EX17 ... 79 F7
WADDETON ... 228 F6
Waddeton Cl TQ4 ... 225 F1
Waddeton Dr TQ3 ... 225 F1
Waddeton Ind Est TQ4 ... 225 F1
Waddeton Rd
Paignton TQ4 ... 225 F1
Stoke Gabriel TQ5 ... 228 D6
Waddeton TQ4 ... 228 E7
WADDICOMBE ... 32 E6
Waddington Cross EX36 ... 31 A3
Waddington La EX18 .. 45 A5
Waddles Down Cross EX4 ... 98 E5
WADDON ... 124 A6
Waddon Cl PL7 ... 250 E7
Waddon La TQ13 ... 124 A6
Waddons Cross TQ9 . 216 C6
Wade Cl EX8 ... 202 E8
Wadham Cross
Knowstone EX36 ... 32 A2
West Anstey EX36 ... 32 A4
Wadham Hill EX36 ... 32 A2
Wadham Ho EX4 ... 173 A1
Wadham Terr 6 PL2 248 A5
Wadlands Mdw EX20 170 D5
Wadley Hill DT7 ... 260 A5
Waggoners Way EX4 177 A8
Waggon Hill PL7 ... 251 A4
WAGGS PLOT ... 88 B4
Waggs Plot EX13 ... 88 B4
Wagtail Ave PL8 ... 256 F8
Waie Cotts EX17 ... 78 C6
Waie Cross EX17 ... 78 B6
Wain La TQ12 ... 207 A4
Wain Pk PL7 ... 250 F4
Wakefield Ave PL5 ... 243 E1
Wakefields Yard 7 TQ13 ... 180 C7
Wakeham Ct EX33 ... 152 E4
Wakehams Cl PL21 ... 137 C2
Wake St PL4 ... 262 B4
Walcot Cl PL6 ... 245 E3
Walcott Way EX14 ... 67 C1
Walden Rd EX14 ... 67 C1
Waldland Gdns 4 TQ12 ... 244 E6
Waldon Cl PL7 ... 251 B6
Waldon Ct TQ2 ... 220 B4
Waldon Ho TQ2 ... 220 B4
Waldon Point TQ2 ... 220 B4
Waldons Cross EX19 .. 57 F1
Waldon Way EX22 ... 164 C6
Waldron's Cross TA21 . 35 E1
Walkers Gate TA21 ... 160 D5
Walker Terr PL1 ... 262 B1
Walkham Bsns Pk PL5 ... 244 B1
Walkham Cl PL19 ... 171 D5
Walkham Mdws PL20 126 F4
WALKHAMPTON ... 127 A4
Walkhampton Rd PL20 ... 126 F4
Walkhampton Wlk PL6 ... 245 E1
Walkham Rise TQ2 ... 219 B8
Walkham Terr 5 PL20 ... 126 F5
Walk La EX36 ... 30 F6
Wallace Ave
Dawlish EX7 ... 204 E7
Exeter EX4 ... 178 B8
Torquay TQ2 ... 219 C8
Wallace La
Lynton EX35 ... 5 A3
West Alvington TQ7 ... 143 F1
West Alvington TQ7 ... 258 B3
Wallace Rd PL7 ... 251 A4
Wallaford Rd TQ11 ... 135 C8
Walland Cross EX32 ... 18 E3
Walland Dr EX39 ... 24 B1
Wallaton Cross TQ9 .. 145 A7
Walled Gdn The EX2 . 182 C7
Wallens La
Lutworthy EX16 ... 46 A3
Meshaw EX17 ... 45 F3
Wallfield Rd TQ13 ... 180 B5
Wallingford Rd TQ7 . 258 D6
Wallis Gr TQ14 ... 209 A8
Wallon Cross TQ13 ... 110 F7
Wallpark Cl PL7 ... 250 F7
Wall Park Cl TQ5 ... 230 E5
Wall Park Rd TQ5 ... 230 E5
Wall Pk TQ9 ... 222 F6
Walls Cl EX8 ... 196 D2
Wallsend Ind Est PL4 263 C1
Walls Hill Rd TQ1 ... 220 D7
Wall St PL1 ... 247 E2
Walnut Cl
9 Chudleigh TQ13 ... 123 F6
Exminster EX6 ... 182 A4
Plymouth PL7 ... 251 B5
Totnes TQ9 ... 223 B6
Walnut Ct
Brixham TQ5 ... 230 D4
Torquay TQ2 ... 219 E4
Walnut Dr
Crediton EX17 ... 165 D6
Plymouth PL7 ... 251 C5
Tiverton EX16 ... 161 F5
Walnut Gdns PL7 ... 251 C5
Walnut Gr EX8 ... 202 C7
Walnut La TQ2 ... 219 E4
Walnut Rd
Exeter EX2 ... 177 F2
Honiton EX14 ... 166 A4
Torquay TQ2 ... 219 E4
Walnut Way EX32 ... 155 D4
Walpole Cl EX4 ... 174 C1
Walreddon Cl PL19 ... 171 B4
Walronds The EX16 ... 161 C2
Walscott Hill
Newtown EX32 ... 18 F3
Popham EX36 ... 19 A3
Walshams EX14 ... 87 A7
Walsingham Ct PL7 .. 251 B6
Walsingham Pl EX2 .. 178 D4
Walsingham Rd EX2 . 178 D4
Walson Cross EX17 ... 78 D3
Walson La EX19 ... 76 E7
Walson Rd EX17 ... 78 D3
Waltacre PL8 ... 257 F3
Walters Field EX31 ... 154 A2
Walters Orch EX15 ... 163 C3
Walters Rd PL5 ... 243 C2
Walter Way EX31 ... 153 E6
Waltham Pl PL2 ... 248 A8
Waltham Rd TQ12 ... 207 A3
Waltham Way PL21 ... 237 E4
Walton Cres PL5 ... 244 C1
Walton Rd EX2 ... 178 C5
Walton Way EX32 ... 155 C5
WAMBROOK ... 69 F3
Wambrook TA20 ... 69 D2
Wandle Pl PL3 ... 249 D5
Wanstead Gr PL5 ... 244 A2
Wantage Gdns PL1 ... 262 A3
Warberry Ce Acad TQ1 ... 220 C5
Warberry Rd W TQ1 .. 220 B5
Warberry Vale 3 TQ1 ... 220 B6
Warboro Terr EX6 ... 201 B8
Warborough Hill EX6 194 E3
Warborough Rd TQ5 . 229 C6
Warbrightsleigh Hill EX16 ... 48 B7
Warbro Ct 1 TQ1 ... 220 B7
Warbro Rd TQ1 ... 220 C7
Warburton Gdns PL5 243 C1
Warcombe La EX34 ... 1 B2
Wardens Cl EX37 ... 43 B7
Ward La EX19 ... 59 A2
Wardleworth Ct TA21 ... 160 C7
Wardleworth Way TA21 ... 160 C7
Wardlow Cl PL6 ... 248 F8
Wardlow Gdns PL6 ... 248 F8
Wardour Wlk PL6 ... 245 B7
Ward Pl PL3 ... 249 B5
Wardrew Rd EX4 ... 176 F5
Wards Cross EX5 ... 99 C8

Ware Cl TQ12 207 F7
Ware Cliff Chalets DT7 260 D2
Warecroft Rd TQ12 207 F7
Ware Cross
Kingsteignton TQ12 207 F7
Ugborough PL21 137 D6
Warecross Gdns TQ12 207 F7
Warefield Rd TQ3 226 C7
Wareham Cross EX13 88 E1
Wareham Rd EX13 88 E2
Ware Hill PL21 137 D6
Ware La DT7 260 B2
Warelwast Cl [1] PL7 250 D5
Waresfoot Dr EX17 165 B6
Warfelton Cres PL12 242 E2
Warfelton Gdns PL12 242 E2
Warfelton Terr PL12 242 E2
Warfield Villas EX34 150 C5
WARFLEET 234 A1
Warfleet Creek Rd TQ6 234 A1
Warfleet Rd TQ6 234 A2
Waring Bowen Ct EX2 177 F1
Waring Rd PL6 244 D7
Warkidons Way EX5 185 A5
WARKLEIGH 29 A2
Warkleigh Cross EX37 29 B1
Warland TQ9 223 C5
Warleigh Ave PL2 247 E5
WARLEIGH BARTON 243 F8
Warleigh Cres PL6 244 F5
Warleigh La PL2 247 E5
Warleigh Rd [2] PL4 248 E4
Warm Hill TQ13 123 B7
Warmwell Rd PL5 243 E4
Warneford Gdns EX8 196 E2
Warne La PL19 117 E6
Warnicombe La EX16 64 D6
Warran La PL19 171 C3
Warraton Cl PL12 242 D3
Warraton Gn PL12 242 D3
Warraton La PL12 242 D3
Warraton Rd PL12 242 D3
Warren Cl
Great Torrington EX38 159 C5
Payhembury EX14 84 C4
Wembury PL9 140 D7
West Hill EX11 168 D4
Warren Cross EX16 161 B7
Warren Dr EX9 198 B2
Warren Hill TQ2 220 B4
Warren La
Bickleigh PL5 243 F8
Chudleigh TQ13 124 A7
Dartington TQ9 216 B3
Exeter EX4 261 B4
Farway EX24 102 A7
Great Torrington EX38 41 C6
Great Torrington EX38 159 C5
Lee Mill PL21 136 D6
Plymouth PL5 244 A8
Wembury PL9 140 E7
Warren Pk
Plymouth PL6 245 D7
West Hill EX11 168 D4
Warren Rd
Bigbury-on-S TQ7 142 E3
Cockwood EX6 201 B5
Dawlish EX7 205 A8
Dawlish Warren EX7 201 B2
Kingsbridge TQ7 258 E3
Mary Tavy PL19 117 E6
Simonsbath TA24 13 D3
Thurlestone TQ7 143 A1
Torquay TQ2 220 B4
Warrens Mead EX10 188 D8
Warren St
Plymouth PL2 247 E4
Rockwell Green TA21 160 A4
Warren The TQ12 206 F3
Warren View EX39 156 E2
Warspite Gdns PL5 244 D2
Warton Cl PL5 244 D3
Warwick Ave
Exeter EX1 178 C5
Plymouth PL5 244 D3
Warwick Cl
Feniton EX14 84 E2
Torquay TQ1 220 E7
Warwick Orchard Cl PL5 244 B3
Warwick Rd EX1 178 C6
Warwick Terr [8] EX32 154 F6
Warwick Way EX4 178 C8
Wasdale Cl PL6 245 D2
Wasdale Gdns PL6 245 D2
WASH 215 B7
Washabrook La TQ7 258 E6
Washabrook Way TQ7 258 E5
WASHBOURNE 139 D5
Washbourne Cl
Brixham TQ5 230 E5
Plymouth PL1 247 E3
Washbourne Cross TQ9 139 D6
Washbrook View EX11 169 E4
Wash Cross TQ11 215 B8
WASHFIELD 48 F2
Washfield La
Calverleigh EX16 48 F2
Tiverton EX16 49 A1
Washfield La *continued*
Tiverton EX16 64 A8
Tiverton EX16 161 B7
WASHFORD PYNE 61 F6
Washford Pyne Cross EX17 61 E4
Washington Cl TQ3 219 B1
Washington Ho [5] EX12 192 A4
Wastor Cross PL21 142 D7
Wastor Pk TQ7 142 D7
WATCHCOMBE 102 F8
Watching Place Cross TQ13 111 B3
Watch The TQ7 143 A2
WATCOMBE 214 B2
Watcombe Beach Rd TQ3 214 C3
Watcombe Heights Rd TQ1 214 C4
Watcombe Prim Sch TQ2 214 B3
WATER 121 F7
Waterbeer St EX4 261 A3
Water Bridge Cross EX17 78 F6
Watercolour Wy PL4 255 B6
Water Cotts TQ13 121 F7
Waterdale Pk TQ12 213 A4
Waterford Cross TQ9 131 E1
Waterford La EX13 103 C5
Water Gate EX2 261 B2
Watergate Cotts PL9 140 D8
Watergate Cross EX20 107 E6
Waterhaynes La TA20 68 F8
WATERHEAD 143 B6
Waterhead Cl TQ6 234 B4
Waterhead Terr TQ6 234 B4
Waterhouse Cross EX17 62 E1
Waterhouse Hill EX20 74 F1
Waterhouse La EX13, EX14 87 C6
Watering Ct EX9 198 E7
Watering La EX9 198 F8
Watering Pk La EX17 60 A7
Water La
Barnstaple EX32 155 B3
Bow EX17 78 C4
Combe Martin EX34 3 A3
Cornworthy TQ9 227 A3
Dartington TQ9 215 B2
Exeter EX2 177 C3
Kingskerswell TQ12 213 A4
Sidmouth EX10 188 B5
Tiverton EX16 161 D4
Torquay TQ2 219 C8
Waterlake La EX31 16 A7
Waterlake Rd TA20 88 C8
Water Lane Cl [2] EX32 155 B3
Water Lane Cotts [4] EX32 155 B3
Water Lane End TQ9 215 B3
Waterlears Cross TQ7 147 D8
Waterleat Ave
Honiton EX14 166 D5
Paignton TQ3 225 E6
Waterleat Cl TQ3 225 F5
Waterleat Ct TQ3 225 F5
Waterleat Rd TQ3 225 E5
Waterleat Way TQ13 130 F6
Waterloo Cl PL1 248 A2
Waterloo Cotts EX15 163 C2
Waterloo Cross EX15 65 F8
Waterloo Ct PL1 248 A2
Waterloo Gdns EX38 159 F6
Waterloo Hill EX16 47 B6
Waterloo Path EX34 150 D6
Waterloo Rd
Exeter EX2 177 A3
Holsworthy EX22 164 D5
Kingsbridge TQ7 258 D6
Torquay TQ1 220 B6
Wellington TA21 160 C6
Waterloo St
Plymouth PL4 263 A4
Plymouth, Stoke PL1 248 A3
[14] Teignmouth TQ14 210 C4
Waterloo Terr [1] EX39 156 F1
Waterloo Yard Flats PL1 248 A2
Watermark Way PL21 237 D6
Water Mdw EX15 163 C2
Watermead TA20 88 D8
Watermill Ct [5] TQ5 230 C4
Watermore Ct [1] EX4 177 E7
Watermouth Castle* EX34 2 D4
Watermouth Rd EX34 150 E6
Waterpark Ct EX10 187 F4
Water Park Rd EX39 156 D2
Water Path TA21 160 A5
Waterpool Rd TQ6 233 E2
WATERROW 35 F4
Waters Edge PL19 171 D6
Waterside
Exeter EX2 261 A1
Kingsbridge TQ7 258 D4
Newton Abbot TQ13 180 D7
Uplyme DT7 260 B5
Waterside Ho
Ivybridge PL21 237 C4
[8] Totnes TQ9 223 D5
Waterside La EX39 157 E6
Waterside Mews PL1 247 D3
Waterside Rd TQ4 226 C1
Waterside Vw TQ4 226 C1
Waterslade Dr PL21 237 F4
Waterslade La EX5 179 E8
Waterslade Way
Clyst Honiton EX1 175 E1
Clyst Honiton EX5 179 E8
Watersmeet House* EX35 5 E5
Watersmeet Rd EX35 151 E4
Waterstream Sq [5] TQ13 123 F6
Water Terr [11] EX34 3 A3
Water Turn TQ13 130 E5
Waterwell La TQ12 213 C8
Waterworks La TQ14 209 D4
Watery La
Axminster EX13 88 A3
Beara EX31 9 A1
Braunton EX33 152 F5
Budlake EX5 82 E3
Colyton EX13, EX24 103 A6
Combe Martin EX34 3 A3
Croyde EX33 7 E2
Great Torrington EX38 159 B4
Hawkridge TA22 21 E3
Milton Combe PL6 240 D6
Parracombe EX31 11 D6
Stoke Canon EX5 81 F3
Tiverton EX16 161 E5
Whiddon EX31 9 C1
Woodbury EX5 184 B4
Watkins Way
Bideford EX39 157 C2
Paignton TQ3 225 D7
Watson Gdns PL4 263 B3
Watson Pl
Exeter EX2 177 E4
Plymouth PL4 263 B2
Watts Park Rd PL2 248 C7
Watts Rd PL19 171 B5
Watts' Rd PL4 263 C3
Waveney Gdns PL5 244 C3
Waverley Ave EX4 261 B4
Waverley Rd
Exmouth EX8 202 A8
Kingsbridge TQ7 258 C4
Newton Abbot TQ12 207 B4
Plymouth PL5 243 D2
Waverley Terr EX35 151 B5
Wavish Pk PL11 246 E3
Waybrook Cotts EX2 181 B7
Waybrook Cres EX2 181 C8
Waybrook La EX2 181 B6
Way Cnr EX16 63 A5
Waycott Wlk PL6 244 D6
Way Cross EX20 107 D8
Way Down Cross TQ13 110 F8
Waye Cross TQ13 110 F5
Wayfaring EX32 155 D3
Way La EX6 98 B5
Wayland Ave EX2 261 C1
Waylands Cnr EX16 161 D7
Waylands Rd
Bolham EX16 49 C1
Tiverton EX16 161 D6
Wayside
Brixham TQ5 230 A4
Ivybridge PL21 237 C4
Wayside Cl TQ5 230 A4
Wayside Cres EX1 178 B7
Way's La EX15 163 C2
WAYTOWN 24 D1
Waytown Cross TQ9 131 D2
WAY VILLAGE 63 A5
Wear Barton Rd EX2 182 B7
Wear Cl EX2 182 C7
WEARDE 242 F2
Wearde Rd PL12 242 E1
WEARE GIFFARD 26 B1
Weatherdon Dr PL21 237 F5
Weatherill Rd EX14 166 C4
Weaver Cross EX15 83 E6
Weaver Ct TQ2 219 B8
Weaver La EX15 83 E7
Weavers Ct EX2 261 A2
Weavers Rd TQ12 123 E5
Weaver's Reach TA21 160 B7
Weavers Way
Dartington TQ9 222 E8
Kingskerswell TQ12 213 A4
Weavers Wlk EX15 163 B2
Webber Cl TQ12 211 F8
Webber La EX17 78 F3
Webbers CE Prim Sch TA21 50 F5
Webbers Cl
Wellington TA21 160 E4
Whimple EX5 99 E8
Webbers Mdw EX5 184 D3
Webbers Way
Dartington TQ9 215 E1
Dartington TQ9 222 F8
Tiverton EX16 161 E6
Willand EX15 162 D4
Webbers Yard Est TQ9 222 E8
Webberton Cross EX2 113 F6
Webbery Cross EX39 26 D4
Webbery Moor Cross EX36 31 A3
Webble Green Cross EX13 87 C8
Webbs Orch EX20 77 C4
Webland La TQ10 135 C3
Webley Rd EX2 176 F3
Webster Cl TQ12 207 C3
Weddicott Cross TQ13 111 A4
Wedding Well La EX33 8 F1
Wedgwood Ct [9] TQ14 210 B4
Wedlake Mews [22] EX7 204 D6
Wedlake Way EX31 154 A2
Weech Cl EX7 204 C6
Weeches The EX16 48 F2
Weech Rd EX7 204 C6
WEEK
Barnstaple 27 E6
North Tawton 77 B4
Totnes 215 D1
Weekaborough Dr TQ3 218 D2
Weekaborough Oak Cross TQ12 217 E4
Week Cross
Bishop's Tawton EX31 27 F6
Bradninch EX5 82 F7
Burrington EX37 43 C5
Chulmleigh EX18 45 D3
Moretonhampstead TQ13 111 C4
Puddington EX16 62 D6
South Zeal EX20 95 B3
Zeal Monachorum EX17 78 C7
Weeke Cross PL21 137 D4
Weeke Hill TQ6 146 C8
Weekes Mdw TA21 51 E6
Week La
Dawlish Warren EX7 201 A1
High Bickington EX37 43 D5
Week Lane End EX31 27 F5
Week Park Cross EX37 43 C5
Weeksland Rd TQ2 219 C6
Weeks Row PL18 125 D6
Weekstone Cross EX22 71 B8
Weir Cl PL6 245 F2
Weirfield Ho EX2 261 B1
Weirfield Rd EX2 261 B1
Weirfields TQ9 223 C6
Weirford La EX20 76 F4
Weir Gdns PL6 245 F2
Weir Head Cotts TA22 33 D7
Weir Rd PL6 245 F2
Weirside Pl EX2 261 B1
Weirside Way EX32 155 B6
Welbeck Ave PL4 262 C4
Welch Cl EX13 167 D5
Welch's La EX31 15 C2
WELCOMBE 37 A5
Welcombe Cross EX39 37 E4
Welcome St EX2 261 A1
Weld Park Ave [4] EX34 150 D5
Welland Gdns PL3 249 C5
Wellands Cl EX15 66 B7
Wellands Cross EX13 87 D4
Wellbrook Gn EX16 161 B4
Wellbrook St EX16 161 C4
Wellbrook Terr
[10] Bideford EX39 157 A1
[8] Tiverton EX16 161 B4
Wellclose Rd EX33 152 D5
Well Cross PL21 137 E6
Welle House Gdns TQ7 258 D6
Weller Rd EX13 167 D4
Wellesley Park Prim Sch TA21 160 E4
Wellesley Pk TA21 160 D4
Wellesley Rd TQ1 220 B6
Wellesley Way TA3 68 D7
Wellfield Cl PL7 251 C5
Wellfield Hill EX13, DT6 88 H2
Well Gdns PL1 262 B3
Wellhay Cl PL9 256 C6
Well Hill TQ7 147 E6
Well Hill Cl TQ7 147 E6
Wellings Cl TA20 88 C8
WELLINGTON 160 D7
Wellington Basin Nature Reserve* TA21 160 B6
Wellington Cl [2] EX2 178 D5
Wellington Com Hospl TA21 160 D5
Wellington Hill TA21 160 F2
Wellington Jun Sch TA21 160 E5
Wellington Mus* TA21 160 D6
Wellington Pl [1] TQ1 220 B6
Wellington Rd
Exeter EX2 177 A3
Torquay TQ1 220 B6
Wellington Relief Rd
Wellington TA21 160 C3
Wellington TA21 160 F4
Wellington Sch TA21 160 E5
Wellington Sports Ctr TA21 160 C6
Wellington Sq [15] TQ10 134 F3
Wellington St
Plymouth PL4 263 A4
Plymouth, Stoke PL1 248 A3
[13] Teignmouth TQ14 210 C4
Torpoint PL11 247 B3
Wellington Way EX5 179 E8
WELLISFORD 51 D8
Well La
Bradworthy EX22 38 E1
Hartland EX39 22 D3
Welcombe EX39 37 B5
Well Mead EX13 87 C1
Well Oak Pk EX2 177 F3
Wellpark Cl EX4 176 F6
Well Park Flats EX38 159 D5
Well Park Pl TQ6 146 A7
Wellpark Rd PL18 125 C5
Well Park Rd
Great Torrington EX38 159 D5
Torpoint PL11 247 B3
Wellparks Hill EX17 165 F4
Well Pk EX22 164 C5
Wells Ave EX14 84 E2
Wellsbourne Pk PL3 249 A6
Wells Cl EX8 196 E4
Wells Ct PL10 252 E4
Well Spring Cl EX39 22 E3
Wellspring Pl PL9 256 D8
Wellsprings La EX20 76 F3
Well St
Exeter EX4 261 C4
Great Torrington EX38 41 E7
Great Torrington EX38 159 D5
Loddiswell TQ7 143 F7
Paignton TQ3 226 B6
Starcross EX6 201 B8
Wells Terr EX17 62 E1
Well Stones Cl PL21 237 E4
WELLSWOOD 220 D5
Wellswood Ave TQ1 220 E5
Wellswood Gdns
Exeter EX4 176 E5
Torquay TQ1 220 E5
Wellswood Manor [3] TQ1 220 D5
Wellswood Path TQ1 220 D5
Wellswood Pk TQ1 220 D5
Well The TA21 160 B5
Welman Rd PL10 252 F6
Welsbere La EX17 62 C3
WELSFORD 37 F8
Welsford Ave PL2 247 F5
Welstor Cross TQ13 130 E7
Welsury Rd TQ2 213 C2
WEMBURY 256 B1
Wembury Dr TQ2 214 B2
Wembury Marine Ctr* PL9 140 C7
Wembury Mdw [1] PL9 140 D8
Wembury Park Rd PL3 248 D6
Wembury Prim Sch PL9 140 D8
Wembury Rd
Plymouth PL9 256 A4
Wembury PL9 140 E8
WEMBWORTHY 59 C4
Wembworthy Down La EX18 59 C4
Wembworthy Learning Ctr EX18 59 C6
Wendover Way EX2 178 B2
Wenlock Gdns PL2 248 B8
Wensum Cl PL7 251 A4
Wentwood Gdns PL6 245 E3
Wentwood Pl PL6 245 E3
Wentworth Gdns
Crediton EX17 165 E4
Exeter EX4 176 E4
Wentworth Pl PL4 249 B2
Wentworth Rd TQ12 180 F3
Wentworth Way PL12 242 C2
Werstan Rd EX1 175 E1
Wesley Ave PL3 248 E5
Wesley Cl
Exeter EX2 177 A3
[3] Tiverton EX16 64 D7
Torquay TQ2 214 A3
Wesley Ct PL11 247 C3
Wesley La PL12 242 F2
Wesley Mews TQ2 214 A2
Wesley Pl
Harberton TQ9 222 D2
Plymouth, Mutley PL3 248 E5
[1] Plymouth, Stoke PL2 248 A4
Wesley Rd
Holsworthy EX22 164 B5
Saltash PL12 242 F2
Wesley Terr
Hartland EX39 22 D3
Ipplepen TQ12 211 D2
Wesley View TQ12 211 D2
Wesley Way EX2 181 B8
Wessex Cl EX3 182 D6
Wessex Est EX4 177 A7
Wessex Ho [1] DT7 260 D3
Wessex Way TQ6 233 C2
Wessiters EX12 192 A5
Westabrook Ave TQ13 130 F5
Westabrook Cl TQ13 130 F5
Westabrook Dr TQ13 130 F5
Westacombe EX31 27 B8
WESTACOTT 155 F4
Westacott Cross
Inwardleigh EX20 75 C3
Meshaw EX36 45 E8
North Tawton EX20 77 E5
Westacott La
Coldridge EX17 59 E2
East Buckland EX32 18 D2
Mariansleigh EX36 45 E8
North Tawton EX20 77 E5
Westacott Mdw EX32 155 E3
Westacott Rd EX32 155 E4
West Acres EX12 191 F7
WEST ALVINGTON 258 B4
West Alvington Butts TQ7 143 E2
West Alvington CE Prim Sch TQ7 258 A4
West Alvington Hill TQ7 258 C5
WEST ANSTEY 32 C6
West Anstey School Cross EX36 32 C5
West Ave
Barnstaple EX31 154 D3
Exeter EX4 177 C8
[4] Tavistock PL19 171 B5
Westaway EX31 153 E5
Westaway Cl EX31 155 A7
Westaway Hts EX31 155 A8
Westawayplain EX31 154 F7
Westaway Plain EX31 155 A8
Westaway Rd [6] EX24 103 A4
West Ball Hill EX39 22 D3
West Barton La EX20 76 E4
West Beckon Cl EX23 37 A1
Westbourne Gr EX34 150 A5
Westbourne Rd
Plymouth PL3 248 D5
Torquay TQ1 220 A7
Westbourne Terr
Budleigh Salterton EX9 203 F8
Saltash PL12 242 F3
Westward Ho! EX39 156 C7
Westbourne Villas EX34 150 B6
Westbridge Cl EX20 170 B5
Westbridge Cotts PL19 171 B4
Westbridge Ct EX2 181 D8
Westbridge Ind Est [3] PL19 171 B4
Westbrook Ave
Teignmouth TQ14 209 E7
Teignmouth TQ14 210 A5
Westbrook Cl EX4 178 B8
Westbrook Pl EX16 161 E4
West Brushford La EX18 59 C2
West Buckeridge TQ14 210 B6
WEST BUCKLAND
Barnstaple 18 B2
Wellington 52 F7
West Buckland Cross EX32 18 B2
West Buckland Prim Sch TA21 52 F7
West Buckland Rd TA21 52 D7
West Buckland Sch EX32 18 C2
West Burridge Cross EX18 60 E7
Westbury Cl PL5 244 B4
West Challacombe La EX34 3 A4
WEST CHARLETON 144 C1
West Charleton Ct TQ7 144 C1
West Cl EX13 167 C5
West Cliff EX7 204 E6
West Cliff Cl EX7 204 D5
West Cliff Park Dr EX7 204 D5
Westcliff Prim Acad EX7 204 C5
Westcliff Rd DT6 104 F4
West Cliff Rd EX7 204 D6
West Cliff Terr [2] EX12 192 A4
Westclyst EX1 175 A3
Westclyst Com Prim Sch EX4 174 F3
Westcombe EX2 181 B8
Westcombe Cres PL9 255 D5
Westcombe La
Bideford EX39 156 F2
Bideford EX39 157 A2
Westcombes EX13 88 B7
West Coombe La TA4 35 D8
Westcots Dr EX19 58 F2
WESTCOTT 83 C7
Westcott Cl PL6 249 A8
Westcott Cross EX14 66 F2
Westcott La
Aylesbeare EX5 99 D4
Beara EX31 9 A1
Bridford EX6 112 C6
Witheridge EX16 61 E7
Westcott Rd [15] EX16 64 D7
West Cotts TA24 13 A2

Westcott Way EX14 . . 166 D6
Westcountry Cl PL2 . . 247 F7
Westcroft Ct 3 EX39 156 F1
Westcroft Rd
Holsworthy TA20 . . . . . . 71 F6
Holsworthy TA20 . . . . . . 164 B4
Plymouth PL5 . . . . 243 D1
West Croft Rd EX22 . . 164 B4
West Croft Sch EX39 . 156 F1
West Cross EX33 . . . . . 152 D6
Westcroyde EX33 . . . . . . 7 D1
WEST CURRY 89 A4
West Devon Bsns Pk
PL19 . . . . 171 B3
WEST DOWN 8 F5
West Down EX16 . . . . . . 65 A6
West Down County Prim
Sch EX34 . . . . 8 F5
West Down Hill EX33,
EX34 . . . . 8 F4
West Down La EX8 . . . 203 A6
West Down Rd PL2 . . . 248 B6
West Down View
EX8 . . . . 203 B6
West & East Putford Prim
Sch EX22 . . . . 39 C2
West Efford La EX17 . . . 81 A4
Westella Rd PL20 . . . . 127 A2
West Emlett La EX17 . . 61 E3
West End Cross EX16 . . 48 D5
West End La EX16 . . . . . 48 D5
West End Rd
Bradninch EX5 . . . . 82 F6
Buckfastleigh TQ11 . . . . 236 B4
West End Terr
Ashburton TQ13 . . . . . . 130 F4
Denbury TQ12 . . . . 211 A6
South Molton EX36 . . . . 158 C4
Westentown TQ7 . . . . . 142 C6
Westeria Terr PL2 . . . 248 C7
WESTERLAND 218 D1
Westerland TQ6 . . . . . 234 B3
Westerland Gn TQ3 . . 218 D2
Westerland La TQ3 . . . 218 D2
Wester-Moor Cl 6
EX31 . . . . 154 A2
Wester-Moor Dr
EX31 . . . . 154 A2
Wester-Moor Way
EX31 . . . . 154 A2
Western App PL1 . . . . 262 B2
Western Ave
Appledore EX39 . . . . 15 A1
Exeter EX2 . . . . 182 D7
Western Bsns Pk
TQ4 . . . . 225 F2
Western By-Pass
TQ9 . . . . 223 B5
Western College Rd
PL4 . . . . 248 F5
WESTERN COMMON . . 19 D7
Western Cotts EX20 . . 107 E1
Western Ct EX10 . . . . . 188 A3
Western Dr
Newton Abbot TQ12 . . . 206 F4
Plymouth PL3 . . . . 249 B4
Starcross EX6 . . . . 201 B8
Western Field EX10 . . 188 A3
Western Gardens Rd
EX34 . . . . 3 A3
Western Ho EX7 . . . . . 204 E7
Westernlea EX17 . . . . . 165 A5
Western Piece La EX31 . 9 D1
Western Pl 4 EX24 . . 103 A4
Western Rd
Ashburton TQ13 . . . . . . 130 F4
Crediton EX17 . . . . 165 A6
Exeter EX4 . . . . 177 A5
Holsworthy EX22 . . . . . 164 C4
Ivybridge PL21 . . . . 237 C4
Newton Abbot TQ12 . . . 207 C3
Torquay TQ1 . . . . 214 B1
Zeal Monachorum EX17 . 78 B6
Western Rise EX34 . . . . . 8 A6
Western Side
Clawton EX22 . . . . 89 E8
Clawton TA20 . . . . 71 F1
Western Terr
Barnstaple EX31 . . . . . . 154 E5
Ilfracombe EX34 . . . . . . 150 A4
Totnes TQ9 . . . . 223 B6
WESTERN TOWN 188 A3
Western Units TQ13 . . 180 D5
Western Villas
Crediton EX17 . . . . 165 B5
Totnes TQ9 . . . . 223 B5
Western Way
Exeter, Barnfield EX1,
EX2 . . . . 261 C3
Exeter, Friars' Green
EX1 . . . . 261 A2
Western Way Ind Est
EX15 . . . . 163 C4
Western Wood Way
PL7 . . . . 251 D5
West Exe N EX16 . . . . . 161 C4
West Exe S EX16 . . . . . 161 C3
West Exe Tech Coll
EX2 . . . . 177 A2
Westfield
Bradninch EX5 . . . . 82 F6
Plymouth PL7 . . . . 251 A6
Westfield Ave
Barnstaple EX31 . . . . . . 154 D4
Plymouth PL9 . . . . 255 C6
Westfield Bsns Pk
TQ3 . . . . 225 E1
Westfield Cl
Brixham TQ5 . . . . 230 B3
Budleigh Salterton
EX9 . . . . 198 A1
Westfield Rd
Budleigh Salterton
EX9 . . . . 198 A1
Tiverton EX16 . . . . 161 C3
West Field Rd EX6 . . . 182 B3
Westfield Terr 8
EX16 . . . . 161 C3
WESTFORD 51 F7
Westford Cl TA21 . . . . 160 A5
Westford Ct TA21 . . . . 160 A5
Westford Dr TA21 . . . . 160 A5
Westford Grange
TA21 . . . . 160 A5
West Garth Ct EX4 . . . 172 F2
West Garth Rd EX4 . . . 173 A3
Westgate EX17 . . . . 60 D3
West Golds Wy TQ12 . 207 B5
West Grove Rd EX2 . . . 261 C2
Westhampnett Pl
PL5 . . . . 243 F4
West Hartley TQ9 . . . . 139 E3
Westhay Cross EX13 . . 88 F3
Westhay Rd TA20 . . . . . 69 C7
Westhays Cl PL9 . . . . . 255 F4
Westhead Rd PL10 . . . 140 H2
WEST HILL 168 E4
West Hill
Budleigh Salterton
EX9 . . . . 203 F8
Heybrook Bay PL9 . . . . . 140 A7
Westhill Ave TQ1 . . . . 220 B7
Westhill Avenue Cl
TQ1 . . . . 220 B7
Westhill Cres TQ3 . . . . 226 B7
West Hill Ct EX9 . . . . . 203 F8
West Hill Gdns EX9 . . . 203 F8
West Hill La
Braunton EX33 . . . . 152 C6
Budleigh Salterton EX9 197 F1
Parracombe EX31 . . . . 4 B2
West Hill Prim Sch
EX11 . . . . 168 D4
Westhill Rd
Paignton TQ3 . . . . 226 A7
Torquay TQ1 . . . . 220 B8
West Hill Rd
Lyme Regis DT7 . . . . . . 260 D3
Ottery St Mary EX11 . . . 169 B2
Plymouth PL4 . . . . 248 F4
West Hill EX10 . . . . 100 B5
West Hill EX11 . . . . 168 D4
West Hill EX11 . . . . 168 E5
Westhill Terr TQ12 . . . 213 A4
West Ho EX13 . . . . 167 D5
WEST HOE 262 B1
West Hoe Rd PL1 . . . . 262 B1
Westholme 6 TQ1 . . . 220 C5
WEST ILKERTON 5 A3
West La
Braunton EX33 . . . . 152 D6
Challacombe EX31 . . . . . 11 D4
Dolton EX19 . . . . 57 E6
Knowle EX33 . . . . 8 C2
Lapford EX17 . . . . 60 C3
Oakford EX16 . . . . 48 A7
Paignton TQ3 . . . . 225 A6
Templeton EX16 . . . . 48 A1
WESTLAKE 136 E4
Westlake Cl PL11 . . . . 246 F3
Westlake Rd PL9 . . . . . 140 A8
Westlake Rise PL9 . . . 140 A8
Westland La EX16 . . . . . 62 C6
Westlands
Exmouth EX8 . . . . 202 C6
Wrafton EX33 . . . . 152 E4
Westlands La TQ1 . . . . 220 B7
Westleat Ave TQ3 . . . . 225 F6
WESTLEIGH
Bideford 157 E6
Wellington 51 A4
WEST LEIGH 77 E8
West Leigh Cross
TQ9 . . . . 135 F1
Westleigh La EX34 . . . . . 3 C2
Westleigh Wy PL9 . . . . 249 D1
West Lodge DT7 . . . . . 193 D5
West Lyn Rd EX35 . . . . 151 C2
West Malling Ave
PL5 . . . . 243 E5
West Manley La EX16 . . 64 E7
Westmead Cl EX33 . . . 152 C6
West Meadow Cl
EX33 . . . . 152 B7
West Meadow Rd
EX33 . . . . 152 A7
West Mill Cross
TQ11 . . . . 236 B4
Westminster Cl
Exmouth EX8 . . . . 196 D3
Feniton EX14 . . . . 84 D2
Westminster Rd EX4 . 176 E6
Westminster Villas
EX34 . . . . 150 D5
West Molland La EX36 31 D7
Westmoor Cl PL7 . . . . 251 C6
West Moor Cl EX39 . . . 156 F8
Westmoor Pk PL19 . . . 171 C4
West Moor Way
EX39 . . . . 156 F8
West Mount TQ12 . . . . 207 D1
West of England Sch &
Coll EX1 . . . . 178 B1
WEST OGWELL 206 A1
West Ogwell Cross
TQ12 . . . . 211 C8
WESTON 189 D6
Weston Cl
Brixham TQ5 . . . . 230 C3
Broadhembury EX14 . . . . 84 D7
Weston Cross
Awliscombe EX14 . . . . . . 85 C3
Sidmouth EX10 . . . . 189 D8
Weston Ct TQ9 . . . . . . 223 F5
Westonfields TQ9 . . . . 223 E5
Weston La
Awliscombe EX14 . . . . . . 85 B4
Totnes TQ9 . . . . 223 E4
WESTON MILL 247 E8
Weston Mill Com Prim
Sch PL2 . . . . 247 E7
Weston Mill Dr PL5 . . 247 F8
Weston Mill Hill PL5 . 243 F1
Weston Mill La PL5 . . . 244 A1
Weston Mill Rd PL5 . . 243 E1
Weston Park Rd PL3 . 248 D6
Weston Rd
Totnes TQ9 . . . . 223 D5
Wambrook TA20 . . . . 69 F3
Weston Terr EX11 . . . . 169 E4
WESTON TOWN 188 A3
Westover Cl
Brixham TQ5 . . . . 230 D4
Ivybridge PL21 . . . . 237 B5
Westover Hill
Charmouth DT6 . . . . 104 F5
Penn DT7 . . . . 260 F8
Westover Ind Est
PL21 . . . . 237 C4
Westover La PL21 . . . . 237 B4
Westown Rd EX2 . . . . . 176 C1
West Pafford Ave
TQ2 . . . . 214 B3
Westpark TA21 . . . . 52 D7
WEST PARK 244 A3
Westpark 26 TA21 . . . . . 52 D7
West Park Dr PL7 . . . . 251 C5
West Park Hill PL7 . . . 251 B7
West Park Rd EX10 . . . 188 A5
Westpark Villas 8
PL20 . . . . 126 F5
West Pk
Braunton EX33 . . . . 152 C6
Outer Hope TQ7 . . . . . . 147 B7
South Molton EX36 . . . . 158 B4
Stoke Fleming TQ6 . . . . 146 B8
Wellington TA21 . . . . . . 160 D7
Westpoint (County
Showground) EX5 . . 179 C3
West Pugsley Cross
EX37 . . . . 29 A2
WEST PUTFORD 39 C2
West Quay PL10 . . . . . 252 E5
West Rd
Roborough EX19 . . . . 42 F4
Sheepwash EX21 . . . . . . 56 C1
Woolacombe EX34 . . . . . . 7 F6
Westridge Cross EX16 63 C4
West Rock Dr EX36 . . . . 30 F2
WEST SANDFORD 79 E5
West Spurway La
EX16 . . . . 48 A8
West St
Ashburton TQ13 . . . . . . 130 F4
Axminster EX13 . . . . . . 167 D5
Bampton EX16 . . . . 34 B1
Bishops Nympton EX36 . . 30 F2
Bishopsteignton TQ14 . . 208 F8
Denbury TQ12 . . . . 211 A6
Exeter EX1, EX4 . . . . . . 261 A2
Hartland EX39 . . . . 22 D3
Millbrook PL10 . . . . 252 E5
Okehampton EX20 . . . . 170 B5
South Molton EX36 . . . . 158 C4
Tavistock PL19 . . . . 171 B5
Torpoint PL10 . . . . 252 E4
Witheridge EX16 . . . . 46 E1
West Terr
Budleigh Salterton
EX9 . . . . 198 A1
Churston Ferrers TQ5 . . 229 E4
Exeter EX1 . . . . 177 F6
WEST TOWN
Crediton 165 B5
Newton St Cyres 98 F8
Woolfardisworthy 38 E8
West Town Cross
EX39 . . . . 38 E8
West Town Mdw
TQ14 . . . . 208 E8
West Town Rd
Newton St Cyres EX5 . . . 98 F8
Newton St Cyres EX5 . . 109 A8
West Ugworthy Cross
EX22 . . . . 53 E3
West Underleys
EX12 . . . . 191 C5
West View
Beer EX12 . . . . 191 D5
Colyford EX24 . . . . 103 A3
Holsworthy EX22 . . . . . 164 C5
Tavistock PL19 . . . . 171 E2
West View Ave EX39 . . 157 B2
Westview Cl EX5 . . . . . . 99 E8
West View Cl TQ12 . . . 206 F1
West View Ct 1
EX32 . . . . 155 B4
West View Rd
5 Bere Alston PL20 . . . 125 E1
Marldon TQ3 . . . . 218 D2
Okehampton EX20 . . . . 170 C5
West View Terr
Exeter EX4 . . . . 261 A2
3 Honiton EX14 . . . . . . 166 B6
Lympstone EX8 . . . . 195 F5
WESTVILLE 258 B5
Westward Bsns Ctr
EX17 . . . . 165 D5
Westward Cl TQ9 . . . . 223 C5
Westward Dr EX8 . . . . 202 B7
WESTWARD HO! 156 D8
Westward View
TQ12 . . . . 208 A2
Westwater Hill EX6 . . . 97 E5
West Waters La EX31 . . . 4 D5
Westway PL9 . . . . 255 B5
Westway Cross EX16 . . 61 F8
WESTWEEKMOOR 91 A4
WESTWOOD
Cockwood 201 A6
Crediton 165 A5
Whimple 83 C1
Westwood Ave PL6 . . . 245 C6
Westwood Cl EX17 . . . 165 A5
Westwood Cleave
TQ12 . . . . 211 F8
Westwood Cotts EX6 . . 98 E2
Westwood Hill EX6 . . . 201 A5
Westwood La EX6 . . . . 176 B4
Westwood Rd
Crediton EX17 . . . . 165 A5
East Ogwell TQ12 . . . . . 212 A8
Westwoods EX6 . . . . . . 98 B4
Westwood Units EX2 177 D1
Westwood Way EX12 192 B7
WEST WORLINGTON . . 61 A8
Westworthy Cross
EX20 . . . . 77 E6
Westyard La EX18 . . . . . 58 E8
West Yelland EX31 . . . . 15 C2
West Yeo Cross EX16 . . 46 C2
West Yeo Moor Hill
EX16 . . . . 46 C3
WEST YOULSTONE . . . 37 E2
Wethered Cl EX16 . . . . 161 C3
Wet La
Christow EX6 . . . . 113 B4
17 Combe Martin EX34 . . . 3 A3
WEYCROFT 88 B2
Weycroft Ave EX13 . . . 167 F7
Weycroft Cl EX1 . . . . . 178 D6
Weymouth Pk TQ7 . . . . 147 B7
Whalley La DT7 . . . . . . 260 B4
Wharf Cotts TA21 . . . . 160 B8
Wharf Rd TQ12 . . . . . . 207 D4
Wharf Road Ind Est
TQ12 . . . . 207 D4
Wharf Theatre & Gall
The★ PL19 . . . . 171 B5
Whatley La TA20 . . . . . . 69 A7
Whatley Mws 4 PL3 . 249 D1
Wheadon Cross EX16 . . 46 D4
Wheal Betsy★ PL19 . . 117 F8
Wheal Maria PL19 . . . . 116 C1
Wheal Maria Cotts
PL19 . . . . 116 B1
Wheal Rd PL19 . . . . . . 117 E6
Wheat Belt Rise 3
EX1 . . . . 178 F8
Wheatclose Cross
EX36 . . . . 20 D2
Wheatcombe Ct TQ2 . 214 B3
Wheatfield Cl EX15 . . . 163 B2
Wheatland Cross
EX16 . . . . 48 D6
Wheatland La EX16 . . . . 48 C6
Wheatlands Rd TQ4 . . 226 B4
Wheatley Cl EX4 . . . . . 176 E5
Wheatley Ct 5 EX1 . . 261 A2
Wheatly Cotts EX17 . . . 78 C4
Wheatly La EX31 . . . . . . 4 B2
Wheat Pk TQ9 . . . . 138 D8
Wheatridge PL7 . . . . . . 250 B7
Wheatridge La TQ2 . . . 219 E2
Wheatsheaf 18 EX5 . . . 99 A6
Wheatsheaf Way
EX2 . . . . 177 A1
Wheelbarrow La EX15 67 C8
Wheel Cl 11 EX31 . . . . 154 A2
Wheel Cross EX34 . . . . . . 2 F1
Wheeldon Off-road Bike
Ctr★ TQ9 . . . . 138 E5
Wheelers Cross EX22 . . 39 B1
Wheelers Yard EX24 . 103 A5
Wheel La EX34 . . . . 2 F1
Wheelwright Ct PL20 127 B4
Whelmstone Cross
EX17 . . . . 78 E3
Whetcombe Cross
PL21 . . . . 137 F6
Whey Cross EX37 . . . . . 28 D3
Whidborne Ave TQ1 . . 221 A4
Whidborne Cl TQ1 . . . 220 F3
Whidborne Mews
TQ14 . . . . 124 D1
WHIDDON
Barnstaple 155 D2
Marwood 9 D1
Whiddon Cross
Abbotskerswell TQ12 . . 212 B4
Whiddon EX31 . . . . 9 D1
WHIDDON DOWN 95 F3
Whiddon Down Rd
TQ13 . . . . 111 E5
Whiddon Dr EX32 . . . . 155 D3
Whiddon La
Ide EX2 . . . . 114 A8
Whiddon EX31 . . . . 9 D1
Whiddon Rd TQ12 . . . . 212 B4
Whiddon Valley Ind Est
EX32 . . . . 155 D3
Whidley La EX6 . . . . . . 112 E8
Whilborough Rd
TQ12 . . . . 212 E2
WHIMBLE 164 E2
Whimble Hill EX22 . . . 164 D3
Whimbrel Ct EX3 . . . . 182 E6
Whimbrels Edge
TQ7 . . . . 143 A1
Whimbrel Way PL9 . . . 256 D8
WHIMPLE 99 E7
Whimple Prim Sch
EX5 . . . . 99 E8
Whimple St PL1 . . . . . . 262 C2
Whimple Sta EX5 . . . . . 99 E8
Whin Bank Rd PL5 . . . 244 E2
WHIPCOTT 51 B5
Whippenscott Hill
EX36 . . . . 46 B8
Whipple's Cross
PL21 . . . . 136 E4
WHIPTON 178 C8
Whipton Barton Ho
EX1 . . . . 178 B7
Whipton Barton Inf Sch
EX1 . . . . 178 B7
Whipton Barton Jun Sch
EX1 . . . . 178 B7
Whipton Barton Rd
EX1 . . . . 178 C7
Whipton La EX1 . . . . . 178 A6
Whipton Rd EX4 . . . . . 178 A8
Whipton Village Rd
EX4 . . . . 178 B8
Whisselwell Cl TQ13 . 122 D4
Whistley Down PL20 . 126 E2
Whistley Hill TQ13 . . . 131 A4
Whistley Hill Cross
TQ13 . . . . 131 A4
Whitaker Cl EX1 . . . . . 174 F3
Whitby Cres PL6 . . . . . 245 A1
Whitby Rd PL6 . . . . 245 A1
WHITCHURCH 171 D3
Whitchurch Ave EX2 . 178 B4
Whitchurch Com Prim
Sch PL19 . . . . 171 D2
Whitchurch Rd
Horrabridge PL20 . . . . . 126 F5
Tavistock PL19 . . . . 171 C3
Whitcott Hill EX36 . . . . 31 A8
Whiteabury Cross
TQ13 . . . . 111 C7
Whitear Cl EX11 . . . . . 124 E1
Whitear's Way TQ12 . 207 E7
White Ash La TA20 . . . . 69 D5
WHITE BALL 51 D6
Whiteball Rd EX16 . . . . 51 E6
Whitebeam Cl
Exeter EX4 . . . . 174 B2
Paignton TQ3 . . . . 225 E7
Whitebeam Gr EX14 . . . 67 B1
Whitebear Cross EX22 . 54 F6
Whiteborough La
Chudleigh TQ13 . . . . 123 D8
Trusham TQ13 . . . . 113 D1
Whitebridges EX14 . . . 166 B4
Whitebrook Terr TA21 . 50 F5
Whitechapel La EX36 . . 30 F6
White Cl
Paignton TQ3 . . . . 219 B2
West Clyst EX4 . . . . 174 E3
Whitecleave Cross
EX37 . . . . 43 F2
White Cliff 8 EX12 . . . 192 B4
White Cross
Aylesbeare EX5 . . . . 99 C1
Cheriton Fitzpaine EX17 . 62 F1
Malborough TQ7 . . . . . . 147 E6
Ottery St Mary EX11 . . . 100 F3
White Cross Ct PL4 . . . 263 A3
Whitecross Gdns
EX12 . . . . 192 B7
White Cross Hill EX17 . 62 F1
White Cross Rd EX5 . . 184 D6
White Ct 11 EX7 . . . . . 204 E6
Whitedown Cross
EX15 . . . . 67 E4
White Down Cross
EX16 . . . . 64 E5
White Farm La
West Hill EX10 . . . . 100 A4
West Hill EX11 . . . . 168 D3
Whitefield EX14 . . . . . . 86 C3
Whitefield Cross
EX36 . . . . 32 D3
Whitefield Hill EX31 . . . . 9 E2
Whitefield La EX32 . . . . 19 A6
Whitefield Terr PL4 . . 263 B4
Whiteford Rd PL3 . . . . 248 E6
White Friars La PL4 . . 263 B3
White Gate EX24 . . . . . 102 E3
Whitegates EX34 . . . . . . 2 F4
White Gates Cross
TQ13 . . . . 110 F7
WHITEHALL 52 A1
Whitehall Cl
Morebath EX16 . . . . 34 B4
South Molton EX36 . . . . 158 C3
Whitehall Dr
9 Bere Alston PL20 . . . 125 E1
Plymouth PL9 . . . . 256 B7
Whitehall La EX3 . . . . 182 F8
Whitehall Manor
TQ7 . . . . 143 E4
White Hart La TA21 . . 160 D6
Whitehaven Way
PL6 . . . . 245 A7
Whitehayes Cl
Kilmington EX13 . . . . 87 C1
Wilmington EX14 . . . . . . 86 D2
Whiteheads Cross
TQ11 . . . . 135 C7
White Heather Terr
TQ13 . . . . 180 D8
Whitehill Cl TQ12 . . . . 207 B5
Whitehill Cotts TQ12 . 206 F5
Whitehill Cross PL15 105 B6
White Hill Dro TA20 . . . 69 F5
Whitehill Gdns PL7 . . . 132 F4
Whitehill La TQ9, TQ9 228 B8
Whitehill Rd TQ12 . . . 207 A5
Whitehorse La EX39 . . 157 A8
Whitehouse Cl 2
EX39 . . . . 15 B1
Whitehouse Cross
EX39 . . . . 156 B3
Whitehouse La EX18 . . 58 D5
White La PL1 . . . . 263 A2
White Ladies TQ6 . . . . 146 B7
White Lady Rd PL9 . . . 255 D5
White Lady Waterfall★
EX20 . . . . 107 E2
Whiteland Head EX20 . 57 B8
Whiteley Ave TQ9 . . . . 222 F6
Whiteley Cross PL21 . 137 B5
White Lodge EX9 . . . . 198 B1
Whitemoor Cross
PL8 . . . . 142 A8
Whitemoor Hill EX32 . . 16 E1
Whitemoor La EX5,
EX17 . . . . 81 C8
Whiteoxen Cross
TQ10 . . . . 135 C4
White Pk TQ9 . . . . 139 A3
White Post EX36 . . . . . . 20 F2
White Rock Cl TQ4 . . . 225 F1
White Rock Ct TQ4 . . . 228 F8
White Rock Prim Sch
TQ4 . . . . 229 A8
White Rock Rd
Paignton TQ4 . . . . 225 F1
Paignton TQ4 . . . . 228 F8
Whiterocks Pk PL18 . . 125 A6
White Rock Wy TQ4 . . 225 F1
Whites Cotts EX20 . . . . 95 B4
Whiteside Cl EX2 . . . . 178 C4
Whites La EX31 . . . . . . 154 F7
White's La
Great Torrington
EX38 . . . . 159 C5
Stockland EX14 . . . . 86 F7
Stockland EX14 . . . . 87 A7
White St EX3 . . . . 182 F4
WHITESTAUNTON 69 D5
Whitestaunton Cross
TA20 . . . . 69 E5
WHITESTONE 98 E4
Whitestone Cross
TQ7 . . . . 145 C5
Whitestone Dr EX16 . . 161 C6
Whitestone La EX33 . . . . 8 D1
Whitestone Orch 2
TQ4 . . . . 226 B5
White Stones EX8 . . . . 202 C6
Whitethorn Cl
Honiton EX14 . . . . 166 C4
Sidmouth EX10 . . . . 187 F8
Whitethorn Pk EX4 . . . 173 C3
White Tor Cl EX20 . . . . 170 E5
Whitewater Ct PL7 . . . 250 E6
Whiteway Cl 6 EX5 . . . 99 E8
Whiteway Dr EX1 . . . . 178 B6
Whiteway La TQ1 . . . . 214 D8
Whiteway Rd TQ12 . . . 207 D7
WHITFORD 103 B6
Whitford Rd EX13 . . . . 103 C6
Whitham Pk PL19 . . . . 171 C4
Whiting Cl EX39 . . . . . . 25 F4
WHITLEIGH 244 C5
Whitleigh Ave PL5 . . . 244 E2
Whitleigh Com Prim Sch
PL5 . . . . 244 D4
Whitleigh Cotts PL5 . . 244 E2
Whitleigh Ct PL5 . . . . . 244 D4
Whitleigh Gn PL5 . . . . 244 C4
Whitleigh Villas PL5 . . 244 E2
Whitleigh Way PL5 . . . 244 C4
Whitleigh Wood Nature
Reserve★ PL6 . . . . . . 244 E4
Whitley Cross TQ7 . . . 143 C3
Whitley Rd
Farway EX24 . . . . 101 F7
Paignton TQ4 . . . . 226 A4
Whitley Rocks EX36 . . . 31 C7
Whitlocks Mews
TQ14 . . . . 210 A6
Whitlow Copse EX2 . . 178 C4
Whitman Cl EX8 . . . . . 196 C4
Whitmore La PL21 . . . 137 C4
Whitmore Way EX14 . 166 A4
WHITNAGE 50 C2
Whitnage La EX16 . . . . . 50 C2
Whitnole Cross EX16 . . 48 A5
Whitnole La
Calverleigh EX16 . . . . . . 48 A4
Rackenford EX16 . . . . . . 47 F4
Whitsam Cross PL20 . 125 D1
Whitsley Cross EX19,
EX38 . . . . 42 C4
Whitson Cross PL5 . . . 244 C7
Whitsoncross La
PL5 . . . . 244 C7
WHITSTONE 70 E1
Whitstone Com Prim Sch
EX22 . . . . 70 E1

Whitstone Head Sch EX22 70 E1
Whitstone La
Bovey Tracey TQ13 180 C8
Meshaw EX36 46 B5
Whitstone Rd TQ4 226 B5
Whittingham Rd
Ilfracombe EX34 150 C5
Yealmpton PL8 141 B8
Whittington St PL3 262 B4
Whitton Ct EX10 187 F7
Whitton Way EX15 163 C4
Whitwell La EX24 103 A3
Whitycombe Way EX4 176 D8
Whity Cross PL12 242 A4
Whympston Cross PL21 137 D1
Wicaford Cross EX36 31 A2
Wicaford La EX36 31 A2
Wick Cross EX14 85 F7
Wicket The EX2 178 C3
Wickham Cl
Bideford EX39 157 C1
East-the-Water EX39 26 A4
Wickington La EX20 95 B7
Widdicombe Cross
Marldon TQ3 218 F5
Paignton TQ3 218 E5
Widdicombe Dr PL21 237 D4
WIDECOMBE IN THE MOOR 121 B4
Widecombe in the Moor Prim Sch TQ13 121 B3
Widecombe Way EX4 173 E1
Widegate Nursery PL9 256 D8
Widepost La EX13 167 C5
WIDEWELL 245 B7
Widewell La PL6 245 C7
Widewell Prim Acad PL6 245 B7
Widewell Rd PL6 245 B7
Widey Court Prim Sch PL6 244 F1
Widey Cross PL6 244 F1
Widey Ct PL6 244 F1
Widey Hill PL8 141 A7
Widey La PL6 244 F1
Widey View PL3 248 F6
Widgery Dr EX36 158 C4
Widgery Rd EX4 178 A8
WIDWORTHY 86 D2
Widworthy Ct EX14 86 C2
Wigeon Rd EX23 70 A8
Wigford Cross TQ7 138 C1
Wigford La TQ7 138 D2
WIGGATON 100 E4
Wiggaton Rd EX10 100 F4
Wigley Cross EX31 16 C8
Wilbarn Rd TQ3 226 C7
Wilburton Cross PL21 136 C3
Wilburt Rd PL3 249 D8
Wilbury Way EX7 204 F7
Wilcocks Rd EX4 174 D1
Wilcombe Cross
Brayford EX32 18 E4
Charles EX32 18 E4
Wilcombe Prim Sch EX16 161 F3
Wilcove PL5 247 A6
Wilcove Cl PL5 247 E8
Wilcove La
Torpoint PL11 246 E5
Wilcove PL5 247 A6
Wilderbrook Way EX34 1 F1
Wilderness La EX14 84 D6
Wilderness Rd PL3 248 E5
Wilder Pk EX34 150 B5
Wilder Rd EX34 150 B6
Wildersmouth Ct EX34 150 B6
Wildmoor La TA21 52 F6
Wildner Top
Barbrook EX35 5 A4
Lynton EX35 4 F4
Wildwoods Cres TQ12 207 F4
Wilford Rd EX2 178 B5
Wilkey Cl EX32 155 C4
Wilkins Dr TQ4 225 E2
Wilkinson Rd PL5 247 D8
Willake Rd TQ12 213 A5
WILLAND
Taunton 68 B8
Tiverton 162 E4
Willand Ind Est EX15 162 D5
WILLAND MOOR 162 E5
Willand Moor Mews EX15 162 E5
Willand Moor Rd EX15 162 E5
Willand Old Village EX15 162 C3
Willand Rd
Braunton EX33 152 C6
Cullompton EX15 163 C4
Willand EX15 162 B6
Willand Sch EX15 162 D4
Willas Rd PL16 105 E4
Willcocks Cl 6 TA21 160 D5
Willet St 3 EX39 157 A2
Willey La EX20 95 A6
Willeys Ave EX2 261 A1
Willeys Ct EX2 261 A1
Willhayes Cross EX6 113 E6
Willhayes Hill EX6 113 E6
Willhayes Pk EX13 167 D6
Willhay La EX13 167 D7
Willhayne La EX24 102 F5
Willhays Cl 15 TQ12 123 F1
William Cl EX11 169 B2
William Evans Cl PL6 244 D5
William Prance Rd PL6 245 A3
Williams Ave
Exeter EX2 177 B4
Exeter EX2 261 A1
Plymouth PL4 249 B1
Williams Cl
Dawlish EX7 204 C5
Wrafton EX33 152 E4
Williams Ct EX31 154 C2
Williams Ct TQ11 236 B5
Williamson Cl EX33 8 A2
Williamson Ho EX31 155 A8
Williamson Way EX36 158 C4
William St 3 EX16 161 D4
Willicombe Rd TQ3 226 A5
Willie La EX17 79 F7
WILLINGCOTT 8 D6
Willingcott Cross EX34 8 C6
Willingcott Hill EX34 8 D4
Willingcott Valley EX34 8 D5
Willing Cross TQ10 135 F5
Willing Gate TQ10 135 E5
Willis Ct 1 TQ1 220 A7
Willis Dr EX4 174 F4
Willis's Cross TQ12 122 D2
Willmott Cl EX8 196 E1
Willoughby Cl EX8 196 C3
Willoughby Ho EX10 187 E2
Willoughby Rd TQ1 220 C6
Willoughby Wy PL1 262 B1
Willow Ave
Exmouth EX8 196 B3
Torquay TQ2 214 A3
Willoway Cl EX33 152 C6
Willoway Gr EX33 152 C6
Willoway La EX33 152 C7
Willowbank Prim Sch EX15 163 B3
Willowbrook Ave 6 EX4 178 C8
Willowbrook Sch EX4 174 B1
Willowby Gdns PL20 127 A2
Willowby Pk PL20 127 A2
Willow Cl
Ilfracombe EX34 150 E4
Newton Abbot TQ12 213 A8
Plymouth PL3 249 E5
Seaton EX12 192 A8
Stoke Canon EX5 173 F8
Willow Cotts PL7 250 D4
Willow Ct
Exeter EX2 178 A4
Plymouth PL6 249 E7
Willowdale Cl 1 EX14 166 B6
Willow Dr EX15 65 F7
Willowfield
Barton TQ2 213 F2
Braunton EX33 152 C7
Willow Gdns EX5 175 C6
Willow Gn PL12 242 D2
Willow Gr
Bideford EX39 25 D4
Stibb Cross EX38 40 D2
Willow La
Cornworthy TQ9 227 B3
Hemyock EX15 52 F2
Willowpark La TQ12 213 C4
Willow Rd PL19 171 C3
Willow Rise EX17 61 E8
Willows Cl TQ7 144 E1
Willow St 2 TQ14 210 B4
Willows The
Chilsworthy EX22 53 E1
Shillingford St George EX2 114 C6
Willows The TQ2 213 D2
Willow Tree Cl EX20 170 C5
Willow Tree Rd EX32 155 B2
Willow View Pk EX5 100 A7
Willow Way
Dawlish Warren EX7 201 A2
Exeter EX4 178 C8
Willow Wlk
Crediton EX17 165 E6
2 Exeter EX4 177 D8
Honiton EX14 166 B4
Plymouth PL6 245 D5
Wills Ave TQ3 219 C1
Wills Cl PL6 244 E7
Willsdown Rd EX2 181 C8
Willshere Rd EX32 155 C4
Wills La EX1 175 A2
Willsland Cl EX6 194 D3
Wills Rd
Bideford EX39 156 D1
Bovey Tracey TQ13 180 B6
Totnes TQ9 223 D6
Willsworthy Dr PL19 171 B7
WILMINGTON 86 D3
Wilmington La EX13, EX14 86 E2
WILMINSTONE 117 D3
Wilminstone Ind Est PL19 171 E7
Wilmot Gdns PL5 244 D3
Wilncote Lodge 6 TQ1 220 A6
WILSHAM 5 F5
Wilsham Cross EX35 6 A5
Wilsham La EX35 5 F5
Wilson Cres PL2 248 B5
Wilson La
Queen Dart EX16 47 B4
Witheridge EX17 46 B1
Wilton Cl TQ12 212 B6
Wilton Rd
Paignton TQ3 219 B2
Plymouth PL1 248 A3
Wilton St PL1 262 A4
Wilton Way
Abbotskerswell TQ12 212 B6
Exeter EX1 178 D6
WILTOWN 52 F3
Wiltown La EX15 52 F3
Wiltshier Cl EX5 175 C7
Wiltshire Cl
Exeter EX4 176 E4
Plymouth PL4 248 F4
Wilway La TA22 33 C6
Wimble Cross EX22 164 D3
Winchester Ave
Exeter EX4 176 F7
Torquay TQ2 213 F1
Winchester Cl EX14 84 D2
Winchester Dr EX8 196 D4
Winchester Gdns PL5 244 A5
Windabout Cross EX39 39 B7
Windard Terr EX20 93 B1
Windbow La EX16 48 D3
Windeatt Sq 4 TQ9 223 D5
Winder Cres EX16 161 B6
Windermere Cl EX4 176 F6
Windermere Cres PL6 244 F4
Windermere Rd TQ1 220 C6
Windford Hill EX31 10 C4
Wind La EX32 18 F7
Windmilland Cross EX21 74 A6
Windmill Ave TQ3 219 A1
Windmill Cl TQ5 230 D4
Windmill Cross EX31 27 A3
Windmill Ct 9 TQ5 230 C4
Windmill Gdns TQ3 219 A1
Windmill Hill
Brixham TQ5 230 D4
Saltash PL12 242 E2
Windmill La
Northam EX39 26 A8
Northam EX39 157 B7
North Whilborough TQ12 212 D1
Paignton TQ3 218 F1
West Hill EX10 100 A5
West Hill EX11 168 D5
Windmill Rd
Brixham TQ5 230 D4
Holsworthy EX22 164 D4
Paignton TQ3 219 A1
Windout La EX6 97 E3
Windrush Rise EX11 169 D3
Windsbatch La 6 PL3 249 D1
Windsor Ave TQ12 207 F3
Windsor Cl
Cullompton EX15 163 C6
Exeter EX4 177 A7
Ivybridge PL21 237 E4
Newton Abbot TQ12 207 C2
Torquay TQ1 220 B6
Windsor Ct
Ilfracombe EX34 150 B5
Kingsbridge TQ7 258 D5
Windsor Dr EX7 200 E2
Windsor Gdns EX31 154 C1
Windsor Ho EX8 202 B7
Windsor La
Saltash PL12 242 E2
Stokenham TQ7 145 B1
Windsor Mead EX10 101 A1
Windsor Pl PL1 262 C2
Windsor Rd
Barnstaple EX31 154 E7
Dartmouth TQ6 233 C3
Kingsbridge TQ7 258 D5
Northam EX39 156 F7
Plymouth PL3 249 B7
Torquay TQ1 220 C6
Windsor Sq EX8 202 A7
Windsor Terr DT7 260 D4
Windsor Villas PL1 262 C2
Windthorn Cross TQ12 218 A7
Windthorn La TQ3, TQ12 218 B7
Windward La EX7 201 B8
Windward Rd TQ2 213 E3
Windway Hill TA4 34 D6
Windwhistle Cross EX5 81 C8
Wind Whistle Cross EX15 66 C1
Windwhistle La EX16 49 B8
Windy Ash Cross EX32 16 F1
Windy Ash Hill EX32 155 C1
Windy Cnr TQ4 229 B6
Windy Cross
Ashford EX31 16 A6
8 Chulmleigh EX18 44 E1
Doddiscombsleigh EX6 113 E7
Great Torrington EX38 159 C5
Windy Cross *continued*
Holsworthy Beacon EX22 54 F2
Windypost Cross EX35 151 C2
Windys Way EX8 202 D7
Wingate La EX20 75 C7
Wingfield TQ7 143 A1
Wingfield Cl 3 EX16 161 C3
Wingfield Mans PL3 248 A3
Wingfield Rd PL3 262 A4
Wingfield Way PL3 262 A4
Winham La EX15 83 B6
Winifred Baker Ct 5 PL4 263 A4
Winifred Cliff Ct 1 EX16 34 B1
WINKLEIGH 58 E2
Winkleigh Cl EX2 177 A2
Winkleigh Com Prim Sch EX19 58 F2
Winkleigh La EX6 184 F8
Winkleigh Moor Cross EX19 58 C7
Winneford La EX14 85 C3
Winner Hill Rd TQ3 226 A6
Winner St TQ3 226 A6
Winnicott Cl PL6 244 E7
Winnings Way TQ1 220 D7
Winnow Cl PL9 255 F4
Winsbeer La
Rockwell Green TA21 160 A6
Runnington TA21 51 F8
Winsbury Ct PL6 245 A1
Winscombe La EX6 96 D3
Winscott Cotts EX5 81 B1
Winscott Cross
Holsworthy EX22 72 A4
Newton St Cyres EX5 81 B1
WINSFORD 156 C2
Winsford La EX21 73 E3
Winsford Rd TQ2 219 C3
Winsford Walled Gdn* EX21 73 F4
WINSHAM 8 E1
Winsham Cross EX33 8 D1
Winsham Rd EX33 8 D1
Winslade Cl TQ7 144 E1
Winslade Ct TQ7 144 E1
WINSLADE PARK 179 B2
Winslade Park Ave EX5 179 B2
Winslade Pk EX5 179 B1
Winslade Rd EX10 188 B6
Winslake Mdw EX6 97 F4
Winsland Ave TQ9 222 E6
Winson Cross EX37 29 A4
Winsor Cross PL8 136 C4
Winsor Meadow EX36 30 D8
Winstanley Wlk PL3 249 D6
Winstitchen Cross TA24 13 C2
Winstitchen La TA24 13 C2
WINSTON 257 B4
Winston Ave PL4 262 C4
Winston Cl TQ12 207 E7
Winston Ct TQ14 210 C6
Winstone Ave TQ2 214 A1
Winstone Cotts PL8 257 B4
Winstone La PL8 257 B4
Winston Ho EX36 158 C5
Winston Pk EX36 158 C5
Winston Rd EX8 196 E2
Winsu Ave TQ3 226 A8
WINSWELL 56 D8
Winswell Water EX38 56 D7
Winswood EX17 165 D4
Winsworthy EX39 23 D3
Winterbourne Rd TQ14 210 C5
Winter Gdn TQ2 220 B4
Winterland La EX22 164 D2
Winters Cross TA4 35 C8
Wintershead Rd
Simonsbath TA24 19 F8
Simonsbath TA24 20 A8
Winters La EX11 169 D3
Winter's La EX11 169 D3
Winward Rise EX7 210 F8
Wiriga Way EX16 46 E1
Wiscombe La TQ7 142 D6
Wishings Rd TQ5 230 D3
Wish Meadow La EX5 175 D3
Wisteria Cl EX19 57 F7
Wisteria Pl TQ7 258 C5
Wistford Cross EX32 18 C4
Wistman's Wood National Nature Reserve* PL20 119 D4
Wiston Cross EX36 32 D2
Witch La EX14 86 F8
Witcombe La EX6 194 D3
WITHACOTT 70 F8
Witham Gdns PL3 249 C5
Witheby EX10 187 F3
Withecombe Cross TQ13 110 F8
Withen Cross EX5 99 C1
Withen La EX5 99 D2
Witherdon Cross EX21 91 D5
WITHERIDGE 46 F1
Witheridge CE Prim Sch EX16 46 E1
Witheridge Cl EX22 38 E1
Witheridge Mill Cross EX16 46 E2
Witheridge Moor Cross (East) EX16 47 E1
Witheridge Moor Cross (West) EX16 47 D1
Witheridge Pl EX34 150 E5
Withey The EX5 99 E8
Withies St PL3 249 D1
WITHLEIGH 63 D7
Withleigh Cross EX16 63 C8
Withleigh La EX16 63 D7
WITHNOE 252 A4
Withnoe La PL10 252 B6
Withy Cl EX16 161 F3
Withycombe Park Dr EX8 196 E2
WITHYCOMBE RALEIGH 196 C2
Withycombe Raleigh CE Prim Sch EX8 196 C1
Withycombe Rd EX8 202 A8
Withycombe Village Rd EX8 202 B8
Withy Cross EX38 42 E6
Withygate La EX32 19 A5
Withy La EX15 52 B1
WITHYPOOL 21 C6
Withypool Cross
Hawkridge TA22 21 C2
Twitchen EX36 20 E4
Withywell La EX33 7 E1
Withywine La TA22 34 C5
Witten Gdns EX39 157 A5
Wixenford Ct PL9 255 F8
Wixon Cross EX18 45 B3
Wixon La EX18 45 B3
Woburn Cl TQ3 225 D7
Woburn Terr PL9 255 C7
WOLBOROUGH 207 B1
Wolborough Church Path TQ12 207 A2
Wolborough Cl TQ12 207 C2
Wolborough Gdns
Brixham TQ5 230 E6
Newton Abbot TQ12 207 C2
Wolborough St TQ12 207 B3
Wolbough CE (Aided) Prim Sch 18 TQ12 207 C3
Wolford Cross EX14 85 B8
WOLLATON 257 B6
Wollaton Cross PL8 257 A6
Wollaton Gr PL5 243 F3
Wolrige Ave PL7 251 B5
Wolrige Way PL7 251 A5
Wolsdon La
Antony PL11 246 A1
St John PL11 252 B8
Wolsdon Pl PL1 262 A3
Wolsdon St PL1 262 B3
Wolseley Bsns Pk 2 PL2 248 A5
Wolseley Cl PL2 248 A5
Wolseley Rd
Plymouth PL5 247 E7
Plymouth, Camels Head PL5 247 F6
Plymouth, St Budeaux PL5 243 C1
Wolseley Road Flats PL2 247 F6
Wolston Cl TQ5 230 B6
WOLVERSTONE 85 A7
Wolverstone Cross EX14 85 A8
Wolverstone Hill EX14 85 A7
Wolverton Dr TQ12 207 D7
Wolverwood Cl PL7 251 C3
Wolverwood La PL7 251 B3
Wombwell Cres PL2 247 E7
Wonders Cnr EX38 40 D2
WONFORD 178 A4
Wonford House Hospl EX2 177 F4
Wonford Rd EX2 261 C2
Wonford Sp Ctr EX1 178 A3
Wonford St EX2 178 A4
Wonnacott's Rd EX20 170 C5
WONSON 110 D8
Wonton Cross TQ9 135 D2
WOODA 157 C8
WOODACOTT 54 E2
Woodacott Cross EX22 54 E2
Wood Acre PL12 242 B4
Woodacre Ct PL12 242 B4
Woodah Rd EX4 176 F5
Wooda Rd EX39 157 C8
Woodberry Down Wy DT7 260 E5
Woodbine Cotts PL7 250 E4
Woodbine Pl 5 EX12 192 A5
Woodbine Terr EX4 261 A4
Woodbridge La
Bondleigh EX18 77 D8
Farway EX24 102 B6
North Tawton EX17 59 E1
Woodbrook Rd TQ9 223 E5
Woodburn Cl PL21 237 B5
Woodburn Cross EX16 32 F2
Woodburn Hill EX16 32 F2
Woodburn Water Cross EX16 32 F1
WOODBURY 184 C3
Woodbury Bsns Pk EX5 184 A1
Woodbury CE Prim Sch EX5 184 C3
Woodbury Ct EX8 202 C6
Woodbury Gdns PL5 244 A3
Woodbury La EX13 167 E3
Woodbury Pk EX13 167 C4
Woodbury Rd EX3, EX5 183 E5
Woodbury Rise TQ6 233 B2
WOODBURY SALTERTON 184 C6
Woodbury Salterton CE Prim Sch EX5 184 C7
Woodbury View
Broadclyst EX5 175 D6
Exeter EX2 177 A2
Woodbury Way EX13 167 D4
Woodbury Wlk EX6 181 F5
Woodchurch PL20 126 E3
Wood Cl
Christow EX6 113 B4
Saltash PL12 242 B3
Wood Cnr EX6 97 C2
Woodcock Cl PL10 253 A6
Woodcock Way EX13 88 B7
Woodcote Ct EX5 184 C3
Wood Cotts TQ12 180 C1
Woodcourt Rd TQ9 139 C7
Woodcroft Cross EX19 76 D7
Woodcroft La EX19 76 D8
Woodcroft Mdws TA20 69 B7
Wood Cross EX14 86 C6
Woodend Rd
Plymouth PL6 245 D7
Torquay TQ1 220 D4
Wooder Wharf 12 EX39 157 A1
Woodfield Cl EX8 196 E2
Woodfield Cres PL21 237 E4
Woodfield Ct TQ1 220 D3
Woodfield Prim Sch PL5 244 C5
Woodfields EX12 192 A7
WOODFORD
Blackawton 139 D2
Plymouth 250 C7
Woodford Ave PL7 250 A7
Woodford Cl PL7 250 A7
Woodford Cres PL7 250 A6
Woodford Gdns EX32 155 C2
Woodford Gn PL7 250 B6
Woodford Prim Sch PL7 250 B6
Woodford Rd PL6 245 D6
WOODGATE 51 E2
Woodhaye Cl 2 TQ10 134 F2
Woodhaye Gdns 5 TQ1 220 D4
Woodhayes Cl EX7 204 F8
Woodhayes Dr EX15 67 C2
Woodhayes La
Whimple EX5 99 F7
Whimple EX5 100 A7
Woodhaye Terr 1 TQ10 134 F2
Woodhead Cross
Branscombe EX12 190 E7
Totnes TQ9 217 D4
Woodhead La
Cheriton Fitzpaine EX16 63 A7
Totnes TQ12 217 E4
Woodhill View EX14 166 B4
Woodhouse Cl TQ7 258 C4
Woodhouse Cross TQ13 122 D3
Woodhouse Fields DT7 104 B4
Woodhouse La
Axminster EX13 88 D1
Uplyme DT7 104 B4
Woodhouse Rd EX13 88 D1
Woodhuish La TQ5, TQ6 235 B7
Wood La
Abbotskerswell TQ12 212 A5
Ashreigney EX18 43 D1
Broadhembury EX14 84 E7
Christow EX6 113 B4
Combe Martin EX34 3 B2
East Buckland EX32 18 F1
Exmouth EX8 196 D1
Kingswear TQ6 234 B3
Monkton EX14 86 C6
Morchard Bishop EX17 61 A2
Slapton TQ7 145 D4
Stockleigh Pomeroy EX17 81 B4
West Alvington TQ7 258 A4
West Down EX34 8 F4
WOODLAND
Ashburton 131 D3
Ivybridge 237 A5
Woodland Ave
Kingskerswell TQ12 212 F5
Plymouth PL9 256 A8
Teignmouth TQ14 210 D7
Woodland Bsns Pk TQ2 219 E8

Woodland Cl
Barnstaple EX32......**155** E4
Braunton EX33.........**8** D1
Denbury TQ12........**131** F3
Gunnislake PL18......**125** C6
Ivybridge PL21.......**237** B6
Staverton TQ9........**216** A4
2 Tiverton EX16 ... **49** B8
Torquay TQ2.........**219** E8
Woodland Cotts
PL21................**237** A5
Woodland Cross EX31. **27** B4
Woodland Ct
10 Barnstaple EX32 ...**155** A4
Ivybridge PL21.......**237** A5
Paignton TQ3........**226** B7
Woodland Dr
Brixton PL8.........**257** B5
Exeter EX1..........**178** E3
Plymouth PL7........**250** B4
WOODLAND HEAD....**97** C7
Woodlandhead Cross
EX17................**97** B7
Woodland Hill
Cheriton Bishop EX17.. **97** B8
Yeoford EX17.........**79** A1
Woodland La TQ9 ...**227** D4
Woodland Mews
Broadclyst EX5.......**175** D6
1 Paignton TQ3.....**226** B7
Woodland Pk
Ivybridge PL21.......**237** A5
Northam EX39........**156** F5
Northam EX39........**157** A5
Paignton TQ3........**226** B7
Woodland Rd
Ashburton TQ13......**130** F4
Broadclyst EX5.......**175** C6
Denbury TQ12........**211** A6
Exeter EX1..........**178** D7
Harbertonford TQ9....**139** C7
Ivybridge PL21.......**237** B5
Lee Mill PL21........**136** D7
Plymouth PL7........**250** C6
Torquay TQ2.........**219** E8
Woodlands
Budleigh Salterton
EX9................**203** E8
Churchstow TQ7......**143** E4
Combe Martin EX34 ....**2** F4
Dousland PL20.......**127** B3
Halwill EX21..........**73** D3
Kingsteignton TQ12 ...**123** E2
Newton St Cyres EX5 .. **98** F8
Plymouth PL9........**255** F6
Sidmouth EX10.......**188** A4
Wellington TA21......**160** F3
Whimple EX5..........**99** E8
Woodlands Bsns Pk
EX16................**51** C3
Woodlands Cl
Churchstow TQ7......**143** E4
Offwell EX14..........**86** B2
Teignmouth TQ14.....**210** C5
Woodlands Ct
Exmouth EX8........**196** B3
Plymouth PL5........**244** A3
Woodlands Dr EX8..**196** B3
Woodlands End PL6. **245** D5
Woodlands Gdns 5
TQ12...............**207** F2
Woodlands La PL6 ..**245** F1
Woodlands L Pk★
TQ9................**139** F3
Woodlands Park Prim
Sch PL21..........**237** A5
Woodlands Pk EX6.. **98** B4
Woodlands Rd TQ12. **207** F2
Woodlands Special Sch
PL5................**244** D4
Woodlands Way EX5 .**179** E3
Woodlands Wlk
TQ13...............**180** C4
Woodland Terr
Ivybridge PL21.......**237** B4
Kingswear TQ6.......**234** A3
Plymouth PL4........**263** B4
Woodland Terr La
PL4................**263** B4
Woodland View
EX22...............**164** C3
Woodland Way
Gunnislake PL18......**125** D6
Torpoint PL11........**246** F3
Woodland Wood Valley
Nature Reserve★
PL5................**244** B4
Woodlark La 2 EX31 **154** A2
Wood Lea EX39......**39** E8
WOODLEIGH.........**144** B7
Woodleigh Cl EX4...**173** A3
Woodleigh Pk TQ14 .**210** B2

Woodleigh Rd TQ12..**206** F3
Woodley Cross EX5 ...**98** F8
Woodley La EX5 .....**98** E8
Woodleys Dr EX10 ..**186** D8
Woodman's Cnr
PL20...............**127** A3
Woodmans Cres 2
EX14...............**166** C5
Woodmans Orch EX5.. **84** A2
WOODMANTON......**196** C8
Woodmead Halls
DT7................**260** D3
Woodmead Rd
Axminster EX13.......**167** C5
Lyme Regis DT7......**260** D3
Woodmere Way
TQ12...............**207** A3
Woodpark Cross EX17 **61** A8
Woodpark La
Molland EX36.........**31** E6
Sidmouth EX10.......**188** B5
Wood Park La EX34 ...**2** D3
Woodpecker Dr
TQ12...............**207** C8
Woodpecker Way
Cheriton Bishop EX6... **97** B4
Tavistock PL19.......**171** D2
Wood Pk
Ivybridge PL21.......**237** D6
Plymouth PL6........**132** A2
Woodplace La
Cruwys Morchard
EX16................**63** D1
Pennymoor EX16......**62** F7
Woodridge Cross
EX19................**57** D6
Wood Rock EX36......**32** C5
Woodroffe Mdw DT7 **260** C4
Woodroffe Sch The
DT7................**260** C4
Woods Cross EX36....**31** D6
Wood's Cross EX36 ...**32** C5
Woods Field EX20....**106** E5
Woodside
Crapstone PL20.......**126** E2
Plymouth PL4........**263** B4
Woodside Ave PL9 ...**255** C6
Woodside Cl
Ivybridge PL21.......**237** D4
Raymond's Hill EX13...**104** C8
Woodside Ct
Lynton EX35.........**151** D5
Plymouth PL7........**250** E4
Woodside Dr TQ1 ...**220** C4
Woodside La PL4.....**263** B4
Woodside Wlk EX14 ..**166** D6
Woods Pasture 17
EX5................**99** A6
Woods The TQ1......**220** E3
Woodstock Gdns
PL5................**243** D1
WOODTOWN
East-the-Water........**26** D4
Fairy Cross..........**25** B2
Woodvale Ct 21
TQ12...............**207** B3
Wood View TQ12.....**207** A3
Woodview Pk PL9....**256** A6
Woodview Rd TQ4 ...**225** E1
Wood View Terr
PL21...............**136** F3
Woodville EX31......**154** C3
Woodville Ave PL20..**128** A8
Woodville Cl EX31....**154** C4
Woodville Cross EX23 . **36** F1
Woodville Rd
Exeter EX2..........**177** B3
Exmouth EX8........**202** A8
Morwenstow EX23......**36** F1
Plymouth PL2........**247** F7
Torquay TQ1.........**220** C4
Woodward Rd
Tiverton EX16........**64** A6
Tiverton EX16........**161** B2
Woodwater Acad
EX2................**178** A4
Woodwater La EX2...**178** B4
Woodway PL9.......**256** A7
Woodway Cl TQ14...**210** C7
Woodway Dr TQ14 ..**210** C6
Woodway Rd TQ14...**210** C6
Woodway St TQ13...**123** E6
WOODY BAY..........**4** D6
Woody Bay Sta★ EX31.. **4** E3
Woody La
Lynton EX35..........**5** C5
West Lyn EX35.......**151** D3
WOOLACOMBE........**7** F7
Woolacombe Cross
PL20...............**125** F1
Woolacombe Ct EX34 .. **8** A6
Woolacombe Rd
PL20...............**125** F1

Woolacombe Rise EX34 **8** B6
Woolacombe Sch EX34. **8** A6
Woolacombe Station Rd
EX34................**8** B6
Woolbarn Lawn
EX32...............**155** D4
Woolbrook Cl EX10 ..**188** A6
Woolbrook Mdws
EX10...............**188** A7
Woolbrook Mead
EX10...............**187** F7
Woolbrook Pk EX10..**188** A7
Woolbrook Rd EX10..**188** A7
Woolbrook Rise
EX10...............**188** A7
Wool Cl EX15........**163** A1
Woolcombe La
Ivybridge PL21.......**237** D4
Ivybridge PL21.......**237** D6
Sidmouth EX10.......**188** B5
Woolcott Way EX15..**163** B2
WOOLFARDISWORTHY
...................**62** A3
Woolfardisworthy Cross
Clovelly EX39.........**23** D2
Woolfardisworthy EX17. **62** A3
WOOLFARDISWORTHY
OR WOOLSERY......**38** E7
WOOLHANGER........**4** F2
Woolhanger's La EX34 . **2** E3
WOOLLATON.........**56** B7
Woollcombe Ave PL7 **250** F4
Woolleigh Cross EX19. **42** B3
WOOLLEY...........**37** D3
Woolms Mdw EX21...**237** A4
Woolpit La TA24......**21** B7
Woolsery Ave EX4....**178** B8
Woolsery Cl EX4.....**178** B8
Woolsery Gr EX4.....**178** B8
Woolsery Prim Sch
EX39................**38** F7
Woolster Ct 7 EX4..**263** A2
Woolfardisworthy EX17. **62** A3
WOOLSTON.........**147** F8
WOOLSTON GREEN..**131** B1
Woolway Ave EX6....**182** B4
Woolwell Cres PL6...**245** C8
Woolwell Dr PL6.....**245** C7
Woolwell Rd PL6.....**245** D7
Wootton Cross EX13 ..**88** F1
Worcester Cres
EX15...............**162** D4
Worden Cross
Milton Damerel EX22 ... **54** E6
Sutcombe EX22.......**54** C8
Wordland Cross EX17 . **80** F8
Wordsworth Ave
Barnstaple EX31......**154** F7
6 Barnstaple EX32 ...**155** A7
Wordsworth Cl
5 Exmouth EX8......**196** C4
Torquay TQ2.........**219** E6
Wordsworth Cres
PL2................**247** F7
Wordsworth Rd PL2..**247** F7
Worham's La EX13.....**86** F2
Works The EX16......**161** C4
World of Country Life★
EX8................**203** B6
WORLINGTON........**15** C1
Worlington Cross
EX39................**15** C1
Worlington Hill EX39. **15** C1
Wormsworthy Hill
EX16................**48** D6
WORSTON..........**136** B3
Worthele Cl PL21....**237** A4
Worthele Cres PL21 **237** B1
Worth La
Hele EX5............**82** E5
Withypool TA22,TA24 ...**21** C4
Worth Rd EX34......**150** C5
Worthy La EX16.......**47** C6
Wotten Way TQ9....**216** D8
WOTTER...........**132** D4
Wotton Cross TQ12 ..**131** E4
Wotton La
Exmouth EX8........**196** B5
Lympstone EX8.......**195** F5
Wotton Pound EX8...**196** A5
Wotton Way TQ9....**131** E1
WRAFTON..........**152** F4
Wrafton Rd EX33....**152** E4
Wragg Dr EX8.......**202** E7
WRANGATON........**137** D8
Wrangaton Bsns Pk
TQ10...............**137** D8
Wrangaton Rd
Bittaford PL21,TQ10...**137** D8
Moorhaven Village
TQ10...............**137** D8
Wrangcombe La TA21. **52** A4
Wrangcombe Rd
Wellington TA21.......**52** A4
Wrangway TA21......**160** A1

WRANGWAY.........**52** A4
Wrangway Rd EX15...**52** A3
Wrangworthy Cross
EX39................**39** E4
Wreford's Cl EX4....**173** A3
Wreford's Dr EX4....**173** A3
Wreford's La EX4....**173** A3
Wreford's Link EX4 ..**173** A3
Wren Cl
Honiton EX14........**166** B4
Northam EX39........**157** A6
Wren Ct 10 TQ5.....**230** C4
Wren Gdns PL7......**250** C6
Wren Ret Pk TQ2....**213** D2
Wrens Gate PL9......**255** E8
Wrentham Bsns Ctr
EX4................**177** D8
Wrentham Est EX4...**177** D8
Wrenwell Cross
TQ12...............**131** F3
Wressing View EX15 ..**66** A3
Wrey Ave EX31......**154** D4
Wright Cl PL1.......**247** E3
Wright Dr EX17.......**79** A5
Wrights La PL8......**140** F7
Wright's La
Exmouth EX8........**196** F6
Torquay TQ1.........**220** A7
Wrigwell Cross
TQ12...............**211** E1
Wrigwell La TQ12....**217** F8
WRINKLEBERRY......**23** D3
Wrinkleberry La EX39. **23** D3
Wroxall Grange TQ1 .**220** C4
Wulphere Cl EX14.... **67** B1
Wyatts La PL19......**171** B6
Wychall Orch EX12...**192** A6
Wychall Pk EX12.....**192** A7
Wych Ct EX13.........**88** E3
Wychwood Cl EX7...**204** E7
Wycliffe Rd PL3.....**249** B4
Wye Gdns PL3......**249** D7
Wyke Cross EX17.....**80** F2
WYKE GREEN.......**167** D1
Wykeham Dr 2 PL2..**248** A7
Wyke Hill EX17........**80** F2
Wyke La EX13.......**167** D2
Wyke Moor Cross
EX20................**95** C8
Wyke Rd EX13.......**167** D3
Wykes Rd EX1.......**177** F7
Wylie Ho EX2........**261** A1
Wynards Cl EX14....**198** B6
Wynards La 2 EX2...**261** B2
Wynards Rd EX9.....**198** B6
Wyndham Ave EX1...**177** F6
Wyndham La PL1....**262** A3
Wyndham Mews 1
PL1................**262** A3
Wyndham Pl PL1....**262** A3
Wyndham Rd EX5.....**82** B6
Wyndham Sq PL1....**262** A3
Wyndham Street E
PL1................**262** B3
Wyndham Street W
PL1................**262** B3
Wyndthorpe Gdns 17
EX34...............**150** C6
Wynford Rd EX4.....**173** F1
Wynstream Sch EX2..**177** F3
Wyoming Cl PL3.....**249** C6
Wyre Cl TQ4.........**226** A2
Wytch Gn EX13.......**88** E3
Wythburn Gdns PL6..**245** D3

Y

Yacht Haven Quay
PL4................**255** C6
YALBERTON........**225** C2
Yalberton Ind Est
TQ4................**225** D3
Yalberton Ind
Management Units
TQ4................**225** E3
Yalberton Rd TQ4....**225** D3
Yalberton Tor Ind Est
TQ4................**225** D3
Yalland Cross TQ10 ..**134** F5
Yallop Way EX14....**166** B4
Yanhey Hill EX16......**32** E4
Yannon Dr TQ14....**210** B5
Yannon La TQ12.....**212** E5
Yannons Ct TQ3.....**225** E2
Yannons Rd TQ4.....**225** E2
Yannons The TQ14...**210** B6
Yannon Terr TQ14...**210** B6
Yapham Cross EX39...**23** A4
YARCOMBE..........**69** A3
Yarda Wlk PL8......**257** A4
Yardbury Hill Rd
EX24...............**102** E7
Yard Cross EX14......**86** B7

Yard Down Cross
EX36................**19** C6
Yard Downs La EX5 ..**188** B7
Yarde Cl EX10.......**188** B7
Yarde Cotts EX38.....**41** D1
Yarde Cross EX32.....**18** A4
Yarde Gate Cross
EX36................**19** B5
Yarde Hill Orch EX10 **188** B7
Yardelands EX10.....**188** B7
Yardelands Cl EX10 ..**188** B7
Yarde Mead EX10....**188** B7
Yarde's Grave Cross
TQ9................**222** F7
Yard Hill TQ13.......**111** D2
Yard La EX36.........**46** B8
Yardleigh Cross EX13 . **88** D4
Yardley Gdns PL6....**245** E3
Yards La
Brixham TQ5.........**230** C1
Brixham TQ5.........**230** C2
Yardwells Cross
EX36................**19** B5
Yarlington Mill EX5...**99** A6
Yarmleigh La EX17....**79** E7
Yarnacott Cnr EX32...**17** E1
Yarnapitts Cross
TQ13...............**110** E7
Yarner Wood Nature
Trail★ TQ13........**122** C5
YARNSCOMBE........**27** E2
Yarrow Mead PL9....**256** D7
YAWL..............**104** B5
Yawl Cres DT7......**104** B5
Yawl Cross DT7.....**104** B6
Yawl Hill DT7.......**104** C6
Yawl Hill La DT7....**104** C5
YEALMBRIDGE......**136** A2
Yealmbury Hill PL8 ..**257** F4
Yealm Gr TQ2.......**219** C7
Yealm Pk PL8.......**257** E4
Yealmpstone Cl PL7..**251** B4
Yealmpstone Dr PL7 **251** B3
Yealmpstone Farm Prim
Sch PL7...........**251** B3
YEALMPTON........**257** E4
Yealmpton Prim Sch
PL8................**257** E4
Yealm Rd PL8........**140** F6
Yealm View Rd PL8 ..**141** A6
Yearlstone Vineyard★
EX16................**63** F3
Yearnor Mill La TA24... **6** F5
Yeats Cl PL5.........**244** C2
Yeatt Cross TQ12....**131** F3
Yellaford Way 1
EX31...............**154** B3
YELLAND...........**153** A4
Yelland Bglws TQ10..**135** E5
Yelland Cross
Challacombe EX31......**11** D4
Rattery TQ10........**135** E5
Yelland EX31........**153** A5
Yelland Rd EX31.....**153** C5
Yellands Pk TQ7.....**142** C6
Yellaton La EX34......**3** B1
Yellowmead Rd PL2..**248** A7
Yellow Tor Ct PL12..**242** C2
Yellow Tor La PL12..**242** C2
Yellow Tor Rd PL12..**242** B2
YELVERTON........**127** A3
Yelverton Bsns Pk
PL20...............**126** E2
Yelverton Cl PL5.....**243** E4
Yelverton Paperweight
Ctr★ PL20..........**126** F2
Yelverton Terr
Tavistock PL19.......**171** D6
Yelverton PL20.......**127** A2
Yendacott La EX17....**81** B3
Yeo Bsns Pk EX5....**179** E3
Yeo Cl PL3..........**249** B5
Yeo Cotts PL21......**133** D3
Yeo Cres EX17......**165** E4
Yeo Dr 20 EX39......**15** A1
YEOFORD...........**79** C1
Yeoford Com Prim Sch
EX17................**79** C1
Yeoford Mdws EX17..**79** C1
Yeoford Sta EX17.....**79** C1
Yeoford Way EX2....**181** D8
Yeo Gate EX36.......**31** C4
Yeo Hill EX36........**30** F1
Yeo La
Molland EX36.........**31** C5
North Tawton EX20....**77** B5
Yeoland Down
Crapstone PL20......**126** F1
Yelverton PL20......**241** E8
Yeoland La
Swimbridge EX32......**17** F1
Yelverton PL20......**126** F1
Yeolands The TQ9 ...**227** F8
Yeolland La PL21....**237** D5
Yeolland Pk PL21....**237** E5

Yeomadon Cross
EX22................**71** D4
Yeomans Way PL7...**251** A4
Yeo Mill Cross EX36...**32** C5
Yeo Pk PL8.........**136** A3
Yeo Rd
Braunton EX31........**15** E5
Zeal Monachorum EX17. **78** D7
Yeotown Cross EX37...**44** C8
Yeo Vale Cross EX17...**60** C2
Yeo Vale Ho 5 EX32 .**154** F6
Yeo Vale Ind Est EX17. **60** C2
Yeo Vale Rd EX32....**154** F6
Yeo Valley Prim Sch
EX32...............**155** A6
Yeo View EX17.......**79** C1
Yerris Rd EX15.......**65** F2
Yetsonais Cross TQ9 .**144** D8
YETTINGTON.......**197** F8
Yettington Rd EX9 ..**198** A4
Yew Cl
Brixham TQ5.........**229** F2
Honiton EX14........**166** A4
Yewdale Gdns PL6 ..**245** D2
Yew Tree Cl
Exeter EX4..........**173** E1
Exmouth EX8........**196** C3
Yew Tree Dr TQ12...**207** E6
Yew Wood Cross
EX15................**66** A4
Yolhey La TQ12......**212** C5
Yonder Acre Way EX5. **99** B6
Yonder Cl EX11......**169** E3
Yonder Cnr EX11....**169** E3
Yonder Hill Cotts
EX13................**88** E7
Yonder Mdw TQ9 ...**227** F8
Yonder Mount EX13..**103** D5
Yonder St
Ottery St Mary EX11...**169** E3
Plymouth PL9........**255** B6
YONDERTOWN......**133** B1
Yon St TQ12........**212** F4
York Cl
Axminster EX13......**167** E6
Exmouth EX8........**196** C3
Feniton EX14.........**84** D2
York Cres
Feniton EX14.........**84** D2
Torquay TQ1.........**220** C8
Yorke Rd TQ6........**233** D3
York Gdns TQ4......**226** B4
York Mews TQ4.....**226** B5
York Pl
Bideford EX39........**157** A3
Cullompton EX15.....**163** C5
Plymouth PL2........**247** F4
York Rd
Exeter EX4..........**261** C4
Paignton TQ4........**226** B4
Plymouth PL5........**247** E8
Seaton EX12........**192** A5
Torpoint PL11........**247** B3
Torquay TQ1.........**220** C8
York Rise EX39......**156** F2
York St
Plymouth PL1........**247** E4
1 Sidmouth EX10....**188** B4
York Terr
Exeter EX4..........**261** C4
7 Plymouth PL2.....**247** F5
Sidmouth EX10......**188** B3
York Villas TQ1......**220** C8
Youings Dr EX31....**155** A7
Youlden La EX20......**95** C7
Youldon Moor Cross
EX22................**53** E4
Youldons Cl TQ9....**139** C7
Youldon Way PL20 ..**126** F4
Youlston Cl EX31......**17** A7
Youltree Cross EX39...**22** E4
Youngaton Rd EX39 .**156** C7
Younghayes Rd EX5...**99** A4
Young's Park La TQ4 **226** C4
Young's Park Rd TQ4 **226** C4

Z

Zeal Cross EX6......**112** F8
Zealley Est TQ12....**207** E6
ZEAL MONACHORUM **78** C7
Zeal Rd
Dunsford EX6........**112** F8
Tedburn St Mary EX6... **97** F1
Zempson Cross TQ10 **135** B5
Zephyr Cres EX32....**155** B5
Zeth Hill La PL21....**136** D8
Zion Pl
Dartmouth TQ6......**233** F4
Ivybridge PL21.......**237** C5
Zion Rd 3 TQ2.....**219** F5
Zion St PL1.........**262** C2